LIFE SAFETY CODE HANDBOOK

Second Edition

LIFE SAFETY
CODE HANDBOOK

Second Edition

Based on the 1981 Edition of the
Life Safety Code®

Edited by

James K. Lathrop

National Fire Protection Association, Inc.
Quincy, Massachusetts

Contents

Foreword

For well over half a century the National Fire Protection Association has been the publisher of the *Life Safety Code*. Formerly known as the *Building Exits Code*, the *Code* is prepared by the NFPA Committee on Safety to Life, one of the more than 170 technical committees operating within the framework of the NFPA's standards-making activities. The Safety to Life Committee is made up of a group of well-qualified individuals who have demonstrated competence in the design and construction of buildings and structures, in the manufacturing and testing of a variety of building components and accessories, and in the enforcement of regulations pertaining to life safety from fire and other perils encountered in buildings and structures.

The *Life Safety Code* is a unique document; its contents address themselves specifically to requirements that have a direct influence on safety to life in both new *and* existing structures and not just in new construction alone. Then, too, although the *Code*'s paramount concern is life safety and not protection of property, per se, there is in observance of *Code* requirements ancillary benefit to property conservation.

What impact application of the *Code* may have on saving lives is a difficult thing to measure; however, it is reasonable to assume that its influence is significant. For example, of the many fatal building fires (other than in one- and two-family dwellings) investigated by the NFPA, invariably, one or more of the features contributing to loss of life from fire were in violation of the requirements of the *Code*.

The NFPA recognizes that a code suitable for enforcement purposes must, by the nature of its purpose, be concise and without explanatory text. And, too, a code cannot be written to cover every situation that will be encountered; thus it must be applied with judgment, and exercised with good sense and with an awareness of the rationale for the requirements that must be enforced. A little help and counsel along the way would make the job a lot easier, hence the reason for this LIFE SAFETY CODE HANDBOOK.

This HANDBOOK gives users of the *Life Safety Code* background information on the reasons for certain *Code* provisions, as recalled by several members of the life safety committee and by NFPA staff members. It also gives some suggestions, through text and illustrations, on how some *Code* requirements can be implemented intelligently. With this kind of information, it is hoped that users of the *Code* will have a better understanding of, and appreciation for, the requirements in the *Code*. The net result should be buildings and structures that are more fire safe than ever in the past. The reader is cautioned, though, to look upon the commentary that appears in the HANDBOOK only as views expressed by the contributors to the HAND-BOOK.

The editor welcomes critiques of the commentary on *Code* requirements appearing in this edition and suggestions on what other *Code* provisions should be discussed. In the sense that the *Life Safety Code* is a standard reflecting a synthesis of the best efforts of a representative committee, so should the LIFE SAFETY CODE HANDBOOK represent the best in thought by fire protection practitioners involved with the *Code* and its requirements. It is knowledge that must be shared.

RICHARD E. STEVENS
Vice President and Chief Engineer
National Fire Protection Association

Preface

The *Life Safety Code* had its origin in the work of the Committee on Safety to Life of the National Fire Protection Association which was appointed in 1913. For the first few years of its existence the Committee devoted its attention to a study of the notable fires involving loss of life and in analyzing the causes of this loss of life. This work led to the preparation of standards for the construction of stairways, fire escapes, etc., for fire drills in various occupancies and for the construction and arrangement of exit facilities for factories, schools, etc., which form the basis of the present *Code*. These reports were adopted by the National Fire Protection Association and published in pamphlet form as "Outside Stairs for Fire Exits" (1916) and "Safeguarding Factory Workers from Fire" (1918). A pamphlet, "Exit Drills in Factories, Schools, Department Stores and Theatres," published in 1912 following its presentation by the late Committee member Mr. R. H. Newbern at the 1911 Annual Meeting of the Association, although antedating the organization of the Committee, is considered as having the status of a Committee publication and had been used with the other pamphlets as a groundwork for the present *Code*. These pamphlets were widely circulated and put into quite general use.

In 1921 the Committee was enlarged to include representation of certain interested groups not previously participating, and work was started on the further development and integration of previous Committee publications to provide a comprehensive guide to exits and related features of life safety from fire in all classes of occupancy, to be known as the *Building Exits Code*. Various drafts were published, circulated and discussed over a period of years and the first edition of the *Building Exits Code* was published by the National Fire Protection Association in 1927. Thereafter the Committee continued its deliberations, adding new material on features not originally covered, and revising various details in the light of fire experience and practical experience in the use of the *Code*. New editions were published in 1929, 1934, 1936, 1938, 1939, 1942, and 1946 to incorporate the amendments adopted by the National Fire Protection Association.

The Cocoanut Grove Night Club fire in Boston in 1942 in which 492 lives were lost focused national attention upon the importance of adequate exits and related fire safety features. Public attention to exit matters was further stimulated by the series of hotel fires in 1946 (LaSalle, Chicago — 61 dead; Canfield, Dubuque — 19 dead; and the Winecoff, Atlanta — 119 dead). The *Building Exits Code* thereafter was used to an increasing extent for legal regulatory purposes. However, the *Code* was not in suitable form for adoption into law, as it had been drafted as a reference document containing many advisory provisions useful to designers of buildings, but not appropriate for legal use. This led to a decision by the Committee to re-edit the entire *Code* limiting the body of the text to requirements suitable for mandatory application and placing advisory and explanatory material in notes. The re-editing also involved adding to the *Code* provisions on many features in order to produce a complete document. Preliminary work was carried on concurrently with development of the 1948, 1949, 1951 and 1952 editions. The results were incorporated in the 1956 edition, and further refined in subsequent editions dated 1957, 1958, 1959, 1960, 1961 and 1963.

In 1955 separate documents, NFPA 101B and NFPA 101C, were published on nursing homes and interior finish, respectively. NFPA 101C was revised in 1956. These publications have since been withdrawn.

In 1963 the Safety to Life Committee was reconstructed. The Committee was decreased in size to include only those having very broad knowledge in fire matters and representing all interested factions. The Committee served as a review and correlating committee for seven Sectional Committees whose personnel included members having a special knowledge and interest in various portions of the *Code.*

Under the revised structure, the Sectional Committees through the Safety to Life Committee prepared the 1966 edition of the *Code* which was a complete revision of the 1963 edition. The *Code* title was changed from *Building Exits Code* to the *Code for Life Safety from Fire in Buildings and Structures,* the text was put in "code language" and all explanatory notes were placed in an appendix. The contents of the *Code* were arranged in the same general order as contents of model building codes because the *Code* is used primarily as a supplement to building codes.

The *Code* was placed on a three-year revision schedule, with new editions adopted in 1967, 1970, 1973, and 1976.

In 1977 the Committee on Safety to Life was reorganized as a Technical Committee with an Executive Committee and eleven standing subcommittees responsible for various chapters and sections. The 1981 edition contains major editorial changes including reorganization within the occupancy chapters to make them parallel to each other and the splitting of requirements for new and existing buildings into separate chapters. New chapters on Detention and Correctional Facilities were added as well as new requirements for Atriums, Apartments for the Elderly, and Ambulatory Health Care Centers.

In all of the work in developing the various sections of the *Code* the groups particularly concerned have been consulted. All public proposals have been reviewed and these proposals along with Committee proposals and the Committee's response to all proposals have been published by the NFPA for review by all concerned and any comments received have been discussed and many have been adopted by the Committee or at meetings of the NFPA. Records of the discussions and action taken by the NFPA will be found in the *Technical Committee Reports* and the *Technical Committee Documentation.*

The Committee welcomes comments and suggestions on the *Life Safety Code.* Any reader may file a request for consideration of changes. Such requests should be filed in writing, giving specific proposals and supporting data.

JAMES K. LATHROP
Editor

Acknowledgments

The editor of this Second Edition of the LIFE SAFETY CODE HANDBOOK acknowledges with gratitude the efforts of the many persons and organizations who contributed to its preparation and development. The following persons deserve special acknowledgment for their extensive work in the compilation, research, writing, and review of the materials contained herein:

Donald W. Belles

Wayne G. Carson

David P. Demers

John A. Sharry

Much of the material in this Second Edition of the LIFE SAFETY CODE HANDBOOK is based on the First Edition edited by John A. Sharry. Included with contributors to that edition of the HANDBOOK were Michael Slifka, Calvin Yuill, James Thompson, Harold Clar, Donald Belles, and Orville (Bud) Slye.

Appreciation is expressed to the NFPA staff members who attended to the countless details that went into the preparation of this HANDBOOK and especially to Keith Tower, Project Manager; Donna Fox, typing; Elizabeth Carmichael, coordination; Sharon Summers and Melissa Evans, composition; Ann Coughlin, proofreading; John Williams and Donald McGonagle, production; and Carmen Johnson, art coordination.

Finally, the editor wishes to express his sincere appreciation to Mary Strother of the NFPA staff for her invaluable assistance not only in preparing this HANDBOOK but also in preparing the 1981 *Code* itself.

Cover Design by Frank Lucas

Artwork within the commentary on the various sections of the LIFE SAFETY CODE HANDBOOK by Kathleen Desmond, Coni Porter, and Visual Presentations.

NOTE: The text and illustrations that make up the commentary on the various sections of the *Life Safety Code* are printed in color. The text of the *Code* itself is printed in black.

1

ADMINISTRATION

SECTION 1-1 TITLE

1-1.1 This *Code* shall be known as the *Life Safety Code*, may be cited as such, and is referred to herein as "this *Code*" or "the *Code*."

As discussed in the Preface to this *Life Safety Code Handbook*, the name of the *Code* was changed from the *Building Exits Code* to the *Life Safety Code* in 1966. What is significant is that the change in title expanded this document beyond a specification code for stairways, doors, and fire escapes (as the *Building Exits Code*) into a performance and specification code dealing with all factors that contribute to or center upon life safety in the event of fire.

SECTION 1-2 PURPOSE

1-2.1 The purpose of this *Code* is to establish minimum requirements that will provide a reasonable degree of safety from fire in buildings and structures.

The purpose of the *Code* is not directed to fire alone, but also covers "similar emergencies" such as explosions, since those "similar emergencies" also involve being able to leave the structure safely. However, the primary motivating forces behind this document are the need to counter the effect of fire upon the occupants of a structure, the need for occupants to find safety, and the need to provide the structural elements that will ensure safety.

1-2.2 The *Code* endeavors to avoid requirements that might involve unreasonable hardships or unnecessary inconvenience or interference with the normal use and occupancy of a building but insists upon compliance with a minimum standard for fire safety consistent with the public interest.

The requirements for existing buildings when compared to those for new construction are frequently less stringent or more flexible. This is partly due to financial considerations and an objective of having at least a minimum level of safety.

SECTION 1-3 SCOPE

1-3.1 This *Code* addresses life safety from fire and similar emergencies.

The *Code* recognizes that panic in a burning building may be uncontrollable. However, its provisions and requirements are designed to prevent the development of panic.

Experience indicates that panic seldom develops, even in the presence of potential danger, as long as occupants of buildings are moving toward exits which they can see within a reasonable distance with no obstructions or undue congestion in the path of travel. However, any uncertainty as to the location or adequacy of means of egress, the presence of smoke, or stoppage of exit travel, which may occur when a person stumbles and falls on stairs, may be conducive to panic. Panic danger is greatest when there is a large number of people in a confined area.

Recent studies focusing on human behavior under the duress of fire have re-examined the question of panic. It is now recognized that actions which the outside observer might consider to be the result of panic are in fact a rational form of behavior on the part of an occupant confronted by a clear and present danger. Human behavior in a dangerous situation may follow one of many courses. The usual choices are: (1) investigate, (2) sound an alarm, (3) rescue, (4) seek help, and (5) flee. Any of these actions would be considered normal behavior, even when done en masse. The object uppermost in the minds of most people is to avoid direct contact with a fire in the course of action taken.

In studies of recent emergency situations supposedly involving "panic," it was found that the occupants performed well. Crowds of people have been found to move through smoke- and heat-contaminated corridors or exits with only slight difficulty or discomfort. Perhaps the provisions and requirements of this *Code* in these investigated incidents were in part responsible for the lack of panic.

1-3.2   The *Code* addresses those construction, protection, and occupancy features necessary to minimize danger to life from fire, smoke, fumes, or panic.

There may not be a great deal of fire incident data or statistics to justify the existence of some of the requirements of the *Code*. However, there is a factor that needs to be considered. It is that certain building features intuitively present potential problems in a fire situation. This has resulted in the limited presence of certain hazardous features and a resulting limited presence in available fire statistics. This, in many cases, indicates that authorities having jurisdiction are doing their job.

1-3.3   The *Code* identifies the minimum criteria for the design of egress facilities so as to permit prompt escape of occupants from buildings or, where desirable, into safe areas within the building.

Evacuation into safe areas (areas of refuge) should not be overlooked as an important aspect in means of egress design. In some cases, it is not practical to consider total evacuation to the exterior. Evacuation to areas of refuge can also increase design flexibility.

1-3.4   The *Code* recognizes that life safety is more than a matter of egress and, accordingly, deals with other considerations that are essential to life safety.

There are numerous elements that impact on the ultimate level of life safety. The *Code* does address many of these items. There are, however, elements that are not dealt with. An example would be public education related to fire safety.

1-3.5 Vehicles, vessels, or other mobile structures shall be treated as buildings in regard to means-of-egress requirements when in fixed locations and occupied as buildings.

1-3.6 The *Code* does not attempt to address those general fire prevention or building construction features that are normally a function of fire prevention and building codes.

1-3.7 The prevention of accidental personal injuries during the course of normal occupancy of buildings, personal injuries incurred by an individual due to his own negligence, and the preservation of property from loss by fire have not been considered as the basis for any of the provisions of this *Code*.

The scope of the *Code* indicates that the *Code* covers only those design elements that relate to life safety from fire; however, accident prevention and the preservation of property may result from adhering to the provisions of the *Code*.

The *Life Safety Code* is not a building code, a fact stated in 1-3.6. It is meant to be used *with* a building code. Further, the *Code* clearly states that it cannot "save" everyone in an occupancy even if all the design and operational requirements of the *Code* are met. In particular, those people who accidentally or deliberately initiate a fire or who are close by the point of ignition are beyond the *Code*'s capability to protect totally or, in some cases, partially.

SECTION 1-4   APPLICATION

1-4.1 The *Code* applies to both new construction and existing buildings. In various chapters there are specific provisions for existing buildings which may differ from those for new construction.

This concept is essential to understanding the intent of the *Code*, which is to achieve at least a minimal level of life safety in all structures and in all occupancies. To this end, there are provisions throughout the document that either specifically apply to existing buildings or that are specifically modified for existing buildings. This represents an attempt to limit the retroactive provisions of the *Code* to existing buildings. If no special provisions are made for existing structures, then the provisions for *new* construction apply, an approach quite different from that of a building code. This applies to the entire text: where life safety is involved, there is no reason for an existing structure not to conform to the *Code*. As a minimum, the *Code* will modify or will alter the "new" requirements as they are applied to "existing" buildings. Yet, in many instances, the *Code* will not alter a basic provision at the expense of life safety, and will call for its application in both "new" and "existing" buildings. In recognition of the fact that the *Life Safety Code* is a general code that applies across the board to all structures and occupancies, the *Code* is designed to be flexible in the event of the extenuating circumstances that may exist in an individual case. Since only the individuals involved can properly assess these extenuating circumstances, the authority having jurisdiction is recognized as the best judge of to what extent the *Code* may be further modified. However, the *Code* does establish the bottom limit so that reasonable life safety against the hazards of fire, explosion, and panic is provided and maintained.

1-4.2 Where specific requirements contained in Chapters 8 through 30 differ from similar requirements contained in Chapters 1 through 7, the requirements of Chapters 8 through 30 shall govern.

Paragraph 1-4.2 indicates the general arrangement of the *Life Safety Code*. The first seven chapters contain administrative definitions and fundamental requirements establishing minimum acceptable criteria for all types of occupancies. Chapters 8 through 30 of the *Code* establish criteria for life safety based upon specific occupancies. If conflicts between the general requirements and specific occupancy requirements occur, the requirements contained in the specific occupancy chapter apply.

1-4.3 Alterations shall not diminish the level of life safety below that which exists prior to the alteration. Life safety features which do not meet the requirements for new buildings but exceed the requirements for existing buildings shall not be further diminished. Life safety features in excess of those required for new construction are not required to be maintained. In no case shall the resulting life safety be less than that required for existing buildings.

It should be recognized that all changes and alterations that are made in occupancies must be in conformance with the minimum provisions of the *Code*. It may not be practical if the structure involved cannot accommodate the design provisions for new construction. For example, an existing hospital may have a corridor 6 ft (1.83 m) wide which, if renovated, is required to be 8 ft (2.44 m) wide. However, if the building's column spacing is 7 ft by 7 ft (4.55 m²) (a dimension common to fire-resistive multistory buildings), there is no way to achieve an 8-ft (2.44-m) corridor width. Therefore, the authority having jurisdiction would have to decide if a 6-ft (1.83-m) wide or even a 7-ft (2.13-m) wide corridor is adequate or if additional provisions may be required to accommodate a corridor less than 8 ft (2.44 m) in width.

The following is an example of what is intended by 1-4.3. In a hospital which has 6-ft (182.8-cm) corridors, these corridors cannot be reduced in width even though the requirements for existing buildings do not require 6-ft (182.8-cm) wide corridors. However, if a hospital had 10-ft (304.8-cm) wide corridors they may be reduced to 8 ft (243.8 cm) which is the requirement for new construction. If the hospital corridor was 3 ft (91.44 cm) wide it would have to be increased to 4 ft (121.9 cm). If alterations require replacement of a portion of a hospital corridor wall, this portion of the wall should be increased to 1-hour fire resistance in accordance with the requirements for new construction. However, it would not be required that the corridor width be increased to 8 ft (243.8 cm) unless it was practical to do so.

Paragraph 1-4.3 does not specify the degree or magnitude of a change or alteration at which conformance with the provisions of the *Code* becomes mandatory. Both minor and major alterations and changes must comply. The authority having jurisdiction may still modify the *Code*'s requirements or accept equivalent design options based on the special circumstances and the technical documentation presented.

1-4.4   Additions shall conform to the provisions for new construction.

1-4.5   Where two or more classes of occupancy occur in the same building or structure, and are so intermingled that separate safeguards are impracticable, means of egress facilities, construction, protection, and other safeguards shall comply with the most restrictive life safety requirements of the occupancies involved.

Exception: As otherwise specified in Chapters 8 through 30.

1-4.6   The authority having jurisdiction shall determine the adequacy of means of egress and other measures for life safety from fire in accordance with the provisions of this *Code*. In existing buildings the authority having jurisdiction may grant exceptions from this *Code*, but only when it is clearly evident that reasonable safety is provided.

In existing buildings it is not always practical to strictly apply the provisions of this *Code*. Physical limitations may require disproportionate effort or expense with little increase in life safety. In such cases the authority having jurisdiction should be satisfied that reasonable life safety is assured.

In existing buildings it is intended that any condition which represents a serious threat to life be mitigated by application of appropriate safeguards.

It is not intended to require modifications for conditions which do not represent a significant threat to life even though the circumstances are not literally in compliance with the *Code*.

1-4.7 Provisions in Excess of Code Requirements.   Nothing in this *Code* shall be construed to prohibit a better type of building construction, more exits, or otherwise safer conditions than the minimum requirements specified in this *Code*.

Because the *Life Safety Code* is a minimum code, it never prohibits the use of a design that exceeds the provisions of the *Code*. In practice, however, economic considerations usually prevent the use of a design that exceeds the written provisions of the *Code*.

There have been situations, however, that by exceeding the *Code* provisions, money was saved or generated. A specific example was a high-rise hotel project that was not required to have complete automatic sprinkler protection. By including sprinklers, a stairway was eliminated due to allowable increases in travel distance, and many revenue-producing guest rooms were put in the vacated space.

SECTION 1-5   EQUIVALENCY CONCEPTS

Section 1-5 helps to establish one of the most sensitive and the most critical design criteria found in the *Code*. It takes the *Life Safety Code* beyond the scope of a typical general specification code into that of a goal-oriented performance code, where state-of-the-art fire protection design is permissible and even desirable.

1-5.1   Nothing in this *Code* is intended to prevent the use of systems, methods, or devices of equivalent or superior quality, strength, fire resistance, effectiveness, durability, and safety to those prescribed by this *Code*, providing technical documentation is submitted to the authority having jurisdiction to demonstrate equivalency and the system, method, or device is approved for the intended purpose.

Paragraph 1-5.1 recognizes that a code can only reflect what is known and commonly practiced in fire protection design. Considering the rate at which technology advances, a major breakthrough or even a simple change in existing hardware can mean the creation of design capabilities not contemplated at the time that the current edition of the *Code* was written. In realization of the limitations of a written code, Section 1-5.1 permits the use of "systems, methods, or devices of equivalent or superior quality, strength, fire resistance, effectiveness, durability, and safety"; the stipulation is that technical documentation be submitted to the authority having jurisdiction, justifying the use of the new approach.

This paragraph is important for two reasons. First, it recognizes that the judgment of the authority having jurisdiction is instrumental in achieving the letter and intent of the *Code*. Secondly, it states that the *Code* is neither limited nor bound by the written provisions of the *Code*. Thus it allows for the development of new technology, new systems, new devices, and new designs not recognized by or written into the *Code*. This permits the designer and the authority having jurisdiction to pursue the state-of-the-art in applying fire protection engineering for the purpose of achieving life safety. It also gives the *Code* a broader perspective than that of a specification code which only concerns itself with the construction details of individual items. In fact, there was little assurance that the elements found in a specification code would necessarily fit together into a design approach that achieved fire safety. The paragraph actually opts for an approach to design that goes beyond the individual elements of the *Code*, providing that technical documentation is available to support the design.

1-5.2 The specific requirements of this *Code* for existing buildings may be modified by the authority having jurisdiction to allow alternative arrangements that will secure as nearly equivalent safety to life from fire as practical, but in no case shall the modification afford less safety to life than compliance with the corresponding provisions contained in this *Code* for existing buildings. (*See also 1-5.1.*)

The allowances made for new technology in 1-5.1 not only affect work on new designs, but may also have a retroactive impact on existing buildings. To further the flexibility of the *Code* requirements in instances where new technology can be effectively incorporated into existing structures, 1-5.2 allows the authority having jurisdiction to modify the requirements applicable to existing buildings. These modifications must result in a level of safety equal or greater to that attained by a strict compliance with those *Code* provisions which would normally apply.

Paragraph 1-5.2 also allows the authority having jurisdiction to exercise some flexibility in dealing with "historically preserved" buildings. These buildings may have numerous design defects such as open stair shafts or highly combustible interior finishes. To attain an equivalent level of safety, the authority having jurisdiction may require the use of sprinkler systems, smoke detection systems, voice alarm systems for staged evacuation, smoke control systems, etc., to overcome the built-in design defects. This would be done in lieu of rebuilding the structure to the written *Code* requirements, which might mean totally destroying the historical character of the structure that is to be preserved. The design alternatives used in such an instance may actually raise the level of safety many times over that which is already found in the existing structure. They must, however, provide equivalent safety to life or greater safety to life than the written *Code* provisions.

SECTION 1-6 OCCUPANCY (*See also Section 30-1.*)

1-6.1 No new construction or existing building shall be occupied in whole or in part in violation of the provisions of this *Code*.

1-6.2 Existing buildings that are occupied at the time of adoption of the *Code* may be continued in use provided:

(a) The occupancy classification remains the same.

(b) No serious life safety hazard exists that would constitute an imminent threat.

(c) Only those requirements whose application would be clearly impractical in the judgment of the authority having jurisdiction shall be modified.

Because the *Code* is to be applied retroactively, 1-6.1 prohibits the use of existing, nonconforming facilities. Paragraph 1-6.2 states that this retroactive enforcement may be modified if the occupancy has not been changed since the adoption of the *Code*, the *Code* requirements prove to be impractical, and no serious life safety hazard exists which would constitute an imminent threat.

1-6.3 Buildings or portions of buildings may be occupied during construction, repair, alterations, or additions only if all means of egress and all fire protection features are in place and continuously maintained for the part occupied.

Paragraph 1-6.3 helps to control a now common practice, the occupying of a partially completed structure (done usually to obtain rent revenue). The *Code* first requires that all exit facilities for the part occupied be complete. In many cases the exit facilities, although completed, may be blocked with supplies and equipment needed for the ongoing construction, or the exits may be locked to limit access to parts of the building still under construction. If any of these conditions are found, occupancy should be absolutely prohibited. One must bear in mind that the incidence of fire is more frequent, and therefore more likely, during construction, alterations, repairs, etc. Fire fatalities may occur because a required stairway has been closed for repairs or removed for rebuilding, or because a required automatic sprinkler system has been shut off to change piping. Extra caution and concern must be exercised to ensure adequate exit capacity and arrangement during periods of construction in any occupied building. Secondly, all fire protection features must also be in place and continuously maintained for similar reasons.

1-6.4 Changes of Occupancy. A change from one occupancy classification to another in any building or structure whether necessitating a physical alteration or not may be made only if such building or structure conforms with the requirements of this *Code* applying to new construction of the proposed new use.

Paragraph 1-6.4 states that whenever an occupancy's classification changes, the building or space used by that occupancy must be in compliance with the provisions for *new* construction for the *new* occupancy. The reason for this can be clearly seen in the example of a shoe store being changed into a restaurant; the restaurant would probably not have adequate exit facilities.

2
FUNDAMENTAL REQUIREMENTS

The goals toward which the provisions of this *Code* are aimed are specified in Chapter 2. The achievement of these goals ensures a reasonable level of life safety in building design and arrangement. Simply stated they are:

1. To provide for adequate exits without dependence on any one single safeguard,
2. To ensure that construction is sufficient to provide structural integrity during a fire while occupants are exiting,
3. To provide exits that have been designed to the size, shape, and nature of the occupancy,
4. To ensure that the exits are clear, unobstructed, and unlocked,
5. To ensure that the exits and routes of escape are clearly marked so that there is no confusion in reaching an exit,
6. To provide adequate lighting,
7. To ensure early warning of fire,
8. To provide for back-up or redundant exit arrangements,
9. To ensure the suitable enclosure of vertical openings, and
10. To make allowances for those design criteria that go beyond the *Code* provisions and are tailored to the normal use and needs of the occupancy in question.

2-1 Every building or structure, new or old, designed for human occupancy shall be provided with exits sufficient to permit the prompt escape of occupants in case of fire or other emergency. The design of exits and other safeguards shall be such that reliance for safety to life in case of fire or other emergency will not depend solely on any single safeguard; additional safeguards shall be provided for life safety in case any single safeguard is ineffective due to some human or mechanical failure.

2-2 Every building or structure shall be so constructed, arranged, equipped, maintained and operated as to avoid undue danger to the lives and safety of its occupants from fire, smoke, fumes, or resulting panic during the period of time reasonably necessary for escape from the building or structure in case of fire or other emergency.

2-3 Every building or structure shall be provided with exits of kinds, numbers, location, and capacity appropriate to the individual building or structure, with due regard to the character of the occupancy, the number of persons exposed, the fire protection available, and the height and type of construction of the building or structure, to afford all occupants convenient facilities for escape.

2-4 In every building or structure, exits shall be so arranged and maintained as to provide free and unobstructed egress from all parts of the building or structure at all times when it is occupied. No lock or fastening shall be installed to prevent free escape from the inside of any building.

Exception: Locks shall be permitted in mental health, detention, or corrective institutions where supervisory personnel are continually on duty and effective provisions are made to remove occupants in case of fire or other emergency.

Problems with locking devices have consistently been a contributing factor in multiple fatality fires in correctional facilities. Some of these problems include malfunctioning locks, inability to locate keys in smoke or in the dark (frequently caused by smoke obscuration of lighting), locks jammed from toothpicks and chewing gum, and locks made inoperative from pushing against the door. All of these problems have shown up in the fire record. Many times, prior to a fire, it might have been assumed that in the event of an emergency there would be effective provisions for unlocking locks and that personnel would be continually on duty. Extreme care must be exercised to ensure that locks can and will be unlocked or that alternate methods of providing life safety, other than total evacuation, are provided.[1,2]

2-5 Every exit shall be clearly visible or the route to reach it shall be conspicuously indicated in such a manner that every occupant of every building or structure who is physically and mentally capable will readily know the direction of escape from any point. Each means of egress, in its entirety, shall be so arranged or marked that the way to a place of safety is indicated in a clear manner. Any doorway or passageway that is not an exit or a way to reach an exit, but is capable of being confused with an exit shall be so arranged or marked to prevent occupant confusion with acceptable exits. Every effort shall be taken to avoid occupants mistakenly traveling into dead end spaces in a fire emergency.

2-6 When artificial illumination is required in a building or structure, exit facilities will be included in the lighting design in an adequate and reliable manner.

2-7 Fire alarm facilities shall be provided, where necessary, to warn occupants of the existence of fire in every building or structure of such size, arrangement, or occupancy that a fire may not itself provide adequate occupant warning. Fire alarms will alert occupants to initiate escape. Fire alarms facilitate the orderly conduct of fire exit drills.

Several multiple fatality fire incidents in recent years, especially in hotels, have shown that fire alarm sounding devices were inadequate to alert building occupants. This was because occupants either could not hear the alarm or did not recognize the alarm as a fire alarm signal. Confusion with telephones or alarm clocks has been reported. Authorities having jurisdiction must ensure that sounding devices can be heard over ambient noise levels and can be recognized as fire alarm signals.[3,4]

2-8 Two means of egress, as a minimum, shall be provided in every building or structure, section, or area where the size, occupancy, and arrangement endangers occupants attempting to use a single means of egress which is blocked by fire or smoke. The two means of egress shall be arranged to minimize the possibility that both may be impassable by the same fire or emergency condition.

2-9 Every vertical way of exit and other vertical opening between floors of a building shall be suitably enclosed or protected, as necessary, to afford reasonable safety to occupants while using exits and to prevent spread of fire, smoke, or fumes through vertical openings from floor to floor before occupants have entered exits.

2-10 Compliance with this *Code* shall not be construed as eliminating or reducing the necessity for other provisions for safety of persons using a structure under normal occupancy conditions. Also no provision of the *Code* shall be construed as requiring or permitting any condition that may be hazardous under normal occupancy conditions.

The provisions of this *Code* will not necessarily provide a building suitable for use by physically handicapped people. Refer to ANSI A117.1.[5]

References Cited in Commentary

[1]Best, Richard, "The Seminole County Jail Fire," *Fire Journal*, Vol. 70, No. 1, January 1976, pp. 5-10, 17.
[2]Demers, David P., "Fire in Prisons," *Fire Journal*, Vol. 72, No. 2, March 1978, pp. 29-42.
[3]————, "Familiar Problems Cause 10 Deaths in Hotel Fire," *Fire Journal*, Vol. 74, No. 1, January 1980, pp. 52-56.
[4]————, "Ten Die in Greece, New York Hotel Fire," *Fire Journal*, Vol. 73, No. 4, July 1979, pp. 25-30.
[5]*Specifications for Making Buildings and Facilities Accessible to, and Usable by, the Physically Handicapped*, ANSI A117.1—1961, American National Standards Institute, 1430 Broadway, New York, NY 10018 (reaff. 1971).

3

DEFINITIONS

SECTION 3-1   GENERAL

3-1.1   The following terms, for the purposes of this *Code*, shall have the meanings given in this chapter, if not otherwise modified for a specific occupancy.

3-1.2   Words used in the present tense include the future; words used in the masculine gender include the feminine and neuter; the singular number includes the plural and the plural the singular.

3-1.3   Where terms are not defined in this chapter, they shall have their ordinarily accepted meanings or such as the context may imply.

SECTION 3-2   DEFINITIONS

Addition.   An extension or increase in floor area or height of a building or structure.

Apartment Building.   *(See Section 18-1 or 19-1.)*

Approved.   Means "acceptable to the authority having jurisdiction."

The National Fire Protection Association does not approve, inspect or certify any installations, procedures, equipment or materials nor does it approve or evaluate testing laboratories. In determining the acceptability of installations or procedures, equipment or materials, the authority having jurisdiction may base acceptance on compliance with NFPA or other appropriate standards. In the absence of such standards, said authority may require evidence of proper installation, procedure or use. The authority having jurisdiction may also refer to the listings or labeling practices of an organization concerned with product evaluations which is in a position to determine compliance with appropriate standards for the current production of listed items.

Area.   See Floor Area.

Arena Stage.   A stage or platform open on at least three sides to audience seating. It may be with or without overhead scene handling facilities.

Atrium.   A floor opening or series of floor openings connecting two or more stories that is covered at the top of the series of openings and is used for purposes other than an enclosed stairway; elevator hoistway; or utility shaft used for plumbing, electrical, air conditioning, or communication facilities.

13

Authority Having Jurisdiction. The "authority having jurisdiction" is the organization, office, or individual responsible for "approving" equipment, an installation, or a procedure.

> The phrase "authority having jurisdiction" is used in NFPA Documents in a broad manner since jurisdictions and "approval" agencies vary as do their responsibilities. Where public safety is primary, the "authority having jurisdiction" may be a federal, state, local, or other regional department or individual such as a fire chief, fire marshal, chief of a fire prevention bureau, labor department, health department, building official, electrical inspector, or others having statutory authority. For insurance purposes, an insurance inspection department rating bureau, or other insurance company representative may be the "authority having jurisdiction." In many circumstances, the property owner or his designated agent assumes the role of the "authority having jurisdiction"; at government installations, the commanding officer or departmental official may be the "authority having jurisdiction."

Automatic. Providing a function without the necessity of human intervention.

Building. Any structure used or intended for supporting or sheltering any use or occupancy. The term building shall be construed as if followed by the words "or portions thereof." (*See Structure.*)

Building, Existing. Any structure erected prior to the adoption of this *Code* or for which a permit for construction has been issued.

Business Occupancy. (*See Section 4-1.*)

Child Day-Care Centers. (*See Section 10-7 or 11-7.*)

Combustible. Capable of undergoing combustion.

Combustion. A chemical process that involves oxidation sufficient to produce light or heat.

Common Atmosphere (Educational Occupancies). (*See Section 10-1 or 11-1.*)

Correctional Occupancies. (*See Section 4-1.*)

Court. An open, uncovered, unoccupied space, unobstructed to the sky, bounded on three or more sides by exterior building walls.

Court, Enclosed. A court bounded on all sides by the exterior walls of a building or exterior walls and lot lines on which walls are allowable.

Critical Radiant Flux. The level of incident radiant heat energy on a floor covering system at the most distant flameout point as determined by the test procedure of *Standard Method of Test for Critical Radiant Flux of Floor Covering Systems Using a Radiant Heat Energy Source*, NFPA 253. The unit of measurement of critical radiant flux is watts per square centimeter (watts/cm^2).

Detention Occupancies. (*See Section 4-1.*)

Dormitories. (*See Section 16-1 or 17-1.*)

Educational Occupancies. (*See Section 10-1 or 11-1.*)

Existing. That which is already in existence at the date when this *Code* goes into effect, as existing buildings, structures, or exit facilities.

Exit.   That portion of a means of egress that is separated from all other spaces of the building or structure by construction or equipment as required in 5-1.3.1 to provide a protected way of travel to the exit discharge.

Exit Access.   That portion of a means of egress which leads to an entrance to an exit.

Exit Discharge.   That portion of a means of egress between the termination of an exit and a public way.

Family Day-Care Home.   (*See Section 10-9 or 11-9.*)

Fire Barrier.   A fire barrier is a continuous membrane, either vertical or horizontal, such as a wall or floor assembly, that is designed and constructed with a specified fire resistance rating to limit the spread of fire and which will also restrict the movement of smoke. Such barriers may have protected openings. (*See 6-2.2.*)

Fire Compartment.   A fire compartment is a space within a building that is enclosed by fire barriers on all sides, including the top and bottom. (*See 6-2.2.*)

When fire compartments utilize the outside walls of a building, it is not intended that the outside walls be specifically fire resistance rated unless required by other standards. Likewise, it is not intended for outside windows or doors to be protected unless specifically required for exposure protection by another section of this *Code* or by other standards.

Fire Resistance Rating.   The time, in minutes or hours, that materials or assemblies have withstood a fire exposure as established in accordance with the test procedures of *Standard Methods of Fire Tests of Building Construction and Materials*, NFPA 251.

Fire Window.   A window assembly, including frame, wired glass, and hardware that under the *Standard for Fire Tests of Window Assemblies*, NFPA 257 meets the fire protective requirements for the location in which it is to be used.

Flame Spread.   The propagation of flame over a surface. (*See Section 6-5.*)

Flexible Plan Educational Buildings.   (*See Section 10-1 or 11-1.*)

Floor Area, Gross.   Gross floor area shall be the floor area within the inside perimeter of the outside walls of the building under consideration with no deduction for hallways, stairs, closets, thickness of interior walls, columns, or other features. Where the term area is used elsewhere in this *Code*, it shall be understood to be gross area unless otherwise specified.

Floor Area, Net.   Net floor area shall be the actual occupied area, not including accessory unoccupied areas or thickness of walls.

The net area is arrived at after deductions have been made for the space that structural features and fixtures occupy. This would include hallways, stairs, closets, interior walls, columns, counters, display racks, tables, bars, dividers, planters, displays, and other items which take up space that might otherwise have been used for human occupancy.

General Industrial Occupancies.   *(See Section 28-1.)*

Group Day-Care Homes.   *(See Section 10-8 or 11-8.)*

Guard.   A vertical protective barrier erected along exposed edges of stairways, balconies, etc.

Handrail.   A bar, pipe, or similar member designed to furnish persons with a handhold. (A handrail, if of suitable design, may also serve as part of a guard.)

Hazardous Areas.   Areas of structures, buildings, or parts thereof used for purposes that involve highly combustible, highly flammable, or explosive products or materials that are likely to burn with extreme rapidity or that may produce poisonous fumes or gases, including highly toxic or noxious alkalies, acids, or other liquids or chemicals that involve flame, fume, explosive, poisonous or irritant hazards; also uses that cause division of material into fine particles or dust subject to explosion or spontaneous combustion, and uses that constitute a high fire hazard because of the form, character, or volume of the material used.

Health Care Occupancies.   *(See Section 4-1.)*

High Hazard Industrial Occupancy.   *(See Section 28-1.)*

Horizontal Exit.   *(See 5-1.2.5.)*

Hospital.   *(See Section 12-1 or 13-1.)*

Hotel.   *(See Section 16-1 or 17-1.)*

Industrial Occupancy.   *(See Section 4-1.)*

Interior Finish.   *(See Section 6-5.)*

Interior Floor Finish.   *(See Section 6-5.)*

Interior Room (Educational Occupancies).   *(See Section 10-1 or 11-1.)*

Limited-Combustible.   As applied to a building construction material, means a material, not complying with the definition of noncombustible material, that, in the form in which it is used, has a potential heat value not exceeding 3500 Btu per lb (8.14 $\times$ 10^6 J/Kg),[1] and complies with one of the following paragraphs (a) or (b).

Materials subject to increase in combustibility or flame spread rating beyond the limits herein established through the effects of age, moisture, or other atmospheric condition shall be considered combustible.

(a) Materials having a structural base of noncombustible material with a surfacing not exceeding a thickness of ⅛ in. (3.175 mm) that has a flame spread rating not greater than 50.

(b) Materials, in the form and thickness used, other than as described in (a), having neither a flame spread rating greater than 25 nor evidence of continued progressive combustion and of such composition that surfaces that would be exposed by cutting through the material on any plane would have neither a flame spread rating greater than 25 nor evidence of continued progressive combustion.

Load, Live.   The weight superimposed by the use and occupancy of the building, not including the wind load, earthquake load, or dead load.

Lodging Homes.   *(See Section 20-1.)*

---

[1]See *Standard Test Method for Potential Heat of Building Materials*, NFPA 259, and *Standard Types of Building Construction*, NFPA 220.

Means of Egress.   (*See Section 5-1.*)

Means of Escape.   A way out of a building or structure that does not conform to the strict definition of means of egress but does provide an alternate way out.

Mercantile Occupancies.   (*See Section 4-1.*)

Noncombustible.   A material which in the form in which it is used and under the conditions anticipated will not aid combustion or add appreciable heat to an ambient fire. Materials, when tested in accordance with *Standard Test Method for Behavior of Materials in a Vertical Tube Furnace at 750°C*, ASTM E136 and conforming to the criteria contained in Section 6 of the referenced standard shall be considered as noncombustible.

Nursing Homes.   (*See Section 12-1 or 13-1.*)

Occupancy.   The purpose for which a building or portion thereof is used or intended to be used.

Occupant Load.   The total number of persons that may occupy a building or portion thereof at any one time.

One- and Two- (1-2-) Family Dwellings.   (*See Section 22-1.*)

Open Industrial Structures.   (*See Section 28-1.*)

Open Plan Educational Buildings.   (*See Section 10-1 or 11-1.*)

Outpatient (Ambulatory) Clinics.   (*See Section 12-1 or 13-1.*)

Outside Stairs.   Outside stairs include stairs in which at least one side is open to the outer air. (*See 5-2.5.*)

Penal Occupancies.   (*See Section 4-1.*)

Place of Assembly.   (*See Section 4-1.*)

Platform, Enclosed (Stage).   (*See Section 8-1 or 9-1.*)

Plenum.   An air compartment or chamber to which one or more ducts are connected and which forms part of an air distribution system.

Proscenium Wall.   (*See Section 8-1 or 9-1.*)

Public Way.   Any street, alley or other similar parcel of land essentially open to the outside air, deeded, dedicated, or otherwise permanently appropriated to the public for public use and having a clear width and height of not less than 10 ft (304.8 cm).

Ramp.   An inclined floor surface. (*See 5-2.6.*)

Residential Occupancies.   (*See Section 4-1.*)

Residential-Custodial Care Facility.   (*See Section 12-1 or 13-1.*)

Room (Educational Occupancies).   (*See Section 10-1 or 11-1.*)

Rooming House.   (*See Section 20-1.*)

Self-closing.   Equipped with an approved device which will ensure closing after having been opened.

Separate Atmosphere (Educational Occupancies).   (*See Section 10-1 or 11-1.*)

Separate Means of Egress (Educational Occupancies).   (*See Section 10-1 or 11-1.*)

Smoke Barrier. A smoke barrier is a continuous membrane, either vertical or horizontal, such as a wall, floor, or ceiling assembly, that is designed and constructed to restrict the movement of smoke. A smoke barrier may or may not have a fire resistance rating. Such barriers may have protected openings. (*See Section 6-3.*)

Smoke Compartment. A smoke compartment is a space within a building enclosed by smoke barriers or fire barriers on all sides, including the top and bottom. (*See Section 6-3.*)

When smoke compartments utilize the outside walls of a building, it is not intended that the outside walls or any doors or windows therein be capable of resisting the passage of smoke.

Smoke Detector. A device which senses visible or invisible particles of combustion.

Special Purpose Industrial Occupancies. (*See Section 28-1.*)

Stage. (*See Section 8-1 or 9-1.*)

Storage Occupancy. (*See Section 4-1.*)

Stores. (*See Section 24-1 or 25-1.*)

Story. That portion of a building included between the upper surface of a floor and the upper surface of the floor or roof next above.

Street. Any public thoroughfare (street, avenue, boulevard) 30 ft (914.4 cm) or more in width that has been dedicated or deeded to the public for public use and is accessible for use by the fire department in fighting fire. Enclosed spaces and tunnels, even though used for vehicular and pedestrian traffic, are not considered as streets for the purposes of the *Code*.

Street Floor. Any story or floor level accessible from the street or from outside the building at ground level with floor level at main entrance not more than three risers above or below ground level at these points, and so arranged and utilized as to qualify as the main floor. Where, due to differences in street levels, there are two or more stories accessible from the street, each is a street floor for the purposes of the *Code*. Where there is no floor level within the specified limits for a street floor above or below ground level, the building shall be considered as having no street floor.

Structure. That which is built or constructed. The term structure shall be construed as if followed by the words "or portion thereof." (*See Building.*)

Thrust Stage. (*See Section 8-1 or 9-1.*)

Unit of Exit Width. (*See Section 5-3.*)

Vertical Opening. An opening through a floor or roof.

Yard. An open, unoccupied space other than a court, unobstructed from the ground to the sky, except where specifically provided by the *Code*, on the lot on which a building is situated.

REFERENCES CITED BY *CODE*

(These publications comprise a part of the requirements to the extent called for by the Code.*)*

NFPA 220, *Standard Types of Building Construction*, NFPA, Boston, 1979.

NFPA 251, *Standard Methods of Fire Tests of Building Construction and Materials*, NFPA, Boston, 1979.

NFPA 253, *Standard Method of Test for Critical Radiant Flux of Floor Covering Systems Using a Radiant Heat Energy Source*, NFPA, Boston, 1978.

NFPA 257, *Standard for Fire Tests of Window Assemblies*, NFPA, Boston, 1980.

NFPA 259, *Standard Test Method for Potential Heat of Building Materials*, NFPA, Boston, 1976.

Standard Test Method for Behavior of Materials in a Vertical Tube Furnace at 750°C, ASTM E136—1979, American Society for Testing and Materials, 1916 Race Street, Philadelphia, PA 19103.

4

CLASSIFICATION OF OCCUPANCY AND HAZARD OF CONTENTS

SECTION 4-1 CLASSIFICATION OF OCCUPANCY

The occupancy groupings found in Chapter 4 are based upon design features and occupancy patterns that are particular to certain types of occupancies, the main concern being to achieve a certain level of life safety for each. These groups are:

Assembly. These occupancies generally house large groups of people who are unfamiliar with the space, and therefore subject to indecision about the best means of escape should an emergency occur.

Educational. Primarily, the *Code* is concerned with the large numbers of young people found in school buildings. In some cases (as with the day-care and preschool ages), they may even have to be carried out.

Health Care. The overriding concern with these occupancies is that no matter how many exits are called for or provided, the occupants are not necessarily able or free to use them. They might be immobile, perhaps wired to monitoring equipment, debilitated, or recovering from surgery; or they might be in some way handicapped. The *Code*, in this instance, calls for a design that stresses horizontal movement and compartmentation. It recognizes that the occupants must be provided enough protection to enable them to survive the fire by staying *in* the structure, at least temporarily, *during* the fire.

Detention and Correctional. Many of the concerns for life safety in detention and correctional facilities are similar to those in health care facilities; however, there are additional special problems. Among these problems are security, inmate population, ignition potential, and training of staff.

The large number of multiple-fatality fires in correctional facilities during the mid-1970s led to the formation of a new subcommittee on correctional facilities and, in the 1981 edition of the *Code*, new chapters for this type of occupancy.

Residential. The main concern is that the occupants will be asleep for a portion (sometimes the major portion) of the time they occupy the building. Thus, they will be unaware of an incipient fire and may be trapped before actions can be taken to exit.

Mercantile. As with places of assembly, large numbers of people are gathered in a space relatively unfamiliar to them, sometimes in the presence of a sizable fuel load.

21

Business. The problems associated with high-rise office occupancies have been recognized. Provisions contained in the *Code* are based on the fact that a rapid evacuation (and possibly any evacuation at all) may not be physically possible in multistory office buildings. As in health care occupancies, occupants may have to survive a fire while located *within* the structure.

Industrial. Because of the special circumstances involved, the *Code* relates the hazard of the occupancy to its incipient fuel load, and considers the hazard of sizable industrial processes (including their unique or unusual features) when determining the requirements for exiting.

Storage. As in the case of industrial occupancies, fuel load and fuel arrangement, as well as a relatively low human population, are the basis for the *Code* provisions.

4-1.1 A building or structure shall be classified as follows, subject to the ruling of the authority having jurisdiction in case of question as to proper classification in any individual case.

A detailed breakdown of occupancy classification is available in NFPA 901, *Uniform Coding for Fire Protection.*[1]

4-1.2 Assembly (*for requirements see Chapters 8 and 9*). Places of assembly include, but are not limited to, all buildings or portions of buildings used for gathering together 50 or more persons for such purposes as deliberation, worship, entertainment, amusement, or awaiting transportation. Assembly occupancies include:

Theaters
Motion picture theaters
Assembly halls
Auditoriums
Exhibition halls
Museums
Libraries
Skating rinks
Gymnasiums
Bowling lanes
Pool rooms
Armories
Restaurants
Churches

Dance halls
Club rooms
Passenger stations and terminals of
    air, surface, underground, and
    marine public transportation facil-
    ities
Recreation piers
Courtrooms
Conference rooms
Drinking establishments
Mortuary chapels
College and university classrooms,
    50 persons and over

Occupancy of any room or space for assembly purposes by less than 50 persons in a building of other occupancy and incidental to such other occupancy shall be classed as part of the other occupancy and subject to the provisions applicable thereto.

Such occupancies are characterized by the presence or potential presence of crowds, with a subsequent panic hazard in case of fire or other emergency. They are generally open to the public or, in some cases, are open to the public only on occasion; the occupants, present voluntarily, are not ordinarily subject to discipline or control. Generally, such buildings are occupied by able-bodied persons and are not used for sleeping purposes. The need for alternate exit routes for small commercial places of assembly (such as restaurants, lounges, theaters, etc.) with capacities of as few as 50 persons is specially treated in this method of classification. Special conference rooms, snack areas, etc., incidental to and under the control of the management of other occupancies (such as offices) fall under the 50-person limitation.

4-1.3 Educational (*for requirements see Chapters 10 and 11*). Educational occupancies include all buildings used for the gathering of groups of 6 or more persons for purposes of instruction. Educational occupancies include:

Schools	Nursery schools
Academies	Kindergartens
	Child day-care facilities

Other occupancies associated with educational institutions shall be in accordance with the appropriate parts of this *Code*.

Exception: Licensed day-care facilities shall include those of any capacity.

In cases where instruction is incidental to some other occupancy, the section of this *Code* governing such other occupancy shall apply.

Educational occupancy is distinguished from assembly occupancy in that the same occupants are regularly present and are subject to discipline and control. Educational occupancies include buildings or portions of buildings used for educational purposes through the twelfth grade by 6 or more persons for 4 hours per day or more than 12 hours per week. College classroom buildings are considered Business Occupancies.

4-1.4 Health Care (*for requirements see Chapters 12 and 13*). Health care occupancies are those used for purposes such as medical or other treatment or care of persons suffering from physical or mental illness, disease or infirmity; and for the care of infants, convalescents, or infirm aged persons. Health care occupancies provide sleeping facilities for the occupants or are occupied by persons who are mostly incapable of self-preservation because of age, physical or mental disability, or because of security measures not under the occupants' control.

Health care occupancies are treated in this *Code* in the following groups.

(a) Health care facilities

Hospitals
Nursing homes

(b) Residential-custodial care

Nurseries
Homes for the infirm aged
Mentally retarded care institutions

(c) Supervisory care facilities

(d) Ambulatory care facilities

4-1.5 Detention and Correctional Occupancies (*for requirements see Chapters 14 and 15*). Detention and correctional occupancies (also known as Residential-Restrained Care Institutions) are those used to house occupants under some degree of restraint or security. Detention and correctional occupancies are occupied by persons who are mostly incapable of self-preservation because of security measures not under the occupants' control.

Detention and correctional occupancies include:
>   Residential-restrained care
>   Penal institutions
>   Reformatories
>   Jails
>   Detention centers
>   Correctional centers

4-1.6 Residential (*for requirements see Chapters 16 through 23*). Residential occupancies are those occupancies in which sleeping accommodations are provided for normal residential purposes and include all buildings designed to provide sleeping accommodations.

Exception: Those classified under Health Care or Detention and Correctional Occupancies.

Residential occupancies are treated separately in this *Code* in the following groups:

(a) Hotels (*Chapters 16 and 17*)
   Motels
(b) Apartments (*Chapters 18 and 19*)
   Apartments for the Elderly
(c) Dormitories (*Chapters 16 and 17*)
   Orphanages for age 6 years and older
(d) Lodging or rooming houses (*Chapter 20*)
(e) One- and two-family dwellings (*Chapter 22*)

4-1.7 Mercantile (*for requirements see Chapters 24 and 25*). Mercantile occupancies include stores, markets, and other rooms, buildings, or structures for the display and sale of merchandise. Included in this occupancy group are:

Supermarkets	Shopping centers
Department stores	Drugstores

Auction rooms

Minor merchandising operations in buildings predominantly of other occupancies, such as a newsstand in an office building, shall be subject to the exit requirements of the predominant occupancy.

Office, storage, and service facilities incidental to the sale of merchandise and located in the same building are included with mercantile occupancy.

4-1.8 Business (*for requirements see Chapters 26 and 27*). Business occupancies are those used for the transaction of business (other than that covered under Mercantile), for the keeping of accounts and records, and similar purposes. Included in this occupancy group are:

Doctors' offices	Outpatient clinics, ambulatory
Dentists' offices	College and university-instructional
City halls	buildings, classrooms under 50
General offices	persons, and instructional
Town halls	laboratories
Courthouses	

Minor office occupancy incidental to operations in another occupancy shall be considered as a part of the predominating occupancy and shall be subject to the provisions of this *Code* applying to the predominating occupancy.

Doctors' and dentists' offices are included unless of such character as to be classified as health care. Service facilities usual to city office buildings (such as newsstands, lunch counters serving fewer than 50 persons, barber shops, and beauty parlors) are included in this occupancy group.
City halls, town halls, and courthouses are included in this occupancy group insofar as their principal function is the transaction of public business and the keeping of books and records; insofar as used for assembly purposes, they are classified as places of assembly.

4-1.9 Industrial (*for requirements see Chapter 28*). Industrial occupancies include factories making products of all kinds and properties devoted to operations such as processing, assembling, mixing, packaging, finishing or decorating, and repairing, including, among others, the following:

Factories of all kinds	Creameries
Laboratories	Gas plants
Dry cleaning plants	Refineries
Power plants	Sawmills
Pumping stations	College and university non-
Smokehouses	instructional laboratories
Laundries	

4-1.10 Storage (*for requirements see Chapter 29*). Storage includes all buildings or structures utilized primarily for the storage or sheltering of goods, merchandise, products, vehicles, or animals. Included in this occupancy group are:

Warehouses	Parking garages
Cold storage	Hangars
Freight terminals	Grain elevators
Truck and marine terminals	Barns
Bulk oil storage	Stables

Minor storage incidental to another occupancy shall be treated as part of the other occupancy.

Storage properties are characterized by the presence of relatively few people in proportion to the area. Any new use which increases the number of occupants to a figure comparable with other classes of occupancy changes the classification of the building to that of the new use.

4-1.11 Unusual Structures. Occupancies in unusual structures include any building or structure which cannot be properly classified in any of the preceding occupancy groups, either by reason of some function not encompassed or some unusual combination of functions necessary to the purpose of the building or structure. Such miscellaneous buildings and structures shall conform to the fundamental principles stated in Chapter 2 of this *Code* and to any specific provisions applicable thereto in Chapter 30.

4-1.12 Mixed Occupancies (*see 1-4.5*).

SECTION 4-2   HAZARD OF CONTENTS

4-2.1 General.

4-2.1.1   The hazard of contents, for the purpose of this *Code*, shall be the relative danger of the start and spread of fire, the danger of smoke or gases generated, and the danger of explosion or other occurrence potentially endangering the lives and safety of the occupants of the building or structure.

To understand the purpose of Section 4-2, one must recognize that the classification of hazard is based on the potential threat to life the contents represent. A fuel load that might be considered as a "low" hazard in terms of its ease of extinguishment by a sprinkler system may in fact produce enough smoke and other toxic products of combustion to threaten the life of the occupants before the sprinklers are even activated. Hence, the *Code* would classify the material as a "high" hazard.

The *Code*'s method of hazard classification is based on life safety. For this reason its provisions are not readily incorporated into the design criteria of other codes where hazard classification is based on property preservation. Thus, for a material considered to be a high hazard by the *Life Safety Code*, there may be no constructive design or system arrangement to compensate for the potential threat to life short of total enclosure and isolation of the material involved. Further, many "ordinary" fuels (from an extinguishment point of view) may be treated as severe hazards under the *Life Safety Code*. For example, an office occupancy may have a "light" hazard classification under NFPA 13, *Standard for the Installation of Sprinkler Systems,*[2] but is considered "ordinary" hazard under the *Life Safety Code*.

4-2.1.2   Hazard of contents shall be determined by the authority having jurisdiction on the basis of the character of the contents and the processes or operations conducted in the building or structure.

Exception: Where the flame spread rating of the interior finish or other features of the building or structure are such as to involve a hazard greater than the hazard of contents, the greater degree of hazard shall govern.

Under this provision, any violation of the interior finish requirements of Section 6-5 would inherently involve violation of other sections of the *Code* unless additional exit facilities appropriate to the higher hazard contents were provided.

4-2.1.3   Where different degrees of hazard of contents exist in different parts of a building or structure, the most hazardous shall govern the classification for the purpose of this *Code*.

Exception: Where hazardous areas are segregated or protected, as specifed in Section 6-4 and the applicable sections of Chapters 8 through 30.

Under this provision, any violation of the requirements of Chapters 8 through 30 for segregation or protection of hazardous operation or storage would inherently involve violation of the other sections of the *Code* unless additional exit facilities appropriate to the higher hazard contents were provided.

4-2.2 Classification of Hazard of Contents.

4-2.2.1 The hazard of contents of any building or structure shall be classified as low, ordinary, or high in accordance with 4-2.2.2, 4-2.2.3 and 4-2.2.4.

These classifications *do not* apply to the application of sprinkler protection classifications. See NFPA 13, *Standard for the Installation of Sprinkler Systems.*[2]

4-2.2.2 Low hazard contents shall be classified as those of such low combustibility that no self-propagating fire therein can occur and that, consequently, the only probable danger requiring the use of emergency exits will be from panic, fumes, smoke, or fire from some external source.

It should be noted that very few occupancies qualify as having low hazard contents.

Chapter 29, "Storage Occupancies," recognizes storage of noncombustible materials as low hazard. In other occupancies it is assumed that even where the actual content hazard may normally be low, there is sufficient likelihood that some combustible material or hazardous operations will be introduced in connection with building repair or maintenance, or that some psychological factor might create conditions conducive to panic, so that the exit facilities cannot safely be reduced below those specified for ordinary hazard contents.

4-2.2.3 Ordinary hazard contents shall be classified as those which are liable to burn with moderate rapidity or to give off a considerable volume of smoke but from which neither poisonous fumes nor explosions are to be feared in case of fire.

This classification represents the conditions found in most buildings, and is the basis for the general requirements of this *Code.*

The fear of poisonous fumes or explosions is necessarily a relative matter to be determined on a judgment basis. All smoke contains some toxic fire gases, but under conditions of ordinary hazard there should be no unduly dangerous exposure during the period necessary to escape from the fire area, assuming proper exits.

4-2.2.4 High hazard contents shall be classified as those which are liable to burn with extreme rapidity or from which poisonous fumes or explosions are to be feared in the event of fire. (*For means of egress requirements see Section 5-11.*)

High hazard contents may include occupancies: (1) where gasoline and other flammable liquids are handled or used or are stored under conditions involving possible release of flammable vapors; (2) where grain dust, wood flour or plastic dusts, aluminum or magnesium dust, or other explosive dusts may be produced; (3) where hazardous chemicals or explosives are manufactured, stored, or handled; (4) where cotton or other combustible fibers are processed or handled under conditions producing flammable flyings; and (5) other situations of similar hazard.

Chapter 28, "Industrial Occupancies," and Chapter 29, "Storage Occupancies," include detailed provisions on high hazard contents.

As can be seen from the definitions, occupancies containing low hazard or high hazard contents are rare. As an aid to the user of the *Code* in deciding which hazard classification applies, it is suggested that the user ask himself the following questions: Do the contents qualify for a low hazard classification? Do the contents qualify for a high hazard classification? If the answer to both of these questions is "no," then the hazard of contents must be in the "ordinary" classification.

REFERENCES CITED IN COMMENTARY

[1]NFPA 901, *Uniform Coding for Fire Protection*, NFPA, Boston, 1976.
[2]NFPA 13, *Standard for the Installation of Sprinkler Systems*, NFPA, Boston, 1980.

5

MEANS OF EGRESS

The purpose of this chapter is to establish minimum requirements for the means of egress, requirements that can be applied to all types of occupancies. Those instances in which these requirements are not specific enough for the needs of a particular situation are noted in the exceptions.

Means of egress is a term defined in 5-1.2.1 as including the exit, the exit access, and the exit discharge. This chapter covers the types, number, and arrangement of exits; their lighting and identification; as well as such key factors as travel distances and exit capacity.

SECTION 5-1   GENERAL

5-1.1 Application.

These requirements apply both to new and to existing buildings. Any change, either in structure or occupancy, that reduces the level of life safety is not permitted. The objective is to provide for an acceptable degree of safety in terms of the present and future use of a building.

5-1.1.1   Means of egress for both new and existing buildings shall comply with this chapter.

Exception: As otherwise provided for in Chapters 8 through 30.

The means of egress must comply with this *Code*. Portable ladders, rope fire escapes, helicopters, and similar emergency escape devices may serve a useful function as a means of escape from a burning building, but they cannot be relied upon to provide a level of safety equivalent to that of a *Code*-complying means of egress. Such devices are quite unsuitable for use by the aged or the physically handicapped or by small children. The sense of security they give is a false one, and their presence in a building cannot be used as an excuse for excluding standard egress facilities.

5-1.1.2   Any alteration or addition that would reduce means of egress below the requirements of this *Code* is prohibited.

5-1.1.3   Any change of occupancy that would result in means of egress below the requirements of this *Code* is prohibited.

Whenever a building is renovated or when additions are made to it, care must be taken not to reduce the means of egress below the level required by the *Code*. Even though a new addition in itself may meet all requirements, it is prohibited to add to an existing building if, by doing so, the means of egress in the existing portion is reduced to a level below that specified by the *Code*. Also, any change in building occupancy requires a review of the means of egress to ensure that the requirements specified for the new occupancy classification are met. See 1-4.3 for additional information regarding application to alterations and 1-6.4 regarding application to changes of occupancy.

5-1.2 Definitions.

5-1.2.1   A **means of egress** is a continuous and unobstructed way of exit travel from any point in a building or structure to a public way and consists of three separate and distinct parts: (a) the way of exit access, (b) the exit, and (c) the way of exit discharge. A means of egress comprises the vertical and horizontal ways of travel and shall include intervening room spaces, doorways, hallways, corridors, passageways, balconies, ramps, stairs, enclosures, lobbies, escalators, horizontal exits, courts, and yards.

From every location in a building there must be a means of egress or path of travel over which a person can move to gain access to the outside, or gain access to a place of safety and refuge should the need arise. Any person who gains entrance to a building (means of entry) has available that same route by which to exit. Yet one important consideration makes exiting something more than just reversing one's route of entry, especially if emergency conditions exist. This reverse route, or any other route chosen for exiting, may present to the person leaving the building features which, though they were not obstacles upon entrance, prove to be such upon exit. For example, a door hinged to swing in the direction of entry becomes an obstacle when one attempts to leave the building in the opposite direction. The door swings against the flow of traffic — a flow that in an emergency situation is greatly increased as compared with the leisurely flow of people entering a building. In such an instance, time is limited, and the way of entry may become blocked by fire. The path of travel must be one easily traversable and recognizable.

The occupant of a building must be protected from obstacles to a safe egress, and to do that the protection of each component in the process of exiting must be considered individually. Clear and concise definitions are needed, definitions which help point to the special needs for that component.

The term *means of egress* has been used for many years in building codes, but it was not until the late 1950s that it took on a more meaningful definition, comprising three separate and distinct parts: (1) the exit access, (2) the exit, and (3) the exit discharge. Until the late 50s the term exit was used more often than not, a fact evidenced by the *Life Safety Code*'s original title — the *Building Exits Code*. Difficulties arose when the Joint Committee on Building Codes (later called the Model Code Standardization Council) reviewed the chapters on means of egress in the model building codes and compared them with the provisions of the *Building Exits Code*. Not only were there no clear cut definitions of some terms, but also no clear descriptions of the parts and portions of buildings were given as a point of reference on which to base a review and comparison. Here is an example of the type of misunderstanding that clouded the picture: exit to one person meant the door out of a building, to another only the stairway, yet to another it meant any path of travel out of the building. The Sectional Committee on Means of Egress developed a proposed definition for "means of egress" and presented it to the NFPA Committee on Safety to Life for consideration. The original definition proposed contained the description of just two parts — an exit access and an exit. The committee saw the need for a third part — the exit discharge. Now when reference is made to any of the three parts, there is a clear understanding of what part of a particular building is being referenced and the function it serves in relation to the total means of egress.

5-1.2.2   Exit access is that portion of a means of egress which leads to an entrance to an exit.

The exit access includes the room or space in a building in which a person is located and the aisles, ramps, passageways, corridors, and doors that must be traversed on the way to an exit. No special protection is required for the exit access beyond that which is normally required by building regulations for compartmentation within the building. For maximum travel distances, see Section 5-6 and the occupancy chapters, Chapters 8 through 30. Some variations in design of ways of exit access are shown in Figure 5-1.

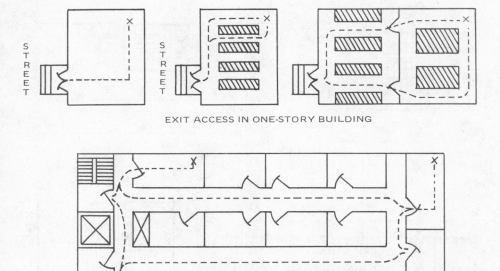

EXIT ACCESS IN ONE-STORY BUILDING

EXIT ACCESS ON UPPER OFFICE FLOOR

Figure 5-1. Variations of Exit Access.

5-1.2.3   Exit is that portion of a means of egress which is separated from all other spaces of the building or structure by construction or equipment as required in 5-1.3.1 to provide a protected way of travel to the exit discharge.

The exit may include parts of corridors, stairs, smokeproof towers, escalators, outside balconies, ramps, and doors. In each case, the exit component must conform to the specifications for fire protection and the maximum or minimum dimensions established by the *Code.* In its simplest form, the exit is simply a door leading to the outside. An example of this is found in the schoolroom having a door or doors opening directly to the outside.

In the case of a stairway, the exit includes the door to the stairway enclosure, stairs and landings inside the enclosure, the door from the stairway enclosure to the street or open air, or any passageway and door necessary to provide a path of travel from the stairway enclosure to the street or open air.

The entrance to an exit (part of the exit) is usually a fire door that provides a protected entrance into a protected area. A fire door, however, does not always signal an entrance to an exit. A door or fire door between a hotel room and a corridor, or a fire door across a corridor or hotel lobby, is not part of an exit unless the corridor or lobby and all other openings into it are protected as required for an exit.

The important fact to remember is that an exit provides a *protected* path of travel from a building.

Several types of exits, as they may actually occur in some buildings, are shown in Figure 5-2.

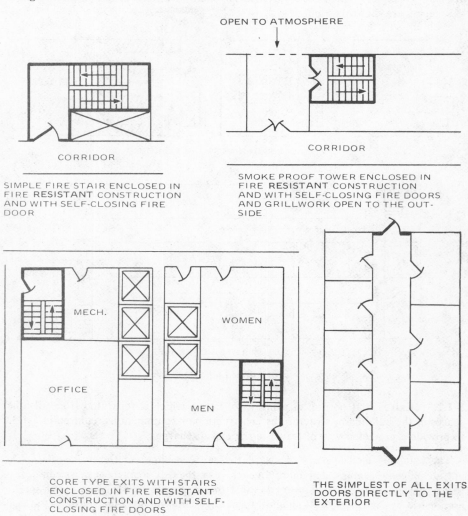

Figure 5-2. Variations of Exits.

5-1.2.4 **Exit discharge** is that portion of a means of egress between the termination of an exit and a public way.

An example of an exit discharge is a partially enclosed entrance to a motion picture theater, open to the street and sidewalk, and leading to the exit discharge doors (the theater entrance). In the example of the schoolroom mentioned before, the door leading directly out of a schoolroom is the exit, while the lawn or other area between the door and the public way is the exit discharge.

Where an exit stair opens onto an alley, court, or yard of size insufficient to accommodate the people using the exit, a safe passageway must be provided to a public way or some other area adequate in size. Such a passageway would constitute a part of the exit discharge.

Even where areas of refuge are provided within buildings, as provided in recent code amendments addressing high-rise structures, provision is made for the ultimate evacuation of such areas. Miscalculation or errors in design, faulty construction, or improper maintenance of a building, as well as other extraneous factors, may result in far greater fire involvement of the area than anticipated, making complete evacuation a necessity. Even here, the exit discharge would involve safe passage to a public way.

Typical plans of various forms of the exit discharge are shown in Figures 5-3, 5-4, and 5-5.

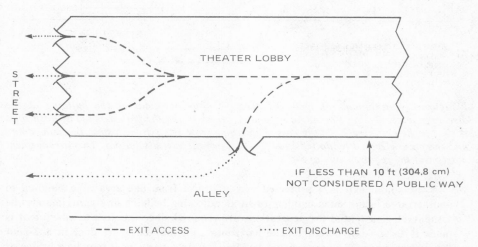

Figure 5-3. An Example of Two Types of Exits from a Theater. If the alley is less than 10 ft (3.05 m) wide, it will not meet the definition of a public way; thus, the exit discharge continues to the street.

5-1.2.5 A **horizontal exit** is a way of passage from one building to an area of refuge in another building on approximately the same level or a way of passage through or around a wall or partition to an area of refuge on approximately the same level in the same building that affords safety from fire or smoke from the area of incidence and areas communicating therewith (*see 5-2.4*).

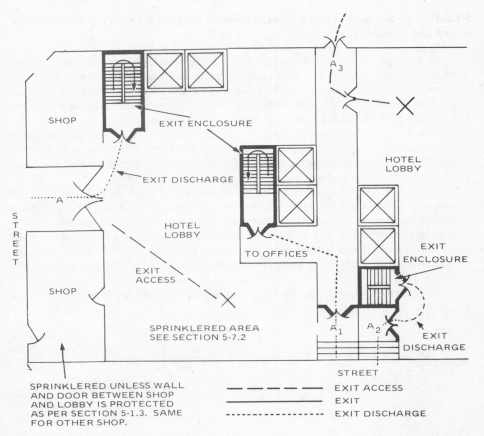

Figure 5-4. Examples of Exit Discharge. To the occupant of the building at the discharge level, the doors at A, A₁, A₂, and A₃ are exits and the path denoted by dash lines (- - - -) is the exit access. To the person emerging from the exit enclosure, the same doors and the paths denoted by dotted lines (. . . . .) are the exit discharges. This arrangement must meet the requirements of 5-7.2.

A horizontal exit is a protected way of travel from one area of a building to another area in the same building or in an adjoining building on approximately the same level. Substantial fire separations are required since the area to which exit is made is to serve as a refuge. The horizontal exit may be a fire door in a 2-hour fire-resistant partition separating a building into two areas, or it may be a bridge or balcony leading to an adjoining building. Examples of horizontal exits are shown in Figure 5-6.

Horizontal exits are useful in health care occupancies. Horizontal exits make it possible to move the patients in their beds, and door and passageway widths in such cases are specified with this in mind.

Horizontal exits should not be confused with egress through doors in smoke partitions. Doors in smoke partitions are designed only for temporary protection against smoke, whereas horizontal exits provide protection against serious fire for a relatively long period of time.

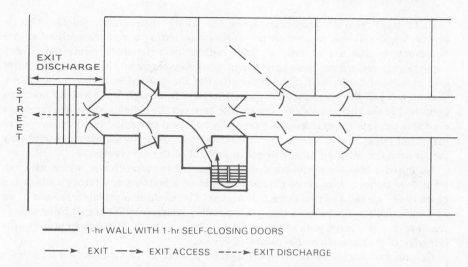

—————— 1-hr WALL WITH 1-hr SELF-CLOSING DOORS

——————► EXIT ——-► EXIT ACCESS - - - -► EXIT DISCHARGE

Figure 5-5. The Exit Discharge from a 2-Story Building of this Configuration Extends from the Exterior Door to the Public Way (Street).

5-1.3 Separation of Means of Egress (*see also Section 6-2*).

5-1.3.1 When an exit is required to be protected by separation from other parts of the building by some requirement of this *Code*, the separating construction shall meet the requirements of Section 6-2 and the following requirements:

The provisions for the enclosure of exits must be considered in conjunction with those contained in Chapter 6 because exceptions to some of these requirements are to be found in both Chapters 5 and 6. And, of course, the occupancy chapters, Chapters 8 through 30, may contain even more restrictive requirements.

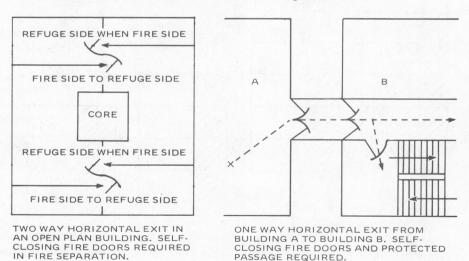

Figure 5-6. Types of Horizontal Exits. See 5-2.4 for more details on horizontal exits.

Exits must provide protection from fire along their entire length. This is accomplished through separation or construction having a designated level of fire resistance, by the use of interior finish within the exit which meets the *Code*'s requirements related to flame spread and smoke development, and by tight control over openings into the exit enclosure itself. (For the discussion of interior finish see Section 6-5 and the occupancy chapters, Chapters 8 through 30.) The only openings permitted in the enclosure walls between the exit and the building space are the doors needed to get into the exit from any normally occupied space and the doors needed to get out of the exit at the level of exit discharge; in other words, openings used only for an occupant wishing escape to get in and out of the exit enclosure.

No opening into the enclosure walls is permitted for pipe chases, which may run from floor to floor throughout the entire height of a building and through which fire could easily spread and render an exit useless. The *Code* also prohibits the use of an exit enclosure for any purpose that could possibly interfere with the exit being able to function as a protected path of travel. Every measure should be taken to preserve the integrity of that portion of the means of egress.

Certain exit access corridors must also be protected. This subsection includes a basic requirement for new buildings. However, many of the occupancy chapters contain more specific provisions.

(a) The separation shall have at least a 1-hour fire resistance rating when the exit connects three stories or less. This applies whether the stories connected are above or below the story at which exit discharge begins.

(b) The separation shall have at least a 2-hour fire resistance rating when the exit connects four or more stories, whether above or below the level of exit discharge. It shall be constructed of an assembly of noncombustible or limited-combustible materials and shall be supported by construction having at least a 2-hour fire resistance rating.

See Figures 5-7 and 5-8.

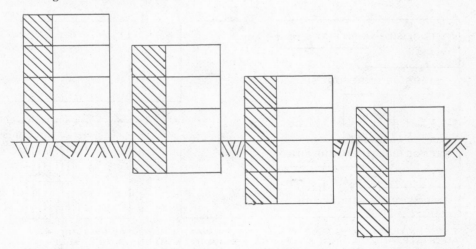

Figure 5-7. With Four Stories or More, Exit Stairs Must Be Enclosed in 2-Hour Noncombustible or Limited-Combustible Construction (Shaded Areas) and Supported by 2-Hour Construction.

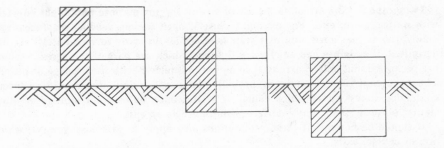

Figure 5-8. With Three Stories or Less, Exit Stairs Must Be Enclosed in 1-Hour Construction (Shaded Areas).

(c) Any opening therein shall be protected by an approved self-closing fire door (*also see 5-2.1.2.3*).

Exception: Fire doors which have been specifically approved as a pair not requiring an astragal at the meeting edges.

The intent of 5-1.3.1(c) is to limit doors into an exit enclosure to single doors. The exception to 5-1.3.1(c) permits a pair of doors to open into the enclosure *only* if the pair of doors is listed for use without an astragal. The reason for this is the need for pairs of doors with an astragal to close in sequence. The use of a coordinator is required to accomplish the sequential closing and the historical record of coordinators properly functioning is poor. To avoid the possibility of doors not properly closing, the *Code* prohibits the use of pairs of doors with an astragal.

(d) Openings in exit enclosures shall be limited to those necessary for access to the enclosure from normally occupied spaces and for egress from the enclosure.

Section 6-2 contains provisions for the protection of floor openings, which include stairs.

The only openings permitted in the exit for the passage of people are at the point of entry and at the exit discharge. These are required to be self-closing fire doors, as described in 5-2.1.2.3. Openings for ventilation of exit stairs and smokeproof towers may be permitted (see 5-2.3). Openings are not allowed, therefore, from storage rooms, closets, electrical equipment rooms, and similar areas.

5-1.3.2 Interior Finish in Exits.   The flame spread of interior finish on walls and ceilings shall be limited to Class A or Class B in exit enclosures. Chapters 8 through 30 governing individual occupancies may impose further limitations.

Except as provided in Chapters 8 through 30, the interior finish in exits is required to be Class A (0-25 flame spread rate, 0-450 smoke development factor) or Class B (26-75 flame spread rate, 0-450 smoke development factor) as defined in Section 6-5. Obviously, the effort is to minimize the possibility of fire spreading into and within the exit.

5-1.3.3   No exit enclosure shall be used for any purpose which would interfere with its use as an exit, such as for storage or similar purposes. (*Also see 5-2.2.2.2.*)

Paragraph 5-1.3.3 prohibits the use of an exit for any purpose that might interfere with its use as an exit. For example, closets, open wiring, vending machines, and maids' rooms that open onto exit stair landings (as in many foreign hotels) are not permitted. Standpipes and emergency lighting, which are part of the egress system, are permitted, but only if arranged so as not to interfere with the passage of people. The paragraph also intends to prohibit the construction of an exit enclosure containing excess space which could, at a later date, be used for storage or other similar purpose which may interfere with its use as an exit.

It should be noted that these prohibitions also apply to exit passageways, which are, of course, exits.

5-1.3.4   Corridors used as exit access and serving an area having an occupant load of more than 30 shall be separated from other parts of the building by construction having at least a 1-hour fire resistance rating. Openings in such separations shall be protected by an approved fire door assembly having a fire protection rating of at least 20 minutes when tested in accordance with *Standard Methods of Fire Tests of Door Assemblies*, NFPA 252 without the hose stream test.

Exception No. 1:   Existing buildings.

Exception No. 2:   Where requirements differ in Chapters 8 through 30.

Paragraph 5-1.3.4 establishes protection of certain exit access corridors in new buildings. It must be noted, however, that many of the occupancy chapters establish exit access corridor protection requirements that supersede these requirements. Paragraph 5-1.3.4 does not require corridors, but does require that where corridors do exist and they serve an area having an occupant load of more than 30, they must be separated. Since openings must be protected by an assembly having a fire protection rating of at least 20 minutes, a closer end latch is required (see Figure 5-9).

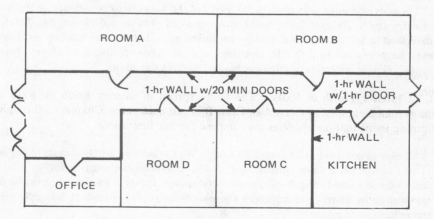

Figure 5-9. Protection of Exit Access Corridors. This plan shows an example of the requirement for protection of exit access corridors required by 5-1.3.4. Note the difference for the protection from the kitchen hazard.

5-1.4 Headroom. Means of egress shall be so designed and maintained as to provide adequate headroom as provided in other sections of this *Code* (*see 5-2.2.1.2*) but in no case shall the ceiling height be less than 7 ft 6 in. (228.6 cm) nor any projection from the ceiling be less than 6 ft 8 in. (203.2 cm) from the floor.

Headroom on stairs is the vertical distance above a plane parallel to and tangent with the most forward projection of the stair tread (see Figure 5-10).

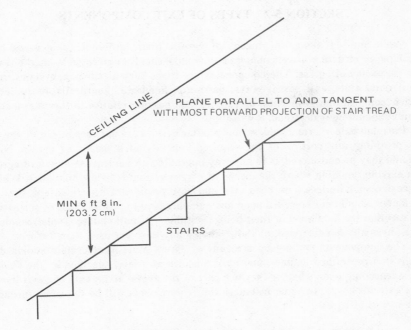

Figure 5-10. The Method of Measuring Headroom on Stairs.

5-1.5 Changes in Elevation. Changes in elevation in areas constituting part of a means of egress shall be by stairs or by ramps.

Exception: Changes in elevation that do not exceed 21 in. (53.34 cm) shall be by ramps.

5-1.6 Workmanship, Impediments to Egress.

5-1.6.1 Doors, stairs, ramps, passageways, signs, and all other components of means of egress shall be of substantial, reliable construction and shall be built or installed in a workmanlike manner.

5-1.6.2 Any device or alarm installed to restrict the improper use of a means of egress shall be so designed and installed that it cannot, even in case of failure, impede or prevent emergency use of such means of egress.

Exception: As provided in Chapters 14 and 15.

5-1.6.3 Means of egress shall be free of obstructions which would prevent its use.

Paragraph 5-1.6.3 is intended to prevent the obstruction or partial obstruction of any portion of the means of egress by construction features, furniture, fixtures, or accumulations of ice and snow. This paragraph is not only a design requirement but also a maintenance requirement. It should be remembered that this provision applies to the entire means of egress, including the exit discharge which may include sidewalks leading to the public way.

SECTION 5-2   TYPES OF EXIT COMPONENTS

While moving along any means of egress, many different components of the building or structure are encountered — components that go to make up the features of the means of egress. The components are items such as the doors, stairs, ramps, horizontal exits, exit passageways, hardware, handrails, guardrails, balconies, etc. Their composition, properties, use, limits, and bearing relative to the total means of egress should be understood.

Portable ladders, rope ladders, and similar devices are not recognized by the *Code* as providing any portion of the required capacity of a means of egress. Neither should they be considered as in any way upgrading an inadequate means of egress in an existing building where the means of egress system is below minimum. While on occasion such devices have been used and have provided a way to safety, they most definitely should not be relied upon and can only lead to a false sense of security, not to mention the likelihood of their being unusable by small children, older people, and the physically handicapped, or those who simply have not used them before.

The components making up a means of egress must meet certain standards, be built in a prescribed manner, and must perform at a level specified by the *Code*, all this depending upon whether they are part of the access to an exit, the exit itself, or the exit discharge. In some instances the requirements will be the same throughout the means of egress.

5-2.1 Doors.

5-2.1.1 General.

Doors serve three purposes related to the comfort and safety of building occupants. They provide protection from:
1. Weather, drafts, the noise and disturbance from adjoining areas;
2. Trespass by unauthorized persons; and
3. Fire and smoke, with which this *Code* is concerned.

There are three broad categories of doors, providing varying degrees of protection from fire. First is the *non-fire-rated door*, such as is used in one- and two-family dwelling construction. While not fire-rated, such doors in fact do provide a limited degree of protection *if closed*. Second is the tested *fire door* that has passed the standard fire test for doors (NFPA 252, *Standard Methods of Fire Tests of Door Assemblies*).[1] These doors will withstand a severe fire and hose stream exposure for a definite period of time, as is specified for various uses and occupancies. Finally, there is the *smoke stop door* that is usually of lighter construction than the fire door. Its function is to provide a temporary barrier against the passage of heat, smoke, and gases.

None of the three types of doors will perform satisfactorily if they are left open in a fire, thus allowing the entry of fire and combustion products into what should have been a safer area. The history of fire is full of tragic examples of those who died because of an open door, and there are many examples of people saved because a door was closed. Less frequent, but nonetheless real, are those situations in which doors needed for escape were blocked or locked, with dire consequences. *Code* requirements take into consideration these possibilities.

Some types of doors, which are designed to prevent spread of fire through wall openings, are not necessarily suitable for use in exits, and there is the hazard of personal injury if they are so used. This category includes various rolling-shutter and sliding-door types.

5-2.1.1.1 Application.

5-2.1.1.1.1 A door assembly, including the doorway, frame, door, and necessary hardware, may be used as a component in a means of egress when it conforms to the general requirements of Section 5-1 and to the special requirements of this section. As such, the assembly is designated as a door.

Paragraph 5-2.1.1.1.1 is alerting the *Code* user that the *Code* uses the term "door" to mean door assembly. Thus, whenever the *Code* refers to a rated door or fire door it is referring to the entire door assembly unless otherwise noted.

5-2.1.1.1.2 Every door and every principal entrance that is required to serve as an exit shall be so designed and constructed that the way of exit travel is obvious and direct. Windows that, because of their physical configuration or design and the materials used in their construction, could be mistaken for doors shall be made inaccessible to the occupants by barriers or railings conforming to the requirements of 5-2.2.3.

5-2.1.1.2 Units of Exit Width.

5-2.1.1.2.1 In determining the units of exit width for a doorway, only the clear width of the doorway when the door is in the full open position shall be measured. Clear width shall be the net, unobstructed width of the door opening without projections into such width.

Exception: In existing buildings, projections into the door opening by stops or by the hinge stile shall be permitted.

Figure 5-11 illustrates the points from which the clear width of a doorway is measured. It should be noted that the "net width" method of measuring clear width is new in this edition of the *Code* and applies only to new buildings.

5-2.1.1.2.2 Where a doorway is divided by mullions, the allowable units of exit width for the entire doorway shall be the sum of the units of exit width calculated separately for each individual door in the opening.

An example of the application of 5-2.1.1.2.2 is two 30-in. (76.2-cm) doors (with a mullion between them). They should not be counted as 60 in. (152.4 cm) or 2½ units of exit width, but rather as 2 units of exit width, 1 unit for each door.

IN <u>NEW</u> BUILDINGS THE ACTUAL NET UNOBSTRUCTED WIDTH OF THE DOOR
OPENING IS MEASURED

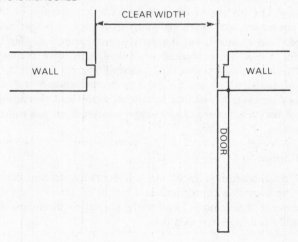

DOOR STOP AND HINGE STILE PROJECTIONS ARE DISREGARDED IN
DETERMINING CLEAR WIDTH IN <u>EXISTING</u> BUILDINGS

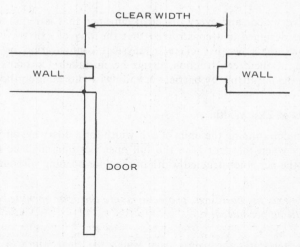

Figure 5-11. How to Measure Clear Width of a Doorway as Described in 5-2.1.1.2.1.

5-2.1.1.3 Width and Floor Level.

5-2.1.1.3.1 No door opening in the means of egress shall be less than 32 in. (81.28 cm) in clear width.

Exception No. 1: In existing buildings no single door in a doorway shall be less than 28 in. (71.12 cm) wide.

Exception No. 2: As provided in Chapters 14 and 15.

5-2.1.1.3.2 No single door in a doorway shall exceed 48 in. (121.92 cm) in width.

Generally, there are doors of varying types along the entire route of a means of egress, and each door must be wide enough to accommodate the number of people expected to move through that doorway during an emergency. This width is based on the occupancy served and on the standard 22-in. (55.88-cm) unit of exit width. A door is considered a level egress component; therefore, it has a capacity equal to that specified for level components (see 5-3.3). No door may be less than 32 in. (81.28 cm) wide; where a particular *Code* section specifies a width greater than 32 in. (81.28 cm), that width must be used. Thus it is the intent of the *Code* that the door not create a bottleneck in the means of egress. But note that though another portion of the means of egress may be larger than required, and create the illusion of a bottleneck, the door width is determined by the occupant load, and this specified width will be sufficient. For example, a door serving a hallway need not be as wide as the hallway since hallway width requirements are determined by other factors in addition to the occupant load (see Figure 5-12). An example of this is a health care facility, where corridor and door widths are much wider than the occupant load would seem to dictate. In this instance, the size of the corridor and doors is governed by the necessity of moving patients in their beds along the means of egress route, and the width is sized accordingly. In any event, the *Code* places a maximum of 48 in. (121.92 cm) on door width. This requirement prevents the possible installation of doors of unwieldly size, a size that would make them difficult to handle, and thus not easily accommodate the load reflected by their width.

Previous editions of the *Code* specified that no single door in a doorway be less than 28 in. (71.12 cm) wide; therefore, an exception is provided for exiting buildings. The new wider width permits the passage of wheelchairs. It should also be noted that the minimum width required may not be adequate for the normal usage of the doorway for purposes other than exiting.

For security and operations purposes, detention and correctional facilities are allowed to have doors of smaller width (see Chapters 14 and 15).

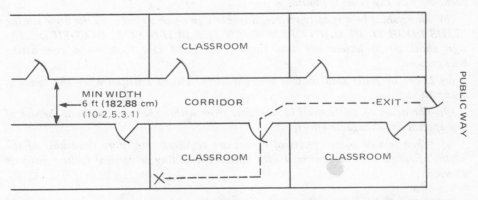

Figure 5-12. Exit Door Need Not Be as Wide as the Corridor Is Required to Be, Because Operational Features of the Occupancy in Addition to the Occupant Load Are Used in Determining Required Corridor Width. In this example of a school, the corridor is required to be 6 ft (182.88 cm) wide while the occupant load served would dictate the size of the exit door.

5-2.1.1.3.3   The floor on both sides of a door shall be substantially level and shall have the same elevation on both sides of the door, for a distance on each side at least equal to the width of the widest single door.

Exception: In existing buildings when the door discharges to the outside or to an exterior balcony, exterior exit, or exterior exit access, the floor level outside the door may be one step lower than the inside but not more than 8 in. (20.32 cm) lower.

Previously the *Code* permitted the floor level outside exterior doors to be one step but not more than 8 in. (20.32 cm) lower than the floor level inside the door. The reason for this was to avoid blocking the outward swing of the door by a build-up of snow or ice. The committee changed the paragraph in this edition to prohibit the one exterior step based on the possible tripping hazard. The committee also noted that other provisions of the *Code* require that the means of egress be maintained free of obstructions or be protected from the weather, thus providing for the removal of snow or ice accumulations. Existing buildings are permitted, of course, to use the one exterior step as noted in the exception to 5-2.1.1.3.3.

5-2.1.1.4 Swing and Force to Open.

5-2.1.1.4.1   Any door in a means of egress shall be of the side-hinged, swinging type. Doors shall swing in the direction of exit travel:

(a) When used in an exit, or

(b) When serving a high hazard area, or

(c) When serving an occupant load of 50 or more.

Exception No. 1:   As provided in Chapters 14, 15, and 22.

Exception No. 2:   Where permitted by Chapters 8 through 30, horizontal or vertical security grills or doors, that are a part of the required means of egress shall conform to the following:

(a) They must remain secured in the full open position during the period of occupancy by the general public.

(b) There shall be a readily visible, durable sign on or adjacent to the door stating "THIS DOOR TO REMAIN OPEN WHEN THE BUILDING IS OCCUPIED." The sign shall be in letters not less than 1 in. (2.54 cm) high on a contrasting background.

(c) Doors or grills shall not be brought to the closed position when the space is occupied.

(d) The doors or grills shall be openable from within the space without the use of any special knowledge or effort.

(e) When two or more means of egress are required, not more than half of the means of egress may be equipped with horizontal sliding or vertical rolling grills or doors.

Ideally, all doors in a means of egress should swing in the direction of exit travel. The *Code* requires that those doors which enter into the exit itself or are themselves an exit, such as a door leading directly to the outside (one- and two-family dwellings exempted) must swing in the direction of exit travel. Doors that may occur along the access to an exit should be considered separately, since there are cases where swing in the direction of travel is not necessary or desirable. Take, for example, a classroom door that provides the passage into a corridor serving as an exit access for several other classrooms. It is felt that, because a student is aware of and accustomed to a door opening into a room, it is better to let the door swing into the room than otherwise. If the door opened into the corridor, it could open against another door or against a flow of people, and possibly restrict or decrease the width of passage in that more critical element of the means of egress. The *Code* recognizes this danger and limits to 50 or fewer the occupant load of such a room, and thus limits the number of people using a door which swings against traffic. But the *Code* does not permit this arrangement in high hazard occupancies.

Paragraph 5-2.1.1.4.1 requires that doors be the side-hinged, swinging type. In designing and planning the means of egress, care must always be taken to check all possibilities of what might happen to the flow of traffic by the swing of a door. Never let the opening of a door which allows for the flow of one portion of the total occupant load completely block the flow of another portion (see Figure 5-13).

Some of the occupancy chapters provide exceptions to these requirements. For example, detention and correctional occupancies allow certain sliding doors. An exception is also allowed for horizontal or vertical security grills on doors provided that the exception is specifically allowed by the occupancy chapter applicable. This

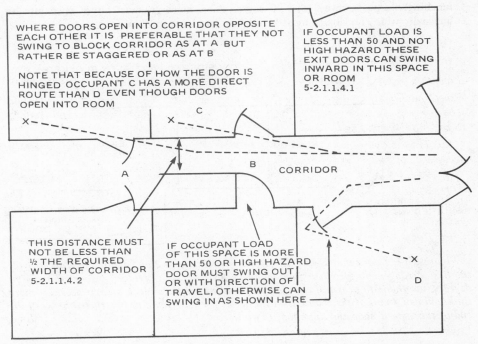

WHERE DOORS OPEN INTO CORRIDOR OPPOSITE EACH OTHER IT IS PREFERABLE THAT THEY NOT SWING TO BLOCK CORRIDOR AS AT A BUT RATHER BE STAGGERED OR AS AT B

NOTE THAT BECAUSE OF HOW THE DOOR IS HINGED OCCUPANT C HAS A MORE DIRECT ROUTE THAN D EVEN THOUGH DOORS OPEN INTO ROOM

IF OCCUPANT LOAD IS LESS THAN 50 AND NOT HIGH HAZARD THESE EXIT DOORS CAN SWING INWARD IN THIS SPACE OR ROOM 5-2.1.1.4.1

CORRIDOR

THIS DISTANCE MUST NOT BE LESS THAN ½ THE REQUIRED WIDTH OF CORRIDOR 5-2.1.1.4.2

IF OCCUPANT LOAD OF THIS SPACE IS MORE THAN 50 OR HIGH HAZARD DOOR MUST SWING OUT OR WITH DIRECTION OF TRAVEL, OTHERWISE CAN SWING IN AS SHOWN HERE

NOTE: ALL DOORS TO STAIRWAYS MUST SWING IN DIRECTION OF EXIT TRAVEL (5-2.1.1.4.2)

Figure 5-13. A Diagramatic Representation of Some of the Considerations Involved in Evaluating the Effect of Various Arrangements of Door Swing at Entrances to Corridors.

exception is to permit the security doors and grills normally found in a covered shopping mall. It should be noted that there is a difference between items (a) and (c) in Exception No. 2. Item (a) requires that the door be fully opened when the space is occupied by the public where item (b) states that the door cannot be closed when the space is occupied. This allows the common practice of the door being partially closed during inventory, closing, etc.

5-2.1.1.4.2 During its swing, any door in a means of egress shall not reduce the effective width of an aisle, passageway, stair or stair landing to less than one-half its required width. When fully open, the door shall not project more than 3½ in. (8.89 cm) into the required width of a stair or stair landing nor more than 7 in. (17.78 cm) into the required width of an aisle or passageway.

Exception: In existing buildings, a door giving access to a stairway shall neither reduce the effective width of a stair or landing to less than one unit of exit width nor, when open, interfere with the full use of the stairs.

Doors that open 180 degrees have a greater utility than those opening only 90 degrees. As shown in Figure 5-14, the former can open into an exit corridor without blocking the passageway. The 90-degree door, however, must either open into an unusually wide corridor or must be set into an alcove as shown.

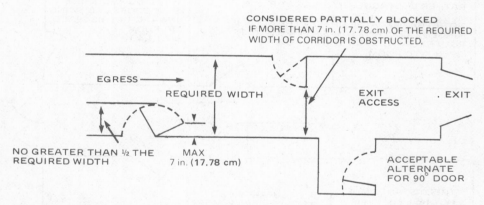

Figure 5-14. Doors that Swing 180 Degrees to Come to Rest Against a Wall Provide the Best Arrangement for Clear Passage in an Exit Access Corridor. A door swinging 90 degrees into the path of travel can be considered to partially block an exit access if more than 7 in. (17.8 cm) of the required width of the corridor remains obstructed between the end of the opened door and the opposite wall.

Doors serving as an entrance to an exit stairway should not block the stair landing or the stairs. It is preferred that the door not reduce the required width either during its swing or at rest. However, the *Code* does allow arrangements similar to Figure 5-15. An acceptable arrangement for a door opening onto a stair landing in an existing building is shown in Figure 5-16.

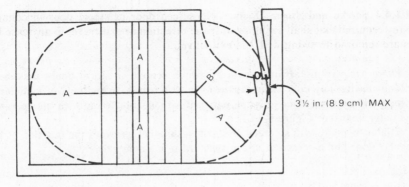

A - REQUIRED WIDTH
B - AT LEAST ½ A

Figure 5-15. A Typical Interior Stairway Showing Clearances that Must Be Observed in New Buildings. For example, if the stairway is required to be 66 in. (167.64 cm) in width, Dimension "B" must be at least 33 in. (83.82 cm).

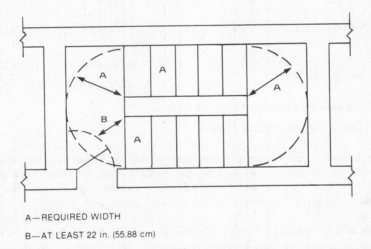

A—REQUIRED WIDTH

B—AT LEAST 22 in. (55.88 cm)

Figure 5-16. A Typical Interior Stairway Showing Clearances that Must Be Observed in Existing Buildings. Stair widths and landing radii (A) are equal; clearance (B) between opening door and stair newel post must be at least 22 in. (55.88 cm) (one unit of exit width).

5-2.1.1.4.3 The force required to fully open any door in the means of egress shall not exceed 50 lb (222 N) applied to the latch stile.

Care must be taken to ensure that the 50 lb force (222 N) limit to open a door in the means of egress is not exceeded for doors opening into a pressurized stair. Many times the volume of air necessary to pressurize a stair may produce sufficient pressure on a stair door to exceed the 50 lb opening force (222 N). The use of barometric relief dampers or other pressure regulating methods may be required.

5-2.1.1.4.4 Screen and Storm Doors.   No screen door or storm door in connection with any required exit shall swing against the direction of exit travel in any case where doors are required to swing with the exit travel.

There are various arrangements by which screen or storm doors may be used without having any door swing against the exit travel. A vestibule of sufficient size will permit the inner door to swing outward without interfering with the operation of the outer door (see Figure 5-17).

A jalousie door, with a screen or storm sash panel, provides the function of both a regular door and a screen or storm sash, all in a single unit.

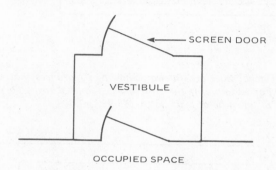

Figure 5-17. A Possible Arrangement of a Vestibule Leading to a Screen Door that Complies with 5-2.1.1.4.4.

5-2.1.2 Hardware for Doors in Means of Egress.

5-2.1.2.1 Locks, Latches, Alarm Devices.

The increase in petty thievery, molestations, and similar actions has led, in some instances, to the practice of locking the doors leading to exits. Such practices, particularly involving the doors to exit stairs and exit discharges, are an open invitation to tragedy in the event of fire or other emergency. Paragraph 5-2.1.2.1 is aimed at preventing locked doors in exit ways or any other unnecessary interference with the orderly movement of people in the event of fire. The Committee on Safety to Life has attempted to accomplish this objective while maintaining those features essential to security within the building.

The basic concerns of this section are:

1. Doors must be able to be easily opened by hand from the side of exit, even in complete darkness. This means no key locks or hard-to-use devices, such as door handles or latches covered with glass that has to be broken. Where panic bars are used, no fastener that might interfere with their operation can be used; however, this does not prevent the use of alarm connections that will indicate that the door is in use.

2. Some form of security must be maintained. The stair side of exit doors may be without door handles or knobs with the exception of the third floor in every three-floor interval. This will discourage the use of stairs in other than emergency situations and, at the same time, permit reentry into the building should a fire cut off the stair on a lower floor.

Requirements for doors leading to exits apply also to doors opening to roofs (where exit stairs terminate at a recognized roof exit) and to exit discharge doors leading to the street or other public way.

5-2.1.2.1.1 A door shall be so arranged as to be readily opened from the side from which egress is to be made at all times when the building served thereby is occupied.

For the purpose of this section, a building is occupied at any time it is open to or accessible to the public or at any other time it is occupied by more than 10 persons, unless otherwise provided by Chapters 8 through 30 for specific occupancies. Locks, if provided, shall not require the use of a key for operation from the inside of the building.

Exception No. 1:   As provided in Chapters 12 through 15.

Exception No. 2:   Exterior doors may have key operated locks from the egress side provided:

(a) There is a readily visible, durable sign on the egress side on or adjacent to the door stating, "THIS DOOR TO REMAIN UNLOCKED WHEN THE BUILDING IS OCCUPIED." The sign shall be in letters not less than 1 in. (2.54 cm) high on a contrasting background, and

(b) The locking device is of a type that is readily distinguishable as locked, and

(c) This Exception is specifically permitted by Chapters 8 through 30 for the specific occupancy.

(d) This Exception may be revoked by the authority having jurisdiction for cause.

Paragraph 5-2.1.2.1.1 establishes the principle that doors must be readily openable from the side from which egress is to be made. It prohibits the provision of locks which require the use of a key to open the door from the inside. The paragraph defines "occupied" for the purpose of this requirement. It should be noted that the paragraph prohibits the provision of such a lock as well as its use when the building is occupied. An exception is provided for key-operated locks under four conditions, one of which is that the appropriate occupancy chapter must specifically allow the exception.

In addition, there is an exception to the paragraph to allow certain provisions in the occupancy chapters for detention and correctional occupancies as well as special health care occupancies to override these requirements.

Doors to the enclosures of interior stair exits should be arranged to open from the stair side at least at every third floor so that it will be possible to leave the stairway at such floor should the fire render the lower part of the stair unusable during egress or should the occupants seek refuge on another floor.

5-2.1.2.1.2 A latch or other fastening device on a door shall be provided with a knob, handle, panic bar, or other simple type of releasing device, the method of operation of which is obvious, even in darkness.

This paragraph requires that when a latch or other similar device is provided, its releasing device must be such that the method of operation is obvious even in the dark. This requires that the method be one that is familiar to the average person. A two-step release such as a knob and an independent slide bolt is not normally acceptable.

This requirement may be satisfied by the use of conventional types of hardware, whereby the door is released by the turning of a knob or handle, or pushing against a panic bar, but not by unfamiliar methods or operation such as a blow to break glass.

5-2.1.2.1.3 Where pairs of doors are required in a means of egress, each leaf of the pair shall be provided with its own releasing device. Devices which depend upon the releasing of one door before the other shall not be used.

Exception: When exit doors are used in pairs and approved automatic flush bolts are used, the door leaf having the automatic flush bolts shall have no door knob or surface-mounted hardware. The unlatching of any leaf shall not require more than one operation.

This applies only to pairs of doors that are required. If the second leaf is provided for moving furniture or equipment and is not required for egress, this provision does not apply. It is recommended that, in the situation where a second leaf is provided for reasons other than egress, the leaf be identified as such by some means.

5-2.1.2.1.4 No lock, padlock, hasp, bar, chain, or other device, or combination thereof shall be installed or maintained at any time on or in connection with any door on which panic hardware is required by this *Code* if such device prevents or is intended to prevent the free use of the door for purposes of egress.

It is not the intent of 5-2.1.2.1.4 to require panic hardware. This requirement is made by the various occupancy chapters.

5-2.1.2.1.5 Special Locking Arrangements.

5-2.1.2.1.5.1 In buildings protected throughout by an approved supervised automatic fire alarm or automatic sprinkler system and when permitted by Chapters 8 through 30, doors in low and ordinary hazard areas, as defined by 4-2.2, may be equipped with approved, listed, locking devices which shall:

  (a) Unlock upon actuation of an approved supervised automatic fire alarm system or fire extinguishing system installed in accordance with Section 7-6 or 7-7, and

  (b) Unlock upon loss of power controlling the locking device, and

  (c) Initiate an irreversible process which will free the latch within 15 seconds whenever a force of not more than 15 lb (66.72 N) is applied to the release device required in 5-2.1.2.1.2 and not relock until the door has been opened. Operation of the release device shall activate a signal in the vicinity of the door for assuring those attempting to exit that the system is functional.

Exception: The authority having jurisdiction may approve a delay not to exceed 30 seconds provided that reasonable life safety is assured.

5-2.1.2.1.5.2 Signs shall be provided on the door adjacent to the release device which read:

"KEEP PUSHING. THIS DOOR WILL OPEN IN 15 SECONDS. ALARM WILL SOUND."

Sign letters shall be at least 1 in. (2.54 cm) high.

5-2.1.2.1.5.3 Emergency lighting in accordance with Section 5-9 shall be provided at the door.

This special locking arrangement is only allowed when specifically permitted by the appropriate occupancy chapter. Paragraph 5-2.1.2.1.5.1(a) *requires* that the building be equipped with *either* a *total automatic fire alarm system* or a *total automatic fire extinguishing system*, and that the devices unlock *upon activation of* the system. Item (c) requires that, once the release device is activated, the door unlock within 15 seconds; this action must be irreversible, and therefore cannot require that the user maintain pressure on the release device.

5-2.1.2.2 Panic Hardware.

5-2.1.2.2.1 Panic hardware consists of a door latching assembly incorporating a device which releases the latch upon the application of a force in the direction of exit travel.

5-2.1.2.2.2 When a door is required to be equipped with panic hardware by some other provision of this *Code* such releasing device shall:

(a) Consist of bars or panels, the actuating portion of which shall extend across not less than one-half of the width of the door leaf, not less than 30 in. (76.2 cm) nor more than 44 in. (111.76 cm) above the floor, and

(b) Cause the door latch to release when a force not to exceed 15 lb (66.72 N) is applied.

5-2.1.2.2.3 Only approved panic hardware shall be used.

5-2.1.2.2.4 Required panic hardware shall not be equipped with any locking or dogging device, set screw, or other arrangement which can be used to prevent the release of the latch when pressure is applied to the bar.

Exception: As permitted in Chapters 14 and 15.

As the name implies, panic hardware should be designed for utility, serviceability, and reliability under conditions which range from the orderly evacuation of building spaces to the panicked, chaotic mob action that can accompany fast-moving fires. Hence, the stress on ease of operation under extreme conditions.

Panic hardware, as specified in 5-2.1.2.2, must be able to be instantly and easily released, except in mental and penal institutions (as provided in Chapters 12 through 14). Panic hardware is to be located at a convenient height above the floor — 30 to 44 in. (76.2 to 111.76 cm) — and the actuating bar is to be at least one-half the width of the door. A force no greater than 15 lb (66.72 N) is needed to operate the device. This is the force needed to release the latching device only; the force needed to open the door itself is governed by 5-2.1.1.4.3. It is a relatively low pressure and well within the capability of small children and elderly people.

Note that 5-2.1.2.2 does not require panic hardware, but sets the requirements for such hardware when called for by the applicable occupancy chapter.

It is the intent of the *Code* to permit the use of the special locking arrangement permitted by 5-2.1.2.1.5 where panic hardware is required if permitted by the occupancy chapters, Chapters 8 through 30.

5-2.1.2.3 Self-Closing Devices. A door designed to be kept normally closed in a means of egress, such as a door to a stair enclosure or horizontal exit, shall be a self-closing door and shall not at any time be secured in the open position. (*Also see 5-10.4.2.2.*)

Exception: In any building of low or ordinary hazard contents, as defined in 4-2.2.2 and 4-2.2.3, where permitted by Chapters 8 through 30, or where the authority having jurisdiction approves the installation and finds that the circumstances are such that reasonable life safety from fire and smoke is not endangered thereby, stairway doors, doors in smoke partitions, and doors on horizontal exits may be automatic closing, where

(a) Upon release, the door becomes self-closing, and

(b) An approved release device is provided, so arranged that any interruption of the hold-open feature will cause the door to be released, and

(c) The release device is so designed that the door may be instantly released manually and upon release become self-closing or the door may be closed by some simple or readily obvious operation, and

(d) The automatic releasing mechanism or medium will be activated by (1) the operation of an approved automatic sprinkler system which protects the entire building, including both sides of any horizontal exit, the door of which is held open by any release so controlled, or (2) the operation of an approved automatic fire detection system installed to protect the entire building, so designed and installed as to provide for actuation of the system so promptly as to preclude the generation of heat or smoke sufficient to interfere with egress before the system operates, or (3) the operation of approved smoke detectors installed in such a way as to detect smoke on either side of the door opening, as detailed in Standard on Automatic Fire Detectors, NFPA 72E, Section 8-2, and

(e) Any sprinkler or fire detection system or smoke detector is provided with such supervision and safeguards as are necessary to assure complete reliability of operation in case of fire. (See also Section 7-6.)

Doors in a means of egress route should be kept in the closed position, particularly those in the entrance to a stair enclosure or horizontal exit; however, it is in these latter two locations that doors so often are blocked open by some type of door-stopping chock. The simple requirement that these doors be self-closing is not enough, since this feature works only when the door can move freely. Often a door is blocked open to aid in the free flow of normal traffic from floor to floor (as in schools, health care occupancies, motels, and office buildings); however, this sets the stage for the easy and rapid spread of fire, smoke, and heat throughout the building — the very thing which the stringent design requirements for the exit enclosure are intended to protect against.

Realizing that the self-closing feature may be tampered with and in an effort to encourage the use of positive measures rather than some printed prohibition likely not to be adhered to, the *Code* makes an exception for doors located in buildings which house contents of low or ordinary hazard, that is if the appropriate occupancy chapter allows it or if the authority having jurisdiction gives approval. The exception to 5-2.1.2.3 allows for doors to be held open by an automatic releasing device. The triggering of the automatic release is done through the operation of an automatic sprinkler or fire detection system protecting the entire building or through the operation of a smoke detection system (see NFPA 72E, *Standard on Automatic Fire*

Detectors, Section 9-2)[2] designed to detect smoke on either side of the door opening. Fusible links are not an acceptable trigger in this system because untenable smoke conditions could very easily render an exit enclosure unusable long before the heat has built up to a point high enough to operate the fusible link.

5-2.1.3 Special Doors, Devices in Means of Egress.

Paragraph 5-2.1.3 covers the basic requirements for doors operated by photoelectric mechanisms or by step-on-plates, and the requirements for revolving doors. These requirements also provide guidance for any other type of power-operated door for which approval may be requested.

5-2.1.3.1 Powered-Operated Doors.

5-2.1.3.1.1 Where required doors are operated by power, such as doors with photoelectric-actuated mechanism to open the door upon the approach of a person or doors with power-assisted manual operation, the design shall be such that in event of power failure the door may be opened manually to permit exit travel or closed where necessary to safeguard means of egress.

5-2.1.3.1.2 If a power-operated door is to be accepted as a required exit, it shall also swing with the exit travel by manual means.

Exception: As provided in Chapters 14 and 15.

Power-operated sliding doors activated by some automatic mechanism are permitted, provided that their movement can be manually overpowered and the door made to swing in the direction of travel, still providing the units of exit width for which it has been given credit. The feature for manual operation must work at all times, even when other features of the door's mechanism (such as the treadle, an electric eye, the sliding rail, etc.) have failed.

5-2.1.3.2 Revolving Doors.

5-2.1.3.2.1 A revolving door shall not be used in a means of egress.

Exception: Where specifically permitted by an occupancy chapter of this Code for an exit from the level of exit discharge directly to the outside, in which case:

(a) Such door(s) shall not be used at the foot or at the top of stairs at the level of exit discharge.

(b) Such door(s) shall not be given credit for more than 50 percent of the required units of exit width.

(c) Such revolving door(s) shall be of approved type(s).

The individual occupancy chapters must be consulted for the permitted use of revolving doors in a means of egress, since generally they are not permitted. If they are permitted, it is under the limited conditions described in the exception to 5-2.1.3.2.1. When permitted, they must comply with 5-2.1.3.2.2 through 5-2.1.3.2.4.

5-2.1.3.2.2 Each allowed revolving door may receive credit as constituting one-half unit of exit width.

The one-half unit rating here specified is based upon operation of the door in normal revolving position, where only one side is used for travel in one direction, and the rotating leaves of the door may slow the rate of travel to about half of that through an unobstructed door opening of the same width as one leaf of the revolving door. Collapsible revolving doors, while better than fixed leaf doors, are not given any increased rating in units of exit width, because if the setting is such as to prevent accidental collapse of leaves in normal operation, their free collapse in case of emergency may be doubtful.

5-2.1.3.2.3   The number of revolving doors used as exit doors shall not exceed the number of swinging doors used as exit doors within 20 ft (609.6 cm) thereof.

Exception: Revolving doors may serve as exits without adjacent swinging doors for street floor elevator lobbies if no stairways or doors from other parts of the building discharge through the lobby and the lobby has no occupancy other than as a means of travel between elevators and street.

5-2.1.3.2.4   Revolving doors shall be equipped with means to prevent their rotation at too rapid a rate to permit orderly egress.

Anyone having used a revolving door can easily anticipate the problems to be encountered should too many people try to use them in too short a period of time. The congestion created is one reason why their use is prohibited at the foot or top of stairs at the level of exit discharge. Because of the potential danger such doors present, they are not permitted to be used in numbers that would have them providing more than 50 percent of the required units of exit width. Where they are used, they receive credit for only one-half a unit of exit width, no matter what the width of the revolving panel.

Satisfying the 50 percent credit provision in item (b) of the exception to 5-2.1.3.2.1 does not also satisfy the one-half unit of exit width stipulation in 5-2.1.3.2.2, and vice versa. The provision in 5-2.1.3.2.3, regarding the number of revolving doors and swinging doors used in conjunction, carefully ensures that revolving doors will not be used unless there are swinging doors located within 20 ft (609.6 cm).

A rate of 12 revolutions per minute is recommended to comply with 5-2.1.3.2.4.

5-2.1.3.3 Turnstiles.

The intent of 5-2.1.3.3 is to give as much guidance as possible on how best to place turnstiles in a building, and to describe the circumstances under which they are permitted, in the hope that this will reduce the probability of their use during an emergency.

5-2.1.3.3.1   No turnstile or similar device to restrict travel to one direction or to collect fares or admission charges shall be so placed as to obstruct any required means of egress.

Exception: Approved turnstiles not over 3 ft (91.44 cm) high, which turn freely in the direction of exit travel, shall be permitted in any occupancy where revolving doors are permitted.

To say in 5-2.1.3.3.1 that no turnstile shall obstruct the means of egress is perhaps inappropriate, and it should be said rather that they shall obstruct no access to an exit. Certainly, the intent is that the turnstiles should not be used in exits, and perhaps not in exit discharges.

Because of similarities, it appears that turnstiles are permitted where revolving doors are permitted, although they are used in some occupancies where revolving doors are generally not found. This is not meant to imply that there is a relationship between revolving doors and turnstiles insofar as their purpose. The revolving door is not meant to restrict traffic in either direction, while the turnstile is often used to do just that, with the restriction or obstruction to traffic movement usually in the direction of entry. Yet, if a turnstile does not "obstruct any required means of egress," it can be looked upon the same as a revolving door.

While most turnstiles will not turn in the direction of entry until coin operated, there are those that are used simply to count numbers of people. Perhaps the most dangerous are those that do not bar entry but specifically bar leaving. An example of this would be in the large discount stores where turnstiles turn freely for entering, but will not turn in the direction of egress, thereby causing patrons to go through a checkout slot. It is likely that the patrons of places using one-way turnstiles are quite aware of this limitation and will know the correct path to be taken in order to leave; however, this cannot be relied on, especially if the turnstiles are placed near the exit doors. In emergencies people do not always stop to think things out, and could head for what appears to be the shortest means of escape — only to find the way blocked by a "wrong way" turnstile.

Some other examples of types of turnstiles are those placed in subways, rapid transit stations, and other places of assembly to prevent the entrance of people who have not paid a fare or admission fee. These, too, may pose a serious obstruction to rapid egress in the case of a fire or other emergency, even though such turnstiles are designed to permit people to leave. Multiple bar turnstiles designed to prevent people from crawling over, under, or around the bars are more objectionable than the single bar turnstiles, such as the coin-operated types, but any type of turnstile involves some interference with egress. Where turnstiles are used, required exit facilities may be provided by alternate exits like the swinging gate, with visual supervision by employees to prevent improper use.

5-2.1.3.3.2 Turnstiles over 3 ft (91.44 cm) high shall be subject to the requirements for revolving doors.

To clarify what appears to be a discrepancy between the exception to 5-2.1.3.3.1 and 5-2.1.3.3.2 concerning the 3-ft (91.44-cm) high turnstile, the following explanation might be helpful. The exception places no restriction on the turnstile except as to *where* it can be used when it measures no more than 3 ft (91.44 cm) high. Paragraph 5-2.1.3.3.2 does place restrictions on the turnstile if it is more than 3 ft (91.44 cm) high, i.e., it is counted only as permitted for revolving doors in terms of capacity, location, etc.

5-2.1.3.3.3 Turnstiles in or furnishing access to required exits shall be of such design as to provide 22 in. (55.88 cm) clear width as the turnstile rotates.

5-2.1.3.3.4 No turnstile shall be placed in any required means of egress.

5-2.1.3.3.5 Turnstiles shall be rated the same as revolving doors as regards units of exit width and rates of travel.

5-2.1.3.4 Doors in Folding Partitions. When permanently mounted folding or movable partitions are used to divide a room into smaller spaces, a swinging door or open doorway shall be provided as a way of exit access from each such space.

Exception: Under the following conditions the swinging door may be omitted and the partition may be used to enclose the space completely.

(a) The subdivided space shall not be used by more than 20 persons at any time.

(b) The use of the space shall be under adult supervision.

(c) The partitions shall be so arranged that they do not extend across any aisle or corridor used as a way of access to the required exits from the floor.

(d) The partitions shall conform to the interior finish and other applicable requirements of this Code.

(e) The partitions shall be an approved type, shall have a simple method of release, and shall be capable of being opened quickly and easily by inexperienced persons in case of emergency.

5-2.2 Interior Stairs.

Stairs, whether interior or exterior, serve three functions: they are a means of communication between the floors and different levels of a building; they serve as an emergency exit in case of fire; and they are essential for the rescue and fire-control operations conducted by fire fighters.

Exterior stairs are discussed in 5-2.5. Here, only interior stairs as a component of the means of egress will be considered. This includes monumental stairs — those stairs, often made of stone or masonry, that are used in public buildings such as libraries, museums, and post offices. This discussion also includes winders, curved stairs, and spiral stairs.

5-2.2.1 General.

5-2.2.1.1 All stairs serving as required means of egress shall be of permanent fixed construction.

5-2.2.1.2 Classification of Stairs. Stairs shall be in accordance with the following table:

New Stairs

Minimum width clear of all obstructions, except handrails which may project not more than 3½ in. (8.89 cm) on each side and stringers which may project not more than 1½ in. (3.81 cm) on each side	44 in. (111.76 cm) 36 in. (91.44 cm), where total occupant load of all floors served by stairways is less than 50.
Maximum height of risers	7 in. (17.78 cm)
Minimum height of risers	4 in. (10.16 cm)
Minimum tread depth	11 in. (27.94 cm)
Winders	See 5-2.2.2.4.
Minimum headroom	6 ft. 8 in. (203.2 cm)
Maximum height between landings	12 ft. (365.76 cm)
Minimum dimension of landings in direction of travel	See 5-2.2.2.5.
Doors opening immediately on stairs, without landing at least width of door	No

Exception: Existing stairs in existing buildings may remain in use or be rebuilt if they meet the requirements shown in the table for existing stairs.

Existing Stairs

	Class A	Class B
Minimum width clear of all obstructions, except handrails which may project not more than 3½ in. (8.89 cm) on each side and stringers which may project not more than 1½ in. (3.81 cm) on each side	44 in. (111.76 cm)	44 in. (111.76 cm) 36 in. (91.44 cm) where total occupant load of all floors served by stairways is less than 50.
Maximum height of risers	7½ in. (19.05 cm)	8 in. (20.32 cm)
Minimum tread depth	10 in. (24.4 cm)	9 in. (22.86 cm)
Winders	See 5-2.2.2.4.	See 5-2.2.2.4.
Minimum headroom	6 ft. 8 in. (203.2 cm)	6 ft. 8 in. (203.2 cm)
Maximum height between landings	12 ft. (365.76 cm)	12 ft. (365.76 cm)
Minimum dimension of landings in direction of travel	44 in. (111.76 cm)	44 in. (111.76 cm)
Doors opening immediately on stairs without landing at least width of door	No	No

Paragraph 5-2.2.1.2 represents a significant change in the 1981 Edition of the *Life Safety Code* from the 1976 Edition. In the 1976 Edition, only the table showing Class A and Class B stairs appeared and each occupancy specified which class of stair could be used. The 1981 Edition requires that all new stairs comply with the first table. The new trend and riser dimensions come from a comprehensive review of stair dimensions published in the *Scientific American* in 1974[3] and NBSIR 78-1554.[4]

The table also now refers to 5-2.2.2.4 for winder provisions rather than just prohibiting them across the board.

Due to the impact of the new dimensions, the *Code* permits existing stairs in existing buildings to comply with previous requirements. It also allows existing stairs to be rebuilt to previous requirements since a new stairway would not fit in an existing stairwell. Therefore existing interior stairs are divided into two classes: Class A and Class B. Actually, there is little difference between the two. As shown in Figure 5-18, the difference lies in the tread width and riser height, with a possible difference in stair width if the total occupant load of all floors served by a Class B stairway is less than 50. In that instance, the minimum width can be reduced from 44 in. (111.76 cm) to 36 in. (91.44 cm). The occupancy chapters specify which class of stair may be used.

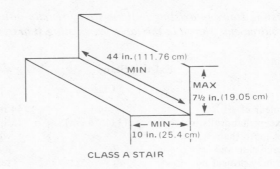

CLASS A STAIR

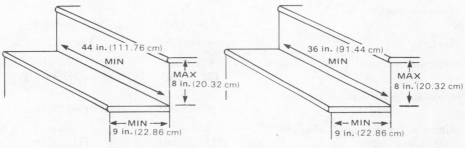

TOTAL OCCUPANT LOAD 50 OR MORE   TOTAL OCCUPANT LOAD LESS THAN 50

CLASS B STAIRS

Figure 5-18. Existing Stairways in Existing Buildings. Class A and B stairs showing maximum and minimum dimensions for each class. Class A stairs have a minimum width of 44 in. (111.76) even if the occupant load is 50 or less.

5-2.2.1.3 Enclosures.   All interior stairs shall be enclosed in accordance with the provisions of Section 5-1 of this *Code.*   5- 1, 3, 1

Exception: Open stairs permitted by 6-2.2.

5-2.2.1.4 Monumental Stairs.   Monumental stairs, either inside or outside, shall be accepted as required exits if all requirements for exit stairs are complied with, including required enclosures and minimum depth of treads.

5-2.2.1.5 Curved Stairs.   Curved stairs may be used in means of egress provided the minimum depth of tread is 10 in. (25.4 cm) and the smallest radius is not less than twice the stair width.

    Paragraph 5-2.2.1.5 is a new paragraph in this edition of the *Code*. Previously, curved stairs were allowed as an exception to 5-2.2.1.4 if the interior radius was 25 ft (762 cm) or more. This edition allows curved stairs, as shown in Figure 5-19.

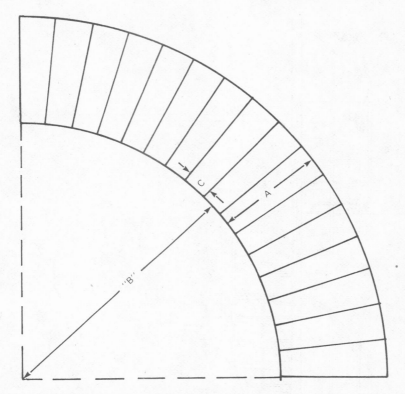

Figure 5-19. Curved Stairs. Dimension A must be at least 44 in. (111.76 cm).
Dimension B must be at least twice A. Dimension C must be at least 10 in. (25.4 cm).

5-2.2.1.6 Spiral Stairs. Where permitted for individual occupancies by Chapters 8 through 30 spiral stairs may be used in a means of egress provided:

(a) The clear width of the stairs is not less than 26 in. (66.04 cm).

(b) The height of riser shall not exceed 9½ in. (24.13 cm).

(c) Headroom shall be not less than 6 ft 6 in. (198.12 cm).

(d) Treads shall have a minimum depth of 7½ in. (19.05 cm) at a point 12 in. (30.48 cm) from the narrowest edge.

(e) All treads shall be identical.

(f) The occupant load served is not more than 5.

The provisions for spiral stairs appear for the first time in this edition of the *Code*. Previously, spiral stairs were not allowed in a required means of egress due to their width and the rise and tread depth.

In addition to setting specifications for the spiral stairs, the *Code* states that they cannot serve as required means of egress for an occupant load of more than five. Also, they can only be used when allowed by the appropriate occupancy chapter (see Figure 5-20).

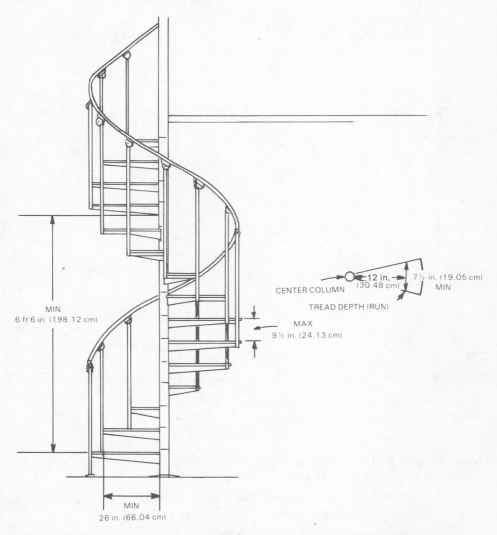

Figure 5-20. Spiral Stairs. Minimum and maximum dimensions for spiral stairs as given in 5-2.2.1.6. All treads must be identical, and the stair can serve a maximum occupant load of five.

5-2.2.2 Stair Details.

5-2.2.2.1   Each new stair and platform, landing, etc., used in conjunction therewith in buildings more than three stories in height and in new buildings required by this *Code* to be of fire-resistive construction, shall be of noncombustible material throughout.

Exception: Handrails are exempted from this requirement.

Paragraph 5-2.2.2.1 covers the types of materials used in the construction of stairs. Stairs serving up to and including three stories may be of combustible construction unless the structure is otherwise required to be of fire-resistive

construction as described in NFPA 220, *Standard Types of Building Construction.*[5] In the latter case the material used for the stair construction must be noncombustible throughout. In all buildings of more than three stories, the stairway construction must be of noncombustible material.

5-2.2.2.2 There shall be no enclosed usable space within an exit enclosure, including under stairs, nor shall any open space within the enclosure, including stairs, and on landings be used for any purpose such as storage or similar use which could interfere with egress. Where there is enclosed usable space under stairs the walls and soffits of the enclosed space shall be protected the same as the stair enclosure.

Although this paragraph may, at first, seem to contradict itself, it does not. First, the paragraph states that *within* an exit enclosure there shall be no enclosed usable space, nor shall any open space be used for any purpose which could interfere with the use of the exit enclosure. An enclosed usable space under a stair can be considered to be *outside* the exit enclosure if the walls and soffits of the enclosed space are protected the same as the stair enclosure, thereby separating the space from the exit enclosure. The door to the space can *not* open into the exit enclosure per 5-1.3.1(d).

5-2.2.2.3 Each stair, platform, landing, balcony, and stair hallway floor shall be designed to carry a live load of 100 lb/sq ft (488.24 kg/sq m), or a concentrated load of 300 lb (136.08 kg), so located as to produce maximum stress conditions.

5-2.2.2.4 Winders are permitted in stairs where allowed by Chapters 8 through 30. Such winders shall have a minimum depth of tread of 6 in. (15.24 cm), and a minimum depth of tread of 9 in. (22.86 cm) at a point 12 in. (30.48 cm) from the narrowest edge.

Previously, 5-2.2.2.4 of the *Code* prohibited winders. In this edition of the *Code*, Chapter 5 sets criteria for winders if the appropriate occupancy permits the use of them (see Figure 5-21).

5-2.2.2.5 Stairways and intermediate landings shall continue with no decrease in width along the direction of exit travel. In new buildings every landing shall have a dimension, measured in direction of travel, equal to the width of the stair. Such dimension need not exceed 4 ft (121.92 cm) when the stair has a straight run.

5-2.2.2.6 Stair treads shall be uniform slip resistant and shall be free of projections or lips that could trip stair users.

When walking up or down stairs, a person's foot exerts a smaller horizontal force against treads than achieved when walking on level floors. Therefore, materials that are acceptable as slip resistant for floors (as described by ASTM) provide adequate slip resistance when used for stair treads, including the important leading edges of treads — the part of the tread which the foot first contacts during descent, the most critical direction of travel. If stair treads are wet there may be an increased danger of slipping just as there may be an increased danger of slipping on wet floors of similar materials. A small wash or drainage slope on exterior stair treads is therefore recommended to shed water. (See NBSIR 78-1554).[4] When environmental conditions

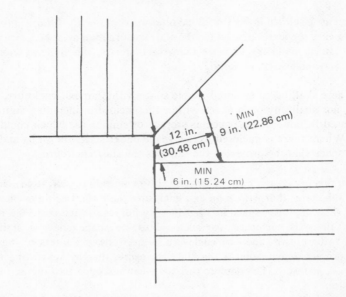

Figure 5-21. Acceptable Winders. When allowed by the occupancy chapter, winders which comply with 5-2.2.2.4 are acceptable in a required means of egress.

(such as illumination levels and directionality, or a complex visual field that draws a person's attention away from stair treads) lead to a hazardous reduction in one's ability to perceive stair treads, the treads should be made of a material that permits ready discrimination of their number and position. In all cases, the leading edges of all treads should be readily visible during both ascent and descent. A major factor in injury-producing stair accidents, and in the ability to use stairs efficiently in conditions such as egress, is the clarity of the stair treads as separate stepping surfaces.

In previous editions of the *Code* there was a requirement that "The height of every riser and the width of every tread shall be so proportioned that the sum of two risers and a tread, exclusive of its nosing or projection, is not less than 24 in. (60.96 cm) nor more than 25 in. (63.5 cm)." This requirement was deleted since it was based on a 300-year-old formula in which the inch represented a different unit of measure. Modern research showed the formula to be invalid.

5-2.2.2.7 The minimum number of risers in any one flight of stairs shall be three.

5-2.2.2.8 Treads of stairs and landing floors shall be solid.

5-2.2.2.9 There shall be no variation exceeding ³/₁₆ in. (.48 cm) in the depth of adjacent treads or in the height of adjacent risers and the tolerance between the largest and smallest riser or between the largest and smallest tread shall not exceed ³/₈ in. (.95 cm) in any flight.

Exception: Where the bottom riser adjoins a sloping public way, walk or driveway having an established grade and serving as a landing, a variation in height of the bottom riser of not more than 3 in. (7.62 cm) in every 3 ft (91.44 cm) of stairway width is permitted.

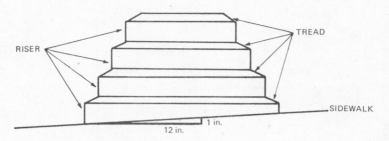

Figure 5-22. Stairway Complying with the Exception to 5-2.2.2.9. This figure illustrates the intent of the exception.

Many accidents have resulted from irregularities in stairs. There should be no design irregularities. Variations due to construction are permitted provided the variation between adjacent treads or adjacent risers does not exceed ³/₁₆ in. (.48 cm) and that the tolerance between the largest and smallest riser in a flight does not exceed ⅜ in. (.95 cm) (see Figures 5-22 and 5-23).

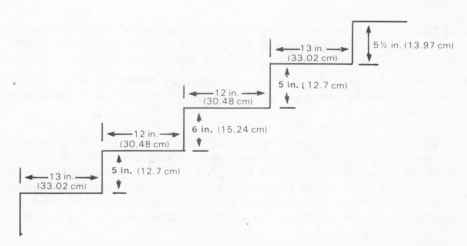

Figure 5-23. Variations in Tread and Riser Dimensions Invite Accidents. This arrangement should not be permitted.

5-2.2.2.10 Tread depth shall be measured horizontally between the vertical planes of the foremost projection of adjacent treads and at a right angle to the tread's leading edge.

Exception: Approved existing stairs.

Tread depth is measured such that the addition of a nosing does not increase tread depth (see Figure 5-24).

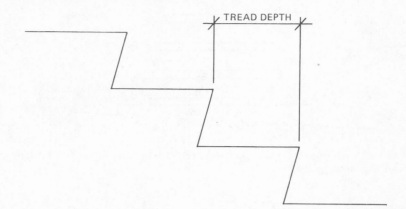

Figure 5-24. Measurement of Tread Depth.

Previous editions of the *Code* required a 1-in. (2.54-cm) tread nosing. This has been deleted from the *Code* since modern research indicates the nosing may be a tripping hazard.

5-2.2.2.11 Stairs and other exits shall be so arranged as to make clear the direction of egress to the street. Exit stairs that continue beyond the floor of discharge shall be interrupted at the floor of discharge by partitions, doors, or other effective means.

Exception: Exit stairs that continue one-half story beyond the level of exit discharge need not be interrupted by physical barriers where the exit discharge is clearly obvious.

Figure 5-25 illustrates an important stair detail (see 5-2.2.2.11) designed to minimize the possibility of a person unknowingly passing through the exit discharge level into a basement or some level below that of the exit discharge. This can be accomplished by the use of a partition, or other physical barrier, that effectively interrupts the flow of travel, causing a person to wonder if the proper direction is being taken. The use of railings to create this barrier and doorway is acceptable. Also see 5-7.3.

5-2.2.3 Guards and Handrails.

5-2.2.3.1 Means of egress such as landings, balconies, corridors, passageways, floor or roof openings, ramps, aisles, porches, or mezzanines that are more than 30 in. (76.2 cm) above the floor or grade below shall be provided with guards to prevent falls over the open side. Stairs that are provided with handrails as specified in 5-2.2.3.4 need not be provided with guards. Each new stair and new ramp shall have handrails on both sides. (*See also 5-2.2.3.4.*)

Handrails are required on each side of new stairs and ramps, but they are not required on landings except as noted in 5-2.2.3.2 and 5-2.2.3.4. They provide support for people using stairs and can serve as a guide when, as sometimes happens, smoke

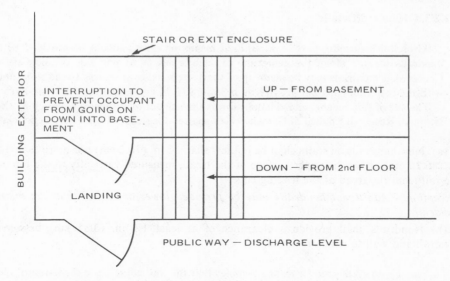

STAIR OR EXIT ENCLOSURE

BUILDING EXTERIOR

INTERRUPTION TO
PREVENT OCCUPANT
FROM GOING ON
DOWN INTO BASE-
MENT

UP — FROM BASEMENT

DOWN — FROM 2nd FLOOR

LANDING

PUBLIC WAY — DISCHARGE LEVEL

Figure 5-25. Interrupting a Passageway from the Exit Discharge Level. This is done by placing a door in the passage to the basement level. It serves to warn occupants in the exit enclosure that they are on the discharge level.

enters the stairway in a quantity sufficient to interfere with one's vision or when the stair lighting system fails. Thus, it is desirable to have railings for each unit of exit width (each file of people), although this is not required except as noted.

Superficially, the design details for guards and handrails may appear to be relatively unimportant. Yet even in normal use, poorly designed and constructed guards and handrails have been the cause of many accidents. In emergency situations, situations which may involve crowding and panic, they become extremely hazardous. Of course the lack of guards and handrails on stairs, ramps, landings, and balconies can be even more disastrous.

5-2.2.3.2 Required guards and handrails shall continue for the full length of each flight of stairs. At turns of stairs inside handrails shall be continuous between flights at landings.

Exception: On existing stairs the handrails are not required to be continuous between flights of stairs at landings.

It is not the intent of this *Code* to require handrails on stair landings. However, the interior handrail on stairs which change direction at a landing shall be continuous. (See **Figure 5-27.**)

5-2.2.3.3 The design of guards and handrails and the hardware for attaching handrails to guards, balusters, or masonry walls shall be such that there are no projecting lugs on attachment devices or nonprojecting corners or members of grills or panels which may engage loose clothing. Openings in guards shall be designed to prevent loose clothing from becoming wedged in such openings.

5-2.2.3.4 Handrail Details.

Aisle stairs forming part of a required means of egress should be provided with handrails located along the centerline of such aisles or at one side of such aisle. Center aisle handrails may be made up of short sections, with returns to the stair, and with the resulting gaps not greater than 36 in. (91.44 cm) measured horizontally.

The use of this recommended handrail was the subject of extensive research by the National Research Council of Canada which showed the handrail to be very beneficial.

(a) New handrails on stairs shall be not less than 30 in. (76.2 cm) nor more than 34 in. (86.36 cm) above the upper surface of the tread, measured vertically to the top of the rail from the tread at the leading edge.

Exception: Additional handrails may be provided lower or higher than the main handrail.

(b) Handrails shall provide a clearance of at least 1½ in. (3.81 cm) between handrail and wall to which fastened.

This 1½-in. (3.81-cm) clearance assumes that the wall adjacent to the handrail is a smooth surface. Where rough wall surfaces are used, greater clearances are recommended.

(c) Handrails shall be of such design and so supported as to withstand a load of not less than 200 lb (889.6 N) applied at any point, downward or horizontally.

(d) New handrails shall be so designed as to be continuously graspable along the entire length.

Handrails should be designed so that they can be grasped firmly with a comfortable grip and so that the hand can be slid along the rail without encountering obstructions. The profile of the rail should comfortably match the hand grips. For example, a round profile such as is provided by the simplest round tubing or pipe having an outside diameter of 1½ to 2 in. (3.81 to 5.08 cm) provides good graspability for adults. Factors such as the use of a handrail by small children and the wall-fixing details should be taken into account in assessing handrail graspability.

It should be noted that handrails are one of the most important components of a stair; therefore, design excesses such as oversized wood handrail sections should be avoided unless there is a readily perceived and easily grasped handhold provided. At all times in handrail design it is useful to remember the effectiveness of a simple round profile that permits some locking action by fingers as they curl around the handrail.

Item (d) introduces a subtle but important requirement for handrails, that of graspability. This would prohibit the use of unshaped lumber for handrails. Figure 5-26 shows examples of acceptable and unacceptable handrails. (See Figure 5-26.)

(e) New handrail ends shall be returned to the wall or floor or shall terminate at newel posts.

(f) New handrails that are not continuous between flights shall be extended horizontally a minimum of 12 in. (30.48 cm) at the required height at the top and bottom landings where a guard or wall exists.

MINIMUM 1½ in. (3.81 cm)

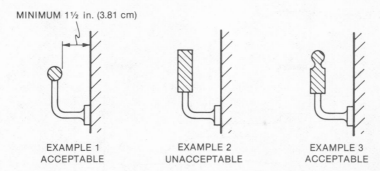

| EXAMPLE 1 | EXAMPLE 2 | EXAMPLE 3 |
| ACCEPTABLE | UNACCEPTABLE | ACCEPTABLE |

Figure 5-26. Handrails. Example 1 shows a typical handrail which is acceptable for graspability. Example 2 shows a handrail not acceptable from a graspability standpoint. Example 3 shows how to modify the handrail in Example 2 to comply with the graspability criteria.

(g) Every stairway required to be more than 88 in. (223.52 cm) in width shall have not less than one intermediate handrail for each 88 in. (223.52 cm) in required width. (*See also 5-2.2.3.1.*)

A reduced intermediate handrail spacing [see 5-2.2.3.4(g)] of approximately 60 in. (152.4 cm), along with a handrail height at the upper limit of permissible heights, is recommended in public assembly, educational, and similar occupancies where crowds of people must simultaneously use a stair for normal access and egress as well as for emergency egress. This permits everyone to reach and grasp one handrail. On monumental stairs the required handrails should be located along the normal path of travel to and from the building.

(h) New handrails on open sides of stairs shall have intermediate rails or an ornamental pattern such that a sphere, 6 in. (15.24 cm) in diameter, cannot pass through any openings in such handrail.

Exception: As provided in Chapters 14 and 15.

Figure 5-27 summarizes most of the handrail requirements.

5-2.2.3.5 Guard Details.

(a) The height of guards required by 5-2.2.3.1 shall be measured vertically to the top of the guard from the surface adjacent thereto.

(b) Guards shall be not less than 42 in. (106.68 cm) high.

Exception: Guards within dwelling units may be 36 in. (91.44 cm) high.

(c) Open guards shall have intermediate rails or ornamental pattern such that a sphere, 6 in. (15.24 cm) in diameter, cannot pass through any opening.

Exception No. 1: As provided in Chapters 14 and 15.

Exception No. 2: Approved existing open guards.

(d) Enclosure walls and guards consisting of masonry, railings, or other construction either shall be designed for loads transmitted by attached handrails or shall be

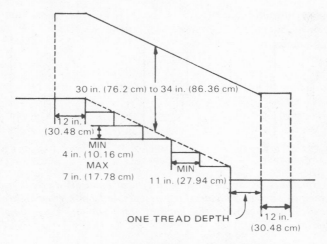

ELEVATION (STRAIGHT STAIR)

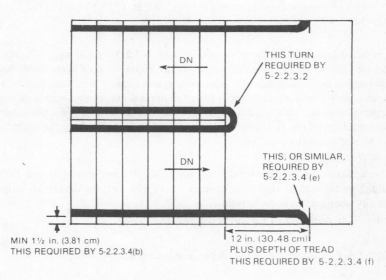

PLAN VIEW (RETURN STAIR)

TYPICAL HANDRAIL DETAILS

Figure 5-27. Typical Handrail Details.

designed to resist a horizontal force of 50 lb/ft (729.7 N/m) applied at the top of the guard, whichever condition produces maximum stresses. For walls or guards higher than minimum height the specified force shall be applied at a height of 42 in. (106.68 cm) above the floor or tread.

(e) Intermediate rails, balusters, and panel fillers shall be designed for a uniform load of not less than 25 lb/sq ft (1197 Pa) over the gross area of the guard (including the area of any openings in the guard) of which they are a part. Reactions due to this loading need not be added to the loading specified by 5-2.2.3.5(d) in designing the main supporting members of guards.

In order to prevent small children, in their inquisitiveness, from making their way through guards and to prevent them from being pushed through a guard by a panicked crowd, the configuration and construction of a guard in its plane must meet certain minimum requirements. Paragraph 5-2.2.3.5(c) represents a significant change from previous editions of the *Code*. Rather than several paragraphs of specifications for intermediate rails, this *Code* sets a performance criterion which allows alternate solutions.

Since pressures against guards may increase with the hurried movement of people in a panicked state, guards are required to withstand a horizontal force of 50 lb (22.68 kg) per lineal ft, and intermediate members, 25 lb per lineal ft (22.1 kg/sq m) (see Figure 5-28).

5-2.3 Smokeproof Towers.

5-2.3.1 A smokeproof tower shall be a stairway enclosure so designed that the movement into the smokeproof tower of products of combustion produced by a fire occurring in any part of the building shall be limited.

A smokeproof tower is a stair enclosure designed to limit the penetration of heat, smoke, and fire gases from a fire in any part of a building. This smoke control system should limit the entrance of products of combustion into the tower to a level where, during a period of 2 hours, the atmosphere of the smokeproof tower will not include a quantity of air emanating from the fire area that is more than 1 percent of the volume of the smokeproof tower. (This criterion is on a 97½ percent basis for the geographical location of the building. The 97½ percent basis for the outside winter temperature may be obtained from the ASHRAE *Handbook of Fundamentals*.)[6]

5-2.3.2 The appropriate design method shall be any system which meets the performance level stipulated in 5-2.3.1, above, or that given in 5-2.3.3 through 5-2.3.8, below.

The intent of 5-2.3.2 is to allow two general types of smokeproof towers. One type meets the performance criteria outlined in 5-2.3.1 and its commentary; thus a pressurized stairway would qualify. The second type meets the specification criteria given in 5-2.3.3 to 5-2.3.8. This second type of tower is characterized by the use of a balcony or vestibule to limit the possible entrance of smoke into the stairway enclosure proper. Either type of tower meets the requirements of 5-2.3.

See Figure 5-29 for examples of smokeproof towers that meet *Code* criteria.

5-2.3.3 A smokeproof tower, as herein specified, shall be a continuous, fire-resistive enclosure protecting a stairway from fire or smoke in the building served, with communication between the buildings and the tower by means of balconies directly open to the outer air.

5-2.3.4 Stairs, enclosure walls, vestibules, balconies, and other components of smokeproof towers shall be of noncombustible materials, and all other requirements specified in 5-2.2 for inside stairs shall apply to stairs in smokeproof towers.

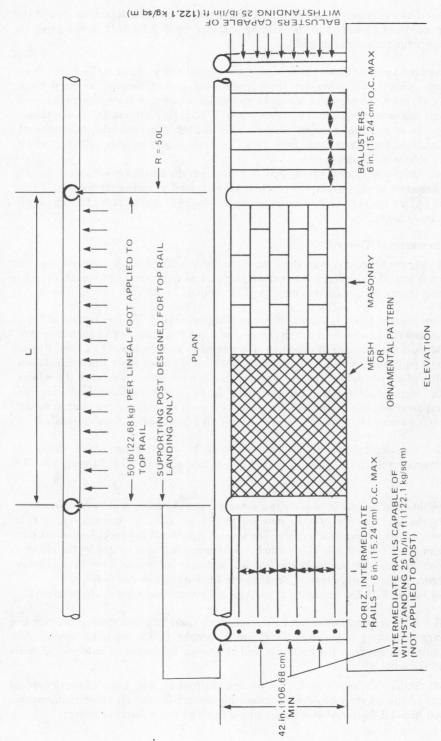

Figure 5-28. Details on the Installation of Guards and the Horizontal Loads They Are Required to Withstand.

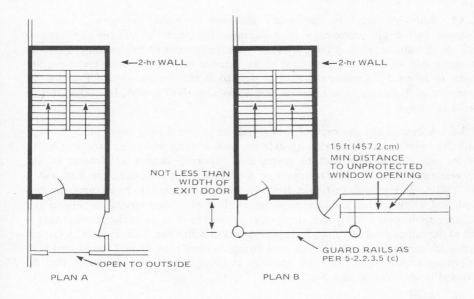

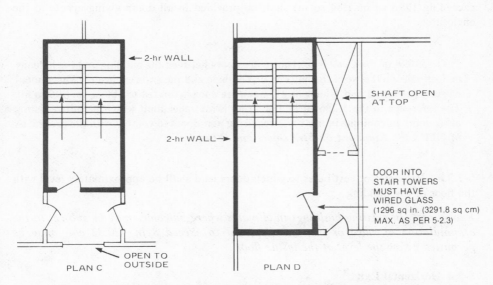

Figure 5-29. Four Variations of Smokeproof Towers Conforming to Code Criteria. Plan A is with a vestibule opening from a corridor. Plan B shows an entrance by way of an outside balcony. Plan C could provide a stair tower entrance common to two buildings. In Plan D, smoke and gases entering the vestibule would be exhausted by natural or induced draft in the open air shaft. In each case a double entrance to the stair tower with at least one side open or vented is characteristic of this type of construction. Pressurization of the stair tower in the event of fire provides an attractive alternate for tall buildings and is a means of eliminating the entrance vestibule.

5-2.3.5 Stairways shall be completely enclosed by walls having a 2-hour fire resistance rating and comprised of noncombustible material. There shall be no openings in walls separating the enclosure from the interior of the building. Fixed or automatic fire windows are permitted in an exterior wall of the stair enclosure not subject to severe fire exposure hazard as defined in the *Recommended Practice for Protection of Buildings from Exterior Fire Exposures*, NFPA 80A, from the same or nearby buildings.

5-2.3.6 Access to the smokeproof tower shall be provided from every story through vestibules open to the outside on an exterior wall or from balconies overhanging an exterior wall but not subject to severe fire exposure hazard as defined in the *Recommended Practice for Protection of Buildings from Exterior Fire Exposures*, NFPA 80A. Every such vestibule, balcony, or landing shall have an unobstructed length and width not less than the required width of exit doors serving same, and exit discharge shall open directly to a street or alley or yard or to an enclosed court that is open at the top and not less than 20 ft (609.6 cm) in width and 1000 sq ft (92.93 sq m) in area. Balconies or vestibules shall have guards not less than 42 in. (106.68 cm) high conforming with 5-2.2.3.5(c). Wall openings exposing balconies or vestibules shall be protected in accordance with 5-2.5.1.3.1.

5-2.3.7 Access from a building to vestibules or balconies shall be through doorways not less than 40 in. (101.6 cm) wide for new and 36 in. (91.44 cm) wide for existing towers. These openings and the entrances to the towers shall be provided with approved, self-closing fire doors swinging with the exit travel. Clear wired glass not exceeding 1296 sq in. (.84 sq m) shall be provided in all doors giving access to the enclosure.

> The intent of the *Code* is to require fire doors between the building and the balcony or vestibule and between the balcony or vestibule and the stair enclosure. The amount of glass permitted in a 1-hour or 1½-hour fire door is limited to 100 sq in. (.06 sq m). The reference to the 1,296 sq in. (84 sq m) is an upper limit which permits existing older doors to continue in use while requiring new doors to comply with the provisions of NFPA 80, *Standard on Fire Doors and Windows*[7].

5-2.3.8 Balconies or vestibules to which doors lead shall be approximately level with the floor of the building.

Exception: In existing buildings in climates where balconies may be subject to the accumulation of snow or ice, one step, not to exceed 8 in. (20.32 cm), may be permitted below the level of the inside floor.

5-2.4 Horizontal Exits.

5-2.4.1 General.

5-2.4.1.1 Application. Horizontal exits may be substituted for other exits to an extent that the total exit capacity of the other exits (stairs, ramps, doors leading outside the building) will not be reduced below half that required for the entire area of the building or connected buildings if there were no horizontal exits.

EXAMPLE: A department store building 270 ft by 210 ft (82 m by 64 m) (occupant load 945 per floor) would be required by this *Code* to have exits from the upper floors sufficient to furnish 16 units of exit width. This would ordinarily require eight 44-in. (111.76-cm) stairways.

Assume that this building is divided by a fire wall into two sections, one 100 ft by 210 ft (30 m by 64 m) and the other 170 ft by 210 ft (52 m by 64 m), with doors through the wall furnishing horizontal exits. The smaller section, considered separately, will require three 2-unit exits and the larger section will require five 2-unit exits. The horizontal exits will serve as one of the three exits required for the smaller section and two of the five exits required for the larger section. Therefore, only two 2-unit stairs from the smaller section and three 2-unit stairs from the larger section will be required, if the exits can be arranged to meet the requirements for the 150-ft (45.7-m) distance from any point, which can be done in a sprinklered building. Thus, the total number of stairways required for the building will be five, as compared with eight if no horizontal exit is provided. Another option would be the use of two 2½-unit stairs from the larger section, which would reduce the total number of stairways required to four. However, if the building were further subdivided by a second fire wall with fire doors in openings, no further reduction in the number of stairways is permitted. Figure 5-30 illustrates how to apply the requirement allowing the substitution of horizontal exits for other exits, a concept outlined in the aforementioned example. Figure 5-31 illustrates how that requirement may be violated.

5-2.4.1.2 Egress from Area of Refuge.

5-2.4.1.2.1 Every fire compartment for which credit is allowed in connection with a horizontal exit shall have in addition to the horizontal exit or exits at least one stairway or doorway leading outside or other exit which is not a horizontal exit. Any fire compartment not having a stairway or doorway leading outside shall be considered as part of an adjoining compartment with stairway.

Exception: As provided in Chapters 14 and 15.

5-2.4.1.2.2 Every horizontal exit for which credit is given shall be so arranged that there are continuously available paths of travel leading from each side of the exit to stairways or other standard means of egress leading to outside the building.

The requirement of 5-2.4.1.2.2 can be complied with only where the entire area from the horizontal exit to the stairway (or other standard means of egress) is occupied by the same tenant or where there are public corridors or other continuously available passageways leading from each side of the exit to the means of egress that will in turn lead to the outside.

5-2.4.1.2.3 Whenever either side of the horizontal exit is occupied, the doors used in connection with the horizontal exit shall be unlocked.

Exception: As provided in Chapters 12 through 15.

5-2.4.1.2.4 The floor area on either side of a horizontal exit shall be sufficient to hold the occupants of both floor areas, allowing not less than 3-sq ft (.28-sq m) clear floor area per person.

Exception: Special floor area requirements as provided in Chapters 12, 13, 14, and 15.

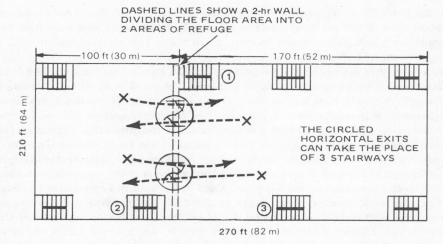

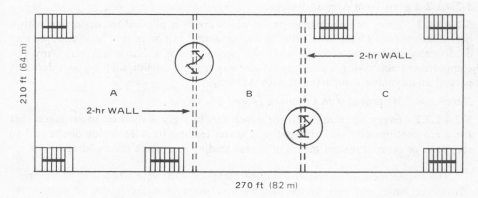

Figure 5-30. An Example of Substituting Horizontal Exits for Other Exits. Note that the horizontal exits (circled) take the place of stair towers as paths of escape for the occupants on either side of the 2-hour wall (shown as a dashed line) dividing the area into two sections. This would permit the elimination of the three stair towers closest to the horizontal exits, stair towers which would be required if the entire area was to be considered as one.

Figure 5-31. An Example of How Horizontal Exits (Circled) Cannot Be Used. The two horizontal exits from area B violate 5-2.4.1.1 in that at least one-half of the required exits must be other than horizontal exits. Area B also does not provide a continuous path of travel by stairway or other type of exit for occupants evacuating either area A or C as required by 5-2.4.1.2.

A horizontal exit is a passage from one building area into another building area, each separated from the other by a wall, space, or other form of protection of such a character that it enables one area to serve as an area of refuge from a fire in the other area. A horizontal exit, however, is not confined to one building. It can be a bridge from one building to another. Just as with other types of exits, the horizontal exit has components consisting of doors and enclosure walls, and often includes structural features, such as bridges and balconies, used in the passage from one area to the other. Because the horizontal exit is usually located on the same level as the area from which escape is desired, there are no stairs or ramps involved.

Although horizontal exits can often provide as fast and as safe a means of reaching an area of refuge as any other exit, they cannot be given credit for providing more than one-half the required exit capacity of the building or buildings connected, except in health care occupancies where they are permitted to provide two-thirds of the exit capacity and in Detention and Correctional Occupancies.

Before an area can be used as an area of refuge in a horizontal exit, it must itself satisfy certain criteria. An area, although protected with 2-hour enclosure walls, cannot be used as an area of refuge unless there is at least one other standard type of exit leading from it (not another horizontal exit) and unless the area is large enough to accommodate the occupants of both the fire area and area of refuge, allowing 3 sq ft (.28 sq m) of floor space per person. This figure is modified in Health Care Occupancies and in Detention and Correctional Occupancies. The nature of a horizontal exit is such that the psychological feeling of being in another area or building, away from the fire, can do much to prevent panic and the disorderly movement of people.

5-2.4.2 Walls for Horizontal Exits.

5-2.4.2.1 Walls or partitions separating buildings or areas between which there are horizontal exits shall be an assembly of noncombustible material having a 2-hour fire resistance rating. They shall provide a separation continuous to ground. (*See also 6-2.2.*)

Exception No. 1:   Such walls or partitions may be omitted on the street floor when they are supported on other construction having at least a 2-hour fire resistance rating continuous to the ground and meet all the conditions in the following Exception No. 2.

Exception No. 2:   Where a fire partition is used to provide a horizontal exit in any story of a building, such partition may be omitted in any lower story under the following conditions:

(a) The open fire area story from which the fire partition is omitted shall be separated from the stories above by construction having at least a 2-hour fire resistance rating.

(b) Required exits from the stories above the open fire area story shall be separated therefrom by construction having a 2-hour fire resistance rating and shall discharge outside without travel through the open fire area story.

(c) Vertical openings between the open fire area story and the stories above shall be enclosed with construction having a 2-hour fire resistance rating. Other details shall be in accordance with the applicable provisions of 6-2.2.

Exception No. 3:   Where a fire partition is used to provide a horizontal exit for any story below the discharge level, such partition may be omitted at the level of exit discharge under the following conditions:

(a) The open fire area story from which the fire partition is omitted shall be separated from the stories below by construction having at least a 2-hour fire resistance rating.

(b) Required exits from stories below the open fire area story shall be separated from the open fire area story by construction having a 2-hour fire resistance rating and shall discharge directly outside without travel through the open fire area story.

(c) Vertical openings between the open fire area story and the floors below shall be enclosed with construction having a 2-hour fire resistance rating. Other details shall be in accordance with the applicable provisions of 6-2.2.

Figure 5-32 illustrates how separation walls can be eliminated from the lower floors of a multistory building and still conform to the basic requirements of 5-2.4.2.

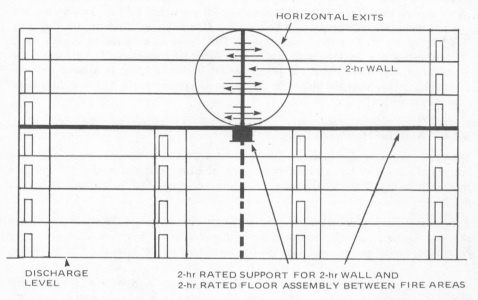

Figure 5-32. A Multistory Building Showing How a 2-Hour Rated Division Wall for Horizontal Exits can Be Stopped at any Lower Floor Rather than Extending to the Ground Floor (as Shown by the Dashed Line), as Required by 5-2.4.2.1. The same arrangement can be provided for basement areas.

5-2.4.2.2   Any opening in such walls, whether or not such opening serves as an exit, shall be adequately protected in an approved manner against the passage of fire or smoke..

NFPA 80, *Standard for Fire Doors and Windows,*[7] *covers the installation of fire doors.*

5-2.4.2.3   Swinging fire doors on horizontal exits shall swing with the exit travel. Where a horizontal exit serves areas on both sides of a wall, there shall be adjacent openings with swinging doors at each, opening in opposite directions, with signs on each side of the wall or partition indicating as the exit the door which swings with the travel from that side, or other approved arrangements providing doors always swinging with any possible exit travel.

The customary building code requirement for having fire doors placed on both sides of an opening in a fire wall may be met by having an automatic sliding fire door on one side, and a self-closing fire door swinging out from the other side of the wall. This arrangement qualifies only as a horizontal exit from the side of the sliding door (see Figure 5-33).

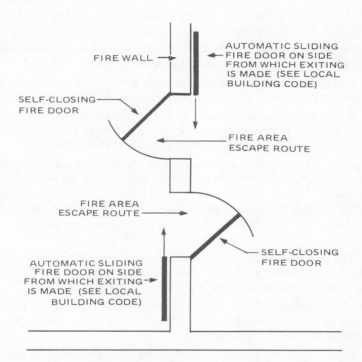

Figure 5-33. Arrangement of Fire Doors on Both Sides of Openings in a Fire Wall That Provides Horizontal Exits. Note that this arrangement only qualifies an opening as a horizontal exit from the side of the sliding door.

5-2.4.2.4 Sliding fire doors shall not be used on a horizontal exit.

Exception No. 1: Where the doorway is protected by a fire door on each side of the wall in which it occurs, one fire door shall be of the swinging type as provided in 5-2.4.2.3, and the other may be an automatic sliding fire door that shall be kept open whenever the building is occupied.

Exception No. 2: As provided in Chapters 14 and 15.

Automatic doors, often installed to cover the entire cross section of a building corridor, do not qualify as horizontal exits under the provisions of 5-2.4.2.4, because dangerous quantities of smoke might pass through the corridor before there is sufficient heat to close the door.

Automatic sliding doors are also difficult to open once they have closed and thus may trap people behind them in the absence of some other available means of escape.

5-2.4.3 Bridges and Balconies.

5-2.4.3.1 Each bridge or balcony utilized in conjunction with horizontal exits shall comply with the structural requirements for outside stairs and shall have guards and handrails in general conformity with the requirements of 5-2.2 for stairs and 5-2.3 for smokeproof towers.

5-2.4.3.2 Every bridge or balcony shall be at least as wide as the door leading to it and not less than 44 in. (111.76 cm) for new construction.

5-2.4.3.3 Every door leading to a bridge or balcony serving as a horizontal exit from a fire area shall swing with the exit travel out of the fire area.

5-2.4.3.4 Where the bridge or balcony serves as a horizontal exit in one direction, only the door from the bridge or balcony into the area of refuge shall swing in.

5-2.4.3.5 Where the bridge or balcony serves as a horizontal exit in both directions, doors shall be provided in pairs swinging in opposite directions. Only the door swinging with the exit travel shall be counted in determination of exit width.

Exception No. 1:   If the bridge or balcony has sufficient floor area to accommodate the occupant load of either connected building or fire area on the basis of 3 sq ft (.28 sq m) per person.

Exception No. 2:   In existing buildings by specific permission of the authority having jurisdiction, doors on both ends of the bridge or balcony may swing out from the building.

5-2.4.3.6 The bridge or balcony floor shall be approximately level with the building floor and in climates subject to the accumulation of snow and ice shall be protected to prevent the accumulation of snow and ice.

Exception: In existing buildings in climates where balconies may be subject to the accumulation of snow or ice, one step, not to exceed 8 in. (20.32 cm), may be permitted below the level of the inside floor.

5-2.4.3.7 Ramps shall be employed where there is a difference in level between connected buildings or floor areas. Steps may be used where the difference in elevation is greater than 21 in. (53.34 cm). Ramps and stairs shall be in accordance with the sections of this *Code* pertaining to ramps, stairs, and outside stairs.

> **One or two steps at a doorway are considered to constitute an accident hazard in emergency use. Stairways with level landings between the door and stair are satisfactory.**

5-2.4.3.8 All wall openings, in both of the connected buildings or fire areas, any part of which is within 10 ft (304.8 cm) of any bridge or balcony as measured horizontally or below, shall be protected with fire doors or fixed metal-frame, wired glass windows.

Exception: Where bridges have solid sides not less than 6 ft (182.88 cm) in height such protection of wall openings may be omitted.

5-2.5 Outside Stairs.

5-2.5.1 General.

5-2.5.1.1 Any permanently installed stair outside of the building served is acceptable in a means of egress under the same condition as an inside stair provided that such stairs comply with all the requirements for inside stairs. (*See 5-2.2.*)

Exception: As modified by the following paragraphs of this subsection.

The safety to life provisions for outside stairs and outside ramps are so alike that they can be covered in the same discussion and by using the same illustrations. The classification of outside stairs and ramps must conform to the provisions in 5-2.2.1.2 for inside stairs (discussed earlier in this chapter) and 5-2.6.1.2 for inside ramps. In general, these two outside components of a means of egress are accepted on the same basis and given the same considerations as their counterparts used inside the building. They must be separated from the interior of the building by walls having the same fire resistance required for walls used in inside enclosures, or a designated horizontal and vertical separation from openings in the walls of the building or adjoining buildings must be used. One advantage of the outside stair or ramp is that a person using it is outside of the building proper and in the open air — a decided psychological advantage in a fire. Also, fire department ladders can be easily used to help people off of outside stairs and ramps. Recognition of these advantages is reflected in 5-2.5.1.3.1 (stairs) and 5-2.6.2.2.1 (ramps) by waiving the fire resistance and separation requirements when the building is less than three stories.

5-2.5.1.2   Subject to the approval of the authority having jurisdiction, outside stairs may be accepted where leading to roofs of other sections of the building or adjoining building, where the construction is fire resistive, where there is a continuous and safe means of exit from the roof, and where all other reasonable requirements for life safety are maintained.

While not covered under the provisions for inside stairs and not likely to be the case for outside ramps, outside stairs leading to the roofs of other sections of the building or onto the roofs of adjoining buildings are acceptable as part of the means of egress, but only upon approval of the authority having jurisdiction. The conditions and settings of such paths of travel are likely to be so varied that it is virtually impossible to cover them by written provisions. Each situation is best judged individually by the authority having jurisdiction.

5-2.5.1.3 Separation and Protection.

5-2.5.1.3.1   Under all conditions where enclosure of inside stairways is required, outside stairs shall be separated from the interior of the building by fire-resistive walls the same as required for inside stairway enclosures with fire doors or fixed wired glass windows protecting any openings therein. When an exterior stairway serves more than two stories all openings below and all openings within a 10-ft (304.8-cm) horizontal projection of the stair and its landings shall be protected by a fixed or self-closing fire assembly having a ¾-hour fire protection rating.

5-2.5.1.3.2   All openings below an outside stair shall be protected:

(a) When located in a court the least dimension of which is less than one-third its height, or

(b) When located in an alcove having a width less than one-third its height and a depth greater than one-fourth its height.

Most important in the consideration of outside stairs and ramps is their proximity to openings in the wall of the building, openings through which fire emerging from the building could render stairs and ramps useless as a means of egress. Protection against this kind of occurrence takes two forms: (1) protection from openings, which is accomplished by distance separation; and (2) protection of openings, which must be done if the openings fall or are placed in a wall in such a way that the separation distances are less than required. The example of the old fire escape arrangement, in which a window access immediately below the fire escape landing leads to fire exposure of the fire escape, is the type of situation which must be avoided. By studying Figures 5-34 to 5-37, the enclosure provisions in 5-2.5.1.3 (outside stairs) and 5-2.6.1.3 (outside ramps) can more easily be understood.

Construction details for outside stairs and ramps are much the same as for inside stairs and ramps, except that attention must be given to providing a means for the inspection and painting of the exposed structural members, which might deteriorate in the weather.

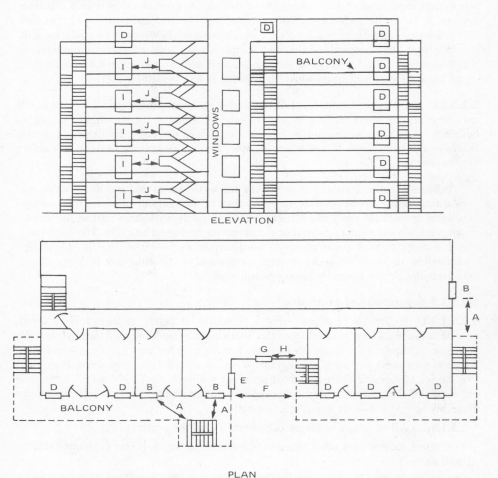

Figure 5-34. Protection of Openings for Outside Stairs — Example 1.
1. If distance A is less than 10 ft (304.8 cm), windows B must be protected.
2. Windows D require no protection.
3. Window E must be protected if distance F is less than 10 ft (304.8 cm).
4. Window G must be protected if distance H is less than 10 ft (304.8 cm).
5. Window I must be protected if distance J is less than 10 ft (304.8 cm).

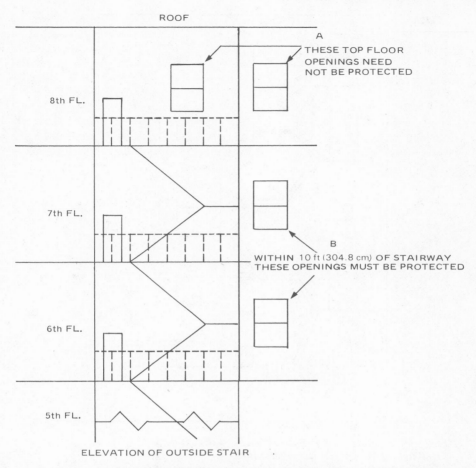

ROOF

A
THESE TOP FLOOR
OPENINGS NEED
NOT BE PROTECTED

8th FL.

7th FL.

B
WITHIN 10 ft (304.8 cm) OF STAIRWAY
THESE OPENINGS MUST BE PROTECTED

6th FL.

5th FL.

ELEVATION OF OUTSIDE STAIR

Figure 5-35. Protection of Openings for Outside Stairs — Example 2. Top floor openings A need not be protected if the outside stair does not go to the roof. If openings B are within 10 ft (304.8 cm) of the outside stairs they must be protected [see 5-2.5.1.3.1(c)].

5-2.5.1.3.3 Visual Enclosure. Outside stairs shall be so arranged as to avoid any handicap to the use of the stairs by persons having a fear of high places. For stairs more than three stories in height any arrangement intended to meet this requirement shall be at least 4 ft (121.92 cm) in height.

Outside stairs frequently have an open side that must be protected by a railing or guard. On high buildings, the fear of height may interfere with use of such stairs, and so 5-2.5.1.3.3 calls for a 4-ft high (121.92-cm high) guard construction to protect against this possibility. Guards required for the unenclosed sides of stairs (see 5-2.2.2) will usually meet this requirement when the stair is not more than three stories high. Special architectural treatment, including the application of such devices as metal or masonry screens and grills, will usually be necessary to accomplish the intent of this requirement for those stairs over three stories in height.

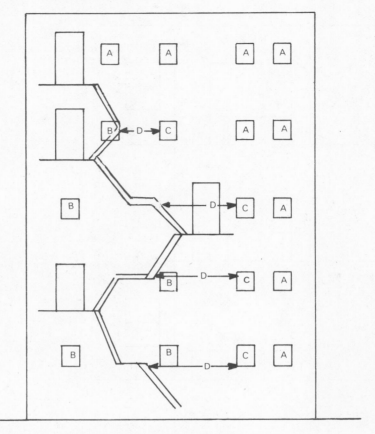

Figure 5-36. Protection of Outside Stairs — Example 3.
1. *Windows A need not be protected.*
2. *Windows B must be protected since they are below the stair.*
3. *Windows C must be protected when Distance D is less than 10 ft (304.8 cm).*

5-2.5.2 Balconies.   Balconies to which access doors lead shall be approximately level with the floor of the building.

Exception: In existing buildings in climates where balconies may be subject to accumulation of snow or ice, one step, not to exceed 8 in. (20.32 cm), may be permitted below the level of the inside floor.

Where snow and ice are a possibility, protection must be given against snow and ice accumulations that could block the free swing of the access doors leading to balconies or prevent full use of the stairs. The 8-in. (20.32-cm) clearance provided in the exception to 5-2.5.2 gives some of that protection; however, protection of the walking surfaces is also required.

5-2.5.3 Stair Details (*see 5-2.5.1.1*).

5-2.5.3.1   Treads shall be solid.

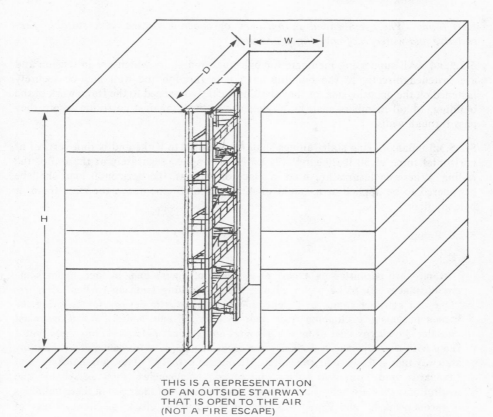

THIS IS A REPRESENTATION
OF AN OUTSIDE STAIRWAY
THAT IS OPEN TO THE AIR
(NOT A FIRE ESCAPE)

Figure 5-37. The Basis for Required Protection at Openings Below Open, Outside Stairs Discharging to a Courtyard.
1. *If D or W is less than one-third of H openings below the open, outside stairs must be protected.*
2. *If D is greater than one-fourth of H and W is more than one-third of H, no protection is required at openings.*

Example 1	*Example 2*
H = 60 ft (18.29 m)	*H = 60 ft (18.29 m)*
D or W < 20 ft (609.6 cm)	*D > 15 ft (457.2 cm) and*
Protection Required	*W = 20 ft (609.6 cm) or more*
	Protection Not Required

5-2.5.3.2 Risers shall be solid.

Exception: The skirt type, having a 1-in. (2.54-cm) space for drainage, shall be permitted.

5-2.5.3.3 No structural metal member shall be employed the entire surface of which is not capable of being inspected and painted.

Exception: Where embedded in masonry or concrete or where a suitable fire-resistive and waterproof covering is provided.

5-2.5.3.4 All supporting members for balconies and stairs which are in tension and are fastened directly to the building shall pass through the wall and be securely fastened on the opposite side, or they shall be securely fastened to the framework of the building. Metal members shall be protected effectively against corrosion where they pass through walls.

5-2.5.3.5 Balcony and stair railings shall be designed to withstand both a vertical or horizontal force of 50 lb/linear ft (729.7 N/m) applied separately at the top of the railing. Where enclosures are used in place of railings, the horizontal load shall be considered to be applied at a height of 42 in. (106.68 cm) above the stair tread or balcony floor.

5-2.6 Ramps.

Ramps are permitted as a part of a means of egress and, in fact, under some circumstances are to be preferred over stairs. Quoting from an earlier reference: "One can consider ramps and steps simply as prosthetic devices for assisting the human organism in climbing from floor to floor....," and, again: "When one must consider the energy cost of both horizontal and vertical movement, one finds that a ramp with a gradient of less than about eight degrees is more economical than any stairway that is likely to be encountered in normal activity."[3] The National Bureau of Standards study states in part: "For certain occupancies, such as schools and institutions, they are believed to be more satisfactory and their use in these buildings is recommended," and again: "...ramps have a rate of discharge between that of stairways and level passageways."[8]

The National Safety Council[9] has suggested the following criteria as a basis for the selection of a straight run of steps, a combination of steps and landings, or ramps:

Grade	Preference
20°-50°	Stairway
7°-20°	Stairway and landings
under 7°	Ramps

5-2.6.1 Inside Ramps.

5-2.6.1.1 General. A ramp shall be permitted as a component in a means of egress when it conforms to the general requirements of Section 5-1 and to the special requirements of this subsection.

5-2.6.1.2 Classification. A ramp shall be designated as Class A or Class B in accordance with the table at the top of p. 85.

Exception: Existing Class A ramps with slopes of 1 to 1³⁄₁₆ in 12 and Existing Class B ramps with slopes of 1³⁄₁₆ to 2 in 12 are permitted subject to the approval of the authority having jurisdiction.

	Class A	Class B
Minimum width	44 in. (111.76 cm)	30 in. (76.2 cm)
Maximum slope	1 in 10	1 in 8
Maximum height between landings	No limit	12 ft. (365.76 cm)

Capacity in persons per unit of exit width (except as modified by Chapters 8 through 30)

	Class A	Class B
Down	100	100
Up	100	60

Paragraph 5-2.6.1.2 establishes two classes of ramps: Class A and Class B. Class A ramps are required to be at least 44 in. (111.76 cm) wide with a maximum slope of 1 in 10, and no limit is placed on the height between landings. Certain health care occupancies are permitted to use these ramps, and their utility for the movement of wheelchairs and beds is obvious. Class B ramps are to be at least 30 in. (76.2 cm) wide, with a slope of 1 in 8, and have a 12-ft (365.76-cm) maximum height between landings. Considerable latitude is given the authority having jurisdiction with regard to the use of Class B ramps in existing buildings.

5-2.6.1.3 Enclosure.

5-2.6.1.3.1   When a ramp inside a building is used as a part of an exit it shall be protected by separation from other parts of the building, as specified in 5-1.3.

5-2.6.1.3.2   Fixed wired glass panels in steel sash may be installed in such a separation in a fully sprinklered building.

5-2.6.1.3.3   There shall be no enclosed usable space under ramps within an exit enclosure nor shall the open space under such ramps be used for any purpose. Where there is enclosed usable space under ramps the walls and soffits of the enclosed space shall be protected the same as the ramp enclosure.

It is the intent of 5-2.6.1.3.3 to prohibit closets and similar spaces under ramps. It is not to be interpreted as prohibiting an enclosed ramp from being located beneath another.

Although this paragraph may at first seem to contradict itself, it does not. First, the paragraph states that *within* an exit enclosure there shall be no enclosed usable space, nor shall any open space be used for any purpose which could interfere with the use of the exit enclosure. An enclosed usable space under a ramp can be considered to be outside of the exit enclosure if the walls and soffits of the enclosed space are protected the same as the ramp enclosure, thereby separating the space and the exit enclosure. The door to the space *cannot* open into the exit enclosure per 5-1.3.1(d).

5-2.6.1.4 Other Details.

5-2.6.1.4.1   A ramp and the platforms and landings associated therewith shall be designed for not less than 100-lb/sq ft (488.24-kg/m^2) live load.

5-2.6.1.4.2   The slope of a ramp shall not vary between landings. Landings shall be level and changes in direction of travel, if any, shall be made only at landings.

5-2.6.1.4.3   A ramp used as a means of egress in a building more than three stories in height or in a building of any height of noncombustible or fire-resistive construction shall be of an assembly of noncombustible or limited-combustible material. The ramp floor and landings shall be solid and without perforations.

5-2.6.1.4.4   A ramp shall have a slip-resistant surface.

5-2.6.1.4.5   Guards and handrails complying with 5-2.2.3 shall be provided in comparable situations for ramps.

5-2.6.2 Outside Ramps.

5-2.6.2.1 General.   Any ramp permanently installed on the outside of the building served shall be accepted as a component in a means of egress under the same conditions as an inside ramp, provided it complies with all requirements for inside ramps as modified by the following provisions of 5-2.6.2.

> Outside ramps may serve as part of a means of egress, subject to the regulations governing access to exits, exits, and exit discharges. When used as an exit, ramps must afford the occupant a protected passage from the point of entrance to the point of discharge. This applies to outside ramps as well as inside ramps. In fact, the same regulations apply here (see 5-2.6.2) as apply to outside stairs (see 5-2.5), including the requirements governing their location in a court or alcove (see 5-2.6.2.2.2).

5-2.6.2.2 Separation and Protection.

5-2.6.2.2.1   Under all conditions where enclosure of inside ramps is required, outside ramps serving as exits shall be separated from the interior of the building by wall construction that has a fire resistance rating equal to that required for such enclosure. When an exterior ramp serves more than two stories, all openings below and all openings within a 10-ft (304.8-cm) horizontal projection of the ramp and its landings shall be protected by a fixed or self-closing fire assembly having a ¾-hour fire protection rating.

5-2.6.2.2.2   All openings below an outside ramp shall be protected:

(a)   When in a court, the least dimension of which is less than one-third of its height, or

(b)   When in an alcove having a width less than one-third of its height and a depth greater than one-fourth of its height.

5-2.6.2.2.3 Visual Protection.   Outside ramps shall be so arranged as to avoid any handicap to their use by persons having a fear of high places. For ramps more than three stories in height, any arrangement intended to meet this requirement shall be at least 4 ft (121.92 cm) in height.

5-2.6.2.2.4   Balconies or landings to which doors lead shall be approximately level with the floor of the building.

Exception: In existing building in climates where balconies or landings may be subject to accumulation of snow or ice, one step, not to exceed 8 in. (20.32 cm), may be permitted below the level of the inside floor.

Paragraph 5-2.6.2.2 sets the same requirements for outside ramps as 5-2.5.1.3 does for outside stairs. See pages 79-83 for discussion of the requirements for outside stairs.

5-2.6.2.3 Ramp Details.

5-2.6.2.3.1 Structural metal members, where used, shall be capable of inspection over their entire length.

Exception: Where embedded in masonry or concrete, where a suitable fire-resistive and waterproof covering is provided, or where corrosion-resistive metals are used.

5-2.6.2.3.2 All supporting members for balconies and ramps that are in tension and are fastened directly to the building shall pass through the wall and be securely fastened on the opposite side or shall be securely fastened to the framework of the building. Metal members shall be protected effectively against corrosion where they pass through walls.

5-2.6.2.3.3 Balcony and ramp railings shall be designed to withstand both a vertical and horizontal force of 50 lb per linear ft (729.7 N/m) applied separately at the top of the railing. Where enclosures are used in place of railings, the horizontal load shall be considered to be applied at a height of 42 in. (106.68 cm) above the stair tread or balcony floor.

5-2.7 Exit Passageways.

An exit passageway serves as a horizontal means of exit travel and is protected from fire in a manner similar to an enclosed interior exit stair. Where it is desired to offset exit stairs in a multistory building, an exit passageway can be used to preserve the continuity of the protected exit by connecting the bottom of one stair to the top of another stair that will continue to the exit discharge. Probably the most important use of an exit passageway is to satisfy the requirement that exit stairs discharge directly to the outside from multistory buildings. Thus, if it is impractical to locate the stair on an exterior wall, an exit passageway can be connected to the bottom of the stair to convey the occupants safely to an outside exit door. In buildings with an extremely large area, such as shopping malls and some factories, the exit passageway can be used to advantage where the distance of travel to reach an exit would otherwise be excessive. Exit passageways are different from access aisles, corridors, and hallways in that the latter are not required to be protected by a fire-resistant enclosure.

The fact that the word *exit* is used in the expression "exit passageway" signals that it is not just any passageway; it is an area providing the same level of protection and safety that is required of any exit. It is a very versatile feature because it can be used to extend an exit, as mentioned before, or as is done in many cases, it can be used to bring an exit closer. As shown in Figure 5-38, by simply extending the protecting enclosure along what would normally be the corridor and then relocating the exit door, the exit can, in effect, be extended. This also gives an advantage to the designer in that it actually increases the travel distance while not changing the permitted travel distance at all. The proper use of an exit passageway can often solve what may seem to be insurmountable problems and very costly solutions in the design of the means of egress. While an exit passageway is for the most part a horizontal means of travel, it must be considered in light of the entire exit and have whatever protection is required for the number of stories that the overall exit serves. Paragraph 5-1.3 details separation requirements. A simple way to remember the protection requirements for exit passageway is that they are the same as for stairs.

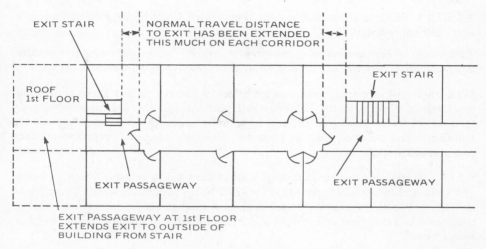

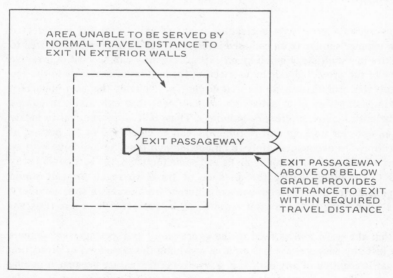

Figure 5-38. *Extending Exits by Use of Exit Passageways.*

5-2.7.1 General. Any hallway, corridor, passage, tunnel, underfloor passageway, or overhead passageway shall be permitted as an exit passageway and as an exit or exit component when conforming to all other requirements of Section 5-1 as modified by the provisions of this section.

5-2.7.2 Enclosure. An exit passageway shall be protected by separation from other parts of the building as specified in 5-1.3.

Exception: Fixed wired glass panels in steel sash may be installed in such a separation in a fully sprinklered building.

5-2.7.3 Width. The width of an exit passageway shall be adequate to accommodate the aggregate capacity of all exits discharging through it.

5-2.7.4 Floor. The floor shall be solid and without perforations.

5-2.8 Escalators and Moving Walks.

5-2.8.1 General.

5-2.8.1.1 An escalator or moving walk may be accepted as a component in a means of egress where permitted by Chapters 8 through 30 when it conforms to the general requirements of Section 5-1 and to the special requirements of this subsection.

As specified in 5-2.8.1.1, escalators and moving walkways may be used as components in a means of egress when allowed by the appropriate occupancy chapter; however, reference must be made to the appropriate occupancy chapter for more detailed information about their proper use. Several of the occupancy chapters (generally in the "2.2" sections such as 12-2.2 or 24-2.2) do not include escalators and moving walkways among the types of exits permitted. This is true of educational, health care, and storage occupancies. If used, escalators and moving walkways must be protected as for any other vertical opening. Even if they are recognized as a required exit, there are limits placed on the credit that can be given to them as exits. Under such conditions economic factors come into play and have a tendency to prevent any excesses in their use.

5-2.8.1.2 Enclosure (*see 6-2.2*).

5-2.8.2 Escalators.

5-2.8.2.1 An escalator shall comply with the applicable requirements for stairs in 5-2.2.

Exception: As modified in 5-2.8.2.2 through 5-2.8.2.7.

5-2.8.2.2 Escalators constituting a means of egress shall operate only in the direction of egress.

Usually escalators are provided in pairs, i.e., one separate stair moving up and another moving down; however, should the electricity fail and both stop, there would actually be two stairs available for downward movement. With this in mind, one might propose that both stairways be accepted as constituting a means of egress, with the idea that the current could intentionally be turned off. The problem is that in an emergency the current might not get turned off, and one stair would continue to move against traffic. For this reason 5-2.8.2.2 specified only those escalators moving in the direction of egress as constituting a means of egress.

5-2.8.2.3 An escalator shall be of the horizontal tread type and shall be of noncombustible construction throughout.

Exception: Step tread surfaces, handrails, and step wheels.

5-2.8.2.4 A single escalator 32 in. (81.28 cm) wide shall be given credit for one unit of exit width. An escalator 48 in. (121.92 cm) wide shall be given credit for two units of exit width.

Even though a person does not have to exert any energy or do any moving while on an escalator, there are many people who are frightened by them and many who are extremely cautious in approaching them, factors which would contribute to a bottleneck. Thus, it is recognized that an escalator would have to be wider than a stair to effectively move the same number of people. Taking this into consideration, the permitted capacity of the escalator is kept the same as for other types of stair exits by requiring a wider unit of exit width, as specified in 5-2.8.2.4.

5-2.8.2.5 There shall be an unobstructed space of at least 4 in. (10.16 cm) outside the handrail and above the handrail for the full length of the escalator.

5-2.8.2.6 No single escalator shall have an uninterrupted vertical travel of more than one story.

5-2.8.2.7 Escalators shall be designed, installed, and operated in accordance with the *Safety Code for Elevators, Dumbwaiters, Escalators, and Moving Walks*, ANSI A17.1.

ANSI A17.1, *Safety Code for Elevators, Dumbwaiters, Escalators, and Moving Walks*,[10] is the source of generally accepted standards of safe engineering practice, and escalators must be designed according to provisions of that code.

5-2.8.3 Moving Walks.

5-2.8.3.1 An inclined moving walk shall comply with the applicable requirements of 5-2.6 for ramps, and a level moving walk shall comply with the applicable requirements of 5-2.7 for exit passageways.

Exception: As modified in 5-2.8.3.2 through 5-2.8.3.3.

5-2.8.3.2 No moving walk capable of being operated in the direction contrary to normal exit travel shall be used in a means of egress.

5-2.8.3.3 Moving walks shall be designed, installed, and operated in accordance with the *Safety Code for Elevators, Dumbwaiters, Escalators, and Moving Walks*, ANSI A17.1.

Most of the same principles which apply to the design and operation of escalators also apply to moving walkways. The major difference is that the moving walkway — moving in the direction of exit travel — can be evaluated in terms of the usual 22-in. (55.9-cm) unit of exit width rather than the larger dimensions specified for escalators in 5-2.8.2.4. (See *Safety Code for Elevators, Dumbwaiters, Escalators, and Moving Walks*, ANSI A17.1.)[10]

5-2.9 Fire Escape Stairs.

5-2.9.1 General.

Fire escape stairs and ladders have fallen into disrepute for a variety of reasons. These include:
1. Unsightly appearance;
2. Possible icing in winter weather;
3. Expense of maintenance (the metal is subject to corrosion);
4. Possibility of users being trapped by a fire below; and
5. Fear of height, and hence an objection to using them.

On the other hand, well-maintained fire escape stairs can and have saved many lives when smoke-filled exit stairs have become impassable. A classic example of this is the June 5, 1946 fire in the 22-story LaSalle Hotel in Chicago. "Hundreds" of people made their escape from the building on outside fire escape stairs.[11] Many other similar examples could be quoted.

There are times when fire fighters have been able to use outside fire escape stairs to advantage. On the other hand, instances could be cited where rusted fire escapes have collapsed or where people have been fatally burned because fire broke out of windows or doors at a lower level. The committee has consistently held that the goal of safety from fire can best be served by the proper internal design of exit ways and the gradual phasing out of fire escape stairs as new buildings replace old.

In summary, the provisions of 5-2.9 on fire escape stairs should be looked upon in this light: if escape stairs must be put in an existing building or are found in an existing building, they must adhere to provisions of the *Code* in order to provide as high a level of safety as might be expected.

5-2.9.1.1 Application.

5-2.9.1.1.1   Fire escape stairs may be used in required means of egress only in existing buildings, subject to the provisions of the applicable occupancy chapter.

Fire escape stairs as specified in this section of the *Code* should not be confused with the outside stairs covered in 5-2.5.

At best, fire escape stairs are regarded as only an expedient in remedying the deficiencies in exits of existing buildings, where it may not be practicable to provide outside stairs or additional inside stairways, properly enclosed and conforming to all other provisions of this *Code*. Fire escape stairs, however, may greatly facilitate fire department rescue and fire fighting operations.

The fire escape stairs specified by this *Code* should not be confused with the inferior fire escapes which are commonly found on old buildings. These utterly inadequate, flimsy, precipitous fire escapes, unshielded against fire in the structure to which they are attached, are positively a menace because they give an occupant a false sense of security. Such escape stairs are not recognized by this *Code* as exits.

Even the fire escape stairs constructed in accordance with this *Code* have limitations which may prevent their effective use in time of fire. Even where window protection is provided, conditions may be such that fire (or the smoke from fire) on lower floors may render the stairs impassable before the occupants of the upper floors have had time to use them. Fire escape stairs may be blocked by snow, ice, or sleet at the time when they are most needed. People using fire escape stairs at a considerable height are likely to be timid and to descend the stairs, if at all, at a rate much slower than that used for inside stairs. This is true even when the solid tread stairs that are specified by the *Code* are used in place of the ordinary slatted-tread construction. Fire escape stairs are not a usual means of egress. Occupants of buildings will not so readily use them in case of fire as they will the usual means of exit, the inside stairway. Because they are an emergency device and not ordinarily used, their proper upkeep may be neglected.

5-2.9.1.1.2   Fire escape stairs shall not constitute more than 50 percent of the required exit capacity in any case.

5-2.9.1.1.3   Fire escape stairs shall not be accepted as constituting any part of the required means of egress for new buildings.

The basic principles of the *Code* regarding fire escape stairs are contained in 5-2.9.1.1.1 to 5-2.9.1.1.3. Absolutely no recognition is given to the use of fire escape stairs in new buildings, for any of the three parts of a means of egress. Only a token recognition of 50 percent is given for existing buildings, and this is simply because the escape stairs have already been installed or because they may be the only economical manner of upgrading a system of means of egress in an existing building. To recognize them in the latter instance is at least better than completely ignoring the limited value of a poor system.

5-2.9.1.2   Fire escape stairs shall provide a continuous unobstructed safe path of travel to the ground or other safe area of refuge to which they lead. Where the fire escape is not continuous, as in cases where stairs lead to an adjoining roof that must be crossed before continuing downward travel, the direction of travel shall be clearly indicated and suitable walkways with handrails shall be provided where necessary. Where a single means of egress consists of a combination of inside stairs and fire escape stairs, each shall comply with the applicable provisions of this *Code*, and the two shall be so arranged and connected as to provide a continuous safe path of travel.

5-2.9.1.3 Types.   The following types of fire escape stairs are recognized by this *Code*:

(a) Return platform type, superimposed runs.

(b) Straight run type with platforms continuing in the same direction.

Either of the above types may be parallel to or at right angles to the building. They may be attached to buildings or erected independently of them and connected by bridges. (*See also 5-2.9.7 for swinging stairs.*)

5-2.9.2 Protection of Openings.

5-2.9.2.1   Fire escape stairs shall be so arranged that they will be exposed by the smallest possible number of window and door openings. There shall be no transoms over doors. Every opening any portion of which is in the limits specified below shall be completely protected by approved fire doors or metal-frame, wired glass windows as follows:

(a) *Horizontally.*   If within 15 ft (457.2 cm) of any balcony, platform, or stairway constituting a part of the escape proper.

Exception No. 1:   This provision does not apply to a platform or walkway leading from the same floor to the escape proper.

Exception No. 2:   Protection need not extend around a right angle corner (outside angle 270 degrees) of the building where stairs are remote from such corner.

(b) *Below.*   If within three stories or 35 ft (10.67 m) of any balcony, platform, walkway, or stairway constituting a part of the escape proper or within two stories or 20 ft (609.6 cm) of a platform or walkway leading from any story to the escape proper.

(c) *Above.*   If within 10 ft (304.8 cm) of any balcony, platform, or walkway as measured vertically or of any stair treads as measured vertically from the face of the outside riser.

(d) *Top Story.*   Protection for wall openings shall not be required where stairs do not lead to the roof.

5-2.9.2.2   All openings below a fire escape stair shall be protected:

(a) When in a court, the least dimension of which is less than one-third of its height, or

(b) When in an alcove having a width less than one-third of its height and depth greater than one-fourth of its height.

Exception: The provisions of 5-2.9.2 may be modified by the authority having jurisdiction in consideration of automatic sprinkler protection, low hazard occupancy, or other special conditions.

5-2.9.3 Access.

5-2.9.3.1   Access to fire escape stairs shall be provided in accordance with 5-2.9.4 and the general provisions of 5-4.1.2.

5-2.9.3.2   Where access is by way of double hung windows, such windows shall be so counterbalanced and maintained that they can be readily opened with a minimum of physical effort. Insect screens, if any, on any type of opening giving access to fire escape stairs shall be of types that may be readily opened or pushed out. No storm sash shall be used on any window providing access to fire escape stairs.

Access to fire escape balconies by doors or by casement windows equivalent to doors, with sills at floor level, is the only way in which fire escape stairs can furnish exit facilities in any way equivalent to inside stairs. Where access requires climbing over window sills, the exit facility is inherently inferior; such arrangements are suitable only for relatively small numbers of people in existing buildings where the provision of doors may be impracticable. Figure 5-39 indicates the more critical measurements for windows opening onto fire escape stairs.

5-2.9.3.3   Fire escape stairs shall extend to the roof in all cases where the roof is subject to occupancy or is constructed and arranged to provide an area of refuge from fire. In all cases where stairs do not extend to the roof, access thereto shall be provided by a ladder in accordance with 5-2.10.

Exception: Such ladders are not required in the case of roofs with pitch steeper than 2 in. to 1 ft (1 m to 6 m).

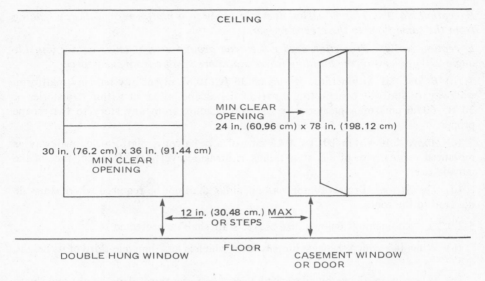

Figure 5-39. Window Openings for Fire Escape Exits.

5-2.9.3.4   Balconies to which access doors lead shall be approximately level with the floor of the building or, in climates where balconies may be subject to accumulation of snow or ice, one step no more than 8 in. (20.32 cm) below the level of the inside floor shall be allowed.

5-2.9.3.5   Balconies to which access is secured through windows with sills above the inside floor level shall be not more than 18 in. (45.72 cm) below the sill. In no case shall the balcony level be above the sill.

5-2.9.4 Stair Details.   Fire escape stairs, depending upon the requirements of Chapters 8 through 30 of this *Code*, shall be in accordance with Table 5-2.9.4 and subsequent paragraphs.

Generally, the requirements for fire escape stairs are similar to those specified for outside stairs which are located on buildings four or more stories in height. The major difference between the two types of stairways lies in the dimensions for fire escape stairs, as shown in Table 5-1. Also shown are the differences between the generally accepted fire escape stair of existing buildings and the lighter fire escape stair acceptable for existing "very small" buildings serving ten or fewer occupants.

The existing stair, with a minimum width of 22 in. (55.88 cm) is a type which may be acceptable for buildings of small or moderate size. Depending upon local conditions, these existing fire escape stairs may generally be accepted.

The existing stair with a minimum width of 18 in. (45.72 cm) represents the absolute minimum that may be accepted in an existing fire escape stairway. Because of access over window sills, steep pitch, and a narrow width, the travel down such stairs will be necessarily slow and may be dangerous. Stairs with spiral stair treads or the stairs which terminate at a balcony above ground level with a fixed or movable ladder going from there down are even worse. These stairs are suitable only in situations where a very small number of people is involved.

Table 5–2.9.4

	Existing Stairs	Existing Stairs Serving 10 or less occupants (very small buildings)
Minimum widths	22 in. (55.88 cm) clear between rails	18 in. (45.72 cm) clear between rails
Minimum horizontal dimension any landing or platform	22 in. (55.88 cm)	18 in. (45.72 cm)
Maximum rise	9 in. (22.86 cm)	12 in. (30.48 cm)
Minimum tread, exclusive of nosing	9 in. (22.86 cm)	6 in. (15.24 cm)
Minimum nosing or projection	1 in. (2.54 cm)	No requirement
Tread construction	Solid, ½-in. (1.27-cm) dia. perforations permitted	Flat metal bars on edge or sq. bars secured against turning, spaced 1¼ in. (3.18 cm) max. on centers
Winders (spiral)	None	Permitted subject to capacity penalty
Risers	None	No requirement
Maximum height between landings	12 ft. (365.76 cm)	No requirement
Headroom, minimum	6 ft. 8 in. (203.2 cm)	6 ft. 8 in. (203.2 cm)
Access to escape	Door or casement windows 24 in. × 6 ft. 6 in. (60.96 cm × 198.12 cm) or double hung windows 30 in. × 36 in. (76.2 cm × 91.44 cm) clear opening	Windows
Level of access opening	Not over 12 in. (30.48 cm) above floor; steps if higher	Same
Discharge to ground	Swinging stair section permitted	Swinging stair, or ladder if approved
Capacity, number of persons	45 per unit,* if access by door; 20 if access by climbing over windowsill	10; if winders or ladder from bottom balcony, 5; if both, 1

*See 5–2.1.1.3 for counting fractions of a unit for stairs more than one unit wide.

Table 5-1. Differences Between Outside Stairs and Fire Escape Stairs.

Design Factor	New Outside Stair	Existing Outside Stair Class A	B	Fire Escape Stair Normal	Small Buildings
Accepted as Exit	Yes	Yes		Existing buildings	
Access openings protected	Yes, over 2 stories	Yes, over 2 stories		Required	
Fire separation	Required	Required		Not required	
Width	44 in.*	44 in.	44 in.*	22 in.	18 in.
Maximum rise	7 in.	7½ in.	8 in.	9 in.	12 in.
Minimum tread	11 in.	10 in.	9 in.	9 in.	6 in.
Tread constitution	solid	solid		solid	metal bars

Metric: 1 in. = 2.54 cm

Note: The capacity of normal fire escape stairs is 45 persons for doors, and 20 for windows where a sill must be climbed over. On small buildings the capacity is 10 persons, 5 if winders or a ladder from bottom landing, 1 if both winders and a ladder from bottom landing.

*36 in. when serving occupant load of 50 or less.

5-2.9.5 Guards and Handrails.

5-2.9.5.1 All fire escapes shall have walls or guards on both sides in accordance with 5-2.2.3.

5-2.9.5.2 All fire escapes shall have handrails on both sides, not less than 30 in. (76.2 cm) nor more than 42 in. (106.68 cm) high measured vertically from a point on the stair tread 1 in. (2.54 cm) back from the leading edge, all in general conformity to the requirements for stair handrails in 5-2.2.3.

5-2.9.5.3 Handrails and guards shall be so constructed as to withstand a force of 200 lb (889.6 N) applied downward or horizontally at any point.

5-2.9.6 Materials and Strength.

5-2.9.6.1 Iron, steel, or concrete, or other approved noncombustible materials shall be used for the construction of fire escape stairs, balconies, railings, and other features appurtenant thereto.

5-2.9.6.2 Balconies and stairs shall be designed to carry a live load of 100 lb/sq ft (488.24 kg/sq m) or a concentrated load of 300 lb (136.08 kg) so located as to produce maximum stress conditions.

5-2.9.6.3 Structural metal members, where used, shall be capable of inspection over their entire length.

Exception: Where embedded in masonry or concrete, where a suitable fire-resistive and waterproof covering is provided, or where corrosion-resistive metals are used.

5-2.9.6.4 All supporting members for balconies and stairs that are in tension and are fastened directly to the buildings shall pass through the wall and be securely fastened on the opposite side or they shall be securely fastened to the framework of the building. Where metal members pass through walls, they shall be protected effectively against corrosion.

5-2.9.6.5 Balcony and stair railings shall be designed to withstand both a vertical and horizontal force of 50 lb per linear ft (729.7 N/m) separately applied at the top of the railing. Where enclosures are used in place of railings, the horizontal load shall be considered to be applied at a height of 42 in. (106.68 cm) above the stair tread or balcony floor.

Exception: As provided in 5-2.9.6.6

5-2.9.6.6 Notwithstanding the provisions of 5-2.9.6.2 and 5-2.9.6.5, the authority having jurisdiction may approve any existing fire escape stair for a very small building when it has been shown by load test or other satisfactory evidence to have adequate strength.

5-2.9.7 Swinging Stairs.

5-2.9.7.1 Swinging stair sections shall not be used for fire escape stairs.

Exception: Where termination over sidewalks, alleys, or driveways makes it impracticable to build stairs permanently to the ground. Where used, swinging stairs shall comply with 5-2.9.7.2 through 5-2.9.7.9.

5-2.9.7.2 Swinging sections of stairs shall not be located over doors, over the path of travel from any other exit, or in any location where there are or are likely to be obstructions.

5-2.9.7.3 Width of swinging sections of stairs shall be at least equal to that of the stairs above.

5-2.9.7.4 The pitch of swinging sections of stairs shall not be steeper than that of the stairs above.

5-2.9.7.5 Railings shall be provided similar in height and construction to those required for the stairs above. Railings shall be designed to prevent any possibility of injury to persons at the head of the stairs or on balconies when stairs swing downward. Minimum clearance between moving sections where hands might be caught shall be 4 in. (10.16 cm).

5-2.9.7.6 If the distance from the lowest platform to ground exceeds 12 ft (365.76 cm), an intermediate balcony not more than 12 ft (365.76 cm) from the ground or less than 7 ft (213.36 cm) in the clear underneath shall be provided with width not less than that of the stairs and length not less than 4 ft (121.92 cm).

5-2.9.7.7 Counterweight shall be provided for swinging stairs and this shall be of a type balancing about a pivot; no cables shall be used. Counterweight shall be securely bolted in place, but sliding ball weights or their equivalent may be used to hold stairs up and to help lower them. Counterbalancing shall be such that a weight of 150 lb (68.04 kg) one step from the pivot shall not start the swinging section downward, and a weight of 150 lb (68.04 kg) one quarter of the length of the swinging stairs from the pivot will positively cause the stairs to swing down.

Where a fire escape stair would block a sidewalk or other public way, or provide ready access for intruders, the discharge may be counterweighted, and the unlocked swinging stair designed so that a 150-lb (68-kg) weight applied one-quarter of the length from the pivot point will cause the stair to drop into the usable position.

5-2.9.7.8 The pivot for swinging stairs shall either have a corrosion-resistant assembly or shall have sufficient clearance to prevent sticking due to corrosion.

5-2.9.7.9 No device to lock the swinging stair section in up position shall be installed.

A latch is desirable, however, to hold the stairs down, once they have swung to the ground.

5-2.10 Fire Escape Ladders.

5-2.10.1 General. No form of ladder shall be used as a fire escape under the provisions of this *Code*.

Exception No 1:   Ladders conforming to the following specifications may be used:

(a) To provide access to unoccupied roof spaces as permitted by 5-2.9.3.3.

(b) To provide a means of escape from boiler rooms, grain elevators, and towers, as permitted by Chapters 29 and 30, and elevated platforms around machinery or similar spaces subject to occupancy only by able-bodied adults, not more than 3 in number.

Exception No. 2:   Existing ladders may be accepted to provide access to the street from the lowest balcony of fire escape stairs for very small buildings if approved by the authority having jurisdiction subject to the limitations in capacity specified in 5-2.9.4.

Although the *Code* contains provisions for fire escape ladders, it does not mean to recommend their use. Note that in 5-2.10.1 reference is made only to their use as a fire escape; nothing is said relative to a means of egress. These ladders, when they are used, are used because they are about the only means of moving from one space to another along what might be a path of egress for some occupants who might frequent certain spaces from time to time. The intent of the *Code* is not to encourage the use of ladders but to provide access to an exit from any regularly occupied area. The provisions of 5-2.10.1, and those contained in Chapters 15 and 16 for storage occupancies and unusual structures, constitute the very minimal recognition given fire escape ladders by this *Code*. The *Code* does specify requirements for ladder construction and installation to ensure their structural integrity and ease of use if they must be installed.

Other requirements for ladders may be imposed by the Occupational Safety and Health Act. Reference should be made to OSHA Regulations.

5-2.10.2 Installation.

5-2.10.2.1 All ladders shall be permanently installed in a fixed position supported by rigid connection to the building or structure at intervals not exceeding 10 ft (304.8 cm).

Counterbalanced ladders, and other forms of movable ladders designed to provide access from the lowest fire escape balcony to the street, are not recognized as exits by this *Code*.

5-2.10.2.2 Where ladders provide access to roofs or elevated platforms, rails shall extend not less than 45 in. (114.3 cm) above the roofline or platform floor or 45 in. (114.3 cm) above the coping or parapet, if there is one. Extension of side rails to roof shall be carried over the coping or parapet to afford a handhold.

5-2.10.2.3 Ladders shall be arranged parallel to buildings or structures with travel either between the ladder and building, in which case minimum clearance between center of rungs and building shall be 27 in. (68.58 cm), or outside of the ladder, in which case minimum clearance between center of rungs and building shall be 6½ in. (165.1 cm).

MEANS OF EGRESS   99

5-2.10.2.4 Ladders shall be vertical or positively inclined. No negative incline (i.e., ladder sloping out over head of person using it) shall be permitted.

5-2.10.3 Construction.

5-2.10.3.1 Ladders shall be constructed of iron, of steel, or of other metal in design having equivalent strength and resistance to corrosion.

5-2.10.3.2 Rails of iron or steel ladders shall be not less than ½ in. × 2 in. (1.27 cm × 5.08 cm) in section, and not less than 16 in. (40.64 cm) apart.

5-2.10.3.3 Rungs shall be not less than ⅞ in. (2.22 cm) in diameter and shall be riveted or welded in position not less than 10 in. (25.4 cm) nor more than 12 in. (30.48 cm) on centers.

5-2.10.3.4 The lowest rung of any ladder shall be not more than 12 in. (30.48 cm) above the level of the ground or balcony floor beneath it.

5-2.11 Slide Escapes.

5-2.11.1 General.

5-2.11.1.1 A slide escape may be used as a component in a means of egress where specifically authorized by Chapters 8 through 30.

5-2.11.1.2 Each slide escape shall be of an approved type.

5-2.11.1.3 Slide escapes used as exits shall comply with the applicable requirements of Chapter 5 for other types of exits subject to the approval of the authority having jurisdiction.

Slide escapes are given more recognition than ladders and fire escapes in that they are permitted as a component in a means of egress and even as exits. Customarily, one thinks of entering a slide escape through a window or special opening in an exterior wall, and from that point on they function as an exit discharge. Should the slide escape be entered from within the building, and thus be considered as an exit, it must be protected as an exit enclosure as required by 5-1.3; that is, until it passes through the exterior wall. It is the *Code*'s intent that slide escapes have the same separation or protection from openings in the exterior walls as do outside stairs and ramps.

A slide pole, of the type found in fire stations, is not considered as a slide escape.

5-2.11.2 Capacity.

5-2.11.2.1 Slide escapes, where permitted as required exits, shall be rated at one exit unit per slide, with rated travel capacity of 60 persons.

5-2.11.2.2 Slide escapes shall not constitute more than 25 percent of the required number of units of exit width from any building or structure or any individual story or floor thereof.

Exception: As permitted for high hazard manufacturing buildings or structures.

The 25 percent limitation on slides as a required exit prohibits designating a slide as one of two exits when two exits are required.

SECTION 5-3   CAPACITY OF MEANS OF EGRESS

5-3.1 Occupant Load. ← *total # of people in the structure at any given time.*

5-3.1.1   The capacity of means of egress for any floor, balcony, tier, or other occupied space shall be sufficient for the occupant load thereof.

The normal occupancy load is not necessarily a suitable criterion for determining the size of the means of egress, as the greatest hazard may occur when an unusually large crowd is present; this is a condition often difficult for the authority having jurisdiction to control by regulatory measures. The principle of this *Code* is to provide exits for the maximum probable number of occupants, rather than to attempt to limit the number of occupants to a figure commensurate with available exits; there are, however, limits of occupancy specified in certain special cases for other reasons.

The geometry of a building, its occupancy and related occupant load, and the travel distance to exits, dictate in a large measure the appropriate location of exits, the number of exits, and the access thereto. As a consequence, the exits themselves profoundly influence the plan and layout of the entire system of means of egress. The ability of the means of egress to accommodate certain volumes of people is proportionately related to the ability of each component within it to accommodate a certain volume of people. It is beyond the scope of this chapter to do more than simply provide the basic stepping stones toward designing a safe and satisfactory system of means of egress from a building, while keeping economic considerations in mind at the same time.

The number of people for which the means of egress will provide a path of travel must be determined first. This number should be based on the maximum number of occupants that can be anticipated to be in the building rooms or spaces at any one given time, under all occasions or unusual circumstances; it must not be based only upon the usual number of normal occupancy. Never, in the planning or design stage, should it be anticipated that the actual number of occupants in a building will be equal to the number used as the permitted capacity of the means of egress. For example, even though 168 sq ft (15.6 sq m) of space may be allocated for a one-person office, the means of egress capacity must be based on what surveys and research have shown to be the more likely, realistic space to be occupied by one person, which for an office occupancy is 100 sq ft (9.29 sq m) per person based on gross area. In this way the probable maximum occupant load is taken into consideration. More detailed discussion follows under 5-3.1.2.

5-3.1.2   The occupant load permitted in any building or portion thereof shall not be assumed to be less than the number determined by dividing the floor area assigned to that use by the occupant load factor as specified in Chapters 8 through 30 for individual occupancies. Where both gross and net area figures are given for the same occupcancy, calculations shall be made applying the gross area figure to the building as a whole and the net area figure to the net area of the specific use.

Table 5-2 provides the occupant load factors taken from the individual occupancy chapters, Chapters 8 through 30. Note that some values are for net area while others are based on gross area. The gross area figure applies to the building as a whole (the area within the exterior confines of the building), while the net area figure applies to actual occupied spaces, such as classroom spaces, and does not include the corridors, the area occupied by walls, or other unoccupied areas. None of the occupancy chapters give values for both the net and gross areas of a building; however, there may be cases of mixed occupancy where, for example, a place of assembly having an occupant load based on net floor area may be located in an office or mercantile building, where the occupancy load is based on gross area.

Note, too, that 5-3.1.2 requires that exit capacity must be provided for *at least* the occupant load determined by dividing the area of the space (gross or net) by the appropriate occupant load factor.

Table 5-2. Occupant Load Factors

Occupancy	Sq Ft	Sq M
Places of assembly (Chapters 8 and 9)		
Concentrated use without fixed seating	15 net	1.39
Less concentrated use without fixed seating	7 net	.65
Waiting space	3 net	.28
Mercantile (Chapters 24 and 25)		
Street floor and sales basement	30 gross	2.79
Other floors	60 gross	5.57
Storage, shipping	300 gross	27.87
Office areas	100 gross	9.29
Malls	See 12-2.3.1(g).	
Educational occupancies (Chapters 10 and 11)		
Classroom area	20 net	1.86
Shops and other vocational areas	50 net	4.65
Day nurseries with sleeping facilities	35 net	3.25
Business, industrial (Chapters 26 through 28)	100 gross	9.29
Hotel and apartment (Chapters 16 through 19)	200 gross	18.58
Health care (Chapters 12 and 13)		
Sleeping departments	120 gross	11.15
Inpatient departments	240 gross	22.30
Detention and correctional occupancies (Chapters 14 and 15)	120 gross	11.15

5-3.1.3 The occupant load permitted in any building or portion thereof may be increased from that number established for the given use as specified in 5-3.1.2 when all other requirements of this *Code* are also met based on such modified number. The authority having jurisdiction may require an approved aisle, seating, or fixed equipment diagram to substantiate any increase in occupant load and may require that such diagram be posted in an approved location.

The concept of 5-3.1.3 is very important. For the most part, the *Code* is not attempting to restrict the occupant load of a building based on square footage. An occupant load is established for later use in determining exit capacity, numbers of exits, aisle and corridor widths, and similar items. If all *Code* provisions can be met using a higher occupant load, this higher occupant load may be used providing that the authority having jurisdiction is satisfied that all corridors, aisles, and other exit access ways can be maintained.

For example, a classroom area of 20,000 sq ft (1,858 sq m) would normally be assigned an occupant load of 1,000. However, it may be increased to 1,200, for example, if all provisions of the *Code* for aisles, corridors, exit capacity, etc., can be met.

Reduction below 3 sq ft (.65 sq m)/person net should be avoided since travel speeds are reduced to a crawl when occupancy exceeds this density. This phenomenon is known as jam-point.

Places of assembly have special, but similar, provisions for increasing occupant load.

5-3.1.4 Where exits serve more than one floor, only the occupant load of each floor considered individually need be used in computing the capacity of the exits at that floor, provided that exit capacity shall not be decreased in the direction of exit travel.

Chapter 6 contains special provisions for open stairs or other unprotected vertical openings, which require the capability for simultaneous exiting of exposed floors.

5-3.1.5 When means of egress from floors above and below converge at an intermediate floor, the capacity of the means of egress from the point of convergence shall be not less than the sum of the two.

Each story or floor level is considered separately when calculating the occupant load to be served by the exits from that floor. The size or width of the exits at a floor level need only be that required to accommodate the floor served; however, in a multistory building, the floor requiring the greatest number of units of exit width dictates the minimum width of exits from that point on in the direction of exit travel. It is not permissible to reduce exit width for the floors below, that is, in the direction of exit travel, simply because the exit must be capable of accommodating that number of people all along its path from the point where they had entered. Exits serving the stories above that critical floor may be the same or less in width as long as their occupant load does not require more units of exit width. These principles are illustrated in Figure 5-40.

Stair size is determined by the exit capacity for each floor, therefore it is not necessary to accumulate occupant loads from floor to floor to determine stair width. The reason for this is based on the theory of "staging," that is, by the time the occupants of the fifth floor reach the fourth floor the occupants from the fourth floor are already gone.

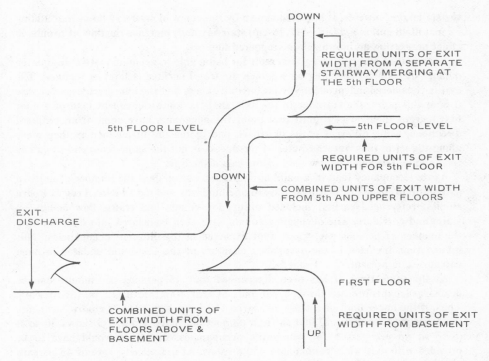

Figure 5-40. Schematic Illustration of Requirements Contained in 5-3.1.4 and 5-3.1.5.

5-3.2 Units of Exit Width.

5-3.2.1 Means of egress shall be measured in units of exit width of 22 in. (55.88 cm). Fractions of a unit less than 12 in. (30.48 cm) shall not be counted. Fractions of a unit comprising 12 in. (30.48 cm) or more, added to one or more full units, shall be counted as ½ unit of exit width.

The basic unit used in egress calculations, including inside and outside stairs, doors, and corridors, is the *unit of exit width*. This is the 22-in. (55.88-cm) width needed for the orderly movement of a single file of people along a passageway, and it is based on studies made more than 40 years ago.[8] In England, 21 in. (53.34 cm) is used in a similar fashion based on studies by the London Transit Board published in 1958.[12] These and other sources agree that the 22-in. or 21-in. (55.88-cm or 53.34-cm) dimension will accommodate the shoulders of an adult male. On this basis, two units of exit width, i.e., a stair of passage 44 in. (111.76 cm) wide, should provide for the movement of two rows of people. This, then, is the background for exit widths as found in the *Life Safety Code* today.

The measurement of exit width in terms of units representing the width occupied by one person, rather than measurement in feet and inches, is an important concept of the *Code*. Measurement in feet may in some cases involve additional expense in building construction without any corresponding increase in safety. For example, a 44-in. (111.76-cm) stairway comfortably accommodates two files of people; adding 4 in. (10.16 cm) to make a 4-ft (121.9-cm) stairway does not increase the capacity of the stairway. However, it has been shown by the count of stairway flows that adding 12 in. (30.48 cm) to a 44-in. (111.76-cm) stairway does increase the flow of people, in effect permitting an intermediate staggered file.

Each unit of exit width is given credit for being able to accommodate a designated number of people, depending on whether the travel surface is level or inclined. The exit is considered independently from the exit access and the exit discharge, because it is at this point, the entrance to the exit, that the known occupant load of a floor first merges together. Up until that point the occupants have come from different directions, using different paths of travel, and increasing in number as they move along the path; thus, the character of the access is not the same from end to end as for an exit. The same can be said of the exit discharge.

As the occupancy load of a building increases, so too does the number of units of exit width needed. The National Bureau of Standards and the London Transit Board studies, referenced earlier, included occupancy counts and traffic flow counts on stairs and corridors. The occupancy counts have been translated into data showing the number of persons per square foot expected in the different occupancies. This information, included in the occupancy chapters of the *Code* and updated in most categories, is presented in Table 5-3.

At the same time, it has been determined that 45 persons per minute can be discharged expeditiously through one unit of exit stair width [22 in. (55.88 cm)]. Thus, if the upper floor of a store measured 150 ft by 180 ft (4572 cm by 5486 cm), the gross area would be 27,000 sq ft (2508.3 sq m). Since Table 5-3 shows 60 sq ft (5.57 sq m) per person for mercantile occupancies, this floor would have to be provided with exits to accommodate 450 persons. At a discharge rate of 45 persons per unit of exit stair width, ten units would be required. Rather than provide ten 22-in. (55.88-cm) stairs, a more economical solution would be to provide five 44-in. (111.76 cm) stairs.

In the example just cited, oversimplified for illustrative purposes, three 66-in. (167.64-cm) and one 22-in. (55.88-cm) stairs would provide the needed exit width as would two 110-in. (279.4-cm) stairs. In the latter case, however, the greater width could induce crowding and contribute to panic on the stairway, while the 22-in. (55.88-cm) stair, mentioned in the first alternative, might induce crowding at the entrance door. A better solution might be to provide four exit stairs of equal width.

An auditorium located on the floor mentioned in the example would be calculated for separately [7 sq ft (.65 sq m) per person], as would a restaurant [15 sq ft (1.39 sq m) per person], if each were to accommodate more than 50 people. In any case, the authority having jurisdiction must use judgment in establishing the occupancy limits for each floor, realizing that the figures in Table 5-3 represent typical numbers for the occupancies listed.

Current studies by the NRCC are disputing the previous work at NBS and the London Transit Board. However, the committee feels that this work needs further verification before any *Code* changes are made due to the magnitude of the impact.

5-3.2.2 Width of means of egress shall be measured in the clear at the narrowest point of the exit component under consideration.

Exception No 1:   A handrail may project inside the measured width on each side not more than 3½ in. (8.89 cm).

Exception No. 2:   A stringer may project inside the measured width on each side not more than 1½ in. (3.81 cm).

Table 5-3. Occupant Load for Determining Exit Requirements.

Occupancy Types	*ft² per person*
Assembly	
Concentrated use (auditorium, dance floor)	7(net area)
Less concentrated (conference, dining, etc.)	15(net area)
Standing or waiting space	3(net area)
Bench-type seating	18 in./person
Fixed seating	see *Code* text
Educational	
Classrooms	20(net area)
Shops	50(net area)
Day nurseries with sleeping facilities and child day care centers . . .	35(net area)
Health Care/Penal	
Sleeping departments	120 (gross)
Inpatient treatment departments	240 (gross)
Residential	
One- and two-family dwellings	no requirement
Apartments	200 (gross)
Hotels	200 (gross)
Dormitories	200 (gross)
Lodging/rooming houses	200 (gross)
Mercantile	
Street floor	30 (gross)
Upper floors	60 (gross)
Office areas	100 (gross)
Storage/shipping areas	300 (gross)
Covered malls	
First floor	30 (gross)
Second floor	60 (gross)
Business	100 (gross)
Industrial	100 (gross)

Note: In calculating exit requirements, open mezzanine or balcony occupant loads shall be added to the occupant load of the floor below.
For occupancy types not listed (group and family day care centers and storage) there are no special requirements.

Handrails, at approximately waist height, do not actually restrict the effective width of exits. Door jambs, on the other hand, do restrict the width. In the case of a narrow stairway or passage, this feeling of restricted space might be conducive to panic under fire conditions. For this reason, any projection — radiator, pipe, or other object that extends into a corridor, irrespective of width — is undesirable, particularly where large crowds must be accommodated.

5-3.3 Capacity per Unit of Width. The capacity in number of persons per unit of width for approved components of means of egress shall be as follows:

(a) Level egress components, and Class A ramps — 100 for travel in either direction.

(b) Class B ramps — 60 for travel in the up direction, 100 for travel in the down direction.

(c) Stairways — 60 for travel in either direction.

A rated capacity of stairs permitting 45 persons for each 22-in. (55.88-cm) unit allows the passage of a single line of 45 physically able people per minute down the stairs. A single line of 60 people per minute can pass through an exit which is on a horizontal plane. Capacities of units of exit width, as given in the *Code*, are therefore based on a time period considered to be a safe exiting time.

Each unit of exit width is credited with being able to accommodate a designated number of reasonably alert and healthy people, the number being dependent on whether they are moving along a level path, a ramp, or on the steps of a stairway. As would be expected, the figure is lower for stairways, which require a different level of agility, watchfulness, and energy to negotiate, and, surprisingly, observations have shown that people are capable of moving up at the same speed in which they move down. This is probably due to the fact that one can better see where to place the feet when going upward, as opposed to the somewhat uncertain feeling of stepping down and placing the feet in a spot somewhat removed from one's vision. Of course, the fear of falling also becomes a factor when going down stairs.

Thus, knowing the occupant load of a floor level, the number of units of exit width can be determined by simple division. How these units of exit width are combined to form the separate exits themselves and then placed in the building becomes the concern of the designer, who must use all the provisions set forth in the *Code* as a basis for the design.

Again, each building has its own particular design needs which must be given consideration; consequently, different solutions are needed to provide a safe and workable means of egress. Actually, every effort is made to write provisions that are flexible, and, as a consequence, the *Code* provides unlimited possibilities to challenge the initiative of the designer in seeking economical exiting consistent with the safety principles contained therein.

5-3.4 Minimum Width.

5-3.4.1 The minimum width of any way of exit access shall be as specified for individual occupancies by Chapters 8 through 30, but in no case shall such width be less than 36 in. (91.44 cm).

Exception No. 1: Doors as provided for in 5-2.1.1.3.1.

Exception No. 2: In existing buildings the minimum width shall not be less than 28 in. (71.12 cm).

5-3.4.2 Where a single way of exit access leads to an exit, its capacity in terms of width shall be at least equal to the required capacity of the exit to which it leads. Where more than one way of exit access leads to an exit, each shall have a width adequate for the number of persons it must accommodate.

The physical makeup of the ways of access to exits is dependent on the occupancy. The minimum width allowed is given in the *Code* chapters for individual occupancies. The widths are based on experience and on observations of the manner in which people move along paths used for exit access purposes. The minimum width permitted for any passageway used as an exit access is 36 in. (91.44 cm), but most occupancies require more. Educational buildings require a width of not less than 6 ft (182.88 cm);

for health care occupancies a width not less than 8 ft (243.84 cm), which reflects the need to be able to move bedridden patients along the path to an exit. Hotels rely on the provisions in Chapter 5, which set the following standard: where an exit has but one way of access to it, the access width cannot be less than that of the exit itself. But under no circumstances is the exit access to be less than 36 in. (91.44 cm).

The exception for existing buildings is in recognition of the previous minimum of 28 in. (71.12 cm).

SECTION 5-4   NUMBER OF EXITS

5-4.1 General.

5-4.1.1   Number of exits shall be as specified for the particular occupancy in Chapters 8 through 30.

5-4.1.2   Exits shall be so located and exit access shall be so arranged that exits are readily accessible at all times (*see 5-5.1.1*). Where exits are not immediately accessible from an open floor area, safe and continuous passageways, aisles, or corridors shall be maintained leading directly to every exit and shall be so arranged as to provide convenient access for each occupant to at least two exits by separate ways of travel.

Exception: Where a single exit or limited dead ends are permitted by other provisions of the Code.

SECTION 5-5   ARRANGEMENT OF MEANS OF EGRESS

5-5.1 General.

5-5.1.1   Exits shall be so located and exit access shall be so arranged that exits are readily accessible at all times.

5-5.1.2   When more than one exit is required from a story, at least two of the exits shall be remote from each other and so arranged and constructed as to minimize any possibility that both may be blocked by any one fire or other emergency condition.

It is a precept of life safety in buildings, repeated many times in the *Code*, that if two exits are required, they should be not only separate but also remote from one another. While the objective of this requirement is clear — if one exit is blocked by smoke or fire the other will be available — the term "remote" cannot always be sharply defined.

When exits are located at each end of a long corridor or at each end or side of a building, there is no problem in providing a remotely located second exit. But the advent of core-type buildings with elevators, service shafts, and stairs in one central or side core has introduced some challenging problems with respect to exits. Figure 5-41 shows two core-type buildings that illustrate the problem. The upper sketch shows the plan of the Rault Center Building in New Orleans where five women were trapped by fire on the fifteenth floor. Both exit stairways were blocked, and the women finally jumped to the roof of an adjacent eight-story building. Four of the five died.[13]

The lower sketch in Figure 5-41 shows the plan of the twentieth floor of a New York City office building. An incendiary device was evidently set off somewhere near the lobby reception area. One of fifteen people on the floor at the time made it to the

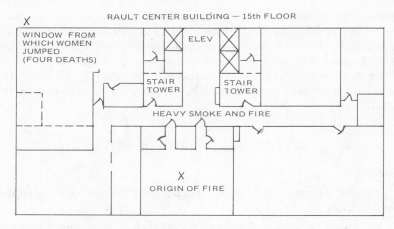

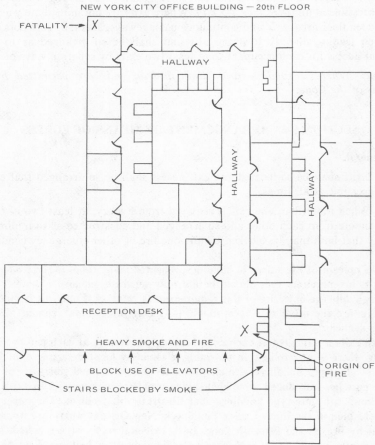

Figure 5-41. Plan Views of Upper Floors of Two Core-type High-Rise Buildings where Fires Occurred. Exit stairs were located in the core areas which became heavily involved in smoke and fire, blocking paths of escape.

stair exit, but the other fourteen were trapped and removed by fire fighters. One of the fourteen died.[14]

In a sense, the exit stairs in each example might be described as being remote from each other, but with more attention given to life safety during the design stage, a much better solution could have been devised. Figure 5-42 was taken from a

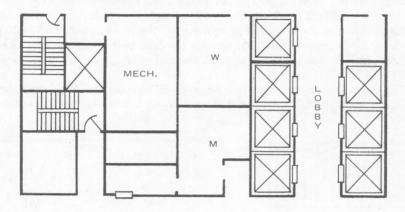

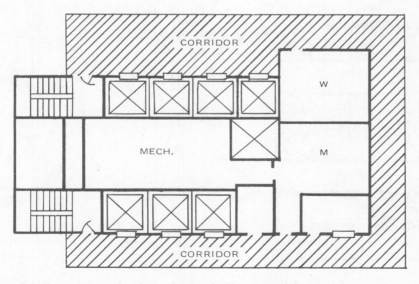

Figure 5-42. An Example of Not-So-Good Planning and Good Planning of Exits in a Core-type Multitenanted Building. In the upper plan view the exit stairs are not as remote from each other as practicable; they are both on the same end of the core, a detriment when tenants, present and future, lay out their own partition arrangements to suit their needs. By removing the elevator lobby from the core, as shown in the lower plan, the designer can, by adding a corridor around three sides of the core, make sure that tenants will have access to two remote exits. This solution also assists in providing two ways out of each tenant space.

discussion of core-type building designs in the NFPA *Fire Journal*.[15] It illustrates how, with a little thought and imagination and little, if any, added expense, a poor design can be greatly improved.

Other model codes have attempted to specify remoteness by formulas; however, the *Life Safety Code* has avoided this and left the determination of remoteness up to the authority having jurisdiction. The key to the *Code*'s intent is that exits should be arranged so that both cannot be blocked by a single fire event. As an aid in assisting authorities in the determination of remoteness, the formula used by the *Uniform Building Code*[16] may be used. The formula indicates that exits from a space should be separated by a distance of at least one-half of the diagonal of the space in question.

The use of scissor-type stairs (see Figure 5-43) must be considered since they are used and are a highly controversial subject. Some believe they are hazardous and

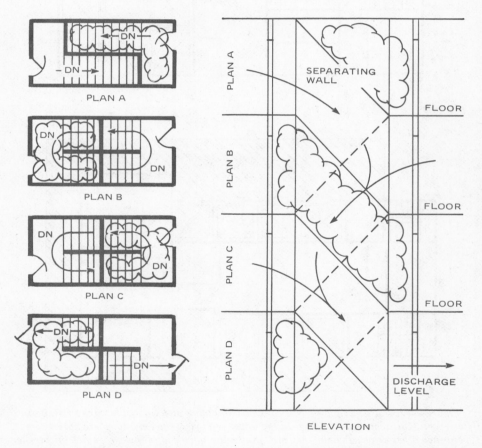

Figure 5-43. Scissor Stairs. Two stairways in the same enclosure but completely separated from each other are called scissor stairs. This results in space saving — two exits are provided in one enclosure. With this arrangement, two entirely independent escape paths are possible even though the two stairs are not remote. Note the continuity of all walls providing a complete separation at all points. Follow arrows for path of travel.

should not be permitted; others believe just the opposite. Generally, the principal objection seems to be that they cannot be reliably built to present an absolute barrier to the passage of smoke and toxic gases. Even if they can be, there is still concern that building settlement or exposure to fire conditions might result in the cracking of the separating wall, which could permit smoke and gases to pass into one exit stairway from the other. On the other hand, those who feel the scissor stairs do not present these problems see advantages because they reduce construction costs and save space. These points can all be seen in the stairs illustrated in Figures 5-43 and 5-44. Even though side by side, scissor stairs can be placed in some locations and still provide the remote placement of exits with the entrances to the exits remote from one another and the exit discharges also remotely placed.

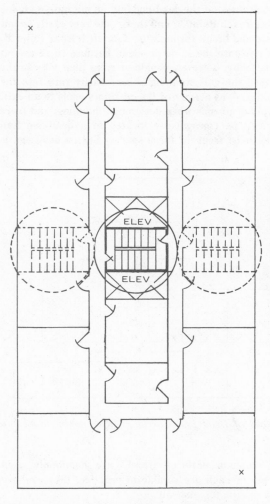

THIS SET OF SCISSORS STAIRS PROVIDES THE SAME DEGREE OF REMOTE EXIT OR ENTRANCE DOORS AS THE CIRCLED STAIRS SHOWN BY DOTTED LINES — TRAVEL DISTANCE FOR ALL OCCUPANTS IS THE SAME, EVEN IF THE DOTTED EXIT STAIRS WERE LOCATED AT OPPOSITE CORNERS DENOTED BY THE CROSS MARK. SPACE IS SAVED, HOWEVER THE INTEGRITY OF THE SEPARATION OF THE 2 SCISSORED STAIRS MAY REMAIN IN QUESTION.

Figure 5-44. Scissor Stairs Versus Conventional Exit Stairs — Advantages and Disadvantages.

5-5.1.3 Means of egress shall be so arranged that there are no dead end pockets, hallways, corridors, passageways, or courts whose depth exceeds the limits specified for individual occupancies by Chapters 8 through 30.

A dead end occurs when a hallway or other space is so arranged that a person standing in it is able to travel in one direction only in order to reach any of the exits. Although relatively short dead ends are permitted by the *Code*, it is better practice to eliminate them as much as possible, for they increase the danger of people being trapped in case of fire. Compliance with the limits on dead ends does not necessarily mean that the requirements for remoteness of exits have been met. This is particularly true in small buildings or buildings with short public hallways.

Figure 5-45 gives examples of two types of dead-end corridors. The one serving the occupied rooms is far more dangerous than the one adjoining the bank of elevators or elevator lobby. The occupants of the rooms off the dead-end hall do not have a choice of two directions to an exit until they reach Point A, and they could very easily be cut off altogether should a fire originate and break through the door such as at Point B. The elevator lobby, Point C, does not pose the same problem, because there are no doors to occupied rooms off of the lobby; however, people groping their way in the dark or smoke-filled corridor toward the exit stair could very easily turn into the dead-end corridors and become confused, as neither of the corridors leads to an exit. Sometimes it is very difficult to avoid dead ends when designing a building, and there are some little-used spaces that can be conveniently located in a dead-end hall without undue hazard to those who must frequent these spaces. But no dead end is ever a desirable feature.

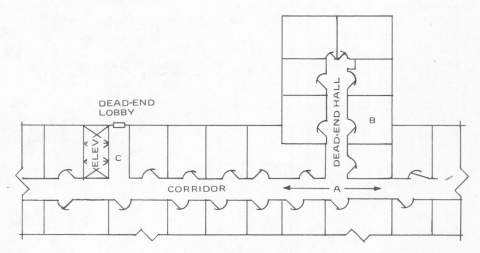

Figure 5-45. Examples of Two Types of Dead-End Corridors. (See commentary for 5-5.1.3.)

The terms "dead end" and "common path of travel" are commonly used interchangeably. While the concepts of each are similar in practice, they are two different concepts [see Figure 5-46 (a), (b), (c), and (d)].

A common path of travel exists when a space is arranged so that occupants within that space are able to travel in only one direction to reach any of the exits or to reach the point at which the occupants have the choice of two paths of travel to remote exits. Figure 5-46(a) is an example of a common path of travel.

While a dead end is similar, a dead end may also occur where there is no path of travel from an occupied space, but where an occupant may enter a corridor or space thinking there is an exit at the end and, finding none, must retrace his/her path to again reach a choice of exits. Figure 5-46(b) is an example of such a dead-end arrangement.

Combining the two concepts, Figure 5-46(c) is an example of a combined dead-end common path of travel problem.

Common paths of travel and dead-end travel are measured using the same principles used to measure travel distance as described in Section 5-6 of the *Code*. Because the room in Figure 5-46(d) is occupied by more than six persons, measurement is made 1 ft (30.48 cm) from the most remote point in the room, Point A, along the natural path of travel, through the doorway along the centerline of the corridor to Point C, located at the centerline of the corridor which provides the choice of two different paths to remote exits; this is the common path of travel. The distance 1 ft (30.48 cm) from the wall at Point B along the centerline of the corridor to Point C is a dead end. If the room had been occupied by six or fewer persons, then the common path of travel would have been measured starting from the door to the room.

5-5.1.4   Exit access shall be so arranged that it will not be necessary to pass through any area identified under "Protection from Hazards" in Chapters 8 through 30.

Although this is a new paragraph, it has been the intent of the *Code* to prohibit such arrangements through the provisions of the now deleted 5-5.2.3.

Paragraph 5-5.1.4 prohibits the exit access from passing through any area identified under "Protection from Hazards" (generally in the "3.2" sections such as 18-3.2 or 24-3.2) in the appropriate occupancy chapter.

5-5.2 Impediments to Egress (*see also 5-1.6 and 5-2.1.2*).

5-5.2.1   In no case shall access to an exit be through kitchens, storerooms, restrooms, workrooms, closets, bedrooms or similar spaces or other rooms subject to locking.

Exception No. 1:   Where the exit is required to serve only the bedroom or other room subject to locking, or adjoining rooms constituting part of the same dwelling or apartment used for single family occupancy.

Exception No. 2:   Exit access may pass through rooms or spaces subject to locking as provided in Chapters 14 and 15.

Paragraph 5-5.2.1 in combination with 5-5.1.4 prevent exit access from going through certain rooms either due to hazard, or to potential blockage or locking.

5-5.2.2   Ways of exit access and the doors to exits to which they lead shall be so designed and arranged as to be clearly recognizable. Hangings or draperies shall not be placed over exit doors or otherwise located so as to conceal or obscure any exit. Mirrors shall not be placed on exit doors. Mirrors shall not be placed in or adjacent to any exit in such a manner as to confuse the direction of exit.

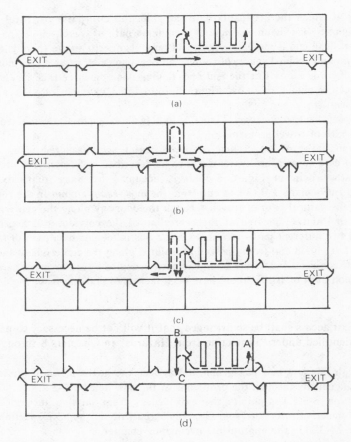

Figure 5-46. "Dead End" and "Common Path of Travel" Concepts.

Doors which lead through wall paneling and which harmonize in appearance with the rest of the wall, so as to avoid detracting from some desired aesthetic or decorative effect, are not acceptable under 5-5.2.2. Casual occupants may not be aware of such exits even though they are actually visible.

5-5.3 Exterior Ways of Exit Access.

5-5.3.1   Access to exit may be by means of any exterior balcony, porch, gallery, or roof that conforms to the requirements of this chapter.

5-5.3.2   A permanent, reasonably straight path of travel shall be maintained over the required exterior way of exit access.

5-5.3.3   There shall be no obstruction by railings, barriers, or gates that divide the open space into sections appurtenant to individual rooms, apartments, or other subdivisions.

5-5.3.4   An exterior way of exit access shall be so arranged that there are no dead ends in excess of 20 ft (609.6 cm).

5-5.3.5   Any gallery, balcony, bridge, porch or other exterior exit access that projects beyond the outside wall of the building shall comply with the requirements of this chapter as to width and arrangement.

5-5.3.6   Exterior ways of exit access shall have smooth, solid, substantially level floors, and shall have guards on the unenclosed sides at least equivalent to those specified in 5-2.2.3.

5-5.3.7   Where accumulation of snow or ice is likely because of the climate, the exterior way of exit access shall be protected by a roof.

The intent of the *Code* is to prevent the accumulation of ice and snow. Any method which accomplishes this and is acceptable to the local authority would be satisfactory. Examples of alternative methods would be snow melting cables or pipes within the floor or radiant heaters.

5-5.3.8   The materials of construction shall be as permitted for the building served.

SECTION 5-6   MEASUREMENT OF TRAVEL DISTANCE TO EXITS

Building codes generally, and the *Life Safety Code* in particular, specify the maximum distance that a person should have to travel from his or her position in a building to the nearest exit. There is no formula by which this distance can be established. Writing in one of the building code journals, one architect said: "Even though exiting has been, and will remain, the fundamental means of surviving building fires and their attendant conditions, the model codes...cannot always agree exactly on the correct methods of determining requirements for successful exiting."[17]

The factors on which the Committee on Safety to Life bases maximum travel distances are:

1. The number, age, and physical condition of building occupants and the rate at which they can be expected to move;
2. The type and number of obstructions — display cases, seating, heavy machinery, etc. — must be circumvented;
3. The number of people in any room or space and the distance from the farthest point in that room to the door;
4. The amount and nature of combustibles expected in a particular occupancy; and
5. The rapidity with which fire might spread — a function of the type of construction, the materials used, the degree of compartmentation, and the presence or absence of automatic fire detection and extinguishing systems.

It is obvious that travel distances will vary with the type and size of occupancy and the degree of hazard present. As given in Table 5-4, maximum travel distances in unsprinklered buildings can vary from 75 ft (22.86 m) in high hazard locations to 200 ft (60.96 m) in low hazard occupancies. This figure may be increased by as much as 100 percent in some cases, if complete sprinkler systems have been installed.

Having provided the occupant with at least two paths of travel to an exit, it becomes important that the time needed to travel those paths not be so long as to put the occupant in further danger. Many factors have been considered and weighed in

Table 5-4
Exit Travel Distance and Dead-End Limits
(By Occupancy)

Type of Occupancy	Dead-End Limit	Travel Limit to an Exit	
		Unsprinklered	Sprinklered
PLACES OF ASSEMBLY			
NEW	20[a] (609.6 cm)	150 (45.72 m)	200 (60.96 m)
EXISTING	20[a] (609.6 cm)	150 (45.72 m)	200 (60.96 m)
EDUCATIONAL			
NEW	20 (609.6 cm)	150 (45.72 m)	200 (60.96 m)
EXISTING	20 (609.6 cm)	150 (45.72 m)	200 (60.96 m)
HEALTH CARE			
NEW	30 (914.4 cm)	100[c] (30.48 m)	150[c] (45.72 m)
EXISTING	N.R.[b]	100[c] (30.48 m)	150[c] (45.72 m)
DETENTION AND CORRECTION			
NEW			
Use Conditions			
II, III, IV	50 (15.24 m)	100[c] (30.48 m)	150[c] (45.72 m)
V	20 (609.6 cm)	100[c] (30.48 m)	150[c] (45.72 m)
EXISTING			
Use Conditions			
II, III, IV, V	N.R.[b]	100[c] (30.48 m)	150[c] (45.72 m)
RESIDENTIAL			
A. Hotels			
NEW	35 (10.67 m)	100[c,d] (30.48 m)	150[c,d] (45.72 m)
EXISTING	35 (10.67 m)	100[c,d] (30.48 m)	150[c,d] (45.72 m)
B. Apartments			
NEW	35 (10.67 m)	100[c,e] (30.48 m)	150[c,e] (45.72 m)
EXISTING	35 (10.67 m)	100[c,e] (30.48 m)	150[c,e] (45.72 m)
C. Dormitories			
NEW	0	100 (30.48 m)	150 (45.72 m)
EXISTING	35 (10.67 m)	100 (30.48 m)	150 (45.72 m)
D. Lodging or Rooming Houses, 1- & 2-Family Dwellings	N.R.[b]	N.R.[b]	N.R.[b]
MERCANTILE			
Class A, B & C			
NEW	50 (15.24 m)	100 (30.48 m)	150 (45.72 m)
EXISTING	50 (15.24 m)	100 (30.48 m)	150 (45.72 m)
Open Air	0	N.R.[b]	N.R.[b]
Covered Mall			
NEW	50 (15.24 m)	100 (30.48 m)	350[c,h] (106.68 m)
EXISTING	50 (15.24 m)	100 (30.48 m)	350[c,h] (106.68 m)
BUSINESS			
NEW	50 (15.24 m)	200 (60.96 m)	300 (91.44 m)
EXISTING	50 (15.24 m)	200 (60.96 m)	300 (91.44 m)
INDUSTRIAL			
A. General, and B. Special Purpose	50 (15.24 m)	100 (30.48 m)	150[i] (45.72 m)
C. High Hazard	0	75 (22.86 m)	75 (22.86 m)
D. Open Structures	N.R.[b]	N.R.[b]	N.R.[b]

Table 5-4 (Continued)

| Type of Occupancy | Dead-End Limit | Travel Limit to an Exit | |
		Unsprinklered	Sprinklered
STORAGE			
Low Hazard	N.R.[b]	N.R.[b]	N.R.[b]
Ordinary Hazard	N.R.[b]	200 (60.96 m)	400 (121.92 m)
High Hazard	0	75 (22.86 m)	100 (30.48 m)
Parking Garages, Open	50 (15.24 m)	200 (60.96 m)	300 (91.44 m)
Parking Garages, Enclosed	50 (15.24 m)	150 (45.72 m)	200 (60.96 m)
Aircraft Hangars, Ground Floor	20 (609.6 cm)	Varies[f]	Varies[f]
Aircraft Hangars, Mezzanine Floor	N.R.[b]	75 (22.86 m)	75 (22.86 m)
Grain Elevators	[f]	N.R.	N.R.
Miscellaneous Occupancies, Towers, Piers & Water Surrounded Structures, Vehicles & Vessels & Emergency Shelters	50 (15.24 m)	100 (30.48 m)	150 (45.72 m)

[a] In aisles. In area and thrust stage theaters dead-end aisles at the stage must not exceed five rows beyond cross aisle.
[b] No requirement or not applicable.
[c] See Section 5-6 when space is subdivided.
[d] See Chapters 16 and 17 for exceptons.
[e] See Chapters 18 and 19 for exceptions.
[f] See Chapter 29 for special requirements.
[g] For existing buildings, see 5-5.1.3 for dead-end limits.
[h] See Chapters 24 and 25 for exceptions and special considerations.
[i] See Chapter 28 for special considerations.

establishing the maximum travel distances, and because there are no formulae or exact criteria for determining these distances, they are the result of observing people in motion, good judgment, and many years of studying the results of fires in which the prefire conditions of a building were known.

5-6.1 The maximum travel distance in any occupied space to at least one exit, measured in accordance with the following requirements, shall not exceed the limits specified for individual occupancies by Chapters 8 through 30.

When studying Table 5-4 it must be kept in mind that the maximum travel distance is that which must not be exceeded to reach at least one of the exits. A fire could very well block passage to the closest exit, causing the occupant to seek out the next available exit, which might mean an almost doubled travel distance.

5-6.2 The travel distance to an exit shall be measured on the floor or other walking surface along the center line of the natural path of travel starting 1 ft (30.48 cm) from the most remote point, curving around any corners or obstructions with a 1-ft

(30.48-cm) clearance therefrom, and ending at the center of the doorway or other point at which the exit begins. Where measurement includes stairs, the measurement shall be taken in the plane of the tread nosing.

The natural exit access (path of travel) will be influenced by the contents and occupancy of the building. Furniture, fixtures, machinery, or storage might considerably increase the length of travel. It is good practice in building design to recognize this by spacing exits at intervals closer than would be needed for a completely open floor area, thus reducing the possibility of excessive travel distances and minimizing the danger of violating the travel distance requirements of this *Code*. Figure 5-47 illustrates the path along which travel distance to an exit is measured.

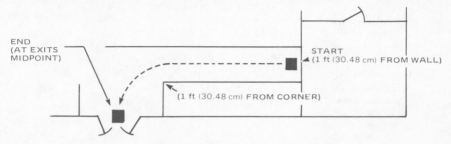

Figure 5-47. Measuring Travel Distance to an Exit.

Where stairs form part of an exit access rather than an exit, they are to be included in the travel distance. The measurement, in such cases, would be taken in the plane of the tread nosing (see Figure 5-48).

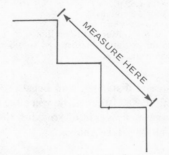

Figure 5-48. Method for Measuring Travel Distance on Stairs.

5-6.3   In the case of open areas, distance to exits shall be measured from the most remote point subject to occupancy.

5-6.4   In the case of individual rooms subject to occupancy by not more than 6 persons, distance to exits shall be measured from the doors of such rooms provided the path of travel from any point in the room to the room door does not exceed 50 ft (15.24 m).

It must be remembered that even though a room may only be occupied by 2 people, its size may be such that it is subject to occupancy by more than 6 people. For example, if an office is 700 sq ft (65.03 sq m) and is to be occupied by 2 people, it is still considered to be subject to occupancy by more than 6 people since the occupant load factor for business occupancies is 100 and the occupant load for the office is 7.

5-6.5   Where open stairways or ramps are permitted as a path of travel to required exits, such as between mezzanines or balconies and the floor below, the distance shall include the travel on the stairway or ramp and the travel from the end of the stairway or ramp to reach an outside door or other exit in addition to the distance to reach the stairway or ramp.

5-6.6   Where any part of an exterior way of exit access is within 15 ft (457.2 cm) horizontal distance of any unprotected building opening, as permitted by 5-2.5.1.3.1 for outside stairs, the distance to the exit shall include the length of travel to ground level.

The intent of this paragraph has been interpreted to mean that if the exterior stair is exposed by unprotected building openings, then it is not considered an exit but exit access and the travel distance is measured down the stair.

SECTION 5-7   DISCHARGE FROM EXITS

5-7.1   All exits shall terminate directly at a public way or at an exit discharge. Yards, courts, open spaces, or other portions of the exit discharge shall be of required width and size to provide all occupants with a safe access to a public way.

Exception No. 1:   As permitted by 5-7.2 and 5-7.5.

Exception No. 2:   Means of egress may terminate in an exterior area of refuge as provided in Chapters 14 and 15.

It is important that ample roadways be available outside of buildings in which there are large numbers of occupants so that the exits will not be blocked by people already outside. Two or more avenues of departure should be available for all but very small places. Location of a large theater on a narrow dead-end street, for example, may properly be prohibited by the authority having jurisdiction, unless some alternate way of travel to another street is shown to be available.

It is not enough to require that exits terminate at the outside of a building, because there may not be a space having a clear width of 10 ft (304.8 cm) to provide safe movement away from the building involved. Also, the terminus cannot be just to the outside in a closed court from which some sort of travel back through the building may be necessary in order to get away from the building. In such a case, an exit passageway at least as wide as the exit itself is required to provide travel from the courtyard to the street. In using an exit passageway, occupants should not have to pass closer to any openings in the burning building than the distance which is required for the unprotected openings of exterior stairs and ramps.

5-7.2   Where permitted for individual occupancies by Chapters 8 through 30, a maximum of 50 percent of the exits may discharge through areas on the level of discharge provided all of the following are met:

(a) Such exits discharge to a free and unobstructed way to the exterior of the building, which way is readily visible and identifiable from the point of discharge from the exit.

(b) The entire area on the level of discharge is separated from areas below by construction having a minimum of 2-hour fire resistance rating.

(c) The level of discharge is protected throughout by an approved automatic sprinkler system and any other portion of the level of discharge with access to the discharge area is protected throughout by an approved automatic sprinkler system or separated from it in accordance with the requirements for the enclosure of exits (*see 5-1.3*).

Exception: The requirements of 5-7.2(c) may be waived if the discharge area is a vestibule or foyer meeting all of the following and where allowed in Chapters 8 through 30:

(a) The depth from the exterior of the building is not greater than 10 ft (304.8 cm) and the length is not greater than 20 ft (609.6 cm).

(b) The foyer is separated from the remainder of the level of discharge by construction providing protection at least the equivalent of wired glass in steel frames.

(c) The foyer serves only for means of egress including exits directly to the outside.

The intent of 5-7.2 is to provide some level of protection for exits discharging through the level of exit discharge. Probably the most often asked question concerning this section concerns the requirements of item (c). The intent of item (c) is to require the entire level of exit discharge and any area connected to the level of discharge with access to the discharge area be protected by automatic sprinkler protection. As an alternative the discharge path must be enclosed or separated from the rest of the level of discharge by construction as required for exits. In other words, create an exit passageway to the exterior. In short there are two solutions: enclose the path of travel in an exit passageway, or provide sprinkler protection for the entire level of exit discharge.

Figure 5-49 illustrates alternate arrangements for the exit discharge required by 5-7.2(b).

5-7.3   The exit discharge shall be so arranged and marked as to make clear the direction of egress to a public way. Exit stairs that continue beyond the level of discharge shall be interrupted at the level of discharge by partitions, doors, or other physical barriers.

Exception: Exit stairs that continue one-half story beyond the level of exit discharge need not be interrupted by physical barriers where the exit discharge is clearly obvious.

See also 5-2.2.2.11 on stair details.

The exception to 5-7.3 is most commonly used in "garden"-type apartment buildings.

5-7.4   Stairs, ramps, bridges, balconies, escalators, moving walks, and other components of an exit discharge shall comply with the detailed requirements of this chapter for such components.

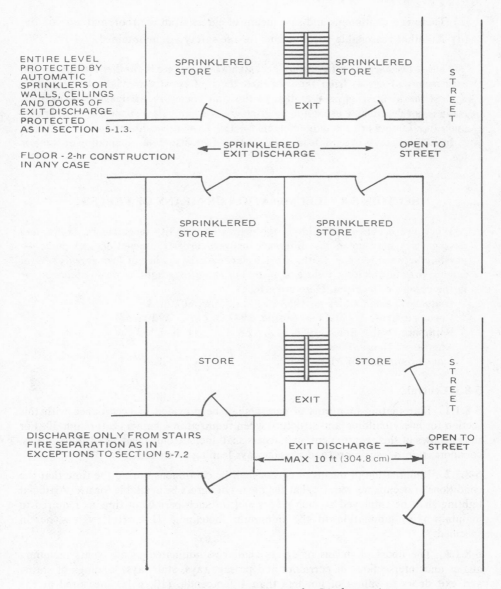

ENTIRE LEVEL
PROTECTED BY
AUTOMATIC
SPRINKLERS OR
WALLS, CEILINGS
AND DOORS OF
EXIT DISCHARGE
PROTECTED
AS IN SECTION 5-1.3.

FLOOR - 2-hr CONSTRUCTION
IN ANY CASE

SPRINKLERED STORE

SPRINKLERED STORE

EXIT

STREET

SPRINKLERED EXIT DISCHARGE

OPEN TO STREET

SPRINKLERED STORE

SPRINKLERED STORE

STORE

STORE

EXIT

STREET

DISCHARGE ONLY FROM STAIRS
FIRE SEPARATION AS IN
EXCEPTIONS TO SECTION 5-7.2

EXIT DISCHARGE ——▶

OPEN TO STREET

——MAX 10 ft (304.8 cm)——

Figure 5-49. Alternate Arrangements for Discharge Areas.

5-7.5 Subject to the approval of the authority having jurisdiction, exits may be accepted where:

(a) They discharge to the roof or other sections of the building or adjoining buildings, and

(b) The roof has a fire resistance rating at least the equivalent of that required for the exit enclosure, and

(c) There is a continuous and safe means of egress from the roof, and

(d) All other reasonable requirements for life safety are maintained.

An exit discharge to a roof is not acceptable unless there is another continuous and safe means of egress from the roof, and the roof construction affords protection against fire at least as good as that of the stair enclosure. Helicopter rescue from roofs is not dependable enough to be given credit as an exit — updrafts, downdrafts, and other factors are too unpredictable for this to be a consideration.

In addition, exits over roofs must be protected against the accumulation of snow or ice.

SECTION 5-8   ILLUMINATION OF MEANS OF EGRESS

When fire occurs in a building, the degree of visibility in corridors, stairs, and passageways may mean the difference between orderly evacuation and panic — possibly between life and death. A brief glance at the history of fires reveals several famous fires in which the failure of normal or emergency lighting was a major factor in the casualties incurred. Here are a few:

Iroquois Theater, Chicago, 1903 . . . . 602 died.[18]
Cocoanut Grove Night Club, Boston, 1942 . . . . 492 died.[18]
Baltimore Oyster Roast, 1956 . . . . 11 died.[18]
Apartment House, Boston, 1971 . . . . 8 died[19]
Summerland, Isle of Man, 1973 . . . . 50 died.[20]

5-8.1 General.

5-8.1.1 Illumination of means of egress shall be provided in accordance with this section for every building and structure when required in Chapters 8 through 30. For the purposes of this requirement, exit access shall include only designated stairs, aisles, corridors, ramps, escalators, and passageways leading to an exit.

5-8.1.2 Illumination of means of egress shall be continuous during the time that the conditions of occupancy require that the means of egress be available for use. Artificial lighting shall be employed at such places and for such periods of time as required to maintain the illumination to the minimum footcandle [Lux (lx)] values herein specified.

5-8.1.3 The floors of means of egress shall be illuminated at all points including angles and intersections of corridors and passageways, stairways, landings of stairs, and exit doors to values of not less than 1 footcandle (10.76 lx) measured at the floor.

Exception: In auditoriums, theatres, concert or opera halls, and other places of assembly, the illumination of the floors of exit access may be reduced during such periods of the performances to values not less than one-fifth footcandle (2.15 lx).

The *Code* requires that there be at least 1.0 footcandle (10.76 lx) of illumination at floor level in all three elements of a means of egress, i.e., the exit access, the exit, and the exit discharge. For the purposes of this section only, the *Code* limits exit *access* to designated stairs, aisles, corridors, and passageways leading to an exit. While motion pictures, slides, and the like are being shown in theaters, auditoriums, and other places of assembly, the level of illumination can be reduced to one-fifth of a footcandle. A good type of exit illumination would be lights recessed in walls about 1 ft (30.48 cm) above the floor; such lights are not likely to be obscured by smoke.

5-8.1.4 Any required illumination shall be so arranged that the failure of any single lighting unit, such as the burning out of an electric bulb, will not leave any area in darkness.

In any case, the arrangement of lights, circuits, or auxiliary power must be such that continuity of egress lighting will be ensured. This can be accomplished in a number of ways — duplicate light bulbs in fixtures, overlapping light patterns, or overlapping dual circuits.

5-8.1.5 The same equipment or units installed to meet the requirements of Section 5-10 may also serve the function of illumination of means of egress, provided that all applicable requirements of this section for such illumination are also met.

5-8.2 Sources of Illumination.

5-8.2.1 Illumination of means of egress shall be from a source of reasonably assured reliability, such as public utility electric service.

5-8.2.2 Where electricity is used as a source of illumination of means of egress, the installation shall be properly made in accordance with the *National Electrical Code®*, NFPA 70.

5-8.2.3 No battery operated electric light nor any type of portable lamp or lantern shall be used for primary illumination of means of egress but may be used as an emergency source to the extent permitted under Emergency Lighting, Section 5-9.

When batteries are used for auxiliary power, they must be the type that will automatically be kept charged and will function for 1½ hours when used.

SECTION 5-9   EMERGENCY LIGHTING

5-9.1 General.

5-9.1.1 Emergency lighting facilities for means of egress shall be provided for every building or structure in accordance with this section when required in Chapters 8 through 30.

5-9.1.2 Where maintenance of illumination depends upon changing from one energy source to another, there shall be no appreciable interruption of illumination during the changeover. Where emergency lighting is provided by a prime mover-operated electric generator, a delay of not more than 10 seconds shall be permitted.

Where auxiliary generators are used, they must be capable of coming on line within 10 seconds after interruption of the main service. Connecting the emergency lighting circuit to the main power line on the "live" side of the main disconnect has the advantage of service continuity should the main switch be thrown by employees or fire fighters as a precautionary measure. The *Code* does not prohibit this practice; however, it should be noted that this method does not meet the requirements for emergency lighting.

Work done on normal or emergency lighting systems must be in accordance with the provisions of NFPA 70, the *National Electrical Code*®.[21]

5-9.2 Performance of System.

5-9.2.1   Emergency lighting facilities shall be arranged to maintain the specified degree of illumination throughout the means of egress, but not less than 1 footcandle (10.76 lx), for a period of 1½ hours in the event of failure of the normal lighting. (*See also 5-8.1.3.*)

5-9.2.2   Battery operated emergency lights shall use only reliable types of rechargeable batteries provided with suitable facilities for maintaining them in properly charged condition. Batteries used in such lights or units shall be approved for their intended use and shall comply with the *National Electrical Code*, NFPA 70.

Automobile-type lead storage batteries are not suitable. They have a relatively short life when not subject to frequent discharge and recharge as occurs in automobile operation.

The former prohibition against dry batteries has been removed provided they can meet performance criteria. For proper selection and maintenance of appropriate batteries, see NFPA 70, the *National Electrical Code*.[21]

5-9.2.3   An emergency lighting system shall be so arranged as to provide the required illumination automatically in the event of any interruption of normal lighting, such as any failure of public utility or other outside electrical power supply, opening of a circuit breaker or fuse, or any manual act(s), including accidental opening of a switch controlling normal lighting facilities.

When approved by the authority having jurisdiction, the requirement of 5-9.2.3 may be met by means such as:

1. Two separate electric lighting systems, with independent wiring, each adequate by itself to provide the specified lighting. One of the systems should be supplied from an outside source, such as a public utility service, and the other from an electric generator on the premises driven by an independent source of power. Both sources of electric power are to be in regular, simultaneous operation whenever the building is occupied during periods of darkness;

2. An electric circuit or circuits used only for means of egress illumination, with two independent electric sources arranged so that on the failure of one the other will come automatically and immediately into operation. One source is to be a connection from a public utility or similar outside power source, and the other an approved storage battery with suitable provision to keep it automatically charged. The battery must also have automatic controls that cause it to come into operation upon failure or shutdown of the primary power

---

®Registered Trademark, The National Fire Protection Association, Inc.

source for the lights. The controls must also cut out the battery when the primary current source is again turned on, and cause it to be automatically recharged in preparation for further service; or

3. Electric battery-operated emergency lighting systems, where permitted, complying with the provisions of 5-9.2.2., operating on a separate circuit and at a voltage different from that of the primary light. Refer to NFPA 70, the *National Electrical Code.*[21]

These requirements are not intended to prohibit the connection of a feeder serving exit lighting and similar emergency functions ahead of the service disconnecting means. Such an arrangement does not constitute an acceptable alternate source of power; however, it does give supplementary protection for emergency electrical functions, particularly when intended to permit the fire department to open the main electrical disconnect without hampering exit lighting. Provision should be made to alert the fire department that certain power and lighting is fed by an emergency generator and will continue operation after the service disconnect is opened.

5-9.2.4 An emergency lighting system shall be either continuously in operation or capable of repeated automatic operation without manual intervention.

SECTION 5-10   EXIT MARKING

5-10.1 General.

5-10.1.1 Where required by the provisions of Chapters 8 through 30, exits shall be marked by an approved sign readily visible from any direction of exit access.

5-10.1.2 Access to exits shall be marked by readily visible signs in all cases where the exit or way to reach it is not immediately visible to the occupants. Sign placement shall be such that no point in the exit access is more than 100 ft (30.48 m) from the nearest visible sign.

Exception: Signs in existing buildings need not meet the 100 ft (30.48 m) distance requirement.

Where a main entrance also serves as an exit, the exit location will usually be sufficiently obvious to occupants and no exit sign is needed.

The character of the occupancy has a practical effect upon the need for signs. In any place of assembly, hotel, department store, or other building subject to transient occupancy, the need for signs will be greater than in a building subject to permanent or semipermanent occupancy. In the latter instance, such as in an apartment house, residents may be presumed to be familiar with exit facilities, such as outside stairs, even though these are not subject to regular use during the normal occupancy of the building.

There are many situations where the actual need for signs may be debatable. In cases of doubt, however, it is best to provide signs; putting the signs up does not ordinarily involve major expense or inconvenience.

The requirement for the locations of exit signs visible from any direction of exit access may be illustrated as in Figure 5-50.

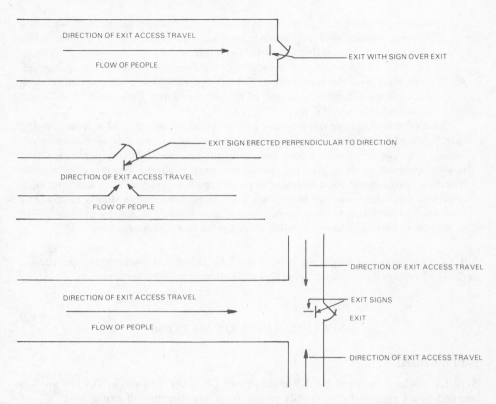

Figure 5-50. Locations of Exit Signs Visible from any Direction of Exit Access.

The 100-ft (30.48-m) distance requirement is established since sign size and illumination levels are now based on visibility from 100 ft (30.48 m).

5-10.1.3 Every required sign designating an exit or way of exit access shall be so located and of such size, distinctive color, and design as to be readily visible and shall provide contrast with decorations, interior finish, or other signs. No decorations, furnishings, or equipment which impair visibility of an exit sign shall be permitted, nor shall there be any brightly illuminated sign (for other than exit purposes), display, or object in or near the line of vision to the required exit sign of such a character as to so detract attention from the exit sign.

In stores, an otherwise adequate exit sign might be made inconspicuous by a high-intensity illuminated advertising sign in the immediate vicinity. For this reason, such distractions are not allowed near the line of vision to an exit sign.

Red is the traditional color for exit signs and is required by law in many places. However, at an early stage in the development of the *Code*, a provision was made that green be the color for exit signs, following the example of traffic lights, where green indicates safety and red is the signal to stop. During the period when green signs were specified by the *Code*, many such signs were installed, but the traditional red signs also persisted. In 1949, the Fire Marshals Association of North America voted to request that red be restored as the required exit sign color, as they found that the provision for green involved difficulties in law enactment out of all proportion to the importance of the subject. The 10th edition of the *Code* accordingly specified "red where not otherwise required by law." The present *Code* text avoids any specific requirement for color, on the assumption that either red or green will be used in most cases, and that there may be some situations where a color other than red or green might actually provide better visibility.

The location of exit signs is not specified. Usually they are placed over the exit entrance or near the ceiling. There are those who argue, with reason, that smoke builds up more rapidly at higher levels and exit signs a foot or so above the floor would be visible for a much longer period in a fire situation. However, when several people are moving toward an exit, those in the back might not be able to see signs located at a low level. Also, in the absence of careful housekeeping, such signs might be damaged or blocked. Thus the *Code* simply states that exit signs be located as to be readily visible and provide contrast with the surroundings.

5-10.2 Size of Signs.   Every "EXIT", directional "EXIT", and "NOT AN EXIT" sign required by Section 5-10 shall have the appropriate wording in plainly legible letters not less than 6 in. (15.24 cm) high with the principal strokes of letters not less than ¾ in. (1.91 cm) wide.

Exception: Existing signs having the required wording in plainly legible letters not less than 4½ in. (11.43 cm) high may be continued in use.

5-10.3 Illumination of Signs.

5-10.3.1   Every exit sign shall be suitably illuminated by a reliable light source. Externally and internally illuminated signs shall be visible in both the normal and emergency lighting mode.

Exit signs may be internally or externally illuminated. Internally illuminated signs are usually provided in occupancies where reduction of normal illumination is permitted, such as in motion picture theaters.

It is not the intent of 5-10.3.1 to require emergency lighting, but that where emergency lighting is provided the signs must be visible in both the normal and emergency lighting mode.

5-10.3.2   Externally illuminated signs shall be illuminated by not less than 5 footcandles (53.82 lx) and shall employ a contrast ratio of not less than 0.5.

Colors providing a good contrast are red or green letters on matte white background. Glossy background and letter colors should be avoided.

5-10.3.3   In an internally illuminated sign with translucent letters and an opaque background the average luminance due to the internal source only of the letters shall be a minimum of 2 footlamberts (6.85 cd/sq m) and a maximum of 3 footlamberts (10.28 cd/sq m). The letters shall be illuminated such that the brightest spot is not more than four times as bright as the darkest spot.

Exception No. 1:   Approved existing signs.

Exception No. 2:   Approved self-luminous signs which provide evenly illuminated letters may have a minimum luminance of .06 footlamberts (.21 cd/sq m).

Two footlamberts (6.85 lx) are required to view the sign in total darkness from a distance of 100 ft (30.48 m) (by a 65-year-old adult with 20/20 vision). With a maximum of 3 footlamberts (10.28 lx), the letters will remain dark against the white background when viewed with high ambient light. The average luminance may be computed by measuring the luminance of ¾-in. (1.91-cm) diameter circular areas at the positions indicated by Xs in the diagram in Figure 5-51.

Self-luminous signs are illuminated by self-contained power sources and operate independently of external power sources. Batteries do not qualify as a self-contained power source under this definition.

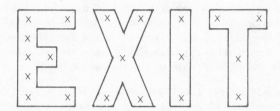

Figure 5-51. Locations to Take Luminance Measurements to Determine Voltage Luminance.

5-10.3.4 In an internally illuminated sign with translucent background and opaque letters the average luminance of the background shall be a minimum of 3 footlamberts (10.28 cd/sq m). The background shall be illuminated such that the brightest spot is not more than four times as bright as the darkest spot. The contrast ratio between letters and background shall be at least 0.5.

Exception: Approved existing signs.

For even background illumination by the internal source, the brightest spot, a ¾ in.-(1.91-cm) diameter circle, should not be more than four times as bright as the darkest spot.

5-10.3.5 In an internally illuminated sign with translucent background and translucent letters the average luminance of the brighter portion shall be a minimum of 6 footlamberts (20.56 cd/sq m) due to internal sources only. The background shall be illuminated such that the brightest spot is not more than four times as bright as the darkest spot. The contrast ratio between letters and background shall be at least 0.5.

Exception: Approved existing signs.

5-10.3.6 Illumination of exit signs shall be continuous as required under the provisions of Section 5-8.

Exception: Illumination for exit signs may flash on and off upon activation of the fire alarm system.

The flashing repetition rate should be approximately 1 cycle per second and the duration of the off-time should not exceed ¼ second per cycle. During on-time, the illumination levels must be provided in accordance with 5-10.3.2, 5-10.3.3, 5-10.3.4, or 5-10.3.5. Flashing signs when activated with the fire alarm system may be of assistance to people with hearing impairments.

5-10.3.7 Where emergency lighting facilities are required by the applicable provisions of Chapters 8 through 30 for individual occupancies, the exit signs, except approved self-luminous signs, shall be illuminated by the emergency lighting facilities. The level of illumination of the exit sign shall be at the levels provided in accordance with 5-10.3.2, 5-10.3.3, 5-10.3.4 or 5-10.3.5 for the required emergency lighting time duration as specified in 5-9.2.1 but may decline to 60 percent of the illumination level at the end of the emergency lighting time duration.

5-10.4 Specific Requirements.

5-10.4.1 Directional Signs.

5-10.4.1.1 A sign reading "EXIT", or similar designation with an arrow indicating the direction shall be placed in every location where the direction of travel to reach the nearest exit is not immediately apparent.

Since, for most occupancies, two exits must be available in separate ways of travel, it is logical to assume that from the point where measurement of travel distance starts, there should always be two exit signs visible.

5-10.4.1.2 Escalators, Moving Walks. A sign complying with 5-10.2 indicating the direction of the nearest approved exit shall be placed at the point of entrance to any escalator or moving walk that is not in a means of egress.

5-10.4.2 Special Signs.

5-10.4.2.1 Any door, passage, or stairway that is neither an exit nor a way of exit access and that is so located or arranged that it is likely to be mistaken for an exit shall be identified by a sign reading "NOT AN EXIT".

The likelihood of mistaking for exit doors, passageways, or stairways which lead to dead-end spaces where occupants might be trapped depends upon the same considerations as govern the need for exit signs. Thus, such areas should be marked with a sign reading, "NOT AN EXIT". Supplementary lettering indicating the character of the area such as "TO BASEMENT," "STOREROOM," "LINEN CLOSET," or the like, may be provided.

5-10.4.2.2 A door designed to be kept normally closed shall bear a sign, visible only in the direction of exit travel, reading substantially as follows:

FIRE EXIT
Keep Door Closed

This edition of the *Code* now specifies that the sign shall only be placed on the side from which egress is made. This is to prevent confusing this sign with an "exit" sign and the possible resulting misdirection.

SECTION 5-11   SPECIAL PROVISIONS FOR
OCCUPANCIES WITH HIGH HAZARD
CONTENTS (*See Section 4-2.*)

5-11.1 In all cases where the contents are classified as high hazard, exits shall be provided of such types and numbers and so arranged as to permit all occupants to escape from the building or structure or from the hazardous area thereof to the outside or to a place of safety with a travel distance of not over 75 ft (22.86 m), measured as specified in 5-6.2.

Seventy-five ft (22.86 m) can be traversed in approximately 10 to 15 seconds, even allowing for some momentary delay in decision as to which way to go; it may be assumed that a normal individual can hold his/her breath for at least that long.

5-11.2 Capacity of exits provided in accordance with 5-11.1 shall be as specified in the applicable section of Chapters 8 through 30 but not less than such as to provide one unit for each 30 persons where exit is by inside or outside stairs or one unit for each 50 persons where exit is by doors at grade level, by horizontal exits, or by Class A ramps.

5-11.3 At least two exits shall be provided from each building or hazardous area thereof.

5-11.4 Means of egress shall be so arranged that there are no dead end pockets, hallways, corridors, passageways, or courts.

It is not the intent of the *Code* to apply the provisions of this section to hazardous areas as defined in each occupancy chapter, but to apply it to an occupancy of high hazard contents. Small areas of high hazard are considered incidental to the main occupancy of the building. The decision as to when a small hazardous area becomes significant enough to warrant application of this section is left to the authority having jurisdiction.

REFERENCES CITED BY *CODE*

(These publications comprise a part of the requirements to the extent called for by the Code.*)*

NFPA 70, *National Electrical Code*, NFPA, Boston, 1981.

NFPA 72E, *Standard on Automatic Fire Detectors*, NFPA, Boston, 1978.

NFPA 80A, *Recommended Practice for Protection of Buildings from Exterior Fire Exposure*, NFPA, Boston, 1980.

NFPA 252, *Standard Methods of Fire Tests of Door Assemblies*, NFPA, Boston, 1979.

ANSI A17.1 — 1978, *Safety Code for Elevators, Dumbwaiters, Escalators, and Moving Walks; and Supplement:* ANSI A17.1a — 1979; American Society of Mechanical Engineers, 345 East 47th Street, New York, NY 10017.

REFERENCES CITED IN COMMENTARY

[1]NFPA 252, *Standard Methods of Fire Tests of Door Assemblies*, NFPA, Boston, 1979.

[2]NFPA 72E, *Standard on Automatic Fire Detectors*, NFPA, Boston, 1978.

[3]J. Fitch, J. Templer, P. Corcoran, "The Dimensions of Stairs," *Scientific American*, October 1974, pp. 82-90.

[4]J. Templer, G. Mullet, J. Archea, and S. Margulis, *An Analysis of the Behavior of Stair Users*, National Bureau of Standards NBSIR 78-1554.

[5]NFPA 220, *Standard Types of Building Construction*, NFPA, Boston, 1979.

[6]*Handbook of Fundamentals*, American Society of Heating, Refrigeration, and Air Conditioning Engineers (ASHRAE), 345 East 47th Street, New York, NY 10017.

[7]NFPA 80, *Standard for Fire Doors and Windows*, NFPA, Boston, 1979.

[8]*Design and Construction of Building Exits*, Miscellaneous Publication M 51, October 10, 1935, National Bureau of Standards, Washington, DC (out of print).

[9]*National Safety Council Safe Practices*, Pamphlet No. 2, National Safety Council, 425 N. Michigan Avenue, Chicago, IL 60611, 1934.

[10]ANSI A17.1 — 1978, *Safety Code for Elevators, Dumbwaiters, Escalators, and Moving Walks; and Supplement:* ANSI A17.1a — 1979; American Society of Mechanical Engineers, 345 East 47th Street, New York, NY 10017.

[11]Paul Robert Lyons, *Fire in America*, NFPA SPP-33, NFPA, Boston, 1976, p. 190.

[12]London Transit Board Research, "Second Report of the Operational Research Team on the Capacity of Footways," Research Report No. 95, August 1958, London.

[13]Laurence D. Watrous, "High-Rise Fire in New Orleans," *Fire Journal*, Vol. 67, No. 3, May 1973, pp. 6-9.

[14]Robert F. Mendes, *Fighting High-Rise Building Fires — Tactics and Logistics*, NFPA FSP-44, NFPA, Boston, 1975.

[15]Richard E. Stevens, "Exits in Core-Type Office Buildings," *Fire Journal*, Vol. 64, No. 3, May 1970, pp. 68-70.

[16]*Uniform Building Code*, International Conference of Building Officials, Whittier, CA

[17]G. R. Fox, "An Architect's View of Exiting and the Codes," *Southern Building*, August 1973.

[18]R. S. Moulton, "Emergency Lighting for Fire Safety," *NFPA Quarterly*, Vol. 50, No. 2, October 1956, pp. 93-96.

[19]A. Elwood Willey, "Unsafe Existing Conditions! Apartment House Fire, Boston, Massachusetts," *Fire Journal*, Vol. 65, No. 4, July 1971, pp. 16-23.

[20]James K. Lathrop, "The Summerland Fire: 50 Die on Isle of Man," *Fire Journal*, Vol. 69, No. 2, March 1975, pp. 5-12.

[21]NFPA 70, *National Electrical Code*, NFPA, Boston, 1981.

6

FEATURES OF
FIRE PROTECTION

This chapter establishes basic requirements for features of fire protection which include such items as protection of vertical openings, fire barriers, smoke barriers, construction, protection of concealed spaces, protection from hazards, and interior finish. For the most part, this chapter sets requirements which are then referenced by the applicable occupancy chapters. However, some requirements apply to all occupancies.

SECTION 6-1 GENERAL

6-1.1 Application.

6-1.1.1 Features of fire protection related to the construction of a building, its subdivision, and interior finishes as detailed in this chapter apply to both new and existing buildings.

Exception: Where specific requirements contained in Chapters 8 through 30 differ from similar requirements contained in this chapter, the requirements of Chapters 8 through 30 shall govern.

Lack of compartmentation and rapid fire development have been found to be primary factors in numerous multiple fatality fires, especially in residential occupancies. In many fire reports, the factors of unprotected vertical openings and highly combustible interior finish appear repeatedly, indicating the need to apply requirements to both new and existing buildings.

SECTION 6-2 CONSTRUCTION AND COMPARTMENTATION

The purpose of Section 6-2 is to set forth, in general terms, how those using exits and other "safe" areas in buildings are to be protected from fire in adjoining areas. This is accomplished by providing wall, ceiling, and floor construction that will be reasonably free from penetration by fire and smoke for a safe period. Because requirements vary for different occupancies, specific details for construction and compartmentation are included in Chapters 8 through 30 of the *Code*.

To be consistent and to preserve the integrity of the "compartment" or safe area, all openings for doors, ducting, and building services, i.e., electric power, telephone, water supply, and waste lines, must also be effectively closed or fitted with automatic closures. Equally important, and sometimes overlooked, are hidden spaces, particularly those above suspended ceilings, that can be, and frequently have been, the means of spreading fire into otherwise protected areas. In some instances, these interstitial spaces may be 8 ft (2.44 m) or more in height; in others, they may serve as supply or return air plenum chambers for air conditioning systems. In any event, provision must be made to treat such spaces as separate fire areas with automatic fire protection and a limit placed on the area dimensions.[1]

In this section and throughout the *Code* a distinction is made between smoke barriers and fire barriers. The function of the former is to restrict the passage of smoke (including fire gases). As such, they must be reasonably airtight even though the air pressure on the fire side may increase due to expansion of the heated air. The fire barrier, on the other hand, must prevent passage of heat and flame for a designated period of time. In other words, it must be capable of withstanding direct impingement of the fire as determined by large-scale tests conducted in accordance with NFPA 251, *Standard Methods of Fire Tests of Building Construction and Materials*,[2] and NFPA 252, *Standard Methods of Fire Tests of Door Assemblies*.[3]

At present there are no standard tests for measuring the resistance of door assemblies or other closures to the passage of smoke. Note that the term "door assemblies" is used. A qualified door is one that has been tested as a system, including frame and sill (where used), and hardware. The doors should have minimum clearances, no louvers or grills, no undercuts, and only approved, transparent wired glass of limited area if a window is needed.

The practice of undercutting doors between rooms and corridors to allow the latter to serve as return or supply air ducts for the air conditioning system, or to allow for easy movement of the door over high pile carpeting, is not consistent with the objectives of this *Code*.

6-2.1 Construction. Buildings or structures occupied or used according to the individual occupancy chapters (*Chapters 8 through 30*), shall meet the minimum construction requirements of those Chapters. The *Standard on Types of Building Construction*, NFPA 220, shall be used to determine the requirements for the construction classification.

In general, the *Life Safety Code* is not a building code. However, in certain occupancies, construction requirements are established in order to increase the probability of maintaining an acceptable minimum level of life safety.

6-2.2 Compartmentation.

6-2.2.1 When required by Chapters 8 through 30, every building shall be divided into compartments to limit the spread of fire and restrict the movement of smoke.

6-2.2.2 Fire compartments shall be formed with fire barriers which are continuous from outside wall to outside wall, from another fire barrier to a fire barrier, or a combination thereof; including continuity through all concealed spaces such as those found above a ceiling, including interstitial spaces.

Exception: Fire barriers are not required in interstitial spaces when such spaces are designed and constructed with ceilings that can provide equivalent resistance to the passage of fire to that provided by fire barriers.

Interstitial spaces, especially in health care occupancies, in some cases contain a considerable fuel load and are readily accessible by people. Over the life of a building, the possibility that an interstitial space will be used for storage cannot be overlooked. These factors must be considered to determine whether or not an interstitial space is in fact another floor.

It must be remembered that normally ceilings are not tested alone and are tested as part of a ceiling/floor or ceiling/roof assembly. This test does not give the performance of the ceiling, but of the total assembly. For example, the ceiling of a 1-hour floor/ceiling assembly may fail after 20 minutes, but the assembly overall passes the 1-hour test. Often an architect or contractor will refer to a 1- or 2-hour ceiling and request to terminate a fire barrier at the ceiling, but in reality the ceiling is part of a 1-hour or 2-hour floor/ceiling or roof/ceiling assembly and therefore the fire barrier should extend from slab to slab. There are tests which indicate that, by using two layers of ⅝-in. fire-rated gypsum board properly installed as a ceiling, a fire barrier of approximately 1 hour can be obtained and therefore termination of the wall fire barrier would be permitted if allowed by the authority having jurisdiction.

It must, however, be pointed out that some occupancies do allow the fire barrier to terminate at the ceiling of a floor/ceiling assembly. For example, Chapters 10 and 11 on educational occupancies allow this for 1-hour corridor walls. Perhaps this is allowed since the occupants are familiar with the building, well-drilled, alert, and mobile. But caution must be exercised, since ceilings of these assemblies are often improperly installed or, once installed, have been violated during routine maintenance. (See Figure 6-1.)

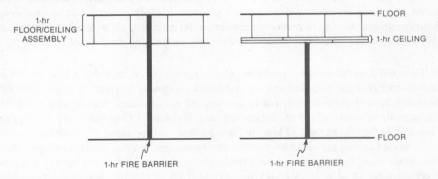

Figure 6-1. Fire Barriers Must Extend Through Ceiling Spaces Unless the Ceiling Is Itself a Fire Barrier.

6-2.2.3 Floor Openings.

6-2.2.3.1   When required by Chapters 8 through 30, floor openings, such as stairways and shaftways used for elevators, light, ventilation, or building services, shall be enclosed with fire barriers (vertical) such as wall or partition assemblies. Such enclosures shall be continuous from floor to floor. Openings shall be protected as appropriate for the fire resistance rating of the fire barrier.

Protection of vertical openings is of extreme importance if fire casualties are to be reduced. In an analysis of 500 fires involving fatalities, the current edition (14th) of the *Fire Protection Handbook* lists the vertical spread of fire in buildings as being the responsible factor in 250 incidents (50 percent of the cases).[4]

Demonstrating a correlation that frequently exists between life loss and monetary loss from fire, the *Handbook* goes on to show that vertical fire spread is a major contributing factor in the extensive property damages of large loss building fires. This relates directly to the lack of protection for vertical openings, i.e., "...the principal structural weakness responsible for vertical spread of fire is the absence of the fire cutoffs at openings between floors."[5]

Exception No. 1: Where permitted by Chapters 8 through 30, unenclosed openings comprising a portion of the total area of the building are permitted for the purpose of communicating between three floor levels, providing the following conditions are met:

(a) The communicating area has a low hazard occupancy, or ordinary hazard occupancy protected throughout by an approved automatic sprinkler system.

(b) The lowest or next to the lowest level of the portion so designated is a street floor.

(c) The entire portion so designated is open and unobstructed in a manner such that it may be assumed that a fire in any part of the space will be readily obvious to the occupants.

(d) Exit capacity is sufficient to provide simultaneously for all the occupants of all levels to egress the portion so designated by considering it to be a single floor area for the determination of required exit capacity.

(e) Each floor level, considered separately, has at least one-half of its individual required exit capacity provided by an exit or exits leading directly out of that level without occupants having to traverse another communicating floor level or be exposed to the smoke or fire spreading from another communicating floor level.

To avoid possible misinterpretation of Exception No. 1 to 6-2.2.3.1, it should be understood that the requirement for automatic sprinkler protection applies only to ordinary hazard occupancies, not to low hazard occupancies. However, as stated in Chapter 4, "Classification of Occupancy and Hazard of Contents," most occupancies are ordinary hazard. Thus, in low hazard occupancies or ordinary hazard occupancies having sprinkler protection, the enclosures may be omitted on up to three communicating floor levels, when permitted by the applicable occupancy chapter. Exception No. 1 of 6-2.2.3.1 may be applied if all of the following conditions have been met:

1. Approval has been given by the authority having jurisdiction;
2. Areas served are open so as to ensure quick discovery of a fire or any other hazardous condition;
3. The lowest level is at or not more than one level below street level;
4. The combined occupant load of all levels served is used in calculating the exit capacity; and
5. One-half the exit capacity on each floor must be provided by exits which lead directly out of the area without traversing the area exposed by the unprotected opening.

Exception No. 2: Where permitted by Chapters 8 through 30, an atrium may be utilized providing the following conditions are met:

When atriums are used, there is an added degree of safety to occupants because of the large volume of space into which smoke can be dissipated. However, there is a need to ensure that dangerous concentrations of smoke are promptly removed from the atrium and the exhaust system needs careful design.

(a) No horizontal dimension between opposite edges of the floor opening is less than 20 ft (609.6 cm) and the opening is a minimum of 1,000 sq ft (92.9 sq m).

As some atriums may be of other than square or rectangular shape, the 20 ft (609.6 cm) obviously cannot be applied where the corners exist. This would necessitate that the designer and the authority having jurisdiction work out equivalent life safety.

(b) The exits are separately enclosed from the atrium in accordance with 6-2.2.3.2. Access to exits may be within the atrium.

(c) The occupancy within the space meets the specifications for classification as low or ordinary hazard contents (see 4-2.2.).

(d) The entire portion so designated is open and unobstructed in a manner such that it may be assumed that a fire in any part of the space will be readily obvious to the occupants prior to the time it becomes a hazard to them.

(e) The entire building is protected throughout by an approved automatic sprinkler system in accordance with Section 7-7.

Exception to (e):   When the ceiling of the atrium is more than 55 ft (16.76 m) above the floor the authority having jurisdiction may permit the omission of sprinklers at the top of the atrium.

(f) In new construction, an engineered smoke control system acceptable to the authority having jurisdiction shall be provided. Factors such as means of egress and smoke control of adjacent spaces shall be considered.

Exception to (f):   In lieu of an engineered smoke control system, a smoke removal system acceptable to the authority having jurisdiction may be considered.

(g) In new construction the required engineered smoke control system or smoke removal system shall be activated by all of the following:

1. Approved smoke detectors located at the top of the atrium, and adjacent to each return air intake from the atrium, and

2. The required automatic sprinkler system, and

3. The required fire alarm system, and

4. Manual controls which are readily accessible to the fire department.

Activation of the ventilation system by manual fire alarms, extinguishing systems, and detection systems can cause unwanted operation of the system, and it is suggested that consideration be given to zoning of the activation functions so the ventilation system operates only when actually needed.

(h) Enclosure of Atriums.   In new construction atriums shall be separated from the adjacent spaces by fire barriers with at least a 1-hour fire resistance rating.

Exception No. 1 to (h):   Any three levels of the building may open directly to the atrium without enclosure.

Exception No. 2 to (h):   Glass walls may be used in lieu of the fire barriers where automatic sprinklers are spaced 6 ft (182.88 cm) apart or less along both sides of the glass wall, not more than 1 ft (30.48 cm) from the glass, and with the automatic sprinklers located so that the surface of the glass is wet upon operation of the sprinklers. The glass shall be float glass held in place by a gasket system which permits the glass framing system to deflect without loading the glass before the sprinklers operate. Automatic sprinklers are not required on the atrium side of the glass wall when there is no walkway or other floor area on the atrium side above the main floor level.

The following information gives guidance for the smoke removal system which may be used in lieu of an engineered smoke control system:

A mechanical exhaust system at the top of the atrium arranged so that the space does not become pressurized.

(1) In atriums 55 ft (16.76 m) or less in height with a volume of 600,000 cu ft (16 992 cu m) or less, the system should exhaust 40,000 cfm (18.88 cu m/s) or six air changes per hour, whichever is greater. Gravity supply inlets should be provided at the lowest level of the atrium and be sized for 75 percent of the exhaust.

(2) In atriums 55 ft (16.76 m) or less in height with a volume in excess of 600,000 cu ft (16 992 cu m), the system should be sized to provide a minimum of four air changes per hour. Gravity supply inlets should be provided at the lowest level of the atrium and be sized for 75 percent of the exhaust.

(3) In atriums in excess of 55 ft (16.76 m) in height (regardless of volume) the exhaust system should be sized to provide a minimum of four air changes per hour. Supply air should be mechanically introduced from near the bottom of the atrium and should be directed vertically toward the top of the atrium at a rate of approximately 75 percent of the exhaust.

For additional information see:

(1) Butcher and Parnell, *Smoke Control in Fire Safety Design.*[6]

(2) See discussion following 15-3.1.3.

Volume Determination. The volume of an atrium is determined by calculating all the space having a common atmosphere. The presence of a fire barrier with protected openings, whether developed by fire barriers or specially designed glass walls with special sprinkler protection, is intended to provide the limits of the common atmosphere.

6-2.2.3.2   The minimum fire resistance rating for the enclosure of floor openings shall be as follows: (*See 5-1.3.1 for enclosure of exits.*)

(a) Enclosures connecting four stories or more in new construction — 2-hour fire barriers.

(b) Other enclosures in new construction — 1-hour fire barriers.

(c) Enclosures in existing buildings — ½-hour fire barriers.

The key to understanding 6-2.2.3.2 is the fact that the *Code*'s concern is with the number of stories connected, not the height of the building. For example, if there is a vertical opening between the second, third, and fourth stories of an eight-story building, the enclosure of the opening must be 1-hour fire-resistant construction, not 2-hour construction.

When dealing with vertical openings, the *Code* does not use the height of buildings or a designated number of floors aboveground as the basis for its requirements. Rather, it refers to the total number of floors connected by the vertical opening. When a vertical opening connects any total of four stories or more, whether they be all above the exit discharge level, all below the exit discharge level, or any combination thereof, the protection afforded must have at least a 2-hour fire resistance rating (see Figures 6-2 and 6-4). When three stories or less are connected by the vertical opening, the rating must be at least 1-hour (see Figures 6-3 and 6-5).

Experience shows that under some circumstances each of the 1- and 2-hour rating levels provides more than a comfortable time for the occupants of a building to get out. On the other hand, there are times when the strength of the construction will be taxed to its limit, e.g., a situation in which a fire that has gone undetected for a long period generates heavy smoke and toxic gases, complicating evacuation by blocking the exit access. Further, allowance should be made for possible combinations of horizontal and vertical travel along the exit way.

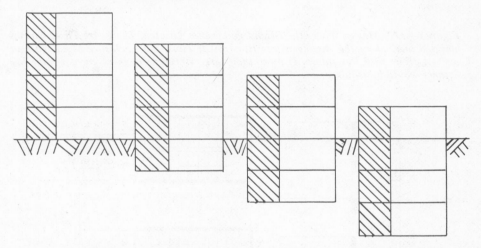

Figure 6-2. With Four Stories or More, Exit Stairs Must Be Enclosed in 2-Hour Noncombustible or Limited-Combustible Construction (Shaded Areas) and Supported by 2-Hour Construction.

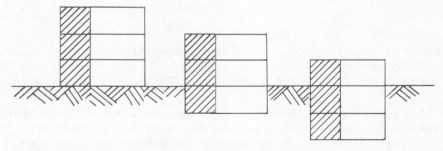

Figure 6-3. With Three Stories or Less, Exit Stairs Must Be Enclosed in 1-Hour Construction (Shaded Areas).

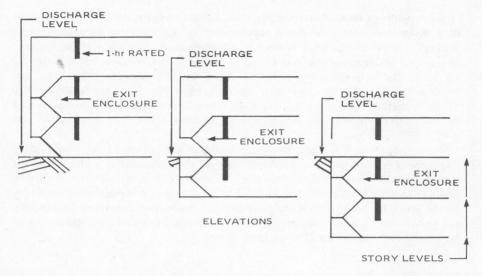

Figure 6-4. No Matter Where the Discharge Level Is Located, There Are Three Stories Connected in Each of the Arrangements Illustrated; Thus, the Enclosure Must Have at Least a 1-Hour Fire Resistance. If more than three stories were involved, a 2-hour fire resistance would be required.

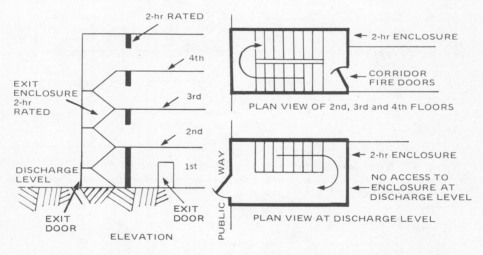

Figure 6-5. While the Stairway Serves Three Stories, the Stairway Does Provide an Opening Between Four Stories; Thus, According to 6-2.2.3.2(a), the Enclosure Must Have at Least a 2-Hour Fire Resistance.

The application of the 2-hour rule, in buildings not divided into stories, may be based on the number of levels of platforms or walkways served by the stairs.

Masonry enclosure walls are generally specified for new construction. For enclosing open stairways in existing buildings, various types of light construction are used, including plaster on metal lath.

6-2.2.3.3   Any escalators or moving walks serving as a required exit shall be enclosed in the same manner as exit stairways.

When used as an exit, an escalator must be completely enclosed with fire-rated construction, including entrance and discharge doors.

6-2.2.3.4   Escalators or moving walks not constituting an exit shall have their floor openings enclosed or protected as required for other vertical openings.

Exception No. 1:   In lieu of such protection, in buildings protected throughout by an approved automatic sprinkler system in accordance with Section 7-7, escalator or moving walk openings may be protected by one of the methods described in Appendix A† or in accordance with the method detailed with Standard for the Installation of Sprinkler Systems, NFPA 13, or in accordance with a method as approved by the authority having jurisdiction.

†The methods referred to in Appendix A of the *Code* are contained in the commentary of this *Handbook*.

Exception No. 2:   Escalators in large open areas such as atriums and enclosed shopping malls.

An important exception contained in 6-2.2.3.4 provides that escalators need not be enclosed if certain provisions are met. Several methods are available to permit the use of unenclosed escalators in completely sprinklered buildings, where the escalators are not used as exits. These include:

(a) A sprinkler-vent method;
(b) A spray nozzle method;
(c) A rolling shutter method; and
(d) A partial enclosure method.

A fifth method of protection, the sprinkler-draft curtain method, is detailed in NFPA 13, *Standard for the Installation of Sprinkler Systems,*[7] (see 4-4.8.2.3 and A-4-4.8.2.3 of that standard). It consists of surrounding the escalator opening with an 18-in. (45.72-cm) deep draft stop located on the underside of the floor to which the escalator ascends. This would serve to delay the heat, smoke, and combustion gases developed in the early stages of a fire on that floor from entering into the escalator well. A row of automatic sprinklers located outside of the draft stop also surrounds the escalator well. When activated by heat, the sprinklers provide a water curtain. (A typical installation is shown in Figure 6-6.) In combination with the sprinkler system in the building, this system should be effective in delaying fire spread and allowing time for use of the escalator stairs as the second means of egress.

(a) Sprinkler-Vent Method. Under the conditions specified, escalator or moving walk openings may be protected by the "sprinkler-vent" method, consisting of a combination of an automatic fire or smoke detection system, automatic exhaust system, and an automatic water curtain meeting the following requirements and of a design meeting the approval of the authority having jurisdiction:

1. The exhaust system must be of such capacity as to create a downdraft through the escalator or moving walk floor opening. The downdraft must have an average velocity of not less than 300 ft/min (1.52 m/s) under normal conditions for a period of not less than 30 minutes.

This requirement can be met by the provisions of an air intake from the outside of the building above the floor opening. The test of the system under "normal"

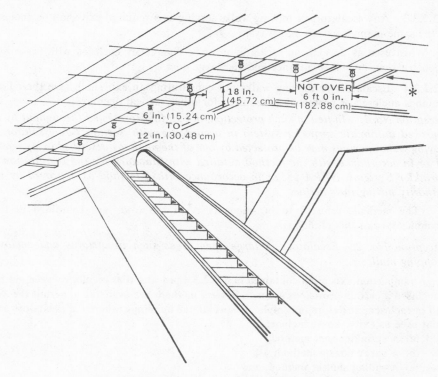

Figure 6-6. Sprinklers Around an Escalator.

conditions requires that the velocity of the downdraft be developed when windows or doors on the several stories normally used for ventilation are open. The size of the exhaust fan and exhaust ducts must be sufficient to meet such ventilation conditions. Experience indicates that fan capacity should be based on a rating of not less than 500 cfm/sq ft (8.33 cu m/s/sq m) of moving stairway opening to obtain the 300 ft/min (1.52 m/s) required. If the building is provided with an air-conditioning system, arranged to be automatically shut down in the event of fire, the test conditions should be met with the air-conditioning system shut down. The 300 ft/min (1.52 m/s) downdraft through the opening provides for the testing of the exhaust system without requiring an expansion of air present under actual fire conditions.

2. Operation of the exhaust system for any floor opening must be initiated by an approved device in the story involved and must be any one of the following means in addition to a manual means for operating and testing the system:

(i) Thermostats — fixed temperature, rate-of-rise, or a combination of both.

(ii) Water flow in the sprinkler system.

(iii) Approved supervised smoke detection. Smoke detection devices, if used, must be so located that the presence of smoke is detected before it enters the stairway.

3. Electric power supply to all parts of the exhaust system and its control devices must be designed and installed for maximum reliability. The electric power supply provisions of NFPA 20, *Standard for the Installation of Centrifugal Fire*

Pumps,[8] may be referred to as a guide to design and installation features to assure maximum reliability.

4. Any fan or duct used in connection with an automatic exhaust system must be of the approved type and must be installed in accordance with the applicable standards listed in the References at the end of this chapter.

5. Periodic tests, not less frequently than quarterly, must be made of the automatic exhaust system to maintain the system and the control devices in good working condition.

6. The water curtain must be formed by open sprinklers or spray nozzles so located and spaced as to form a complete and continuous barrier along all exposed sides of the floor opening and reaching from the ceiling to the floor. Water intensity for water curtain must be not less than approximately 3 gal per min per lineal ft (6.2 x 10^{-4} cu m/sec/m) of water curtain, measured horizontally around the opening.

7. The water curtain must operate automatically from thermal responsive elements of fixed temperature type so placed with respect to the ceiling (floor) opening that the water curtain comes into action upon the advance of heat toward the escalator or moving walk opening.

8. Every automatic exhaust system, including all motors, controls and automatic water curtain system, must be supervised in an approved manner, similar to that specified for automatic sprinkler system supervision.

(b) Spray Nozzle Method. Under the conditions specified, escalator openings may be protected by the spray nozzle method, consisting of a combination of an automatic fire or smoke detection system and a system of high velocity water spray nozzles meeting the following requirements and of a design meeting the approval of the authority having jurisdiction.

1. Spray nozzles must be of the open type and must have a solid conical spray pattern with discharge angles between 45 and 90 degrees. The number of nozzles, their discharge angles, and their location must be such that the escalator or moving walk opening between the top of the wellway housing and the treadway will be completely filled with dense spray on operation of the system.

2. The number and size of nozzles and water supply must be sufficient to deliver a discharge of 2 gal of water/sq ft/min (.27 cu m/sq m/m) through the wellway, area to be figured perpendicular to treadway. (See Figure 6-7.)

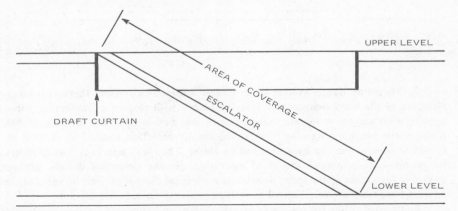

Figure 6-7. Area of Coverage for the Spray Nozzle Method of Protecting Vertical Openings.

3. Spray nozzles must be so located as to effectively utilize the full advantage of the cooling and counterdraft effect. They must be so positioned that the center line of spray discharge is as closely as possible in line with the slope of the escalator or moving walk, not more than an angle of 30 degrees with the top slope of the wellway housing. Nozzles must be positioned, also, so that the center line of discharge is at an angle of not more than 30 degrees from the vertical sides of the wellway housing.

4. Spray nozzles must discharge at a minimum pressure of at least 25 lb/sq in. (1.72 x 10^5 Pa). Water supply piping may be taken from the sprinkler system, provided that in so doing an adequate supply of water will be available for the spray nozzles and the water pressure at the sprinkler farthest from the supply riser is not reduced beyond the required minimum. Supply taken from the sprinkler system is designed to provide protection to the wellway opening for life hazard during the exit period, but may not be relied upon to provide an effective floor cutoff.

5. Control valves must be readily accessible to minimize water damage.

6. A noncombustible or limited-combustible draft curtain must be provided extending at least 20 in. (50.8 cm) below and around the opening, and a solid noncombustible wellway housing at least 5 ft (152.4 cm) long, measured parallel to the handrail and extending from the top of the handrail enclosure to the soffit of the stairway or ceiling above, at each escalator floor opening. When necessary, spray nozzles must be protected against mechanical injury or tampering that might interfere with proper discharge. (See Figure 6-8.)

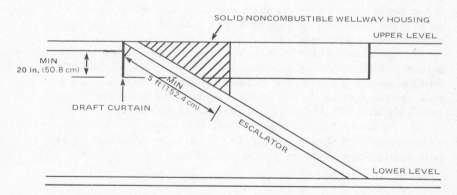

Figure 6-8. The Draft Curtain and Wellway Housing Method of Protecting Vertical Openings.

7. The spray nozzle system must operate automatically from thermal response elements of the fixed temperature type, so placed with respect to the ceiling (floor) opening that the spray nozzle system comes into action upon the advance of heat towards the escalator opening. Supervised smoke detection located in or near the escalator opening may be used to sound an alarm. The spray nozzle system must also be provided with manual means of operation. Smoke detection devices are not desirable for action of the spray nozzles as accidental discharge must be safeguarded against from both a panic hazard as well as property damage standpoint.

8. Control valves for the spray nozzle system and approved smoke detection or thermostatic devices must be supervised in accordance with the applicable provisions of Section 7-6.

(c) Rolling Shutter Method. Under the conditions specified, escalator or moving walk openings above the street floor only may be protected by the rolling shutter method, consisting of an automatic self-closing rolling shutter which completely encloses the top of each escalator or moving walk, meets the following requirements, and the design of which meets the approval of the authority having jurisdiction. The use of an automatic rolling shutter to protect moving stairway or moving walk wellways between street floors and floors below is not acceptable for the reason that the normal path of travel to reach a place of safety in an emergency is usually that used for access to the area. Persons seeking egress from a floor below the street floor served by moving stairways or moving walk could be trapped by fully closed rolling shutters at the street floor level. Observation of rolling shutters in use indicates the likelihood that under emergency conditions there is a quite different psychological reaction by those facing its operation from upper floors than could be expected when the rolling shutter is closed above a person seeking egress from a basement. On upper floors, the operation of an automatic rolling shutter will be clearly visible to persons seeking egress and other means of egress (i.e., stairways) can be readily found and used if the requirements of the *Code* are followed.

1. The shutter must close off the wellway opening immediately upon the automatic detection, by an approved heat-actuated or smoke-sensitive device, of fire or smoke in the vicinity of the escalator. In addition, there must be provided a manual means of operating and testing the operation of the shutter.

2. The shutter assembly must be capable of supporting a weight of 200 lb (90.72 kg) applied on any 1 sq ft (.09 sq m) of area and must be not less resistant to fire or heat than 24 gage steel.

3. The shutter must operate at a speed of not greater than 30 ft/min (.15 m/s). It must be equipped with a sensitive leading edge, which must arrest the progress of the moving shutter and cause it to retract a distance of approximately 6 in. (15.24 cm) upon the application of a force not in excess of 20 lb (9.07 kg) applied on the surface of the leading edge. The shutter, following retraction, must continue to close immediately.

4. Automatic rolling shutters must be provided with an electric contact which will disconnect the power supply from the escalator or moving walk and apply the brakes as soon as the shutter starts to close and will prevent further operation of the escalator or moving walk until the rolling shutter is again in the open position.

5. The electrical supply to the control devices for actuation of the automatic rolling shutter must be so designed and installed as to provide maximum reliability. The electric power supply provisions of NFPA 20, *Standard for the Installation of Centrifugal Fire Pumps*,[8] may be referred to as a guide to design and installation features to assume maximum reliability.

6. Rolling shutters must be operated at least once a week in order to make sure that they remain in proper operating condition.

(d) Partial Enclosure Method. Under the conditions specified, escalator or moving walk openings may be protected by a partial enclosure, or so-called kiosk, so designed as to provide an effective barrier to the spread of smoke from floor to floor.

1. Partial enclosures must be of construction providing fire resistance equivalent to that specified for stairway enclosures in the same building, with openings therein protected by approved self-closing fire doors, or may be of approved wired glass and metal frame construction with wired glass panel doors.

2. Such doors may be equipped with electric opening mechanism to open the

door automatically upon the approach of a person. The mechanism must be such as to return the door to its closed position upon any interruption of electric current supply, and the adjustment must be such that the pressure of smoke will not cause opening of the door.

6-2.2.4 Fire barriers used to provide enclosure of floor openings or used for subdivision of stories shall be classified in accordance with their fire resistance rating as follows:

(a) 2-hour fire resistance rating.

(b) 1-hour fire resistance rating.

(c) ¾-hour fire resistance rating.

(d) ½-hour fire resistance rating.

(e) 20-minute fire resistance rating.

The fire resistance of a fire barrier is determined by the test method described in NFPA 251, *Standard Methods of Fire Tests of Building Construction and Materials.*[2] These tests are commonly done by testing laboratories which normally issue a report of the test and then list the assembly. It is important that the assembly in the field be the same as that listed. For example, if a floor/ceiling assembly calls for clips on the ceiling tiles, these must be installed and maintained. Another example is the special treatment often required for lights or air ducts in suspended ceilings. A common problem in walls is the installation of an untested material between the wallboard and the studs or the installation of recessed wall fixtures which requires the removal of wallboard.

6-2.2.5 Every opening in a fire barrier shall be protected to limit the spread of fire and restrict the movement of smoke from one side of the fire barrier to the other. The fire protection rating for opening protectives shall be as follows:

(a) 2-hour fire barrier — 1½-hour fire protection rating.

(b) 1-hour fire barrier — 1-hour fire protection rating when used for vertical openings or ¾-hour fire protection rating when used for other than vertical openings.

Exception No. 1:   When a lesser fire protection rating is specified by Chapter 5 or Chapters 8 through 30.

Exception No. 2:   Where the fire barrier is provided as a result of a requirement that corridor walls be of 1-hour fire-resistive construction, the opening protectives shall have a fire protection rating of not less than 20 minutes when tested in accordance with Standard Methods of Fire Tests of Door Assemblies, NFPA 252 without the hose stream test.

Exception No. 3:   Where special requirements for doors in 1-hour fire rated corridor walls and 1-hour fire rated smoke barriers are specified in Chapters 12 and 13.

In general, 1-hour fire barriers for vertical openings require doors with a 1-hour fire protection rating and 1-hour fire barriers for other than vertical openings require doors with a ¾-hour fire protection rating.

Exception No. 1 allows Chapter 5 and the occupancy chapters to alter this general rule. For the most part though this is usually only done in regard to the requirements in several chapters that corridor walls be of a 1-hour fire resistance rating. Exception No. 2 specifically deals with this subject.

Exception No. 3 recognizes the special requirements contained in Chapters 12 and 13 for Health Care Occupancies which recognize the functional needs and abilities unique to these facilities.

(c) ¾-hour fire barrier — 20-minute fire protection rating.

(d) ½-hour fire barrier — 20-minute fire protection rating.

(e) 20-minute fire barrier — 20-minute fire protection rating.

Longer ratings may be required where doors are provided for property protection as well as life safety.

NFPA 80, *Standard for Fire Doors and Windows,*[9] may be consulted for standard practice in the selection and installation of fire doors.

A 1¾-in. (4.45-cm) solid bonded wood core door has been considered the equivalent to a door with a 20-minute fire protection rating.

6-2.2.6 Fire door assemblies in fire barriers shall comply with the provisions of 5-2.1.

6-2.2.7 Openings in fire barriers for air handling ductwork or air movement shall be protected in accordance with the *Standard for the Installation of Air Conditioning and Ventilating Systems*, NFPA 90A. When a fire barrier also serves as a smoke barrier, an approved damper designed to resist the passage of smoke shall be provided in accordance with 6-3.5.

Exception: This requirement need not apply for ductwork which is part of an engineered smoke control system.

In engineered smoke control systems, the designers should consider the use of fire dampers having high temperature links where air handling ductwork penetrates fire barriers.

6-2.2.8 Passages of pipes, conduits, buss ducts, cables, wires, air ducts, pneumatic ducts, and similar building service equipment through fire barriers shall be protected as follows:

(a) The space between the penetrating item and the fire barrier shall:

1. be filled with a material capable of maintaining the fire resistance of the fire barrier, or

2. be protected by an approved device designed for the specific purpose.

(b) Where the penetrating item uses a sleeve to penetrate the fire barrier, the sleeve shall be solidly set in the fire barrier and the space between the item and the sleeve shall be:

1. filled with a material capable of maintaining the fire resistance of the fire barrier, or

2. be protected by an approved device designed for the specific purpose.

(c) Where designs take transmission of vibration into consideration, any vibration isolation:

1. shall be made on either side of the fire barrier, or

2. shall be by an approved device designed for the specific purpose.

Over the life of a building, it is important to maintain the integrity of barriers to fire spread. Renovations or any changes to building utilities will tend to violate the compartmentation provided when a building is first occupied.

6-2.2.9   The enclosing walls (fire barriers) of floor openings serving stairways or ramps that are required exits shall be so arranged as to provide a continuous path of escape, including landings and passageways, in accordance with 5-2.2, providing protection for persons using the stairway or ramp against fire, or smoke therefrom, in other parts of the building.

One of the purposes of 6-2.2.9 is to prevent a required stair or ramp design which requires a person to leave the exit, enter a floor, and then reenter the exit to continue down. Figure 6-9 shows an unacceptable arrangement.

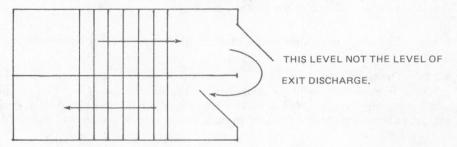

THIS LEVEL NOT THE LEVEL OF
EXIT DISCHARGE.

Figure 6-9. An Unacceptable Arrangement for Enclosing a Stairway Serving as a Required Exit.

6-2.2.10   Floor-ceiling assemblies; and bearing and nonbearing wall or partition assemblies, used as fire barriers to form fire compartments; and columns, beams, girders, or trusses supporting such assemblies shall be of a design which has been tested to meet the conditions of acceptance of *Standard Methods of Fire Tests of Building Construction and Materials*, NFPA 251.

Not only is it necessary to provide the proper fire barriers, but the structural integrity of those barriers must be maintained. This is not only for evacuation of occupants but for the safety of fire fighters during search and rescue operations.

6-2.2.11   Door or window assemblies in fire barriers shall be of an approved type with appropriate rating for the location in which installed. Fire doors and windows shall be installed in accordance with the *Standard for Fire Doors and Windows*, NFPA 80. Fire doors shall be of a design that has been tested to meet the conditions of acceptance of *Standard Methods of Fire Tests of Door Assemblies*, NFPA 252. Fire windows shall be of a design which has been tested to meet the conditions of acceptance of *Standard for Fire Tests of Window Assemblies*, NFPA 257.

6-2.3 Concealed Spaces.

6-2.3.1   In new construction, any concealed space in which materials having a flame-spread rating greater than Class A, as defined in Section 6-5, are exposed shall be effectively firestopped with approved materials, as provided below:

Exception: If the space is protected throughout by an approved automatic sprinkler system in accordance with Section 7-7.

The vertical spread of fire through shafts, chases, and hollow wall construction and the horizontal spread of fire through plenums and open attics are phenomena common to many serious fires. Where such spaces are protected with automatic sprinklers, the risk of unseen fires is minimized. Where this protection is not installed in new buildings and the materials used have a flame spread rating of more than 25 (Class A), certain additional precautions are required.

(a) Every exterior and interior wall and partition shall be firestopped at each floor level, at the top story ceiling level, and at the level of support for roofs.

(b) Every unoccupied attic space shall be subdivided by firestops into areas not to exceed 3,000 sq ft (279 sq m).

(c) Any concealed space between the ceiling and the floor or roof above shall be firestopped for the full depth of the space along the line of support for the floor or roof structural members and, if necessary, at other locations to form areas not to exceed 1,000 sq ft (93 sq m) for any space between the ceiling and floor and 3,000 sq ft (279 sq m) for any space between the ceiling and roof.

Firestopping of attic spaces is particularly important in one-story-and-attic shopping centers and in two-story apartments or row housing. Experience has shown that a fire starting in one of these occupancy units and breaking into the attic space can spread through the attic and travel down into adjoining units, and frequently this has been the case.

Numerous fires in garden apartments have demonstrated two common weaknesses relating to the lack of adequate firestopping. The areas frequently not firestopped are between the underside of the roof deck and the top of fire walls that do not extend above roof line and in the pipe chase that contains the plumbing vent stack. The vent stack is of particular concern because it frequently is between two mirror-image apartment units and interconnects all the floors of the apartment unit. A fire that develops into this concealed space can spread to the attic and soon involve the entire structure.

The area limitations specified are based on life safety considerations and are not intended to suggest that changes should be made in local building codes having similar or more restrictive requirements that are based on other considerations. Building codes generally contain detailed information on the proper selection and installation of firestopping materials.

6-2.3.2   In every existing building, firestopping shall be provided as required by the provisions of Chapters 8 through 30.

SECTION 6-3   SMOKE BARRIERS

6-3.1   Where required by Chapters 8 through 30, smoke barriers shall be provided to subdivide building spaces for the purpose of restricting the movement of smoke.

6-3.2   Smoke barriers required by this *Code* shall be continuous from outside wall to outside wall, from a fire barrier to a fire barrier, from a floor to a floor, from a smoke barrier to a smoke barrier, or a combination thereof; including continuity through all concealed spaces such as those found above a ceiling, including interstitial spaces.

Exception: Smoke barriers are not required in interstitial spaces when such spaces are designed and constructed with ceilings that can provide resistance to the passage of smoke equivalent to that provided by smoke barriers.

In occupancies where evacuation is a last resort or is expected to be otherwise delayed, smoke partitions and doors therein will require a degree of fire resistance as specified by the requirements found in the occupancy chapters (Chapters 8 through 30) of the *Code.*

Other openings in smoke and fire partitions must be protected as well. Heating, air conditioning, and ventilation ducts provide a ready path for smoke and fire to travel from one area to another unless carefully protected. Penetrations in walls and ceiling construction for utility lines and other building services must be firestopped to prevent smoke spread. The hidden spaces behind suspended ceilings and attic spaces are out of sight and easily overlooked.

The exception to 6-3.2 must be used with extreme care for several reasons. First, several chapters require the smoke barrier to have some fire resistance rating and therefore could only terminate at the ceiling if the ceiling could also obtain this rating (see discussion of 6-2.2.2). Also, even if no fire resistance was required, it is difficult to assure that a ceiling is smoketight unless it is of monolithic construction without air handling penetrations. However, this kind of construction is often found in apartment buildings, hotels, and dormitories, and consequently the exception can be useful.

6-3.3   Doors in smoke barriers shall be of a swinging type that close the opening with only a minimum clearance necessary for proper operation and shall be without undercuts, louvers, or grills. When a fire resistance rating is specified elsewhere in the *Code* for smoke barriers, the doors in the smoke barriers shall have a fire protection rating of at least twenty minutes. If vision panels are used in the doors, such glass shall be approved transparent wired glass.

Exception No. 1:   If a different fire protection rating for smoke barrier doors is specified by Chapters 8 through 30.

Exception No. 2:   Latching hardware is not required when so indicated by Chapters 8 through 30.

Doors in smoke partitions, while not the equivalent of fire doors, and not completely smoketight, are effective in restricting the spread of smoke and reducing drafts which might otherwise spread fire rapidly. And, since there is no performance standard for the passage of smoke through door assemblies, a 20-minute fire-rated door assembly in a smoke partition has been accepted by the Committee on Safety to Life as a reasonable barrier. It has been shown by tests that the commonly used 1¾-in. (4.45-cm) solid wood core door assembly can be expected to fail in 22 to 24 minutes, and has performed well in actual fires *when closed*.[10] The use of the 20-minute designation replaces a specification standard with a performance standard. The same reference emphasizes that even fully rated fire doors will not keep out smoke because of the clearances needed to have the door work properly. Gasketing will help, but a tight-fitting door should keep out enough smoke so that orderly exiting may proceed. The clearance for proper operation of smoke doors has been defined as ⅛ in. (.32 cm).

Doors in a fire separation, horizontal exit, or smoke partition should be closed at all times to impede the travel of smoke and fire gases. Functionally, however, this involves decreased efficiency and, for example, limits patient observation by the professional staff of a health care occupancy. To accommodate these necessities, it is practical to presume that the doors will be kept open even to the extent of employing wood chocks and other makeshift devices. When, because of operational necessity, it is desired to have smoke barrier doors normally open, such doors should be provided with hold-open devices which are activated to close the doors by the operation of smoke detectors and other alarm functions.

6-3.4   Door assemblies in smoke barriers shall comply with the provisions of 5-2.1.

6-3.5   An approved damper designed to resist the passage of smoke shall be provided at each point a duct penetrates a required smoke barrier. The damper shall close upon detection of smoke by an approved smoke detector located within the duct.

Exception No. 1:   Ductwork which is part of an engineered smoke control system.

Exception No. 2:   Dampers are not required in ducts where the air continues to move and the air handling system to which the ducts are connected is arranged to prevent recirculation of exhaust or return air upon detection of smoke in the system.

Exception No. 2 to 6-3.5 can only be used in very limited cases. It can only be used on small ventilation systems since NFPA 90A, *Standard for Air Conditioning and Ventilating Systems,*[11] requires that systems over 15,000 cfm (7.1 cu m/sec) that are not part of a smoke control system shut down upon detection of smoke (see NFPA 90A, paragraph 4-3.2). Exception No. 1 to 6-3.5 addresses smoke control exceptions. Even without the restriction of NFPA 90A it is difficult to ensure that the air handling system will be in continuous operation. In this day of energy conservation many systems are either cycled or shut down during parts of the day, or this feature could be added later without knowing that it was causing a problem.

However, the exception can be useful for ductwork for small ventilation systems such as for bathrooms or small suites.

6-3.6   Passages of pipes, conduits, buss ducts, cables, wires, air ducts, pneumatic ducts, and similar building service equipment through smoke barriers shall be protected as follows:

(a) The space between the penetrating item and the smoke barrier shall:

1. be filled with a material capable of maintaining the smoke resistance of the smoke barrier, or

2. be protected by an approved device designed for the specific purpose.

(b) Where the penetrating item uses a sleeve to penetrate the smoke barrier, the sleeve shall be solidly set in the smoke barrier and the space between the item and the sleeve shall be:

1. filled with a material capable of maintaining the smoke resistance of the smoke barrier, or

2. be protected by an approved device designed for the specific purpose.

(c) Where designs take transmission of vibration into consideration, any vibration isolation:

    1. shall be made on either side of the smoke barrier, or

    2. shall be by an approved device designed for the specific purpose.

As with fire barriers, it is important to maintain the integrity of smoke barriers over the life of a building.

SECTION 6-4   SPECIAL HAZARD PROTECTION

6-4.1   Protection shall be provided from any area having a degree of hazard greater than that normal to the general occupancy of the building or structure, such as storage of combustibles or flammables, heat producing appliances, or maintenance purposes, as follows:

(a) Enclosure with construction in accordance with Section 6-2 with a fire resistance rating as specified by Chapters 8 through 30, but not less than 1 hour, or

(b) Protection with automatic extinguishing systems in accordance with Section 7-7 as required by Chapters 8 through 30, or

(c) Both (a) and (b) above when specified by Chapters 8 through 30.

Exception: In existing buildings or structures, as permitted by Chapters 8 through 30, an automatic fire or smoke detection system in accordance with Section 7-6 may be substituted for the automatic extinguishing system if the enclosure above is achieved.

Here, the *Code* attempts to minimize the chance of fire or the need for evacuation by isolating those areas that have a high potential for fire or a high fuel load. The committees responsible for the occupancy chapters identified the particular hazards against which protection was to be provided. The authority having jurisdiction is responsible for the final determining of what are and are not hazardous areas. This approach represents the fundamental fire protection step of either protecting against the known hazards via automatic extinguishment systems or isolating the known hazards by construction.

6-4.2   Where hazardous processes or storage are of such a character as to introduce an explosion potential, explosion venting or an explosion suppression system specifically designed for the hazard involved shall be provided.

If the potential hazard is of an explosive nature, explosion venting or explosion suppression systems are required safeguards. NFPA 68, *Guide for Explosion Venting*,[12] contains details of acceptable venting systems, and NFPA 69, *Standard on Explosion Prevention Systems*,[13] covers suppression systems. NFPA 63, *Standard for the Prevention of Dust Explosions in Industrial Plants*,[14] is useful where explosive dusts are encountered.

6-4.3   A hazardous operation or process may be conducted in a detached structure sufficiently remote from other buildings to avoid any danger to occupants of other buildings. Protection for the safety of any occupants of the detached structure shall be provided.

SECTION 6-5   INTERIOR FINISH

6-5.1 General.

6-5.1.1 Interior finish means the exposed interior surfaces of buildings including, but not limited to, fixed or movable walls and partitions, columns, and ceilings. For requirements on decorations and furnishings see 31-1.2 and 31-1.4.

The faster a fire develops, the greater a threat it represents to the occupants of a building and the more difficult it will be to control. The wall and ceiling surfaces of a building have a major influence on how fast a fire develops. In establishing restrictions for the use of interior finish materials, the intention is to slow the early growth of fire and to limit the speed at which flame will travel across the interior surfaces of a building. Further, the restrictions are imposed on interior finish materials to minimize the contribution of "fuel" to the early growth of a fire and to limit the generation of smoke and toxic gases.

Interior finishes are the interior surfaces of a building which are secured in place prior to occupancy. Thus, wall, ceiling, and column coverings would be considered interior finishes. Movable walls or folding partitions would also be treated as interior finish. However, this section uses the expression "but not limited to" which allows the authority having jurisdiction to exercise judgment in determining what constitutes interior finish. For example, a tapestry would not normally be construed as interior finish. However, a large tapestry which is secured to and covers a major portion of a wall could promote the rapid growth of fire and may warrant regulation.

Furnishings are not normally considered as interior finish even in the case where the furnishings are fixed in place. However, if the furnishings are judged to represent a hazard, they may be regulated as interior finish by the authority having jurisdiction.

6-5.1.2 Interior floor finish means the exposed floor surfaces of buildings including coverings which may be applied over a normal finished floor. A finished floor or floor covering on floors shall be exempt from requirements of this section as interior finish provided, however, that (1) in any case where the authority having jurisdiction finds a floor surface of unusual hazard; or (2) where floor finish requirements are specified elsewhere in this *Code* for specific occupancies, the floor surface shall be regulated in accordance with the interior floor finish requirements of this section. (*See Chapters 8 through 30 for specific occupancy requirements.*)

Experience has shown that traditional floor coverings such as wood flooring and resilient tile do not contribute to the early growth of fire. Paragraph 6-5.1.2 acknowledges the satisfactory performance of traditional floor coverings and exempts such materials from the restrictions which would otherwise be applicable. However, the authority having jurisdiction is empowered to require substantiation for the performance of any floor covering which may be of a type or nature with which they are not familiar. For example, "plastic" imitation wood floors, artificial turf, artificial surfaces of athletic fields, and carpeting are types of products which may merit substantiation. When the authority having jurisdiction judges that a floor covering warrants testing and substantiation or when an occupancy chapter imposes restrictions as is the case in Chapters 10 and 11, dealing with Day-Care Centers; Chapters 12 and 13, dealing with Health Care Occupancies; Chapters 14 and 15, dealing with Detention and Correctional Occupancies; and Chapters 18 and 19, dealing with Residential Occupancies, the floor covering would be treated as interior floor finish and would be regulated on the basis of tests conducted within the Flooring Radiant Panel as required in 6-5.2.

6-5.1.3   Cellular or foamed plastic materials shall not be used as interior finish.

Exception No. 1:   Cellular or foamed plastic materials may be permitted on the basis of fire tests that substantiate on a reasonable basis their combustibility characteristics, for the use intended, in actual fire conditions.

Exception No. 2:   Cellular or foamed plastic may be used for trim, not in excess of 10 percent of the wall or ceiling area, provided it is not less than 20 lb/cu ft (320 kg/m³) in density, is limited to ½ in. (1.27 cm) in thickness, 4 in. (10.16 cm) in width and complies with the requirements for Class A or B interior finish; however, the smoke rating is not limited.

Cellular or foamed plastic material implies a heterogenous system comprised of at least two phases, one of which is a continuous polymeric organic material, and the second of which is a material deliberately introduced for the purpose of distributing gas into voids throughout the material. The system also includes foamed and unfoamed polymeric or monomeric precursors (prepolymer, if used), plasticizers, fillers, extenders, catalysts, blowing agents, colorants, stabilizers, lubricants, surfactants, pigments, reaction control agents, processing aids, and flame retardants.

This section sets forth the fundamental premise that foamed plastics should not be used exposed within buildings. This prohibition is based upon actual fire experience in which foam plastics have contributed to very rapid fire development. It is also acknowledged that tunnel testing may not accurately assess the potential hazard of "plastics" in general. Therefore, if cellular or foamed plastic are to be used within a building, their use should be substantiated on the basis of full-scale fire tests or fire testing which simulates conditions of actual use.

Exception No. 2 addresses the limited use of plastics as a substitute for traditional wood trim. The exception suggests that foamed or cellular plastic materials may be used as trim assuming the performance under fire exposure will be comparable to that of wood. In establishing a minimum density of 20 lb/cu ft (320.4 kg/cu m), it is intended to prohibit the use of light 1 to 3 lb/cu ft (16.02 to 48.06 kg/cu m) foam plastics as trim. To control the "mass" of the material which can be used, limits have been established on width and thickness.

Plastic trim is limited to Class A or B materials which, in combination with the 10 percent area limit of walls and ceiling, forms a more restrictive position than would be applicable to wood. This more restrictive position is established to assure the performance of the plastic trim will be equivalent to, or better than, that of traditional materials.

In establishing the 10 percent limit, it is intended that the trim will be used around doors and windows. Therefore, the trim will be uniformly distributed throughout the room. There would be a significant difference in the probable performance if the 10 percent is concentrated in one area and this exception intends to prohibit such a condition.

6-5.1.4 The classification of interior finish materials specified in 6-5.1.5 shall be that of the basic material used by itself or in combination with other materials.

Exception No. 1: Subsequently applied paint or wall covering not exceeding ¹/₂₈ in. (.09 cm) in thickness.

Exception No. 2: The authority having jurisdiction shall include such finishes in the determination of classification in any case where in the opinion of the authority having jurisdiction they are of such character or thickness or so applied as to affect materially the flame spread or smoke development characteristics.

Interior finish classifications apply to the basic materials used such as wood, gypsum board, plaster, or any combination of the materials. Exception No. 1 notes that thin coverings — not exceeding ¹/₂₈ in. (.09 cm) in thickness — will not significantly affect the performance of the basic wall or ceiling material. Thin paint and wallpaper coverings when secured to a noncombustible substrate will not significantly alter the performance of the substrate during a fire. However, thicker coverings, such as multiple layers of wallpaper, can and have contributed to rapid fire growth in actual fires. For example, multiple layers of wall coverings contributed to rapid fire growth in the multiple death fire in The Holiday Inn in Cambridge, Ohio which occurred on July 31, 1979.[15] Exception No. 1 would cause any wall or ceiling covering in excess of ¹/₂₈ in. (.09 cm) in thickness to be treated as interior finish.

Exception No. 2 permits the authority having jurisdiction to designate finish materials not normally considered interior finish as interior finish if the materials are of a character which would materially affect the smoke or fire characteristics of the basic material involved. In making this determination, consideration should be given not only to smoke but to decomposition products likely to be produced by the finish or the combination of the finish and substrate.

6-5.1.5 Interior finish materials shall be grouped in the following classes in accordance with their flame spread and smoke development:

Class A Interior Finish. Flame spread 0-25, smoke developed 0-450. Includes any material classified at 25 or less on the flame spread test scale and 450 or less on the smoke test scale described in 6-5.1.6. Any element thereof when so tested shall not continue to propagate fire.

Class B Interior Finish. Flame spread 26-75, smoke developed 0-450. Includes any material classified at more than 25 but not more than 75 on the flame spread test scale and 450 or less on the smoke test scale described in 6-5.1.6.

Class C Interior Finish. Flame spread 76-200, smoke developed 0-450. Includes any material classified at more than 75 but not more than 200 on the flame spread test scale and 450 or less on the smoke test scale described in 6-5.1.6.

Exception: Existing interior finishes complying with the above flame spread ratings only may be continued in use.

6-5.1.6 Interior finish materials as specified in 6-5.1.5 shall be classified in accordance with *Method of Test of Surface Burning Characteristics of Building Materials*, NFPA 255.

Although flame spread and smoke development are both recorded in the results of a test conducted in accordance with NFPA 255, *Method of Test of Surface Burning*

Characteristics of Building Materials,[16] there is not a direct relationship between these measurements. Fuel contributed values are no longer recorded as a required portion of the test procedure.

Materials are classed on the basis of various flame spread ratings; however, the same smoke development level is used for all three flame spread classifications. Flame spread ratings offer a general indication of the speed with which fire may spread across the surface of a material. In assessing the hazard presented by a material on the basis of flame spread, it is assumed a person may be in close proximity to the fire and would thereby be directly exposed to the energy associated with the actual flames. Smoke developed ratings, on the other hand, provide a general indication of the amount of smoke produced by a material during a fire. Smoke may affect occupants of a building in the vicinity of a fire and in remote locations. Smoke may spread to spaces remote from the fire as a result of stack effect, action of air handling systems, open vertical shafts, and the like.

Flame spread limits applicable to building materials vary on the basis of location. Different classes of materials are specified for an office area, for example, as compared to an exit or exit access corridor. The different classes recognize that in escaping a building a person must move away from the flames as he/she travels through the means of egress toward an exit. The classes of interior finishes that are considered acceptable within an open office are, therefore, different from those which are required for exits.

The same smoke developed limit is used for all three flame spread classifications. This limit recognizes that smoke generated during a fire may affect persons both in the vicinity and remote from the fire. Large building volumes can be quickly filled with smoke as a result of a fire. An upper limit has been established, therefore, which applies to interior finish materials irrespective of where the materials are located.

An exception is created for existing buildings. In existing buildings, interior finish materials are restricted only on the basis of flame spread. Editions of the *Life Safety Code* prior to 1976 did not regulate interior finish materials based upon smoke development. As a general rule, replacement of existing materials which were previously approved on the basis only of flame spread is not warranted. However, 6-5.1.7 provides the authority having jurisdiction with the authority to regulate materials on the basis of "products of decomposition" when, in the authority's judgment, a material constitutes an unreasonable life hazard due to the nature or quantity of such products.

The smoke developed limit of 450 was developed on the basis of research conducted at Underwriters Laboratories Inc.[17] Smoke from the tunnel test chamber was distributed into a 5,000-cu ft (141.6-cu m) room. The room was equipped with illuminated exit signs. The time required to reach various stages of exit sign obscuration was recorded and compared to the smoke developed rating for the various materials involved. The report states "materials having smoke developed ratings above 325 showed 'good' to 'marginal' visibility (scale readings of 3 - 4.8) in a few cases; other materials produced conditions of 'marginal' to obscuration in the six minute period."

Considering both time and smoke levels, the 450 limit on smoke ratings as used in the *Code* is what has been judged to be a "reasonable" limit. In considering flame spread and smoke development, it should be emphasized that there is no direct relationship between such data. In the report referenced above, for example, one material had a flame spread rating of 490 and a smoke developed factor of 57 while another had a flame spread rating of 44 and a smoke developed factor of 1,387.

It should be emphasized that the 450 smoke developed limit is based solely on obscuration. Other important factors in evaluations of materials based on smoke generation involve irritability and toxicity of gases. The adverse physiological effects on the human body resulting from exposure to heat and the effects from inhaling hot gases must also be considered.

6-5.1.7 Any interior finish material shown by test to present an unreasonable life hazard due to the character of the products of decomposition shall be used only with the approval of the authority having jurisdiction.

Restrictions limiting the use of interior finish materials are based upon smoke development and the obscuration of light. Products of decomposition of interior finish materials may act as irritants further reducing visibility and may additionally have a debilitating physiological effect on persons attempting to escape from a building. This provision gives the authority having jurisdiction the latitude needed to regulate materials which are not accurately assessed by flame spread and smoke developed ratings and which may create a hazard to life .

6-5.1.8 Classification of interior finish materials shall be in accordance with tests made under conditions simulating actual installations, provided that the authority having jurisdiction may by rule establish the classification of any material on which a rating by standard test is not available.

Samples are tested in accordance with NFPA 255, *Method of Test of Surface Burning Characteristics of Building Materials,*[16] with a noncombustible backing. Specimens are tested with adhesives, joints, and other conditions which would simulate the actual installation of a product in a building. NFPA 255[16] will provide a general indication of product performance only if the product is installed in a fashion similar to that which was tested. Data is available to show that the performance of interior finish materials varies on the basis of mounting conditions.[18] For example, a product installed over a combustible substrate will tend to propagate fire more readily than would be typical of the same product installed over a noncombustible substrate. Further, a wall covering installed with air space behind the covering would tend to spread flame more readily than would one installed in contact with a noncombustible substrate. Mounting techniques, therefore, must be carefully considered in the evaluation of probable product performance.

This section gives the authority having jurisdiction latitude to exercise personal judgment where specific test data is not available for a specific assembly. This judgment should be rendered only after a careful review of background data.

Some interior finish materials, such as fabrics not applied to a solid backing, may not lend themselves to tests made in accordance with NFPA 255, *Method of Test of Surface Burning Characteristics of Building Materials.*[16] In these cases, materials might better be evaluated on the basis of tests conducted in accordance with NFPA 701, *Standard Methods of Fire Tests for Flame-Resistant Textiles and Films.*[19]

6-5.2 Interior Floor Finish.

Experience and full-scale fire test data have shown that floor coverings of modest resistance to flame spread are unlikely to become involved in the early growth of a fire. Regulation of flooring materials based upon flammability considerations should, therefore, be approached with care. Regulation of flooring materials excepting those which are judged to represent an unusual hazard is usually not warranted.

When the judgment is made to regulate floor coverings, the evaluation is to be made based upon tests conducted in accordance with NFPA 253, *Standard Method of Test for Critical Radiant Flux of Floor Covering Systems Using a Radiant Heat Energy Source.*[20] The Flooring Radiant Panel Test was specifically developed to evaluate the tendency of a floor covering material to propagate flame.

Fire tests have been conducted by the National Bureau of Standards — see NBSIR 76-1013 entitled "Flame Spread of Carpet Systems Involved in Room Fires" by King-Mon Tu and Sanford Davis, June 1976[21] — to demonstrate that carpet which passes the Federal Flammability Standard FF-1-70 "Pill Test"[22] is not likely to become involved in a fire until a room reaches or approaches flashover. Since all carpet manufactured for sale in the United States has been required since April 1971 to meet the "Pill Test," no further regulation is necessary for carpet located within rooms.

On the other hand, it has been shown that floor coverings may propagate flame under the influence of a sizeable exposure fire. For example, it has been shown carpet located in a corridor may spread flame when subjected to the energy of a fully developed room fire. The fire discharges flame and hot gases into the corridor causing a radiant heat energy exposure to the floor. It has been shown that the level of energy radiating on to the floor is a significant determinant as to whether or not progressive flaming will occur. NFPA 253, *Standard Method of Test for Critical Radiant Flux of Floor Covering Systems Using a Radiant Heat Energy Source,*[20] measures the minimum energy required in watts per square centimeter (critical radiant flux) on the floor covering to sustain flame. The Flooring Radiant Panel Test, therefore, provides a measure of a floor covering's tendency to spread flames when located in the corridor and exposed to the flame and hot gases from a room fire.

In summary, the Flooring Radiant Panel Test Method is to be used as a basis for estimating the fire performance of a floor covering installed in the building corridor. Floor coverings in open building spaces and in rooms within buildings merit no further regulation providing the floor covering is at least as resistant to flame spread as a material which will meet the Federal Flammability Standard, FF-1-70, "Pill Test."[22]

Interior floor finishes should be tested as proposed for use. For example, where a carpet is to be used with a separate underlayment, the carpet should be evaluated with a separate underlayment. The Flooring Radiant Panel Test specifies a carpet may be tested either using the "standard" underlayment as defined in NFPA 253, *Standard Method of Test for Critical Radiant Flux of Floor Covering Systems Using a Radiant Heat Energy Source,*[20] or the carpet may be tested over the actual underlayment proposed for use. Testing using the "standard" underlayment would allow the carpet tested to be used over any separate underlayment.

Floor coverings are not regulated on the basis of smoke generation. Smoke development limits are not believed to be necessary. As indicated in the foregoing discussion, floor coverings generally will not contribute to a fire until the fire has grown to large proportions. Under the circumstances, the minimal benefits achieved by imposing smoke development limits does not generally warrant such regulation.

6-5.2.1   Interior floor finishes shall be grouped in the following Classes, in accordance with the critical radiant flux ratings:

Class I Interior Floor Finish. Critical radiant flux, minimum of 0.45 watts per square centimeter as determined by the test described in 6-5.2.2.

Class II Interior Floor Finish. Critical radiant flux, minimum of 0.22 watts per square centimeter as determined by the test described in 6-5.2.2.

6-5.2.2   Critical radiant flux test ratings, as specified in 6-5.2.1, shall be classified in accordance with *Standard Method of Test for Critical Radiant Flux of Floor Covering Systems Using a Radiant Heat Energy Source*, NFPA 253.

6-5.3 Fire Retardant Paints.

6-5.3.1   The required flame spread or smoke developed classification of surfaces may be secured by applying approved fire retardant paints or solutions to surfaces having a higher flame spread rating than permitted. Such treatments shall conform to the requirements of *Standard for Fire Retardant Treatments of Building Materials*, NFPA 703.

6-5.3.2   Fire retardant paints or solutions shall be renewed at such intervals as necessary to maintain the necessary fire retardant properties.

Fire retardant paints, coatings, and penetrants are sometimes used to improve the flame spread ratings of materials or assemblies used as interior finishes within buildings. Fire retardant treatments may be used to satisfy the flame spread requirements for materials both in new construction and within existing buildings. It should be recognized, however, that fire retardants are a surface treatment which, through intumescence or other chemical reaction, will delay ignition of a material and slow flame spread. The basic nature of the material (to which the treatment has been applied) is not changed. Fire exposures of sufficient duration or intensity can ultimately result in burning of a treated material. Therefore, as a fundamental premise, materials with favorable intrinsic performance characteristics are preferred over those which achieve a satisfactory level of performance via externally applied treatments. However, externally applied treatments properly applied and maintained can be effective in achieving reasonable fire performance.

Application of fire retardant paints, coatings, and penetrants must be performed strictly according to the manufacturer's instructions and in conformance with the specimens evaluated by fire tests. With most paints and coatings, this requires an application rate three to four times greater than that of ordinary paints. Application is usually by brush, spray, immersion, or pressure treatment. The treatment should be reapplied or renewed at periodic intervals. Treatments which may be removed by normal maintenance, washing, or cleaning procedures will require periodic examination and renewal to maintain the required level of performance.

The use of fire retardants can improve the performance of some Class C materials to a Class B category and, similarly, Class B materials can, in some cases, be upgraded to Class A. Likewise, materials, having flame spread ratings in excess of 200, can sometimes be upgraded into the Class C category.

Finally, in approving fire retardant treatments, the authority having jurisdiction should give consideration to the type and quantity of decomposition products likely to be produced by the treatment during a fire. Further, it should be noted that in reducing flame spread, a treatment may increase smoke generation of a material which in new construction is required to have a smoke developed factor of 450 or less.

6-5.4 Automatic Sprinklers.

6-5.4.1 Where a complete standard system of automatic sprinklers is installed, Class C interior finish materials may be used in any location where Class B is normally specified, and Class B interior finish materials may be used in any location where Class A is normally specified.

Exception: Unless specifically prohibited elsewhere in this Code.

6-5.4.2 Where a complete standard system of automatic sprinklers is installed, Class II interior floor finish may be used in any location where Class I interior floor finish is normally specified, and where Class II is normally specified, no critical radiant flux rating is required.

Fire testing and actual fire experience has shown that automatic sprinklers are able to prevent flame spread across the surface of a wall, ceiling, or floor covering. Flame spread (wall and ceiling) and critical radiant flux (floor covering) limits are reduced in buildings which are completely protected by an automatic sprinkler system. However, there is a value beyond which the potential for flame spread becomes unacceptably high. For example, even in fully sprinklered buildings, walls and ceiling finishes must meet the criteria for Class C materials.

6-5.5 Trim and Incidental Finish.   Interior finish not in excess of 10 percent of the aggregate wall and ceiling areas of any room or space may be Class C materials in occupancies where interior finish of Class A or Class B is required.

This paragraph is intended to allow the use of wood trim around doors, windows, as a decoration or functional molding, as chair rails, and the like. Wood trim (see 6-5.1.3, Exception No. 2 for restrictions applicable to plastic trim) must meet the criteria for Class C materials. Where such trim is used in rooms or spaces requiring the use of Class A or B products, the trim may constitute not more than 10 percent of the aggregate wall or ceiling area. It is intended in establishing the 10 percent area limit that the trim will be more or less uniformly distributed throughout the room or space. It should be noted if the trim is concentrated in one sizeable continuous pattern, for example on one wall of a room, the materials could contribute to rapid fire growth and application of this paragraph as substantiation for such a practice would be in error.

6-5.6 Use of Interior Finishes.

6-5.6.1 Interior finish material shall be used in accordance with requirements for individual classes of occupancy specified elsewhere in the *Code*. Wherever the use of Class C interior finish material is specified, Class A or B shall be permitted; where Class B interior finish is specified, Class A shall be permitted; and similarly, where Class II floor finish is specified, Class I materials shall be permitted.

6-5.6.2 Materials such as carpeting having a napped, tufted, looped, or similar surface, when applied on walls or ceilings, shall meet the requirements of Class A interior finish.

Carpet-like materials having a napped, tufted, or looped surface, when applied to walls and ceilings and having a flame spread rating higher than 50 to 75, could contribute to a fast developing fire. This paragraph intends to restrict the application of carpet-like materials to walls and ceilings to those materials meeting the criteria for Class A in accordance with 6-5.1.5.

Table 6-1. Interior Finish Requirements of the Occupancy Chapters.

Occupancy	Exits	Access to Exits	Other Spaces
Places of assembly — New***	A	A or B	A, B, or C
Places of assembly — Existing***	A	A or B	A, B, or C
Educational — New	A	A or B	A, B, or C
Educational — Existing	A	A or B	A, B, or C
Open plan and Flexible plan***	A	A	A or B C on movable partitions not over 5 ft (1.5 m) high
Child Day-Care Centers—New	A I or II	A or B I or II	A or B
Child Day-Care Centers—Existing	A or B I or II	A or B I or II	A or B
Group Day-Care Homes	A or B	A or B	A, B, or C
Family Child Day-Care Homes	A or B	A or B	A, B, or C
Health Care — New	A I	A I	A B in individual room with capacity not more than four persons
Health Care — Existing	A or B	A or B	A or B
Detention & Correctional — New*	A I	A I	A, B, or C
Detention & Correctional — Existing*	A or B I or II	A or B I or II	A, B, or C
Residential, hotels — New	A I or II	A or B I or II	A, B, or C
Residential, hotels — Existing*	A or B I or II	A or B I or II	A, B, or C
Residential, apartment buildings — New	A I or II	A or B I or II	A, B, or C
Residential, apartment buildings — Existing	A or B I or II	A or B I or II	A, B, or C
Residential, dormitories — New	A I or II	A or B I or II	A, B, or C
Residential, dormitories — Existing*	A or B I or II	A or B I or II	A, B or C
Residential, 1- and 2-family, lodging or rooming houses		A, B, or C	

continued on next page

Table 6-1 Continued

Occupancy	Exits	Access to Exits	Other Spaces
Mercantile — New***	A or B	A or B	A or B
Mercantile — Existing Class A or B***	A or B	A or B	ceilings — A or B existing on walls — A, B, or C
Mercantile — Existing Class C***	A, B, or C	A, B, or C	A, B, or C
Office — New and Existing	A or B	A or B	A, B, or C
Industrial	A or B	A, B, or C	A, B, or C
Storage	A, B, or C	A, B, or C	A, B, or C
Unusual Structures**	A or B	A, B, or C	A, B, or C

* See Chapters for details.
** See Section 30-1 for occupancy classification.
***Exposed portions of structural members complying with the requirements for heavy timber construction may be permitted.

Notes:
Class A Interior Finish — flame spread 0-25, smoke developed 0-450.
Class B Interior Finish — flame spread 26-75, smoke developed 0-450.
Class C Interior Finish — flame spread 76-200, smoke developed 0-450.
Class I Interior Floor Finish — minimum 0.45 watts per sq cm.
Class II Interior Floor Finish — minimum 0.22 watts per sq cm.
Automatic Sprinklers — where a complete standard system of automatic sprinklers is installed, interior finish with flame spread rating not over Class C may be used in any location where Class B is normally specified and with rating of Class B in any location where Class A is normally specified. Similarly, Class II interior floor finish may be used in any location where Class I is normally specified and no critical radiant flux rating is required where Class II is normally specified.

REFERENCES CITED BY CODE

(These publications comprise a part of the requirements to the extent called for by the Code.)

NFPA 13, *Standard for the Installation of Sprinkler Systems*, NFPA, Boston, 1980.

NFPA 80, *Standard for Fire Doors and Windows*, NFPA, Boston, 1979.

NFPA 90A, *Standard for the Installation of Air Conditioning and Ventilating Systems*, NFPA, Boston, 1978.

NFPA 220, *Standard Types of Building Construction*, NFPA, Boston, 1979.

NFPA 251, *Standard Methods of Fire Tests of Building Construction and Materials*, NFPA, Boston, 1979.

NFPA 252, *Standard Methods of Fire Tests on Door Assemblies*, NFPA, Boston, 1979.

NFPA 253, *Standard Method of Test for Critical Radiant Flux of Floor Covering Systems Using a Radiant Heat Energy Source*, NFPA, Boston, 1978.

NFPA 255, *Method of Test of Surface Burning Characteristics of Building Materials*, NFPA, Boston, 1979.

NFPA 257, *Standard for Fire Tests of Window Assemblies*, NFPA, Boston, 1980.

NFPA 703, *Standard for Fire-Retardant Impregnated Wood and Fire-Retardant Coatings for Building Materials*, NFPA, Boston, 1979.

REFERENCES CITED IN COMMENTARY

[1]*Designing Buildings for Fire Safety*, NFPA SPP-24, NFPA, Boston, 1975, pp. 72-74.

[2]NFPA 251, *Standard Methods of Fire Tests of Building Construction and Materials*, NFPA, Boston, 1979.

[3]NFPA 252, *Standard Methods of Fire Tests of Door Assemblies*, NFPA, Boston, 1979.

[4]*Fire Protection Handbook*, 14th ed., NFPA, Boston, 1976, Table 1-2C, pp. 1-9 to 1-10.

[5]————, 14th ed., NFPA, Boston, 1976, p. 1-24.

[6]E. G. Butcher and A. C. Parnell, *Smoke Control in Fire Safety Design*, NFPA, Boston, 1979.

[7]NFPA 13, *Standard for the Installation of Sprinkler Systems*, NFPA, Boston, 1980.

[8]NFPA 20, *Standard for the Installation of Centrifugal Fire Pumps*, NFPA, Boston, 1978.

[9]NFPA 80, *Standard for Fire Doors and Windows*, NFPA, Boston, 1979.

[10]J. Degenkolb, "The 20-Minute Door and Other Considerations," *Building Standards*, Vol. XLV, No. 1, January-February 1976.

[11]NFPA 90A, *Standard for the Installation of Air Conditioning and Ventilating Systems*, NFPA, Boston, 1978.

[12]NFPA 68, *Guide for Explosion Venting*, NFPA, Boston, 1978.

[13]NFPA 69, *Standard on Explosion Prevention Systems*, NFPA, Boston, 1978.

[14]NFPA 63, *Standard for the Prevention of Dust Explosions in Industrial Plants*, NFPA, Boston, 1975.

[15]David D. Demers, "Familiar Problems Cause 10 Deaths in Hotel Fire," *Fire Journal*, Vol. 74, No. 1, January 1980, pp. 52-56.

[16]NFPA 255, *Method of Test of Surface Burning Characteristics of Building Materials*, NFPA, Boston, 1979.

[17]Underwriters Laboratories Inc., "Study of Smoke Ratings Developed in Standard Fire Tests in Relation to Visual Observations," Bulletin of Research, No. 56, April 1965.

[18]David Waksman and John B. Ferguson, "Fire Tests of Building Interior Covering Systems," *Fire Technology*, Vol. 10, No. 3, pp. 211-220.

[19]NFPA 701, *Standard Methods of Fire Tests for Flame-Resistant Textiles and Films*, NFPA, Boston, 1977.

[20]NFPA 253, *Standard Method of Test for Critical Radiant Flux of Floor Covering Systems Using a Radiant Heat Energy Source*, NFPA, Boston, 1978.

[21]King-Mon Tu and Sanford Davis, "Flame Spread of Carpet Systems Involved in Room Fires," NBSIR 76-1013, June 1976.

[22]Federal Flammability Standard FF-1-70, *Standard for the Surface Flammability of Carpets and Rugs* (Pill Test).

7

BUILDING SERVICE
AND FIRE PROTECTION
EQUIPMENT

Primarily, Chapter 7 serves to provide the user of the *Code* with cross references to other codes and standards that provide design guidance for building service equipment. The provisions of these various codes and standards must be adhered to and met in order for the facility to comply with the *Life Safety Code*. Referencing within the main body of the *Code* is meant to reinforce the fact that compliance with these codes is *mandatory*.

SECTION 7-1   UTILITIES

7-1.1   Equipment utilizing gas and related gas piping shall be installed in accordance with the *National Fuel Gas Code*, NFPA 54, or the *Standard for Storage and Handling of Liquefied Petroleum Gases*, NFPA 58.

Exception: Existing installations may be continued in service, subject to approval by the authority having jurisdiction.

7-1.2   Electrical wiring and equipment installed shall be in accordance with the *National Electrical Code*, NFPA 70.

Exception: Existing installations may be continued in service subject to approval by the authority having jurisdiction.

Because the installation of natural gas piping or electrical wiring may require a complicated system or array involving many specifications and design details, the *Life Safety Code* does not repeat them; rather, it provides a reference to the appropriate code or standard in which the necessary design guidance can be found.

SECTION 7-2   HEATING, VENTILATING, AND AIR
CONDITIONING

7-2.1   Air conditioning, heating, ventilating ductwork, and related equipment shall be installed in accordance with the *Standard for the Installation of Air Conditioning and*

165

Ventilating Systems, NFPA 90A, or *Standard for the Installation of Warm Air Heating and Air Conditioning Systems*, NFPA 90B, as applicable.

Exception: Existing installations may be continued in service, subject to approval by the authority having jurisdiction.

Paragraph 7-2.1 refers *Code* users to either NFPA 90A, *Standard for Air Conditioning and Ventilating Systems*,[1] or 90B, *Standard for Warm Air Heating and Air Conditioning Systems*,[2] for the proper installation of HVAC systems.

7-2.2 Ventilating or heat producing equipment shall be installed in accordance with: *Standard for the Installation of Blower and Exhaust Systems*, NFPA 91; *Standard for Chimneys, Fireplaces, and Vents*, NFPA 211; *Standard for Oil Burning Equipment*, NFPA 31; *National Fuel Gas Code*, NFPA 54; *National Electrical Code*, NFPA 70, as applicable.

Exception: Existing installations may be continued in service, subject to approval by the authority having jurisdiction.

7-2.3 Commercial cooking equipment for use in occupancies shall be installed in accordance with the *Standard for the Installation of Equipment for the Removal of Smoke and Grease-Laden Vapors from Commercial Cooking Equipment*, NFPA 96.

Exception: Existing installations may be continued in service, subject to approval by the authority having jurisdiction.

NFPA 96, *Standard for Removal of Smoke and Grease-Laden Vapors from Commercial Cooking Equipment*,[3] also provides design guidance on the safe arrangement of hoods, ducting, and exhaust systems.

SECTION 7-3   SMOKE CONTROL

7-3.1 In accordance with the provisions of Chapters 8 through 30, smoke control systems may be designed and installed in lieu of other specific requirements.

Exception: Where occupancies necessitate alternative smoke control provisions, the designers shall furnish information fully supporting the system to the authority having jurisdiction.

For guidance on designing and installing engineered smoke control systems, see Appendix B of NFPA 90A, *Standard for the Installation of Air Conditioning and Ventilating Systems*.[1] An extensive and authoritative discussion on smoke control is contained in *Smoke Control in Fire Safety Design*, by Butcher and Parnell.[4]

SECTION 7-4   ELEVATORS, DUMBWAITERS, AND VERTICAL CONVEYORS

7-4.1 Elevators shall not be considered an exit component.

In the past, the exit capacity of elevators has been figured on the basis of 3 average elevators being roughly equivalent to 1 unit of stairway width, and in this way they have been accepted as required exits under certain limited conditions by prior editions of the *Code*. No such credit has been given since 1956 because of some inherent characteristics which may make elevators unsuitable for emergency exit use. These characteristics are accentuated in modern automatic elevators where no operator is available to exercise judgment in the control of the elevator in case of fire or other emergency. Some of the reasons why elevators are not recognized as required exits are summarized in the following paragraphs:

1. People seeking to escape from a fire by means of an elevator may have to wait at the elevator door for some time, during which they may be exposed to fire or smoke or be overtaken by panic.

2. Automatic elevators respond to the pressing of buttons in such a way that it would be quite possible for an elevator being used to descend from floors above a fire to stop automatically at the floor of the fire, and for the doors to open automatically, thus exposing occupants to fire and smoke.

A further consideration is that an elevator shaft will act as a built-in "chimney" in a high-rise building. It will carry heat and smoke from a fire and expose passengers to toxic levels of both, even though the elevator does not stop at the floor of the fire and continues to function.

3. Modern elevators cannot start until the doors are fully closed. In an emergency situation, a large number of people may try to crowd into an elevator and make it impossible for the elevator to start.

4. Any power failure, such as the burning out of electric supply cables during a fire, may render the elevators inoperative or may cause people to become trapped in elevators stopped between floors. Under fire conditions there might not be time to permit rescue of the trapped occupants through emergency escape hatches or doors.

Notwithstanding the dangers of using elevators for emergency exit purposes, they may serve an important function as a supplemental facility, particularly in occupancies such as hospitals. Elevators are also an important consideration in exiting from very high buildings or deep underground spaces, where travel over considerable vertical distance on stairs might cause people not accustomed to such physical effort to collapse before they reach the street. In these instances, required exits such as stairs or horizontal exits may be used for the initial escape from the area of immediate danger during a fire, and the elevators used to complete the travel to the street. It may be reasonably assumed that in all buildings of a height sufficient to indicate the need for elevators as supplementary exit facilities, elevators will be provided for normal use; thus, no requirement for the installation of elevators is included in the *Code*.

Elevators for emergency evacuation purposes, when operated by trained emergency service personnel (building personnel, fire personnel, etc.) in accordance with the *Safety Code for Elevators, Dumbwaiters, Escalators, and Moving Walks*, ANSI A17.1, Rule 211.3[5], may be utilized in the building evacuation program.

7-4.2 Elevators shall be installed in accordance with the *Safety Code for Elevators, Dumbwaiters, Escalators, and Moving Walks*, ANSI A17.1.

Exception: Existing installations may be continued in service, subject to approval by the authority having jurisdiction.

The *Life Safety Code* references ANSI A17.1[6] because of the automatic recall provisions and the fire fighter's override provisions that this document contains. These provisions make possible the recall of elevators to the ground floor during a fire, thus taking them out of service, or permit fire fighters to manually override the controls and use the elevators as necessary.

7-4.3 Vertical conveyors, including dumbwaiters and pneumatic conveyors serving various stories in a building, shall be separately enclosed by walls or partitions in accordance with the provisions of Section 6-2. Service openings shall not open to an exit. Service openings, when required to be open on several stories at the same time for purposes of operation of the conveyor, shall be provided with closing devices that will close all service doors upon activation of smoke detectors that are located inside and outside the shaft enclosure in locations acceptable to the authority having jurisdiction.

SECTION 7-5 RUBBISH CHUTES, INCINERATORS, AND LAUNDRY CHUTES

7-5.1 Each rubbish chute shall be separately enclosed by walls or partitions in accordance with the provisions of Section 6-2. Inlet openings serving chutes shall be protected in accordance with Section 6-2. Doors for such chutes shall open only to a separate room which is designed exclusively for that purpose. The room shall be separated from other spaces in accordance with Section 6-4.

Exception: Existing installations with properly enclosed service chutes and with properly installed and maintained service openings may open to a corridor or normally occupied room, subject to approval by the authority having jurisdiction.

According to the provisions of 7-5.1 and those of Chapter 6, rubbish chutes must be enclosed in fire-rated shafts and the openings to the chutes must be located in enclosed fire-rated room constructions as a back-up design feature. This redundant design prevents the possibility of an open incinerator chute directly exposing an exit access corridor to fire. Further, it prevents a fire in an incinerator chute from blocking exit access corridors with either smoke or flames before evacuation or corrective action can be taken. This arrangement also recognizes the fact that frequently occupants pile rubbish in front of the incinerator door rather than put it into the chute.

Standard good practice for the installation and maintenance of incinerator flues is to be found in the NFPA standard, referenced in 7-5.2, which also covers rubbish chutes and linen or laundry chutes, as the last named have hazards similar to those of rubbish chutes.

7-5.2 Rubbish chutes, laundry chutes, and incinerators shall be installed and maintained in accordance with the *Standard on Incinerators, Waste and Linen Handling Systems and Equipment*, NFPA 82.

Exception: Existing installations may be continued in service, subject to approval by the authority having jurisdiction.

7-5.3 Laundry chutes shall be enclosed and any opening protected as specified for rubbish chutes in 7-5.1.

Exception: Existing installations may be continued in service, subject to approval by the authority having jurisdiction.

SECTION 7-6 DETECTION, ALARM, AND COMMUNICATIONS SYSTEMS

7-6.1 General.

7-6.1.1 The provisions of this section cover the basic functions of a complete protective signaling and control system including fire alarm. These systems are primarily intended to provide the indication and warning of abnormal conditions, the summoning of appropriate aid, and the control of occupancy facilities to enhance protection of life.

The intent of this section of the *Code* is to cover general provisions related to all protective signaling systems, not to indicate where any particular type is required.

The provision for early warning of fire, accompanied by notification of appropriate authorities, is a key element of a fire protection program. Where people are involved, protective signaling assumes even greater importance.

A review of the "Bimonthly Fire Record," included in each issue of the NFPA's *Fire Journal*, time and again emphasizes the need for such equipment and the sometimes tragic consequences of being without it. Among the more common problems encountered are:

1. Fire burned or smoldered for some time before discovery (the night watchman passed by "twenty minutes" before);
2. Fire was observed, but everyone assumed that someone else had turned in the alarm;
3. People didn't know who to notify, were confused, gave the wrong address;
4. Persons present were asleep, bedridden, or otherwise unable to act;
5. Worker attempted extinguishment rather than admit a careless act had started the fire; or
6. Person in position of responsibility went or sent someone to investigate before sounding an alarm.

In schools, stores, and offices there are usually enough people present, at least during a part of the day, to discover an incipient fire. Such circumstances are recognized by the *Code* by providing less rigid requirements for protective signaling systems. The installation of an automatic extinguishing system with an integral alarm obviously obviates the need for an independent signaling system.

Fire detection without warning is not enough. People must be alerted to the existence of an emergency in order to take appropriate action.

7-6.1.2 All occupancies shall, when required by Chapters 8 through 30, provide a fire alarm system for life safety that shall be installed, tested and maintained in accordance with applicable requirements of the following: *Standard for the Installation, Maintenance and Use of Central Station Signaling Systems*, NFPA 71; *Standard for the Installation, Maintenance and Use of Local Protective Signaling Systems for Watchman, Fire Alarm and Signaling Service*, NFPA 72A; *Standard for the Installation, Maintenance and Use of Auxiliary Protective Signaling Systems for Fire Alarm Service*, NFPA 72B; *Standard for the Installation, Maintenance and Use of Remote Station Protective Signaling Systems*, NFPA 72C; *Standard for the Installation, Maintenance and Use of Proprietary Protective Signaling Systems for Guard, Fire Alarm and Supervisory Service*, NFPA 72D; *Standard on Automatic Fire Detectors*, NFPA 72E; *Household Fire Warning Equipment*, NFPA 74; and *Public Fire Service Communications*, NFPA 1221.

Exception: Existing installations may be continued in use, subject to the approval of the authority having jurisdiction.

7-6.1.3   All systems and components shall be approved for the purpose for which installed.

Approval by the authority having jurisdiction of both the system as a whole and its components is required. Substantiating data could be in the form of test reports, listings in approval lists issued by such organizations as the Factory Mutual System or Underwriters Laboratories Inc., or approval by another recognized source.

7-6.1.4   For the purposes of this *Code* a protective signaling and control system is used for initiation, notification and control.

(a) *Initiation.*   The initiation function provides the input signal to the system.

Both automatic and manual signal initiation is considered. See 7-6.2.

(b) *Notification.*   The notification function is the means by which the system advises that human action is required in response to a particular condition.

This covers all forms of notification whether audible or audible and visual (see 7-6.3). It includes both notification of occupants (see 7-6.3.3) and notification of the fire department where required (see 7-6.3.4).

(c) *Control.*   The control function provides outputs to control building facilities to enhance protection of life.

This covers functions which the system may actuate to make the building safer, such as elevator recall and door closing (see 7-6.4).

7-6.2 Signal Initiation.

7-6.2.1   As required in Chapters 8 through 30, actuation of the protective system shall occur by any or all of the following means of initiation but not limited thereto:

(a) Manual fire alarm initiation

(b) Automatic heat detection

(c) Automatic smoke detection

(d) Extinguishing system operation

(e) Automatic detection of hazardous condition which could cause fire or explosion.

The location of detector system components is of prime importance. If they are too close to a wall/ceiling intersection, particularly over a door, air currents may cause heat and smoke to bypass the unit completely. Likewise, location with respect to a dropped beam or other construction can have a similar nullifying effect. This can pose problems when partitions are moved without regard to the location of detector units. The problem is illustrated in Figure 7-1. NFPA 72E, *Standard on Automatic Fire Detectors,*[7] gives extensive guidance in this area.

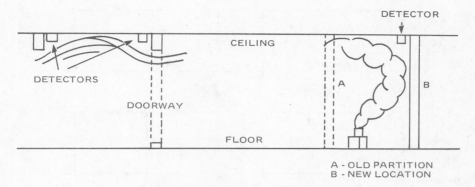

Figure 7-1. Problems to Avoid in Detector Location.

Where both manual and automatic systems are in use, they should be complementary. If, due to poor maintenance, abuse, or mechanical failure, one system becomes inoperative, the second will provide backup support.

Any automatic fire detection system for life safety from fire should have a high degree of reliability. This indicates the need for such features as:

1. An electric current supply independent of the electric power source for the building;
2. Trouble signals to give warning in case of short circuits or breaks in wires, or other conditions which might interfere with the proper operation of the system;
3. Gongs or other such signals located so as to ensure warning even to those sleeping; and
4. Above all, a regular maintenance program.

There is a very considerable diversity in types of automatic fire detection and alarm equipment commercially available, and selection of types suitable for any given situation calls for the exercise of judgment based upon experience.

7-6.2.2 Manual fire alarm stations shall be used only for fire protective signaling purposes.

7-6.2.3 A manual fire alarm station shall be provided in the natural path of escape near each required exit from an area unless modified by Chapters 8 through 30.

Where manual fire alarm boxes are required by Chapters 8 through 30 of the *Code*, they are required to be located near an exit, in the natural path of escape, and in a position of maximum visibility. The purpose is to expedite the turning in of an alarm in a time of stress and to reduce the possibility of the person involved being caught by the fire between a remotely located alarm and an exit. While the designer may not wish to detract from some special effect at the end of a corridor, the advantage from the life safety point of view is obvious, as shown in Figure 7-2.

7-6.2.4 Additional fire alarm stations shall be so located that, from any part of the building, not more than 200 ft (60.96 m) horizontal distance on the same floor shall be traversed in order to reach a fire alarm station.

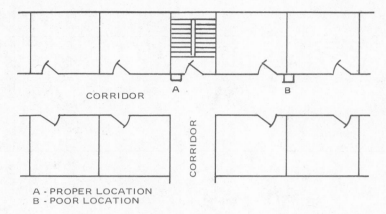

A - PROPER LOCATION
B - POOR LOCATION

Figure 7-2. Proper and Improper Location of an Alarm Box.

7-6.2.5 Each manual fire alarm station on a system must be accessible, unobstructed, visible, and of the same general type.

7-6.2.6 Where a sprinkler system provides automatic detection and alarm system initiation it shall be provided with an approved alarm initiation device that will operate when the flow of water is equal to or greater than that from a single automatic sprinkler.

7-6.3 Signal Notification.

7-6.3.1 As required in Chapters 8 through 30, actuation of the system shall provide signal notification of fire or other emergency as required by the authority having jurisdiction.

(a) Alert occupants

(b) Notify local fire brigade

(c) Notify fire departments.

Acceptable means of transmitting an alarm to the fire department are:
(a) A connection of the building alarm to the municipal fire system.
(b) A connection of the building alarm to an approved central station.
(c) An approved remote station connection to a municipal or other alarm headquarters which is manned 24 hours a day.
Fire alarm equipment installed for the notification of occupants of a building, in localities under the protection of a regularly organized fire department or private fire brigade, can be arranged to give automatic transmission of alarms (either directly or through an approved central office) to the fire department or brigade upon operation of an alarm-sending station or system. When no such connection is provided, a fire alarm box arranged to signal the fire department could be installed either at the main entrance to the building, at the telephone switchboard, or somewhere outside the building plainly visible day or night and conveniently accessible from the main entrance. (Note that while this arrangement is desirable, it is not required by 7-6.3.1 unless the occupancy chapter specifically requires this feature.)

7-6.3.2 Signal notification shall be a presignal or general audible alarm-type system as required by the authority having jurisdiction. When permitted by the authority having jurisdiction, notification may also be by visual signals or permanently recorded printout.

Exception: Presignal systems are not permitted where prohibited by Chapters 8 through 30.

7-6.3.3 Notification of Occupants.

7-6.3.3.1 Notification signals for occupants to evacuate shall be by audible signals and, where deemed necessary by the authority having jurisdiction, shall also be by visual signals.

Visible alarm devices, in addition to the audible alarms, are desirable in buildings occupied by deaf persons.

7-6.3.3.2 The general evacuation alarm signal shall operate throughout the entire building.

Exception No. 1: Where a building is divided by: (1) 2-hour fire barriers into separate fire compartments, or (2) by other means with adequate safeguards against the spread of fire or smoke from one compartment to another, each compartment may be considered a separate building.

Exception No. 2: When total evacuation of occupants is not practical due to building configuration, only the occupants in the affected zones shall be initially notified. Provisions shall be made to selectively notify occupants in other zones to afford orderly evacuation of the entire building.

Exception No. 2 to 7-6.3.3.2 normally applies to high-rise buildings. It makes provisions for zoned staged evacuation. This exception is closely related to Exception No. 1 in that 2-hour fire separation is usually provided between floors of high-rise buildings.

Exception No. 3: Where occupants are incapable of evacuating themselves because of age, physical/mental disabilities, or physical restraint, only the attendants and other personnel required to evacuate occupants from a zone, area, floor, or building are required to be notified. This notification shall include means to readily identify the zone, area, floor, or building in need of evacuation.

Exception No. 3 commonly applies to health care and detention and correctional occupancies. It is a common application in these occupancies to use coded chimes or a similar method of announcing throughout the facility the location of the fire emergency. Notification by telephone would *not* be acceptable for this purpose.

7-6.3.3.3 Audible alarm indicating devices shall be of such character and so distributed as to be effectively heard above the ambient noise level obtained under normal conditions of occupancy.

The authority having jurisdiction needs to carefully review the types and locations of alarm indicating devices. A balance must be achieved between being able to hear

devices, and having sound close to decibel levels that could damage hearing and economics.

7-6.3.3.4 Audible alarm indicating devices shall produce signals that are distinctive from audible signals used for other purposes in the same building.

Where the provisions of Chapters 8 through 30 require an evacuation alarm signal, the uniform fire alarm evacuation signal described in NFPA 72A, *Standard on Local Protective Signaling Systems*,[8] should be used.

The manner of sounding alarms should be standardized with a view to obtaining uniformity throughout as large a geographic area as practicable. In that way, people moving from one locality to another will not be misled and confused by differences in the manner of sounding alarms.

Two multiple fatality fires in hotel occupancies that occurred in late 1978 and 1979 illustrate the need for standardized adequate fire alarm signals. In both incidents, which were in the middle of the night, many survivors reported not hearing any alarm device or mistaking the alarm for telephones or alarm clocks. An additional multiple fatality fire in a hotel in 1978 showed the special problems with alarm notification when hearing is impaired. In this fire, several elderly occupants removed hearing aids before going to bed, thus creating severe evacuation problems.

7-6.3.3.5 Pre-recorded or live voice evacuation instructions to occupants shall be permitted. Pre-recorded instructions shall be preceded by not less than 5 seconds or more than 10 seconds of a continuous alerting signal. Upon completion or failure of pre-recorded instructions, the fire alarm evacuation signal shall sound. Pre-recorded instructions shall be repeated two or more times. Live voice instructions shall be permitted to interrupt the pre-recorded message or the fire alarm evacuation signal.

7-6.3.3.6 Audible and visual fire alarm devices required by Chapters 8 through 30 shall be used only for fire alarm system or other emergency purposes.

Exception No. 1:   When a system has a continuously manned central control room with trained operators, selective paging is permitted.

Exception No. 2:   Where otherwise permitted by Chapters 8 through 30.

7-6.3.3.7 Alarm notification signals shall take precedence over all other signals.

7-6.3.4 Notification of Fire Department.

7-6.3.4.1 When required by Chapters 8 through 30, a system shall be arranged to automatically transmit an alarm directly to the municipal fire department or, if such service is not available, to such other outside service as may be available.

See discussion of 7-6.3.1(c).

7-6.4 Emergency Control.

7-6.4.1 A signaling system shall, where required by Chapters 8 through 30, be arranged to automatically actuate control functions necessary to make the protected premises safer for building occupants.

7-6.4.2 When required by Chapters 8 through 30, the following functions shall be permitted to be actuated by the fire alarm system:

(a) Elevator capture and control

(b) Release of automatic door closers

(c) Stairwell pressurization

(d) Control of building environmental systems to provide smoke control

(e) Control of fire and smoke dampers

(f) Initiation of automatic fire extinguishing equipment

(g) Emergency lighting control

(h) Unlocking of doors

(i) Emergency shut off of gas and fuel supplies that may be hazardous providing the continuation of service is not essential to the preservation of life.

7-6.4.3   The performance of emergency control functions shall not, in any way, impair the effective response of all required alarm notification functions.

7-6.5 Location of Controls.

7-6.5.1   Operator controls, visual alarm annunciators, and manual communications capability shall be installed in a control center at a convenient location. Controls used by the fire department shall be located adjacent to an entrance as designated by the authority having jurisdiction.

SECTION 7-7   AUTOMATIC SPRINKLERS AND OTHER EXTINGUISHING EQUIPMENT

7-7.1 Automatic Sprinklers.

7-7.1.1   Each automatic sprinkler system shall be installed in accordance with *Standard for the Installation of Sprinkler Systems*, NFPA 13, where specified by the requirements of this *Code*.

Experience shows that automatic sprinklers, properly installed and maintained, are the most effective of the various safeguards against loss of life by fire. Their value is psychological as well as physical, in that they give a sense of security to the occupant of a building and tend to minimize the possibility of panic in case of fire. There is no case in the NFPA records of over 100,000 fires in sprinklered buildings in which water from automatic sprinklers in any way contributed to panic.

The requirements in the *Code* for automatic sprinklers have been carefully based on the sprinkler experience record, which shows that a sprinkler system is the most effective device, when installed properly, for protecting and safeguarding against loss of life and property. Occupants of a building who are aware of the presence of sprinkler protection can feel secure because they know that any fire will be detected and *fought* at its origin, and that an alarm will be given; they know that it is probable that they will have time to evacuate a burning building before fire can cut off their escape.

There have been claims made by the uninformed that water in a sprinkler system can be heated to scalding temperatures and literally sprayed out onto occupants, thus causing injury and panic. Another fallacy is the belief that merely the spraying of large quantities of water will itself cause panic. As stated before, NFPA records of over a hundred thousand cases of sprinklers operating in building fires show no instances of this happening. The small quantity of water in the system piping over the fire that might be heated before the time the eutectic metal on the sprinkler melts and opens the flow will quickly be dissipated, and cool water will begin to flow. Other misconceptions about sprinkler systems, such as that occupants of a room might be drowned, electrocuted, or scalded by steam, have not been shown by fire record data to exist and thus should be discounted.

NFPA 13, *Standard for the Installation of Sprinkler Systems*,[9] covers installation details for standard automatic sprinkler systems. It will generally be found most desirable to provide a complete standard automatic sprinkler installation to protect the entire property, in the interest of both life safety from fire and the protection of property, even in situations where the *Code* requires sprinklers only for hazardous areas.

NFPA 13[9] is the so-called "bible" for sprinkler systems insofar as design, installation, and character and adequacy of water supply are concerned. Even though there are usually some areas in a building where fires are more likely to start than in others, it is impossible to predict where a fire might start and hence protect those areas only. Thus, it is recommended that when sprinklers are installed, they be installed throughout a building.

NFPA 13, *Standard for the Installation of Sprinkler Systems*,[9] provides for the installation of systems of various types appropriate for the individual building protected, subject to the approval of the authority having jurisdiction.

Where automatic sprinklers are installed for life safety in buildings of small or moderate size in areas where no adequate public water supplies are available, pressure tank supply will usually be found satisfactory. Pressure tanks may be filled from any small domestic water supply.

NFPA 13A, *Recommended Practice for the Care and Maintenance of Sprinkler Systems*,[10] gives detailed information on maintenance procedures.

7-7.1.2   In areas protected by automatic sprinklers, automatic heat detection devices required by other sections of this *Code* may be deleted.

Properly designed automatic sprinkler systems provide the dual function of both automatic alarms and automatic extinguishment. Because the operation of an automatic sprinkler system is initiated by a heat sensing device and works on the same principle as an automatic heat detection and alarm system, the sprinkler system is judged to be capable of serving the same purpose. Even though some sprinkler systems may not give an alarm on activation, most properly designed systems do. Furthermore, while a system may not give an alarm, it does begin immediate extinguishment, a feature which is equally as valuable, if not more so, as one which sounds an alarm only.

Detection of smoke, on the other hand, can be accomplished at the incipient stages of a fire and give rise to an earlier warning than that provided by heat detection, so it is considered in a somewhat different light. This is the case with health care occupancy provisions (Chapters 12 and 13), which generally require both sprinklers and smoke detectors in nursing homes. There are two schools of thought on the matter: some feel that a system that starts suppression of a fire immediately upon detection is better than one that simply detects the fire and gives an alarm, even though the latter is quicker in initiation of signal indication. Others believe, however, that an early alarm system is the more advantageous form, particularly in some health care occupancies. The first group is concerned with immediate arrest or containment of fire — it may take a considerable amount of time for fire fighters to arrive; the second group stresses immediate notification of occupants.

7-7.1.3 Where automatic sprinkler protection is provided, other requirements of this *Code* may be modified to such extent as permitted by the provisions of this *Code*.

Standard automatic sprinkler protection provides a high degree of life safety from fire. This *Code*, however, does not rely on any one feature as the sole safeguard for life, and specifies other additional safeguards in recognition of the fact that automatic sprinkler systems may, in rare instances, be inoperative. This *Code* also recognizes the fact that some quantity of smoke may be produced before fire is extinguished by automatic sprinklers, and that any smoke may create a panic hazard even though there may be no actual danger.

When buildings are equipped with sprinklers there are usually *Code* provisions permitting an increase in allowable area, an increase in travel distance, and some possible reduction in fire resistance requirements, although not below a specified level.

7-7.2 Supervision.

7-7.2.1 When supervised automatic sprinkler protection is specified in this *Code*, a distinct supervisory signal shall be provided to indicate a condition that will impair the satisfactory operation of the sprinkler system. This shall include but not be limited to monitoring of control valves, fire pump power supplies and running conditions, water tank levels and temperatures, pressure of pressure tanks, and air pressure on dry-pipe valves.

NFPA 71, *Standard for the Installation, Maintenance, and Use of Central Station Signaling Systems*,[11] gives details of standard practice in sprinkler supervision.

Subject to the approval of the authority having jurisdiction, sprinkler supervision may also be provided by direct connection to municipal fire departments or, in the case of very large establishments, to a private headquarters providing similar functions.

NFPA 72A, *Standard on Local Protective Signaling Systems*[8]; NFPA 72B, *Standard on Auxiliary Protective Signaling Systems*[12]; NFPA 72C, *Standard on Remote Station Protective Signaling Systems*[13]; and NFPA 72D, *Standard on Proprietary Protective Signaling Systems*[14], cover such matters. Where municipal fire alarm systems are involved, reference should also be made to NFPA 1221, *Public Fire Service Communications*.[15]

One reason why the automatic sprinkler system has attained a high level of satisfactory performance and response to fire conditions is the fact that, through supervision, it can be kept in operative condition. Of course, keeping the system operative is dependent upon routine maintenance and the owner's willingness to repair the system when there are indications of some impairment. Features of the system can be automatically monitored, such as the opening and closing of water control valves, the power supplies for needed pumps, water tank levels, etc. If an undesirable situation develops, a signal is given in the protected building or relayed to a central station.

A supervisory system will also indicate or activate a waterflow alarm which, in addition to being transmitted to proprietary or control stations, can be transmitted directly to the fire department. The signals for mechanical problems need not burden the fire department unnecessarily, whereas those indicating a fire can be received directly.

7-7.2.2 Supervisory signals for sprinkler systems shall terminate in a location within the protected building or premises which is constantly attended by qualified personnel in the employ of the owner or shall terminate in an approved remote receiving facility.

7-7.2.3 When supervised automatic sprinkler protection is specified in this *Code*, waterflow alarms shall be transmitted to an approved proprietary alarm receiving facility, remote station, central station, or the fire department. Such connections shall be installed in accordance with appropriate NFPA standards listed in Section 7-6 (NFPA 71 and 72 series).

7-7.3 Other Automatic Extinguishing Equipment. In any occupancy where the character of the potential fuel for fire is such that extinguishment or control of fire may be more effectively accomplished by a type of automatic extinguishing system other than an automatic sprinkler system such as carbon dioxide, dry chemical, foam, Halon 1301, or water spray, a standard extinguishing system of other type may be installed in lieu of an automatic sprinkler system. Such systems shall be installed in accordance with appropriate NFPA standards.

Use of special types of extinguishing systems is a matter of engineering judgment on the part of the designer, working in collaboration with the owner and the authorities concerned. Various NFPA standards are available to provide guidance in installation and maintenance procedures. Automatic extinguishing systems other than automatic sprinklers are covered by the following NFPA standards:

NFPA 11, *Standard for Foam Extinguishing Systems*[16]

NFPA 12, *Standard on Carbon Dioxide Extinguishing Systems*[17]

NFPA 12A, *Standard on Halogenated Fire Extinguishing Agent Systems - Halon 1301*[18]

NFPA 12B, *Standard on Halogenated Fire Extinguishing Agent Systems - Halon 1211*[19]

NFPA 15, *Standard for Water Spray Fixed Systems*[20]

NFPA 17, *Standard on Dry Chemical Extinguishing Systems*[21]

7-7.4 Manual Extinguishing Equipment.

7-7.4.1 When required by the provisions of Chapters 8 through 30, portable fire extinguishers shall be installed in accordance with *Standard for the Installation of Portable Fire Extinguishers*, NFPA 10.

7-7.4.2 When required by the provisions of Chapters 8 through 30, standpipe and hose systems shall be provided in accordance with *Standard for the Installation of Standpipe and Hose Systems*, NFPA 14.

The *Code* does not always have requirements for standpipes or extinguishers listed in the individual occupancy chapters. When it does, the number, types, and locations required are beyond the scope of the *Code*; guidance can be found in NFPA 10, *Standard for Portable Fire Extinguishers*,[22] and NFPA 14, *Standard for Standpipe and Hose Systems*.[23]

For a description of standard types of extinguishers and their installation, maintenance, and use, see NFPA 10, *Standard for the Installation of Portable Fire Extinguishers*.[22] The labels of recognized testing laboratories on extinguishers provide evidence of tests indicating reliability and suitability of the extinguisher for its intended use. Many unlabeled extinguishers are offered for sale which are substandard by reason of insufficient extinguishing capacity, questionable reliability, or which contain extinguishing agents not effective on fires in ordinary combustible materials, or which involve a personal hazard to the user.

REFERENCES CITED BY *CODE*

(These publications comprise a part of the requirements to the extent called for by the Code.)

NFPA 10, *Standard for Portable Fire Extinguishers*, NFPA, Boston, 1978.

NFPA 13, *Standard for the Installation of Sprinkler Systems*, NFPA, Boston, 1980.

NFPA 14, *Standard for the Installation of Standpipes and Hose Systems*, NFPA, Boston, 1980.

NFPA 31, *Standard for the Installation of Oil Burning Equipment*, NFPA, Boston, 1978.

NFPA 54, *National Fuel Gas Code*, NFPA, Boston, 1980.

NFPA 58, *Standard for Storage and Handling of Liquefied Petroleum Gases*, NFPA, Boston, 1979.

NFPA 70, *National Electrical Code*, NFPA, Boston, 1981.

NFPA 71, *Standard for the Installation, Maintenance and Use of Central Station Signaling Systems*, NFPA, Boston, 1977.

NFPA 72A, *Standard for the Installation, Maintenance and Use of Local Protective Signaling Systems*, NFPA, Boston, 1979.

NFPA 72B, *Standard for the Installation, Maintenance and Use of Auxiliary Protective Signaling Systems*, NFPA, Boston, 1979.

NFPA 72C, *Standard for the Installation, Maintenance and Use of Remote Station Protective Signaling Systems*, NFPA, Boston, 1975.

NFPA 72D, *Standard for the Installation, Maintenance and Use of Proprietary Protective Signaling Systems*, NFPA, Boston, 1979.

NFPA 72E, *Standard on Automatic Fire Detectors*, NFPA, Boston, 1978.

NFPA 74, *Standard for the Installation, Maintenance and Use of Household Fire Warning Equipment*, NFPA, Boston, 1980.

NFPA 82, *Standard on Incinerators, Waste and Linen Handling Systems and Equipment*, NFPA, Boston, 1977.

NFPA 90A, *Standard for the Installation of Air Conditioning and Ventilating Systems*, NFPA, Boston, 1978.

NFPA 90B, *Standard for the Installation of Warm Air Heating and Air Conditioning Systems*, NFPA, Boston, 1980.

NFPA 91, *Standard for the Installation of Blower and Exhaust Systems*, NFPA, Boston, 1973.

NFPA 96, *Standard for the Installation of Equipment for the Removal of Smoke and Grease-Laden Vapors from Commercial Cooking Equipment*, NFPA, Boston, 1980.

NFPA 211, *Standard for Chimneys, Fireplaces, Vents and Solid Fuel Burning Appliances*, NFPA, Boston, 1980.

NFPA 1221, *Standard for the Installation, Maintenance and Use of Public Fire Service Communications*, NFPA, Boston, 1980.

ANSI A17.1 — 1978, *Safety Code for Elevators, Dumbwaiters, Escalators, and Moving Walks; and Supplement:* ANSI A17.1a — 1979; American Society of Mechanical Engineers, 345 East 47th Street, New York, NY 10017.

REFERENCES CITED IN COMMENTARY

[1]NFPA 90A, *Standard for the Installation of Air Conditioning and Ventilating Systems*, NFPA, Boston, 1978.

[2]NFPA 90B, *Standard for the Installation of Warm Air Heating and Air Conditioning Systems*, NFPA, Boston, 1980.

[3]NFPA 96, *Standard for the Installation of Equipment for the Removal of Smoke and Grease-Laden Vapors from Commercial Cooking Equipment*, NFPA, Boston, 1980.

[4]E. G. Butcher and A. C. Parnell, *Smoke Control in Fire Safety Design*, NFPA, Boston, 1979.

[5]ANSI A17.1 — 1978, *Safety Code for Elevators, Dumbwaiters, Escalators, and Moving Walks; and Supplement:* ANSI A17.1a — 1979, Rule 211.3, American Society of Mechanical Engineers, 345 East 47th Street, New York, NY 10017.

[6]ANSI A17.1 — 1978, *Safety Code for Elevators, Dumbwaiters, Escalators, and Moving Walks; and Supplement:* ANSI A17.1a — 1979, American Society of Mechanical Engineers, 345 East 47th Street, New York, NY 10017.

[7]NFPA 72E, *Standard on Automatic Fire Detectors*, NFPA, Boston, 1978.

[8]NFPA 72A, *Standard for the Installation, Maintenance and Use of Local Protective Signaling Systems*, NFPA, Boston, 1979.

[9]NFPA 13, *Standard for the Installation of Sprinkler Systems*, NFPA, Boston, 1980.

[10]NFPA 13A, *Recommended Practice for the Care and Maintenance of Sprinkler Systems*, NFPA, Boston, 1978.

[11]NFPA 71, *Standard for the Installation, Maintenance and Use of Central Station Signaling Systems*, NFPA, Boston, 1977.

[12]NFPA 72B, *Standard for the Installation, Maintenance and Use of Auxiliary Protective Signaling Systems*, NFPA, Boston, 1979.

[13]NFPA 72C, *Standard for the Installation, Maintenance and Use of Remote Station Protective Signaling Systems*, NFPA, Boston, 1975.

[14]NFPA 72D, *Standard for the Installation, Maintenance and Use of Proprietary Protective Signaling Systems*, NFPA, Boston, 1979.

[15]NFPA 1221, *Standard for the Installation, Maintenance and Use of Public Fire Service Communications*, NFPA, Boston, 1980.

[16]NFPA 11, *Standard on Foam Extinguishing Systems*, NFPA, Boston, 1978.

[17]NFPA 12, *Standard on Carbon Dioxide Extinguishing Systems*, NFPA, Boston, 1980.

[18]NFPA 12A, *Standard on Halon 1301 Fire Extinguishing Systems*, NFPA, Boston, 1980.

[19]NFPA 12B, *Standard on Halon 1211 Fire Extinguishing Agent Systems*, NFPA, Boston, 1980.

[20]NFPA 15, *Standard for Water Spray Fixed Systems for Fire Protection*, NFPA, Boston, 1979.

[21]NFPA 17, *Standard for Dry Chemical Extinguishing Systems*, NFPA, Boston, 1980.

[22]NFPA 10, *Standard for Portable Fire Extinguishers*, NFPA, Boston, 1978.

[23]NFPA 14, *Standard for the Installation of Standpipe and Hose Systems*, NFPA, Boston, 1980.

8

NEW PLACES
OF ASSEMBLY

(See also Chapter 31.) page 745

Places of assembly include, but are not limited to, all buildings or portions of buildings used for gathering together 50 or more people for such purposes as deliberation, worship, entertainment, amusement, or awaiting transportation. Assembly occupancies include, but are not limited to:

Theaters	Restaurants
Motion picture theaters	Churches
Assembly halls	Dance halls
Auditoriums	Club rooms
Exhibition halls	Passenger stations and terminals of
Museums	air, surface, underground, and
Skating rinks	marine public transportation
Gymnasiums	facilities
Bowling establishments	Recreation piers
Pool rooms	Courtrooms
Armories	Conference rooms
Mortuary chapels	Drinking establishments
Libraries	

Chapter 31 specifies the life safety requirements for the operation of places of assembly.

SECTION 8-1   GENERAL REQUIREMENTS

8-1.1 Application.   The requirements of this chapter apply to new places of assembly. *(See 8-1.3 for definition.)*

This 1981 Edition of the *Code* has divided most occupancies into separate chapters for new and existing. The provisions for existing places of assembly are found in Chapter 9.

It should be noted that if an existing building of some other occupancy were to change occupancies to a place of assembly, the portion of the building housing the assembly occupancy must comply with this chapter for new places of assembly even though it is in an existing building. (See 1-6.4 of the *Code*.)

8-1.2 Mixed Occupancies.

8-1.2.1 Any place of assembly and its access to exits in buildings of other occupancy, such as ballrooms in hotels, restaurants in stores, rooftop places of assembly, or assembly rooms in schools, shall be so located, separated, or protected as to avoid any undue danger to the occupants of the place of assembly from a fire originating in the other occupancy or smoke therefrom.

> Generally, division by a partition with a fire resistance of at least 1 hour is recommended to establish a degree of separation between the place of assembly and the remainder of the building. If possible, 2-hour fire resistance should be pursued. The partition should extend totally around the assembly space and should be continuous from the floor slab through any interstitial space to the slab of the floor or roof above. Instead of separation, protection of the other occupancy by automatic sprinklers or other appropriate measures might be sufficient.
>
> In buildings of fire-resistive construction where the hazard of the other occupancy is low or moderate (as in schools or hotels), separation of the place of assembly may not be necessary.

8-1.2.2 Occupancy of any room or space for assembly purposes by less than 50 persons in a building of other occupancy and incidental to such other occupancy shall be classed as part of the other occupancy and subject to the provisions applicable thereto.

> Fifty has traditionally been considered the lowest number of people assembled in one space for which the *Code* requires special provisions, such as a door having to swing in the direction of exit travel (see 5-2.1.1.4.1). Therefore, in Chapter 8, 50 people constitute a sufficiently high level of risk to life safety to require classifying an occupancy as a place of assembly and, consequently, to subject the occupancy to the special design requirements found within this chapter.

8-1.2.3 Places of assembly in buildings of other occupancy may use exits common to the place of assembly and the other occupancy provided that the assembly area and the other occupancy considered separately each have exits sufficient to meet the requirements of this *Code*.

8-1.2.4 Exits shall be sufficient for simultaneous occupancy of both the place of assembly and other parts of the building.

Exception: Where the authority having jurisdiction determines that the conditions are such that simultaneous occupancy will not occur, such as in certain schools as specified in Chapter 10.

> Here, the *Code* requires that each occupancy, considered separately, have sufficient exits and that, when it is possible for simultaneous occupancy to occur, the exits be sufficient for the combined occupant load. An example of a situation in which simultaneous occupancy of a place of assembly and another occupancy does not usually occur is that of an assembly room for the inmates of a detention or correctional occupancy.

8-1.3 Special Definitions.

Arena Stage.   A stage or platform open on at least three sides to audience seating. It may be with or without overhead scene-handling facilities.

Theater-in-the-round is an example of an arena stage.

Places of Assembly.   Include, but are not limited to, all buildings or portions of buildings used for gathering together 50 or more persons for such purposes as deliberation, worship, entertainment, dining, amusement, or awaiting transportation.

The definition for places of assembly stresses the need for alternate exit routes in small places of assembly, such as restaurants, lounges, or theaters, with capacities for as few as 50 people.

Platform, Enclosed.   A partially enclosed portion of an assembly room, the ceiling of which is not more than 5 ft (152.4 cm) above the proscenium opening, that is designed or used for the presentation of plays, demonstrations, or other entertainment wherein scenery, drops, decorations, or other effects may be installed or used.

Proscenium Wall.   A fire-resistive wall that separates a stage or enclosed platform from the public or spectators' area of an auditorium or theater.

Stage.   A partially enclosed portion of an assembly building that is designed or used for the presentation of plays, demonstrations, or other entertainment wherein scenery, drops, or other effects may be installed or used and where the distance between the top of the proscenium opening and the ceiling above the stage is more than 5 ft (152.4 cm).

As shown in Figure 8-1A, the criterion for distinguishing between an enclosed platform and a stage is the distance from the top of the proscenium opening to the ceiling of the platform or stage. The 5-ft (1.52-m) criterion limits the quantity and type of fuel load (such as combustible scenery or lights) which the proscenium arch of an enclosed platform can realistically conceal. The other portion of a stage (significant to life safety but not discussed in this portion of the *Code*) is the fly galleries located to the rear and sides of the stage. If fly galleries are incorporated in the stage construction, significant amounts of combustible fuel in the form of scenery and backdrops should be expected. Automatic extinguishment systems should be provided for these areas.

Thrust Stage.   That portion of a stage that projects into the audience on the audience side of a proscenium wall or opening.

An arena stage is illustrated in Figure 8-1B. A typical example of a thrust stage is the so-called "runway" at Atlantic City that is used annually for the Miss America Pageant. See Figure 8-1C.

8-1.4 Classification of Occupancy.   (*See 4-1.2.*)

8-1.4.1 Classification of Places of Assembly.   Each place of assembly shall be classified according to its capacity, as follows: Class A, capacity 1000 persons or more; Class B, capacity 300 to 1000 persons; Class C, capacity 50 to 300 persons.

As each increment of population is reached, the level of risk to life safety from exposure to fire rises. In view of this, the stringency of the requirements found in this chapter increases to counter each higher risk level.

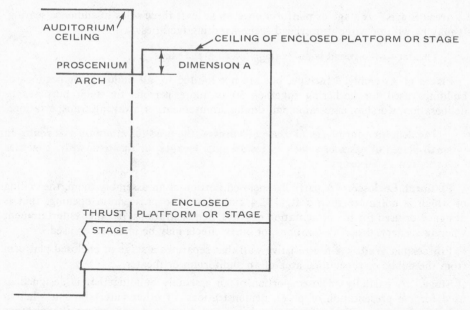

Figure 8-1A. Difference Between an Enclosed Platform and a Stage. If Dimension A < 5 ft (1.52 m), construction is classed as an "enclosed platform"; if Dimension A > 5 ft (1.52 m), construction is classed as a "stage."

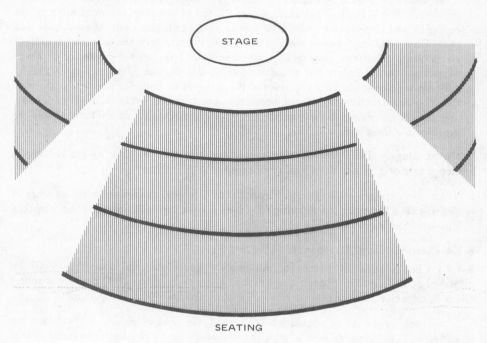

Figure 8-1B. Arena Stage.

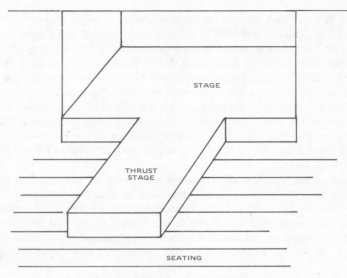

Figure 8-1C. Thrust Stage.

8-1.5 Classification of Hazard of Contents. Contents of assembly occupancies shall be classified in accordance with the provisions of Section 4-2.

8-1.6 Location of Places of Assembly. The location of a place of assembly shall be limited as follows:

Type of Construction	Below LED	LED	Number of Levels Above LED			
			1	**2**	**3**	**4 & Above**
I (443)	A†B†C†	ABC	ABC	ABC	ABC	A†B†C
I (332)	Any Number					
II (222)	of Levels					
II (111)	A†B†C† One Level Below LED	ABC	ABC	A†BC	B†C†	N.P.
III (211)	A†B†C† One Level Below LED	ABC	ABC	A†B†C	B†C†	N.P.
IV (2HH)						
V (111)						
II (000)	B†C† One Level Below LED	BC	C†	N.P.	N.P.	N.P.
III (200)						
V (000)						

†Allowed if the level of the place of assembly and any story intervening between that level and the level of exit discharge are protected throughout by an approved automatic sprinkler system. If there are any openings between the level of exit discharge and the exits serving the place of assembly, the level of exit discharge shall also be protected throughout by an approved automatic sprinkler system (*see Section 7-7*).

N.P. — Not Permitted

LED — Level of Exit Discharge

It should be noted that the chart is arranged based on levels above the level of exit discharge (LED). Thus, in a normal building with the level of exit discharge at grade, the column "1" in the table refers to the second story of the building.

Since the Cocoanut Grove Night Club fire in Boston (1942), much emphasis has been placed by the Committee on Assembly and Educational Occupancies on limiting the number of occupants in those places of assembly that provide only a minimum level of life safety because of the nature of the construction. The Cocoanut Grove fire illustrated the effect that a combustible structure (as well as combustible interior finish) and a multilevel location for a place of assembly had on the severity of the fire and its high death count. More recently the Beverly Hills Supper Club fire (1977) also illustrated these factors.

Paragraph 8-1.6 restricts the location of places of assembly. Fire-resistive construction, with its "built-in-place" structural survivability (under fire attack), is acceptable for any place of assembly (hence, for any number of occupants) at the level of exit discharge and up to the fourth story. As the fire resistivity of the structure diminishes from protected noncombustible to wood-frame construction, the location of places of assembly (and the permitted number of occupants) is restricted.

The chart contained in 8-1.6 is new in the 1981 Edition of the *Code*. The chart represents a revision of the *Code* requirements and recognizes the value of automatic sprinklers as a life safety device. Note that the chart deals with the location of the place of assembly in relation to the level of exit discharge. Thus, for example, if the building in question was a seven-story, fire-resistive (Type I) building with the level of exit discharge at the first floor, a Class A place of assembly could be located at the fourth floor without sprinkler protection. If the Class A place of assembly were located at the fifth floor, automatic sprinkler protection would be required for the fifth floor as well as for the first through fourth floors. (See note to chart.) If the first floor of the building was so arranged that the exit stairs servicing the assembly floor were enclosed to the outside with no door openings into the first story or level of exit discharge, then sprinklers would not be required at that level.

Any place of assembly located below the level of exit discharge requires automatic sprinkler protection, as do all levels intervening between the assembly level and the level of exit discharge. The same rule concerning openings into the stair at the level of exit discharge applies.

Also note that in unrated construction (000), only Class B and C places of assembly are permitted at the level of discharge.

8-1.7 Occupant Load.

8-1.7.1 The occupant load permitted in any assembly building, structure, or portion thereof shall be determined by dividing the net floor area or space assigned to that use by the square foot (square meter) per occupant as follows:

(a) An assembly area of concentrated use without fixed seats such as an auditorium, church, chapel, dance floor, or lodge room — 7 sq ft (.65 sq m) per person.

(b) An assembly area of less concentrated use such as a conference room, dining room, drinking establishment, exhibit room, gymnasium, or lounge — 15 sq ft (1.39 sq m) per person.

(c) Standing room or waiting space — 3 sq ft (.28 sq m) per person.

See 8-1.7.3 for locations where this occupant load factor can be used.

(d) Bleachers, pews, and similar bench-type seating — 18 linear in. (45.72 linear cm) per person.

(e) Fixed seating. The occupant load of an area having fixed seats shall be determined by the number of fixed seats installed. Required aisle space serving the fixed seats shall not be used to increase the occupant load.

(f) Libraries.   In stack areas — 100 sq ft (9.3 sq m) per person; in reading rooms — 50 sq ft (4.7 sq m) per person.

The occupant load factors of 8-1.7.1 reflect the data developed from surveys of typical occupancies.

Figure 8-2A illustrates a room or area with two 36-in. (91.44-cm) doors, each providing one-and-a-half exit units, or a total of three exit units. Using only the criterion of exit capacity, such a room would be permitted 300 occupants. However, since this room has an area of 2,500 sq ft (232.25 sq m), at 15 sq ft (1.39 sq m) per person, the area will permit only 167 occupants. However, 8-1.7.2 makes provisions for possibly increasing this figure.

Both criteria (exit capacity and occupant load) must be considered in establishing the permissible occupant load for a room or area. For example, the exit capacity of

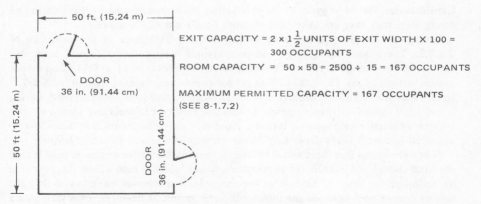

Figure 8-2A. Determination of Maximum Permitted Occupant Load for a Place of Assembly by Room Capacity.

the room in Figure 8-2B is sufficient for an occupant load of 300 people. An occupant load calculated on the basis of the room size (3,600 sq ft ÷ 7) would permit 514 people. Therefore, the exit capacity must be increased to five-and-a-half units of exit width in accordance with 5-3.1.2 since exit capacity must be provided for the occupant load determined by application of the occupant load factor.

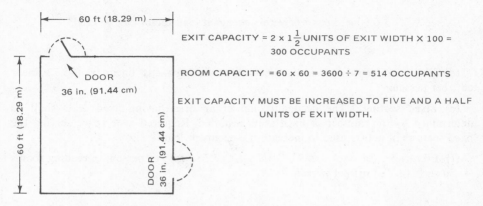

Figure 8-2B. Determination of Minimum Exit Capacity for a Place of Assembly.

8-1.7.2 The occupant load permitted in a building or portion thereof may be increased above that specified in 8-1.7.1 if the necessary aisles and exits are provided. To increase the occupant load, a diagram indicating placement of equipment, aisles, exits, and seating shall be provided to and approved by the authority having jurisdiction prior to any increase in occupant load.

The accessibility of room exits is as important as the exit capacity. Therefore, when an increase is permitted over the occupant load established by 8-1.7.1, it must be demonstrated that adequate aisles and access ways are provided leading to the room exits. Spacing of tables must provide for occupied chairs plus an aisle. Consideration should be given to the probability that when occupants leave during an emergency, they may not take time to move chairs out of the aisles.

Dining and drinking areas most frequently take advantage of the provision of 8-1.7.2. There have been large banquet layouts where the occupant load was successfully increased to reflect a population density factor of 11 sq ft (1.02 sq m) per person instead of the 15 sq ft (1.39 sq m) per person specified by item (b) of 8-1.7.1. In all cases where an increase in the occupant load is permitted, the authority having jurisdiction should insist on complete fixture and furniture layouts and should strictly enforce adherence to approved layouts. Note that the same room may have several approved occupant loads depending on the various fixture and furniture layouts.

When situations like these arise, another governing factor for occupant load is that the load should not exceed the maximum amount which would affect the practical operation of the place of assembly. For example, a restaurant so crowded that the servers cannot pass between the tables will soon go out of business. This serves as a controlling factor in limiting the expected population of a space.

Finally, the authority having jurisdiction cannot permit a population which would crowd a space to the point where the people would not have ready and quick access to exits. It has been shown in research at the National Research Council in Canada and by the London Transport Board that if people are crowded into a space so that each person is occupying less than 7 sq ft (.65 sq m), then movement is approaching a "shuffle"; when each person is occupying less than 3 sq ft (.28 sq m), "jam point" is approached and all movement by the occupants is effectively stopped. These figures should also be used by the authority having jurisdiction when making a decision concerning the maximum permitted occupant load.

See Figures 8-3A and 8-3B for two examples of increasing occupant load.

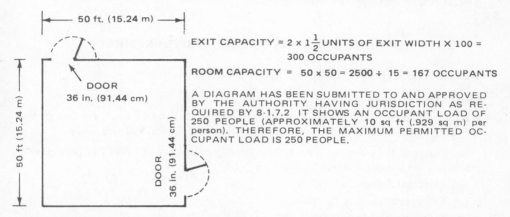

Figure 8-3A. Determination of Maximum Permitted Occupant Load for a Place of Assembly. Note that a practical upper limit for the room's population, which will still ensure rapid and orderly movement to an exit, may be 357 people (2,500 ÷ 7) based on research by the London Transport Board. Since the exit capacity provides for 300 people, the authority having jurisdiction could conceivably allow a maximum permitted occupant load of 300.

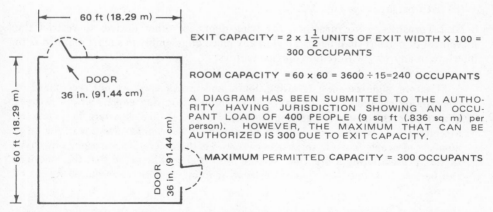

Figure 8-3B. Determination of Maximum Permitted Occupant Load for a Place of Assembly by Exit Capacity. Note that a practical upper limit for the room's population, which will still ensure rapid and orderly movement to an exit, may be 514 people (3,600 ÷ 7) based on research by the London Transport Board. However, the exit capacity of 300 must determine the maximum permitted occupant load.

8-1.7.3 Waiting Spaces. In theaters and similar places of public assembly where persons are admitted to the building at times when seats are not available for them and are allowed to wait in a lobby or similar space until seats are available, such use of lobby or similar space shall not encroach upon the required clear width of exits. Such waiting shall be restricted to areas other than the required means of egress. Exits shall be provided for such waiting spaces on the basis of one person for each 3 sq ft (.28 sq m) of waiting space area. Such exits shall be in addition to the exits specified for the main auditorium area and shall conform in construction and arrangement to the general rules for exits given in this chapter.

SECTION 8-2 MEANS OF EGRESS REQUIREMENTS

8-2.1 General. (*See 8-1.2, Mixed Occupancies.*)

8-2.2 Types of Exits.

8-2.2.1 Exits of the specified number and width shall be of one or more of the following types, in accordance with the provisions of Chapter 5 of this *Code*:

(a) Doors of the swinging type leading directly outside or to a lobby or passageway leading to the outside of the building (*see 5-2.1*)

(b) Horizontal exits (*see 5-2.4*)

(c) Smokeproof towers (*see 5-2.3*)

(d) Interior stairs (*see 5-2.2*)

(e) Outside stairs. Same requirements as for interior stairs, including intermediate handrails on monumental stairs serving main entrance doors (*see 5-2.5*)

(f) Ramps. Class A for Class A places of assembly; Class B for Class B and Class C places of assembly (*see 5-2.6*)

(g) Escalators (*see 5-2.8*)

(h) Exit passageways (*see 5-2.7*).

8-2.2.2 Turnstiles. No turnstiles, revolving doors, or other devices to restrict the movement of persons shall be installed in any place of assembly in such a manner as to interfere in any way with required exit facilities.

Elevators, slide escapes, revolving doors, and fire escapes are not recognized as constituting required exits in places of assembly. Revolving doors and fire escapes have frequently shown up as contributing factors to fire disasters in places of assembly. Slide escapes and elevators are not suited for rapid evacuation of the large numbers of people found in these occupancies. Further, elevators introduce other risk factors if used during a fire. (See Section 7-4.) It should be noted that these devices can be installed, but they cannot obstruct or interfere with the required means of egress.

8-2.3 Capacity of Means of Egress.

8-2.3.1 Every place of assembly, every tier or balcony, and every individual room used as a place of assembly shall have exits sufficient to provide for the total capacity thereof as determined in accordance with 8-1.7 and as follows:

(a) No individual unit of exit width shall serve more than 100 persons.

(b) Doors leading outside the building at grade level or not more than three risers above or below grade, Class A ramps, or horizontal exits — 100 persons per exit unit adjusted according to location of exits as required in 8-2.3.2 and 8-2.3.3.

(c) Stairs or other type of exit not specified in (b) above — 75 persons per exit unit.

The difference between the requirements for doors at ground level and for stairs is based on their rated capacity: 60 persons per minute per unit of exit width for level exit through doors, 45 down stairs. These figures provide an evacuation time of 1 minute 40 seconds, assuming the rated capacity and travel rate, exclusive of the time for the first person to reach the exit and for the last person to reach a place of safety after entering the exit.

The provisions of 8-2.3.1 are based on the assumption that all the occupants of a place of assembly may start for the exits at the same moment. The situation is different in other types of occupancies where it is assumed that only the occupants of a single floor will rush to the exits at the immediate outbreak of fire and that occupants of other floors can use the same stairways afterwards.

8-2.3.2 Main Exit.   Every assembly occupancy shall be provided with a main exit. The main exit shall be of sufficient width to accommodate one-half of the total occupant load but shall be not less than the total required width of all aisles, exit passageways, and stairways leading thereto and shall be at the level of exit discharge or shall connect to a stairway or ramp leading to a street.

Exception No. 1: A bowling establishment shall have a main exit of sufficient capacity to accommodate 50 percent of the total occupant load without regard to the number of aisles which it serves.

Exception No. 2: In assembly occupancies such as stadiums, sports arenas, and passenger stations, exits may be distributed around the perimeter of the building provided the total exit width provides 116⅔ percent of the width needed to accommodate the permitted occupant load.

The usual entrance to an assembly occupancy also generally serves as its main exit. As a rule, people leave a building by way of their entrance to the structure. Therefore, the main exit should be sized to accommodate at least 50 percent of the occupants; however, it must not be less in width than the sum of the *required* widths of the aisles which it serves.

Bowling establishments usually have relatively few rows of seats for spectators, but are necessarily wide to accommodate the alleys. Due to the limitation of not more than 6 seats intervening between any seat and an aisle, many more aisles are required than in other types of assembly occupancies. Exception No. 1 to 8-2.3.2 modifies what would be the excessive main exit width required to accommodate the sum of the required aisle widths served by the exit. Exception No. 2 clarifies the intent of the *Code* to provide the 16⅔ percent increase in exit capacity in buildings having no main exit. The intent is to distribute the extra width reasonably equally to all exits.

Figures 8-4A and 8-4B demonstrate how to calculate the required aisle widths and also provide for width increases as the number of seats (and the number of people) increases; how to split the occupant load (seating) between the main exit (50 percent must be assigned to the main exit) and the side exits; how to provide sufficient lobby depth to accommodate 50 percent of the aisles; and how to size the exits without effectively reducing the width of the aisles leading to them.

8-2.3.3 Other Exits.   Each level of an assembly occupancy shall have access to the main exit *and* shall be provided with exits of sufficient width to accommodate two-thirds of the total occupant load served by that level. Such exits shall discharge directly to a street or into an exit court, enclosed stairway, outside stairway, or exit passageway leading to a street. Such exits shall be located as far apart as practicable and as far from the main exit as practicable. Such exits shall be accessible from a cross aisle or a side aisle. (*See 8-2.3.2.*)

Exception: Where only two exits are required, each exit shall be of sufficient width to accommodate not less than half the total occupant load.

As an example of the requirements of 8-2.3.3, if a place of assembly had an occupant load of 300, the main exit would have to accommodate 150 people (50

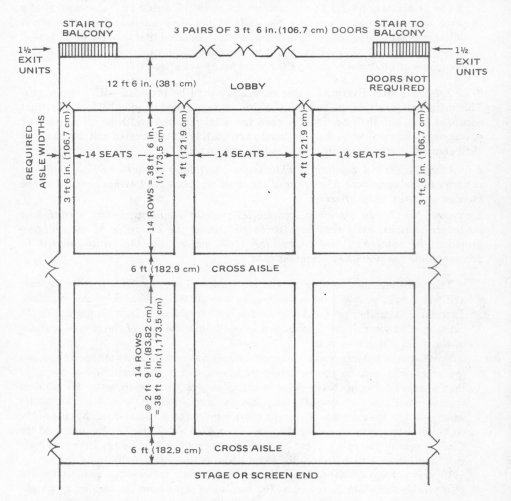

Figure 8-4A. Calculation of the Capacity of Means of Egress for a Place of Assembly with Fixed Seating. The illustrated example has an occupant load of 1,176 calculated by multiplying the number of seats in a row by the number of rows [see 8-1.7.1(e)]. The number of seats in a row between aisles (14) is the maximum allowed by 8-2.5.3(b).

percent). If there were two additional exits, together they would have to accommodate 200 people (two-thirds of the occupant load). Essentially, where more than two exits are required, the sum of the exit capacity must be at least one-sixth greater than (or 116⅔ percent of) the total required by the occupant load. Also, 8-2.4.2 requires that in a Class B place of assembly with a capacity of more than 600 people, at least three exits must be provided and no exit may be less than two units of exit width [44 in. (111.76 cm)]. The arrangement illustrated in Figure 8-4A incorporates these principles. Calculations for required exit capacities and aisle widths for this place of assembly are shown in Figure 8-4B.

REQUIRED AISLE WIDTH   38 ft 6 in. x ½ = 19 ft 3 in. ÷ 5 = 4 INCREMENTS @ 1½ in. = 6 in.

[8-2.5.4(a)]   19 ft 3 in. IS THE GREATEST DISTANCE BETWEEN ANY POINT IN AN AISLE AND AN EXIT, CROSS AISLE, OR FOYER.
4 INCREMENTS ARE THE NUMBER OF 5-ft INCREMENTS FOR WHICH 1½ in. MUST BE ADDED TO THE AISLE WIDTH.

SIDE AISLE   3 ft 0 in. + 6 in. = 3 ft 6 in.
OTHER AISLE   3 ft 6 in. + 6 in. = 4 ft 0 in.

CAPACITY OF MAIN EXIT   ½ OCCUPANT LOAD = $\frac{1176}{2}$ = 588 OCCUPANTS = 6 EXIT UNITS (100 OCCUPANTS EACH) = 6 x 22 in. = 11 ft 0 in.

(8-2.3.2)   SUM OF REQUIRED AISLES AND EXITS:

AISLES   2 @ 3 ft 6 in. + 2 @ 4 ft 0 in. =   15 ft 0 in.
BALCONY EXITS   2 @ 1½ EXIT UNITS = 3 x 22 in. =   5 ft 6 in.
                                                          20 ft 6 in.

20 ft 6 in. GOVERNS THE CAPACITY SINCE THE MAIN EXIT CANNOT BE LESS THAN THE WIDTH OF THE AISLES AND STAIRWAYS LEADING TO IT. PROVIDING 3 PAIRS OF 3 ft 6 in. DOORS (21 ft 0 in.) WOULD MEET THE CODE'S REQUIREMENTS.

CROSS AISLES   1 @ 4 ft 0 in. =   4 ft 0 in.
                  ½(4 ft 0 in.) =   2 ft 0 in.
[8-2.5.4(c)]   6 ft 0 in.

SIDE AISLES LEADING DIRECTLY TO AN EXIT NEED NOT BE CONSIDERED WHEN CALCULATING THE WIDTH OF THE CROSS AISLE.

LOBBY WIDTH   AISLES: 1 @ 4 ft 0 in. =   4 ft 0 in.
                              ½(4 ft 0 in. + 3 ft 6 in. + 3 ft 6 in.) =   5 ft 6 in.
[8-2.5.4(c)]   9 ft 6 in.
                 BALCONY: ½(2 ft 10 in. + 2 ft 10 in.) =   2 ft 10 in.
                                                                      12 ft 6 in.

CAPACITY OF SIDE EXITS   TOTAL OCCUPANT LOAD = 1176

(8-2.3.3)   THE 4 EXITS MUST PROVIDE 2/3 OF TOTAL OCCUPANT LOAD (784 OCCUPANTS). 784 ÷ 4 = 196 OCCUPANT LOAD EACH SIDE EXIT = 2 EXIT UNITS. CAN BE SATISIFED BY 1 DOOR 44 in. WIDE. HOWEVER, FROM A PRACTICAL STANDPOINT, THIS WOULD NOT TAKE FULL ADVANTAGE OF THE WIDTH OF THE CROSS AISLE. RECOMMEND USING AS A MINIMUM, 1 PAIR OF 3 ft 0 in. DOORS.

1 in. = 2.54 cm; 1 ft = 30.48 cm

Figure 8-4B. Calculations for the Required Aisle Widths and Exit Capacities for the Place of Assembly Illustrated in Figure 8-4A.

These requirements provide some relief from the congestion which would result if an exit should become unusable during a fire.

8-2.4 Number of Exits.

8-2.4.1   Every Class A place of assembly (capacity over 1,000 persons or more) shall have at least four separate exits as remote from each other as practicable.

8-2.4.2   Every Class B place of assembly (capacity over 300 to 1,000 persons) shall have at least two separate exits as remote from each other as practicable and, if of a capacity of over 600, at least three separate exits, each not less than two exit units wide.

8-2.4.3   Every Class C place of assembly (capacity 50 to 300 persons) shall have at least two means of egress consisting of separate exits or doors leading to a corridor or other spaces giving access to two separate and independent exits in different directions.

As the concentration or number of people increases in a place of assembly, the chance of a simultaneous exiting by a sizable group of occupants increases. Therefore, to reduce jamming at doorways (which leads to panic and disorder), more exits at a variety of locations are needed. Paragraphs 8-2.4.1 through 8-2.4.3 provide for this design requirement.

Since 8-1.2.2 specifies that assembly areas with individual occupant loads of fewer than 50 people in buildings of occupancies other than assembly shall be classed as part of the other occupancy, no criteria are given for the number and location of exits in such an occupancy by 8-2.4.

8-2.5 Arrangement of Means of Egress.

8-2.5.1   Exits shall be remote from each other and shall be arranged to minimize the possibility that they may be blocked by any emergency.

Exception: A common path of travel may be permitted for the first 20 ft (609.6 cm) from any point.

Separation of exits as far as practicable cannot be overemphasized. Two or more exits which are located too close to each other can become unusable during the same incident. The fundamental principles of this *Code*, as expressed in Chapter 2, require remoteness of exits to the point that a single fire event will not simultaneously block both exits.

Revolving rooftop places of assembly need special consideration; as the structure revolves, exit signs are often lost from view. To provide an unobstructed panoramic view, the exterior element revolves around a small stationary interior core in which the exits are often located. In many cases the two exits are too close to each other to avoid involving both exits in case of fire. Usually at least one stairway must transfer from its position in the stationary core to the normal location of the building stairways. This transfer, since it is a continuation of the stairway, must be made in an exit passageway possessing a fire resistance equal to that required for the stair enclosure.

8-2.5.2   Means of egress shall not be permitted through kitchens, storerooms, restrooms, closets, or hazardous areas as described in 8-3.2.

The purpose of this requirement, which is new in the 1980 Edition of the *Code*, is to make clear that exit access travel is not permitted to pass through areas subject to locking or areas possessing a hazard higher than that normal for the occupancy.

8-2.5.3 Seating.

(a) The spacing of rows of seats shall provide a space of not less than 12 in. (30.48 cm) from the back of one seat to the front of the most forward projection of the seat immediately behind it, when the seat is in the down position, as measured horizontally between vertical planes.

(b) Rows of seats between aisles shall have not more than 14 seats.

(c) Rows of seats opening onto an aisle at one end only shall have not more than seven seats.

(d) Seats without dividing arms shall have their capacity determined by allowing 18 in. (45.72 cm) per person.

In other than continental seating, not more than six seats may intervene between any seat in a row and an aisle. This permits a maximum of 14 seats in a row which terminates with an aisle at each end. Where seats are served by an aisle at one end only, not more than seven seats may be provided in any such row. Figure 8-5A illustrates these requirements, which are specified in 8-2.5.3(b) and (c).

The requirement for the spacing between rows of seats [see 8-2.5.3(a)] is illustrated in Figure 8-5B. Note that when seats with self-storing table arms, as found in schools, are used, the distance required in 8-2.5.3(a) should be measured with the table arm in the up or in-use position (see Figure 8-5C).

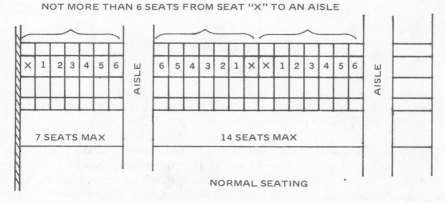

Figure 8-5A. Arrangement of Seats and Aisles in Place of Assembly Without Continental Seating.

Paragraph 8-2.5.3(d) applies to bench-type seats or to pews without dividing arms. Benches or pews may be 21 ft (6.4 m) long between aisles (14 persons × 18 in.) and 10½ ft (3.2 m) long (7 persons × 18 in.) where an aisle occurs at one end only. Small increases in these lengths [less than 18 in. (45.72 cm)] may be approved in order to provide more comfort for occupants.

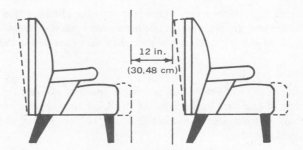

Figure 8-5B. Correct Measurement of Minimum Spacing Between Rows of Seats in Place of Assembly Without Continental Seating [see 8-2.5.3(a)].

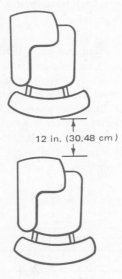

Figure 8-5C. Minimum Spacing Between Rows of Seats with Self-Storing Table Arms. Measure with the table arm in the up (in-use) position. There must be 12 in. (30.48 cm) between the back of a seat and the leading edge of a table arm.

(e) Where bleacher or grandstand seating without backs is used indoors, rows of seats shall be spaced not less than 22 in. (55.88 cm) nor more than 30 in. (76.2 cm) back to back. Vertical aisles shall be provided when such seating is more than eleven rows high. Vertical aisles, where provided, shall not have a dead end in excess of sixteen rows. The rise per row shall not exceed 12 in. (30.48 cm).

Exception: Folding or telescopic seating shall comply with Standard for Tents, Grandstands and Air-Supported Structures Used for Places of Assembly, NFPA 102 with a limit of dead ends in vertical aisles of sixteen rows.

The elimination of backs allows the entire bleacher to be a path of exit access. People can simultaneously evacuate a bleacher upward or downward without using aisles. This compensates for the openness of bleacher-type structures which can expose the entire population to a single fire either under or adjacent to the structure.

The provisions of the Code concerning bleacher or grandstand seating and folding or telescopic seating have been modified to coordinate requirements with NFPA 102, Standard for Assembly Seating, Tents, and Air-Supported Structures.[1]

(f) Continental seating.

1. With continental seating, the spacing of rows of unoccupied seats shall provide a clear width between rows measured horizontally as follows (automatic or self-rising seats shall be measured in the seat-up position; other seats shall be measured in the seat-down position): 18-in. (45.72-cm) clear width between rows of 18 seats or less; 20-in. (50.8-cm) clear width between rows of 35 seats or less; 21-in. (53.34-cm) clear width between rows of 45 seats or less; 22-in. (55.88-cm) clear width between rows of 46 seats or more, and

2. There shall be not more than 100 seats in a row between aisles at both sides of the seating area, and

3. Exit doors shall be provided along each side aisle of the row of seats at the rate of one pair of exit doors for each five rows of seats. There shall be not more than five seat rows between pairs of doors. Such exit doors shall provide a minimum clear width of 66 in. (167.64 cm) discharging into a foyer, lobby, or to the exterior of the building.

With continental seating, up to 100 seats may be provided in a row. This large number of seats requires a full exit unit of clear width between the rows of seats. Lesser widths between the rows reduce the permissible number of seats in a row. Because continental seating feeds so many occupants into the side aisles, frequent exits from the side aisles are required. Therefore, the Code requires that there be one pair of doors 66 in. (167.64 cm) wide for every five rows of seats, and that not more than five rows of seats occur between pairs of doors leading from the side aisles to an exit access or an exit. Figures 8-6A and 8-6B illustrate these requirements.

8-2.5.4 Aisles.   Every portion of any assembly building that contains seats, tables, displays, equipment, or other materials shall be provided with aisles leading to exits as follows:

(a) When serving more than 60 seats, every aisle shall be not less than 3 ft (91.44 cm) wide when serving seats on one side only, and not less than 3 ft 6 in. (106.68 cm) wide when serving seats on both sides. Such minimum width shall be measured at the point farthest from an exit, cross aisle, or foyer and shall be increased in width by 1½ in. (3.81 cm) for each 5 ft (152.4 cm) in length toward the exit, cross aisle, or foyer.

(b) When serving 60 seats or less, aisles shall be not less than 30 in. (76.2 cm) wide.

When determining the number of seats served, the entire block of seats on each side of the aisle is to be counted.

(c) Aisles shall terminate in a cross aisle, foyer, or exit. The width of such cross aisle, foyer, or exit shall be not less than the sum of the required width of the widest aisle plus 50 percent of the total required width of the remaining aisles that it serves.

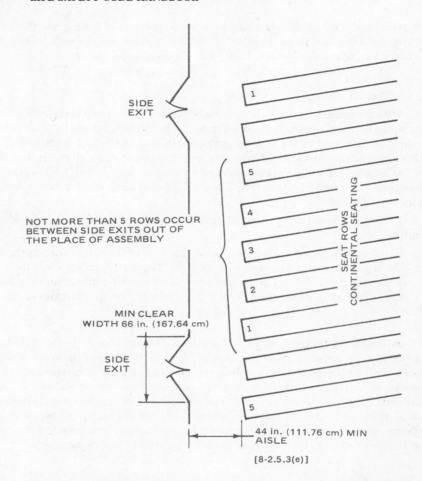

Figure 8-6A. Arrangement of Continental Seating in Place of Assembly. Each row may contain up to 100 seats.

(d) No dead-end aisle shall be greater than 20 ft (609.6 cm) in length. In arena or thrust stage theaters, dead-end aisles at the stage shall not exceed five rows beyond a cross aisle.

(e) With continental seating as set forth in 8-2.5.3(f), side aisles shall be not less than 44 in. (111.76 cm) in width.

(f) Steps shall not be placed in aisles to overcome differences in level unless the gradient exceeds 1 ft (1 m) of rise in 8 ft (8 m) of run. Steps in aisles shall conform to the requirements for stairs as to rise and run.

Exception: In balconies and galleries, rise and run shall be as for stairs, but one tread in each seat platform width may have a greater width to accommodate access to seats. Seating platforms shall be of uniform width.

(g) The gradient of sloping aisles shall not exceed 1 ft (1 m) of rise in 8 ft (8 m) of run.

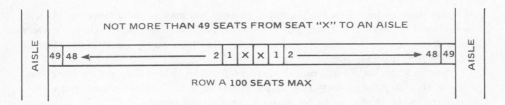

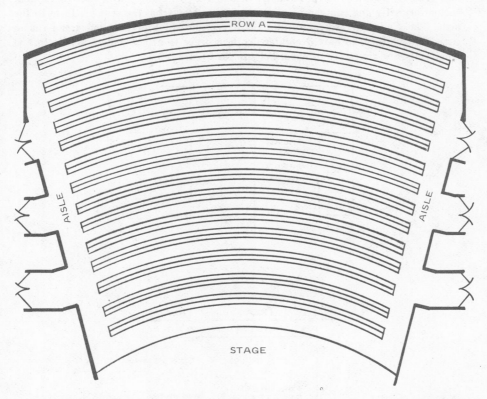

Figure 8-6B. Arrangement of Seats and Aisles in Place of Assembly with Continental Seating. Note that 100 seats is the maximum number for one row and that the maximum number of intervening seats between any one seat and an aisle is 49 seats. Note, too, the frequency of the exits from the side aisles in the depicted theater arrangement.

In addition to exits, it is necessary to provide clearly visible aisles sufficient in number and arranged to provide safe access to exits or protected exit accesses.

When serving seating areas, aisle widths are required to increase in the direction of travel based on the distance to an exit, cross aisle, or foyer. Since most aisles are required to provide access in two directions to an exit, cross aisle, or foyer, the minimum width is applied to the midpoint of the aisle and the aisle width increased in both directions. In practice, of course, most designers simply maintain the maximum width for the entire length. See Figure 8-4A.

Only those aisles which are permitted to dead end may actually increase in width away from the dead end. Dead ends are limited to 20 ft (6.1 m) in length. In theaters with arena or thrust stages, dead-end aisles at the stage may not exceed five rows of seats beyond a cross aisle.

Steps in aisles should be avoided wherever possible. Where they are necessary due to the aisle slope exceeding 1 ft (.3 m) of rise in 8 ft (2.44 m) of run, steps must conform to the requirements for stairs as to rise and run (see 5-2.2.1.2). Balconies and galleries pose a problem in choice of hazards. To comply with the requirement for uniform rise and run can create a dangerous step from the seat platform to the aisle. The *Code*, therefore, provides the exception which permits one tread run in each seat platform to have a greater depth in order to accommodate access to and from seats; the risers are of equal height. See Figure 8-7.

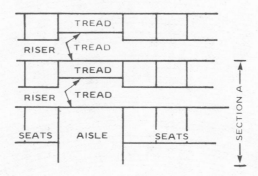

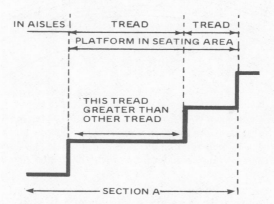

Figure 8-7. Steps in Aisles Complying with the Exception to 8-2.5.4(f). The limits are built in by the rise/run relationship for stairs. The uniformity is required to prevent people from tripping and stumbling when different depths are introduced.

8-2.6 Measurement of Travel Distance to Exits.   Exits shall be so arranged that the total length of travel from any point to reach an exit will not exceed 150 ft (45.72 m) in any place of assembly.

Exception: The travel distance may be increased to 200 ft (60.96 m) in assembly occupancies protected throughout by an approved automatic sprinkler system.

Travel distance to exits from balconies or galleries which are served by unenclosed stairways must be measured to include the distance on the slope of the stair in the plane of the nosings. Travel distance would be measured as illustrated in Figure 8-8.

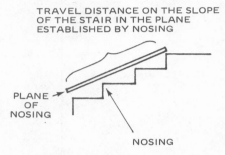

Figure 8-8. Measurement of Travel Distance to Exit when Balconies Are Served by Unenclosed Stairs.

8-2.7 Discharge from Exits.

8-2.7.1 The level of exit discharge shall be measured at the point of principal entrance to the building.

8-2.7.2 Where the principal entrance to a place of assembly is via a depressed terrace, the terrace shall be at least as wide as the exit that it serves, but not less than 5 ft (152.4 cm) wide, and it shall be increased in width by 50 percent of any other exits tributary thereto. The level of the terrace shall be considered the level of exit discharge for the purpose of 8-1.6 above.

The requirements of 8-2.7.2 are illustrated in Figure 8-9.

8-2.7.3 A maximum of 50 percent of the exits may discharge through areas on the level of exit discharge in accordance with 5-7.2

8-2.8 Illumination of Means of Egress.

8-2.8.1 Illumination of means of egress in places of assembly shall be provided in accordance with Section 5-8.

8-2.8.2 In every auditorium or other place of assembly where pictures, motion pictures, or other projections are made by means of directed light, the illumination of the floors of exit access may be reduced during such period of projection to values of not less than ⅕ footcandle (2.15 lx).

8-2.9 Emergency Lighting. All places of assembly and their means of egress shall be provided with emergency lighting in accordance with Section 5-9.

Exception: Churches that are Class C places of assembly, used exclusively for religious worship, shall not be required to have emergency lighting.

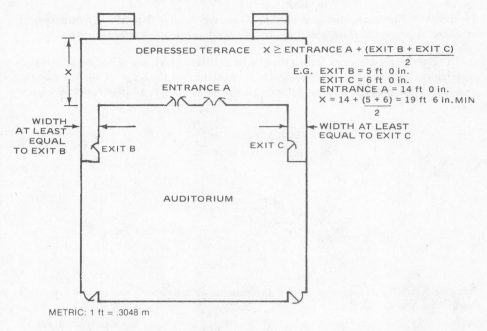

DEPRESSED TERRACE $X \geq$ ENTRANCE A + $\dfrac{(EXIT\ B + EXIT\ C)}{2}$

E.G. EXIT B = 5 ft 0 in.
EXIT C = 6 ft 0 in.
ENTRANCE A = 14 ft 0 in.
$X = 14 + \dfrac{(5 + 6)}{2} = 19$ ft 6 in. MIN

ENTRANCE A

X

WIDTH AT LEAST EQUAL TO EXIT B

EXIT B

EXIT C

WIDTH AT LEAST EQUAL TO EXIT C

AUDITORIUM

METRIC: 1 ft = .3048 m

Figure 8-9. Place of Assembly with Depressed Terrace as Principal Entrance.

The exception to the requirement for emergency lighting is intended to apply only to Class C places of assembly (50 to 300 people) which are not likely to be used for any purpose except religious worship because they contain permanently fixed furnishings such as pews, pulpits, or altars.

8-2.10 Marking of Means of Egress.   Means of egress shall have signs in accordance with Section 5-10.

8-2.11 Special Features.

8-2.11.1 Panic Hardware.   An exit door from a place of assembly having an occupant load of 100 or more persons may be provided with a latch or lock only if it is panic hardware.

Exception No. 1:   In places of assembly having an occupant load of less than 600, panic hardware may be omitted from the main exit when the main exit consists of a single door or a pair of doors. Any locking device on this door(s) shall meet the requirements of Exception No. 2 to 5-2.1.2.1.1.

This new exception to 8-2.11.1 is in recognition of new provisions contained in Chapter 5, Means of Egress. These new provisions recognize the need to lock doors for security purposes and provide limits on how this can be done. These provisions also recognize, in fact, that in order for the business to function the main door must be open; thus, this exception is to coordinate with the changes in Chapter 5.

Exception No. 2:   Special locking arrangements complying with 5-2.1.2.1.5 are permitted on doors other than main exit doors.

This exception allows delayed release panic hardware meeting the requirements of 5-2.1.2.1.5 to be used on all but the main exit.

8-2.11.2   Class C places of assembly in covered malls (*see 24-4.3.1 Exception*) may have horizontal or vertical security grills or doors on the main entrance/exits in accordance with the provisions of Exception No. 2 to 5-2.1.1.4.1.

This provision allows small restaurants in malls to use the security grills or doors provided for in 5-2.1.1.4.1 Exception No. 2.

8-2.11.3 Railings.

(a) The fasciae of boxes, balconies, and galleries shall not be less than 26 in. (66.04 cm) high above the adjacent floor or have substantial railings not less than 26 in. (66.04 cm) high above the adjacent floor.

(b) The height of the rail above footrests on the adjacent floor immediately in front of a row of seats shall be no less than 26 in. (66.04 cm). Railings at the ends of aisles shall not be less than 36 in. (91.44 cm) high for the full width of the aisle and shall be not less than 42 in. (106.68 cm) high for the width of the aisle where steps occur.

(c) Cross aisles shall be provided with railings not less than 26 in. (66.04 cm) high above the adjacent floor.

Exception: Where the backs of seats on the front of the aisle project 24 in. (60.96 cm) or more above the adjacent floor of the aisle.

Figure 8-10A illustrates the requirements of 8-2.11.3(a) and (b). Rail height at the fascia end of a sloping aisle must not be less than 36 in. (91.44 cm). However, when the aisle is not ramped but has steps, the rail height must be at least 42 in. (106.68 cm). There is more danger of people tripping on steps than on a sloping surface with a maximum gradient of 1 ft (.3 m) of rise to 8 ft (2.44 m) of run.

The *Code* requires a barrier along the downhill side of a cross aisle [see 8-2.11.3(c)]. The barrier may be a rail or the backs of the seats which abut the downhill side of the aisle when the backs project 24 in. (60.96 cm) or more above the cross aisle. The difference between the 24 in. (60.96 cm) back height and the required 26-in. (66.04-cm) railing is insignificant. See Figure 8-10B.

SECTION 8-3   PROTECTION

8-3.1 Protection of Vertical Openings.   All interior stairways and other vertical openings shall be enclosed and protected as provided in Section 6-2.

Exception No. 1:   Unprotected openings connecting not more than three floors may be permitted provided that they comply with the requirements of 6-2.2.3.1 Exception No. 1.

Exception No. 2:   Stairs may be open between balconies and main assembly floors in theaters, churches, or auditoriums where the travel distance is within the allowable limits (see 8-2.6).

8-3.2 Protection from Hazards.

8-3.2.1 Stage and Enclosed Platform.   (*See 8-1.3.*)

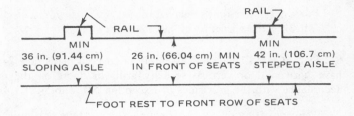

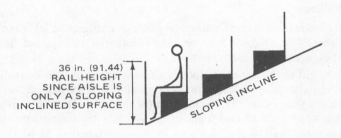

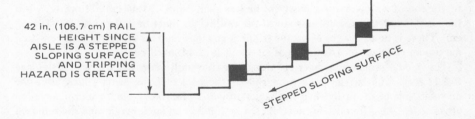

Figure 8-10A. Railings Installed in Accordance with 8-2.11.3(a) and (b).

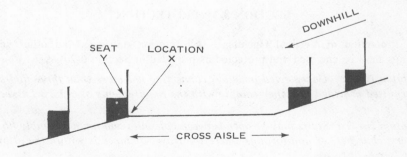

Figure 8-10B. Barrier for Cross Aisles in Accordance with 8-2.11.3(c). A railing [< 26 in. (66.04 cm)] is required at Location X if the back of Seat Y is less than 24 in. (60.96 cm) high.

8-3.2.1.1 Every stage equipped with fly galleries, gridirons, and rigging for movable theater-type scenery and every enclosed platform larger than 500 sq ft (46.45 sq m) in area shall have a system of automatic sprinklers at the ceiling, under the gridiron, in usable spaces under the stage or platform, and in auxiliary spaces and dressing rooms, storerooms, and workshops. Where the distance from the back of the stage to the proscenium wall is less than 30 ft (914.4 cm), in lieu of sprinklers under the entire gridiron area, complete peripheral sidewall sprinklers with baffle plates may be substituted. Such sidewall sprinklers shall be not more than 30 in. (76.2 cm) below the gridiron or 6 in. (15.24 cm) below the baffle plates.

When openings are provided in the stage floor for stage lifts, trap doors, or stairs, sprinklers spaced 5 ft (152.4 cm) on centers shall be provided around the opening at the ceiling below the stage, and baffles at least 12 in. (30.48 cm) in depth shall be installed around the perimeter of the opening.

8-3.2.1.2 Every stage and every enclosed platform larger than 500 sq ft (46.45 sq m) shall have a ventilator or ventilators in or above it, operable from the stage floor by hand and also opening by fusible links or other approved automatic heat actuated device, or heat and smoke actuated device, to give a free opening equal to at least five percent of the area of the floor of the stage or enclosed platform.

Where mechanical ventilation is provided it shall be so arranged that natural ventilation, at least equal to the above, will be available. Makeup air for mechanical ventilation shall not be obtained from the audience (seating) areas.

8-3.2.1.3 The proscenium opening of every stage shall be provided with a curtain constructed and mounted so as to intercept hot gases, flames, and smoke and to prevent glow from a severe fire on the stage showing on the auditorium side within a 5-minute period. The curtain shall be automatic closing without the use of applied power.

Exception: In lieu of the protection required herein, all the following may be provided:

(a) A noncombustible opaque fabric curtain so arranged that it will close automatically, and

(b) An automatic dry-pipe system of spray heads on both sides of the curtain. Discharge and spacing shall be such that the entire curtain will be wet. Water supply shall be controlled by a deluge valve and shall be sufficient to keep the curtain completely wet for 30 minutes or until valve is closed by fire department personnel, and

(c) Curtain, spray heads, stage sprinklers, and vents shall be automatically operated in case of fire, by rate-of-rise and fixed temperature detectors. Spacing, number, and location of detectors shall be as required by the devices used, with maximum center-to-center distance of 10 ft (304.8 cm). Detectors shall completely cover the periphery of the sprinklered and protected area, and

(d) Operation of a sprinkler or spray head deluge valve shall automatically activate the emergency ventilating system and close the curtain.

Modern stages pose problems which didn't exist in the past. Scenery may be shifted horizontally, vertically, or both ways. The use of thrust stages and arena stages creates other problems.

The classic stage of the past had great height above the proscenium opening to accommodate the rigid asbestos curtain. The high void was a natural place to house combustible scenery for a performance, along with the rigging necessary for handling scene changes. This vertical storage area represented both a high fuel load and a difficult space to reach in case of a fire. Many new theaters use a flexible noncombustible curtain which does not require much height to accommodate it. Scenery on these stages is moved horizontally, thus reducing the distance necessary for storage between the top of the proscenium opening and the stage ceiling. Most combustible scenery is now stored in areas adjacent to the stage. All rigging and lighting is condensed in less vertical space.

Both stage arrangements require sprinklers and vents installed in accordance with 8-3.2.1.1 and 8-3.2.1.2. It is important that if mechanical ventilation for evacuating smoke from the stage is provided in lieu of openable vents, the natural air supply must be provided from a source other than the auditorium seating area.

If, instead of the fire-resistant curtain specified in 8-3.2.1.3, a flexible proscenium curtain is used, the *Code* requires an automatic dry-pipe system with spray nozzles on both sides of the curtain. This system must be capable of completely wetting both sides of the curtain and of maintaining it wet for at least 30 minutes or until the deluge valve is closed by the fire department. *Automatic Sprinkler and Standpipe Systems*[2] by Dr. John L. Bryan contains a detailed explanation of the design and operation of dry-pipe sprinkler systems and of deluge valves. Specifications for the installation of sprinkler systems in general are found in NFPA 13, *Standard for the Installation of Sprinkler Systems*.[3] Of course, for any sprinkler system to effectively minimize the hazards from fire to life safety or property, regular inspection and maintenance of the system is essential. NFPA 13A, *Recommended Practice for the Care and Maintenance of Sprinkler Systems*,[4] provides recommendations for ensuring that an extinguishing system will not fail in an emergency.

The spray nozzles for the curtain, and the sprinklers and vents for the stage are required to operate automatically by heat detectors capable of monitoring an abnormally high temperature or rate-of-temperature rise. NFPA 72E, *Standard on Automatic Fire Detectors*,[5] and its appendix contain specifications and recommendations on the installation of heat detectors.

To complete the protection system, operation of the sprinkler or spray nozzle deluge valve must also automatically close the proscenium curtain and activate the emergency ventilating system.

8-3.2.1.4 Auxiliary stage spaces such as understage areas, dressing rooms, workshops, and similar spaces associated with the functioning of a stage shall comply with the following:

(a) No point within any auxiliary space shall be more than 50 ft (15.24 m) from a door providing access to an exit.

(b) There shall be at least two exits available from every auxiliary stage space, one of which shall be available within a travel distance of 75 ft (22.86 m). A common path of travel of 20 ft (609.6 cm) to the two exits shall be permitted.

(c) Auxiliary stage spaces shall be equipped with automatic sprinklers when required by the provisions of 8-3.2.1.1.

(d) No workshop involving the use of combustible or flammable paint, liquids, or gases, or their storage shall open directly upon a stage.

Auxiliary stage spaces are sources of serious hazards. It is therefore necessary to provide automatic fire protection and adequate exits within a short travel distance from such spaces. All workshops must be separated from the stage area by construction having a fire resistance of at least 1 hour, with any openings between a workshop and the stage area protected by 1-hour rated fire assemblies.

8-3.2.1.5 Where automatic sprinkler protection is not provided, the proscenium wall of every theater using movable scenary or decorations shall not have more than two openings entering the stage, exclusive of the proscenium opening. Such openings shall not exceed 21 sq ft (1.95 sq m) each and shall be fitted with self-closing fire doors.

The limitations of 8-3.2.1.5 apply only to enclosed platforms with a maximum area of 500 sq ft (46.45 sq m) or to stages without fly galleries, gridirons, or rigging for movable scenery. Other configurations must have the automatic sprinkler protection specified in 8-3.2.1.1.

8-3.2.1.6 Each stage shall be equipped with a standpipe located on each side of the stage, equipped with a 2½-in. (6.35-cm) fire department connection, and a 1½-in. (3.8-cm) hose for occupant use, installed in accordance with *Standard for the Installation of Standpipe and Hose Systems*, NFPA 14.

There must be a standpipe located on each side of a stage to provide the stage hands and the responding fire department with a manual fire fighting capability at the area of a theater where a fire is most likely to occur. The installation of the standpipes must comply with NFPA 14, *Standard for the Installation of Standpipe and Hose Systems.*[6] NFPA 13E, *Recommendations for Fire Department Operations in Properties Protected by Sprinkler and Standpipe Systems,*[7] should also be consulted for a discussion of the necessity of a properly installed standpipe system. Standpipes are required whether or not the stage has automatic sprinkler protection.

8-3.2.2 Projection Booth.

8-3.2.2.1 Every place of assembly where an electric arc, Xenon, or other light source that generates hazardous gases, dust, or radiation is used shall have a projection room that complies with 8-3.2.2.2, from which the projection shall be made. Where cellulose nitrate film is used, the projection room shall comply with *Standard for the Storage and Handling of Cellulose Nitrate Motion Picture Film*, NFPA 40. (*See also Chapter 31.*)

The requirements for projection booths were developed jointly with those of NFPA 40, *Standard for the Storage and Handling of Cellulose Nitrate Motion Picture Film,*[8] and the motion picture industry at the height of movie popularity when cellulose nitrate film was still being used. Although only safety film is now used (except at film festivals or revivals) and the risk level has been reduced, the primary function of these requirements is to build a shelter around the projection booth, eliminating it as an exposure threat to the theater audience.

The intent of 8-3.2.2.1 is to protect the audience from the dangers associated with light sources such as electric arc or Xenon. Where incandescent light is used, projection booths are not required in places of assembly. Note the booth is required based on the light source, not on the projection of film.

Paragraph 31-2.7 requires that unless the construction of a projection booth complies with NFPA 40, *Standard for the Storage and Handling of Cellulose Nitrate Motion Picture Film,*[8] a conspicuous sign must be posted on the door of the projection booth and also inside the booth. The sign must state: "Safety Film Only Permitted in This Room". The intent is to ensure that cellulose nitrate film is projected only with adequate safeguards.

8-3.2.2.2 Projection Rooms for Safety Film.

8-3.2.2.2.1 Every projection room shall be of permanent construction consistent with the construction requirements for the type of building in which the projection room is located. Openings need not be protected. The room shall have a floor area of not less than 80 sq ft (7.43 sq m) for a single machine and at least 40 sq ft (3.72 sq m) for each additional machine. Each motion picture projector, floodlight, spotlight, or similar piece of equipment shall have a clear working space of not less than 30 in. (76.2 cm) on each side and at its rear, but only one such space shall be required between adjacent projectors.

The projection room and the rooms appurtenant thereto shall have a ceiling height of not less than 7 ft 6 in. (228.6 cm).

8-3.2.2.2.2 Each projection room shall have at least one out-swinging, self-closing door not less than 2 ft 6 in. (76.2 cm) wide by 6 ft 8 in. (203.2 cm) high.

8-3.2.2.2.3 The aggregate of ports and openings for projection equipment shall not exceed 25 percent of the area of the wall between the projection room and the auditorium.

All openings shall be provided with glass or other approved material so as to completely close the opening.

It should be emphasized that 8-3.2.2.2.1 through 8-3.2.2.2.6 apply only to booths for the projection of cellulose acetate or other safety film. Although openings in the booth do not need to be protected, they must be provided with glass or other approved material which will completely close the opening and prevent gas, dust, or radiation from contaminating the audience or seating area.

8-3.2.2.2.4 Projection booth room ventilation shall be not less than the following:

(a) *Supply Air.* Each projection room shall be provided with two or more separate fresh air inlet ducts with screened openings terminating within 12 in. (30.48 cm) of the floor and located at opposite ends of the room. Such air inlets shall be of sufficient size to permit an air change every 3 minutes. Fresh air may be supplied from the general building air conditioning system, providing it is so arranged that the projection booth will continue to receive one change of air every 3 minutes when no other air is supplied by the general air conditioning system.

(b) *Exhaust Air.* Each projection room shall be provided with one or more exhaust air outlets that may be manifolded into a single duct outside the booth. Such outlets shall be so located as to ensure circulation throughout the room. Projection room exhaust air systems shall be independent of any other air systems in the buildings. Exhaust air ducts shall terminate at the exterior of the building in such a location that the exhaust air cannot be readily recirculated into the supply air system. The exhaust system shall be mechanically operated and of such a capacity as to provide a minimum of one change of air every 3 minutes. The blower motor shall be outside the duct system.

The projection room ventilation system may also serve appurtenant rooms, such as the generator room and the rewind room.

The requirements for the ventilation of a projection booth are designed to effectively "isolate" the booth from the theater so that any products of combustion created by a fire in a projection booth would not be circulated into the theater. This is accomplished by having an independent exhaust system for the booth by ensuring that the exhaust outlet on the exterior of the building is located at a point where the air intake for the theater cannot recirculate the exhausted air.

If fresh air for the projection booth's ventilation system is supplied from the general system of the building, it is essential that the combined system be arranged to ensure the required 3-minute air change in the booth when no other air is supplied to the general system of the building. To further minimize the risk to the life safety of the audience from a fire or explosion in the projection booth, the blower motor of the exhaust must be located outside of the duct system.

8-3.2.2.2.5 Each projection machine shall be provided with an exhaust duct that will draw air from each lamp and exhaust it directly to the outside of the building in such a fashion that it will not be picked up by supply inlets. Such a duct shall be of rigid materials, except for a continuous flexible connector approved for the purpose. The lamp exhaust system shall not be interconnected with any other system.

(a) *Electric Arc Projection Equipment.* The exhaust capacity shall be 200 cfm (.09 cu m/s) for each lamp connected to the lamp exhaust system, or as recommended by the equipment manufacturer. Auxiliary air may be introduced into the system through a screened opening to stabilize the arc.

(b) *Xenon Projection Equipment.* The lamp exhaust system shall exhaust not less than 300 cfm (.14 cu m/s) per lamp, or not less than that exhaust volume required or recommended by the equipment manufacturer, whichever is the greater. The external temperature of the lamp housing shall not exceed 130°F (54.4°C) when operating.

The *Code* sets forth the minimum capacity for the exhaust system of a projection machine; however, a greater capacity must be provided when recommended by the manufacturer of the projection equipment. This system must be independent of any other ventilation system in the building housing the theater.

8-3.2.2.2.6 Miscellaneous Equipment and Storage.

(a) Each projection room shall be provided with rewind and film storage facilities.

The intent of the requirement for the storage and rewinding of film is to prevent these operations from occurring outside the projection booth at some less protected location where, if a fire occurred, the exposure to the theater would be significantly greater. All operations which relate to projection activities must be kept within the protected enclosure afforded by the projection booth.

(b) A maximum of four containers for flammable liquids of not greater than 16 oz (4.7 × 10⁻⁴ cu m) capacity and of a nonbreakable type may be permitted in each projection booth.

(c) Appurtenant electrical equipment such as rheostats, transformers, and generators may be located within the booth or in a separate room of equivalent construction.

8-3.2.3 Service Equipment, Hazardous Operations or Processes, and Storage Facilities.

8-3.2.3.1 Rooms containing high-pressure boilers, refrigerating machinery of other than domestic refrigerator type, large transformers, or other service equipment subject to possible explosion shall not be located directly under or adjacent to required exits. All such rooms shall be separated by a 1-hour fire barrier from other parts of the building.

> **The preservation of the integrity of exits in any building is one of the principal concerns of the *Code*. Therefore, hazardous areas, even if enclosed with the required fire-resistant construction, must never be located where they might directly expose a required exit to fire.**

8-3.2.3.2 All openings between the balance of the building and rooms or enclosures for hazardous operations or processes shall be protected by standard self-closing or smoke-actuated fire doors and shall be provided with adequate vents to the outer air, in accordance with Section 6-4 of this *Code*.

8-3.2.3.3 Rooms or spaces for the storage, processing, or use of the materials specified in this section shall be protected in accordance with the following:

(a) Rooms or spaces used for the storage of combustible supplies in quantities deemed hazardous by the authority having jurisdiction, hazardous materials in quantities deemed hazardous by recognized standards, or fuel shall be separated from the remainder of the building by construction having not less than a 1-hour fire-resistive rating with all openings protected by self-closing or smoke-actuated fire doors, or such rooms or spaces may be protected by an automatic extinguishing system as set forth in Section 6-4.

(b) Rooms or spaces used for processing or use of combustible supplies in quantities considered hazardous by the authority having jurisdiction, hazardous materials, or flammable or combustible liquids in quantities deemed hazardous by recognized standards shall be separated from the remainder of the building by construction having not less than a 1-hour fire-resistive rating with all openings protected by self-closing or smoke-actuated fire doors and shall also be protected by an automatic extinguishing system as set forth in Section 6-4.

(c) Boiler and furnace rooms, laundries, and maintenance shops, including woodworking and painting areas, shall be separated from the remainder of the building by construction having not less than a 1-hour fire-resistive rating with all openings protected by self-closing or smoke-actuated fire doors.

Exception: Rooms enclosing air-handling equipment.

(d) When automatic extinguishing systems are used to meet the requirements of this section, the rooms or spaces shall be separated from the remainder of the building by a smoke barrier.

> **The intent of 8-3.2.3.3 is to specify the degree of protection necessary for certain hazardous areas. It has been divided into three sections based on the degree of**

hazard. The hazards noted in item (a) are required to be enclosed in 1-hour construction or protected by sprinklers. If the sprinkler option is chosen, an enclosure is still required; however, the enclosure need not be rated, but only form a membrane against the passage of smoke.

The hazards noted in item (b) must be enclosed in 1-hour construction *and* be protected by automatic sprinklers.

The hazards noted in item (c) are required to be enclosed in 1-hour construction with no option for a sprinkler equivalency for the enclosure. The exception to item (c) pertains to rooms housing air-handling equipment *only*. If the room is used for other purposes, then the provisions of item (a) or (b) apply.

8-3.2.4 Special Provisions for Food Service Establishments.

8-3.2.4.1 All devices in connection with the preparation of food shall be so installed and operated as to avoid hazard to the safety of occupants.

8-3.2.4.2 All devices in connection with the preparation of food shall be of an approved type and shall be installed in an approved manner.

An "approved type" of device means that, from the standpoint of potential fire hazards, the unit is acceptable to the authority having jurisdiction. An "approved manner" of installation means installation in accordance with the requirements of the authority having jurisdiction.

8-3.2.4.3 Food preparation facilities shall be protected in accordance with *Vapor Removal Cooking Equipment*, NFPA 96, and are not required to have openings protected between food preparation areas and dining areas.

The intent of 8-3.2.4.3 is to provide some barrier between cooking areas and dining areas of restaurants. The intent of the barrier is to screen possible flash fires from the view of the patrons in an attempt to prevent panic. Openings in this barrier are not restricted and do not need to be protected. The *Code* is counting on the automatic extinguishing system to control any fire on the cooking surfaces, and thus no longer requires enclosure by rated construction. The degree of screening required, and thus the size of the barrier required, is left to the judgment of the authority having jurisdiction.

8-3.3 Interior Finish.

8-3.3.1 The interior finish requirements of this section shall be in accordance with Section 6-5.

8-3.3.2 Interior finish in all corridors and lobbies shall be Class A or B and in enclosed stairways Class A.

8-3.3.3 Interior finish in general assembly areas shall be Class A, B, or C.

Exception: In any place of assembly, exposed portions of structural members complying with the requirements for Type IV (2HH) construction may be permitted.

8-3.3.4 Screens on which pictures are projected shall comply with requirements of Class A or Class B interior finish.

A structural member is a column, a beam, a girder, or an arch. It can be located wherever it is needed to bear the weight of the structure. Heavy timber construction is defined in NFPA 220, *Standard Types of Building Construction.*[9] The NFPA *Fire Protection Handbook*[10] discusses the principal features of the construction.

8-3.4 Alarm and Communication Systems.

8-3.4.1   Every Class A or B place of assembly shall be provided with a manual fire alarm system in accordance with 7-6.1.2.

8-3.4.2   The alarm system shall not automatically sound an alarm in the audience or seating portion of the place of assembly but shall sound an alarm in a constantly manned location.

Exception: Places of assembly in educational occupancies.

8-3.4.3   Provisions shall be made for transmitting voice messages by a public address system throughout the assembly area. Reliability of the public address system shall be assured by testing the system prior to allowing occupants into the assembly room.

Exception: Places of assembly in educational occupancies.

8-3.4.4   The public address system shall be provided with an emergency power source.

Exception: Places of assembly in educational occupancies.

The intent of the provisions of 8-3.4 is to provide an alarm system which will not produce a panic reaction from the occupants. Previous editions of the *Code* required no alarm system. The intent of this section is to provide a system which will permit activation of the system by pull stations as required by 7-6.1.2, but that an audible alarm will not be sounded in the seating or audience areas of the place of assembly. In lieu of the audible alarm throughout the place of assembly, the system must sound an alarm in a constantly manned location. (Constantly manned, in this case, means during the time the place of assembly is in use, the alarm panel must be manned.) From that constantly manned location, voice messages instructing the occupants can be issued via a public address system. This method allows for the orderly evacuation of the occupants and permits the issuance of proper instructions on how to evacuate rather than simply sounding an evacuation alarm which may produce panic.

8-3.5 Extinguishment Requirements.   (*See 8-1.6, 8-2.6, and 8-3.2.*)

8-3.5.1 Fire Suppression Systems.   Every Class A and B place of assembly shall be protected throughout by an approved automatic sprinkler system.

Exception No. 1:   Auditoriums with fixed seating.

Exception No. 2:   Multipurpose educational occupancy auditoriums of less than 12,000 sq ft (1115 sq m) area.

Exception No. 3:   Passenger terminals at or above grade.

Exception No. 4:   Gymnasiums used for no other purpose.

Exception No. 5:   Skating rinks and swimming pools used exclusively for participant sport and no audience facilities for more than 300.

Exception No. 6:   Class B places of assembly used as restaurants.

This is a new requirement in the *Code* and results from recent fires involving places of assembly, most notably the Beverly Hills Supper Club fire (1977). The exceptions to the general requirement are important in that they limit the areas or buildings needing the protection.

Exception No. 1 exempts auditoriums with fixed seating from the requirement. However, other areas in the auditorium may require automatic suppression systems by other provisions of this *Code*. For example, stage areas, auxiliary stage spaces, and certain hazardous areas would still require this protection.

Exception No. 2 exempts multipurpose rooms in educational occupancies when the multipurpose room is less than 12,000 sq ft (1114.8 sq m). Multipurpose rooms larger than 12,000 sq ft (1114.8 sq m) require the protection because the size of the space indicates it may be used for other, more hazardous purposes.

Exception No. 3 exempts passenger terminals at or above grade from the requirement. In essence, this requires any below grade passenger terminal to be protected by an automatic suppression system.

Exception No. 4 exempts gymnasiums from the requirements if the gymnasium is used for no other purpose. If the gymnasium functions as a multipurpose room, then the 12,000 sq ft (1114.58 sq m) limitation applies.

Exception No. 5 exempts skating rinks (including ice or roller) and swimming pools where there is an audience or spectator gallery having an occupant load of 300 or less. If the skating rink or swimming pool can be floored over and used for other purposes, then the multipurpose room requirements apply. If the spectator gallery has an occupant load greater than 300, then an automatic system is required.

Exception No. 6 exempts Class B and C places of assembly (occupant load 50-1,000) used as restaurants. This exception recognizes the reasonably good life safety record of properly designed restaurants. However, the protection would be required in a restaurant with an occupant load over 1,000.

It should also be noted that automatic suppression systems may be required by 8-1.6 based on the location of the place of assembly, even though this paragraph would not normally require this protection.

SECTION 8-4   SPECIAL PROVISIONS

8-4.1 Windowless or Subterranean Buildings.   The requirements of places of assembly shall be in accordance with this chapter and Section 30-7 of this *Code*.

Many buildings which house places of assembly are windowless by design. In theaters, opera halls, concert halls, etc., windows are detrimental to operations. In recent years, large exhibition halls have also been constructed without windows.

Windowless buildings with an occupant load of 100 or more must be provided with a complete automatic extinguishing system — usually sprinklers. All windowless assembly occupancies must be provided with emergency lighting in accordance with Section 5-9 of the *Code*. By formal interpretation, the audience chambers of movie theaters are not required to be sprinklered since the committee does not consider them truly windowless if they have exits directly to the outside from the seating area.

Subterranean places of assembly require special consideration. Although they are similar to windowless buildings, additional problems of access for fire fighting and rescue are created when they are located in basements or subbasements of buildings. Exits, and where possible the exit accesses, must be adequately cut off from the assembly area by construction of partitions, walls, and doors of sufficient fire resistance. Positive means must be provided to prevent smoke from contaminating the exits. Like any windowless building, a subterranean place of assembly requires automatic sprinkler protection, emergency lighting, and a smoke evacuation system.

8-4.2 Outdoor Assembly.

8-4.2.1   All grandstands, tents, and other places of outdoor assembly shall comply with the requirements of *Tents, Grandstands and Air-Supported Structures*, NFPA 102.

When an outdoor place of assembly is created in an enclosed court so that exits can only be provided through a surrounding building, the requirements for exits, seating, and aisles must be the same as for an indoor assembly area.

8-4.3 Special Provisions for Exhibition Halls.

Exhibition halls have problems which differ from those of theaters, restaurants, or other places of assembly. They are large, multiuse facilities and have high ceilings appropriate to their size. Combustible materials are frequently displayed, and the containers in which the exhibits are shipped contribute to the fuel load. Due to the size of exhibition halls, most are required to be protected by automatic sprinklers by 8-3.5.

8-4.3.1   No display or exhibit shall be so installed or operated as to interfere in any way with access to any required exit or with visibility of any required exit or of any required exit sign nor shall any display block access to fire fighting equipment.

It is advisable to have prepared plans or diagrams to show the arrangement of displays or exhibits, including any which are to be suspended from the ceiling or an overhead structure. Displays or exhibits must never interfere in any way with access to any required exit, and they must not conceal exit signs. See Figure 8-11. A display should not block access to fire fighting equipment nor interfere with the normal operation of automatic extinguishing equipment or devices for smoke evacuation.

8-4.3.2   All displays or exhibits of combustible material or construction and all booths and temporary construction in connection therewith shall be so limited in combustibility or protected as to avoid any undue hazard of fire that might endanger occupants before they have the opportunity to use available exits, as determined by the authority having jurisdiction.

Displays or exhibits of combustible material must be limited in quantity in order to reduce the fuel load to an acceptable level. Excess combustible display material and all other combustible materials which are not in use should be kept in a separate storage room until needed. A separation with a fire resistance of 2 hours is required between such a storage room and all other parts of the building, and the room must be protected by an automatic sprinkler system.

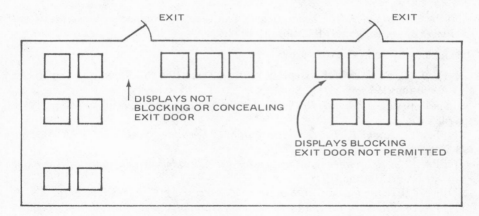

Figure 8-11.. Arrangement of Displays in an Exhibition Hall.

Rows of booths become exit accesses; therefore, booths and other temporary construction should be of minimal combustible construction or protected to avoid undue hazard of fire which might endanger occupants before they can reach available exits.

8-4.3.3 A storage room having an enclosure with a fire resistance rating of at least 2 hours and protected by an automatic fire extinguishing system shall be provided for combustible materials not on display.

SECTION 8-5   BUILDING SERVICES

8-5.1   Utilities shall comply with the provisions of Section 7-1.

8-5.2   Heating, ventilating, and air conditioning equipment shall comply with the provisions of Section 7-2.

8-5.3   Elevators, dumbwaiters, and vertical conveyors shall comply with the provisions of Section 7-4.

8-5.4   Rubbish chutes, incinerators, and laundry chutes shall comply with the provisions of Section 7-5.

REFERENCES CITED BY CODE

(These publications comprise a part of the requirements to the extent called for by the Code.)

NFPA 14, Standard for the Installation of Standpipe and Hose Systems, NFPA, Boston, 1980.

NFPA 40, Standard for the Storage and Handling of Cellulose Nitrate Motion Picture Film, NFPA, Boston, 1974.

NFPA 96, Standard for the Installation of Equipment for the Removal of Smoke and Grease-Laden Vapors from Commercial Cooking Equipment, NFPA, Boston, 1980.

NFPA 102, *Standard for Tents, Grandstands and Air-Supported Structures Used for Places of Assembly*, NFPA, Boston, 1978.

REFERENCES CITED IN COMMENTARY

[1] NFPA 102, *Standard for Assembly Seating, Tents, and Air-Supported Structures*, NFPA, Boston, 1978.

[2] John L. Bryan, *Automatic Sprinkler and Standpipe Systems*, NFPA, Boston, 1976, pp. 248-307.

[3] NFPA 13, *Standard for the Installation of Sprinkler Systems*, NFPA, Boston, 1980.

[4] NFPA 13A, *Recommended Practice for the Care and Maintenance of Sprinkler Systems*, NFPA, Boston, 1978.

[5] NFPA 72E, *Standard on Automatic Fire Detectors*, NFPA, Boston, 1978.

[6] NFPA 14, *Standard for the Installation of Standpipe and Hose Systems*, NFPA, Boston, 1980.

[7] NFPA 13E, *Recommendations for Fire Department Operations in Properties Protected by Sprinkler and Standpipe Systems*, NFPA, Boston, 1978.

[8] NFPA 40, *Standard for the Storage and Handling of Cellulose Nitrate Motion Picture Film*, NFPA, Boston, 1974.

[9] NFPA 220, *Standard Types of Building Construction*, NFPA, Boston, 1979.

[10] *Fire Protection Handbook*, 14th ed., NFPA, Boston, 1976, pp. 6-39 to 6-41.

9

EXISTING PLACES
OF ASSEMBLY

(See also Chapter 31.)

SECTION 9-1   GENERAL REQUIREMENTS

Places of assembly include, but are not limited to, all buildings or portions of buildings used for gathering together 50 or more people for such purposes as deliberation, worship, entertainment, amusement, or awaiting transportation. Assembly occupancies include, but are not limited to:

Theaters	Restaurants
Motion picture theaters	Churches
Assembly halls	Dance halls
Auditoriums	Club rooms
Exhibition halls	Passenger stations and terminals of
Museums	air, surface, underground, and
Skating rinks	marine public transportation
Gymnasiums	facilities
Bowling establishments	Recreation piers
Pool rooms	Courtrooms
Armories	Conference rooms
Mortuary chapels	Drinking establishments
Libraries	

Chapter 31 specifies the life safety requirements for the operation of places of assembly.

9-1.1 Application.   The requirements of this chapter apply to existing places of assembly. *(See 9-1.3 for definition.)*

This 1981 Edition of the *Code* has divided most occupancies into separate chapters for new and existing. The provisions for new places of assembly are found in Chapter 8.

It should be noted that if an existing building of some other occupancy were to change occupancies to a place of assembly, the portion of the building housing the assembly occupancy must comply with Chapter 8 for new places of assembly even though it is in an existing building. (See 1-6.4 of the *Code*.)

217

Exception: An existing building housing an assembly occupancy established prior to the effective date of this Code may have its use continued if it conforms to or is made to conform to the provisions of this Code to the extent that, in the opinion of the authority having jurisdiction, reasonable life safety against the hazards of fire, explosions, and panic is provided and maintained.

It is not the intent of the *Code* to make existing places of assembly conform precisely to the requirements for new occupancies. It is, however, the intent of the *Code* that existing places of assembly comply to the extent that reasonable life safety is provided.

A place of assembly for which plans and specifications were approved and a permit was issued prior to the adoption of this *Code* may be considered to have been legally established prior to the adoption of the *Code*. However, if the authority having jurisdiction believes that there is an adequate level of life safety in an existing or previously approved place of assembly, he or she may require intermediate design measures which, while not meeting all the requirements for new construction, will raise the level of life safety to an equivalent level. Automatic sprinklers, detection systems, compartmentation (subdivision of the space), or additional exits may serve this purpose.

9-1.2 Mixed Occupancies.

9-1.2.1   Any place of assembly and its access to exits in buildings of other occupancy, such as ballrooms in hotels, restaurants in stores, rooftop places of assembly, or assembly rooms in schools shall be so located, separated, or protected as to avoid any undue danger to the occupants of the place of assembly from a fire originating in the other occupancy or smoke therefrom.

Generally, division by a partition with a fire resistance of at least 1 hour is recommended to establish a degree of separation between the place of assembly and the remainder of the building. If possible, 2-hour fire resistance should be pursued. The partition should extend totally around the assembly space and should be continuous from the floor slab through any interstitial space to the slab of the floor or roof above. Instead of separation, protection of the other occupancy by automatic sprinklers or other appropriate measures might be sufficient.

In buildings of fire-resistive construction where the hazard of the other occupancy is low or moderate (as in schools or hotels), separation of the place of assembly may not be necessary.

9-1.2.2   Occupancy of any room or space for assembly purposes by less than 50 persons in a building of other occupancy and incidental to such other occupancy shall be classed as part of the other occupancy and subject to the provisions applicable thereto.

Fifty has traditionally been considered the lowest number of people assembled in one space for which the *Code* requires special provisions, such as a door having to swing in the direction of exit travel (see 5-2.1.1.4.1). Therefore, in Chapter 9, 50 people constitute a sufficiently high level of risk to life safety to require classifying an occupancy as a place of assembly and, consequently, to subject the occupancy to the special design requirements found within this chapter.

9-1.2.3 Places of assembly in buildings of other occupancy may use exits common to the place of assembly and the other occupancy provided that the assembly area and the other occupancy considered separately each have exits sufficient to meet the requirements of this *Code*.

9-1.2.4 Exits shall be sufficient for simultaneous occupancy of both the place of assembly and other parts of the building.

Exception: Where the authority having jurisdiction determines that the conditions are such that simultaneous occupancy will not occur, such as in certain schools as designated in Chapter 11.

Here, the *Code* requires that each occupancy, considered separately, have sufficient exits and that, when it is possible for simultaneous occupancy to occur, the exits be sufficient for the combined occupant load. An example of a situation in which simultaneous occupancy of a place of assembly and another occupancy does not usually occur is that of an assembly room for the inmates of a detention or correctional occupancy.

9-1.3 Special Definitions.

Arena Stage. A stage or platform open on at least three sides to audience seating. It may be with or without overhead scene handling facilities.

Theater-in-the-round is an example of an arena stage.

Places of Assembly. Include but are not limited to all buildings or portions of buildings used for gathering together 50 or more persons for such purpose as deliberation, worship, entertainment, dining, amusement, or awaiting transportation.

Platform, Enclosed. A partially enclosed portion of an assembly room, the ceiling of which is not more than 5 ft (152.4 cm) above the proscenium opening, that is designed or used for the presentation of plays, demonstrations, or other entertainment wherein scenery, drops, decorations, or other effects may be installed or used.

Proscenium Wall. A fire-resistive wall that separates a stage or enclosed platform from the public or spectators' area of an auditorium or theater.

Stage. A partially enclosed portion of an assembly building that is designed or used for the presentation of plays, demonstrations, or other entertainment wherein scenery, drops, or other effects may be installed or used and where the distance between the top of the proscenium opening and the ceiling above the stage is more than 5 ft (152.4 cm).

As shown in Figure 9-1A, the criterion for distinguishing between an enclosed platform and a stage is the distance from the top of the proscenium opening to the ceiling of the platform or stage. The 5-ft (152.4-cm) criterion limits the quantity and type of fuel load (such as combustible scenery or lights) which the proscenium arch of an enclosed platform can realistically conceal. The other portion of a stage (significant to life safety but not discussed in this portion of the *Code*) is the fly galleries located to the rear and sides of the stage. If fly galleries are incorporated in the stage construction, significant amounts of combustible fuel in the form of scenery and backdrops should be expected. Automatic extinguishment systems should be provided for these areas.

Thrust Stage. That portion of a stage that projects into the audience on the audience side of a proscenium wall or opening.

An arena stage is illustrated in Figure 9-1B. A typical example of a thrust stage is the so-called "runway" at Atlantic City that is used annually for the Miss America Pageant. See Figure 9-1C.

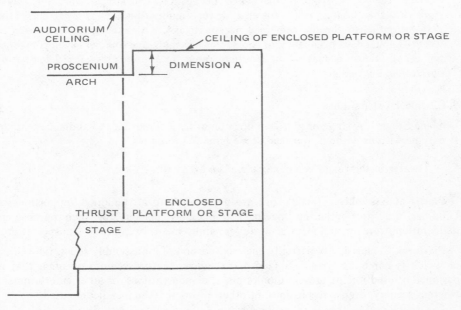

Figure 9-1A. Difference Between an Enclosed Platform and a Stage. If Dimension A < 5 ft (152.4 cm), construction is classed as an "enclosed platform"; if Dimension A > 5 ft (152.4 cm), construction is classed as a "stage."

9-1.4 Classification of Occupancy. *(See 4-1.2.)*

9-1.4.1 Classification of Places of Assembly. Each place of assembly shall be classified according to its capacity, as follows: Class A, capacity 1000 persons or more; Class B, capacity 300 to 1000 persons; Class C, capacity 50 to 300 persons.

As each increment of population is reached, the level of risk to life safety from exposure to fire rises. In view of this, the stringency of the requirements found in this chapter increases to counter each higher risk level.

9-1.5 Classification of Hazard of Contents. Contents of assembly occupancies shall be classified in accordance with the provisions of Section 4-2.

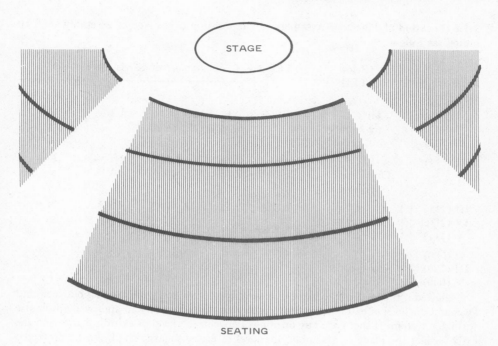

Figure 9-1B. Arena Stage.

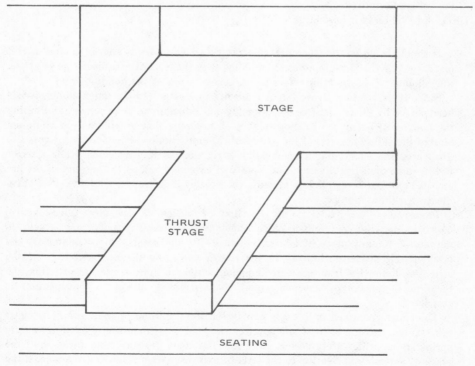

Figure 9-1C. Thrust Stage.

9-1.6 Location of Places of Assembly. The location of a place of assembly shall be limited as follows:

Type of Construction	Below LED	LED	Number of Levels Above LED			
			1	2	3	4 & Above
I (443) I (332) II (222)	A†B†C† Any Number of Levels	ABC	ABC	ABC	ABC	A†BC
II (111)	A†B†C† One Level Below LED	ABC	ABC	A†BC	B†C†	N.P.
III (211) IV (2HH) V (111)	A†B†C† One Level Below LED	ABC	ABC	A†B†C	B†C†	N.P.
II (000) III (200) V (000)	B†C† One Level Below LED	BC	C†	N.P.	N.P.	N.P.

†Allowed if the level of the place of assembly and any story intervening between that level and the level of exit discharge are protected throughout by an approved automatic sprinkler system. If there are any openings between the level of exit discharge and the exits serving the place of assembly, the level of exit discharge shall also be protected throughout by an approved automatic sprinkler system (*see Section 7-7*).

N.P. — Not Permitted
LED — Level of Exit Discharge

It should be noted that the chart is arranged based on levels above the level of exit discharge (LED). Thus, in a normal building with the level of exit discharge at grade, the column "1" in the table refers to the second story of the building.

Since the Cocoanut Grove Night Club fire in Boston (1942), much emphasis has been placed by the Committee on Assembly and Educational Occupancies on limiting the number of occupants in those places of assembly that provide only a minimum level of life safety because of the nature of the construction. The Cocoanut Grove fire illustrated the effect that a combustible structure (as well as combustible interior finish) and a multilevel location for a place of assembly had on the severity of the fire and its high death count. More recently the Beverly Hills Supper Club fire (1977) also illustrated these factors.

Paragraph 9-1.6 restricts the location of places of assembly. Fire-resistive construction, with its "built-in-place" structural survivability (under fire attack), is acceptable for any place of assembly (hence, for any number of occupants) at the level of exit discharge and up to the fourth story. As the fire resistivity of the structure diminishes from protected noncombustible to wood-frame construction, the location of places of assembly (and the permitted number of occupants) is restricted.

The chart contained in 9-1.6 is new in the 1981 Edition of the *Code*. The chart represents a revision of the *Code* requirements and recognizes the value of automatic sprinklers as a life safety device. Note that the chart deals with the location of the place of assembly in relation to the level of exit discharge. Thus, for example, if the building in question was a seven-story, fire-resistive (Type I) building with the level of exit discharge at the first floor, a Class A place of assembly could be located at the fourth floor without sprinkler protection. If the Class A place of assembly were located at the fifth floor, automatic sprinkler protection would be required for the fifth floor, as well as for the first through fourth floors. (See note to chart.) If the first floor of the building was so arranged that the exit stairs servicing the assembly floor were enclosed to the outside with no door openings into the first story or level of exit discharge, then sprinklers would not be required at that level.

Any place of assembly located below the level of exit discharge requires automatic sprinkler protection, as do all levels intervening between the assembly level and the level of exit discharge. The same rule concerning openings into the stair at the level of exit discharge applies.

Also note that in unrated construction (000), only Class B and C places of assembly are permitted at the level of discharge.

9-1.7 Occupant Load.

9-1.7.1   The occupant load permitted in any assembly building, structure, or portion thereof shall be determined by dividing the net floor area or space assigned to that use by the square foot (square meter) per occupant as follows:

(a) An assembly area of concentrated use without fixed seats such as an auditorium, church, chapel, dance floor, or lodge room — 7 sq ft (.65 sq m) per person.

(b) An assembly area of less concentrated use such as a conference room, dining room, drinking establishment, exhibit room, gymnasium, or lounge — 15 sq ft (1.39 sq m) per person.

(c) Standing room or waiting space — 3 sq ft (.28 sq m) per person.

See 9-1.7.3 for locations where this occupant load factor can be used.

(d) Bleachers, pews, and similar bench-type seating — 18 linear in. (45.72 linear cm) per person.

(e) Fixed seating. The occupant load of an area having fixed seats shall be determined by the number of fixed seats installed. Required aisle space serving the fixed seats shall not be used to increase the occupant load.

(f) Libraries. In stack areas — 100 sq ft (9.3 sq m) per person; in reading rooms — 50 sq ft (4.7 sq m) per person.

Exception: The authority having jurisdiction may permit occupancy by number of persons not to exceed that for which the existing means of egress are adequate, provided that measures are established to prevent occupancy by any greater number of persons than permitted by room area or by fixed seating.

The occupant load factors of 9-1.7.1 reflect the data developed from surveys of typical occupancies.

Figure 9-2A illustrates a room or area with two 36-in. (91.44-cm) doors, each providing one-and-a-half exit units, or a total of three exit units. Using only the criterion of exit capacity, such a room would be permitted 300 occupants. However, since this room has an area of 2,500 sq ft (232.25 sq m) per person, the area will permit only 167 occupants. However, 9-1.7.2 makes provisions for possibly increasing this figure.

Both criteria (exit capacity and occupant load) must be considered in establishing the permissible occupant load for a room or area. For example, the exit capacity of the room in Figure 9-2B is sufficient for an occupant load of 300 people. An occupant load calculated on the basis of the room size (3,600 sq ft ÷ 7) would permit 514 people. The exit capacity of 300 must govern. This is allowed because of the special exception for existing buildings; in new construction, the exit capacity would be required to increase to five-and-a-half units of exit width in accordance with 5-3.1.2 since exit capacity must be provided for the occupant load determined by application of the occupant load factor.

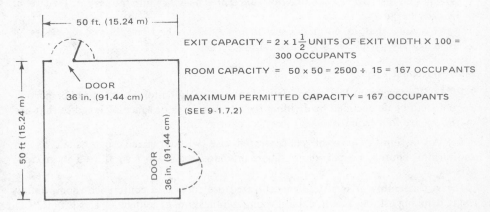

Figure 9-2A. Determination of Maximum Permitted Occupant Load for an Existing Place of Assembly by Room Capacity.

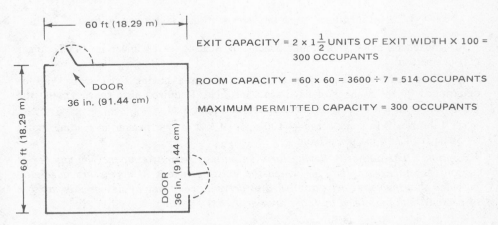

Figure 9-2B. Determination of Occupant Load for an Existing Place of Assembly by Exit Capacity.

9-1.7.2 The occupant load permitted in a building or portion thereof may be increased above that specified in 9-1.7.1 if the necessary aisles and exits are provided. To increase the occupant load a diagram indicating placement of equipment, aisles, exits, and seating shall be provided to and approved by the authority having jurisdiction prior to any increase in occupant load.

The accessibility of room exits is as important as the exit capacity. Therefore, when an increase is permitted over the occupant load established by 9-1.7.1, it must be demonstrated that adequate aisles and access ways are provided leading to the room exits. Spacing of tables must provide for occupied chairs plus an aisle. Consideration should be given to the probability that when occupants leave during an emergency, they may not take time to move chairs out of the aisles.

Dining and drinking areas most frequently take advantage of the provision of 9-1.7.2. There have been large banquet layouts where the occupant load was successfully increased to reflect a population density factor of 11 sq ft (1.02 sq m) per person instead of the 15 sq ft (1.39 sq m) per person specified by item (b) of 9-1.7.1. In all cases where an increase in the occupant load is permitted, the authority having jurisdiction should insist on complete fixture and furniture layouts and should strictly enforce adherence to approved layouts. Note that the same room may have several approved occupant loads depending on the various fixture and furniture layouts.

When situations like these arise, another governing factor for occupant load is that the load should not exceed the maximum amount which would affect the practical operation of the place of assembly. For example, a restaurant so crowded that the servers cannot pass between the tables will soon go out of business. This serves as a controlling factor in limiting the expected population of a space.

Finally, the authority having jurisdiction cannot permit a population which would crowd a space to the point where the people would not have ready and quick access to exits. It has been shown in research at the National Research Council in Canada and by the London Transport Board that if people are crowded into a space so that each person is occupying less than 7 sq ft (.65 sq m), then movement is approaching a "shuffle"; and when each person is occupying less than 3 sq ft (.28 sq m), "jam point" is approached and all movement by the occupants is effectively stopped. These figures should also be used by the authority having jurisdiction in making a decision concerning the maximum permitted occupant load.

See Figures 9-3A and 9-3B for two examples of increasing occupant load.

9-1.7.3 Waiting Spaces.   In theaters and similar places of public assembly where persons are admitted to the building at times when seats are not available for them and are allowed to wait in a lobby or similar space until seats are available, such use of lobby or similar space shall not encroach upon the required clear width of exits. Such waiting shall be restricted to areas other than the required means of egress. Exits shall be provided for such waiting spaces on the basis of one person for each 3 sq ft (.28 sq m) of waiting space area. Such exits shall be in addition to the exits specified for the main auditorium area and shall conform in construction and arrangement to the general rules for exits given in this chapter.

SECTION 9-2   MEANS OF EGRESS REQUIREMENTS

9-2.1 General.   (*See 9-1.2, Mixed Occupancies.*)

9-2.2 Types of Exits.

9-2.2.1   Exits of the specified number and width shall be of one or more of the following types, in accordance with the provisions of Chapter 5 of this *Code*:

(a) Doors of the swinging type leading directly outside or to a lobby or passageway leading to the outside of the building (*see 5-2.1*)

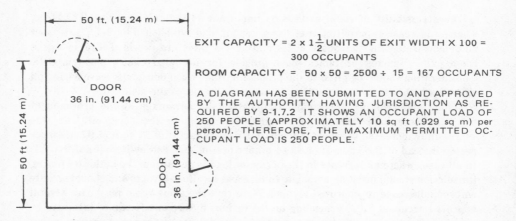

EXIT CAPACITY = 2 x 1½ UNITS OF EXIT WIDTH X 100 = 300 OCCUPANTS

ROOM CAPACITY = 50 x 50 = 2500 ÷ 15 = 167 OCCUPANTS

A DIAGRAM HAS BEEN SUBMITTED TO AND APPROVED BY THE AUTHORITY HAVING JURISDICTION AS REQUIRED BY 9-1.7.2 IT SHOWS AN OCCUPANT LOAD OF 250 PEOPLE (APPROXIMATELY 10 sq ft (.929 sq m) per person). THEREFORE, THE MAXIMUM PERMITTED OCCUPANT LOAD IS 250 PEOPLE.

Figure 9-3A. Determination of Maximum Permitted Occupant Load for an Existing Place of Assembly by Room Capacity. Note that a practical upper limit for the room's population, which will still ensure rapid and orderly movement to an exit, may be 2,500 ÷ 7 = 357 people, based on research by the London Transport Board. Since the exit capacity provides for 300 people, the authority having jurisdiction could conceivably allow a maximum permitted occupant load of 300.

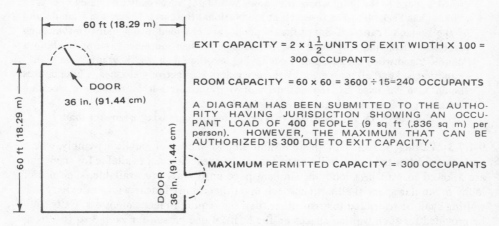

EXIT CAPACITY = 2 x 1½ UNITS OF EXIT WIDTH X 100 = 300 OCCUPANTS

ROOM CAPACITY = 60 x 60 = 3600 ÷ 15 = 240 OCCUPANTS

A DIAGRAM HAS BEEN SUBMITTED TO THE AUTHORITY HAVING JURISDICTION SHOWING AN OCCUPANT LOAD OF 400 PEOPLE (9 sq ft (.836 sq m) per person). HOWEVER, THE MAXIMUM THAT CAN BE AUTHORIZED IS 300 DUE TO EXIT CAPACITY.

MAXIMUM PERMITTED CAPACITY = 300 OCCUPANTS

Figure 9-3B. Determination of Maximum Permitted Occupant Load for an Existing Place of Assembly by Exit Capacity. Note that a practical upper limit for the room's population, which will still ensure rapid and orderly movement to an exit, may be 3,600 ÷ 7 = 514 people, based on research by the London Transport Board. However, the exit capacity of 300 must determine the maximum permitted occupant load.

(b) Horizontal exits (*see 5-2.4*)

(c) Smokeproof towers (*see 5-2.3*)

(d) Interior stairs, Class A or Class B (*see 5-2.2*)

(e) Outside stairs. Same requirements as for interior stairs, including intermediate handrails on monumental stairs serving main entrance doors (*see 5-2.5*)

(f) Ramps, Class A or Class B (*see 5-2.6*)

(g) Escalators (*see 5-2.8*)

(h) Exit passageways (*see 5-2.7*)

(i) Fire escape stairs (*see 5-2.9*).

9-2.2.2 Turnstiles. No turnstiles, revolving doors, or other devices to restrict the movement of persons shall be installed in any place of assembly in such a manner as to interfere in any way with required exit facilities.

Elevators, slide escapes, and revolving doors are not recognized as constituting required exits in existing places of assembly. Revolving doors and fire escapes have frequently shown up as contributing factors to fire disasters in places of assembly. Slide escapes and elevators are not suited for rapid evacuation of the large numbers of people found in these occupancies. Further, elevators introduce other risk factors if used during a fire. (See Section 7-4.) It should be noted that these devices can be installed, but cannot obstruct or interfere with the required means of egress.

9-2.3 Capacity of Means of Egress.

9-2.3.1 Every place of assembly, every tier or balcony, and every individual room used as a place of assembly shall have exits sufficient to provide for the total capacity thereof as determined in accordance with 9-1.7 and as follows:

(a) No individual unit of exit width shall serve more than 100 persons.

(b) Doors leading outside the building at grade level or not more than three risers above or below grade, Class A ramps, or horizontal exits — 100 persons per exit unit adjusted according to location of exits as required in 9-2.3.2 and 9-2.3.3.

(c) Stairs or other type of exit not specified in (b) above — 75 persons per exit unit.

The difference between the requirements for doors at ground level and for stairs is based on their rated capacity: 60 persons per minute per unit of exit width for level exit through doors, 45 down stairs. These figures provide an evacuation time of 1 minute 40 seconds, assuming the rated capacity and travel rate, exclusive of the time for the first person to reach the exit and for the last person to reach a place of safety after entering the exit.

The provisions of 9-2.3.1 are based on the assumption that all the occupants of a place of assembly may start for the exits at the same moment. The situation is different in other types of occupancies where it is assumed that only the occupants of a single floor will rush to the exits at the immediate outbreak of fire, and that occupants of other floors can use the same stairways afterwards.

9-2.3.2 Main Exit. Every assembly occupancy shall be provided with a main exit. The main exit shall be of sufficient width to accommodate one-half of the total occupant load but shall be not less than the total required width of all aisles, exit passageways, and stairways leading thereto and shall be at the level of exit discharge or shall connect to a stairway or ramp leading to a street.

Exception No. 1: A bowling establishment shall have a main exit of sufficient capacity to accommodate 50 percent of the total occupant load without regard to the number of aisles that it serves.

Exception No. 2:   In assembly occupancies such as stadiums, sports arenas, and passenger stations, exits may be distributed around the perimeter of the building provided the total exit width provides 116⅔ percent of the width needed to accommodate the permitted occupant load.

The usual entrance to an assembly occupancy also generally serves as its main exit. As a rule, people leave a building by way of their entrance to the structure. Therefore, the main exit should be sized to accommodate at least 50 percent of the occupants; however, it must not be less in width than the sum of the *required* widths of the aisles which it serves.

Bowling establishments usually have relatively few rows of seats for spectators, but are necessarily wide to accommodate the alleys. Due to the limitation of not more than six seats intervening between any seat and an aisle, many more aisles are required than in other types of assembly occupancies. Exception No. 1 to 9-2.3.2 modifies what would be the excessive main exit width required to accommodate the sum of the required aisle widths served by the exit. Exception No. 2 clarifies the intent of the *Code* to provide the 16⅔ percent increase in exit capacity in buildings having no main exit. The intent is to distribute the extra width reasonably equally to all exits.

Figures 9-4A and 9-4B demonstrate how to calculate the required aisle widths and also provide for width increases as the number of seats (and the number of people) increases; how to split the occupant load (seating) between the main exit (50 percent must be assigned to the main exit) and the side exits; how to provide sufficient lobby depth to accommodate 50 percent of the aisles; and how to size the exits without effectively reducing the width of the aisles leading to them.

9-2.3.3 Other Exits.   Each level of an assembly occupancy shall have access to the main exit *and* shall be provided with exits of sufficient width to accommodate two-thirds of the total occupant load served by that level. Such exits shall discharge directly to a street or into an exit court, enclosed stairway, outside stairway, or exit passageway leading to a street. Such exits shall be located as far apart as practicable and as far from the main exit as practicable. Such exits shall be accessible from a cross aisle or a side aisle (*see 9-2.3.2*).

Exception: Where only two exits are required, each exit shall be of sufficient width to accommodate not less than half the total occupant load.

As an example of the requirements of 9-2.3.3, if a place of assembly had an occupant load of 300, the main exit would have to accommodate 150 people (50 percent). If there were two additional exits, together they would have to accommodate 200 people (two-thirds of the occupant load). Essentially, where more than two exits are required, the sum of the exit capacity must be at least one-sixth greater than (or 116⅔ percent of) the total required by the occupant load. Also, 9-2.4.2 requires that in a Class B place of assembly with a capacity of more than 600 people, at least three exits must be provided and no exit may be less than two units of exit width [44 in. (111.76 cm)]. The arrangement illustrated in Figure 9-4A incorporates these principles. Calculations for required exit capacities and aisle widths for this place of assembly are shown in Figure 9-4B.

These requirements provide some relief from the congestion which would result if an exit should become unusable during a fire.

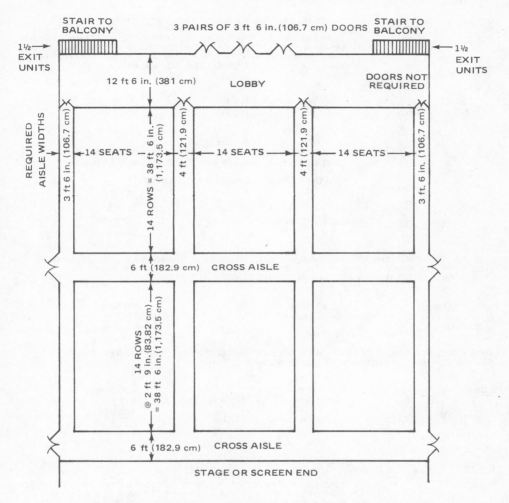

Figure 9-4A. Calculation of the Capacity of Means of Egress for a Place of Assembly with Fixed Seating. The illustrated example has an occupant load of 1,176 calculated by multiplying the number of seats in a row by the number of rows [see 9-1.7.1(e)]. The number of seats in a row between aisles (14) is the maximum allowed by 9-2.5.3(b).

9-2.4 Number of Exits.

9-2.4.1   Every Class A place of assembly (capacity over 1,000 persons or more) shall have at least four separate exits as remote from each other as practicable.

9-2.4.2   Every Class B place of assembly (capacity over 300 to 1,000 persons) shall have at least two separate exits as remote from each other as practicable, and if of a capacity of over 600, at least three separate exits, each not less than two exit units wide.

9-2.4.3   Every Class C place of assembly (capacity 50 to 300 persons) shall have at least two means of egress, consisting of separate exits or doors leading to a corridor or

REQUIRED AISLE WIDTH   38 ft 6 in. x ½ = 19 ft 3 in. ÷ 5 = 4 INCREMENTS @ 1½ in. = 6 in.

[9-2.5.4(a)]   19 ft 3 in. IS THE GREATEST DISTANCE BETWEEN ANY POINT
IN AN AISLE AND AN EXIT, CROSS AISLE, OR FOYER.
4 INCREMENTS ARE THE NUMBER OF 5-ft INCREMENTS FOR
WHICH 1½ in. MUST BE ADDED TO THE AISLE WIDTH.

SIDE AISLE   3 ft 0 in. + 6 in. = 3 ft 6 in.
OTHER AISLE   3 ft 6 in. + 6 in. = 4 ft 0 in.

CAPACITY OF MAIN EXIT   ½ OCCUPANT LOAD = $\frac{1176}{2}$ = 588 OCCUPANTS = 6 EXIT
UNITS (100 OCCUPANTS EACH) = 6 x 22 in. = 11 ft 0 in.

(9-2.3.2)   SUM OF REQUIRED AISLES AND EXITS:

AISLES   2 @ 3 ft 6 in. + 2 @ 4 ft 0 in. =   15 ft 0 in.
BALCONY EXITS   2 @ 1½ EXIT UNITS = 3 x 22 in. =   <u>5 ft 6 in.</u>
                                      20 ft 6 in.

20 ft 6 in. GOVERNS THE CAPACITY SINCE THE MAIN EXIT CANNOT BE LESS THAN THE
WIDTH OF THE AISLES AND STAIRWAYS LEADING TO IT. PROVIDING 3 PAIRS OF
3 ft 6 in. DOORS (21 ft 0 in.) WOULD MEET THE CODE'S REQUIREMENTS.

CROSS AISLES   1 @ 4 ft 0 in. =   4 ft 0 in.
              ½(4 ft 0 in.) =   <u>2 ft 0 in.</u>
[9-2.5.4(c)]   6 ft 0 in.

SIDE AISLES LEADING DIRECTLY TO AN EXIT NEED NOT BE CONSIDERED WHEN
CALCULATING THE WIDTH OF THE CROSS AISLE.

LOBBY WIDTH   AISLES: 1 @ 4 ft 0 in. =   4 ft 0 in.
                      ½(4 ft 0 in. + 3 ft 6 in. + 3 ft 6 in.) =   <u>5 ft 6 in.</u>
[9-2.5.4(c)]   9 ft 6 in.
            BALCONY: ½(2 ft 10 in. + 2 ft 10 in.) =   <u>2 ft 10 in.</u>
                                      12 ft 6 in.

CAPACITY OF SIDE EXITS   TOTAL OCCUPANT LOAD = 1176

(9-2.3.3)   THE 4 EXITS MUST PROVIDE 2/3 OF TOTAL OCCUPANT LOAD
(784 OCCUPANTS). 784 ÷ 4 = 196 OCCUPANT LOAD EACH
SIDE EXIT = 2 EXIT UNITS. CAN BE SATISFIED BY 1 DOOR
44 in. WIDE. HOWEVER, FROM A PRACTICAL STANDPOINT, THIS
WOULD NOT TAKE FULL ADVANTAGE OF THE WIDTH OF THE
CROSS AISLE. RECOMMEND USING AS A MINIMUM,
1 PAIR OF 3 ft 0 in. DOORS.

1 in. = 2.54 cm; 1 ft = 30.48 cm

Figure 9-4B. Calculations for the Required Aisle Widths and Exit Capacities for the Place of Assembly Illustrated in Figure 9-4A.

other spaces giving access to two separate and independent exits in different directions.

As the concentration or number of people increases in a place of assembly, the chance of a simultaneous exiting by a sizable group of occupants increases. Therefore, to reduce jamming at doorways (which leads to panic and disorder), more exits at a variety of locations are needed. Paragraphs 9-2.4.1 to 9-2.4.3 provide for this design requirement.

Since 9-1.2.2 specifies that assembly areas with individual occupant loads of fewer than 50 people in buildings of occupancies other than assembly shall be classed as part of the other occupancy, no criteria are given for the number and location of exits in such an occupancy by 9-2.4.

9-2.5 Arrangement of Means of Egress.

9-2.5.1 Exits shall be remote from each other and shall be arranged to minimize the possibility that they may be blocked by any emergency.

Exception: A common path of travel may be permitted for the first 20 ft (609.6 cm) from any point.

Separation of exits as far as practicable cannot be overemphasized. Two or more exits which are located too close to each other can become unusable during the same incident. The fundamental principles of this *Code*, as expressed in Chapter 2, require remoteness of exits to the point that a single fire event will not simultaneously block both exits.

Revolving rooftop places of assembly need special consideration; as the structure revolves, exit signs are often lost from view. To provide an unobstructed panoramic view, the exterior element revolves around a small stationary interior core in which the exits are often located. In many cases the two exits are too close to each other to avoid involving both exits in case of fire. Usually at least one stairway must transfer from its position in the stationary core to the normal location of the building stairways. This transfer, since it is a continuation of the stairway, must be made in an exit passageway possessing a fire resistance equal to that required for the stair enclosure.

9-2.5.2 Means of egress shall not be permitted through kitchens, storerooms, restrooms, closets, or hazardous areas as described in 9-3.2.

The purpose of this requirement, which is new in the 1981 Edition of the *Code*, is to make clear that exit access travel is not permitted to pass through areas subject to locking or areas possessing a hazard higher than that normal for the occupancy.

9-2.5.3 Seating.

(a) The spacing of rows of seats shall provide a space of not less than 12 in. (30.48 cm) from the back of one seat to the front of the most forward projection of the seat immediately behind it, when the seat is in the down position as measured horizontally between vertical planes.

(b) Rows of seats between aisles shall have not more than 14 seats.

(c) Rows of seats opening onto an aisle at one end only shall have not more than seven seats.

(d) Seats without dividing arms shall have their capacity determined by allowing 18 in. (45.72 cm) per person.

In other than continental seating, not more than six seats may intervene between any seat in a row and an aisle. This permits a maximum of 14 seats in a row which terminates with an aisle at each end. Where seats are served by an aisle at one end only, not more than seven seats may be provided in any such row. Figure 9-5A illustrates these requirements, which are specified in 9-2.5.3(b) and (c).

The requirement for the spacing between rows of seats [see 9-2.5.3(a)] is illustrated in Figure 9-5B. Note that when seats with self-storing table arms, as found in schools, are used, the distance required in 9-2.5.3(a) should be measured with the table arm in the up or in-use position (see Figure 9-5C).

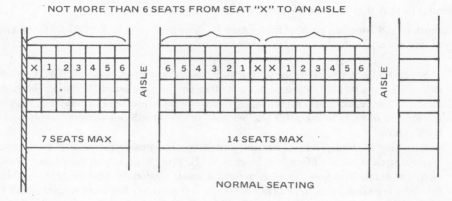

Figure 9-5A. Arrangement of Seats and Aisles in Place of Assembly Without Continental Seating.

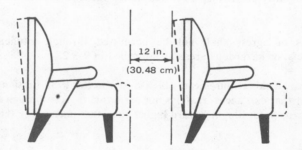

Figure 9-5B. Correct Measurement of Minimum Spacing Between Rows of Seats in Place of Assembly Without Continental Seating [see 9-2.5.3(a)].

Paragraph 9-2.5.3(d) applies to bench-type seats or to pews without dividing arms. Benches or pews may be 21 ft (6.4 m) long (14 persons × 18 in.) between aisles and 10½ ft (3.2 m) long (7 persons × 18 in.) where an aisle occurs at one end only. Small increases in these lengths [less than 18 in. (45.72 cm)] may be approved in order to provide more comfort for occupants.

(e) Where bleacher or grandstand seating without backs is used, indoors rows of seats shall be spaced not less than 22 in. (55.88 cm) nor more than 30 in. (76.2 cm) back to back. Vertical aisles shall be provided when such seating is more than eleven

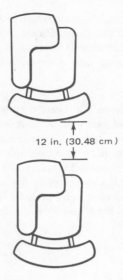

Figure 9-5C. Minimum Spacing Between Rows of Seats with Self-Storing Table Arms. Measure with the table arm in the up (in-use) position. There must be 12 in. (30.48 cm) between the back of a seat and the leading edge of a table arm.

rows high. Vertical aisles, where provided, shall not have a dead end in excess of sixteen rows. The rise per row shall not exceed 12 in. (30.48 cm).

Exception: Folding or telescopic seating shall comply with Standard for Tents, Grandstands and Air-Supported Structures Used for Places of Assembly, NFPA 102, with a limit of dead ends in vertical aisles of sixteen rows.

The elimination of backs allows the entire bleacher to be a path of exit access. People can simultaneously evacuate a bleacher upward or downward without using aisles. This compensates for the openness of bleacher-type structures which can expose the entire population to a single fire either under or adjacent to the structure. The provisions of the *Code* concerning bleachers or graduated seating and folding or telescopic seating have been modified to coordinate requirements with NFPA 102, *Standard for Assembly Seating, Tents, and Air-Supported Structures*.[1]

(f) Continental seating.

1. With continental seating, the spacing of rows of unoccupied seats shall provide a clear width between rows measured horizontally as follows (automatic or self-rising seats shall be measured in the seat-up position; other seats shall be measured in the seat-down position); 18-in. (45.72-cm) clear width between rows of 18 seats or less; 20-in. (50.8-cm) clear width between rows of 35 seats or less; 21-in. (53.34-cm) clear width between rows of 45 seats or less; 22-in. (55.88-cm) clear width between rows of 46 seats or more, and

2. There shall be not more than 100 seats in a row between aisles at both sides of the seating areas, and

3. Exit doors shall be provided along each side aisle of the row of seats at the rate of one pair of exit doors for each five rows of seats. There shall be not more than five seat rows between pairs of doors. Such exit doors shall provide a minimum clear width of 66 in. (167.64 cm) discharging into a foyer, lobby, or to the exterior of the building.

With continental seating, up to 100 seats may be provided in a row. This large number of seats requires a full exit unit of clear width between the rows of seats. Lesser widths between the rows reduce the permissible number of seats in a row. Because continental seating feeds so many occupants into the side aisles, frequent exits from the side aisles are required. Therefore, the *Code* requires that there be one pair of doors 66 in. (167.64 cm) wide for every five rows of seats, and that not more than five rows of seats occur between pairs of doors leading from the side aisles to an exit access or an exit. Figures 9-6A and 9-6B illustrate these requirements.

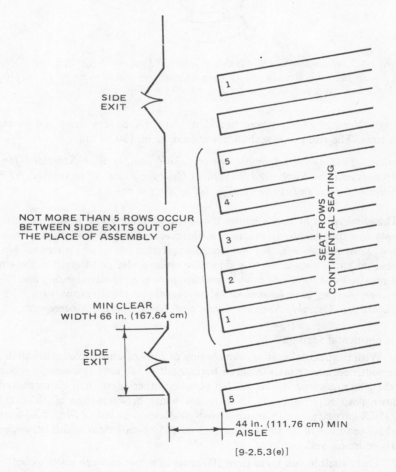

Figure 9-6A. Arrangement of Continental Seating in Place of Assembly. Each row may contain up to 100 seats.

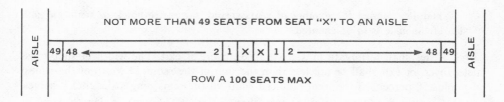

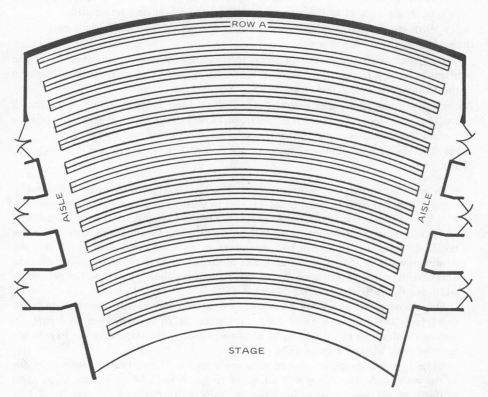

Figure 9-6B. Arrangement of Seats and Aisles in Place of Assembly with Continental Seating. Note that 100 seats is the maximum number for one row and that the maximum number of intervening seats between any one seat and an aisle is 49 seats. Note, too, the frequency of the exits from the side aisles in the depicted theater arrangement.

9-2.5.4 Aisles. Every portion of any assembly building that contains seats, tables, displays, equipment, or other materials shall be provided with aisles leading to exits as follows:

(a) When serving more than 60 seats, every aisle shall be not less than 3 ft (91.44 cm) wide when serving seats on one side only and not less than 3 ft 6 in. (106.68 cm) wide when serving seats on both sides. Such minimum width shall be measured at the point farthest from an exit, cross aisle, or foyer and shall be increased in width by 1½ in. (3.81 cm) for each 5 ft (152.4 cm) in length toward the exit, cross aisle, or foyer.

(b) When serving 60 seats or less, aisles shall be not less than 30 in. (76.2 cm) wide.

When determining the number of seats served, the entire block of seats on each side of the aisle is to be counted.

(c) Aisles shall terminate in a cross aisle, foyer, or exit. The width of such cross aisle, foyer, or exit shall be not less than the sum of the required width of the widest aisle plus 50 percent of the total required width of the remaining aisles that it serves.

(d) Existing dead-end aisles greater than 20 ft (609.6 cm) in length may be continued in use subject to the approval of the authority having jurisdiction.

(e) With continental seating as set forth in 9-2.5.3(f), side aisles shall be not less than 44 in. (111.76 cm) in width.

(f) Steps shall not be placed in aisles to overcome differences in level unless the gradient exceeds 1 ft (1 cm) of rise in 8 ft (8 cm) of run. Steps in aisles shall conform to the requirements for Class A stairs as to rise and run.

Exception: In balconies and galleries rise and run shall be as for Class A or Class B stairs, but one tread in each seat platform width may have a greater width to accommodate access to seats. Seating platforms shall be of uniform width.

(g) The gradient of sloping aisles shall not exceed 1 ft (1 cm) of rise in 8 ft (8 cm) of run.

In addition to exits, it is necessary to provide clearly visible aisles sufficient in number and arranged to provide safe access to exits or protected exit accesses.

When serving seating areas, aisle widths are required to increase in the direction of travel based on the distance to an exit, cross aisle, or foyer. Since most aisles are required to provide access in two directions to an exit, cross aisle, or foyer, the minimum width is applied to the midpoint of the aisle and the aisle width increases in both directions. In practice, of course, most designers simply maintain the maximum width for the entire length. See Figure 9-4A.

Only those aisles which are permitted to dead end may actually increase in width away from the dead end. Dead ends are limited to 20 ft (609.6 cm) in length. In theaters with arena or thrust stages, dead-end aisles at the stage may not exceed five rows of seats beyond a cross aisle.

Steps in aisles should be avoided wherever possible. Where they are necessary due to the aisle slope exceeding 1 ft (.3 m) of rise in 8 ft (2.44 m) of run, steps must conform to the requirements for Class A stairs as to rise and run (see 5-2.2.1.2). Balconies and galleries pose a problem in choice of hazards. To comply with the requirement for uniform rise and run can create a dangerous step from the seat platform to the aisle. The *Code* therefore provides the exception which permits one tread run in each seat platform to have a greater depth in order to accommodate access to and from seats; the risers are of equal height. See Figure 9-7.

9-2.6 Measurement of Travel Distance to Exits.   Exits shall be so arranged that the total length of travel from any point to reach an exit will not exceed 150 ft (45.72 m) in any place of assembly.

Exception: The travel distance may be increased to 200 ft (60.96 m) in assembly occupancies protected throughout by an automatic sprinkler system.

Travel distance to exits from balconies or galleries which are served by unenclosed stairways must be measured to include the distance on the slope of the stair in the plane of the nosings. Travel distance would be measured as illustrated in Figure 9-8.

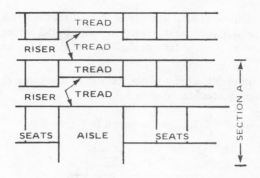

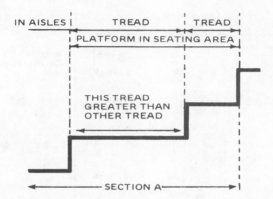

Figure 9-7. Steps in Aisles Complying with the Exception to 9-2.5.4(f). The limits are built in by the rise/run relationship for stairs. The uniformity is required to prevent people from tripping and stumbling when different depths are introduced.

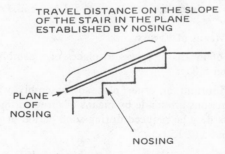

Figure 9-8. Measurement of Travel Distance to Exit when Balconies Are Served by Unenclosed Stairs.

9-2.7 Discharge from Exits.

9-2.7.1 The level of exit discharge shall be measured at the point of principal entrance to the building.

9-2.7.2 Where the principal entrance to a place of assembly is via a depressed terrace, the terrace shall be at least as wide as the exit that it serves but not less than 5 ft (152.4 cm) wide, and it shall be increased in width by 50 percent of any other exits tributary thereto. The level of the terrace shall be considered the level of exit discharge for the purpose of 9-1.6 above.

9-2.7.3 A maximum of 50 percent of the exits may discharge through areas on the level of exit discharge in accordance with 5-7.2.

The requirements of 9-2.7.2 are illustrated in Figure 9-9.

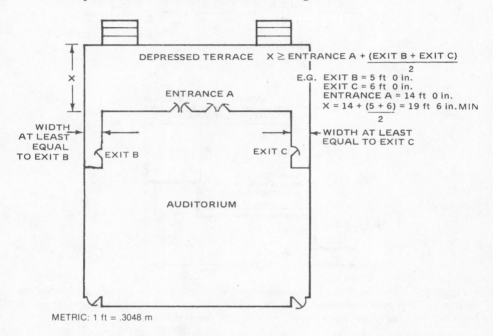

Figure 9-9. Place of Assembly with Depressed Terrace as Principal Entrance.

9-2.8 Illumination of Means of Egress.

9-2.8.1 Illumination of means of egress in places of assembly shall be provided in accordance with Section 5-8.

9-2.8.2 In every auditorium or other place of assembly where pictures, motion pictures, or other projections are made by means of directed light, the illumination of the floors of exit access may be reduced during such period of projection to values of not less than ⅕ footcandle (2.15 lx).

9-2.9 Emergency Lighting. All places of assembly and their means of egress shall be provided with emergency lighting in accordance with Section 5-9.

Exception: Churches that are Class C places of assembly, used exclusively for religious worship, shall not be required to have emergency lighting.

The exception to the requirement for emergency lighting is intended to apply only to Class C places of assembly (50 to 300 people) which are not likely to be used for any purpose except religious worship because they contain permanently fixed furnishings such as pews, pulpits, or altars.

9-2.10 Marking of Means of Egress.   Means of egress shall have signs in accordance with Section 5-10.

9-2.11 Special Features.

9-2.11.1 Panic Hardware.   An exit door from a place of assembly having an occupant load of 100 or more persons may be provided with a latch or lock only if it is panic hardware.

Exception No. 1:   In places of assembly having an occupant load of less than 600, panic hardware may be omitted from the main exit when the main exit consist of a single door or a pair of doors. Any locking device on this door(s) shall meet the requirements of Exception No. 2 to 5-2.1.2.1.1.

This new exception to 9-2.11.1 is in recognition of new provisions contained in Chapter 5, Means of Egress. These new provisions recognize the need to lock doors for security purposes and provide limits on how this can be done. These provisions also recognize, in fact, that in order for the business to function the main door must be open; thus, this exception is to coordinate with the changes in Chapter 5.

Exception No. 2:   Special locking arrangements complying with 5-2.1.2.1.5 are permitted on doors other than main exit doors.

This exception allows delayed release panic hardware meeting the requirements of 5-2.1.2.1.5 to be used on all but the main exit.

9-2.11.2   Class C places of assembly in covered malls (*see 25-4.3.1 Exception*) may have horizontal or vertical security grills or doors on the main entrance/exits in accordance with the provisions of Exception No. 2 to 5-2.1.1.4.1.

This provision allows small restaurants in malls to use the security grills or doors provided for in 5-2.1.1.4.1 Exception No. 2.

9-2.11.3 Railings.

(a) The fasciae of boxes, balconies, and galleries shall not be less than 26 in. (66.04 cm) high above the adjacent floor or have substantial railings not less than 26 in. (66.04 cm) high above the adjacent floor.

(b) The height of the rail above footrests on the adjacent floor immediately in front of a row of seats shall be not less than 26 in. (66.04 cm). Railings at the ends of aisles shall be not less than 36 in. (91.44 cm) high for the full width of the aisle and shall be not less than 42 in. (106.68 cm) high for the width of the aisle where steps occur.

(c) Cross aisles shall be provided with railings not less than 26 in. (66.04 cm) high above the adjacent floor.

Exception No. 1:   Where the backs of seats on the front of the aisle project 24 in. (60.96 cm) or more above the adjacent floor of the aisle.

Exception No. 2:   Existing railings 36 in. (91.44 cm) high at the ends of aisles where steps occur may continue to be used.

Figure 9-10A illustrates the requirements of 9-2.11.3(a) and (b). Rail height at the fascia end of a sloping aisle must not be less than 36 in. (91.44 cm). However, when the aisle is not ramped but has steps, the rail height must be at least 42 in. (106.68 cm). There is more danger of people tripping on steps than on a sloping surface with a maximum gradient of 1 ft (.3 m) of rise to 8 ft (2.44 m) of run. Exception No. 2 permits continued use of existing 36-in. (91.44-cm) high railings. This avoids the hardship that would be placed on existing facilities if the railing had to be raised 6 in. (15.24 cm).

The *Code* requires a barrier along the downhill side of a cross aisle [see 9-2.11.3(c)]. The barrier may be a rail or the backs of the seats which abut the downhill side of the aisle when the backs project 24 in. (60.96 cm) or more above the cross aisle. The difference between the 24 in. (60.96 cm) back height and the required 26-in. (66.04-cm) railing is insignificant. See Figure 9-10B.

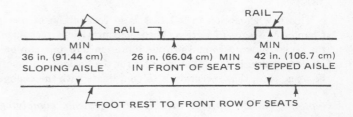

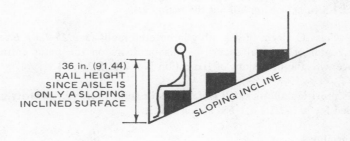

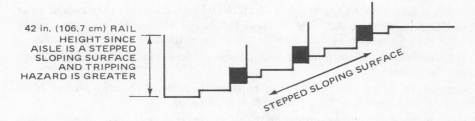

Figure 9-10A. Railings Installed in Accordance with 9-2.11.3 (a) and (b).

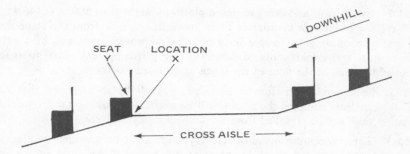

Figure 9-10B. Barrier for Cross Aisles in Accordance with 9-2.11.3(c). A railing [< 26 in. (66.04 cm)] is required at Location X if the back of Seat Y is less than 24 in. (60.96 cm) high.

SECTION 9-3   PROTECTION

9-3.1 Protection of Vertical Openings.   All interior stairways and other vertical openings shall be enclosed and protected as provided in Section 6-2.

Exception No. 1:   Stairs may be open between balconies and main assembly floors in theaters, churches, or auditoriums where the travel distance is within the allowable limits (see 9-2.6).

Exception No. 2:   Existing wood lath and plaster, existing ½-in. (1.27-cm) gypsum wallboard, existing installations of ¼-in. (.64-cm) thick wired glass that are, or are rendered, inoperative and fixed in the closed position, or other existing materials having similar fire-resistive capabilities shall be acceptable. All such assemblies shall be in good repair and free of any condition that would diminish their original fire-resistive characteristics.

Exception No. 3:   Unprotected openings connecting not more than three floors may be permitted provided that they comply with the requirements of 6-2.2.3.1 Exception No. 1.

9-3.2 Protection from Hazards.

9-3.2.1 Stage and Enclosed Platform.   *(See 9-1.3.)*

9-3.2.1.1   Every stage equipped with fly galleries, gridirons, and rigging for movable theater-type scenery, and every enclosed platform larger than 500 sq ft (46.45 sq m) in area shall have a system of automatic sprinklers at the ceiling, under the gridiron, in usable spaces under the stage or platform and in auxiliary spaces and dressing rooms, storerooms, and workshops. Where the distance from the back of the stage to the proscenium wall is less than 30 ft (914.4 cm), in lieu of sprinklers under the entire gridiron area, complete peripheral sidewall sprinklers with baffle plates may be substituted. Such sidewall sprinklers shall be not more than 30 in. (76.2 cm) below the gridiron or 6 in. (15.24 cm) below the baffle plates.

When openings are provided in the stage floor for stage lifts, trap doors, or stairs, sprinklers spaced 5 ft (152.4 cm) on centers shall be provided around the opening at the ceiling below the stage, and baffles at least 12 in. (30.48 cm) in depth shall be installed around the perimeter of the opening.

9-3.2.1.2 Every stage and every enclosed platform larger than 500 sq ft (46.45 sq m) shall have a ventilator or ventilators in or above it, operable from the stage floor by hand and also opening by fusible links or other approved automatic heat actuated device or heat and smoke actuated device to give a free opening equal to at least 5 percent of the area of the floor of the stage or enclosed platform.

Where mechanical ventilation is provided, it shall be so arranged that natural ventilation, at least equal to the above, will be available. Makeup air for mechanical ventilation shall not be obtained from the audience (seating) areas.

9-3.2.1.3 The proscenium opening of every stage shall be provided with a curtain constructed and mounted so as to intercept hot gases, flames, and smoke, and to prevent glow from a severe fire on the stage showing on the auditorium side within a 5-minute period. The curtain shall be automatic closing without the use of applied power.

Exception: In lieu of the protection required herein, all the following may be provided:

(a) A noncombustible opaque fabric curtain so arranged that it will close automatically, and

(b) An automatic dry-pipe system of spray heads on both sides of the curtain. Discharge and spacing shall be such that the entire curtain will be wet. Water supply shall be controlled by a deluge valve and shall be sufficient to keep the curtain completely wet for 30 minutes or until valve is closed by fire department personnel, and

(c) Curtain, spray heads, stage sprinklers, and vents shall be automatically operated in case of fire by rate-of-rise and fixed temperature detectors. Spacing, number, and location of detectors shall be as required by the devices used, with maximum center to center distance of 10 ft (304.8 cm). Detectors shall completely cover the periphery of the sprinklered and protected area, and

(d) Operation of a sprinkler or spray head deluge valve shall automatically activate the emergency ventilating system and close the curtain.

Modern stages pose problems which didn't exist in the past. Scenery may be shifted horizontally, vertically, or both ways. The use of thrust stages and arena stages creates other problems.

The classic stage of the past had great height above the proscenium opening to accommodate the rigid asbestos curtain. The high void was a natural place to house combustible scenery for a performance, along with the rigging necessary for handling scene changes. This vertical storage area represented both a high fuel load and a difficult space to reach in case of a fire. Many new theaters use a flexible noncombustible curtain which does not require much height to accommodate it. Scenery on these stages is moved horizontally, thus reducing the distance necessary for storage between the top of the proscenium opening and the stage ceiling. Most combustible scenery is now stored in areas adjacent to the stage. All rigging and lighting is condensed in less vertical space.

Both stage arrangements require sprinklers and vents installed in accordance with 9-3.2.1.1 and 9-3.2.1.2. It is important that if mechanical ventilation for evacuating smoke from the stage is provided in lieu of openable vents, the natural air supply must be provided from a source other than the auditorium seating area.

If, instead of the fire-resistant curtain specified in 9-3.2.1.3, a flexible proscenium curtain is used, the *Code* requires an automatic dry-pipe system with spray nozzles on both sides of the curtain. This system must be capable of completely wetting both sides of the curtain and of maintaining it wet for at least 30 minutes or until the deluge valve is closed by the fire department. *Automatic Sprinkler and Standpipe Systems*[2] by Dr. John L. Bryan contains a detailed explanation of the design and operation of dry-pipe sprinkler systems and of deluge valves. Specifications for the installation of sprinkler systems in general are found in NFPA 13, *Standard on Installation of Sprinkler Systems*.[3] Of course, for any sprinkler system to effectively minimize the hazards from fire to life safety or property, regular inspection and maintenance of the system is essential. NFPA 13A, *Recommended Practice for the Care and Maintenance of Sprinkler Systems*,[4] provides recommendations for ensuring that an extinguishing system will not fail in an emergency.

The spray nozzles for the curtain, and the sprinklers and vents for the stage are required to operate automatically by heat detectors capable of monitoring an abnormally high temperature or rate-of-temperature rise. NFPA 72E, *Standard on Automatic Fire Detectors*,[5] and its appendix contain specifications and recommendations on the installation of heat detectors.

To complete the protection system, operation of the sprinkler or spray nozzle deluge valve must also automatically close the proscenium curtain and activate the emergency ventilating system.

9-3.2.1.4 Auxiliary stage spaces such as understage areas, dressing rooms, workshops, and similar spaces associated with the functioning of a stage shall comply with the following:

(a) No point within any auxiliary space shall be more than 50 ft (15.24 m) from a door providing access to an exit.

(b) There shall be at least two exits available from every auxiliary stage space, one of which shall be available within a travel distance of 75 ft (22.86 m). A common path of travel of 20 ft (609.6 cm) to the two exits shall be permitted.

(c) Auxiliary stage spaces shall be equipped with automatic sprinklers when required by the provisions of 9-3.2.1.1.

(d) No workshop involving the use of a combustible or flammable paint, liquids, or gases, or their storage shall open directly upon a stage.

Auxiliary stage spaces are sources of serious hazards. It is therefore necessary to provide automatic fire protection and adequate exits within a short travel distance from such spaces. All workshops must be separated from the stage area by construction having a fire resistance of at least 1 hour, with any openings between a workshop and the stage area protected by 1-hour-rated fire assemblies.

9-3.2.1.5 Where automatic sprinkler protection is not provided, the proscenium wall of every theater using movable scenery or decorations shall not have more than two openings entering the stage, exclusive of the proscenium opening. Such openings shall not exceed 21 sq ft (1.95 sq m) each and shall be fitted with self-closing fire doors.

The limitations of 9-3.2.1.5 apply only to enclosed platforms with a maximum area of 500 sq ft (46.45 sq m) or to stages without fly galleries, gridirons, or rigging for movable scenery. Other configurations must have the automatic sprinkler protection specified in 9-3.5.1.1.

9-3.2.1.6 Each stage shall be equipped with a standpipe located on each side of the stage, equipped with a 2½-in. (6.35-cm) fire department connection, and a 1½-in. (3.81-cm) hose for occupant use, installed in accordance with *Standard for the Installation of Standpipe and Hose Systems*, NFPA 14.

There must be a standpipe located on each side of a stage to provide the stage hands and the responding fire department with a manual fire fighting capability at the area of a theater where a fire is most likely to occur. The installation of the standpipes must comply with NFPA 14, *Standard on Standpipe and Hose Systems*,[6]. NFPA 13E, *Recommendations for Fire Department Operations in Properties Protected by Sprinkler and Standpipe Systems*,[7] should also be consulted for a discussion of the necessity of a properly installed standpipe system. Standpipes are required whether or not the stage has automatic sprinkler protection.

9-3.2.2 Projection Booth.

9-3.2.2.1 Every place of assembly where an electric arc, Xenon, or other light source that generates hazardous gases, dust, or radiation is used shall have a projection room that complies with 9-3.2.2.2 from which the projection shall be made. Where cellulose nitrate film is used, the projection room shall comply with *Standard for the Storage and Handling of Cellulose Nitrate Motion Picture Film*, NFPA 40. (*See also Chapter 31.*)

The requirements for projection booths were developed jointly with those of NFPA 40, *Standard for the Storage and Handling of Cellulose Nitrate Motion Picture Film*,[8] and the motion picture industry at the height of movie popularity when cellulose nitrate film was still being used. Presently, only safety film is used (except at film festivals or revivals) and the risk level has been reduced. The primary function of these requirements is to build a shelter around the projection booth, eliminating it as an exposure threat to the theater audience.

The intent of 9-3.2.2.1 is to protect the audience from the dangers associated with light sources such as electric arc or Xenon. Where incandescent light is used, projection booths are not required in places of assembly. Note the booth is required based on the light source, not on the projection of film.

Paragraph 17-2.7 requires that unless the construction of a projection booth complies with NFPA 40, *Standard for the Storage and Handling of Cellulose Nitrate Motion Picture Film*,[8] a conspicuous sign must be posted on the door of the projection booth and also inside the booth. The sign must state: "Safety Film Only Permitted in This Room". The intent is to ensure that cellulose nitrate film is projected only with adequate safeguards.

9-3.2.2.2 Projection Rooms for Safety Film.

9-3.2.2.2.1 Every projection room shall be of permanent construction consistent with the construction requirements for the type of building in which the projection room is located. Openings need not be protected. The room shall have a floor area of not less than 80 sq ft (7.43 sq m) for a single machine and at least 40 sq ft (3.72 sq m) for each additional machine. Each motion picture projector, floodlight, spotlight, or similar piece of equipment shall have a clear working space not less than 30 in. (76.2 cm) on each side and at the rear thereof, but only one such space shall be required between adjacent projectors.

The projection room and the rooms appurtenant thereto shall have a ceiling height of not less than 7 ft 6 in. (228.6 cm).

9-3.2.2.2.2 Each projection room shall have at least one out-swinging, self-closing door not less than 2 ft 6 in. (76.2 cm) wide by 6 ft 8 in. (203.2 cm) high.

9-3.2.2.2.3 The aggregate of ports and openings for projection equipment shall not exceed 25 percent of the area of the wall between the projection room and the auditorium.

All openings shall be provided with glass or other approved material, so as to completely close the opening.

It should be emphasized that 9-3.2.2.2.1 through 9-3.2.2.2.6 apply only to booths for the projection of cellulose acetate or other safety film. Although openings in the booth do not need to be protected, they must be provided with glass or other approved material which will completely close the opening and prevent gas, dust, or radiation from contaminating the audience or seating area.

9-3.2.2.2.4 Projection booth room ventilation shall be not less than the following:

(a) *Supply Air.* Each projection room shall be provided with two or more separate fresh air inlet ducts with screened openings terminating within 12 in. (30.48 cm) of the floor, and located at opposite ends of the room. Such air inlets shall be of sufficient size to permit an air change every three minutes. Fresh air may be supplied from the general building air conditioning system, providing it is so arranged that the projection booth will continue to receive one change of air every three minutes, when no other air is supplied by the general air conditioning system.

(b) *Exhaust Air.* Each projection room shall be provided with one or more exhaust air outlets that may be manifolded into a single duct outside the booth. Such outlets shall be so located as to ensure circulation throughout the room. Projection room exhaust air systems shall be independent of any other air systems in the buildings. Exhaust air ducts shall terminate at the exterior of the building in such a location that the exhaust air cannot be readily recirculated into the supply air system. The exhaust system shall be mechanically operated and of such a capacity as to provide a minimum of one change of air every 3 minutes. The blower motor shall be outside the duct system.

The projection room ventilation system may also serve appurtenant rooms, such as the generator room and the rewind room.

The requirements for the ventilation of a projection booth are designed to effectively "isolate" the booth from the theater so that any products of combustion created by a fire in a projection booth would not be circulated into the theater. This is accomplished by having an independent exhaust system for the booth by ensuring that the exhaust outlet on the exterior of the building is located at a point where the air intake for the theater cannot recirculate the exhausted air.

If fresh air for the projection booth's ventilation system is supplied from the general system of the building, it is essential that the combined system be arranged to ensure the required 3-minute air change in the booth when no other air is supplied to the general system of the building. To further minimize the risk to the life safety of the audience from a fire or explosion in the projection booth, the blower motor of the exhaust must be located outside of the duct system.

9-3.2.2.2.5 Each projection machine shall be provided with an exhaust duct that will draw air from each lamp and exhaust it directly to the outside of the building in such a fashion that it will not be picked up by supply inlets. Such a duct shall be of rigid materials, except for a continuous flexible connector approved for the purpose. The lamp exhaust system shall not be interconnected with any other system.

(a) *Electric Arc Projection Equipment.*   The exhaust capacity shall be 200 cfm (.09 cu m/s) for each lamp connected to the lamp exhaust system, or as recommended by the equipment manufacturer. Auxiliary air may be introduced into the system through a screened opening to stabilize the arc.

(b) *Xenon Projection Equipment.*   The lamp exhaust system shall exhaust not less than 300 cfm (.14 cu m/s) per lamp, not less than that exhaust volume required or recommended by the equipment manufacturer, whichever is the greater. The external temperature of the lamp housing shall not exceed 130°F (54.4°C) when operating.

The *Code* sets forth the minimum capacity for the exhaust system of a projection machine; however, a greater capacity must be provided when recommended by the manufacturer of the projection equipment. This system must be independent of any other ventilation system in the building housing the theater.

9-3.2.2.2.6 Miscellaneous Equipment and Storage.

(a) Each projection room shall be provided with rewind and film storage facilities.

The intent of the requirement for the storage and rewinding of film is to prevent these operations from occurring outside the projection booth at some less protected location where, if a fire occurred, the exposure to the theater would be significantly greater. All operations which relate to projection activities must be kept within the protected enclosure afforded by the projection booth.

(b) A maximum of four containers for flammable liquids not greater than 16 oz (4.7 × 10⁻⁴ cu m) capacity and of a nonbreakable type may be permitted in each projection booth.

(c) Appurtenant electrical equipment such as rheostats, transformers, and generators may be located within the booth or in a separate room of equivalent construction.

9-3.2.3 Service Equipment, Hazardous Operations or Processes, and Storage Facilities.

9-3.2.3.1 Rooms containing high pressure boilers, refrigerating machinery of other than domestic refrigerator type, large transformers, or other service equipment subject to possible explosion shall not be located directly under or adjacent to required exits. All such rooms shall be separated by a 1-hour fire barrier from other parts of the building.

The preservation of the integrity of exits in any building is one of the principal concerns of the *Code*. Therefore, hazardous areas, even if enclosed with the required fire-resistant construction, must never be located where they might directly expose a required exit to fire.

9-3.2.3.2 All openings between the balance of the building and rooms or enclosures for hazardous operations or processes shall be protected by standard self-closing or smoke-actuated fire doors and shall be provided with adequate vents to the outer air, in accordance with Section 6-4 of this *Code*.

9-3.2.3.3 Rooms or space for the storage, processing, or use of the materials specified in this section shall be protected in accordance with the following:

(a) Rooms or spaces used for the storage of combustible supplies in quantities deemed hazardous by the authority having jurisdiction, hazardous materials in quantities deemed hazardous by recognized standards, or fuel shall be separated from the remainder of the building by construction having not less than a 1-hour fire-resistive rating with all openings protected by self-closing or smoke-actuated fire doors, or such rooms or spaces may be protected by an automatic extinguishing system as set forth in Section 6-4.

(b) Rooms or spaces used for processing or use of combustible supplies in quantities considered hazardous by the authority having jurisdiction, hazardous materials, or for flammable or combustible liquids in quantities deemed hazardous by recognized standards shall be separated from the remainder of the building by construction having not less than a 1-hour fire-resistive rating with all openings protected by self-closing or smoke-actuated fire doors and shall also be protected by an automatic extinguishing system as set forth in Section 6-4.

(c) Boiler and furnace rooms, laundries, and maintenance shops, including woodworking and painting areas, shall be separated from the remainder of the building by construction having not less than a 1-hour fire-resistive rating with all openings protected by self-closing or smoke-actuated fire doors.

Exception: Rooms enclosing air-handling equipment.

(d) When automatic extinguishing systems are used to meet the requirements of this section, the rooms or spaces shall be separated from the remainder of the building by a smoke barrier.

The intent of 9-3.2.3.3 is to specify the degree of protection necessary for certain hazardous areas. It has been divided into three sections based on the degree of hazard. The hazards noted in item (a) are required to be enclosed in 1-hour construction or protected by sprinklers. If the sprinkler option is chosen, an enclosure is still required; however, the enclosure need not be rated, but only form a membrane against the passage of smoke.

The hazards noted in item (b) must be enclosed in 1-hour construction *and* be protected by automatic sprinklers.

The hazards noted in item (c) are required to be enclosed in 1-hour construction with no option for a sprinkler equivalency for the enclosure. The exception to item (c) pertains to rooms housing air-handling equipment *only*. If the room is used for other purposes, then the provisions of item (a) or (b) apply.

9-3.2.4 Special Provisions for Food Service Establishments.

9-3.2.4.1   All devices in connection with the preparation of food shall be so installed and operated as to avoid hazard to the safety of occupants.

9-3.2.4.2   All devices in connection with the preparation of food shall be of an approved type and shall be installed in an approved manner.

> An "approved type" of device means that, from the standpoint of potential fire hazards, the unit is acceptable to the authority having jurisdiction. An "approved manner" of installation means installation in accordance with the requirements of the authority having jurisdiction.

9-3.2.4.3   Food preparation facilities shall be protected in accordance with *Vapor Removal Cooking Equipment*, NFPA 96 (*see Appendix B*), and are not required to have openings protected between food preparation areas and dining areas.

> The intent of 9-3.2.4.3 is to provide some barrier between cooking areas and dining areas of restaurants. The intent of the barrier is to screen possible flash fires from the view of the patrons in an attempt to prevent panic. Openings in this barrier are not restricted and do not need to be protected. The *Code* is counting on the automatic extinguishing system to control any fire on the cooking surfaces, and thus no longer requires enclosure by rated construction. The degree of screening required, and thus the size of the barrier required, is left to the judgment of the authority having jurisdiction.

9-3.3 Interior Finish.

9-3.3.1   The interior finish requirements of this section shall be in accordance with Section 6-5.

9-3.3.2   Interior finish in all corridors and lobbies shall be Class A or B and in enclosed stairways Class A.

9-3.3.3   Interior finish in general assembly areas, shall be Class A, B, or C.

Exception: In any place of assembly, exposed portions of structural members complying with the requirements for Type IV (2HH) construction may be permitted.

9-3.3.4   Screens on which pictures are projected shall comply with requirements of Class A or Class B interior finish.

> Interior finish requirements for new places of assembly are unequivocal and are subject to rigid interpretation. Evaluation of interior finish in existing facilities is sometimes difficult. Where flame spread characteristics cannot be readily determined using the test procedure in NFPA 255, *Method of Test of Surface Burning Characteristics of Building Materials*,[9] the questionable material should be removed or treated with approved flame retardants. When treatment cannot reduce flame spread to required limits, automatic sprinklers may be provided to compensate for the remaining deficiency.
>
> A structural member is a column, a beam, a girder, or an arch. It can be located wherever it is needed to bear the weight of the structure. Heavy timber construction is defined in NFPA 220, *Standard Types of Building Construction*.[10] The NFPA *Fire Protection Handbook*[11] discusses the principal features of the construction.

9-3.4 Alarm and Communication Systems.

9-3.4.1   Every Class A or B place of assembly shall be provided with a manual fire alarm system in accordance with 7-6.1.2.

9-3.4.2   The alarm system shall not automatically sound an alarm in the audience or seating portion of the place of assembly but shall sound an alarm in a constantly manned location.

Exception: Places of assembly in educational occupancies.

9-3.4.3   Provisions shall be made for transmitting voice messages by a public address system throughout the assembly area. Reliability of the public address system shall be assured by testing the system prior to allowing occupants into the assembly room.

Exception: Places of assembly in educational occupancies.

9-3.4.4   The public address system shall be provided with an emergency power source.

Exception: Places of assembly in educational occupancies.

The intent of the provisions of 9-3.4 is to provide an alarm system which will not produce a panic reaction from the occupants. Previous editions of the *Code* required no alarm system. The intent of this section is to provide a system which will permit activation of the system by pull stations as required by 7-6.1.2, but that an audible alarm will not be sounded in the seating or audience areas of the place of assembly. In lieu of the audible alarm throughout the place of assembly, the system must sound an alarm in a constantly manned location. (Constantly manned, in this case, means during the time the place of assembly is in use, the alarm panel must be manned.) From that constantly manned location, voice messages instructing the occupants can be issued via a public address system. This method allows for the orderly evacuation of the occupants and permits the issuance of proper instructions on how to evacuate rather than simply sounding an evacuation alarm which may produce panic.

9-3.5 Extinguishment Requirements.   *(See 9-1.6, 9-2.6, and 9-3.2.)*

9-3.5.1 Fire Suppression Systems.   Any place of assembly used or capable of being used for exhibition or display purposes shall be protected throughout by an approved automatic sprinkler system in accordance with Section 7-7 when the exhibition or display area exceeds 15,000 sq ft (1,394 sq m).

This requirement applies to places of assembly used or *capable* of being used for exhibition or display purposes. This would apply to many facilities over 15,000 sq ft (1,394 sq m) unless fixed seating or similar obstruction to this use is provided.

SECTION 9-4   SPECIAL PROVISIONS

9-4.1 Windowless or Subterranean Buildings.   The requirements of places of assembly shall be in accordance with this chapter and Section 30-7 of this *Code*.

Many buildings which house places of assembly are windowless by design. In theaters, opera halls, concert halls, etc., windows are detrimental to operations. In recent years, large exhibition halls have also been constructed without windows.

Windowless buildings with an occupant load of 100 or more must be provided with a complete automatic extinguishing system, usually sprinklers. All windowless assembly occupancies must be provided with emergency lighting in accordance with Section 5-9 of the *Code*. By formal interpretation, the audience chambers of a movie theater are not required to be sprinklered since the committee does not consider them truly windowless if they have exits directly to the outside from the seating area.

Subterranean places of assembly require special consideration. Although they are similar to windowless buildings, additional problems of access for fire fighting and rescue are created when they are located in basements or subbasements of buildings. Exits, and where possible the exit accesses, must be adequately cut off from the assembly area by construction of partitions, walls, and doors of sufficient fire resistance. Positive means must be provided to prevent smoke from contaminating the exits. Like any windowless building, a subterranean place of assembly requires automatic sprinkler protection, emergency lighting, and a smoke evacuation system.

9-4.2 Outdoor Assembly.

9-4.2.1 All grandstands, tents, and other places of outdoor assembly shall comply with the requirements of *Tents, Grandstands and Air-Supported Structures*, NFPA 102.

When an outdoor place of assembly is created in an enclosed court so that exits can only be provided through a surrounding building, the requirements for exits, seating, and aisles must be the same as for an indoor assembly area.

9-4.3 Special Provisions for Exhibition Halls.

Exhibition halls have problems which differ from those of theaters, restaurants, or other places of assembly. They are large, multiuse facilities and have high ceilings appropriate to their size. Combustible materials are frequently displayed, and the containers in which the exhibits are shipped contribute to the fuel load. Paragraph 9-3.5 requires most exhibition halls to be protected by automatic sprinklers.

9-4.3.1 No display or exhibit shall be so installed or operated as to interfere in any way with access to any required exit or with visibility of any required exit or of any required exit sign, nor shall any display block access to fire fighting equipment.

It is advisable to have prepared plans or diagrams to show the arrangement of displays or exhibits, including any which are to be suspended from the ceiling or an overhead structure. Displays or exhibits must never interfere in any way with access to any required exit, and they must not conceal exit signs. See Figure 9-11. A display should not block access to fire fighting equipment nor interfere with the normal operation of automatic extinguishing equipment or devices for smoke evacuation.

9-4.3.2 All displays or exhibits of combustible material or construction and all booths and temporary construction in connection therewith shall be so limited in combustibility or protected as to avoid any undue hazard of fire that might endanger occupants before they have the opportunity to use available exits, as determined by the authority having jurisdiction.

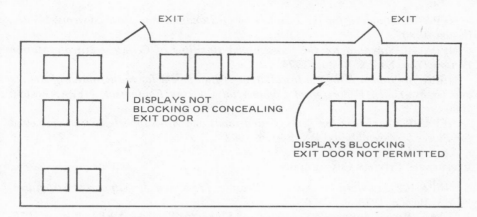

Figure 9-11. Arrangement of Displays in an Exhibition Hall.

Displays or exhibits of combustible material must be limited in quantity in order to reduce the fuel load to an acceptable level. Excess combustible display material and all other combustible materials which are not in use should be kept in a separate storage room until needed. A separation with a fire resistance of 2 hours is required between such a storage room and all other parts of the building, and the room must be protected by an automatic sprinkler system.

Rows of booths become exit accesses; therefore, booths and other temporary construction should be of minimal combustible construction or protected to avoid undue hazard of fire which might endanger occupants before they can reach available exits.

9-4.3.3 A storage room having an enclosure with a fire resistance rating of at least 2 hours and protected by an automatic fire extinguishing system shall be provided for combustible materials not on display.

SECTION 9-5 BUILDING SERVICES

9-5.1 Utilities shall comply with the provisions of Section 7-1.

9-5.2 Heating, ventilating, and air conditioning equipment shall comply with the provisions of Section 7-2.

9-5.3 Elevators, dumbwaiters, and vertical conveyors shall comply with the provisions of Section 7-4.

9-5.4 Rubbish chutes, incinerators, and laundry chutes shall comply with the provisions of Section 7-5.

REFERENCES CITED BY CODE

(These publications comprise a part of the requirements to the extent called for by the Code.)

NFPA 14, *Standard for the Installation of Standpipe and Hose Systems*, NFPA, Boston, 1980.

NFPA 40, *Standard for the Storage and Handling of Cellulose Nitrate Motion Picture Film*, NFPA, Boston, 1974.

NFPA 96, *Standard for the Installation of Equipment for the Removal of Smoke and Grease-Laden Vapors from Commercial Cooking Equipment*, NFPA, Boston, 1980.

NFPA 102, *Standard for Tents, Grandstands and Air-Supported Structures Used for Places of Assembly*, NFPA, Boston, 1978.

REFERENCES CITED IN COMMENTARY

[1]NFPA 102, *Standard for Assembly Seating, Tents, and Air-Supported Structures*, NFPA, Boston, 1978.

[2]John L. Bryan, *Automatic Sprinkler and Standpipe Systems*, NFPA, Boston, 1976, pp. 248-307.

[3]NFPA 13, *Standard for the Installation of Sprinkler Systems*, NFPA, Boston, 1980.

[4]NFPA 13A, *Recommended Practice for the Care and Maintenance of Sprinkler Systems*, NFPA, Boston, 1978.

[5]NFPA 72E, *Standard on Automatic Fire Detectors*, NFPA, Boston, 1978.

[6]NFPA 14, *Standard for the Installation of Standpipe and Hose Systems*, NFPA, Boston, 1980.

[7]NFPA 13E, *Recommendations for Fire Department Operations in Properties Protected by Sprinkler and Standpipe Systems*, NFPA, Boston, 1978.

[8]NFPA 40, *Standard for the Storage and Handling of Cellulose Nitrate Motion Picture Film*, NFPA, Boston, 1974.

[9]NFPA 255, *Method of Test of Surface Burning Characteristics of Building Materials*, NFPA, Boston, 1979.

[10]NFPA 220, *Standard Types of Building Construction*, NFPA, Boston, 1979.

[11]*Fire Protection Handbook*, 14th ed., NFPA, Boston, 1976, pp. 6-39 to 6-41.

10

NEW EDUCATIONAL OCCUPANCIES

(See also Chapter 31.)   31.3 page 752

Educational occupancies include all buildings used for the gathering of groups of six or more people for purposes of instruction. Educational occupancies include:

Schools	Kindergartens
Academies	Child day-care facilities
	Nursery schools

Other occupancies associated with educational institutions must be in accordance with the appropriate parts of this *Code.*

Operational features for educational occupancies are specified in Chapter 31, Operating Features.

SECTION 10-1 GENERAL REQUIREMENTS

10-1.1 Application.

10-1.1.1 The requirements of this chapter apply to new buildings.

Existing educational occupancies are dealt with in Chapter 11.

10-1.1.2 Rooms used for preschool, kindergarten, or first-grade pupils shall not be located above or below the level of exit discharge. Rooms used for second-grade pupils shall not be located more than one story above the level of exit discharge.

The restrictions on the location of rooms used by preschool, kindergarten, or first- or second-grade pupils were developed to avoid the danger of older (and larger) children overrunning the very young on stairs or ramps during a fire or other incident requiring rapid evacuation of a building. Paragraph 10-1.1.2 also recognizes that young children may need assistance or have to be rescued.

10-1.1.3 Educational occupancies shall make provisions for the physically handicapped.

Federal and state laws governing financial assistance for education emphasize that public educational institutions must provide equal access to education for the physically handicapped. In addition, many states specifically prohibit segregating handicapped students from other pupils which makes it impossible to locate all physically handicapped pupils at the level of exit discharge. Unfortunately, these laws and related standards do not address the need for emergency egress of the handicapped during fires or similar events. In winning the right to equal access to educational facilities, the handicapped have placed themselves "at risk" in many buildings.

To minimize the level of risk created by interspersing the handicapped at all levels and locations within an educational building, horizontal exits, permitting horizontal movement away from the area of a fire, can easily be designed into new construction. This parallels the design concept in Chapter 12, New Health Care Occupancies, for the evacuation of litter-borne, bedridden, or handicapped patients from health care occupancies. Standards for the construction of elevators are discussed in Chapter 7 and in ANSI A17.1.[1] Standards for making buildings accessible to the handicapped are presented in ANSI A117.1.[2]

10-1.1.4   Educational occupancies housing classes over the twelfth grade need not comply with this chapter, but shall comply with the following requirements:

(a) Instructional Building — Business Occupancy
(b) Classrooms under 50 persons — Business Occupancy
(c) Classrooms 50 persons and over — Place of Assembly
(d) Laboratories, Instructional — Business Occupancy
(e) Laboratories, Non-Instructional — Industrial.

The provisions of 10-1.1.4 recognize that colleges and universities do not have the same problem as elementary and high schools. Because of the maturity of the occupants, college buildings more properly resemble office occupancies. Thus, this paragraph identifies those uses and refers to other appropriate provisions of the *Code*.

10-1.2 Mixed Occupancies.   (*See also 10-1.4.*)

10-1.2.1 General.   In case two or more classes of occupancy occur in the same building or structure so intermingled that separate safeguards are impracticable, the means of egress shall be sufficient to meet the requirements for each individual room or section and for the maximum occupant load of the entire building. Construction, protection, and other safeguards shall meet requirements of the most hazardous occupancy.

Exception: As otherwise specified in this chapter.

Many times it is difficult to determine what is the "most hazardous occupancy." The intent of the *Code* is to apply the requirements which provide the highest level of life safety for the building occupants.

10-1.2.2 Assembly and Educational.   Any auditorium, assembly room, cafeteria, or gymnasium used for assembly purposes such as athletic events with provisions for seating of spectators, or other spaces subject to assembly occupancy, shall comply with Chapter 8, including Special Provisions for Places of Assembly in Buildings of Other

Occupancy, which provides that where auditorium and gymnasium exits lead through corridors or stairways also serving as exits for other parts of the building, the exit capacity shall be sufficient to permit simultaneous exit from auditorium and classroom sections.

Exception: In the case of an auditorium and gymnasium of a type suitable only for use of the school occupant load (and therefore not subject to simultaneous occupancy), the same exit capacity may serve both sections.

The point of this requirement is that if classrooms and places of assembly are likely to be occupied simultaneously, the exit capacity of the building must be designed and arranged for the combined use. For example, classrooms are often used during the evening for adult or remedial education while a school's gymnasium or auditorium is being used by another group. In such cases, the exception would not apply even though during the day the place of assembly would be used only by the school's population.

10-1.2.3 Dormitory and Classrooms.   Any building used for both classroom and dormitory purposes shall comply with the applicable provisions of Chapter 16 in addition to complying with Chapter 10. Where classroom and dormitory sections are not subject to simultaneous occupancy, the same exit capacity may serve both sections.

10-1.2.4 Other Combined Occupancies.

10-1.2.4.1   Any other combinations of occupancy not covered in 10-1.2.2 and 10-1.2.3 shall comply with all applicable chapters of this *Code*, with means of egress adequate to serve all occupancies simultaneously.

10-1.3 Special Definitions.

Common Atmosphere.   A common atmosphere exists between rooms, spaces or areas within a building, which are not separated by an approved smoke partition.

Flexible Plan and Open Plan Educational Buildings.   Include every building or portion of a building not having corridors which comply with 10-3.6.1 and are designed for multiple teaching stations.

(a) Flexible plan buildings have movable corridor walls and movable partitions of full-height construction with doors leading from rooms to corridors.

The intent of the *Code* in referring to movable corridor walls is the use of demountable partitions or partitions which are designed to be easily removed and reinstalled at a different location.

(b) Open plan buildings have rooms and corridors delineated by use of tables, chairs, desks, bookcases, counters, low-height 5-ft (152.4-cm) partitions, or similar furnishings.

Although corridors in flexible plan or open plan buildings do not comply with 10-3.6.1 by not having a fire resistance of at least 1 hour, they must be divided at least every 300 ft (91.44 m) by a smoke partition (see 10-3.7.1).

Flexible plan buildings without exit access doors between rooms and corridors shall be classified as open plan buildings.

This paragraph is not meant to prohibit interior rooms in flexible plan buildings. The intent is to emphasize that all rooms adjoining a corridor in flexible plan buildings must have a door. Simply removing the doors from rooms in a flexible plan building does not make the building open plan. The concept of open plan involves openness to be able to observe a fire in its early stages. Thus, by applying the definition of open plan, partitions cannot be higher than 5 ft (152.4 cm).

Interior Room.   A room whose only means of egress is through an adjoining or intervening room which is not an exit.

Note that this definition of interior room does not imply a windowless room. See Figure 10-1.

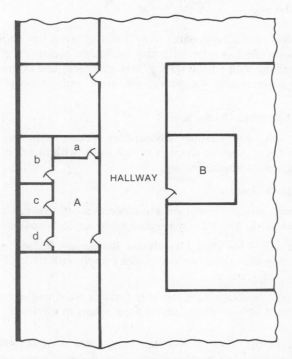

Figure 10-1. Examples of Interior Rooms. Rooms a, b, c, and d are interior rooms because they must pass through Room A before reaching the corridor. An example would be music practice rooms off a large music room. Room B, although windowless, is not an interior room as defined in Chapter 10 because the means of egress is from the room directly to the corridor.

Room.   For the purposes of this section, a room is a space or area bounded by any obstructions to egress which at any time enclose more than 80 percent of the perimeter of the space or area. Openings of less than 3 ft (91.44 cm) clear width and less than 6 ft 8 in. (203.2 cm) high shall not be considered in computing the unobstructed perimeter.

Separate Atmosphere. A separate atmosphere exists between rooms, spaces or areas that are separated by an approved smoke partition.

Separate Means of Egress. A means of egress separated in such a manner from other required means of egress as to provide an atmospheric separation which precludes contamination of both means of egress by the same fire. (*See Section 6-3.*)

Smoke Partition. (*See Section 6-3.*) For purposes of this section, smoke partitions shall also include floors and openings therein.

The definition for "smoke partition" emphasizes that floors are an integral part of a smoke control system designed to provide separate atmospheres. For a smoke partition to be effective, there cannot be any unprotected vertical openings (such as unenclosed stairs) in the area which is to serve as a compartment in case of a fire. See 10-6.3.8.2(a).

10-1.4 Classification of Occupancy. (*See 4-1.3.*)

10-1.4.1 Educational occupancies shall include all buildings used for educational purposes through the twelfth grade by six or more persons for 4 hours per day or more than 12 hours per week.

Educational occupancies for students of high school age and below are distinguished from assembly occupancies in that the same occupants are regularly present and they are subject to discipline and control. Sunday schools or church schools which are not used for daily classes throughout the week are considered to fall within the scope of assembly occupancies.

10-1.4.2 Educational occupancy includes part-day, nursery schools, kindergartens, and other schools whose purpose is primarily educational even though the children are of preschool age.

The *Code* classifies part-day and nursery school facilities as educational occupancies because they provide education in addition to "baby sitting" services. This parallels federal guidelines for subsidizing day-care/educational activities at both the federal and state levels. By requiring educational criteria and related activities, it was hoped that a higher quality of staff would be provided for these facilities by these standards. A day-care "baby sitting" service with no, or limited, educational activities is beyond the scope of Sections 10-1 through 10-6. Sections 10-7, 10-8, and 10-9 set forth special requirements for day-care facilities.

10-1.4.3 Other occupancies associated with educational institutions shall be in accordance with the appropriate parts of this *Code*. (*See Chapters 12, 16, 18, 20, 28, 29, and 30, and 1-4.4.*)

The fact that education or instruction takes place in an occupancy affects the life safety requirements because, particularly in a school for students of high school age and below, the same occupants are regularly present and they are subject to discipline and control, even though many areas of school buildings (gymnasiums, auditoriums, rooms with fixed or movable furniture) resemble places of assembly.

10-1.4.4 In cases where instruction is incidental to some other occupancy, the section of this *Code* governing such other occupancy shall apply.

When instruction is incidental to other occupancies, the requirements for the occupancy in which the instruction occurs are applicable. Church schools which are used for religious instruction for a few hours on one or two days of the week are generally classed as places of assembly. In an office building or factory a few rooms may be used for orientation or instruction in the work requirements; these rooms are subject to the *Code* requirements for offices or factories. Barber colleges and beauty schools frequently are located in commercial buildings and should be governed by the requirements of the buildings in which they occur. The revision to 10-1.4.1 helps in classifying an educational occupancy.

10-1.5 Classification of Hazard of Contents.   Contents of educational occupancies shall be classified in accordance with the provisions of Section 4-2.

In general, educational occupancies will contain ordinary hazard contents.

10-1.6 Minumum Construction Required.   No Requirements.

Fire-resistive construction is not generally specified in this chapter of the *Code*, though it is obviously desirable and should be used wherever feasible.

10-1.7 Occupant Load.

10-1.7.1   The occupant load of educational buildings or any individual story or section thereof for the purpose of determining exits shall be as determined by the authority having jurisdiction but not less than one person for each 20 sq ft (1.86 sq m) of net classroom area or 50 sq ft (4.65 sq m) of net area of shops, laboratories, and similar vocational rooms. In day nurseries where sleeping facilities are provided, the occupant load shall be not less than one person for each 35 sq ft (3.25 sq m) of net area.

10-1.7.2   The occupant load of an area having fixed seats shall be determined by the number of fixed seats installed. Required aisle space serving the fixed seats shall not be used to increase the occupant load.

10-1.7.3   The capacity of an educational occupancy or a portion thereof may be modified from that specified above if the necessary aisles and exits are provided. An approved aisle or seating diagram shall be required by the authority having jurisdiction to substantiate such a modification.

Figure 10-2 illustrates a classroom designed in conformance with 10-1.7.2. Its population is 35. This figure is determined by the room's number of fixed seats related to the required aisle space serving the room, not by the criterion of 20 sq ft (1.86 sq m) of net classroom area per person (see 10-1.7.1). Figure 10-3 demonstrates how a classroom with the same floor area can safely contain nearly 40 percent more students if the necessary aisles and exits are provided. In Figure 10-3, the bookcase has been eliminated and a row of seats placed directly against the window wall. The desks in the other rows have been placed front to front. The result adds 13 additional students to the room. This rearrangement of the furniture conforms with 10-1.7.3 and is one of many examples of how the *Code* requirements may still be met while adding to the occupant load of a building.

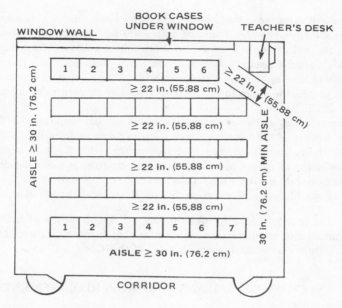

Figure 10-2. Classroom Arranged to Comply with 10-1.7.2. Room area = 594 sq ft (22 by 27 ft) 55.18 sq m; at 20 sq ft (1.86 sq m)/person, occupant load = 29. Layout allows 35 occupants (4 rows of 7 seats, 1 row of 6, plus the teacher). Note that the maximum number of seats permitted in a row is 7.

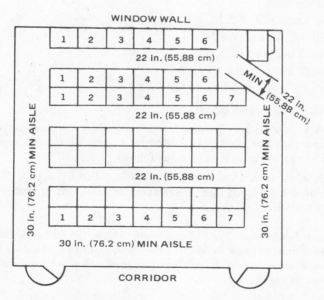

Figure 10-3. Modified Arrangement of Classroom Complying with 10-1.7.2 and 10-1.7.3. Room area = 594 sq ft (22 by 27 ft); at 20 sq ft/person, occupant load = 29. Layout allows 48 occupants (5 rows of 7 seats, 2 rows of 6, plus the teacher).

In both illustrations, the 22-in. (55.88-cm) access by the teacher's desk and between the rows provides 1 unit of exit width for ease of movement at all times. Placing the desks front to front so that 2 rows share a 22-in. (55.88-cm) access meets the *Code*'s requirements. Note that if the room contained more than 60 seats, the aisles would have to be 36 in. (91.44 cm) wide. Also, since both rooms contain fewer than 50 people, the doors to the corridor would be allowed to swing into the rooms (see 10-2.5.5).

Separate tables and chairs create problems not encountered with the illustrated seating. Instead of fixed seating which leads to predictable egress patterns, separate movable chairs and tables may lead to temporary blockage or restriction of the designed means of egress. Where this style of furniture is used, additional emphasis must be placed on the daily operational procedures followed by the facility's staff to minimize any blockage, obstruction, or restriction of the required means of egress.

10-1.7.4 The occupant load for determining exit requirements of individual lecture rooms, gymnasiums, or cafeterias used for assembly purposes of more than 50 persons shall be determined in accordance with 8-1.7 of this *Code*.

SECTION 10-2   MEANS OF EGRESS REQUIREMENTS

10-2.1 General. Every aisle, corridor, balcony, other means of access to exits, and discharge from exits shall be in accordance with Chapter 5.

10-2.2 Types of Exits. Exits of the specified number and width shall be one or more of the following types, in accordance with the provisions of Chapter 5 of this *Code*.

(a) Doors.(*See 5-2.1.*)

(b) Interior Stairs.(*See 5-2.2.*)

(c) Smokeproof Towers.(*See 5-2.3.*)

(d) Outside Stairs.(*See 5-2.5.*)

(e) Horizontal Exits.(*See 5-2.4.*)

(f) Ramps — Class A or Class B.(*See 5-2.6.*)

10-2.3 Capacity of Means of Egress.

10-2.3.1 Every educational building, and every floor, section or room thereof considered separately shall have exits sufficient to provide for the capacity thereof, comprised of one or more types of exits, as follows:

(a) Any door, in accordance with 5-2.1, leading directly outside the building at ground level, or not to exceed three risers above or below the ground — 100 persons per unit of exit width.

Paragraph 5-3.2 defines "unit of exit width" [22 in. (55.88 cm)], tells how to count fractions of a unit, and how to measure the width of an exit. If a door has more than three risers inside or outside to reach ground level, the stair is calculated separately to determine its capacity.

(b) Any door leading outside the building but requiring steps of over three risers to reach the ground — 100 persons per unit of exit width; steps must have one-third more units of width than doors to allow for slower travel rate.

(c) Stairs, smokeproof towers or outside stairs, in accordance with 5-2.2, 5-2.3 and 5-2.5 — 60 persons per unit of exit width.

(d) Ramps, in accordance with 5-2.6.

    1. Class A — 100 persons per unit of exit width.

    2. Class B — 60 persons per unit of exit width.

(e) Horizontal exits, in accordance with 5-2.4 — 100 persons per unit of exit width.

10-2.3.2 The same exit units or fraction thereof required for any individual floor may be counted as simultaneously serving all floors above the first story or floor of exit discharge.

> For example, in the case of enclosed interior stairways, where the capacity of the third floor requires three stairways, and the capacity of the second floor also requires three stairways, the second floor may utilize the stairways which serve the third floor so that the total number of stairways required is three, not six.
>
> The street floor and basement, however, must either have their required exit capacity provided by separate exits or, if the path of exit from the street floor or basement is through a part of the same stair tower serving the upper floors, the total exit capacity must provide the required exit facilities for the street floor and basement without encroaching upon the stair capacity required for the upper floors. This assumes that, due to a greater travel distance, people on floors above the second will require more time to reach the street and will not exit simultaneously with the occupants of the basement, the street floor, or the second floor.

10-2.4 Number of Exits.

10-2.4.1 There shall be at least two exits available from every floor area.

10-2.4.2 Every room or space with a capacity of over 50 persons or over 1,000 sq ft (92.9 sq m) in area shall have at least two doorways as remote from each other as practicable. Such doorways shall provide access to separate exits, but, where egress is through corridors, may open upon a common corridor leading to separate exits in opposite directions.

10-2.5 Arrangement of Means of Egress.

10-2.5.1 Exits shall be so arranged that at least two separate exits will be available from every floor area. Exits shall be as remote from each other as practicable, so arranged that there will be no pockets or dead ends of appreciable size in which occupants may be trapped, and in no case shall any dead-end corridor extend more than 20 ft (609.6 cm) beyond the stairway of other means of exit therefrom.

> A school plan with outside doors or stairways at both ends of a central corridor meets the requirements of 10-2.5.1. Pockets may be created where stairways are not located at the end of corridors but at intermediate points. See Figure 10-4.

10-2.5.2 Every classroom or room used for educational purposes or student occupancy below the floor of exit discharge shall have access to at least one exit which leads directly to the exterior at level of discharge without entering the floor above.

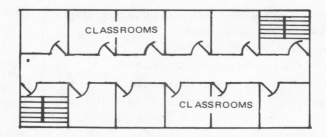

PREFERRED ARRANGEMENT OF EXITS WITHOUT DEAD ENDS

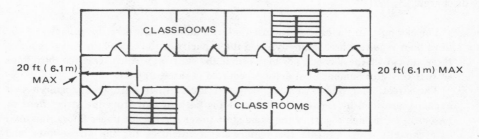

20 ft (6.1 m)
MAX

20 ft(6.1 m) MAX

ACCEPTABLE ARRANGEMENT OF EXITS WITH DEAD ENDS
UP TO 20 ft (6.1 m)

Figure 10-4. Stair Placement in Accordance with 10-2.5.1.

Figures 10-5 and 10-6 illustrate two types of exits which will satisfy the requirements of 10-2.5.2. The enclosed stairs in Figure 10-6 may serve floors other than the floor above the basement.

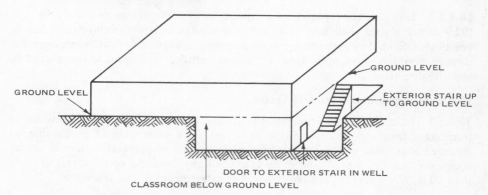

GROUND LEVEL

GROUND LEVEL

EXTERIOR STAIR UP
TO GROUND LEVEL

DOOR TO EXTERIOR STAIR IN WELL

CLASSROOM BELOW GROUND LEVEL

Figure 10-5. Exit from Classroom Below Floor of Exit Discharge.

10-2.5.3 Minimum Corridor Width.

10-2.5.3.1   Exit access corridors shall be not less than 6 ft (182.88 cm) wide in the clear.

This paragraph applies to exit access corridors and not to nonrequired corridors that are provided for convenience only.

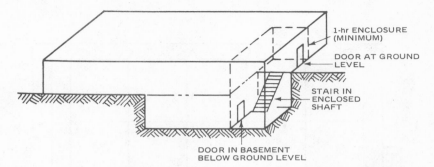

Figure 10-6. Exit from Classroom Below Floor of Exit Discharge. The enclosed stair could be located on the outside of the building. If so, the shaft enclosure would have to be of the same construction as the exterior construction of the building.

10-2.5.3.2   Drinking fountains or other equipment, fixed or movable, shall not be so placed as to obstruct the required minimum 6 ft (182.88 cm) corridor width.

"In the clear" means a 6-ft (1.83-m) wide clear space with no furniture or other obstructions the full length of the corridor.

10-2.5.3.3   Doors which swing into an exit access corridor shall be recessed to prevent interference with corridor traffic; any doors not so recessed shall open 180 degrees to stop against wall. Doors in any position shall not reduce the required corridor width by more than one half.

See 10-2.11.2 for further information on door swing.

10-2.5.4   When there are more than 60 seats, every aisle shall be not less than 3 ft (91.44 cm) wide when serving seats on one side only and not less than 3 ft 6 in. (106.68 cm) when serving seats on both sides. When serving 60 seats or less, aisles shall not be less than 30 in. (76.2 cm) wide. Within a classroom where there are rows of seats with room access to the seats between individual rows, this space does not constitute an aisle. No more than six seats shall intervene between any seat and an aisle.

See Figures 10-2 and 10-3.

10-2.5.5 Exterior Corridors or Balconies.

10-2.5.5.1   Where exterior corridors or balconies are provided as means of exit, they shall open to the outside air except for railings or balustrades with stairs or level exits to grade not over the allowable travel distance apart, so located that an exit will be available in either direction from the door to any individual room or space, with dead ends not to exceed 20 ft (609.6 cm). If balconies are enclosed by glass or in any other manner, they shall be treated as interior corridors.

From the standpoint of life safety, the preferable school design provides classroom exits directly to the outside or to exterior balconies open to the outside air with exterior stairways to ground level available in either direction. See Figure 10-7. Conventional designs incorporate interior corridors, which can become untenable from the accumulation of smoke and heat.

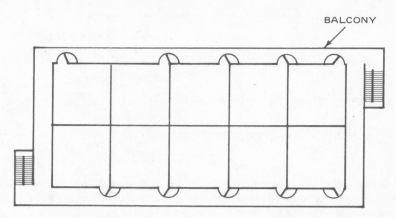

Figure 10-7. Stair Placement, Exterior Balcony. Distance between stairs must not be greater than the allowable travel distance would permit. Balcony width must be at least as wide as the door leading to it or the stair leading away from it.

10-2.5.5.2 The floors of balconies (exterior corridors) and stairs shall be solid, without openings, and shall comply with requirements for outside stairs as regards balustrades or railings, width and pitch of stairs, and other details, but are not required to be shielded from fire within the building by blank walls, wired glass windows or the like where the stairs are located on the side of the balcony or corridor away from the building and are separated from the building by the full required width of the balcony or corridor. Regardless of other provisions, exterior balconies and stairs may be of the same type of construction as the building which they serve.

Stairs from exterior balconies must not pass or come close to windows or other openings in stories below. Preferable stair placements complying with 10-2.5.5.1 and 10-2.5.5.2 are illustrated in Figures 10-8 and 10-9.

10-2.6 Measurement of Travel Distance to Exits.   Travel distance to an exit shall not exceed 150 ft (45.72 cm) from any point in a building.

Exception No. 1:   For travel distance in open plan buildings, see 10-6.2.2.

Exception No. 2:   The travel distance may be increased to 200 ft (60.96 m) in educational occupancies protected throughout by an approved automatic sprinkler system.

10-2.7 Discharge from Exits.   Discharge from exits shall be arranged in accordance with the provisions of Section 5-7.

10-2.8 Illumination of Means of Egress.   All educational buildings shall have adequate exit illumination in accordance with Section 5-8.

10-2.9 Emergency Lighting.   Emergency lighting in accordance with Section 5-9 shall be provided:

(a) In all interior stairs and corridors

(b) In all normally occupied spaces

Exception to (b):

1. Administrative areas.

2. General classrooms.

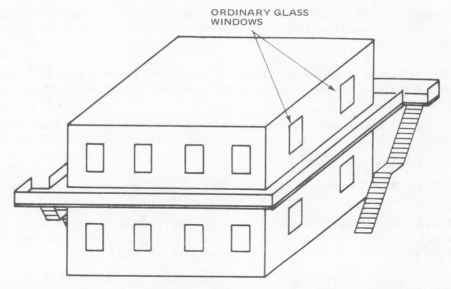

Figure 10-8. Stair Placement, Exterior Balcony. Since stairs are separated from the building by the full width of the balcony, blank walls or wired glass windows are not required near the stairs.

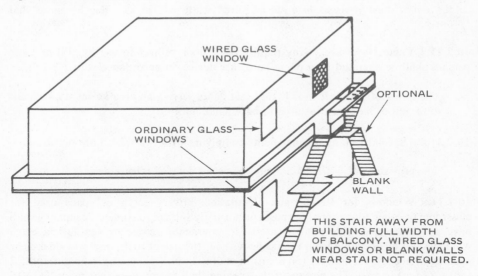

Figure 10-9. Stair Placement, Exterior Balcony. The stair placed directly against the building must not pass near unprotected openings.

3. *Mechanical rooms and storage areas.*

(c) In flexible and open plan buildings

(d) In all portions of buildings that are interior or windowless.

The changes to 10-2.9 in this edition are to make clear the intent of the *Code* as to where emergency lighting is required. The exceptions to item (b) indicate that normal classrooms, offices, and storage or mechanical spaces do not require emergency lighting. Shops, laboratories, and assembly rooms would require emergency lighting.

10-2.10 Marking of Means of Egress. All educational buildings shall have signs designating the location of exits or the path of travel to reach them, in accordance with Section 5-10.

Exception: Signs are not required in situations where location of exits is otherwise obvious and familiar to all occupants, such as in small elementary school buildings.

10-2.11 Special Features.

10-2.11.1 Door Closure. All exit doors designed to be kept normally closed shall conform with 5-2.1.2.3.

10-2.11.2 Door Swing. If a room or space is subject to occupancy by more than 50 persons, exit doors shall swing out. Only one locking or latching device shall be permitted on a door or a leaf of a pair of doors. (*See also 10-2.5.3.*)

Paragraph 10-2.11.2 relates to the requirement in 5-2.1.1.4.1 that doors must swing in the direction of exit travel if they serve a room occupied by more than 50 people. Paragraph 10-2.5.3.3 requires that doors which swing into an exit access corridor either be recessed or open 180 degrees to stop against the wall. The swing of the doors must never reduce the required width of the corridor by more than one-half.

10-2.11.3 Panic Hardware. Any required exit door subject to use by 100 or more persons shall be operated by a panic hardware device, in accordance with 5-2.1.2.2.

The intent of the *Code* here is that exit doors serving an area having an occupant load of 100 or more are required to have panic hardware.

10-2.11.4 Special locking arrangements complying with 5-2.1.2.1.5 are permitted.

The provisions of 5-2.1.2.1.5 apply to special delayed release devices.

10-2.11.5 Windows for Rescue and Ventilation. Every room or space used for classroom or other educational purposes or normally subject to student occupancy shall have at least one outside window used for emergency rescue or ventilation. Such window shall be openable from the inside without the use of tools, and provide a clear opening of not less than 20 in. (50.8 cm) in width, 24 in. (60.96 cm) in height and 5.7 sq ft (.5 sq m) in area. The bottom of the opening shall be not more than 44 in. (111.16 cm) above the floor, and any latching device shall be capable of being operated from not more than 54 in. (137.16 cm) above the finished floor.

Exception No. 1: In buildings protected throughout by an approved automatic sprinkler system in accordance with Section 7-7.

Exception No. 2: Where the room or space has a door leading directly to the outside of the building.

The dimensions specified for windows used for emergency rescue or for ventilation are based on simulations of emergency rescue conducted by the San Diego Fire Department. Windows providing clear openings of identical dimensions are also required for rescue or ventilation in one- and two-family dwellings. Figure 10-10 illustrates two configurations which achieve the required area of 5.7 sq ft (.53 sq m).

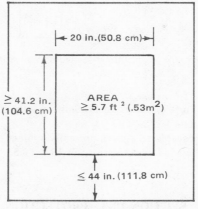

REQUIRED CLEAR OPENING

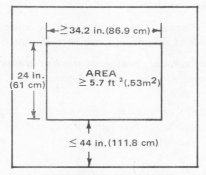

REQUIRED CLEAR OPENING

Figure 10-10. Windows for Rescue or Ventilation, Required Dimensions.

Although the *Code* intends the fire department or others to assist students, particularly over ladders, if these windows must be used as a supplementary means of escape, the windows should permit small children in the lower grades to escape unaided. Therefore, storm sashes, screens, or devices in front of the windows must be easy to open or remove and the sills must be low enough for the children to reach.

Where the location of windows precludes their use for rescue or escape, they may still provide trapped children with air for breathing in smoke-filled rooms. If awning or hopper-type windows are installed solely for emergency ventilation, they should be hinged or subdivided to provide a clear opening of at least 600 sq in. (3,871 sq cm) with no dimension less than 22 in. (55.88 cm). See Figure 10-11.

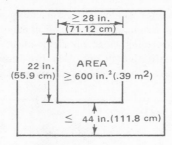

Figure 10-11. Windows for Ventilation (Awning or Hopper-type), Recommended Dimensions.

Exception No. 2 allows windows to be omitted only if a classroom has a door leading directly to ground level.

Bathrooms are not considered spaces normally subject to student occupancy and, thus, do not require the window referred to in 10-2.11.5.

SECTION 10-3   PROTECTION

10-3.1 Protection of Vertical Openings.

10-3.1.1 Any interior stairway and other vertical opening in educational buildings shall be enclosed and protected in accordance with Section 6-2.

Exception: Unprotected vertical openings connecting not more than three floors may be permitted in accordance with 6-2.2.3.1, Exception No. 1.

Since a school normally would be considered ordinary hazard, 6-2.2.3.1, Exception No. 1 requires that complete approved automatic sprinkler protection be provided in addition to other requirements.

10-3.1.2 Stairs shall be enclosed in accordance with Section 6-2.

Exception: Stairway enclosure will not be required for a stairway serving only one adjacent floor except a basement and not connected with corridors or stairways serving other floors.

The exception to 10-3.1.2 would allow a two-story school building to have open stairs between the first floor and the second floor. Since basements usually contain hazardous areas with high fuel loads, such as storage rooms, boiler rooms, or workshops, the use of open stairs as a connection between the basement and the upper floors is prohibited. The intent is to reduce the probability of children on upper floors being exposed to the vertical spread of a fire originating in the basement of a building. Figures 10-12 and 10-13 illustrate acceptable examples of the exception to 10-3.1.2 in a multistory school.

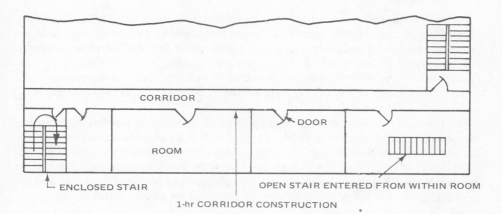

CORRIDOR

DOOR

ROOM

ENCLOSED STAIR

OPEN STAIR ENTERED FROM WITHIN ROOM

1-hr CORRIDOR CONSTRUCTION

Figure 10-12. Open Stair Complying with 10-3.1.2.

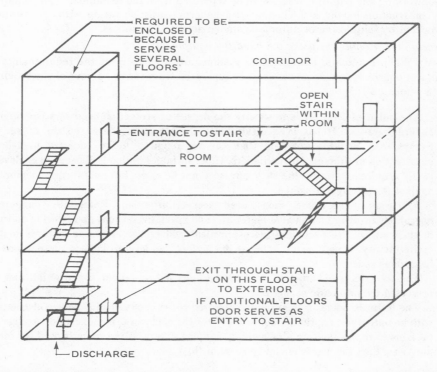

REQUIRED TO BE ENCLOSED BECAUSE IT SERVES SEVERAL FLOORS

CORRIDOR

OPEN STAIR WITHIN ROOM

ENTRANCE TO STAIR

ROOM

EXIT THROUGH STAIR ON THIS FLOOR TO EXTERIOR

IF ADDITIONAL FLOORS DOOR SERVES AS ENTRY TO STAIR

DISCHARGE

Figure 10-13. Open Stair Complying with 10-3.1.2. Stair serves only one floor and is not connected to a corridor.

10-3.2 Protection from Hazards.

10-3.2.1 Rooms or spaces for the storage, processing, or use of the materials specified in this section shall be protected in accordance with the following:

(a) Rooms or spaces used for the storage of combustible supplies in quantities deemed hazardous by the authority having jurisdiction, hazardous materials in quantities deemed hazardous by recognized standards, or fuel shall be separated from the remainder of the building by construction having not less than a 1-hour fire-resistive rating with all openings protected by self-closing or smoke-actuated fire doors, or such rooms or spaces may be protected by an automatic extinguishing system as set forth in Section 6-4.

(b) Rooms or spaces used for processing or use of combustible supplies in quantities considered hazardous by the authority having juridiction, hazardous materials, or for flammable or combustible liquids in quantities deemed hazardous by recognized standards shall be separated from the remainder of the building by construction having not less than a 1-hour fire-resistive rating with all openings protected by self-closing or smoke-actuated fire doors and shall also be protected by an automatic extinguishing system as set forth in Section 6-4.

(c) Boiler and furnace rooms, laundries, and maintenance shops, including woodworking and painting areas, shall be separated from the remainder of the building by construction having not less than a 1-hour fire-resistive rating with all openings protected by self-closing or automatic smoke-actuated fire doors.

Exception: Rooms enclosing air-handling equipment.

(d) When automatic extinguishing systems are used to meet the requirements of this section, the rooms or spaces shall be separated from the remainder of the building by a smoke barrier.

The intent of 10-3.2.1 is to specify the degree of protection necessary for certain hazardous areas. It has been divided into three sections based on the degree of hazard. The hazards noted in item (a) are required to be enclosed in 1-hour construction or protected by sprinklers. If the sprinkler option is chosen, an enclosure is still required; however, the enclosure need not be rated, but only form a membrane against the passage of smoke.

Art rooms and some shops need special attention. Potentially dangerous operations involving flammable materials, and specialized ovens and ignition sources in these areas, are becoming more prevalent and create increased hazards to the entire facility. It may be advisable at the high school level to include these rooms as hazardous spaces.

The hazards noted in item (b) must be enclosed in 1-hour construction *and* be protected by automatic sprinklers.

The hazards noted in item (c) are required to be enclosed in 1-hour construction with no option for a sprinkler equivalency for the enclosure. The exception to item (c) pertains to rooms housing air-handling equipment *only*. If the room is used for other purposes, then the provisions of item (a) or (b) apply.

10-3.2.2 Food preparation facilities shall be protected in accordance with *Removal of Smoke and Grease-Laden Vapors from Commercial Cooking Equipment*, NFPA 96, and are not required to have openings protected between food preparation areas and dining areas.

The intent of 10-3.2.2 is to provide some barrier between cooking areas and dining areas. The intent of the barrier is to screen possible flash fires from view in an attempt to prevent panic. Openings in this barrier are not restricted and do not need to be protected. The *Code* is counting on the automatic extinguishing system to control any fire on the cooking surfaces, and, thus, no longer requires enclosure by rated construction. The degree of screening required, and thus the size of the barrier required, is left to the judgment of the authority having jurisdiction.

10-3.2.3 Janitor closets shall be protected by an automatic sprinkler system which may be supplied by the domestic water supply system serving no more than six sprinklers and having a water supply sufficient to provide 0.15 gpm per sq ft (1.02 × 10^{-4} cu m/s/sq m) of floor area. Doors to janitor closets may have ventilating louvers.

Where janitor closets are located off of corridors, a louvered door is usually provided for ventilation. It is necessary to provide these spaces with automatic sprinkler protection since the louvered door offers little fire resistance and permits a fire in the closet to directly affect the corridor. To accomplish this at reasonable cost, these sprinklers (not more than six in number) may be supplied from the domestic water supply to the closet if the supply is capable of providing the required quantity of water. It is advisable to provide a water-flow switch (see Chapter 6) to initiate an alarm when a sprinkler is opened.

The minimum flow of 0.15 gpm/sq ft (1.02 × 10^{-4} cu m/s/sq m) is based on the requirements in NFPA 13, *Standard for the Installation of Sprinkler Systems*[3], for protecting buildings containing ordinary hazards. This criterion, when multiplied by the floor area of the largest closet, leads to a gross flow rate that *must* be provided by the domestic water supply.

10-3.2.4 Laboratories that use chemicals shall comply with *Standard on Fire Protection for Laboratories Using Chemicals*, NFPA 45.

10-3.3 Interior Finish.

10-3.3.1 Interior finish shall be Class A in stairways and Class A or B in corridors and lobbies and Class A, B or C elsewhere, in accordance with the provisions of Section 6-5.

10-3.3.2 Interior Floor Finish. No Requirements.

Section 6-5 permits the use of fire retardant or intumescent paints and surface coatings to reduce the *surface flame spread* of an interior finish. These coatings *will not* render a finish noncombustible. They will simply delay the eventual ignition of a finish exposed to fire.

Some coatings have a short life and require frequent reapplication. Over the useful life of a building, all coatings may eventually have to be renewed. Also, some coatings will severely mar or alter the appearance of the finish. Due to these liabilities, the option of using coatings and paints may not provide the best fire protection at a reasonable cost in all cases.

10-3.4 Detection, Alarm, and Communication Systems.

10-3.4.1 Approved manually operated fire alarm facilities in accordance with 7-6.1.2 shall be provided in every educational building. When acceptable to the authority having jurisdiction the fire alarm system may be used to designate class change provided the fire alarm is distinctive in signal and overrides all other use.

10-3.4.2   In buildings provided with automatic sprinkler protection, the operation of the sprinkler system shall automatically actuate the fire alarm system.

10-3.5 Extinguishment Requirements.   Every portion of educational buildings below the floor of exit discharge shall be protected throughout by an approved automatic sprinkler system in accordance with Section 7-7.

> Levels below the level of exit discharge are not necessarily below grade.

10-3.6 Interior Corridors.

10-3.6.1   Every interior corridor shall be of construction having not less than a 1-hour fire resistance rating. Such corridor walls shall extend from floor slab to floor slab or when the ceiling of the entire story is an element of a 1-hour fire-resistive floor or ceiling system, the corridor wall may terminate at the ceiling. All openings shall be protected with doors, frames and hardware, including closers, that shall all have a fire protection rating of at least 20 minutes.

Exception No. 1:   Such corridor protection shall not be required when all classrooms served by such corridors have at least one door directly to the outside or to an exterior balcony or corridor as in 10-2.5.4.

Exception No. 2:   The corridor protection may be reduced to a ½-hour fire resistance rating providing the building is protected throughout by an approved automatic sprinkler system.

> The intent of Exception No. 1 is to delete the requirement for a rated corridor wall; however, a wall and doors with closers providing a smoke barrier are still required.

10-3.7 Subdivision of Building Spaces.

10-3.7.1   When the aggregate length of interior corridors, including dead-end corridors and cross corridors, exceeds 300 ft (91.44 m), the corridor shall be divided into reasonably equal sections not exceeding 300 ft (91.44 m) in length by smoke barriers installed in accordance with Section 6-3.

> The 300-ft (91.44-m) limit bears a direct relationship to the travel distance criteria in Chapter 10 and reflects the committee's concern about the maximum area within an educational facility that would be immediately contaminated by products of combustion from a fire. Travel distance for this occupancy is limited to 150 ft (45.72 m) from *any point* in the building (see 10-2.6). Extrapolated to travel distance in a corridor (ignoring the distance from any room or space of the corridor), this criterion would lead to the exit arrangement shown in Figure 10-14, with no point in the corridor being more than 150 ft (45.72 m) from at least one exit.
>
> The committee, in viewing this relationship, felt it was reasonable and prudent to require smoke partitions across a corridor at maximum intervals of 300 ft (91.44 m) so that the products of combustion would affect a limited number of exits at one time. Figure 10-15 illustrates how the partition location dovetails with the travel distance criterion and minimizes the area of a building immediately affected by a fire.

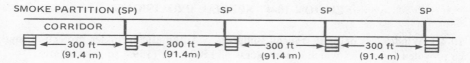

Figure 10-14. Smoke Partitions in Interior Corridors.

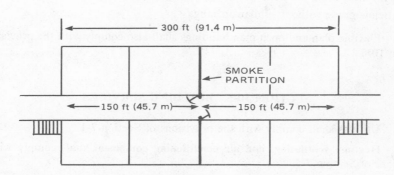

Figure 10-15. Smoke Partitions in Interior Corridors.

For purposes of this requirement (see 10-3.7.1), the measurement of the length of the interior corridor does include side corridors. In Figure 10-16, the distance governing the installation of a smoke partition is 360 ft (109.7 m); thus, a smoke partition is required.

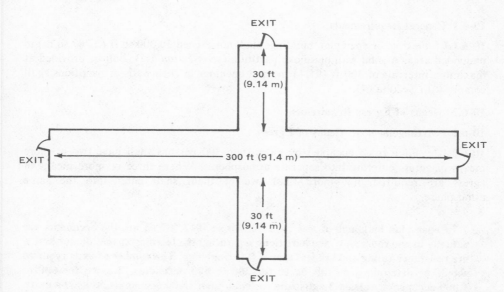

Figure 10-16. Measurement of Interior Corridor Length for Purposes of Complying with 10-3.7.1. Count the side corridors. In this example, a smoke partition is required because the aggregate corridor length is greater than 300 ft (91.44 m).

SECTION 10-4   SPECIAL PROVISIONS

10-4.1 Windowless or Subterranean Buildings. Automatic sprinkler protection shall be provided for stories which are in excess of 1500 sq ft (139.4 sq m) and are:

(a) Without windows or other openings directly to the exterior at the rate of 20 sq ft (1.9 sq m) of opening per 50 linear ft (15.24 m) in any two walls or,

(b) Below grade without similar openings.

10-4.2 Flexible plan and open plan buildings shall also comply with the provisions of Section 10-6.

SECTION 10-5   BUILDING SERVICES

10-5.1 Utilities shall comply with the provisions of Section 7-1.

10-5.2 Heating, ventilating, and air conditioning equipment shall comply with the provisions of Section 7-2.

10-5.3 Elevators, dumbwaiters, and vertical conveyors shall comply with the provisions of Section 7-4.

10-5.4 Rubbish chutes, incinerators, and laundry chutes shall comply with the provisions of Section 7-5.

SECTION 10-6   FLEXIBLE PLAN AND OPEN PLAN BUILDINGS

10-6.1 General Requirements.

10-6.1.1 Flexible or open plan buildings shall not exceed 30,000 sq ft (2,787 sq m) in undivided area. A solid wall or smoke partition (*see Section 6-3*) shall be provided at maximum intervals of 300 ft (91.44 m) and openings in such walls or partitions shall comply with Section 6-3.

10-6.2 Means of Egress Requirements.

10-6.2.1 Arrangement of Means of Egress.

10-6.2.1.1 Each room occupied by more than 300 persons shall have two or more means of egress entering into separate atmospheres. Where three or more means of egress are required, not more than two of them shall enter into the same atmosphere.

In open plan buildings of less than 30,000 sq ft (2,787 sq m), the occupants are actually in one room since the partitions separating the learning spaces do not have a fire resistance rating and are less than 5 ft (1.5 m) high. The number of exits required should be determined on this basis: for 200 to 600 occupants, 2 exits; for 600 to 1,000 occupants, at least 3 exits; and for more than 1,000 occupants, at least 4 exits. Exits from rooms or areas which have an occupant load in excess of 300 must be through separate atmospheres as required by 10-6.2.1.1 and illustrated in Figure 10-17.

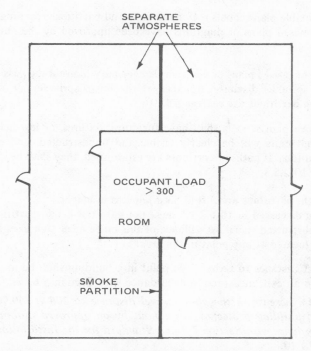

SEPARATE
ATMOSPHERES

OCCUPANT LOAD
> 300

ROOM

SMOKE
PARTITION →

Figure 10-17. Example of Room in Open Plan Building Requiring Two or More Means of Egress into Separate Atmospheres.

10-6.2.1.2 Exit access from interior rooms may pass through an adjoining or an intervening room, provided that the travel distances do not exceed those set forth in 10-6.2.2. Foyers and lobbies constructed as required for corridors shall not be construed as intervening rooms.

10-6.2.1.3 Where the only means of egress from an interior room or rooms is through an adjoining or intervening room, smoke detectors shall be installed in the area of the common atmosphere through which the means of egress must pass. The detectors shall actuate alarms audible in the interior room and shall be connected to the school fire alarm system.

Exception No. 1: Smoke detectors are not required where the aggregate occupant load is less than ten.

Exception No. 2: Interior rooms used exclusively for mechanical and public utility service to the buildings.

Exception No. 3: Where the building is protected throughout by an approved automatic sprinkler system.

If the only means of egress from a room is through an adjoining or intervening room, smoke detectors must be installed in the room through which the means of egress must pass because occupants of the interior room may not be aware of a fire or smoke condition in the intervening room, the room which provides their only means of egress. Alarm-sounding smoke detectors provide the occupants with an early warning so that they can safely pass through the room.

10-6.2.1.4   Flexible plan schools may have walls and partitions rearranged periodically, only after revised plans or diagrams have been approved by the authority having jurisdiction.

Approval of revised plans or diagrams is necessary to avoid the possibility of either obstructing sprinkler discharge or excessive spacing of sprinklers or other life safety devices when partitions are rearranged.

10-6.2.1.5   Open plan schools shall have furniture, fixtures, or low-height partitions so arranged that exits will be clearly visible and unobstructed, and exit paths are direct, not circuitous. If paths or corridors are established, they shall be at least as wide as required by 10-2.5.3.

Low-height partitions are 5 ft (1.53 m) or less in height.
Corridors discussed in 10-6.2.1.5 must not have full-height partitions in order to provide unobstructed visual surveillance of the entire open plan area by members of the faculty located at any point in the area.

10-6.2.2 Travel Distance to Exits.   No point in a building shall be more than 150 ft (45.72 m) from an exit, measured in accordance with Section 5-6.

Exception: An increase in the above travel distance to 200 ft (60.96 m) shall be permitted in a building protected throughout by an approved automatic sprinkler system in accordance with Section 7-7 and Standard for the Installation of Sprinkler Systems, NFPA 13.

10-6.3 Protection.

10-6.3.1 Vertical Openings.

10-6.3.1.1   All exit stairs shall be enclosed in accordance with Section 6-2.

10-6.3.1.2   Vertical openings other than exits shall be enclosed as required by Section 6-2. (*See 10-3.1.2 for enclosure of exits.*)

Enclosures around interior vertical penetrations (openings) must not reduce the clear surveillance of an entire floor from any position on the floor. It is generally advisable to locate the required enclosing shafts at the building periphery to minimize potential visual obstruction.

10-6.3.2 Protection from Hazards.

10-6.3.2.1   Stages in places of assembly shall be separated from school areas by construction having at least a 1-hour fire resistance rating and shall comply with 8-3.2. Openings shall be protected by self-closing or smoke-activated fire doors having a fire protection rating of ¾ hours.

10-6.3.2.2   Shops, laboratories, and similar vocational rooms, as well as storage rooms, shall be separated from school areas by construction having at least a 1-hour fire resistance rating. They shall have exits independent from other areas.

Facilities referenced by 10-6.3.2.2 should be separated from each other as well as from the remainder of the facility. This would avoid such hazards as welding in one shop area while glass fiber-reinforced plastic is being worked on (molded, shaped, sanded, or glued) in another area. This can create a very hazardous interaction between open flame and flammable vapors.

10-6.3.3 Interior Finish.   Interior finish, in accordance with Section 6-5, in flexible plan and open plan buildings shall be as follows:

(a) Corridors in flexible plan buildings — Class A, on rigid material that will not deform at temperatures below 450°F (232°C).

(b) Other than corridor walls — Class A or Class B.

Exception No. 1:   Fixtures and low-height partitions not over 5 ft (152.4 cm) high may be Class C.

Exception No. 2:   In one-story buildings the exposed portions of structural members complying with the requirements for Type IV (2HH) construction may be permitted.

> Heavy timber construction is defined in NFPA 220, *Standard Types of Building Construction*⁴. Essential to the definition of heavy timber construction is that the bearing walls be of noncombustible or limited-combustible material and that the wood of the floors and roofs be without concealed spaces.

10-6.3.4 Reserved.

10-6.3.5 Automatic Fire Extinguishing Systems.

10-6.3.5.1   Any flexible plan building or open plan building in which the travel distance to exits exceeds 150 ft (45.72 m) shall be protected throughout by an approved automatic sprinkler system in accordance with Section 7-7. Extinguishing systems shall be electrically interconnected with the school fire alarm system.

10-6.3.5.2   Automatic fire extinguishing systems shall be modified to conform with partition changes. Modification plans shall have prior approval of the authority having jurisdiction.

10-6.3.6 Reserved.

10-6.3.7 Reserved.

10-6.3.8 Smoke Control.

10-6.3.8.1   The specific requirements of this section are not intended to prevent the design or use of other systems, equipment or techniques that will effectively prevent the products of combustion from breaching the atmospheric separation.

> The intent of the requirements for separate atmospheres is to provide at least one uncontaminated egress path when a fire occurs in any part of a building. Guidance on meeting the provisions of 10-6.3.8.2(c) will be found in NFPA 90A, *Standard for the Installation of Air Conditioning and Ventilating Systems.*⁵ Also refer to 12-3.7.9.

10-6.3.8.2   The provisions of this subsection shall apply only to the requirements for providing separate atmospheres. The fire resistance requirements shall comply with other provisions of the *Code*.

(a) Walls, partitions and floors forming all of or part of an atmospheric separation shall be of materials consistent with the requirements for the type of construction, but of construction not less effective than a smoke barrier. Glass lights of approved wired glass set in steel frames may be installed in such walls or partitions.

(b) Every door opening therein shall be protected with a fire assembly as required elsewhere in the *Code*, but not less than a self-closing or automatic-closing, tight-fitting smoke assembly having a fire protection rating of not less than 20 minutes.

(c) Ducts penetrating atmospheric separation walls, partitions, or doors shall be equipped with an approved automatic-closing smoke damper when having openings into more than one atmosphere, or the atmospheric separation shall be maintained by an approved method of smoke control.

(d) All automatic-closing fire assemblies installed in the atmospheric separation shall be activated by approved smoke detectors.

(e) Janitor closets and storage rooms shall be enclosed by materials having 1-hour fire resistance. Stages and enclosed platforms shall be constructed in accordance with Chapter 8.

Exception: Doors to janitor closets may have ventilating louvers.

Janitor closets are required to be sprinklered by 10-3.2.3.

SECTION 10-7   CHILD DAY-CARE CENTERS

(See also Sections 10-8 and 10-9.)

10-7.1 General Requirements.

Table 10-1 summarizes the *Code*'s requirements for the three types of day-care centers.

10-7.1.1 Application.

10-7.1.1.1   The requirements detailed in Section 10-7, Child Day-Care Centers (more than 12 children), are based on the minimum staff-to-child ratios which follow:

Staff Ratio	Age
1:3	0 to 2
1:5	2 to 3
1:10	3 to 5
1:12	5 to 7
1:15	7 and over

10-7.1.1.2   This section establishes life safety requirements for child day-care centers in which more than 12 children receive care, maintenance, and supervision for 24 hours or less per day. The provisions of Sections 10-2 through 10-6 shall not apply to this section unless a specific requirement is referenced by this section.

The intent of 10-7.1.1.2 is to differentiate between institutions where children are in residence 24 hours a day (such as orphanages) and day-care facilities where children, who normally reside at another location with at least one parent, are cared for during the parent's absence. A facility supplying "total care" for each child would provide laundries, dormitories, cafeterias, and other ancillary services not found in a day-care center. The life safety requirements of such a facility would not be governed by Chapter 10.

Table 10-1. Minimum Requirements For Day Care Centers

	Child	*Group*	*Family*
Number of Children	Any	7 to 12	6
Number of Children under Two Years	Any	3	2
Recommended Staff to Child Ratio	Age (yrs) Ratio < 2 1:3 2-3 1:5 3-5 1:10 5-7 1:12 >7 1:15	2:12	1:6
Occupant Load Factor	1 person/35 sq. ft.*	NR†	NR
Area of Refuge	If center above fifth floor	NR	NR
Number of Exits	2 remote (see 10-7.2.4)	2 remote (see 10-8.2.4)	2 remote (see 10-9.2.4)
Travel Distance to Exit‡ (ft)*	100 (from room door) 150 (from any point in a room)	150 (from any point)	150 (from any point)
Exit Discharge	To outside	At least one directly to outside	At least one directly to outside
Door Latches (closet)	Child opens from inside	Child opens from inside	Child opens from inside
Door Locks (bathroom)	Staff unlocks	Staff unlocks	Staff unlocks
Illumination of Means of Egress	If used after daylight hours	If used after daylight hours	If used after daylight hours
Emergency Lighting	See 5-9	See 31-3.5	See 31-3.6
Protection of Vertical Openings	See 6-2	See 10-8.3.1	NR
Class of Interior Finish	A (stairways, corridors, lobbies) B (other areas)	B (means of egress) C (all other spaces)	B (means of egress and rooms into which exits discharge) C (all other spaces)
Class of Interior Floor Finish	I or II (corridors, lobbies, exits)		
Alarm System	Manual (direct connection to fire department if > 100 children)	NR	NR
Smoke Detectors	See 10-7.3.4.2	See 10-8.3.4	See 10-9.3.4
Extinguishers	Portable (standpipes if building ≥ 6 stories)	Portable (in kitchens and cooking areas)	Portable (in kitchens and cooking areas)
Hazard Protection	1-hr enclosure or automatic sprinklers (see 10-7.3.2)	NR	NR
Building Construction (permissible height vs. age of children)	See 10-7.1.6.1	Must meet applicable building codes	Must meet applicable building codes
Compartmentation	See 10-7.3.7	NR	NR
Electric Equipment	See NFPA 70 (receptacle covers required, Chapter 7)	See NFPA 70 (receptacle covers required, Chapter 7)	See NFPA 70 (receptacle covers required, Chapter 7)
HVAC	See Chapter 7	Separated from spaces by screens/partitions	See 10-9.5.2

*Metric: 1 ft. = .3048 meter   †No requirement.   ‡50% increase if sprinklered.

10-7.1.1.3   The text principally applies to centers in which children 5 years old or less may be sleeping during their time in the facility, but the provisions are for all facilities unless otherwise indicated.

The *Code* recognizes that children under 5 years of age usually take naps during the day and that, if they do not have to be carried, they are not easily led as a group. The staffing levels recommended in Table 10-1, as well as the other provisions for day-care centers, are designed to allow the children to be awakened and evacuated in case of fire.

10-7.1.1.4   Centers housing children 6 years of age and older shall conform to the requirements for educational occupancies, except as noted herein.

Centers which only provide care for children of school age are required to conform to the requirements for educational occupancies and to the special requirements for such facilities when they are located in buildings of other occupancies.

10-7.1.1.5   Where a facility houses more than one age group, the requirements for the younger children shall apply, unless the area housing the younger children is maintained as a separate fire area.

A separate fire area is usually constructed with walls which have a fire resistance of 2 hours. Most facilities governed by this chapter will be maintained as separate atmospheres through smoke partitions of a 1-hour fire resistance.

10-7.1.2 Mixed Occupancies.

(a) Where centers are located in a building containing mixed occupancies, the separation requirements of the locally applicable building code or, if none exists, a nationally recognized model code shall be satisfied.

(b) Centers in apartment buildings.

1. If the two exit accesses from the center enter the same corridor as the apartment occupancy, the exit accesses shall be separated in the corridor by a smoke barrier having not less than a 1-hour fire resistance rating. The smoke barrier shall be so located that there is an exit on each side of it.

2. The door in the smoke barrier shall be not less than 36 in. (91.44 cm) wide.

3. The door and frame assembly in the smoke barrier shall have a fire protection rating of at least 20 minutes and shall be equipped with a self-closing device, a latch, and an automatic hold-open device activated by a smoke detector. (*See also 5-2.1.2.3.*)

When a center is located in a building housing another occupancy, the operators of the center usually have no control of the safety procedures and precautions practiced outside the center. Paragraph 10-7.1.2 requires additional protection to minimize the children's exposure to potential hazards outside the center.

The rationale for the protection with a 20-minute door is the same as that used in Chapters 12 and 13 for health care facilities. The fuel load of the occupancy is not considered great enough to provide a severe attack on the door. This minimum construction will provide sufficient protection against flame and a good seal against smoke spread. The 20-minute door, coupled with the 1-hour wall, provides a barrier which will either contain a fire within a space for a limited time after it has been evacuated or will prevent a fire from entering an occupied space for a period of time.

10-7.1.3 Special Definitions.   (None.)

10-7.1.4 Classification of Occupancy.   For the purposes of this section, children are classified in age groups, as follows: children under 3 years of age, children from 3 through 5 years of age, and children 6 years of age and older.

10-7.1.5 Classification of Hazard of Contents.   (Not specifically classified.)

10-7.1.6 Minimum Construction Standards.

10-7.1.6.1   Centers shall not be located above the heights indicated for the types of construction given in Table 10-7.1.6.1.

Table 10–7.1.6.1   Height and Construction Limits

Type of Construction	Age Group	Number of Stories (Stories are counted starting at floor of exit discharge)			
		1	2	3	4 and over
I (443) I (332) II (222) II (111)	0 to 3 3 thru 5 6 and older	X X X	X X X	X X X	X X X
III (211) V (111)	0 to 3 3 thru 5 6 and older	X X X	See Note 1 X X	Not Permitted See Note 1 See Note 1	
IV (2HH)	0 to 3 3 thru 5 6 and older	X X X	See Note 1 See Note 1 See Note 1		
II (000)	0 to 3 3 thru 5 6 and older	X X X	See Note 1 See Note 1 See Note 1		
III (200) V (000)	0 thru 3 3 thru 5 6 and older			Not Permitted See Note 2 See Note 2	

NOTE 1: Permitted if entire building is protected throughout by an approved automatic sprinkler system.

NOTE 2: May be permitted for children 3 years of age and older if the children are limited to the first floor and the number of children is limited to 50 and there are two remote exits; or if they are limited to the first floor and the number of children is limited to 100 and each room has an exit directly to the outside.

10-7.1.6.2 Location. The story below the level of exit discharge may be used in buildings of any type other than Type II (000), Type III (200), and Type V (000). (*See 10-7.2.4.2.*)

10-7.1.7 Occupant Load. The occupant load for which means of egress shall be provided for any floor shall be the maximum number of persons intended to occupy that floor but not less than one person for each 35 sq ft (3.25 sq m) of net floor area used by the children.

When a center occupies a portion of a floor on which another occupancy exists, the occupant load for that floor is the sum of the occupant loads of the two occupancies. For example:

Net Floor Area (ft²)		Population Density Factor (ft²/person)		Occupant Load
Day Care Center 1,750	÷	35	=	50
Place of Assembly 3,000	÷	7	=	429

By addition, the total occupant load for which means of egress must be provided would be 479.

10-7.2 Means of Egress Requirements.

10-7.2.1 General.   (None.)

10-7.2.2 Types of Exits.   (*See 10-2.2.*)

10-7.2.2.1 Stairs.

(a) Exit stairs shall be enclosed in accordance with 10-3.1.2.

(b) There shall be no enclosed usable space under stairs in an exit enclosure nor shall the open space within the enclosure either under or adjacent to the stairs be used for any purpose.

10-7.2.2.2 Areas of Refuge.   In buildings over five stories above ground level, areas of refuge shall be provided for occupants of child day-care centers, either by smokeproof towers or horizontal exits.

In all cases where day-care centers are found on upper floors of tall buildings, areas of refuge (smokeproof towers or horizontal exits) should be designed so that the children will survive a fire. Five stories or approximately 75 ft (22.86 m) is the maximum height at which the fire department can be expected to rescue the occupants of a building from outside. However, many fire departments do not have the equipment to reach this height, and, in such locations, areas of refuge are necessary at lower levels.

In any event, dependence on rescue by the fire department is not prudent. The time, number of personnel, and effort involved in rescuing one person down an extension ladder is so great that it is not possible to rescue a large number of children by this method.

10-7.2.3 Capacity of Means of Egress.   (*See 10-2.3.*)

10-7.2.4 Number of Exits.

10-7.2.4.1 Each floor occupied by children shall have not less than two remote exits.

10-7.2.4.2 When the story below the exit discharge is used (*see 10-7.1.6.2*), the following conditions shall be met:

(a) For up to 30 children there shall be two remote exits. One exit shall discharge directly outside and the vertical travel to ground level shall not exceed 8 ft (243.84 cm). There shall be no unprotected opening into the enclosure of the second exit.

(b) For over 30 children a minimum of two exits shall be provided directly outside with one of the two exiting at ground level.

Exception No. 1:   The exit directly to ground level is not required if the exits are protected in accordance with 5-1.3. There shall be no openings into the exit other than for ingress and egress. Smoke detectors shall be provided in that story and the story of discharge.

Exception No. 2:   The exit directly to ground level is not required if one exit complies with Exception No. 1 and sprinklers are used in that story and the story of exit discharge.

The intent of 10-7.2.4.2 is to permit the use of basements for child day-care centers only if protected exits with relatively short upward travel are provided. The committee recognized the level of risk involved in children occupying rooms below ground level. First, children of this age have difficulty in traveling up stairs, particularly at a fast speed. This is why the maximum vertical travel is 8 ft (2.44 m). Second, spaces below ground level have limited numbers of windows (or none) for emergency ventilation or for rescue. Third, a fire in a basement space will cause products of combustion to rise rapidly and block any means of egress that travels up the interior or exterior of a building. Finally, a fire on the upper floors of a facility may be undetected until exits leading from the basement have been blocked.

This section of the *Code* also recognizes that the level of risk to life safety increases with the number of children who may be exposed to a fire in a basement. In both Figures 10-18 and 10-19, an exterior stair (not likely to be lost to fire or be filled with smoke) is required. In Figure 10-18, with fewer than 30 children subject to fire exposure, the second means of egress may be an enclosed stair, without any unprotected openings, leading to ground level. With the case of the greater risk (more than 30 children), the second exit must lead directly to ground level. As the number of children potentially exposed to fire increases, the emphasis of the *Code* shifts to horizontal travel and to horizontal means of egress for two principal reasons. Even in organized groups, children of preschool age are difficult to lead and (as previously stated) have difficulty in climbing stairs.

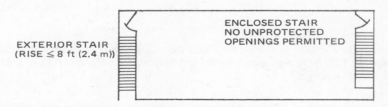

Figure 10-18. Exit Requirements for Child Day-Care Center in Basement Occupied by 30 or Fewer Children.

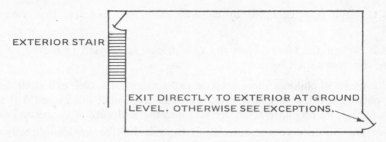

Figure 10-19. Exit Requirements for Child Day-Care Center in Basement Occupied by More than 30 Children.

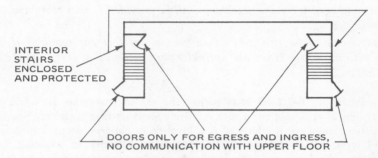

Figure 10-20. Exit Requirements for Child Day-Care Center in Basement Occupied by More than 30 Children, Smoke Detectors Installed on Occupied Floor and Upper Floor of Exit Discharge.

If the potential for the children's exposure to fire is reduced, the *Code* permits reliance on upward travel in lieu of horizontal movement. In Figure 10-20, per Exception No. 1, two enclosed interior stairs are permitted because smoke detectors have been installed. In Figure 10-21, per Exception No. 2, only one enclosed exit is necessary since automatic sprinklers have been installed in the basement and on the floor of exit discharge.

Figure 10-21. Exit Requirements for Child Day-Care Center in Basement Occupied by More than 30 Children, Automatic Sprinklers Installed on Occupied Floor and Upper Floor of Exit Discharge.

10-7.2.5 Arrangement of Means of Egress. (*When the story below the exit discharge is used, see also 10-7.2.4.2.*)

10-7.2.6 Measurement of Travel Distance to Exits.

10-7.2.6.1   Travel distance shall be measured in accordance with Section 5-6.

10-7.2.6.2   Travel distance (a) between any room door intended as exit access and an exit shall not exceed 100 ft (30.48 m); (b) between any point in a room and an exit shall not exceed 150 ft (45.72 m); (c) between any point in a sleeping room or suite and an exit access door of that room or suite shall not exceed 50 ft (15.24 m).

Exception: The travel distance in (a) and (b) above may be increased by 50 ft (15.24 m) in buildings protected throughout by an approved automatic sprinkler system in accordance with Section 7-7.

Paragraph 10-7.2.6.2 is structured to say the same thing several different ways. As shown in Figure 10-22, the maximum travel distance from a room door (exit access to the corridor) to an exit door is 100 ft (30.48 m). The *total* travel distance from any point (such as in a room) to an exit is 150 ft (45.72 m). By subtraction, it follows that the maximum travel distance from a point in a room to an exit access door is 50 ft (15.24 m). This distance may not be increased even if the building is sprinklered.

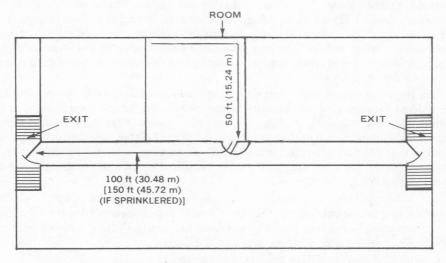

Figure 10-22. Maximum Travel Distance to Exit, Child Day-Care Center.

10-7.2.6.3   The travel distance to exits in open plan centers for children 3 years of age and older shall be in accordance with 10-6.2.2 for open plan schools.

10-7.2.7 Discharge from Exits.   (*When the story below the exit discharge is used, see also 10-7.2.4.2.*) All such exits shall discharge directly to the outside.

10-7.2.8 Illumination of Means of Egress.   If the facility is used after daylight hours, it shall comply with Section 5-8.

10-7.2.9 Emergency Lighting.   Means of egress in each day-care center shall be provided with emergency lighting, in accordance with Section 5-9.

10-7.2.10 Marking of Means of Egress.   (No additional special requirements.) (*See Section 5-10.*)

10-7.2.11 Special Features.

10-7.2.11.1 Doors in means of egress shall swing in the direction of exit travel and shall meet the requirements of 10-2.11.2.

10-7.2.11.2 Every closet door latch shall be such that children can open the door from inside the closet.

10-7.2.11.3 Every bathroom door lock shall be designed to permit opening of the locked door from the outside in an emergency, and the opening device shall be readily accessible to the staff.

10-7.3 Protection.

10-7.3.1 Protection of Vertical Openings. Any vertical opening in centers shall be enclosed and protected in accordance with Section 6-2.

10-7.3.2 Protection from Hazards. Rooms or spaces for the storage, processing, or use of the materials specified in this section shall be protected in accordance with the following:

(a) Rooms or spaces used for the storage of combustible supplies in quantities deemed hazardous by the authority having jurisdiction, hazardous materials in quantities deemed hazardous by recognized standards, or fuel shall be separated from the remainder of the building by construction having not less than a 1-hour fire-resistive rating with all openings protected by self-closing or smoke-actuated fire doors, or such rooms or spaces may be protected by an automatic extinguishing system as set forth in Section 6-4.

(b) Rooms or spaces used for processing or use of combustible supplies in quantities considered hazardous by the authority having jurisdiction, hazardous materials, or for flammable or combustible liquids in quantities deemed hazardous by recognized standards shall be separated from the remainder of the building by construction having not less than a 1-hour fire-resistive rating with all openings protected by self-closing or smoke-actuated fire doors and shall also be protected by an automatic extinguishing system as set forth in Section 6-4.

(c) Boiler and furnace rooms, laundries, and maintenance shops, including woodworking and painting areas, shall be separated from the remainder of the building by construction having not less than a 1-hour fire-resistive rating with all openings protected by self-closing or smoke-actuated fire doors.

Exception: Rooms enclosing air-handling equipment.

(d) When automatic extinguishing systems are used to meet the requirements of this section, the rooms or spaces shall be separated from the remainder by a physical barrier of such construction so as to contain the heat or smoke generated by a fire to allow for ready extinguishing system activation.

Exception: Food preparation facilities protected in accordance with Removal of Smoke and Grease-Laden Vapors from Commercial Cooking Equipment, NFPA 96, are not required to have openings protected between food preparation areas and dining areas. Where domestic cooking equipment is used for food warming or limited cooking, protection or segregation of food preparation facilities is not required if approved by the authority having jurisdiction.

The intent of 10-7.3.2 is to specify the degree of protection necessary for certain hazardous areas. It has been divided into three sections based on the degree of hazard. The hazards noted in item (a) are required to be enclosed in 1-hour construction or protected by sprinklers. If the sprinkler option is chosen, an enclosure is still required; however, the enclosure need not be rated, but only form a membrane against the passage of smoke.

The hazards noted in item (b) must be enclosed in 1-hour construction *and* be protected by automatic sprinklers.

The hazards noted in item (c) are required to be enclosed in 1-hour construction with no option for a sprinkler equivalency for the enclosure. The exception to item (c) pertains to rooms housing air-handling equipment *only*. If the room is used for other purposes, then the provisions of item (a) or (b) apply.

The intent of the exception to 10-7.3.2 is to provide some barrier between cooking areas and dining areas. The intent of the barrier is to screen possible flash fires from view in an attempt to prevent panic. Openings in this barrier are not restricted and do not need to be protected. The *Code* is counting on the automatic extinguishing system to control any fire on the cooking surfaces, and, thus, no longer requires enclosure by rated construction. The degree of screening required, and thus the size of the barrier required, is left to the judgment of the authority having jurisdiction.

10-7.3.3 Interior Finish.

Page 155 6-5.1.5

10-7.3.3.1   Interior finish for all walls and ceilings shall be Class A or Class B in accordance with Section 6-5. Interior finish in stairways, corridors, and lobbies shall be Class A.

10-7.3.3.2   In all centers, floor coverings within corridors and exitways shall be Class I or Class II in accordance with Section 6-5.

10-7.3.3.3   Decorations and furnishings shall be in accordance with Chapter 31.

10-7.3.4 Detection, Alarm, and Communications.

10-7.3.4.1   There shall be a manually operated fire alarm system in accordance with Section 7-6 on each floor of the center. In centers with more than 100 children, the fire alarm system shall be installed to transmit an alarm by the most direct and reliable method approved by local regulations to the fire department that is legally committed to serve the area in which the center is located.

Exception: When the child day-care center is housed in one room.

In all child day-care centers, manually operated fire alarm systems should be directly connected to the fire department. The committee felt compelled to emphasize that in centers which serve more than 100 children, this arrangement is essential. There are fire departments which will not accept direct alarms. In such cases, positive provisions must be made for rapid notification of the fire department by remote or central station systems.

10-7.3.4.2   Smoke detectors shall be installed on the ceiling of each story in front of the doors to the stairways and at no greater than 30 ft (914.4 cm) spacing in the corridors of all floors containing the center. Detectors shall also be installed in lounges and recreation areas in centers. The detectors may be single station units with an integral alarm having a decibel rating of at least 85.

Exception: Detectors are not required in centers housing children 6 years of age and older, if no sleeping facilities are provided.

The purpose of this requirement is obvious, but worth noting. In centers housing children younger than 6, naps and sleep time are provided. The smoke detectors in selected areas provide early warning of an impending fire.

10-7.3.5 Extinguishment Requirements.

10-7.3.5.1 Portable fire extinguishers suitable for Class B fires shall be installed in kitchens and cooking areas, and extinguishers suitable for Class A fires shall be installed throughout the remainder of the center. (*See Section 7-7.*)

NFPA 10, *Standard for Portable Fire Extinguishers,*[6] should be consulted concerning installation and maintenance of portable fire extinguishers.

10-7.3.5.2 Standpipes for fire department use shall be installed in all buildings of six stories or more housing child day-care centers.

10-7.3.6 Corridors.   (*See 10-7.1.2.*)

10-7.3.7 Subdivision into Compartments.

(a) When sleeping areas in centers housing children under 3 years of age are divided into rooms, room dividers shall have a minimum of 1-hour fire resistance, and glass in wall areas shall not exceed 25 percent of the wall area and shall be glazed with fixed wire glass in steel frames.

(b) When interior room doors are provided between adjacent rooms they shall be not less than 3 ft (91.44 cm) wide. Doors and frames shall have a 20-minute fire protection rating and shall have self-closing devices, latches, and automatic hold-open devices as specified in 5-2.1.2.3.

The purpose of 10-7.3.7 is to provide a minimum level of compartmentation. Note that both items (a) and (b) say "when." In other words, these paragraphs do not require the compartments, but set minimums if they are provided.

10-7.4 Special Provisions.   (None.)

10-7.5 Building Services.

10-7.5.1 Utilities.

10-7.5.1.1   Utilities shall comply with the provisions of Section 7-1.

10-7.5.1.2   Receptacles and outlets serviced by extension cord-type wiring are prohibited. Electrical appliances shall be grounded in accordance with *National Electrical Code*, NFPA 70.

10-7.5.1.3   Special protective receptacle covers shall be installed in all areas occupied by children in centers for children under 5 years of age.

Children are subject to serious injury if they insert foreign objects into electrical receptacles. Protective covers must be provided and maintained in order to avoid such accidents.

10-7.5.2   Heating, ventilating, and air conditioning equipment shall be in accordance with Section 7-2.

10-7.5.3   Elevators, dumbwaiters, and vertical conveyors shall comply with the provisions of Section 7-4.

10-7.5.4 Rubbish chutes, incinerators, and laundry chutes shall comply with the provisions of Section 7-5.

SECTION 10-8   GROUP DAY-CARE HOMES

10-8.1 General Requirements.

10-8.1.1 Application.

10-8.1.1.1 This section establishes life safety requirements for group day-care homes in which at least seven but not more than twelve children receive care, maintenance, and supervision by other than their parent(s) or legal guardian(s) for 24 hours per day or less (generally within a dwelling unit). The provisions of Sections 10-2 through 10-6 shall not apply to this section unless a specific requirement is referenced by this section.

The requirements detailed in Section 10-8 (Group Day-Care Homes, for fewer than 13 children) are based on the minimum staff-to-child ratio of two staff for up to 12 children with no more than three children under the age of 2.

Group day-care homes are often found in buildings housing occupancies such as apartments, stores, or places of assembly. In such buildings, exit accesses usually open into a corridor. Paragraph 10-8.1.2(b) describes the requirements for safeguarding the integrity of at least one egress path from such a facility.

10-8.1.1.2 The text principally applies to centers in which children 5 years old or less may be sleeping during their time in the facility, but the provisions are for all facilities unless otherwise indicated.

10-8.1.1.3 Where a facility houses more than one age group, the requirements for the younger age group shall apply, unless the area housing the younger children is maintained as a separate fire area.

10-8.1.2 Mixed Occupancies.

(a) When a group home is located in a building containing mixed occupancies, the separation requirements of the locally applicable building code or, if none exists, a nationally recognized model code shall be satisfied.

(b) Homes in apartment buildings.

1. If the two exit accesses from the home enter the same corridor as the apartment occupancy, the exit accesses shall be separated in the corridor by a smoke barrier having not less than a 1-hour fire resistance rating. The smoke barrier shall be so located that there is an exit on each side of it.

2. The door in the smoke barrier shall be not less than 36 in. (91.44 cm) wide.

3. The doors and frames in the smoke barrier shall have a fire protection rating of at least 20 minutes and shall be equipped with a self-closing device, a latch, and an automatic hold-open device as specified in 5-2.1.2.3.

10-8.1.3 Special Definitions.   (None.)

10-8.1.4 Classification of Occupancy.   For purposes of this section, children are classified in age groups as follows: children under 3 years of age, children from 3 through 5 years of age, and children 6 years of age and older.

10-8.1.5 Classification of Hazard of Contents.   (Not specifically classified.)

10-8.1.6 Minimum Construction Standards.

Each building used as a group day-care home should meet the local minimum housing code and fire prevention code for the applicable class of residential construction or, if none exists, a nationally recognized model code.

10-8.1.7 Occupant Load.   No Special Requirements.

10-8.2 Means of Egress Requirements.

10-8.2.1 General.   (None.)

10-8.2.2 Types of Exits.   (*See 10-8.2.4.*)

10-8.2.3 Capacity of Means of Egress.   (*See 10-2.3.*)

10-8.2.4 Number of Exits.

10-8.2.4.1   Each floor occupied by children shall have not less than two remote means of egress.

10-8.2.4.2   Where spaces on the floor above the floor of exit discharge are used for sleeping purposes by children, at least one exit shall lead directly, or through an enclosed stairway, to the outside.

10-8.2.4.3   Where children are located on a story below the level of exit discharge (basement) at least one exit directly to the outside at ground level shall be provided. No facility shall be located more than one story below the ground. Any stairway to the story above shall be cut off by a fire barrier containing a door of at least a 20-minute fire protection rating, equipped with a self-closing device and a latch.

As illustrated in Figure 10-23, there must be an exit directly to ground level from a group day-care center in a basement. If a stairway were provided, it would have to be cut off from the basement by a fire barrier containing a door with a fire protection rating of at least 20 minutes. As discussed in 10-8.2.4.2, the committee drafted these provisions to stress the necessity for horizontal exiting to ground level. The factors underlying this concern were the age of the children (up to three children in a group day-care center may be under 2 years of age); the difficulty in leading children of preschool age; and the physical difficulty encountered by small children in climbing stairs.

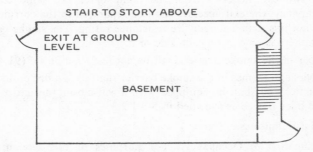

STAIR TO STORY ABOVE

EXIT AT GROUND
LEVEL

BASEMENT

Figure 10-23. Exit Requirements for Group Day-Care Center in Basement.

10-8.2.5 Arrangement of Means of Egress. *(When a story above or below the exit discharge is used, see 10-8.2.4.)*

10-8.2.6 Measurement of Travel Distance to Exits. *(See 10-2.6.)*

10-8.2.7 Discharge from Exits. *(When the story above or below the exit discharge is used, see 10-8.2.4.)*

10-8.2.8 Illumination of Means of Egress. *(See 10-7.2.8.)*

10-8.2.9 Emergency Illumination. No Requirements.

10-8.2.10 Marking of Means of Egress. *(See 10-7.2.10.)*

10-8.2.11 Special Requirements.

10-8.2.11.1 Every closet door latch shall be such that children can open the door from inside the closet.

10-8.2.11.2 Every bathroom door lock shall be designed to permit opening of the locked door from outside in an emergency, and the opening device shall be readily accessible to the staff.

10-8.3 Protection.

10-8.3.1 Protection of Vertical Openings. The doorway between the floor of exit discharge and any floor below shall be equipped with a self-closing door plus frame and hardware all of at least a 20-minute fire protection rating. Where the floor above the floor of exit discharge is used for sleeping purposes, there shall be a self-closing door plus frame and hardware all of at least a 20-minute fire protection rating at the top or bottom of each stairway.

10-8.3.2 Protection from Hazards. No Requirements.

10-8.3.3 Interior Finish.

10-8.3.3.1 The interior finish in means of egress shall be Class A or B.

10-8.3.3.2 Interior finish in occupied spaces in the home shall be Class A, B or C, in accordance with Section 6-5.

10-8.3.4 Detection Systems. Where the floor above the floor of exit discharge is used for sleeping purposes there shall be a smoke detector at the top of the stairs in a building three stories or less in height or inside the dwelling unit used as a day-care facility in a multiple-dwelling building.

10-8.3.5 Extinguishers. A portable fire extinguisher suitable for Class B fires shall be provided for the kitchens and cooking areas.

10-8.4 Special Provisions. (None.)

10-8.5 Building Services.

10-8.5.1 Electrical Services.

10-8.5.1.1 Electrical wiring in new construction shall be installed in accordance with Section 7-1.

10-8.5.1.2 Electrical appliances shall be grounded in accordance with *National Electrical Code*, NFPA 70. Receptacles and outlets serviced by extension cord-type wiring are prohibited.

10-8.5.1.3   Special protective receptacle covers shall be installed in all areas occupied by children in homes for children under 5 years of age.

10-8.5.2 Heating Equipment.

10-8.5.2.1   Any heaters in spaces occupied by children shall be separated from the space by partitions, screens, or other means.

> Screens which separate heating equipment from spaces occupied by children must be of closely spaced wire or expanded metal, of heavy gage, and must be securely attached to elements of the building. The purpose is to prevent the children from bending the screens or inserting their fingers through the mesh.

10-8.5.2.2   If solid partitions are used to provide the separation required in 10-8.5.2.1, provision shall be made to assure adequate air for combustion and ventilation for the heating equipment.

SECTION 10-9   FAMILY CHILD DAY-CARE HOMES

10-9.1 General Requirements.

10-9.1.1 Application.

10-9.1.1.1   This section establishes life safety requirements for licensed family child day-care homes in which fewer than seven children receive care, maintenance, and supervision by other than their parent(s) or legal guardian(s) for less than 24 hours per day (usually a dwelling unit). The provisions of Sections 10-2 through 10-6 shall not apply to this section unless a specific requirement is referenced by this section.

> The requirements detailed in Section 10-9 (Family Child Day-Care Homes) are based on the minimum staff-to-child ratio of one staff for up to six children, including the caretaker's own children under the age of 6, with no more than two children under the age of 2.
>
> Family day-care homes are usually situated in single-family dwellings or in apartment houses. If they occur in apartment houses, they must also comply with the applicable requirements of 10-9.1.2.

10-9.1.1.2   The text principally applies to centers in which children 5 years old or less may be sleeping during their time in the facility, but the provisions are for all facilities unless otherwise indicated.

10-9.1.1.3   Where a facility houses more than one age group, the requirements for the younger children shall apply, unless the area housing the younger children is maintained as a separate fire area.

10-9.1.2 Mixed Occupancies.   Where family child day-care homes are located in a building containing mixed occupancies, the separation requirements of the locally applicable building code or, if none exists, a nationally recognized model code shall be satisfied.

10-9.1.3 Special Definitions.   (None.)

10-9.1.4 Classification of Occupancies.   For the purposes of this section, children are classified in age groups as follows: children under 3 years of age, children from 3 through 5 years of age, and children 6 years of age and older.

10-9.1.5 Classification of Hazard of Contents.   (Not specifically classified.)

10-9.1.6 Minimum Construction Standards.

Each building used as a family child day-care home should meet the local minimum housing code and fire prevention code for the applicable class of residential construction or, if none exists, a nationally recognized model code.

10-9.1.7 Occupant Load.   No Special Requirements.

10-9.2 Means of Egress Requirements.

10-9.2.1 General.   (None.)

10-9.2.2 Types of Exits.   *(See 10-9.2.4.)*

10-9.2.3 Capacity of Means of Egress.   *(See 10-2.3.)*

10-9.2.4 Number of Exits.

10-9.2.4.1   In a one- or two-family dwelling or building of unprotected wood frame construction used for child care purposes, every room used for sleeping, living, or dining purposes shall have at least two means of escape, at least one of which shall be a door or stairway providing a means of unobstructed travel to the outside of the building at street or ground level. No room or space shall be occupied for living or sleeping purposes which is accessible only by a ladder, folding stairs, or through a trap door.

This paragraph reflects the requirements for one- and two-family dwellings. The change from means of egress to means of escape also recognizes a window of proper size as one method of escaping a fire.

10-9.2.4.2   Where children are located on a floor (basement) below the floor of exit discharge, at least one exit shall be provided directly to the outside at ground level. No facility shall be located more than one story below the ground.

10-9.2.4.3 Stairs.   Every stairway shall comply at least with the minimum requirements for stairs as described in 5-2.2 in respect to width, risers, and treads and shall be maintained free of items of storage.

10-9.2.5 Arrangement of Means of Egress.   *(See 10-9.2.4.)*

10-9.2.6 Measurement of Travel Distance to Exits.   *(See 10-2.6.)*

10-9.2.7 Discharge from Exits.   *(See 10-9.2.4.)*

10-9.2.8 Illumination of Means of Egress.   *(See 10-7.2.8.)*

10-9.2.9 Emergency Lighting.   No Requirements.

10-9.2.10 Marking of Means of Egress.   *(See 10-7.2.10.)*

10-9.2.11 Special Features.

10-9.2.11.1   Each door in a means of egress shall not be less than 24 in. (60.96 cm) wide.

10-9.2.11.2   Every closet door latch shall be such that children can open the door from inside the closet.

10-9.2.11.3   Every bathroom door lock shall be designed to permit the opening of the locked door from the outside in an emergency and the opening device shall be readily accessible to the staff.

10-9.3 Protection.

10-9.3.1 Protection of Vertical Openings.   (No additional special provisions.)

10-9.3.2 Protection from Hazards.   No Requirements.

10-9.3.3 Interior Finish.

10-9.3.3.1   The interior finish in corridors, stairways and lobbies and in rooms into which exits discharge shall be Class A or B.

10-9.3.3.2   Interior finish in occupied spaces in the home shall be Class A, B or C, in accordance with Section 6-5.

10-9.3.4 Detection Systems.   Where the floor above the level of exit discharge is used for sleeping purposes there shall be a smoke detector at the top of the stairs in a building three stories or less with open stairways, or inside the dwelling unit used as a day-care facility in a multiple dwelling.

10-9.3.5 Extinguishers.   A portable fire extinguisher suitable for Class B fires shall be provided for the kitchens and cooking areas.

10-9.4 Special Provisions.   No Requirements.

10-9.5 Building Services.

10-9.5.1 Electrical Services.

10-9.5.1.1   Electrical wiring in new construction shall be installed in accordance with Chapter 7.

10-9.5.1.2   Electrical appliances shall be grounded in accordance with *National Electrical Code*, NFPA 70. Receptacles and outlets serviced by extension cord-type wiring are prohibited.

10-9.5.1.3   Special protective receptacle covers shall be installed in all areas occupied by children in homes for children under 5 years of age.

10-9.5.2 Heating Equipment.

10-9.5.2.1   Unvented room heaters shall not be permitted. Oil- and gas-fired room heaters shall be installed in accordance with the applicable standards cited by this *Code*. A guard shall be provided to protect the children from hot surfaces and open flames.

10-9.5.2.2   No stove or combustion heater shall be so located as to block escape in case of malfunctioning of the stove or heater.

REFERENCES CITED BY *CODE*

(These publications comprise a part of the requirements to the extent called for by the Code.)

NFPA 13, *Standard for the Installation of Sprinkler Systems*, NFPA, Boston, 1980.

NFPA 70, *National Electrical Code*, NFPA, Boston, 1981.

NFPA 45, *Fire Protection for Laboratories Using Chemicals*, NFPA, Boston, 1975.

NFPA 96, *Standard for the Installation of Equipment for the Removal of Smoke and Grease-Laden Vapors from Commercial Cooking Equipment*, NFPA, Boston, 1980.

REFERENCES CITED IN COMMENTARY

[1]*American National Standard Safety Code for Elevators, Dumbwaiters, Escalators, and Moving Walks*, ANSI A17.1 — 1978, (and supplement, ANSI A17.1a — 1979), American Society of Mechanical Engineers, 345 East 47th Street, New York, NY 10017.

[2]*Specifications for Making Buildings and Facilities Accessible to, and Usable by, the Physically Handicapped*, ANSI A117.1 — 1961, American National Standards Institute, 1430 Broadway, New York, NY 10018 (reaff. 1971).

[3]NFPA 13, *Standard for the Installation of Sprinkler Systems*, NFPA, Boston, 1980.

[4]NFPA 220, *Standard Types of Building Construction*, NFPA, Boston, 1979.

[5]NFPA 90A, *Standard for the Installation of Air Conditioning and Ventilating Systems*, NFPA, Boston, 1978.

[6]NFPA 10, *Standard for Portable Fire Extinguishers*, NFPA, Boston, 1978.

11

EXISTING EDUCATIONAL OCCUPANCIES

(See also Chapter 31.)

Educational occupancies include all buildings used for the gathering of groups of six or more people for purposes of instruction. Educational occupancies include:

Schools   Kindergartens
Academies   Child day-care facilities
                    Nursery schools

Other occupancies associated with educational institutions must be in accordance with the appropriate parts of this *Code*.

Operational features for educational occupancies are specified in Chapter 31, Operating Features.

SECTION 11-1   GENERAL REQUIREMENTS

11-1.1 Application.

11-1.1.1   The requirements of this chapter apply to existing buildings.

11-1.1.2   Existing buildings, built and in use prior to the effective date of this *Code*, may have their use continued provided that, in the opinion of the authority having jurisdiction, reasonable life safety against the hazards of fire, explosion, and panic is provided and maintained. The authority having jurisdiction may accept such equivalent alternatives as: reduction of the occupant load, a complete automatic extinguishing system, provide additional exits, install doors from the classroom discharging directly outside, or in lieu of direct exit discharge to the outside from classrooms, communicating doors between classrooms or student-occupied areas that provide access to at least one exit stair without passing through interior corridors, additional stairs, or balconies with stairs.

Acceptance of existing buildings must be made on an individual case basis by the authority having jurisdiction. Life safety deficiencies may be corrected in an existing

297

building by providing additional means of egress, automatic sprinkler protection, or area separations. Whether these or alternate methods of protection are used to achieve reasonable life safety from fire and panic, sufficient technical documentation must be submitted for the authority having jurisdiction to render a decision. A code establishing minimum criteria for life safety cannot evaluate every proposed design solution to specific deficiencies. The responsibility to develop and to justify alternate design approaches with technical documentation rests with engineers and architects. See the discussion of Equivalency Concepts (Section 1-5).

Automatic sprinklers, specified in the *Code* to achieve life safety, also provide a substantial degree of protection for property. Sprinkler protection, to be effective, must be complete and cover all portions of a building. Partial automatic sprinkler systems covering only corridors, stairs, and points of special hazard are effective only when fires start in the protected area; they will not prevent the spread of fire or the dangerous spread of smoke or other products of combustion from fires starting in areas not protected by automatic sprinklers. In no case is reliance placed solely on automatic sprinklers or on any other single safeguard.

11-1.1.3 Rooms used for preschool, kindergarten, or first-grade pupils shall not be located above or below the level of exit discharge. Rooms used for second-grade pupils shall not be located more than one story above the level of exit discharge.

The restrictions on the location of rooms used by preschool, kindergarten, first-grade or second-grade pupils were developed to avoid the danger of older (and larger) children overrunning the very young on stairs or ramps during a fire or other incident requiring rapid evacuation of a building. Paragraph 11-1.1.3 also recognizes that young children may need assistance or have to be rescued.

11-1.1.4 Educational occupancies shall make provisions for the physically handicapped.

Federal and state laws governing financial assistance for education emphasize that public educational institutions must provide equal access to education for the physically handicapped. In addition, many states specifically prohibit segregating handicapped students from other pupils which makes it impossible to locate all physically handicapped pupils at the level of exit discharge. Unfortunately, these laws and related standards do not address the need for emergency egress of the handicapped during fires or similar events. In winning the right to equal access to educational facilities, the handicapped have placed themselves "at risk" in many buildings.

To minimize the level of risk created by interspersing the handicapped at all levels and locations within an educational building, horizontal exits, permitting horizontal movement away from the area of a fire, can easily be designed into new construction. This parallels the design concept in Chapter 12 for the evacuation of litter-borne, bedridden, or handicapped patients from health care occupancies. In existing buildings, it will probably be necessary to provide long ramps or to protect the elevators and their shafts and lobbies. Standards for the construction of elevators are discussed in Chapter 7 and in ANSI A17.1.[1] Standards for making buildings accessible to the handicapped are presented in ANSI A117.1.[2]

11-1.1.5 Educational occupancies housing classes over the twelfth grade need not comply with this chapter, but shall comply with the following requirements:

(a) Instructional Building — Business Occupancy

(b) Classrooms under 50 persons — Business Occupancy

(c) Classrooms 50 persons and over — Place of Assembly

(d) Laboratories, Instructional — Business Occupancy

(e) Laboratories, Non-Instructional — Industrial.

The provisions of 11-1.1.5 recognize that colleges and universities do not have the same problems as elementary and high schools. Because of the maturity of the occupants, college buildings more properly resemble office occupancies. Thus, this paragraph identifies those uses and refers to other appropriate provisions of the *Code*.

11-1.2 Mixed Occupancies.   (*See also 11-1.4.*)

11-1.2.1 General.   In case two or more classes of occupancy occur in the same building or structure so intermingled that separate safeguards are impracticable, the means of egress shall be sufficient to meet the requirements for each individual room or section and for the maximum occupant load of the entire building. Construction, protection, and other safeguards shall meet requirements of the most hazardous occupancy.

Exception: As otherwise specified in this chapter.

Many times it is difficult to determine what is the "most hazardous occupancy." The intent of the *Code* is to apply the requirements which provide the highest level of life safety for the building occupants.

11-1.2.2 Assembly and Educational.   Any auditorium, assembly room, cafeteria, or gymnasium used for assembly purposes such as athletic events with provisions for seating of spectators, or other spaces subject to assembly occupancy, shall comply with Chapter 9, including Special Provisions for Places of Assembly in Buildings of Other Occupancy, which provides that where auditorium and gymnasium exits lead through corridors or stairways also serving as exits for other parts of the building, the exit capacity shall be sufficient to permit simultaneous exit from auditorium and classroom sections.

Exception: In the case of an auditorium and gymnasium of a type suitable only for use of the school occupant load (and therefore not subject to simultaneous occupancy), the same exit capacity may serve both sections.

The point of this requirement is that if classrooms and places of assembly are likely to be occupied simultaneously, the exit capacity of the building must be designed and arranged for the combined use. For example, classrooms are often used during the evening for adult or remedial education while a school's gymnasium or auditorium is being used by another group. In such cases, the exception would not apply even though during the day the place of assembly would be used only by the school's population.

11-1.2.3 Dormitory and Classrooms. Any building used for both classroom and dormitory purposes shall comply with the applicable provisions of Chapter 17 in addition to complying with Chapter 11. Where classroom and dormitory sections are not subject to simultaneous occupancy, the same exit capacity may serve both sections.

11-1.2.4 Other Combined Occupancies.

11-1.2.4.1 Any other combinations of occupancy not covered in 11-1.2.2 and 11-1.2.3 shall comply with all applicable chapters of this *Code*, with means of egress adequate to serve all occupancies simultaneously.

11-1.3 Special Definitions.

Common Atmosphere. A common atmosphere exists between rooms, spaces or areas within a building, which are not separated by an approved smoke partition.

Flexible Plan and Open Plan Educational Buildings. Include every building or portion of a building not having corridors which comply with 11-3.6.1 and are designed for multiple teaching stations.

(a) Flexible plan buildings have movable corridor walls and movable partitions of full-height construction with doors leading from rooms to corridors.

The intent of the *Code* in referring to moveable corridor walls is the use of demountable partitions which are designed to be easily removed and reinstalled at a different location.

(b) Open plan buildings have rooms and corridors delineated by use of tables chairs, desks, bookcases, counters, low-height 5-ft (152.4-cm) partitions, or similar furnishings.

Although corridors in flexible plan or open plan buildings do not comply with 11-3.6.1 by not having a fire resistance of at least 1 hour, they must be divided at least every 300 ft (91.44 m) by a solid wall or a smoke partition (see 11-3.7.1).

Flexible plan buildings without exit access doors between rooms and corridors shall be classified as open plan buildings.

This paragraph is not meant to prohibit interior rooms in flexible plan buildings. The intent is to emphasize that all rooms adjoining a corridor in flexible plan buildings must have a door. Simply removing the doors from rooms in a flexible plan building does not make the building open plan. The concept of open plan involves openness to be able to observe a fire in its early stages. Thus, by applying the definition of open plan, partitions cannot be higher than 5 ft (152.4 cm).

Interior Room. A room whose only means of egress is through an adjoining or intervening room which is not an exit.

Note that this definition of interior room does not imply a windowless room. See Figure 11-1.

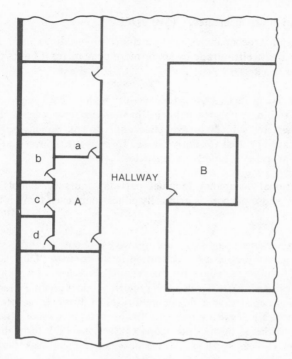

Figure 11-1. Examples of Interior Rooms. Rooms a, b, c, and d are interior rooms because they must pass through Room A before reaching the corridor. An example would be music practice rooms off a large music room. Room B, although windowless, is not an interior room as defined in Chapter 10 because the means of egress is from the room directly to the corridor.

Room. For the purposes of this section, a room is a space or area bounded by any obstructions to egress which at any time enclose more than 80 percent of the perimeter of the space or area. Openings of less than 3 ft (91.44 cm) clear width and less than 6 ft 8 in. (203.2 cm) high shall not be considered in computing the unobstructed perimeter.

Separate Atmosphere. A separate atmosphere exists between rooms, spaces or areas that are separated by an approved smoke partition.

Separate Means of Egress. A means of egress separated in such a manner from other required means of egress as to provide an atmospheric separation which precludes contamination of both means of egress by the same fire. (*See Section 6-3.*)

Smoke Partition. (*See Section 6-3.*) For purposes of this section, smoke partitions shall also include floors and openings therein.

The definition for "smoke partition" emphasizes that floors are an integral part of a smoke control system designed to provide separate atmospheres. For a smoke partition to be effective, there cannot be any unprotected vertical openings (such as unenclosed stairs) in the area which is to serve as a compartment in case of a fire. See 11-6.3.8.2(a).

11-1.4 Classification of Occupancy. (*See 4-1.3.*)

11-1.4.1 Educational occupancies shall include all buildings used for educational purposes through the twelfth grade by six or more persons for 4 hours per day or more than 12 hours per week.

Educational occupancies for students of high school age and below are distinguished from assembly occupancies in that the same occupants are regularly present and they are subject to discipline and control. Sunday schools or church schools which are not used for daily classes throughout the week are considered to fall within the scope of assembly occupancies.

11-1.4.2 Educational occupancy includes part-day, nursery schools, kindergartens, and other schools whose purpose is primarily educational even though the children are of preschool age.

The *Code* classifies part-day and nursery school facilities as educational occupancies because they provide education in addition to "baby sitting" services. This parallels federal guidelines for subsidizing day-care/educational activities at both the federal and state levels. By requiring educational criteria and related activities, it was hoped that a higher quality of staff would be provided for these facilities by these standards. A day-care "baby sitting" service with no, or limited, educational activities is beyond the scope of Sections 11-1 through 11-6. Sections 11-7, 11-8, and 11-9 set forth special requirements for day-care facilities.

11-1.4.3 Other occupancies associated with educational institutions shall be in accordance with the appropriate parts of this *Code*. (*See Chapters 13, 17, 19, 20, 28, 29, and 30, and 1-4.4.*)

The fact that education or instruction takes place in an occupancy affects the life safety requirements because, particularly in a school for students of high school age and below, the same occupants are regularly present and they are subject to discipline and control, even though many areas of school buildings (gymnasiums, auditoriums, rooms with fixed or movable furniture) resemble places of assembly.

11-1.4.4 In cases where instruction is incidental to some other occupancy, the section of this *Code* governing such other occupancy shall apply.

When instruction is incidental to other occupancies, the requirements for the occupancy in which the instruction occurs are applicable. Church schools which are used for religious instruction for a few hours on one or two days of the week are generally classed as places of assembly. In an office building or factory a few rooms may be used for orientation or instruction in the work requirements; these rooms are subject to the *Code* requirements for offices or factories. Barber colleges and beauty schools frequently are located in commercial buildings and should be governed by the requirements of the buildings in which they occur. The revision to 11-1.4.1 helps in classifying an educational occupancy.

11-1.5 Classification of Hazard of Contents. Contents of educational occupancies shall be classified in accordance with the provisions of Section 4-2.

In general, educational occupancies will contain ordinary hazard contents.

11-1.6 Minimum Construction.   No Requirements.

Fire-resistive construction is not generally specified in this chapter of the *Code*, though it is obviously desirable and should be used wherever feasible.

11-1.7 Occupant Load.

11-1.7.1   The occupant load of educational buildings or any individual story or section thereof for the purpose of determining exits shall be as determined by the authority having jurisdiction but not less than one person for each 20 sq ft (1.86 sq m) of net classroom area or 50 sq ft (4.65 sq m) of net area of shops, laboratories, and similar vocational rooms. In day nurseries where sleeping facilities are provided, the occupant load shall be not less than one person for each 35 sq ft (3.25 sq m) of net area.

11-1.7.2   The occupant load of an area having fixed seats shall be determined by the number of fixed seats installed. Required aisle space serving the fixed seats shall not be used to increase the occupant load.

11-1.7.3   The capacity of an educational occupancy or a portion thereof may be modified from that specified above if the necessary aisles and exits are provided. An approved aisle or seating diagram shall be required by the authority having jurisdiction to substantiate such a modification.

Figure 11-2 illustrates a classroom designed in conformance with 11-1.7.2. Its population is 35. This figure is determined by the room's number of fixed seats related to the required aisle space serving the room, not by the criterion of 20 sq ft (1.86 sq m) of net classroom area per person (see 11-1.7.1). Figure 11-3 demonstrates how a classroom with the same floor area can safely contain nearly 40 percent more students if the necessary aisles and exits are provided. In Figure 11-3, the bookcase has been eliminated and a row of seats placed directly against the window wall. The desks in the other rows have been placed front to front. The result adds 13 additional students to the room. This rearrangement of the furniture conforms with 11-1.7.3 and is one of many examples of how the *Code* requirements may still be met while adding to the occupant load of a building.

In both illustrations, the 22-in. (55.88-cm) access by the teacher's desk and between the rows provides 1 unit of exit width for ease of movement at all times. Placing the desks front to front so that 2 rows share a 22-in. (55.88-cm) access meets the *Code*'s requirements. Note that if the room contained more than 60 seats, the aisles would have to be 36 in. (91.44 cm) wide. Also, since both rooms contain fewer than 50 people, the doors to the corridor would be allowed to swing into the rooms (see 11-2.5.5).

Separate tables and chairs create problems not encountered with the illustrated seating. Instead of fixed seating which leads to predictable egress patterns, separate movable chairs and tables may lead to temporary blockage or restriction of the designed means of egress. Where this style of furniture is used, additional emphasis must be placed on the daily operational procedures followed by the facility's staff to minimize any blockage, obstruction, or restriction of the required means of egress.

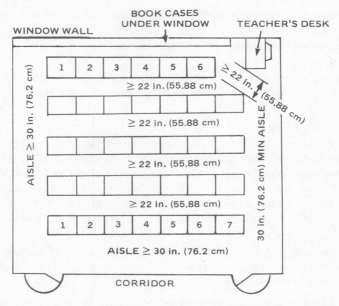

Figure 11-2. Classroom Arranged to Comply with 11-1.7.2. Room area = 594 sq ft (22 by 27 ft) 55.18 sq m (6.71 m by 8.23 m); at 20 sq ft (1.86 sq m)/person, occupant load = 29. Layout allows 35 occupants (4 rows of 7 seats, 1 row of 6, plus the teacher). Note that the maximum number of seats permitted in a row is 7.

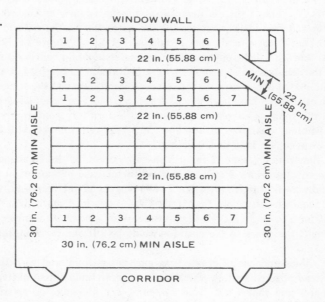

Figure 11-3. Modified Arrangement of Classroom Complying with 11-1.7.2 and 11-1.7.3. Room area = 594 sq ft (22 by 27 ft); at 20 sq ft/person, occupant load = 29. Layout allows 48 occupants (5 rows of 7 seats, 2 rows of 6, plus the teacher).

11-1.7.4   The occupant load for determining exit requirements of individual lecture rooms, gymnasiums, or cafeterias used for assembly purposes of more than 50 persons shall be determined in accordance with 9-1.7 of this *Code*.

SECTION 11-2   MEANS OF EGRESS REQUIREMENTS

11-2.1 General.   Every aisle, corridor, balcony, other means of access to exits, and discharge from exits shall be in accordance with Chapter 5.

11-2.2 Types of Exits.   Exits of the specified number and width shall be one or more of the following types, in accordance with the provisions of Chapter 5 of this *Code*.

(a) Doors. (*See 5-2.1.*)

(b) Interior Stairs, Class A or Class B. (*See 5-2.2.*)

NOTE: Class B stairs shall not be used for student access.

(c) Smokeproof Towers. (*See 5-2.3.*)

(d) Outside Stairs — Class A. (*See 5-2.5*).

(e) Horizontal Exits. (*See 5-2.4.*)

(f) Ramps — Class A or Class B. (*See 5-2.6.*)

11-2.3 Capacity of Means of Egress.

11-2.3.1   Every educational building, and every floor, section or room thereof considered separately shall have exits sufficient to provide for the capacity thereof, comprised of one or more types of exits, as follows:

(a) Any door, in accordance with 5-2.1, leading directly outside the building at ground level, or not to exceed three risers above or below the ground — 100 persons per unit of exit width.

> Paragraph 5-3.2 defines "unit of exit width" [22 in. (55.88 cm)], tells how to count fractions of a unit, and how to measure the width of an exit. If a door has more than three risers inside or outside to reach ground level, the stair is calculated separately to determine its capacity.

(b) Any door leading outside the building but requiring steps of over three risers to reach the ground — 100 persons per unit of exit width; steps must have one-third more units of width than doors to allow for slower travel rate.

(c) Stairs, smokeproof towers or outside stairs, in accordance with 5-2.2, 5-2.3 and 5-2.5 — 60 persons per unit of exit width.

(d) Ramps, in accordance with 5-2.6.

1. Class A — 100 persons per unit of exit width.

2. Class B — 60 persons per unit of exit width.

(e) Horizontal exits, in accordance with 5-2.4 — 100 persons per unit of exit width.

11-2.3.2   The same exit units or fraction thereof required for any individual floor may be counted as simultaneously serving all floors above the first story or level of exit discharge.

For example, in the case of enclosed interior stairways, where the capacity of the third floor requires three stairways, and the capacity of the second floor also requires three stairways, the second floor may utilize the stairways which serve the third floor so that the total number of stairways required is three, not six.

The street floor and basement, however, must either have their required exit capacity provided by separate exits or, if the path of exit from the street floor or basement is through a part of the same stair tower serving the upper floors, the total exit capacity must provide the required exit facilities for the street floor and basement without encroaching upon the stair capacity required for the upper floors. This assumes that, due to a greater travel distance, people on floors above the second will require more time to reach the street and will not exit simultaneously with the occupants of the basement, the street floor, or the second floor.

11-2.4 Number of Exits.

11-2.4.1   There shall be at least two exits available from every floor area.

11-2.4.2   Every room or space with a capacity of over 50 persons or over 1,000 sq ft (92.9 sq m) in area shall have at least two doorways as remote from each other as practicable. Such doorways shall provide access to separate exits, but, where egress is through corridors, may open upon a common corridor leading to separate exits in opposite directions.

11-2.5 Arrangement of Means of Egress.

11-2.5.1   Exits shall be so arranged that at least two separate exits will be available from every floor area. Exits shall be as remote from each other as practicable, so arranged that there will be no pockets or dead ends of appreciable size in which occupants may be trapped, and in no case shall any dead-end corridor extend more than 20 ft (609.6 cm) beyond the stairway or other means of exit therefrom.

A school plan with outside doors or stairways at both ends of a central corridor meets the requirements of 11-2.5.1. Pockets may be created where stairways are not located at the end of corridors but at intermediate points. See Figure 11-4.
A school plan using alternate methods of correcting means of egress deficiencies is shown in Figure 11-5.

11-2.5.2   Every classroom or room used for educational purposes or student occupancy below the floor of exit discharge shall have access to at least one exit which leads directly to the exterior at level of discharge without entering the floor above.

Figures 11-6A and 11-6B illustrate two types of exits which will satisfy the requirements of 11-2.5.2. The enclosed stair in Figure 11-6B serves floors other than the floor above the basement.

11-2.5.3 Minimum Corridor Width.

11-2.5.3.1   Exit access corridors shall be not less than 6 ft (182.88 cm) wide in the clear.

This paragraph applies to exit access corridors and not to unrequired corridors that are provided for convenience only.

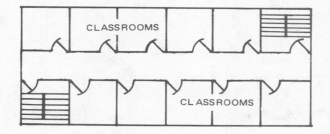

PREFERRED ARRANGEMENT OF EXITS WITHOUT DEAD ENDS

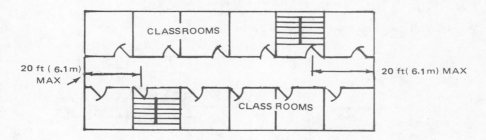

ACCEPTABLE ARRANGEMENT OF EXITS WITH DEAD ENDS
UP TO 20 ft (6.1 m)

Figure 11-4. Stair Placement in Accordance with 11-2.5.1.

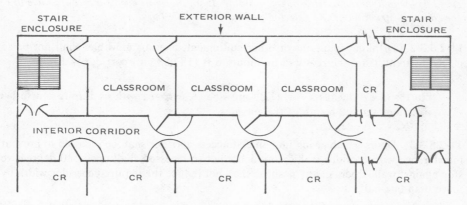

*Figure 11-5. Correction of Deficiencies in the Means of Egress in an Existing Building
in Accordance with 11-1.1.2. Doors communicating between classrooms provide exit access
without passing through an interior corridor. The construction requirements for the walls
and doors of the corridor could also be "corrected" if all the classrooms had a door
leading directly to ground level or to an exterior corridor or balcony (see 11-3.6.1.1,
Exception No. 1).*

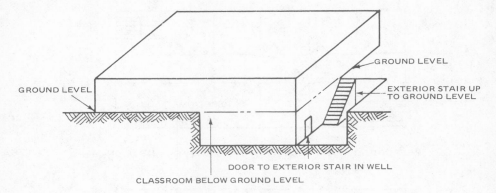

Figure 11-6A. Exit from Classroom Below Floor of Exit Discharge.

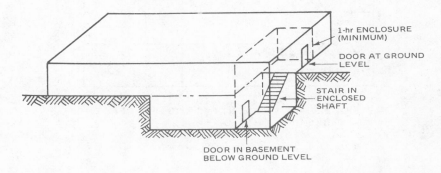

Figure 11-6B. Exit from Classroom Below Floor of Exit Discharge. The enclosed stair could be located on the outside of the building. If so, the shaft enclosure would have to be the same construction as the exterior construction of the building.

11-2.5.3.2   Drinking fountains or other equipment, fixed or movable, shall not be so placed as to obstruct the required minimum 6 ft (182.88 cm) corridor width.

"In the clear" means a 6-ft (1.83-m) wide clear space with no furniture or other obstructions the full length of the corridor.

11-2.5.3.3   Doors which swing into an exit access corridor shall be recessed to prevent interference with corridor traffic; any doors not so recessed shall open 180 degrees to stop against wall. Doors in any position shall not reduce the required corridor width by more than one-half.

See 11-2.11.2 for further information on door swing.

11-2.5.4   When there are more than 60 seats, every aisle shall be not less than 3 ft (91.44 cm) wide when serving seats on one side only and not less than 3 ft 6 in. (106.68 cm) when serving seats on both sides. When serving 60 seats or less, aisles shall not be less than 30 in. (76.2 cm) wide. Within a classroom where there are rows of seats with room access to the seats between individual rows, this space does not constitute an aisle. No more than six seats shall intervene between any seat and an aisle.

See Figures 11-2 and 11-3.

11-2.5.5 Exterior Corridors or Balconies.

11-2.5.5.1   Where exterior corridors or balconies are provided as means of exit, they shall open to the outside air except for railings or balustrades with stairs or level exits to grade not over the allowable travel distance apart, so located that an exit will be available in either direction from the door to any individual room or space, with dead ends not to exceed 20 ft (609.6 cm). If balconies are enclosed by glass or in any other manner, they shall be treated as interior corridors.

From the standpoint of life safety, the preferable school design provides classroom exits directly to the outside or to exterior balconies open to the outside air with exterior stairways to ground level available in either direction. See Figure 11-7. Conventional designs incorporate interior corridors, which can become untenable from the accumulation of smoke and heat.

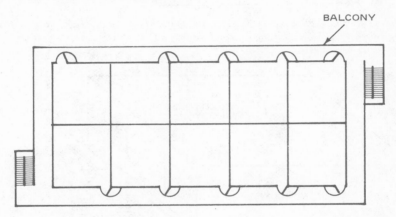

Figure 11-7. Stair Placement, Exterior Balcony. Distance between stairs must not be greater than the allowable travel distance would permit. Balcony width must be at least as wide as the door leading to it or the stair leading away from it.

11-2.5.5.2   The floors of balconies (exterior corridors) and stairs shall be solid, without openings, and shall comply with requirements for outside stairs as regards balustrades or railings, width and pitch of stairs, and other details, but are not required to be shielded from fire within the building by blank walls, wired glass windows or the like where the stairs are located on the side of the balcony or corridor away from the building and are separated from the building by the full required width of the balcony or corridor. Regardless of other provisions, exterior balconies and stairs may be of the same type of construction as the building which they serve.

Stairs from exterior balconies must not pass or come close to windows or other openings in stories below. Preferable stair placements complying with 11-2.5.5.1 and 11-2.5.5.2 are illustrated in Figures 11-8 and 11-9.

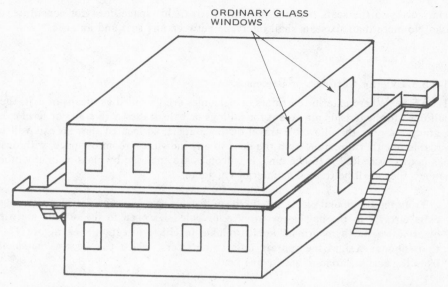

Figure 11-8. Stair Placement, Exterior Balcony. Since stairs are separated from the building by the full width of the balcony, blank walls or wired glass windows are not required near the stairs.

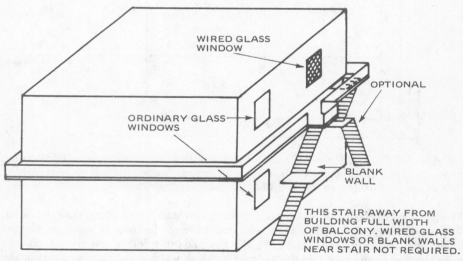

Figure 11-9. Stair Placement, Exterior Balcony. The stair placed directly against the building must not pass near unprotected openings.

11-2.6 Measurement of Travel Distance to Exits.   Travel distance to an exit shall not exceed 150 ft (45.72 m) from any point in a building.

Exception No. 1:   For travel distance in open plan buildings, see 11-6.2.2.

Exception No. 2:   The travel distance may be increased to 200 ft (60.96 m) in educational occupancies protected throughout by an approved automatic sprinkler system.

11-2.7 Discharge from Exits.   Discharge from exits shall be arranged in accordance with the provisions of Section 5-7.

11-2.8 Illumination of Means of Egress.   All educational buildings shall have adequate exit illumination in accordance with Section 5-8.

11-2.9 Emergency Lighting.   Emergency lighting in accordance with Section 5-9 shall be provided:

(a) In all interior stairs and corridors

(b) In all normally occupied spaces

Exception to (b):

   1. Administrative areas.

   2. General classrooms.

   3. Mechanical rooms and storage areas.

(c) In flexible and open plan buildings

(d) In all portions of buildings that are interior or windowless.

The changes to 11-2.9 in this edition are to make clear the intent of the *Code* as to where emergency lighting is required. The exceptions to item (b) indicate that normal classrooms, offices, and storage or mechanical spaces do not require emergency lighting. Shops, laboratories, and assembly rooms would require emergency lighting.

11-2.10 Marking of Means of Egress.   All educational buildings shall have signs designating the location of exits or the path of travel to reach them, in accordance with Section 5-10.

Exception: Signs are not required in situations where location of exits is otherwise obvious and familiar to all occupants, such as in small elementary school buildings.

11-2.11 Special Features.

11-2.11.1 Door Closure.   All exit doors designed to be kept normally closed shall conform with 5-2.1.2.3.

11-2.11.2 Door Swing.   If a room or space is subject to occupancy by more than 50 persons, exit doors shall swing out. Only one locking or latching device shall be permitted on a door or a leaf of a pair of doors. (*See also 11-2.5.3.*)

Paragraph 11-2.11.2 relates to the requirement in 5-2.1.1.4.1 that doors must swing in the direction of exit travel if they serve a room occupied by more than 50 people. Paragraph 11-2.5.3.3 requires that doors which swing into an exit access corridor either be recessed or open 180 degrees to stop against the wall. The swing of the doors must never reduce the required width of the corridor by more than one-half.

11-2.11.3 Panic Hardware.   Any required exit door subject to use by 100 or more persons shall be operated by a panic hardware device, in accordance with 5-2.1.2.2.

The intent of the *Code* here is that exit doors serving an area having an occupant load of 100 or more are required to have panic hardware.

11-2.11.4   Special locking arrangements complying with 5-2.1.2.1.5 are permitted.

The provisions of 5-2.1.2.1.5 apply to special delayed release devices.

11-2.11.5 Windows for Rescue and Ventilation. Every room or space used for classroom or other educational purposes or normally subject to student occupancy shall have at least one outside window used for emergency rescue or ventilation. Such window shall be openable from the inside without the use of tools, and provide a clear opening of not less than 20 in. (50.8 cm) in width, 24 in. (60.96 cm) in height and 5.7 sq ft (.5 sq m) in area. The bottom of the opening shall be not more than 44 in. (111.76 cm) above the floor.

Exception No. 1:   In buildings protected throughout by an approved automatic sprinkler system in accordance with Section 7-7.

Exception No. 2:   Where the room or space has a door leading directly to the outside of the building.

The dimensions specified for windows used for emergency rescue or for ventilation are based on simulations of emergency rescue conducted by the San Diego Fire Department. Windows providing clear openings of identical dimensions are also required for rescue or ventilation in one- and two-family dwellings. Figure 11-10 illustrates two configurations which achieve the required area of 5.7 sq ft (.53 sq m).

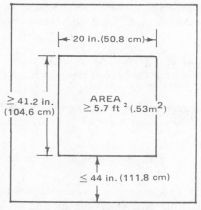

REQUIRED CLEAR OPENING

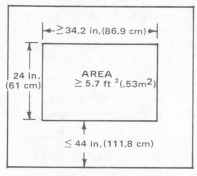

REQUIRED CLEAR OPENING

Figure 11-10. Windows for Rescue or Ventilation, Required Dimensions.

Although the *Code* intends the fire department or others to assist students, particularly over ladders, if these windows must be used as a supplementary means of escape, the windows should permit small children in the lower grades to escape unaided. Therefore, storm sashes, screens, or devices in front of the windows must be easy to open or remove and the sills must be low enough for the children to reach.

Where the location of windows precludes their use for rescue or escape, they may still provide trapped children with air for breathing in smoke-filled rooms. If awning or hopper-type windows are installed solely for emergency ventilation, they should be hinged or subdivided to provide a clear opening of at least 600 sq in. (3,871 sq cm) with no dimension less than 22 in. (55.88 cm). See Figure 11-11.

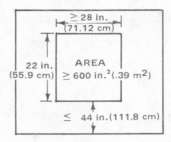

Figure 11-11. Windows for Ventilation (Awning or Hopper-type), Recommended Dimensions.

Exception No. 2 allows windows to be omitted only if a classroom has a door leading directly to ground level.

Bathrooms are not considered spaces normally subject to student occupancy and, thus, do not require the windows referred to in 11-2.11.5.

SECTION 11-3   PROTECTION

11-3.1 Protection of Vertical Openings.

11-3.1.1   Any interior stairway and other vertical opening in educational buildings shall be enclosed and protected in accordance with Section 6-2.

Exception: Unprotected vertical openings connecting not more than three floors may be permitted in accordance with 6-2.2.3.1, Exception No. 1.

Since a school normally would be considered ordinary hazard, 6-2.2.3.1, Exception No. 1 requires that complete automatic sprinkler protection be provided in addition to other requirements.

11-3.1.2   Stairs shall be enclosed in accordance with Section 6-2.

Exception: Stairway enclosure will not be required for a stairway serving only one adjacent floor except a basement and not connected with corridors or stairways serving other floors.

The exception to 11-3.1.2 would allow a two-story school building to have open stairs between the first floor and the second floor. Since basements usually contain hazardous areas with high fuel loads, such as storage rooms, boiler rooms, or workshops, the use of open stairs as a connection between the basement and the upper floors is prohibited. The intent is to reduce the probability of children on upper floors being exposed to the vertical spread of a fire originating in the basement of a building. Figures 11-12 and 11-13 illustrate acceptable examples of the exception to 11-3.1.2 in a multistory school.

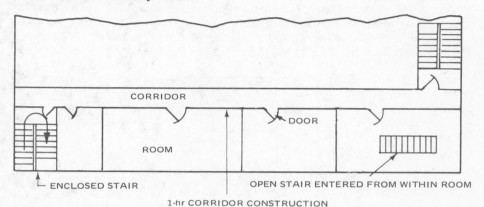

Figure 11-12. Open Stair Complying with 11-3.1.2.

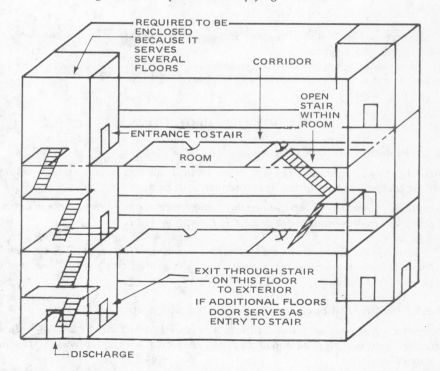

Figure 11-13. Open Stair Complying with 11-3.1.2. Stair serves only one floor and is not connected to a corridor.

11-3.2 Protection from Hazards.

11-3.2.1 Rooms or spaces used for the storage, processing, or use of the materials specified in this section shall be protected in accordance with the following:

(a) Rooms or spaces used for the storage of combustible supplies in quantities deemed hazardous by the authority having jurisdiction, hazardous materials in quantities deemed hazardous by recognized standards, or fuel shall be separated from the remainder of the building by construction having not less than a 1-hour fire-resistive rating with all openings protected by self-closing or smoke-actuated fire doors, or such rooms or spaces may be protected by an automatic extinguishing system as set forth in Section 6-4.

(b) Rooms or spaces used for processing or use of combustible supplies in quantities considered hazardous by the authority having jurisdiction, hazardous materials, or for flammable or combustible liquids in quantities deemed hazardous by recognized standards shall be separated from the remainder of the building by construction having not less than a 1-hour fire-resistive rating with all openings protected by self-closing or smoke-actuated fire doors and shall also be protected by an automatic extinguishing system as set forth in Section 6-4.

(c) Boiler and furnace rooms, laundries, and maintenance shops, including woodworking and painting areas, shall be separated from the remainder of the building by construction having not less than a 1-hour fire-resistive rating with all openings protected by self-closing or smoke-actuated fire doors.

Exception: Rooms enclosing air-handling equipment.

(d) When automatic extinguishing systems are used to meet the requirements of this section, the rooms or spaces shall be separated from the remainder of the building by a smoke barrier.

The intent of 11-3.2.1 is to specify the degree of protection necessary for certain hazardous areas. It has been divided into three sections based on the degree of hazard. The hazards noted in item (a) are required to be enclosed in 1-hour construction or protected by sprinklers. If the sprinkler option is chosen, an enclosure is still required; however, the enclosure need not be rated, but only form a membrane against the passage of smoke.

Art rooms and some shops need special attention. Potentially dangerous operations involving flammable materials, and specialized ovens and ignition sources in these areas, are becoming more prevalent and create increased hazards to the entire facility. It may be advisable at the high school level to include these rooms as hazardous spaces.

The hazards noted in item (b) must be enclosed in 1-hour construction *and* be protected by automatic sprinklers.

The hazards noted in item (c) are required to be enclosed in 1-hour construction with no option for a sprinkler equivalency for the enclosure. The exception to item (c) pertains to rooms housing air-handling equipment *only*. If the room is used for other purposes, then the provisions of item (a) or (b) apply.

11-3.2.2 Food preparation facilities shall be protected in accordance with *Removal of Smoke and Grease-Laden Vapors from Commercial Cooking Equipment*, NFPA 96, and are not required to have openings protected between food preparation areas and dining areas.

The intent of 11-3.2.2 is to provide some barrier between cooking areas and dining areas. The intent of the barrier is to screen possible flash fires from view in an attempt to prevent panic. Openings in this barrier are not restricted and do not need to be protected. The *Code* is counting on the automatic extinguishing system to control any fire on the cooking surfaces, and, thus, no longer requires enclosure by rated construction. The degree of screening required, and thus the size of the barrier required, is left to the judgment of the authority having jurisdiction.

11-3.2.3   Janitor closets shall be protected by an automatic sprinkler system, which may be supplied by the domestic water supply system serving no more than six sprinklers and having a water supply sufficient to provide 0.15 gpm per sq ft (1.02 × 10^{-4} cu m/s/sq m) of floor area. Doors to janitor closets may have ventilating louvers.

Where janitor closets are located off of corridors, a louvered door is usually provided for ventilation. It is necessary to provide these spaces with automatic sprinkler protection since the louvered door offers little fire resistance and permits a fire in the closet to directly affect the corridor. To accomplish this at reasonable cost, these sprinklers (not more than six in number) may be supplied from the domestic water supply to the closet if the supply is capable of providing the required quantity of water. It is advisable to provide a water-flow switch (see Chapter 6) to initiate an alarm when a sprinkler is opened.

The minimum flow of 0.15 gpm/sq ft (1.02 × 10^{-4} cu m/s/sq m) is based on the requirements in NFPA 13, *Standard for the Installation of Sprinkler Systems*[3], for protecting buildings containing ordinary hazards. This criterion, when multiplied by the floor area of the largest closet, leads to a gross flow rate that *must* be provided by the domestic water supply.

11-3.2.4   Laboratories that use chemicals shall comply with *Standard on Fire Protection for Laboratories Using Chemicals*, NFPA 45.

11-3.3 Interior Finish.

11-3.3.1   Interior finish shall be Class A in stairways and Class A or B in corridors and lobbies and Class A, B or C elsewhere, in accordance with the provisions of Section 6-5.

Section 6-5 permits the use of fire retardant or intumescent paints and surface coatings to reduce the *surface flame spread* of an interior finish. These coatings *will not* render a finish noncombustible. They will simply delay the eventual ignition of a finish exposed to fire.

Some coatings have a short life and require frequent reapplication. Over the useful life of a building, all coatings may eventually have to be renewed. Also, some coatings will severely mar or alter the appearance of the finish. Due to these liabilities, the option of using coatings and paints may not provide the best fire protection at a reasonable cost in all cases.

11-3.3.2 Interior Floor Finish.   No Requirements.

11-3.4 Detection, Alarm, and Communication Systems.

11-3.4.1   Approved manually operated fire alarm facilities in accordance with 7-6.1.2 shall be provided in every educational building. When acceptable to the authority having jurisdiction the fire alarm system may be used to designate class change provided the fire alarm is distinctive in signal and overrides all other use.

Exception: In buildings where all normally occupied spaces are provided with a two-way communication system between all normally occupied spaces and a manned location where a general alarm can be sounded, the manual fire pull stations may be omitted except in locations specifically designated by the authority having jurisdiction.

The purpose of the exception to 11-3.4.1 is to allow the deletion of manual pull stations in schools to prevent a false alarm problem. Where there is a two-way communication system between classrooms and a manned location where a general alarm can be sounded, the need for pull stations is obviated. To qualify to use this exception, it is intended that the "manned location" be manned continuously while school is in session.

11-3.4.2   In buildings provided with automatic sprinkler protection, the operation of the sprinkler system shall automatically actuate electrical school fire alarm systems.

11-3.4.3   Requirements for fire alarm systems for existing educational buildings shall conform to those for new educational buildings subject to the approval of the authority having jurisdiction.

11-3.5 Extinguishment Requirements.   Every portion of educational buildings below the floor of exit discharge shall be protected throughout by an approved automatic sprinkler system in accordance with Section 7-7.

Levels below the level of exit discharge are not necessarily below grade.

11-3.6 Interior Corridors.

11-3.6.1   Every interior corridor shall be of construction having not less than a 1-hour fire resistance rating, and all openings protected with doors, frames and hardware, including closers, that shall all have a fire protection rating of at least 20 minutes.

Exception No. 1:   Such corridor protection shall not be required when all classrooms served by such corridors have at least one door directly to the outside or to an exterior balcony or corridor as in 11-2.5.4.

Exception No. 2:   The corridor protection may be reduced to a ½-hour fire resistance rating providing the building is protected throughout by an approved automatic sprinkler system.

Exception No. 3:   Existing doors may be 1¾ in. (4.45-cm) solid bonded wood core doors or the equivalent.

The intent of Exception No. 1 is to delete the requirement for a rated corridor wall; however, a wall and doors with closers providing a smoke barrier are still required.

11-3.7 Subdivision of Building Spacers.

11-3.7.1   When the aggregate length of interior corridors, including dead-end corridors and cross corridors, exceeds 300 ft (91.44 m), the corridor shall be divided into reasonably equal sections not exceeding 300 ft (91.44 m) in length by smoke partitions installed in accordance with Section 6-3.

   The 300-ft (91.44-m) limit bears a direct relationship to the travel distance criteria in Chapter 11 and reflects the committee's concern about the maximum area within an educational facility that would be immediately contaminated by products of combustion from a fire. Travel distance for this occupancy is limited to 150 ft (45.72 m) from *any point* in the building (see 11-2.6). Extrapolated to travel distance in a corridor (ignoring the distance from any room or space of the corridor), this criterion would lead to the exit arrangement shown in Figure 11-14, with no point in the corridor being more than 150 ft (45.72 m) from at least one exit.

   The committee, in viewing this relationship, felt it was reasonable and prudent to require smoke partitions across a corridor at maximum intervals of 300 ft (91.44 m) so that the products of combustion would affect a limited number of exits at one time. Figure 11-15 illustrates how the partition location dovetails with the travel distance criterion and minimizes the area of a building immediately affected by a fire.

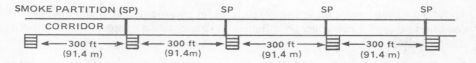

Figure 11-14. Smoke Partitions in Interior Corridors.

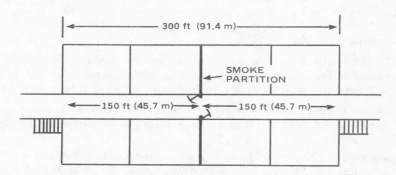

Figure 11-15. Smoke Partitions in Interior Corridors.

   For purposes of this requirement (see 11-3.7.1), the measurement of the length of the interior corridor does include side corridors. In Figure 11-16, the distance governing the installation of a smoke partition is 360 ft (109.7 m); thus, a smoke partition is required.

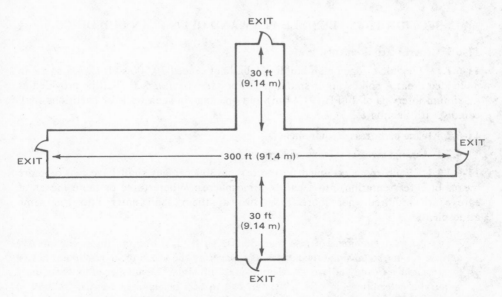

Figure 11-16. Measurement of Interior Corridor Length for Purposes of Complying with 11-3.7.1. Count the side corridors. In this example, a smoke partition is required because the aggregate corridor length is greater than 300 ft (91.44 m).

SECTION 11-4   SPECIAL PROVISIONS

11-4.1 Windowless or Subterranean Buildings. Automatic sprinklers shall be provided for stories which are in excess of 1500 sq ft (139.35 sq m) and are:

(a) Without windows or other openings directly to the exterior at the rate of 20 sq ft (1.86 sq m) of opening per 50 linear ft (15.24 m) in any two walls or,

(b) Below grade without similar openings.

11-4.2 Flexible plan and open plan buildings shall also comply with the provisions of Section 11-6.

SECTION 11-5   BUILDING SERVICES

11-5.1 **Utilities** shall comply with the provisions of Section 7-1.

11-5.2 **Heating, ventilating, and air conditioning equipment** shall comply with the provisions of Section 7-2.

11-5.3 **Elevators, dumbwaiters, and vertical conveyors** shall comply with the provisions of Section 7-4.

11-5.4 **Rubbish chutes, incinerators, and laundry chutes** shall comply with the provisions of Section 7-5.

SECTION 11-6   FLEXIBLE PLAN AND OPEN PLAN BUILDINGS

11-6.1 General Requirements.

11-6.1.1   Flexible or open plan buildings shall not exceed 30,000 sq ft (2,787 sq m) in undivided area. A solid wall or smoke partition (*see Section 6-3*) shall be provided at maximum intervals of 300 ft (91.44 m) and openings in such walls or partitions shall comply with Section 6-3.

11-6.2 Means of Egress Requirements.

11-6.2.1 Arrangement of Means of Egress.

11-6.2.1.1   Each room occupied by more than 300 persons shall have two or more means of egress entering into separate atmospheres. Where three or more means of egress are required, not more than two of them shall enter into the same atmosphere.

In open plan buildings of less than 30,000 sq ft (2,787 sq m), the occupants are actually in one room since the partitions separating the learning spaces do not have a fire resistance rating and are less than 5 ft (1.5 m) high. The number of exits required should be determined on this basis: for 200 to 600 occupants, 2 exits; for 600 to 1,000 occupants, at least 3 exits; and for more than 1,000 occupants, at least 4 exits. Exits from rooms or areas which have an occupant load in excess of 300 must be through separate atmospheres as required by 11-6.2.1.1 and illustrated in Figure 11-17.

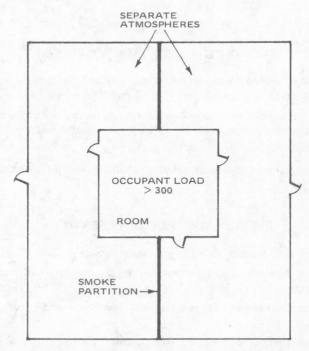

Figure 11-17. Example of Room in Open Plan Building Requiring Two or More Means of Egress into Separate Atmospheres.

11-6.2.1.2   Exit access from interior rooms may pass through an adjoining or an intervening room, provided that the travel distances do not exceed those set forth in 11-6.2.2. Foyers and lobbies constructed as required for corridors shall not be construed as intervening rooms.

11-6.2.1.3   Where the only means of egress from an interior room or rooms is through an adjoining or intervening room, smoke detectors shall be installed in the area of the common atmosphere through which the means of egress must pass. The detectors shall actuate alarms audible in the interior room and shall be connected to the school fire alarm system.

Exception No. 1:   Smoke detectors are not required where the aggregate occupant load is less than ten.

Exception No. 2:   Interior rooms used exclusively for mechanical and public utility service to the buildings.

Exception No. 3:   Where the building is protected throughout by an approved automatic sprinkler system.

If the only means of egress from a room is through an adjoining or intervening room, smoke detectors must be installed in the room through which the means of egress must pass because occupants of the interior room may not be aware of a fire or smoke condition in the intervening room, the room which provides their only means of egress. Alarm-sounding smoke detectors provide the occupants with an early warning so that they can safely pass through the room.

11-6.2.1.4   Flexible plan schools may have walls and partitions rearranged periodically, only after revised plans or diagrams have been approved by the authority having jurisdiction.

Approval of revised plans or diagrams is necessary to avoid the possibility of either obstructing sprinkler discharge or excessive spacing of sprinklers or other life safety devices when partitions are rearranged.

11-6.2.1.5   Open plan schools shall have furniture, fixtures, or low-height partitions so arranged that exits will be clearly visible and unobstructed, and exit paths are direct, not circuitous. If paths or corridors are established, they shall be at least as wide as required by 11-2.5.3.

Low-height partitions are 5 ft (1.53 m) or less in height.
Corridors discussed in 11-6.2.1.5 must not have full-height partitions in order to provide unobstructed visual surveillance of the entire open plan area by members of the faculty located at any point in the area.

11-6.2.2 Travel Distance to Exits.   No point in a building shall be more than 150 ft (45.72 m) from an exit, measured in accordance with Section 5-6.

Exception: An increase in the above travel distance to 200 ft (60.96 m) shall be permitted in a building protected throughout by an approved automatic sprinkler system in accordance with Section 7-7 and Standard for the Installation of Sprinkler Systems, NFPA 13.

11-6.3 Protection.

11-6.3.1 Vertical Openings.

11-6.3.1.1 All exit stairs shall be enclosed in accordance with Section 6-2.

11-6.3.1.2 Vertical openings other than exits shall be enclosed as required by Section 6-2. (*See 11-3.1.2 for enclosure of exits.*)

Enclosures around interior vertical penetrations (openings) must not reduce the clear surveillance of an entire floor from any position on the floor. It is generally advisable to locate the required enclosing shafts at the building periphery to minimize potential visual obstruction.

11-6.3.2 Protection from Hazards.

11-6.3.2.1 Stages in places of assembly shall be separated from school areas by construction having at least a 1-hour fire resistance rating and shall comply with 9-3.2. Openings shall be protected by self-closing or smoke-activated fire doors having a fire protection rating of ¾ hours.

11-6.3.2.2 Shops, laboratories, and similar vocational rooms, as well as storage rooms, shall be separated from school areas by construction having at least a 1-hour fire resistance rating. They shall have exits independent from other areas.

Facilities referenced by 11-6.3.2.2 should be separated from each other as well as from the remainder of the facility. This would avoid such hazards as welding in one shop area while glass fiber-reinforced plastic is being worked on (molded, shaped, sanded, or glued) in another area. This can create a very hazardous interaction between open flame and flammable vapors.

11-6.3.3 Interior Finish.   Interior finish, in accordance with Section 6-5, in flexible plan and open plan buildings shall be as follows:

(a) Corridors in flexible plan buildings — Class A, on rigid material that will not deform at temperatures below 450°F (232°C).

(b) Other than corridor walls — Class A or Class B.

Exception No. 1:   Fixtures and low-height partitions not over 5 ft (152.4 cm) high may be Class C.

Exception No. 2:   In one-story buildings the exposed portions of structural members complying with the requirements for Type IV (2HH) construction may be permitted.

Heavy timber construction is defined in NFPA 220, *Standard Types of Building Construction.*[4] Essential to the definition of heavy timber construction is that the bearing walls be of noncombustible or limited-combustible material and that the wood of the floors and roofs be without concealed spaces

11-6.3.4 Reserved.

11-6.3.5 Automatic Fire Extinguishing Systems.

11-6.3.5.1 Any flexible plan building or open plan building in which the travel distance to exits exceeds 150 ft (45.72 m) shall be protected throughout by an approved automatic sprinkler system in accordance with Section 7-7. Extinguishing systems shall be electrically interconnected with the school fire alarm system.

11-6.3.5.2 Automatic fire extinguishing systems shall be modified to conform with partition changes. Modification plans shall have prior approval of the authority having jurisdiction.

11-6.3.6 Reserved.

11-6.3.7 Reserved.

11-6.3.8 Smoke Control.

11-6.3.8.1 The specific requirements of this section are not intended to prevent the design or use of other systems, equipment or techniques that will effectively prevent the products of combustion from breaching the atmospheric separation.

> The intent of the requirements for separate atmospheres is to provide at least one uncontaminated egress path when a fire occurs in any part of a building. Guidance on meeting the provisions of 11-6.3.8.2(c) will be found in NFPA 90A, *Standard for the Installation of Air Conditioning and Ventilating Systems.*[5] Also refer to 13-3.7.7.

11-6.3.8.2 The provisions of this subsection shall apply only to the requirements for providing separate atmospheres. The fire resistance requirements shall comply with other provisions of the *Code*.

(a) Walls, partitions, and floors forming all of or part of an atmospheric separation shall be of materials consistent with the requirements for the type of construction, but of construction not less effective than a smoke barrier. Glass lights of approved wired glass set in steel frames may be installed in such walls or partitions.

(b) Every door opening therein shall be protected with a fire assembly as required elsewhere in the *Code*, but not less than a self-closing or automatic-closing, tight-fitting smoke assembly having a fire protection rating of not less than 20 minutes.

(c) Ducts penetrating atmospheric separation walls, partitions, or doors shall be equipped with an approved automatic-closing smoke damper when having openings into more than one atmosphere, or the atmospheric separation shall be maintained by an approved method of smoke control.

(d) All automatic-closing fire assemblies installed in the atmospheric separation shall be activated by approved smoke detectors.

(e) Janitor closets and storage rooms shall be enclosed by materials having 1-hour fire resistance. Stages and enclosed platforms shall be constructed in accordance with Chapter 9.

Exception: Doors to janitor closets may have ventilating louvers.

> Janitor closets are required to be sprinklered by 11-3.2.3.

SECTION 11-7   CHILD DAY-CARE CENTERS
(See also Sections 11-8 and 11-9.)

11-7.1 General Requirements.

Table 11-1 summarizes the *Code*'s requirements for the three types of day-care centers.

11-7.1.1 Application.

11-7.1.1.1   The requirements detailed in Section 11-7, Child Day-Care Centers (more than 12 children), are based on the minimum staff-to-child ratios given below:

Staff Ratio	Age
1:3	0 to 2
1:5	2 to 3
1:10	3 to 5
1:12	5 to 7
1:15	7 and over

11-7.1.1.2   This section establishes life safety requirements for child day-care centers in which more than 12 children receive care, maintenance, and supervision for 24 hours or less per day. The provisions of Sections 11-2 through 11-6 shall not apply to this section unless a specific requirement is referenced by this section.

The intent of 11-7.1.1.2 is to differentiate between institutions where children are in residence 24 hours a day (such as orphanages) and day-care facilities where children, who normally reside at another location with at least one parent, are cared for during the parent's absence. A facility supplying "total care" for each child would provide laundries, dormitories, cafeterias, and other ancillary services not found in a day-care center. The life safety requirements of such a facility would not be governed by Chapter 11.

11-7.1.1.3   The text principally applies to centers in which children 5 years old or less may be sleeping during their time in the facility, but the provisions are for all facilities unless otherwise indicated.

The *Code* recognizes that children under 5 years of age usually take naps during the day and that, if they do not have to be carried, they are not easily led as a group. The staffing levels recommended in Table 11-1, as well as the other provisions for day-care centers, are designed to allow the children to be awakened and evacuated in case of fire.

11-7.1.1.4   Centers housing children 6 years of age and older shall conform to the requirements for educational occupancies, except as noted herein.

Cf Table 10-1 page 279

Table 11-1. Minimum Requirements For Day Care Centers

	Child	Group	Family
Number of Children	Any	7 to 12	6
Number of Children under Two Years	Any	3	2
Recommended Staff to Child Ratio	Age (yrs) Ratio <2 1:3 2-3 1:5 3-5 1:10 5-7 1:12 >7 1:15	2:12	1:6
Occupant Load Factor	1 person/35 sq. ft.*	NR†	NR
Area of Refuge	If center above fifth floor	NR	NR
Number of Exits	2 remote (see 11-7.2.4)	2 remote (see 11-8.2.4)	2 remote (see 11-9.2.4)
Travel Distance to Exit‡ (ft)*	100 (from room door) 150 (from any point in a room)	150 (from any point)	150 (from any point)
Exit Discharge	To outside	At least one directly to outside	At least one directly to outside
Door Latches (closet)	Child opens from inside	Child opens from inside	Child opens from inside
Door Locks (bathroom)	Staff unlocks	Staff unlocks	Staff unlocks
Illumination of Means of Egress	If used after daylight hours	If used after daylight hours	If used after daylight hours
Emergency Lighting	See 5-9	See 31-3.5	See 31-3.6
Protection of Vertical Openings	See 6-2	See 11-8.3.1	NR
Class of Interior Finish	B (all areas)	B (means of egress) C (all other spaces)	B (means of egress and rooms into which exits discharge) C (all other spaces)
Class of Interior Floor Finish	I or II (corridors, lobbies, exits)		
Alarm System	Manual (direct connection to fire department if >100 children)	NR	NR
Smoke Detectors	See 11-7.3.4.2	See 11-8.3.4	See 11-9.3.4
Extinguishers	Portable (standpipes if building ≥ 6 stories)	Portable (in kitchens and cooking areas)	Portable (in kitchens and cooking areas)
Hazard Protection	1-hr enclosure or automatic sprinklers (see 11-7.3.2)	NR	NR
Building Construction (permissible height vs. age of children)	See 11-7.1.6.1	Must meet applicable building codes	Must meet applicable building codes
Compartmentation	See 11-7.3.7	NR	NR
Electric Equipment	See NFPA 70 (receptacle covers required, Chapter 7)	See NFPA 70 (receptacle covers required, Chapter 7)	See NFPA 70 (receptacle covers required, Chapter 7)
HVAC	See Chapter 7	Separated from spaces by screens/partitions	See 11-9.5.2

*Metric: 1 ft. = .3048 meter   †No requirement.   ‡50% increase if sprinklered.

Centers which only provide care for children of school age are required to conform to the requirements for educational occupancies and to the special requirements for such facilities when they are located in buildings of other occupancies.

11-7.1.1.5 Where a facility houses more than one age group, the requirements for the younger children shall apply, unless the area housing the younger children is maintained as a separate fire area.

A separate fire area is usually constructed with walls which have a fire resistance of 2 hours. Most facilities governed by this chapter will be maintained as separate atmospheres through smoke partitions of a 1-hour fire resistance.

11-7.1.2 Mixed Occupancies.

(a) Where centers are located in a building containing mixed occupancies, the separation requirements of the locally applicable building code or, if none exists, a nationally recognized model code shall be satisfied.

(b) Centers in apartment buildings.

1. If the two exit accesses from the center enter the same corridor as the apartment occupancy, the exit accesses shall be separated in the corridor by a smoke barrier having not less than a 1-hour fire resistance rating. The smoke barrier shall be so located that there is an exit on each side of it.

2. The door in the smoke barrier shall be not less than 36 in. (91.44 cm) wide.

Exception: Existing doors not less than 32 in. (81.28 cm) wide may be accepted.

3. The door and frame assembly in the smoke barrier shall have a fire protection rating of at least 20 minutes and shall be equipped with a self-closing device, a latch, and an automatic hold-open device activated by a smoke detector. (*See also 5-2.1.2.3.*)

When a center is located in a building housing another occupancy, the operators of the center usually have no control of the safety procedures and precautions practiced outside the center. Paragraph 11-7.1.2 requires additional protection to minimize the children's exposure to potential hazards outside the center.

The rationale for the protection with a 20-minute door is the same as that used in Chapters 12 and 13 for health care facilities. The fuel load of the occupancy is not considered great enough to provide a severe attack on the door. This minimum construction will provide sufficient protection against flame and a good seal against smoke spread. The 20-minute door, coupled with the 1-hour wall, provides a barrier which will either contain a fire within a space for a limited time after it has been evacuated or will prevent a fire from entering an occupied space for a period of time.

11-7.1.3 Special Definitions.   (None.)

11-7.1.4 Classification of Occupancy.   For the purposes of this section, children are classified in age groups, as follows: children under 3 years of age, children from 3 through 5 years of age, and children 6 years of age and older.

11-7.1.5 Classification of Hazard of Contents.   (Not specifically classified.)

11-7.1.6 Minimum Construction Standards.

11-7.1.6.1   Centers shall not be located above the heights indicated for the types of construction given in Table 11-7.1.6.1.

(handwritten: Cf 187).1.6.1 p. 281)

Table 11-7.1.6.1   Height and Construction Limits

Type of Construction	Age Group	Number of Stories (Stories are counted starting at floor of exit discharge)			
		1	2	3	4 and over
I (443) I (332) II (222) II (111)	0 to 3 3 thru 5 6 and older	X X X	X X X	X X X	X X X
III (211) V (111)	0 to 3 3 thru 5 6 and older	X X X	See Note 1 X X	Not Permitted See Note 1 See Note 1	
IV (2HH)	0 to 3 3 thru 5 6 and older	X X X	See Note 1 See Note 1 See Note 1		
II (000)	0 to 3 3 thru 5 6 and older	X X X	See Note 1 See Note 1 See Note 1		
III (200) V (000)	0 thru 3 3 thru 5 6 and older			Not Permitted See Note 2 See Note 2	

NOTE 1:   Permitted if entire building is protected throughout by an approved automatic sprinkler system.

NOTE 2:   May be permitted for children 3 years of age and older if the children are limited to the first floor and the number of children is limited to 50 and there are two remote exits; or if they are limited to the first floor and the number of children is limited to 100 and each room has an exit directly to the outside.

11-7.1.6.2 Location.   The story below the level of exit discharge may be used in buildings of any type other than Type II (000), Type III (200), and Type V (000). (*See 11-7.2.4.2.*)

11-7.1.7 Occupant Load.   The occupant load for which means of egress shall be provided for any floor shall be the maximum number of persons intended to occupy that floor but not less than one person for each 35 sq ft (3.25 sq m) of net floor area used by the children.

When a center occupies a portion of a floor on which another occupancy exists, the occupant load for that floor is the sum of the occupant loads of the two occupancies. For example:

Net Floor Area (ft²)		Population Density Factor (ft²/person)		Occupant Load
Day Care Center 1,750	÷	35	=	50
Place of Assembly 3,000	÷	7	=	429

By addition, the total occupant load for which means of egress must be provided would be 479.

11-7.2 Means of Egress Requirements.

11-7.2.1 General. (None.)

11-7.2.2 Types of Exits. (*See 11-2.2.*)

11-7.2.2.1 Stairs.

(a) Exit stairs shall be enclosed in accordance with 11-3.1.2.

(b) There shall be no enclosed usable space under stairs in an exit enclosure nor shall the open space within the enclosure either under or adjacent to the stairs be used for any purpose.

11-7.2.2.2 Areas of Refuge.   In buildings over five stories above ground level, areas of refuge shall be provided for occupants of child day-care centers, either by smokeproof towers or horizontal exits.

In all cases where day-care centers are found on upper floors of tall buildings, areas of refuge (smokeproof towers or horizontal exits) should be designed so that the children will survive a fire. Five stories or approximately 75 ft (22.86 m) is the maximum height at which the fire department can be expected to rescue the occupants of a building from outside. However, many fire departments do not have the equipment to reach this height, and, in such locations, areas of refuge are necessary at lower levels.

In any event, dependence on rescue by the fire department is not prudent. The time, number of personnel, and effort involved in rescuing one person down an extension ladder is so great that it is not possible to rescue a large number of children by this method.

11-7.2.3 Capacity of Means of Egress.   (*See 11-2.3.*)

11-7.2.4 Number of Exits.

11-7.2.4.1   Each floor occupied by children shall have not less than two remote exits.

11-7.2.4.2   When the story below the exit discharge is used (*see 11-7.1.6.2*), the following conditions shall be met:

(a) For up to 30 children there shall be two remote exits. One exit shall discharge directly outside and the vertical travel to ground level shall not exceed 8 ft (243.84 cm). There shall be no unprotected opening into the enclosure of the second exit.

(b) For over 30 children a minimum of two exits shall be provided directly outside with one of the two exiting at ground level.

Exception No. 1:   The exit directly to ground level is not required if the exits are protected in accordance with 5-1.3. There shall be no openings into the exit other than for ingress and egress. Smoke detectors shall be provided in that story and the story of discharge.

Exception No. 2:   The exit directly to ground level is not required if one exit complies with Exception No. 1 and sprinklers are used in that story and the story of exit discharge.

The intent of 11-7.2.4.2 is to permit the use of basements for child day-care centers only if protected exits with relatively short upward travel are provided. The committee recognized the level of risk involved in children occupying rooms below ground level. First, children of this age have difficulty in traveling up stairs, particularly at a fast speed. This is why the maximum vertical travel is 8 ft (2.44 m). Second, spaces below ground level have limited numbers of windows (or none) for emergency ventilation or for rescue. Third, a fire in a basement space will cause products of combustion to rise rapidly and block any means of egress that travels up the interior or exterior of a building. Finally, a fire on the upper floors of a facility may be undetected until exits leading from the basement have been blocked.

This section of the *Code* also recognizes that the level of risk to life safety increases with the number of children who may be exposed to a fire in a basement. In both Figures 11-18 and 11-19, an exterior stair (not likely to be lost to fire or be filled with smoke) is required. In Figure 11-18, with fewer than 30 children subject to fire exposure, the second means of egress may be an enclosed stair, without any unprotected openings, leading to ground level. With the case of the greater risk (more than 30 children), the second exit must lead directly to ground level. As the number of children potentially exposed to fire increases, the emphasis of the *Code* shifts to horizontal travel and to horizontal means of egress for two principal reasons. Even in organized groups, children of preschool age are difficult to lead and (as previously stated) have difficulty in climbing stairs.

Figure 11-18. Exit Requirements for Child Day-Care Center in Basement Occupied by 30 or Fewer Children.

Figure 11-19. Exit Requirements for Child Day-Care Center in Basement Occupied by More than 30 Children.

If the potential for the children's exposure to fire is reduced, the *Code* permits reliance on upward travel in lieu of horizontal movement. In Figure 11-20, per Exception No. 1, two enclosed interior stairs are permitted because smoke detectors have been installed. In Figure 11-21, per Exception No. 2, only one enclosed exit is necessary since automatic sprinklers have been installed in the basement and on the floor of exit discharge.

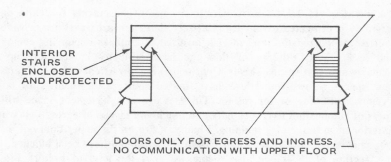

Figure 11-20. Exit Requirements for Child Day-Care Center in Basement Occupied by More than 30 Children, Smoke Detectors Installed on Occupied Floor and Upper Floor of Exit Discharge.

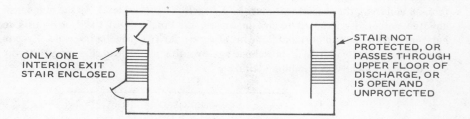

Figure 11-21. Exit Requirements for Child Day-Care Center in Basement Occupied by More than 30 Children, Automatic Sprinklers Installed on Occupied Floor and Upper Floor of Exit Discharge.

11-7.2.5 Arrangement of Means of Egress.   (*When the story below the exit discharge is used, see also 11-7.2.4.2.*)

11-7.2.6 Measurement of Travel Distance to Exits.

11-7.2.6.1   Travel distance shall be measured in accordance with Section 5-6.

11-7.2.6.2   Travel distance (a) between any room door intended as exit access and an exit shall not exceed 100 ft (30.48 m); (b) between any point in a room and an exit shall not exceed 150 ft (45.72 m); (c) between any point in a sleeping room or suite and an exit access door of that room or suite shall not exceed 50 ft (15.24 m).

Exception: The travel distance in (a) and (b) above may be increased by 50 ft (15.24 m) in buildings protected throughout by an approved automatic sprinkler system in accordance with Section 7-7.

Paragraph 11-7.2.6.2 is structured to say the same thing several different ways. As shown in Figure 11-22, the maximum travel distance from a room door (exit access to the corridor) to an exit door is 100 ft (30.48 m). The *total* travel distance from any point (such as in a room) to an exit is 150 ft (45.72 m). By subtraction, it follows that the maximum travel distance from a point in a room to an exit access door is 50 ft (15.24 m). This distance may not be increased even if the building is sprinklered.

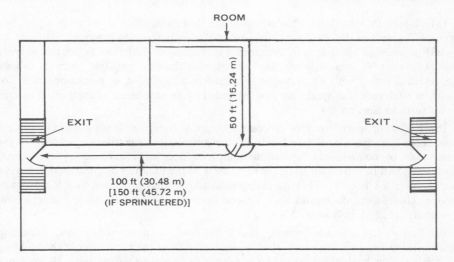

Figure 11-22. Maximum Travel Distance to Exit, Child Day-Care Center.

11-7.2.6.3 The travel distance to exits in open plan centers for children 3 years of age and older shall be in accordance with 11-6.2.2 for open plan schools.

11-7.2.7 Discharge from Exits. (*When the story below the exit discharge is used, see also 11-7.2.4.2.*) All such exits shall discharge directly to the outside.

11-7.2.8 Illumination of Means of Egress. If the facility is used after daylight hours, it shall comply with Section 5-8.

11-7.2.9 Emergency Lighting. Means of egress in each day care center shall be provided with emergency lighting, in accordance with Section 5-9.

11-7.2.10 Marking of Means of Egress. (No additional special requirements.) (*See Section 5-10.*)

11-7.2.11 Special Features.

11-7.2.11.1 Doors in means of egress shall swing in the direction of exit travel and shall meet the requirements of 11-2.11.2.

Exception: Doors from an existing center to an exit access in apartment buildings.

11-7.2.11.2 Every closet door latch shall be such that children can open the door from inside the closet.

11-7.2.11.3 Every bathroom door lock shall be designed to permit opening of the locked door from the outside in an emergency, and the opening device shall be readily accessible to the staff.

11-7.3 Protection.

11-7.3.1 Protection of Vertical Openings. Any vertical opening in centers shall be enclosed and protected in accordance with Section 6-2.

11-7.3.2 Protection from Hazards. Rooms or spaces for the storage, processing, or use of the materials specified in this section shall be protected in accordance with the following:

(a) Rooms or spaces used for the storage of combustible supplies in quantities deemed hazardous by the authority having jurisdiction, hazardous materials in quantities deemed hazardous by recognized standards, or fuel shall be separated from the remainder of the building by construction having not less than a 1-hour fire-resistive rating with all openings protected by self-closing or smoke-actuated fire doors, or such rooms or spaces may be protected by an automatic extinguishing system as set forth in Section 6-4.

(b) Rooms or spaces used for processing or use of combustible supplies in quantities considered hazardous by the authority having jurisdiction, hazardous materials, or for flammable or combustible liquids in quantities deemed hazardous by recognized standards shall be separated from the remainder of the building by construction having not less than a 1-hour fire-resistive rating with all openings protected by self-closing or smoke-actuated fire doors and shall also be protected by an automatic extinguishing system as set forth in Section 6-4.

(c) Boiler and furnace rooms, laundries, and maintenance shops, including woodworking and painting areas, shall be separated from the remainder of the building by construction having not less than a 1-hour fire-resistive rating with all openings protected by self-closing or smoke-actuated fire doors.

Exception: Rooms enclosing air-handling equipment.

(d) When automatic extinguishing systems are used to meet the requirements of this section, the rooms or spaces shall be separated from the remainder by a physical barrier of such construction so as to contain the heat or smoke generated by a fire to allow for ready extinguishing system activation.

Exception: Food preparation facilities protected in accordance with Removal of Smoke and Grease-Laden Vapors from Commercial Cooking Equipment, NFPA 96, are not required to have openings protected between food preparation areas and dining areas. Where domestic cooking equipment is used for food warming or limited cooking, protection or segregation of food preparation facilities is not required if approved by the authority having jurisdiction.

The intent of 11-7.3.2 is to specify the degree of protection necessary for certain hazardous areas. It has been divided into three sections based on the degree of hazard. The hazards noted in item (a) are required to be enclosed in 1-hour construction or protected by sprinklers. If the sprinkler option is chosen, an enclosure is still required; however, the enclosure need not be rated, but only form a membrane against the passage of smoke.

The hazards noted in item (b) must be enclosed in 1-hour construction *and* be protected by automatic sprinklers.

The hazards noted in item (c) are required to be enclosed in 1-hour construction with no option for a sprinkler equivalency for the enclosure. The exception to item (c) pertains to rooms housing air-handling equipment *only*. If the room is used for other purposes, then the provisions of item (a) or (b) apply.

The intent of the exception to 11-7.3.2 is to provide some barrier between cooking areas and dining areas. The intent of the barrier is to screen possible flash fires from view in an attempt to prevent panic. Openings in this barrier are not restricted and do not need to be protected. The *Code* is counting on the automatic extinguishing system to control any fire on the cooking surfaces, and, thus, no longer requires enclosure by rated construction. The degree of screening required, and thus the size of the barrier required, is left to the judgment of the authority having jurisdiction.

11-7.3.3 Interior Finish.

11-7.3.3.1   Interior finish for all walls and ceilings shall be Class A or Class B in accordance with Section 6-5.

11-7.3.3.2   In all centers, floor coverings within corridors and exitways shall be Class I or Class II in accordance with Section 6-5.

11-7.3.3.3   Decorations and furnishings shall be in accordance with Chapter 31.

11-7.3.4 Detection, Alarm, and Communications.

11-7.3.4.1   There shall be a manually operated fire alarm system in accordance with Section 7-6 on each floor of the center. In centers with more than 100 children, the fire alarm system shall be installed to transmit an alarm by the most direct and reliable method approved by local regulations to the fire department that is legally committed to serve the area in which the center is located.

Exception: When the child day-care center is housed in one room.

In all child day-care centers, manually operated fire alarm systems should be directly connected to the fire department. The committee felt compelled to emphasize that in centers which serve more than 100 children, this arrangement is essential. There are fire departments which will not accept direct alarms. In such cases, positive provisions must be made for rapid notification of the fire department by remote or central station systems.

11-7.3.4.2   Smoke detectors shall be installed on the ceiling of each story in front of the doors to the stairways and at no greater than 30-ft (914.4-cm) spacing in the corridors of all floors containing the center. Detectors shall also be installed in lounges and recreation areas in centers. The detectors may be single station units with an integral alarm having a decibel rating of at least 85.

Exception: Detectors are not required in centers housing children 6 years of age and older, if no sleeping facilities are provided.

The purpose of this requirement is obvious, but worth noting. In centers housing children younger than 6 years old, naps and sleep time are provided. The smoke detectors in selected areas provide early warning of an impending fire.

11-7.3.5 Extinguishment Requirements.

11-7.3.5.1   Portable fire extinguishers suitable for Class B fires shall be installed in kitchens and cooking areas, and extinguishers suitable for Class A fires shall be installed throughout the remainder of the center. (*See Section 7-7.*)

NFPA 10, *Standard for Portable Fire Extinguishers,*[6] **should be consulted concerning installation and maintenance of portable fire extinguishers.**

11-7.3.5.2   Standpipes for fire department use shall be installed in all buildings of six stories or more housing child day-care centers.

11-7.3.6 Corridors.   (*See 10-7.1.2.*)

11-7.3.7 Subdivision into Compartments.

(a) When sleeping areas in centers housing children under 3 years of age are divided into rooms, room dividers shall have a minimum of 1-hour fire resistance, and glass in wall areas shall not exceed 25 percent of the wall area and shall be glazed with fixed wire glass in steel frames.

(b) When interior room doors are provided between adjacent rooms they shall be not less than 32 in. (81.28 cm) wide. Doors and frames shall have a 20-minute fire protection rating and shall have self-closing devices, latches, and automatic hold-open devices as specified in 5-2.1.2.3.

The purpose of 11-7.3.7 is to provide a minimum level of compartmentation. Note that both items (a) and (b) say "when." In other words, these paragraphs do not require the compartments, but set minimums if they are provided.

11-7.4 Special Provisions.   (None.)

11-7.5 Building Services.

11-7.5.1 Utilities.

11-7.5.1.1   Utilities shall comply with the provisions of Section 7-1.

11-7.5.1.2   In existing buildings, the electrical wiring shall be sized to provide for the load. Receptacles and outlets serviced by extension cord-type wiring are prohibited. Electrical appliances shall be grounded in accordance with *National Electrical Code,* NFPA 70.

11-7.5.1.3   Special protective receptacle covers shall be installed in all areas occupied by children in centers for children under 5 years of age.

Children are subject to serious injury if they insert foreign objects into electrical receptacles. Protective covers must be provided and maintained in order to avoid such accidents.

11-7.5.2 Heating, ventilating, and air conditioning equipment shall be in accordance with Section 7-2.

11-7.5.3 Elevators, dumbwaiters, and vertical conveyors shall comply with the provisions of Section 7-4.

11-7.5.4 Rubbish chutes, incinerators, and laundry chutes shall comply with the provisions of Section 7-5.

SECTION 11-8   GROUP DAY-CARE HOMES

11-8.1 General Requirements.

11-8.1.1 Application.

11-8.1.1.1   This section establishes life safety requirements for group day-care homes in which at least seven but not more than twelve children receive care, maintenance, and supervision by other than their parent(s) or legal guardian(s) for 24 hours per day or less (generally within a dwelling unit). The provisions of Sections 11-2 through 11-6 shall not apply to this section unless a specific requirement is referenced by this section.

> The requirements detailed in Section 11-8 (Group Day-Care Homes, for fewer than 13 children) are based on the minimum staff-to-child ratio of two staff for up to 12 children with no more than three children under the age of 2.
> Group day-care homes are often found in buildings housing occupancies such as apartments, stores, or places of assembly. In such buildings, exit accesses usually open into a corridor. Paragraph 11-8.1.2(b) describes the requirements for safeguarding the integrity of at least one egress path from such a facility.

11-8.1.1.2   The text principally applies to centers in which children 5 years old or less may be sleeping during their time in the facility, but the provisions are for all facilities unless otherwise indicated.

11-8.1.1.3   Where a facility houses more than one age group, the requirements for the younger age group shall apply, unless the area housing the younger children is maintained as a separate fire area.

11-8.1.2 Mixed Occupancies.

(a)   When a group home is located in a building containing mixed occupancies, the separation requirements of the locally applicable building code or, if none exists, a nationally recognized model code shall be satisfied.

(b)   Homes in apartment buildings.

1. If the two exit accesses from the home enter the same corridor as the apartment occupancy, the exit accesses shall be separated in the corridor by a smoke barrier having not less than a 1-hour fire resistance rating. The smoke barrier shall be so located that there is an exit on each side of it.

2. The door in the smoke barrier shall be not less than 36 in. (91.44 cm) wide.

Exception: Existing doors not less than 32 in. (81.28 cm) wide may be accepted.

3. The doors and frames in the smoke barrier shall have a fire protection rating of at least 20 minutes and shall be equipped with a self-closing device, a latch, and an automatic hold-open device as specified in 5-2.1.2.3.

11-8.1.3 Special Definitions.   (None.)

11-8.1.4 Classification of Occupancy.   For purposes of this section, children are classified in age groups as follows: children under 3 years of age, children from 3 through 5 years of age, and children 6 years of age and older.

11-8.1.5 Classification of Hazard of Contents.   (Not specifically classified.)

11-8.1.6 Minimum Construction Standards.

Each building used as a group day-care home should meet the local minimum housing code and fire prevention code for the applicable class of residential construction or, if none exists, a nationally recognized model code.

11-8.1.7 Occupant Load.   No Special Requirements.

11-8.2 Means of Egress Requirements.

11-8.2.1 General.   (None.)

11-8.2.2 Types of Exits.   (*See 11-8.2.4.*)

11-8.2.3 Capacity of Means of Egress.   (*See 11-2.3.*)

11-8.2.4 Number of Exits.

11-8.2.4.1   Each floor occupied by children shall have not less than two remote means of egress.

11-8.2.4.2   Where spaces on the floor above the floor of exit discharge are used for sleeping purposes by children, at least one exit shall lead directly, or through an enclosed stairway, to the outside.

11-8.2.4.3   Where children are located on a story below the level of exit discharge (basement) at least one exit directly to the outside at ground level shall be provided. No facility shall be located more than one story below the ground. Any stairway to the story above shall be cut off by a fire barrier containing a door of at least a 20-minute fire protection rating, equipped with a self-closing device and a latch.

As illustrated in Figure 11-23, there must be an exit directly to ground level from a group day-care center in a basement. If a stairway were provided, it would have to be cut off from the basement by a fire barrier containing a door with a fire protection rating of at least 20 minutes. As discussed in 11-8.2.4.3, the committee drafted these provisions to stress the necessity for horizontal exiting to ground level. The factors underlying this concern were the age of the children (up to three children in a group day-care center may be under 2 years of age); the difficulty in leading children of preschool age; and the physical difficulty encountered by small children in climbing stairs.

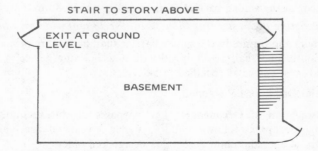

STAIR TO STORY ABOVE

EXIT AT GROUND
LEVEL

BASEMENT

Figure 11-23. Exit Requirements for Group Day-Care Center in Basement.

11-8.2.5 Arrangement of Means of Egress. *(When a story above or below the exit discharge is used, see 11-8.2.4.)*

11-8.2.6 Measurement of Travel Distance to Exits. *(See 11-2.6.)*

11-8.2.7 Discharge from Exits. *(When the story above or below the exit discharge is used, see 11-8.2.4.)*

11-8.2.8 Illumination of Means of Egress. *(See 11-7.2.8.)*

11-8.2.9 Emergency Illumination. No Requirements.

11-8.2.10 Marking of Means of Egress. *(See 11-7.2.10.)*

11-8.2.11 Special Requirements.

11-8.2.11.1 Every closet door latch shall be such that children can open the door from inside the closet.

11-8.2.11.2 Every bathroom door lock shall be designed to permit opening of the locked door from outside in an emergency, and the opening device shall be readily accessible to the staff.

11-8.3 Protection.

11-8.3.1 Protection of Vertical Openings. The doorway between the floor of exit discharge and any floor below shall be equipped with a self-closing door plus frame and hardware all of at least a 20-minute fire protection rating. Where the floor above the floor of exit discharge is used for sleeping purposes, there shall be a self-closing door plus frame and hardware all of at least a 20-minute fire protection rating at the top or bottom of each stairway.

Exception: Existing self-closing 1¾-in. (4.45-cm) solid bonded wood core doors without rated frames may be accepted by the authority having jurisdiction.

11-8.3.2 Protection from Hazards. No Requirements.

11-8.3.3 Interior Finish.

11-8.3.3.1 The interior finish in means of egress shall be Class A or B.

11-8.3.3.2 Interior finish in occupied spaces in the home shall be Class A, B or C, in accordance with Section 6-5.

11-8.3.4 Detection Systems. Where the floor above the floor of exit discharge is used for sleeping purposes there shall be a smoke detector at the top of the stairs in a building three stories or less in height or inside the dwelling unit used as a day-care facility in a multiple-dwelling building.

11-8.3.5 Extinguishers. A portable fire extinguisher suitable for Class B fires shall be provided for the kitchens and cooking areas.

11-8.4 Special Provisions. (None.)

11-8.5 Building Services.

11-8.5.1 Electrical Services.

11-8.5.1.1 Electrical wiring in new construction shall be installed in accordance with Section 7-1.

11-8.5.1.2   In existing buildings the electrical wiring shall be sized to provide for the load. Electrical appliances shall be grounded in accordance with *National Electrical Code*, NFPA 70. Receptacles and outlets serviced by extension cord-type wiring are prohibited.

11-8.5.1.3   Special protective receptacle covers shall be installed in all areas occupied by children in homes for children under 5 years of age.

11-8.5.2 Heating Equipment.

11-8.5.2.1   Any heaters in spaces occupied by children shall be separated from the space by partitions, screens, or other means.

> **Screens which separate heating equipment from spaces occupied by children must be of closely spaced wire or expanded metal, of heavy gage, and must be securely attached to elements of the building. The purpose is to prevent the children from bending the screens or inserting their fingers through the mesh.**

11-8.5.2.2   If solid partitions are used to provide the separation required in 11-8.5.2.1, provision shall be made to assure adequate air for combustion and ventilation for the heating equipment.

SECTION 11-9   FAMILY CHILD DAY-CARE HOMES

11-9.1 General Requirements.

11-9.1.1 Application.

11-9.1.1.1   This section establishes life safety requirements for licensed family child day-care homes in which fewer than seven children receive care, maintenance and supervision by other than their parent(s) or legal guardian(s) for less than 24 hours per day (usually a dwelling unit). The provisions of Sections 11-2 through 11-6 shall not apply to this section unless a specific requirement is referenced by this section.

> **The requirements detailed in Section 11-9 (Family Child Day-Care Homes) are based on the minimum staff-to-child ratio of one staff for up to six children, including the caretaker's own children under the age of 6, with no more than two children under the age of 2.**
> **Family day-care homes are usually situated in single-family dwellings or in apartment houses. If they occur in apartment houses, they must also comply with the applicable requirements of 11-9.1.2.**

11-9.1.1.2   The text principally applies to centers in which children 5 years old or less may be sleeping during their time in the facility, but the provisions are for all facilities unless otherwise indicated.

11-9.1.1.3   Where a facility houses more than one age group, the requirements for the younger children shall apply, unless the area housing the younger children is maintained as a separate fire area.

11-9.1.2 Mixed Occupancies.   Where family child day-care homes are located in a building containing mixed occupancies, the separation requirements of the locally applicable building code or, if none exists, a nationally recognized model code shall be satisfied.

11-9.1.3 Special Definitions.   (None.)

11-9.1.4 Classification of Occupancies.   For the purposes of this section, children are classified in age groups as follows: children under 3 years of age, children from 3 through 5 years of age, and children 6 years of age and older.

11-9.1.5 Classification of Hazard of Contents.   (Not specifically classified.)

11-9.1.6 Minimum Construction Standards.

Each building used as a family child day-care home should meet the local minimum housing code and fire prevention code for the applicable class of residential construction or, if none exists, a nationally recognized model code.

11-9.1.7 Occupant Load.   No Special Requirements.

11-9.2 Means of Egress Requirements.

11-9.2.1 General.   (None.)

11-9.2.2 Types of Exits.   (*See 11-9.2.4.*)

11-9.2.3 Capacity of Means of Egress.   (*See 11-2.3.*)

11-9.2.4 Number of Exits.

11-9.2.4.1   In a one- or two-family dwelling or building of unprotected wood frame construction used for child care purposes, every room used for sleeping, living, or dining purposes shall have at least two means of escape, at least one of which shall be a door or stairway providing a means of unobstructed travel to the outside of the building at street or ground level. No room or space shall be occupied for living or sleeping purposes which is accessible only by a ladder, folding stairs, or through a trap door.

This paragraph reflects the requirements for one- and two-family dwellings. The change from means of egress to means of escape also recognizes a window of proper size as one method of escaping a fire.

11-9.2.4.2   Where children are located on a floor (basement) below the floor of exit discharge, at least one exit shall be provided directly to the outside at ground level. No facility shall be located more than one story below the ground.

11-9.2.4.3 Stairs.   Every stairway shall comply at least with the minimum requirements for Class B stairs, as described in 5-2.2, in respect to width, risers, and treads and shall be maintained free of items of storage.

11-9.2.5 Arrangement of Means of Egress.   (*See 11-9.2.4.*)

11-9.2.6 Measurement of Travel Distance to Exits.   (*See 11-2.6.*)

11-9.2.7 Discharge from Exits.   (*See 11-9.2.4.*)

11-9.2.8 Illumination of Means of Egress.   (*See 11-7.2.8.*)

11-9.2.9 Emergency Lighting.   No Requirements.

11-9.2.10 Marking of Means of Egress.   (*See 11-7.2.10.*)

11-9.2.11 Special Features.

11-9.2.11.1 Each door in a means of egress shall not be less than 24 in. (60.96 cm) wide.

11-9.2.11.2 Every closet door latch shall be such that children can open the door from inside the closet.

11-9.2.11.3 Every bathroom door lock shall be designed to permit the opening of the locked door from the outside in an emergency and the opening device shall be readily accessible to the staff.

11-9.3 Protection.

11-9.3.1 Protection of Vertical Openings.   (No additional special provisions.)

11-9.3.2 Protection from Hazards.   No Requirements.

11-9.3.3 Interior Finish.

11-9.3.3.1 The interior finish in corridors, stairways and lobbies and in rooms into which exits discharge shall be Class A or B.

11-9.3.3.2 Interior finish in occupied spaces in the home shall be Class A, B or C, in accordance with Section 6-5.

11-9.3.4 Detection Systems.   Where the floor above the level of exit discharge is used for sleeping purposes there shall be a smoke detector at the top of the stairs in a building three stories or less with open stairways, or inside the dwelling unit used as a day-care facility in a multiple dwelling.

11-9.3.5 Extinguishers.   A portable fire extinguisher suitable for Class B fires shall be provided for the kitchens and cooking areas.

11-9.4 Special Provisions.   No Requirements.

11-9.5 Building Services.

11-9.5.1 Electrical Services.

11-9.5.1.1 Electrical wiring in new construction shall be installed in accordance with Chapter 7.

11-9.5.1.2 In existing buildings, the electrical wiring shall be sized to provide for the load. Electrical appliances shall be grounded in accordance with *National Electrical Code*, NFPA 70.

Receptacles and outlets serviced by extension cord-type wiring are prohibited.

11-9.5.1.3 Special protective receptacle covers shall be installed in all areas occupied by children in homes for children under 5 years of age.

11-9.5.2 Heating Equipment.

11-9.5.2.1 Unvented room heaters shall not be permitted. Oil- and gas-fired room heaters shall be installed in accordance with the applicable standards cited by this *Code*. A guard shall be provided to protect the children from hot surfaces and open flames.

11-9.5.2.2 No stove or combustion heater shall be so located as to block escape in case of malfunctioning of the stove or heater.

REFERENCES CITED BY *CODE*

(These publications comprise a part of the requirements to the extent called for by the Code.)

NFPA 13, Standard for the Installation of Sprinkler Systems, NFPA, Boston, 1980.

NFPA 45, *Standard on Fire Protection for Laboratories Using Chemicals*, NFPA, Boston, 1975.

NFPA 70, *National Electrical Code*, NFPA, Boston, 1981.

NFPA 96, *Standard for the Installation of Equipment for the Removal of Smoke and Grease-Laden Vapors from Commercial Cooking Equipment*, NFPA, Boston, 1980.

REFERENCES CITED IN COMMENTARY

[1]*American National Standard Safety Code for Elevators, Dumbwaiters, Escalators, and Moving Walks*, ANSI A17.1 — 1978 (and supplement, ANSI A17.1a — 1979), American Society of Mechanical Engineers, 345 East 47th Street, New York, NY 10017.

[2]*Specifications for Making Buildings and Facilities Accessible to, and Usable by, the Physically Handicapped*, ANSI A117.1 — 1961, American National Standards Institute, 1430 Broadway, New York, NY 10018 (reaff. 1971).

[3]NFPA 13, *Standard for the Installation of Sprinkler Systems*, NFPA, Boston, 1980.

[4]NFPA 220, *Standard Types of Building Construction*, NFPA, Boston, 1979.

[5]NFPA 90A, *Standard for the Installation of Air Conditioning and Ventilating Systems*, NFPA, Boston, 1978.

[6]NFPA 10, *Standard for Portable Fire Extinguishers*, NFPA, Boston, 1978.

12

NEW HEALTH CARE OCCUPANCIES

(See also Chapter 31.)

This chapter covers the requirements for new health care occupancies. In previous editions of the *Code* these occupancies were known as "Institutional Occupancies."

Detention and correctional occupancies are now discussed in Chapters 14 and 15.

Health care occupancies are those used for purposes such as medical or other treatment or care of persons suffering from physical or mental illness, disease, or infirmity, and for the care of infants, convalescents, or infirm aged persons. Health care occupancies provide sleeping facilities for the occupants and are occupied by persons who are mostly incapable of self-preservation because of age, physical or mental disability, or because of security measures not under the occupants' control.

Health care occupancies treated in this chapter include:
- (a) Hospitals and
  Nursing homes
- (b) Residential-custodial care
  Nurseries
  Homes for aged
  Mentally retarded care facilities
  Facilities for social rehabilitation
- (c) Supervisory care facilities
- (d) Ambulatory health care centers

SECTION 12-1   GENERAL REQUIREMENTS

12-1.1 Application.

12-1.1.1 General.

12-1.1.1.1   New health care facilities shall comply with the provisions of this chapter. *(See Chapter 31 for operating features.)*

Exception: Hospitals and nursing homes found to have equivalent safety. One such method for determining this equivalency is given in Appendix C.

Appendix C is an equivalency system which uses numerical values to analyze the fire safety effectiveness of a building design. The system provides a methodology by which alternative designs can be evaluated as options to literal *Code* compliance. In providing the Appendix C equivalency system, it is not intended to limit equivalency evaluations to solely this one system. The authority having jurisdiction retains the authority as expressed within 1-5.1 to evaluate and approve alternative designs on the basis of appropriate supporting data. Appendix C may be used to assist in this evaluation.

12-1.1.1.2   This chapter establishes life safety requirements for the design of all new hospitals, nursing homes, residential-custodial care, and supervisory care facilities. Where requirements vary, the specific occupancy is named in the paragraph pertaining thereto. Section 12-6 establishes life safety requirements for the design of all new ambulatory health care centers.

Chapter 13 provides the requirements for existing health care facilities.

12-1.1.1.3   Health care occupancies are those used for purposes such as medical or other treatment or care of persons suffering from physical or mental illness, disease or infirmity; for the care of infants, convalescents, or infirm aged persons.

12-1.1.1.4   Health care facilities provide sleeping accommodations for the occupants and are occupied by persons who are mostly incapable of self-preservation because of age, physical or mental disability, or because of security measures not under the occupants' control.

12-1.1.1.5   This chapter also covers ambulatory health care centers as defined in 12-1.3(e). See Section 12-6 for requirements.

12-1.1.1.6   Buildings or sections of buildings which house, or in which care is rendered to, mental patients, including the mentally retarded, who are capable of judgment and appropriate physical action for self-preservation under emergency conditions in the opinion of the governing body of the facility and the governmental agency having jurisdiction, may come under other chapters of the *Code* instead of Chapter 12.

12-1.1.1.7   It shall be recognized that, in buildings housing certain types of patients or having detention rooms or a security section, it may be necessary to lock doors and bar windows to confine and protect building inhabitants. In such instances, the authority having jurisdiction shall make appropriate modifications to those sections of this *Code* which would otherwise require the keeping of exits unlocked.

12-1.1.1.8   It shall be also recognized that some mental health patients are not capable of seeking safety without guidance.

12-1.1.1.9   Buildings or sections of buildings which house older persons and which provide activities that foster continued independence but do not include those services distinctive to residential-custodial care facilities [as defined in 12-1.3(c)] shall be subject to the requirements of other sections of this *Code*, such as Chapter 18.

12-1.1.1.10   Health care occupancies shall include all buildings or parts thereof with occupancy as described in this chapter under Special Definitions, 12-1.3.

Paragraphs 12-1.1.1.2 through 12-1.1.1.10 contain explanatory material indicating some general characteristics of the occupants of health care occupancies. A few fundamental safeguards are also set forth. Formal definitions are established in 12-1.3.

Implied by the definitions of 12-1.3 and stated in 12-1.1.1.4, health care facilities are buildings which provide sleeping facilities (24-hour care) for occupants. Occupants in a health care facility may be restrained, but are housed primarily for treatment of mental or physical infirmities. Where occupants are restrained for penal or corrective purposes, the building would be classified as a detention and correctional occupancy which is treated in Chapters 14 and 15.

Where a building is used for the treatment or housing of mental patients (see 12-1.1.1.6) or aged persons (see 12-1.1.1.9) where:
1) Occupants are not restrained by locked doors or other devices, and
2) The patients are ambulatory, and
3) The occupants are capable of perceiving threat and taking appropriate action for self-preservation,
then the building may be classed as an occupancy other than health care.

Occupants of health care facilities are considered to be *incapable of self-preservation* (see 12-1.1.1.4) because of age, because of physical or mental disability, or because of security measures not under the occupant's control. A significant number of occupants in health care facilities are assumed to be nonambulatory or bedridden. Other occupants, who are capable of self-movement, may have impaired judgment (see 12-1.1.1.8).

Although locking exit doors and barring windows is always undesirable from the viewpoint of life safety, the *Code* recognizes that in some cases it is necessary to restrain people. In these instances, provision should be made for the continuous supervision and prompt release of restrained persons (see 12-1.1.1.7). Release of occupants should be accomplished by a system capable of automatically unlocking the doors in the means of egress, or by the presence of attendants who are continuously available and equipped with keys. In any event, continuous supervision is considered essential (see 12-2.11.4).

12-1.1.2 Objective. The objective of this chapter is to provide a reasonable level of safety by reducing the probability of injury and loss of life from the effects of fire with due consideration for functional requirements. This is accomplished by limiting the development and spread of a fire emergency to the room of fire origin and reducing the need for occupancy evacuation, except from the room of fire origin.

It should be recognized that only through control of a person's environment can the well-being of an individual be reasonably ensured. That is, only through complete control of the environment, including building members, building finishes, furnishings, decorations, clothing, linens, bedding, and the like, can the individual be protected against fire. However, no code can prevent injury resulting from a person's careless actions.

Although an effort should be made to protect the individual through prevention efforts, the primary objective of the requirements of Chapter 12 is to prevent fire from escaping the room of origin and thereby limit threats posed to individuals *outside* the room of origin.

12-1.1.3 Total Concept. All health care facilities shall be so designed, constructed, maintained, and operated as to minimize the possibility of a fire emergency requiring the evacuation of occupants. Because the safety of health care occupants cannot be assured adequately by dependence on evacuation of the building, their protection from fire shall be provided by appropriate arrangement of facilities, adequate staffing, and careful development of operating and maintenance procedures composed of the following:

(a) Proper design, construction, and compartmentation;

(b) Provision for detection, alarm, and extinguishment; and

(c) Fire prevention and the planning, training, and drilling in programs for the isolation of fire, transfer of occupants to areas of refuge, or evacuation of the building.

Vertical movement of patients within a health care facility is an inefficient, time-consuming process. In one study, it was shown through the simulated evacuation of patients from a second-story ward to ground level that more than 30 minutes may be required for evacuation during a fire.

The provisions of Chapter 12, therefore, are based upon a "defend in place" philosophy which minimizes the probability of a fire necessitating vertical movement of occupants. Patients in critical care areas may be connected to life support equipment which makes movement difficult and, in some cases, impossible. Barriers are required to provide for the horizontal movement of patients to safe areas of refuge on a single floor level and to limit to a manageable number the number of occupants exposed to any single fire. Vertical means of egress (stairs or ramps) are specified by Chapter 12 as escape routes for visitors and staff and as a "last line of defense" for the movement of patients.

12-1.1.4   Additions, Conversions, Modernization, Renovation, and Construction Operations.

12-1.1.4.1   Additions shall be separated from any existing structure not conforming to the provisions within Chapter 13 by a fire barrier having at least a 2-hour fire resistance rating constructed of materials as required for the addition.

Paragraph 12-1.1.4.1 establishes separation criteria for additions to existing structures where existing structures do not conform to the provisions of Chapter 13. It should be emphasized where an existing building meets the provisions of Chapter 13, the building would be in compliance with the *Code* and the addition would not require separation.

Where additions must be separated, partitions must be constructed of assemblies providing 2-hours fire resistance. Where the structural framing of the addition or the existing buildings are of assemblies of less than 2-hours fire resistance, special provision should be made to assure the necessary separation will be maintained for the 2-hour period.

Materials used in the construction of the partition should be "constructed to the standards of the addition." That is, if the addition is required to be constructed of noncombustible or limited-combustible materials (Construction Types I or II) then the materials used in the partition must be limited-combustible or noncombustible as defined in NFPA 220, *Standard Types of Building Construction*[1]. Conversely, if the addition may be constructed of combustible materials, then combustible materials may be used as a portion of the partition.

12-1.1.4.2 Communicating openings in dividing fire barriers required by 12-1.1.4.1 shall occur only in corridors and shall be protected by approved self-closing fire doors. (*See also Section 6-2.*)

12-1.1.4.3 Doors in barriers required by 12-1.1.4.1 shall normally be kept closed.

Exception: Doors may be held open only if they meet the requirements of 12-2.11.6.

Openings in barriers separating additions from nonconforming existing structures are limited to corridors (see 12-1.1.4.2). Openings are required to be protected by 1½ hour, "B" labeled, fire door assemblies. The fire doors are required to be self-closing and maintained closed, or may be held open by an automatic device in accordance with 12-2.11.6. See Figure 12-1.

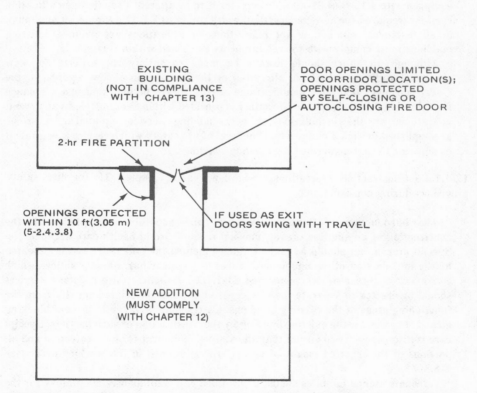

Figure 12-1. Separation of New Addition from Existing Building Not in Compliance with Chapter 13. If the addition is of fire-resistive or noncombustible construction, use noncombustible or limited-combustible materials in the 2-hour fire partition (see NFPA 220, Standard Types of Building Construction.*)*[1]

12-1.1.4.4 Conversions. An existing building may be converted to a hospital, nursing home, or residential-custodial care facility only if it complies with all requirements for new health care buildings prior to occupancy as a health care facility.

12-1.1.4.5 Modernization or Renovation. Alterations shall not diminish the level of life safety below that which exists prior to the alterations except that life safety features in excess of those required for new construction are not required to be maintained. In no case shall the resulting life safety be less than that required for existing buildings. Alterations or installations of new building services equipment shall be accomplished as nearly as possible in conformance with the requirements for new construction.

Alterations may not reduce the level of life safety below that which exists prior to the alterations; however, provisions in excess of the requirements for new construction are not required to be maintained. Suppose, for example, an existing hospital has a 6-ft (1.83-m) wide corridor, and a portion of the hospital was to be renovated. Even though the building is existing, a minimum 6-ft (1.83-m) wide corridor must be maintained. Conversely, suppose a portion of an existing hospital equipped with a 10-ft (3.05-m) wide corridor is to be altered. The minimum allowable corridor (required for new construction) width would be 8 ft (2.44 m). As a minimum, in all instances, whether or not renovations or alterations are planned, existing buildings must comply with the requirements contained within Chapter 13.

Although an effort should always be made to satisfy the criteria for new construction during a building alteration or the installation of new equipment, the *Code* recognizes that such modifications cannot always be accomplished. Guidance for achieving "equivalency" to life safety is provided within Section 1-5. In any event, alterations or the installation of new building service equipment must be accomplished in such a manner that the level of life safety which results is equivalent or superior to that prescribed for existing buildings.

12-1.1.4.6 Construction Operations. See 1-6.3 and Chapter 31 for life safety provisions during construction.

The introduction of "outside" workers and activities associated with the construction of an addition creates unusual risks of fire in health care occupancies. Special precautions should be taken to guard against the potential exposure created by the introduction of flammable substances or by other hazardous practices which could pose a threat to occupants (see 31-1.1.2). Temporary fire-resistant barriers should be erected to separate the new construction and associated activity from the functioning areas of the existing buildings. Care should be taken to prevent blocking means of egress for the existing building by the construction of such barriers. Special care is also necessary to ensure that all existing equipment for fire protection and all portions of the required means of egress are maintained in full working order (see 1-6.3).

Adequate escape facilities should be provided and continuously maintained for the use of construction workers. (See 31-1.1.1 and NFPA 241, *Standard for Safeguarding Building Construction and Demolition Operations.)*[2]

12-1.2 Mixed Occupancies.

12-1.2.1 Sections of health care facilities may be classified as other occupancies if they meet all of the following conditions:

(a) They are not intended to serve health care occupants for purposes of housing, treatment or customary access.

(b) They are adequately separated from areas of health care occupancies by construction having a fire resistance rating of at least 2 hours.

12-1.2.2 Ambulatory care (*see Section 12-6*), medical clinics and similar facilities which are contiguous to health care occupancies but are primarily intended to provide outpatient services may be classified as a business or ambulatory care occupancy provided the facilities are separated from health care occupancies by not less than 2-hour fire-resistive construction.

Exception: When the business occupancy or similar facility is intended to provide:

(a) Services for hospital patients who are litter borne, or,

(b) General anesthesia services,

the section shall meet all requirements for health care facilities.

Paragraphs 12-1.2.1 and 12-1.2.2 set forth criteria for classifying spaces as "other" occupancies, although they are located in buildings primarily used for health care purposes. Paragraph 12-1.2.1 would allow offices to be classified as business occupancies, cafeterias to be classified as places of assembly, dormitories to be classified as residential, etc., if both items (a) and (b) of 12-1.2.1 are met. If either item (a) or (b) is not met, then the area would be considered "mixed occupancy" and the provisions of 1-4.5 apply and require that the more restrictive life safety provisions apply. (See 1-4.5.)

Paragraph 12-1.2.2 covers a similar subject as 12-1.2.1, but specifically discusses ambulatory care centers, medical clinics, and similar areas which primarily provide outpatient services. If these facilities are separated by 2-hour fire-resistive construction, then they may be classified as ambulatory health care centers or as business occupancies, whichever applies. If, however, litter-borne inpatients are treated or general anesthesia is used, then the facility must meet the requirements for health care occupancies. The provisions of business occupancies and ambulatory health care centers were written around the concept that most people walk in and out.

Note that the 1981 Edition of the *Code* dropped the prohibition against using these spaces as part of the means of egress. Paragraph 12-1.2.4 will now allow this under certain conditions.

12-1.2.3 Health care occupancies in buildings housing other occupancies shall be completely separated from them by construction having a fire resistance rating of at least 2 hours as provided for additions in 12-1.1.4.

Paragraph 12-1.2.3 requires that if a health care occupancy is located in a building of another classification (such as business, storage, mercantile, or industrial), the health care occupancy must be separated from the other occupancy by construction having a fire resistance of 2 hours, as detailed in 12-1.1.4. Also see the discussion following 12-1.1.4.

Note that 12-1.2.3 deals with occupancy classification and *not* with hazard of contents. Hazard of contents is treated in 12-1.2.6 and 12-1.2.7.

12-1.2.4   All means of egress from health care occupancies that traverse non-health care spaces shall conform to requirements of this *Code* for health care occupancies.

Exception: It is permissible to exit through a horizontal exit into other contiguous occupancies which do not conform to health care egress provisions but which do comply with requirements set forth in the appropriate occupancy chapter of this Code, as long as the occupancy does not have high hazard contents. The horizontal exit must comply with the requirements of 12-2.2.5.

Paragraph 12-1.2.4 specifies that the means of egress from health care occupancies which traverses non-health care spaces must conform to requirements for health care occupancies. However, an exception is provided where a 2-hour barrier is provided and such barrier is used as a horizontal exit. Where a 2-hour barrier serves as a horizontal exit, it is acceptable to exit into a different occupancy providing the "other" occupancy complies with the provisions of the *Code* which would be applicable thereto, and the "other" occupancy does not have high hazard contents. For example, if a horizontal exit is provided between a health care facility and a business occupancy, inpatients may exit into the business occupancy through a horizontal exit. In this instance, corridor width, corridor partitions, stairway details, and the like must conform to the provisions set forth within either Chapters 26 or 27 which deal with business occupancies. However, the horizontal exit must comply with all the requirements of 12-2.2.5.

12-1.2.5   Auditoriums, chapels, staff residential areas or other occupancies provided in connection with health care facilities shall have exits provided in accordance with other applicable sections of the *Code*.

Auditoriums, chapels, and other areas separated by 2-hour construction and meeting the criteria of 12-1.2.1 and 12-1.2.2 for other occupancies are required to be designed in accordance with the appropriate occupancy chapter governing their use.

Nontypical health care spaces should have means of egress features designed in accordance with the use of the space. For example, if a space located in a health care facility is used as a chapel or auditorium with an occupant load in excess of 50, then it is considered a place of assembly. In such circumstances, doors in the means of egress should be sidehinged swinging doors, arranged to swing in the direction of exit travel (see 5-2.1.1.4.1), and should not be equipped with a latch or lock unless such a latch or lock is operated by panic hardware (see 8-2.11.1).

12-1.2.6   Any area with a hazard of contents classified higher than that of the health care occupancy and located in the same building shall be protected as required in 12-3.2.

Paragraph 12-1.2.6 regulates spaces in a health care facility which, although comprising only a portion of the facility, contain more hazardous materials (in quantity or type) than are usually found in most other spaces.

Spaces such as rooms used for the storage of combustible materials, trash collection rooms, gift shops, and paint shops must be protected in accordance with 12-3.2.

12-1.2.7 Non-health care related occupancies classified as containing high-hazard contents shall not be permitted in buildings housing health care occupancies.

Paragraph 12-1.2.7 prohibits another occupancy (such as storage) with highly hazardous contents (such as flammable liquids) from being located in a building housing health care occupancies.

This paragraph limits use based upon *occupancy classification* with regard to hazard of contents. For example, the paragraph is *not* meant to exclude laboratory operations as a portion of a health care facility. The intent is to prevent a portion of a hospital from being converted or designed for use as an educational or research facility (classed as an educational or possibly an industrial occupancy) and having laboratories using and storing sizable quantities of flammable liquids larger than would be expected in a health care laboratory.

12-1.3 Special Definitions.

(a) **Hospital.** A building or part thereof used for the medical, psychiatric, obstetrical or surgical care, on a 24-hour basis, of four or more inpatients. Hospital, wherever used in this *Code*, shall include general hospitals, mental hospitals, tuberculosis hospitals, children's hospitals, and any such facilities providing inpatient care.

(b) **Nursing Home.** A building or part thereof used for the lodging, boarding and nursing care, on a 24-hour basis, of four or more persons who, because of mental or physical incapacity, may be unable to provide for their own needs and safety without the assistance of another person. Nursing home, wherever used in this *Code*, shall include nursing and convalescent homes, skilled nursing facilities, intermediate care facilities, and infirmaries in homes for the aged.

(c) **Residential-Custodial Care Facility.** A building, or part thereof, used for the lodging or boarding of four or more persons who are incapable of self-preservation because of age or physical or mental limitation. The following types of facilities, when accommodating persons of the above description, shall be classified as residential-custodial care facilities:

1. Nursery facilities that provide full-time care for children under 6 years of age.

2. Mentally retarded care facilities, including specialized intermediate care facilities for the mentally retarded.

3. Facilities in a home for the aging, that contain a group housing arrangement for older persons, that provide at least two meals per day and such social and personal care services needed by their residents, but that do not provide intermediate or skilled nursing care.

4. Facilities for social rehabilitation, such as those used for the treatment of alcoholism, drug abuse, or mental health problems, that contain a group housing arrangement, and that provide at least two meals per day and personal care services for their residents, but do not provide intermediate or skilled nursing care.

Facilities housing older persons, or mental patients, including the mentally retarded, who are judged to be capable of self-preservation with minimal staff assistance in an emergency, are covered by other chapters of the *Code*. (*See 12-1.1.1.6 and 12-1.1.1.9.*)

Children's facilities that do not provide lodging or boarding for their occupants are classified as Child Day-Care Centers, Group Day-Care Centers, or Family Child Day-Care Homes.

(d) **Supervisory Care Facility.** A building or part thereof used for the lodging or boarding of four or more mental health patients who are capable of self-preservation and who require supervison and who are receiving therapy, training or other health related care and who may have imposed upon them security measures not under their control.

(e) **Ambulatory Health Care Centers.** A building or part thereof used to provide services or treatment to four or more patients at the same time and meeting either (1) or (2) below.

1. Those facilities which provide, on an outpatient basis, treatment for patients which would render them incapable of taking action for self-preservation under emergency conditions without assistance from others, such as hemodialysis units or freestanding emergency medical units.

2. Those facilities which provide, on an outpatient basis, surgical treatment requiring general anesthesia.

Paragraph 12-1.3(a) through (e) defines the characteristics of the occupancies covered by Chapter 12. To be classed as a health care occupancy, a building must house four or more *people incapable of self-preservation* on a 24-hour basis.

Occupants of hospitals or nursing homes are assumed to be nonambulatory and incapable of self-preservation. In making this judgment, due consideration should be given to the use of physical restraints and tranquilizing drugs which can render occupants immobile. Different staffing criteria and levels of care make differentiation between hospitals and nursing homes apparent. The difference between nursing homes and residential-custodial care facilities is not so clear.

Although residential-custodial care facilities house four or more occupants incapable of self-preservation, either because of age or physical or mental limitations, occupants are generally considered to be ambulatory and would require only limited assistance during emergency evacuation. Buildings which house mentally retarded occupants or persons being treated for alcohol or drug abuse who are ambulatory and may be expected to evacuate a structure with limited assistance would meet the criteria for residential-custodial care facilities. Day-care facilities which provide care for the aged, children, mentally retarded, or others would be classified as other than health care if the care or treatment is not provided on a 24-hour basis.

Although age, in itself, is not sufficient justification to develop a classification for a health care occupancy, it should be recognized that the elderly represent a unique fire problem. Experiences in buildings where the elderly are housed reveal that the reaction of the elderly to a fire may not be directed toward self-preservation. On discovering a fire, the elderly patient may ignore it, be transfixed by it, or seek refuge from it in his or her room and fail to notify anyone else of the fire. In some cases, the

elderly have resisted efforts to remove them from the building and familiar surroundings.

A supervisory care facility houses occupants on a 24-hour basis who *are* capable of self-preservation and are receiving therapy, training, or other health-related care, but who may have imposed upon them security measures which restrict freedom of escape. Where occupants are mobile but are housed for mental treatment and may at times be incapable of perceiving threat and taking action for self-preservation, such facilities should be classed as residential-custodial care facilities.

The intent of the definition of a supervisory care facility is to describe a condition where the patients involved can, with the unlocking of any locked doors and/or the assistance and guidance of the staff, rapidly evacuate the building or move to an internal area of refuge. The authority having jurisdiction may require additional safeguards if this intent is not being met, or may classify as supervisory care those occupancy facilities involving some patients who are not individually capable of self-preservation, if it is demonstrated to his or her satisfaction that the intent of the ability to rapidly evacuate all patients is present at all times.

In previous editions of the *Code*, occupancies which offered medical services on an outpatient basis would have been regulated within the chapter dealing with business occupancies. The threat to life in an outpatient facility where four or more patients may be subject to medical procedures requiring general anesthesia, treatments such as hemodialysis, or free-standing emergency service is significantly greater than that typical of a business occupancy. Conversely, application of the requirements expressed for health care facilities which contemplate 24-hour care would be inappropriate and would be unnecessarily restrictive. In establishing the occupancy classification of an ambulatory health care center, it was intended to develop requirements which fall between the restrictions applicable to business occupancies and the health care facilities in terms of level of life safety achieved.

12-1.4 Classification of Occupancy.   See Definitions, 12-1.3.

12-1.5 Classification of Hazard of Contents.   The classification of hazard of contents shall be as defined in Section 4-2.

12-1.6 Minimum Construction Requirements.

12-1.6.1   For the purpose of 12-1.6, stories shall be counted starting at the primary level of exit discharge and ending at the highest occupiable level. For the purposes of this section, the primary level of exit discharge of a building shall be that floor which is level with or above finished grade of the exterior wall line for 50 percent or more of its perimeter. Building levels below the primary level shall not be counted as a story in determining the height of a building.

Allowable building construction types are a function of the number of stories in a building. In determining the number of stories, the first story is considered to be the level of exit discharge. Only "occupiable levels" are counted in determining story height. For example, unoccupied attics would not constitute a story.

Difficulties have been experienced in determining story height where a building is located on a sloping grade. Paragraph 12-1.6.1 notes that a story on a sloping site which is partially below grade should be counted as a story if the floor is level with or above grade for 50 percent or more of the perimeter of the building at the exterior wall. See Figure 12-2.

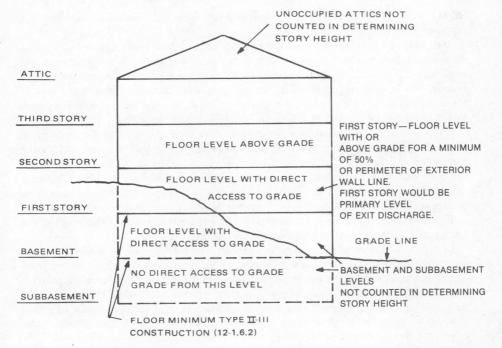

Figure 12-2. Building Section — Illustrates Application of 12-1.6.1 and 12-1.6.2.

12-1.6.2 Health care buildings of one story in height only may be constructed of Type I (443), I (332), II (222), II (111), II (000), III (211), IV (2HH), or V (111) construction. All buildings with more than one level below the level of exit discharge shall have all such lower levels separated from the level of exit discharge by at least Type II (111) construction. (*See 12-3.5 for automatic extinguishment requirements.*)

Exception: Any building of Type I or Type II (222 or 111) construction may include roofing systems involving combustible supports, decking, or roofing provided: (1) the roof covering meets Class A requirements in accordance with Fire Tests for Roof Coverings, NFPA 256, and (2) the roof is separated from all occupied portions of the building by a noncombustible floor assembly having at least a 2-hour fire resistance rating which includes at least 2½ in. (6.35 cm) of concrete or gypsum fill. To qualify for this exception, the attic or other space so developed shall either be unoccupied or protected throughout by an approved automatic sprinkler system.

Construction types permitted in new health care facilities are summarized within Table 12-1. See NFPA 220, *Standard Types of Building Construction*,[1] for definitions of construction types. An exception is provided for certain roof constructions under limited conditions.

12-1.6.3 Health care buildings two stories or more in height shall be of Type I (443), I (332) or II (222) construction.

Exception No. 1:   Health care buildings up to and including three stories in height may be of Type II (111) construction if protected throughout by an approved automatic sprinkler system.

Exception No. 2:   Any building of Type I or Type II (222 or 111) construction may include roofing systems involving combustible supports, decking, or roofing provided: (1) the roof covering meets Class A requirements in accordance with NFPA 256, Fire Tests for Roof Coverings, and (2) the roof is separated from all occupied portions of the building by a noncombustible floor assembly having at least a 2-hour fire resistance rating which includes at least 2½ in. (6.35 cm) of concrete or gypsum fill. To qualify for this exception, the attic or other space so developed shall either be unoccupied or protected throughout by an approved automatic sprinkler system.

Multistory, nonsprinklered health care facilities are required to be constructed of noncombustible materials with a minimum 2-hour fire resistance rating. It is recognized that movement of patients may not be possible, and occupants of a health care facility may be required to remain in the structure for the duration of the fire. In specifying 2-hours fire resistance, it is intended that building members be adequately protected against fire effects to assure building stability for the projected fire duration.

An exception is allowed for buildings *completely* protected by automatic sprinklers. Type II (111) structures can be erected to a maximum of three stories where a complete system of electrically supervised automatic sprinklers is provided.

An exception is provided for certain roof constructions under limited conditions.

12-1.6.4 For construction requirements of enclosures of vertical openings between floors, see 12-3.1.

Table 12–1.   Construction Types Permitted in New
Health Care Occupancies

| | Stories | | | |
Construction Type	1	2	3	Over 3
Types I-443, I-332, II-222 (Fire Resistive and Protected Noncombustible)	X	X	X	X
Type II-111 (Protected Noncombustible)	X	X*	X*	
Type II-000 (Unprotected Noncombustible)	X*			
Type III-211 (Protected Ordinary)	X*			
Type IV-2HH (Heavy Timber)	X*			
Type V-111 (Protected Wood Frame)	X*			

X = Construction types allowed.
* = Automatic sprinkler protection required.

12-1.6.5 All interior walls and partitions in buildings of Type I or Type II construction shall be of noncombustible or limited-combustible materials.

NFPA 220, *Standard Types of Building Construction*,[1] establishes restrictions relative to the use of combustible building materials within structures required to be constructed of noncombustible or limited-combustible materials. NFPA 220[1] should be consulted for specific limitations. The terms noncombustible and limited-combustible are defined within NFPA 220[1] and are repeated in Chapter 3 of the *Code* for quick reference.

12-1.6.6 Openings for the passage of pipes or conduit in walls or partitions that are required to have fire or smoke resisting capability shall be protected in accordance with 6-2.2.8 or 6-3.6.

Fire and smoke may spread across a fire-rated barrier or fire-rated wall via openings created by the passage of pipes, conduit, or other building services. Paragraph 12-1.6.6 specifies where such penetrations occur, suitable appliances such as metal plates, masonry fill, or other products approved for the purpose should be installed to maintain the fire and smoke resisting capability of the partition.

12-1.6.7 Firestopping. Each exterior wall of Type V construction and interior stud partitions shall be firestopped so as to cut off all concealed draft openings, both horizontal and vertical, between any cellar or basement and the first floor. Such firestopping shall consist of wood at least 2 in. (nominal) (5.1 cm) thick, or of suitable noncombustible material.

12-1.7 Occupant Load. The occupant load for which means of egress shall be provided for any floor shall be the maximum number of persons intended to occupy that floor, but not less than one person for each 120 sq ft (11.15 sq m) gross floor area in health care sleeping departments and not less than one person for each 240 sq ft (22.30 sq m) of gross floor area of inpatient health care treatment departments. Gross floor areas shall be measured within the exterior building walls with no deductions. (*See Chapter 3.*)

Paragraph 12-1.7 sets forth criteria for projecting occupant loads. The minimum occupant load for which exits must be provided in all buildings may not be less than that established by projections involving one person for each 120 sq ft (11.15 sq m) of gross floor area in health care sleeping areas, and not less than one person for each 240 sq ft (22.3 sq m) of gross floor area in inpatient health care treatment areas. However, if by actual count the number of persons exceeds that number projected by area calculations, then the actual number of persons present becomes the minimum population load for which exits must be provided.

The maximum number of people allowed to occupy a space is limited on the basis of available exit capacity and other functional considerations. It is not intended to limit populations based upon the area projections contained in this paragraph.

SECTION 12-2   MEANS OF EGRESS REQUIREMENTS

12-2.1 General. Every aisle, passageway, corridor, exit discharge, exit location and access shall be in accordance with Chapter 5.

Exception No. 1:   As modified in the following paragraphs.

Exception No. 2:   The requirements of Chapter 5 specifying net clear door width do not apply. Projections into the door opening by stops or by hinge stiles shall be permitted.

Means of egress details are to conform to the fundamental provisions expressed in Chapter 5, except as modified in Chapter 12. For example, see Exception No. 2 to 12-2.1. Exception No. 2 would continue to allow the width of exit doors to be measured on the basis of actual door leaf width. Projections into the door opening by the hinge stile and stops are to be ignored in health care facilities. This is done since the larger widths specified in Chapter 12 were developed taking these projections into consideration. In addition, these larger widths inherently meet the requirements of Chapter 5.

12-2.2 Types of Exits.   Exits shall be restricted to the permissible types described in 12-2.2.1 through 12-2.2.7.

Ramps are undesirable in hospitals and nursing homes due to the potential for accidents in both normal and emergency traffic, the exception being ramps with very gradual slopes which require so much space as to be impracticable in most building designs. Ramps are, however, the only practicable method of moving patients in beds from one story to another, except for elevators which may not be available during a fire. The best plan is to provide for horizontal egress to another section of the building, minimizing the need for complete evacuation.

12-2.2.1 Doors Leading Directly Outside the Building.   *(See 5-2.1.)*

12-2.2.2 Interior Stairs.   *(See 5-2.2.)*

12-2.2.3 Smokeproof Towers.   *(See 5-2.3.)*

12-2.2.4 Outside Stairs.   *(See 5-2.5.)*

12-2.2.5 Horizontal Exits.   A horizontal exit shall be in conformance with 5-2.4, modified as below.

(a) At least 30 net sq ft (2.79 sq m) per patient in a hospital or nursing home or 15 net sq ft (1.39 sq m) per resident in a residential-custodial care facility shall be provided within the aggregated area of corridors, patient rooms, treatment rooms, lounge or dining areas and other low hazard areas on each side of the horizontal exit. On stories not housing bed or litter patients and in supervisory care facilities at least 6 net sq ft (.56 sq m) per occupant shall be provided on each side of the horizontal exit for the total number of occupants in adjoining compartments.

(b) A single door leaf may be used as a horizontal exit if it serves one direction only and is at least 44 in. (111.76 cm) wide.

Exception: A door leaf a minimum of 36 in. (91.44 cm) wide may be provided within residential-custodial care facilities, mental hospitals, and supervisory care facilities.

(c) A horizontal exit in a hospital or nursing home in a corridor 8 ft (243.84 cm) or more in width serving as a means of egress from both sides of the doorway shall have the opening protected by a pair of swinging doors arranged to swing in the opposite direction from the other, with each door leaf being at least 44 in. (111.76 cm) wide.

(d) A horizontal exit in a residential-custodial care facility, mental hospital, or supervisory care facility in a corridor 6 ft (182.88 cm) or more in width serving as a means of egress from both sides of the doorway shall have the opening protected by a pair of swinging doors, arranged to swing in the opposite direction from each other, with each door being at least 32 in. (81.28 cm) wide.

(e) An approved vision panel is required in each horizontal exit door. Center mullions are prohibited.

(f) The total exit capacity of the other exits (stairs, ramps, doors leading outside the building) shall not be reduced below one-third that required for the entire area of the building.

The requirements for horizontal exits in 12-2.2.5(a) through (f) are illustrated in Figures 12-3 and 12-4.

In planning exits, arrangements should be made so that patients confined to their beds may be transferred from one section of a floor to another section of the same floor separated by a fire or smoke barrier. Where the building design will permit, the section of the corridor containing an entrance or elevator lobby should be separated from adjoining corridors by fire or smoke barriers. Such an arrangement, where the lobby is centrally located, will produce a smoke lock, placing a double barrier between the area to which patients may be taken and the area from which they must be evacuated because of threatening smoke and fire. Note that this is not required by the *Life Safety Code*, but is considered as good fire protection design.

Ramps may be the best means for providing egress from doors two or three steps above or below ground level (see 5-1.5), and may also compensate for minor differences in floor levels between adjoining sections of buildings (also see 5-1.5). Such ramps should be constructed in accordance with 12-2.2.6.

Doors in horizontal exits are required to swing in the direction of exit travel. In the case of a fire wall serving as a horizontal exit for two adjoining fire areas, a pair of doors arranged with each leaf to swing in a direction opposite from the other, or some other equivalent arrangement, must be used. If a fire wall serves as a horizontal exit from just one fire area, the door opening may be protected by a single door [44 in. (111.76 cm) wide in a hospital and nursing homes, or 36 in. (91.44 cm) wide in residential-custodial care facilities] arranged to swing in the direction of exit travel [see 12-2.2.5(b)].

Because of practical difficulties involving vertical exit travel in health care facilities, special recognition is given to horizontal travel and the use of horizontal exits. Up to two-thirds of the total required exit capacity for a given fire area may be provided by horizontal exits [see 12-2.2.5(f)]. It should be noted, however, that every floor or fire section must be equipped with at least one exit consisting of a door leading directly outside the building, an interior stair, an outside stair, a smokeproof tower, a ramp, or an exit passageway (see 12-2.4.2). In other words, no fire area can be served only by horizontal exits. In the event a horizontal exit also serves as a smoke barrier, see discussion following 12-2.4.2 and 12-3.7.

12-2.2.6 Class A Ramps. (*See 5-2.6.*) Ramps enclosed as exits shall be of sufficient width to provide exit capacity in accordance with 12-2.3.2.

Exception: A Class B ramp may be used where the height of the ramp is 1 ft (30.48 cm) or less.

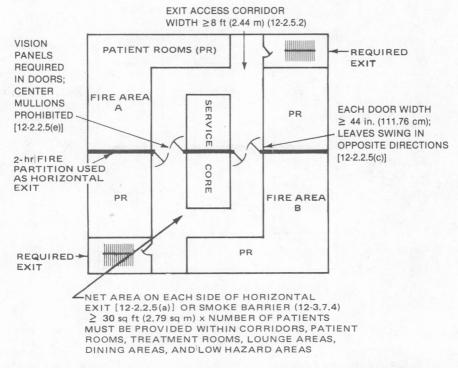

Figure 12-3. Horizontal Exits in a Hospital or Nursing Facility, New Construction. At least one exit for each fire area must be an interior stair, smokeproof tower, outside stair, Class A ramp, exit passageway, or door to outside (see 12-2.4.2). Such an exit must provide at least one-third the required exit capacity of the fire area which it serves. [see 12-2.2.5(f)].

Ramps enclosed and otherwise arranged and used as exits must be of sufficient width to adequately accommodate the required exit capacity on the basis of 30 persons per unit of exit width (see 12-2.3.2). For example, if a Class A ramp is to be used as an exit for 60 persons, the ramp must be a minimum of 44 in. (111.76 cm) wide.

12-2.2.7 Exit Passageways. *(See 5-2.7.)*

12-2.3 Capacity of Means of Egress. *(See also 12-2.5.2, 12-2.5.3 and 12-2.5.4.)*

12-2.3.1 The capacity of any required means of egress shall be based on its width as defined in Section 5-3.

12-2.3.2 The capacity of means of egress providing travel by means of stairs shall be 22 persons per exit unit; and the capacity of means of egress providing horizontal travel (without stairs) such as doors, ramps, or horizontal exits, shall be 30 persons per exit unit.

Exception: The capacity of means of egress in health care occupancies protected

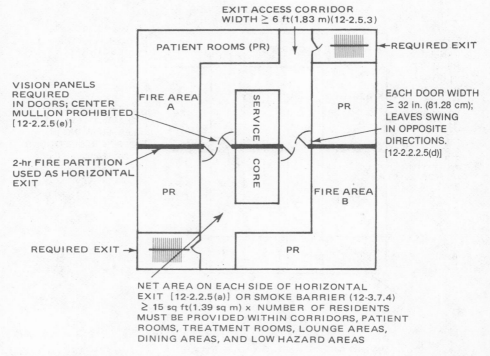

EXIT ACCESS CORRIDOR
WIDTH ≥ 6 ft(1.83 m)(12-2.5.3)

PATIENT ROOMS (PR)

◄─REQUIRED EXIT

VISION PANELS
REQUIRED
IN DOORS; CENTER
MULLION PROHIBITED.
[12-2.2.5(e)]

FIRE AREA
A

SERVICE CORE

PR

EACH DOOR WIDTH
≥ 32 in. (81.28 cm);
LEAVES SWING
IN OPPOSITE
DIRECTIONS.
[12-2.2.2.5(d)]

2-hr FIRE PARTITION
USED AS HORIZONTAL
EXIT

PR

FIRE AREA
B

REQUIRED EXIT ►

PR

NET AREA ON EACH SIDE OF HORIZONTAL
EXIT [12-2.2.5(a)] OR SMOKE BARRIER (12-3.7.4)
≥ 15 sq ft(1.39 sq m) x NUMBER OF RESIDENTS
MUST BE PROVIDED WITHIN CORRIDORS, PATIENT
ROOMS, TREATMENT ROOMS, LOUNGE AREAS,
DINING AREAS, AND LOW HAZARD AREAS

Figure 12-4. Horizontal Exits in a Residential-Custodial Care Facility, New Construction. At least 1 exit for each fire area must be an interior stair, smokeproof tower, outside stair, Class A ramp, exit passageway, or door to outside (12-2.4.2). Such an exit must provide at least one-third the required exit capacity of the fire area which it serves [see 12-2.2.5(f)].

throughout by an approved automatic sprinkler system may be increased to 35 persons per exit unit for travel by means of stairs, and to 45 persons per exit unit for horizontal travel without stairs.

The exit capacities in 12-2.3.2 are substantially less than those specified in other parts of the *Code* dealing with exits for people in good health. In health care occupancies, it is assumed that some patients will not be able to escape from a fire without assistance, and that others will have to be transported on beds, mattresses, litters, or in wheelchairs.

12-2.4 Number of Exits.

12-2.4.1 At least two exits of the types described in 12-2.2.1 through 12-2.2.7, located remotely from each other, shall be provided for each floor or fire section of the building.

12-2.4.2 At least one exit from each floor, fire section or smoke compartment shall be a door leading directly outside the building, interior stair, outside stair, smokeproof tower, ramp or exit passageway. Any fire section, floor or smoke compartment not meeting these requirements shall be considered as part of an adjoining zone. Egress shall not require return through the zone of fire origin.

Figure 12-5 illustrates the application of 12-2.4.2. Each space created as a place of refuge by the provision of a smoke barrier or a horizontal exit must be provided with an exit which is arranged to discharge directly to the outside. If a fire section or smoke compartment is not provided with such an exit, the compartment would then be considered as a portion of an adjacent zone. The adjacent zone would be required to be equipped with a stair, smokeproof tower, ramp, or exit passageway which discharges to the outside. This arrangement will allow a person to escape without requiring travel back into the compartment of fire origin.

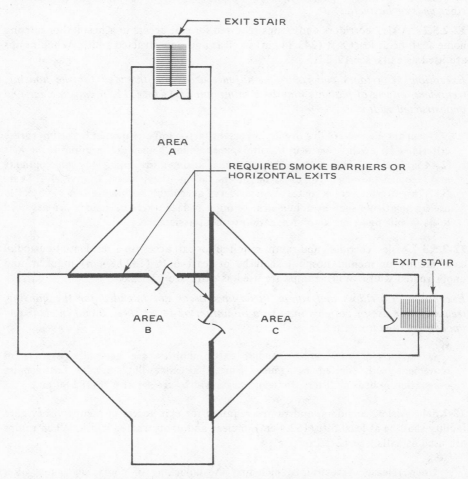

Figure 12-5. Arrangement of Exits in a New Health Care Occupancy Complying with 12-2.4.2. At least one exit is required from Area B consisting of a door to outside, interior stair, outside stair, smokeproof tower, ramp, or exit passageway, or Area B is considered a part of Area A or C. Areas A and C would require an exit which discharges directly to the outside.

12-2.5 Arrangement of Means of Egress.

12-2.5.1 Every patient sleeping room shall have an exit access door leading directly to an exit access corridor.

Exception No. 1:   If there is an exit door opening directly to the outside from the room at ground level.

Exception No. 2:   One adjacent room, such as a sitting or anteroom, may intervene, if all doors along the means of egress are equipped with nonlockable hardware other than provided in 12-2.11, and if the intervening room is not used to serve as an exit access for more than eight patient sleeping beds.

Exception No. 3:   Exception No. 2 above shall apply to special nursing suites permitted in 12-2.5.6 and suites in supervisory care facilities without being limited to eight beds or basinettes.

12-2.5.2   Aisles, corridors and ramps required for exit access in a hospital or nursing home shall be at least 8 ft (243.84 cm) in clear and unobstructed width. When ramps are used as exits, see 12-2.2.6.

Exception: Corridors and ramps in adjunct areas not intended for the housing, treatment, or use of patients may be a minimum of 44 in. (111.76 cm) in clear and unobstructed width.

Occupant characteristics are an important factor to be evaluated in setting egress criteria. Exit access routes in hospitals and nursing homes are required to be 8 ft (2.44 m) in clear width on the assumption that during a fire emergency some patients may require movement in beds, on litters, or in wheelchairs. Conversely, 44-in. (111.76-cm) wide access routes are considered acceptable within areas not subject to use by inpatients such as administrative office spaces where occupants are assumed to be mobile and capable of evacuation without assistance.

12-2.5.3   Aisles, corridors and ramps required for exit access in a residential-custodial care facility or mental hospital shall be at least 6 ft (182.88 cm) in clear and unobstructed width. When ramps are used as exits, see 12-2.2.6.

Exception: Corridors and ramps in adjunct areas not intended for the housing, treatment, or use of patients may be a minimum of 44 in. (111.76 cm) in clear and unobstructed width.

Occupants of residential-custodial care facilities are generally capable of movement with limited assistance. Since patients will generally not require evacuation in beds or litters, the exit access widths are set at 6 ft (182.88 cm).

12-2.5.4   Aisles, corridors, and ramps required for exit access in a supervisory care facility shall be at least 5 ft (152.4 cm) in clear and unobstructed width. When ramps are used as exits, see 12-2.2.6.

Upon release of restraints, including the unlocking of doors, occupants of a supervisory care facility are assumed to be mobile and capable of a rapid evacuation with the assistance or guidance of staff.

12-2.5.5   Any room, and any suite of rooms as permitted in 12-2.5.1, of more than 1,000 sq ft (92.9 sq m) shall have at least two exit access doors remote from each other.

It is the intent that this apply to any room exceeding 1,000 sq ft (92.9 sq m), even if that room complies with a single exit access door having a travel distance of 50 ft (15.24 m) maximum. The exit access doors may lead to a common corridor.

12-2.5.6 Any patient sleeping room which complies with the requirements previously set forth in this section may be subdivided with non-fire-rated, noncombustible or limited-combustible partitions, provided that the arrangement allows for direct and constant visual supervision by nursing personnel. Rooms which are so subdivided shall not exceed 5,000 sq ft (464.5 sq m).

Exception: In supervisory care facilities, such spaces continuously monitored by staff do not require direct visual supervision providing the space is equipped with an electrically supervised smoke detection system.

It is permissible to use sliding doors on individual cubicles within the suite.

In supervisory care facilities, the direct and constant supervision by staff is waived in consideration of functional requirements when a complete, electrically supervised smoke detection system is provided.

12-2.5.7 Every corridor shall provide access to at least two approved exits in accordance with Section 5-4. Means of egress shall be in accordance with Section 5-5 without passing through any intervening rooms or spaces other than corridors or lobbies.

12-2.5.8 Every exit or exit access shall be so arranged that no corridor, aisle or passageway has a pocket or dead end exceeding 30 ft (914.4 cm).

The requirements of 12-2.5.1 through 12-2.5.8 are illustrated in Figures 12-6A through 12-10.

12-2.6 Measurement of Travel Distance to Exits.

12-2.6.1 Travel distance shall be measured in accordance with Section 5-6.

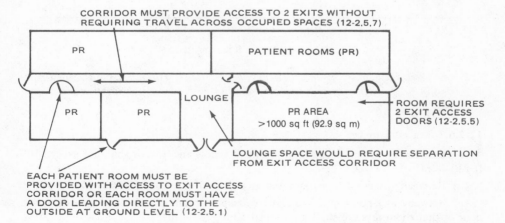

Figure 12-6A. Incorrect Arrangement of Exit Access in New Health Care Occupancy. Lounge must not interfere with exit access.

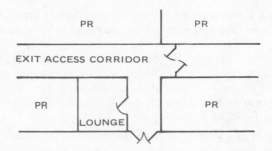

Figure 12-6B. Corrected Arrangement of Exit Access in New Health Care Occupancy. Lounge is separated from exit access corridor as required by 12-2.5.7. See also 12-3.6.1, Exception Nos. 3, 4, and 5 where a lounge or waiting space may be open to an exit access corridor.

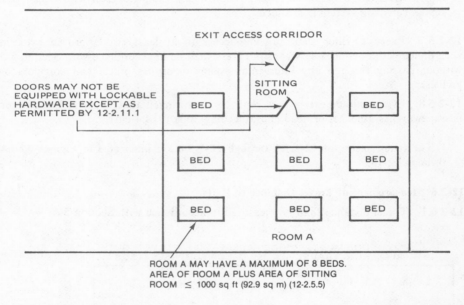

Figure 12-7. Exit Access from a Patient Sleeping Room Through an Adjacent Room, New Health Care Occupancy. Illustration complies with 12-2.5.1, Exception No. 2, and 12-2.5.5.

12-2.6.2 Travel distance:

(a) Between any room door required as exit access and an exit shall not exceed 100 ft (30.48 m);

(b) Between any point in a room and an exit shall not exceed 150 ft (45.72 m);

(c) Between any point in a health care sleeping room or suite and an exit access door of that room or suite shall not exceed 50 ft (15.24 m).

Exception: The travel distance in (a) or (b) above may be increased by 50 ft (15.24 m) in buildings protected throughout by an approved automatic sprinkler system.

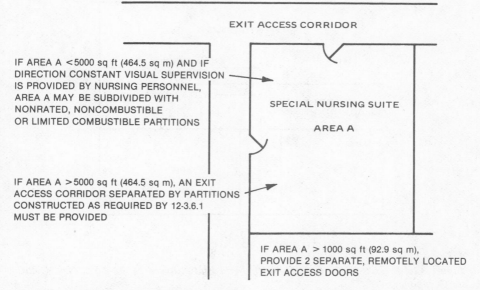

EXIT ACCESS CORRIDOR

IF AREA A <5000 sq ft (464.5 sq m) AND IF
DIRECTION CONSTANT VISUAL SUPERVISION
IS PROVIDED BY NURSING PERSONNEL,
AREA A MAY BE SUBDIVIDED WITH
NONRATED, NONCOMBUSTIBLE
OR LIMITED COMBUSTIBLE PARTITIONS

SPECIAL NURSING SUITE

AREA A

IF AREA A >5000 sq ft (464.5 sq m), AN EXIT
ACCESS CORRIDOR SEPARATED BY PARTITIONS
CONSTRUCTED AS REQUIRED BY 12-3.6.1
MUST BE PROVIDED

IF AREA A > 1000 sq ft (92.9 sq m),
PROVIDE 2 SEPARATE, REMOTELY LOCATED
EXIT ACCESS DOORS

*Figure 12-8. Exit Access from a Special Nursing Suite, New Health Care Occupancy.
See 12-2.5.1, 12-2.5.5, and 12-2.5.6.*

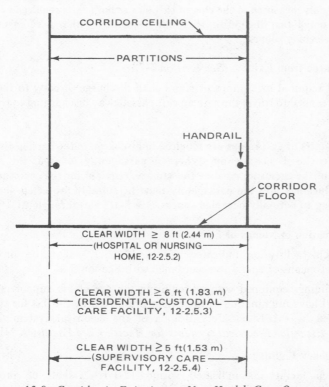

CORRIDOR CEILING

PARTITIONS

HANDRAIL

CORRIDOR
FLOOR

CLEAR WIDTH ≥ 8 ft (2.44 m)
(HOSPITAL OR NURSING
HOME, 12-2.5.2)

CLEAR WIDTH ≥ 6 ft (1.83 m)
(RESIDENTIAL-CUSTODIAL
CARE FACILITY, 12-2.5.3)

CLEAR WIDTH ≥ 5 ft (1.53 m)
(SUPERVISORY CARE
FACILITY, 12-2.5.4)

Figure 12-9. Corridor in Exit Access, New Health Care Occupancy.

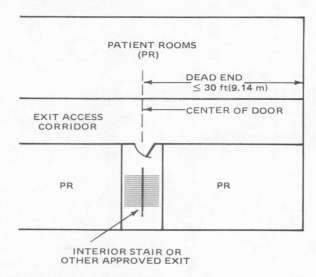

Figure 12-10. Exit Access Corridor with Dead End Allowed by 12-2.5.8, New Health Care Occupancy.

The requirements of 12-2.6.1 and 12-2.6.2 are illustrated in Figure 12-11. Travel distance is only measured to the closest exit, not to both exits required by 12-2.5.7. It should be noted that the 50-ft (15.24-m) restriction within a room or suite only applies to sleeping rooms.

12-2.7 Discharge from Exits.   *(See Section 5-7.)*

12-2.7.1   All required exit ramps or stairs shall discharge directly to the outside at grade or be arranged to travel through an exit passageway discharging to the outside at grade.

All exit stairs or exit ramps are required to discharge to the outside either directly or by an enclosed passageway. Where a passageway is used, the fire-resistive separation of the enclosure must be the same as required for the enclosure of a stair or ramp. Openings into the passageway must be suitably protected and limited to doors leading to normally occupied spaces. See 5-1.3.1(a) through (d).

12-2.8 Illumination of Means of Egress.

12-2.8.1   Each facility as indicated within 12-1.1.1.2 shall be provided with illumination of means of egress in accordance with Section 5-8.

12-2.8.2   Buildings equipped with or requiring the use of life support systems (*see 12-5.1.3*) shall have illumination to the extent prescribed by 5-8.1.3 for the means of egress supplied by the Life Safety Branch of the electrical system described in *Standard for Essential Electrical Systems for Health Care Facilities*, NFPA 76A.

12-2.9 Emergency Lighting.

12-2.9.1   Each facility as indicated within 12-1.1.1.2 shall be provided with emergency lighting in accordance with Section 5-9.

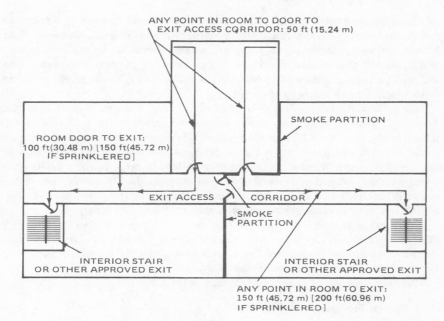

ANY POINT IN ROOM TO DOOR TO
EXIT ACCESS CORRIDOR: 50 ft (15.24 m)

SMOKE PARTITION

ROOM DOOR TO EXIT:
100 ft(30.48 m) [150 ft(45.72 m)
IF SPRINKLERED]

EXIT ACCESS   CORRIDOR

SMOKE
PARTITION

INTERIOR STAIR
OR OTHER APPROVED EXIT

INTERIOR STAIR
OR OTHER APPROVED EXIT

ANY POINT IN ROOM TO EXIT:
150 ft (45.72 m) [200 ft(60.96 m)
IF SPRINKLERED]

Figure 12-11. Maximum Travel Distance to Exits, New Health Care Occupancy. The distance is measured along the natural path of travel (see 5-6.2). "Sprinklered" means that the entire building is protected by a complete approved automatic extinguishing system. (Note that a room door in a smoke partition must meet the requirements of 6-3.3 and 12-3.7.6 and be self-closing.)

12-2.9.2 Buildings equipped with or requiring the use of life support systems (*see 12-5.1.3*) shall have emergency lighting equipment supplied by the Life Safety Branch of the electrical system described in *Standard for Essential Electrical Systems for Health Care Facilities*, NFPA 76A.

12-2.10 Marking of Means of Egress.

12-2.10.1 Each facility as indicated within 12-1.1.1.2 shall be provided with exit marking in accordance with Section 5-10.

12-2.10.2 Buildings equipped with or requiring the use of life support systems (*see 12-5.1.3*) shall have illumination of the required exit and directional signs supplied by the Life Safety Branch of the electrical system as described in *Standard for Essential Electrical Systems for Health Care Facilities*, NFPA 76A.

Each health care facility equipped with or requiring the use of life support systems is required to have illumination, and the marking of the means of egress and emergency lighting supplied by the Life Safety Branch of the electrical systems described in NFPA 76A, *Standard for Essential Electrical Systems for Health Care Facilities*.[3]

A facility would not be required to comply with NFPA 76A[3] if the building is a free-standing unit which is independent of any facility providing 24-hour care and, as a normal practice, (1) management maintains admitting and discharge policies that preclude the provision of care for any patient or resident who may need to be

sustained by electromechanical means such as respirators, suction apparatus, etc., and (2) the building offers no surgical treatment requiring general anesthesia, and (3) battery operated systems or equipment are provided which would maintain power to exit lights and illumination of exit corridors, stairways, medical preparation areas, and the like, for a minimum of 4 hours. Additionally, battery power would be required to be supplied to all alarm systems.

NFPA 76A, *Standard for Essential Electrical Systems for Health Care Facilities*,[3] requires emergency power supplies be arranged and protected so as to minimize the possibility of a single incident affecting both normal and emergency power supplies simultaneously. Circuits are to be run separately. Emergency and normal circuits are "joined" at the transfer switch. Damage to the transfer switch would interrupt normal and emergency power supplies simultaneously. The transfer switch is therefore a critical item and should be separated from any potential source of fire, including the emergency generator and attendant fuel supply.

Emergency generators should preferably be started and exercised weekly. NFPA 76A, *Standard for Essential Electrical Systems for Health Care Facilities*,[3] specifies emergency generators, as a minimum, must be inspected weekly and exercised for 30 minutes a month under load.

Minimum duration of emergency supplies is 1½ hours (see 5-9.2.1).

12-2.11 Special Features.

12-2.11.1   Locks shall not be permitted on patient sleeping room doors.

Exception No. 1:   Key locking devices which restrict access to the room from the corridor may be permitted. Such devices shall not restrict egress from the room.

Exception No. 2:   Doors in homes for the aged may be lockable by the occupant, if they can be unlocked from the opposite side and keys are carried by attendants at all times. (See also 5-2.1.2.1.1 and 5-2.1.2.1.2.)

Exception No. 3:   Special door locking arrangements are permitted in mental health facilities. (See 12-1.1.1.7 and 12-2.11.4.)

12-2.11.2   Doors leading directly to the outside of the building may be subject to locking from the room side.

12-2.11.3   Doors within the means of egress shall not be equipped with a latch or lock which requires the use of a key from the inside of the building. (*See 5-2.1.2.*)

Exception No. 1:   Door locking arrangements are permitted in mental health facilities. (See 12-2.11.4.)

Exception No. 2:   Special locking arrangements in accordance with 5-2.1.2.1.5 on exterior doors are permitted.

Paragraph 5-2.1.2.1.5 sets minimum requirements for delayed release panic hardware.

12-2.11.4   In buildings in which doors are locked, provisions shall be made for the rapid removal of occupants by such reliable means as the remote control of locks or by keying all locks to keys readily available to staff who are in constant attendance.

In buildings where it is necessary to lock doors, continuous supervision by staff must be provided. Provisions should be made for the prompt release of restrained persons either by equipping staff with keys or by providing remote unlocking capabilities for doors. Where reliance is placed on the use of keys, consideration should be given to a master key system which would facilitate the quick release of occupants.

12-2.11.5 Exit access doors from hospital and nursing home sleeping rooms; diagnostic and treatment areas, such as X-ray, surgery, or physical therapy; all door leaves between these spaces and the required exits; and all exit door leaves serving these spaces shall be at least 44 in. (111.76 cm) wide. Door leaves from residential-custodial sleeping rooms and door leaves from nursery rooms; and door leaves between these spaces and the required exits; and all exit door leaves serving these spaces shall be at least 36 in. (91.44 cm) wide.

Exception No. 1: Exit door leaves which are so located as not to be subject to use by any health care occupant may be not less than 34 in. (86.36 cm) wide.

Exception No. 2: Door leaves in exit stair enclosures shall not be less than 36 in. (91.44 cm) wide.

Provisions of 12-2.11.5 are illustrated in Figures 12-12A through 12-12D.

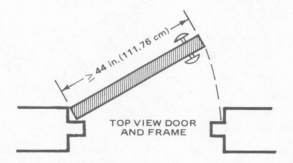

Figure 12-12A. Minimum Width of Doors for Exit and Exit Access from Sleeping Rooms, Diagnostic and Treatment Areas in New Hospitals and Nursing Homes. Maximum width is 48 in. (121.92 cm) (see 5-2.1.1.3.2).

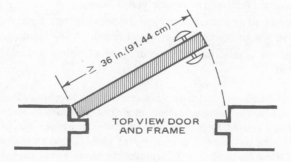

Figure 12-12B. Minimum Width of Doors for Exit and Exit Access from Sleeping Rooms in New Residential-Custodial Care Facilities and from Nursery Rooms in Health Care Occupancies. Maximum width is 48 in. (121.92 cm) (see 5-2.1.1.3.2).

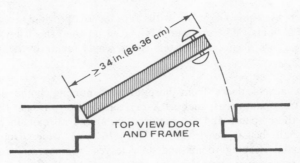

Figure 12-12C. Minimum Width of Doors for Exit and Exit Access not Subject to Use by Institutional Occupants, New Health Care Occupancies. Maximum width is 48 in. (121.92 cm) (see 5-2.1.1.3.2).

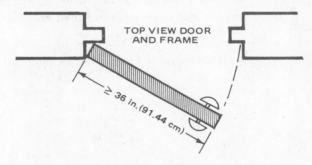

Figure 12-12D. Minimum Width of Doors for Access to Exit Stair Enclosures, New Health Care Occupancies. Maximum width is 48 in. (121.92 cm) (see 5-2.1.1.3.2). Doors must swing in direction of exit travel (see 5-2.1.1.4.1).

12-2.11.6   Any door in an exit passageway, horizontal exit, a required enclosure of a hazardous area (except boiler rooms, heater rooms, and mechanical equipment rooms) or smoke barrier may be held open only by an automatic release device which complies with 5-2.1.2.3. Each of the following systems shall be arranged so as to initiate the closing action of all such doors by zone or throughout the entire facility:

(a) The required manual alarm system (*see 12-3.4*),

(b) The required and approved automatic smoke detection system (*see 12-3.4.6*) or a local device designed to detect smoke on either side of the opening, and

(c) A complete automatic fire extinguishing or complete automatic fire detection system, if provided.

It is desirable to keep doors in exit enclosures, in required enclosures around hazardous areas, and in smoke barriers closed at all times to impede the spread of smoke and gases caused by a fire. Functionally, however, this involves decreased efficiency and limits patient observation by the professional staff of an institution. To accommodate these necessities, it is practical to assume that such doors will be kept open even to the extent of employing wood chocks and other makeshift devices. All doors described in 12-2.11.6 should, therefore, be equipped with automatic hold-open devices activated by the methods described in items (a), (b), and (c). It should be noted that doors protecting openings in stair towers are required to be self-closing and maintained closed (see 12-3.1.2).

Where doors are held open, the automatic device must cause the doors to close upon operation of the manual fire alarm system. Smoke detectors designed to detect smoke on either side of the door opening must be provided and arranged to cause the door to close in the event of actuation. Further, if a complete automatic fire extinguishing or complete automatic fire detection system is provided, actuation of such systems must also be arranged to cause the doors to close.

SECTION 12-3   PROTECTION

12-3.1 Protection of Vertical Openings.

12-3.1.1   Any stairway, ramp, elevator hoistway, light or ventilation shaft, chute, and other vertical opening between stories shall be enclosed in accordance with 6-2.2 with construction having a 2-hour fire resistance rating.

Exception No. 1:   One-hour rated enclosures are permitted in buildings required to be of 1-hour construction.

Exception No. 2:   Stairs that do not connect to a corridor, do not connect more than two levels, and do not serve as a means of egress need not comply with these regulations.

Exception No. 3:   The fire resistance rating of enclosures in health care occupancies protected throughout by an approved automatic sprinkler system may be reduced to 1 hour in buildings up to, and including, three stories in height.

Exception No. 4:   Duct penetrations of floor assemblies which are protected in accordance with Standard for the Installation of Air Conditioning and Ventilating Systems, NFPA 90A.

Exception No. 5:   Floor and ceiling openings for pipes or conduits when the opening around the pipes or conduits is sealed in an approved manner. (See 6-2.2.8.)

Paragraph 12-3.1 specifies protection levels required to maintain floor-to-floor separation in health care facilities. Two-hour enclosures are required around vertical openings in all buildings that must be of fire-resistive construction (see 12-1.6.2 and 12-1.6.3). One-hour enclosure of vertical openings is required in all other buildings.

Exception No. 2 to 12-3.1.1 is illustrated in Figure 12-13.

Air-handling ducts which transfer from floor to floor should be protected as specified in NFPA 90A, *Standard for the Installation of Air Conditioning and Ventilating Systems.*[4] Note that 3-3.3.1 of NFPA 90A[4] permits elimination of vertical shaft enclosures and allows provision of a fire damper at each point a floor is pierced only if air-handling ducts extend through only *one floor.*

Exception No. 5 will allow piping and conduit to penetrate floors without requiring an enclosed shaft. Floor penetrations, however, must be adequately protected in an approved manner to maintain the required fire resistance of the floor system. The penetrations should be sealed in a fashion which would minimize the transfer of smoke.

12-3.1.2   A door in a stair enclosure shall be self-closing, shall normally be kept in a closed position, and shall be marked in accordance with 5-10.4.2.

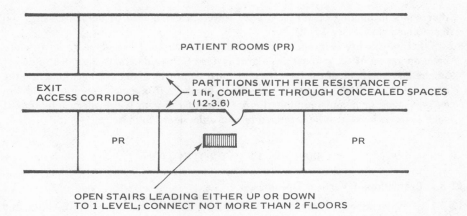

Figure 12-13. Open Stairs in Accordance with 12-3.1.1, Exception No. 2, New Health Care Occupancies.

Paragraph 12-3.1.2 requires fire doors protecting openings in stairway enclosures to be self-closing and normally maintained in a closed position. Automatic closing devices permitted in 12-2.11.6 are not permitted to be used on doors protecting openings in stair tower enclosures. Stair tower doors should be equipped with a sign substantially stating "Fire Exit — Keep Door Closed" (see 5-10.4.2).

12-3.2 Protection from Hazards.

12-3.2.1 Any hazardous area shall be safeguarded by a fire barrier of 1-hour fire resistance rating or provided with an automatic extinguishing system in accordance with 6-4.1. Hazardous areas include, but are not restricted to, the following. Those areas accompanied by a dagger (†) in the list shall have both fire-resistant separation and a complete extinguishment system.

Boiler and heater rooms
Laundries
Kitchens
Repair shops
Handicraft shops
Employee locker rooms
†Soiled linen rooms
†Paint shops
†Trash collection rooms
Gift shops

†Rooms or spaces, including repair shops, used for the storage of combustible supplies and equipment in quantities deemed hazardous by the authority having jurisdiction.
Laboratories employing quantities of flammable, or combustible materials less than that which would be considered severe.

Hazardous areas are spaces with contents which, because of their basic nature (as in the case of flammable liquids) or because of the quantity of combustible materials involved, represent a significantly higher hazard than would otherwise be typical of health care facilities.

A listing of typical hazardous areas is included in 12-3.2.1. Hazardous areas must be separated from other areas by 1-hour fire-resistant construction, complete with approved fire doors protecting door openings; otherwise, automatic sprinkler protection must be installed. In those instances where the hazard is judged to be severe, such as in rooms used to store soiled linen, paint shops, trash collection rooms, repair shops, large storage areas, and the like, both fire-resistant separation and automatic sprinkler protection are required. Where automatic sprinkler protection is provided and the hazard is not severe, the hazardous area may be separated by nonrated partitions designed to resist the passage of smoke. See comments under the exceptions to automatic sprinkler protection in 12-3.6.1. Although 12-3.2.1 lists typical hazardous and high hazard areas, it is the responsibility of the authority having jurisdiction to determine which areas are hazardous and high hazard.

Provisions for the enclosure of rooms used for charging linen and waste chutes, or for the rooms into which chutes empty, are provided in Chapter 7. In addition to the fire-resistant cutoff of rooms into which linen chutes and waste chutes discharge, automatic sprinkler protection is considered essential.

Where flammable liquids are handled or stored, NFPA 30, *Flammable and Combustible Liquids Code*,[5] should be consulted to establish the minimum criteria necessary to mitigate this hazard. Rooms in clinical laboratories in which the unattended automatic processing of specimens with flammable solvents is likely to take place present a limited hazard which may be protected through use of sprinklers connected to the domestic water supply. Provisions for the use and storage of flammable gases and oxygen are covered in NFPA 56A, *Standard for the Use of Inhalation Anesthetics (Flammable and Nonflammable)*,[6] and NFPA 56F, *Standard for Nonflammable Medical Gas Systems*.[7]

See commentary on 12-3.2.2 for discussion of laboratories.

12-3.2.2 Laboratories employing quantities of flammable, combustible, or hazardous materials which are considered as severe hazard shall be protected in accordance with *Laboratories in Health-Related Institutions*, NFPA 56C.

Laboratories which contain "ordinary" combustibles and flammable liquids in sufficient quantity to threaten a 1-hour fire separation — wood equivalent fuel loads in the range of 5 to 10 lb/sq ft (24.41 to 48.82 kg/sq m) — are considered a severe hazard. Laboratories representing a severe hazard must be protected in accordance with NFPA 56C, *Safety Standard for Laboratories in Health-Related Institutions*.[8] Protection would include 1-hour fire resistance separation and automatic sprinkler protection.

Where fuel loads of lesser amounts are involved and quantities of flammable liquids are limited, laboratories would be simply considered a hazardous area, and would require either 1-hour separation or automatic sprinkler protection as indicated in 12-3.2.1 and Section 6-4.

12-3.2.3 Cooking facilities shall be protected in accordance with 7-2.3.

Commercial cooking equipment must be installed and protected in accordance with NFPA 96, *Standard for the Installation of Equipment for the Removal of Smoke and Grease-Laden Vapors from Commercial Cooking Equipment*.[9] A regularly serviced, fixed, automatic fire extinguishing system would be required for the protection of cooking surfaces and exhaust and duct systems where cooking operations involve the potential for grease-laden vapors.

This paragraph would not apply to a room used as a staff lounge equipped with a domestic-type range or hot plate. Such a room would be considered similar to a treatment room and would require separation as indicated in 12-3.6.1.

12-3.3 Interior Finish.

12-3.3.1 Interior finish of walls and ceilings throughout shall be Class A in accordance with Section 6-5.

Exception: Walls and ceilings may have Class A or B interior finish in individual rooms of not over four persons in capacity.

Interior finishes on walls and ceilings are limited to Class A materials, except in rooms of four or fewer persons where Class B materials are allowed.

Where automatic sprinkler protection is provided, Class B materials can be used where Class A is normally required, and similarly Class C materials are allowed where Class B materials would otherwise be required. See Section 6-5.

12-3.3.2 Interior floor finish in corridors and exitways shall be Class I in accordance with Section 6-5.

Interior floor finish within corridors and exits is required to be of Class I materials as determined in accordance with Section 6-5. Class I materials are those having a critical radiant flux of not less than 0.45 watts/sq m as determined by tests conducted in accordance with NFPA 253, *Standard Method of Test for Critical Radiant Flux of Floor Covering Systems Using a Radiant Heat Energy Source.*[10] See commentary on 6-5.2.

Regulation of interior floor finish within rooms is not considered necessary.

Where automatic sprinkler protection is provided, Class II materials can be used where Class I is normally specified.

12-3.4 Detection, Alarm and Communication Systems.

12-3.4.1 Required fire detection and signaling devices and systems shall be in accordance with Section 7-6.

12-3.4.2 Every building shall have a manually operated fire alarm system in accordance with Section 7-6, and such system shall be electrically supervised.

12-3.4.3 Operation of any fire alarm activating device shall automatically, without delay, accomplish the following:

(a) General alarm indication

(b) Control functions required to be performed by that device.

Zoned, coded systems shall be permitted.

12-3.4.4 The fire alarm system shall be arranged to transmit an alarm automatically to the fire department legally committed to serve the area in which the health care facility is located, by the most direct and reliable method approved by local regulations.

12-3.4.5 Internal audible alarm devices shall be provided and shall be installed in accordance with Section 7-6.

12-3.4.6 An approved automatic smoke detection system shall be installed in all corridors of new nursing homes, new custodial and new supervisory care facilities. Such systems shall be installed in accordance with Section 7-6 and with the applicable standards listed in Section 7-6, but in no case shall smoke detectors be spaced further apart than 30 ft (914.4 cm) on centers or more than 15 ft (457.2 cm) from any wall. All automatic smoke detection sytems required by this section shall be electrically interconnected to the fire alarm system.

Exception: Where each patient sleeping room is protected by such an approved detection system and a local detector is provided at the smoke barrier and horizontal exits, such corridor systems will not be required on the patient sleeping room floors.

12-3.4.7 Any fire detection device or system required by this section shall be electrically interconnected with the fire alarm system.

12-3.4.8 Any alarm system(s) and any detection system(s) required in any health care occupancy shall be provided with an alternative power supply in accordance with *Standard for the Installation, Maintenance, and Use of Local Protective Signaling Systems*, NFPA 72A.

Paragraphs 12-3.4.1 through 12-3.4.8 deal with required fire alarm equipment. Reliability is of prime importance; therefore, electrical supervision of the system and system components is specified. In the event of circuit fault, component failure, or other "trouble," continuous "trouble indication" is required and should be provided at a constantly attended location.

A manual fire alarm system is required by 12-3.4.2. Manual pull stations should be located along the natural routes of egress and located so as to adequately cover all portions of the building. Manual pull stations should always be located so that anyone qualified to send an alarm may summon aid without having to leave the zone of his or her ordinary activities or pass out of the sight and hearing of people immediately exposed to or in direct view of a fire. The operation of a manual fire alarm station should automatically summon attendants who can assist in removing physically helpless occupants and in controlling mentally incompetent occupants.

The system required by 12-3.4.2 may be incorporated into an automatic system equipped to detect a fire and initiate an alarm.

Actuation of any required fire or smoke detector, activation of a required sprinkler system, or operation of a manual pull station should *automatically*, without delay, sound *audible alarm devices* within the building. Presignal systems are not permitted.

The alarm must automatically transmit to a point outside the facility. Where automatic transmission of alarms to the fire department legally committed to serve the facility is not permitted, arrangements should be made for the prompt notification of the fire department or such other assistance as may be available in the case of fire or other emergency. Acceptable means of automatic transmission of an alarm are, in the order of preference:

(a) A direct connection of the building alarm to the municipal fire alarm system

(b) Auxiliary connect by municipal alarm system

(c) A direct connection of the building alarm to an approved central station

(d) A telephone connection to a municipal or other alarm headquarters.

Paragraph 12-3.4.6 requires smoke detectors to be located in all corridors of new supervisory care, new nursing homes, and residential-custodial care facilities. As an option to locating smoke detectors in corridors, smoke detectors may be installed in each patient's room and at smoke barriers and horizontal exits. In recognition of different staffing criteria, smoke detectors are not required in hospitals.

Actuation of the fire alarm must cause audible alerting devices to sound throughout the affected zone or building as appropriate. Visible alerting devices may be used but may not serve as a substitute for audible devices.

12-3.5 Extinguishment Requirements.

12-3.5.1 All health care facilities shall be protected throughout by an approved automatic sprinkler system. (*See 12-1.6 for construction types permitted.*)

Exception: Buildings of Type I (443), I (332) or II (222) construction of any height or Type II (111) construction not over one story in height.

Requirements for automatic sprinkler protection in new health care occupancies are summarized in Table 12-1. See NFPA 220, *Standard Types of Building Construction*,[1] for definitions of construction type. Where sprinkler protection is specified, complete building coverage, in accordance with the provisions of NFPA 13, *Standard on Installation of Sprinkler Systems*,[11] is required.

12-3.5.2 Where exceptions are stated in the provisions of the *Code* for health care occupancies protected throughout by an approved automatic sprinkler system, and where such systems are required, the systems shall be in complete accordance with Section 7-7 for systems in light hazard occupancies and shall be electrically interconnected with the fire alarm system.

12-3.5.3 The main sprinkler control valve(s) shall be electrically supervised so that at least a local alarm will sound at a constantly attended location when the valve is closed.

12-3.5.4 Sprinkler piping serving not more than six sprinklers for any isolated hazardous area may be connected directly to a domestic water supply system having a capacity sufficient to provide 0.15 gal per minute per sq ft (1.02×10^{-4} cu m/s/sq m) of floor area throughout the entire enclosed area. An indicating shut-off valve shall be installed in an accessible location between the sprinklers and the connection to the domestic water supply. Where more than two sprinklers are installed in a single area, waterflow detection shall be provided to sound the building fire alarm system in the event of sprinkler operation. (*For sprinkler requirements for hazardous areas, see 12-3.2 and for sprinkler requirements for chutes, see 12-5.4.*)

12-3.5.5 Portable fire extinguishers shall be provided in all health care occupancies in accordance with 7-7.4.1.

12-3.6 Construction of Corridor Walls.

12-3.6.1 Corridors shall be separated from all other areas by partitions. Such partitions shall be continuous from the floor slab to the underside of the roof or floor slab above, through any concealed spaces such as those above the suspended ceilings, and through interstitial structural and mechanical spaces, and shall have a fire resistance rating of at least 1 hour.

Exception No. 1: In health care occupancies protected throughout by an approved automatic sprinkler system, a corridor may be separated from all other areas by non-fire-rated partitions, and where suspended ceilings are provided, the partitions may be terminated at the suspended ceiling.

Exception No. 2:   Corridor partitions may terminate at ceilings which are not an integral part of a floor construction if there exists 5 ft (152.4 cm) or more of space between the top of the ceiling subsystem and the bottom of the floor or roof above, provided:

(a) The ceiling shall have been tested as a part of a fire-rated assembly in accordance with Standard Methods of Fire Tests of Building Construction and Materials, NFPA 251, for a test period of 1 hour or more, and

(b) Corridor partitions form smoketight joints with the ceilings (joint filler, if used, shall be noncombustible) and,

(c) Each compartment of interstitial space which constitutes a separate smoke area is vented, in case of smoke emergency, to the outside by mechanical means having sufficient capacity to provide at least two air changes per hour, but in no case having a capacity less than 5,000 cfm (2.36 cu m/s), and

(d) The interstitial space shall not be used for storage, and

(e) The space shall not be used as a plenum for supply, exhaust or return air except as noted in (c).

Exception No. 3:   Waiting areas on a patient sleeping floor may be open to the corridor, provided:

(a) The area does not exceed 250 sq ft (23.23 sq m), and

(b) The area is located to permit direct supervision by the facility staff, and

(c) The area is equipped with an electrically supervised automatic smoke detection system installed in accordance with 12-3.4, and

(d) Not more than one such waiting area is permitted in each smoke compartment, and

(e) The area is arranged not to obstruct access to required exits.

Exception No. 4:   Waiting areas on floors other than health care sleeping floors may be open to the corridor, provided:

(a) Each area does not exceed 600 sq ft (55.74 sq m), and

(b) The area is located to permit direct supervision by the facility staff, and

(c) The area is arranged not to obstruct access to required exits, and

(d) The area is equipped with an electrically supervised, automatic smoke detection system installed in accordance with 12-3.4.

Exception No. 5:   Buildings protected throughout by an approved automatic sprinkler system may have spaces which are unlimited in size open to the corridor provided:

(a) The spaces are not used for patient sleeping rooms, treatment rooms or hazardous areas, and

(b) Each space is located to permit direct supervision by the facility staff, and

(c) The space and corridors which the space opens onto in the same smoke compartment are protected by an electrically supervised automatic smoke detection system installed in accordance with 12-3.4, and

(d) The space is arranged not to obstruct access to required exits.

Exception No. 6: Space for doctors' and nurses' charting, communications, and related clerical areas may be open to the corridor.

Exception No. 7: In a supervisory care facility, group meeting or multipurpose therapeutic spaces, other than hazardous areas, under continuous supervision by facility staff may be open to the corridor provided:

(a) Each area does not exceed 1,500 sq ft (139.35 sq m), and

(b) The area is located to permit direct supervision by the facility staff, and

(c) The area is arranged not to obstruct any access to required exits, and

(d) The area is equipped with an electrically supervised, automatic smoke detection system installed in accordance with 12-3.4, and

(e) Not more than one such space is permitted per smoke compartment.

12-3.6.2 Fixed wired glass vision panels shall be permitted in corridor walls provided they do not exceed 1,296 sq in. (.84 sq m) in area and are mounted in steel or other approved metal frames.

Exception: There shall be no restrictions in area and fire resistance of glass and frames in buildings protected throughout by an approved automatic sprinkler system.

12-3.6.3 Doors protecting corridor openings, in other than required enclosures of exits or hazardous areas, shall be substantial doors, such as 1¾-in. (4.45-cm) solid bonded core wood or of construction that will resist fire for at least 20 minutes. Doors shall be provided with latches suitable for keeping the door tightly closed and acceptable to the authority having jurisdiction. Fixed view panels of wired glass in steel frames or other approved construction shown acceptable by fire test, limited to 1,296 sq in. (.84 sq m) in area, may be installed in these doors.

Exception No. 1: In buildings protected throughout by an approved automatic sprinkler system, the door construction requirements noted above are not required but the doors shall be constructed to resist the passage of smoke. Doors shall be provided with latches of a type suitable for keeping the door tightly closed and acceptable to the authority having jurisdiction.

Exception No. 2: In buildings protected throughout by an approved automatic sprinkler system, there is no restriction on the area of vision panels in such doors, the vision panels do not need to be wired glass, and there is no restriction in the type of frames.

Exception No. 3: Door closing devices are not required on doors in corridor wall openings other than those serving exits or required enclosures of hazardous area.

Exception No. 4: Labeled door frames are not required on openings other than those serving exits or required enclosures of hazardous areas, providing the door frames and stops are of steel construction or other approved construction shown acceptable by fire test.

Exception No. 5: Doors to toilet rooms, bathrooms, shower rooms, sink closets, and similar auxiliary spaces which do not contain flammable or combustible materials are exempt from these requirements.

12-3.6.4 Transfer grills, whether or not protected by fusible link operated dampers, shall not be used in these walls or doors.

Exception: Doors to toilet rooms, bathrooms, shower rooms, sink closets and similar auxiliary spaces which do not contain flammable or combustible materials may have ventilating louvers or may be undercut.

The requirements of 12-3.6.1 through 12-3.6.4 essentially stipulate that all areas which contain combustibles in sufficient quantities to produce a life-threatening fire must be separated from exit access corridors by partitions. The details of constructing such partitions depend principally on whether complete automatic sprinkler protection is provided.

In nonsprinklered buildings, corridor partitions must be constructed of 1-hour fire-resistant assemblies using materials selected on the basis of the construction types allowed by 12-1.6.2 and 12-1.6.3. All construction materials in buildings of Type I or Type II construction must satisfy the criteria for noncombustible or limited-combustible materials (see 12-1.6.5). Corridor partitions must be constructed continuously through all concealed spaces (for example, to the floor or roof deck above a suspended "lay-in" ceiling).

Openings in corridor partitions in nonsprinklered buildings must be suitably protected to maintain corridor separation. Glazing is limited to a maximum of 1,296 sq in. (8,362 sq cm) of wired glass set in steel or approved metal frames. Each wired glass panel must be limited to a maximum dimension of 54 in. (137.16 cm). The glass must be labeled, must be ¼ in. (.64 cm) thick, and must be well-embedded in putty with all exposed joints between the metal and glass struck and pointed. (See NFPA 80, *Standard for Fire Doors and Windows.*[12].) A number of wired glass panels may be used in a single partition provided that each 1,296-sq in. (8,362-sq m) section is separated from adjacent panels by a metal mullion. It must be recognized that the use of wired glass panels in a partition will reduce the fire-resistive capability of the partition, in that there will be radiant energy transfer through the glass panel. Therefore, excessive use of wired glass panels should be avoided.

Doors protecting openings in partitions are required to be 1¾-in. (4.45-cm) solid bonded core wood, or of construction capable of resisting fire for at least 20 minutes. Doors must be equipped with a positive latch which cannot be held in the retracted position. The latch must be capable of holding the door in a closed position when subjected to stresses imposed by exposure to fire. Such doors are required to be installed in approved steel frames or frames of such other construction proven acceptable by fire tests. Fixed wired glass vision panels installed in these doors may not exceed an area of 1,296 sq in. (8,362 sq cm) and must be set in steel or approved metal frames. Labeled door frames and door-closing devices are not required except on doors protecting openings in exit enclosures or required enclosures of hazardous areas.

The use of exit access corridors as an exhaust, supply, or return air plenum for a building's air-handling system is not permitted. Corridor doors may not be undercut to facilitate transfer of air, nor are transfer grills allowed in corridor partitions (see 12-3.6.4) or corridor doors. See also 2-2.2 of NFPA 90A, *Standard for the Installation of Air Conditioning and Ventilating Systems.*[4] However, sink closets, bathrooms, and toilets may have doors equipped with a fixed grill or louver to allow exhaust air to be "made up" from the corridor. Where a door to a sink closet, bathroom, or toilet is equipped with a grill or louver, such spaces may not be used for the storage of flammable or combustible supplies.

Air-handling ducts penetrating corridor partitions should be adequately protected to preserve separation of exit access routes. In general, steel ducts will not require a fire damper. In any event, the possible movement of air from space to space under conditions of system operation and conditions of system shutdown should be evaluated. If there is a significant potential for transferring contaminants from an occupied space to a corridor, consideration should be given to providing a fire damper even though the *Code* does not explicitly require such protection.

Where complete automatic sprinkler protection is provided, corridor partitions need not be rated but must still be constructed to resist the passage of smoke. The materials for constructing the partitions must be selected on the basis of the construction types allowed by 12-1.6.2 and 12-1.6.3. Where suspended ceilings are provided, partitions may be terminated at the suspended ceiling without any additional special protection if the suspended ceiling will resist the passage of smoke. The ability to resist the passage of smoke must be *carefully* evaluated. Doors protecting openings in partitions must be installed to resist the passage of smoke, but are not required to have a fire protection rating. Finally, there are no restrictions in terms of area or fire resistance for glazing used in corridor partitions in sprinklered buildings.

Exception No. 2 to 12-6.3.1 sets forth additional criteria for terminating corridor partitions at ceilings, including the "lay-in" type. Partitions may be terminated at a ceiling which has been tested as a portion of an assembly having a fire resistance rating of 1 hour or more. Each compartment located above such a ceiling must be equipped with an automatic mechanical smoke exhaust system, capable of providing a minimum of two air changes per hour but exhausting not less than 5,000 cu ft/min (2.36 cu m/sec). See the additional criteria in items (a) through (e) of Exception No. 2.

Subject to certain restrictions, a specific area may be open to a corridor. It is assumed that spaces which are not separated by partitions will have limited fuel loads in terms of quantity and continuity, inherently limiting the risk of exposing the corridor to fire. Exception Nos. 3, 4, 5, 6, and 7 of 12-3.6.1 set forth specific areas which may be open to corridors.

Waiting areas, which are subject to area limitations, may be open to the corridor under the following conditions. Each waiting area must be located to permit direct visual supervision by the staff and must be equipped with an electrically supervised automatic smoke detection system. Not more than one open waiting area is permitted in each smoke compartment on floors with rooms where patients sleep. On other floors, multiple waiting areas which comply with the preceding restrictions are permitted in each smoke compartment. In all cases, waiting spaces must be arranged so as not to obstruct access to exits.

Exception No. 5 has been added to make provision for spaces such as recreation/lounge/waiting areas which may be open to the corridor but not subject to the area restrictions imposed on waiting spaces in previous editions of the *Code*. Exception No. 5 may be applied only within buildings fully protected by automatic sprinklers. The open space must be visually supervised by staff. The open space and interconnected corridors which are not separated from the space must be equipped with an electrically supervised smoke detection system.

Areas used for charting and communication by doctors and nurses may be open to the corridor.

12-3.7 Subdivision of Building Spaces.

12-3.7.1 Smoke barriers shall be provided, regardless of building construction type, as follows:

(a) To divide every story used by inpatients for sleeping or treatment, or any story having an occupant load of 50 or more persons, into at least two compartments, and

Item (a) requires subdivision of *any* floor used by inpatients for sleeping or treatment. It also requires subdivision of *any other* floor which has an occupant load of 50 or more.

(b) To limit on any story the length and width of each smoke compartment to no more than 150 ft (45.72 m).

It is *not* the intent of item (b) to require that the length and width be added together with the resulting sum being 150 ft (45.72 m) or less. It is the intent that the length be 150 ft (45.72 m) or less and that the width be 150 ft (45.72 m) or less.

Exception: Protection may be accomplished in conjunction with the provision of horizontal exits.

12-3.7.2 Smoke barriers shall be provided on stories which are usable but unoccupied.

12-3.7.3 Any required smoke barrier shall be constructed in accordance with Section 6-3 except as provided in 12-3.7.9 and shall have a fire resistance rating of at least 1 hour.

12-3.7.4 At least 30 net sq ft (2.79 sq m) per patient in a hospital or nursing home or 15 net sq ft (1.39 sq m) per resident in a residential-custodial care facility shall be provided within the aggregate area of corridors, patient rooms, treatment rooms, lounge or dining areas and other low hazard areas on each side of the smoke barrier. On stories not housing bed or litter patients or in supervisory care facilities, at least 6 net sq ft (.56 sq m) per occupant shall be provided on each side of the smoke barrier for the total number of occupants in adjoining compartments.

12-3.7.5 Doors in smoke barriers shall be substantial doors such as 1¾-in. (4.45-cm) thick solid bonded core wood or construction that will resist fire for at least 20 minutes. Corridor openings in smoke barriers shall be protected by a pair of swinging doors, each door to swing in a direction opposite from the other. The minimum door leaf width shall be as follows:

(a) Hospitals and nursing homes: 44 in. (111.76 cm).

(b) Residential-custodial care institutions: 32 in. (81.28 cm).

12-3.7.6 Doors in smoke barriers shall comply with 6-3.3 and shall be self-closing.

Exception: Doors may be held open only if they meet the requirements of 12-2.11.6.

12-3.7.7 Vision panels of approved transparent wired glass not exceeding 1,296 sq in. (.84 sq m) in approved metal frames shall be provided in each door in a smoke barrier.

12-3.7.8 Rabbets, bevels, or astragals are required at the meeting edges, and stops are required at the head and sides of door frames in smoke barriers. Positive latching hardware is not required. Center mullions are prohibited.

Exception: Protection at the meeting edges of doors and stops at the head and sides of door frames may be omitted in buildings equipped with an approved engineered smoke control system. The engineered smoke control system shall respond automatically, preventing the transfer of smoke across the barrier, and shall be designed in accordance with Standard for the Installation of Air Conditioning and Ventilating Systems, NFPA 90A.

Openings between the meeting edges of pairs of doors and between the doors and frames must be closed to retard the transfer of smoke. Since 12-3.7.5 requires these doors to swing in opposite directions to each other, the protection at the meeting edge does not create a coordination problem and, therefore, is simple to provide.

When an engineered smoke control system is provided, and the smoke control system is designed to respond automatically preventing smoke transfer across the smoke barrier, protection at the meeting edges of the doors and at the head and sides of the door may be omitted.

12-3.7.9   An approved damper designed to resist the passage of smoke shall be provided at each point a duct penetrates a smoke barrier required by 12-3.7.1. The damper shall close upon detection of smoke by an approved smoke detector, located within the duct. (*See also Section 6-3.*)

Exception No. 1:   In lieu of an approved smoke detector located within the duct, ducts which penetrate smoke barriers above smoke barrier doors (required by 12-3.7.5) may have the approved damper arranged to close upon detection of smoke by the local device designed to detect smoke on either side of the smoke barrier door opening.

Exception No. 2:   Dampers may be omitted in buildings equipped with an approved engineered smoke control system. The smoke control system shall respond automatically, preventing the transfer of smoke across the smoke barrier, and shall be designed in accordance with Standard for the Installation of Air Conditioning and Ventilating Systems, NFPA 90A.

Exception No. 3:   Dampers may be omitted where the openings in ducts are limited to a single smoke compartment and the ducts are of steel construction.

The requirements of 12-3.7.1 through 12-3.7.9 for subdividing building spaces through smoke barriers are illustrated in Figures 12-14 through 12-16. Paragraph 12-2.2.5 discusses horizontal exits.

In planning exits, arrangements should be made to transfer patients from one section of a floor to another section of the same floor separated by a fire barrier or smoke barrier in such a manner that patients confined to their beds may be transferred in their beds. Where the building design will permit, the section of the corridor containing an entrance or elevator lobby should be separated from corridors leading from it by fire or smoke barriers. Such an arrangement, where the lobby is centrally located, will, in effect, produce a smoke lock, placing a double barrier between the area to which patients may be taken and the area from which they must be evacuated because of threatening smoke and fire.

During a fire the emergency evacuation of patients in a health care facility is an inefficient, time-consuming process. Realistically, if patients must be moved, only through horizontal travel can sizable numbers of occupants be relocated. Smoke barriers and horizontal exits used to subdivide a building serve three purposes fundamental to the protection of inpatients in that they:

1. Limit the spread of fire and fire-produced contaminants,
2. Limit the number of occupants exposed to a single fire, and
3. Provide for horizontal relocation of patients by creating an area of refuge on the same floor level.

Note that the combination fire/smoke dampers required in 12-3.7.9 may be omitted in buildings equipped with an engineered smoke control system which is designed to limit smoke transfer across the smoke barriers.

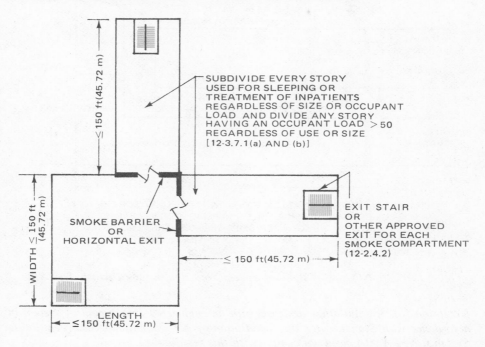

Figure 12-14. Subdivision of Building Spaces, New Health Care Occupancies. (See also Figures 12-3, 12-4, and 12-5.)

12-3.8 Special Features.

12-3.8.1 Every patient sleeping room shall have an outside window or outside door arranged and located so that it can be opened from the inside to permit the venting of products of combustion and to permit any occupant to have direct access to fresh air in case of emergency. (*See 12-1.1.1.7 for detention screen requirements.*) The maximum allowable sill height shall not exceed 36 in. (91.44 cm) above the floor. Where windows require the use of tools or keys for operation, the tools or keys shall be located on the floor involved at a prominent location accessible to staff.

Exception No. 1:   The window sill in special nursing care areas such as those housing ICU, CCU, hemodialysis, and neo-natal patients may be 60 in. (152.4 cm) above the floor.

Exception No. 2:   Rooms intended for occupancy of less than 24 hours, such as those housing obstetrical labor beds, recovery beds and observation beds in the emergency department; and newborn nurseries need not comply with this requirement.

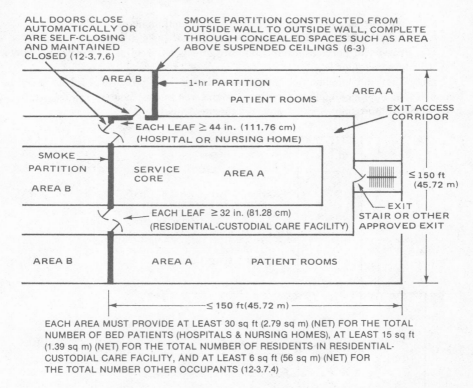

ALL DOORS CLOSE AUTOMATICALLY OR ARE SELF-CLOSING AND MAINTAINED CLOSED (12-3.7.6)

SMOKE PARTITION CONSTRUCTED FROM OUTSIDE WALL TO OUTSIDE WALL, COMPLETE THROUGH CONCEALED SPACES SUCH AS AREA ABOVE SUSPENDED CEILINGS (6-3)

AREA B

1-hr PARTITION

PATIENT ROOMS

AREA A

EXIT ACCESS CORRIDOR

EACH LEAF ≥ 44 in. (111.76 cm) (HOSPITAL OR NURSING HOME)

SMOKE PARTITION

AREA B

SERVICE CORE

AREA A

≤ 150 ft (45.72 m)

EACH LEAF ≥ 32 in. (81.28 cm) (RESIDENTIAL-CUSTODIAL CARE FACILITY)

EXIT STAIR OR OTHER APPROVED EXIT

AREA B

AREA A

PATIENT ROOMS

≤ 150 ft (45.72 m)

EACH AREA MUST PROVIDE AT LEAST 30 sq ft (2.79 sq m) (NET) FOR THE TOTAL NUMBER OF BED PATIENTS (HOSPITALS & NURSING HOMES), AT LEAST 15 sq ft (1.39 sq m) (NET) FOR THE TOTAL NUMBER OF RESIDENTS IN RESIDENTIAL-CUSTODIAL CARE FACILITY, AND AT LEAST 6 sq ft (56 sq m) (NET) FOR THE TOTAL NUMBER OTHER OCCUPANTS (12-3.7.4)

Figure 12-15. Subdivision of Building Spaces, New Health Care Occupancies.

Exception No. 3: Buildings designed with an engineered smoke control system in accordance with Standard for the Installation of Air Conditioning and Ventilating Systems, NFPA 90A, need not comply with this requirement.

Paragraph 12-3.8.1 requires an outside door or outside window in each room where patients sleep unless the building is equipped with an engineered smoke control system. The window must be equipped with an operable section to be opened in an emergency to provide access to fresh air. The maximum allowable sill height is specified as 36 in. (91.44 cm), except in special nursing care areas (recovery rooms, intensive care units, coronary care units, and dialysis units) where the sill height may not be more than 60 in. (152.4 cm) above the floor. Sill heights are limited to ensure access to window latches so that the operable section may be opened without special equipment.

To install windows with a latching arrangement which requires special knowledge to operate, or to place the latches at a level which requires the use of a chair or ladder for access would not meet the intent of this section, even if the criteria for sill height were satisfied. Conversely, a window with a sill height exceeding that specified by this section, but equipped with a mechanical linkage permitting operation of the window from floor level without special tools, special knowledge, or other special equipment, could satisfy the intent of this section.

It is desirable to have operable windows which have the capability of being opened

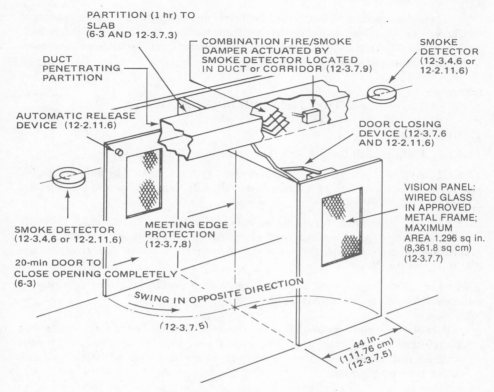

PARTITION (1 hr) TO
SLAB
(6-3 AND 12-3.7.3)

DUCT
PENETRATING
PARTITION

COMBINATION FIRE/SMOKE
DAMPER ACTUATED BY
SMOKE DETECTOR LOCATED
IN DUCT or CORRIDOR (12-3.7.9)

SMOKE
DETECTOR
(12-3.4.6 or
12-2.11.6)

AUTOMATIC RELEASE
DEVICE (12-2.11.6)

DOOR CLOSING
DEVICE (12-3.7.6
AND 12-2.11.6)

VISION PANEL:
WIRED GLASS
IN APPROVED
METAL FRAME;
MAXIMUM
AREA 1.296 sq in.
(8,361.8 sq cm)
(12-3.7.7)

SMOKE DETECTOR
(12-3.4.6 or 12-2.11.6)

MEETING EDGE
PROTECTION
(12-3.7.8)

20-min DOOR TO
CLOSE OPENING COMPLETELY
(6-3)

SWING IN OPPOSITE DIRECTION

(12-3.7.5)

44 in.
(111.76 cm)
(12-3.7.5)

Figure 12-16. Smoke Barrier for New Health Care Occupancy Installed in Accordance with 12-3.7.

without requiring a tool or a key. However, windows may be locked, providing keys are readily available. The *Code* recognizes that detention screens are sometimes necessary. Rooms so equipped should be limited in number to those where such precautions are deemed necessary. Continuous supervision should be provided for such areas. (See 12-1.1.1.7)

Rooms which are occupied for less than 24 hours, such as those used for recovery, child delivery, or emergency care, or rooms used for newborn nurseries, need not be provided with a window. In excepting these rooms from the requirements for windows, the committee felt that the high incidence of direct nursing supervision of all patients in these areas reduces the likelihood that patients will be trapped in a smoky fire. However, when it is not possible to provide windows, a conservative design should provide some added protection such as individual sprinkler protection of enclosed areas (closets and pantries), early warning by smoke detectors, or high-volume exhaust ventilation.

SECTION 12-4   SPECIAL PROVISIONS

12-4.1 Windowless Buildings.   See Section 30-7 for requirements for windowless buildings.

Windowless portions of health care facilities must comply with the requirements of Chapter 12 in addition to the criteria set forth for such structures in Section 30-7. Paragraph 12-4.1 does not obviate the requirements for openable patient room windows contained within 12-3.8.1.

SECTION 12-5   BUILDING SERVICES

12-5.1 Utilities.

12-5.1.1   Utilities shall comply with the provisions of Section 7-1.

12-5.1.2   Alarms, emergency communication systems and the illumination of generator set locations shall be as described in the Life Safety Branch of the *National Electrical Code*, NFPA 70.

12-5.1.3   Any health care occupancy as indicated within 12-1.1.1.2 which normally utilizes life support devices shall have electrical systems designed and installed in accordance with *Standard for Essential Electrical Systems for Health Care Facilities*, NFPA 76A.

Exception: This requirement does not apply to a facility that has life support equipment for emergency purposes only.

It is not uncommon to lose all or some power supplies during a fire emergency. Therefore, it is important that life support equipment be supplied by properly designed and installed electrical systems so as not to create additional problems during the emergency.

12-5.2 Heating, Ventilating, and Air Conditioning.

12-5.2.1   Heating, ventilating, and air conditioning shall comply with the provisions of Section 7-2 and shall be installed in accordance with the manufacturer's specifications.

Exception: As modified in 12-5.2.2 following.

12-5.2.2   Portable space heating devices are prohibited. Any heating device other than a central heating plant shall be so designed and installed that combustible material will not be ignited by it or its appurtenances. If fuel fired, such heating devices shall be chimney or vent connected, shall take air for combustion directly from outside, and shall be so designed and installed to provide for complete separation of the combustion system from the atmosphere of the occupied area. Any heating device shall have safety features to immediately stop the flow of fuel and shut down the equipment in case of either excessive temperatures or ignition failure.

Exception No. 1:   Approved suspended unit heaters may be used in locations other than means of egress and patient sleeping areas, provided such heaters are located high enough to be out of the reach of persons using the area and provided they are equipped with the safety features called for above.

Exception No. 2.:   Fireplaces may be installed and used only in areas other than patient sleeping areas, provided that these areas are separated from patient sleeping spaces by construction having a 1-hour fire resistance rating and they comply with Standard for Chimneys, Fireplaces and Vents, NFPA 211. In addition thereto, the fireplace shall be equipped with a hearth that shall be raised at least 4 in. (10.16 cm), and a heat tempered glass, or other approved material, fireplace enclosure guaranteed against breakage up to a temperature of 650°F (343.33°C). If, in the opinion of the authority having jurisdiction, special hazards are present, a lock on the enclosure and other safety precautions may be required.

Exception No. 3: Portable space heating devices shall be permitted to be used in nonsleeping staff and employee areas when the heating elements of such a device are limited to not more than 212°F (100°C).

It is generally agreed that the maximum acceptable temperature to which combustible materials may be exposed for prolonged periods of time is on the order of 160°F (71°C) to 190°F (88°C).

Paragraphs 12-5.2.1 and 12-5.2.2 specify safeguards for air conditioning, ventilating, heating, and other service equipment to minimize the possibility of such devices serving as a source of ignition. Fuel-fired heating devices, except central heating systems, must be designed to provide complete separation of the combustion system from the occupied spaces. Air for combustion must be taken directly from the outside.

A major concern of the *Code* is to prevent the ignition of clothing, bedclothes, furniture, and other furnishings by a heating device. Therefore, 12-5.2.2 prohibits portable heating devices in areas used by patients.

12-5.3 Elevators, dumbwaiters and vertical conveyors shall comply with the provisions of Section 7-4.

Elevators. (See Section 7-4.)

Although not counted as a required exit, elevators may constitute a valuable supplemental facility for evacuating patients from health care buildings. In some cases, movement of critically ill patients or patients in restraining devices may be realistically accomplished only by an elevator.

Elevators, however, have many inherent weaknesses which tend to limit reliability. Elevator access doors are designed with operating tolerances which permit smoke transfer into the shaft. Power failure during a fire could result in trapping persons on elevators which stop between floors. Elevators may, during their descent from upper floors, stop automatically at the floor of the fire, allow the doors to open, and expose the occupants.

Many of these weaknesses can be minimized by providing emergency power, separating the elevator lobby from other building spaces by rated construction, designing detection and alarm equipment to prevent elevators from stopping at a floor exposed to a fire, providing an emergency smoke control system, and by pressurizing the elevator shaft and adjacent lobbies (see Section 7-3). This represents good fire protection judgment, but is not the result of any requirements of this *Code*.

Through emergency planning and staff training, crowding of elevators (another potential problem) may be avoided. Emergency plans may make effective use of elevators by transferring patients through a horizontal exit, for example, to a separate fire area. Within the separate fire area, a staged evacuation program could be instituted, the elevators ultimately taking patients to the outside at ground level.

12-5.4 Rubbish Chutes, Incinerators, and Laundry Chutes.

12-5.4.1 Rubbish chutes, incinerators, and laundry chutes shall comply with the provisions of Section 7-5.

12-5.4.2 Any rubbish chute or linen chute, including pneumatic rubbish and linen systems, shall be provided with automatic extinguishing protection installed in accordance with *Standard for the Installation of Sprinkler Systems*, NFPA 13. (*See Section 7-5.*)

12-5.4.3 Any trash chute shall discharge into a trash collecting room used for no other purpose and protected in accordance with Section 6-4.

12-5.4.4 An incinerator shall not be directly flue-fed nor shall any floor charging chute directly connect with the combustion chamber.

SECTION 12-6   NEW AMBULATORY HEALTH CARE CENTERS

12-6.1 General Requirements.

12-6.1.1 Application.

12-6.1.1.1 Ambulatory health care centers shall comply with the provisions of both Chapter 26 and (this) Section 12-6, as may be more stringent.

12-6.1.1.2 This section establishes life safety requirements, in addition to those required in Chapter 26, for the design of all ambulatory health care centers and outpatient surgical centers which meet the requirements of 12-1.3(e).

Ambulatory health care centers exhibit some of the occupancy characteristics of business occupancies and some of the characteristics of health care facilities. In developing Section 12-6, it was intended to prescribe a level of life safety from fire which would be greater than that typically specified for business occupancies, but less than that typically found in health care facilities. See commentary for 12-1.3.

Ambulatory health care centers are required to comply with the provisions of Chapter 26 pertaining to business occupancies, except as more restrictive provisions are established within Section 12-6.

12-6.1.2 Reserved.

12-6.1.3 Special Definitions.   (*See 12-1.3*)

2-6.1.4 Classification of Occupancy.   (*See 12-1.3*)

12-6.1.5 Reserved.

12-6.1.6 Minimum Construction Requirements.

12-6.1.6.1 For purposes of 12-6.1.6, stories shall be counted starting at the primary level of exit discharge and ending at the highest occupiable level. For the purposes of this section, the primary level of exit discharge of a building shall be that floor which is level with or above finished grade of this exterior wall line for 50 percent or more of its perimeter.

Allowable building construction types are a function of the number of stories in a building. In determining the number of stories, the first story is considered to be the level of exit discharge. Only "occupiable levels" are counted in determining story height. For example, unoccupied attics would not constitute a story.

Difficulties have been experienced in determining story height where a building is located on a sloping grade. Paragraph 12-6.1.6.1 notes that a story on a sloping site which is partially below grade should be counted as a story if the floor is level with or above grade for 50 percent or more of the perimeter of the building at the exterior wall. See Figures 12-2 and 12-17.

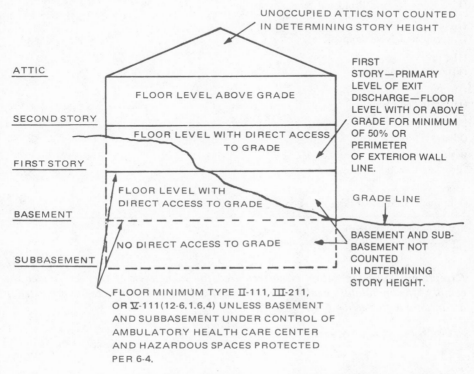

Figure 12-17. Illustration of the Application of 12-6.1.6.1 and 12-6.1.6.4.

12-6.1.6.2 Buildings of one story in height housing ambulatory health care centers may be of Type I, II, III, IV or V construction.

12-6.1.6.3 Buildings of two or more stories in height housing ambulatory health care centers may be of Type I (443), I (332), or II (222), Type II (111), Type III (211), Type IV (2HH) or Type V (111) construction.

Exception: Such buildings may be constructed of Type II (000), III (200) or V (000) if equipped throughout with an approved automatic extinguishing system.

Construction types permitted in ambulatory health care centers are summarized in Table 12-2. See NFPA 220, *Standard Types of Building Construction.*[1].

12-6.1.6.4 Any level below the level of exit discharge shall be separated from the level of exit discharge by at least Type II (111), Type III (211) or Type V (111) construction.

Table 12–2.   Construction Types Permitted in Ambulatory
Health Care Occupancies

Construction Type	Stories	
	1	*2 or more*
I-443, I-332, II-222, II-111 (Fire Resistive and Protected Noncombustible)	X	X
II-000 (Unprotected Noncombustible)	X	X*
III-211 (Protected Ordinary)	X	X
III-200 (Unprotected Ordinary)	X	X*
IV-2HH (Heavy Timber)	X	X
V-111 (Protected Wood Frame)	X	X
V-000 (Unprotected Wood Frame)	X	X*

X = Construction types allowed.
* = Automatic sprinkler protection required.

Exception: Such separation is not required for such levels if they are under the contol of the ambulatory health care center and any hazardous spaces are protected in accordance with Section 6-4.

Refer to Figure 12-17.

12-6.1.6.5 When new ambulatory health care centers are located in existing buildings, the authority having jurisdiction may accept construction systems of lesser fire resistance than required above if it can be demonstrated to his satisfaction that in cases of fire, prompt evacuation of the center can be made or that the exposing occupancies and materials of construction present no threat of fire penetration from such occupancy into the ambulatory health care center or collapse of the structure.

This paragraph is meant to liberalize the construction requirements applicable to a new ambulatory health care center which is to be placed in an existing building. Adequate supporting data must be supplied to the authority having jurisdiction to justify such a reduction.

12-6.1.7 Occupant Load.

12-6.2 Means of Egress Requirements.

12-6.2.1 General.   Every aisle, passageway, corridor, exit discharge, exit location and access shall be in accordance with Chapter 5.

Exception No. 1:   As modified in the following paragraphs.

Exception No. 2:   The requirements of Chapter 5 specifying net clear door width do not apply. Projections into the door opening by stops or by hinge stiles shall be permitted.

Means of egress details are to conform to the fundamental provisions expressed in Chapter 5, except as modified in Chapter 12. For example, Exception No. 2 to 12-2.1 would allow the width of exit doors to be measured on the basis of the actual door leaf width. Projections into the door opening by the hinge stile and door stops are ignored.

12-6.2.2 Types of Exits.   Exits shall be restricted to the permissible types described in 26-2.2.

12-6.2.3 Capacity of Means of Egress.

12-6.2.3.1   The minimum width of any corridor or passageway required for exit access shall be 44 in. (111.76 cm) clear.

Corridors or passageways within ambulatory health care centers used in moving patients who are temporarily nonambulatory from one room to another room or area should be of adequate width to meet the functional needs of the facility. Widths greater than 44 in. (111.76 cm) will be required in many instances. However, the minimum width for public corridors used as common exit access corridors or passageways is 44 in. (111.76 cm). The 44 in. (111.76 cm) width is stipulated on the assumption that most occupants will be ambulatory.

12-6.2.3.2   The capacity of any required means of egress shall be determined in accordance with the provisions of 26-2.3 and shall be based on its width as defined in Section 5-3.

The capacity of the means of egress in ambulatory health care centers is determined on the basis of provisions within Chapter 26 dealing with business occupancies. For example, 26-2.3.1 allows level exit components to serve 100 people per unit of exit width, whereas stairs are allowed to serve 60 persons per unit. These capacities are much higher than would be typically allowed for a health care center, and are considered permissible on the basis that the majority of occupants will be ambulatory.

12-6.2.4 Number of Exits.

12-6.2.4.1   At least two exits of the types described in 26-2.2 (Business Occupancy) located remote from each other shall be provided for each floor or fire section of the building.

12-6.2.4.2   Any room and any suite of rooms of more than 1,000 sq ft (92.9 sq m) shall have at least two exit access doors located remote from each other.

12-6.2.5 Arrangement of Means of Egress.   *(See 26-2.5.)*

12-6.2.6 Measurement of Travel Distance to Exits.

12-6.2.6.1   Travel distance shall be measured in accordance with Section 5-6.

12-6.2.6.2 Travel distance:

(a) Between any room door required as exit access and an exit shall not exceed 100 ft (30.48 m); and

(b) Between any point in a room and an exit shall not exceed 150 ft (45.72 m).

Exception: The travel distance in (a) or (b) above may be increased by 50 ft (15.24 m) in buildings protected throughout by an approved automatic sprinkler system.

Travel distance is measured only to the closest exit, not to both exits required by 12-6.2.4.1. The requirements of 12-6.2.6.2 are illustrated in Figure 12-18.

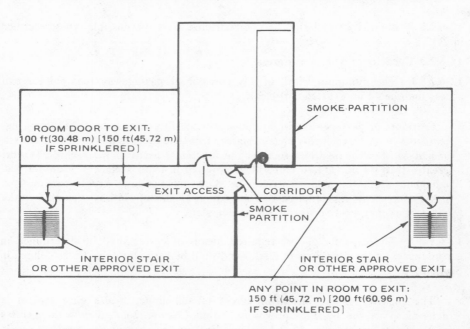

Figure 12-18. Maximum Travel Distance to Exits, New Ambulatory Health Care Occupancy. The distance is measured along the natural path of travel (see 5-6.2). "Sprinklered" means that the entire building is protected by a complete approved automatic extinguishing system. (Note that a room door in a smoke partition must meet the requirements of 6-3.3 and 12-3.7.6 and be self-closing.)

12-6.2.7 Discharge from Exits.   (*See 26-2.7.*)

12-6.2.8 Illumination of Means of Egress.   Each ambulatory health care center shall be provided with illumination of means of egress in accordance with Section 5-8.

12-6.2.9 Emergency Lighting and Essential Electrical Systems.

12-6.2.9.1   Each ambulatory health care center shall be provided with emergency lighting in accordance with Section 5-9.

12-6.2.9.2   Where general anesthesia or life support equipment is used, each ambulatory health care center shall be provided with an essential electrical system in accordance with *Essential Electrical Systems for Health Care Facilities*, NFPA 76A.

Exception: Where battery operated equipment is provided, a generator is not required for emergency power.

All ambulatory health care centers are required to be equipped with emergency lighting. If medical procedures requiring general anesthesia are practiced, or if life support equipment is required, ambulatory health care centers are required to be served by electrical systems meeting the criteria for essential electrical systems as detailed in NFPA 76A, *Standard for Essential Electrical Systems for Health Care Facilities.*[3].

A facility would not be required to comply with NFPA 76A[3] if the building is a free-standing unit which is independent of any facility providing 24-hour care and, as a normal practice, (1) management maintains admitting and discharge policies that preclude the provision of care for any patient or resident who may need to be sustained by electromechanical means such as respirators, suction apparatus, etc., and (2) the building offers no surgical treatment requiring general anesthesia, and (3) battery operated systems or equipment are provided which would maintain power to exit lights and illumination of exit corridors, stairways, medical preparation areas, and the like, for a minimum of 4 hours. Additionally, battery power would be required to be supplied to all alarm systems.

12-6.2.10 Marking of Means of Egress.   Signs designating exits and ways of travel thereto shall be provided in accordance with Section 5-10.

12-6.2.11 Special Features.

12-6.2.11.1   Locks installed on patient treatment, diagnostic, or recovery room doors shall be so arranged that they can be locked only from the corridor side. All such locks shall be arranged to permit exit from the room by a simple operation without the use of a key.

12-6.2.11.2   Doors leading directly to the outside of the buildings may be subject to locking from the room side.

12-6.2.11.3   Special locking arrangements in accordance with 5-2.1.2.1.5 are permitted on exterior doors.

Paragraph 5-2.1.2.1.5 establishes minimum requirements for delayed release panic hardware.

12-6.2.11.4   Exit access door leaves from diagnostic or treatment areas, such as X-ray, surgical or physical therapy; all door leaves between these spaces and the required exits; and all exit door leaves serving these spaces shall be at least 34 in. (86.36 cm) wide.

Doors within ambulatory health care centers which are used in moving patients who are temporarily nonambulatory should be of adequate width to meet the functional needs of the facility. In many instances, doors wider than 34 in. (86.36 cm) will be required. This paragraph intends to address doors used by the public or those doors which provide access to public hallways and corridors. The 34 in. (86.36 cm) minimum width is specified for doors on the basis that most occupants will be ambulatory.

12-6.2.11.5 Any door in an exit passageway, stair enclosure, horizontal exit, a required enclosure of a hazardous area, or a smoke partition may be held open only by an automatic device which complies with 5-2.1.2.3. The device shall be so arranged that the operation of the following will initiate the self-closing action:

(a) The manual alarm system required in 12-6.3.4 and either (b) or (c) below.

(b) A local device designed to detect smoke on either side of the opening, or

(c) A complete automatic fire extinguishing or complete automatic fire detection system.

12-6.2.11.6 Where doors in a stair enclosure are held open by an automatic device as permitted in 12-6.2.11.5, initiation of a door closing action on any level shall cause all doors at all levels in the stair enclosure to close.

It is desirable to keep doors in exit enclosures, stair enclosures, horizontal exits, smoke barriers, and hazardous areas closed at all times to impede the spread of smoke and gases caused by a fire. However, some doors will be kept open, either for reasons of operating efficiency or comfort. Where doors in required fire or smoke barriers are to be held open, such doors must be equipped with automatic devices which are arranged to close the doors by the methods described within 12-6.2.11.5.

The automatic device must cause the doors to close upon operation of the manual fire alarm system. The doors must also be designed to close by actuation of a smoke detector located to detect smoke on either side of the door opening or by actuation of a complete automatic fire extinguishing or complete automatic fire detection system.

It is especially important in facilities providing health care to maintain floor-to-floor separation. Doors protecting openings in a stair tower enclosure may be held open by an automatic device only if arranged to close as specified above. Initiation of any automatic action which causes a door to close at one level must cause all doors at all levels protecting openings within the stair enclosure to close and latch.

12-6.3 Protection.

12-6.3.1 Protection of Vertical Openings.   (*See 26-3.1.*)

12-6.3.2 Protection from Hazards.   (*See 26-3.2.*)

12-6.3.2.1 Laboratories employing quantities of flammable, combustible, or hazardous materials which are considered as severe hazard shall be protected in accordance with *Laboratories in Health Related Institutions*, NFPA 56C.

Laboratories which contain "ordinary" combustibles and flammable liquids in sufficient quantity to threaten a 1-hour fire separation — wood equivalent fuel loads in the range of 5 to 10 lb/sq ft (24.41 to 48.82 kg/sq m) — are considered a severe hazard. Laboratories representing a severe hazard must be protected in accordance with NFPA 56C, *Safety Standard for Laboratories in Health-Related Institutions*.[8] Protection would include 1-hour fire resistance separation and automatic sprinkler protection.

Where fuel loads of lesser amounts are involved and quantities of flammable liquids are limited, laboratories would be simply considered hazardous areas, and would require either 1-hour separation or automatic sprinkler protection.

12-6.3.2.2 Anesthetizing locations shall be protected in accordance with *Inhalations Anesthetics in Ambulatory Care Facilities*, NFPA 56G.

12-6.3.3 Interior Finish. (*See 26-3.3.*)

12-6.3.4 Detection, Alarm and Communication Systems.

12-6.3.4.1 Other than as noted below, required fire detection and signaling devices or systems shall be in accordance with Section 7-6.

12-6.3.4.2 Every building shall have a manually operated fire alarm system, in accordance with Section 7-6. Pre-signal systems are not allowed within an ambulatory surgical care center.

12-6.3.4.3 Operation of any fire alarm activating device shall automatically, without delay, accomplish general alarm indication and control functons. Zoned, coded systems shall be permitted.

12-6.3.4.4 The fire alarm system shall be arranged to transmit an alarm automatically to the fire department legally committed to serve the area in which the health care facility is located, by the most direct and reliable method approved by local regulations.

12-6.3.4.5 Internal audible alarm devices shall be provided and shall be installed in accordance with Section 7-6.

12-6.3.4.6 Any fire detection device or system required by this section shall be electrically interconnected with the fire alarm system.

Paragraphs 12-6.3.4.1 through 12-6.3.4.6 deal with required fire alarm equipment. Reliability is of prime importance; therefore, electrical supervision of the system and system components is specified by the standards referenced in Section 7-6. In the event of circuit fault, component failure, or other "trouble," a continuous "trouble indication" signal is required and must be provided at a constantly attended location.

A manual fire alarm system is required by 12-6.3.4.2. Manual pull stations should be located along the natural routes of egress and located so as to adequately cover all portions of the building. Manual pull stations should always be located so that anyone qualified to send an alarm may summon aid without having to leave the zone of his or her ordinary activities, or pass out of the sight and hearing of people immediately exposed to, or in direct view of, a fire. The operation of a manual fire alarm station must automatically summon attendants who can assist in removing physically helpless occupants.

The system required by 12-6.3.4.2 may be incorporated into an automatic system equipped to detect a fire and initiate an alarm.

Actuation of any required fire or smoke detector, activation of a required sprinkler system, or operation of a manual pull station must *automatically,* without delay, sound *audible alarm devices* within the building. Presignal systems are not permitted.

The fire alarm system is required by 12-6.3.4.4 to *automatically* notify the public fire department legally committed to serve the facility. The preferred arrangement is direct transmission to the fire department fire alarm headquarters. If such an arrangement is not permitted, the next best option is notification by an approved central station alarm system. If a central station alarm system is not available, the alarm should be transmitted by an electrically supervised system to a constantly attended location with the capability of alerting the public fire department.

Actuation of the fire alarm must cause audible alerting devices to sound throughout the affected zone or building as appropriate. Visible alerting devices may be used, but may not serve as a substitute for audible devices.

12-6.3.5 Extinguishment Requirements.   (See 26-3.5.)

12-6.3.5.1   The sprinkler piping, serving no more than six sprinklers for any isolated hazardous area, may be connected directly to a domestic water supply system having a capacity sufficient to provide 0.15 gal per minute per sq ft (1.02 × 10⁻⁴ cu m/s/sq m) of floor area throughout the entire enclosed area. An indicating shutoff valve shall be installed in an accessible location between the sprinklers and the connection to the domestic water supply. Where more than two sprinklers are installed in a single area, waterflow detection shall be provided to sound the building fire alarm system in the event of sprinkler operation. (*For sprinkler requirements for hazardous areas, see 12-6.3.2.*)

12-6.3.5.2   Portable fire extinguishers shall be provided in ambulatory health care occupancies in accordance with 7-7.4.1.

12-6.3.6 Corridors.   (See 26-3.6.)

12-6.3.7 Subdivision of Building Space.

12-6.3.7.1   Ambulatory health care occupancies shall be separated from other tenants and occupancies by walls having at least a 1-hour fire-resistive construction. Such walls shall extend from the floor slab below to the floor or roof slab above. Doors shall be at least 1¾-in. (4.45-cm) solid bonded wood core or the equivalent and equipped with positive latches. These doors shall be self-closing and normally kept in the closed position except when in use. Any vision panels shall be of fixed wired glass set in approved metal frames and limited in size to 1,296 sq in. (.84 sq m).

Ambulatory health care centers are frequently located within buildings used for a variety of purposes. Location within buildings having hazardous occupancies should be avoided. Where ambulatory health care centers are located within buildings of mixed use, the ambulatory health care center must be separated from adjacent tenants and occupancies by at least 1-hour fire-rated partitions. Doors protecting openings in such partitions must be a minimum of 1¾-in. (4.45-cm) solid bonded wood core, or of other equivalent construction which will resist fire for a minimum of 20 minutes. The doors must be equipped with positive latching hardware of a type which cannot be held in the retracted position. These doors must be self-closing and normally maintained closed or, if the doors are to be held open, an automatic device must be used as indicated in 12-6.2.11.4.

Glazing within doors and partitions is limited to a maximum of 1,296 sq in. (8,362 sq cm) of wired glass, set in approved metal frames. Each wired glass panel must be limited to a maximum dimension of 54 in. (137.16 cm). The glass must be labeled, ¼ in. (.64 cm) thick, and well-embedded in putty with all exposed joints between the metal and the glass struck and pointed. (See NFPA 80, *Standard for Fire Doors and Windows.*[12]) A number of wired glass panels may be used in a single partition provided that each 1,296-sq in. (8,362-sq cm) section is separated from adjacent panels by a metal mullion. The excessive use of wired glass panels should be avoided. It must be recognized that the use of wired glass panels in a partition reduces the effectiveness of the partition in that radiant energy transfer will readily occur through the glass panel..

Partitions separating ambulatory health care centers from other occupancies must extend from the floor to the floor or roof deck above, complete through concealed spaces above suspended ceilings, for example. The partition must form a continuous barrier. Openings around penetrations involving building services must be adequately protected to maintain the 1-hour separation. Special attention should be paid to penetrations involving air-handling ducts. In general, steel ducts will not require a fire damper. Penetrations involving nonmetallic ducts or aluminum ducts should be carefully evaluated. Fire dampers should be provided to protect duct penetrations where the projected fire exposure is judged sufficient to jeopardize the required separation because of the duct penetration. The possible movement of air from space to space under conditions of system operation and conditions of system shutdown should both be evaluated. If there is a significant potential for transferring contaminants from an adjacent space to the ambulatory health care center or from the center to a corridor, fire dampers should be provided for duct penetrations, even though the *Code* does not specifically require such protection.

See Figure 12-19.

12-6.3.7.2 The ambulatory health care facility shall be divided into at least two smoke compartments.

Exception: Facilities less than 2,000 sq ft (185.8 sq m) and protected by an approved automatic smoke detection system need not be divided.

12-6.3.7.3 Walls separating the smoke compartments shall be of at least a 1-hour construction, and shall extend from the floor slab below to the floor or roof slab above.

12-6.3.7.4 Vision panels in the smoke barrier shall be of fixed wired glass set in approved metal frames and shall be limited in size to 1,296 sq in. (.84 sq m).

12-6.3.7.5 Doors in smoke barriers shall be at least 1¾-in. (4.45-cm) solid bonded wood core or the equivalent and shall be self-closing. A vision panel is required.

12-6.3.7.6 Doors in smoke barriers shall normally be kept closed or if held open, they shall be equipped with automatic devices which will release the doors upon activation of:

(a) The fire alarm system, and either

(b) A local smoke detector, or,

(c) A complete automatic fire extinguishing system or complete automatic fire detection system.

12-6.3.7.7 An approved damper designed to resist the passage of smoke shall be provided at each point a duct penetrates a smoke barrier required by 12-6.3.7.1. The damper shall close upon detection of smoke by an approved smoke detector, located within the duct. (*See Section 6-3.*)

Exception No. 1:   In lieu of an approved smoke detector located within the duct, ducts which penetrate smoke barriers above smoke barrier doors (required in 12-6.3.7.5) may have the approved damper arranged to close upon detection of smoke by the local device designed to detect smoke in either side of the smoke barrier door opening.

Exception No. 2:   Dampers may be omitted in buildings equipped with an approved engineered smoke control system. The smoke control system shall respond automatically, preventing the transfer of smoke across the barrier, and shall be designed in accordance with Standard for the Installation of Air Conditioning and Ventilating Systems, NFPA 90A.

The requirements of 12-6.3.7.1 through 12-6.3.7.7 for subdividing building spaces through smoke barriers are illustrated in Figures 12-19 and 12-20.

During a fire the emergency evacuation of patients in an ambulatory health care facility could be an inefficient, time-consuming process. Realistically, if nonambulatory patients must be moved, only through horizontal travel can any number of occupants be relocated. Smoke barriers and horizontal exits used to subdivide a building serve three purposes fundamental to the protection of inpatients in that they:

1. Limit the spread of fire and fire-produced contaminants,
2. Limit the number of occupants exposed to a single fire, and
3. Provide for horizontal relocation of patients by creating an area of refuge on the same floor level.

Note that the combination fire/smoke dampers required in 12-6.3.7.7 may be omitted in buildings equipped with an engineered smoke control system which is designed to limit smoke transfer across the smoke barriers.

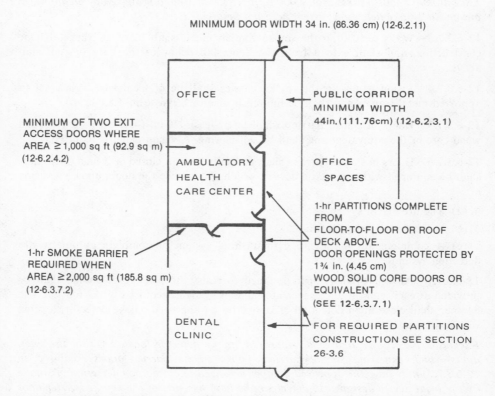

Figure 12-19. Subdivision Requirements for an Ambulatory Health Care Center.

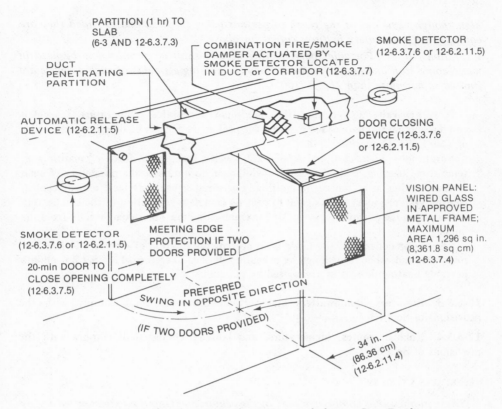

PARTITION (1 hr) TO SLAB (6-3 AND 12-6.3.7.3)

DUCT PENETRATING PARTITION

COMBINATION FIRE/SMOKE DAMPER ACTUATED BY SMOKE DETECTOR LOCATED IN DUCT or CORRIDOR (12-6.3.7.7)

SMOKE DETECTOR (12-6.3.7.6 or 12-6.2.11.5)

AUTOMATIC RELEASE DEVICE (12-6.2.11.5)

DOOR CLOSING DEVICE (12-6.3.7.6 or 12-6.2.11.5)

SMOKE DETECTOR (12-6.3.7.6 or 12-6.2.11.5)

20-min DOOR TO CLOSE OPENING COMPLETELY (12-6.3.7.5)

MEETING EDGE PROTECTION IF TWO DOORS PROVIDED

VISION PANEL: WIRED GLASS IN APPROVED METAL FRAME; MAXIMUM AREA 1,296 sq in. (8,361.8 sq cm) (12-6.3.7.4)

PREFERRED SWING IN OPPOSITE DIRECTION (IF TWO DOORS PROVIDED)

34 in. (86.36 cm) (12-6.2.11.4)

Figure 12-20. Smoke Barrier for a New Ambulatory Care Facility.

12-6.4 Special Provisions.   *(See Section 26-4.)*

12-6.5 Building Services.

12-6.5.1 Utilities.   Utilities shall comply with the provisions of Section 7-1.

12-6.5.2 Heating, Ventilating and Air Conditioning.

12-6.5.2.1   Heating, ventilating and air conditioning shall comply with the provisions of Section 7-2 and shall be installed in accordance with the manufacturer's specifications.

Exception: As modified in 12-6.5.2.2 following.

12-6.5.2.2   Portable space heating devices are prohibited. Any heating device other than a central heating plant shall be so designed and installed that combustible material will not be ignited by it or its appurtenances. If fuel fired, such heating devices shall be chimney or vent connected, shall take air for combustion directly from the outside, and shall be so designed and installed to provide for complete separation of the combustion system from the atmosphere of the occupied area. Any heating device shall have safety features to immediately stop the flow of fuel and shut down the equipment in case of either excessive temperature or ignition failure.

Exception No. 1:   Approved suspended unit heaters may be used in locations other than means of egress and patient treatment areas, provided such heaters are located high enough to be out of the reach of persons using the area and provided they are equipped with the safety features called for above.

Exception No. 2: Portable space heating devices shall be permitted to be used in nonsleeping staff and employee areas when the heating elements of such a device are limited to not more than 212° F (100° C).

It is generally agreed that the maximum acceptable temperature to which combustible materials may be exposed for prolonged periods of time is on the order of 160°F (71°C) to 190°F (88°C).

Paragraphs 12-6.5.2.1 and 12-6.5.2.2 specify safeguards for air conditioning, ventilating, heating, and other service equipment to minimize the possibility of such devices serving as a source of ignition. Fuel-fired heating devices, except central heating systems, must be designed to provide complete separation of the combustion system from the occupied spaces. Air for combustion must be taken directly from the outside.

The major concern of the *Code* is to prevent the ignition of clothing, bedclothes, furniture, and other furnishings by a heating device. Therefore, 12-6.5.2.2 prohibits portable heating devices in areas used by patients.

12-6.5.3 Elevators, dumbwaiters and vertical conveyors shall comply with the provisions of Section 7-4.

12-6.5.4 Rubbish chutes, incinerators, and laundry chutes shall comply with the provisions of Section 7-5.

REFERENCES CITED BY *CODE*

(These publications comprise a part of the requirements to the extent called for by the Code.*)*

NFPA 56C, *Safety Standard for Laboratories in Health-Related Institutions*, NFPA, Boston, 1980.

NFPA 56G, *Standard for Inhalation Anesthetics in Ambulatory Care Facilities*, NFPA, Boston, 1980.

NFPA 72A, *Standard for the Installation, Maintenance, and Use of Local Protective Signaling Systems*, NFPA, Boston, 1979.

NFPA 76A, *Standard for Essential Electrical Systems for Health Care Facilities*, NFPA, Boston, 1977.

NFPA 90A, *Standard for the Installation of Air Conditioning and Ventilating Systems*, NFPA, Boston, 1978.

NFPA 211, *Standard for Chimneys, Fireplaces, Vents, and Solid Fuel Burning Appliances*, NFPA, Boston, 1980.

NFPA 251, *Standard Methods of Fire Tests of Building Construction and Materials*, NFPA, Boston, 1979.

NFPA 256, *Standard Methods of Fire Tests of Roof Coverings*, NFPA, Boston, 1976.

REFERENCES CITED IN COMMENTARY

[1]NFPA 220, *Standard Types of Building Construction*, NFPA, Boston, 1979.

[2]NFPA 241, *Standard for Safeguarding Building Construction and Demolition Operations,* NFPA, Boston, 1980.

[3]NFPA 76A, *Standard for Essential Electrical Systems for Health Care Facilities,* NFPA, Boston, 1977.

[4]NFPA 90A, *Standard for the Installation of Air Conditioning and Ventilating Systems,* NFPA, Boston, 1978.

[5]NFPA 30, *Flammable and Combustible Liquids Code,* NFPA, Boston, 1981.

[6]NFPA 56A, *Standard for the Use of Inhalation Anesthetics (Flammable and Nonflammable),* NFPA, Boston, 1978.

[7]NFPA 56F, *Standard for Nonflammable Medical Gas Systems,* NFPA, Boston, 1977.

[8]NFPA 56C, *Safety Standard for Laboratories in Health-Related Institutions,* NFPA, Boston, 1980.

[9]NFPA 96, *Standard for the Installation of Equipment for the Removal of Smoke and Grease-Laden Vapors from Commercial Cooking Equipment,* NFPA, Boston, 1980.

[10]NFPA 253, *Standard Method of Test for Critical Radiant Flux of Floor Covering Systems Using a Radiant Heat Energy Source,* NFPA, Boston, 1978.

[11]NFPA 13, *Standard on Installation of Sprinkler Systems,* NFPA, Boston, 1980.

[12]NFPA 80, *Standard for Fire Doors and Windows,* NFPA, Boston, 1979.

13

EXISTING
HEALTH CARE
OCCUPANCIES

(See also Chapter 31.)

This chapter covers the requirements for existing health care occupancies. In previous editions of the *Code* these occupancies were known as "Institutional Occupancies."

Detention and correctional occupancies are now discussed in Chapters 14 and 15.

Health care occupancies are those used for purposes such as medical or other treatment or care of persons suffering from physical or mental illness, disease, or infirmity, and for the care of infants, convalescents, or aged persons. Health care occupancies provide sleeping facilities for the occupants and are occupied by persons who are mostly incapable of self-preservation because of age, physical or mental disability, or because of security measures not under the occupants' control.

Health care occupancies treated in this chapter include:

(a) Hospitals and
    Nursing homes
(b) Residential-custodial care
    Nurseries
    Homes for aged
    Mentally retarded care facilities
    Facilities for social rehabilitation
(c) Supervisory care facilities
(d) Ambulatory health care centers

SECTION 13-1   GENERAL REQUIREMENTS

13-1.1 Application.

13-1.1.1 General.

13-1.1.1.1   Existing health care facilities shall comply with the provisions of this chapter. (*See Chapter 31 for operating features.*)

Exception: Hospitals and nursing homes found to have equivalent safety. One such method for determining this equivalency is given in Appendix C.

Chapter 13 has been prepared for application solely to existing buildings. In previous editions of the *Code*, the sections dealing with existing health care occupancies made reference to provisions contained within the section dealing with new construction. In this edition, the sections dealing with existing facilities are complete and are intended to be applied without reference to the requirements for new construction.

This section is to be applied retroactively. Due consideration has been given to the practical difficulties of making alterations in existing, functioning facilities. The specified provisions, viewed as a whole, establish *minimum* acceptable criteria for life safety which reasonably minimize the likelihood of a life-threatening fire.

The requirements of Chapter 13 may be modified in instances of practical difficulty or where alternate, but equal, provisions are proposed. The modifications must provide an equivalent level of protection as would have been achieved by compliance with the corresponding *Code* provisions. An equivalency system has been incorporated in this edition in the *Code* and is located in Appendix C.

The equivalency system located within Appendix C uses numerical values to analyze the fire safety effectiveness of existing building arrangements or improvements proposed within existing structures. The system provides a method by which alternative improvement programs can be evaluated as options to literal *Code* compliance. In providing the Appendix C equivalency system, it is not intended to limit equivalency evaluations to solely this one system. The authority having jurisdiction retains the authority as expressed within Section 1-5 to evaluate and approve alternative improvement programs on the basis of appropriate supporting data. Appendix C may be used to assist in this evaluation.

13-1.1.1.2   This chapter establishes life safety requirements for the design of all existing hospitals, nursing homes, residential-custodial care and supervisory care facilities. Where requirements vary, the specific occupancy is named in the paragraph pertaining thereto. Section 13-6 establishes life safety requirements for the design of all existing ambulatory health care centers.

13-1.1.1.3   Health care occupancies are those used for purposes such as medical or other treatment or care of persons suffering from physical or mental illness, disease or infirmity; for the care of infants, convalescents or infirm aged persons.

13-1.1.1.4   Health care facilities provide sleeping accommodations for the occupants and are occupied by persons who are mostly incapable of self-preservation because of age, physical or mental disability, or because of security measures not under the occupants' control.

13-1.1.1.5   This chapter also covers ambulatory health care centers as defined in 13-1.3(e). See Section 13-6 for requirements.

13-1.1.1.6   Buildings or sections of buildings which house, or in which care is rendered to, mental patients, including the mentally retarded, who are capable of judgment and appropriate physical action for self-preservation under emergency conditions in the opinion of the governing body of the facility and the governmental agency having jurisdiction, may come under other chapters of the *Code* instead of Chapter 13.

13-1.1.1.7 It shall be recognized that, in buildings housing certain types of patients or having detention rooms or a security section, it may be necessary to lock doors and bar windows to confine and protect building inhabitants. In such instances, the authority having jurisdiction shall make appropriate modifications to those sections of this *Code* which would otherwise require the keeping of exits unlocked.

13-1.1.1.8 It shall be also recognized that some mental health patients are not capable of seeking safety without guidance.

13-1.1.1.9 Buildings or sections of buildings which house older persons and which provide activities that foster continued independence but do not include those services distinctive to residential-custodial care facilities [as defined in 13-1.3(c)] shall be subject to the requirements of other Sections of this *Code*, such as Chapter 19.

13-1.1.1.10 Health care occupancies shall include all buildings or parts thereof with occupancy as described in this chapter under Special Definitions, 13-1.3.

Paragraphs 13-1.1.1.2 through 13-1.1.1.10 contain explanatory material indicating some general characteristics of the occupants of health care occupancies. A few fundamental safeguards are also set forth. Formal definitions are established in 13-1.3.

Implied by the definitions of 13-1.3 and stated in 13-1.1.1.4, health care facilities are buildings which provide sleeping facilities (24-hour care) for occupants. Occupants in a health care facility may be restrained, but are housed *primarily* for treatment of mental or physical infirmities. Where occupants are restrained for penal or corrective purposes, the building would be classified as a detention and correctional occupancy which is treated in Chapters 14 and 15.

Where a building is used for the treatment or housing of mental patients (see 13-1.1.1.6) or aged persons (see 13-1.1.1.9) where:

1) Occupants are not restrained by locked doors or other devices, and
2) The patients are ambulatory, and
3) The occupants are capable of perceiving threat and taking appropriate action for self-preservation,

then the building may be classed as an occupancy other than health care.

Occupants of health care facilities are considered to be *incapable of self-preservation* (see 13-1.1.1.4) because of age, because of physical or mental disability, or because of security measures not under the occupant's control. A significant number of occupants in health care facilities are assumed to be nonambulatory or bedridden. Other occupants, who are capable of self-movement, may have impaired judgment (see 13-1.1.1.8).

Although locking exit doors and barring windows is always undesirable from the viewpoint of life safety, the *Code* recognizes that in some cases it is necessary to restrain people. In these instances, provision should be made for the continuous supervision and prompt release of restrained persons (see 13-1.1.1.7). Release of occupants should be accomplished by a system capable of automatically unlocking the doors in the means of egress, or by the presence of attendants who are continuously available and equipped with keys. In any event, continuous supervision is considered essential (see 13-2.11.4).

13-1.1.2 Objective. The objective of this chapter is to provide a reasonable level of safety by reducing the probability of injury and loss of life from the effects of fire with due consideration for functional requirements. This is accomplished by limiting the development and spread of a fire emergency to the room of fire origin and reducing the need for occupancy evacuation, except from the room of fire origin.

It should be recognized that only through control of a person's environment can the well-being of an individual be reasonably ensured. That is, only through complete control of the environment, including building members, building finishes, furnishings, decorations, clothing, linens, bedding, and the like, can the individual be protected against fire. However, no code can prevent injury resulting from a person's careless actions.

Although an effort should be made to protect the individual through prevention efforts, the primary objective of the requirements of Chapter 13 is to prevent fire from escaping the room of origin and thereby limit threats posed to individuals *outside* the room of origin.

13-1.1.3 Total Concept.   All health care facilities shall be so designed, constructed, maintained, and operated as to minimize the possibility of a fire emergency requiring the evacuation of occupants. Because the safety of health care occupants cannot be assured adequately by dependence on evacuation of the building, their protection from fire shall be provided by appropriate arrangement of facilities, adequate staffing, and careful development of operating and maintenance procedures composed of the following:

(a) Proper design, construction, and compartmentation;

(b) Provision for detection, alarm, and extinguishment; and

(c) Fire prevention and the planning, training, and drilling in programs for the isolation of fire, transfer of occupants to areas of refuge, or evacuation of the building.

Vertical movement of patients within a health care facility is an inefficient, time-consuming process. In one study, it was shown through the simulated evacuation of patients from a second-story ward to ground level that more than 30 minutes may be required for evacuation during a fire.

The provisions of Chapter 13, therefore, are based upon a "defend in place" philosophy which minimizes the probability of a fire necessitating vertical movement of occupants. Patients in critical care areas may be connected to life support equipment which makes movement difficult and, in some cases, impossible. Barriers are required to provide for the horizontal movement of patients to safe areas of refuge on a single floor level and to limit to a manageable number the number of occupants exposed to any single fire. Vertical means of egress (stairs or ramps) are specified by Chapter 13 as escape routes for visitors and staff and as a "last line of defense" for the movement of patients.

13-1.1.4 Additions, Conversions, Modernization, Renovation, and Construction Operations.

13-1.1.4.1   Additions shall be separated from any existing structure not conforming to the provisions within Chapter 13 by a fire barrier having at least a 2-hour fire resistance rating constructed of materials as required for the addition.

Paragraph 13-1.1.4.1 establishes separation criteria for additions to existing structures where existing structures do not conform to the provisions of Chapter 13. It should be emphasized where an existing building meets the provisions of Chapter 13, the building would be in compliance with the *Code* and the addition would not require separation.

Where additions must be separated, partitions must be constructed of assemblies providing 2-hours fire resistance. Where the structural framing of the addition or the existing buildings are of assemblies of less than 2-hours fire resistance, special provision should be made to assure the necessary separation will be maintained for the 2-hour period.

Materials used in the construction of the partition should be "constructed to the standards of the addition." That is, if the addition is required to be constructed of noncombustible or limited-combustible materials (Construction Types I or II), then the materials used in the partition must be limited-combustible or noncombustible as defined in NFPA 220, *Standard Types of Building Construction*[1]. Conversely, if the addition may be constructed of combustible materials, then combustible materials may be used as a portion of the partition. The addition must conform to the requirements of Chapter 12.

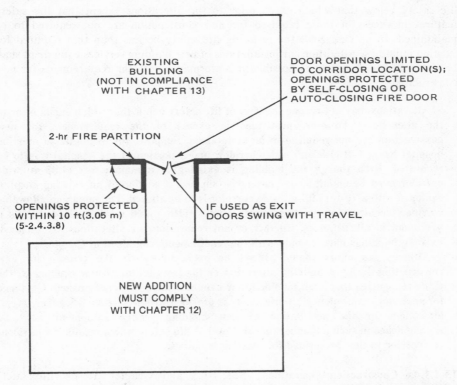

Figure 13-1. Separation of New Addition from Existing Building Not in Compliance with Chapter 13. If the addition is of fire-resistive or noncombustible construction, use noncombustible or limited-combustible materials in the 2-hour fire partition (see NFPA 220, Standard Types of Building Construction.)[1]

13-1.1.4.2 Communicating openings in dividing fire barriers required by 13-1.1.4.1 shall occur only in corridors and shall be protected by approved self-closing fire doors. (*See also Section 6-2.*)

13-1.1.4.3 Doors in barriers required by 13-1.1.4.1 shall normally be kept closed.

Exception: Doors may be held open only if they meet the requirements of 13-2.11.5.

Openings in barriers separating additions from nonconforming existing structures are limited to corridors (see 13-1.1.4.2). Openings are required to be protected by 1½-hour, "B" labeled, fire door assemblies. The fire doors are required to be self-closing and maintained closed, or may be held open by an automatic device in accordance with 13-2.11.5. See Figure 13-1.

13-1.1.4.4 Conversions. An existing building may be converted to a hospital, nursing home, or residential-custodial care facility only if it complies with all requirements for new health care buildings prior to occupancy as a health care facility. (*See Chapter 12.*)

13-1.1.4.5 Modernization or Renovation. Alterations shall not diminish the level of life safety below that which exists prior to the alterations except that life safety features in excess of those required for new construction are not required to be maintained. In no case shall the resulting life safety be less than that required for existing buildings. Alterations or installations of new building services equipment shall be accomplished as nearly as possible in conformance with the requirements for new construction.

Alterations may not reduce the level of life safety below that which exists prior to the alterations; however, provisions in excess of the requirements for new construction are not required to be maintained. Suppose, for example, an existing hospital has a 6-ft (1.83-m) wide corridor, and a portion of the hospital was to be renovated. Even though the building is existing, a minimum 6-ft (1.83-m) wide corridor must be maintained. Conversely, suppose a portion of an existing hospital equipped with a 10-ft (3.05-m) wide corridor is to be altered. The minimum allowable corridor (required for existing construction) width would be 8 ft (2.44 m). As a minimum, in all instances, whether or not renovations or alterations are planned, existing buildings must comply with the requirements contained in Chapter 13.

Although an effort should always be made to satisfy the criteria for new construction during a building alteration or the installation of new equipment, the *Code* recognizes that such modifications cannot always be accomplished. Guidance for achieving "equivalency" to life safety is provided within Section 1-5. In any event, alterations or the installation of new building service equipment must be accomplished in such a manner that the level of life safety which results is equivalent or superior to that prescribed for existing buildings.

13-1.1.4.6 Construction Operations. See 1-6.3 and Chapter 31 for life safety provisions during construction.

The introduction of "outside" workers and activities associated with the construction of an addition creates unusual risks of fire in health care occupancies.

Special precautions should be taken to guard against the potential exposure created by the introduction of flammable substances or by other hazardous practices which could pose a threat to occupants (see 31-1.1.2). Temporary fire-resistant barriers should be erected to separate the new construction and associated activity from the functioning areas of the existing buildings. Care should be taken to prevent blocking means of egress for the existing building by the construction of such barriers. Special care is also necessary to ensure that all existing equipment for fire protection and all portions of the required means of egress are maintained in full working order (see 1-6.3).

Adequate escape facilities should be provided and continuously maintained for the use of construction workers. See 31-1.1.1 and NFPA 241, *Standard on Safeguarding Building Construction and Demolition Operations.*[2]

13-1.1.5 Modification of Retroactive Provisions.

13-1.1.5.1 The requirements of this section may be modified if their application clearly would be impractical in the judgment of the authority having jurisdiction and if the resulting arrangement could be considered as presenting minimum hazard to the life safety of the occupants. The requirements may be modified by the authority having jurisdiction to allow alternative arrangements that will secure as nearly equivalent safety to life from fire as practical; but in no case shall the modification afford less safety than compliance with the corresponding provisions contained in the following part of this *Code*.

13-1.1.5.2 A limited but reasonable time shall be allowed for compliance with any part of this section, commensurate with the magnitude of expenditure and the disruption of services.

In some cases, appreciable cost may be involved in bringing an existing occupancy into compliance with Chapter 13. Where this is true, it would be appropriate for the authority having jurisdiction to formulate a schedule, determined jointly with the institution, which will allow suitable periods of time for correcting various deficiencies, and will give due consideration to the ability of the owner to secure the necessary funds.

13-1.1.5.3 Alternative protection, installed and accepted, shall be considered as conforming for purposes of this *Code*.

13-1.2 Mixed Occupancies.

13-1.2.1 Sections of health care facilities may be classified as other occupancies if they meet all of the following conditions:

(a) They are not intended to serve health care occupants for purposes of housing, treatment or customary access.

(b) They are adequately separated from areas of health care occupancies by construction having a fire resistance rating of at least 2 hours.

13-1.2.2 Ambulatory care (*see Section 13-6*), medical clinics and similar facilities which are contiguous to health care occupancies but are primarily intended to provide outpatient services may be classified as a business or ambulatory care occupancy provided the facilities are separated from health care occupancies by not less than 2-hour fire-resistive construction.

Exception: When the business occupancy or similar facility is intended to provide:

   (a) Services for hospital patients who are litter borne, or,

   (b) General anesthesia services,

the section shall meet all requirements for health care facilities.

Paragraphs 13-1.2.1 and 13-1.2.2 set forth criteria for classifying spaces as "other" occupancies, although they are located in buildings primarily used for health care purposes. Paragraph 13-1.2.1 would allow offices to be classified as business occupancies, cafeterias to be classified as places of assembly, dormitories to be classified as residential, etc., if both items (a) and (b) of 13-1.2.1 are met. If either item (a) or (b) is not met, then the area would be considered "mixed occupancy" and the provisions of 1-4.5 apply and require that the more restrictive life safety provisions apply. (See 1-4.5.)

Paragraph 13-1.2.2 covers a similar subject as 13-1.2.1, but specifically discusses ambulatory care centers, medical clinics, and similar areas which primarily provide outpatient services. If these facilities are separated by 2-hour fire-resistive construction, then they may be classified as ambulatory health care centers or as business occupancies, whichever applies. If, however, litter-borne inpatients are treated or general anesthesia is used, then the facility must meet the requirements for health care occupancies. The provisions of business occupancies and ambulatory health care centers were written around the concept that most people walk in and out.

Note that the 1981 Edition of the *Code* dropped the prohibition against using these spaces as part of the means of egress. Paragraph 13-1.2.4 will now allow this under certain conditions.

13-1.2.3   Health care occupancies in buildings housing other occupancies shall be completely separated from them by construction having a fire resistance rating of at least 2 hours; as provided for additions in 13-1.1.4.

Paragraph 13-1.2.3 requires that if a health care occupancy is located in a building of another classification (such as business, storage, mercantile, or industrial), the health care occupancy must be separated from the other occupancy by construction having a fire resistance of 2 hours, as detailed in 13-1.1.4. Also see the discussion following 13-1.1.4.

Note that 13-1.2.3 deals with occupancy classification and *not* with hazard of contents. Hazard of contents is treated in 13-1.2.6 and 13-1.2.7.

13-1.2.4   All means of egress from health care occupancies that traverse non-health care spaces shall conform to requirements of this *Code* for health care occupancies.

Exception: It is permissible to exit through a horizontal exit into other contiguous occupancies which do not conform with health care egress provisions but which do comply with requirements set forth in the appropriate occupancy chapter of this Code, as long as the occupancy does not have high hazard contents. The horizontal exit must comply with the requirements of 13-2.2.5.

Paragraph 13-1.2.4 specifies that the means of egress from health care occupancies which traverses non-health care spaces must conform to requirements for health care occupancies. However, an exception is provided where a 2-hour barrier is provided and such barrier is used as a horizontal exit. Where a 2-hour barrier serves as a horizontal exit, it is acceptable to exit into a different occupancy providing the "other" occupancy complies with the provisions of the *Code* which would be applicable thereto. For example, if a horizontal exit is provided between a health care facility and a business occupancy, inpatients may exit into the business occupancy through a horizontal exit. In this instance, corridor width, corridor partitions, stairway details, and the like must conform to the provisions set forth in either Chapters 26 or 27 which deal with business occupancies.

13-1.2.5 Auditoriums, chapels, staff residential areas or other occupancies provided in connection with health care facilities shall have exits provided in accordance with other applicable sections of the *Code*.

Auditoriums, chapels, and other areas separated by 2-hour construction and meeting the criteria of 13-1.2.1 and 13-1.2.2 for other occupancies are required to be designed in accordance with the appropriate occupancy chapter governing their use.

Nontypical health care spaces should have means of egress features designed in accordance with the use of the space. For example, if a space located in a health care facility is used as a chapel or auditorium with an occupant load in excess of 50, then it is considered a place of assembly. In such circumstances, doors in the means of egress should be sidehinged swinging doors, arranged to swing in the direction of exit travel (see 5-2.1.1.4.1), and should not be equipped with a latch or lock unless such a latch or lock is operated by panic hardware (see 9-2.11.1).

13-1.2.6 Any area with a hazard of contents classified higher than that of the health care occupancy and located in the same building shall be protected as required in 13-3.2.

Paragraph 13-1.2.6 regulates spaces in a health care facility which, although comprising only a portion of the facility, contain more hazardous materials (in quantity or type) than are usually found in most other spaces.

Spaces such as rooms used for the storage of combustible materials, trash collection rooms, gift shops, and paint shops must be protected in accordance with 13-3.2.

13-1.2.7 Non-health care related occupancies classified as containing high hazard contents shall not be permitted in buildings housing health care occupancies.

Paragraph 13-1.2.7 prohibits another occupancy (such as storage) with highly hazardous contents (such as flammable liquids) from being located in a building housing health care occupancies.

This paragraph limits use based upon *occupancy classification* with regard to hazard of contents. For example, the paragraph is *not* meant to exclude laboratory operations as a portion of a health care facility. The intent is to prevent a portion of a hospital from being converted or designed for use as an educational or research facility (classed as an educational or possibly an industrial occupancy) and having laboratories using and storing sizable quantities of flammable liquids larger than would be expected in a health care laboratory.

13-1.3 Special Definitions.

(a) **Hospital.** A building or part thereof used for the medical, psychiatric, obstetrical or surgical care, on a 24-hour basis, of four or more inpatients. Hospital, wherever used in this *Code*, shall include general hospitals, mental hospitals, tuberculosis hospitals, children's hospitals, and any such facilities providing inpatient care.

(b) **Nursing Home.** A building or part thereof used for the lodging, boarding and nursing care, on a 24-hour basis, of four or more persons who, because of mental or physical incapacity, may be unable to provide for their own needs and safety without the assistance of another person. Nursing home, wherever used in this *Code*, shall include nursing and convalescent homes, skilled nursing facilities, intermediate care facilities, and infirmaries in homes for the aged.

(c) **Residential-Custodial Care Facility.** A building, or part thereof, used for the lodging or boarding of four or more persons who are incapable of self-preservation because of age or physical or mental limitation. The following types of facilities, when accommodating persons of the above description, shall be classified as residential-custodial care facilities:

1. Nursery facilities that provide full-time care for children under 6 years of age.

2. Mentally retarded care facilities, including specialized intermediate care facilities for the mentally retarded.

3. Facilities in a home for the aging, that contain a group housing arrangement for older persons, that provide at least two meals per day and such social and personal care services needed by their residents, but that do not provide intermediate or skilled nursing care.

4. Facilities for social rehabilitation, such as those used for the treatment of alcoholism, drug abuse, or mental health problems, that contain a group housing arrangement, and that provide at least two meals per day and personal care services for their residents, but do not provide intermediate or skilled nursing care.

Facilities housing older persons, or mental patients, including the mentally retarded, who are judged to be capable of self-preservation with minimal staff assistance in an emergency, are covered by other chapters of the *Code*. (*See 13-1.1.1.6 and 13-1.1.1.9.*)

Children's facilities that do not provide lodging or boarding for their occupants are classified as Child Day-Care Centers, Group Day-Care Centers, or Family Child Day-Care Homes.

(d) **Supervisory Care Facility.** A building or part thereof used for the lodging or boarding of four or more mental health patients who are capable of self-preservation and who require supervison and who are receiving therapy, training or other health related care and who may have imposed upon them security measures not under their control.

(e) **Ambulatory Health Care Centers.** A building or part thereof used to provide services or treatment to four or more patients at the same time and meeting either (1) or (2) below.

1. Those facilities which provide, on an outpatient basis, treatment for patients which would render them incapable of taking action for self-preservation under

emergency conditions without assistance from others, such as hemodialysis units or freestanding emergency medical units.

2. Those facilities which provide, on an outpatient basis, surgical treatment requiring general anesthesia.

Paragraph 13-1.3(a) through (e) defines the characteristics of the occupancies covered by Chapter 13. To be classed as a health care occupancy, a building must house four or more *people incapable of self-preservation* on a 24-hour basis.

Occupants of hospitals or nursing homes are assumed to be nonambulatory and incapable of self-preservation. In making this judgment, due consideration should be given to the use of physical restraints and tranquilizing drugs which can render occupants immobile. Different staffing criteria and levels of care make differentiation between hospitals and nursing homes apparent. The difference between nursing homes and residential-custodial care facilities is not so clear.

Although residential-custodial care facilities house four or more occupants incapable of self-preservation, either because of age or physical or mental limitations, occupants are generally considered to be ambulatory and would require only limited assistance during emergency evacuation. Buildings which house mentally retarded occupants or persons being treated for alcohol or drug abuse who are ambulatory and may be expected to evacuate a structure with limited assistance would meet the criteria for residential-custodial care facilities. Day-care facilities which provide care for the aged, children, mentally retarded, or others would be classified as other than health care if the care or treatment is not provided on a 24-hour basis.

Although age, in itself, is not sufficient justification to develop a classification for a health care occupancy, it should be recognized that the elderly represent a unique fire problem. Experiences in buildings where the elderly are housed reveal that the reaction of the elderly to a fire may not be directed toward self-preservation. On discovering a fire, the elderly patient may ignore it, be transfixed by it, or seek refuge from it in his or her room and fail to notify anyone else of the fire. In some cases, the elderly have resisted efforts to remove them from the building and familiar surroundings.

A supervisory care facility houses occupants on a 24-hour basis who *are* capable of self-preservation and who are receiving health-related care, but who may have imposed upon them security measures which restrict freedom of escape. Where occupants are mobile but are housed for mental treatment and may at times be incapable of perceiving threat and taking action for self-preservation, such facilities should be classed as residential-custodial care facilities.

The intent of the definition of a supervisory care facility is to describe a condition where the patients involved can, with the unlocking of any locked doors, and/or the assistance and guidance of the staff, rapidly evacuate the building or move to an internal area of refuge. The authority having jurisdiction may require additional safeguards if this intent is not being met, or may classify as supervisory care those occupancy facilities involving some patients who are not individually capable of self-preservation if it is demonstrated to his or her satisfaction that the intent of the ability to rapidly evacuate all patients is present at all times.

In previous editions of the *Code*, occupancies which offered medical services on an outpatient basis would have been regulated within the chapter dealing with business occupancies. The threat to life in an outpatient facility where four or more patients may be subject to medical procedures requiring general anesthesia, treatments such as hemodialysis, or free-standing emergency service is significantly greater than that typical of a business occupancy. Conversely, application of the requirements expressed for health care facilities which contemplate 24-hour care would be inappropriate and would be unnecessarily restrictive. In establishing the occupancy classification of an ambulatory health care center, it was intended to develop requirements which fall between the restrictions applicable to business occupancies and the health care facilities in terms of level of life safety achieved.

13-1.4 Classification of Occupancy.   See Definitions 13-1.3.

13-1.5 Classification of Hazard of Contents.   The classification of hazard of contents shall be as defined in Section 4-2.

13-1.6 Minimum Construction Requirements.

Construction types permitted in existing health care facilities are summarized in Table 13-1. See NFPA 220, *Standard Types of Building Construction,*[1] for definitions of construction types. See Table 13-1.

Table 13–1.   Construction Types Permitted in Existing
Health Care Occupancies

	Stories			
Construction Type	1	2	3	Over 3
Types I-443, I-332, II-222 (Fire Resistive)	X	X	X	X
Type II-111 (Protected Noncombustible)	X	X*	X*	
Type II-000 (Unprotected Noncombustible)	X*	X*		
Type III-211 (Protected Ordinary)	X*	X*		
Type III-200 (Unprotected Ordinary)	X*			
Type IV-2HH (Heavy Timber)	X*	X*		
Type V-111 (Protected Wood Frame)	X*	X*		
Type V-000 (Unprotected Wood Frame)	X*			

X = Construction types allowed.
* = Automatic sprinkler protection required.

13-1.6.1   For the purpose of 13-1.6, stories shall be counted starting at the primary level of exit discharge and ending at the highest occupiable level. For the purposes of this section, the primary level of exit discharge of a building shall be that floor which is level with or above finished grade of the exterior wall line for 50 percent or more of its perimeter. Building levels below the primary level shall not be counted as a story in determining the height of a building.

Allowable building construction types are a function of the number of stories in a building. In determining the number of stories, the first story is considered to be the level of exit discharge. Only "occupiable levels" are counted in determining story height. For example, unoccupied attics would not constitute a story.

Difficulties have been experienced in determining story height where a building is located on a sloping grade. Paragraph 13-1.6.1 notes that a story on a sloping site which is partially below grade should be counted as a story if the floor is level with or above grade for 50 percent or more of the perimeter of the building at the exterior wall. See Figure 13-2.

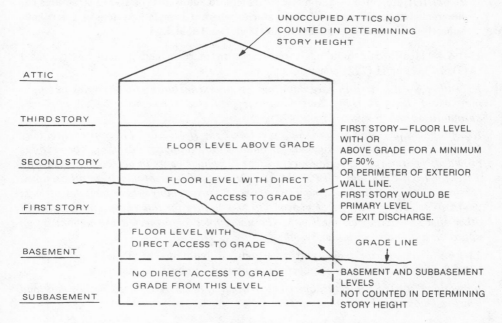

Figure 13-2. Building Section — Illustrates Application of 13-1.6.1.

13-1.6.2 Health care buildings of one story in height only may be of any type of construction. (*See 13-3.5 for automatic extinguishment requirements.*)

13-1.6.3 Health care buildings up to and including two stories in height may be constructed of Type I (443), I (332) or II (222) construction, Type II (111) construction, Type III (211) construction, Type V (111) construction, Type IV (2HH) construction, or Type II (000) construction. (*See 13-3.5 for automatic extinguishment requirements.*)

Exception: Any building of Type I or Type II (222 or 111) construction may include roofing systems involving combustible supports, decking, or roofing provided: (1) the roof covering meets Class C requirements in accordance with Fire Tests for Roof

Coverings, NFPA 256 and (2) the roof is separated from all occupied portions of the building by a noncombustible floor assembly which includes at least 2½ in. (6.35 cm) of concrete or gypsum fill. To qualify for this exception, the attic or other space so developed shall either be unoccupied or protected throughout by an approved automatic sprinkler system.

Multistory, nonsprinklered, health care facilities are required to be constructed of noncombustible materials with a minimum 2-hour fire resistance rating. It is recognized that movement of patients may not be possible and occupants of a health care facility may be required to remain in the structure for the duration of the fire. In specifying 2-hour fire resistance, it is intended that building members be adequately protected against fire effects to assure building stability for the projected fire duration.

An exception is allowed for two story buildings of "1-hour" construction *completely* protected by automatic sprinklers. In addition Type II-111 structures can be erected to a maximum of three stories where a complete system of electrically supervised automatic sprinklers is provided. See Table 13-1.

13-1.6.4 Health care buildings three stories or more in height shall be of Type I (443), I (332) or II (222) construction.

Exception No. 1:   Health care buildings up to and including three stories in height may be of Type II (111) construction if protected throughout by an approved automatic sprinkler system.

Exception No. 2:   Any building of Type I or Type II (222 or 111) construction may include roofing systems involving combustible supports, decking, or roofing provided: (1) the roof covering meets Class C requirements in accordance with Fire Tests for Roof Coverings, NFPA 256 and (2) the roof is separated from all occupied portions of the building by a noncombustible floor assembly which includes at least 2½ in. (6.35 cm) of concrete or gypsum fill. To qualify for this exception, the attic or other space so developed shall either be unoccupied or protected throughout by an approved automatic sprinkler system.

13-1.6.5 All interior walls and partitions in buildings of Type I or Type II construction shall be of noncombustible or limited-combustible materials.

Exception: Listed fire retardant treated wood studs may be used within non-load bearing 1-hour fire-rated partitions.

NFPA 220, *Standard Types of Building Construction,*[1] establishes restrictions relative to the use of combustible building materials within structures required to be constructed of noncombustible or limited-combustible materials. NFPA 220[1] should be consulted for specific limitations. The terms noncombustible and limited-combustible are defined within NFPA 220[1] and are repeated in Chapter 3 of the *Code* for quick reference.

Note that the exception allows listed fire-retardant treated wood studs within non-load bearing 1-hour fire-rated partitions. It does not allow them in 20-minute or 30-minute partitions since the studs would be exposed to fire sooner.

13-1.6.6 Openings for the passage of pipes or conduit in walls or partitions that are required to have fire or smoke resisting capability shall be protected in accordance with 6-2.2.8 or 6-3.6.

Fire and smoke may spread across a fire-rated barrier or fire-rated wall via openings created by the passage of pipes, conduit, or other building services. Paragraph 13-1.6.6 specifies where such penetrations occur, suitable appliances such as metal plates, masonry fill, or other products approved for the purpose must be installed to maintain the fire and smoke resisting capability of the partition.

13-1.6.7 Firestopping. Each exterior wall of frame construction and interior stud partitions shall be firestopped so as to cut off all concealed draft openings, both horizontal and vertical, between any cellar or basement and the first floor. Such firestopping shall consist of wood at least 2 in. (5.1 cm) (nominal) thick, or of suitable noncombustible material.

13-1.7 Occupant Load. The occupant load for which means of egress shall be provided for any floor shall be the maximum number of persons intended to occupy that floor, but not less than one person for each 120 sq ft (11.15 sq m) gross floor area in health care sleeping departments and not less than one person for each 240 sq ft (22.3 sq m) of gross floor area of inpatient health care treatment departments. Gross floor areas shall be measured within the exterior building walls with no deductions. (*See Chapter 3.*)

Paragraph 13-1.7 sets forth criteria for projecting occupant loads. The minimum occupant load for which exits must be provided in all buildings may not be less than that established by projections involving one person for each 120 sq ft (11.15 sq m) of gross floor area in health care sleeping areas, and not less than one person for each 240 sq ft (22.3 sq m) of gross floor area in inpatient health care treatment areas. However, if by actual count the number of persons exceeds that number projected by area calculations, then the actual number of persons present becomes the minimum population load for which exits must be provided.

The maximum number of people allowed to occupy a space is limited on the basis of available exit capacity and other functional considerations. It is not intended to limit populations based upon the area projections contained in this paragraph.

SECTION 13-2   MEANS OF EGRESS REQUIREMENTS

13-2.1 General. Every aisle, passageway, corridor, exit discharge, exit location and access shall be in accordance with Chapter 5.

Exception No. 1:   As modified in the following paragraphs.

Exception No. 2:   The requirements of Chapter 5 specifying net clear door width do not apply. Projections into the door opening by stops or by hinge stiles shall be permitted.

Means of egress details are to conform to the fundamental provisions expressed in Chapter 5, except as modified in Chapter 13. For example, see Exception No. 2 to 13-2.1. Exception No. 2 would continue to allow the width of exit doors to be measured on the basis of actual door leaf width. Projections into the door opening by the hinge stile and door stops are to be ignored in health care facilities. This is done since the larger widths specified in Chapter 13 were developed taking these projections into consideration. In addition, these larger widths inherently meet the requirements of Chapter 5.

13-2.2 Types of Exits. Exits shall be restricted to the permissible types described in 13-2.2.1 through 13-2.2.7.

Ramps are undesirable in hospitals and nursing homes due to the potential for accidents in both normal and emergency traffic, the exception being ramps with very gradual slopes which require so much space as to be impracticable in most building designs. Ramps are, however, the only practicable method of moving patients in beds from one story to another, except for elevators which may not be available during a fire. The best plan is to provide for horizontal egress to another section of the building, minimizing the need for complete evacuation.

13-2.2.1 Doors Leading Directly Outside the Building.   (*See 5-2.1.*)

13-2.2.2 Class A or B Interior Stairs.   (*See 5-2.2.*)

Exception: Any existing interior stair not complying with 5-2.2 may be continued in use subject to the approval of the authority having jurisdiction.

13-2.2.3 Smokeproof Towers.   (*See 5-2.3.*)

13-2.2.4 Outside Stairs.   (*See 5-2.5.*)

13-2.2.5 Horizontal Exits. A horizontal exit shall be in conformance with 5-2.4, modified as below:

(a) At least 30 net sq ft (2.79 sq m) per patient in a hospital or nursing home or 15 net sq ft (1.39 sq m) per resident in a residential-custodial care facility shall be provided within the aggregate area of corridors, patient rooms, treatment rooms, lounge or dining areas and other low hazard areas on each side of the horizontal exit. On stories not housing bed or litter patients, or in supervisory care facilities, at least 6 net sq ft (.56 sq m) per occupant shall be provided on each side of the horizontal exit for the total number of occupants in adjoining compartments.

(b) A door in a horizontal exit is not required to swing with exit travel as specified in 5-2.4.2.3.

(c) The total exit capacity of the other exits (stairs, ramps, doors leading outside the building) shall not be reduced below one-third that required for the entire area of the building.

In planning exits, arrangements should be made so that patients confined to their beds may be transferred from one section of a floor to another section of the same floor separated by a fire or smoke barrier. Where the building design will permit, the section of the corridor containing an entrance or elevator lobby should be separated from adjoining corridors by fire or smoke barriers. Such an arrangement, where the lobby is centrally located, will produce a smoke lock, placing a double barrier between the area to which patients may be taken and the area from which they must be evacuated because of threatening smoke and fire. Note that this is not required by the *Life Safety Code*, but is considered as good fire protection design.

Ramps may be the best means for providing egress from doors two or three steps above or below ground level (see **5-1.5**), and may also compensate for minor differences in floor levels between adjoining sections of buildings (also see **5-1.5**). Such ramps should be constructed in accordance with 13-2.2.6.

Because of practical difficulties involving vertical exit travel in health care facilities, special recognition is given to horizontal travel and the use of horizontal exits. Up to two-thirds of the total required exit capacity for a given fire area may be provided by horizontal exits [see 13-2.2.5(c)]. It should be noted, however, that every floor or fire section must be equipped with at least one exit consisting of a door leading directly outside the building, an interior stair, an outside stair, a smokeproof tower, a ramp, or an exit passageway (see 13-2.4.2). In other words, no fire area can be served only by horizontal exits. In the event a horizontal exit also serves as a smoke barrier, see the discussion of 13-2.4.2 and 13-3.7.

Paragraph 13-2.2.5(b) allows doors in horizontal exits in existing buildings to swing in the direction opposite of exit travel. This modification is based upon the assumption that in health care occupancies, there will be little possibility of a panic rush which might prevent opening the doors which swing against exit travel.

Further, it is recognized that corridors in existing health care occupancies may be 4 ft (1.22 m) wide, and it is therefore impossible in many instances to install a pair of doors in a horizontal exit. However, the 4-ft (1.22-m) corridor width will permit the opening of a single door against the flow of travel with minimal difficulty.

In the case of a fire barrier serving as a horizontal exit for two adjoining fire areas and where corridor widths will permit, a pair of doors arranged with each leaf to swing in a direction opposite from the other should be used. Each leaf in the pair of doors should be a minimum of 34 in. (86.36 cm) wide.

New horizontal exits in an existing facility are considered a renovation and must be installed in accordance with Chapter 12 to the extent feasible (see 13-1.1.4.5). The requirements for horizontal exits in 13-2.2.5(a) to (c) are illustrated in Figure 13-3.

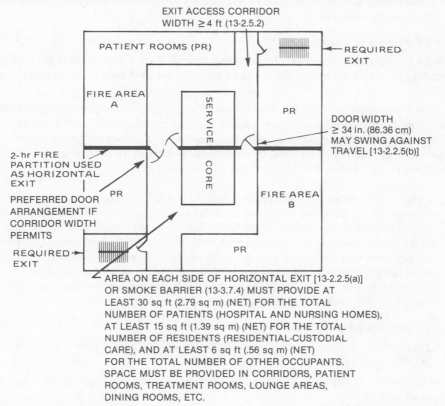

Figure 13-3. Horizontal Exits in an Existing Health Care Facility. If corridor width permits, the door arrangement as required by 13-2.2.5 should be provided.

13-2.2.6 Class A or B Ramps.   (*See 5-2.6.*) Ramp width shall be as specified in 13-2.5.2.

13-2.2.7 Exit Passageways.   (*See 5-2.7.*)

13-2.3 Capacity of Means of Egress.   (*See also 13-2.5.2.*)

13-2.3.1   The capacity of any required means of egress shall be based on its width as defined in Section 5-3.

13-2.3.2   The capacity of means of egress providing travel by means of stairs shall be 22 persons per exit unit; and the capacity of means of egress providing horizontal travel (without stairs); such as doors, ramps, or horizontal exits, shall be 30 persons per exit unit.

Exception: The capacity of means of egress in health care occupancies protected throughout by an approved automatic sprinkler system may be increased to 35 persons per exit unit for travel by means of stairs, and to 45 persons per exit unit for horizontal travel without stairs.

The exit capacities in 13-2.3.2 are substantially less than those specified in other parts of the *Code* dealing with exits for people in good health. In health care occupancies, it is assumed that some patients will not be able to escape from a fire without assistance, and that others will have to be transported on beds, mattresses, litters, or in wheelchairs.

13-2.4 Number of Exits.

13-2.4.1   At least two exits of the types described in 13-2.2.1 through 13-2.2.7, located remotely from each other, shall be provided for each floor or fire section of the building.

13-2.4.2   At least one exit from each floor, fire section or smoke compartment shall be a door leading directly outside the building, interior stair, outside stair, smokeproof tower, ramp or exit passageway. Any fire section, floor or smoke compartment not meeting these requirements shall be considered as part of an adjoining zone. Egress shall not require return through the zone of fire origin.

Figure 13-4 illustrates the application of 13-2.4.2. Each space created as a place of refuge by the provision of a smoke barrier or a horizontal exit must be provided with an exit which is arranged to discharge directly to the outside. If a fire section or smoke compartment is not provided with such an exit, the compartment would then be considered as a portion of an adjacent zone. The adjacent zone would be required to be equipped with a stair, smokeproof tower, ramp, or exit passageway which discharges to the outside. This arrangement will allow a person to escape without requiring travel back into the compartment of fire origin.

13-2.5 Arrangement of Means of Egress.

13-2.5.1   Every patient sleeping room shall have an exit access door leading directly to an exit access corridor.

Exception No. 1:   If there is an exit door opening directly to the outside from the room at ground level.

Exception No. 2:   One adjacent room, such as a sitting or anteroom, may intervene, if all doors along the means of egress are equipped with nonlockable hardware other

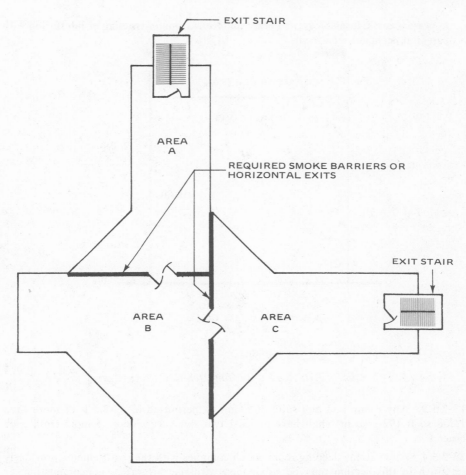

Figure 13-4. Arrangement of Exits in an Existing Health Care Occupancy Complying with 13-2.4.2. At least one exit is required from Area B consisting of a door to the outside, interior stair, outside stair, smokeproof tower, ramp, or exit passageway, or Area B is considered a part of Area A or C. Areas A and C would require an exit which discharges directly to the outside.

than provided in 13-2.11, and if the intervening room is not used to serve as an exit access for more than eight patient sleeping beds.

Exception No. 3:   Exception No. 2 above shall apply to special nursing suites permitted in 13-2.5.4 and suites in supervisory care facilities without being limited to eight beds or basinettes.

13-2.5.2   Any required aisle, corridor, or ramp shall be not less than 48 in. (121.92 cm) in clear width when serving as means of egress from patient sleeping rooms. It shall be so arranged as to avoid any obstructions to the convenient removal of nonambulatory persons carried on stretchers or on mattresses serving as stretchers.

Figure 13-5 illustrates an exit access corridor which complies with 13-2.5.2. The specified minimum of 48 in. (121.92 cm) leaves little safety margin. Care is necessary

to prevent carts, furnishings, and other materials from obstructing or interfering with potential occupant movement.

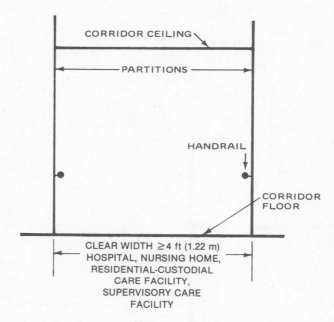

CORRIDOR CEILING

PARTITIONS

HANDRAIL

CORRIDOR FLOOR

CLEAR WIDTH ≥ 4 ft (1.22 m)
HOSPITAL, NURSING HOME,
RESIDENTIAL-CUSTODIAL
CARE FACILITY,
SUPERVISORY CARE
FACILITY

Figure 13-5. Corridor in Exit Access, Existing Health Care Occupancy (see 13-2.5.2).

13-2.5.3 Any room, and any suite of rooms as permitted in 13-2.5.1, of more than 1,000 sq ft (92.9 sq m) shall have at least two exit access doors remote from each other.

13-2.5.4 Any patient sleeping room which complies with the requirements previously set forth in this section may be subdivided with non-fire-rated, noncombustible or limited-combustible partitions, provided that the arrangement allows for direct and constant visual supervision by nursing personnel. Rooms which are so subdivided shall not exceed 5,000 sq ft (464.5 sq m).

Exception: In supervisory care facilities, such spaces continuously monitored by staff do not require direct visual supervision providing the space is equipped with an electrically supervised smoke detection system.

It is permissible to use sliding doors on individual cubicles within the suite.

In supervisory care facilities, the direct and constant supervision by staff is waived in consideration of functional requirements when a complete, electrically supervised smoke detection system is provided.

13-2.5.5 Every corridor shall provide access to at least two approved exits in accordance with Sections 5-4 and 5-5 without passing through any intervening rooms or spaces other than corridors or lobbies.

Exception: Existing dead-end corridors may be continued in use if it is not practical and feasible to alter them so that exits will be accessible in at least two different directions from all points in aisles, passageways and corridors.

Exit access corridors, aisles, and passageways should preferably be arranged so that exits will be accessible in at least two different directions from all points in the aisle, passageway, and corridor. However, in many buildings, dead-end corridors exist. The *Code* intends to allow dead-end corridors of moderate length to remain without correction.

In all instances, dead-end corridors up to 30 ft (9.14 m) may remain in use without correction. For dead-end corridors in excess of 30 ft (9.14 m), considerable judgment must be exercised in determining what constitutes an excessive dead-end pocket. Where a dead-end corridor is judged excessive, corrective action should be taken either by provision of additional egress facilities or by provision of other safeguards which result in an equivalent degree of safety. Alternative approaches might involve application of additional detectors, sprinklers, provision of smoke control and the like.

The provisions of 13-2.5.1 through 13-2.5.5 are illustrated in Figures 13-6, 13-7, and 13-8.

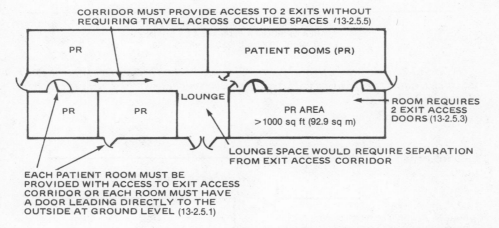

Figure 13-6A. Incorrect Arrangement of Exit Access in an Existing Health Care Facility. Lounge must not interfere with exit access.

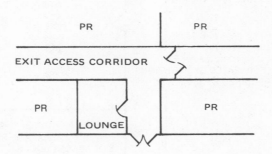

Figure 13-6B. Corrected Arrangement of Exit Access in an Existing Health Care Facility. Lounge is separated from exit access corridor as required by 13-2.5.5. See also 13-3.6.1, Exception Nos. 3 and 4 where a lounge or waiting space may be open to an exit access corridor.

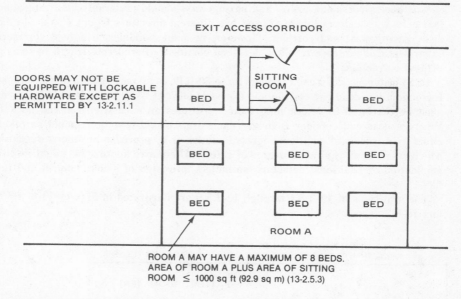

Figure 13-7. Exit Access from a Patient Sleeping Room Through an Adjacent Room, Existing Health Care Occupancy. This arrangement complies with 13-2.5.1, Exception No. 2, and 13-2.5.3.

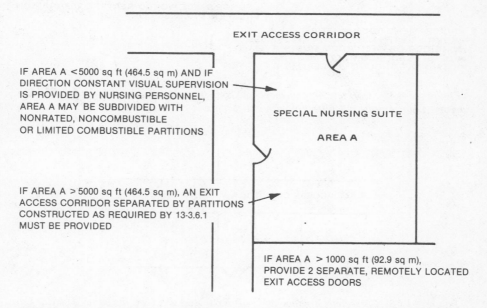

Figure 13-8. Exit Access From a Special Nursing Suite, Existing Health Care Occupancy. See 13-2.5.1, 13-2.5.3, and 13-2.5.4.

13-2.6 Measurement of Travel Distance to Exits.

13-2.6.1   Travel distance shall be measured in accordance with Section 5-6.

13-2.6.2   Travel distance:

(a) Between any room door required as exit access and an exit shall not exceed 100 ft (30.48 m);

(b) Between any point in a room and an exit shall not exceed 150 ft (45.72 m);

(c) Between any point in a health care sleeping room or suite and an exit access door of that room or suite shall not exceed 50 ft (15.24 m).

Exception: The travel distance in (a) or (b) above may be increased by 50 ft (15.24 m) in buildings protected throughout by an approved automatic sprinkler system.

Travel distance is only measured to the closest exit. It is not measured to the second exit required by 13-2.4.1. The requirements of 13-2.6.1 and 13-2.6.2 are illustrated in Figure 13-9. It should be noted that the 50-ft (15.24-cm) restriction within a room or suite only applies to sleeping rooms.

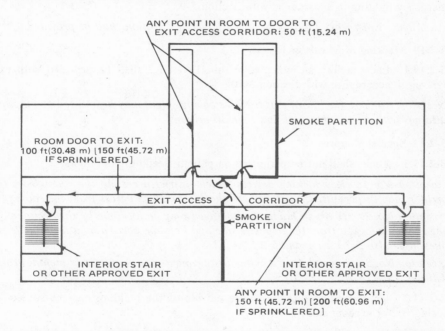

Figure 13-9. Maximum Travel Distance to Exits, Existing Health Care Occupancy. The distance is measured along the natural path of travel (see 5-6.2). "Sprinklered" means that the entire building is protected by a complete approved automatic extinguishing system. (Note that a room door in a smoke barrier must meet the requirements of 6-3.3 and 13-3.7.6 and be self-closing.)

13-2.7 Discharge from Exits.   *(See Section 5-7.)*

13-2.7.1   The exit discharge shall be arranged and marked to make clear the direction of egress. Required exit stairs that continue beyond the level of discharge shall be interrupted at the level of discharge by partitions, doors, physical barriers, or other effective means.

13-2.7.2   A maximum of 50 percent of the exits may discharge through areas on the floor of exit discharge in accordance with 5-7.2.

Exits should be continuously enclosed and should preferably be arranged to discharge directly to the outside at a grade. However, it is considered reasonable to discharge up to 50 percent of the required exit capacity from upper floor levels through the level of exit discharge subject to the qualifications expressed in 5-7.2.

13-2.8 Illumination of Means of Egress.

13-2.8.1   Each facility as indicated within 13-1.1.1.2 shall be provided with illumination of means of egress in accordance with Section 5-8.

13-2.9 Emergency Lighting.

13-2.9.1   Each facility as indicated within 13-1.1.1.2 shall be provided with emergency lighting in accordance with Section 5-9.

Exception: Emergency lighting of at least 1-hour duration shall be provided.

13-2.10 Marking of Means of Egress.

13-2.10.1   Each facility as indicated within 13-1.1.1.2 shall be provided with exit marking in accordance with Section 5-10.

Exception: Where the line of exit travel is obvious signs may be omitted in one story buildings with an occupancy of less than 30 persons.

13-2.11 Special Features.

13-2.11.1   Locks shall not be permitted on patient sleeping room doors.

Exception No. 1:   Key locking devices which restrict access to the room from the corridor may be permitted. Such devices shall not restrict egress from the room.

Exception No. 2:   Doors in homes for the aged may be lockable by the occupant, if they can be unlocked from the opposite side and keys are carried by attendants at all times. (See also 5-2.1.2.1.1 and 5-2.1.2.1.2.)

Exception No. 3:   Special door locking arrangements are permitted in mental health facilities. (See 13-1.1.1.7 and 13-2.11.4.)

13-2.11.2   Doors leading directly to the outside of the building may be subject to locking from the room side.

13-2.11.3   Doors within the means of egress shall not be equipped with a latch or lock which requires the use of a key from the inside of the building. (See 5-2.1.2.)

Exception No. 1:   Door locking arrangements are permitted in mental health facilities. (See 13-1.1.1.7.)

Exception No. 2:   Special locking arrangements in accordance with 5-2.1.2.1.5 are permitted on exterior doors.

Paragraph 5-2.1.2.1.5 sets minimum requirements for delayed release panic hardware.

13-2.11.4 The minimum width for evacuation purposes only for exit access door leaves from hospital, nursing home and residential custodial sleeping rooms, diagnostic and treatment areas, such as X-ray, surgery, or physical therapy; all door leaves between the spaces and the required exits; and all exit door leaves serving these spaces shall be at least 34 in. (86.36 cm) wide.

See Figure 13-10.

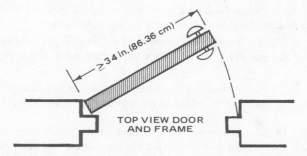

Figure 13-10. Minimum Width of Doors of Exit and Exit Access in Existing Health Care Facilities.

13-2.11.5 Any door in an exit passageway, stair enclosure, horizontal exit, a required enclosure of a hazardous area, or a smoke barrier may be held open only by an automatic release device which complies with 5-2.1.2.3. The following systems shall be arranged so as to initiate the closing action of all such doors by zone or throughout the entire facility:

(a) The manual alarm system required in 13-3.4 and either (b) or (c) below.

(b) A local device designed to detect smoke on either side of the opening, or

(c) A complete automatic fire extinguishing or complete automatic fire detection system.

13-2.11.6 Where doors in a stair enclosure are held open by an automatic device as permitted in 13-2.11.5, initiation of a door closing action on any level shall cause all doors at all levels in the stair enclosure to close.

Fire doors protecting openings in fire-resistant enclosures should preferably be maintained in the closed position. In existing buildings, fire doors protecting openings in exit enclosures, stair enclosures, horizontal exits, smoke barriers, or required enclosures for hazardous areas may be held open only by a device arranged to close the door automatically (see 13-2.11.5). The automatic closer must cause the doors to close upon operation of the manual fire alarm system and the activation of either a local device designed to detect smoke on each side of the opening or a complete automatic fire extinguishing or fire detection system.

It is especially important in health care facilities to maintain floor-to-floor separation. Doors protecting openings in a stair tower enclosure in an existing building may be held open as permitted above. Initiation of any automatic action which causes a door to close at one level must cause all doors at all levels in the stair enclosure to close and latch (see 13-2.11.6).

SECTION 13-3   PROTECTION

13-3.1 Protection of Vertical Openings.

13-3.1.1   Any stairway, ramp, elevator hoistway, light or ventilation shaft, chute, and other vertical opening between stories shall be enclosed in accordance with Section 6-2.2 with construction having a 1-hour fire resistance rating.

Exception No. 1:   Where a full enclosure of a stairway that is not a required exit is impracticable, the required enclosure may be limited to that necessary to prevent a fire originating in any story from spreading to any other story.

Exception No. 2:   Stairs that do not connect to a corridor, do not connect more than two levels, and do not serve as a means of egress need not comply with these regulations.

Exception No. 3:   Floor and ceiling openings for pipes or conduits when the opening around the pipes or conduits is sealed in an approved manner. (See 6-2.2.8.)

Paragraph 13-3.1.1 requires that vertical shafts (including stairways, ramp enclosures, elevators, light and ventilation shafts, chutes, and other vertical openings connecting stories) must be enclosed with barriers providing a minimum fire resistance of 1 hour. Openings must be protected by approved fire doors, complete with a closing device and a positive latch. Doors in stair tower enclosures may be held open as specified by 13-2.11.4 and 13-2.11.5.

When a stairway is not used as a portion of the means of egress, and full enclosure is not possible, the enclosure may be limited to that necessary to prevent fire or smoke originating in any one story from spreading to another story. For example, in a two-story building, the stair tower might be enclosed at the second floor level and open at the first floor level.

Exception No. 2 is illustrated in Figure 13-11.

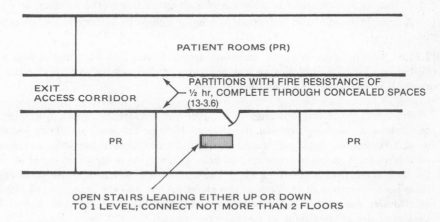

Figure 13-11. Open Stairs in Accordance with 13-3.1.1, Exception No. 2, Existing Health Care Occupancies.

Exception No. 3 will allow piping and conduit to penetrate floors without requiring an enclosed shaft. The floor penetration, however, must be adequately protected in an approved manner to maintain the required fire resistance of the floor system. The penetration must be sealed in a fashion which would minimize the transfer of smoke.

13-3.1.2 A door in a stair enclosure shall be self-closing, shall normally be kept in a closed position and shall be marked in accordance with 5-10.4.2.

Exception: Doors in stair enclosures may be held open under the conditions specified by 13-2.11.5.

13-3.2 Protection from Hazards.

13-3.2.1 Any hazardous areas shall be safeguarded by a fire barrier of 1-hour fire resistance rating or provided with an automatic extinguishing system in accordance with 6-4.1. Hazardous areas include, but are not restricted to, the following:

Boiler and heater rooms
Laundries
Kitchens
Repair shops
Handicraft shops
Employee locker rooms
Soiled linen rooms
Paint shops
Trash collection rooms
Gift shops

Rooms or spaces, including repair shops, used for storage of combustible supplies and equipment in quantities deemed hazardous by the authority having jurisdiction

Laboratories employing quantities of flammable or combustible materials less than that which would be considered severe.

Hazardous areas are spaces with contents which, because of their basic nature (as in the case of flammable liquids) or because of the quantity of combustible materials involved, represent a significantly higher hazard than would otherwise be typical of health care facilities.

A listing of typical hazardous areas is included in 13-3.2.1. Hazardous areas must be separated from other areas by 1-hour fire-resistant construction, complete with approved fire doors protecting door openings; otherwise, automatic sprinkler protection must be installed. Where automatic sprinkler protection is provided and the hazard is not severe, the hazardous area may be separated by nonrated partitions designed to resist the passage of smoke. See comments under the exceptions to automatic sprinkler protection in 13-3.6.1.

Provisions for the enclosure of rooms used for charging linen and waste chutes, or for the rooms into which chutes empty, are provided in Chapter 7. In addition to the fire-resistant cutoff of rooms into which linen chutes and waste chutes discharge, automatic sprinkler protection is considered essential.

Where flammable liquids are handled or stored, NFPA 30, *Flammable and Combustible Liquids Code*,[3] should be consulted to establish the minimum criteria necessary to mitigate this hazard. Rooms in clinical laboratories in which the unattended automatic processing of specimens with flammable solvents is likely to take place present a limited hazard which may be protected through use of sprinklers connected to the domestic water supply. Provisions for the use and storage of flammable gases and oxygen are covered in NFPA 56A, *Standard on Inhalation Anesthetics*,[4] and NFPA 56F, *Standard on Nonflammable Medical Gas Systems*.[5]

See commentary on 13-3.2.2 for discussion of laboratories.

13-3.2.2 Laboratories employing quantities of flammable, combustible, or hazardous materials which are considered as severe hazard shall be protected in accordance with *Laboratories in Health-Related Institutions*, NFPA 56C.

Laboratories which contain "ordinary" combustibles and flammable liquids in sufficient quantity to threaten a 1-hour fire separation — wood equivalent fuel loads in the range of 5 to 10 lb/sq ft (24.41 to 48.82 kg/sq m) — are considered a severe hazard. Laboratories representing a severe hazard must be protected in accordance with NFPA 56C, *Standard for Laboratories in Health-Related Institutions.*[6] Protection would include 1-hour fire resistance separation and automatic sprinkler protection.

Where fuel loads of lesser amounts are involved and quantities of flammable liquids are limited, laboratories would be simply considered a hazardous area, and would require either 1-hour separation or automatic sprinkler protection, as indicated in 13-3.2.1 and Section 6-4.

13-3.2.3 Cooking facilities shall be protected in accordance with 7-2.3.

Commercial cooking equipment must be installed and protected in accordance with NFPA 96, *Standard for the Installation of Equipment for the Removal of Smoke and Grease-Laden Vapors from Commercial Cooking Equipment.*[7] A regularly serviced, fixed, automatic fire extinguishing system would be required for the protection of cooking surfaces and exhaust and duct systems where cooking operations involve the potential for grease-laden vapors.

This paragraph would not apply to a room used as a staff lounge equipped with a domestic-type range or hot plate. Such a room would be considered similar to a treatment room and would require separation as indicated in 13-3.6.1.

13-3.3 Interior Finish.

13-3.3.1 Interior finish on walls and ceilings throughout shall be Class A or Class B, in accordance with Section 6-5.

Exception: In buildings equipped with a complete approved automatic sprinkler system, Class C interior finish may be continued in use on all walls and ceilings within rooms separated in accordance with 13-3.6 from the exit access corridors.

Existing interior finishes on walls and ceilings are limited solely on the basis of flame spread. Paragraph 6-5.1.5 exempts existing interior finishes from the limitations based upon smoke development.

Paragraph 6-5.3 makes provision for application of approved flame-retardant coatings to reduce flame spread characteristics of certain types of existing interior finish materials to an acceptable level. Refer to the commentary on 6-5.3 for additional guidance.

Where rooms are separated from corridors by barriers designed to retard the transfer of smoke and a building is completely protected by an automatic sprinkler system, Class C interior finish materials may be continued in use on walls and ceilings within the rooms so separated and protected.

13-3.3.2 Newly installed interior floor finish in corridors and exits shall be Class I in accordance with Section 6-5. No restrictions shall apply to existing interior floor finish.

Any new interior floor finish to be installed in corridors and exits within existing health care facilities is required to meet the criteria for Class I materials as indicated within 6-5.2.1. However, existing floor finish materials which have been previously evaluated and judged acceptable may be continued in use.

No restrictions apply to existing floor finish materials in areas equipped with an approved automatic sprinkler system. For example, if corridors are sprinklered, interior floor finish within the corridor is not subject to any flame spread restrictions.

13-3.4 Detection, Alarm, and Communication Systems.

13-3.4.1   Other than as noted below, required fire detection and signalling devices or systems shall be in accordance with Section 7-6.

13-3.4.2   Every building shall have a manually operated fire alarm system, in accordance with Section 7-6.

13-3.4.3   Operation of any fire alarm activating device shall automatically, without delay, accomplish the following:

(a) General alarm indication

(b) Control functions required to be performed by that device.

Zoned, coded systems shall be permitted.

13-3.4.4   The fire alarm system shall be arranged to transmit an alarm automatically to the fire department legally committed to serve the area in which the health care facility is located, by the most direct and reliable method approved by local regulations.

The alarm must automatically transmit to a point outside the facility. Where automatic transmission of alarms to the fire department legally committed to serve the facility is not permitted, arrangements should be made for the prompt notification of the fire department or for summoning other available assistance in the case of fire or other emergency. Acceptable means of automatic transmission of alarm are in the order of preference:
   a) A direct connection of the building alarm to the municipal fire alarm system
   b) Auxiliary contact to municipal alarm system
   c) A direct connection of the building alarm to an approved central station
   d) A telephone connection to a municipal or other alarm headquarters.

13-3.4.5   Internal audible alarm devices shall be provided and shall be installed in accordance with Section 7-6.

Exception: Where visual alarm devices have been installed in patient sleeping areas, they may be accepted by the authority having jurisdiction.

Internal, audible alarm devices are required by 13-3.4.5, but visual alarm devices may continue to be used in areas where the patients sleep, subject to the approval of the authority having jurisdiction. This exception assumes adequate continuous supervision by the staff to ensure that the alarm is recognized. The use of visual devices places heavy reliance upon the staff to sound the alert.

13-3.4.6   An approved automatic smoke detection system shall be installed in all corridors of supervisory care facilities. Such systems shall be installed in accordance with Section 7-6 and with the applicable standards listed in Section 7-6, but in no case shall smoke detectors be spaced further apart than 30 ft (914.4 cm) on centers or more than 15 ft (457.2 cm) from any wall. All automatic smoke detection systems required by this section shall be electrically interconnected to the fire alarm system.

Exception: Where each patient sleeping room is protected by such an approved detection system and a local detector is provided at the smoke barrier and horizontal exits, such corridor systems will not be required on the patient sleeping room floors.

13-3.4.7   Any fire detection device or system required by this section shall be electrically interconnected with the fire alarm system.

13-3.5 Extinguishment Requirements.

13-3.5.1   All health care facilities shall be protected throughout by an approved automatic sprinkler system. (*See 13-1.6 for construction types permitted.*)

Exception: Buildings of Type I (443), I (332) or II (222) construction of any height or Type II (111) construction not over 1 story in height.

> Requirements for automatic sprinkler protection in existing health care occupancies are summarized in Table 13-1. See NFPA 220, *Standard Types of Building Construction,*[1] for definitions of construction type. Where sprinkler protection is specified, complete building coverage, in accordance with the provisions of NFPA 13, *Standard for the Installation of Sprinkler Systems,*[8] is required.

13-3.5.2   Where exceptions are stated in the provisions of the *Code* for health care occupancies protected throughout by an approved automatic sprinkler system, and where such systems are required, the systems shall be in complete accordance with Section 7-7 for systems in light hazard occupancies and shall be electrically interconnected with the fire alarm system.

13-3.5.3   The main sprinkler control valve(s) shall be electrically supervised so that at least a local alarm will sound at a constantly attended location when the valve is closed.

13-3.5.4   Sprinkler piping serving not more than six sprinklers for any isolated hazardous area may be connected directly to a domestic water supply system having a capacity sufficient to provide 0.15 gal per minute per sq ft (1.02×10^{-4} cu m/s/sq m) of floor area throughout the entire enclosed area. An indicating shut-off valve shall be installed in an accessible location between the sprinklers and the connection to the domestic water supply. New installations in existing buildings where more than two sprinklers are installed in a single area, waterflow detection shall be provided to sound the building fire alarm system in the event of sprinkler operation. (*For sprinkler requirements for hazardous areas, see 13-3.2 and for sprinkler requirements for chutes, see 13-5.4.*)

13-3.5.5   Portable fire extinguishers shall be provided in all health care occupancies in accordance with 7-7.4.1.

13-3.6 Construction of Corridor Walls.

13-3.6.1 Corridors shall be separated from all other areas by partitions. Such partitions shall be continuous from the floor slab to the underside of the roof or floor slab above, through any concealed spaces such as those above the suspended ceilings, and through interstitial structural and mechanical spaces, and shall have a fire resistance rating of at least 20 minutes.

Exception No. 1:   In health care occupancies protected throughout by an approved automatic sprinkler system, a corridor may be separated from all other areas by non-fire-rated partitions, and where suspended ceilings are provided, the partitions may be terminated at the suspended ceiling.

Exception No. 2:   Corridor partitions may terminate at ceilings which are not an integral part of a floor construction if there exists 5 ft (152.4 cm) or more of space between the top of the ceiling subsystem and the bottom of the floor or roof above, provided:

(a) The ceiling shall have been tested as a part of a fire-rated assembly in accordance with Standard Methods of Fire Tests of Building Construction and Materials, NFPA 251, for a test period of 1 hour or more, and

(b) Corridor partitions form smoketight joints with the ceilings (joint filler, if used, shall be noncombustible), and

(c) Each compartment of interstitial space which constitutes a separate smoke area is vented, in case of smoke emergency, to the outside by mechanical means having sufficient capacity to provide at least two air changes per hour, but in no case having a capacity less than 5,000 cfm (2.36 cu m/s), and

(d) The interstitial space shall not be used for storage, and

(e) The space shall not be used as a plenum for supply, exhaust or return air except as noted in (c).

Exception No. 3:   Waiting areas may be open to the corridor, provided:

(a) Each area does not exceed 600 sq ft (55.74 sq m), and

(b) The area is located to permit direct supervision by the facility staff, and

(c) The area is arranged not to obstruct any access to required exits, and

(d) The area is equipped with an electrically supervised, automatic smoke detection system installed in accordance with 13-3.4.

Exception No. 4:   Spaces other than patient sleeping rooms, treatment rooms and hazardous areas may be open to the corridor and may be unlimited in area provided:

(a) Each space is located to permit direct supervision by the facility staff, and

(b) The space and corridors which the space opens onto in the same smoke compartment are protected by an electrically supervised automatic smoke detection system installed in accordance with 13-3.4, and

(c) Each space is protected by automatic sprinklers or the furnishings and furniture in combination with all other combustibles within the area are of such a minimum quantity and are so arranged that a fully developed fire is unlikely to occur, and

(d) The space is arranged not to obstruct access to required exits.

Exception No. 5:   Space for doctors' and nurses' charting, communications, and related clerical areas may be open to the corridor.

Exception No. 6:   Corridor partitions may terminate at monolithic ceilings which are designed and constructed to resist the passage of smoke and there is a smoketight joint between the top of the partition and the bottom of the ceiling.

Exception No. 7:   In a supervisory care facility, group meeting or multipurpose therapeutic spaces, other than hazardous areas, under continuous supervision by facility staff may be open to the corridor provided:

(a) Each area does not exceed 1,500 sq ft (139.35 sq m), and

(b) The area is located to permit direct supervision by the facility staff, and

(c) The area is arranged not to obstruct any access to required exits, and

(d) The area is equipped with an electrically supervised, automatic smoke detection system installed in accordance with 13-3.4, and

(e) Not more than one such space is permitted per smoke compartment.

13-3.6.2   Fixed wired glass vision panels shall be permitted in corridor walls provided they do not exceed 1,296 sq in. (.84 sq m) in area and are mounted in steel or other approved metal frames.

Exception: There shall be no restrictions in area and fire resistance of glass and frames in buildings protected throughout by an approved automatic sprinkler system.

13-3.6.3   Doors protecting corridor openings, in other than required enclosures of exits or hazardous areas, shall be substantial doors, such as 1¾-in. (4.45-cm) solid bonded core wood or of construction that will resist fire for at least 20 minutes. Doors shall be provided with latches suitable for keeping the door tightly closed and acceptable to the authority having jurisdiction. Fixed view panels of wired glass in approved steel frames, or other approved construction shown acceptable by fire test, limited to 1,296 sq in. (.84 sq m) in area, may be installed in these doors.

Exception No. 1:   In buildings protected throughout by an approved automatic sprinkler system, the door construction requirements noted above are not required but the doors shall be constructed to resist the passage of smoke. Doors shall be provided with latches of a type suitable for keeping the door tightly closed and acceptable to the authority having jurisdiction.

Exception No. 2:   In buildings protected throughout by an approved automatic sprinkler system, there is no restriction on the area of the vision panels in such doors, and the vision panels do not need to be wired glass, and there is no restriction in the type of frames.

Exception No. 3:   Door-closing devices are not required on doors in corridor wall openings other than those serving exits or required enclosure of hazardous areas.

Exception No. 4:   Doors to toilet rooms, bathrooms, shower rooms, sink closets and similar auxiliary spaces which do not contain flammable or combustible materials are exempt from these requirements.

13-3.6.4   Transfer grills, whether or not protected by fusible link-operated dampers, shall not be used in these walls or doors.

Exception: Doors to toilet rooms, bathrooms, shower rooms, sink closets and similar auxiliary spaces which do not contain flammable or combustible materials may have ventilating louvers or may be undercut.

The requirements of 13-3.6.1 to 13-3.6.4 essentially stipulate that all areas containing combustibles in sufficient quantity to produce a life-threatening fire must be separated from exit access corridors by partitions designed to resist the passage of smoke. The details of construction for such partitions vary depending upon whether or not automatic sprinkler protection is provided.

In nonsprinklered buildings, corridor partitions must be constructed of assemblies having a minimum fire resistance rating of 20 minutes. In establishing the 20 minute fire-resistive rating for corridor partitions, it is intended to require a nominal fire rating for assemblies where the fire rating of existing partitions cannot be documented. Examples of acceptable partition assemblies would include, but are not limited to, ½-in. (1.27-cm) ordinary core gypsum board, wood lath and plaster, gypsum lath, or metal lath and plaster.

Materials used in the construction of partitions are limited on the basis of the construction types allowed by 13-1.6.2, 13-1.6.3, and 13-1.6.4. All material used in the construction of Type I or Type II buildings must satisfy the criteria for noncombustible or limited-combustible materials (see 13-1.6.5).

Corridor partitions must be constructed continuously through all concealed spaces (e.g., to the floor or roof deck above a suspended "lay-in" ceiling). Where a monolithic ceiling is provided composed of noncombustible materials such as plaster or gypsum board having seams or cracks permanently sealed, thus forming a continuous horizontal membrane, partitions may be terminated at the underside of the ceiling (refer to Exception No. 6 to 13-3.6.1).

Openings in corridor partitions in nonsprinklered buildings must be suitably protected to maintain corridor separation. Glazing is limited to a maximum of 1,296 sq in. (8,362 sq cm) of wired glass set in approved metal frames. Preferably, but not required, each wired-glass panel should be limited to a maximum dimension of 54 in. (137.16 cm). The glass must be labeled ¼ in. (.635 cm) thick, and be well-embedded in putty with all exposed joints between the metal and the glass struck and pointed. See NFPA 80, *Standard for Fire Doors and Windows*.[9] A number of wired glass panels may be used in a single partition provided that each 1,296 sq in. (8,362 sq m) section is separated from adjacent panels by a metal mullion. The use of wired glass panels in a partition will reduce the fire-resistive capability of the partition in that there will be radiant energy transfer through the glass panel. The excessive use of wired glass panels, therefore, should be avoided.

Doors in corridor partitions are required to resist the penetration of fire for at least 20 minutes, be constructed of 1¾-in. (4.45-cm) solid bonded wood core, or be of equivalent construction. Doors must be equipped with a positive latch which cannot be held in the retracted position. The latch must be capable of holding the door in a closed position when subjected to stresses imposed by exposure to fire. Such doors are required to be installed in approved metal or "heavy wood" frames. Fixed wired glass vision panels installed in these doors may not exceed an area of 1,296 sq in. (8,362 sq cm) [maximum dimension of 54 in. (137.2 cm)], and must be set in approved metal frames. Labeled door frames and closing devices are not required except on doors protecting openings in exit enclosures or required enclosures of hazardous areas.

The use of exit access corridors as an exhaust, supply, or return air plenum for a building's air-handling system is prohibited. Corridor doors may not be undercut to facilitate transfer of air, nor are transfer grills allowed in corridor partitions (see 13-3.6.4) or corridor doors. See also 2-2.2 of NFPA 90A, *Standard for the Installation of Air Conditioning and Ventilating Systems*.[10] However, sink closets, bathrooms, and toilets may have doors equipped with a fixed grill or louver to provide make up air from the corridor for room exhaust systems. Where the door is equipped with a grill or louver, such spaces may not be used for the storage of flammable or combustible supplies.

Air-handling ducts penetrating corridor partitions should be adequately protected to preserve the 20-minute separation of exit access routes. Any space existing around ducts at the point of penetration of corridor partitions should be tightly sealed with a noncombustible material.

Where complete automatic sprinkler protection is provided, corridor partitions need not be rated, but must still be constructed to resist the passage of smoke. The materials for constructing the partitions must be selected on the basis of the construction types allowed by 13-1.6.2, 13-1.6.3, and 13-1.6.4. Where suspended ceilings are provided, partitions may be terminated at the suspended ceiling without any additional special protection if the suspended ceiling will resist the passage of smoke. The ability to resist the passage of smoke must be carefully evaluated. Doors protecting openings in partitions must be installed to resist the passage of smoke, but are not required to have a fire protection rating. Finally, there are no restrictions in terms of area or fire resistance for glazing used in corridor partitions in sprinklered buildings.

Exception No. 2 to 13-3.6.1 sets forth additional criteria for terminating corridor partitions at ceilings, including the "lay-in" type. Partitions may be terminated at a ceiling which has been tested as a portion of an assembly having a fire resistance rating of 1 hour or more. Each compartment located above such a ceiling must be equipped with an automatic mechanical smoke exhaust system, capable of providing a minimum of two air changes per hour but exhausting not less than 5,000 cu ft/min (2.36 cu m/sec). See the additional criteria in items (a) through (e) of Exception No. 2.

Subject to certain restrictions, a few specific areas may be open to the corridor. It is assumed that these spaces will have limited fuel loads in terms of quantity and continuity so as to inherently limit fire exposure. Exception Nos. 3, 4, 5, and 7 to 13-3.6.1 set forth specific areas which may be open to corridors. However, patient sleeping rooms, treatment rooms, and hazardous areas must be separated by partitions.

For example, Exception No. 4 says that waiting spaces, lounges, and other similar spaces may be open to corridors on floors with rooms where patients sleep, or on floors used for other purposes. Each waiting space must be located to permit direct visual supervision by staff. A waiting space must also be located and arranged so that its furnishing will not interfere with or obstruct access to any required exits. The number of waiting areas open to the corridor in each smoke compartment is not limited. The spaces and the corridor to which the spaces open within each smoke compartment must be equipped with an electrically supervised, automatic, smoke detection system. The area of the open space is not limited. However, each space must be provided with automatic sprinkler protection or the furnishings and furniture in combination with all other available fuels (combustibles) must be adequately restricted so a fire will be self-limiting. In making use of the fuel limiting technique, combustibles must be of a minimum quantity and adequately separated so that a fire will remain limited to the object of origin. Combustibles must be arranged and limited to a type to prevent full room involvement.

Areas used for charting and communication by doctors and nurses may be open to the corridor.

It is important to note that the installation of new corridor walls is considered a renovation, and such walls must comply with Chapter 12 to the extent feasible (see 13-1.1.4.5).

13-3.7 Subdivision of Building Spaces.

13-3.7.1 Smoke barriers shall be provided, regardless of building construction, as follows:

(a) To divide every story, used for sleeping rooms for more than 30 health care occupants, into at least two compartments, and

(b) To limit on any story the maximum area of each smoke compartment to no more than 22,500 sq ft (2090 sq m), of which both length and width shall be no more than 150 ft (45.72 m).

It is *not* the intent of item (b) to require that the length and width be added together with the resulting sum being 150 ft (45.72 m) or less. It is the intent that the length be 150 ft (45.72 m) or less, and that the width be 150 ft (45.72 m) or less.

Exception: Protection may be accomplished in conjunction with the provision of horizontal exits.

13-3.7.2 Smoke barriers shall be provided on stories which are usable but unoccupied.

13-3.7.3 Any required smoke barrier shall be constructed in accordance with Section 6-3 and shall have a fire resistance rating of at least ½ hour.

13-3.7.4 At least 30 net sq ft (2.79 sq m) per patient in a hospital or nursing home or 15 net sq ft (1.39 sq m) per resident in a residential-custodial care facility shall be provided within the aggregate area of corridors, patient rooms, treatment rooms, lounge or dining areas and other low hazard areas on each side of the smoke barrier. On stories not housing bed or litter patients or in supervisory care facilities at least 6 net sq ft (.56 sq m) per occupant shall be provided on each side of the smoke barrier for the total number of occupants in adjoining compartments.

13-3.7.5 Openings in smoke barriers shall be protected by wired glass panels in steel frames, by doors of 20-minute fire protection rating, or by 1¾-in. (4.45-cm) solid bonded wood core doors as a minimum.

Exception: Doors may have wired glass vision panels installed in approved metal frames not exceeding 1,296 sq in. (.84 sq m).

13-3.7.6 Doors in smoke barriers shall comply with Section 6-3 and shall be self-closing. Such doors in smoke barriers shall not be required to swing with exit travel.

Exception: Doors may be held open only if they meet the requirements of 13-2.11.5.

13-3.7.7 An approved damper designed to resist the passage of smoke shall be provided at each point a duct penetrates a smoke barrier required by 13-3.7.1. The damper shall close upon detection of smoke by an approved smoke detector, located within the duct. (*See also Section 6-3.*)

Exception No. 1: In lieu of an approved smoke detector located within the duct, ducts which penetrate smoke barriers above smoke barrier doors (required by

13-3.7.5) may have the approved damper arranged to close upon detection of smoke by the local device designed to detect smoke on either side of the smoke barrier door opening.

Exception No. 2:   Dampers may be omitted in buildings equipped with an approved engineered smoke control system. The smoke control system shall respond automatically, preventing the transfer of smoke across the smoke barrier and shall be designed in accordance with Standard for the Installation of Air Conditioning and Ventilating Systems, NFPA 90A.

Exception No. 3:   Dampers may be omitted where openings in ducts are limited to a single smoke compartment and the ducts are of steel construction.

The requirements of 13-3.7.1 through 13-3.7.7 for subdividing building spaces through smoke barriers are illustrated in Figures 13-12 through 13-14. Paragraph 13-2.2.5 discusses horizontal exits.

During the fire the emergency evacuation of patients in a health care facility is an inefficient, time-consuming process. Realistically, if patients must be moved, only through horizontal travel can sizable numbers of occupants be relocated. Smoke barriers and horizontal exits used to subdivide a building serve three purposes fundamental to the protection of inpatients in that they:

1. Limit the spread of fire and fire-produced contaminants,
2. Limit the number of occupants exposed to a single fire, and
3. Provide for horizontal relocation of patients by creating an area of refuge on the same floor level.

Note that the combination fire/smoke dampers required in 13-3.7.7 may be omitted in buildings equipped with an engineered smoke control system which is designed to limit smoke transfer across the smoke barriers.

A few noteworthy differences exist between the requirements of 12-3.7 and 13-3.7. In existing health care occupancies:

1. Each story, with sleeping accommodations for more than 30 health care occupants, must be divided into at least two compartments by a smoke barrier.
2. Each story must be subdivided by a smoke barrier into areas of not more than 22,500 sq ft (2,090 sq m), both the length and the width not exceeding 150 ft (45.72 m). Such subdivision is required throughout all portions of a building classed as either a hospital, nursing home, residential-custodial care, or supervisory care facility.
3. Smoke barriers must be constructed of assemblies providing a fire resistance of at least ½ hour, constructed continuously from outside wall to outside wall through concealed spaces; for example, above suspended ceilings.
4. Doors protecting openings in smoke barriers must, as a minimum, have a 20-minute fire protection rating, or be of 1¾-in. (4.45-cm) solid bonded wood core construction. Latching hardware is not required.
5. Openings in smoke barriers may be protected by fixed wired glass panels set in metal frames. Such panels may not exceed a maximum of 1,296 sq in. (8,362 sq cm).
6. Doors in smoke barriers are required to be self-closing, but may be held open if the criteria of 13-2.11.4 are satisfied. Doors in smoke barriers are not required to swing in the direction of exit travel, although this is desirable.
7. Vision panels are not required in existing smoke barrier doors. However, if provided, they must be of wired glass in approved metal frames.

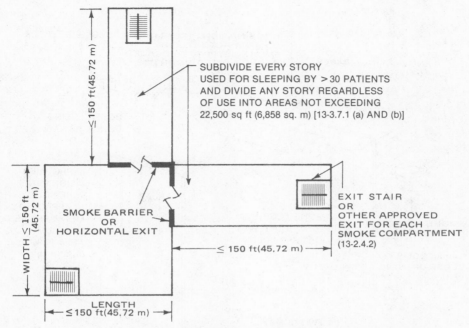

Figure 13-12. Subdivision of Building Spaces, Existing Health Care Occupancies.

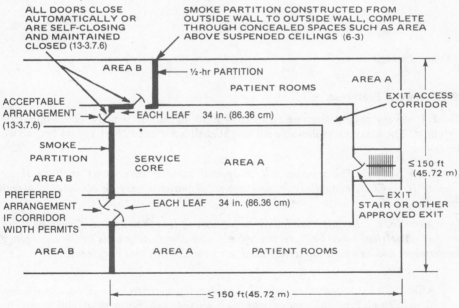

Figure 13-13. Subdivision of Building Spaces, Existing Health Care Occupancies.

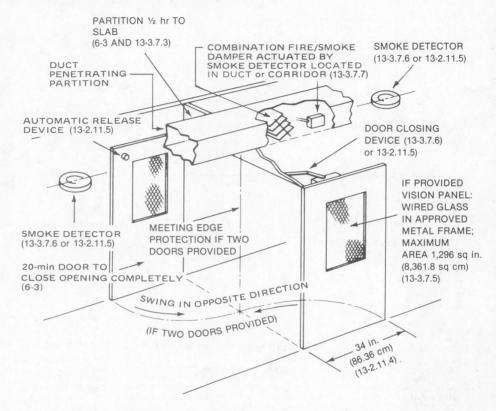

PARTITION ½ hr TO
SLAB
(6-3 AND 13-3.7.3)

DUCT
PENETRATING
PARTITION

COMBINATION FIRE/SMOKE
DAMPER ACTUATED BY
SMOKE DETECTOR LOCATED
IN DUCT or CORRIDOR (13-3.7.7)

SMOKE DETECTOR
(13-3.7.6 or 13-2.11.5)

AUTOMATIC RELEASE
DEVICE (13-2.11.5)

DOOR CLOSING
DEVICE (13-3.7.6)
or 13-2.11.5)

IF PROVIDED
VISION PANEL:
WIRED GLASS
IN APPROVED
METAL FRAME;
MAXIMUM
AREA 1,296 sq in.
(8,361.8 sq cm)
(13-3.7.5)

SMOKE DETECTOR
(13-3.7.6 or 13-2.11.5)

MEETING EDGE
PROTECTION IF TWO
DOORS PROVIDED

20-min DOOR TO
CLOSE OPENING COMPLETELY
(6-3)

SWING IN OPPOSITE DIRECTION

(IF TWO DOORS PROVIDED)

34 in.
(86.36 cm)
(13-2.11.4)

Figure 13-14. Smoke Barrier for Existing Health Care Occupancy.

13-3.8 Special Features.

13-3.8.1   Every patient sleeping room shall have an outside window or outside door with light. The maximum allowable sill height shall not exceed 36 in. (91.44 cm) above the floor.

Exception No. 1:   The window sill in special nursing care areas such as those housing ICU, CCU, hemodialysis, and neo-natal patients may be 60 in. (152.4 cm) above the floor.

Exception No. 2:   Rooms intended for occupancy of less than 24 hours, such as those housing obstetrical labor beds, recovery beds, and observation beds in the emergency department; and newborn nurseries, need not comply with this requirement.

Although 13-3.8.1 requires each patient sleeping room to have an outside window or door with glazing, the window may have a fixed sash. Security glazing should be avoided. Glazing should be of a type which can be broken out should such action become necessary in a fire emergency. Glazing should be limited to a type which, if broken out, will not develop sharp edges posing a threat to occupants outside the building at grade.

SECTION 13-4   SPECIAL PROVISIONS

13-4.1 Windowless Buildings. See Section 30-7 for requirements for windowless buildings.

Windowless portions of health care facilities must comply with the requirements of Chapter 13 in addition to the criteria set forth for such structures in Section 30-7. Paragraph 13-4.1 does not obviate the requirements for patient room windows contained within 13-3.8.1.

SECTION 13-5   BUILDING SERVICES

13-5.1 Utilities.   Utilities shall comply with the provisions of Section 7-1.

13-5.2 Heating, Ventilating and Air Conditioning.

13-5.2.1   Heating, ventilating and air conditioning shall comply with the provisions of Section 7-2 and shall be installed in accordance with the manufacturer's specifications.

Exception: As modified in 13-5.2.2 following.

13-5.2.2   Portable space heating devices are prohibited. Any heating device other than a central heating plant shall be so designed and installed that combustible material will not be ignited by it or its appurtenances. If fuel fired, such heating devices shall be chimney or vent connected, shall take air for combustion directly from the outside, and shall be so designed and installed to provide for complete separation of the combustion system from the atmosphere of the occupied area. Any heating device shall have safety features to immediately stop the flow of fuel and shut down the equipment in case of either excessive temperature or ignition failure.

Exception No. 1:   Approved suspended unit heaters may be used in locations other than means of egress and patient sleeping areas, provided such heaters are located high enough to be out of the reach of persons using the area and provided they are equipped with the safety features called for above.

Exception No. 2:   Fireplaces may be installed and used only in areas other than patient sleeping areas, provided that these areas are separated from patient sleeping spaces by construction having a 1-hour fire resistance rating and they comply with Standard for Chimneys, Fireplaces and Vents, NFPA 211. In addition thereto, the fireplace shall be equipped with a heat tempered glass, or other approved material, fireplace enclosure guaranteed against breakage up to a temperature of 650°F (343.33°C). If, in the opinion of the authority having jurisdiction, special hazards are present, a lock on the enclosure and other safety precautions may be required.

Exception No. 3:   Portable space heating devices shall be permitted to be used in nonsleeping staff and employee areas when the heating elements of such a device are limited to not more than 212°F (100°C).

It is generally agreed that the maximum acceptable temperature to which combustible materials may be exposed for prolonged periods of time is on the order of 160°F (71°C) to 190°F (88°C).

Paragraphs 13-5.2.1 and 13-5.2.2 specify safeguards for air conditioning, ventilating, heating, and other service equipment to minimize the possibility of such devices serving as a source of ignition. Fuel-fired heating devices, except central heating systems, must be designed to provide complete separation of the combustion system from the occupied spaces. Air for combustion must be taken directly from the outside.

A major concern of the *Code* is to prevent the ignition of clothing, bedclothes, furniture, and other furnishings by a heating device. Therefore, 13-5.2.2 prohibits portable heating devices in areas used by patients.

13-5.3 Elevators, dumbwaiters, and vertical conveyors shall comply with the provisions of Section 7-4.

Although not counted as a required exit, elevators may constitute a valuable supplemental facility for evacuating patients from health care buildings. In some cases, movement of critically ill patients or patients in restraining devices may be realistically accomplished only by an elevator.

Elevators, however, have many inherent weaknesses which tend to limit reliability. Elevator access doors are designed with operating tolerances which permit smoke transfer into the shaft. Power failure during a fire could result in trapping persons on elevators which stop between floors. Elevators may, during their descent from upper floors, stop automatically at the floor of the fire, allow the doors to open, and expose the occupants.

Many of these weaknesses can be minimized by providing emergency power, separating the elevator lobby from other building spaces by rated construction, designing detection and alarm equipment to prevent elevators from stopping at a floor exposed to a fire, providing an emergency smoke control system, and by pressurizing the elevator shaft and adjacent lobbies (see Section 7-3). This represents good fire protection judgment, but is not the result of any requirements of this *Code*.

Through emergency planning and staff training, crowding of elevators (another potential problem) may be avoided. Emergency plans may make effective use of elevators by transferring patients through a horizontal exit, for example, to a separate fire area. Within the separate fire area, a staged evacuation program could be instituted, the elevators ultimately taking patients to the outside at ground level.

13-5.4 Rubbish Chutes, Incinerators and Laundry Chutes.

13-5.4.1 Any existing linen and trash chute, including pneumatic rubbish and linen systems, which opens directly onto any corridor shall be sealed by fire-resistive construction to prevent further use or shall be provided with a fire door assembly suitable for a Class B location and having a fire protection rating of 1½ hours. All new chutes shall comply with Section 7-5.

13-5.4.2 Any rubbish chute or linen chute, including pneumatic rubbish and linen systems, shall be provided with automatic extinguishing protection installed in accordance with *Standard for the Installation of Sprinkler Systems*, NFPA 13 (*see Section 7-5*).

13-5.4.3 Any trash chute shall discharge into a trash collecting room used for no other purpose and protected in accordance with Section 6-4.

13-5.4.4 Existing flue-fed incinerators shall be sealed by fire-resistive construction to prevent further use.

SECTION 13-6   EXISTING AMBULATORY HEALTH CARE CENTERS

13-6.1 General Requirements.

13-6.1.1 Application.

13-6.1.1.1   Existing ambulatory health care centers shall comply with the provisions of both Chapter 27 and (this) Section 13-6, as may be more stringent.

13-6.1.1.2   This section establishes life safety requirements, in addition to those required in Chapter 27, for the design of all ambulatory health care centers and outpatient surgical centers which meet the requirements of 13-1.3(e).

Ambulatory health care centers exhibit some of the occupancy characteristics of business occupancies and some of the characteristics of health care facilities. In developing Section 13-6, it was intended to prescribe a level of life safety from fire which would be greater than that typically specified for business occupancies, but less than that typically found in health care facilities. See commentary for 13-1.3.

Ambulatory health care centers are required to comply with the provisions of Chapter 27 pertaining to business occupancies, except as more restrictive provisions are established within Section 13-6.

13-6.1.1.3 Modification of Retroactive Provisions.

13-6.1.1.3.1   The requirements of this section may be modified if their application clearly would be impractical in the judgment of the authority having jurisdiction and if the resulting arrangement could be considered as presenting minimum hazard to the life safety of the occupants. The requirements may be modified by the authority having jurisdiction to allow alternative arrangements that will secure as nearly equivalent safety to life from fire as practical; but in no case shall the modification afford less safety than compliance with the corresponding provisions contained in the following part of this *Code*.

Chapter 13 has been prepared for application solely to existing buildings. In previous editions of the *Code*, the sections dealing with existing health care occupancies made reference to provisions contained within the section dealing with new construction. In this edition, the sections dealing with existing facilities are complete and are intended to be applied without reference to the requirements for new construction.

This section is to be applied retroactively. Due consideration has been given to the practical difficulties of making alterations in existing, functioning facilities. The specified provisions, viewed as a whole, establish *minimum* acceptable criteria for life safety which reasonably minimizes the likelihood of a life-threatening fire.

The requirements of Chapter 13 may be modified in instances of practical difficulty or where alternate, but equal, provisions are proposed. The modifications must provide an equivalent level of protection as would be achieved by compliance with the corresponding *Code* provisions.

13-6.1.1.3.2   A limited but reasonable time shall be allowed for compliance with any part of this section, commensurate with the magnitude of expenditure and the disruption of services.

In some cases appreciable cost may be involved in bringing an existing occupancy into compliance with Section 13-1. Where this is true, it would be appropriate for the authority having jurisdiction to formulate a schedule, determined jointly with the institution, which will allow suitable periods of time for correcting various deficiencies, and which gives due consideration to the ability of the owner to secure the necessary funds.

13-6.1.1.3.3 Alternative protection installed and accepted shall be considered as conforming for the purposes of this *Code*.

13-6.1.2 Reserved.

13-6.1.3 Special Definitions. *(See 13-1.3.)*

13-6.1.4 Classification of Occupancy. *(See 13-1.3.)*

13-6.1.5 Reserved.

13-6.1.6 Minimum Construction Requirements.

13-6.1.6.1 For purposes of 13-6.1.6, stories shall be counted starting at the primary level of exit discharge and ending at the highest occupiable level. For the purposes of this section, the primary level of exit discharge of a building shall be that floor which is level with or above finished grade of this exterior wall line for 50 percent or more of its perimeter.

Allowable building construction types are a function of the number of stories in a building. In determining the number of stories, the first story is considered to be the level of exit discharge. Only "occupiable levels" are counted in determining story height. For example, unoccupied attics would not constitute a story.

Difficulties have been experienced in determining story height where a building is located on a sloping grade. Paragraph 13-6.1.6.1 notes that a story on a sloping site which is partially below grade should be counted as a story if the floor is level with or above grade for 50 percent or more of the perimeter of the building at the exterior wall. See Figure 13-15.

13-6.1.6.2 Buildings of one story in height housing ambulatory health care centers may be of Type I, II, III, IV or V construction.

13-6.1.6.3 Buildings of two or more stories in height housing ambulatory health care centers may be of Type I (443), I (332), or II (222), Type II (111), Type III (211), Type IV (2HH) or Type V (111) construction.

Exception: Such buildings may be constructed of Type II (000), III (200) or V (000) if equipped throughout with an approved automatic extinguishing system.

Construction types permitted in ambulatory health care centers are summarized in Table 13-2. See NFPA 220, *Standard Types of Building Construction.*[1].

13-6.1.6.4 Any level below the level of exit discharge shall be separated from the level of exit discharge by at least Type II (111), Type III (211) or Type V (111) construction.

Exception: Such separation is not required for such levels if they are under the control of the ambulatory health care center and any hazardous spaces are protected in accordance with Section 6-4.

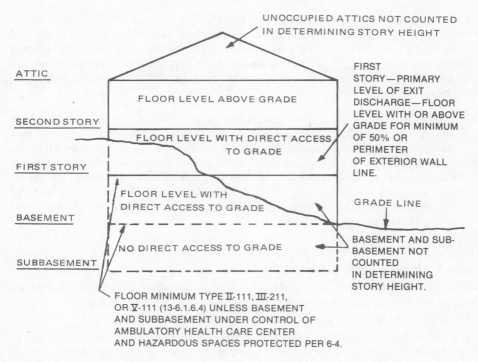

Figure 13-15. Illustration of the Application of 13-6.1.6.1 and 13-6.1.6.4.

**Table 13–2.   Construction Types Permitted in Ambulatory
Health Care Occupancies**

Construction Type	Stories	
	1	2 or more
I-443, I-332, II-222, II-111 (Fire Resistive and Protected Noncombustible)	X	X
II-000 (Unprotected Noncombustible)	X	X*
III-211 (Protected Ordinary)	X	X
III-200 (Unprotected Ordinary)	X	X*
IV-2HH (Heavy Timber)	X	X
V-111 (Protected Wood Frame)	X	X
V-000 (Unprotected Wood Frame)	X	X*

X = Construction types allowed.
* = Automatic sprinkler protection required.

13-6.1.6.5 In existing buildings, the authority having jurisdiction may accept construction systems of lesser fire resistance than required above if it can be demonstrated to his satisfaction that in cases of fire, prompt evacuation of the center can be made or that the exposing occupancies and materials of construction present no threat of fire penetration from such occupancy into the ambulatory health care center or collapse of the structure.

This paragraph allows the authority having jurisdiction to accept lesser construction types than those specified above, providing it can be demonstrated that the occupants of the ambulatory health care center are capable of evacuating the building promptly. If lesser construction types are to be accepted, potential exposures from adjacent occupancies or tenants must be provided with appropriate safeguards such as sprinklers, fire detectors, or fire-resistive separation. Structural stability must be maintained for the time required to evacuate the building, plus an additional period of time as a safety margin.

13-6.1.7 Occupant Load.

13-6.2 Means of Egress Requirements.

13-6.2.1 General.   Every aisle, passageway, corridor, exit discharge, exit location and access shall be in accordance with Chapter 5.

Exception No. 1:   As modified in the following paragraphs.

Exception No. 2:   The requirements of Chapter 5 specifying net clear door width do not apply. Projections into the door opening by stops or by hinge stiles shall be permitted.

· **Means of egress details are to conform to the fundamental provisions expressed in Chapter 5, except as modified in Chapter 27 and Chapter 13. For example, Exception No. 2 to 13-2.1 would allow the width of exit doors to be measured on the basis of the actual door leaf width. Projections into the door opening by the hinge stile and door stops are ignored.**

13-6.2.2 Types of Exits.   Exits shall be restricted to the permissible types described in 27-2.2.

13-6.2.3 Capacity of Means of Egress.

13-6.2.3.1 The minimum width of any corridor or passageway required for exit access shall be 44 in. (111.76 cm) clear.

Corridors or passageways within ambulatory health care centers used in moving patients who are temporarily nonambulatory from one room to another room or area should be of adequate width to meet the functional needs of the facility. Widths greater than 44 in. (111.76 cm) will be required in many instances. However, the minimum width for public corridors used as common exit access corridors or passageways is 44 in. (111.76 cm). The 44 in. (111.76 cm) width is stipulated on the assumption that most occupants will be ambulatory.

13-6.2.3.2 The capacity of any required means of egress shall be determined in accordance with the provisions of 27-2.3 and shall be based on its width as defined in Section 5-3.

The capacity of the means of egress in ambulatory health care centers is determined on the basis of provisions within Chapter 27 dealing with business occupancies. For example, 27-2.3.1 allows level exit components to serve 100 people per unit of exit width, whereas stairs are allowed to serve 60 persons per unit. These capacities are much higher than would be typically allowed for a health care center, and are considered permissible on the basis that the majority of occupants will be ambulatory.

13-6.2.4 Number of Exits.

13-6.2.4.1   At least two exits of the types described in 27-2.2 (Business Occupancy) located remote from each other shall be provided for each floor or fire section of the building.

13-6.2.4.2   Any room and any suite of rooms of more than 1,000 sq ft (92.9 sq m) shall have at least two exit access doors located remote from each other.

13-6.2.5 Arrangement of Means of Egress.   (*See 27-2.5.*)

13-6.2.6 Measurement of Travel Distance to Exits.

13-6.2.6.1   Travel distance shall be measured in accordance with Section 5-6.

13-6.2.6.2   Travel distance:

(a) Between any room door required as exit access and an exit shall not exceed 100 ft (30.48 m); and

(b) Between any point in a room and an exit shall not exceed 150 ft (45.72 m).

Exception: The travel distance in (a) or (b) above may be increased by 50 ft (15.24 m) in buildings protected throughout by an approved automatic sprinkler system.

Travel distance is measured to the closest exit, not to both exits required by 13-6.2.4.1. The requirements of 13-6.2.6.2 are illustrated in Figure 13-16.

13-6.2.7 Discharge from Exits.   (*See 27-2.7.*)

13-6.2.8 Illumination of Means of Egress.   Each ambulatory health care center shall be provided with illumination of means of egress in accordance with Section 5-8.

13-6.2.9 Emergency Lighting and Essential Electrical Systems.

13-6.2.9.1   Each ambulatory health care center shall be provided with emergency lighting in accordance with Section 5-9.

13-6.2.9.2   Where general anesthesia or life support equipment is used, each ambulatory health care center shall be provided with an essential electrical system in accordance with *Essential Electrical System for Health Care Facilities*, NFPA 76A.

Exception: Where battery operated equipment is provided, a generator is not required for emergency power.

All ambulatory health care centers are required to be equipped with emergency lighting. If medical procedures requiring general anesthesia are practiced, or if life support equipment is required, ambulatory health care centers are required to be served by electrical systems meeting the criteria for essential electrical systems as detailed in NFPA 76A, *Standard for Essential Electrical Systems for Health Care Facilities.*[11]

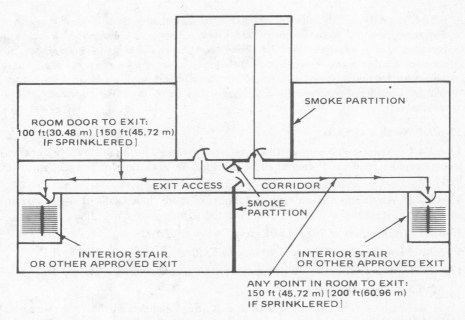

Figure 13-16. Maximum Travel Distance to Exits, Existing Ambulatory Health Care Occupancy.

A facility would not be required to comply with NFPA 76A[11], if the building is a free-standing unit which is independent of any facility providing 24-hour care and, as a normal practice, (1) management maintains admitting and discharge policies that preclude the provision of care for any patient or resident who may need to be sustained by electromechanical means such as respirators, suction apparatus, etc., and (2) the building offers no surgical treatment requiring general anesthesia, and (3) battery operated systems or equipment are provided which would maintain power to exit lights and illumination of exit corridors, stairways, medical preparation areas, and the like, for a minimum of 4 hours. Additionally, battery power would be required to be supplied to all alarm systems.

13-6.2.10 Marking of Means of Egress. Signs designated exits and ways of travel thereto shall be provided in accordance with Section 5-10.

13-6.2.11 Special Features.

13-6.2.11.1 Locks installed on patient treatment, diagnostic, or recovery room doors shall be so arranged that they can be locked only from the corridor side. All such locks shall be arranged to permit exit from the room by a simple operation without the use of a key.

13-6.2.11.2 Doors leading directly to the outside of the buildings may be subject to locking from the room side.

13-6.2.11.3 Special locking arrangements in accordance with 5-2.1.2.1.5 are permitted on exterior doors.

Paragraph 5-2.1.2.1.5 establishes minimum requirements for delayed release panic hardware.

13-6.2.11.4 Exit access door leaves from diagnostic or treatment areas, such as X-ray, surgical or physical therapy; all door leaves between these spaces and the required exits; and all exit door leaves serving these spaces shall be at least 34 in. (86.36 cm) wide.

Doors within ambulatory health care centers which are used in moving patients who are temporarily nonambulatory should be of adequate width to meet the functional needs of the facility. In many instances, doors wider than 34 in. (86.36 cm) will be required. This paragraph intends to address doors used by the public or those doors which provide access to public hallways and corridors. The 34 in. (86.36 cm) minimum width is specified for doors on the basis that most occupants will be ambulatory.

13-6.2.11.5 Any door in an exit passageway, stair enclosure, horizontal exit, a required enclosure of a hazardous area, or a smoke partition may be held open only by an automatic device which complies with 5-2.1.2.3. The device shall be so arranged that the operation of the following will initiate the self-closing action:

(a) The manual alarm system required in 13-6.3.4 and either (b) or (c) below.

(b) A local device designed to detect smoke on either side of the opening, or

(c) A complete automatic fire extinguishing or complete automatic fire detection system.

13-6.2.11.6 Where doors in a stair enclosure are held open by an automatic device as permitted in 13-6.2.11.5, initiation of a door closing action on any level shall cause all doors at all levels in the stair enclosure to close.

It is desirable to keep doors in exit enclosures, stair enclosures, horizontal exits, smoke barriers, and hazardous areas closed at all times to impede the spread of smoke and gases caused by a fire. However, some doors will be kept open, either for reasons of operating efficiency or comfort. Where doors in required fire or smoke barriers are to be held open, such doors must be equipped with automatic devices which are arranged to close the doors by the methods described within 13-6.2.11.5.

The automatic device must cause the doors to close upon operation of the manual fire alarm system. The doors must also be designed to close by actuation of a smoke detector located to detect smoke on either side of the door opening or by actuation of a complete automatic fire extinguishing or complete automatic fire detection system.

It is especially important in facilities providing health care to maintain floor-to-floor separation. Doors protecting openings in a stair tower enclosure may be held open by an automatic device only if arranged to close as specified above. Initiation of any automatic action which causes a door to close at one level must cause all doors at all levels protecting openings within the stair enclosure to close and latch.

13-6.3 Protection.

13-6.3.1 Protection of Vertical Openings. (*See 27-3.1.*)

13-6.3.2 Protection from Hazards. (*See 27-3.2.*)

13-6.3.2.1 Laboratories employing quantities of flammable, combustible, or hazardous materials which are considered as severe hazard shall be protected in accordance with *Laboratories in Health Related Institutions*, NFPA 56C.

Laboratories which contain "ordinary" combustibles and flammable liquids in sufficient quantity to threaten a 1-hour fire separation — wood equivalent fuel loads in the range of 5 to 10 lb/sq ft (24.41 to 48.82 kg/sq m) — are considered a severe hazard. Laboratories representing a severe hazard must be protected in accordance with NFPA 56C, *Standard for Laboratories in Health-Related Institutions*.[6] Protection would include 1-hour fire resistance separation and automatic sprinkler protection.

Where fuel loads of lesser amounts are involved and quantities of flammable liquids are limited, laboratories would be simply considered hazardous areas, and would require either 1-hour separation or automatic sprinkler protection as indicated within 13-6.3.2.1 and Section 6-4.

13-6.3.2.2 Anesthetizing locations shall be protected in accordance with *Inhalation Anesthetics in Ambulatory Care Facilities*, NFPA 56G.

13-6.3.3 Interior Finish.   (*See 27-3.3.*)

13-6.3.4 Detection, Alarm and Communication Systems.

13-6.3.4.1 Other than as noted below, required fire detection and signaling devices or systems shall be in accordance with Section 7-6.

13-6.3.4.2 Every building shall have a manually operated fire alarm system, in accordance with Section 7-6. Pre-signal systems are not allowed within an ambulatory surgical care center.

13-6.3.4.3 Operation of any fire alarm activating device shall automatically, without delay, accomplish general alarm indication and control functions. Zoned, coded systems shall be permitted.

13-6.3.4.4 The fire alarm system shall be arranged to transmit an alarm automatically to the fire department legally committed to serve the area in which the health care facility is located, by the most direct and reliable method approved by local regulations.

13-6.3.4.5 Internal audible alarm devices shall be provided and shall be installed in accordance with Section 7-6.

13-6.3.4.6 Any fire detection device or system required by this section shall be electrically interconnected with the fire alarm system.

Paragraphs 13-6.3.4.1 through 13-6.3.4.6 deal with required fire alarm equipment. Reliability is of prime importance; therefore, electrical supervision of the system and system components is specified by the standards referenced in Section 7-6. In the event of circuit fault, component failure, or other "trouble," a continuous "trouble indication" signal is required and should be provided at a constantly attended location.

A manual fire alarm system is required by 13-6.3.4.2. Manual pull stations should be located along the natural routes of egress and located so as to adequately cover all portions of the building. Manual pull stations should always be located so that anyone qualified to send an alarm may summon aid without having to leave the zone of his or her ordinary activities, or pass out of the sight and hearing of people immediately exposed to, or in direct view of, a fire. The operation of a manual fire alarm station should automatically summon attendants who can assist in removing physically helpless occupants.

The system required by 13-6.3.4.2 may be incorporated into an automatic system equipped to detect a fire and initiate an alarm.

Actuation of any required fire or smoke detector, activation of a required sprinkler system, or operation of a manual pull station must *automatically*, without delay, sound *audible alarm devices* within the building. Presignal systems are not permitted.

The fire alarm system is required by 13-6.3.4.4 to *automatically* notify the public fire department legally committed to serve the facility. The preferred arrangement is direct transmission to the fire department fire alarm headquarters. If such an arrangement is not permitted, the next best option is notification by an approved central station alarm system. If a central station alarm system is not available, the alarm should be transmitted by an electrically supervised system to a constantly attended location with the capability of alerting the public fire department.

Actuation of the fire alarm must cause audible alerting devices to sound throughout the affected zone or building as appropriate. Visible alerting devices may be used, but may not serve as a substitute for audible devices.

13-6.3.5 Extinguishment Requirements.   (*See 27-3.5.*)

13-6.3.5.1   The sprinkler piping, serving no more than six sprinklers for any isolated hazardous area, may be connected directly to a domestic water supply system having a capacity sufficient to provide 0.15 gal per minute per sq foot (1.02×10^{-4} cu m/s/sq m) of floor area throughout the entire enclosed area. An indicating shutoff valve shall be installed in an accessible location between the sprinklers and the connection to the domestic water supply. Where more than two sprinklers are installed in a single area, waterflow detection shall be provided to sound the building fire alarm system in the event of sprinkler operation. (*For sprinkler requirements for hazardous areas, see 13-6.3.2.*)

13-6.3.5.2   Portable fire extinguishers shall be provided in ambulatory health care occupancies in accordance with 7-7.4.1.

13-6.3.6 Corridors.

13-6.3.7 Subdivision of Building Space.

13-6.3.7.1   Ambulatory health care occupancies shall be separated from other tenants and occupancies by walls having at least a 1-hour fire-resistive construction. Such walls shall extend from the floor slab below to the floor or roof slab above. Doors shall be at least 1¾-in. (4.45-cm) solid bonded wood core or the equivalent and equipped with positive latches. These doors shall be self-closing and normally kept in the closed position except when in use. Any vision panels shall be of fixed wired glass set in approved metal frames and limited in size to 1,296 sq in. (.84 sq m).

Ambulatory health care centers are frequently located within buildings used for a variety of purposes. Location within buildings having hazardous occupancies should be avoided. Where ambulatory health care centers are located within buildings of mixed use, the ambulatory health care center must be separated from adjacent tenants and occupancies by at least 1-hour fire-rated partitions. Doors protecting openings in such partitions must be a minimum of 1¾-in. (4.45-cm) solid bonded wood core, or of other equivalent construction which will resist fire for a minimum of 20 minutes. The doors must be equipped with positive latching hardware of a type which cannot be held in the retracted position. These doors must be self-closing and normally maintained closed or, if the doors are to be held open, an automatic device must be used as indicated in 13-6.2.11.5.

Glazing within doors and partitions is limited to a maximum of 1,296 sq in. (8,362 sq cm) of wired glass, set in approved metal frames. Each wired glass panel must be limited to a maximum dimension of 54 in. (137.16 cm). The glass must be labeled ¼ in. (.64 cm) thick, and be well-embedded in putty with all exposed joints between the metal and the glass struck and pointed. (See NFPA 80, *Standard for Fire Doors and Windows.*) A number of wired glass panels may be used in a single partition provided that each 1,296-sq in. (8,362-sq cm) section is separated from adjacent panels by a metal mullion. The excessive use of wired glass panels should be avoided. It must be recognized that the use of wired glass panels in a partition reduces the effectiveness of the partition in that radiant energy transfer will readily occur through the glass panel.

Partitions separating ambulatory health care centers from other occupancies must extend from the floor to the floor or roof deck above, complete through concealed spaces above suspended ceilings, for example. The partition must form a continuous barrier. Openings around penetrations involving building services must be adequately protected to maintain the 1-hour separation. Special attention must be paid to penetrations involving air-handling ducts. In general, steel ducts will not require a fire damper. Penetrations involving nonmetallic ducts or aluminum ducts should be carefully evaluated. Fire dampers should be provided to protect duct penetrations where the projected fire exposure is judged sufficient to jeopardize the required separation because of the duct penetration. The possible movement of air from space to space under conditions of system operation and conditions of system shutdown should both be evaluated. If there is a significant potential for transferring contaminants from an adjacent space to the ambulatory health care center or from the center to a corridor, fire dampers should be provided for duct penetrations, even though the *Code* does not specifically require such protection.

See Figure 13-17.

13-6.3.7.2   The ambulatory health care facility shall be divided into at least two smoke compartments.

Exception: Facilities less than 2,000 sq ft (185.8 sq m) and protected by an approved automatic smoke detection system need not be divided.

13-6.3.7.3   Walls separating the smoke compartments shall be of at least a 1-hour construction, and shall extend from the floor slab below to the floor or roof slab above.

13-6.3.7.4   Vision panels in the smoke barrier shall be of fixed wired glass set in approved metal frames and shall be limited in size to 1,296 sq in. (.84 sq m).

13-6.3.7.5   Doors in smoke barriers shall be at least 1¾-in. (4.45-cm) solid bonded wood core or the equivalent and shall be self-closing. A vision panel is required.

13-6.3.7.6   Doors in smoke barriers shall normally be kept closed or, if held open, they shall be equipped with automatic devices which will release the doors upon activation of:

(a) The fire alarm system, and either

(b) A local smoke detector, or,

(c) A complete automatic fire extinguishing system or complete automatic fire detection system.

13-6.3.7.7 An approved damper designed to resist the passage of smoke shall be provided at each point a duct penetrates a smoke barrier required by 13-6.3.7.1. The damper shall close upon detection of smoke by an approved smoke detector located within the duct. (*See Section 6-3.*)

Exception No. 1:   In lieu of an approved smoke detector located within the duct, ducts which penetrate smoke barriers above smoke barrier doors (required in 13-6.3.7.5) may have the approved damper arranged to close upon detection of smoke by the local device designed to detect smoke in either side of the smoke barrier door opening.

Exception No. 2:   Dampers may be omitted in buildings equipped with an approved engineered smoke control system. The smoke control system shall respond automatically, preventing the transfer of smoke across the barrier, and shall be designed in accordance with Standard for the Installation of Air Conditioning and Ventilating Systems, NFPA 90A.

The requirements of 13-6.3.7.1 through 13-6.3.7.7 for subdividing building spaces through smoke barriers are illustrated in Figures 13-17 and 13-18.

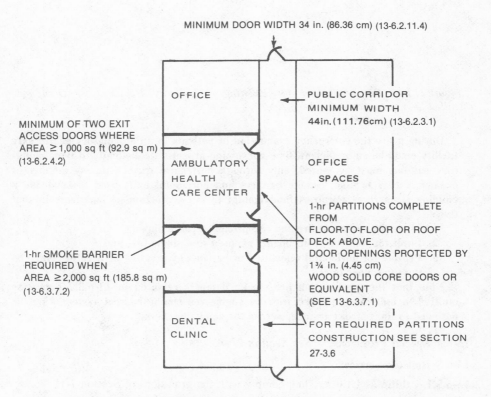

Figure 13-17. Building Subdivision, Existing Ambulatory Health Care Center.

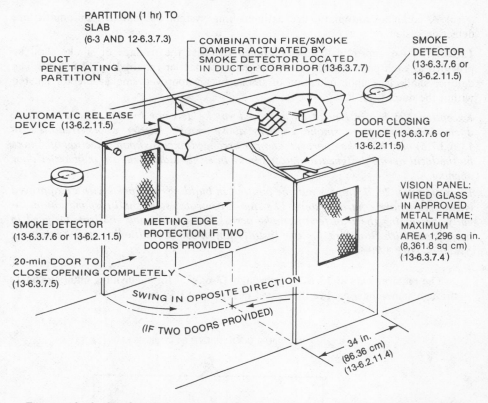

PARTITION (1 hr) TO
SLAB
(6-3 AND 12-6.3.7.3)

DUCT
PENETRATING
PARTITION

COMBINATION FIRE/SMOKE
DAMPER ACTUATED BY
SMOKE DETECTOR LOCATED
IN DUCT or CORRIDOR (13-6.3.7.7)

SMOKE
DETECTOR
(13-6.3.7.6 or
13-6.2.11.5)

AUTOMATIC RELEASE
DEVICE (13-6.2.11.5)

DOOR CLOSING
DEVICE (13-6.3.7.6 or
13-6.2.11.5)

SMOKE DETECTOR
(13-6.3.7.6 or 13-6.2.11.5)

MEETING EDGE
PROTECTION IF TWO
DOORS PROVIDED

VISION PANEL:
WIRED GLASS
IN APPROVED
METAL FRAME;
MAXIMUM
AREA 1,296 sq in.
(8,361.8 sq cm)
(13-6.3.7.4)

20-min DOOR TO
CLOSE OPENING COMPLETELY
(13-6.3.7.5)

SWING IN OPPOSITE DIRECTION
(IF TWO DOORS PROVIDED)

34 in.
(86.36 cm)
(13-6.2.11.4)

Figure 13-18. Smoke Barrier for Existing Ambulatory Health Care Occupancy Installed in Accordance with 13-6.3.7.

During a fire the emergency evacuation of patients in an ambulatory health care facility could be an inefficient, time-consuming process. Realistically, if nonambulatory patients must be moved, only through horizontal travel can any number of occupants be relocated. Smoke barriers and horizontal exits used to subdivide a building serve three purposes fundamental to the protection of inpatients in that they:

1. Limit the spread of fire and fire-produced contaminants,
2. Limit the number of occupants exposed to a single fire, and
3. Provide for horizontal relocation of patients by creating an area of refuge on the same floor level.

Note that the combination fire/smoke dampers required in 13-6.3.7.7 may be omitted in buildings equipped with an engineered smoke control system which is designed to limit smoke transfer across the smoke barriers.

13-6.4 Special Provisions.   *(See Section 27-4.)*

13-6.5 Building Services.

13-6.5.1 Utilities.   Utilities shall comply with the provisions of Section 7-1.

13-6.5.2 Heating, Ventilating and Air Conditioning.

13-6.5.2.1 Heating, ventilating and air conditioning shall comply with the provisions of Section 7-2 and shall be installed in accordance with the manufacturer's specifications.

Exception: As modified in 13-6.5.2.2 following.

13-6.5.2.2 Portable space heating devices are prohibited. Any heating device other than a central heating plant shall be so designed and installed that combustible material will not be ignited by it or its appurtenances. If fuel fired, such heating devices shall be chimney or vent connected, shall take air for combustion directly form the outside, and shall be so designed and installed to provide for complete separation of the combustion system from the atmosphere of the occupied area. Any heating device shall have safety features to immediately stop the flow of fuel and shut down the equipment in case of either excessive temperature or ignition failure.

Exception No. 1: Approved suspended unit heaters may be used in locations other than means of egress and patient treatment areas, provided such heaters are located high enough to be out of the reach of persons using the area and provided they are equipped with the safety features called for above.

Exception No. 2: Portable space heating devices shall be permitted to be used in nonsleeping staff and employee areas when the heating elements of such a device are limited to not more than 212° F (100° C).

It is generally agreed that the maximum acceptable temperature to which combustible materials may be exposed for prolonged periods of time is on the order of 160°F (71°C) to 190°F (88°C).

Paragraphs 13-6.5.2.1 and 13-6.5.2.2 specify safeguards for air conditioning, ventilating, heating, and other service equipment to minimize the possibility of such devices serving as a source of ignition. Fuel-fired heating devices, except central heating systems, must be designed to provide complete separation of the combustion system from the occupied spaces. Air for combustion must be taken directly from the outside.

The major concern of the *Code* is to prevent the ignition of clothing, bedclothes, furniture, and other furnishings by a heating device. Therefore, 13-6.5.2.2 prohibits portable heating devices in areas used by patients.

13-6.5.3 Elevators, dumbwaiters and vertical conveyors shall comply with the provisions of Section 7-4.

13-6.5.4 Rubbish chutes, incinerators, and laundry chutes shall comply with the provisions of Section 7-5.

REFERENCES CITED IN *CODE*

(These publications comprise a part of the requirements to the extent called for by the Code.)

NFPA 13, *Standard for the Installation of Sprinkler Systems,* NFPA, Boston, 1980.

NFPA 56A, *Standard for the Use of Inhalation Anesthetics (Flammable and Nonflammable),* NFPA, Boston, 1978.

NFPA 56C, *Safety Standard for Laboratories in Health-Related Institutions,* NFPA, Boston, 1980.

NFPA 56G, *Standard for Inhalation Anesthetics in Ambulatory Care Facilities*, NFPA, Boston, 1980.

NFPA 76A, *Standard for Essential Electrical Systems for Health Care Facilities*, NFPA, Boston, 1977.

NFPA 90A, *Standard for the Installation of Air Conditioning and Ventilating Systems*, NFPA, Boston, 1978.

NFPA 211, *Standard for Chimneys, Fireplaces, Vents, and Solid Fuel Burning Appliances*, NFPA, Boston, 1978.

NFPA 251, *Standard Methods of Fire Tests of Building Construction and Materials*, NFPA, Boston, 1979.

NFPA 256, *Standard Methods of Fire Tests of Roof Coverings*, NFPA, Boston, 1976.

REFERENCES CITED IN COMMENTARY

[1]NFPA 220, *Standard Types of Building Construction*, NFPA, Boston, 1979.

[2]NFPA 241, *Standard for Safeguarding Building Construction and Demolition Operations*, NFPA, Boston, 1980.

[3]NFPA 30, *Flammable and Combustible Liquids Code*, NFPA, Boston, 1981.

[4]NFPA 56A, *Standard for the Use of Inhalation Anesthetics (Flammable and Nonflammable)*, NFPA, Boston, 1978.

[5]NFPA 56F, *Standard for Nonflammable Medical Gas Systems*, NFPA, Boston, 1977.

[6]NFPA 56C, *Safety Standard for Laboratories in Health-Related Institutions*, NFPA, Boston, 1980.

[7]NFPA 96, *Standard for the Installation of Equipment for the Removal of Smoke and Grease-Laden Vapors from Commercial Cooking Equipment*, NFPA, Boston, 1980.

[8]NFPA 13, *Standard for the Installation of Sprinkler Systems*, NFPA, Boston, 1980.

[9]NFPA 80, *Standard for Fire Doors and Windows*, NFPA, Boston, 1979.

[10]NFPA 90A, *Standard for the Installation of Air Conditioning and Ventilating Systems*, NFPA, Boston, 1978.

[11]NFPA 76A, *Standard for Essential Electrical Systems for Health Care Facilities*, NFPA, Boston, 1977.

14

NEW DETENTION
AND CORRECTIONAL
OCCUPANCIES

(See also Chapter 31.)

In this, the 1981 Edition of the *Life Safety Code*, detention and correctional occupancies now are covered in their own chapters, Chapters 14 and 15. In previous editions these occupancies were discussed in the chapter on institutional occupancies, later renamed health care occupancies (Chapters 12 and 13 of this edition).

In 1974 the Committee on Safety to Life decided to establish a Sectional Committee on Penal Occupancies. It was, however, too late to prepare a report for the 1976 Edition of the *Code*, and in 1977 the Committee on Safety to Life was reorganized as a Technical Committee with subcommittees. The Subcommittee on Penal Occupancies was appointed with its first working meeting in January of 1978. It was soon renamed the Subcommittee on Detention and Correctional Occupancies. During this period, there were several major detention and correctional occupancy fires which added emphasis to the need for the Subcommittee and provided information for its use. These included:

October 1974	Youth Correctional Center Cranston, RI	2 dead[1]
June 1975	Seminole County Jail Sanford, FL	11 dead[1]
November 1975	Lycoming County Jail Williamsport, PA	3 dead[1]
June 1976	Marion State Prison Marion, NC	9 dead[1]
June 1977	Maury County Jail Columbia, IN	42 dead[1]
June 1977	St. John City Detention Center St. John, NB, Canada	21 dead[1]
July 1977	Federal Correctional Institution Danbury, CT	5 dead[1]
December 1979	Lancaster County Jail Lancaster, SC	11 dead[2]

No list of prison fires would be complete without mentioning the Ohio State Penitentiary fire in Columbus, Ohio, in April 1930 in which 320 were killed, and the State Road Camp fire in Berrydale, Florida, in July 1967 in which 38 were killed.[1]

SECTION 14-1   GENERAL

14-1.1 Application.

14-1.1.1   New detention and correctional facilities shall comply with the provisions of this chapter. They shall also comply with the applicable requirements of Chapter 31.

> **Provisions for existing detention and correctional occupancies are contained in Chapter 15.**

14-1.1.2   This chapter establishes life safety requirements for the design of all new detention and correctional facilities.

Exception: Use Condition I requirements are those stated in the applicable requirements of Chapters 16, 18, or 20.

> **See 14-1.4 for definition of use condition.**

14-1.1.3   Detention and correctional occupancies are those used for purposes such as jails, detention centers, correctional institutions, reformatories, houses of correction, pre-release centers, and other residential-restrained care facilities where occupants are confined or housed under some degree of restraint or security.

14-1.1.4   Detention and correctional occupancies provide sleeping facilities for four or more residents and are occupied by persons who are generally prevented from taking self-preservation action because of security measures not under the occupants' control.

14-1.1.5 Total Concept.   All detention and correctional facilities shall be so designed, constructed, maintained and operated as to minimize the possibility of a fire emergency. Because the safety of all occupants in all detention and correctional facilities cannot be adequately assured solely by a dependence on evacuation of the building, their protection from fire shall be provided by appropriate arrangement of facilities, adequate trained staff, and careful development of operating, security, and maintenance procedures composed of the following:

(a) Proper design, construction and compartmentation,

(b) Provision for detection, alarm and extinguishment,

(c) Fire prevention and planning, training, and drilling in programs for the isolation of fire and transfer of occupants to areas of refuge or evacuation of the building, or protection of the occupants in place,

(d) Provision of security to the degree necessary for the safety of the public and the occupants of the facility.

> **It is important to note that the occupants' safety is dependent upon the effective management of his or her environment, including building structure, interior finish, furnishings, decorations, clothing, bedding, and all other materials which make up that environment. No code can prevent injury resulting from a person's careless or intentional actions. The best means of protection is to prevent the fire. Obviously, this is not always practical. The primary objective of the requirements of this chapter is to prevent fire from escaping the room of origin, thereby limiting the effects of the fire to occupants outside the room of origin.**

14-1.1.6 Additions.   Additions shall be separated from any existing structure not conforming with the provisions within Chapter 15 by a fire barrier having at least a 2-hour fire resistance rating constructed to the standards of the addition. Doors in these partitions shall normally be kept closed.

Exception: Doors may be held open if they meet the requirements of the exception to 5-2.1.2.3.

Note that doors may be located anywhere in the separating partition, but must be kept closed unless they meet the requirements for closing in the exception to 5-2.1.2.3.

Figure 14-1 illustrates requirements of 14-1.1.6.

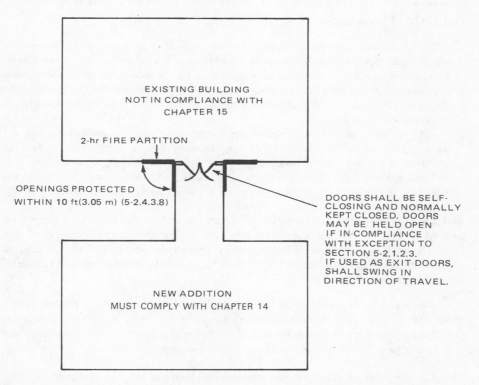

Figure 14-1. Separation of New Addition from Existing Building Not in Compliance with Chapter 15 (see 14-1.1.6).

14-1.1.7 Modernization or Renovation.

14-1.1.7.1   No construction in either modernization or renovation projects shall diminish the fire safety features of the facility below the level of new construction as described elsewhere in this *Code*. Alterations or installations of new building services equipment shall be accomplished as nearly as possible in conformance with the requirements for new construction.

Alterations may not reduce the level of life safety in an existing building below that required for new construction. If, however, an existing design exceeds the *Code* provisions for new construction, it is *not* required that the building's fire-safety features in excess of the *Code* be maintained. It *is* required that the provisions for existing construction be met.

Although every effort should be made to satisfy the criteria for new construction during a building alteration or the installation of new equipment, the *Code* recognizes that such modifications cannot always be accomplished. Guidance for achieving "equivalency to life safety" is provided in Section 1-5. In any event, alterations, or installation of new building service equipment, may *not* reduce a building's level of life safety below that provided for existing buildings, nor may it be reduced below that which existed before the alteration (see Section 1-5).

14-1.1.7.2   See 1-6.3 and Chapter 31 for life safety provisions during construction.

14-1.2 Mixed Occupancies.

Detention and correctional occupancies are a complex of structures, each serving a definite and usually different purpose. For instance, in all probability there will be represented in many institutions an example of all, or almost all, of the occupancy type classifications found in this *Code*. Exits and other features shall be governed by the type of occupancy classification and the hazard of occupancy unless specific exceptions are made.

All buildings and structures shall be classified using this chapter and Section 4-1 as a guide, subject to the ruling of the authority having jurisdiction in case of question as to the proper classification of any individual building or structure.

Use condition classification of the institution, as well as individual areas within the complex, shall always be considered by the authority having jurisdiction.

14-1.2.1   Egress provisions for areas of detention and correctional facilities which correspond to other occupancies shall meet the corresponding requirements of this *Code* for such occupancies. Where security operations necessitate the locking of required means of egress, necessary staff shall be provided for the supervised release of occupants during all times of use.

Release of occupants should be accomplished by a manually activated system capable of unlocking all doors in the means of egress or by a sufficient number of attendants who are *continuously* on duty in the immediate area of the exit doors, and who are provided with keys. Continuous supervision is essential.

14-1.2.2   Sections of detention and correctional facilities may be classified as other occupancies if they meet all of the following conditions:

(a) They are not intended to serve residents for purpose of housing, customary access or means of egress.

(b) They are adequately separated from areas of detention or correctional occupancies by construction having a fire resistance rating of at least 2 hours.

For example, administrative offices, maintenance areas, etc., which are not customarily used by the inmates, are not part of the egress system from the inmate occupied areas, and are separated by 2-hour rated fire resistance construction, may be classified as another occupancy such as business or industrial.

14-1.2.3   Detention and correctional occupancies in buildings housing other occupancies shall be completely separated from the other occupancies by construction having a fire resistance rating of at least 2 hours, as provided for additions in 14-1.1.6.

> Paragraph 14-1.2.3 requires that if a detention or correctional occupancy is located in a building of another classification (such as business or assembly), the detention or correctional occupancy must be separated from the other occupancy by construction having a fire resistance of 2 hours, as detailed in 14-1.1.6.
> Note that 14-1.2.3 deals with occupancy classification only, and not with hazard of contents. Hazard of contents is treated in 14-1.2.5.

14-1.2.4   All means of egress from detention and correctional occupancies that traverse other use areas shall, as a minimum, conform to requirements of this *Code* for detention and correctional occupancies.

> The means of egress from detention and correctional occupancies which traverse non-detention and non-correctional spaces must conform to the requirements for detention and correctional occupancies. For example, if an opening in a 2-hour barrier between a detention or correctional occupancy and a business occupancy (offices) is used as a horizontal exit, then elements such as corridor widths, details of corridor protection, and stairway details in the business occupancy must conform to the appropriate requirements set forth in this chapter for new, or Chapter 15 for existing, detention and correctional occupancies.

14-1.2.5   Any area with a hazard of contents classified higher than that of the detention or correctional occupancy and located in the same building shall be protected, as required in 14-3.2.

> This paragraph regulates those spaces in a detention or correctional occupancy which contain more hazardous materials (in quantity or type) than are usually found in this occupancy. Spaces such as rooms used for the storage of combustible materials, trash collection rooms, and paint shops must be protected in accordance with 14-3.2.

14-1.2.6   Non-detention or non-correctional related occupancies classified as containing high hazard contents shall not be permitted in buildings housing detention or correctional occupancies.

> This paragraph prohibits another occupancy (such as storage) with highly hazardous contents (such as flammable liquids) from being located in a building housing detention and correctional occupancies. This paragraph limits the use of the building based upon occupancy classification with regard to hazard of contents. For example, this paragraph is not meant to exclude the storage of linens in a detention and correctional occupancy. The intent is to prevent a portion of a detention and correctional facility from being converted to a warehouse and having a larger quantity of combustibles than would be expected in a detention and correctional occupancy.

14-1.3 Special Definitions.

(a) **Sallyport (Security Vestibule).**   A compartment provided with two or more doors where the intended purpose is to prevent the continuous and unobstructed passage by allowing the release of only one door at a time.

(b) **Fire Barrier.**   See Chapter 6.

(c) **Fire Compartment.**   See Chapter 6.

(d) **Smoke Barrier.**   See Chapter 6.

(e) **Smoke Compartment.**   See Chapter 6.

14-1.4 Classification of Occupancy.

14-1.4.1   Users and occupants of detention and correctional facilities at various times can be expected to include staff, visitors, and residents. The extent and nature of facility utilization by members of each of these groups will vary according to type of facility, its function and programs. For applications of the life safety requirements which follow, the resident user category is divided into five groups:

Use Condition I — Free Egress

Free movement is allowed from sleeping areas, and other spaces where access or occupancy is permitted, to the exterior via means of egress meeting the requirements of the *Code.*

> **In Use Condition I, there are no physical restrictions, such as locks, on the means of egress. The occupants are capable of self-preservation. An example might be a work release center where the doors are not locked.**

Use Condition II — Zoned Egress

Free movement is allowed from sleeping areas and any other occupied smoke compartment to one or more other smoke compartments.

> **The occupants are free to move within the building, including free access across the smoke barrier. See Figure 14-2.**

Use Condition III — Zoned Impeded Egress

Free movement is allowed within individual smoke compartments, such as within a residential unit comprised of individual sleeping rooms and group activity space, with egress impeded by remote control release of means of egress from such smoke compartment to another smoke compartment.

> **The important item to note in Use Condition III is that the smoke barrier door can be remotely unlocked. See Figure 14-2.**

Use Condition IV — Impeded Egress

Free movement is restricted from an occupied space. Remote controlled release is provided to permit movement from all sleeping rooms, activity spaces and other occupied areas within the smoke compartment to other smoke compartment(s).

> **In Use Condition IV, occupants are locked in their cells. However, both the cell doors and the smoke barrier door can be remotely unlocked. See Figure 14-2.**

Use Condition V — Contained

Free movement is restricted from an occupied space. Staff controlled manual release at each door is provided to permit movement from all sleeping rooms, activity spaces and other occupied areas within the smoke compartment to other smoke compartment(s).

All locks must be manually unlocked at the door to each cell and the smoke barrier door. See Figure 14-2.

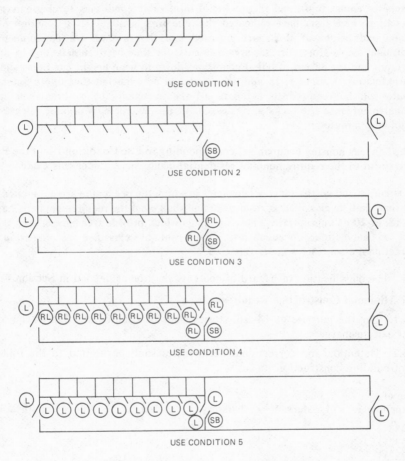

DETENTION AND CORRECTIONAL USE CONDITIONS

ⓛ LOCKED

®ⓁⓇⓁ LOCKED—REMOTE RELEASE OR EQUIVALENT

⑤ⓈⒷ SMOKE BARRIER OR HORIZONTAL EXIT

Figure 14-2. Classification of Occupancy by Use Condition (see 14-1.4.1).

14-1.4.2 To classify as Use Condition III or IV the arrangement, accessibility and security of the release mechanism(s) used for emergency egress shall be such that the minimum available staff, at any time, can promptly release the locks.

The important requirement noted in this section is that the area must be under continuous supervision and that a sufficient number of staff must be available for, and capable of, releasing the locks.

Prompt operation is intended to be accomplished in the period of time following detection of fire by either the smoke detector(s) required by 14-3.4 or by other means (whichever comes first), and the advent of intolerable conditions forcing emergency evacuation. Fire tests have indicated that the time available is a function of the volume and height of the space involved and the rate of fire development. In traditional single-story corridor arrangements, the time between detection by smoke detectors and the advent of lethal conditions down to head height can be as short as approximately 3 minutes. In addition, it should be expected that approximately 1 minute will be required to evacuate all the occupants of a threatened smoke compartment once the locks are released. In this example, a prompt release time would be 2 minutes.

14-1.4.3   Areas housing occupancies corresponding to Use Condition I — Free Egress shall conform to the requirements of residential occupancies under this *Code*.

Detention and correctional occupancies in which the occupants are not locked in at any time shall be classified as residential and shall meet the requirements of Chapters 16, 18, or 20 as appropriate. Those buildings which provide free egress, even though used as correctional occupancies, should not be classified as detention and correctional occupancies under this *Code*.

14-1.5   The classification of hazard of contents shall be as defined in Section 4-2.

14-1.6 Minimum Construction Requirements.

14-1.6.1   For the purpose of 14-1.6, stories shall be counted starting at the lowest level of exit discharge.

14-1.6.2   Detention and correctional occupancies shall be limited to the following types of building construction:

Type of Construction	Below 1st story	1st story	2nd	3rd	4th & above
I (433) I (332) II (222)	X	X	X	X	X
II (111)	X†	X	X†	N.P.	N.P.
III (211) IV (2HH) V (111)	X†	X	X†	N.P.	N.P.
II (000) III (200) V (000)	A.S.	A.S.	A.S.	N.P.	N.P.

A.S.: Permitted if the entire building is protected throughout by an approved automatic sprinkler system in accordance with Section 7-7.

X: Permitted

N.P.: Not permitted

†: A.S. required in buildings where Use Condition V is used.

The table contained in 14-1.6.2 establishes minimum construction types for detention and correctional occupancies. Under some conditions, certain construction types are prohibited even if protected by automatic sprinklers. It should be noted that the automatic sprinkler requirements contained in this table are determined on construction type. Even though not required here, automatic sprinkler protection may be required by 14-3.8.1 due to separation requirements by use conditions.

See NFPA 220, *Standard Types of Building Construction*,[3] for definition of types of construction.

14-1.7 Occupant Load. The occupant load for which means of egress shall be provided for any floor shall be the maximum number of persons intended to occupy that floor, but not less than one person for each 120 sq ft (11.15 sq m) gross floor area.

This paragraph sets forth criteria for projecting occupant loads. The number of people for whom *exits must be provided* may be based upon an actual count of persons intended to occupy a space. However, the occupant load *may not* be less than that established by projections involving one person for each 120 sq ft (11.15 sq m) of gross floor area.

The maximum number of people occupying a space is limited on the basis of exit capacity and other functional considerations. The *Code* does not intend to limit population based upon the area projections contained in this paragraph.

SECTION 14-2   MEANS OF EGRESS

14-2.1 General. The provisions of Chapter 5 of the *Code* apply to this chapter with the following exceptions:

Exception No. 1:   14-2.11.3.

Exception No. 2:   Doors in a means of egress may be of the horizontal sliding type provided the force to slide the door to its fully open position does not exceed 50 lb (222 N) with a perpendicular force against the door of 50 lb (222 N).

Paragraph 5-2.1.1.4.1 requires that all doors in a means of egress be side-hinged and swinging. This exception allows the use of sliding doors if they meet the specified requirements.

Exception No. 3:   Horizontal exits may be substituted for other exits provided the maximum exit travel distance specified in 14-2.6 is not exceeded. Horizontal exits may comprise 100 percent of the exits required. Every fire compartment for which credit is allowed in connection with a horizontal exit shall not be required to have a stairway or door leading directly outside, provided the adjoining fire compartments have stairways or doors leading directly outside.

Exception No. 3 permits horizontal exits to comprise 100 percent of the exits, provided exit travel distance is not exceeded and the adjacent fire compartments do have egress directly to the outside. See Figure 14-3.

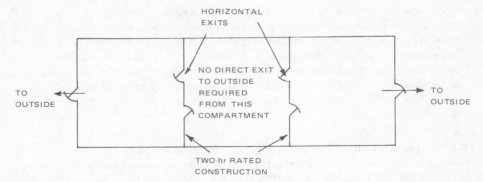

Figure 14-3. Horizontal Exits Comprising 100 Percent of Total Exits (see 14-2.1, Exception No. 3).

Exception No. 4:   Exit access from a cell or room may be through a dayroom.

Exception No. 5:   Exit discharge may terminate directly at the building's exterior, or at a horizontal exit, and may discharge into a fenced or walled courtyard, provided that not more than two walls of the courtyard are the building walls from which exit is being made. Enclosed yards or courts shall be of sufficient size to accommodate all occupants, a minimum of 50 ft (15.24 m) from the building with a net area of 15 sq ft (1.39 sq m) per person.

Figure 14-4 illustrates Exception No. 5.

Exception No. 6:   The provisions of 5-2.2.3.4(h) and 5-2.2.3.5(c) do not apply.

These two paragraphs in Chapter 5 require intermediate rails, etc., on handrails and guardrails. Since these may seriously interfere with the supervision of sleeping rooms, the requirement is exempted in detention and correctional occupancies.

14-2.2 Types of Exits.

14-2.2.1   Exits of the specified number and width shall be one or more of the following types, in accordance with the provision of Chapter 5.

(a) *Doors.   (See 5-2.1.)*

(b) *Interior Stairs.   (See 5-2.2.)*

(c) *Smokeproof Towers.   (See 5-2.3.)*

(d) *Horizontal Exits.   (See 5-2.4.)* A horizontal exit shall be in conformance with 5-2.4, modified as below:

1. At least 6 sq ft (.56 sq m) of accessible space per occupant shall be provided on each side of the horizontal exit for the total number of people in adjoining compartments.

Section 5-2.4 requires at least 3 sq ft (.28 sq m) per occupant. This section requires 6 sq ft (.56 sq m) per occupant due to several factors, including nature of the occupants, permission of 100 percent horizontal exiting, duration in area, etc.

Doors in horizontal exits are required to swing in the direction of exit travel. In the

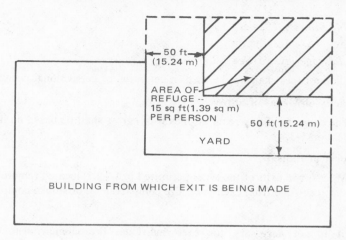

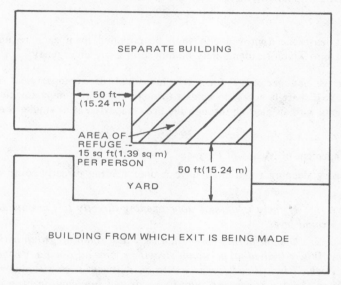

Figure 14-4. Exit Discharge into an Enclosed Yard (see 14-2.1, Exception No. 5).

case of a fire wall serving as a horizontal exit for two adjoining fire areas, a pair of doors arranged with each leaf to swing in a direction opposite from the other or some other equivalent arrangement must be used. If the fire wall serves as a horizontal exit from just one fire area, the door opening may be protected by a single door [32 in. (81.28 cm) wide — minimum] arranged to swing in the direction of exit travel.

Because of practical difficulties involving vertical exit travel in detention and correctional occupancies, special recognition is given to horizontal travel and the use of horizontal exits. One hundred percent of the total required exit capacity for a given fire area may be provided by horizontal exits (see 14-2.1, Exception No. 3). In the event a horizontal exit also serves as a smoke barrier, see 14-2.4 and 14-3.7.

(e) *Outside Stairs.* *(See 5-2.5.)*

(f) *Ramps.* *(See 5-2.6.)*

(g) *Exit Passageways.* *(See 5-2.7.)*

14-2.2.2 Slide escapes shall not be used in detention or correctional occupancies.

14-2.3 Capacity of Means of Egress.

14-2.3.1 The capacity of any required means of egress shall be based on its width as defined in Section 5-3.

14-2.4 Number of Exits.

14-2.4.1 At least two exits of the types permitted in 14-2.2, located remote from each other, shall be accessible from each floor, fire compartment, or smoke compartment of the building.

An exit is not necessary for each individual fire compartment or smoke compartment if there is access to an exit through other fire compartments or smoke compartments without passing through the fire compartment or smoke compartment of origin.

14-2.4.2 At least one approved exit shall be provided from each required smoke compartment into which residents may be moved in a fire emergency.

An exit is not necessary for each individual fire compartment or smoke compartment if there is access to an exit through other fire compartments or smoke compartments without passing through the fire compartment or smoke compartment of origin.

14-2.5 Arrangement of Means of Egress.

14-2.5.1 Every sleeping room shall have a door leading directly to an exit access corridor.

Exception No. 1: If there is an exit door opening directly to the outside from the room at the ground level.

Exception No. 2: One adjacent room, such as a day room or group activity space, may intervene. Where individual occupant sleeping rooms adjoin a day room or group activity space which is utilized for access to an exitway, such sleeping rooms may open directly to the day space and may be separated in elevation by a one-half or full-story height (see 14-3.7).

Figure 14-5 illustrates the requirements of Exception No. 2.

14-2.5.2 All exits may discharge through the level of exit discharge. The requirements of 5-7.2 may be waived provided that not more than 50 percent of the exits discharge into a single fire compartment.

14-2.5.3 No exit or exit access shall contain a corridor, hallway or aisle having a pocket or dead end exceeding 50 ft (15.24 m) for Use Conditions II, III or IV and 20 ft (6.1 m) for Use Condition V.

Figure 14-6 illustrates the requirements of 14-2.5.3.

EXIT ACCESS CORRIDOR

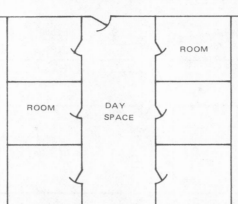

Figure 14-5. One Adjacent Room May Intervene Between Sleeping Room and Exit Access Corridor. Sleeping rooms may be separated in elevation by ½ to 1 story (see 14-2.5.1, Exception No. 2).

14-2.5.4 A sallyport may be permitted in a means of egress where there are provisions for continuous and unobstructed passage through the sallyport during an emergency exit condition.

Figure 14-7 illustrates the requirements of 14-2.5.4.

14-2.5.5 Aisles, corridors, and ramps required for access or exit shall be at least 4 ft (121.92 cm) in width.

14-2.6 Measurement of Travel Distance to Exits.

14-2.6.1   Travel distance:

(a) Between any room door required as exit access and an exit shall not exceed 100 ft (30.48 m);

(b) Between any point in a room and an exit shall not exceed 150 ft (45.72 m); and

(c) Between any point in a sleeping room or suite and an exit access door of that room or suite shall not exceed 50 ft (15.24 m).

Exception: The travel distance in (a) or (b) above may be increased by 50 ft (15.24 m) in buildings protected throughout by an approved automatic sprinkler system or smoke control system.

Travel distance is measured to the closest exit, not to both exits required by 14-2.4. Figure 14-8 illustrates the requirements of 14-2.6.1.

14-2.7 Discharge from Exits.   (*See 14-2.1 and 14-2.5.*)

14-2.8 Illumination of Means of Egress.   Illumination shall be in accordance with Section 5-8.

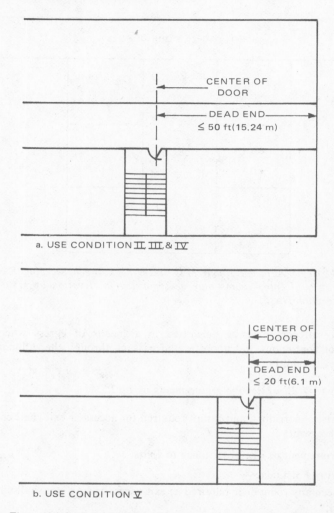

a. USE CONDITION II, III, & IV

b. USE CONDITION V

Figure 14-6. Dead-End Corridor Requirements (see 14-2.5.3).

14-2.9 Emergency Lighting.   Emergency lighting shall be in accordance with Section 5-9.

14-2.10 Marking of Means of Egress.   Exit marking shall be provided in areas accessible to the public in accordance with Section 5-10.

Exception: Exit signs may be omitted in sleeping room areas.

14-2.11 Special Features.

14-2.11.1   Doors within means of egress shall be as required in Chapter 5.

Exception: As provided in 14-2.11.2 through 14-2.11.7.

14-2.11.2   Doors to resident sleeping rooms shall be at least 28 in. (71.12 cm) in clear width.

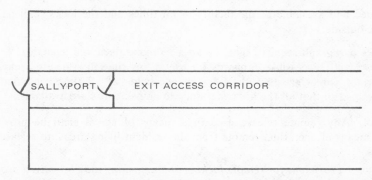

Figure 14-7. Requirements for Sallyport or Security Vestibule. Both doors of sallyport must be capable of being opened at the same time to provide unobstructed egress (see 14-2.5.4).

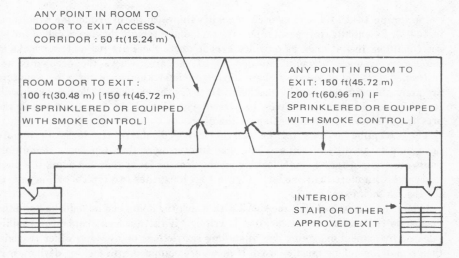

Figure 14-8. Maximum Travel Distance to Exits, New Detention and Correctional Occupancies (see 14-2.6.1). The travel distance is measured along the natural path of travel (see 5-6.2). "Sprinklered" means that the entire building is protected by a complete approved automatic extinguishing system. "Smoke Control" means that the entire building or fire area is equipped with a system to control the movement of smoke in accordance with NFPA 90A, Standard for the Installation of Air Conditioning and Ventilating Systems.[4]

It may be necessary to provide a certain number of resident sleeping rooms with doors providing a minimum clear width of 32 in. (81.28 cm) (see 5-2.1.1.2.1) in order to comply with the requirements for the physically handicapped. Such sleeping rooms should be located where there is a direct accessible access to the exterior or to an area of safe refuge (see 14-3.7).

14-2.11.3   Doors from areas of refuge to the exterior may be locked with key lock in lieu of locking methods described in 14-2.11.4. The keys to unlock such doors shall be maintained and available at the facility at all times and the locks shall be operable from the outside.

This paragraph requires that the keys be maintained and available. "Available" means readily accessible to guards for use at any time to evacuate occupants. The important points are that the keys be accessible at all times and that they be maintained so that all the keys necessary to unlock doors are available.

14-2.11.4   Any remote release used in a means of egress shall be provided with reliable means of operation, remote from the resident living areas, to release locks on all doors.

Exception: Provisions for remote locking and unlocking may be waived provided not more than ten doors are necessary to be unlocked in order to move all occupants from one smoke compartment to an area of refuge as promptly as required for remote unlocking. The opening of all necessary doors shall be accomplished with no more than two separate keys.

Paragraph 14-2.11.4 is to be used in conjunction with the use condition definitions in 14-1.3. Essentially, this paragraph says that where remote locking is called for by use condition, then it must be provided except where there are ten or fewer locks in the egress system. "Remote" means out of the area where the occupants are restrained. It is *not* necessary to have the remote unlocking mechanism in a separate fire area, although this may be beneficial. Doors in the exit should be unlocked prior to unlocking sleeping room doors to prevent jamming of the exit door due to the pressure of several persons pushing on the door.

The exception permits the manual unlocking of up to ten locks to remove occupants to an area of refuge. This may involve more than ten doors if multiple doors are secured with a single locking mechanism, or fewer than ten doors if a door is secured with more than one lock. Figure 14-9 illustrates two typical arrangements for the ten lock exception.

It must be recognized that the speed with which the doors can be unlocked and the occupants removed to a safe location is critical. If the ten locks cannot be rapidly released by manual unlocking due to staffing restrictions or whatever other reasons, then remote unlocking must be used. If doors are equipped with locking devices, it is assumed that the locks will be used and must be counted in the total number of locks.

14-2.11.5   All power-operated sliding doors or power-operated locks for swinging doors shall be so constructed that in the event of power interruption or power failure a manual mechanical means operable from a remote location or by key and lock mechanism at the door shall be provided to manually release locks and move sliding doors to a full open position.

14-2.11.6   Doors remotely unlocked under emergency conditions shall not automatically relock when closed unless specific action is taken at the remote location to enable doors to relock.

Paragraph 14-2.11.6 requires that once doors are remotely unlocked under emergency conditions, they cannot automatically relock should they reclose unless specific action is taken to lock them. This specific action can be at the individual door or at the remote location.

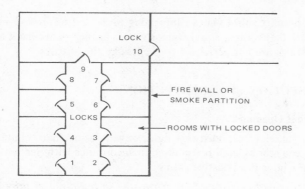

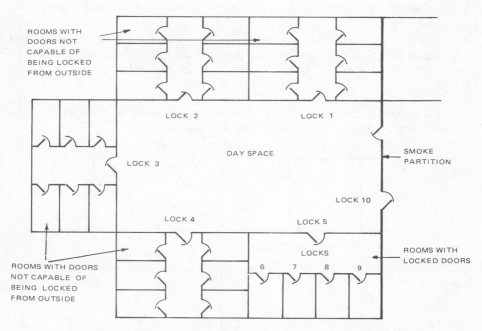

Figure 14-9. Maximum of Ten Manually Unlocked Doors or Locks (see 14-2.11.4, Exception).

14-2.11.7 Standby emergency power shall be provided for all electrically power-operated sliding doors and power-operated locks. Power shall be arranged to automatically operate upon failure of normal power within 10 seconds and to maintain the necessary power source for at least 1½ hours.

Exception: This provision is not applicable for facilities with ten locks or less complying with the exception in 14-2.11.4.

14-2.11.8 Spiral stairs meeting the requirements of 5-2.2.1.6 are permitted for access to and between staff locations.

Paragraph 14-2.11.8 permits spiral stairs conforming to 5-2.2.1.6 for staff only. Note that Chapter 5 restricts the use of spiral stairs to areas having an occupant load of five or fewer. Spiral stairs are not permitted for access by the inmates.

SECTION 14-3   PROTECTION

14-3.1 Protection of Vertical Openings.

14-3.1.1   Any stairway, ramp, elevator, hoistway, light, or ventilation shaft, chute, or other vertical opening between stories shall be enclosed in accordance with Section 6-2 with construction having a 2-hour fire-resistive rating.

Exception No. 1:   One-hour rated enclosures are permitted in buildings required to be of Type II (111).

Exception No. 2:   Stairs that do not connect a corridor, do not connect more than two levels, and do not serve as a means of egress need not comply with these regulations.

Exception No. 3:   The fire resistance rating of enclosures in detention and correctional occupancies protected throughout by an approved automatic sprinkler system may be reduced to 1 hour in buildings up to, and including, three stories in height.

Paragraph 14-3.1.1 specifies protection levels required to maintain floor-to-floor separation. Exception No. 2 is illustrated in Figure 14-10.

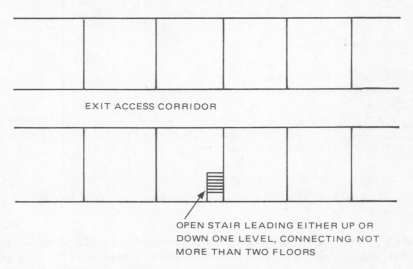

EXIT ACCESS CORRIDOR

OPEN STAIR LEADING EITHER UP OR DOWN ONE LEVEL, CONNECTING NOT MORE THAN TWO FLOORS

Figure 14-10. Open Stairs in Accordance with 14-3.1.1, Exception No. 2.

14-3.1.2   Two communicating floor levels are permitted without enclosure protection between levels provided all the following conditions are met:

(a) The entire normally occupied area, including all communicating floor levels, is sufficiently open and unobstructed so that it may be assumed that a fire or other dangerous condition in any part will be immediately obvious to the occupants or supervisory personnel in the area.

(b) Exit capacity is sufficient to provide simultaneously for all the occupants of all communicating levels and areas, all communicating levels in the same fire area being considered as a single floor area for purposes of determination of required exit capacity.

(c) Each floor level, considered separately, has at least one-half of its individual required exit capacity accessible by exit access leading directly out of that level without transversing another communicating floor level.

Paragraph 14-3.1.2 permits open communication between two floors. The space must be sufficiently open to permit supervisory personnel to immediately recognize a potential fire problem; the total exit capacity must be sufficient to handle the entire occupant load of both floors; and each level must have exit access directly out of that level without travel on the communicating level to handle one-half its occupant load.

14-3.2 Protection from Hazards.

14-3.2.1   An area used for general storage, boiler or furnace rooms, fuel storage, janitor's closets, maintenance shops including woodworking and painting areas, laundries and kitchens shall be separated from other parts of the building with construction having not less than a 1-hour fire resistance rating and all openings shall be protected with self-closing fire doors, or such area shall be provided with automatic sprinkler protection. Where the hazard is severe, both the fire resistance separation and automatic sprinklers shall be provided.

Hazardous areas are spaces with contents which, because of their basic nature (as in the case of flammable liquids) or because of the quantity of combustible materials involved, represent a significantly higher hazard than would otherwise be typical of detention and correctional occupancies.

Hazardous areas must be separated from other areas by 1-hour fire-resistant construction complete with approved fire doors protecting door openings and dampers in any ducts which penetrate the enclosure, or the area may be protected by automatic sprinklers. In those instances where the hazard is judged to be severe by the authority having jurisdiction, both the fire-resistant separation and automatic sprinkler protection are required. Where automatic sprinkler protection is provided and the hazard is not severe, the hazardous area may be separated by nonrated barriers designed to resist the passage of smoke.

Where flammable liquids are handled or stored, NFPA 30, Flammable and Combustible Liquids Code,[5] should be consulted to establish the minimum criteria necessary to mitigate this hazard.

14-3.2.2   Padded cells are severe hazard areas.

Padded cells are considered severe hazard areas due to high heat release, the speed of combustion, and the quantity of smoke produced by the padding materials. Due to this, padded cells must be protected by automatic sprinklers and separated by 1-hour construction.

14-3.2.3 Cooking facilities shall be protected in accordance with 7-2.3.

14-3.3 Interior Finish.

14-3.3.1 Interior finish of walls and ceilings in corridors, exits and any space not separated from corridors and exits by a partition capable of retarding the passage of smoke shall be Class A. All other areas shall be Class A, B or C in accordance with Section 6-5.

14-3.3.2 Interior floor finish in corridors and exits and any space not separated from corridors and exits by a partition capable of retarding the passage of smoke shall be Class I in accordance with Section 6-5.

Paragraphs 14-3.3.1 and 14-3.3.2 require only that the separating partition be capable of retarding the passage of smoke. The partition must be of substantial construction, but is not required to have a fire resistance. See Chapter 6 for definition of "smoke barrier."

14-3.4 Detection, Alarm and Communication Systems.

14-3.4.1 Required fire detection and signaling devices and systems shall be in accordance with Section 7-6.

Exception: Except as provided in this section.

14-3.4.2 Every building shall have a manually operated fire alarm system in accordance with Section 7-6, and such system shall be electrically supervised.

Exception No. 1:   Manual fire alarm boxes may be locked.

Exception No. 2:   Manual fire alarm boxes may be located at staff locations in lieu of being located in the sleeping room areas.

Paragraph 14-3.4.2 permits locking of the fire alarm boxes. However, where manual stations are locked, staff must be present on a 24-hour basis, and must have keys readily available to unlock the manual stations. Where a continuously manned staff location is provided in the sleeping area, the manual station may be provided within the locked staff location.

14-3.4.3 Operation of any fire alarm activating device shall automatically, without delay, accomplish general alarm indication and control functions. Zoned or coded systems shall be permitted to be used.

The use of presignal systems is prohibited by 14-3.4.3.

14-3.4.4 The fire alarm system shall be arranged to transmit an alarm automatically to the fire department legally committed to serve the area in which the facility is located by the most direct and reliable method approved by the local regulations.

Exception: Smoke detectors may be arranged to alarm locally and at a constantly attended location only and are not required to be connected to the fire alarm or to the fire department.

Where the fire department is not equipped to receive such alarms or direct transmission to the fire department is not permitted, arrangements should be made

for the prompt notification of the fire department. The next best option is notification by an approved central station alarm system. Where smoke detectors are provided, they are not required to sound the fire alarm or to transmit a signal to the fire department, but are required to sound an alarm at a constantly attended location, unless specifically noted otherwise.

14-3.4.5 An approved automatic smoke detection system shall be installed in all sleeping areas and areas not separated from sleeping areas by fire-resistive construction in Use Condition IV and V areas and in sleeping rooms occupied by more than four people in Use Condition III. Such systems shall be installed in accordance with Section 7-6 and with the applicable standards listed in Section 7-6, but in no case shall smoke detectors be spaced further apart than 30 ft (914.4 cm) on centers or more than 15 ft (457.2 cm) from any wall. All automatic smoke detection systems required by this section shall be electrically interconnected to the fire alarm system.

Exception No. 1: Buildings protected by a complete automatic fire extinguishing system in accordance with 14-3.5 shall install a smoke detection system in all corridors with smoke detectors spaced no further apart than 30 ft (914.4 cm) on centers or more than 15 ft (457.2 cm) from any wall.

Exception No. 2: Other arrangements and positioning of smoke detectors may be used to prevent damage or tampering or for other purposes provided the function of detecting any fire is fulfilled and the siting of detectors is such that the speed of detection will be equivalent to that provided by the spacing and arrangements described above. This may include the location of detectors in exhaust ducts from cells, behind grills, or in other locations. The equivalent performance of the design, however, must be acceptable to the authority having jurisdiction in accordance with the Equivalency Concepts specified in Section 1-5 of this Code.

14-3.4.6 An approved automatic smoke detection system shall be installed in all corridors and common spaces of Use Condition II and III detention and correctional facilities. Such systems shall be installed in accordance with Section 7-6 and with the applicable standards listed in Section 7-6, but in no case shall smoke detectors be spaced further apart than 30 ft (914.4 cm) on centers or more than 15 ft (457.2 cm) from any wall.

Exception: Other arrangements and positioning of smoke detectors may be used to prevent damage or tampering or for other purposes provided the function of detecting any fire is fulfilled and the siting of detectors is such that the speed of detection will be equivalent to that provided by the spacing and arrangements described above. This may include the location of detectors in exhaust ducts from cells, behind grills, or in other locations. The equivalent performance of the design, however, must be acceptable to the authority having jurisdiction in accordance with the Equivalency Concepts specified in Section 1-5 of this Code.

14-3.4.7 Any fire detection device or system required by this section shall be electrically interconnected with the fire alarm system.

14-3.4.8 Any alarm system(s) and any detection system(s) required in this section shall be provided with a secondary power supply in accordance with 2-3.4.2 of *Standard for the Installation, Maintenance, and Use of Local Protective Signaling Systems*, NFPA 72A.

14-3.5 Extinguishment Requirements.

14-3.5.1 When required by 14-1.6, facilities shall be protected throughout by an approved automatic sprinkler system in accordance with Section 7-7.

14-3.5.2 Where exceptions are stated in the provisions of this *Code* (*including those specified in 14-3.8.1*) for detention and correctional occupancies equipped with an approved automatic extinguishing system, and where such systems are required, the systems shall be in complete accordance with Section 7-7 for systems in light hazard occupancies and shall be electrically interconnected with the fire alarm system.

14-3.5.3 The main sprinkler control valve(s) shall be electrically supervised so that at least a local alarm will sound at a constantly attended location when the valve is closed.

14-3.5.4 The sprinkler piping, serving no more than six sprinklers for any isolated hazardous area, may be connected directly to a domestic water supply system having a capacity sufficient to provide 0.15 gal per minute per sq ft (1.02×10^{-4} cu m/s/sq m) of floor area throughout the entire enclosed area. An indicating shutoff valve shall be installed in an accessible location between the sprinklers and the connection to the domestic water supply. (*For sprinkler requirements for hazardous areas see 14-3.2 and for sprinkler requirements for chutes see 14-5.4.*)

14-3.5.5 Portable fire extinguishers shall be provided in all detention and correctional occupancies in accordance with 7-7.4.1.

Exception No. 1: Access to portable fire extinguishers may be locked.

Exception No. 2: Portable fire extinguishers may be located at staff locations only.

The exceptions to 14-3.5.5 permit locking of the fire extinguishers. Where extinguishers are locked, staff must be present on a 24-hour basis, and the staff must have keys readily available to unlock the extinguishers. Time is of the essence in using extinguishers; therefore, keys must be carried by the staff or be readily accessible.

14-3.5.6 Standpipe and hose systems shall be provided in accordance with 7-7.4.2 as follows:

(a) Class III standpipe and hose systems shall be provided for buildings over 75 ft (22.86 m) in height.

(b) Class II or III standpipe and hose systems shall be provided for any unsprinklered building over three stories in height.

Exception No. 1: One-in. (2.54-cm) diameter formed hose in lieu of hose requirements of Standard for the Installation of Standpipes and Hose Systems, NFPA 14, may be used.

Exception No. 2: Separate Class I and Class II systems may be used in place of Class III.

Exception No. 1 permits the use of 1-in. (2.54-cm) formed rubber hose in place of fabric-jacket rubber-lined hose normally required in standpipe systems. The rubber hose is normally stored on reels and is somewhat easier to use.

14-3.6 Corridors. [*See 14-3.8, Special Features (Subdivision of Resident Housing Spaces).*]

14-3.7 Subdivision of Building Spaces.

14-3.7.1 Smoke barriers shall be provided, regardless of building construction type, as follows:

(a) To divide every story used by residents for sleeping, or any other story having an occupant load of 50 or more persons, into at least two compartments, and

(b) To limit the housing of a maximum of 200 residents in any smoke compartment, and

(c) To limit the travel distance to a door in a smoke barrier:

1. From any room door required as exit access to 100 ft (30.48 m),
2. From any point in a room to 150 ft (45.72 m).

Exception No. 1: Protection may be accomplished with horizontal exits (see 5-2.4).

Exception No. 2: Spaces having direct exit to (a) a public way, (b) a building separated from the resident housing area by 2-hour fire resistance or 50 ft (15.24 m) of open space, or (c) an enclosed area having a holding space 50 ft (15.24 m) from the housing area that provided 6 sq ft (.56 sq m) or more of refuge area per person (resident, staff, visitors, etc.) that may be present at the time of the fire fulfills the requirement for subdivision of such spaces provided the locking arrangement of doors involved meets the requirements for doors at the compartment barrier for the use condition involved.

Smoke barriers and horizontal exits used to subdivide a building serve three purposes fundamental to the protection of occupants in that they:

1. Limit the spread of fire and fire-produced contaminants,
2. Limit the number of occupants exposed to a single fire, and
3. Provide for horizontal relocation of occupants by creating an area of refuge on the same floor.

The requirements of 14-3.7.1 for subdividing building spaces are illustrated in Figure 14-11.

Figure 14-12 illustrates the requirements of Exception No. 2 to 14-3.7.1.

14-3.7.2 Any required smoke barrier shall be constructed in accordance with Section 6-3. Barriers shall be of substantial construction and shall have structural fire resistance. Fixed wired glass vision panels shall be permitted in such barriers provided they do not individually exceed 1,296 sq in. (.84 sq m) in area and are mounted in approved steel frames. There is no restriction on the total number of such vision panels in any barrier (e.g., a smoke barrier may consist of wire glass panels mounted in a security grill arrangement).

Paragraph 14-3.7.2 requires smoke barriers to have structural fire resistance. The specific fire resistance is omitted. The intent is to eliminate highly combustible or flimsy materials which could possibly limit smoke movement but have little structural integrity, such as plastic sheeting. Structural fire resistance is defined as the ability of the assembly to stay in place and maintain structural integrity without consideration of heat transmission. Twelve-gage steel plate suitably framed and stiffened meets this requirement. This paragraph does permit the entire smoke

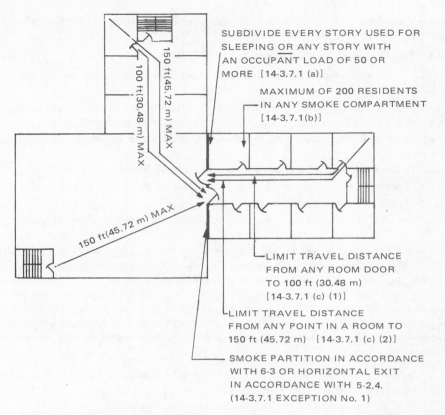

SUBDIVIDE EVERY STORY USED FOR
SLEEPING OR ANY STORY WITH
AN OCCUPANT LOAD OF 50 OR
MORE [14-3.7.1 (a)]

MAXIMUM OF 200 RESIDENTS
IN ANY SMOKE COMPARTMENT
[14-3.7.1(b)]

100 ft(30.48 m) MAX

150 ft(45.72 m) MAX

150 ft(45.72 m) MAX

LIMIT TRAVEL DISTANCE
FROM ANY ROOM DOOR
TO 100 ft (30.48 m)
[14-3.7.1 (c) (1)]

LIMIT TRAVEL DISTANCE
FROM ANY POINT IN A ROOM TO
150 ft (45.72 m) [14-3.7.1 (c) (2)]

SMOKE PARTITION IN ACCORDANCE
WITH 6-3 OR HORIZONTAL EXIT
IN ACCORDANCE WITH 5-2.4.
(14-3.7.1 EXCEPTION No. 1)

Figure 14-11. Subdivision of Building Spaces, New Detention and Correctional Occupancies.

barrier to be constructed of wired glass panels not exceeding 1,296 sq in. (.84 sq m) each in steel frames.

14-3.7.3   At least 6 net sq ft (.56 sq m) per occupant shall be provided on each side of the smoke barrier for the total number of occupants in adjoining compartments.

14-3.7.4   Doors in smoke barriers shall swing in the direction of egress. In those applications where egress may be in either direction, a pair of swinging doors shall be provided. The minimum clear width of exit in the direction of exit travel shall be 32 in. (81.28 cm).

Exception: Doors in a means of egress may be of the horizontal sliding type provided the force to slide the door to its fully open position does not exceed 50 lb (222 N) with a perpendicular force against the door of 50 lb (222 N).

14-3.7.5   Doors in smoke barriers shall be self-closing or automatic closing as required in 5-2.1.2.3. Swinging doors shall be self-latching.

14-3.7.6   Doors in smoke barriers shall conform with the requirements for doors in means of egress as specified in Section 14-2 and shall have locking and release arrangements according to the use condition as follows:

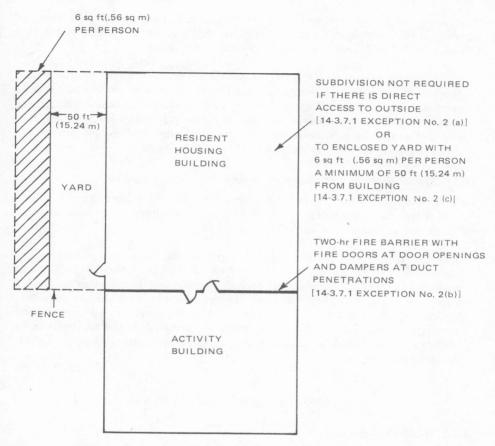

6 sq ft(.56 sq m)
PER PERSON

50 ft
(15.24 m)

RESIDENT
HOUSING
BUILDING

YARD

FENCE

ACTIVITY
BUILDING

SUBDIVISION NOT REQUIRED
IF THERE IS DIRECT
ACCESS TO OUTSIDE
[14-3.7.1 EXCEPTION No. 2 (a)]
OR
TO ENCLOSED YARD WITH
6 sq ft (.56 sq m) PER PERSON
A MINIMUM OF 50 ft (15.24 m)
FROM BUILDING
[14-3.7.1 EXCEPTION No. 2 (c)]

TWO-hr FIRE BARRIER WITH
FIRE DOORS AT DOOR OPENINGS
AND DAMPERS AT DUCT
PENETRATIONS
[14-3.7.1 EXCEPTION No. 2(b)]

Figure 14-12. Alternatives to Subdivision by Smoke Barriers.

(a) For Use Conditions I (Free Egress) and II (Zoned Egress) there shall be no locks or other arrangement to prevent free egress through the doors in the smoke partition.

(b) For Use Conditions III (Zoned Impeded Egress) and IV (Impeded Egress) the doors may be locked to prevent free egress provided there is remote release control conforming with the requirements for such control as specified in 14-2.11.4.

(c) For Use Condition V (Contained) the doors in smoke barriers may be locked with a key provided the keying arrangement meets the requirements specified for locked egress doors in 14-2.11.

14-3.7.7 Vision panels of approved transparent wired glass not exceeding 720 sq in. (.46 sq m) in steel frames shall be provided in each door in a smoke barrier.

14-3.7.8 An approved damper designed to resist the passage of smoke shall be provided at each point a duct penetrates a smoke barrier required by 14-3.7.1. The damper shall close upon detection of smoke. (*Also see Section 6-3.*)

Exception: Buildings designed with an engineered smoke control system in accordance with Standard for the Installation of Air Conditioning and Ventilating Systems, NFPA 90A, need not comply with this requirement.

The current state-of-the-art on smoke control technology is limited to systems and approaches that limit or prevent the migration of smoke from one compartment to another. Exhaust fans, smoke vents, and other means of relieving smoke from the fire area to the outside can assist in this, but cannot be expected to make the fire area safe and cannot be substituted for the compartmentation, detection, evacuation, extinguishment, and other criteria applicable to safety in the space of fire origin.

14-3.8 Special Features.   (Subdivision of Resident Housing Spaces.)

14-3.8.1   Any individual cell, dormitory, or other space where residents are housed shall be separated from all other spaces by substantial construction of noncombustible materials in accordance with Table 14-3.8.1.

Paragraph 14-3.8.1 provides for the separation of areas where residents are housed. This separation provides for two basic items: (1) keeping the fire and its products contained to the area of origin, and (2) protecting those outside the area of origin. The table establishes different requirements based on the use condition involved. Within each use condition, different provisions are required depending upon whether automatic sprinkler protection is or is not provided. Note 4 also provides an additional method which, in combination with the locking options previously stated, can be quite useful.

SECTION 14-4   SPECIAL PROVISIONS

14-4.1 Windowless Buildings.

14-4.1.1   For the purposes of this chapter a windowless building or portion of a building is one with nonopenable windows, windows not readily breakable, or with no windows.

14-4.1.2   Windowless buildings shall be provided with vent openings, smoke shafts, or an engineered smoke control system to provide ventilation (mechanical or natural) for each windowless smoke compartment.

Paragraph 14-4.1.2 does not require venting or smoke control for those areas (smoke compartments) which are provided with operable windows.

14-4.2 Underground Buildings.

14-4.2.1   See Chapter 30 for requirements for underground buildings.

SECTION 14-5   BUILDING SERVICES

14-5.1 Utilities.

14-5.1.1   Utilities shall comply with the provisions of Section 7-1.

Table 14-3.8.1

USE CONDITION	II		III		IV		V	
Feature	NS	AS	NS	AS	NS	AS	NS	AS
Room to Room Separation	NR	NR	NR	NR	ST	NR	FR(½)	ST
Room Face to Corridor Separation	ST	NR	ST	NR	ST	NR	FR	ST
Room Face to Common Space Separation	NR	NR	NR <50 ft* (15.24 m) / ST >50 ft* (15.24 m)	NR <50 ft* (15.24 m) / ST >50 ft* (15.24 m)	ST	NR	FR	ST
Common Space to Corridor Separation	FR	NR	FR	NR	FR	NR	FR	ST
Total Openings in Solid Room Face	120 sq in. (.08 sq m)		120 sq in. (.08 sq m)		120 sq in. (.08 sq m)		120 sq in. (.08 sq m) Closable from inside or 120 sq in. (.08 sq m) w/smoke control	

AS — Protected by automatic sprinklers
NS — Not protected by automatic sprinklers
NR — No requirement

ST — Smoketight
FR — Fire Rated — 1 hour
FR(½) — Fire Rated — ½ hour

*This is the travel distance through the common space to the exit access corridor.

NOTE 1: Doors in openings in partitions required to be fire resistive by this chart in other than required enclosures of exits or hazardous areas shall be substantial doors, of construction that will resist fire for at least 20 minutes. Wire glass vision panels are permitted. Latches and door closers are not required on cell doors.

NOTE 2: Doors in openings in partitions required to be smoketight by the chart shall be substantial doors, of construction that will resist the passage of smoke. Latches and door closers are not required on cell doors.

NOTE 3: "Total Openings in Solid Room Face" includes all openings (undercuts, food passes, grills, etc.), the total of which will not exceed 120 sq in. (.08 sq m). All openings shall be 36 in. (91.44 cm) or less above the floor.

NOTE 4: Under Use Condition II, III, or IV, a space housing not more than 16 persons and subdivided by open construction (any combination of grating doors and grating walls or solid walls) may be considered one room. The perimeter walls of such space shall be of smoketight construction. Smoke detection shall be provided in such space. Under Use Condition IV, common walls between sleeping areas within the space shall be smoketight and grating doors and fronts may be used.

14-5.1.2 Alarms, emergency communication systems and the illumination of generator set locations shall be as described in the Life Safety Branch of the *National Electrical Code*, NFPA 70.

14-5.2 Heating, Ventilating and Air Conditioning.

14-5.2.1 Heating, ventilating and air conditioning equipment shall comply with the provisions of Section 7-2 and shall be installed in accordance with manufacturer's specifications.

Exception: As modified in 14-5.2.2 following.

14-5.2.2 Portable space heating devices are prohibited. Any heating device other than a central heating plant shall be so designed and installed that combustible material will not be ignited by it or its appurtenances. If fuel-fired, such heating devices shall be chimney or vent connected, shall take air for combustion directly from outside, and shall be so designed and installed to provide for complete separation of the combustion system from the atmosphere of the occupied area. The heating system shall have safety devices to immediately stop the flow of fuel and shut down the equipment in case of either excessive temperatures or ignition failure.

Exception: Approved suspended unit heaters may be used in locations other than means of egress and sleeping areas provided such heaters are located high enough to be out of the reach of persons using the area and provided they are vent connected and equipped with the safety devices called for above.

14-5.2.3 Combustion and ventilation air for boiler, incinerator or heater rooms shall be taken directly from and discharged directly to the outside air.

14-5.3 Elevators, dumbwaiters, and vertical conveyors shall comply with the provisions of Section 7-4.

14-5.4 Rubbish Chutes, Incinerators and Laundry Chutes.

14-5.4.1 Rubbish chutes, incinerators and laundry chutes shall comply with the provisions of Section 7-5.

14-5.4.2 Any rubbish chute or linen chute, including pneumatic rubbish and linen systems, shall be provided with automatic extinguishing protection installed in accordance with *Standard for the Installation of Sprinkler Systems*, NFPA 13.

14-5.4.3 Any trash chute shall discharge into a trash collecting room used for no other purpose and protected in accordance with Section 6-4.

14-5.4.4 Any incinerator shall not be directly flue-fed nor shall any floor chute directly connect with the combustion chamber.

REFERENCES CITED IN *CODE*

(These publications comprise a part of the requirements to the extent called for by the Code.)

NFPA 13, *Standard for the Installation of Sprinkler Systems*, NFPA, Boston, 1980.

NFPA 14, *Standard for the Installation of Standpipes and Hose Systems*, NFPA, Boston, 1980.

NFPA 70, *National Electrical Code*, NFPA, Boston, 1981.

NFPA 72A, *Standard for the Installation, Maintenance and Use of Local Protective Signaling Systems,* NFPA, Boston, 1979.

NFPA 90A, *Standard for the Installation of Air Conditioning and Ventilating Systems,* NFPA, Boston, 1978.

REFERENCES CITED IN COMMENTARY

[1]"A Study of Penal Institution Fires," NFPA FR 78-1.

[2]James Bell, "Eleven Die in Jail Fire," *Fire Journal,* Vol. 74, No. 4, July 1980, pp. 23-25, 90.

[3]NFPA 220, *Standard Types of Building Construction,* NFPA, Boston, 1979.

[4]NFPA 90A, *Standard for the Installation of Air Conditioning and Ventilating Systems,* NFPA, Boston, 1978.

[5]NFPA 30, *Flammable and Combustible Liquids Code,* NFPA, Boston, 1981.

15

EXISTING DETENTION AND CORRECTIONAL OCCUPANCIES

(See also Chapter 31.)

In this, the 1981 Edition of the *Life Safety Code*, detention and correctional occupancies now are covered in their own chapters, Chapters 14 and 15. In previous editions these occupancies were discussed in the chapter on institutional occupancies, later renamed health care occupancies (Chapters 12 and 13 of this edition).

In 1974 the Committee on Safety to Life decided to establish a Sectional Committee on Penal Occupancies. It was, however, too late to prepare a report for the 1976 Edition of the *Code*, and in 1977 the Committee on Safety to Life was reorganized as a Technical Committee with subcommittees. The Subcommittee on Penal Occupancies was appointed with its first working meeting in January of 1978. It was soon renamed the Subcommittee on Detention and Correctional Occupancies. During this period, there were several major detention and correctional occupancy fires which added emphasis to the need for the Subcommittee and provided information for its use. These included:

October 1974	Youth Correctional Center Cranston, RI	2 dead[1]
June 1975	Seminole County Jail Sanford, FL	11 dead[1]
November 1975	Lycoming County Jail Williamsport, PA	3 dead[1]
June 1976	Marion State Prison Marion, NC	9 dead[1]
June 1977	Maury County Jail Columbia, IN	42 dead[1]
June 1977	St. John City Detention Center St. John, NB, Canada	21 dead[1]
July 1977	Federal Correctional Institution Danbury, CT	5 dead[1]
December 1979	Lancaster County Jail Lancaster, SC	11 dead[2]

No list of prison fires would be complete without mentioning the Ohio State Penitentiary fire in Columbus, Ohio, in April 1930 in which 320 were killed, and the State Road Camp fire in Berrydale, Florida, in July 1967 in which 38 were killed.[1]

SECTION 15-1   GENERAL

15-1.1 Application.

15-1.1.1 Existing detention and correctional facilities shall comply with the provisions of this chapter. Provisions of Chapter 14 do not apply to existing detention and correctional facilities. Existing facilities shall also comply with the applicable requirements of Chapter 31.

15-1.1.2 This section establishes life safety requirements for all existing detention and correctional facilities.

Exception: Use Condition I requirements are those stated in the applicable requirements for existing buildings of Chapters 17, 19, or 20.

See 15-1.4.1 for definition of use condition.

15-1.1.3 Detention and correctional occupancies are those used for purposes such as jails, detention centers, correctional institutions, reformatories, houses of correction, pre-release centers, and other residential-restrained care facilities where occupants are confined or housed under some degree of restraint or security.

15-1.1.4 Detention and correctional occupancies provide sleeping facilities for four or more residents and are occupied by persons who are generally prevented from taking self-preservation action because of security measures not under the occupants' control.

15-1.1.5 Total Concept. All detention and correctional facilities shall be so designed, constructed, maintained and operated as to minimize the possibility of a fire emergency.

Because the safety of all occupants in all detention and correctional facilities cannot be adequately assured solely by a dependence on evacuation of the building, their protection from fire shall be provided by appropriate arrangement of facilities, adequate trained staff, and careful development of operating, security, and maintenance procedures composed of the following:

(a) Proper design, construction and compartmentation,

(b) Provision for detection, alarm and extinguishment,

(c) Fire prevention and planning, training, and drilling in programs for the isolation of fire and transfer of occupants to areas of refuge or evacuation of the building, or protection of the occupants in place,

(d) Provision security to the degree necessary for the safety of the public and the occupants of the facility.

It is important to note that the occupants' safety is dependent upon the effective management of his or her environment, including building structure, interior finish, furnishings, decorations, clothing, bedding, and all other materials which make up that environment. No code can prevent injury resulting from a person's careless or intentional actions. The best means of protection is to prevent the fire. Obviously, this is not always practical. The primary objective of the requirements of this chapter is to prevent fire from escaping the room of origin, thereby limiting the effects of the fire to occupants outside the room of origin.

15-1.1.6 Additions. Additions shall be separated from any existing structure not conforming with the provisions within Chapter 15 by a fire barrier having at least a 2-hour fire resistance rating constructed to the standards of the addition. Doors in these partitions shall normally be kept closed.

Exception: Doors may be held open if they meet the requirements of the exception to 5-2.1.2.3.

Note that doors may be located anywhere in the separating partition, but must be kept closed unless they meet the requirements for closing in the exception to 5-2.1.2.3.

Additions must comply with the provisions of Chapter 14. This paragraph, 15-1.1.6, makes provisions for the separation of the new construction from the existing occupancy when the existing occupancy does not comply with Chapter 15.

Figure 15-1 illustrates the requirements of 15-1.1.6.

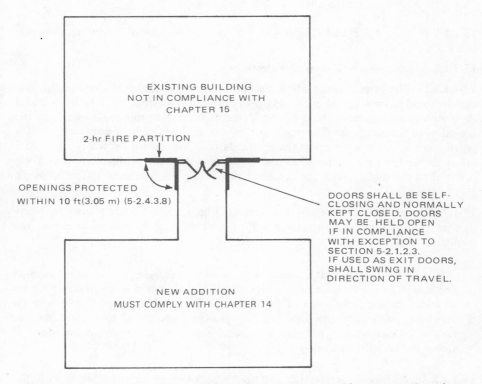

Figure 15-1. Separation of New Addition from Existing Building Not in Compliance with Chapter 15 (see 15-1.1.6).

15-1.1.7 Modernization or Renovation.

15-1.1.7.1 No construction in either modernization or renovation projects shall diminish the fire safety features of the facility below the level of new construction as described elsewhere in this *Code*. Alterations or installations of new building services equipment shall be accomplished as nearly as possible in conformance with the requirements for new construction.

Alterations may not reduce the level of life safety in an existing building below that required for new construction. If, however, an existing design exceeds the *Code* provisions for new construction, it is *not* required that the building's fire safety features in excess of the *Code* be maintained. It *is* required that the provisions for existing construction be met.

Although every effort should be made to satisfy the criteria for new construction during a building alteration or the installation of new equipment, the *Code* recognizes that such modifications cannot always be accomplished. Guidance for achieving "equivalency to life safety" is provided in Section 1-5. In any event, alterations, or installation of new building service equipment, may *not* reduce a building's level of life safety below that provided for existing buildings, nor may it reduce it below that which existed before the alteration (see Section 1-5).

15-1.1.7.2 (*See 1-6.3 and Chapter 31 for life safety provisions during construction.*)

15-1.1.8 Modification of Retroactive Provisions.

15-1.1.8.1 The requirements of this section may be modified if their application clearly would be impractical in the judgment of the authority having jurisdiction and if the resulting arrangement could be considered as presenting minimum hazard to the life safety of the occupants. The requirements may be modified by the authority having jurisdiction to allow alternative arrangements that will secure as nearly equivalent safety to life from fire as practical; but in no case shall the modification afford less safety than compliance with the corresponding provisions contained in the following part of this *Code*.

15-1.1.8.2 A limited but reasonable time shall be allowed for compliance with any part of this section, commensurate with the magnitude of expenditure and the disruption of services.

In some cases, appreciable cost may be involved in bringing an existing occupancy into compliance with the *Code*. Where this is true, it would be appropriate for the authority having jurisdiction to formulate a schedule, determined jointly with the occupancy management, which will allow suitable periods of time for correcting various deficiencies and will give due consideration to the ability of the owner to secure the necessary funds.

15-1.1.8.3 Alternative protection installed and accepted in accordance with the provisions of Section 1-5 shall be considered conforming for the purposes of this *Code*.

15-1.2 Mixed Occupancies.

Detention and correctional occupancies are a complex of structures, each serving a definite and usually different purpose. For instance, in all probability there will be represented in many institutions an example of all, or almost all, of the occupancy type classifications found in this *Code*. Exits and other features shall be governed by the type of occupancy classification and the hazard of occupancy unless specific exceptions are made.

All buildings and structures shall be classified using this chapter and 4-1.1 as a guide, subject to the ruling of the authority having jurisdiction in case of question as to the proper classification of any individual building or structure.

Use condition classification of the institution, as well as individual areas within the complex, shall always be considered by the authority having jurisdiction.

15-1.2.1 Egress provisions for areas of detention and correctional facilities which correspond to other occupancies shall meet the corresponding requirements of this *Code* for such occupancies. Where security operations necessitate the locking of required means of egress, necessary staff shall be provided for the supervised release of occupants during all times of use.

Release of occupants should be accomplished by a manually activated remote system capable of unlocking all doors in the means of egress or by a sufficient number of attendants who are *continuously* on duty in the immediate area of the exit doors, and who are provided with keys. Continuous supervision is essential.

15-1.2.2 Sections of detention and correctional facilities may be classified as other occupancies if they meet all of the following conditions:

(a) They are not intended to serve residents for purpose of housing, customary access or means of egress.

(b) They are adequately separated from areas of detention or correctional occupancies by construction having a fire resistance rating of at least 2 hours.

For example, administrative offices, maintenance areas, etc., which are not customarily used by the inmates, are not part of the egress system from the inmate occupied areas, and are separated by 2-hour rated fire-resistive construction, may be classified as another occupancy, such as business or industrial.

15-1.2.3 Detention and correctional occupancies in buildings housing other occupancies shall be completely separated from the other occupancies by construction having a fire resistance rating of at least 2 hours as provided for additions in 15-1.1.6.

Paragraph 15-1.2.3 requires that if a detention or correctional occupancy is located in a building of another classification (such as business or assembly), the detention or correctional occupancy must be separated from the other occupancy by construction having a fire resistance of 2 hours, as detailed in 15-1.1.6.

Note that 15-1.2.3 deals with occupancy classification only, and not with the hazard of contents. Hazard of contents is treated in 15-1.2.5.

15-1.2.4 All means of egress from detention and correctional occupancies that traverse other use areas shall, as a minimum, conform to requirements of this *Code* for detention and correctional occupancies.

The means of egress from detention and correctional occupancies which traverse non-detention and non-correctional spaces must conform to the requirements for detention and correctional occupancies. For example, if an opening in a 2-hour barrier between a detention or correctional occupancy and a business occupancy (offices) is used as a horizontal exit, then elements such as corridor widths, details of corridor protection, and stairway details in the business occupancy must conform to the appropriate requirements set forth in this chapter for existing detention and correctional occupancies.

15-1.2.5   Any area with a hazard of contents classified higher than that of the detention or correctional occupancy and located in the same building shall be protected, as required in 15-3.2.

This paragraph regulates those spaces in a detention and correctional occupancy which contain more hazardous materials (in quantity or type) than are usually found in this occupancy. Spaces such as rooms used for the storage of combustible materials, trash collection rooms, and paint shops must be protected in accordance with 15-3.2.

15-1.2.6   Non-detention or non-correctional related occupancies classified as containing high hazard contents shall not be permitted in buildings housing detention or correctional occupancies.

This paragraph prohibits another occupancy (such as storage) with highly hazardous contents (such as flammable liquids) from being located in a building housing detention and correctional occupancies. This paragraph limits the use of the building based upon occupancy classification with regard to hazard of contents. For example, this paragraph is not meant to exclude the storage of linens in a detention and correctional occupancy. The intent is to prevent a portion of a detention and correctional facility from being converted to a warehouse and having a larger quantity of combustibles than would be expected in a detention and correctional occupancy.

15-1.3 Special Definitions.

(a) **Sallyport (Security Vestibule).** A compartment provided with two or more doors where the intended purpose is to prevent the continuous and unobstructed passage by allowing the release of only one door at a time.

(b) **Fire Barrier.**   See Chapter 6.

(c) **Fire Compartment.**   See Chapter 6.

(d) **Smoke Barrier.**   See Chapter 6.

(e) **Smoke Compartment.**   See Chapter 6.

15-1.4 Classification of Occupancy.

15-1.4.1   Users and occupants of detention and correctional facilities at various times can be expected to include staff, visitors, and residents. The extent and nature of facility utilization by members of each of these groups will vary according to type of facility, its function and programs. For applications of the life safety requirements which follow, the resident user category is divided into five groups:

Use Condition I — Free Egress

Free movement is allowed from sleeping areas, and other spaces where access or occupancy is permitted, to the exterior via means of egress meeting the requirements of the *Code*.

In Use Condition I, there are no physical restrictions, such as locks, on the means of egress. The occupants are capable of self-preservation. An example might be a work release center where the doors are not locked.

Use Condition II — Zoned Egress

Free movement is allowed from sleeping areas and any other occupied smoke compartment to one or more other smoke compartments.

The occupants are free to move within the building, including free access across the smoke barrier. See Figure 15-2.

Use Condition III — Zoned Impeded Egress

Free movement is allowed within individual smoke compartments, such as within a residential unit comprised of individual sleeping rooms and group activity space, with egress impeded by remote control release of means of egress from such smoke compartment to another smoke compartment.

The important item to note in Use Condition III is that the smoke barrier door can be remotely unlocked. See Figure 15-2.

Use Condition IV — Impeded Egress

Free movement is restricted from an occupied space. Remote controlled release is provided to permit movement from all sleeping rooms, activity spaces and other occupied areas within the smoke compartment to other smoke compartment(s).

In Use Condition IV, occupants are locked in their cells. However, both the cell doors and the smoke barrier door can be remotely unlocked. See Figure 15-2.

Use Condition V — Contained

Free movement is restricted from an occupied space. Staff controlled manual release at each door is provided to permit movement from all sleeping rooms, activity spaces and other occupied areas within the smoke compartment to other smoke compart-ment(s).

All locks must be manually unlocked at the door to each cell and the smoke barrier door. See Figure 15-2.

15-1.4.2   To classify as Use Condition III or IV the arrangement, accessibility and security of the release mechanism(s) used for emergency egress shall be such that the minimum available staff, at any time, can promptly release the locks.

The important requirement noted in this paragraph is that the area must be under continuous supervision and that a sufficient number of staff must be available for, and capable of, releasing the locks.
Prompt operation is intended to be accomplished in the period of time following detection of fire by either the smoke detector(s) required by 15-3.4 or by other means

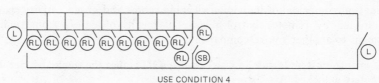

USE CONDITION 1

USE CONDITION 2

USE CONDITION 3

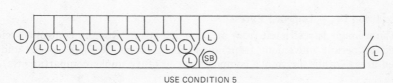

USE CONDITION 4

USE CONDITION 5

DETENTION AND CORRECTIONAL USE CONDITIONS

(L)   LOCKED

(RL)   LOCKED—REMOTE RELEASE OR EQUIVALENT

(SB)   SMOKE BARRIER OR HORIZONTAL EXIT

Figure 15-2. Classification of Occupancy by Use Condition (see 15-1.4.1).

(whichever comes first) and the advent of intolerable conditions forcing emergency evacuation. Fire tests have indicated that the time available is a function of the volume and height of the space involved and the rate of fire development. In traditional single-story corridor arrangements, the time between detection by smoke detectors and the advent of lethal conditions down to head height can be as short as approximately 3 minutes. In addition, it should be expected that approximately 1 minute will be required to evacuate all the occupants of a threatened smoke compartment once the locks are released. In this example, a prompt release time would be 2 minutes.

15-1.4.3   Areas housing occupancies corresponding to Use Condition I Free Egress shall conform to the requirements of residential occupancies under this *Code*.

Detention and correctional occupancies in which the occupants are not locked in at any time shall be classified as residential and shall meet the requirements of Chapters 17, 19, or 20 as appropriate. Those buildings which provide free egress, even though used as correctional occupancies, should not be classified as detention and correctional occupancies under this *Code*.

15-1.5   The classification of hazard of contents shall be as defined in Section 4-2.

15-1.6 Minimum Construction Requirement.

15-1.6.1   For the purpose of 15-1.6, stories shall be counted starting at the lowest level of exit discharge.

15-1.6.2   Detention and correctional occupancies shall be limited to the following types of building construction.

Type of Construction	Below 1st story	1st story	2nd	3rd	4th & above
I (443) I (332) II (222)	X	X	X	X	X
II (111)	X†	X	X†	A.S.	A.S.
III (211) IV (2HH) V (111)	X†	X	X†	A.S.	A.S.
II (000) III (200) V (000)	X†	X†	A.S.	A.S.	A.S.

A.S.: Permitted if the entire building is protected throughout by an approved automatic sprinkler system in accordance with Section 7-7.
  X: Permitted
N.P.: Not permitted
  †: A.S. required in buildings where Use Condition V is used.

Exception No. 1:   Any building of Type I or Type II (222 or 111) construction may include roofing systems involving combustible or steel supports, decking or roofing provided:

(a) The roof covering at least meets Class C requirements in accordance with Fire Tests for Roof Coverings, NFPA 256, and

(b) The roof is separated from all occupied portions of the building by a noncombustible floor assembly which includes at least 2½ in. (6.35 cm) of concrete or gypsum fill. To qualify for this exception, the attic or other space so developed shall either be unoccupied or protected throughout by an approved automatic sprinkler system.

Exception No. 2:   In determining building construction type, exposed steel roof members located 16 ft (487.68 cm) or more above the floor of the highest cell may be disregarded.

Table 15-1.6.2 establishes minimum construction types for detention and correctional occupancies. Certain construction types require automatic sprinkler protection no matter what their use condition. Others only require such protection when Use Condition V is involved. It should be noted that the automatic sprinkler requirements contained in this table are determined on construction type. Even though not required here, automatic sprinkler protection may be required by 14-3.8.1 due to separation requirements by use conditions.

See NFPA 220, *Standard Types of Building Construction*,[3] for definition of types of construction.

15-1.7 Occupant Load. The occupant load for which means of egress shall be provided for any floor shall be the maximum number of persons intended to occupy that floor, but not less than one person for each 120 sq ft (11.15 sq m) gross floor area.

This paragraph sets forth criteria for projecting occupant loads. The number of people for whom *exits must be provided* may be based upon an actual count of persons intended to occupy a space. However, the occupant load *may not* be less than that established by projections involving one person for each 120 sq ft (11.15 sq m) of gross floor area.

The maximum number of people occupying a space is limited on the basis of exit capacity and other functional considerations. The *Code* does not intend to limit population based upon the area projections contained in this paragraph.

SECTION 15-2   MEANS OF EGRESS

15-2.1 General. The provisions of Chapter 5 of the *Code* apply to this chapter with the following exceptions:

Exception No. 1:   15-2.11.3.

Exception No. 2:   Doors in a means of egress may be of the horizontal sliding type provided the force to slide the door to its fully open position does not exceed 50 lb (222 N) with a perpendicular force against the door of 50 lb (222 N).

Paragraph 5-2.1.1.4.1 requires that all doors in a means of egress be side-hinged and swinging. This exception allows the use of sliding doors if they meet the specified requirements.

Exception No. 3:   Horizontal exits may be substituted for other exits provided the maximum exit travel distance specified in 15-2.6 is not exceeded. Horizontal exits may comprise 100 percent of the exits required.

Exception No. 3 permits horizontal exits to comprise 100 percent of the required exits, provided exit travel distance is not exceeded. See Figure 15-3.

Exception No. 4:   Exit access from a cell or room may be through a dayroom.

Exception No. 5:   Exit discharge may terminate directly at the building's exterior, or at a horizontal exit, and may discharge into a fenced or walled courtyard, provided

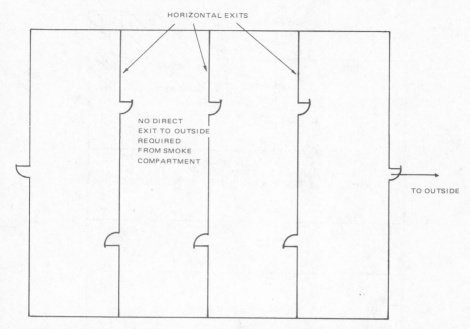

Figure 15-3. Horizontal Exits Comprising 100 Percent of Total Exits (see 15-2.1, Exception No. 3).

that not more than two walls of the courtyard are the building walls from which exit is being made. Enclosed yards or courts shall be of sufficient size to accomodate all occupants, a minimum of 50 ft (15.24 m) from the building with a net area of 15 sq ft (1.39 sq m) per person.

Figure 15-4 illustrates Exception No. 5.

Exception No. 6:   The provisions of 5-2.2.3.4(h) and 5-2.2.3.5(c) do not apply.

These two paragraphs in Chapter 5 require intermediate rails, etc., on handrails and guardrails. Since these may seriously interfere with the supervision of sleeping rooms, the requirement is exempted in detention and correctional occupancies.

15-2.2 Types of Exits.

15-2.2.1   Exits of the specified number and width shall be one or more of the following types, in accordance with the provisions of Chapter 5.

(a) *Doors.   (See 5-2.1.)*

(b) *Interior Stairs.   (See 5-2.2.)*

(c) *Smokeproof Towers.   (See 5-2.3.)*

(d) *Horizontal Exits.*   A horizontal exit shall be in conformance with 5-2.4 modified as below:

1. At least 6 sq ft (.56 sq m) of accessible space per occupant shall be provided on each side of the horizontal exit for the total number of people in adjoining compartments.

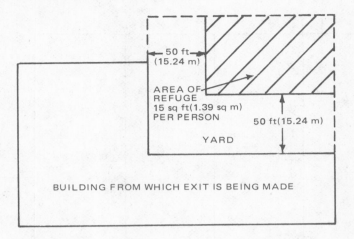

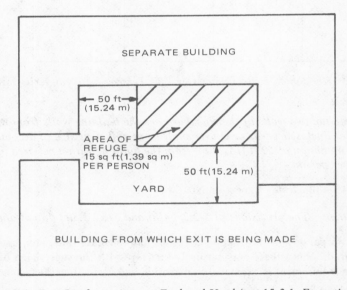

Figure 15-4. Exit Discharge into an Enclosed Yard (see 15-2.1, Exception No. 5).

Section 5-2.4 requires at least 3 sq ft (.28 sq m) per occupant. This section requires 6 sq ft (.56 sq m) per occupant due to several factors, including nature of the occupants, permission of 100 percent horizontal exiting, duration in area, etc.

2. A door in a horizontal exit is not required to swing with travel as specified in 5-2.4.2.3.

Although doors in horizontal exits are not required to swing in the direction of exit travel, it is considered good practice to do so where possible.

Because of practical difficulties involving vertical exit travel in detention and correctional occupancies, special recognition is given to horizontal travel and the use of horizontal exits. One hundred percent of the total required exit capacity for a given fire area may be provided by horizontal exits (see 15-2.1, Exception No. 3). In the event a horizontal exit also serves as a smoke barrier, see 15-2.4 and 15-3.7.

(e) *Outside Stairs. (See 5-2.5.)*

(f) *Ramps. (See 5-2.6.)*

(g) *Exit Passageways. (See 5-2.7.)*

(h) *Fire Escape Stairs. (See Section 5-9.)*

15-2.2.2 Slide escapes shall not be used in detention or correctional occupancies.

15-2.3 Capacity of Means of Egress.

15-2.3.1 The capacity of any required means of egress shall be based on its width as defined in Section 5-3.

15-2.4 Number of Exits.

15-2.4.1 At least two exits of the types permitted in 15-2.2, located remote from each other, shall be accessible from each floor, fire compartment or smoke compartment of the building.

An exit is not necessary for each individual fire compartment or smoke compartment if there is access to an exit through other fire compartments or smoke compartments without passing through the fire compartment or smoke compartment of origin.

15-2.5 Arrangement of Means of Egress.

15-2.5.1 Every sleeping room shall have a door leading directly to an exit access corridor.

Exception No. 1: If there is an exit door opening directly to the outside from the room at the ground level.

Exception No. 2: One adjacent room, such as a dayroom or group activity space, may intervene, subject to the travel distance limitations in 15-2.6. Where individual occupant sleeping rooms adjoin a dayroom or group activity space which is utilized for access to an exitway, such sleeping room may open directly to the day space and may be separated in elevation by a one-half or full-story height (also see 15-3.7).

Figure 15-5 illustrates the requirements of Exception No. 2.

15-2.5.2 All exits may discharge through the level of exit discharge. The requirements of 5-7.2 may be waived provided that not more than 50 percent of the exits discharge into a single fire section.

Exception: Where all exits discharge through areas on the level of discharge, a smoke barrier shall be provided to divide that level into at least two compartments with at least one exit discharging into each compartment and each smoke compartment shall have an exit discharge to the building exterior. The level of discharge shall be provided with automatic sprinkler protection and any other portion of the level of discharge area with access to the discharge area shall be provided with automatic sprinkler protection or separated from it in accordance with the requirements for the enclosure of exits (see 5-1.3.1).

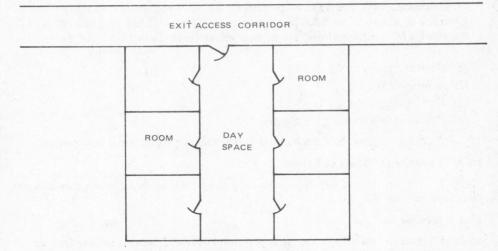

Figure 15-5. One Adjacent Room May Intervene Between Sleeping Room and Exit Access Corridor. Sleeping rooms may be separated in elevation by ½ to 1 story. (See 15-2.5.1, Exception No. 2.)

15-2.5.3 Existing dead-end corridors are undesirable and shall be altered wherever possible so that exits will be accessible in at least two different directions from all points in aisles, passageways, and corridors.

Every exit or exit access *should* be so arranged, *if feasible*, that no corridor or aisle has a pocket or dead end exceeding 50 ft (15.24 m) for Use Conditions II, III, and IV, and 20 ft (609.6 cm) for Use Condition V.

15-2.5.4 A sallyport may be permitted in a means of egress where there are provisions for continuous and unobstructed travel through the sallyport during an emergency exit condition.

Figure 15-6 illustrates the requirements of 15-2.5.4.

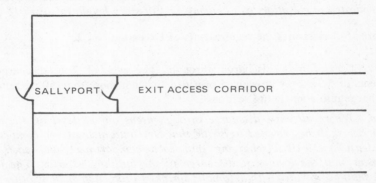

Figure 15-6. Requirements for Sallyport or Security Vestibule. Both doors of sallyport must be capable of being opened at the same time to provide unobstructed egress (see 15-2.5.4).

15-2.5.5 Aisles, corridors, and ramps required for access or exit shall be at least 3 ft (91.44 cm) wide.

15-2.6 Measurement of Travel Distance to Exits.

15-2.6.1 Travel distance:

(a) Between any room door required as exit access and an exit or smoke partition shall not exceed 100 ft (30.48 m);

(b) Between any point in a room and an exit or smoke partition shall not exceed 150 ft (45.72 m); and

(c) Between any point in a sleeping room or suite and an exit access door of that room or suite shall not exceed 50 ft (15.24 m).

Exception No. 1:   The travel distance in (a) or (b) above may be increased by 50 ft (15.24 m) in buildings protected throughout by an approved automatic sprinkler system or smoke control system.

Exception No. 2:   Where travel distance to the exit access door from any point within any sleeping room through the intervening space exceeds 50 ft (15.24 m), at least two exit access doors, remote from each other, shall be provided.

Figure 15-7 illustrates the requirements of 15-2.6.1.

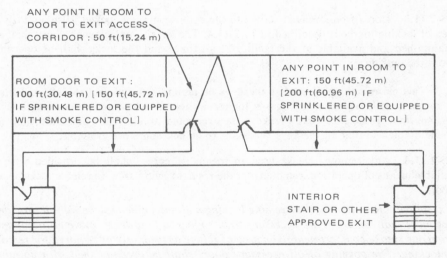

Figure 15-7. Maximum Travel Distance to Exits, Existing Detention and Correctional Occupancies (see 15-2.6.1). The travel distance is measured along the natural path of travel (see 5-6.2). "Sprinklered" means that the entire building is protected by a complete approved automatic extinguishing system. "Smoke Control" means that the entire building or fire area is equipped with a system to control the movement of smoke in accordance with NFPA 90A, Standard for the Installation of Air Conditioning and Ventilating Systems[4].

15-2.7 Discharge from Exits.   *(See 15-2.1 and 15-2.5.)*

15-2.8 Illumination of Means of Egress.   Illumination shall be in accordance with Section 5-8.

15-2.9 Emergency Lighting.   Emergency lighting shall be in accordance with Section 5-9.

Exception: Emergency lighting of at least 1-hour duration may be provided.

15-2.10 Marking of Means of Egress.   Exit marking shall be provided in areas accessible to the public in accordance with Section 5-10.

Exception: Exit signs may be omitted in sleeping areas.

15-2.11 Special Features.

15-2.11.1   Doors within means of egress shall be as required in Chapter 5 except as noted in 15-2.11.2 through 15-2.11.8.

15-2.11.2   Doors to resident sleeping rooms shall be at least 28 in. (71.12 cm) in clear width.

Exception: Existings doors to resident sleeping rooms housing four or less residents may be 19 in. (48.26 cm) in clear width.

It may be necessary to provide a certain number of resident sleeping rooms with doors providing a minimum clear width of 32 in. (81.28 cm) (see 5-2.1.1.2.1) in order to comply with the requirements for the physically handicapped. Such sleeping rooms should be located where there is a direct accessible access to the exterior or to an area of safe refuge (see 15-3.7).

15-2.11.3   Doors from areas of refuge to the exterior may be locked with key lock in lieu of locking methods described in 15-2.11.4. The keys to unlock such doors shall be maintained and available at the facility at all times and the locks shall be operable from the outside.

This paragraph requires that the keys be maintained and available. "Available" means readily accessible to guards for use at any time to evacuate occupants. The important points are that the keys be accessible at all times and that they be maintained so that all the keys necessary to unlock doors are available.

15-2.11.4   Any remote release used in means of egress shall be provided with a reliable means of operation, remote from the resident living area, to release locks on all doors.

Exception: Requirements for remote locking and unlocking may be waived provided not more than ten doors are necessary to be unlocked in order to move all occupants from one smoke compartment to an area of refuge as promptly as required for remote unlocking. The opening of all necessary doors shall be accomplished with no more than two separate keys.

Paragraph 15-2.11.4 is to be used in conjunction with the use condition definitions in 15-1.3. Essentially, this paragraph says that where remote locking is called for by use condition, then it must be provided except where there are ten or fewer locks in the egress system. "Remote" means out of the area where the occupants are restrained. It is *not* necessary to have the remote unlocking mechanism in a separate fire area, although this may be beneficial. Doors in the exit should be unlocked prior to unlocking sleeping room doors to prevent jamming of the exit door due to the pressure of several persons pushing on the door.

The exception permits the manual unlocking of up to ten locks to remove occupants to an area of refuge. This may involve more than ten doors if multiple doors are secured with a single locking mechanism, or fewer than ten doors if a door is secured with more than one lock. Figure 15-8 illustrates two typical arrangements for the ten lock exception.

It must be recognized that the speed with which the doors can be unlocked and the occupants removed to a safe location is critical. If the ten locks cannot be rapidly released by manual unlocking due to staffing restrictions or whatever other reasons, then remote unlocking must be used. If doors are equipped with locking devices, it is assumed that the locks will be used and must be counted in the total number of locks.

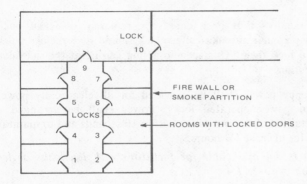

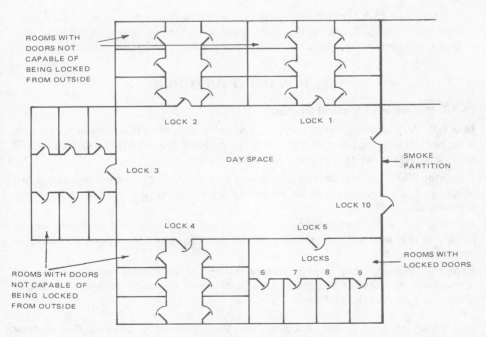

Figure 15-8. Maximum of Ten Manually Unlocked Doors or Locks (see 15-2.11.4, Exception).

15-2.11.5 Doors in smoke barriers shall be self-closing or automatic closing as required in 5-2.1.2.3. Swinging doors shall be self-latching.

15-2.11.6 All power-operated sliding doors or power-operated locks for swinging doors shall be so constructed that in the event of power interruption or power failure a manual mechanical means operable from a remote location or by key and lock mechanism at the door shall be provided to manually release locks and move sliding doors to full open position.

15-2.11.7 Doors remotely unlocked under emergency conditions shall not automatically relock when closed unless specific action is taken at the remote location to enable doors to relock.

> **Paragraph 15-2.11.7 requires that once doors are remotely unlocked under emergency conditions, they cannot automatically relock should they reclose unless specific action is taken to lock them. This specific action can be at the individual door or at the remote location.**

15-2.11.8 Standby emergency power shall be provided for all electrically power-operated sliding doors and power operated locks. Power shall be arranged to automatically operate upon failure of normal power within 10 seconds and to maintain the necessary power source for at least 1½ hours.

Exception: This provision is not applicable for facilitites with ten locks or less complying with the exception in 15-2.11.4.

15-2.11.9 Spiral stairs meeting the requirements of 5-2.2.1.6 are permitted for access to and between staff locations.

> **Paragraph 15-2.11.9 permits spiral stairs conforming to 5-2.2.1.6 for staff only. Note that Chapter 5 restricts the use of spiral stairs to areas having an occupant load of five or fewer. Spiral stairs are not permitted for access by the inmates.**

SECTION 15-3   PROTECTION

15-3.1 Protection of Vertical Opening.

15-3.1.1 Any stairway, ramp, elevator, hoistway, light, or ventilation shaft, chute, or other vertical opening between stories shall be enclosed in accordance with Section 6-2 with construction having a 2-hour fire-resistive rating.

Exception No. 1: Stairs that do not connect a corridor, do not connect more than two levels, and do not serve as a means of egress need not comply with these regulations.

Exception No. 2: Where full enclosure is impractical, the required enclosure may be limited to that necessary to prevent a fire originating in any story from spreading to any other story.

Exception No. 3: The fire resistance rating of enclosures in detention and correctional occupancies protected throughout by an approved automatic sprinkler system may be reduced to 1 hour.

> **Paragraph 15-3.1.1 specifies protection levels required to maintain floor-to-floor separation. Exception No. 1 is illustrated in Figure 15-9.**

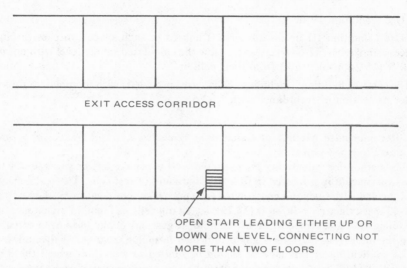

EXIT ACCESS CORRIDOR

OPEN STAIR LEADING EITHER UP OR
DOWN ONE LEVEL, CONNECTING NOT
MORE THAN TWO FLOORS

Figure 15-9. Open Stairs in Accordance with 15-3.1.1, Exception No. 1.

15-3.1.2 Two full communicating floor levels are permitted without enclosure protection between levels provided all the following conditions are met:

(a) The entire normally occupied area, including all communicating floor levels, is sufficiently open and unobstructed so that it may be assumed that a fire or other dangerous condition in any part will be immediately obvious to the occupants or supervisory personnel in the area.

(b) Exit capacity is sufficient to provide simultaneously for all the occupants of all communicating levels and areas, all communicating levels in the same fire area being considered as a single floor area for purposes of determination of required exit capacity.

(c) Each floor level, considered separately, has at least one-half of its individual required exit capacity accessible by exit access leading directly out of that level without transversing another communicating floor level.

Paragraph 15-3.1.2 permits open communication between two floors. The space must be sufficiently open to permit supervisory personnel to immediately recognize a potential fire problem; the total exit capacity must be sufficient to handle the entire occupant load of both floors; and each level must have exit access directly out of that level without travel on the communicating level to handle one-half its occupant load.

15-3.1.3 A multitiered open cell block may be considered as a single-story building provided that either:

1. A smoke control system is provided (*see recommended design criteria*) to maintain the level of smoke filling, from potential cell fires, at least 5 ft (152.4 cm) above the floor level of any occupied tier involving space that is:

(a) Use Condition IV or V.

(b) Use Condition III unless all persons housed in such space can pass through a free access smoke barrier or freely pass below the calculated smoke level with not more than 50 ft (15.24 m) of travel from their cell, or

2. The entire building, including cells, are provided with complete automatic sprinkler protection in accordance with 15-3.5.

A Recommended Method of Calculating Expected Level of Smoke in a Smoke Removal Equipped Cell Block.

This method for calculating the expected level of smoke has been developed from data experimentally produced in full-scale burnouts of test cells. The test cells were sized, loaded with fuel, and constructed to represent severe conditions of heavily fuel loaded [approximately 6 lb/sq ft (22.292 kg/sq m)] cells as found in prison locations. The filling rate and temperature of the effluent gas and smoke have been calculated using the data from these tests and established formulae from plume dynamics.

The application of this method should be limited to situations where there is at least 10 ft (3.05 m) from the floor level to the lowest acceptable level of smoke accumulation (Z); the reservoir above the lowest acceptable level for Z is at least 20 percent of the Z dimension, the length of the cell block is at least equal to Z, and the fan is at least 10 ft (3.05 m) higher than the floor of the highest cell.

The determination of smoke removal requirements is based on the dimensions of the cell opening. Where more than one cell opening is involved, the larger size on the level being calculated should be used.

The fan size, temperature rating, and operations means may be determined by the following procedure:

1. *Acceptable smoke level.* Determine the lowest acceptable level of smoke accumulation in accordance with 15-3.1.3. The vertical distance between that level and the floor level of the lowest open cell is the value of Z to be used in connection with Figure 15-10.

2. *Characteristic cell opening.* Determine the opening of the cell face. Where there is more than one size of cell opening use the largest. Match the actual opening to those shown in Figure 15-11 and use the corresponding curve on Figure 15-10. If there is no match between the size and shape of opening and Figure 15-11, then interpolate between the curves. If the opening exceeds 6 ft by 6 ft (3.34 sq m), use the curve for a 6 ft by 6 ft (3.34 sq m) opening. This curve is considered to represent the maximum burning situation and increasing the size of the opening will not increase the actual burning rate.

3. *Exhaust fan rate.* Determine the exhaust fan capacity needed to extract smoke at a rate that will maintain the smoke level at a point higher than Z. This is the rate shown on the baseline of Figure 15-10 corresponding to the level of Z on the vertical axis for the solid line (ventilation rate) curve appropriate to the cell door size. This exhaust capability must be provided at a point higher than Z.

4. *Intake air.* Provide intake air openings that are either present or automatically provided at times of emergency smoke removal. These are to be located at or near the baseline of the cell block to allow for intake air at the rate to be vented by the fan. The openings provided shall be sufficient to avoid a friction

load that can reduce the exhaust efficiency. Standard air-handling design criteria are used in making this calculation.

5. *Fan temperature rating.* Determine the potential temperature of gases that the fan may be required to handle. To do this, determine the distance from the floor of the highest cell to the centerline of the fan (or fan ports if the fan is in a duct or similar arrangement). Determine the intersection of this new "Z" value with the appropriate ventilation rate curve (solid line) on Figure 15-10. Estimate the temperature rise by interpolating along the appropriate ventilation rate curve and between the constant temperature rise curves (dashed lines) on Figure 15-10. Provide all elements of the exhaust system that are to be above the acceptable smoke level with the capability to effectively operate with the indicated increase in temperature.

6. *Operation of Exhaust System.* The emergency exhaust system should be arranged to initiate automatically on detection of smoke, operation of a manual fire alarm system, or direct manual operation. The capability to manually start the automatic exhaust system should be provided in a guard post in the cell block and/or at another control location. When appropriate, the emergency exhaust fans may be used for comfort ventilation as well as serving their emergency purposes.

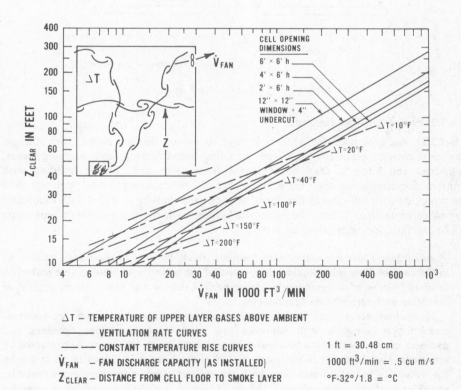

ΔT – TEMPERATURE OF UPPER LAYER GASES ABOVE AMBIENT

——— VENTILATION RATE CURVES

— — — CONSTANT TEMPERATURE RISE CURVES

$\dot{V}_{FAN}$ – FAN DISCHARGE CAPACITY (AS INSTALLED)

Z_{CLEAR} – DISTANCE FROM CELL FLOOR TO SMOKE LAYER

1 ft = 30.48 cm

1000 ft^3/min = .5 cu m/s

°F-32°/1.8 = °C

Figure 15-10. Cell Block Smoke Control Ventilation Curves.

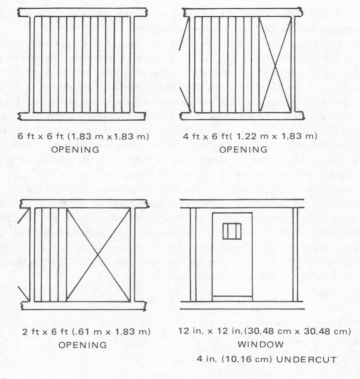

6 ft x 6 ft (1.83 m x1.83 m)   4 ft x 6 ft(1.22 m x 1.83 m)
          OPENING   OPENING

2 ft x 6 ft (.61 m x 1.83 m)   12 in. x 12 in.(30.48 cm x 30.48 cm)
          OPENING   WINDOW
                                    4 in. (10.16 cm) UNDERCUT

Figure 15-11. Typical Cell Openings.

15-3.2 Protection from Hazards.

15-3.2.1   An area used for general storage, boiler or furnace rooms, fuel storage, janitor's closets, maintenance shops including woodworking and painting areas, laundries and kitchens shall be separated from other parts of the building with construction having not less than a 1-hour fire resistance rating and all openings shall be protected with self-closing fire doors, or such area shall be provided with automatic sprinkler protection. Where the hazard is severe, both the fire resistance separation and automatic sprinklers shall be provided.

Hazardous areas are spaces with contents which, because of their basic nature (as in the case of flammable liquids) or because of the quantity of combustible materials involved, represent a significantly higher hazard than would otherwise be typical of detention and correctional occupancies.

Hazardous areas must be separated from other areas by 1-hour fire-resistant construction complete with approved fire doors protecting door openings and dampers in any ducts which penetrate the enclosure, *or* the area may be protected by automatic sprinklers. In those instances where the hazard is judged to be severe by the authority having jurisdiction, both the fire-resistant separation and automatic sprinkler protection are required. Where automatic sprinkler protection is provided and the hazard is not severe, the hazardous areas may be separated by nonrated barriers designed to resist the passage of smoke.

Where flammable liquids are handled or stored, NFPA 30, *Flammable and Combustible Liquids Code*,[5] should be consulted to establish the minimum criteria necessary to mitigate this hazard.

15-3.2.2   Padded cells are severe hazard areas.

Padded cells are considered severe hazard areas due to high heat release, the speed of combustion, and the quantity of smoke produced by the padding materials. Due to this, padded cells must be protected by automatic sprinklers and separated by 1-hour construction.

15-3.2.3   Cooking facilities shall be protected in accordance with 7-2.3.

15-3.3 Interior Finish.

15-3.3.1   Interior finish of walls and ceilings in corridors and exits and any space not separated from the corridors and exits by a partition capable of retarding the passage of smoke shall be Class A or B. All other areas shall be Class A, B or C, in accordance with Section 6-5.

Paragraph 15-3.3.1 requires only that the separating partition be capable of retarding the passage of smoke. The partition must be of substantial construction, but is not required to have a fire resistance. See Chapter 6 for definition of "smoke barrier."

15-3.3.2   Interior floor finish material in corridors and exits shall be Class II in accordance with Section 6-5.

Exception: Existing floor finish material of Class A or B in nonsprinklered buildings and Class A, B or C in sprinklered buildings, which have been evaluated based upon tests in accordance with Method of Test of Surface Burning Characteristics of Building Materials, NFPA 255, may be continued in use.

Previous to this edition of the *Code*, floor finish was tested in accordance with NFPA 255, *Method of Test of Surface Burning Characteristics of Building Materials*[6]. This exception allows material which was tested and approved by this method to remain in use.

15-3.4 Detection, Alarm and Communication Systems.

15-3.4.1   Required fire detection and signaling devices and systems shall be in accordance with Section 7-6 except as provided in this section.

15-3.4.2   Every building shall have a manually operated fire alarm system in accordance with Section 7-6, and such system shall be electrically supervised.

Exception No. 1:   Manual fire alarm boxes may be locked.

Exception No. 2:   Manual fire alarm boxes may be located at guard locations in lieu of being located in the sleeping room areas.

Paragraph 15-3.4.2 permits locking of the fire alarm boxes. However, where manual stations are locked, staff must be present on a 24-hour basis and must have keys readily available to unlock the manual stations. Where a continuously manned staff location is provided in the sleeping area, the manual station may be provided within the locked staff location.

Exception No. 3: Existing nonelectrically supervised systems may be allowed in buildings protected by an automatic extinguishing system.

15-3.4.3 Operation of any fire alarm activating device shall automatically, without delay, accomplish general alarm indication and control functions. Zoned or coded systems shall be permitted to be used.

15-3.4.4 The fire alarm system shall be arranged to transmit an alarm automatically to the fire department legally commmitted to serve the area in which the facility is located by the most direct and reliable method approved by local regulations.

Exception: Smoke detectors may be arranged to alarm locally and at a constantly attended location only and are not required to be connected to the fire alarm system nor the fire department.

Where the fire department is not equipped to receive such alarms or direct transmission to the fire department is not permitted, arrangements should be made for the prompt notification of the fire department. The next best option is notification by an approved central station alarm system. Where smoke detectors are provided, they are not required to sound the fire alarm or to transmit a signal to the fire department, but are required to sound an alarm at a constantly attended location, unless specifically noted otherwise.

15-3.4.5 An approved automatic smoke detection system shall be installed in all sleeping areas and areas not separated from sleeping areas by fire-resistive construction in Use Condition IV and V areas and sleeping rooms occupied by more than four people in Use Condition III facilities. Such systems shall be installed in accordance with Section 7-6 and with the applicable standards listed in Section 7-6, but in no case shall smoke detectors be spaced further apart than 30 ft (914.4 cm) on centers or more than 15 ft (457.2 cm) from any wall.

Exception: Buildings protected by a complete automatic fire extinguishing system in accordance with 15-3.5.

15-3.4.6 Any fire detection device or system required by this section shall be electrically interconnected with the fire alarm system.

15-3.4.7 Any alarm system(s) and any detection system(s) required in this section shall be provided with a secondary power supply in accordance with 2-3.4.2 of *Standard for the Installation, Maintenance, and Use of Local Protective Signaling Systems*, NFPA 72A.

15-3.5 Extinguishment Requirements.

15-3.5.1 When required by 15-1.6, facilities shall be protected throughout by an approved automatic sprinkler system in accordance with Section 7-7.

15-3.5.2 Where exceptions are stated in the provisions of this *Code* (*including those specified in 15-3.8.1*) for detention and correctional occupancies equipped with an approved automatic extinguishing system, and where such systems are required, the systems shall be in complete accordance with Section 7-7 for systems in light hazard occupancies and shall be electrically interconnected with the fire alarm system.

15-3.5.3 The main sprinkler control valve(s) shall be electrically supervised so that at least a local alarm will sound at a constantly attended location when the valve is closed.

15-3.5.4 The sprinkler piping, serving no more than six sprinklers for any isolated hazardous area, may be connected directly to a domestic water supply system having a capacity sufficient to provide 0.15 gal per minute per sq ft (1.02×10^{-4} cu m/s/sq m) of floor area throughout the entire enclosed area. An indicating shutoff valve shall be installed in an accessible location between the sprinklers and the connection to the domestic water supply. (*For sprinkler requirements for hazardous areas see 15-3.2 and for sprinkler requirements for chutes see 15-5.4.*)

15-3.5.5 Portable fire extinguishers shall be provided in accordance with 7-7.4.1.

Exception No. 1: Access to portable fire extinguishers may be locked.

Exception No. 2: Portable fire extinguishers may be located at staff locations only.

The exceptions to 15-3.5.5 permit locking of the fire extinguishers. Where extinguishers are locked, staff must be present on a 24-hour basis and the staff must have keys readily available to unlock the extinguishers. Time is of the essence in using extinguishers; therefore, keys must be carried by the staff or be readily accessible.

15-3.5.6 Standpipe and hose systems shall be provided in accordance with 7-7.4.2 as follows:

(a) Class III standpipe and hose systems shall be provided for buildings over 75 ft (22.86 m) in height and all combustible buildings over two stories in height.

(b) Class II or III standpipes and hose systems shall be provided for any unsprinklered building over three stories in height.

Exception No. 1: One-in. (2.54-cm) diameter formed hose in lieu of hose requirements of Standard for the Installation of Standpipes and Hose Systems, NFPA 14, may be used.

Exception No. 1 permits the use of 1-in. (2.54-cm) formed rubber hose in place of fabric jacket rubber-lined hose normally required in standpipe systems. The rubber hose is normally stored on reels and is somewhat easier to use.

Exception No. 2: Separate Class I and Class II systems may be used in place of Class III.

15-3.6 Corridors. [*See 15-3.8, Special Features (Subdivision of Resident Housing Spaces).*]

15-3.7 Subdivision of Building Spaces.

15-3.7.1 Smoke barriers shall be provided, regardless of building construction type, as follows:

(a) To divide every story used by residents for sleeping, or any other story having an occupant load of 50 or more persons, into at least two compartments, and

(b) To limit the travel distance to a door in a smoke barrier:

1. From any room door required as exit access to 200 ft (60.96 m),

2. From any point in a room to 250 ft (76.20 m).

Exception No. 1: Protection may be accomplished with horizontal exits (see 5-2.4).

Exception No. 2: Spaces having direct exit to (a) a public way, (b) a building separated from the resident housing area by 2-hour fire resistance or 50 ft (15.24 m) of open space, or (c) an enclosed area having a holding space 50 ft (15.24 m) from the housing area that provided 6 sq ft (.56 sq m) or more of refuge area per person (resident, staff, visitors, etc.) that may be present at the time of the fire fulfills the requirement for subdivision of such spaces provided the locking arrangement of doors involved meets the requirements for doors at the compartment barrier for the use condition involved.

Smoke barriers and horizontal exits used to subdivide a building serve three purposes fundamental to the protection of occupants in that they:
1. Limit the spread of fire and fire-produced contaminants,
2. Limit the number of occupants exposed to a single fire, and
3. Provide for horizontal relocation of occupants by creating an area of refuge on the same floor.

Consideration can be given for large open areas which may function as smoke sinks as an alternative to the installation of more than one barrier as required by this section. Vertical movement downward to an area of refuge may be accepted by the authority having jurisdiction in lieu of horizontal movement. Consideration should be given to increasing the travel distance to a smoke barrier to coincide with existing range lengths and exits.

The requirements of 15-3.7.1 for subdividing building spaces are illustrated in Figures 15-12 and 15-13.

15-3.7.2   Any required smoke barrier shall be constructed in accordance with Section 6-3. Barriers shall be of substantial construction and shall have a structural fire resistance. Fixed wired glass vision panels shall be permitted in such partitions provided they do not individually exceed 1,296 sq in. (.84 sq m) in area and are mounted in approved steel frames. There is no restriction on the total number of such vision panels in any partition, (e.g., a smoke barrier may consist of wire glass panels mounted in a security grill arrangement).

Paragraph 15-3.7.2 requires smoke barriers to have structural fire resistance. The specific fire resistance is omitted. The intent is to eliminate highly combustible or flimsy materials which could possibly limit smoke movement but have little structural integrity, such as plastic sheeting. Structural fire resistance is defined as the ability of the assembly to stay in place and maintain structural integrity without consideration of heat transmission. Twelve-gage steel plate suitably framed and stiffened meets this requirement. This paragraph does permit the entire smoke barrier to be constructed of wired glass panels not exceeding 1,296 sq in (.84 sq m) each in steel frames.

15-3.7.3   At least 6 net sq ft (.56 sq m) per occupant shall be provided on each side of the smoke barrier for the total number of occupants in adjoining compartments.

15-3.7.4   Doors in smoke barriers shall comply with Section 6-3 and shall be self-closing or automatic closing as required in 5-2.1.2.3. Swinging doors shall be

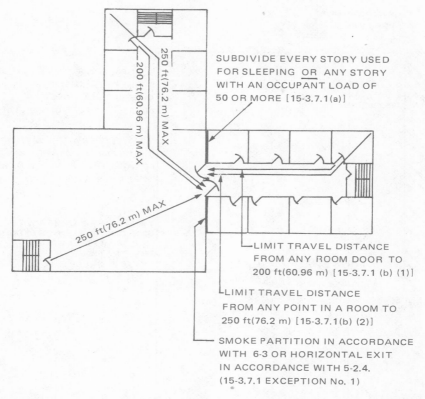

Figure 15-12. Subdivision of Building Spaces, Existing Detention and Correctional Occupancies.

self-latching. Such doors in smoke partitions shall not be required to swing with exit travel. The minimum door width shall be 32 in. (81.28 cm).

Exception No. 1:   See 15-2.1.

Exception No. 2:   Doors may be held open if they meet the requirements of 5-2.1.2.3.

Exception No. 3:   Doors in a means of egress may be of the horizontal sliding type provided the force to slide the door to its fully open position does not exceed 50 lb (222 N) with a perpendicular force against the door of 50 lb (222 N).

15-3.7.5   Doors in smoke barriers shall provide resistance to the passage of smoke.

15-3.7.6   Vision panels of approved transparent wired glass or other material approved by the authority having jurisdiction not exceeding 720 sq in. (.46 sq m) in steel frames shall be provided in each door in a smoke barrier.

15-3.7.7   An approved damper designed to resist the passage of smoke shall be provided at each point a duct penetrates a smoke barrier required by 15-3.7.1. The damper shall close upon detection of smoke.

Exception No. 1:   Buildings designed with an engineered smoke control system in accordance with Standard for the Installation of Air Conditioning and Ventilating Systems, NFPA 90A, need not comply with this requirement.

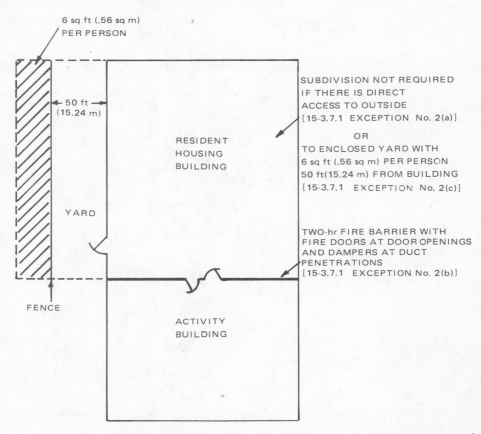

Figure 15-13. Subdivision of Building Spaces, Existing Detention and Correctional Occupancies.

Exception No. 2: Other arrangements and positioning of smoke detectors may be used to prevent damage or tampering or for other purposes provided the function of detecting any fire is fulfilled and the siting of detectors is such that the speed of detection will be equivalent to that provided by the spacing and arrangements described above. This may include the location of detectors in exhaust ducts from cells, behind grills, or in other locations. The equivalent performance of the design, however, must be acceptable to the authority having jurisdiction in accordance with the Equivalency Concepts specified in Section 1-5 of this Code.

The current state-of-the-art on smoke control technology is limited to systems and approaches that limit or prevent the migration of smoke from one compartment to another. Exhaust fans, smoke vents, and other means of relieving smoke from the fire area to the outside can assist in this but cannot be expected to make the fire area safe and cannot be substituted for the compartmentation, detection, evacuation, extinguishment, and other criteria applicable to safety in the space of fire origin.

15-3.8 Special Features.   (Subdivision of Resident Housing Spaces.)

15-3.8.1   Subdivision of facility spaces shall comply with Table 15-3.8.1.

Table 15-3.8.1

USE CONDITION	II		III		IV		V	
Feature	NS	AS	NS	AS	NS	AS	NS	AS
Room to Room Separation	NR	NR	NR	NR	ST	NR	ST	ST*
Room Face to Corridor Separation	NR	NR	ST**	NR	ST**	NR	FR**	ST*
Room Face to Common Space Separation	NR	NR	NR <50 ft*** (15.24 m) / ST >50 ft*** (15.24 m)	NR <50 ft*** (15.24 m) / ST >50 ft*** (15.24 m)	ST**	NR	ST**	ST*
Common Space to Corridor Separation	ST	NR	ST	NR	ST	NR	FR	ST*
Total Openings in Solid Room Face	120 sq in. (.08 sq m)		120 sq in. (.08 sq m)		120 sq in. (.08 sq m)		120 sq in. (.08 sq m) Closable from inside or 120 sq in. (.08 sq m) w/smoke control	

AS — Protected by automatic sprinklers
NS — Not protected by automatic sprinklers
NR — No requirement

ST — Smoketight
FR — Fire Rated — 1 hour

*May be NR where there is either
(a) an approved automatic smoke detection system installed in all corridors and common spaces, or,
(b) multi-tiered cell blocks meeting the requirements of 15-3.1.3
**May be NR in multi-tiered open cell blocks meeting the requirements of f5-3.1.3
***This is the travel distance through the common space to the exit access corridor

NOTE 1: Doors in openings in partitions required to be fire resistive by this chart in other than required enclosures of exits or hazardous areas shall be substantial doors, of construction that will resist fire for at least 20 minutes. Wire glass vision panels are permitted. Latches and door closers are not required on cell doors.

NOTE 2: Doors in openings in partitions required to be smoketight by the chart shall be substantial doors, of construction that will resist the passage of smoke. Latches and door closers are not required on cell doors.

NOTE 3: "Total Openings in Solid Room Face" includes all openings (undercuts, food passes, grills, etc.), the total of which will not exceed 120 sq in. (.08 sq m).

NOTE 4: Under Use Condition II, III, or IV, a space housing not more than 16 persons and subdivided by open construction (any combination of grating doors and grating walls or solid walls) may be considered one room. The perimeter walls of such space shall be of smoketight construction. Smoke detection shall be provided in such space. Under Use Condition IV, common walls between sleeping areas within the space shall be smoketight and grating doors and fronts may be used.

Paragraph 15-3.8.1 provides for the separation of areas where residents are housed. This separation provides for two basic items: (1) keeping the fire and its products contained to the area of origin, and (2) protecting those outside the area of origin. The table establishes different requirements based on the use condition involved. Within each use condition, different provisions are required depending upon whether automatic sprinkler protection is or is not provided. The table, in combination with the notes and asterisked items, as well as the locking options previously mentioned, open up a wide variety of options.

SECTION 15-4   SPECIAL PROVISIONS

15-4.1 Windowless Buildings.

15-4.1.1   For purposes of this chapter a windowless building or portion of a building is one with nonopenable windows, windows not readily breakable, or with no windows.

15-4.1.2   Windowless buildings shall be provided with vent openings, smoke shafts, or an engineered smoke control system to provide ventilation (mechanical or natural) for each windowless smoke compartment.

Paragraph 15-4.1.2 does not require venting or smoke control for those areas (smoke compartments) which are provided with operable windows.

15-4.2 Underground Buildings.

15-4.2.1   See Chapter 30 for requirements for underground buildings.

SECTION 15-5   BUILDING SERVICES

15-5.1 Utilities.

15-5.1.1   Utilities shall comply with the provisions of Section 7-1.

15-5.1.2   Alarms, emergency communication systems, emergency illumination and generator set installations shall be as described in accordance with the *National Electrical Code*, NFPA 70.

Exception: Systems complying with earlier editions of NFPA 70 and not presenting a life safety hazard may be continued in use.

15-5.2 Heating, Ventilating and Air Conditioning.

15-5.2.1   Heating, ventilating and air conditioning equipment shall comply with the provisions of Section 7-2 and shall be installed in accordance with the manufacturer's specifications.

Exception No. 1:   As modified in 15-5.2.2 following.

Exception No. 2:   Systems complying with earlier editions of the applicable codes and not presenting a life safety hazard may be continued in use.

15-5.2.2   Portable space heating devices are prohibited. Any heating device other than a central heating plant shall be so designed and installed that combustible material will not be ignited by it or its appurtenances. If fuel-fired, such heating devices shall be chimmney or vent connected, shall take air for combustion directly from outside, and shall be so designed and installed to provide for complete separation of the combustion system from the atmosphere of the occupied area. The heating system shall have safety devices to immediately stop the flow of fuel and shut down the equipment in case of either excessive temperatures or ignition failure.

Exception: Approved suspended unit heaters may be used in locations other than means of egress and sleeping areas, provided such heaters are located high enough to be out of reach of persons using the area and provided they are vent connected and equipped with the safety devices called for above.

15-5.2.3 Combustion and ventilation air for boiler, incinerator or heater rooms shall be taken directly from and discharged directly to the outside air.

15-5.3 Elevators, dumbwaiters and vertical conveyors shall comply with the provisions of Section 7-4.

15-5.4 Rubbish Chutes, Incinerators and Laundry Chutes.

15-5.4.1 Rubbish chutes, incinerators and laundry chutes shall comply with the provisions of Section 7-5.

15-5.4.2 Any rubbish chute or linen chute, including pneumatic rubbish and linen systems, shall be provided with automatic extinguishing protection installed in accordance with *Standard for the Installation of Sprinkler Systems*, NFPA 13.

15-5.4.3 Any trash chute shall discharge into a trash collecting room used for no other purpose and protected in accordance with Section 6-4.

15-5.4.4 Any incinerator shall not be directly flue-fed nor shall any floor chute directly connect with the combustion chamber.

REFERENCES CITED IN *CODE*

(These publications comprise a part of the requirements to the extent called for by the Code.)

NFPA 13, *Standard for the Installation of Sprinkler Systems*, NFPA, Boston, 1980.

NFPA 14, *Standard for the Installation of Standpipes and Hose Systems*, NFPA, Boston, 1980.

NFPA 70, *National Electrical Code*, NFPA, Boston, 1981.

NFPA 72A, *Standard for the Installation, Maintenance and Use of Local Protective Signaling Systems*, NFPA, Boston, 1979.

NFPA 90A, *Standard for the Installation of Air Conditioning and Ventilating Systems*, NFPA, Boston, 1978.

NFPA 255, *Method of Test of Surface Burning Characteristics of Building Materials*, NFPA, Boston, 1979.

NFPA 256, *Standard Methods of Fire Tests of Roof Coverings*, NFPA, Boston, 1976.

REFERENCES CITED IN COMMENTARY

[1]"A Study of Penal Institution Fires," NFPA FR 78-1.

[2]James Bell, "Eleven Die in Jail Fire," *Fire Journal*, Vol. 74, No. 4, July 1980, pp. 23-25, 90.

[3]NFPA 220, *Standard Types of Building Construction*, NFPA, Boston, 1979.
[4]NFPA 90A, *Standard for the Installation of Air Conditioning and Ventilating Systems*, NFPA, Boston, 1978.
[5]NFPA 30, *Flammable and Combustible Liquids Code*, NFPA, Boston, 1981.
[6]NFPA 255, *Method of Test of Surface Burning Characteristics of Building Materials*, NFPA, Boston, 1979.

16

NEW HOTEL
OCCUPANCIES

(*See also Chapter 31.*)

Prior to the 1981 Edition of the *Code*, all residential occupancies were treated in one chapter. In this edition they have been split into several chapters in order to simplify and clarify the *Code*, resulting in a document that is easier to use.

SECTION 16-1 GENERAL REQUIREMENTS

16-1.1 Application.

16-1.1.1 This *Code* has differing requirements for the several types of residential occupancies; thus, the *Code* has several residential occupancy chapters, Chapters 16 through 23.

Residential occupancies are ones in which sleeping accommodations are provided for normal residential purposes, and include all buildings designed to provide sleeping accommodations. They are treated separately in the *Code* in the following groups:

Hotels/motels (Chapters 16 and 17)

Apartments (Chapters 18 and 19)

Dormitories (including orphanages for age six years and older) (Section 16-6 and 17-6)

Lodging or rooming houses (Chapter 20)

1- and 2-family dwellings (Chapter 22)

Exceptions to the groups listed above are health care occupancies which are covered in Chapters 12 and 13 and detention and correctional occupancies which are covered in Chapters 14 and 15. In earlier editions of the *Code* they were classified as "institutional occupancies."

A review of 4-1.6 underscores a common principle of life safety with which the *Code* is concerned in all the residential occupancies considered by Chapters 16 through 23. Paragraph 4-1.6 states: "Residential occupancies are ones in which *sleeping accommodations* are provided for normal residential purposes and include all buildings designed to provide *sleeping accommodations*." This use of residential occupancies is central to the *Code*'s provisions in Chapters 16 through 23 because people who are asleep will be unaware of a rapidly developing fire and, when alerted, may be somewhat confused because of being awakened suddenly. Other factors on which the provisions of Chapters 16 through 23 were developed are the presence of hazards (such as cooking and heating equipment) and the degree of familiarity of the occupant with his or her living space (ranging from transients with little or no familiarity, as in hotels, to total familiarity in single-family dwellings).

16-1.1.2 This chapter establishes life safety requirements for all new hotels, and for modified buildings according to the provisions of Section 1-4. Section 16-6 contains special provisions for new dormitories. (*See Chapter 31 for operating features.*)

Hotels are defined in 16-1.3.1. It should be noted that lodging or rooming houses which contain more than 15 people are considered hotels and must comply with Chapter 16. Existing hotels are covered in Chapter 17.

16-1.2 Mixed Occupancies.

16-1.2.1 Where another type of occupancy occurs in the same building as a residential occupancy, the requirements of 1-4.5 of this *Code* shall be applicable.

16-1.2.2 For requirements on mixed mercantile and residential occupancies, see 24-1.2.

16-1.2.3 Any ballroom, assembly or exhibition hall, and other space used for purposes of public assembly shall be in accordance with Chapter 8. Dining areas having a capacity of 50 or more persons shall be treated as places of assembly.

Note that Chapter 8 has stringent requirements for both the exit capacity and the permissible location within a building for place of assembly occupancies. In many cases, the location of a place of assembly on either the upper floors (such as a penthouse restaurant), or on lower sublevels (such as a "club" or rathskeller) is in violation of the criteria in Chapter 8.

16-1.3 Definitions.

16-1.3.1 Terms applicable to this chapter are defined in Chapter 3 of this *Code*; where necessary, other terms will be defined in the text as they may occur.

Dormitories. Includes buildings or spaces in buildings where group sleeping accommodations are provided for persons not members of the same family group in one room or in a series of closely associated rooms under joint occupancy and single management, as in college dormitories, fraternity houses, military barracks; with or without meals, but without individual cooking facilities.

In 16-1.3.1, the phrase "without individual cooking facilities" refers to the absence of cooking equipment in any room or unit of a dormitory. If this equipment is present throughout a facility, the occupancy should be classed as an apartment. The phrase "with or without meals" connotes the *Code*'s acceptance of a central cafeteria used to serve meals for the occupants of a dormitory.

Hotels. Includes buildings or groups of buildings under the same management in which there are more than 15 sleeping accommodations for hire, primarily used by transients who are lodged with or without meals, whether designated as a hotel, inn, club, motel, or by any other name. So-called apartment hotels shall be classified as hotels because they are potentially subject to transient occupancy like that of hotels.

Lodging or rooming houses containing more than 15 people are treated as hotels.

Mezzanine. An intermediate level between the floor and ceiling of any story and covering not more than one-third of the floor area of the room in which it is located.

16-1.4 Classification of Occupancy. (*See 16-1.3.*)

16-1.5 Classification of Hazard of Contents.

16-1.5.1 Building contents shall be classified according to the provisions of 4-2.1 of this *Code*. For design of sprinkler systems, the classification of contents in *Standard for the Installation of Sprinkler Systems*, NFPA 13, shall apply.

The contents of living units in residential occupancies fall into the ordinary hazard classification, under the definitions of 4-2.1 of the *Code*. Characteristics of "ordinary" hazards are moderately rapid burning and considerable smoke generation, with the added hazard of the possible presence of toxic combustion products.

NFPA 13, *Standard for the Installation of Sprinkler Systems*,[1] would classify the contents as "light" for the design of extinguishing systems. The difference in classification is based on the threat to life or life safety (ordinary) versus the threat to the extinguishing capability of the automatic sprinkler system (light).

16-1.6 Minimum Construction Requirements. No special requirements.

16-1.7 Occupant Load.

16-1.7.1 The occupant load in numbers of persons for whom exits are to be provided shall be determined on the basis of one person per 200 sq ft (18.58 sq m) gross floor area, or the maximum probable population of any room or section under consideration, whichever is greater. The occupant load of any open mezzanine or balcony shall be added to the occupant load of the floor below for the purpose of determining exit capacity.

A dormitory-type occupancy, particularly where 2- or 3-tier bunks are used with close spacing, may produce an occupant load substantially greater than one person per 200 sq ft (18.58 sq m) of gross floor area. However, even though sleeping areas are densely populated, the building as a whole may not necessarily exceed one person per 200 sq ft (18.58 sq m) of gross area, owing to the space taken for toilet facilities, halls, closets, and living rooms not used for sleeping purposes.

This discussion does not preclude the need for providing exit capability from concentrated sleeping areas (bunk rooms) based on the "maximum probable population" rather than the design figure. If the actual population of a bunk room exceeds one person per 200 sq ft (18.58 sq m), the exit capacity (door widths, etc.) will have to be designed to the actual population load. See 5-3.1 for further details on the use of occupant load for determining capacity of the means of egress.

SECTION 16-2   MEANS OF EGRESS REQUIREMENTS

16-2.1 General.

16-2.1.1 Any floor below the level of exit discharge occupied for public purposes shall have exits arranged in accordance with 16-2.4.1 and 16-2.6.1.

The purpose of 16-2.1.1 is to tie together exit access, exit arrangement, and exit discharge requirements in the referenced paragraphs at one location in the *Code*. Any floor below the level of exit discharge used by or for the public must have exits arranged in the following manner:
1. They provide two separate exits (see 16-2.4.1).
2. At least one exit is within 100 ft (30.48 m) from the door of any room (see 16-2.6.1).

Note that travel distance to these exits may be increased to the following (per the exceptions to 16-2.6.1):
1. *200 ft (60.96 m)*, if the exit and exit access are arranged on the exterior of the building (see 5-5.4).
2. *150 ft (45.72 m)*, if the exit access and the building portions leading to the access are sprinklered, and the building portion where this 150-ft (45.72-m) distance is permitted is separated from the remainder of the facility by 1-hour construction (for buildings three stories or less in height) or 2-hour construction (for buildings four or more stories in height).

16-2.1.2 Any floor below the level of exit discharge not open to the public and used only for mechanical equipment, storage, and service operations (other than kitchens which are considered part of the hotel occupancy) shall have exits appropriate to its actual occupancy in accordance with other applicable sections of the *Code*.

The key point in 16-2.1.2 is that the provisions apply to nonpublic areas of a hotel. The committee felt that nonpublic areas provided a lower level of risk since there are fewer people in these areas, and that those who are in these spaces presumably are familiar with them. With a reduced level of risk, the provisions of occupancy chapters other than Chapter 16 are appropriate.

16-2.1.3 The same stairway or other exit required to serve any one upper floor may also serve other upper floors.

Exception: No inside open stairway, escalator, or ramp may serve as a required egress from more than one floor, unless it conforms with 6-2.2.3.1, Exception No. 1.

Under 16-2.1.3, if the second and third floor are each required to have three stairways, the second floor may use the stairways serving the third floor so that the total number of stairways required is three, not six. This provision avoids the cumulative addition of stair widths leading to increasingly wider stairs in the descent through a building from the uppermost floor to ground level. The committee felt that a fire on one floor will pose a need for the evacuation of that floor first, followed by staged evacuation of the other floors; thus, a stair designed to handle the floor with the largest population will handle the staged evacuation of any other floor. There is a strict prohibition (in the exception) to open stairs, escalators, and ramps being used for more than one floor.

16-2.2 Types of Exits.

16-2.2.1 Exits, or exit components, arranged in accordance with Chapter 5, shall be of one or more of the following types:

(a) Doors to outside at ground level, as per 5-2.1.

(b) Revolving doors, as per 5-2.1 (not at foot of stairs).

(c) Doors to subways, only if the subway meets the requirements of exit passageways or tunnels as specified in 5-2.7.

(d) Interior stairs, in accordance with 5-2.2.

(e) Outside stairs, in accordance with 5-2.5.

(f) Smokeproof towers, in accordance with 5-2.3.

(g) Ramps, Class A or Class B, in accordance with 5-2.6.

(h) Escalators, in accordance with 5-2.8.

(i) Horizontal exits, in accordance with 5-2.4.

(j) Exit passageways, in accordance with 5-2.7.

16-2.3 Capacity of Means of Egress.

16-2.3.1 Exits, arranged as specified elsewhere in this section of the *Code*, shall be sufficient to provide for the occupant load in numbers of persons as determined in accordance with 16-1.7, on the following basis:

(a) Doors, including those three risers or 24 in. (60.96 cm) above or below ground level, Class A ramps and horizontal exits—100 persons per unit of exit width.

(b) Stairs and other types of exits not included in (a) above—75 persons per unit of exit width.

16-2.3.2 Street-floor exits shall provide units of exit width, as follows, occupant load being determined in accordance with 16-1.7.

(a) One unit for each 100 persons street floor capacity for doors and other level exits, including those 24 in. (60.96 cm) or three risers above or below ground level.

(b) One unit for each 75 persons street-floor capacity for stair or other exit requiring descent to ground level.

(c) One and one-half units for each two-unit required stair from upper floors discharging through the street floor.

(d) One and one-half exit units for each two-unit required stair from floors below the street floor discharging through the street floor.

Paragraph 16-2.3.2 requires street-floor exit designs that have sufficient width to provide for the intermingling of exits from the street floor with exits discharging down from the upper floors and discharging up from the lower floors. This is the traditional grand lobby design found in many hotels and in many sizable mercantile occupancies where stairs and street-floor exits converge at one or two exterior door locations. Similar discussion on this matter is found in Chapter 24. Paragraph 16-2.7.2 restricts the number and arrangement of stairs which discharge through the street floor.

Figure 16-1 shows a typical arrangement of multiple exits discharging on the street floor.

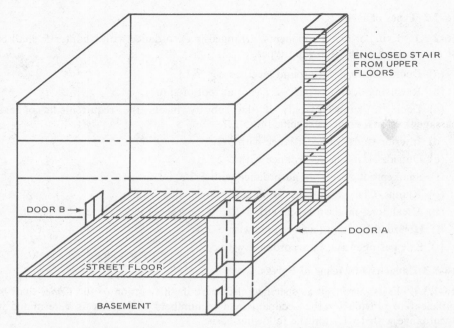

ENCLOSED STAIR
FROM UPPER
FLOORS

DOOR B →

STREET FLOOR

DOOR A

BASEMENT

Figure 16-1. Capacity of Means of Egress in Accordance with 16-2.3.2. Required widths of Doors A and B are based on the number of people expected to use them: 1 unit of exit width [22 in. (55.88 cm)] for every 100 people on the street floor, and 1½ units for every 150 people traveling down from the upper floors, and 1½ units for every 150 people traveling up from the lower floors. (Also see 16-2.7.2.)

16-2.3.3   Every floor below the level of exit discharge shall have exits sufficient to provide for the occupant load of that floor as determined in accordance with 16-1.7 on the basis of 100 persons per exit unit for travel on the same level, 75 persons for upward travel, as up stairs.

   Paragraph 16-2.3.3 simply requires that floors below ground level have their exit capacity provided for on the same basis as upper floors (see 16-2.3.1 and 16-2.3.4).

16-2.3.4   Upper-floor exits shall provide numbers of units of exit width sufficient to meet the requirements of 16-2.3.1

16-2.4 Number of Exits.

16-2.4.1   Not less than two exits shall be accessible from every floor, including floors below the level of exit discharge and occupied for public purposes.

16-2.4.2   Any room having a capacity of less than 50 persons with an outside door at street or ground level may have such outside door as a single exit provided that no part of the room or area is more than 50 ft (15.24 m) from the door measured along the natural path of travel.

   As stated in 16-2.4.2, a room may have a single exit consisting of a door to the outside if *all* of the following conditions are met:

1. The occupant capacity is 49 or less.
2. The room and room door are at street or ground level.
3. The travel distance from all points in the room to the exit door is 50 ft (15.24 m) or less.

16-2.5 Arrangement of Exits.

16-2.5.1 Access to all required exits shall be in accordance with Section 5-5, shall be unobstructed, and shall not be blocked from open view by ornamentation, curtain, or other appurtenance.

Highly decorative interior hotel designs that are currently popular may often lead to ornamentation, curtains, mirrors, or other devices that may obstruct or confuse the location of exits. Care should be taken in new hotel designs to meet the requirements of 16-2.5.1 and avoid these problem areas.

16-2.5.2 Exits shall be so arranged that, from any corridor room door, exits will be accessible in at least two different directions.

Exception: Up to the first 35 ft (10.67 m) of exit travel from a corridor room door may be along a corridor with exit access only in one direction (dead end).

16-2.6 Measurement of Travel Distance to Exits.

16-2.6.1 Any exit as indicated in 16-2.4.1 shall be such that it will not be necessary to travel more than 100 ft (30.48 m) from the door of any room to reach the nearest exit. Travel distance to exits shall be measured in accordance with Section 5-6.

Exception No. 1: Travel distance to exits may be increased to 200 ft (60.96 m) for exterior ways of exit access arranged in accordance with 5-5.3.

Exception No. 2: Travel distance to exits may be increased to 150 ft (45.72 m) if the exit access and any portion of the building which is tributary to the exit access are protected throughout by an approved automatic sprinkler system. In addition, the portion of the building in which the 150-ft (45.72-m) travel distance is permitted shall be separated from the remainder of the building by construction having a fire resistance rating of not less than 1 hour for buildings up to four stories in height, and 2 hours for buildings four or more stories in height.

See Figure 16-2.

16-2.6.2 Travel distance from the door of a room in a suite or living unit to a corridor door shall not exceed 50 ft (15.24 m).

Exception: One-hundred-ft (30.48-m) travel distance is allowed in buildings protected throughout by an approved automatic sprinkler system in accordance with Section 7-7, or an approved single station smoke detector in each habitable area in the suite or living unit.

The committee developed 16-2.6.2 to clarify the point from where travel distances should be measured in suites or apartments in hotels. Note that sprinklered facilities are allowed a 100 percent increase in travel distance, from 50 ft (15.24 m) to 100 ft (30.48 m). See Figure 16-2.

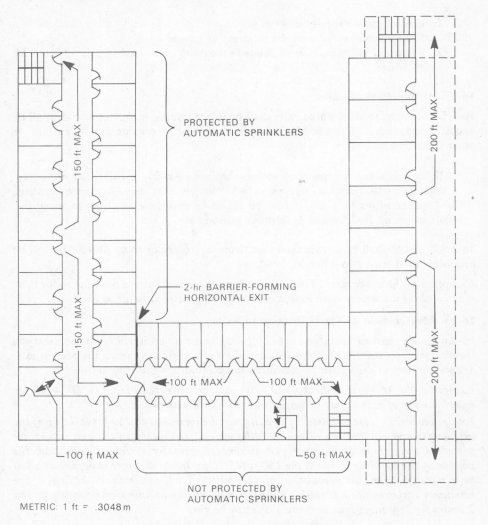

Figure 16-2. Travel Distance in Hotels.

16-2.7 Discharge from Exits.

16-2.7.1   At least half of the required number of units of exit width from upper floors, exclusive of horizontal exits, shall lead directly to the street or through a yard, court, or passageway with protected openings and separated from all parts of the interior of the building.

   Paragraph 16-2.7.1 should be read jointly with the provisions of 16-2.7.2. A *minimum* of 50 percent of the exits from upper floors must discharge directly to the exterior. If less than 50 percent of the exits are arranged (per 16-2.7.2) to discharge through the floor of exit discharge, the remaining exits must be arranged to discharge directly to the exterior.

16-2.7.2 A maximum of 50 percent of the exits may discharge through areas on the floor of exit discharge in accordance with 5-7.2.

See Figures 16-3 and 16-4. (Also see discussion following 5-7.2.)

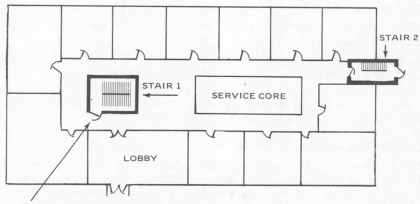

ROUTE FROM STAIR THROUGH LOBBY TO EXTERIOR MUST BE READILY VISIBLE, IDENTIFIED, CLEAR, AND UNOBSTRUCTED.

Figure 16-3. Arrangement of Means of Egress in Accordance with 16-2.7.2 (see 5-7.2). Stair 1 (50 percent of the total number of exits) discharges through the first floor. Stair 2 discharges directly to the exterior. Since other areas on the first floor (the level of exit discharge) are not separated from the path which a person leaving Stair 1 must follow to exit through the lobby, the entire first floor must be completely sprinklered. If the rest of the floor were separated, only the path to the exit discharge would have to be sprinklered.

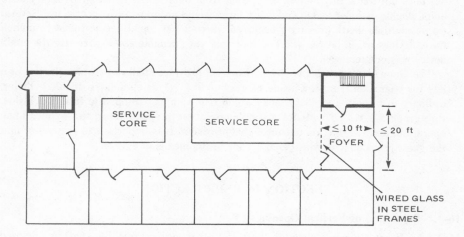

METRIC: 1 ft = .3048 m

Figure 16-4. Foyer Constructed in Compliance with 16-2.7.2 (see 5-7.2). The foyer must serve only as a means of egress.

16-2.8 Illumination of Means of Egress.

16-2.8.1   Each public space, hallway, stairway, or other means of egress shall have illumination in accordance with Section 5-8. Access to exits shall be continuously illuminated at all times.

16-2.9 Emergency Lighting.

16-2.9.1   Any hotel with 26 or more rooms shall have emergency lighting in accordance with Section 5-9.

Exception: Where each guest room has a direct exit to the outside of the building at ground level (as in motels), no emergency lighting shall be required.

The exception to 16-2.9.1 does not apply to motels with exterior balconies and stairs, but only to those with doors directly to grade.

16-2.10 Marking of Means of Egress.

16-2.10.1   Every exit access door from public hallways or from corridors on floors with sleeping accommodations shall have an illuminated sign in accordance with Section 5-10. Where exits are not visible in a hallway or corridor, illuminated directional signs shall be provided to indicate the direction to exits.

16-2.11 Special Features.

16-2.11.1   No door in any means of egress shall be locked against egress when the building is occupied (*see 5-2.1.2*).

Paragraph 16-2.11.1 prohibits a hotel from having any door locked "against egress" while the building is occupied. This requirement permits a door to have a locking device that allows the door to be opened from within the building for egress, but does not allow the door to be opened from outside the building. Ordinary dead bolts, double cylinder locks, and chain locks would not meet these provisions. Several tragic multiple-death fires have occurred where a key could not be found to unlock these devices or, in haste, where a door was not openable simply because the chain device was not removed.

The language of 5-2.1.2 is clear. "Locks if provided shall not require the use of a key for operation from the inside of the building." This eliminates double cylinder, ordinary dead bolt, and chain locks which require a key to operate from the inside. Paragraph 5-2.1.2.1.2 calls for a simple operation to open a door; two-handed knob operation, and the like, do not meet this provision. It is important to remember that the guest room door is considered a door in the means of egress.

SECTION 16-3   PROTECTION

16-3.1 Protection of Vertical Openings.

16-3.1.1   Every stairway, elevator shaft and other vertical opening shall be enclosed or protected in accordance with 6-2.2.

Exception No. 1:   Unprotected vertical openings connecting not more than three floors used for hotel occupancy only may be permitted in accordance with the conditions of 6-2.2.3.1, Exception No. 1.

Exception No. 2:   An atrium may be utilized in accordance with 6-2.2.3.1, Exception No. 2.

Exception No. 3:   Stairway enclosures shall not be required where a one-story stair connects two levels within a single dwelling unit, guest room or suite located above the level of exit discharge.

Concerning Exception No. 1 to 16-3.1.1, it should be noted that 6-2.2.3.1, Exception No. 1 requires total automatic sprinkler protection for "ordinary hazard" occupancies. In the requirements for atriums, 6-2.2.3.1, Exception No. 2 also requires total automatic sprinkler protection. Therefore, unless complying with Exception No. 3, total automatic sprinkler protection must be provided in hotels with unprotected vertical openings.

16-3.1.2   Any required exit stair which is so located that it is necessary to pass through the lobby or other open space to reach the outside of the building shall be continuously enclosed down to the lobby level, or to a mezzanine within the lobby (*see 16-2.7*).

Where open stairways or escalators are permitted, they are considered as *exit accesses* to exits, rather than as exits, and requirements for distance to exits include the travel on such stairs. (See 5-6.5.)

16-3.1.3   No floor below the level of exit discharge, used only for storage, heating equipment, or other purposes other than hotel occupancy open to guests or the public, shall have unprotected openings to floors used for hotel purposes.

16-3.2 Protection from Hazards.

16-3.2.1   Any room containing high-pressure boilers, refrigerating machinery, transformers, or other service equipment subject to possible explosion shall not be located directly under or directly adjacent to exits. All such rooms shall be effectively cut off from other parts of the building as specified in Section 6-4.

16-3.2.2   Every hazardous area shall be separated from other parts of the building by construction having a fire resistance rating of at least 1 hour and communicating openings shall be protected by approved self-closing fire doors, or such area shall be equipped with automatic fire extinguishing system. Hazardous areas include, but are not limited to:

Boiler and heater rooms
Laundries
Repair shops

Rooms or spaces used for storage of combustible supplies and equipment in quantities deemed hazardous by the authority having jurisdiction.

The list in 16-3.2.2 is not all-inclusive. It is the responsibility of the authority having jurisdiction to determine which areas are hazardous.

16-3.3 Interior Finish.

16-3.3.1   Interior finish on walls and ceilings, in accordance with Section 6-5 and subject to the limitations and modifications therein specified, shall be as follows:

(a) Vertical exits [*see 5-1.2.1(b)*] — Class A.

(b) Exit access [*see 5-1.2.1(a)*] — Class A or B.

(c) Lobbies, corridors that are not exit access — Class A or B.

(d) Places of assembly (*see 8-3.3*).

(e) Individual guest rooms and other rooms — Class A, B, or C.

16-3.3.2 Interior floor finish in corridors and exitways shall be Class I or Class II in accordance with Section 6-5.

The provisions for interior finish in 16-3.3 were rewritten for the 1976 Edition of the *Code* to reflect the elimination of the Class D and E categories of interior finish and to provide more specific guidance on where in a hotel these requirements apply. In this, the 1981 Edition, the interior floor finish requirements were modified to reflect changes in Section 6-5.

16-3.4 Detection, Alarm and Communication Systems.

16-3.4.1 An alarm system, in accordance with Section 7-6, shall be provided for any hotel having accommodations for 15 or more guests.

Exception: Where each guest room has a direct exit to the outside of the building and the building is three or less stories in height.

16-3.4.2 Every sounding device shall be of such character and so located as to alert all occupants of the building or section thereof endangered by fire.

This paragraph, although appearing quite basic, is one that apparently needs emphasizing. In several recent multiple-death hotel fires, reports listed inaudible or unrecognized alarms as contributing factors.

16-3.4.3 Buildings shall have a corridor smoke detection system (*see Section 7-6*) connected to the alarm initiation system.

Exception No. 1: Where each guest room has direct exit to the outside of the building and the building is not over three stories in height.

Exception No. 2: Buildings protected throughout by an approved automatic sprinkler system.

The most important element of 16-3.4 is that for *new* hotels, a corridor smoke detection system is required. This was inserted by the committee as a positive response to both the nature and types of deaths by fire occurring in hotels. Since these involved, in the majority of cases, smoke inhalation while the victim was sleeping, the corridor smoke detection system requirement was developed. Note that buildings fewer than four stories in height with direct exit to the outside of the building and totally sprinklered buildings are exempted from this requirement.

16-3.4.4 A manual fire alarm station shall be provided at the hotel desk or other convenient central control point under continuous supervision of responsible employees. Additional manual alarms (*as specified in Section 7-6*) may be waived where there are other effective means (such as complete automatic sprinkler or automatic fire detection systems) for notification of fire as required in 16-3.4.2.

Paragraph 16-3.4.4 eliminates the requirements for fire alarm boxes located so that all portions of a building are within 200 ft (60.96 m) of a box (see Section 7-6) if an automatic sprinkler system or an automatic detection system is provided throughout the building. This does not eliminate the need for the alarm system; it only deletes the requirement for additional manual pull stations.

16-3.4.5 Buildings seven or more stories in height shall have an annunciator panel connected with the alarm system to visually indicate the floor of fire involvement. The location of the annunciator panel shall be approved by the authority having jurisdiction.

16-3.4.6 Provisions shall be made for the immediate notification of the public fire department by either telephone or other means in case of fire. Where there is no public fire department this notification shall go to the private fire brigade.

This paragraph does not require a direct fire alarm connection to the fire department; however, that would be the best method to comply with 16-3.4.6. The telephone required would have to be equipped for direct outside dial without going through a switchboard and it could not be a pay phone.

16-3.4.7 In buildings seven or more stories in height, in addition to a manual fire alarm system, an approved means of voice communication between an accessible central point approved by the authority having jurisdiction and the corridors, elevators, elevator lobbies and exits shall be provided.

16-3.5 Extinguishment Requirements.

16-3.5.1 Where an automatic sprinkler system is installed, either for total or partial building coverage, the system shall be in accordance with the requirements of *Standard for the Installation of Sprinkler Systems*, NFPA 13.

Exception: Sprinkler installation may be omitted in small compartmented areas such as closets not over 24 sq ft (2.23 sq m) and bathrooms not over 55 sq ft (5.11 sq m).

The exception for omitting sprinklers from closets 24 sq ft (2.23 sq m) or less in area and bathrooms 55 sq ft (5.11 sq m) or less follows a pattern in NFPA 13, *Standard for the Installation of Sprinkler Systems*,[1] for allowing (under "light hazard" sprinkler guidelines) certain nonsprinklered areas to exist due to their low fuel loads, lack of ignition sources, and low hazard levels.

16-3.5.2 Hand portable fire extinguishers shall be provided in hazardous areas. When provided, hand portable fire extinguishers shall be installed and maintained as specified in *Standard for Portable Fire Extinguishers*, NFPA 10. (*See Section 31-6.*)

16-3.6 Minimum Fire Resistance Requirements for Protection of Guest Rooms (Corridors).

16-3.6.1 Every interior corridor shall be separated from guest rooms by partitions having at least a 1-hour fire resistance rating.

The criteria in 16-3.6.1 parallel the requirements in Chapter 12 for health care occupancies. In both chapters, the committee's concern for providing safety for the occupant in his or her room, during a fire, led to a minimum corridor wall construction either to block fire movement into a room from the corridor or to block fire in a room from entering the corridor. The common concern in Chapters 12 and 16 is the presence of occupants on a 24-hour-a-day basis with sleeping accommodations.

Exception: Buildings protected throughout by an approved automatic sprinkler system may have partitions having a ½-hour fire resistance rating.

16-3.6.2   Each guest room door which opens onto an interior corridor shall have a fire protection rating of at least 20 minutes. Openings shall resist the passage of smoke.

The door required by 13-3.6.2 provides a level of protection commensurate with the expected fuel load in the room and the fire resistance of the corridor wall construction. The purpose is to box a fire out of a room, or to box it within the room by corridor wall and door construction criteria. (See 16-3.6.3.) It has been shown in fuel load studies conducted by the National Bureau of Standards that residential occupancies will have fuel loads in the 20- to 30-minute range.

Contrary to the general rule (see 5-2.1.1.1.1), the door referred to in 16-3.6.2 applies to the leaf only. In other words, the frame, hinges, latch, closers, etc., do not have to be rated. By requiring the 20-minute door, the committee was attempting to establish a minimum quality of construction, not to provide for a complete listed fire door assembly.

16-3.6.3   Doors between guest rooms and corridors shall be self-closing, and shall meet the requirements of 16-3.6.2.

16-3.6.4   Unprotected openings other than door openings shall be prohibited in partitions of corridors serving as exit access from guest rooms.

Paragraph 2-2.2 of NFPA 90A, *Standard for the Installation of Air Conditioning and Ventilating Systems,*[2] prohibits public corridors from being used as a portion of the supply, return, or exhaust air system.

16-3.6.5   No transom shall be installed in partitions of sleeping rooms.

Transoms have been prohibited for many years in hotels due to tragic fires where the presence of transoms led to the transmission of fire and smoke down corridors and directly into occupied rooms, thus causing multiple deaths.

16-3.7 Subdivision of Building Spaces.   No special requirements.

16-3.8 Special Features.

16-3.8.1   Smokeproof towers shall be provided in accordance with 5-2.3 in buildings seven or more stories in height.

Exception: Buildings protected throughout by an approved automatic sprinkler system.

There is no minimum or maximum number of smokeproof towers required by 16-3.8.1. Conceivably, one smokeproof tower installed in a new seven-story, or higher, hotel would be sufficient.

The ultimate success of achieving a smokeproof tower by use of mechanical means is, in many applications, a direct function of the number of "open stairway doors" at any given time during the emergency period. Depending upon the mechanical pressurization technique, the optimum solution in most cases would be to initially notify occupants of the immediate fire-affected floors on a "selective" or "staged" system of alarming, as compared to a general alarm of the total building. This could be initiated, subject to the authority having jurisdiction, by the utilization of water flow alarms at each floor or smoke detection at each floor, or by manual pull stations or any combination of the above which: (1) instantaneously activates the alarm of the floor of initial hazard and floors immediately above and below; (2) after a reasonable delay (perhaps 90 seconds maximum), alerts other building floors on a zoned mode; and (3) subsequently activates a building general alarm.

It is important that each situation should be individually considered. The approach utilized for a very tall building could differ from the approach in a limited high-rise structure.

SECTION 16-4   SPECIAL PROVISIONS

SECTION 16-5   BUILDING SERVICES

16-5.1 Utilities.   Utilities shall comply with the provisions of Section 7-1.

16-5.2 Heating, Ventilating, and Air Conditioning.   Heating, ventilating and air conditioning equipment shall comply with the provisions of Section 7-2, except as otherwise required in this chapter.

16-5.3 Elevators, Dumbwaiters and Vertical Conveyors.   Elevators, dumbwaiters, and vertical conveyors shall comply with the provisions of Section 7-4. In buildings over six stories one elevator shall be provided with a protected power supply and be available for use by the fire department in case of emergency.

"Protected Power Supply" means a source of electrical energy of sufficient capacity to permit proper operation of the elevator and its associated control and communications systems, and whose point of origin, system of distribution, type and size of over-current protection, degree of isolation from other portions of the building electrical system, and degree of mechanical protection are such that it is unlikely that the supply would be disrupted at any but the advanced stages of building fire involvement or structural collapse.

A "Protected Power Supply" need not incorporate an emergency generating capability nor automatic transfer capability from a "normal" to an "emergency" source, e.g., an alternate set of service conductors. A "Protected Power Supply" should provide at least the level of reliability associated with, and may consist of, an electrical distribution system whose service equipment is located and installed in accordance with Sections 230-72(b) and 230-82, Exception No. 5 of NFPA 70, *National Electrical Code*,[3] and which has no other connection to the "normal" building electrical distribution system.

The number and type of elevators to be connected to a "Protected Power Supply" should be limited, or the characteristics of the "Protected Power Supply" should be selected, so as to ensure conformance with Section 230-95 of NFPA 70, *National Electrical Code*,[3] without the provision of ground-fault protection for the supply.

An elevator installation supplied by a "Protected Power Supply" should comply with Article 620 of NFPA 70, *National Electrical Code*,[3] except that the "energy absorption means" required by Section 620-91 should always be connected on the load side of the disconnecting means and should not consist of loads likely to become inoperative or disconnected under the conditions assumed to exist when the elevator is under the control of fire department personnel, e.g., light and power loads external to the elevator equipment room.

16-5.4 Rubbish Chutes, Incinerators, and Laundry Chutes.   Rubbish chutes, incinerators, and laundry chutes shall comply with the provisions of Section 7-5.

SECTION 16-6   NEW DORMITORIES

16-6.1 Application.

16-6.1.1   New dormitories shall comply with the requirements for new hotels, except as modified in the following paragraphs.

Exception: Any dormitory divided into suites of rooms, with one or more bedrooms opening into a living room or study which has a door opening into a common corridor serving a number of suites, shall be classified as an apartment building.

The exception to 16-6.1.1 recognizes that the now popular dormitory design of a group of bedrooms clustered around a living room duplicates a typical apartment design of several bedrooms clustered around a living room (or a kitchen). Since the design and the risk of fire are the same, the *Code* treats this arrangement the same as that of an apartment building. (See Figure 16-5.)

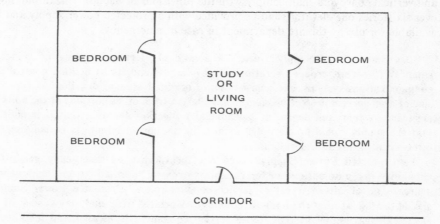

Figure 16-5. Arrangement of Dormitory Suite Treated as an Apartment Under the Exception to 16-6.1.1. More than one bedroom opens into a study or living room which has a door opening into a corridor. The corridor serves a number of suites.

16-6.1.2 Every individual living unit covered by this section shall at least comply with the minimum provisions of Chapter 22, One- and Two-Family Dwellings.

Exception: The requirement of Section 22-2 for means of window egress shall be applicable to buildings of six stories or less.

16-6.2 Means of Egress Requirements.

16-6.2.1 Types and Capacities of Exits.

16-6.2.1.1 Exits of the same types and capacities as required for hotels (*see 16-2.2 and 16-2.3*) shall be provided.

Exception: Each street floor door shall be sufficient to provide one unit of exit width for each 50 persons capacity of the street floor, plus one unit for each unit of required stairway width discharging through the street floor.

The exception to 16-6.2.1.1 follows the approach found in Chapters 16, 24, and 26 for sizing the exits to accommodate the intermingling of the population of the street floor with people using upper floor exits which discharge into areas on the street floor.

16-6.2.2 Arrangement of Means of Egress.

16-6.2.2.1 In any dormitory having sleeping rooms or areas containing more than four occupants, there shall be access to two separate and distinct exits in different directions from the room door, with no common path of travel.

Exception: One exit may be accepted where the room or space is subject to occupancy by not more than ten persons and has a door opening directly to the outside of the building at street or ground level or to an outside stairway.

Note that there is *no dead end permitted* in the arrangement of dormitory space. (This is one of the few occupancies in which the *Code* does not permit a dead end.) The committee was concerned about the crowded conditions found in dormitories, the varying types and ages of dormitory construction, and the fact that (given the varied class schedules and activities of students) a good portion of the occupants are sleeping day or night.

16-6.2.3 Measurement of Travel Distance to Exits.

16-6.2.3.1 Exits shall be so arranged that it will not be necessary to travel more than 100 ft (30.48 m) from any point, or 150 ft (45.72 m) in a building protected throughout by an approved automatic sprinkler system in accordance with Section 7-7, to reach the nearest outside door or exit, nor to traverse more than a one-story flight of inside, unenclosed stairs.

16-6.3 Protection.

16-6.3.1 Protection of Vertical Openings.

16-6.3.1.1 Every exit stair and other vertical openings shall be enclosed or protected in accordance with Section 6-2.

Exception: If every sleeping room or area has direct access to an outside exit without the necessity of passing through any corridor or other space exposed to any unprotected vertical opening and the building is equipped with an automatic fire detection system in accordance with Section 7-6, unprotected openings may be permitted by the authority having jurisdiction.

Note that the *Exception* carries no height limit. The construction of outside exits with outside exit access balconies (plus the required automatic fire detection system) is an acceptable way of taking multistory (more than two stories) facilities and making them *Code*-conforming, even though provided with an open stairway.

16-6.3.2 Alarm and Detection Systems.

16-6.3.2.1   Every dormitory shall have a manual fire alarm system in accordance with Section 7-6.

Exception No. 1: Buildings protected throughout by an approved automatic sprinkler system in accordance with Section 7-7.

Exception No. 2: Buildings protected throughout by an approved automatic fire detection system in accordance with Section 7-6.

16-6.3.2.2   Approved smoke detectors shall be installed on each floor by either:

(a) Using single station smoke detectors in all habitable rooms, or

(b) Using corridor detectors connected to the building fire alarm system and at not over 30 ft (914.4 cm) spacing.

Approved single station smoke detector(s) may be provided in habitable rooms, or corridor smoke detectors interconnected with the building fire alarm system may be provided, whichever is most suitable for early warning purposes. Where unusual factors such as room configuration, air movement, stagnant air pockets, etc., require consideration, the authority having jurisdiction, the designer, and listing information of the testing laboratory should determine the placement of the detectors.

16-6.4 Special Provisions.   Reserved.

16-6.5 Building Services.

16-6.5.1 Utilities.

16-6.5.1.1   Building service equipment shall be installed in accordance with Section 7-1.

16-6.5.2 Heating/Air Conditioning.

16-6.5.2.1   Heating and air conditioning equipment shall meet the requirements of Section 7-2.

REFERENCES CITED BY *CODE*

(These publications comprise a part of the requirements to the extent called for by the Code.)

NFPA 10, *Standard for Portable Fire Extinguishers*, NFPA, Boston, 1978.

NFPA 13, *Standard for the Installation of Sprinkler Systems*, NFPA, Boston, 1980.

REFERENCES CITED IN COMMENTARY

[1]NFPA 13, *Standard for the Installation of Sprinkler Systems*, NFPA, Boston, 1980.

[2]NFPA 90A, *Standard for the Installation of Air Conditioning and Ventilating Systems*, NFPA, Boston, 1978.

[3]NFPA 70, *National Electrical Code*, NFPA, Boston, 1981.

17

EXISTING HOTELS

(See also Chapter 31.)

SECTION 17-1   GENERAL REQUIREMENTS

17-1.1 Application.

17-1.1.1 This *Code* has differing requirements for the several types of residential occupancies; thus, the *Code* has several residential occupancy chapters, Chapters 16 through 23.

Residential occupancies are ones in which sleeping accommodations are provided for normal residential purposes, and include all buildings designed to provide sleeping accommodations. They are treated separately in the *Code* in the following groups:

Hotels/motels (Chapters 16 and 17)

Apartments (Chapters 18 and 19)

Dormitories (including orphanages for age six years and older) (Sections 16-6 and 17-6)

Lodging or rooming houses (Chapter 20)

1- and 2-family dwellings (Chapter 22)

Exceptions to the groups listed above are health care occupancies which are covered in Chapters 12 and 13 and detention and correctional occupancies which are covered in Chapters 14 and 15. In earlier editions of the *Code* they were classified as "institutional occupancies."

A review of 4-1.6 underscores a common principle of life safety with which the *Code* is concerned in all the residential occupancies considered by Chapters 16 through 23. Paragraph 4-1.6 states: "Residential occupancies are ones in which *sleeping accommodations* are provided for normal residential purposes and include all buildings designed to provide *sleeping accommodations*." This use of residential occupancies is central to the *Code*'s provisions in Chapters 16 through 23 because people who are asleep will be unaware of a rapidly developing fire and, when alerted, may be somewhat confused because of being awakened suddenly. Other factors on which the provisions of Chapters 16 through 23 were developed are the presence of hazards (such as cooking and heating equipment) and the degree of familiarity of the occupant with his or her living space (ranging from transients with little or no familiarity, as in hotels, to total familiarity in single-family dwellings).

17-1.1.2 This chapter establishes life safety requirements for all existing hotels. Section 17-6 contains special provisions for existing dormitories. (*See Chapter 31 for operating features.*)

> **Hotels are defined in 17-1.3.1. It should be noted that lodging or rooming houses which contain more than 15 people are considered hotels and must comply with Chapter 17. New hotels are covered in Chapter 16.**

17-1.2 Mixed Occupancies.

17-1.2.1 Where another type of occupancy occurs in the same building as a residential occupancy, the requirements of 1-4.5 of this *Code* shall be applicable.

17-1.2.2 For requirements on mixed mercantile and residential occupancies, see 25-1.2.

17-1.2.3 Public Assembly Occupancies. Any ballroom, assembly or exhibition hall, and other space used for purposes of public assembly shall be in accordance with Chapter 9. Dining areas having a capacity of 50 or more persons shall be treated as places of assembly.

> **Note that Chapter 9 has stringent requirements for both the exit capacity and the permissible location within a building for place of assembly occupancies. In many cases, the location of a place of assembly on either the upper floors (such as a penthouse restaurant), or on lower sublevels (such as a "club" or rathskeller) is in violation of the criteria in Chapter 9.**

17-1.3 Definitions.

17-1.3.1 Terms applicable to this chapter are defined in Chapter 3 of this *Code*; where necessary, other terms will be defined in the text as they may occur.

Dormitories. Includes buildings or spaces in buildings where group sleeping accommodations are provided for persons not members of the same family group in one room or in a series of closely associated rooms under joint occupancy and single management, as in college dormitories, fraternity houses, military barracks; with or without meals, but without individual cooking facilities.

> **In 17-1.3.1, the phrase "without individual cooking facilities" refers to the absence of cooking equipment in any room or unit of a dormitory. If this equipment is present throughout a facility, the occupancy should be classed as an apartment. The phrase "with or without meals" connotes the *Code*'s acceptance of a central cafeteria used to serve meals for the occupants of a dormitory.**

Hotels. Includes buildings or groups of buildings under the same management in which there are more than 15 sleeping accommodations for hire, primarily used by transients who are lodged with or without meals, whether designated as a hotel, inn, club, motel, or by any other name. So-called apartment hotels shall be classified as hotels because they are potentially subject to transient occupancy like that of hotels.

> **Lodging or rooming houses containing more than 15 people are treated as hotels.**

Mezzanine. An intermediate level between the floor and ceiling of any story and covering not more than one-third of the floor area of the room in which it is located.

17-1.4 Classification of Occupancy. (*See 17-1.3.*)

17-1.5 Classification of Hazard of Contents.

17-1.5.1 Building contents shall be classified according to the provisions of 4-2.1 of this *Code.* For design of sprinkler systems, the classification of contents in *Standard for the Installation of Sprinkler Systems*, NFPA 13, shall apply.

The contents of living units in residential occupancies fall into the ordinary hazard classification, under the definitions of 4-2.1 of the *Code*. Characteristics of "ordinary" hazards are moderately rapid burning and considerable smoke generation, with the added hazard of the possible presence of toxic combustion products.

NFPA 13, *Standard for the Installation of Sprinkler Systems*,[1] would classify the contents as "light" for the design of extinguishing systems. The difference in classification is based on the threat to life or life safety (ordinary) versus the threat to the extinguishing capability of the automatic sprinkler system (light).

17-1.6 Minimum Construction Requirements. No special requirements.

17-1.7 Occupant Load.

17-1.7.1 The occupant load in numbers of persons for whom exits are to be provided shall be determined on the basis of one person per 200 sq ft (18.58 sq m) gross floor area, or the maximum probable population of any room or section under consideration, whichever is greater. The occupant load of any open mezzanine or balcony shall be added to the occupant load of the floor below for the purpose of determining exit capacity.

A dormitory-type occupancy, particularly where 2- or 3-tier bunks are used with close spacing, may produce an occupant load substantially greater than one person per 200 sq ft (18.58 sq m) of gross floor area. However, even though sleeping areas are densely populated, the building as a whole may not necessarily exceed one person per 200 sq ft (18.58 sq m) of gross area, owing to the space taken for toilet facilities, halls, closets, and living rooms not used for sleeping purposes.

This discussion does not preclude the need for providing exit capability from concentrated sleeping areas (bunk rooms) based on the "maximum probable population" rather than the design figure. If the actual population of a bunk room exceeds one person per 200 sq ft (18.58 sq m), the exit capacity (door widths, etc.) will have to be designed to the actual population load. See 5-3.1 for further details on the use of occupant load for determining capacity of the means of egress.

SECTION 17-2   MEANS OF EGRESS REQUIREMENTS

17-2.1 General.

17-2.1.1 Any floor below the level of exit discharge occupied for public purposes shall have exits arranged in accordance with 17-2.4.1 and 17-2.6.1.

The purpose of 17-2.1.1 is to tie together exit access, exit arrangement, and exit discharge requirements in the referenced paragraphs at one location in the *Code*. Any floor below the level of exit discharge used by or for the public must have exits arranged in the following manner:

1. They provide two separate exits (see 17-2.4.1).
2. At least one exit is within 100 ft (30.48 m) from the door of any room (see 17-2.6.1).

Note that travel distance to these exits may be increased to the following (per the exceptions to 17-2.6.1):

1. *200 ft (60.96 m)*, if the exit and exit access are arranged on the exterior of the building (see 5-5.4).
2. *150 ft (45.72 m)*, if the exit access and the building portions leading to the access are sprinklered, and the building portion where this 150-ft (45.72-m) distance is permitted is separated from the remainder of the facility by 1-hour construction (for buildings three stories or less in height) or 2-hour construction (for buildings four or more stories in height).

17-2.1.2   Any floor below the level of exit discharge not open to the public and used only for mechanical equipment, storage, and service operations (other than kitchens which are considered part of the hotel occupancy) shall have exits appropriate to its actual occupancy in accordance with other applicable sections of this *Code*.

The key point in 17-2.1.2 is that the provisions apply to nonpublic areas of a hotel. The committee felt that nonpublic areas provided a lower level of risk since there are fewer people in these areas, and that those who are in these spaces presumably are familiar with them. With a reduced level of risk, the provisions of occupant chapters other than Chapter 17 are appropriate.

17-2.1.3   The same stairway or other exit required to serve any one upper floor may also serve other upper floors.

Exception: No inside open stairway, escalator, or ramp may serve as a required egress from more than one floor, unless it conforms to 6-2.2.3.1, Exception No. 1.

Under 17-2.1.3, if the second and third floor are each required to have three stairways, the second floor may use the stairways serving the third floor so that the total number of stairways required is three, not six. This provision avoids the cumulative addition of stair widths leading to increasingly wider stairs in the descent through a building from the uppermost floor to ground level. The committee felt that a fire on one floor will pose a need for the evacuation of that floor first, followed by staged evacuation of the other floors; thus, a stair designed to handle the floor with the largest population will handle the staged evacuation of any other floor. There is a strict prohibition (in the exception) to open stairs, escalators, and ramps being used for more than one floor.

17-2.2 Types of Exits.

17-2.2.1   Exits or exit components, arranged in accordance with Chapter 5, shall be of one or more of the following types:

(a) Doors to outside at ground level, as per 5-2.1.

(b) Revolving doors, as per 5-2.1 (not at foot of stairs).

(c) Doors to subways only if the subway meets the requirements of exit passageways or tunnels as specified in 5-2.7.

(d) Interior stairs, Class A or Class B, in accordance with 5-2.2.

(e) Outside stairs, in accordance with 5-2.5.

(f) Smokeproof towers, in accordance with 5-2.3.

(g) Ramps, Class A or Class B, in accordance with 5-2.6.

(h) Escalators, in accordance with 5-2.8.

(i) Horizontal exits, in accordance with 5-2.4.

(j) Exit passageways, in accordance with 5-2.7.

17-2.2.2 Any existing interior stair or fire escape not complying with 5-2.2 or 5-2.9 may be continued in use subject to the approval of the authority having jurisdiction.

Paragraph 17-2.2.2 allows fire escapes to be continued in use only for *existing* buildings, subject to the approval of the authority having jurisdiction.

17-2.3 Capacity of Means of Egress.

17-2.3.1 Exits, arranged as specified elsewhere in this section of the *Code*, shall be sufficient to provide for the occupant load in numbers of persons as determined in accordance with 17-1.7, on the following basis:

(a) Doors, including those three risers or 24 in. (60.96 cm) above or below ground level, Class A ramps and horizontal exits—100 persons per unit of exit width.

(b) Stairs and other types of exits not included in (a) above—75 persons per unit of exit width.

17-2.3.2 Street-floor exits shall provide units of exit width as follows, occupant load being determined in accordance with 17-1.7.

(a) One unit for each 100 persons street-floor capacity for doors and other level exits, including those 24 in. (60.96 cm) or three risers above or below ground level.

(b) One unit for each 75 persons street-floor capacity for stair or other exit requiring descent to ground level.

(c) One and one-half exit units for each two-unit required stair from upper floors discharging through the street floor.

(d) One and one-half exit units for each two-unit required stair from floors below the street floor discharging through the street floor.

Paragraph 17-2.3.2 requires street-floor exit designs that have sufficient width to provide for the intermingling of exits from the street floor with exits discharging down from the upper floors and discharging up from the lower floors. This is the traditional grand lobby design found in many hotels and in many sizable mercantile occupancies where stairs and street-floor exits converge at one or two exterior door locations. Similar discussion on this matter is found in Chapter 24.

Paragraph 17-2.7.2 restricts the number and arrangement of stairs which discharge through the street floor.

Figure 17-1 shows a typical arrangement of multiple exits discharging on the street floor.

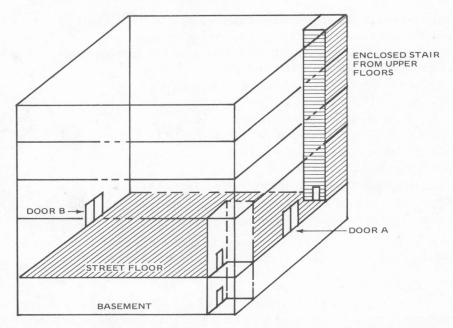

Figure 17-1. Capacity of Means of Egress in Accordance with 17-2.3.2. Required widths of Doors A and B are based on the number of people expected to use them: 1 unit of exit width [22 in. (55.88 cm)] for every 100 people on the street floor, and 1½ units for every 150 people traveling down from the upper floors, and 1½ units for every 150 people traveling up from the lower floors. (Also see 17-2.7.2.)

17-2.3.3 Every floor below the level of exit discharge shall have exits sufficient to provide for the occupant load of that floor as determined in accordance with 17-1.7 on the basis of 100 persons per exit unit for travel on the same level, 75 persons for upward travel, as up stairs.

> **Paragraph 17-2.3.3 simply requires that floors below ground level have their exit capacity provided for on the same basis as upper floors (see 17-2.3.1 and 17-2.3.4).**

17-2.3.4 Upper-floor exits shall provide numbers of units of exit width sufficient to meet the requirements of 17-2.3.1.

17-2.4 Number of Exits.

17-2.4.1 Not less than two exits shall be accessible from every floor, including floors below the level of exit discharge and occupied for public purposes.

17-2.4.2 Any room having a capacity of less than 50 persons with an outside door at street or ground level may have such outside door as a single exit provided that no part of the room or area is more than 50 ft (15.24 m) from the door measured along the natural path of travel.

> **As stated in 17-2.4.2, a room may have a single exit consisting of a door to the outside if *all* of the following conditions are met:**

1. The occupant capacity is 49 or less.
2. The room and room door are at street or ground level.
3. The travel distance from all points in the room to the exit door is 50 ft (15.24 m) or less.

17-2.5 Arrangement of Exits.

17-2.5.1   Access to all required exits shall be in accordance with Section 5-5, shall be unobstructed, and shall not be blocked from open view by ornamentation, curtain, or other appurtenance.

Highly decorative interior hotel designs that are currently popular may often lead to ornamentation, curtains, mirrors, or other devices that may obstruct or confuse the location of exits. Care should be taken to meet the requirements of 17-2.5.1 and avoid these problem areas.

17-2.5.2   Exits shall be so arranged that, from any corridor room door, exits will be accessible in at least two different directions.

Exception: Up to the first 35 ft (10.67 m) of exit travel from a corridor room door may be along a corridor with exit access only in one direction (dead end).

17-2.6 Measurement of Travel Distance to Exits.

17-2.6.1   Any exit as indicated in 17-2.4.1 shall be such that it will not be necessary to travel more than 100 ft (30.48 m) from the door of any room to reach the nearest exit. Travel distance to exits shall be measured in accordance with Section 5-6.

Exception No. 1:   Travel distance to exits may be increased to 200 ft (60.96 m) for exterior ways of exit access arranged in accordance with 5-5.4.

Exception No. 2:   Travel distance to exits may be increased to 150 ft (45.72 m) if the exit access and any portion of the building which is tributary to the exit access are protected throughout by an approved automatic sprinkler system. In addition, the portion of the building in which the 150-ft (45.72-m) travel distance is permitted shall be separated from the remainder of the building by construction having a fire resistance rating of not less than 1 hour for buildings up to four stories in height, and 2 hours for buildings four or more stories in height.

See Figure 17-2.

17-2.6.2   Travel distance from the door of the most remote room in a suite or in an apartment to a corridor door shall not exceed 50 ft (15.24 m).

Exception: One-hundred-ft (30.48-m) travel distance is allowed in buildings protected throughout by an approved automatic sprinkler system in accordance with Section 7-7, or an approved single station smoke detector in each habitable area in the suite or living unit.

The committee developed 17-2.6.2 to clarify the point from where travel distances should be measured in suites or apartments in hotels. Note that sprinklered facilities are allowed a 100 percent increase in travel distance, from 50 ft (15.24 m) to 100 ft (30.48 m). See Figure 17-2.

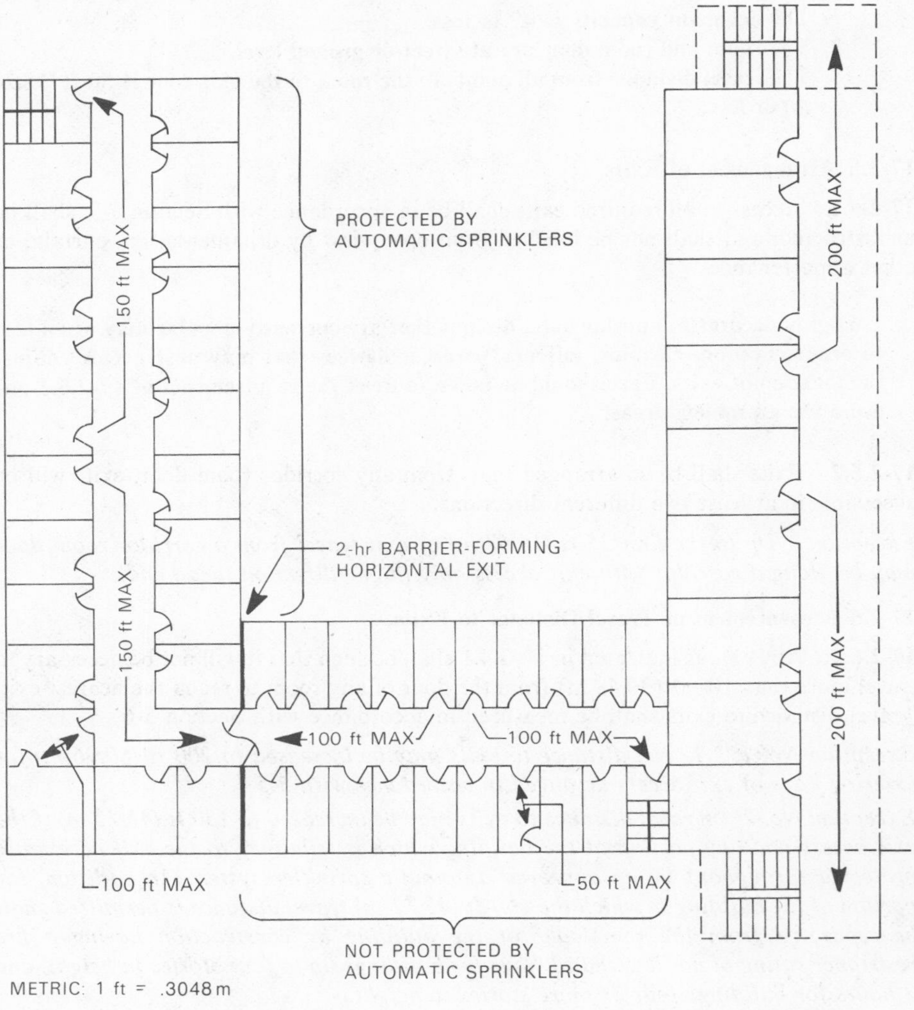

Figure 17-2. Travel Distance in Hotels.

17-2.7 Discharge from Exits.

17-2.7.1   At least half of the required number of units of exit width from upper floors, exclusive of horizontal exits, shall lead directly to the street or through a yard, court, or passageway with protected openings and separated from all parts of the interior of the building.

Paragraph 17-2.7.1 should be read jointly with the provisions of 17-2.7.2. A *minimum* of 50 percent of the exits from upper floors must discharge directly to the exterior. If less than 50 percent of the exits are arranged (per 17-2.7.2) to discharge through the floor of exit discharge, the remaining exits must be arranged to discharge directly to the exterior.

17-2.7.2   If any exits discharge through areas on the level of exit discharge, the conditions of 5-7.2 shall be met.

See Figures 17-3 and 17-4. (Also see discussion of 5-7.2.)

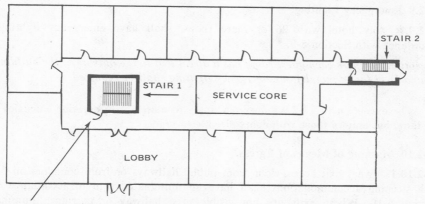

ROUTE FROM STAIR THROUGH LOBBY TO EXTERIOR MUST BE READILY VISIBLE, IDENTIFIED, CLEAR, AND UNOBSTRUCTED.

Figure 17-3. Arrangement of Means of Egress in Accordance with 17-2.7.2 (see 5-7.2). Stair 1 (50 percent of the total number of exits) discharges through the first floor. Stair 2 discharges directly to the exterior. Since other areas on the first floor (the level of exit discharge) are not separated from the path which a person leaving Stair 1 must follow to exit through the lobby, the entire first floor must be completely sprinklered. If the rest of the floor were separated, only the path to the exit discharge would have to be sprinklered.

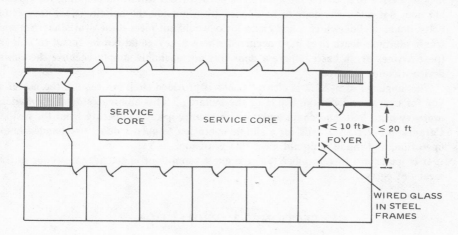

METRIC: 1 ft = .3048 m

Figure 17-4. Foyer Constructed in Compliance with 17-2.7.2 (see 5-7.2). The foyer must serve only as a means of egress.

17-2.8 Illumination of Means of Egress.

17-2.8.1   Each public space, hallway, stairway, or other means of egress shall have illumination in accordance with Section 5-8. Access to exits shall be continuously illuminated at all times.

17-2.9 Emergency Lighting.

17-2.9.1   Any hotel with 26 or more rooms shall have emergency lighting in accordance with Section 5-9.

Exception: Where each guest room has a direct exit to the outside of the building at ground level (as in motels), no emergency lighting shall be required.

The exception to 17-2.9.1 does not apply to motels with exterior balconies and stairs, but only to those with doors directly to grade.

17-2.10 Marking of Means of Egress.

17-2.10.1   Every exit access door from public hallways or from corridors on floors with sleeping accommodations shall have an illuminated sign in accordance with Section 5-10. Where exits are not visible in a hallway or corridor, illuminated directional signs shall be provided to indicate the direction to exits.

17-2.11 Special Features.

17-2.11.1   No door in any means of egress shall be locked against egress when the building is occupied (*see 5-2.1.2.*).

Paragraph 17-2.11.1 prohibits a hotel from having any door locked "against egress" while the building is occupied. This requirement permits a door to have a locking device that allows the door to be opened from within the building for egress, but does not allow the door to be opened from outside the building. Ordinary dead bolts, double cylinder locks, and chain locks would not meet these provisions. Several tragic multiple-death fires have occurred where a key could not be found to unlock these devices or, in haste, where a door was not openable simply because the chain device was not removed.

The language of 5-2.1.2 is clear. "Locks if provided shall not require the use of a key for operation from the inside of the building." This eliminates double cylinder, ordinary dead bolt, and chain locks which require a key to operate from the inside. Paragraph 5-2.1.2.1.2 calls for a simple operation to open a door; two-handed knob operation, and the like, do not meet this provision.

It is important to remember that the guest room door is considered a door in the means of egress.

SECTION 17-3   PROTECTION

17-3.1 Protection of Vertical Openings.

17-3.1.1   Every stairway, elevator shaft and other vertical opening shall be enclosed or protected in accordance with 6-2.2 or provide means of satisfying the requirements of Section 2-9.

Exception No. 1:   Unprotected vertical openings connecting not more than three floors used for hotel occupancy only may be permitted in accordance with the conditions of 6-2.2.3.1, Exception No. 1.

Exception No. 2:   An atrium may be utilized in accordance with 6-2.2.3.1, Exception No. 2.

Exception No. 3:   In any building protected throughout by an approved automatic sprinkler system in accordance with Section 7-7, and where exits and required ways of travel thereto are adequately safeguarded against fire and smoke within the building or where every individual room has direct access to an exterior exit without passing through any public corridor, the protection of vertical openings not part of required exits may be waived by the authority having jurisdiction to such extent as such openings do not endanger required means of egress.

Exception No. 4:   Stairway enclosures shall not be required where a one-story stair connects two levels within a single dwelling unit, guest room or suite located above the level of exit discharge.

Paragraph 17-3.1.1 provides for the enclosure of vertical openings in existing hotels by a performance approach, i.e., either enclose them per 6-2.2 or satisfy the objectives of Section 2-9.

Concerning Exception No. 1 to 17-3.1.1, it should be noted that 6-2.2.3.1, Exception No. 1 requires total automatic sprinkler protection for "ordinary hazard" occupancies which hotels are considered. Exception No. 2 to 6-2.2.3.1 requires buildings with atriums to also be protected throughout by automatic sprinklers.

Exception No. 3, simply stated, allows unprotected openings under the following conditions, subject to the approval of the authority having jurisdiction:

1. The building is totally sprinklered;
2. Exits and exit accesses are adequately separated from the remainder of the building;
3. In lieu of the preceding condition (No. 2), every room has direct access to an exterior exit without going through a public corridor; and
4. Shafts enclosing required exit stairs are protected.

Therefore, unless the unprotected vertical opening complies with Exception No. 4, the building which contains the opening is required to be sprinklered.

17-3.1.2 Any required exit stair which is so located that it is necessary to pass through the lobby or other open space to reach the outside of the building shall be continuously enclosed down to the lobby level, or to a mezzanine within the lobby (*see 17-2.7*).

Where open stairways or escalators are permitted, they are considered as *exit accesses* to exits, rather than as exits, and requirements for distance to exits include the travel on such stairs. (See 5-6.5.)

17-3.1.3 No floor below the level of exit discharge, used only for storage, heating equipment, or other purpose other than hotel occupancy open to guests or the public, shall have unprotected openings to floors used for hotel purposes.

17-3.2 Protection from Hazards.

17-3.2.1 Any room containing high pressure boilers, refrigerating machinery, transformers, or other service equipment subject to possible explosion shall not be located directly under or directly adjacent to exits. All such rooms shall be effectively cut off from other parts of the building as specified in Section 6-4.

17-3.2.2 Every hazardous area shall be separated from other parts of the building by construction having a fire resistance rating of at least 1 hour and communicating openings shall be protected by approved self-closing fire doors, or such area shall be equipped with automatic fire extinguishing system. Hazardous areas include, but are not limited to:

Boiler and heater rooms	Rooms or spaces used for storage of
Laundries	combustible supplies and equip-
Repair shops	ment in quantities deemed hazard-
	ous by the authority having juris-
	diction.

The list in 17-3.2.2 is not all-inclusive. It is the responsibility of the authority having jurisdiction to determine which areas are hazardous.

17-3.3 Interior Finish.

17-3.3.1 Interior finish on walls and ceilings, in accordance with Section 6-5 and subject to the limitations and modifications therein specified, shall be as follows:

  (a) Vertical exits [see 5-1.2.1(b)] — Class A or B.

  (b) Exit access [see 5-1.2.1(a)] — Class A or B.

  (c) Lobbies, corridors that are not exit access — Class A, B, or C.

  (d) Places of assembly (see 9-3.3).

  (e) Individual guest rooms and other rooms — Class A, B, or C.

17-3.3.2 Interior floor finish in corridors and exitways shall be Class I or Class II in accordance with Section 6-5.

Exception: Previously installed floor coverings may be continued in use, subject to the approval of the authority having jurisdiction.

The provisions for interior finish in 17-3.3 were rewritten for the 1976 Edition of the *Code* to reflect the elimination of the Class D and E categories of interior finish and to provide more specific guidance on where in a hotel these requirements apply. In this, the 1981 Edition, the interior floor finish requirements were modified to reflect changes in Section 6-5.

17-3.4 Alarm and Communication Systems.

17-3.4.1 An alarm system, in accordance with Section 7-6, shall be provided for any hotel having accommodations for 15 or more guests.

Exception: Where each guest room has a direct exit to the outside of the building and the building is three or less stories in height.

17-3.4.2 Every sounding device shall be of such character and so located as to alert all occupants of the building or section thereof endangered by fire.

This paragraph, although appearing quite basic, is one that apparently needs emphasizing. In several recent multiple-death hotel fires, reports listed inaudible or unrecognized alarms as contributing factors.

17-3.4.3 A manual fire alarm station shall be provided at the hotel desk or other convenient central control point under continuous supervision of responsible employees. Additional manual alarms (*as specified in Section 7-6*) may be waived where there are other effective means (such as complete automatic sprinkler or automatic fire detection systems) for notification of fire as required in 17-3.4.2.

Paragraph 17-3.4.3 eliminates the requirements for fire alarm boxes located so that all portions of a building are within 200 ft (60.96 m) of a box (see Section 7-6) if an automatic sprinkler system or an automatic detection system is provided throughout the building. This does not eliminate the need for the alarm system; it only deletes the requirement for additional manual pull stations.

17-3.4.4 Provisions shall be made for the immediate notification of the public fire department by either telephone or other means in case of fire. Where there is no public fire department this notification shall go to the private fire brigade.

This paragraph does not require a direct fire alarm connection to the fire department; however, that would be the best method to comply with 17-3.4.4. The telephone required would have to be equipped for direct outside dial without going through a switchboard and it could not be a pay phone.

17-3.5 Extinguishment Requirements.

17-3.5.1 Where an automatic sprinkler system is installed, either for total or partial building coverage, the system shall be in accordance with the requirements of *Standard for the Installation of Sprinkler Systems*, NFPA 13.

Exception: Sprinkler installation may be omitted in small compartmented areas such as closets not over 24 sq ft (2.23 sq m) and bathrooms not over 55 sq ft (5.11 sq m).

The exception for omitting sprinklers from closets 24 sq ft (2.23 sq m) or less in area and bathrooms 55 sq ft (5.11 sq m) or less follows a pattern in NFPA 13, *Standard for the Installation of Sprinkler Systems*,[1] for allowing (under "light hazard" sprinkler guidelines) certain nonsprinklered areas to exist due to their low fuel loads, lack of ignition sources, and low hazard levels.

17-3.5.2 Hand portable fire extinguishers shall be provided in hazardous areas. When provided, hand portable fire extinguishers shall be installed and maintained as specified in *Standard for Portable Fire Extinguishers*, NFPA 10. (*See Section 31-6.*)

17-3.6 Minimum Fire Resistance Requirements for Protection of Guest Rooms (Corridors).

17-3.6.1 Fire resistance for interior corridors shall be 30 minutes.

Exception No. 1:   Where a corridor sprinkler system is provided as outlined in 19-3.5.1 through 19-3.5.3, in which case there will be no fire resistance rating required, but all openings shall resist the passage of smoke.

Exception No. 2:   Where interior corridor walls have openings from transfer grills, see 17-3.6.6.

The criteria in 17-3.6 parallel the requirements in Chapter 13 for health care occupancies. In both chapters, the committee's concern for providing safety for the occupant in his or her room, during a fire, led to a minimum corridor wall construction either to block fire movement into a room from the corridor or to block fire in a room from entering the corridor. The common concern in Chapters 13 and 17 is the presence of occupants on a 24-hour-a-day basis with sleeping accommodations.

Corridor partitions in sprinklered and nonsprinklered facilities are intended to be constructed to resist the passage of smoke.

The intent of the 30-minute fire-resistive rating for corridor partitions is to require a nominal fire rating, particularly where the fire rating of existing partitions cannot be documented. Examples of acceptable partition assemblies would include, but are not limited to, ½-in. (1.27-cm) gypsum board, wood lath and plaster, gypsum lath, or metal lath and plaster.

17-3.6.2   Each guest room door which opens onto an interior corridor shall have a fire protection rating of at least 20 minutes.

The door required by 17-3.6.2 provides a level of protection commensurate with the expected fuel load in the room and the fire resistance of the corridor wall construction. The purpose is to box a fire out of a room, or to box it within the room by corridor wall and door construction criteria. (See 17-3.6.3.) It has been shown in fuel load studies conducted by the National Bureau of Standards that residential occupancies will have fuel loads in the 20- to 30-minute range.

Contrary to the general rule (see 5-2.1.1.1.1), the door referred to in 17-3.6.2 applies to the leaf only. In other words, the frame, hinges, latch, closers, etc., do not have to be rated. By requiring the 20-minute door, the committee was attempting to establish a minimum quality of construction, not to provide for a complete listed fire door assembly.

Exception No. 1:   Previously approved 1¾-in. (4.45-cm) solid bonded wood core doors may remain in use.

Exception No. 2:   In buildings protected throughout by an approved automatic sprinkler system, doors shall be so constructed as to resist the passage of smoke. Doors shall be equipped with latches for keeping doors tightly closed, but may be provided with glass vision panels without restriction.

17-3.6.3   Doors between guest rooms and corridors shall be self-closing, and shall meet the requirements of 17-3.6.2.

17-3.6.4   Unprotected openings shall be prohibited in partitions of interior corridors serving as exit access from guest rooms.

17-3.6.5   Existing transoms installed in corridor partitions of sleeping rooms shall be fixed in the closed position and shall be covered or otherwise protected to provide a fire resistance rating at least equivalent to that of the wall in which they are installed.

Transoms have been prohibited for many years in hotels due to tragic fires where the presence of transoms led to the transmission of fire and smoke down corridors and directly into occupied rooms, thus causing multiple deaths.

17-3.6.6   Transfer grills, whether protected by fusible link operated dampers or not, shall not be used in these walls or doors.

Exception No. 1:   Where a corridor smoke detection system is provided which when sensing smoke will sound the building alarm and shut down return or exhaust fans which draw air into the corridor from the guest rooms. The grills shall be located in the lower one-third of the wall or door height.

Exception No. 2:   Where automatic sprinkler protection is provided in the corridor in accordance with 19-3.5.1 and where the transfer grill is located in the lower one-third of the wall or door height.

Paragraph 2-2.2 of NFPA 90A, *Standard for the Installation of Air Conditioning and Ventilating Systems,*[2] prohibits public corridors from being used as a portion of the supply return or exhaust air system.

17-3.7 Subdivision of Building Spaces.   No special requirements.

17-3.8 Special Features.

17-3.8.1 Smokeproof towers, if provided, shall comply with 5-2.3.

SECTION 17-4   SPECIAL PROVISIONS

SECTION 17-5   BUILDING SERVICES

17-5.1 Utilities.   Utilities shall comply with the provisions of Section 7-1.

17-5.2 Heating, Ventilating and Air Conditioning.   Heating, ventilating and air conditioning equipment shall comply with the provisions of Section 7-2, except as otherwise required in this chapter.

17-5.3 Elevators, Dumbwaiters, and Vertical Conveyors.   Elevators, dumbwaiters and vertical conveyors shall comply with the provisions of Section 7-4.

17-5.4 Rubbish Chutes, Incinerators, and Laundry Chutes.   Rubbish chutes, incinerators, and laundry chutes shall comply with the provisions of Section 7-5.

SECTION 17-6   EXISTING DORMITORIES

17-6.1 Application.

17-6.1.1   Existing dormitories shall comply with the requirements for existing hotels, except as modified in the following paragraphs.

Exception: Any dormitory divided into suites of rooms, with one or more bedrooms opening into a living room or study which has a door opening into a common corridor serving a number of suites, shall be classified as an apartment building.

The exception to 17-6.1.1 recognizes that the now popular dormitory design of a group of bedrooms clustered around a living room duplicates a typical apartment design of several bedrooms clustered around a living room (or a kitchen). Since the design and the risk of fire are the same, the *Code* treats this arrangement the same as that of an apartment building. (See Figure 17-5.)

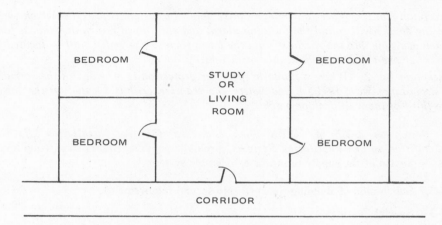

Figure 17-5. Arrangement of Dormitory Suite Treated as an Apartment Under the Exception to 17-6.1.1. More than one bedroom opens into a study or living room which has a door opening into a corridor. The corridor serves a number of suites.

17-6.1.2   Every individual living unit covered by this section shall at least comply with the minimum provisions of Chapter 22, One- and Two-Family Dwellings.

Exception: The requirement of Section 22-2 for means of window egress shall be applicable to buildings of six stories or less.

17-6.2 Means of Egress Requirements.

17-6.2.1 Types and Capacities of Exits.

17-6.2.1.1   Exits of the same types and capacities as required for hotels (*see 17-2.2 and 17-2.3*) shall be provided.

Exception: Each street floor door shall be sufficient to provide one unit of exit width for each 50 persons capacity of the street floor, plus one unit for each unit of required stairway width discharging through the street floor.

The exception to 17-6.2.1.1 follows the approach found in Chapters 17, 25, and 27 for sizing the exits to accommodate the intermingling of the population of the street floor with people using upper floor exits which discharge into areas on the street floor.

17-6.2.2 Arrangement of Means of Egress.

17-6.2.2.1   In any dormitory having sleeping rooms or areas containing more than four occupants, there shall be access to two separate and distinct exits in different directions from the room door, with no common path of travel.

Exception No. 1: One exit may be accepted where the room or space is subject to occupancy by not more than ten persons and has a door opening directly to the outside of the building at street or ground level or to an outside stairway.

Exception No. 2: In existing buildings a common path of travel not exceeding 35 ft (10.67 m) is permitted.

17-6.2.3 Measurement of Travel Distance to Exits.

17-6.2.3.1 Exits shall be so arranged that it will not be necessary to travel more than 100 ft (30.48 m) from any point, or 150 ft (45.72 m) in a building protected throughout by an approved automatic sprinkler system in accordance with Section 7-7, to reach the nearest outside door or exit, nor to traverse more than a one-story flight of inside, unenclosed stairs.

17-6.3 Protection.

17-6.3.1 Protection of Vertical Openings.

17-6.3.1.1 Every exit stair and other vertical openings shall be enclosed or protected in accordance with Section 6-2.

Exception No. 1: In existing buildings not more than two stories in height of any type of construction, unprotected openings may be permitted by the authority having jurisdiction if the building is protected by automatic sprinklers in accordance with Section 7-7.

Exception No. 2: If every sleeping room or area has direct access to an outside exit without the necessity of passing through any corridor or other space exposed to any unprotected vertical opening and the building is equipped with an automatic fire detection system in accordance with Section 7-6, unprotected openings may be permitted by the authority having jurisdiction.

Exception No. 1 to 17-6.3.1.1 was developed to provide some assurance that there would be safe space and a minimum level of life safety in older, non-*Code*-conforming dormitories found at many of the older universities. However, the committee did limit the height of buildings with unprotected openings to two stories, maximum.

Note that Exception No. 2 carries no height limit. The construction of outside exits with outside exit access balconies (plus the required automatic fire detection system) is an acceptable way of taking existing multistory (more than two stories) facilities and making them *Code*-conforming.

17-6.3.2 Alarm and Detection Systems.

17-6.3.2.1 Every dormitory shall have a manual fire alarm system in accordance with Section 7-6.

Exception No. 1: Buildings protected throughout by an approved automatic sprinkler system in accordance with Section 7-7.

Exception No. 2: Buildings protected throughout by an approved automatic fire detection system in accordance with Section 7-6.

17-6.3.2.2 Approved smoke detectors shall be installed on each floor by either:

(a) Using single station smoke detectors in all habitable rooms, or

(b) Using corridor detectors connected to the building fire alarm system and at not over 30 ft (914.4 cm) spacing.

Approved single station smoke detector(s) may be provided in habitable rooms, or corridor smoke detectors interconnected with the building fire alarm system may be provided, whichever is most suitable for early warning purposes. Where unusual factors such as room configuration, air movement, stagnant air pockets, etc., require consideration, the authority having jurisdiction, the designer, and listing information of the testing laboratory should determine the placement of the detectors.

17-6.4 Special Provisions.   Reserved.

17-6.5 Building Services.

17-6.5.1 Utilities.

17-6.5.1.1 Building service equipment shall be installed in accordance with Section 7-1.

17-6.5.2 Heating/Air Conditioning.

17-6.5.2.1 Heating and air conditioning equipment shall meet the requirements of Section 7-2.

REFERENCES CITED BY *CODE*

(These publications comprise a part of the requirements to the extent called for by the Code.*)*

NFPA 10, *Standard for Portable Fire Extinguishers*, NFPA, Boston, 1978.
NFPA 13, *Standard for the Installation of Sprinkler Systems*, NFPA, Boston, 1980.

REFERENCES CITED IN COMMENTARY

[1]NFPA 13, *Standard for the Installation of Sprinkler Systems*, NFPA, Boston, 1980.
[2]NFPA 90A, *Standard for the Installation of Air Conditioning and Ventilating Systems*, NFPA, Boston, 1978.

18

NEW APARTMENT BUILDINGS

(See also Chapter 31.)

Prior to the 1981 Edition of the *Code*, all residential occupancies were treated in one chapter. In this edition they have been split into several chapters in order to simplify and clarify the *Code*, resulting in a document that is easier to use.

SECTION 18-1   GENERAL REQUIREMENTS

18-1.1 Application.

18-1.1.1   This *Code* has differing requirements for the several types of residential occupancies; thus, the *Code* has several residential occupancy chapters, Chapters 16 through 23.

Residential occupancies are ones in which sleeping accommodations are provided for normal residential purposes, and include all buildings designed to provide sleeping accommodations. They are treated separately in the *Code* in the following groups:

Hotels/motels (Chapters 16 and 17)

Apartments (Chapters 18 and 19)

Dormitories (including orphanages for age six years and older) (Section 16-6 and 17-6)

Lodging or rooming houses (Chapter 20)

1- and 2-family dwellings (Chapter 22)

Exceptions to the groups listed above are health care occupancies which are covered in Chapters 12 and 13 and detention and correctional occupancies which are covered in Chapters 14 and 15. In earlier editions of the *Code* they were classified as "institutional occupancies."

A review of 4-1.6 underscores a common principle of life safety with which the *Code* is concerned in all the residential occupancies considered by Chapters 16 through 23. Paragraph 4-1.6 states: "Residential occupancies are ones in which *sleeping accommodations* are provided for normal residential purposes and include all buildings designed to provide *sleeping accommodations*." This use of residential occupancies is central to the *Code*'s provisions in Chapters 16 through 23 because people who are asleep will be unaware of a rapidly developing fire and, when alerted,

557

may be somewhat confused because of being awakened suddenly. Other factors on which the provisions of Chapters 16 through 23 were developed are the presence of hazards (such as cooking and heating equipment) and the degree of familiarity of the occupant with his or her living space (ranging from transients with little or no familiarity, as in hotels, to total familiarity in single-family dwellings).

18-1.1.2 All new buildings classified as apartment buildings by 18-1.3.1 shall conform to the provisions of this chapter, and shall meet the requirements of one of the following options (*see Table 18-1*):

Option 1:   Buildings without fire suppression or detection systems;

Single station smoke detectors in each unit are required per 18-3.4.1.1.

Option 2:   Buildings provided with a complete automatic fire detection and notification system;

Option 3:   Buildings provided with automatic sprinkler protection in selected area;

Option 4:   Buildings protected throughout by an approved automatic sprinkler system.

Paragraph 18-1.1.2 identifies four different ways of arranging apartment buildings for life safety that are acceptable to the *Code*. These four systems are:
1. Buildings without fire suppression or detection systems;
2. Buildings with an automatic fire detection system;
3. Buildings provided with an automatic sprinkler system in corridors only; and
4. Buildings protected by a total automatic sprinkler system.

In the 1976 Edition of the *Code*, Section 11-3 covered both new and existing apartment buildings, with 11-3.1 to 11-3.4 providing general requirements for all apartment buildings, and 11-3.5 through 11-3.8 each covering one of the four options. In that edition, every apartment building was required to meet 11-3.1 through 11-3.4 and any one of 11-3.5 through 11-3.8. This arrangement resulted in a considerable amount of cross-referencing — not only in Section 11-3, but also in Sections 11-1, 11-2, and Chapter 6 — and a sometimes very confusing text resulted. Since the 1981 Edition was undergoing extensive editorial revision to provide separate chapters for new and existing buildings and also to split up the residential chapter, it was decided to reorganize the apartment chapters to make them easier to use and eliminate cross-referencing where possible. As a result of this restructuring, all sections of Chapter 18 apply to all new apartment buildings. There are various paragraphs and parts of paragraphs that apply to different options, or only to housing for the elderly. Every apartment building, whether or not it contains apartments for the elderly, must meet one of the four options.

The best approach in using this portion of the *Code* is to base a design on *Code* Table 18-1 or 18-2 and, when necessary, to refer to the appropriate paragraph to verify specific details. Either Table 18-1 or 18-2 provides almost all the design information needed to meet this portion of the *Code* and both may be found at the end of this chapter.

The committee, recognizing the equivalency provisions found in Section 1-5 of the *Code*, saw a need to establish in advance four equivalent *Code*-acceptable schemes to provide a high degree of design flexibility. The equivalencies developed were based on the committee's professional judgment, the results of full-scale fire tests conducted at the National Bureau of Standards, and a review of the most recent fire experiences. These designs are considered to be equivalent to each other in providing a minimum level of life safety for apartments. Because some systems have additional protective capability (detectors, automatic sprinklers, etc.), higher building heights and larger building areas were permitted. Where the design provided only the minimum level of safety called for in the *Code*, lower building heights and smaller building areas were specified.

This overall approach provides one of the first "system" design attempts to be codified. Whereas a total system would have many design approaches, this is a more limited, or bounded, system in that only four different approaches are available. Yet, a designer can identify an appropriate design from the four approaches based on the building's size, height, and arrangement. This provides the designer an opportunity to put together a safety approach that best fits the building, rather than fitting a building to a single codified design criterion. However, this system works only when the designer and the authority having jurisidiction agree on the plan selected at the earliest design phase.

18-1.1.3 Apartments for the elderly as defined in 18-1.3.1 shall meet the requirements for apartment houses as provided in this section unless otherwise noted.

As given in 18-1.3.1, apartments for the elderly are apartment buildings *specifically designed* for housing elderly people; however, these people *must be capable of self-preservation.* If the occupants are not capable of self-preservation, the building must comply with health care occupancy requirements.

Apartments for the elderly must comply with all the requirements for apartment buildings, using one of the four options, in addition to special provisions for apartments for the elderly which are given where appropriate throughout the chapter.

18-1.1.4 Every individual living unit covered by this section shall at least comply with the minimum provisions for windows of Chapter 22, One- and Two-Family Dwellings.

Exception: The requirements of Section 22-2 for a second means of escape may be waived for buildings over six stories provided that an approved means of smoke control is provided throughout the building as described in Appendix B of Standard for the Installation of Air Conditioning and Ventilating Systems, NFPA 90A.

It would probably be better stated to say "for guidance on a smoke control system see Appendix B of NFPA 90A, *Standard for the Installation of Air Conditioning and Ventilating Systems,*[1]" since that Appendix is more of a discussion of the subject and does not set requirements. *Smoke Control in Fire Safety Design*[2] provides an in-depth comprehensive discussion of smoke control.

18-1.2 Mixed Occupancies.

18-1.2.1 Where another type of occupancy occurs in the same building as a residential occupancy, the requirements of 1-4.5 of this *Code* shall be applicable.

18-1.2.2   For requirements on mixed mercantile and residential occupancies, see 24-1.2.

18-1.3 Definitions.

18-1.3.1   Terms applicable to this chapter are defined in Chapter 3 of this *Code*; where necessary, other terms will be defined in the text as they may occur.

Apartment Buildings.   Includes buildings containing three or more living units with independent cooking and bathroom facilities, whether designated as apartment house, tenement, garden apartment, or by any other name.

Apartments for the Elderly.   An apartment building specifically designed for housing elderly individuals who are capable of self-preservation.

> It is not the intent that these special requirements apply to apartment buildings that just happen to be occupied by the elderly, but only to those apartment buildings specifically intended to house elderly residents. This is usually not difficult to determine since they often come under certain local, state, or federal funding, or apply for tax breaks. In addition, the name, advertising, or facilities provided usually provide ample evidence of the intent.
>
> If individual cooking facilities are not provided, then the building would more accurately be classified as a dormitory. If, however, the residents (four or more) are not capable of self-preservation, then health care requirements would apply.

Complete Automatic Fire Detection and Notification System.   A supervised system which will initiate a trouble signal. It consists of smoke detectors so installed as to provide fire detection in sleeping and living areas, means of egress and mechanical and electrical equipment rooms.

Mezzanine.   An intermediate level between the floor and ceiling of any story and covering not more than one-third of the floor area of the room in which it is located.

18-1.4 Classification of Occupancy.   (*See 18-1.3.1.*)

18-1.5 Classification of Hazard of Contents.

18-1.5.1   Building contents shall be classified according to the provisions of 4-2.1 of this *Code*. For design of sprinkler systems, the classification of contents in *Standard for the Installation of Sprinkler Systems*, NFPA 13, shall apply.

> Under the definitions of 4-2.1 of the *Code*, the contents of living units in residential occupancies fall into the ordinary hazard classification. Characteristics of "ordinary" hazards are moderately rapid burning and considerable smoke generation, with the added hazard of the possible presence of toxic combustion products.
>
> NFPA 13, *Standard for the Installation of Sprinkler Systems*,[3] would classify the contents as "light" for the design of extinguishing systems. The difference in classification is based on the threat to life or life safety (ordinary) versus the threat to the extinguishing capability of the automatic sprinkler system (light).

18-1.6 Minimum Construction Requirements.   No special requirements.

18-1.7 Occupant Load.

18-1.7.1   The occupant load in numbers of persons for whom exits are to be provided shall be determined on the basis of one person per 200 sq ft (18.58 sq m) gross floor area, or the maximum probable population of any room or section under consideration, whichever is greater. The occupant load of any open mezzanine or balcony shall be added to the occupant load of the floor below for the purpose of determining exit capacity.

A dormitory-type occupancy, particularly where 2- or 3-tier bunks are used with close spacing, may produce an occupant load substantially greater than one person per 200 sq ft (18.58 sq m) of gross floor area. However, even though sleeping areas are densely populated, the building as a whole may not necessarily exceed one person per 200 sq ft (18.58 sq m) of gross area, owing to the space taken for toilet facilities, halls, closets, and living rooms not used for sleeping purposes.

This discussion does not preclude the need for providing exit capability from concentrated sleeping areas (bunk rooms) based on the "maximum probable population" rather than the design figure. If the actual population of a bunk room exceeds one person per 200 sq ft (18.58 sq m), the exit capacity (door widths, etc.) will have to be designed to the actual population load. See 5-3.1 for further details on the use of occupant load for determining capacity of the means of egress.

SECTION 18-2   MEANS OF EGRESS REQUIREMENTS

18-2.1 General.

18-2.2 Types of Exits.

18-2.2.1   Exits, or exit components, arranged in accordance with Chapter 5, shall be of one or more of the following types:

(a) Doors, as per 5-2.1.

(b) Revolving doors, as per 5-2.1 (not at foot of stairs).

(c) Doors to subways, only if the subway meets the requirements of exit passageways or tunnels as specified in 5-2.7.

(d) Interior stairs, in accordance with 5-2.2.

(e) Outside stairs, in accordance with 5-2.5.

(f) Smokeproof towers, in accordance with 5-2.3.

(g) Ramps, Class A or Class B, in accordance with 5-2.6.

(h) Escalators, in accordance with 5-2.8.

(i) Horizontal exits, in accordance with 5-2.4.

(j) Exit passageways, in accordance with 5-2.7.

18-2.2.2   In apartments for the elderly horizontal exits are required.

Exception No. 1:   Where exterior exit balconies are provided.

Exception No. 2:   Where a single exit building is acceptable under 18-2.4.1.

Exception No. 3:   Where buildings are three or less stories in height.

Exception No. 4:   Where smoke barriers are permitted by 18-3.7.2(b).

At least one horizontal exit is required on each level of a building four stories or more in height housing apartments for the elderly. Smoke barriers may be used in lieu of the horizontal exits per 18-3.7.2(b) in buildings using Option 4 (total automatic sprinkler protection). Buildings using exterior exit access or having a single exit per 18-2.4.1 are exempted from the horizontal exit requirement.

18-2.3 Capacity of Means of Egress.

18-2.3.1   Exits, arranged as specified elsewhere in this section of the *Code*, shall be sufficient to provide for the occupant load in numbers of persons as determined in accordance with 18-1.7, on the following basis:

(a) Doors, including those three risers or 24 in. (60.96 cm) above or below ground level, Class A ramps and horizontal exits—100 persons per unit of exit width.

(b) Stairs and other types of exits not included in (a) above—75 persons per unit of exit width.

18-2.3.2   Street-floor exits shall provide units of exit width, as follows, occupant load being determined in accordance with 18-1.7.

(a) One unit for each 100 persons street-floor capacity for doors and other level exits, including those 24 in. (60.96 cm) or three risers above or below ground level.

(b) One unit for each 75 persons street-floor capacity for stair or other exit requiring descent to ground level.

(c) One and one-half units for each two-unit required stair from upper floors discharging through the street floor.

(d) One and one-half exit units for each two-unit required stair from floors below the street floor discharging through the street floor.

> Paragraph 18-2.3.2 requires street-floor exit designs that have sufficient width to provide for the intermingling of exits from the street floor with exits discharging down from the upper floors and discharging up from the lower floors. This is the traditional grand lobby design found in many hotels and in many sizable mercantile occupancies where stairs and street-floor exits converge at one or two exterior door locations. Similar discussion on this matter is found in Chapter 24. Paragraph 18-2.7.2 restricts the number and arrangement of stairs which discharge through the street floor.
>
> Figure 18-1 shows a typical arrangement of multiple exits discharging on the street floor.

18-2.3.3   Every floor below the level of exit discharge shall have exits sufficient to provide for the occupant load of that floor as determined in accordance with 18-1.7 on the basis of 100 persons per exit unit for travel on the same level, 75 persons for upward travel, as up stairs.

18-2.3.4   Upper-floor exits shall provide numbers of units of exit width sufficient to meet the requirements of 18-2.3.1.

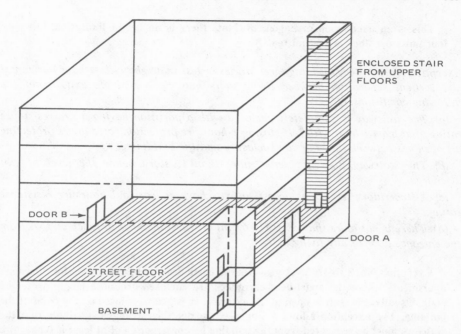

ENCLOSED STAIR
FROM UPPER
FLOORS

DOOR B →

DOOR A

STREET FLOOR

BASEMENT

Figure 18-1. Capacity of Means of Egress in Accordance with 18-2.3.2. Required widths of Doors A and B are based on the number of people expected to use them: 1 unit of exit width [22 in. (55.88 cm)] for every 100 people on the street floor, and 1½ units for every 150 people traveling down from the upper floors, and 1½ units for every 150 people traveling up from the lower floors. (Also see 18-2.7.2.)

18-2.4 Number of Exits.

18-2.4.1 Every living unit shall have access to at least two separate exits remote from each other as required by 5-5.1.

Exception No. 1: Any living unit which has an exit directly to the street or yard at ground level or by way of an outside stairway, or an enclosed stairway with fire resistance rating of 1 hour or more serving that apartment only and not communicating with any floor below the level of exit discharge or other area not a part of the apartment served, may have a single exit.

This is common in a townhouse or row house arrangement. This permits the front door to be the only required exit, and therefore the rear door, which is often provided, would not be required and could be a sliding door to a porch or patio.

Exception No. 2: A building of any height with not more than four living units per floor with a smokeproof tower or outside stair in accordance with the requirements of 5-2.3 as the exit, immediately accessible to all living units served thereby, may have a single exit. ["Immediately accessible" means there is not more than 20 ft (609.6 cm) of travel distance to reach an exit from the entrance door of any living unit.]

This is an uncommon arrangement. Note there is no height limitation, but only four units per floor are permitted.

Exception No. 3:   Any building three stories or less in height with ¾-hour horizontal and vertical separation between living units may have a single exit, under the following conditions:

(a) The stairway is completely enclosed with a partition having a fire resistance rating of at least 1 hour with self-closing 1-hour fire protection rated doors protecting all openings between the stairway enclosure and the building.

(b) The stairway does not serve more than ½ story below the level of exit discharge.

(c) All corridors serving as access to exits have at least a 1-hour fire resistance rating.

(d) There is not more than 35 ft (10.67 m) of travel distance to reach an exit from the entrance door of any living unit.

Exception No. 3 to 18-2.4.1 provides the basic design approach used for "garden" apartments where the apartment entrances are enclosed around a single protected stair. Usually, the stair is open to the exterior, or is glass-enclosed on the front of the building. The exception allows a single exit under this arrangement. Note that the stairway must be separated from the building by construction of at least a 1-hour fire resistance rating, and the doors must be 1-hour rated and self-closing.

These provisions apply to any of the four options summarized in Tables 18-1 and 18-2.

18-2.5 Arrangement of Exits.

18-2.5.1   Access to all required exits shall be in accordance with Section 5-5, shall be unobstructed, and shall not be blocked from open view by ornamentation, curtain, or other appurtenance.

18-2.6 Measurement of Travel Distance to Exits.

18-2.6.1   Travel distance from the door of a room in a suite or living unit to a corridor door shall not exceed the following limits:

(a) For buildings using Option 1 or 3 — 50 ft (15.24 m).

(b) For buildings using Option 2 or 4 — 100 ft (30.48 m).

(c) For apartments for the elderly using Option 1 or 3 — 50 ft (15.24 m).

(d) For apartments for the elderly using Option 2 — 75 ft (22.86 m).

(e) For apartments for the elderly using Option 4 — 100 ft (30.48 m).

18-2.6.2   Maximum single path corridor length of 35 ft (10.67 m) is permitted.

18-2.6.3   The travel distance from a living unit entrance door to the nearest exit shall not exceed the following limits:

(a) For buildings using Option 1 — 100 ft (30.48 m).

(b) For buildings using Option 2, 3 or 4 — 150 ft (45.72 m).

(c) In apartments for the elderly using Option 1 — 75 ft (22.86 m).

(d) In apartments for the elderly using Option 2, 3, or 4 — 100 ft (30.48 m).

Table 18-2.6.3
Travel Distance from Living Unit
Entrance Door to Nearest Exit

Occupancy	Options			
	No. 1	No. 2	No. 3	No. 4
Residential	100 ft (30.48 m)	150 ft (45.72 m)	150 ft (45.72 m)	150 ft (45.72 m)
Apartments for Elderly	75 ft (22.86 m)	100 ft (30.48 m)	100 ft (30.48 m)	100 ft (30.48 m)

18-2.7 Discharge from Exits.

18-2.7.1 At least half of the required number of units of exit width from upper floors, exclusive of horizontal exits, shall lead directly to the street or through a yard, court, or passageway with protected openings and separated from all parts of the interior of the building.

Paragraph 18-2.7.1 should be read jointly with the provisions of 18-2.7.2. A *minimum* of 50 percent of the exits from upper floors must discharge directly to the exterior. If less than 50 percent of the exits are arranged (per 18-2.7.2) to discharge through the floor of exit discharge, the remaining exits must be arranged to discharge directly to the exterior.

18-2.7.2 A maximum of 50 percent of the exits may discharge through areas on the floor of exit discharge in accordance with 5-7.2.

See Figures 18-2 and 18-3. (Also see discussion of 5-7.2.)

18-2.8 Illumination of Means of Egress.

18-2.8.1 Every public space, hallway, stairway, and other means of egress shall have illumination in accordance with Section 5-8.

18-2.9 Emergency Lighting.

18-2.9.1 Any apartment building with more than twelve living units or four or more stories in height shall have emergency lighting in accordance with Section 5-9.

Exception: Where every living unit has a direct exit to the outside at grade level.

This exception does not apply to all buildings with exterior exit access, but only to those where each unit has direct exit to grade.

18-2.10 Marking of Means of Egress.

18-2.10.1 Signs in accordance with Section 5-10 shall be provided in all apartment buildings requiring more than one exit.

18-2.11 Special Features.

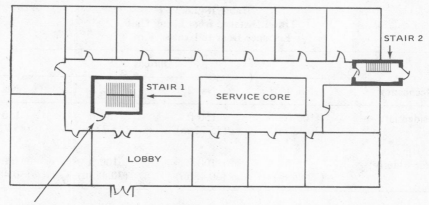

ROUTE FROM STAIR THROUGH LOBBY TO EXTERIOR MUST BE READILY VISIBLE,
IDENTIFIED, CLEAR, AND UNOBSTRUCTED.

*Figure 18-2. Arrangement of Means of Egress in Accordance with 18-2.7.2 (see 5-7.2).
Stair 1 (50 percent of the total number of exits) discharges through the first floor. Stair 2
discharges directly to the exterior. Since other areas on the first floor (the level of exit
discharge) are not separated from the path which a person leaving Stair 1 must follow to
exit through the lobby, the entire first floor must be completely sprinklered. If the rest of
the floor were separated, only the path to the exit discharge would have to be
sprinklered.*

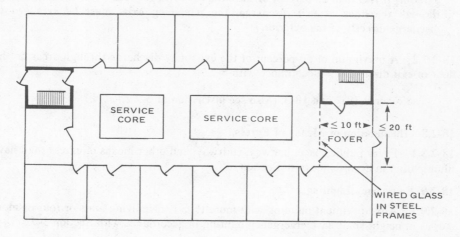

METRIC: 1 ft = .3048 m

*Figure 18-3. Foyer Constructed in Compliance with 18-2.7.2 (see 5-7.2). The foyer must
serve only as a means of egress.*

18-2.11.1 Within any individual living unit, stairs more than one story above or
below the entrance floor level of the living unit shall not be permitted.

Also see **18-2.11.4** and **18-3.1.1, Exception No. 1.**

18-2.11.2   Smokeproof towers shall be provided in accordance with 5-2.3 in buildings seven or more stories in height using Option 1, 2, or 3.

18-2.11.3   No door in any means of egress shall be locked against egress when the building is occupied (*see 5-2.1.2.*).

Paragraph 18-2.11.3 prohibits an apartment building from having any door locked "against egress" while the building is occupied. This requirement permits a door to have a locking device that allows the door to be opened from within the building for egress, but does not allow the door to be opened from outside the building. Ordinary dead bolts, double cylinder locks, and chain locks would not meet these provisions. Several tragic multiple-death fires have occurred where a key could not be found to unlock these devices or, in haste, where a door was not openable simply because the chain device was not removed.

The language of 5-2.1.2 is clear: "Locks if provided shall not require the use of a key for operation from the inside of the building." This eliminates double cylinder, ordinary dead bolt, and chain locks which require a key to operate from the inside. Paragraph 5-2.1.2.1.2 calls for a simple operation to open a door; two-handed knob operations and the like do not meet this provision.

18-2.11.4   Spiral stairs in accordance with 5-2.2.1.6 are permitted within a single living unit.

Exception: Not permitted in apartments for the elderly.

Paragraph 18-2.11.4 in combination with 18-2.11.1 and 18-3.1.1, Exception No. 1 allows a "penthouse" design with the classic spiral staircase (or a regular staircase) for up to one level above or below the entrance to the apartment.

18-2.11.5   Winders in accordance with 5-2.2.2.4 are permitted within a single living unit.

Exception: Not permitted in apartments for the elderly.

SECTION 18-3   PROTECTION

18-3.1 Protection of Vertical Openings.

18-3.1.1   Every stairway, elevator shaft and other vertical opening shall be enclosed or protected in accordance with Section 6-2.2.

Exception No. 1:   Stairway enclosures shall not be required where a one-story stair connects two levels within a single dwelling unit, guest room or suite located above the level of exit discharge.

Also see 18-2.11.1 and 18-2.11.4.

Exception No. 2:   There shall be no unprotected vertical opening in any building or fire section with only one exit.

Exception No. 3:   Vertical exits shall be protected as follows:

(a) In buildings using Option 1, 2, or 3 — Fire resistance of walls in buildings of one to three stories shall be 1 hour; four or more stories, 2 hours.

Fire protection rating of doors in buildings of one to three stories shall be 1 hour; four or more stories, 1½ hours.

These are the normal requirements for the protection of vertical openings as given in Chapter 6.

(b) In buildings using Option 4 — Fire resistance of walls in buildings of one to three stories shall be ¾ hour; four or more stories, 1 hour.

Fire protection rating of doors in buildings of one to three stories in height shall be ¾ hour; four or more stories, 1 hour.

These ratings are a reduction from those specified in Chapter 6 due to the requirements in Chapter 18 for buildings using Option 4 (total sprinkler protection).

Exception No. 4:   An atrium may be utilized in accordance with 6-2.2.3.1, Exception No. 2.

Since 6-2.2.3.1, Exception No. 2 requires total automatic sprinkler protection, the exception could only be used in buildings using Option 4.

18-3.1.2   Any required exit stair which is so located that it is necessary to pass through the lobby or other open space to reach the outside of the building shall be continuously enclosed down to the lobby level, or to a mezzanine within the lobby. (*See Section 18-2.7.*)

18-3.1.3   No floor below the level of exit discharge, used only for storage, heating equipment, or other purposes other than residential occupancy open to the public, shall have unprotected openings to floors used for residential purposes.

18-3.2 Protection from Hazards.

18-3.2.1   In buildings using Option 1, 2, or 3, every hazardous area shall be separated from other parts of the building by construction having a fire resistance rating of at least 1 hour and communicating openings shall be protected by approved smoke-actuated automatic, or self-closing fire doors, or such area shall be equipped with automatic extinguishing system. Hazardous areas include, but are not limited to:

Boiler and heater rooms
Laundries
Repair shops

Rooms or spaces used for storage of combustible supplies and equipment in quantities deemed hazardous by the authority having jurisdiction.

18-3.2.2   In buildings using Option 4, the enclosure for hazardous areas may be of any reasonably smoke resisting construction with or without a fire resistance rating.

18-3.3 Interior Finish.

18-3.3.1   Interior finish on walls and ceilings, in accordance with Section 6-5, and subject to the limitations and modifications therein specified, shall be as follows:

(a) In buildings using Option 1, 2 or 3
  1. Vertical Exits — Class A

   2. Exit Access — Class A or B

   3. Lobbies, corridors that are not exit access — Class A or B

   4. Individual apartments and other habitable spaces — Class A, B, or C.

 (b) In buildings using Option 4

   1. Vertical exits — Class A or Class B

   2. Exit access — Class A, B or C

   3. Lobbies, corridors that are not exit access — Class A, B or C

   4. Individual apartments and other habitable spaces — Class A, B or C.

18-3.3.2 Interior floor finish within corridors and exits of buildings using Option 1 or 2 shall be Class I or Class II in accordance with Section 6-5.

18-3.4 Detection, Alarm and Communication Systems.

18-3.4.1 Smoke Detectors.

18-3.4.1.1 An approved single station smoke detector, continuously powered by the house electrical service, shall be installed in an approved manner in every living unit within the apartment building. When activated, the detector shall initiate an alarm which is audible in the sleeping rooms of that unit. This individual unit detector shall be in addition to any sprinkler system or other detection system that may be installed in the building.

   The detector(s) required by 18-3.4.1.1 should usually be located in the hall area(s) giving access to rooms used for sleeping. In multiple-level living units a detector should usually be located at the top of the stairs. The detector(s) should be mounted on the ceiling or on the wall within 12 in. (30.48 cm) of, but no closer than 6 in. (15.24 cm) to, the ceiling. The detector should be placed remotely from the cooking area. Where unusual factors such as room configuration, air movement, or stagnant air pockets require consideration, the authority having jurisdiction and the designer should determine the placement of the detectors.

   Note that the detector must be powered by "house current" either through direct wiring of the detector or by using plug-in type detectors. Battery-powered units will not meet the provision of 18-3.4.1.1.

   It is not the intent of the paragraph to prohibit interconnecting detectors within a single apartment if the apartment needs more than one detector; in fact, this is required by the second sentence.

   Also note that this requirement is *in addition* to any other detection or suppression system required.

18-3.4.1.2 In apartments for the elderly in buildings seven stories and higher, in addition to being tied into the 24-hour manned location, the detectors shall be tied into an annunciator panel which will provide indication of the floor where the detector is activated.

18-3.4.1.3 In buildings using Option 2 a total automatic smoke detection system is required. An automatic smoke detection system is one which is designed to give complete coverage with smoke detectors in accordance with the spacings and layouts given in *Standard on Automatic Fire Detectors*, NFPA 72E, and laboratory test data and is one in which the detectors are tied together to initiate the alarm and other automatic fire protection devices.

18-3.4.2 Alarms.

18-3.4.2.1 Every apartment building of four or more stories in height, or with 12 or more apartment units, shall have a manual fire alarm system in accordance with Section 7-6.

18-3.4.2.2 In apartments for the elderly, buildings of two or more stories in height, or with 12 or more living units, shall have a manual fire alarm system in accordance with Section 7-6.

Exception: Where all units in a one-story building have direct access to outside at grade.

18-3.4.2.3 Buildings seven or more stories in height shall have an annunciator panel connected with the alarm system to visually indicate the floor of fire involvement. The location of the annunciator panel at an accessible location shall be approved by the authority having jurisdiction.

18-3.4.3 In buildings seven or more stories using Option 1 or 3, in addition to a manual fire alarm system, an approved means of voice communication between an accessible central point approved by the authority having jurisdiction and the corridors, elevators, elevator lobbies and exits shall be provided.

18-3.4.4 In apartments for the elderly located in buildings seven or more stories in height using Option 2, an approved means of voice communication between an accessible central point approved by the authority having jurisdiction and the corridors, elevators, elevator lobbies and exits shall be provided.

Note that 18-3.4.3 requires this same system for Options 1 and 3.

18-3.4.5 In buildings using Option 2, four stories or more in height, or with 12 or more units, the alarm system shall be initiated by the automatic smoke detection system, as well as being capable of manual initiation.

18-3.4.6 In buildings using Option 3, the audible alarm shall be activated upon operation of the sprinkler system as well as manually.

18-3.4.7 In buildings using Option 4, four stories or more in height, or with 12 or more units, the alarm system shall be activated upon operation of the automatic sprinkler system as well as being capable of manual initiation.

18-3.4.8 In apartments for the elderly located in buildings four or more stories in height the fire alarm system shall be arranged to transmit an alarm automatically to the fire department legally committed to serve the area in which the building is located by the most direct and reliable method approved by local regulations in accordance with 7-6.3.4.

Where automatic transmission of alarms to the fire department legally committed to serve the facility is not permitted, arrangements should be made for the prompt notification of the fire department or such other assistance as may be available in the case of fire or other emergency. Acceptable means of transmitting an alarm are, in order of preference:

(a) A direct connection of the building alarm to the municipal fire alarm system

(b) A direct connection of the building alarm to an approved central station

(c) A telephone connection to a municipal or other alarm headquarters which is manned 24 hours a day.

18-3.5 Extinguishment Requirements.

18-3.5.1 In buildings using Option 3 automatic sprinklers shall be installed in corridors along the corridor ceiling, and one sprinkler head shall be opposite the center of and inside any living unit door opening onto the corridor.

18-3.5.2 The sprinkler installation required in 18-3.5.1 shall meet the requirements of Section 7-7 and *Standard for the Installation of Sprinkler Systems*, NFPA 13, in terms of workmanship and materials.

18-3.5.3 The installation of the corridor sprinklers required by 18-3.5.1 shall meet the spacing and protection area requirements of *Standard for the Installation of Sprinkler Systems*, NFPA 13.

18-3.5.4 Buildings using Option 4 shall be protected throughout by an approved automatic sprinkler system. The automatic sprinkler system shall meet the requirements of Section 7-7, including requirements for supervision.

Exception: Sprinkler installation may be omitted in small compartmented areas such as closets not over 24 sq ft (2.23 sq m) and bathrooms not over 55 sq ft (5.11 sq m).

18-3.5.5 Hand portable fire extinguishers shall be provided in hazardous areas. When provided, hand portable fire extinguishers shall be installed and maintained as specified in Section 7-7 and *Standard for Portable Fire Extinguishers*, NFPA 10.

18-3.6 Corridors.

18-3.6.1 Exit access corridors shall be protected as follows:

(a) In buildings using Option 1 — Fire resistance of corridor walls shall be 1 hour; fire protection rating of doors from living units to corridor, 20 minutes.

(b) In buildings using Option 2 or 3 — Fire resistance of corridor walls shall be ¾ hour; fire protection rating of doors from living unit to corridor, 20 minutes.

(c) In buildings using Option 4 — Fire resistance of corridor walls shall be ½ hour; fire protection rating of doors from living unit to corridor, 20 minutes.

The criteria in 18-3.6.1 parallel the requirements in Chapter 12 for health care occupancies. In both chapters, the committee's concern for providing safety for the occupant in his or her room, during a fire, led to a minimum corridor wall construction either to block fire movement into a room from the corridor, or to block fire in a room from entering the corridor. The common concern in Chapters 12 and 18 is the presence of occupants on a 24-hour-a-day basis with sleeping accommodations.

18-3.6.2 Doors between apartments and corridors shall be self-closing.

Requiring doors between apartments and corridors to be self-closing will lead to a significant reduction in fatalities caused by fire in apartment buildings. Studies of typical apartment fires have shown that the cause of fire spreading beyond the apartment or room of origin was due to the door being left open as the occupant fled the fire.

In other cases, a person suspecting a fire died after opening the door to a room fully involved with fire or after causing full involvement of the room through

introducing oxygen by opening the door. A spring-loaded hinge or a closer would have caused these doors to close, preventing smoke or fire from spreading down the corridor and exposing other occupants.

18-3.6.3 The fire resistance rating of living unit/corridor doors shall be 20 minutes.

The door required by 18-3.6.3 provides a level of protection commensurate with the expected fuel load in the room and the fire resistance of the corridor wall construction. The purpose is to box a fire out of a room or to box it within the room by corridor wall and door construction criteria. It has been shown in fuel load studies conducted by the National Bureau of Standards that residential occupancies will have fuel loads in the 20- to 30-minute range.

Contrary to the general rule (see 5-2.1.1.1.1), the door referred to in 18-3.6.3 applies to the leaf only. In other words the frame, hinges, latch, closers, etc., do not have to be rated. By requiring the 20-minute door, the committee was attempting to establish a minimum quality of construction, not to provide for a complete listed fire door assembly.

Ratings longer than those specified by 18-3.6.3 may be required where doors are provided for property protection as well as for life safety. NFPA 80, *Standard for Fire Doors and Windows*,[4] may be consulted for standard practice in the selection and installation of fire doors.

A 1¾-in. (4.45-cm) solid bonded wood core door has been considered the equivalent to a door with a 20-minute fire protection rating.

18-3.7 Subdivisions of Building Spaces.

18-3.7.1 Horizontal Exits. Sufficient horizontal exits are required to limit the maximum gross area per story between horizontal exits to that specified below:

(a) The gross area per story between horizontal exits shall not be limited for the purposes of this *Code* for buildings three stories or less.

(b) In buildings using Option 1 or 2, the gross area per story between horizontal exits shall be a maximum of 20,000 sq ft (1,858 sq m) for buildings four to six stories in height.

(c) The gross area per story between horizontal exits for buildings seven or more stories in height shall be a maximum of 10,000 sq ft (929 sq m) in buildings using Option 1; 15,000 sq ft (1394 sq m) in Option 2; and 20,000 sq ft (1858 sq m) in Option 3.

18-3.7.2 Protection of horizontal exits shall be as follows:

(a) In buildings using Option 1, 2, or 3 — Fire resistance of walls, 2 hours; fire protection rating of doors, 1½ hours.

These are the standard requirements for horizontal exits per 5-2.4.

(b) In apartments for the elderly using Option 4, smoke barriers may be used in lieu of horizontal exits. Smoke barriers shall be constructed in accordance with the provisions of Section 6-3 and shall have a fire resistance rating of at least 1 hour.

18-3.7.3 Smoke Barriers. Smoke barriers in accordance with Section 6-3 shall be provided in exit access corridors between stairs as follows:

(a) In buildings using Option 1 when stairs are spaced greater than 50 ft (15.24 m) apart

(b) In buildings using Option 2 or 3 when exit stairs are spaced greater than 100 ft (30.48 m) apart

(c) In apartments for the elderly using Option 1 when exit stairs are spaced greater than 50 ft (15.24 m) apart

(d) In apartments for the elderly using Option 2 or 3 when exit stairs are spaced greater than 75 ft (22.86 m) apart

(e) In apartments for the elderly using Option 4 when exit stairs are greater than 125 ft (38.10 m) apart.

Protection may be accomplished in conjunction with the provisions for horizontal exits.

Table 18-3.7.3
Smoke Barriers Are Required Where
Exit Stair Spacing Is in Excess of:

Occupancy	Options			
	No. 1	No. 2	No. 3	No. 4
Residential	50 ft (15.24 m)	100 ft (30.48 m)	100 ft (30.48 m)	NR
Apartments for Elderly	50 ft (15.24 m)	75 ft (22.86 m)	75 ft (22.86 m)	125 ft (38.10 m)

Note: When required, there shall be a smoke barrier between stairs.

It should be noted that this does not require smoke barriers every 50 ft (15.24 m) or 100 ft (30.48 m), etc., but only requires a smoke barrier between stairs when the stair spacing exceeds the given lengths. The provision of a horizontal exit can substitute for a smoke barrier and can also be beneficial for travel distance and eliminating a stairway.

18-3.7.4 In apartments for the elderly the minimum width of smoke barrier doors is 32 in. (81.28 cm) and may be a single door that will swing in either direction. Side lights or a vision panel are required in smoke doors.

18-3.8 Special Features.

18-3.8.1 Interior exit access corridors in buildings seven or more stories in height using Option 1 or 2, and in all apartments for the elderly using Option 1, 2, or 3 over three stories in height, shall be continuously pressurized at a minimum of 0.01 in. (2.49 Pa) water, measured at any living unit door.

SECTION 18-4   SPECIAL PROVISIONS

SECTION 18-5   BUILDING SERVICES

18-5.1 Utilities.   Utilities shall comply with the provisions of Section 7-1.

18-5.2 Heating, Ventilating, and Air Conditioning.   Heating, ventilating, and air conditioning equipment shall comply with the provisions of Section 7-2.

> Paragraph 2-2.2 of NFPA 90A, *Standard for the Installation of Air Conditioning and Ventilating Systems,*[1] prohibits the use of public corridors in residential occupancies as part of the supply, return, or exhaust air system.

18-5.3 Elevators, Dumbwaiters, and Vertical Conveyors.

18-5.3.1   Elevators, dumbwaiters, and vertical conveyors shall comply with the provisions of Section 7-4.

18-5.3.2   In apartments for the elderly of seven or more stories, vestibules designed in accordance with the smoke partition requirements of Section 6-3 shall be provided at each floor.

18-5.4 Rubbish Chutes, Incinerators, and Laundry Chutes.   Rubbish chutes, incinerators, and laundry chutes shall comply with the provisions of Section 7-5.

Table 18-1
Alternate Requirements for New Apartment Buildings
According to Protection Provided

	No Suppression or Detection System Option No. 1	Total Automatic Smoke Detection Option No. 2	Sprink. Prot. in Select. Areas Option No. 3	Auto Ext. NFPA 13 (with exceptions) Option No. 4
Max. Gross Area per Story Between Horizontal Exits				
1-3 Stories	NR	NR	NR	NR
4-6 Stories	20,000 sq ft (1,858 sq m)	20,000 sq ft (1,858 sq m)	NR	NR
>6 Stories	10,000 sq ft (929 sq m)	15,000 sq ft (1,394 sq m)	20,000 sq ft (1,858 sq m)	NR
Exit Access				
Travel Distance	100 ft (30.48 m)	150 ft (45.72 m)	150 ft (45.72 m)	150 ft (45.72 m)
Smoke Barrier Req. for Stair Spacing	>50 ft (15.24 m)	>100 ft (30.48 m)	>100 ft (30.48 m)	NR
Max. Single Path Corridor Distance	35 ft (10.67 m)	35 ft (10.67 m)	35 ft (10.67 m)	35 ft (10.67 m)
Max. Dead End	35 ft (10.67 m)	35 ft (10.67 m)	35 ft (10.67 m)	35 ft (10.67 m)
Fire Resistance				
Walls	1 hr	¾ hr	¾ hr	½ hr
Doors (Fire Protection Rating)	20 min	20 min	20 min	20 min

Table 18-1 (Continued)

	No Suppression or Detection System Option No. 1	Total Automatic Smoke Detection Option No. 2	Sprink. Prot. in Select. Areas Option No. 3	Auto Ext. NFPA 13 (with exceptions) Option No. 4
Exit Access (Continued)				
Flame Spread				
Walls & Ceilings	A or B	A or B	A or B	A, B, or C
Floors	I or II	I or II	NR	NR
Exits—Vertical				
Fire Resistance Walls				
1-3 Stories	1 hr	1 hr	1 hr	¾ hr
>3 Stories	2 hr	2 hr	2 hr	1 hr
Smokeproof Towers				
1-6 Stories	NR	NR	NR	NR
>6 Stories	Req.	Req.	Req.	NR
Doors				
1-3 Stories	1 hr	1 hr	1 hr	¾ hr
>3 Stories	1½ hr	1½ hr	1½ hr	1 hr
Flame Spread				
Walls & Ceilings	A	A	A	A or B
Floors	I or II	I or II	NR	NR
Bedroom Windows, 1- to 6-Story Bldg. Ref. 18–1.1.4	Req.	Req.	Req.	Req.
Exits—Horizontal				
Fire Resistance				
Walls	2 hr	2 hr	2 hr	NA
Doors	1½ hr	1½ hr	1½ hr	NA
Habitable Spaces				
Max. Distance from any Room Door to Corridor	50 ft (15.24 m)	100 ft (30.48 m)	50 ft (15.24 m)	100 ft (30.48 m)
Flame Spread				
Walls & Ceilings	A, B, or C	A, B, or C	A, B, or C	A, B, or C
Smoke Detector Indiv. in Unit	Req.	Req.	Req.	Req.
Door to Corridor Self-closing	Req.	Req.	Req.	Req.
Alarm System				
>3 Stories or >11 Units	manual	manual & auto	manual & auto	manual & auto
>6 Stories	annunciator panel and voice communication	annunciator panel	annunciator panel and voice communication	annunciator panel
HVAC				
>6 Stories Pressurized Corridor, 0.01 in. Water (2.49 Pa), min.	Req.	Req.	NR	NR
Elevator—ANSI	A17.1	A17.1	A17.1	A17.1

NL=No Limit.
NR=No Requirements.
NA=Not Applicable.

Table 18-2
Alternate Requirements for New Apartments for the Elderly
According to Protection Provided

	No Suppression or Detection System Option No. 1	Total Automatic Smoke Detection Option No. 2	Sprink. Prot. in Select. Areas Option No. 3	Auto Ext. NFPA 13 (with exceptions) Option No. 4
Max. Gross Area per Story Between Horizontal Exits				
1-3 Stories	NL	NL	NL	NL
4-6 Stories	20,000 sq ft (1,858 sq m)	20,000 sq ft (1,858 sq m)	NL	NL
>6 Stories	10,000 sq ft (929 sq m)	15,000 sq ft (1,394 sq m)	20,000 sq ft (1,858 sq m)	NL
Exit Access				
Travel Distance	75 ft (22.86 m)	100 ft (30.48 m)	100 ft (30.48 m)	100 ft (30.48 m)
Smoke Barrier Req. for Stair Spacing	>50 ft (15.24 m)	>75 ft (22.86 m)	>75 ft (22.86 m)	>125 ft (38.10 m)
Max. Single Path Corridor Distance	35 ft (10.67 m)	35 ft (10.67 m)	35 ft (10.67 m)	35 ft (10.67 m)
Max. Dead End	35 ft (10.67 m)	35 ft (10.67 m)	35 ft (10.67 m)	35 ft (10.67 m)
Fire Resistance Walls	1 hr	¾ hr	¾ hr	½ hr
Doors (Fire Protection Rating)	20 min	20 min	20 min	20 min
Flame Spread Walls & Ceilings	A or B	A or B	A or B	A, B, or C
Floors	I or II	I or II	NR	NR
Exits—Vertical				
Fire Resistance Walls				
1-3 Stories	1 hr	1 hr	1 hr	¾ hr
>3 Stories	2 hr	2 hr	2 hr	1 hr
Smokeproof Towers				
1-6 Stories	NR	NR	NR	NR
>6 Stories	Req.	Req.	Req.	NR
Doors				
1-3 Stories	1 hr	1 hr	1 hr	¾ hr
>3 Stories	1½ hr	1½ hr	1½ hr	1 hr
Flame Spread Walls & Ceilings	A	A	A	A or B
Floors	I or II	I or II	NR	NR
Bedroom Windows, 1- to 6-Story Bldg. Ref. 18–1.1.4	Req.	Req.	Req.	Req.
Exits—Horizontal				
Fire Resistance Walls	2 hr	2 hr	2 hr	NR
Doors	1½ hr	1½ hr	1½ hr	NR
Habitable Spaces Max. Distance from any Room Door to Corridor	50 ft (15.24 m)	75 ft (22.86)	50 ft (15.24 m)	100 ft (30.48 m)

Table 18-2 (Continued)

	No Suppression or Detection System Option No. 1	Total Automatic Smoke Detection Option No. 2	Sprink. Prot. in Select. Areas Option No. 3	Auto Ext. NFPA 13 (with exceptions) Option No. 4
Habitable Spaces (Continued)				
Flame Spread				
Walls & Ceilings	A, B, or C	A, B, or C	A, B, or C	A, B, or C
Smoke Detector				
Indiv. in Unit	Req.	Req.	Req.	Req.
Door to Corridor				
Self-closing	Req.	Req.	Req.	Req.
Alarm System				
2 Stories or more, or				
>11 Units	manual	manual	manual & auto	manual
4 Stories or more	auto to FD	auto* & auto to FD	auto* & auto to FD	auto* & auto to FD
>6 Stories	annunciator and voice communication	annunciator and voice communication	annunciator and voice communication	annunciator
HVAC				
>3 or more, Stories Pressurized Corridor, 0.01 in. Water (2.49 Pa), min.	Req.	Req.	Req.	NR
Elevator—ANSI	A17.1	A17.1	A17.1	A17.1
Vestibule	Req.	Req.	Req.	Req.

NL=No Limit.
NR=No Requirements.
NA=Not Applicable.
*=Also req. in buildings with 12 or more living units.

The following are two examples of how to use Table 18-1.

Example 1: What are the interior finish requirements in exit enclosures for a five-story apartment building equipped with an automatic detection system?

Answer: Enter the table under the column heading "Total Automatic Smoke Detection Option No. 2." In the section "Exits — Vertical," find the heading "Flame Spread (Walls and Ceilings)." The requirement for this building is "A" interior finish for the exits.

Example 2: What is the maximum dead-end (single path of exit travel) distance permitted in an apartment building equipped with sprinklers located only in corridors and inside the doors leading into each living unit?

Answer: Enter the table under the column heading "Sprinkler Protection in Selected Areas Option No. 3." Across from the row headed "Maximum Single Path Corridor Distance" you will find 35 ft (10.67 m) as the answer.

After reviewing the instructions on how to use Tables 18-1 and 18-2, it is necessary to discuss why certain design features were incorporated in the four design approaches.

Height and Area Limitations

Note that the area limitation in Tables 18-1 and 18-2 is for maximum area *between* horizontal exits. Its purpose is to establish the maximum potential area that would be directly exposed to a fire; thus, limiting the number of occupants that would be directly exposed. This parallels the philosophy codified in Chapter 12, which also limits the area of exposure for patients to 22,500 sq ft (2,090 sq m) between smoke barriers. Chapter 18 is similar to Chapter 12 in that both deal with *sleeping* or *bedridden* occupants. Also note that as the fire protection features become more substantial, the area limit is increased. However, as the building becomes greater in height, the maximum area (except for a sprinklered building) becomes less.

Required Smoke Barrier for Stair Spacing

This function dovetails the height and area limits. As the stair spacing exceeds either 50 ft (15.24 m) (for Option No. 1) or 100 ft (30.48 m) (for Option Nos. 2 and 3) in Table 18-1 or 75 ft (22.86 m) (for Option Nos. 2 and 3) or 125 ft (38.10 m) (for Option No. 4) in Table 18-2, smoke barriers are required to isolate a fire and to prevent its products of combustion from contaminating all access to stair shafts by interposing a smoke barrier *between* two separate stair shafts. In this way, at least one stair, relatively free from smoke, will be provided.

Exits — Vertical — Smokeproof Towers

Smokeproof towers are required in apartment designs over six stories in height (except totally sprinklered buildings). This was the committee's requirement, additional to the height and area limits and the specification of interior smoke barriers (both discussed above), to limit the possibility of smoke contaminating exits to the point of impassibility and, therefore, to ensure a safe, protected means of egress from a fire.

Habitable Spaces — Maximum Distance from any Room Door to Corridor

This set of criteria establishes the maximum distance from the farthest interior room door of an apartment suite (usually the rear bedroom) to the entrance door of the apartment. In so doing, it realistically imposes a maximum design dimension (usually width) on the apartment unit.

HVAC

The requirement for 0.01 in. (2.49 Pa) of water in Tables 18-1 and 18-2 should be achieved by any form of a mechanical system that discharges air into the corridor for supply purposes for the apartments (usually via an undercut on the apartment door). Since 0.01 in. (2.49 Pa) is an extremely low value, virtually any design system should achieve it.

REFERENCES CITED BY *CODE*

(These publications comprise a part of the requirements to the extent called for by the Code.)

NFPA 10, *Standard for Portable Fire Extinguishers*, NFPA, Boston, 1978.

NFPA 13, *Standard for the Installation of Sprinkler Systems*, NFPA, Boston, 1980.

NFPA 72E, *Standard on Automatic Fire Detectors*, NFPA, Boston, 1978.

NFPA 90A, *Standard for the Installation of Air Conditioning and Ventilating Systems*, NFPA, Boston, 1978.

REFERENCES CITED IN COMMENTARY

[1]NFPA 90A, *Standard for the Installation of Air Conditioning and Ventilating Systems*, NFPA, Boston, 1978.

[2]E. G. Butcher and A. C. Parnell, *Smoke Control in Fire Safety Design*, NFPA, Boston, 1979.

[3]NFPA 13, *Standard for the Installation of Sprinkler Systems*, NFPA, Boston, 1980.

[4]NFPA 80, *Standard for Fire Doors and Windows*, NFPA, Boston, 1979.

19

EXISTING APARTMENT BUILDINGS

(See also Chapter 31.)

SECTION 19-1 GENERAL REQUIREMENTS

19-1.1 Application.

19-1.1.1 This *Code* has differing requirements for the several types of residential occupancies; thus, the *Code* has several residential occupancy chapters, Chapters 16 through 23.

Residential occupancies are ones in which sleeping accommodations are provided for normal residential purposes and include all buildings designed to provide sleeping accommodations. They are treated separately in the *Code* in the following groups:

Hotels/motels (Chapters 16 and 17)

Apartments (Chapters 18 and 19)

Dormitories (including orphanages for age six years and older) (Section 16-6 and 17-6)

Lodging or rooming houses (Chapter 20)

1- and 2-family dwellings (Chapter 22)

Exceptions to the groups listed above are health care occupancies which are covered in Chapters 12 and 13, and detention and correctional occupancies which are covered in Chapters 14 and 15. In earlier editions of the *Code* they were classified as "institutional occupancies."

A review of 4-1.6 underscores a common principle of life safety with which the *Code* is concerned in all the residential occupancies considered by Chapters 16 through 23. Paragraph 4-1.6 states: "Residential occupancies are ones in which *sleeping accommodations* are provided for normal residential purposes and include all buildings designed to provide *sleeping accommodations*." This use of residential occupancies is central to the *Code*'s provisions in Chapters 16 through 23 because people who are asleep will be unaware of a rapidly developing fire and when alerted may be somewhat confused because of being awakened suddenly. Other factors on which the provisions of Chapters 16 through 23 were developed are the presence of hazards (such as cooking and heating equipment) and the degree of familiarity of the occupant with his or her living space (ranging from transients with little or no familiarity, as in hotels, to total familiarity in single-family dwellings).

19-1.1.2 All existing buildings classified as apartment buildings by 19-1.3 shall conform to the provisions of this chapter, and shall meet the requirements of one of the following options:

Option 1: Buildings without fire suppression or detection systems;
Option 2: Buildings provided with a total automatic smoke detection system;

Single station smoke detectors in each unit are required per 19-3.4.1.1.

Option 3: Buildings provided with automatic sprinkler protection in selected areas;
Option 4: Buildings protected throughout by an approved automatic sprinkler system.

Paragraph 19-1.1.2 identifies four different ways of arranging apartment buildings for life safety that are acceptable to the *Code*. These four systems are:

1. Buildings without fire suppression or detection systems;
2. Buildings with an automatic fire detection system;
3. Buildings provided with an automatic sprinkler system in corridors only; and
4. Buildings protected by a total automatic sprinkler system.

In the 1976 Edition of the *Code*, Section 11-3 covered both new and existing apartment buildings, with 11-3.1 to 11-3.4 providing general requirements for all apartment buildings, and 11-3.5 through 11-3.8 each covering one of the four options. In that edition, every apartment building was required to meet 11-3.1 through 11-3.4, and any one of 11-3.5 through 11-3.8. This arrangement resulted in a considerable amount of cross-referencing — not only in Section 11-3, but also in Sections 11-1, 11-2, and Chapter 6 — and a sometimes very confusing text resulted. Since the 1981 Edition was undergoing extensive editorial revision to provide separate chapters for new and existing buildings and also to split up the residential chapter, it was decided to reorganize the apartment chapters to make them easier to use and eliminate cross-referencing where possible. As a result of this restructuring, all sections of Chapter 19 apply to all existing apartment buildings. There are various paragraphs and parts of paragraphs that apply to different options, or only to housing for the elderly. Every apartment building, whether or not it contains apartments for the elderly, must meet one of the four options.

The best approach in using this portion of the *Code* is to base a design on *Code* Table 19-1 or 19-2 and, when necessary, to refer to the appropriate paragraph to verify specific details. Either Table 19-1 or 19-2 provides almost all the design information needed to meet this portion of the *Code* and both may be found at the end of this chapter.

The committee, recognizing the equivalency provisions found in Section 1-5 of the *Code*, saw a need to establish in advance, four equivalent *Code*-acceptable schemes to provide a high degree of design flexibility. The equivalencies developed were based on the committee's professional judgment, the results of full-scale fire tests conducted at the National Bureau of Standards, and a review of the most recent fire experiences.

These designs are considered to be equivalent to each other in providing a minimum level of life safety for apartments. Because some systems have additional protective capability (detectors, automatic sprinklers, etc.), higher building heights and larger building areas were permitted. Where the design provided only the minimum level of safety called for in the *Code*, lower building heights and smaller building areas were specified.

This overall approach provides one of the first "system" design attempts to be codified. Whereas a total system would have many design approaches, this is a more limited, or bounded, system in that only four different approaches are available. Yet, a designer can identify an appropriate design from the four approaches based on the building's size, height, and arrangement. This provides the designer an opportunity to put together a safety approach that best fits the building, rather than fitting a building to a single codified design criterion. However, this system works only when the designer and the authority having jurisidiction agree on the plan selected at the earliest design phase.

19-1.1.3 Existing apartments for the elderly as defined in 19-1.3.1 shall meet the requirements for existing apartment houses as provided in this section unless otherwise noted.

As given in 19-1.3.1, apartments for the elderly are apartment buildings *specifically designed* for housing elderly people; however, these people *must be capable of self-preservation*. If the occupants are not capable of self-preservation, the building must comply with health care occupancy requirements.

Apartments for the elderly must comply with all the requirements for apartment buildings, using one of the four options, in addition to special provisions for apartments for the elderly which are given where appropriate throughout the chapter.

19-1.1.4 Every individual living unit covered by this section shall at least comply with the minimum provisions for windows of Chapter 22, One- and Two-Family Dwellings.

Exception: The requirement of Section 22-2 for a second means of escape may be waived for buildings over six stories provided that adequate means for smoke ventilation are employed.

19-1.2 Mixed Occupancies.

19-1.2.1 Where another type of occupancy occurs in the same building as a residential occupancy, the requirements of 1-4.4 of this *Code* shall be applicable.

19-1.2.2 For requirements on mixed mercantile and residential occupancies, see 25-1.2.

19-1.3 Definitions.

19-1.3.1 Terms applicable to this chapter are defined in Chapter 3 of this *Code*; where necessary, other terms will be defined in the text as they may occur.

Apartment Buildings. Includes buildings containing three or more living units with independent cooking and bathroom facilities, whether designated as apartment house, tenement, garden apartment, or by any other name.

Apartments for the Elderly. An apartment building specifically designed for housing elderly individuals who are capable of self-preservation.

It is not the intent that these special requirements apply to apartment buildings that just happen to be occupied by the elderly, but only to those apartment buildings specifically intended to house elderly residents. This is usually not difficult to determine since they often come under certain local, state, or federal funding, or apply for tax breaks. In addition, the name, advertising, or facilities provided usually provide ample evidence of the intent.

If individual cooking facilities are not provided, then the building would more accurately be classified as a dormitory. If, however, the residents (four or more) are not capable of self-preservation, then health care requirements would apply.

Mezzanine. An intermediate level between the floor and ceiling of any story and covering not more than one-third of the floor area of the room in which it is located.

19-1.4 Classification of Occupancy. (*See 19-1.3.1.*)

19-1.5 Classification of Hazard of Contents.

19-1.5.1 Building contents shall be classified according to the provisions of 4-2.1 of this *Code*. For design of sprinkler systems, the classification of contents in *Standard for the Installation of Sprinkler Systems*, NFPA 13, shall apply.

Under the definitions of 4-2.1 of the *Code*, the contents of living units in residential occupancies fall into the ordinary hazard classification. Characteristics of "ordinary" hazards are moderately rapid burning and considerable smoke generation, with the added hazard of the possible presence of toxic combustion products.

NFPA 13, *Standard for the Installation of Sprinkler Systems*,[1] would classify the contents as "light" for the design of extinguishing systems. The difference in classification is based on the threat to life or life safety (ordinary) versus the threat to the extinguishing capability of the automatic sprinkler system (light).

19-1.6 Minimum Construction Requirements. No special requirements.

19-1.7 Occupant Load.

19-1.7.1 The occupant load in numbers of persons for whom exits are to be provided shall be determined on the basis of one person per 200 sq ft (18.58 sq m) gross floor area, or the maximum probable population of any room or section under consideration, whichever is greater. The occupant load of any open mezzanine or balcony shall be added to the occupant load of the floor below for the purpose of determining exit capacity.

A dormitory-type occupancy, particularly where 2- or 3-tier bunks are used with close spacing, may produce an occupant load substantially greater than one person per 200 sq ft (18.58 sq m) of gross floor area. However, even though sleeping areas are densely populated, the building as a whole may not necessarily exceed one person per 200 sq ft (18.58 sq m) of gross area owing to the space taken for toilet facilities, halls, closets, and living rooms not used for sleeping purposes.

This discussion does not preclude the need for providing exit capability from concentrated sleeping areas (bunk rooms) based on the "maximum probable population" rather than the design figure. If the actual population of a bunk room exceeds one person per 200 sq ft (18.58 sq m), the exit capacity (door widths, etc.) will have to be designed to the actual population load. See 5-3.1 for further details on the use of occupant load for determining capacity of the means of egress.

SECTION 19-2   MEANS OF EGRESS REQUIREMENTS

19-2.1 General.

19-2.2 Types of Exits.

19-2.2.1   Exits, or exit components, arranged in accordance with Chapter 5, shall be of one or more of the following types:

(a) Doors, as per 5-2.1.

(b) Revolving doors, as per 5-2.1 (not at foot of stairs).

(c) Doors to subways, only if the subway meets the requirements of exit passageways or tunnels as specified in 5-2.7.

(d) Interior stairs, Class A or Class B, in accordance with 5-2.2.

(e) Outside stairs, in accordance with 5-2.5.

(f) Smokeproof towers, in accordance with 5-2.3.

(g) Ramps, Class A or Class B, in accordance with 5-2.6.

(h) Escalators, in accordance with 5-2.8.

(i) Horizontal exits, in accordance with 5-2.4.

(j) Exit passageways, in accordance with 5-2.7.

(k) Fire escape stairs, in accordance with 5-2.9.

19-2.2.2   In apartments for the elderly, smoke barriers are required.

Exception No. 1:   Where exterior exit balconies are provided.

Exception No. 2:   Where a single exit building is acceptable under 19-2.4.1.

Exception No. 3:   Where buildings are three or less stories in height.

At least one smoke barrier is required on each level of a building four stories or more in height housing apartments for the elderly. Buildings using exterior exit access or having a single exit per 19-2.4.1 are exempted from this requirement for smoke barriers.

19-2.2.3   Any existing interior stair or fire escape not complying with 5-2.2 or 5-2.9 may be continued in use subject to the approval of the authority having jurisdiction.

19-2.3 Capacity of Means of Egress.

19-2.3.1   Exits, arranged as specified elsewhere in this section of the *Code*, shall be sufficient to provide for the occupant load in numbers of persons as determined in accordance with 19-1.7, on the following basis:

(a) Doors, including those three risers or 24 in. (60.96 cm) above or below ground level, Class A ramps and horizontal exits—100 persons per unit of exit width.

(b) Stairs and other types of exits not included in (a) above—75 persons per unit of exit width.

19-2.3.2   Street-floor exits shall provide units of exit width as follows, occupant load being determined in accordance with 19-1.7.

(a) One unit for each 100 persons street-floor capacity for doors and other level exits, including those 24 in. (60.96 cm) or three risers above or below ground level.

(b) One unit for each 75 persons street-floor capacity for stair or other exit requiring descent to ground level.

(c) One and one-half exit units for each two-unit required stair from upper floors discharging through the street-floor.

(d) One and one-half exit units for each two-unit required stair from floors below the street-floor discharging through the street-floor.

Paragraph 19-2.3.2 requires street-floor exit designs that have sufficient width to provide for the intermingling of exits from the street floor with exits discharging down from the upper floors and discharging up from the lower floors. This is the traditional grand lobby design found in many hotels and in many sizable mercantile occupancies where stairs and street-floor exits converge at one or two exterior door locations. Similar discussion on this matter is found in Chapter 24. Paragraph 19-2.7.2 restricts the number and arrangement of stairs which discharge through the street floor.

Figure 19-1 shows a typical arrangement of multiple exits discharging on the street floor.

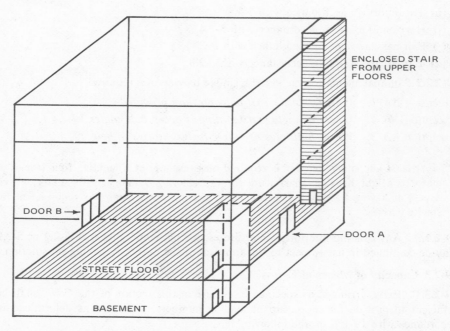

Figure 19-1. Capacity of Means of Egress in Accordance with 19-2.3.2. Required widths of Doors A and B are based on the number of people expected to use them: 1 unit of exit width [22 in. (55.88 cm)] for every 100 people on the street floor, and 1½ units for every 150 people traveling down from the upper floors, and 1½ units for every 150 people traveling up from the lower floors. (Also see 19-2.7.2.)

19-2.3.3 Every floor below the level of exit discharge shall have exits sufficient to provide for the occupant load of that floor as determined in accordance with 19-1.7 on the basis of 100 persons per exit unit for travel on the same level, 75 persons for upward travel, as up stairs.

19-2.3.4 Upper-floor exits shall provide numbers of units of exit width sufficient to meet the requirements of 19-2.3.1.

19-2.3.5 In apartments for the elderly the minimum width of exit access corridors is controlled by 19-3.7.3.

19-2.4 Number of Exits.

19-2.4.1 Every living unit shall have access to at least two separate exits remote from each other as required by 5-5.1.

Exception No. 1: Any living unit which has an exit directly to the street or yard at ground level or by way of an outside stairway, or an enclosed stairway with fire resistance rating of 1 hour or more serving that apartment only and not communicating with any floor below the level of exit discharge or other area not a part of the apartment served, may have a single exit.

This is common in a townhouse or row house arrangement. This permits the front door to be the only required exit, and therefore the rear door, which is often provided, would not be required and could be a sliding door to a porch or patio.

Exception No. 2: A building of any height with not more than four living units per floor with a smokeproof tower or outside stair in accordance with the requirements of 5-2.3 as the exit, immediately accessible to all living units served thereby, may have a single exit. ["Immediately accessible" means there is not more than 20 ft (609.6 cm) of travel distance to reach an exit from the entrance door of any living unit.]

This is an uncommon arrangement. Note there is no height limitation, but only four units per floor are permitted.

Exception No. 3: Any building three stories or less in height, with ¾-hour horizontal and vertical separation between living units, may have a single exit, under the following conditions:

(a) The stairway is completely enclosed, with a partition having a fire resistance rating of at least 1 hour with self-closing 1-hour fire protection rated doors protecting all openings between the stairway enclosure and the building.

(b) The stairway does not serve more than one-half story below the level of exit discharge.

(c) All corridors serving as access to exits have at least a 1-hour fire resistance rating.

(d) There is not more than 35 ft (10.67 m) of travel distance to reach an exit from the entrance door of any living unit.

Exception No. 3 to 19-2.4.1 provides the basic design approach used for "garden" apartments where the apartment entrances are enclosed around a single protected stair. Usually, the stair is open to the exterior, or is glass enclosed on the front of the building. The exception allows a single exit under this arrangement. Note that the

stairway must be separated from the building by construction of at least a 1-hour fire resistance rating, and the doors must be 1-hour rated and self-closing.

These provisions apply to any of the four options summarized in Tables 19-1 and 19-2.

19-2.5 Arrangement of Exits.

19-2.5.1 Access to all required exits shall be in accordance with Section 5-5, shall be unobstructed, and shall not be blocked from open view by ornamentation, curtain, or other appurtenance.

19-2.6 Measurement of Travel Distance to Exits.

19-2.6.1 Travel distance from the door of a room in a suite or living unit to a corridor door shall not exceed the following limits:

(a) For buildings using Option 1 or 3 — 50 ft (15.24 m).

(b) For buildings using Option 2 or 4 — 100 ft (30.48 m).

19-2.6.2 Maximum single path corridor length of 35 ft (10.67 m) permitted.

19-2.6.3 The travel distance from a living unit entrance door to the nearest exit shall not exceed the following limits:

(a) For buildings using Option 1 — 100 ft (30.48 m).

(b) For buildings using Option 2, 3 or 4 — 150 ft (45.72 m).

(c) In apartments for the elderly using Option 1 — 75 ft (22.86 m).

(d) In apartments for the elderly using Option 2, 3 or 4 — 100 ft (30.48 m).

Table 19-2.6.3
Travel Distance from Living Unit
Entrance Door to Nearest Exit

Occupancy	Options			
	No. 1	No. 2	No. 3	No. 4
Residential	100 ft (30.48 m)	150 ft (45.72 m)	150 ft (45.72 m)	150 ft (45.72 m)
Apartments for Elderly	75 ft (22.86 m)	100 ft (30.48 m)	100 ft (30.48 m)	100 ft (30.48 m)

19-2.7 Discharge from Exits.

19-2.7.1 At least half of the required number of units of exit width from upper floors, exclusive of horizontal exits, shall lead directly to the street or through a yard, court, or passageway with protected openings and separated from all parts of the interior of the building.

Paragraph 19-2.7.1 should be read jointly with the provisions of 19-2.7.2. A *minimum* of 50 percent of the exits from upper floors must discharge directly to the exterior. If less than 50 percent of the exits are arranged (per 19-2.7.2) to discharge through the floor of exit discharge, the remaining exits must be arranged to discharge directly to the exterior.

19-2.7.2 If any exits discharge through areas on the level of exit discharge, the conditions of 5-7.2 shall be met.

See **Figures 19-2 and 19-3.** (Also see discussion of 5-7.2.)

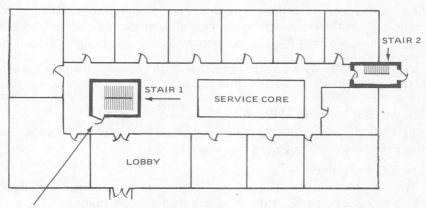

ROUTE FROM STAIR THROUGH LOBBY TO EXTERIOR MUST BE READILY VISIBLE,
IDENTIFIED, CLEAR, AND UNOBSTRUCTED.

Figure 19-2. Arrangement of Means of Egress in Accordance with 19-2.7.2 (see 5-7.2). Stair 1 (50 percent of the total number of exits) discharges through the first floor. Stair 2 discharges directly to the exterior. Since other areas on the first floor (the level of exit discharge) are not separated from the path which a person leaving Stair 1 must follow to exit through the lobby, the entire first floor must be completely sprinklered. If the rest of the floor were separated, only the path to the exit discharge would have to be sprinklered.

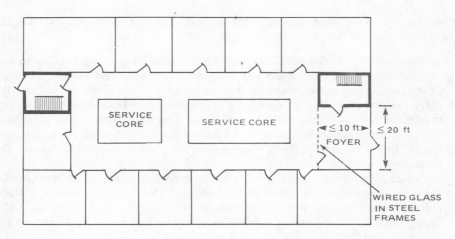

METRIC: 1 ft = .3048 m

Figure 19-3. Foyer Constructed in Compliance with 19-2.7.2 (see 5-7.2). The foyer must serve only as a means of egress.

19-2.8 Illumination of Means of Egress.

19-2.8.1 Every public space, hallway, stairway, and other means of egress shall have illumination in accordance with Section 5-8.

19-2.9 Emergency Lighting.

19-2.9.1 Any apartment building with more than 12 living units or four or more stories in height shall have emergency lighting in accordance with Section 5-9.

Exception: Where every living unit has a direct exit to the outside at grade level.

This exception does not apply to all buildings with exterior exit access, but only to those where each unit has direct exit to grade.

19-2.10 Marking of Means of Egress.

19-2.10.1 Exit signs in accordance with Section 5-10 shall be provided in all apartment buildings requiring more than one exit.

19-2.11 Special Features.

19-2.11.1 Within any individual living unit, stairs more than one story above or below the entrance floor level of the living unit shall not be permitted.

Also see 19-2.11.4 and 19-3.1.1, Exception No. 3.

19-2.11.2 In buildings using Option 1, 2 or 3, smokeproof towers shall be provided in accordance with 5-2.3 in buildings seven or more stories in height.

In 19-2.11.2, the committee recognizes the need to provide some degree of smoke control in existing buildings. Smokeproof towers can be constructed without the use of a vestibule, in accordance with 5-2.3.

19-2.11.3 No door in any means of egress shall be locked against egress when the building is occupied (*see 5-2.1.2*).

Paragraph 19-2.11.3 prohibits an apartment building from having any door locked "against egress" while the building is occupied. This requirement permits a door to have a locking device that allows the door to be opened from within the building for egress, but does not allow the door to be opened from outside the building. Ordinary dead bolts, double cylinder locks, and chain locks would not meet these provisions. Several tragic multiple-death fires have occurred where a key could not be found to unlock these devices or, in haste, where a door was not openable simply because the chain device was not removed.

The language of 5-2.1.2 is clear: "Locks if provided shall not require the use of a key for operation from the inside of the building." This eliminates double cylinder, ordinary dead bolt, and chain locks which require a key to operate from the inside. Paragraph 5-2.1.2.1.2 calls for a simple operation to open a door; two-handed knob operations and the like do not meet this provision.

19-2.11.4 Spiral stairs in accordance with 5-2.2.1.6 are permitted within a single living unit.

Exception: Not permitted in apartments for the elderly.

Paragraph 18-2.11.4 in combination with 19-2.11.1 and 19-3.1.1, Exception No. 3 allows a "penthouse" design with the classic spiral staircase (or a regular staircase) for up to one level above or below the entrance to the apartment.

19-2.11.5   Winders in accordance with 5-2.2.2.4 are permitted.

Exception: Not permitted in apartments for the elderly.

SECTION 19-3   PROTECTION

19-3.1 Protection of Vertical Openings.

19-3.1.1   Every stairway, elevator shaft and other vertical opening shall be enclosed or protected in accordance with 6-2.2 or provide means of satisfying the requirements of Section 2-9.

Exception No. 1:   Unprotected vertical openings connecting not more than three floors may be permitted in accordance with the conditions of 6-2.2.3.1, Exception No. 1.

Since 6-2.2.3.1, Exception No. 1 requires total automatic sprinkler protection, the exception could only be used in buildings using Option 4.

Exception No. 2:   In any building provided with a complete automatic sprinkler system in accordance with Section 7-7, and where exits and required ways of travel thereto are adequately safeguarded against fire and smoke within the building or where every individual room has direct access to an exterior exit without passing through any public corridor, the protection of vertical openings not part of required exits may be waived by the authority having jurisdiction to such extent as such openings do not endanger required means of egress.

Exception No. 3:   Stairway enclosures shall not be required where a one-story stair connects two levels within a single dwelling unit, guest room or suite located above the level of exit discharge.

See also 19-2.11.1 and 19-2.11.4.

Exception No. 4:   An atrium may be utilized in accordance with 6-2.2.3.1, Exception No. 2.

Since 6-2.2.3.1, Exception No. 2 requires total automatic sprinkler protection, the exception could only be used in buildings using Option 4.

19-3.1.2   Any required exit stair which is so located that it is necessary to pass through the lobby or other open space to reach the outside of the building shall be continuously enclosed down to the lobby level, or to a mezzanine within the lobby. (*See 19-2.7.*)

19-3.1.3   No floor below the level of exit discharge used only for storage, heating equipment, or other purpose other than residential occupancy open to the public shall have unprotected openings to floors used for residential purposes.

19-3.2 Protection from Hazards.

19-3.2.1 Hazardous areas, including but not limited to boiler and heater rooms, laundries, repair shops, and rooms or spaces used for storage of combustible supplies and equipment deemed hazardous by the authority having jurisdiction, shall be protected as follows:

(a) In buildings using Option 1, 2 or 3, every hazardous area shall be separated from other parts of the building by construction having a fire resistance rating of at least 1 hour. Communicating openings shall be protected by approved smoke-activated automatic, or self-closing, fire doors with a fire protection rating of ¾ hour.

(b) In buildings using Option 4, the enclosure for hazardous areas may be of any reasonably smoke resisting construction with or without a fire resistance rating.

19-3.3 Interior Finish.

19-3.3.1 Interior finish on walls and ceilings, in accordance with Section 6-5, and subject to the limitations and modifications therein specified, shall be as follows:

(a) In buildings using Option 1, 2 or 3
   1. Vertical exits — Class A or B
   2. Exit access — Class A or B
   3. Lobbies, corridors that are not exit access — Class A or B
   4. Individual living units and other habitable spaces — Class A, B, or C
(b) In buildings using Option 4
   1. Vertical exits — Class A, B, or C
   2. Exit access — Class A, B or C
   3. Lobbies, corridors that are not exit access — Class A, B or C
   4. Individual living units and other habitable spaces — Class A, B or C

19-3.3.2 Interior Floor Finish.   In buildings using Option 1 or 2, interior floor finish in corridors and exitways shall be Class I or Class II in accordance with Section 6-5.

Exception: Previously installed floor coverings may be continued in use, subject to the approval of the authority having jurisdiction.

19-3.4 Detection, Alarm and Communication Systems.

19-3.4.1 Smoke Detectors.

19-3.4.1.1 An approved single station smoke detector, continuously powered by the house electrical service, shall be installed in an approved manner in every living unit within the apartment building. When activated, the detector shall initiate an alarm which is audible in the sleeping rooms of that unit. This individual unit detector shall be in addition to any sprinkler system or other detection system that may be installed in the building.

The detector(s) required by 19-3.4.1.1 should usually be located in the hall area(s) giving access to rooms used for sleeping. In multiple-level living units a detector should usually be located at the top of the stairs. The detector(s) should be mounted on the ceiling or on the wall within 12 in. (30.48 cm) of, but no closer than 6 in. (15.24 cm) to, the ceiling. The detector should be placed remotely from the cooking area. Where unusual factors such as room configuration, air movement, or stagnant air pockets require consideration, the authority having jurisdiction and the designer should determine the placement of the detectors.

Note that the detector must be powered by "house current" either through direct wiring of the detector or by using plug-in type detectors. Battery-powered units will not meet the provision of 11-3.3.3.1.

It is not the intent of the paragraph to prohibit interconnecting detectors within a single apartment if the apartment needs more than one detector; in fact, this is required by the second sentence.

Also note that this requirement is *in addition* to any other detection or suppression system required.

19-3.4.1.2 In apartments for the elderly in buildings seven stories and higher, in addition to being tied into the 24-hour manned location, the detectors shall be tied into an annunciator panel which will provide indication of the floor where the detector is activated.

19-3.4.1.3 In buildings using Option 2, a total automatic smoke detection system is required. An automatic smoke detection system is one which is designed to give complete coverage with smoke detectors in accordance with the spacing and layouts given in *Standard on Automatic Fire Detectors*, NFPA 72E, and laboratory test data, and is one in which the detectors are tied together to initiate the alarm and other automatic fire protection devices.

19-3.4.2 Alarms.

19-3.4.2.1 Every apartment building of four or more stories in height or 12 or more apartment units shall have a manual fire alarm system in accordance with Section 7-6.

19-3.4.2.2 In apartments for the elderly, buildings of two or more stories in height or 12 or more living units shall have a manual fire alarm system in accordance with Section 7-6.

Exception: Where all units in a one-story building have direct access to outside at grade.

19-3.4.2.3 Buildings seven or more stories in height shall have an annunciator panel connected with the alarm system to visually indicate the floor of fire involvement. The location of the annunciator panel at an accessible location shall be approved by the authority having jurisdiction.

19-3.4.3 In apartments for the elderly using Option 1 or 3, in buildings seven or more stories in height, in addition to a manual fire alarm system, an approved means of voice communication between an accessible central point approved by the authority having jurisdiction and the corridors, elevators, elevator lobbies and exits shall be provided.

The purpose of the voice communication system is to provide a means for the fire department to contact the building occupants. The system can be used by the building management during nonemergency periods and can consist of speakers at the designated locations. The system can also be used as part of the alarm system if it can provide more than 85 db at the speakers.

19-3.4.4 In buildings using Option 2, four stories or more in height, or with 12 or more units, the alarm system shall be initiated by the automatic fire or smoke detection system, as well as being capable of manual initiation.

19-3.4.5 In buildings using Option 3, the audible alarm shall be activated upon operation of the sprinkler system as well as manually.

19-3.4.6 In buildings using Option 4, four stories or more in height, or with 12 or more units, the alarm system shall be activated upon operation of the automatic sprinkler system as well as being capable of manual initiation.

19-3.4.7 In apartments for the elderly located in buildings four or more stories in height the fire alarm system shall be arranged to transmit an alarm automatically to the fire department legally committed to serve the area in which the building is located by the most direct and reliable method approved by local regulations in accordance with 7-6.3.4.

> **Where automatic transmission of alarms to the fire department legally committed to serve the facility is not permitted, arrangements should be made for the prompt notification of the fire department or such other assistance as may be available in the case of fire or other emergency. Acceptable means of transmitting an alarm are, in order of preference:**
> **(a) A direct connection of the building alarm to the municipal fire alarm system**
> **(b) A direct connection of the building alarm to an approved central station**
> **(c) A telephone connection to a municipal or other alarm headquarters which is manned 24 hours a day.**

19-3.5 Extinguishment Requirements.

19-3.5.1 In buildings using Option 3, automatic sprinklers shall be installed in corridors along the corridor ceiling, and one sprinkler head shall be opposite the center of and inside any living unit door opening into the corridor.

Exception: The sprinkler head inside living units may be omitted if the door to the living unit has 20 minutes or greater fire resistance and is self-closing.

19-3.5.2 The sprinkler installation required in 19-3.5.1 shall meet the requirements of Section 7-7 and *Standard for the Installation of Sprinkler Systems*, NFPA 13, in terms of workmanship and materials.

19-3.5.3 The installation of the corridor sprinklers required in 19-3.5.1 shall not exceed the maximum spacing and protection area requirements of *Standard for the Installation of Sprinkler Systems*, NFPA 13.

19-3.5.4 Buildings using Option 4 shall be protected throughout by an approved automatic sprinkler system. The automatic sprinkler system shall meet the requirements of Section 7-7 and the requirements for supervision, for buildings over six stories in height.

19-3.5.5 Automatic sprinkler system installations required by 19-3.5.4 shall meet the requirements of Section 7-7 and *Standard for the Installation of Sprinkler Systems*, NFPA 13.

Exception: Sprinkler installation may be omitted in small compartmented areas such as closets not over 24 sq ft (2.23 sq m) and bathrooms not over 55 sq ft (5.11 sq m).

19-3.5.6 Hand portable fire extinguishers shall be provided in hazardous areas. When provided, hand portable fire extinguishers shall be installed and maintained as specified in Section 7-7 and *Standard for Portable Fire Extinguishers*, NFPA 10.

19-3.6 Corridors.

19-3.6.1 Exit access corridors shall be protected as follows:

(a) In buildings using Option 1 or 2, corridor walls shall have fire resistance rating of not less than 30 minutes; doors from living units to corridor shall have 20 minutes fire resistance rating or shall be previously approved 1¾-in. (4.45-cm) solid bonded wood core doors.

(b) In buildings using Option 3, fire resistance of corridor walls shall be ¾ hour; doors and frames shall be constructed to resist passage of smoke. Doors shall be equipped with latches for keeping doors tightly closed.

(c) In buildings using Option 4, fire resistance of corridor walls shall be ½ hour; doors and frames shall be constructed to resist the passage of smoke. Doors shall be equipped with latches for keeping doors tightly closed.

> The criteria in 19-3.6.1 parallel the requirements in Chapter 13 for health care occupancies. In both chapters, the committee's concern for providing safety for the occupant in his or her room, during a fire, led to a minimum corridor wall construction either to block fire movement into a room from the corridor, or to block fire in a room from entering the corridor. The common concern in Chapters 13 and 17 is the presence of occupants on a 24-hour-a-day basis with sleeping accommodations.

19-3.6.2 Doors between living units and corridors shall be self-closing. Doors shall be equipped with latches for keeping doors tightly closed.

> Requiring doors between apartments and corridors to be self-closing will lead to a significant reduction in fatalities caused by fire in apartment buildings. Studies of typical apartment fires have shown that the cause of fire spreading beyond the apartment or room of origin was due to the door being left open as the occupant fled the fire.
>
> In other cases, a person suspecting a fire died after opening the door to a room fully involved with fire or after causing full involvement of the room through introducing oxygen by opening the door. A spring-loaded hinge or a closer would have caused these doors to close, preventing smoke or fire from spreading down the corridor and exposing other occupants.

19-3.6.3 The fire resistance rating of living unit/corridor doors shall be minimum 20 minutes.

Exception No. 1: Previously approved 1¾-in. (4.45-cm) solid bonded wood core doors may continue in use.

Exception No. 2: In buildings using Option 3 or 4, doors shall be so constructed as to resist the passage of smoke.

> The door required by 19-3.6.3 provides a level of protection commensurate with the expected fuel load in the room and the fire resistance of the corridor wall construction. The purpose is to box a fire out of a room or to box it within the room by corridor wall and door construction criteria. It has been shown in fuel load studies conducted by the National Bureau of Standards that residential occupancies will have fuel loads in the 20- to 30-minute range.

Contrary to the general rule (see 5-2.1.1.1.1), the door referred to in 19-3.6.3 applies to the leaf only. In other words the frame, hinges, latch, closers, etc., do not have to be rated. By requiring the 20-minute door, the committee was attempting to establish a minimum quality of construction, not to provide for a complete listed fire door assembly.

Ratings longer than those specified by 19-3.6.3 may be required where doors are provided for property protection as well as for life safety. NFPA 80, *Standard for Fire Doors and Windows*,[2] may be consulted for standard practice in the selection and installation of fire doors.

A 1¾-in. (4.45-cm) solid bonded wood core door has been considered the equivalent to a door with a 20-minute fire protection rating.

19-3.6.4 Transfer grills, whether protected by fusible link operated dampers or not, shall not be permitted in these walls or doors.

Paragraph 2-2.2 of NFPA 90A, *Standard for the Installation of Air Conditioning and Ventilating Systems*,[3] prohibits the use of public corridors in residential occupancies as part of the supply, return, or exhaust air system.

19-3.7 Subdivision of Building Spaces.

19-3.7.1 Horizontal Exit Requirements. No requirements.

Chapter 19 does not require the installation of horizontal exits.

Protection of horizontal exits, if provided, shall be as follows:

(a) In buildings using Option 1, 2 or 3 — Fire resistance of walls: 2 hours; Fire protection rating of doors: 1½ hours.

These are the standard requirements for horizontal exits per 5-2.4.

(b) In apartments for the elderly using Option 4, smoke barriers may be used in lieu of horizontal exits. Smoke barriers shall be constructed in accordance with the provisions in Section 6-3 and shall have a fire resistance rating of at least 1 hour.

19-3.7.2 Smoke Barriers. Smoke barriers in accordance with Section 6-3 shall be provided in exit access corridors between stairs as follows:

(a) In buildings using Option 1 when exit stairs are spaced greater than 50 ft (15.24 m) apart.

(b) In buildings using Option 2 or 3 when exit stairs are spaced greater than 100 ft (30.48 m) apart.

(c) In apartments for the elderly using Option 1 when exit stairs are greater than 50 ft (15.24 m) apart.

(d) In apartments for the elderly using Option 2 or 3 when exit stairs are greater than 75 ft (22.86 m) apart.

(e) In apartments for the elderly using Option 4 when exit stairs are greater than 150 ft (45.72 m) apart.

Protection may be accomplished in conjunction with the provisions for horizontal exits.

Table 19-3.7.2
Smoke Barriers Are Required Where
Exit Stair Spacing Is in Excess of:

Occupancy	Options			
	No. 1	No. 2	No. 3	No. 4
Residential	50 ft (15.24 m)	100 ft (30.48 m)	100 ft (30.48 m)	NR
Apartments for Elderly	50 ft (15.24 m)	75 ft (22.86 m)	75 ft (22.86 m)	150 ft (45.72 m)

Note: When required, there shall be a smoke barrier between stairs.

It should be noted that this does not require smoke barriers every 50 ft (15.24 m) or 100 ft (30.48 m) etc., but only requires a smoke barrier between stairs when the stair spacing exceeds the given lengths. The provision of a horizontal exit can substitute for a smoke barrier and can also be beneficial for travel distance and eliminating a stairway.

19-3.7.3   In apartments for the elderly the minimum width of smoke barrier doors is 32 in. (81.28 cm) and may be a single door that will swing in either direction. Side lights or a vision panel are required in smoke doors.

SECTION 19-4   SPECIAL PROVISIONS

SECTION 19-5   BUILDING SERVICES

19-5.1 Utilities.   Utilities shall comply with the provisions of Section 7-1.

19-5.2 Heating, Ventilating, and Air Conditioning.   Heating, ventilating and air conditioning equipment shall comply with the provisions of Section 7-2.

Paragraph 2-2.2 of NFPA 90A, *Standard for the Installation of Air Conditioning and Ventilating Systems,*[3] **prohibits the use of public corridors in residential occupancies as part of the supply, return, or exhaust air system.**

19-5.3 Elevators, Dumbwaiters and Vertical Conveyors.   Elevators, dumbwaiters and vertical conveyors shall comply with the provisions of Section 7-4.

19-5.4 Rubbish Chutes, Incinerators, and Laundry Chutes.   Rubbish chutes, incinerators and laundry chutes shall comply with the provisions of Section 7-5.

Table 19-1
**Alternate Requirements for Existing Apartment Buildings
According to Protection Provided**

	No Suppression or Detection System Option No. 1	Total Automatic Smoke Detection Option No. 2	Sprink. Prot. in Select. Areas Option No. 3	Auto Ext. NFPA 13 (with exceptions) Option No. 4
Max. Gross Area per Story Between Horizontal Exits				
1-3 Stories	NR	NR	NR	NR
4-6 Stories	NR	NR	NR	NR
>6 Stories	NR	NR	NR	NR
Exit Access				
Travel Distance	100 ft (30.48 m)	150 ft (45.72 m)	150 ft (45.72 m)	150 ft (45.72 m)
Smoke Barrier Req. for Stair Spacing	>50 ft (15.24 m)	>100 ft (30.48 m)	>100 ft (30.48 m)	NR
Max. Single Path Corridor Distance	35 ft (10.67 m)	35 ft (10.67 m)	35 ft (10.67 m)	35 ft (10.67 m)
Max. Dead End	35 ft (10.67 m)	35 ft (10.67 m)	35 ft (10.67 m)	35 ft (10.67 m)
Fire Resistance				
Walls	½ hr	½ hr	¾ hr	½ hr
Doors (Fire Protection Rating)	20 min	20 min	N/A	N/A
Flame Spread				
Walls & Ceilings	A or B	A or B	A or B	A, B, or C
Floors	I or II	I or II	NR	NR
Exits—Vertical				
Fire Resistance Walls				
1-3 Stories	1 hr	1 hr	1 hr	1 hr
>3 Stories	2 hr	2 hr	2 hr	2 hr
Smokeproof Towers				
1-6 Stories	NR	NR	NR	NR
>6 Stories	Req.	Req.	Req.	NR
Doors				
1-3 Stories	1 hr	1 hr	1 hr	1 hr
>3 Stories	1½ hr	1½ hr	1½ hr	1½ hr
Flame Spread				
Walls & Ceilings	A or B	A or B	A or B	A, B, or C
Floors	I or II	I or II	NR	NR
Bedroom Windows, 1- to 6-Story Bldg. Ref. 18–1.1.4	Req.	Req.	Req.	Req.
Exits—Horizontal				
Fire Resistance				
Walls	2 hr	2 hr	2 hr	NA
Doors	1½ hr	1½ hr	1½ hr	NA
Habitable Spaces				
Max. Distance from any Room Door to Corridor	50 ft (15.24 m)	100 ft (30.48 m)	50 ft (15.24 m)	100 ft (30.48 m)
Flame Spread				
Walls & Ceilings	A, B, or C	A, B, or C	A, B, or C	A, B, or C
Smoke Detector				
Indiv. in Unit	Req.	Req.	Req.	Req.
Door to Corridor				
Self-closing	Req.	Req.	Req.	Req.

Table 19-1 (Continued)

	No Suppression or Detection System Option No. 1	Total Automatic Smoke Detection Option No. 2	Sprink. Prot. in Select. Areas Option No. 3	Auto Ext. NFPA 13 (with exceptions) Option No. 4
Alarm System				
>3 Stories or				
>11 Units	manual	manual & auto	manual & auto	manual & auto
>6 Stories	annunciator panel	annunciator panel	annunciator panel	annunciator panel
HVAC				
>6 Stories Pressurized Corridor, 0.01 in. Water (2.49 Pa), min.	NR	NR	NR	NR
Elevator—ANSI	A17.1	A17.1	A17.1	A17.1

NL=No Limit.
NR=No Requirements.
NA=Not Applicable.

Table 19-2
Alternate Requirements for Existing Apartments for the Elderly
According to Protection Provided

	No Suppression or Detection System Option No. 1	Total Automatic Smoke Detection Option No. 2	Sprink. Prot. in Select. Areas Option No. 3	Auto Ext. NFPA 13 (with exceptions) Option No. 4
Max. Gross Area per Story Between Horizontal Exits				
1-3 Stories	NR	NR	NR	NR
4-6 Stories	NR	NR	NR	NR
>6 Stories	NR	NR	NR	NR
Exit Access				
Travel Distance	75 ft (22.86 m)	100 ft (30.48 m)	100 ft (30.48 m)	100 ft (30.48 m)
Smoke Barrier Req. for Stair Spacing	>50 ft (15.24 m)	>75 ft (22.86 m)	>75 ft (22.86 m)	>150 ft (45.72 m)
Max. Single Path Corridor Distance	35 ft (10.67 m)	35 ft (10.67 m)	35 ft (10.67 m)	35 ft (10.67 m)
Max. Dead End	35 ft (10.67 m)	35 ft (10.67 m)	35 ft (10.67 m)	35 ft (10.67 m)
Fire Resistance				
Walls	½ hr	½ hr	¾ hr	½ hr
Doors (Fire Protection Rating)	20 min	20 min	N/A	N/A
Flame Spread				
Walls & Ceilings	A or B	A or B	A or B	A, B, or C
Floors	I or II	I or II	NR	NR
Exits—Vertical Fire Resistance Walls				
1-3 Stories	1 hr	1 hr	1 hr	¾ hr
>3 Stories	2 hr	2 hr	2 hr	1 hr

Table 19-2 (Continued)

	No Suppression or Detection System Option No. 1	Total Automatic Smoke Detection Option No. 2	Sprink. Prot. in Select. Areas Option No. 3	Auto Ext. NFPA 13 (with exceptions) Option No. 4
Exits—Vertical (Continued)				
Smokeproof Towers				
1-6 Stories	NR	NR	NR	NR
>6 Stories	Req.	Req.	Req.	NR
Doors				
1-3 Stories	1 hr	1 hr	1 hr	¾ hr
>3 Stories	1½ hr	1½ hr	1½ hr	1 hr
Flame Spread				
Walls & Ceilings	A or B	A or B	A or B	A, B, or C
Floors	I or II	I or II	NR	NR
Bedroom Windows, 1- to 6-Story Bldg. Ref. 18–1.1.4	Req.	Req.	Req.	Req.
Exits—Horizontal				
Fire Resistance				
Walls	2 hr	2 hr	2 hr	1 hr
Doors	1½ hr	1½ hr	1½ hr	NR
Habitable Spaces				
Max. Distance from any Room Door to Corridor	50 ft (15.24 m)	100 ft (30.48 m)	50 ft (15.24 m)	100 ft (30.48 m)
Flame Spread				
Walls & Ceilings	A, B, or C	A, B, or C	A, B, or C	A, B, or C
Smoke Detector				
Indiv. in Unit	Req.	Req.	Req.	Req.
Door to Corridor				
Self-closing	Req.	Req.	Req.	Req.
Alarm System				
2 Stories or more, or >11 Units	manual	manual	manual & auto	manual
4 Stories or more, or >11 Units	auto to FD	auto* & auto to FD	auto & auto to FD	auto* & auto to FD
>6 Stories	annunciator and voice communication	annunciator	annunciator and voice communication	annunciator
HVAC				
>6 Stories Pressurized Corridor, 0.01 in. Water (2.49 Pa), min.	NR	NR	NR	NR
Elevator—ANSI	A17.1	A17.1	A17.1	A17.1

NL=No Limit.
NR=No Requirements.
NA=Not Applicable.
*=Also req. in buildings with 12 or more living units.

The following are two examples of how to use Table 19-1.

Example 1: **What are the interior finish requirements in an exit stairway for a five-story apartment building equipped with an automatic detection system?**

Answer: Enter the table under the column heading "Total Automatic Smoke Detection Option No. 2." In the section "Exits — Vertical," find the heading "Flame Spread (Walls and Ceilings)." The requirement for this building is "A" or "B" interior finish for the exits.

Example 2: What is the maximum dead-end (single path of exit travel) distance permitted in an existing apartment building equipped with sprinklers located only in corridors and inside the doors leading into each living unit?

Answer: Enter the table under the column heading "Sprinkler Protection in Selected Areas Option No. 3." Across from the row headed "Maximum Single Path Corridor Distance" you will find 35 ft (10.67 m) as the answer.

After reviewing the instructions on how to use Tables 19-1 and 19-2, it is necessary to discuss why certain design features were incorporated in the four design approaches.

Height and Area Limitations

Note that there is no limitation in Tables 19-1 and 19-2 for maximum area *between* horizontal exits.

Required Smoke Barrier for Stair Spacing

As the stair spacing exceeds either 50 ft (15.24 m) (Option No. 1) or 100 ft (30.48 m) (Option Nos. 2 or 3 in Table 19-1), or 75 ft (22.86 m) (Option Nos. 2 or 3) or 150 ft (45.72 m) (Option No. 4 in Table 19-2), smoke barriers are required to isolate a fire and to prevent its products of combustion from contaminating all access to stair shafts by interposing a smoke barrier *between* two separate stair shafts. In this way, at least one stair, relatively free from smoke, will be provided.

Exits — Vertical — Smokeproof Towers

Smokeproof towers are required in apartment designs over six stories in height (except totally sprinklered buildings). This was the committee's requirement, additional to the specification of interior smoke barriers (discussed above), to limit the possibility of smoke contaminating exits to the point of impassability and, therefore, to ensure a safe, protected means of egress from a fire.

Habitable Spaces — Maximum Distance from any Room Door to Corridor

This set of criteria establishes the maximum distance from the farthest interior room door of an apartment suite (usually the rear bedroom) to the entrance door of the apartment. In so doing, it realistically imposes a maximum design dimension (usually width) on the apartment unit.

HVAC

The provision for 0.01 in. (2.49 Pa) of water is not required in Table 19-1 or 19-2.

REFERENCES CITED BY *CODE*

(These publications comprise a part of the requirements to the extent called for by the Code.*)*

NFPA 10, *Standard for Portable Fire Extinguishers*, NFPA, Boston, 1978.

NFPA 13, *Standard for the Installation of Sprinkler Systems*, NFPA, Boston, 1980.

NFPA 72E, *Standard on Automatic Fire Detectors*, NFPA, Boston, 1978.

REFERENCES CITED IN COMMENTARY

[1]NFPA 13, *Standard for the Installation of Sprinkler Systems*, NFPA, Boston, 1980.

[2]NFPA 80, *Standard for Fire Doors and Windows*, NFPA, Boston, 1979.

[3]NFPA 90A, *Standard for the Installation of Air Conditioning and Ventilating Systems*, NFPA, Boston, 1978.

20

LODGING OR ROOMING HOUSES

SECTION 20-1 GENERAL REQUIREMENTS

20-1.1 Application.

20-1.1.1 This *Code* has differing requirements for the several types of residential occupancies; thus, the *Code* has several residential occupancy chapters, Chapters 16 through 23.

> See commentary following 18-1.1.1.

20-1.1.2 This chapter applies only to lodging or rooming houses providing sleeping accommodations for 15 or less persons. Lodging or rooming houses include buildings in which separate sleeping rooms are rented providing sleeping accommodations for a total of 15 or less persons on either a transient or permanent basis, with or without meals but without separate cooking facilities for individual occupants, except as provided in Chapter 22.

> If sleeping accommodations for more than 15 people are present, the occupancy should be classed as a hotel. The reference to Chapter 22 refers to the *maximum* of three rooms allowed to be rented to "outsiders" in one- and two-family dwellings.

20-1.1.3 The requirements of this chapter are applicable to new buildings, and to existing or modified buildings according to the provisions of Section 1-4 of this *Code*.

20-1.1.4 In addition to the following provisions, every lodging or rooming house shall comply with the minimum requirements for one- and two-family dwellings.

20-1.2 Mixed Occupancies.

20-1.2.1 Where another type of occupancy occurs in the same building as a residential occupancy, the requirements of 1-4.5 of this *Code* shall be applicable.

20-1.2.2 For requirements on mixed mercantile and residential occupancies, see 24-1.2 or 25-1.2.

20-1.3 Definitions.

20-1.3.1 Terms applicable to this chapter are defined in Chapter 3 of this *Code*; where necessary, other terms will be defined in the text as they may occur.

20-1.4 Classification of Occupancy. (*See 20-1.1.2.*)

20-1.5 Classification of Hazard of Contents.

20-1.5.1 Building contents shall be classified according to the provisions of 4-2.1 of this *Code*. For design of sprinkler systems, the classification of contents in *Standard for the Installation of Sprinkler Systems*, NFPA 13, shall apply.

> Under the definitions of 4-2.1 of the *Code*, the contents of living units in residential occupancies fall into the ordinary hazard classification. Characteristics of "ordinary" hazards are moderately rapid burning and considerable smoke generation, with the added hazard of the possible presence of toxic combustion products.
>
> NFPA 13, *Standard for the Installation of Sprinkler Systems*,[1] would classify the contents as "light" for the design of extinguishing systems. The difference in classification is based on the threat to life or life safety (ordinary) versus the threat to the extinguishing capability of the automatic sprinkler system (light).

20-1.6 Minimum Construction Requirements.   No special requirements.

20-1.7 Occupant Load. (*See 20-1.1.2.*)

SECTION 20-2   MEANS OF ESCAPE

20-2.1 Number and Means of Escape.

20-2.1.1 Every sleeping room above or below the level of exit discharge shall have access to two separate means of escape one of which shall be either an enclosed interior stairway, an exterior stairway, or a horizontal exit.

Exception: In existing buildings a fire escape stair is acceptable.

> In 20-2.1.1, the phrase *means of escape* is separate and distinct from *means of egress* and indicates the committee's acceptance of slightly less than a *Code*-conforming means of egress for evacuating a lodging or rooming house during a fire. Note that the *Code* requires at least one means of escape to be an enclosed interior stairway, an exterior stairway, or a horizontal exit (or a fire escape in an existing building). No guidance is given on what the other means of escape must be. The committee intended at least one means of escape to be of some degree of quality, but was reluctant to tie the criteria directly to the *Code* because most rooming or lodging houses are converted homes where a *Code*-conforming exit arrangement is seldom found. However, the committee recognized the aspect of public liability represented by lodging guests, and intended a level of escape quality higher than that normally found in a single-family home.

20-2.1.2 At least one means of escape shall be located to provide a safe path of travel to the outside of the building without traversing any corridor or space exposed to an unprotected vertical opening.

Exception: Unprotected vertical openings may be permitted in buildings three stories or less in height protected throughout by an approved automatic sprinkler system designed in accordance with Section 7-7 and Standard for the Installation of Sprinkler Systems, NFPA 13, or Standard for the Installation of Sprinkler Systems in One- and Two-Family Dwellings and Mobile Homes, NFPA 13D.

Paragraph 20-2.1.2 relates to the discussion on 20-2.1.1. By eliminating exposure to unprotected vertical openings (normally found in single-family dwellings), the committee requires a quality of exit arrangement which is a level above that normally found in a single-family dwelling. Figures 20-1, 20-2, and 20-3 illustrate three possible methods of complying with 20-2.1.

20-2.1.3 Every sleeping room located on the level of exit discharge shall have access to two separate means of escape, one of which may be an operable window. (*See Section 22-2.*)

Exception: One-story buildings with rooms having direct access to the exterior at grade.

20-2.2 Winders in accordance with 5-2.2.2.4 are permitted.

20-2.3 No door in any means of egress shall be locked against egress when the building is occupied (*see 5-2.1.2*).

Paragraph 20-2.3 prohibits a lodging or rooming house from having any door locked "against egress" while the building is occupied. This requirement permits a door to have a locking device that allows the door to be opened from within the building for egress, but does not allow the door to be opened from outside the building. Ordinary dead bolts, double cylinder locks, and chain locks would not meet these provisions. Several tragic multiple-death fires have occurred where a key could not be found to unlock these devices or, in haste, where a door was not openable simply because the chain device was not removed.

The language of 5-2.1.2 is clear: "Locks if provided shall not require the use of a key for operation from the inside of the building." This eliminates double cylinder, ordinary dead bolt, and chain locks which require a key to operate from the inside. Paragraph 5-2.1.2.1.2 calls for a simple operation to open a door; two-handed knob operations and the like do not meet this provision.

SECTION 20-3   PROTECTION

20-3.1 Alarm System.

20-3.1.1 A manual fire alarm system shall be provided in accordance with Section 7-6.

20-3.2 Detection System.

20-3.2.1 Approved smoke detectors, meeting the requirements of *Standard for Household Fire Warning Equipment*, NFPA 74, and powered by the house electrical service, shall be installed on each floor level including basements and excluding crawl spaces and unfinished attics. When activated, the detectors shall initiate an alarm which shall be audible in all sleeping areas.

The last sentence of 20-3.2.1 essentially requires that the detectors be interconnected with each other so that when one sounds, they all sound.

SECTION 20-4   SPECIAL PROVISIONS

SECTION 20-5   BUILDING SERVICES

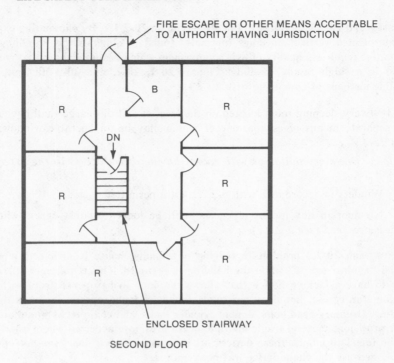

FIRE ESCAPE OR OTHER MEANS ACCEPTABLE
TO AUTHORITY HAVING JURISDICTION

ENCLOSED STAIRWAY

SECOND FLOOR

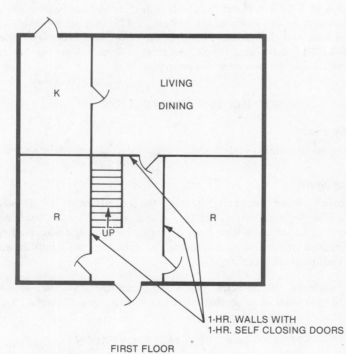

1-HR. WALLS WITH
1-HR. SELF CLOSING DOORS

FIRST FLOOR

Figure 20-1. Means of Escape — Lodging and Rooming House — Example 1. This example provides an enclosed interior stair discharging directly outside (see 20-2.1.1). Access to the interior stair is via an interior corridor which is not exposed to an unprotected vertical opening (see 20-2.1.2). The second means of escape could be a fire escape or any other means acceptable to the authority having jurisdiction. Note that the first floor bedrooms and living room have windows per 20-1.1.4 and 20-2.1.3. The enclosure at the bottom of the stair can be done several ways; this is only one example.

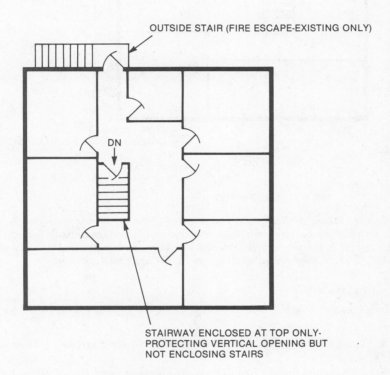

OUTSIDE STAIR (FIRE ESCAPE-EXISTING ONLY)

DN

STAIRWAY ENCLOSED AT TOP ONLY-
PROTECTING VERTICAL OPENING BUT
NOT ENCLOSING STAIRS

SECOND FLOOR

Figure 20-2. Means of Escape — Lodging and Rooming House — Example 2. This example provides an exterior stair complying with 5-2.5 (see 20-2.1.1). The exterior stair has access to it via the interior corridor which is not exposed to an unprotected vertical opening (see 20-2.1.2). The second means of escape is via the stairway which discharges through the first floor.

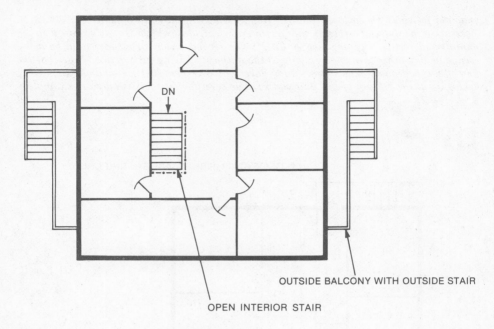

OUTSIDE BALCONY WITH OUTSIDE STAIR

OPEN INTERIOR STAIR

SECOND FLOOR

Figure 20-3. Means of Escape — Lodging and Rooming House — Example 3. This example provides an outside stair with exterior exit access complying with 5-2.5 (see 20-2.1.1). Access is not through the interior corridor which is exposed by the open stair (see 20-2.1.2). The second means of escape is via the open interior stair.

REFERENCES CITED BY *CODE*

(These publications comprise a part of the requirements to the extent called for by the Code.)

NFPA 13, *Standard for the Installation of Sprinkler Systems*, NFPA, Boston, 1980.

NFPA 74, *Standard for the Installation, Maintenance and Use of Household Fire Warning Equipment*, NFPA, 1980.

NFPA 13D, *Standard for the Installation of Sprinkler Systems in One- and Two-Family Dwellings and Mobile Homes*, NFPA, Boston, 1980.

REFERENCES CITED IN COMMENTARY

[1]NFPA 13, *Standard for the Installation of Sprinkler Systems*, NFPA, Boston, 1980.

CHAPTER 21   (RESERVED)

The Committee on Safety to Life has reserved this chapter number for future use.

22

ONE- AND TWO-FAMILY DWELLINGS

SECTION 22-1   GENERAL REQUIREMENTS

22-1.1 Application.

22-1.1.1   This chapter establishes life safety requirements for all one- and two-family private dwellings. One- and two-family dwellings include buildings containing not more than two dwelling units in which each living unit is occupied by members of a single family with no more than three outsiders, if any, accommodated in rented rooms.

> See commentary following 18-1.1.1. If more than three outsiders are accommodated, then the requirements of Chapter 20 apply.

22-1.1.2   The requirements of this chapter are applicable to new buildings, and to existing or modified buildings according to the provisions of Section 1-4 of this *Code*.

22-1.2 Mixed Occupancies.

22-1.2.1   Where another type of occupancy occurs in the same building as a residential occupancy, the requirements of 1-4.5 of this *Code* shall be applicable.

22-1.2.2   For requirements on mixed mercantile and residential occupancies, see 24-1.2 or 25-1.2.

22-1.3 Definitions.

22-1.3.1   Terms applicable to this chapter are defined in Chapter 3 of this *Code*; where necessary, other terms will be defined in the text as they may occur.

22-1.4 Classification of Occupancy.   (*See 22-1.1.1.*)

22-1.5 Classification of Hazard of Contents.

22-1.5.1   Building contents shall be classified according to the provisions of 4-2.1 of this *Code*. For design of sprinkler systems, the classification of contents in *Standard for the Installation of Sprinkler Systems*, NFPA 13, shall apply.

> Under the definitions of 4-2.1 of the *Code*, the contents of living units in residential occupancies fall into the ordinary hazard classification. Characteristics of

"ordinary" hazards are moderately rapid burning and considerable smoke generation, with the added hazard of the possible presence of toxic combustion products.

NFPA 13, *Standard for the Installation of Sprinkler Systems,*[1] would classify the contents as "light" for the design of extinguishing systems. The difference in classification is based on the threat to life or life safety (ordinary) versus the threat to the extinguishing capability of the automatic sprinkler system (light).

It is not the intent of this paragraph to prohibit the use of NFPA 13D, *Standard for the Installation of Sprinkler Systems in One- and Two-Family Dwellings and Mobile Homes.*[2]

22-1.6 Minimum Construction Requirements.   No special requirements.

22-1.7 Occupant Load.

SECTION 22-2   MEANS OF ESCAPE REQUIREMENTS

22-2.1 Number of Exits.

22-2.1.1   In any dwelling of more than two rooms, every bedroom and living room area shall have at least two means of escape, at least one of which shall be a door or stairway providing a means of unobstructed travel to the outside of the building at street or ground level. No bedroom or living room area shall be accessible by only a ladder or folding stairs, or through a trap door.

> The committee adopted the phrase *means of escape* to indicate a way out of a residential unit which, although not conforming to the strict definition of *means of egress*, does provide a safe way out of a building. The committee, recognizing that it is rare to find a *Code*-complying exit in a single-family dwelling (let alone an enclosed vertical opening), called for the quality of egress that is normally found in dwelling design. Note that a "door or stairway providing a means of unobstructed travel to the outside" covers just about every egress arrangement found in a dwelling today.
>
> Paragraph 22-2.1.1 prohibits the addition of a bedroom or den in an attic if the space is accessible only by a trap door or folding ladder. Direct stair access is required.

22-2.2 Type of Second Means of Escape.

22-2.2.1   The second means of escape shall be either:

(a) A door or stairway providing a means of unobstructed travel to the outside of the building at street or ground level, or

(b) An outside window operable from the inside without the use of tools and providing a clear opening of not less than 20 in. (50.8 cm) in width, 24 in. (60.96 cm) in height, and 5.7 sq ft (.53 sq m) in area. The bottom of the opening shall not be more than 44 in. (111.76 cm) above the floor.

Exception No. 1:   If the room has a door leading directly outside of the building to grade, a second means of escape shall not be required.

Exception No. 2:   If buildings are protected throughout by an approved automatic sprinkler system installed in accordance with Standard for the Installation of

Sprinkler Systems, NFPA 13, or Standard for the Installation of Sprinkler Systems in One- and Two-Family Dwellings and Mobile Homes, NFPA 13D, a second means of escape shall not be required.

The requirement of 22-2.2.1 is identical to the criterion for a means of escape specified in 22-2.1.1.

The second way out of most bedrooms, acceptable to the *Code*, is a window meeting the dimensions stated in 22-2.2.1(b). Both the minimum width and minimum height can not be used simultaneously as the minimum area could not be achieved.

22-2.3 Arrangement of Means of Egress.

22-2.3.1   No required path of travel to the outside from any room shall be through another room or apartment not under the immediate control of the occupant of the first room or his family, nor through a bathroom or other space subject to locking.

Paragraph 22-2.3.1 was drafted to reflect that one- and two-family dwellings can have up to three rooms rented to outsiders, or can be arranged so that a second family must egress through the living space of another family. (This is found in older homes not originally designed as duplexes, but later converted to such.) In either case, egress for the renters or for the second family must be independent of any other family's living space.

22-2.4 Doors.

22-2.4.1   No door in the path of travel of a means of escape shall be less than 28 in. (71.12 cm) wide.

Exception: Bathroom doors may be 24 in. (60.96 cm) wide.

The 28-in. (71.12-cm) doors specified in 22-2.4.1 are found in dwelling designs, but ease of access and the need to move furniture and appliances usually dictate a larger size, reflecting prudent architectural design.

22-2.4.2   Every closet door latch shall be such that children can open the door from inside the closet.

22-2.4.3   Every bathroom door lock shall be designed to permit the opening of the locked door from the outside in an emergency.

Paragraphs 22-2.4.2 and 22-2.4.3 reflect the fact that during a fire younger children will often seek refuge in bathrooms or closets (or under beds). Providing for the unlocking of such doors permits ease of rescue by the fire department or by parents.

22-2.4.4   Exterior exit doors may be swinging or sliding and are exempt from the requirements of 5-2.1.1.4.1.

22-2.5 Vertical Means of Escape, Stairs.

22-2.5.1   The width, risers, and treads of every stair shall comply with the minimum requirements for stairs, as described in 5-2.2. Winders and spiral stairs in accordance with Chapter 5 are permitted within a single living unit.

22-2.6 No door in any means of egress shall be locked against egress when the building is occupied (*see 5-2.1.2*).

Paragraph 22-2.6 prohibits a one- or two-family dwelling from having any door locked "against egress" while the building is occupied. This requirement permits a door to have a locking device that allows the door to be opened from within the building for egress, but does not allow the door to be opened from outside the building. Ordinary dead bolts, double cylinder locks, and chain locks would not meet these provisions. Several tragic multiple-death fires have occurred where a key could not be found to unlock these devices or, in haste, where a door was not openable simply because the chain device was not removed.

The language of 5-2.1.2 is clear: "Locks if provided shall not require the use of a key for operation from the inside of the building." This eliminates double cylinder, ordinary dead bolt, and chain locks which require a key to operate from the inside. Paragraph 5-2.1.2.1.2 calls for a simple operation to open a door; two-handed knob operations and the like do not meet this provision.

SECTION 22-3   PROTECTION

22-3.1 Interior Finish.

22-3.1.1 Interior finish on walls and ceilings of occupied spaces shall be Class A, B, or C as defined in Section 6-5.

Note that Class D interior finish (flame spread 200-500) is no longer permitted in one- or two-family dwellings. It was the intent of the committee that this reduction in combustible finishes would increase the level of life safety from fire in dwellings. The use of high flame spread interior decorative paneling has been a factor in many fatal residential fires.

22-3.1.2 Interior Floor Finish.   No requirements.

22-3.2 Detection and Alarm.

22-3.2.1 At least one approved smoke detector powered by the house electric service shall be installed in an approved manner in every dwelling unit. When activated, the detector shall initiate an alarm which is audible in the sleeping rooms.

Exception: In existing construction approved smoke detectors powered by batteries may be used.

Note that directly wired or plug-in type detectors are required in lieu of battery units. However, to avoid expensive installation changes, existing dwellings are permitted to use battery-powered units.

The detector(s) should usually be located in the hall area(s) giving access to rooms used for sleeping purposes. In multiple-level living units a detector should usually be located at the top of the stairs. The detector(s) should be mounted on the ceiling or on the wall within 12 in. (30.48 cm) of, but not closer than 6 in. (15.24 cm) to, the ceiling. The detector should be placed remotely from the cooking area. Where unusual factors such as room configuration, air movement, stagnant air pockets, etc., require consideration, the authority having jurisdiction and the designer should determine the placement of the detectors. See NFPA 74, *Standard for the Installation, Maintenance and Use of Household Fire Warning Equipment*.[3]

This paragraph only requires one detector; however, it is highly recommended that more be installed where needed. For further guidance see NFPA 74, *Standard for the Installation, Maintenance and Use of Household Fire Warning Equipment*.[3]

SECTION 22-4   (RESERVED)

SECTION 22-5   BUILDING SERVICES

22-5.1 Heating Equipment.

22-5.1.1   No stove or combustion heater shall be so located as to block escape in case of fire arising from malfunctioning of the stove or heater.

This requirement takes on even added meaning with today's high energy costs resulting in alternative fuels being used in the home.

REFERENCES CITED BY *CODE*

(These publications comprise a part of the requirements to the extent called for by the Code.)

NFPA 13, *Standard for the Installation of Sprinkler Systems*, NFPA, Boston, 1980.

NFPA 13D, *Standard for the Installation of Sprinkler Systems in One- and Two-Family Dwellings and Mobile Homes*, NFPA, Boston, 1980.

REFERENCES CITED IN COMMENTARY

[1]NFPA 13, *Standard for the Installation of Sprinkler Systems*, NFPA, Boston, 1980.

[2]NFPA 13D, *Standard for the Installation of Sprinkler Systems in One- and Two-Family Dwellings and Mobile Homes*, NFPA, Boston, 1980.

[3]NFPA 74, *Standard for the Installation, Maintenance and Use of Household Fire Warning Equipment*, NFPA, Boston, 1980.

CHAPTER 23   (RESERVED)

The Committee on Safety to Life has reserved this chapter number for future use.

24

NEW MERCANTILE OCCUPANCIES

(See also Chapter 31.)

Mercantile occupancies include stores, markets, and other rooms, buildings, or structures for the display and sale of merchandise. Included in this occupancy group are:

Supermarkets   Auction rooms
Department stores   Shopping centers
Drugstores

Minor merchandising operations in buildings predominantly of other occupancies, such as a newsstand in an office building, must meet the exit requirements of the predominant occupancy.

SECTION 24-1 GENERAL REQUIREMENTS

24-1.1 Application.

24-1.1.1 New mercantile occupancies shall comply with the provisions of Chapter 24. (*See Chapter 31 for operating features.*)

Existing mercantile occupancies must now comply with Chapter 25 of the *Code*.

24-1.1.2 This chapter establishes life safety requirements for the design of all new mercantile buildings. Specific requirements for sub-occupancy groups such as Class A, B and C stores and covered malls are contained in paragraphs pertaining thereto.

24-1.1.3 Additions to existing buildings shall conform to the requirements for new construction. Existing portions of the structure need not be modified, provided that the new construction has not diminished the fire safety features of the facility.

Exception: Existing portions must be upgraded if the addition results in a change of mercantile classification.

Paragraph 24-1.1.3 and its exception are intended to indicate that additions to existing mercantile occupancies must conform to the requirements for new occupancies, while the existing portion of the occupancy may continue in use as long as it complies with the provisions for existing mercantile occupancies contained in

615

Chapter 25 of the *Code*. If, however, the addition results in the mercantile occupancy changing classifications, such as moving from a Class C mercantile to a Class B mercantile, then the existing occupancy must also be upgraded to meet the provisions for new occupancies.

24-1.2 Mixed Occupancies.

24-1.2.1 Combined Mercantile and Residential Occupancies.

24-1.2.1.1 No dwelling unit shall have its sole means of egress through any mercantile occupancy in the same building.

24-1.2.1.2 No multiple dwelling occupancy shall be located above a mercantile occupancy.

Exception No. 1: Where the dwelling occupancy and exits therefrom are separated from the mercantile occupancy by construction having a fire resistance of at least 1 hour.

Exception No. 2: Where the mercantile occupancy is protected by automatic sprinklers in accordance with Section 7-7.

The requirements for mixed occupancies were developed by the committee on mercantile and business occupancies to deal with a then common (but now slowly disappearing) occupancy, the corner tavern, grocery store, or retail store which had a dwelling occupancy on the upper floors. The committee divided this type of combined occupancy into two classes.

Where there is a single dwelling occupancy above the mercantile operation, the *Code* prohibits (see 24-1.2.1.1) the dwelling occupancy from having its sole means of egress through the mercantile occupancy. If the dwelling occupancy has an exit through the mercantile occupancy, it must have a second exit that is *independent of* and does not travel through the mercantile occupancy.

The *Code* prohibits a multiple dwelling occupancy above a mercantile occupancy unless one of the following conditions is met:

1. The dwellings and their exits are separated from the mercantile occupancy by construction with a fire resistance of 1 hour.
2. The mercantile occupancy is protected by an automatic sprinkler system. See Section 6-4 of the *Code*, NFPA 13, *Standard for the Installation of Sprinkler Systems*,[1] and 13A, *Recommended Practice for the Care and Maintenance of Sprinkler Systems*.[2]

The committee established these requirements because of the long historical record of many deaths and injuries where fire originated in mercantile occupancies and spread to unsuspecting families occupying dwelling units above the mercantile occupancy.

24-1.3 Special Definitions.

(a) **Class A Stores.** See 24-1.4.2.1(a).

(b) **Class B Stores.** See 24-1.4.2.1(b).

(c) **Class C Stores.** See 24-1.4.2.1(c).

(d) **Covered Mall.** A covered or roofed interior area used as a pedestrian way and connecting building(s) or portions of a building housing single and/or multiple tenants.

(e) **Open-Air Mercantile Operations.**   Operations conducted outside of all structures with the operations area devoid of all walls and roofs except for small individual weather canopies.

(f) **Gross Leasable Area.**   The total floor area designated for tenant occupancy and exclusive use, expressed in square feet, measured from centerlines of adjoining partitions and exteriors of outside walls.

(g) **Anchor Store.**   A department store or major merchandising center having direct access to the covered mall but having all required means of egress independent of the covered mall.

24-1.4 Classification of Occupancy.

24-1.4.1   Mercantile occupancies shall include all buildings and structures or parts thereof with occupancy as described in 4-1.7.

It is important to review again the *Code*'s definition (see **4-1.7**) of what constitutes a mercantile occupancy. Note that this definition *does not include* "minor merchandising operations in buildings predominantly of other occupancies, such as a newsstand in an office building..." Paragraph 4-1.7 requires that such occupancies be subject to the exit requirements of the predominant (major) occupancy.

24-1.4.2 Subclassification of Occupancy.

24-1.4.2.1   Mercantile occupancies shall be classified as follows:

(a) *Class A.*   All stores having aggregate gross area of 30,000 sq ft (2,787 sq m) or more, or utilizing more than three floor levels for sales purposes.

(b) *Class B.*   All stores of less than 30,000 sq ft (2,787 sq m) aggregate gross area, but over 3,000 sq ft (279 sq m), or utilizing any balconies, mezzanines (*see 24-1.4.2.3*), or floors above or below the street floor level for sales purposes.

Exception: If more than three floors are utilized, the store shall be Class A, regardless of area.

(c) *Class C.*   All stores of 3,000 sq ft (279 sq m) or less gross area used for sales purposes on the street floor only. (*Balcony permitted, see 24-1.4.2.3.*)

The following table summarizes the requirements of 24-1.4.2.1 for qualifying a store as Class A, B, or C. This classification process is important because it leads to specific life safety criteria which apply to each class of store. The criteria vary in degree of stringency dependent upon a store's classification.

Table 24–1. Subclassification of Mercantile Occupancies

Store Class	By Height		By Aggregate Gross Area† (sq ft)
A	>3 Floors‡	or	≥30,000
B	≤3 Floors‡	and	>3,000 and <30,000
C	Street Floor Only§	and	≤3,000

†Sections of floors not used for sales are not counted in the area classification.
‡Floors not used for sales above or below a sales floor are not counted in the height classification.
§A balcony or mezzanine < ½ the area of the sales floor is permitted.

24-1.4.2.2   For the purpose of the classification in 24-1.4.2.1, the aggregate gross area shall be the total gross area of all floors used for mercantile purposes and, where a store is divided into sections, regardless of fire separation, shall include the area of all sections used for sales purposes. Areas of floors not used for sales purposes, such as an area used only for storage and not open to the public, shall not be counted for the purposes of the above classifications, but exits shall be provided for such nonsales areas in accordance with their occupancy, as specified by other chapters of this *Code*.

24-1.4.2.3   A balcony or mezzanine floor having an area less than one-half of the floor below shall not be counted as a floor level for the purpose of applying the classification of 24-1.4.2.1, but if there are two balcony or mezzanine floors, one shall be counted.

Although 24-1.4.2.3 allows the omission of one balcony from the count of the number of floor levels, this does not waive any of the exit requirements applying to balconies.

24-1.4.2.4   Where a number of stores under different management are located in the same building or in adjoining buildings with no fire wall or other standard fire separations between, the aggregate gross area of all such stores shall be used in determining classification per 24-1.4.2.1.

Exception: Covered malls (see 24-4.3).

Paragraphs 24-1.4.2.1 through 24-1.4.2.4 further clarify the classification of stores as Class A, B, or C. Most of these provisions are included in the footnotes to Table 24-1. The following should be noted for emphasis:
1. The aggregate gross area is the sum of the gross areas of all floors used for mercantile (sales) purposes.
2. If the store is divided into sections by fire walls, *only the sales sections* should be included in the aggregate gross area.
3. If there are sections or floors used for sales that are considered as separate "stores" (because they are under different management), with no separation (fire walls or fire barriers) between each "store," the aggregate gross area of all such "stores" is to be used in classifying the occupancy as Class A, B, or C, except as provided for covered malls. (See 24-4.3.)

24-1.5 Classification of Hazard of Contents.   Mercantile occupancies contents shall be classed as ordinary hazard in accordance with Section 4-2.

Exception: Mercantile occupancies shall be classified as high hazard if high hazard commodities are displayed or handled without protective wrappings or containers, in which case the following additional provisions shall apply:

(a) Exits shall be located so that not more than 75 ft (22.86 m) of travel from any point is required to reach the nearest exit.

(b) From every point there shall be at least two exits accessible by travel in different directions (no common path of travel).

(c) All vertical openings shall be enclosed.

Some procedures which would require classifying a mercantile occupancy as highly hazardous are: displaying unwrapped articles fabricated from thin sheets of pyroxylin plastic such as artificial flowers or toys; dispensing gunpowder or other explosives in bulk; sales of polyurethane foam; or dispensing gasoline or flammable solvents by pouring them into open containers. Figure 24-1 illustrates an arrangement of exits from a highly hazardous area in a mercantile occupancy.

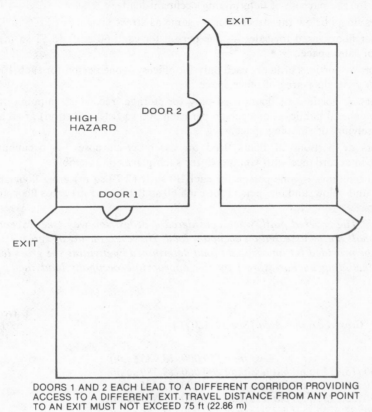

DOORS 1 AND 2 EACH LEAD TO A DIFFERENT CORRIDOR PROVIDING ACCESS TO A DIFFERENT EXIT. TRAVEL DISTANCE FROM ANY POINT TO AN EXIT MUST NOT EXCEED 75 ft (22.86 m)

Figure 24-1. Exit Arrangement from an Area of a Mercantile Occupancy Defined as Highly Hazardous by 24-1.5.

24-1.6 Minimum Construction Requirements.   No special requirements.

The phrase "minimum construction" is used in the *Code* to describe the construction of the building housing the occupancy. Since there are no special requirements, the provisions of the local building code would apply.

24-1.7 Occupant Load.

24-1.7.1   For purposes of determining required exits, the occupant load of mercantile buildings or parts of buildings used for mercantile purposes shall be not less than the following:

(a) Street floor, one person for each 30 sq ft (2.79 sq m) gross floor area of sales space. In stores with no street floor, as defined in Chapter 3, but with access directly from the street by stairs or escalators, the principal floor at the point of entrance to the store shall be considered the street floor. In stores where, due to differences in grade of streets on different sides, there are two or more floors directly accessible from streets (not including alleys or similar back streets), each such floor shall be considered a street floor for the purpose of determining occupant load.

(b) Sales floors below the street floor — same as street floor.

(c) Upper floors, used for sales — one person for each 60 sq ft (5.57 sq m) gross floor area of sales space.

(d) Floors or portions of floors used only for offices — one person for each 100 sq ft (9.29 sq m) gross floor area of office space.

(e) Floors or portions of floors used only for storage, receiving, shipping and not open to the general public — one person per each 300 sq ft (27.87 sq m) gross area of storage, receiving, or shipping space.

(f) Floors or portions of floors used for assembly purposes — occupant load determined in accordance with Chapter 8 for such places of assembly.

(g) Mall buildings — one person for each 30 sq ft (2.79 sq m) gross floor area for street level and below, and one person for each 60 sq ft (5.57 sq m) gross floor area for upper floors.

Exception: The covered mall, when considered a pedestrian way (see Exception to 24-4.3.1), shall not be assessed an occupant load. However, means of egress from the mall shall be provided for an occupant load determined by dividing the gross leasable area (not including anchor stores) by the appropriate occupant load factor listed below:

Gross Leasable Area [See 24-1.3(f).] *(sq ft)*	*Occupant Load Factor*
Less than 150,000 (13,935 sq m)	*30*
Over 150,000 (13,935 sq m) but less than 200,000 (18,580 sq m)	*35*
Over 200,000 (18,580 sq m) but less than 250,000 (23,225 sq m)	*40*
Over 250,000 (23,225 sq m) but less than 300,000 (27,870 sq m)	*45*
Over 300,000 (27,870 sq m) but less than 400,000 (37,160 sq m)	*50*
Over 400,000 (37,160 sq m)	*55*

Each individual tenant space shall have means of egress to the outside and/or to the mall based on occupant loads figured utilizing 24-1.7.1 (a) through (f).

Each individual anchor store shall have means of egress independent of the covered mall.

The occupant load factors given in 24-1.7.1 to calculate the occupant load were established on the basis of population counts of typical stores during periods of maximum occupancy, such as before Christmas or during special sales. The values show that during normal use of a mercantile occupancy the public will congregate, for the most part, on the street floor or in a basement "sales" area. In some cases, an individual store may be more densely populated than these figures indicate, but it may be reasonably assumed that, in any large mercantile building, all areas will not be crowded at the same time and the average occupant load will seldom exceed these figures.

In some types of stores, the occupant load will normally be much less than indicated, e.g., in furniture stores. However, the character of mercantile operations is subject to such rapid change that it is not prudent in designing exit facilities to assume that any store will never be crowded, and for this reason the same figures are used to calculate the occupant load for all types of stores.

In differentiating between street floors and other sales floors, the street floor is *any* floor which has an entrance/exit directly accessible from the street. If differences in the ground level on different sides of a store create several floors of this nature, the *Code* treats them *all* as street floors. It is important to note that, if access to a store from the street is only by stairs or escalators, the principal floor at the point of entrance to the store must be considered the street floor. The *Code* is recognizing merchandising techniques in assigning a higher occupant load to the street floor since these floors have the merchandise conducive to high traffic and thus larger numbers of occupants.

The table used in determining the occupancy load for covered mall shopping centers of varying sizes is arrived at empirically in surveying over 270 covered mall shopping centers, in the study of mercantile occupancy parking requirements, and the observed number of occupants per vehicle during peak seasons.

These studies show that with increasing shopping center size there is a decrease in the number of occupants per square foot of gross leasable area.

This phenomenon is explained when one considers that above a certain shopping center gross leasable area [approx. 600,000 sq ft (55 740 sq m)], a multiplicity of the same types of stores starts to occur: the purpose being to increase the choices available to a customer for any given type of merchandise. Therefore, with increasing shopping center size, the occupant load increases as well, but at a declining rate. In using the table, the occupant load factor is applied to only the gross leasable area utilizing the covered mall as a means of egress.

24-1.7.2 In case of mezzanines or balconies open to the floor below or other unprotected vertical openings between floors as permitted by the Exceptions to 24-3.1, the occupant load (or area) of the mezzanine or other subsidiary floor level shall be added to that of the street floor for the purpose of determining required exits, provided, however, that in no case shall the total number of exit units be less than would be required if all vertical openings were enclosed.

Figures 24-2 and 24-3 illustrate the requirements of 24-1.7.2. Figure 24-2 shows the case where a mezzanine (or balcony) is open to the street floor (which by the definition in Chapter 3 contains the main exit to the exterior or public way). The exits from the street floor must accommodate the people expected to be occupying the street floor, the mezzanine, and the capacity of the stairs from the upper floors discharging through the street floor.

In Figure 24-3, when the mezzanine is not open to the street floor, the capacity of the exits on the street floor must be able to accommodate the people expected to occupy the street floor and the capacity of the stairs from the upper floors discharging through the street floor. The enforcing official should note that the calculations required for the arrangement in Figure 24-3 will establish the *minimum* units of exit width which the *Code* will allow when exits from upper floors discharge into a street floor, whether or not the mezzanine is open to the street floor.

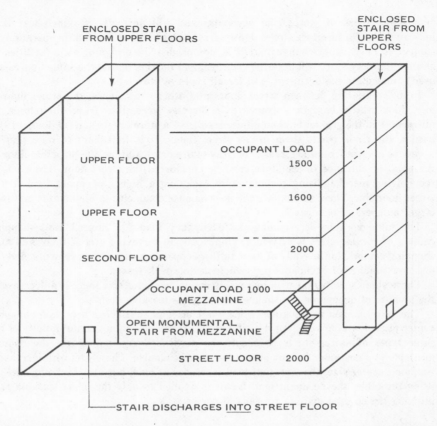

ENCLOSED STAIR FROM UPPER FLOORS

ENCLOSED STAIR FROM UPPER FLOORS

UPPER FLOOR

OCCUPANT LOAD 1500

1600

UPPER FLOOR

2000

SECOND FLOOR

OCCUPANT LOAD 1000 MEZZANINE

OPEN MONUMENTAL STAIR FROM MEZZANINE

STREET FLOOR 2000

STAIR DISCHARGES INTO STREET FLOOR

Figure 24-2. Mercantile Occupancy with a Mezzanine Open to the Street Floor. To determine the exit capacity for the street floor, the occupant load of the mezzanine (1,000) is added to the occupant load of the street floor (2,000). Since a unit of exit width [22 in. (55.88 cm)] can accommodate 100 people traveling horizontally, the doors on the street floor must provide 30 units of exit width (3,000 ÷ 100). In addition, since one-half of the exits from the upper floors discharge through the street floor, the exit capacity of the street floor must be able to accommodate the capacity of the stair exits discharging through it. Since a unit of exit width can accommodate 60 people traveling up or down stairs, 34 units of exit stair width would be required for the upper floors (2,000 ÷ 60 = 33⅓ or 34). However, 24-2.7 permits only one-half of the exits to discharge through the street floor. Thus, 17 units of exit width can discharge through the street floor (34 ÷ 2 = 17). Under the provisions of 24-2.3.2, 13 units of exit door width would be required on the street floor (17 ÷ 2 = 8½ × 1½ = 12¾ or 13). Thus, the street floor must have exit discharge doors which provide 43 units of exit width (13 for stairs discharging through the street floor plus 30 units for the street floor and the mezzanine).

SECTION 24-2 MEANS OF EGRESS REQUIREMENTS

24-2.1 General.

24-2.1.1 All means of egress shall be in accordance with Chapter 5 and this chapter. Only types of exits specified in 24-2.2 shall be used as required exit facilities in any mercantile occupancy.

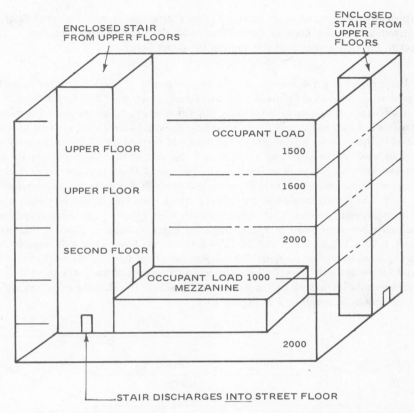

Figure 24-3. Mercantile Occupancy with a Mezzanine Not Open to the Street Floor. The street floor requires 33 units of exit width in exit discharge doors (20 for the street floor and 13 for stairs discharging through the street floor).

24-2.1.2 Where a stairway, escalator, outside stair or ramp serves two or more upper floors, the same stairway or other exit required to serve any one upper floor may also serve other upper floors.

Exception: No inside open stairway, escalator, or ramp may serve as a required egress facility from more than one floor.

As an example of 24-2.1.2, if the second and third floors of a store are each required to have three stairways, the second floor may use the stairways serving the third floor so that the total number of stairways required is three, not six.

Note the exception which prohibits the use of open stairways, escalators, or ramps as an egress facility for more than one floor.

24-2.1.3 Where there are two or more floors below the street floor, the same stairway or other exit may serve all floors (same principle as stated in 24-2.1.2 for upper floors), but all required exits from such areas shall be independent of any open stairways between the street floor and the floor below it.

24-2.1.4 Where a level outside exit from upper floors is possible owing to hills, such outside exits may serve instead of horizontal exits. If, however, such outside exits from the upper floor also serve as an entrance from a principal street, the upper floor shall be classed as a street floor in accordance with the definition in Chapter 3, and is subject to the requirements of this section for street floors.

Paragraph 24-2.1.4 reconfirms the requirements of 24-1.7.1(a) for classifying floors as street floors. Figure 24-4 illustrates a case where two street floors are at ground level at one side of a building, but either above or below ground level at the other side. As a result, these floors must have their exits arranged to allow horizontal travel to the exterior on one end of the floor and vertical travel (either up or down to ground level) at the other end of the floor. This means that the exit capacity to the exterior must be able to accommodate, in the case of Floor 1, people from the higher floors who may need to travel down to and through the exits to the exterior from Floor 1. The reverse holds true for Floor 2, which must size its exterior exit capacity to accommodate occupants who may travel up from Floor 1 as well as occupants who may have to travel down to and through the exterior exits on Floor 2. Paragraphs 5-3.1.4, 24-1.7.2, 24-2.3.2, and 26-2.3.3 demonstrate how to add exit capacity based on expected occupant use from floors above the street floor. (This method is equally valid for adding exit capacity based on expected occupant use from floors *below* the street floor.) Figure 24-5 provides an example of how to calculate exit capacity for a street floor such as Floor 2 in Figure 24-4.

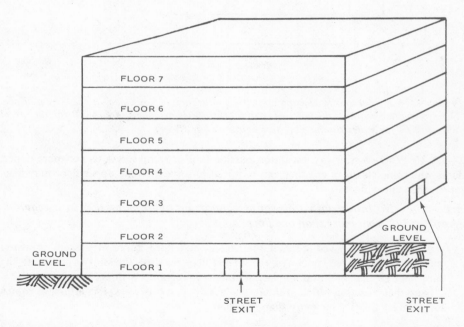

Figure 24-4. Mercantile Occupancy with Two Street Floors. The exit capacity of Floor 1 must be able to accommodate the expected population of Floors 2 through 7. The exit capacity of Floor 2 must be able to accommodate the expected population of Floors 3 through 7 plus the population of Floor 1 which may choose to exit through the second floor's street exit.

24-2.1.5 For special considerations with contents of high hazard, see 24-1.5.

24-2.2 Types of Exits.

24-2.2.1 Exits shall be restricted to the following permissible types:

(a) *Doors (see 5-2.1).*

(b) *Interior stairs (see 5-2.2).*

(c) *Smokeproof towers (see 5-2.3).*

(d) *Outside stairs (see 5-2.5).*

(e) *Horizontal exits (see 5-2.4).*

(f) *Ramps (see 5-2.6).*

(g) *Exit passageways (see 5-2.7).*

(h) *Escalators (see 5-2.8).*

(i) *Revolving doors (see 5-2.1).*

Paragraph 24-2.2.1 prohibits as required exits: fire escape stairs, slide escapes, fire escape ladders, and any other exit facility not in accordance with the applicable provisions of the *Code*.

24-2.3 Capacity of Means of Egress.

24-2.3.1 The capacity of a unit of exit width shall be as follows:

(a) Doors including those leading to outside the building at the ground level or three risers above or below the ground level — 100 persons per unit of exit width.

(b) Interior stairs, smokeproof towers, or outside stairs — 60 persons per unit of exit width.

(c) Ramps: Class A — one unit for 100 persons; Class B — one unit for 60 persons.

(d) Escalators — same as stairs if qualifying as required exits.

Note that to qualify as required exits, the escalators must be enclosed and meet the requirements of 5-2.2, Interior Stairs.

(e) Horizontal exits — 100 persons per unit of exit width.

24-2.3.2 In Class A and Class B stores, street floor exit doors or horizontal exit doors, located as required by 24-2.5 and 24-2.6, shall be sufficient to provide the following numbers of units of exit width:

(a) One unit for each 100 persons capacity of street floor, plus

(b) One and one-half units for each two units of required stairways discharging through the street floor from floors below, plus

(c) One and one-half units for each two units of required stairways discharging through the street floor, plus

(d) One and one-half units for each two units of escalator width discharging through the street floor where escalators qualify as required exits or as means of access to required exits.

(e) If ramps are used instead of stairways, street floor doors shall be provided on the same basis as for stairways, with door width appropriate to the rated discharge of ramps, per 5-2.6.

The committee, in 24-2.3.2, was attempting to provide the exit discharge for the street floor of a Class A or B store with sufficient capacity to handle the people who, in exiting the building during an emergency, must travel up from the basement sales area, down from the upper sales floors, and mix with the customers already on the first or street floor.

Since people move more quickly in the horizontal than in the vertical direction (by a factor of 4 to 3, i.e., 60 people a minute through a horizontal exit as opposed to 45 a minute down stairs; see commentary for 5-3.3), it is permissible to provide *less* door width than stair width. Thus, the *Code* requires doors of 1½ exit units for every two units of exit width provided by stairs, ramps, or escalators which discharge into the street floor. (Note that 2 to 1½ = 4 to 3.) Figure 24-5 provides an example of how to calculate the required exit capacity for the street floor.

An alternative method is to total the units of exit width for any stairs, ramps, or escalators (where the escalators conform to the requirements of 5-2.2) which discharge through the street floor. Multiply the total by ¾ and add the results to the units of exit width (at 100 people per unit) required to handle the population of the street floor. This total will provide a door capacity for the street floor which meets the requirements of 24-2.3.2.

24-2.4 Number of Exits.

24-2.4.1   In Class A and Class B stores, at least two separate exits shall be accessible from every part of every floor, including floors below the street floor.

24-2.4.2   In Class C stores, at least two separate exits shall be provided as specified by 24-2.4.1.

Exception: Where no part of the Class C store is more than 50 ft (15.24 m) from the street door, measured in accordance with 5-6.2, a single exit shall be permitted.

The *Code* allows the exception to the basic requirement that there must be at least two remote exits from an occupancy in the instance of very small Class C mercantile stores, such as tobacco shops, shoe shine stands, and newsstands. If the travel distance from any point in such a store to an exit is 50 ft (15.24 m) or less, the probability is low that a fire might surprise and overcome the customers before they could escape.

24-2.5 Arrangement of Means of Egress.

24-2.5.1   Exits shall be arranged in accordance with Section 5-5.

24-2.5.2   No dead-end corridor shall exceed 50 ft (15.24 m).

Exception: A common path of travel may be permitted for the first 50 ft (15.24 m) from any point. (See 24-1.5 if high hazard contents.)

The purpose of 24-2.5.2 is to protect against pockets or dead ends large enough to trap people in case of fire. It permits small areas such as rooms or alcoves with only one way out if the distance to an exit is short enough to minimize the likelihood that

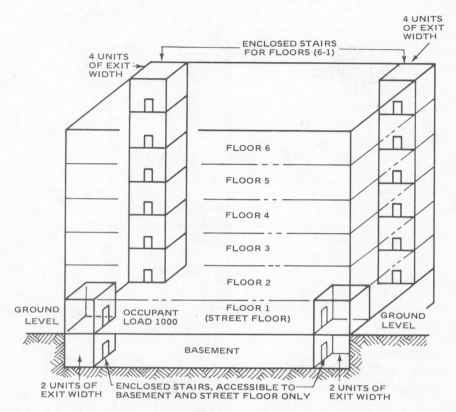

Figure 24-5. Calculation of Exit Capacity for a Class A Mercantile Occupancy Street Floor in Accordance with 24-2.3.2. Capacity for street floor: 10 units of exit width (occupant load of 1,000 ÷ 100 people per unit)
Capacity for upper floors: 6 units of exit width (8 units of stairs ÷ 2 × 1½)
Capacity for basement: 3 units of exit width (4 units of stairs ÷ 2 × 1½)
Total capacity of street floor: 19 units of exit width (10 + 6 + 3)

a fire might develop and block escape before the occupants were aware of the fire and made their way out.

24-2.5.3 The aggregate width of all aisles leading to each exit shall be equal to at least the required width of the exit.

24-2.5.4 In no case shall any aisle be less than 28 in. (71.12 cm) in clear width.

24-2.5.5 In Class A stores, at least one aisle of 5 ft (152.4 cm) minimum width shall lead directly to an exit.

The intent of 24-2.5.3 through 24-2.5.5 is to ensure that the interior arrangement of counters, racks, and displays of merchandise does not block or obscure accesses to an exit. Figure 24-6 illustrates an arrangement that meets the requirements for a Class A store. Essentially, the width of the exit determines the minimum width of the aisle, except that one of the aisles must be at least 5 ft (152.4 cm) wide.

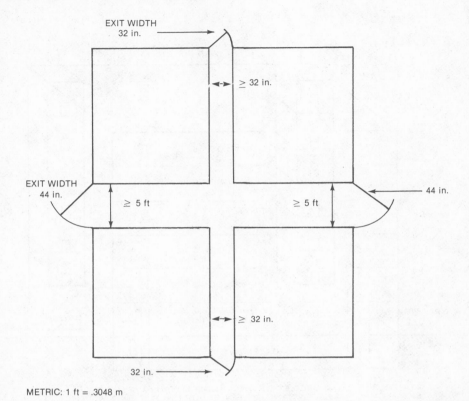

EXIT WIDTH
32 in.

≥ 32 in.

EXIT WIDTH
44 in.

≥ 5 ft

≥ 5 ft

44 in.

≥ 32 in.

32 in.

METRIC: 1 ft = .3048 m

Figure 24-6. Relation Between the Widths of Aisles and Exits in a Class A Mercantile Occupancy.

24-2.5.6   If the only means of customer entrance is through one exterior wall of the building, two-thirds of the required exit width shall be located in this wall.

   In establishing 24-2.5.6, the committee was concerned about the arrangement of many discount and variety stores which have one large main exit/entrance located in the front of the store, and the other exits (which cannot be used as entrances) situated at points unfamiliar to the public. In these cases, the main exit/entrance must be sized to handle two-thirds of the required exit capacity of the store because most of the customers will instinctively try to use this exit during a fire.

24-2.5.7   At least one-half of the required exits shall be so located as to be reached without going through check-out stands. In no case shall check-out stands or associated railings or barriers obstruct exits, required aisles or approaches thereto.

   This is the most frequently violated provision of Chapter 24. (See Figure 24-7.) Most supermarkets, discount, and variety stores are arranged so that it is necessary to pass through checkout counters, around shopping carts, and through turnstiles in order to exit from the facility. Obviously, this causes congestion or blockage during an emergency. Note that the *Code* requires at least one-half of all exits to be located so that people can avoid having to pass through or around these impediments to egress.

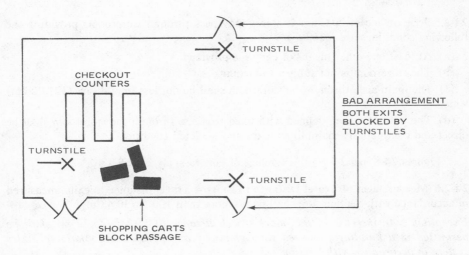

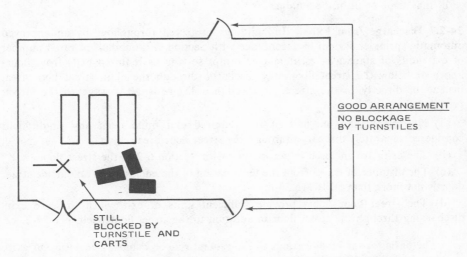

Figure 24-7. Impediments to Egress from a Mercantile Occupancy.

24-2.5.8   Where wheeled carts or buggies are used by customers, adequate provision shall be made for the transit and parking of such carts to minimize the possibility that they may obstruct means of egress.

It is the intent to provide adequate area for transit and parking of wheeled carts or buggies used by customers to eliminate the obstruction to the means of egress of the interior exit access and the exterior exit discharge. This includes corral areas adjacent to exits that are constructed to restrict the movement of wheeled carts or buggies therefrom.

24-2.5.9   Exit access in Class C stores may pass through storerooms providing the following conditions are met:

(a) At least one other means of egress is provided.

(b) The storeroom is not subject to locking.

(c) The main aisle through the storeroom shall be not less than 48 in. (121.92 cm) wide.

(d) The path of travel, defined with fixed barriers, through the storeroom shall be direct and continuously maintained in an unobstructed condition.

Figures 24-8 and 24-9 give examples of how to apply 24-2.5.9.

24-2.6 Measurement of Travel Distance to Exits.   Travel distance to exits, measured in accordance with Section 5-6, shall be no more than 100 ft (30.48 m).

Exception: An increase in the above travel distance to 150 ft (45.72 m) shall be permitted in a building protected throughout by an approved automatic sprinkler system in accordance with Section 7-7.

A review of 5-6.2 will show that the travel distance requirements apply to only the first (or nearest) exit from a point in the building. In other words, the 100-ft (30.48-m) travel distance limit means that at least one exit must be within 100 ft (30.48 m) of a point in the building, not that all exits must be within 100 ft (30.48 m) of that same point in the building.

24-2.7 Discharge from Exits.   In buildings protected throughout by an approved automatic sprinkler system in accordance with Section 7-7, one-half of rated number of exit units of stairways, escalators or ramps serving as required exits from floors above or below the street floor may discharge through the main street floor area, instead of directly to the street, or through a fire-resistive passage to the street, provided that:

(a) Not more than one-half of the required exit units from any single floor considered separately discharge through the street floor area.

(b) The exits are enclosed in accordance with Section 6-2 to the street floor.

(c) The distance of travel from the termination of the enclosure to an outside street door is not more than 50 ft (15.24 m).

(d) The street floor doors provide sufficient units of exit width to serve exits discharging through the street floor in addition to the street floor itself, per 24-2.3.2.

The basis for the modifications to the general rule on complete enclosure of exits up to their point of discharge to the outside of the building is that, with the specified safeguards, reasonable safety is maintained. Note that a limit is applied to this arrangement so that no more than 50 percent of the exits from either the entire building or from any floor can be arranged to discharge to the street floor. Further, this can only be done if the building is sprinklered throughout. Also note that the path of travel on the first floor from the stair enclosure to the outside door cannot exceed 50 ft (15.24 m). The remaining 50 percent of the exits must discharge directly to the exterior.

A stairway is not considered to discharge through the main area of the street floor if it leads to the street through a fire-resistive enclosure separating it from the main

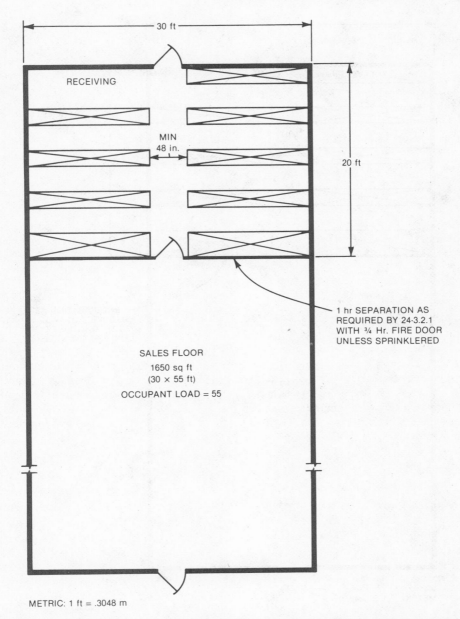

RECEIVING

MIN
48 in.

30 ft

20 ft

1 hr SEPARATION AS
REQUIRED BY 24-3.2.1
WITH ¾ Hr. FIRE DOOR
UNLESS SPRINKLERED

SALES FLOOR
1650 sq ft
(30 × 55 ft)
OCCUPANT LOAD = 55

METRIC: 1 ft = .3048 m

*Figure 24-8. Example of Exit Access Through Storeroom as Permitted by 24-2.5.9.
The aisle within the storeroom must be defined by fixed barriers, such as formed by the
ends of shelving. The aisle must be kept unobstructed.*

area, even though there are doors between the first floor stairway landing and the
main area.

The provisions of 24-2.7 should not be confused with those permitting open
stairways in 24-3.1, Exception No. 1.

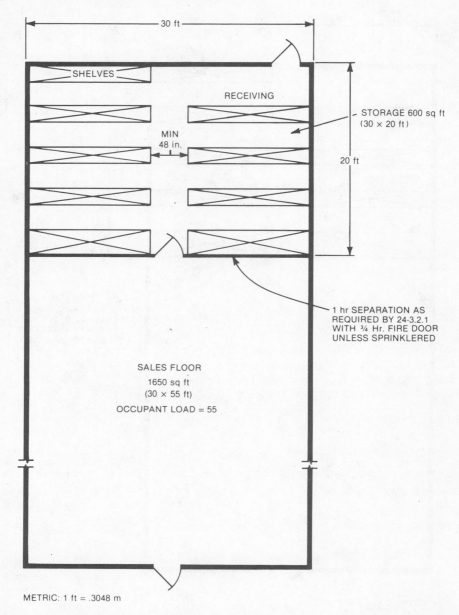

METRIC: 1 ft = .3048 m

Figure 24-9. Example of Exit Access Through Storeroom Which Will Be a Constant Problem Because of Relationship of Receiving Area.

24-2.8 Illumination of Means of Egress. Every mercantile occupancy shall have exit illumination and signs in accordance with Section 5-8.

Note that illumination for the means of egress is not the same as emergency lighting; failure of the building power supply will cause failure of the means of egress illumination system, which is not required to have a back-up, auxiliary, or secondary power supply.

24-2.9 Emergency Lighting.   Every Class A and Class B store shall have emergency lighting facilities conforming to Section 5-9.

Class C stores, due to their small size and small occupant load, are not required by the *Code* to have emergency lighting facilities.

24-2.10 Marking of Means of Egress.   Every mercantile occupancy shall have exit signs in accordance with Section 5-10.

Exception: Where an exit is immediately apparent from all portions of the sales area, the exit marking may be omitted.

The intent of the exception to the provision for marking the means of egress is to avoid requiring exit signs in small areas where the exit is readily apparent. For example, exit signs would not be required in the office of a service station, the purchase and eating areas of a small "fast food" restaurant, or in a Class C store whose size and arrangement complied with the exception to 24-2.4.2.

24-2.11 Special Features.

24-2.11.1   Every street floor door shall be in accordance with 5-2.1, and a horizontal exit door, if used, in accordance with 5-2.4.

24-2.11.2   Where revolving doors are used to provide part of the required number of units of street floor exit width, such doors shall be used in accordance with the provisions of Section 5-2.

If revolving doors are used, 5-2.1.3.2 requires adjoining swinging doors, prohibits revolving doors at the foot of stairs, and rates each revolving door at one-half unit of exit width regardless of the actual total width of the revolving door.

24-2.11.3   All doors at the foot of stairs from upper floors or at the head of stairs leading to floors below the street floor shall swing with the exit travel.

24-2.11.4   Locks in accordance with the Exception stated in 5-2.1.2.1.1 shall be permitted only on principal entrance/exit doors.

This new provision permits doors to be equipped with a key-operated lock in accordance with the provisions of Chapter 5. The term principal entrance/exit doors is intended to imply doors which the authority having jurisdiction can be reasonably assured will be unlocked in order for the facility to do business.

24-2.11.5   Special locking arrangements in accordance with 5-2.1.2.1.5 are permitted.

This permits the use of the time delay lock as provided in Chapter 5.

24-2.11.6   Where horizontal or vertical security grills or doors are used as a part of the required means of egress from a tenant space, such grills or doors shall be used in accordance with the provisions of 5-2.1.1.4.1.

24-2.11.7   Spiral stairs in accordance with 5-2.2.1.6 are permitted.

Note that 5-2.2.1.6 only permits spiral stairs to serve an occupant load of five or fewer. They may be effectively used in storage areas having a small occupant load.

SECTION 24-3   PROTECTION

24-3.1 Protection of Vertical Openings.   Each stairway, elevator shaft, escalator opening or other vertical opening shall be enclosed or protected in accordance with Section 6-2.

Exception No. 1:   As permitted in Class A stores where:

(a) Openings may be unprotected between any two floors, such as open stairs or escalators between the street floor and the floor below, or open stairs to the second floor or balconies or mezzanines above the street floor level.

(b) In stores protected throughout by an approved automatic sprinkler system in accordance with Section 7-7, openings may be unprotected both to the floor below and to the floor above the street floor, or to balconies or mezzanines above the street floor.

(c) In stores protected throughout by an approved automatic sprinkler system in accordance with Section 7-7, openings may be unprotected under the conditions permitted by 6-2.2.3.1 Exception No. 1, or between the street floor and the floor below the street floor and between the street floor and the second floor or, if no openings to the floor below the street floor, between the street floor, street floor balcony or mezzanine, and second floor, but not between more than three floor levels.

Follow the provisions of 24-1.7 on properly assessing the occupant load to develop sufficient exit capacity for a store in which floors, balconies, or mezzanines are open to the street floor. Exception No. 1 to 24-3.1 specifies under which conditions such openings are permitted in Class A stores.

Item (a) allows the floor immediately above the street floor (mezzanines in this case count as floors) or immediately below the street floor to be open to the street floor, *but not both at the same time* unless the special precautions of items (b) or (c) are taken.

Item (b) allows the floors immediately above and immediately below the street floor to be open to the street floor *at the same time* if the store is protected by a complete automatic sprinkler system installed and maintained according to NFPA 13, *Standard for the Installation of Sprinkler Systems,*[1] and NFPA 13A, *Recommended Practice for the Care and Maintenance of Sprinkler Systems.*[2]

In lieu of item (b), item (c) allows a store that is fully sprinklered to have unprotected openings between the street floor and a maximum of two floor levels above it *if there is no unprotected opening between the street floor and the floors below the street floor.* However, in either case, the precautions required by 6-2.2.3.1, Exception No. 1 must be strictly followed, especially the requirement of 6-2.2.3.1, Exception No. 1(e) that at least 50 percent of the people expected to occupy a floor (the occupant load) be able to exit without being exposed to any products of combustion from a fire on a communicating floor. Note that a mezzanine or a balcony would constitute a floor level.

Exception No. 2: As permitted in Class B stores where:

(a) Openings may be unprotected between any two floors, such as open stairs or escalators between the street floor and the floor below, or between the street floor and the mezzanine or second floor.

(b) In stores protected throughout by an approved automatic sprinkler system in accordance with Section 7-7, openings may be unprotected both to the floor below and to the floor above the street floor, or to balconies or mezzanines above the street floor.

(c) In stores protected throughout by an approved automatic sprinkler system in accordance with Section 7-7, openings may be unprotected under the conditions permitted in 6-2.2.3.1 Exception No. 1, or between the floor below the street floor and the street floor, and between the street floor and balcony or mezzanine and second floor.

The cases in which Exception No. 2 permits unprotected vertical openings in Class B stores are based on the scheme used for Class A stores. In fact, items (a), (b), and (c) contain requirements identical to those of Exception No. 1. Item (c) is phrased differently from item (c) of Exception No. 1 because the maximum height of a Class B store is three floors (used for sales). However, if the street floor, a mezzanine, and the second floor of a Class B store were connected by unenclosed stairs, openings between the street floor and the basement of the building would have to be protected.

It is important to note that neither Exception No. 1 nor Exception No. 2 to 24-3.1 intend to allow an arrangement of unprotected openings which would violate the requirement of 6-2.2.3.1 that "the lowest or the next to the lowest" level of a connected series of unprotected vertical openings be a street floor.

Exception No. 3: As permitted in Class C stores where:

(a) In any store, openings may be unprotected between the street floor and balcony.

Exception No. 3 to 24-3.1 recognizes the limited size and probable small population of Class C stores. For these reasons, any Class C store may have unprotected openings to a mezzanine or balcony.

24-3.2 Protection from Hazards.

24-3.2.1 An area used for general storage, boiler or furnace rooms, fuel storage, janitor closets, maintenance shops including woodworking and painting areas, and kitchens shall be separated from other parts of the building by an assembly(ies) having a fire resistance rating of not less than 1 hour, and all openings shall be protected with self-closing fire doors.

Exception: Areas protected by an automatic extinguishing system.

24-3.2.2 Areas with high hazard contents as defined in Section 4-2 shall be provided with both fire-resistive separation and automatic sprinkler protection.

Paragraphs 24-3.2.1 and 24-3.2.2 reflect the intent of Section 6-4 which requires separation of a hazardous area from the rest of a building by suitable construction, or mandates the installation of an automatic extinguishing system in the hazardous area.

24-3.3 Interior Finish.

24-3.3.1 Interior finish on walls and ceilings shall be Class A or B, in accordance with Section 6-5.

Exception: In any mercantile occupancy, exposed portions of structural members complying with the requirements for heavy timber construction may be permitted. Laminated wood shall not delaminate under the influence of heat.

24-3.3.2 Interior Floor Finish. No requirements.

The committee limited the use of exposed heavy timber construction to *only the structural members of a building*, such as columns, beams, girders, or trusses. Panels between supporting columns and wall surfaces *may not* be of exposed heavy timber construction. These panels or wall surfaces must be sheathed with Class A or B interior finish material. Heavy timber construction is discussed in NFPA 220, *Standard Types of Building Construction*,[3] and the NFPA *Fire Protection Handbook*.[4]

24-3.4 Alarm Systems. Class A and Class B stores shall be provided with a manual fire alarm system in accordance with Section 7-6.

Exception No. 1: Buildings protected throughout by an approved automatic fire detection and alarm initiation system in accordance with Section 7-6.

Exception No. 2: Buildings protected throughout by an approved automatic sprinkler system in accordance with Section 7-7 which provides alarm initiation in accordance with Section 7-6.

The intent of the exceptions to 24-3.4 is to eliminate the manual pull stations, but retain the alerting function of the alarm system.

24-3.5 Extinguishment Requirements. Approved automatic sprinkler protection shall be installed in accordance with Section 7-7 in all mercantile occupancies as follows:

(a) In all buildings with a story over 15,000 sq ft (1,394 sq m) in area.

(b) In all buildings exceeding 30,000 sq ft (2,787 sq m) in gross area.

(c) Throughout stories below the level of exit discharge when such stories have an area exceeding 2,500 sq ft (232 sq m) when used for the sale, storage, or handling of combustible goods and merchandise.

For discussions of what constitutes an "approved automatic sprinkler protection system," see NFPA 13, *Standard for the Installation of Sprinkler Systems*,[1] NFPA 13A, *Recommended Practice for the Care and Maintenance of Sprinkler Systems*,[2] and *Automatic Sprinkler and Standpipe Systems*.[5]

Under the provisions of item (a), a store with a total gross area of less than 30,000 sq ft (2,787 sq m) (Class B or C), but with any one floor greater than 15,000 sq ft (1,394 sq m) in area would have to be protected with a complete automatic sprinkler system. A store with a total gross area of less than 30,000 sq ft (2,787 sq m) would not be required to be sprinklered, as long as the area of any floor did not exceed 15,000 sq ft (1,394 sq m).

The intent of item (b) is to require that all stores with a total gross area greater than 30,000 sq ft (2,787 sq m) be protected with a complete automatic sprinkler system.

The committee developed item (c) to ensure that all basement areas larger than 2,500 sq ft (232 sq m) (whether the space is used for sales, storage, or the handling of combustible merchandise) be sprinklered to avoid the potential threat to the occupants of the street floor and to fire fighters. Studies have shown that there is a higher rate of fire incidence in basements than in other areas of stores. Because smoke and heat rise, a fire in a basement can quickly cause exits and exit discharges located on the street floor to be unusable.

24-3.6 Corridors. No special requirements.

The provisions of 5-1.3.4 apply if corridors are present.

24-3.7 Subdivision of Building Spaces. No special requirements.

24-3.8 Special Features.

SECTION 24-4 SPECIAL PROVISIONS

24-4.1 Windowless or Underground Buildings. (*See Section 30-7.*)

24-4.2 Open-Air Mercantile Operations.

24-4.2.1 Open-air mercantile operations, such as open-air markets, gasoline filling stations, roadside stands for the sale of farm produce, and other outdoor mercantile operations shall be so arranged and conducted as to maintain free and unobstructed ways of travel at all times to permit prompt escape from any point of danger in case of fire or other emergency, with no dead ends in which persons might be trapped due to display stands, adjoining buildings, fences, vehicles, or other obstructions.

Paragraph 24-4.2.1 is virtually an open-ended provision which provides guidance for the arrangement, use, and display of merchandise for sales in open-air mercantile operations. The phrase "ways of travel" is purposely used by the committee to avoid confusion with "means of egress" which is strictly defined and whose use implies the minimum requirements of Chapter 5. "Ways of travel" is not defined and implies no specific minimum *Code* provisions. Most open-air mercantile operations have unlimited ways for entering and evacuating the areas used to display goods. For this reason, the committee did not find it necessary to provide specific *Code* requirements beyond the precautionary measures expressed in this paragraph.

24-4.2.2 If mercantile operations are conducted in roof-over areas, they shall be treated as mercantile buildings, provided that canopies over individual small stands to protect merchandise from the weather shall not be construed to constitute buildings for the purpose of this *Code*.

The intent of 24-4.2.2 is to exempt small merchandise stands with canopies from being classed as mercantile occupancies. All other "roofed-over" areas should be treated as buildings, classified by area and height as Class A, B, or C, and subject to the appropriate provisions of Chapter 24.

24-4.3 Covered Malls. The purpose of this section is to establish minimum standards of life safety for covered malls having not more than three levels.

24-4.3.1 The covered mall and all buildings connected thereto shall be treated as a single building for the purposes of calculation of means of egress and shall be subject to the requirements for appropriate occupancies. The covered mall shall be at least of sufficient clear width to accommodate egress requirements as set forth in other sections of this *Code.*

Exception: The covered mall may be considered to be a pedestrian way, in which case the distance of travel within a tenant space to an exit or to the covered mall shall be a maximum of 150 ft (45.72 m) (see Exception to 24-2.6), or shall be the maximum for the appropriate occupancy; plus an additional 200 ft (60.96 m) shall be permitted for travel through the covered mall space if all the following requirements are met:

(a) The covered mall shall be at least of sufficient clear width to accommodate egress requirements as set forth in other sections of this chapter, but in no case less than 20 ft (609.6 cm) wide in its narrowest dimension.

(b) The covered mall shall be provided with an unobstructed exit access on each side of the mall floor area of not less than 10 ft (304.8 cm) in clear width parallel to and adjacent to the mall tenant front. Such exit access shall lead to an exit having a minimum of three units of exit width. (See 24-4.3.2.)

(c) The covered mall and all buildings connected thereto shall be protected throughout by an approved electrically supervised automatic sprinkler system in accordance with Section 7-7.

(d) Walls dividing stores from each other shall extend from the floor to the underside of the roof deck or floor deck above. No separation is required between a tenant space and the covered mall.

(e) The covered mall shall be provided with a smoke control system.

In recent years, covered mall shopping areas have increased in both number and size. The committee developed two options or approaches for dealing with the life safety aspects of these complexes. The first approach (described in 24-4.3.1) considers the mall and the attached stores as essentially one large Class A store subject to all the provisions of Chapter 24. In this view, the covered mall would be treated as an aisle of a store.

The other approach, new in the 1976 Edition of the *Life Safety Code* and essentially unchanged in this 1981 Edition, permits the mall to be considered as a "pedestrian way" by which occupants of the attached stores may egress during a fire. The phrase "pedestrian way" was chosen by the committee both to convey the meaning of the term "exit access" and to allow the mall to be treated as if it were an area of refuge.

The exception to 24-4.3.1 reflects the committee's recognition that if the mall and all the buildings attached to the mall were protected by automatic sprinklers, people fleeing into the mall from a fire in a store would have moved into a space whose volume, size, and arrangement afforded most of the benefits provided by an enclosed stair or a horizontal exit. The exception considers the mall as being virtually an area of refuge for the buildings attached to it even though the mall is not separated from these attached buildings by the type of construction normally provided for an exit as required by 5-1.2.3.

When considering a covered mall as a pedestrian way, the maximum travel distance to an exit or to the mall from any point within a store attached to the mall is 150 ft (45.72 m). This reflects the committee's estimation that using the mall for egress is as acceptable (or as safe) as using an exit. An additional travel distance of up to 200 ft (60.96 m) is permitted within the mall [in addition to the 150 ft (45.72 m) already allowed] if the following conditions are met:

1. The mall and all buildings attached to it must be sprinklered. Note that if the shopping complex were considered as one building, sprinkler protection would almost always be required under the 30,000-sq ft (2,787-sq m) gross area criterion of 24-3.5(b).

2. The clear width of the mall must be at least 20 ft (609.6 cm), wider if the required exit capacity demands it. Note that when considering the covered mall of a shopping center as a pedestrian way, no occupant load is calculated for the mall. The required capacity of the means of egress is calculated on the basis of aggregate gross area of the attached stores, excluding anchor stores.

3. At least 10 ft (304.8 cm) of clear unobstructed space must be available for exit access in front of, adjacent to, and parallel to all store fronts. This requirement is designed to prohibit displays of merchandise, kiosks, or small sales stands from being placed within 10 ft (304.8 cm) of the store fronts and, if enforced, will ensure that the mall will have a minimum clear width of 20 ft (609.6 cm).

4. Each exit access must terminate at an exit whose capacity is a minimum of three units of exit width [66 in. (167.64 cm)]. This requirement is related to 24-2.5.5, which mandates that at least one aisle leading to an exit in a Class A store have a minimum clear width of 5 ft (152.4 cm).

5. Walls separating stores must run continuously from the floor slab to the roof slab (but not necessarily through the roof). The store front need not be separated by construction from the mall.

6. The mall must have a smoke control system. Since the individual stores are open to the mall, this requirement is essential if the mall is to be used as a safe means of egress. Smoke control systems for covered malls are necessary to maintain the mall reasonably free of products of combustion for at least the duration required to evacuate the building and to minimize migration of products of combustion from one tenant to another. Systems that can be engineered to accomplish this include: (a) separate mechanical exhaust or control systems, (b) mechanical exhaust or control systems in conjunction with the heating, ventilating, and air conditioning systems, (c) automatically or manually released gravity roof vent devices such as skylights, relief dampers, or smoke vents, (d) combinations of (a), (b), and (c), or any other engineered system designed to accomplish the purpose of this section.

If these six conditions are not met, the mall may still be considered a "pedestrian way," but the additional travel distance to an exit would not be allowed. In other words, for each store there would be a limit of 100 ft (30.48 m) of travel distance [150 ft (45.72 m) if the store and mall were sprinklered] from a point in the store through the mall to an exit to the exterior. In the majority of configurations, this restriction would preclude the use of the mall as an exit access.

The *Fire Protection Handbook*[6] contains a comprehensive discussion of the hazards to life safety specific to covered mall shopping centers.

24-4.3.2 Exit Details.

24-4.3.2.1 Every floor of a covered mall shall have no less than two exits located remote from each other.

Paragraph 24-5.4.3.1 reaffirms the fundamental *Code* requirement of always providing at least two ways out.

24-4.3.2.2   No less than one-half the required exit widths for each Class A or Class B store connected to a covered mall shall lead directly outside without passage through the mall.

Note that the larger stores (Class A and B) must still have 50 percent of their exits arranged to be independent of the mall.

24-4.3.2.3   Each individual anchor store shall have means of egress independent of the covered mall.

It is not the intent of this paragraph to require that large stores be considered anchor stores. A store not considered in determining the occupant load of the mall must be arranged so that all of its means of egress will be independent of the covered mall.

24-4.3.2.4   Every covered mall shall be provided with unobstructed exit access, parallel to and adjacent to the connected buildings. This exit access shall extend to each mall exit.

Paragraph 24-4.3.2.4 reiterates the provisions of item (b) of the exception to 24-4.3.1 without mentioning that the exit access must have a clear width of at least 10 ft (304.8 cm).

24-4.4 Atriums.

24-4.4.1   Atriums are permitted provided they comply with Section 6-2 and 24-4.4.2 through 24-4.4.6.

24-4.4.2   The occupancy within the atrium meets the specifications for classification as low hazard contents. (*See 4-2.2.2.*)

Note that this is more restrictive than 6-2.2.3.1, Exception No. 2(c).

24-4.4.3   The automatic sprinkler system required by 6-2.2.3.1 Exception No. 2(e) shall be electrically supervised.

24-4.4.4   The atrium is provided with an automatic ventilation system operated by all of the following:

(a) Approved smoke detectors located at the top of the space and adjacent to each return air intake from the atrium, and

(b) The required automatic fire extinguishing system, and

(c) Manual controls which are readily accessible to the fire department.

The intent of 24-4.4.4 is to require a smoke control system as noted in 6-2.2.3.1(f) and to modify the provisions of 6-2.2.3.1(g) to *not* permit the manual alarm to activate the smoke control system. Note that 24-4.4.5 does not require manual pull stations.

The reason for not permitting the manual alarm to activate the system is the possibility of persons pulling a manual alarm on other than the fire floor, thus possibly causing the smoke control system to improperly function.

24-4.4.5 Fire Alarm System. A fire alarm system shall be provided for the building in accordance with Section 7-6.

(a) The initiation of the fire alarm shall be by the activation of any smoke detector or the automatic sprinkler system.

(b) Manual pull stations are not required.

24-4.4.6 All electrical equipment essential for smoke control or automatic extinguishing equipment for buildings more than six stories or 75 ft (22.86 m) in height containing an atrium shall be provided with an emergency source of power in accordance with *National Electrical Code*, NFPA 70, Section 700-12(b), or equivalent.

Note that emergency power complying with Section 700-12(b) of NFPA 70, *National Electrical Code*,[7] requires a generator set.

SECTION 24-5 BUILDING SERVICES

24-5.1 Utilities shall comply with the provisions of Section 7-1.

24-5.2 Heating, ventilating and air conditioning equipment shall comply with the provision of Section 7-2.

24-5.3 Elevators, dumbwaiters and vertical conveyors shall comply with the provisions of Section 7-4.

24-5.4 Rubbish chutes, incinerators and laundry chutes shall comply with the provisions of Section 7-5.

REFERENCES CITED BY *CODE*

(This publication comprises a part of the requirements to the extent called for by the Code.)

NFPA 70, *National Electrical Code*, NFPA, Boston, 1981.

REFERENCES CITED IN COMMENTARY

[1]NFPA 13, *Standard for the Installation of Sprinkler Systems*, NFPA, Boston, 1980.

[2]NFPA 13A, *Recommended Practice for the Care and Maintenance of Sprinkler Systems*, NFPA, 1978.

[3]NFPA 220, *Standard Types of Building Construction*, NFPA, Boston, 1979.

[4]*Fire Protection Handbook*, 14th ed., NFPA, Boston, 1976, pp. 6-39 to 6-41.

[5]John L. Bryan, *Automatic Sprinkler and Standpipe Systems*, NFPA, Boston, 1976.

[6]*Fire Protection Handbook*, 14th ed., NFPA, Boston, 1976, pp. 8-31 to 8-36.

[7]NFPA 70, *National Electrical Code*, NFPA, Boston, 1981.

25

EXISTING MERCANTILE OCCUPANCIES

(See also Chapter 31.)

Mercantile occupancies include stores, markets, and other rooms, buildings, or structures for the display and sale of merchandise. Included in this occupancy group are:

Supermarkets

Department stores

Drugstores

Auction rooms

Shopping centers

Minor merchandising operations in buildings predominantly of other occupancies, such as a newsstand in an office building, must meet the exit requirements of the predominant occupancy.

SECTION 25-1   GENERAL REQUIREMENTS

25-1.1 Application.

25-1.1.1   Existing mercantile occupancies shall comply with the provisions of Chapter 25 (*see Chapter 31 for operating features*).

In understanding the full intent and scope of 25-1.1.1, it is necessary to review it concurrently with Sections 1-4, 1-5, and 1-6. While a building code may exclude existing buildings from coverage under some form of a "grandfather" clause, the *Life Safety Code*, because of its very interest in life safety, does not forgive existing non-*Code*-complying building arrangements except under a very narrow and strict set of guidelines. These guidelines are contained in this chapter.

25-1.1.2   This chapter establishes life safety requirements for existing buildings. Specific requirements for sub-occupancy groups such as Class A, B and C stores and covered malls are contained in paragraphs pertaining thereto.

25-1.1.3 Modernization or Renovation.   No construction in either modernization or renovation projects shall diminish the fire safety features of the building below the level of new construction as described elsewhere in this *Code*. Alterations or installations of new building services equipment shall be accomplished as nearly as possible in conformance with the requirements for new construction. (*See Section 1-5 for equivalency concepts.*)

25-1.1.4 Additions to existing buildings shall conform to the requirements for new construction. Existing portions of the structure need not be modified, provided that the new construction has not diminished the fire safety features of the facility.

Exception: Existing portions must be upgraded if the addition results in a change of mercantile classification.

> Paragraph 25-1.1.4 and its exception are intended to indicate that additions to existing mercantile occupancies must conform to the requirements for new occupancies, while the existing portion of the occupancy may continue in use as long as it complies with the provisions for existing mercantile occupancies contained in this chapter. If, however, the addition results in the mercantile occupancy changing classifications, such as moving from a Class C mercantile to a Class B mercantile, then the existing occupancy must also be upgraded to meet the provisions for new occupancies.

25-1.2 Mixed Occupancies.

25-1.2.1 Combined Mercantile and Residential Occupancies.

25-1.2.1.1 No dwelling unit shall have its sole means of egress through any mercantile occupancy in the same building.

25-1.2.1.2 No multiple dwelling occupancy shall be located above a mercantile occupancy.

Exception No. 1: Where the dwelling occupancy and exits therefrom are separated from the mercantile occupancy by construction having a fire resistance of at least 1 hour.

Exception No. 2: Where the mercantile occupancy is protected by automatic sprinklers in accordance with Section 7-7.

Exception No. 3: As permitted in 25-1.2.1.3.

25-1.2.1.3 A building with not more than two dwelling units above a mercantile occupancy shall be permitted provided that the mercantile occupancy is protected by an automatic fire detection system in accordance with Section 7-6.

> The requirements for mixed occupancies were developed by the subcommittee on mercantile and business occupancies to deal with a then common (but now slowly disappearing) occupancy, the corner tavern, grocery store, or retail store which had a dwelling occupancy on the upper floors. The committee divided this type of combined occupancy into two classes.
>
> Where there is a single dwelling occupancy above the mercantile operation, the *Code* prohibits (see 25-1.2.1.1) the dwelling occupancy from having its sole means of egress through the mercantile occupancy in the same building. If the dwelling occupancy has an exit through the mercantile occupancy, it must have a second exit that is *independent of* and does not travel through the mercantile occupancy.

The *Code* prohibits a multiple dwelling occupancy above a mercantile occupancy unless one of the following conditions is met:

1. The dwellings and their exits are separated from the mercantile occupancy by construction with a fire resistance of 1 hour.
2. The mercantile occupancy is protected by an automatic sprinkler system. See Section 6-4 of the *Code*, NFPA 13, *Standard for the Installation of Sprinkler Systems*,[1] and 13A, *Recommended Practice for the Care and Maintenance of Sprinkler Systems*.[2]
3. There are no more than two dwelling occupancies and the entire building is protected by an automatic fire detection system which must be capable of sounding an alarm in the dwelling occupancies as required by Sections 2-7 and 7-6.

The committee established these requirements because of the long historical record of many deaths and injuries where fire originated in mercantile occupancies and spread to unsuspecting families occupying dwelling units above the mercantile occupancy.

25-1.3 Special Definitions.

(a) **Class A Stores.**   See 25-1.4.2.1(a).

(b) **Class B Stores.**   See 25-1.4.2.1(b).

(c) **Class C Stores.**   See 25-1.4.2.1(c).

(d) **Covered Mall.**   A covered or roofed interior area used as a pedestrian way and connecting building(s) or portions of a building housing single and/or multiple tenants.

(e) **Open-Air Mercantile Operations.**   Operations conducted outside of all structures with the operations area devoid of all walls and roofs except for small individual weather canopies.

(f) **Gross Leasable Area.**   The total floor area designated for tenant occupancy and exclusive use, expressed in square feet, measured from centerlines of joining partitions and exteriors of outside walls.

(g) **Anchor Store.**   A department store or major merchandising center having direct access to the covered mall but having all required means of egress independent of the covered mall.

25-1.4 Classification of Occupancy.

25-1.4.1   Mercantile occupancies shall include all buildings and structures or parts thereof with occupancy as described in 4-1.7.

It is important to review again the *Code*'s definition (see 4-1.7) of what constitutes a mercantile occupancy. Note that this definition *does not include* "minor merchandising operations in buildings predominantly of other occupancies, such as a newsstand in an office building..." Paragraph 4-1.7 requires that such occupancies be subject to the exit requirements of the predominant (major) occupancy.

25-1.4.2 Subclassification of Occupancy.

25-1.4.2.1   Mercantile occupancies shall be classified as follows:

(a) *Class A.*   All stores having aggregate gross area of 30,000 sq ft (2,787 sq m) or more, or utilizing more than three floor levels for sales purposes.

(b) *Class B.*   All stores of less than 30,000 sq ft (2,787 sq m) aggregate gross area, but over 3,000 sq ft (279 sq m), or utilizing any balconies, mezzanines (*see 25-1.4.2.3*), or floors above or below the street floor level for sales purposes.

Exception: If more than three floors are utilized, the store shall be Class A, regardless of area.

(c) *Class C.*   All stores of 3,000 sq ft (279 sq m) or less gross area used for sales purposes on the street floor only. (*Balcony permitted, see 25-1.4.2.3.*)

The following table summarizes the requirements of 25-1.4.2.1 for qualifying a store as Class A, B, or C. This classification process is important because it leads to specific life safety criteria which apply to each class of store. The criteria vary in degree of stringency dependent upon a store's classification.

Table 25–1. Subclassification of Mercantile Occupancies

Store Class	By Height		By Aggregate Gross Area† (sq ft)
A	>3 Floors‡	or	≥30,000
B	≤3 Floors‡	and	>3,000 and <30,000
C	Street Floor Only§	and	≤3,000

†Sections of floors not used for sales are not counted in the area classification.
‡Floors not used for sales above or below a sales floor are not counted in the height classification.
§A balcony or mezzanine < ½ the area of the sales floor is permitted.

25-1.4.2.2   For the purpose of the classification in 25-1.4.2.1, the aggregate gross area shall be the total gross area of all floors, used for mercantile purposes and, where a store is divided into sections, regardless of fire separation, shall include the area of all sections used for sales purposes. Areas of floors not used for sales purposes, such as an area used only for storage and not open to the public, shall not be counted for the purposes of the above classifications, but exits shall be provided for such nonsales areas in accordance with their occupancy, as specified by other chapters of this *Code.*

25-1.4.2.3   A balcony or mezzanine floor having an area less than one-half of the floor below shall not be counted as a floor level for the purpose of applying the classification of 25-1.4.2.1, but if there are two balcony or mezzanine floors, one shall be counted.

Although 25-1.4.2.3 allows the omission of one balcony from the count of the number of floor levels, this does not waive any of the exit requirements applying to balconies.

25-1.4.2.4   Where a number of stores under different management are located in the same building or in adjoining buildings with no fire wall or other standard fire separations between, the aggregate gross area of all such stores shall be used in determining classification per 25-1.4.2.1.

Exception: Covered malls (see 25-4.3).

Paragraphs 25-1.4.2.2 through 25-1.4.2.4 further clarify the classification of stores as Class A, B, or C. Most of these provisions are included in the footnotes to Table 25-1. The following should be noted for emphasis:

1. The aggregate gross area is the sum of the gross areas of all floors used for mercantile (sales) purposes.
2. If the store is divided into sections by fire walls, *only the sales sections* should be included in the aggregate gross area.
3. If there are sections or floors used for sales that are considered as separate "stores" (because they are under different management), with no separation (fire walls or fire barriers) between each "store," the aggregate gross area of all such "stores" is to be used in classifying the occupancy as Class A, B, or C, except as provided for covered malls. (See 25-4.3.)

25-1.5 Classification of Hazard of Contents.   Mercantile occupancies contents shall be classed as ordinary hazard in accordance with Section 4-2.

Exception: Mercantile occupancies shall be classified as high hazard if high hazard commodities are displayed or handled without protective wrappings or containers, in which case the following additional provisions shall apply:

(a) Exits shall be located so that not more than 75 ft (22.86 m) of travel from any point is required to reach the nearest exit.

(b) From every point there shall be at least two exits accessible by travel in different directions (no common path of travel).

(c) All vertical openings shall be enclosed.

Some procedures which would require classifying a mercantile occupancy as highly hazardous are: displaying unwrapped articles fabricated from thin sheets of pyroxylin plastic such as artificial flowers or toys; dispensing gunpowder or other explosives in bulk; sales of polyurethane foam; or dispensing gasoline or flammable solvents by pouring them into open containers. Figure 25-1 illustrates an arrangement of exits from a highly hazardous area in a mercantile occupancy.

25-1.6 Minimum Construction Requirements.   No special requirements.

The phrase "minimum construction" is used in the *Code* to describe the construction of the building housing the occupancy. Since there are no special requirements, the provisions of the local building code would apply.

25-1.7 Occupant Load.

25-1.7.1   For purposes of determining required exits, the occupant load of mercantile buildings or parts of buildings used for mercantile purposes shall be not less than the following:

(a) Street floor, one person for each 30 sq ft (2.79 sq m) gross floor area of sales space. In stores with no street floor as defined in Chapter 3, but with access directly from the street by stairs or escalators, the principal floor at the point of entrance to the store shall be considered the street floor. In stores where, due to differences in grade of streets on different sides, there are two or more floors directly accessible from streets (not including alleys or similar back streets), each such floor shall be considered a street floor for the purpose of determining occupant load.

(b) Sales floors below the street floor — same as street floor.

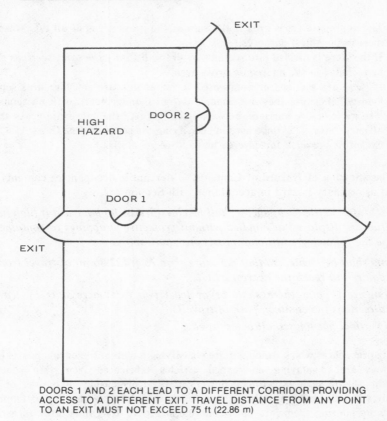

DOORS 1 AND 2 EACH LEAD TO A DIFFERENT CORRIDOR PROVIDING
ACCESS TO A DIFFERENT EXIT. TRAVEL DISTANCE FROM ANY POINT
TO AN EXIT MUST NOT EXCEED 75 ft (22.86 m)

*Figure 25-1. Exit Arrangement from an Area of a Mercantile Occupancy Defined as
Highly Hazardous by 25-1.5.*

(c) Upper floors, used for sales — one person for each 60 sq ft (5.57 sq m) gross
floor area of sales space.

(d) Floors or portions of floors used only for offices — one person for each 100 sq ft
(9.29 sq m) gross floor area of office space.

(e) Floors or portions of floors used only for storage, receiving, shipping and not
open to the general public — one person per each 300 sq ft (27.87 sq m) gross area of
storage, receiving, or shipping space.

(f) Floors or portions of floors used for assembly purposes — occupant load
determined in accordance with Chapter 9 for such places of assembly.

(g) Mall buildings — one person for each 30 sq ft (2.79 sq m) gross floor area for
street level and below, and one person for each 60 sq ft (5.57 sq m) gross floor area for
upper floors.

*Exception: The covered mall, when considered a pedestrian way (see Exception to
25-4.3.1), shall not be assessed an occupant load. However, means of egress from the
mall shall be provided for an occupant load determined by dividing the gross leasable
area (not including anchor stores) by the appropriate occupant load factor listed
in the following chart:*

Gross Leasable Area [See 25-1.3(f).] *(sq ft)*	*Occupant* *Load* *Factor*
Less than 150,000 (13,935 sq m)	*30*
Over 150,000 (13,935 sq m) but less than 200,000 (18,580 sq m)	*35*
Over 200,000 (18,580 sq m) but less than 250,000 (23,225 sq m)	*40*
Over 250,000 (23,225 sq m) but less than 300,000 (27,870 sq m)	*45*
Over 300,000 (27,870 sq m) but less than 400,000 (37,160 sq m)	*50*
Over 400,000 (37,160 sq m)	*55*

Each individual tenant space shall have means of egress to the outside and/or to the mall based on occupant loads figured utilizing 25-1.7.1 (a) through (f).

Each individual anchor store shall have means of egress independent of the covered mall.

The occupant load factors given in 25-1.7.1 to calculate the occupant load were established on the basis of population counts of typical stores during periods of maximum occupancy, such as before Christmas or during special sales. The values show that during normal use of a mercantile occupancy the public will congregate, for the most part, on the street floor or in a basement "sales" area. In some cases, an individual store may be more densely populated than these figures indicate, but it may be reasonably assumed that, in any large mercantile building, all areas will not be crowded at the same time and the average occupant load will seldom exceed these figures.

In some types of stores, the occupant load will normally be much less than indicated, e.g., in furniture stores. However, the character of mercantile operations is subject to such rapid change that it is not prudent in designing exit facilities to assume that any store will never be crowded, and for this reason the same figures are used to calculate the occupant load for all types of stores.

In differentiating between street floors and other sales floors, the street floor is *any* floor which has an entrance/exit directly accessible from the street. If differences in the ground level on different sides of a store create several floors of this nature, the *Code* treats them *all* as street floors. It is important to note that, if access to a store from the street is only by stairs or escalators, the principal floor at the point of entrance to the store must be considered the street floor. The *Code* is recognizing merchandising techniques in assigning a higher occupant load to the street floor since these floors have the merchandise conducive to high traffic and thus larger numbers of occupants.

The table used in determining the occupancy load for covered mall shopping centers of varying sizes is arrived at empirically in surveying over 270 covered mall shopping centers, in the study of mercantile occupancy parking requirements, and the observed number of occupants per vehicle during peak seasons.

These studies show that with increasing shopping center size there is a decrease in the number of occupants per square foot of gross leasable area.

This phenomenon is explained when one considers that above a certain shopping center gross leasable area [approx. 600,000 sq ft (55 740 sq m)], a multiplicity of the same types of stores starts to occur: the purpose being to increase the choices available to a customer for any given type of merchandise. Therefore, with increasing shopping center size, the occupant load increases as well, but at a declining rate. In using the table, the occupant load factor is applied to only the gross leasable area utilizing the covered mall as a means of egress.

25-1.7.2 In case of mezzanines or balconies open to the floor below or other unprotected vertical openings between floors as permitted by the Exceptions to 25-3.1 the occupant load (or area) of the mezzanine or other subsidiary floor level shall be added to that of the street floor for the purpose of determining required exits, provided, however, that in no case shall the total number of exit units be less than would be required if all vertical openings were enclosed.

Figures 25-2 and 25-3 illustrate the requirements of 25-1.7.2. Figure 25-2 shows the case where a mezzanine (or balcony) is open to the street floor (which by the definition in Chapter 3 contains the main exit to the exterior or public way). The exits from the street floor must accommodate the people expected to be occupying the street floor, the mezzanine, and the capacity of the stairs from the upper floors discharging through the street floor.

In Figure 25-3, when the mezzanine is not open to the street floor, the capacity of the exits on the street floor must be able to accommodate the people expected to occupy the street floor and the capacity of the stairs from the upper floors discharging through the street floor. The enforcing official should note that the calculations required for the arrangement in Figure 25-3 will establish the *minimum* units of exit width which the *Code* will allow when exits from upper floors discharge into a street floor, whether or not the mezzanine is open to the street floor.

SECTION 25-2   MEANS OF EGRESS REQUIREMENTS

25-2.1 General.

25-2.1.1   All means of egress shall be in accordance with Chapter 5 and this chapter. Only types of exits specified in 25-2.2 shall be used as required exit facilities in any mercantile occupancy.

25-2.1.2   Where a stairway, escalator, outside stair, or ramp serves two or more upper floors, the same stairway or other exit required to serve any one upper floor may also serve other upper floors.

Exception: No inside open stairway, escalator, or ramp may serve as a required egress facility from more than one floor.

As an example of 25-2.1.2, if the second and third floors of a store are each required to have three stairways, the second floor may use the stairways serving the third floor so that the total number of stairways required is three, not six.

Note the exception which prohibits the use of open stairways, escalators, or ramps as an egress facility for more than one floor.

25-2.1.3   Where there are two or more floors below the street floor, the same stairway or other exit may serve all floors (same principle as stated in 25-2.1.2 for upper floors), but all required exits from such areas shall be independent of any open stairways between the street floor and the floor below it.

25-2.1.4   Where a level outside exit from upper floors is possible owing to hills, such outside exits may serve instead of horizontal exits. If, however, such outside exits from the upper floor also serve as an entrance from a principal street, the upper floor shall be classed as a street floor in accordance with the definition of Chapter 3, and is subject to the requirements of this section for street floors.

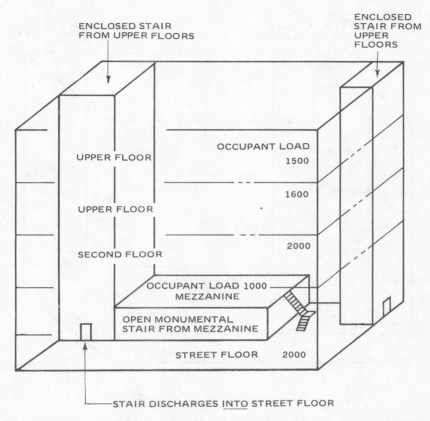

ENCLOSED STAIR
FROM UPPER FLOORS

ENCLOSED
STAIR FROM
UPPER
FLOORS

UPPER FLOOR

OCCUPANT LOAD
1500

1600

UPPER FLOOR

2000

SECOND FLOOR

OCCUPANT LOAD 1000
MEZZANINE

OPEN MONUMENTAL
STAIR FROM MEZZANINE

STREET FLOOR   2000

STAIR DISCHARGES INTO STREET FLOOR

Figure 25-2. Mercantile Occupancy with a Mezzanine Open to the Street Floor. To determine the exit capacity for the street floor, the occupant load of the mezzanine (1,000) is added to the occupant load of the street floor (2,000). Since a unit of exit width [22 in. (55.88 cm)] can accommodate 100 people traveling horizontally, the doors on the street floor must provide 30 units of exit width (3,000 ÷ 100). In addition, since one-half of the exits from the upper floors discharge through the street floor, the exit capacity of the street floor must be able to accommodate the capacity of the stair exits discharging through it. Since a unit of exit width can accommodate 60 people traveling up or down stairs, 34 units of exit stair width would be required for the upper floors (2,000 ÷ 60 = 33⅓ or 34). However, 25-2.7 permits only one-half of the exits to discharge through the street floor. Thus, 17 units of exit width can discharge through the street floor (34 ÷ 2 = 17). Under the provisions of 25-2.3.2, 13 units of exit door width would be required on the street floor (17 ÷ 2 = 8½ × 1½ = 12¾ or 13). Thus, the street floor must have exit discharge doors which provide 43 units of exit width (13 for stairs discharging through the street floor plus 30 units for the street floor and the mezzanine).

Paragraph 25-2.1.4 reconfirms the requirements of 25-1.7.1(a) for classifying floors as street floors. **Figure 25-4** illustrates a case where two street floors are at ground level at one side of a building, but either above or below ground level at the other side. As a result, these floors must have their exits arranged to allow horizontal travel to the exterior on one end of the floor and vertical travel (either up or down to ground level) at the other end of the floor. This means that the exit capacity to the exterior must be able to accommodate, in the case of Floor 1, people from the higher

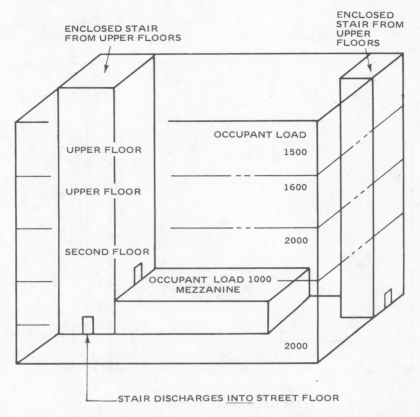

ENCLOSED STAIR
FROM UPPER FLOORS

ENCLOSED
STAIR FROM
UPPER
FLOORS

OCCUPANT LOAD

UPPER FLOOR   1500

UPPER FLOOR   1600

SECOND FLOOR   2000

OCCUPANT LOAD 1000
MEZZANINE

2000

STAIR DISCHARGES INTO STREET FLOOR

Figure 25-3. Mercantile Occupancy with a Mezzanine Not Open to the Street Floor. The street floor requires 33 units of exit width in exit discharge doors (20 for the street floor and 13 for stairs discharging through the street floor).

floors who may need to travel down to and through the exits to the exterior from Floor 1. The reverse holds true for Floor 2, which must size its exterior exit capacity to accommodate occupants who may travel up from Floor 1 as well as occupants who may have to travel down to and through the exterior exits on Floor 2. Paragraphs 5-3.1.4, 25-1.7.2, 25-2.3.2, and 26-2.3.3 demonstrate how to add exit capacity based on expected occupant use from floors above the street floor. (This method is equally valid for adding exit capacity based on expected occupant use from floors *below* the street floor.) Figure 25-5 provides an example of how to calculate exit capacity for a street floor such as Floor 2 in Figure 25-4.

25-2.1.5   For special considerations with contents of high hazard, see 25-1.5.

25-2.2 Types of Exits.

25-2.2.1   Exits shall be restricted to the following permissible types:

(a) *Doors (see 5-2.1).*

(b) *Interior stairs, Class A or B (see 5-2.2).*

(c) *Smokeproof towers (see 5-2.3).*

(d) *Outside stairs (see 5-2.5).*

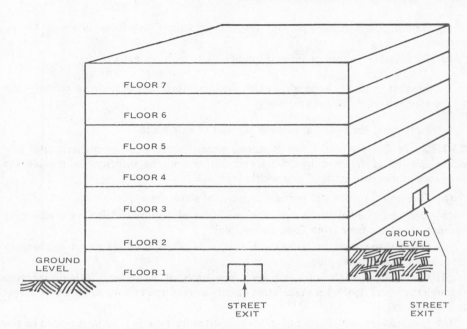

Figure 25-4. Mercantile Occupancy with Two Street Floors. The exit capacity of Floor 1 must be able to accommodate the expected population of Floors 2 through 7. The exit capacity of Floor 2 must be able to accommodate the expected population of Floors 3 through 7 plus the population of Floor 1 which may choose to exit through the second floor's street exit.

(e) *Horizontal exits (see 5-2.4).*

(f) *Ramps (see 5-2.6).*

(g) *Exit passageways (see 5-2.7).*

(h) *Escalators (see 5-2.8).*

(i) *Revolving doors (see 5-2.1).*

(j) *Fire escape stair (see 5-2.9).*

Note that **5-2.9.1.1.1** permits *existing* buildings to use or continue to use fire escape stairs for no more than **50 percent of their required exit capacity.**

25-2.2.2   An existing interior stair or outside stair not complying with 5-2.2 or 5-2.5 may be continued in use, subject to the approval of the authority having jurisdiction.

The authority must determine if equivalent life safety is being provided.

25-2.3 Capacity of Means of Egress.

25-2.3.1   The capacity of a unit of exit width shall be as follows:

(a) Doors including those leading to outside the building at the ground level or three risers above or below the ground level — 100 persons per unit of exit width.

(b) Class A or Class B interior stairs, smokeproof towers, or outside stairs — 60 persons per unit of exit width.

(c) Ramps: Class A — one unit for 100 persons; Class B — one unit for 60 persons.

(d) Escalators — same as stairs if qualifying as required exits.

Note that to qualify as required exits, the escalators must be enclosed and meet the requirements of 5-2.2, Interior Stairs.

(e) Horizontal exits — 100 persons per unit of exit width.

25-2.3.2 In Class A and Class B stores, street floor exit doors or horizontal exit doors, located as required by 25-2.5 and 25-2.6 shall be sufficient to provide the following numbers of units of exit width:

(a) One unit for each 100 persons capacity of street floor, plus

(b) One and one-half units for each two units of required stairways discharging through the street floor from floors below, plus

(c) One and one-half units for each two units of required stairways discharging through the street floor, plus

(d) One and one-half units for each two units of escalator width discharging through the street floor where escalators qualify as required exits or as means of access to required exits.

(e) If ramps are used instead of stairways, street floor doors shall be provided on the same basis as for stairways, with door width appropriate to the rated discharge of ramps, per 5-2.6.

The committee, in 25-2.3.2, was attempting to provide the exit discharge for the street floor of a Class A or B store with sufficient capacity to handle the people who, in exiting the building during an emergency, must travel up from the basement sales area, down from the upper sales floors, and mix with the customers already on the first or street floor.

Since people move more quickly in the horizontal than in the vertical direction (by a factor of 4 to 3, i.e., 60 people a minute through a horizontal exit as opposed to 45 a minute down stairs; see commentary for 5-3.3), it is permissible to provide *less* door width than stair width. Thus, the *Code* requires doors of 1½ exit units for every two units of exit width provided by stairs, ramps, or escalators which discharge into the street floor. (Note that 2 to 1½ = 4 to 3.) Figure 25-5 provides an example of how to calculate the required exit capacity for the street floor.

An alternative method is to total the units of exit width for any stairs, ramps, or escalators (where the escalators conform to the requirements of 5-2.2) which discharge through the street floor. Multiply the total by ¾ and add the results to the units of exit width (at 100 people per unit) required to handle the population of the street floor. This total will provide a door capacity for the street floor which meets the requirements of 25-2.3.2.

25-2.4 Number of Exits.

25-2.4.1 In Class A and Class B stores, at least two separate exits shall be accessible from every part of every floor, including floors below the street floor.

25-2.4.2 In Class C stores, at least two separate exits shall be provided as specified by 25-2.4.1.

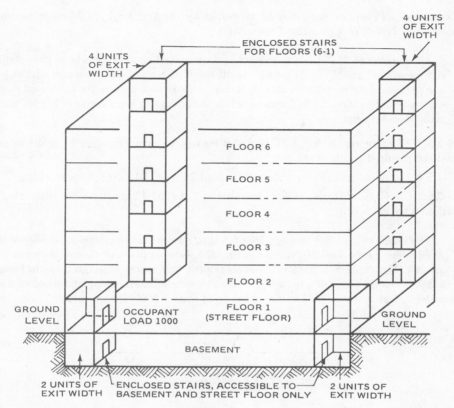

Figure 25-5. Calculation of Exit Capacity for a Class A Mercantile Occupancy Street Floor in Accordance with 25-2.3.2. Capacity for street floor: 10 units of exit width (occupant load of 1,000 ÷ 100 people per unit)
Capacity for upper floors: 6 units of exit width (8 units of stairs ÷ 2 × 1½)
Capacity for basement: 3 units of exit width (4 units of stairs ÷ 2 × 1½)
Total capacity of street floor: 19 units of exit width (10 + 6 + 3)

Exception: Where no part of the Class C store is more than 50 ft (15.24 m) from the street door, measured in accordance with 5-6.2, a single exit shall be permitted.

The *Code* allows the exception to the basic requirement that there must be at least two remote exits from an occupancy in the instance of very small Class C mercantile stores, such as tobacco shops, shoe shine stands, and newsstands. If the travel distance from any point in such a store to an exit is 50 ft (15.24 m) or less, the probability is low that a fire might surprise and overcome the customers before they could escape.

25-2.5 Arrangement of Means of Egress.

25-2.5.1   Exits shall be arranged in accordance with Section 5-5.

25-2.5.2   No dead-end corridor shall exceed 50 ft (15.24 m).

Exception: A common path may be permitted for the first 50 ft (15.24 m) from any point. (See 25-1.5, if high hazard content.)

The purpose of 25-2.5.2 is to protect against pockets or dead ends large enough to trap people in case of fire. It permits small areas such as rooms or alcoves with only one way out if the distance to an exit is short enough to minimize the likelihood that a fire might develop and block escape before the occupants were aware of the fire and made their way out.

25-2.5.3 The aggregate width of all aisles leading to each exit shall be equal to at least the required width of the exit.

25-2.5.4 In no case shall any aisle be less than 28 in. (71.12 cm) in clear width.

25-2.5.5 In Class A stores, at least one aisle of 5 ft (152.4 cm) minimum width shall lead directly to an exit.

The intent of 25-2.5.3 through 25-2.5.5 is to ensure that the interior arrangement of counters, racks, and displays of merchandise does not block or obscure accesses to an exit. Figure 25-6 illustrates an arrangement that meets the requirements for a Class A store. Essentially, the width of the exit determines the minimum width of the aisle, except that one of the aisles must be at least 5 ft (152.4 cm) wide.

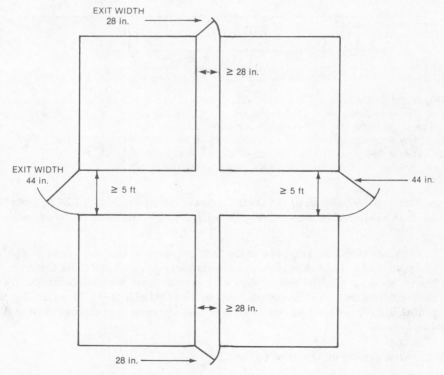

METRIC: 1 ft = .3048 m

Figure 25-6. Relation Between the Widths of Aisles and Exits in a Class A Mercantile Occupancy.

25-2.5.6 If the only means of customer entrance is through one exterior wall of the building, two-thirds of the required exit width shall be located in this wall.

In establishing 25-2.5.6, the committee was concerned about the arrangement of many discount and variety stores which have one large main exit/entrance located in the front of the store, and the other exits (which cannot be used as entrances) situated at points unfamiliar to the public. In these cases, the main exit/entrance must be sized to handle two-thirds of the required exit capacity of the store because most of the customers will instinctively try to use this exit during a fire.

25-2.5.7 At least one-half of the required exits shall be so located as to be reached without going through check-out stands. In no case shall check-out stands or associated railings or barriers obstruct exits, required aisles or approaches thereto.

This is the most frequently violated provision of Chapter 25. (See Figure 25-7.) Most supermarkets, discount, and variety stores are arranged so that it is necessary to pass through checkout counters, around shopping carts, and through turnstiles in order to exit from the facility. Obviously, this causes congestion or blockage during an emergency. Note that the *Code* requires at least one-half of all exits to be located so that people can avoid having to pass through or around these impediments to egress.

25-2.5.8 Where wheeled carts or buggies are used by customers, adequate provision shall be made for the transit and parking of such carts to minimize the possibility that they may obstruct means of egress.

It is the intent to provide adequate area for transit and parking of wheeled carts or buggies used by customers to eliminate the obstruction to the means of egress of the interior exit access and the exterior exit discharge. This includes corral areas adjacent to exits that are constructed to restrict the movement of wheeled carts or buggies therefrom.

25-2.5.9 Exit access in Class B and Class C stores may pass through storerooms providing the following conditions are met:

(a) At least one other means of egress is provided.

(b) The storeroom is not subject to locking.

(c) The main aisle through the storeroom shall be not less than 48 in. (121.92 cm) wide.

(d) The path of travel defined with fixed barriers through the storeroom shall be direct and continuously maintained in an unobstructed condition.

Figures 25-8 and 25-9 give examples of how to apply 25-2.5.9.

25-2.6 Measurement of Travel Distance to Exits. Travel distance to exits, measured in accordance with Section 5-6, shall be no more than 100 ft (30.48 m).

Exception: An increase in the above travel distance to 150 ft (45.72 m) shall be permitted in a building protected throughout by an approved automatic sprinkler system in accordance with Section 7-7.

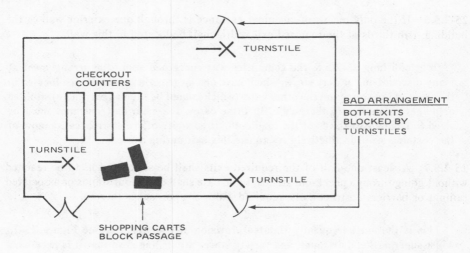

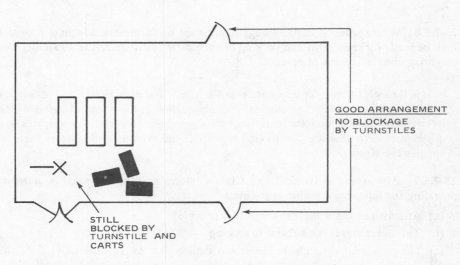

Figure 25-7. Impediments to Egress from a Mercantile Occupancy.

A review of 5-6.2 will show that the travel distance requirements apply to only the first (or nearest) exit from a point in the building. In other words, the 100-ft (30.48-m) travel distance limit means that at least one exit must be within 100 ft (30.48 m) of a point in the building, not that all exits must be within 100 ft (30.48 m) of that same point in the building.

25-2.7 Discharge from Exits. In buildings protected throughout by an approved automatic sprinkler system in accordance with Section 7-7, one-half of rated number of exit units of stairways, escalators or ramps serving as required exits from floors

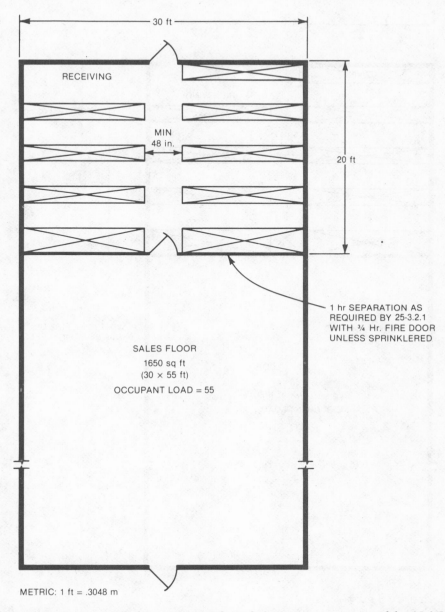

RECEIVING

MIN
48 in.

30 ft

20 ft

1 hr SEPARATION AS
REQUIRED BY 25-3.2.1
WITH ¾ Hr. FIRE DOOR
UNLESS SPRINKLERED

SALES FLOOR
1650 sq ft
(30 × 55 ft)
OCCUPANT LOAD = 55

METRIC: 1 ft = .3048 m

Figure 25-8. Example of Exit Access Through Storeroom as Permitted by 25-2.5.9.
The aisle within the storeroom must be defined by fixed barriers, such as formed by the
ends of shelving. The aisle must be kept unobstructed.

above or below the street floor may discharge through the main street floor area,
instead of directly to the street, or through a fire-resistive passage to the street,
provided that:

(a) Not more than one-half of the required exit units from any single floor
considered separately discharge through the street floor area.

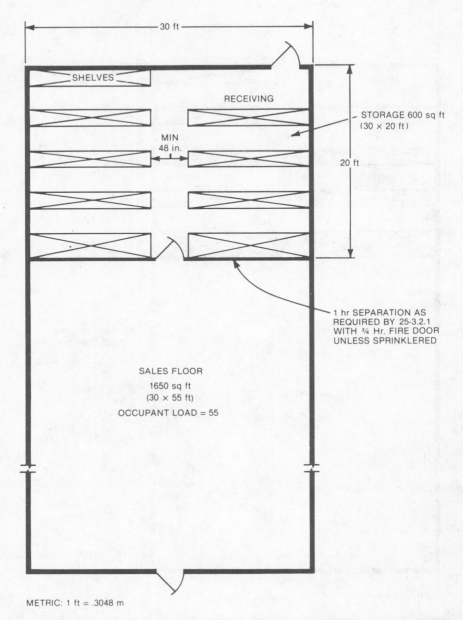

Figure 25-9. Example of Exit Access Through Storeroom Which Will Be a Constant Problem Because of Relationship of Receiving Area.

(b) The exits are enclosed in accordance with Section 6-2 to the street floor.

(c) The distance of travel from the termination of the enclosure to an outside street door is not more than 50 ft (15.24 m).

(d) The street floor doors provide sufficient units of exit width to serve exits discharging through the street floor in addition to the street floor itself, per 25-2.3.2.

The basis for the modifications to the general rule on complete enclosure of exits up to their point of discharge to the outside of the building is that, with the specified safeguards, reasonable safety is maintained. Note that a limit is applied to this arrangement so that no more than 50 percent of the exits from either the entire building or from any floor can be arranged to discharge to the street floor. Further, this can only be done if the building is sprinklered throughout. Also note that the path of travel on the first floor from the stair enclosure to the outside door cannot exceed 50 ft (15.24 m). The remaining 50 percent of the exits must discharge directly to the exterior.

A stairway is not considered to discharge through the main area of the street floor if it leads to the street through a fire-resistive enclosure separating it from the main area, even though there are doors between the first floor stairway landing and the main area.

The provisions of 25-2.7 should not be confused with those permitting open stairways in 25-3.1, Exception No. 1.

25-2.8 Illumination of Means of Egress.   Every mercantile occupancy shall have exit illumination and signs in accordance with Section 5-8.

Note that illumination for the means of egress is not the same as emergency lighting; failure of the building power supply will cause failure of the means of egress illumination system, which is not required to have a back-up, auxiliary, or secondary power supply.

25-2.9 Emergency Lighting.   Every Class A and Class B store shall have emergency lighting facilities conforming to Section 5-9.

Class C stores, due to their small size and small occupant load, are not required by the *Code* to have emergency lighting facilities.

25-2.10 Marking of Means of Egress.   Every mercantile occupancy shall have exit signs in accordance with Section 5-10.

Exception: Where an exit is immediately apparent from all portions of the sales area, the exit marking may be omitted.

The intent of the exception to the provision for marking the means of egress is to avoid requiring exit signs in small areas where the exit is readily apparent. For example, exit signs would not be required in the office of a service station, the purchase and eating areas of a small "fast food" restaurant, or in a Class C store whose size and arrangement complied with the exception to 25-2.4.2.

25-2.11 Special Features.

25-2.11.1   Every street floor door shall be in accordance with 5-2.1, and a horizontal exit door, if used, in accordance with 5-2.4.

25-2.11.2   In Class C mercantile occupancies, doors may swing inward where such doors serve only the street floor area.

25-2.11.3   Where revolving doors are used to provide part of the required number of units of street floor exit width, such doors shall be used in accordance with the provisions of Section 5-2.

If revolving doors are used, 5-2.1.3.2 requires adjoining swinging doors, prohibits revolving doors at the foot of stairs, and rates each revolving door at one-half unit of exit width regardless of the actual total width of the revolving door.

25-2.11.4 All doors at the foot of stairs from upper floors or at the head of stairs leading to floors below the street floor shall swing with the exit travel.

25-2.11.5 Locks in accordance with the Exception stated in 5-2.1.2.1.1 shall be permitted only on principal entrance/exit doors.

This new provision permits doors to be equipped with a key-operated lock in accordance with the provisions of Chapter 5. The term principal entrance/exit doors is intended to imply doors which the authority having jurisdiction can be reasonably assured will be unlocked in order for the facility to do business.

25-2.11.6 Special locking arrangements in accordance with 5-2.1.2.1.5 are permitted.

This permits the use of the time delay lock as provided in Chapter 5.

25-2.11.7 Spiral stairs in accordance with 5-2.2.1.6 are permitted.

Note that 5-2.2.1.6 only permits spiral stairs to serve an occupant load of five or fewer. They may be effectively used in storage areas having a small occupant load.

25-2.11.8 Where horizontal or vertical security grills or doors are used as a part of the required means of egress from a tenant space, such grills or doors shall be used in accordance with the provisions of 5-2.1.1.4.1.

25-2.11.9 Winders in stairs in accordance with 5-2.2.2.4 are permitted.

SECTION 25-3   PROTECTION

25-3.1 Protection of Vertical Openings. Each stairway, elevator shaft, escalator opening or other vertical opening shall be enclosed or protected in accordance with Section 6-2.

Exception No. 1:   As permitted in Class A stores where:

(a) Openings may be unprotected between any two floors, such as open stairs or escalators between the street floor and the floor below, or open stairs to the second floor or balconies or mezzanines above the street floor level.

(b) In stores protected throughout by an approved automatic sprinkler system in accordance with Section 7-7, openings may be unprotected both to the floor below and to the floor above the street floor, or to balconies or mezzanines above the street floor.

(c) In stores protected throughout by an approved automatic sprinkler system in accordance with Section 7-7, openings may be unprotected under the conditions permitted by 6-2.2.3.1 Exception No. 1 or between the street floor and the floor below the street floor and between the street floor and the second floor or, if no openings to the floor below the street floor, between the street floor, street floor balcony or mezzanine, and second floor, but not between more than three floor levels.

(d) One floor above those otherwise permitted may be open if such floor is not used for sales purposes and the entire building is sprinklered.

Follow the provisions of 25-1.7 on properly assessing the occupant load to develop sufficient exit capacity for a store in which floors, balconies, or mezzanines are open to the street floor. Exception No. 1 to 25-3.1 specifies under which conditions such openings are permitted in Class A stores.

Item (a) allows the floor immediately above the street floor (mezzanines in this case count as floors) or immediately below the street floor to be open to the street floor, *but not both at the same time* unless the special precautions of item (b) or (c) are taken.

Item (b) allows the floors immediately above and immediately below the street floor to be open to the street floor *at the same time* if the store is protected by a complete automatic sprinkler system installed and maintained according to NFPA 13, *Standard for the Installation of Sprinkler Systems,*[1] and NFPA 13A, *Recommended Practice for the Care and Maintenance of Sprinkler Systems.*[2]

In lieu of item (b), item (c) allows a store that is fully sprinklered to have unprotected openings between the street floor and a maximum of two floor levels above it *if there is no unprotected opening between the street floor and the floors below the street floor.* However, in either case, the precautions required by 6-2.2.3.1, Exception No. 1 must be strictly followed, especially the requirement of 6-2.2.3.1, Exception No. 1(e) that at least 50 percent of the people expected to occupy a floor (the occupant load) be able to exit without being exposed to any products of combustion from a fire on a communicating floor. Note that a mezzanine or a balcony would constitute a floor level.

Item (d) represents a special provision allowing an existing Class A store to have one additional floor level connected to the street floor by unprotected vertical openings if the store is fully sprinklered and if the additional floor is not used for sales purposes.

Exception No. 2:   As permitted in Class B stores where:

(a) Openings may be unprotected between any two floors, such as open stairs or escalators between the street floor and the floor below, or between the street floor and mezzanine or the second floor.

(b) All floors permitted under Class B may have unprotected openings if the building is protected throughout by an approved automatic sprinkler system in accordance with Section 7-7.

The cases in which Exception No. 2 permits unprotected vertical openings in Class B stores are based on the scheme used for Class A stores. However, if the street floor, a mezzanine, and the second floor of a Class B store were connected by unenclosed stairs, openings between the street floor and the basement of the building would have to be protected.

Item (b) allows all the floor levels of an existing Class B store to be connected by unprotected vertical openings (if the building is completely sprinklered) because a Class B store may have a maximum of four floor levels (basement, street floor, balcony, second floor; or street floor, balcony, second floor, third floor).

It is important to note that neither Exception No. 1 nor Exception No. 2 to 25-3.1 intend to allow an arrangement of unprotected openings which would violate the requirement of 6-2.2.3.1 that "the lowest or the next to the lowest" level of a connected series of unprotected vertical openings be a street floor.

Exception No. 3:   As permitted in Class C stores where:

(a) In any store, openings may be unprotected between the street floor and balcony.

(b) Openings may be unprotected between the street floor and the floor below or the second floor if not used for sales purposes.

Exception No. 3 to 25-3.1 recognizes the limited size and probable small population of Class C stores. For these reasons, any existing Class C store may have unprotected openings to the floor below the street floor and to the second floor. However, if either the basement or the second floor is used for sales, the store would be considered as Class B and be subject to the provisions of Exception No. 2. Also, if the Class C store does not have control of the space represented by the second floor or the basement, the vertical openings to such a floor should be protected.

25-3.2 Protection from Hazards.

25-3.2.1   An area used for general storage, boiler or furnace rooms, fuel storage, janitor closets, maintenance shops including woodworking and painting areas, and kitchens shall be separated from other parts of the building by an assembly(ies) having a fire resistance rating of not less than 1 hour, and all openings shall be protected with self-closing fire doors.

Exception: Areas protected by an automatic extinguishing system.

25-3.2.2   Areas with high hazard contents as defined in Section 4-2 shall be provided with both fire-resistive separation and automatic sprinkler protection.

Paragraphs 25-3.2.1 and 25-3.2.2 reflect the intent of Section 6-4 which requires separation of a hazardous area from the rest of a building by suitable construction, or mandates the installation of an automatic extinguishing system in the hazardous area.

25-3.3 Interior Finish.

25-3.3.1   Interior finish on walls and ceilings shall be Class A or B, in accordance with Section 6-5.

Exception No. 1:   Existing Class C interior finish shall be permitted as follows:

(a) On walls.

(b) Throughout Class C stores.

Exception No. 2:   In any mercantile occupancy, exposed portions of structural members complying with the requirements for heavy timber construction may be permitted. Laminated wood shall not delaminate under the influence of heat.

25-3.3.2 Interior Floor Finish.   No requirements.

Essentially, 25-3.3, Exception No. 1 states that *in existing Class C stores only,* all the interior finish (walls, ceilings, and floors) may be rated as Class C (flame spread of 0-200). All existing stores (Class A, B, or C) may have Class C interior finish on the walls.

The committee limited the use of exposed heavy timber construction to *only the structural members of a building,* such as columns, beams, girders, or trusses.

Panels between supporting columns and wall surfaces *may not* be of exposed heavy timber construction. These panels or wall surfaces must be sheathed with appropriate interior finish material. Heavy timber construction is discussed in NFPA 220, *Standard Types of Building Construction,*[3] and in the NFPA *Fire Protection Handbook.*[4]

25-3.4 Alarm Systems. Class A and Class B stores shall be provided with a manual fire alarm system in accordance with Section 7-6.

Exception No. 1: Buildings protected throughout by an approved automatic fire detection and alarm initiation system in accordance with Section 7-6.

Exception No. 2: Buildings protected throughout by an approved automatic sprinkler system in accordance with Section 7-7 which provides alarm initiation in accordance with Section 7-6.

The intent of the exceptions to 25-3.4 is to eliminate the manual pull stations, but retain the alerting function of the alarm system.

25-3.5 Extinguishment Requirements. Approved automatic sprinkler protection shall be installed in accordance with Section 7-7 in all mercantile occupancies as follows:

(a) In all buildings with a story over 15,000 sq ft (1,394 sq m) in area.

(b) In all buildings exceeding 30,000 sq ft (2,787 sq m) in gross area.

(c) Throughout stories below the level of exit discharge when such stories have an area exceeding 2,500 sq ft (232 sq m) when used for the sale, storage, or handling of combustible goods and merchandise.

For discussions of what constitutes an "approved automatic sprinkler protection system," see NFPA 13, *Standard for the Installation of Sprinkler Systems,*[1] NFPA 13A, *Recommended Practice for the Care and Maintenance of Sprinkler Systems,*[2] and *Automatic Sprinkler and Standpipe Systems.*[5]

Under the provisions of item (a), a store with a total gross area of less than 30,000 sq ft (2,787 sq m) (Class B or C), but with any one floor greater than 15,000 sq ft (1,394 sq m) in area would have to be protected with a complete automatic sprinkler system. A store with a total gross area of less than 30,000 sq ft (2,787 sq m) would not be required to be sprinklered, as long as the area of any floor did not exceed 15,000 sq ft (1,394 sq m).

The intent of item (b) is to require that all stores with a total gross area greater than 30,000 sq ft (2,787 sq m) be protected with a complete automatic sprinkler system.

The committee developed item (c) to ensure that all basement areas larger than 2,500 sq ft (232 sq m) (whether the space is used for sales, storage, or the handling of combustible merchandise) be sprinklered to avoid the potential threat to the occupants of the street floor and to fire fighters. Studies have shown that there is a higher rate of fire incidence in basements than in other areas of stores. Because smoke and heat rise, a fire in a basement can quickly cause exits and exit discharges located on the street floor to be unusable.

25-3.6 Corridors. No special requirements.

The provisions of 5-1.3.4 apply if corridors are present.

25-3.7 Subdivision of Building Spaces. No special requirements.

25-3.8 Special Features.

SECTION 25-4   SPECIAL PROVISIONS

25-4.1 Windowless or Underground Buildings. *(See Section 30-7.)*

25-4.2 Open-Air Mercantile Operations.

25-4.2.1 Open-air mercantile operations, such as open-air markets, gasoline filling stations, roadside stands for the sale of farm produce, and other outdoor mercantile operations shall be so arranged and conducted as to maintain free and unobstructed ways of travel at all times to permit prompt escape from any point of danger in case of fire or other emergency, with no dead ends in which persons might be trapped due to display stands, adjoining buildings, fences, vehicles, or other obstructions.

Paragraph 25-4.2.1 is virtually an open-ended provision which provides guidance for the arrangement, use, and display of merchandise for sales in open-air mercantile operations. The phrase "ways of travel" is purposely used by the committee to avoid confusion with "means of egress" which is strictly defined and whose use implies the minimum requirements of Chapter 5. "Ways of travel" is not defined and implies no specific minimum *Code* provisions. Most open-air mercantile operations have unlimited ways for entering and evacuating the areas used to display goods. For this reason, the committee did not find it necessary to provide specific *Code* requirements beyond the precautionary measures expressed in this paragraph.

25-4.2.2 If mercantile operations are conducted in roof-over areas, they shall be treated as mercantile buildings, provided that canopies over individual small stands to protect merchandise from the weather shall not be construed to constitute buildings for the purpose of this *Code*.

The intent of 25-4.2.2 is to exempt small merchandise stands with canopies from being classed as mercantile occupancies. All other "roofed-over" areas should be treated as buildings, classified by area and height as Class A, B, or C, and subject to the appropriate provisions of Chapter 25.

25-4.3 Covered Malls.

25-4.3.1 The covered mall and all buildings connected thereto shall be treated as a single building for the purposes of calculation of means of egress and shall be subject to the requirements for appropriate occupancies. The covered mall shall be at least of sufficient clear width to accommodate egress requirements as set forth in other sections of this *Code*.

Exception: The covered mall may be considered to be a pedestrian way, in which case the distance of travel within a tenant space to an exit or to the covered mall shall be a maximum of 150 ft (45.72 m) (see Exception to 25-2.6), or shall be the maximum for the appropriate occupancy; plus an additional 200 ft (60.96 m) shall be permitted for travel through the covered mall space if all the following requirements are met:

(a) The covered mall shall be at least of sufficient clear width to accommodate egress requirements as set forth in other sections of this chapter, but in no case less than 20 ft (609.6 cm) wide in its narrowest dimension.

(b) The covered mall shall be provided with an unobstructed exit access on each side of the mall floor area of not less than 10 ft (304.8 cm) in clear width parallel to and adjacent to the mall tenant front. Such exit access shall lead to an exit having a minimum of three units of exit width. (See 25-4.3.2.1.)

(c) The covered mall and all buildings connected thereto shall be protected throughout by an approved electrically supervised automatic sprinkler system in accordance with Section 7-7.

(d) Walls dividing stores from each other shall extend from the floor to the underside of the roof deck or floor deck above. No separation is required between a tenant space and the covered mall.

(e) The covered mall shall be provided with a smoke control system.

In recent years, covered mall shopping areas have increased in both number and size. The committee developed two options or approaches for dealing with the life safety aspects of these complexes. The first approach (described in 25-4.3.1) considers the mall and the attached stores as essentially one large Class A store subject to all the provisions of Chapter 25. In this view, the covered mall would be treated as an aisle of a store.

The other approach, new in the 1976 Edition of the *Life Safety Code* and essentially unchanged in this 1981 Edition, permits the mall to be considered as a "pedestrian way" by which occupants of the attached stores may egress during a fire. The phrase "pedestrian way" was chosen by the committee both to convey the meaning of the term "exit access" and to allow the mall to be treated as if it were an area of refuge.

The exception to 25-4.3.1 reflects the committee's recognition that if the mall and all the buildings attached to the mall were protected by automatic sprinklers, people fleeing into the mall from a fire in a store would have moved into a space whose volume, size, and arrangement afforded most of the benefits provided by an enclosed stair or a horizontal exit. The exception considers the mall as being virtually an area of refuge for the buildings attached to it even though the mall is not separated from these attached buildings by the type of construction normally provided for an exit as required by 5-1.2.3.

When considering a covered mall as a pedestrian way, the maximum travel distance to an exit or to the mall from any point within a store attached to the mall is 150 ft (45.72 m). This reflects the committee's estimation that using the mall for egress is as acceptable (or as safe) as using an exit. An additional travel distance of up to 200 ft (60.96 m) is permitted within the mall [in addition to the 150 ft (45.72 m) already allowed] if the following conditions are met:

1. The mall and all buildings attached to it must be sprinklered. Note that if the shopping complex were considered as one building, sprinkler protection would almost always be required under the 30,000-sq ft (2,787-sq m) gross area criterion of 25-3.5(b).
2. The clear width of the mall must be at least 20 ft (609.6 cm), wider if the required exit capacity demands it. Note that when considering the covered mall of a shopping center as a pedestrian way, no occupant load is calculated

for the mall. The required capacity of the means of egress is calculated on the basis of aggregate gross area of the attached stores, excluding anchor stores.

3. At least 10 ft (304.8 cm) of clear unobstructed space must be available for exit access in front of, adjacent to, and parallel to all store fronts. This requirement is designed to prohibit displays of merchandise, kiosks, or small sales stands from being placed within 10 ft (304.8 cm) of the store fronts and, if enforced, will ensure that the mall will have a minimum clear width of 20 ft (609.6 cm).

4. Each exit access must terminate at an exit whose capacity is a minimum of three units of exit width [66 in. (167.64 cm)]. This requirement is related to 25-2.5.5, which mandates that at least one aisle leading to an exit in a Class A store have a minimum clear width of 5 ft (152.4 cm).

5. Walls separating stores must run continuously from the floor slab to the roof slab (but not necessarily through the roof). The store front need not be separated by construction from the mall.

6. The mall must have a smoke control system. Since the individual stores are open to the mall, this requirement is essential if the mall is to be used as a safe means of egress. Smoke control systems for covered malls are necessary to maintain the mall reasonably free of products of combustion for at least the duration required to evacuate the building and to minimize migration of products of combustion from one tenant to another. Systems that can be engineered to accomplish this include: (a) separate mechanical exhaust or control systems, (b) mechanical exhaust or control systems in conjunction with the heating, ventilating, and air conditioning systems, (c) automatically or manually released gravity roof vent devices such as skylights, relief dampers, or smoke vents, (d) combinations of (a), (b), and (c), or any other engineered system designed to accomplish the purpose of this section.

If these six conditions are not met, the mall may still be considered a "pedestrian way," but the additional travel distance to an exit would not be allowed. In other words, for each store there would be a limit of 100 ft (30.48 m) of travel distance [150 ft (45.72 m) if the store and mall were sprinklered] from a point in the store through the mall to an exit to the exterior. In the majority of configurations, this restriction would preclude the use of the mall as an exit access.

The *Fire Protection Handbook*[6] contains a comprehensive discussion of the hazards to life safety specific to covered mall shopping centers.

25-4.3.2 Exit Details.

25-4.3.2.1   Every floor of a covered mall shall have no less than two exits located remote from each other.

Paragraph 25-4.3.2.1 reaffirms the fundamental *Code* requirement of always providing at least two ways out.

25-4.3.2.2   No less than one-half the required exit widths for each Class A or Class B store connected to a covered mall shall lead directly outside without passage through the mall.

Note that the larger stores (Class A and B) must still have 50 percent of their exits arranged to be independent of the mall.

25-4.3.2.3   Each individual anchor store shall have means of egress independent of the covered mall.

It is not the intent of this paragraph to require that large stores be considered anchor stores. A store not considered in determining the occupant load of the mall must be arranged so that all of its means of egress will be independent of the covered mall.

25-4.3.2.4   Every covered mall shall be provided with unobstructed exit access, parallel to and adjacent to the connected buildings. This exit access shall extend to each mall exit.

Paragraph 25-4.3.2.4 reiterates the provisions of item (b) of the exception to 25-4.3.1 without mentioning that the exit access must have a clear width of at least 10 ft (304.8 cm).

25-4.4 Atriums.

25-4.4.1   Atriums are permitted provided they comply with Section 6-2 and 25-4.4.2 through 25-4.4.6.

25-4.4.2   The occupancy within the atrium meets the specifications for classification as low hazard contents. (*See 4-2.2.2.*)

Note that this is more restrictive than 6-2.2.3.1, Exception No. 2(c).

25-4.4.3   The automatic sprinkler system required by 6-2.2.3.1 Exception No. 2(e) shall be electrically supervised.

25-4.4.4   The atrium is provided with an automatic ventilation system operated by all of the following:

(a) Approved smoke detectors located at the top of the space and adjacent to each return air intake from the atrium, and

(b) The required automatic fire extinguishing system, and

(c) Manual controls which are readily accessible to the fire department.

The intent of 25-4.4.4 is to require a smoke control system as noted in 6-2.2.3.1(f) and to modify the provisions of 6-2.2.3.1(g) to *not* permit the manual alarm to activate the smoke control system. Note that 25-4.4.5 does not require manual pull stations.

The reason for not permitting the manual alarm to activate the system is the possibility of persons pulling a manual alarm on other than the fire floor, thus possibly causing the smoke control system to improperly function.

25-4.4.5 Fire Alarm System.   A fire alarm system shall be provided for the building in accordance with Section 7-6.

(a) The initiation of the fire alarm shall be by the activation of any smoke detectors or the automatic sprinkler system.

(b) Manual pull stations are not required.

25-4.4.6 All electrical equipment essential for smoke control or automatic extinguishing equipment for buildings more than six stories or 75 ft (22.86 m) in height containing an atrium shall be provided with an emergency source of power in accordance with *National Electrical Code*, NFPA 70, Section 700-12(b), or equivalent.

Note that emergency power complying with Section 700-12(b) of NFPA 70, *National Electrical Code,*[7] requires a generator set.

SECTION 25-5   BUILDING SERVICES

25-5.1   Utilities shall comply with the provisions of Section 7-1.

25-5.2   Heating, ventilating, and air conditioning equipment shall comply with the provisions of Section 7-2.

25-5.3   Elevators, dumbwaiters and vertical conveyors shall comply with the provisions of Section 7-4.

25-5.4   Rubbish chutes, incinerators, and laundry chutes shall comply with the provisions of Section 7-5.

REFERENCES CITED BY *CODE*

(This publication comprises a part of the requirements to the extent called for by the Code.)

NFPA 70, *National Electrical Code*, NFPA, Boston, 1981.

REFERENCES CITED IN COMMENTARY

[1]NFPA 13, *Standard for the Installation of Sprinkler Systems*, NFPA, Boston, 1980.

[2]NFPA 13A, *Recommended Practice for the Care and Maintenance of Sprinkler Systems*, NFPA, 1978.

[3]NFPA 220, *Standard Types of Building Construction*, NFPA, Boston, 1979.

[4]*Fire Protection Handbook*, 14th ed., NFPA, Boston, 1976, pp. 6-39 to 6-41.

[5]John L. Bryan, *Automatic Sprinkler and Standpipe Systems*, NFPA, Boston, 1976.

[6]*Fire Protection Handbook*, 14th ed., NFPA, Boston, 1976, pp. 8-31 to 8-36.

[7]NFPA 70, *National Electrical Code*, NFPA, Boston, 1981.

26

NEW BUSINESS OCCUPANCIES

(See also Chapter 31.)

Business occupancies are those used for the transaction of business, for the keeping of accounts and records, and similar purposes. Minor office occupancies incidental to operations in another occupancy are considered as part of the predominating occupancy and are subject to the provisions of this *Code* as they apply to the predominating occupancy. The commentary for 26-1.4 in this chapter discusses classification of business occupancies in more detail.

SECTION 26-1 GENERAL REQUIREMENTS

26-1.1 Application.

26-1.1.1 New construction shall comply with the provisions of this chapter. (*See Chapter 31 for operating features.*)

See Section 1-4 for application provisions.

26-1.1.2 This section establishes life safety requirements for the design of all new business buildings. Specific requirements for high-rise buildings [buildings over 75 ft (22.86 m) in height] are contained in paragraphs pertaining thereto.

Existing buildings are discussed in Chapter 27.

26-1.1.3 Additions to existing buildings shall conform to the requirements for new construction. Existing portions of the structure need not be modified, provided that the new construction has not diminished the fire safety features of the facility.

26-1.2 Mixed Occupancies.

26-1.2.1 Combined Business and Mercantile Occupancy.

26-1.2.1.1 In any building occupied for both business and mercantile purposes, the entire building shall have exits in accordance with 1-4.5.

Exception: If mercantile occupancy sections are effectively segregated from business sections, exit facilities may be treated separately.

The exception to 26-1.2.1.1 is for emphasis only. A review of 1-4.5 shows that only if two different occupancies are "so intermingled that separate safeguards are impracticable," is it necessary for special consideration to be taken beyond the requirements of Chapter 26. Those considerations involve two steps:

1. The exit capacity of each room and section and of the entire building must be determined by careful calculations of the maximum occupant load applicable based on whether a room or section is used primarily for mercantile or business purposes.
2. The *Code*'s requirements for construction, protection, and related safeguards must meet those requirements imposed for the more hazardous occupancy. Or, to phrase it differently, the more stringent requirements for construction, protection, and for safeguards (extinguishing systems, emergency lighting, etc.) must apply *to the entire facility*.

Note that the exception to 26-1.2.1.1 *applies only to the means of egress* and permits designs based on a clearly defined separation of the mercantile portion from the business portion of a mixed occupancy. No. 2 above would still apply to the entire building.

26-1.3 Special Definitions.   None.

26-1.4 Classification of Occupancy.

26-1.4.1   Business occupancies shall include all buildings and structures or parts thereof with occupancy described in 4-1.8.

In reviewing the *Code*'s definition (see 4-1.8) of what constitutes a business occupancy, note that the definition *does not include* types of stores which, though a "business," are covered under the provisions of Chapter 24; e.g., supermarkets, department stores, and other occupancies which display and sell merchandise to large numbers of people. Doctors' offices, and treatment and diagnostic facilities not meeting the definition of a health care occupancy are included in business occupancies. (See Chapter 12.) Also not included are the public assembly portions of city halls, town halls, and courthouses which are covered under Chapter 8.

The following constitute business occupancies and are covered by the provisions of Chapter 26:

1. Those occupancies used for the transaction of business (other than those classified as mercantile occupancies).
2. Occupancies used for the keeping of accounts and records and for similar purposes.

Included in (1) and (2) are: doctors' offices, dentists' offices, general offices, and outpatient clinics, as well as city halls, town halls, and courthouses, all of which have areas for keeping books, records, and transacting public business. Other occupancies included under the definition of business occupancies are service facilities usual to office buildings such as newsstands, lunch counters (serving fewer than 50 people), barber shops, and beauty parlors.

Also, by reference from Chapter 10, college classroom buildings are considered office buildings.

26-1.5 Classification of Hazard of Contents.

26-1.5.1   The contents of business occupancies shall be classified as ordinary hazard in accordance with Section 4-2.

It should be pointed out that the classification of hazard of contents under the definitions in Section 4-2 of the *Life Safety Code* has no bearing or relationship to the hazard classification in NFPA 13, *Standard for the Installation of Sprinkler Systems.*[1]

26-1.5.2   For purposes of the design of an automatic sprinkler system, a business occupancy shall be classified as "light hazard occupancy," as identified by *Standard for the Installation of Sprinkler Systems*, NFPA 13.

Paragraph 26-1.5.2 was placed in the *Code* to show that contents classed as ordinary under the *Code* for life safety purposes are not classified as ordinary under NFPA 13, *Standard for the Installation of Sprinkler Systems.*[1] As indicated in 26-1.5.2, for purposes of sprinkler design, the anticipated fuel load of business occupancies in Chapter 26 is classed as "light hazard."

26-1.6 Minimum Construction Requirements.   No requirements.

The provisions of a local building code may apply.

26-1.7 Occupant Load.

26-1.7.1   For purposes of determining required exits, the occupant load of business buildings or parts of buildings used for business purposes shall be no less than one person per 100 sq ft (9.29 sq m) of gross floor area.

26-1.7.2   In the case of a mezzanine or balcony open to the floor below or other unprotected vertical openings between floors as permitted by 26-3.1, the occupant load of the mezzanine or other subsidiary floor level shall be added to that of the street floor for the purpose of determining required exits. However, in no case shall the total number of exit units be less than would be required if all vertical openings were enclosed.

Since the number of people expected to occupy certain types of office buildings can be determined with a great degree of accuracy, e.g., through a company's detailed arrangement of its office space, it may prove beneficial to compare such a figure with one calculated on the basis of one person per 100 sq ft (9.29 sq m) of gross floor area (see 26-1.7.1). In concentrated office occupancies (particularly those used for government operations), the actual number of people found in a space may exceed the figure calculated by gross area. As emphasized in Section 5-3, when this is the case, the exit capacity must be designed on the basis of the actual occupant load. Note that the converse is not true; namely, if the actual occupant load is less than the gross area calculation, the *Code* still requires that the gross area calculation be used to determine the required exit capacity.

The requirements of 26-1.7.2 are identical to those of 24-1.7.2 for mercantile occupancies. The examples in Figures 24-2 and 24-3 of how to determine the exit capacity for the street floor of a mercantile occupancy apply equally well to a business occupancy. Note that 26-2.3.3 is consonant with 24-2.3.2; in both mercantile and business occupancies, the street floor needs to provide 1½ units of exit width for every 2 units required for stairways discharging through the street floor.

SECTION 26-2   MEANS OF EGRESS REQUIREMENTS

26-2.1 General.

26-2.1.1   All means of egress shall be in accordance with Chapter 5 and this chapter. However, only types of exits specified in 26-2.2 may be used as required exit facilities in any business occupancy with access thereto and ways of travel therefrom in accordance with Chapter 5.

26-2.1.2   If, owing to differences in grade, any street floor exits are at points above or below the street or ground level, such exits shall comply with the provisions for exits from upper floors or floors below the street floor.

Figure 24-4 illustrates a case where two street floors of a mercantile occupancy are at ground level at one side of a building, but either above or below ground level at the other side. Many business occupancies have a similar configuration. The two "street" floors must have their exits arranged to allow horizontal travel to the exterior on one end of the floor and vertical travel (either up or down to ground level) at the other end of the floor. This means that the exit capacity to the exterior must be able to accommodate, in the case of Floor 1, people from the higher floors who may need to travel down to and through the exits to the exterior on Floor 1. The reverse holds true for Floor 2, which must size its exterior exit capacity to accommodate occupants who may travel up from Floor 1 as well as occupants who may have to travel down to, and through, the exterior exits on Floor 2. Paragraphs 5-3.1.4, 26-1.7.2, and 26-2.3.3 demonstrate how to add exit capacity based on expected occupant use from floors above the street floor. (This method is equally valid for adding exit capacity based on expected occupant use from floors below the street floor.) Figure 24-5 provides an example of how to calculate exit capacity for a street floor, such as Floor 2 in Figure 24-4.

26-2.1.3   Where a stairway, escalator, outside stair or ramp serves two or more upper floors, the same stairway or other exit required to serve any one upper floor may also serve other upper floors.

Exception: No inside open stairway, escalator, or ramp may serve as a required egress facility from more than one floor.

Under 26-2.1.3, if the second and third floor of a business occupancy were each required to have three stairways, the second floor could use the stairways serving the third floor so that the total number of stairways required would be three, not six.

Note that the exception prohibits the use of *open* stairways, escalators, or ramps as an egress facility for more than one floor.

26-2.1.4   Where two or more floors below the street floor are occupied for business use, the same stairways, escalators or ramps may serve each.

Exception: No inside open stairway, escalator, or ramp may serve as a required egress facility from more than one floor level.

The explanation to 26-2.1.3 also applies to 26-2.1.4. The only difference is that these floors are *below* the street floor. In both 26-2.1.3 and 26-2.1.4, it is important to remember to base the width of the stair, escalator, or ramp on the floor with the largest occupant load. In this way it can be expected that a stair or other component of a means of egress will accommodate the population of *any* floor it serves. Again, note the prohibition in 26-2.1.4 against open stairs, escalators, or ramps serving more than one floor.

26-2.1.5 Floor levels below the street floor used only for storage, heating, and other service equipment, and not subject to business occupancy, shall have exits in accordance with Chapter 29.

A significant reduction in the number and size of exits is allowed for floors used for the purposes specified in 26-2.1.5, since the expected population of such floors will be well below that of the typical business floor.

26-2.2 Types of Exits.

26-2.2.1 Exits shall be restricted to the following permissible types:

(a) *Doors (see 5-2.1).*

(b) *Interior stairs (see 5-2.2).*

(c) *Smokeproof towers (see 5-2.3).*

(d) *Outside stairs (see 5-2.5).*

(e) *Horizontal exits (see 5-2.4).*

(f) *Ramps (see 5-2.6).*

(g) *Exit passageways (see 5-2.7).*

(h) *Escalators (see 5-2.8).*

(i) *Revolving doors (see 5-2.1).*

26-2.2.2 Slide escapes, elevators or other types of exit facility not specified in 26-2.2.1 shall not be used to provide required exits from any business occupancy.

26-2.3 Capacity of Means of Egress.

26-2.3.1 The minimum width of any corridor or passageway shall be 44 in. (111.76 cm) in the clear.

26-2.3.2 The capacity of a unit of exit width shall be as follows:

(a) Doors, including those leading outside the building at the ground level or three risers above or below the ground level — one unit for 100 persons.

(b) Stairs, outside stairs or smokeproof towers — one unit for 60 persons.

(c) Ramps: Class A — one unit for 100 persons; Class B — one unit for 60 persons.

(d) Escalators — one unit for 60 persons.

(e) Horizontal exits — one unit for 100 persons, but no more than 50 percent of the required exit capacity.

For an escalator to count as a means of egress and be assigned a capacity of 1 unit of exit width for 60 people, it is required that the escalator be enclosed in the same manner as an interior exit stair. (See 5-2.8 and Section 6-2.) Note that escalators protected in accordance with the sprinkler-vent method, the spray nozzle method, the rolling shutter method, or the partial enclosure method do not constitute an acceptable exit and cannot be used in calculating the required exit capacity.

26-2.3.3 Any street floor exit, arranged as required by 26-2.4 and 26-2.6, shall be sufficient to provide the following numbers of units of exit width.

(a) One unit for each 100 persons capacity of the street floor, plus

(b) One and one-half units for each two units of stairway, ramp or escalator from upper floors discharging through the street floor, plus

(c) One and one-half units for each two units of stairway, ramp or escalator from the floor levels below the street floor.

Refer to 26-1.7.2 and 26-2.1.2 when considering the requirements of 26-2.3.3. The committee, in 26-2.3.3, was attempting to provide the exit discharge for the street floor of a business occupancy with sufficient capacity to handle the people who, in exiting the building during an emergency, must travel up from the basement or down from the upper floors, and mix with the occupants who are already on the first, or street, floor.

Since people move more quickly in the horizontal than in the vertical direction (by a factor of 4 to 3, i.e., 60 people a minute through a horizontal exit as opposed to 45 a minute down stairs — see commentary for 5-3.3), it is permissible to provide *less* door width than stair width. Thus, the *Code* requires doors of 1½ exit units for every 2 units of exit width provided by stairs, ramps, or escalators which discharge into the street floor. (Note that 2 to 1½ = 4 to 3.) Figure 24-5 provides an example of how to calculate the required exit capacity for the street floor.

An alternative method is to total the units of exit width for any stairs, ramps, or escalators (where the escalators conform to the requirements of 5-2.2) which discharge through the street floor. Multiply the total by ¾ and add the results to the units of exit width (at 100 people per unit) required to handle the population of the street floor. This total will provide a door capacity for the street floor which meets the requirements of 26-2.3.3.

26-2.4 Number of Exits.   Not less than two exits shall be accessible from every part of every floor, including floor levels below the street floor occupied for business purposes or uses incidental thereto.

Paragraph 26-2.4 would require the 19 units calculated in Figure 24-5 to be divided into at least two groupings of 9½ units located at opposite or remote points on the street floor. Similarly, the required stair capacity from the upper and lower floors must be separated into at least two groupings remote from each other.

Exception No. 1:   For a room or area with a total occupant load of less than 100 persons (or less than 50 if a place of assembly — see Chapter 8), having direct exit to the street or to an open area outside the building at the ground level, with a total distance from any point of not over 100 ft (30.48 m), a single exit may be permitted. Such travel shall be on the same floor level or, if the traversing of stairs is required, such stairs shall not be more than 15 ft (457.2 cm) in height, and they shall be provided with complete enclosures to separate them from any other part of the building, with no door openings therein.

Figures 26-1 and 26-2 illustrate two cases where a single exit is allowed from a room or area in a business occupancy (see Exception No. 1 to 26-2.4). In the first case, the travel distance from the area is on the same floor level as the exit. In the second, stairs must be traversed.

The criteria for allowing the single exit are:

1. Occupant load less than 100 (less than 50 if a place of assembly),
2. Direct exit to a street or to an open exterior area at ground level,
3. Total travel distance no more than 100 ft (30.48 m) from anywhere in the room to the exterior,
4. Any stairs no more than 15 ft (457.2 cm) in height, and
5. Any stairs completely enclosed with no door openings between the stair enclosure and the rest of the building.

If *any* of Conditions 1 to 5 are not met, two exits are required from the room or space in question.

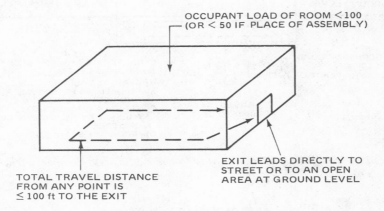

Figure 26-1. *Single Exit from an Area or Room in a Business Occupancy. Travel from area to exit is horizontal.*

Exception No. 2: Any business occupancy not over three stories and not exceeding 3,000 sq ft (279 sq m) gross floor area per floor may be permitted with a single separate exit to each floor if the total travel distance to the outside of the building does not exceed 100 ft (30.48 m) and if such exit is enclosed in accordance with 5-1.3 and serves no other levels and discharges directly to the outside. A single outside stairway in accordance with 5-2.5 may serve all floors.

Figure 26-3 illustrates a single exit from the third floor of a business occupancy. To be permitted, *all* of the following conditions must be met:

1. The building is not more than three stories high,
2. Each floor is no more than 3,000 sq ft (279 sq m) in gross area,
3. Travel distance from any point on any floor to the exterior at ground level is no more than 100 ft (30.48 m),
4. The stair is not used by, nor has an opening to, any other floor,
5. The stair is totally enclosed or is classified as an outside stair (see 5-2.5).

If any of these conditions are not met, the floor must have two exits.

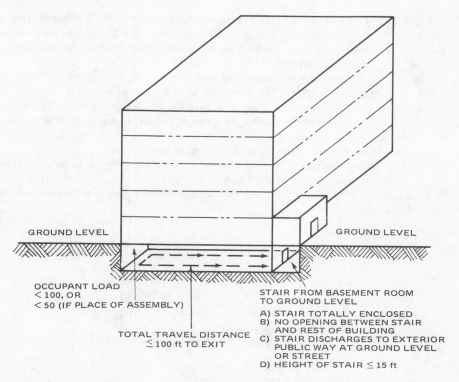

GROUND LEVEL

GROUND LEVEL

OCCUPANT LOAD
< 100, OR
< 50 (IF PLACE OF ASSEMBLY)

STAIR FROM BASEMENT ROOM
TO GROUND LEVEL

A) STAIR TOTALLY ENCLOSED
B) NO OPENING BETWEEN STAIR
   AND REST OF BUILDING
C) STAIR DISCHARGES TO EXTERIOR
   PUBLIC WAY AT GROUND LEVEL
   OR STREET
D) HEIGHT OF STAIR ≤ 15 ft

TOTAL TRAVEL DISTANCE
≤ 100 ft TO EXIT

Figure 26-2. Single Exit from an Area or Room in a Business Occupancy Where Stairs Must Be Traversed.

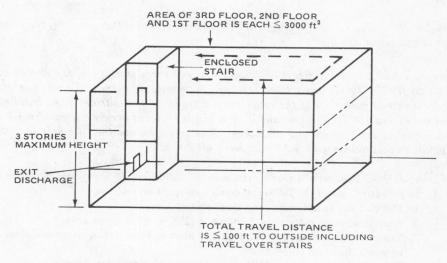

AREA OF 3RD FLOOR, 2ND FLOOR
AND 1ST FLOOR IS EACH ≤ 3000 ft²

ENCLOSED
STAIR

3 STORIES
MAXIMUM HEIGHT

EXIT
DISCHARGE

TOTAL TRAVEL DISTANCE
IS ≤ 100 ft TO OUTSIDE INCLUDING
TRAVEL OVER STAIRS

Figure 26-3. Single Exit from Third Floor of a Business Occupancy. Stair is totally enclosed, has opening only at third floor, and discharges directly to street with no communication at second and first floors. A similar arrangement could be provided for the second floor of the same building.

26-2.5 Arrangement of Means of Egress.

26-2.5.1   Exits shall be arranged in accordance with Section 5-5.

Required exits must be suitably located to allow access without passage through areas which might be locked.

26-2.5.2   No dead-end corridor shall exceed 50 ft (15.24 m).

Exception: A common path may be permitted for the first 50 ft (15.24 m) from any point.

The exception to 26-2.5.2 allows room to be located along the ends of corridors so that travel to an exit is possible in only one direction for the first 50 ft (15.24 m) from the doorway of a room. After the 50-ft (15.24-m) point the corridor, or exit access, must provide at least two paths to two separate exits. This assumes that, in accordance with 5-6.4, each room will not be occupied by more than six people and that the distance between any point in a room and the door to the corridor does not exceed 50 ft (15.24 m). Common paths of travel are illustrated in Figures 26-4A and 26-4B.

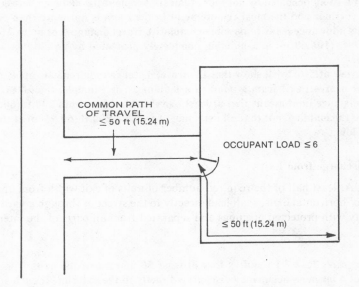

Figure 26-4A. Allowed Common Path of Travel in a Business Occupancy. Measure from room door to point where corridor provides access to two separate exits. The travel distance from any point in the room to the corridor door must not exceed 50 ft (15.24 m) and the occupant load must be six or fewer.

26-2.6 Measurement of Travel Distance to Exits.   Travel distance to exits, measured in accordance with Section 5-6, shall be no more than 200 ft (60.96 m).

Exception: An increase in the above travel distance to 300 ft (91.44 m) shall be permitted in a building protected throughout by an approved automatic sprinkler system in accordance with Section 7-7.

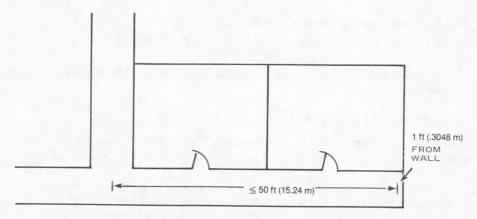

Figure 26-4B. Allowed Dead End in a Business Occupancy. Measure from a point 1 ft (30.48 cm) in from end of corridor to point where access to two separate and remote exits is provided. Measurement is made in the same fashion as travel distance (see 5-6.2).

Paragraph 5-6.4 allows travel distance to an exit to be measured from the corridor door of a room occupied by not more than six people if the distance between the door to the corridor and the most remote point in the room is not more than 50 ft (15.24 m). This allowance leads to possible cumulative travel distances of up to 250 ft (76.20 m) [350 ft (106.68 m) in a building completely protected by an automatic sprinkler system].

A review of 5-6.2 will show that the travel distance requirements apply to only the first (or nearest) exit from a point in a building. For example, the 200-ft (60.96-m) travel distance limit means that at least one exit must be within 200 ft (60.96 m) of a point in the building, not that all exits must be within 200 ft (60.96 m) of that point in the building.

26-2.7 Discharge from Exits.

26-2.7.1 At least half of the required number of units of exit width from upper floors, exclusive of horizontal exits, shall lead directly to the street or through a yard, court, or passageway with protected openings and separated from all parts of the interior of the building.

Paragraph 26-2.7.1 requires that at least 50 percent of the exits from the upper floors of a business occupancy discharge directly to the exterior. If such an exit does not discharge directly to a "public way," 26-2.7.1 requires an exit passageway. For the remaining exits (of which there can be a maximum of 50 percent) which do not discharge directly to the exterior or through an enclosed passageway, see 26-2.7.2.

26-2.7.2 A maximum of 50 percent of the exits may discharge through areas on the level of discharge, provided:

(a) Such exits discharge to a free and unobstructed way to the exterior of the building which way is readily visible and identifiable from the point of discharge from the exit.

(b) The floor into which the exit discharges is protected throughout by an approved automatic sprinkler system and any other area with access to the level of discharge is provided with automatic sprinkler protection or separated from it in accordance with the requirements for the enclosure of exits (*see 5-1.3*).

(c) The entire area on the floor of discharge is separated from areas below by an assembly(ies) having a minimum of 2-hour fire resistance rating.

It is important to note that *all three* of the conditions in 26-2.7.2 must be met for any exit (of which there may be a maximum of 50 percent of the total required for the upper floors of the building) to discharge through a street floor *in less than a protected enclosed passageway*. These conditions are:
1. Free unobstructed passage through the floor of discharge from the base of the stair, ramp, or other allowed type of exit,
2. Automatic sprinkler protection for the floor of discharge and all spaces with direct access to the floor of discharge, or separation of the exit by means of an exit passageway, and
3. Separation of lower floors (basements) from the floor of discharge by 2-hour fire-resistant construction (see NFPA 220, *Standard Types of Building Construction*).[2]

26-2.8 Illumination of Means of Egress.   Exit illumination shall be provided in accordance with Section 5-8. For the purposes of this requirement, exit access shall include only designated aisles, corridors, and passageways leading to an exit.

26-2.9 Emergency Lighting.

26-2.9.1   Emergency lighting in accordance with Section 5-9 shall be required in any business occupancy building where:

(a) The building is two or more stories in height above the level of exit discharge, or

(b) The occupancy is subject to 100 or more occupants above or below the level of exit discharge, or

(c) The occupancy is subject to 1,000 or more total occupants.

For the purposes of this requirement, exit access shall include only designated aisles, corridors, and passageways leading to an exit.

If any of the three conditions of 26-2.9.1 are met, emergency lighting as specified in Section 5-9 is required for the building. Note that in item (a), the provision states that the building have two floors *above* the level of exit discharge or a minimum of three floors.

26-2.9.2   Emergency lighting in accordance with Section 5-9 shall be provided for all windowless or underground structures meeting the definition of 30-1.3.

26-2.10 Marking of Means of Egress.   Signs designating exits and ways of travel thereto shall be provided in accordance with Section 5-10.

26-2.11 Special Features.

26-2.11.1   Locks in accordance with the Exception stated in 5-2.1.2.1.1 shall be permitted only on principal entrance/exit doors.

The term principal entrance/exit doors is intended to imply doors which the authority having jurisdiction can be reasonably assured will be unlocked in order for the facility to do business.

26-2.11.2   Special locking arrangements in accordance with 5-2.1.2.1.5 are permitted.

This paragraph permits the time delay lock.

26-2.11.3   Where horizontal or vertical security grills or doors are used as a part of the required means of egress from a tenant space, such grills or doors shall be used in accordance with the provisions of 5-2.1.1.4.1.

26-2.11.4   Spiral stairs in accordance with 5-2.2.1.6 are permitted.

Note that spiral stairs can only serve an occupant load of five or fewer.

SECTION 26-3   PROTECTION

26-3.1 Protection of Vertical Openings.

26-3.1.1   Every stairway, elevator shaft, escalator opening, and other vertical opening shall be enclosed or protected in accordance with Section 6-2.

Exception No. 1:   Unprotected vertical openings connecting not more than three floors used for business occupancy only may be permitted in accordance with the conditions of Section 6-2.2.3.1 Exception No. 1.

Note that one of the requirements of 6-2.2.3.1, Exception No. 1 is that occupancies with ordinary hazard contents must be protected throughout by automatic sprinklers. Per 26-1.5, business occupancies are considered ordinary hazard.
See 26-4.3 for atrium provisions.

Exception No. 2:   A vertical opening enclosure will not be required for a vertical opening where:

(a) The vertical opening connects only two adjacent floors, neither of which is a basement, and

(b) The vertical opening is not a required means of egress, and

(c) The vertical opening is not connected with corridors or other stairways, and

(d) The building is protected throughout by an approved automatic sprinkler system, or the connected floors are protected throughout by an approved automatic smoke detection system installed in accordance with Section 7-6.

Exception No. 2 to 26-3.1.1 allows the two-level office or reference library in an office building. Item A restricts the use to only two levels. Item B requires that the stairs not be part of the means of egress; therefore, the space would have to have access to exits on both levels. Item C requires that the areas connected by the opening be separated from corridors and other stairways. Item D requires either total building sprinkler protection or total smoke detection on the levels connected.

26-3.1.2 Floors below the street floor used for storage or other than business occupancy shall have no unprotected openings to business occupancy floors.

Enforcing 26-3.1.2 prevents the possibility that a fire in a hazardous area with a high fuel load, e.g., areas used for shops, repairs, storage of maintenance supplies, files, or records, might directly expose the floor of exit discharge through an unprotected vertical opening. Studies have shown that there is a higher rate of fire incidence in basements than in other areas of business occupancies. Because smoke and heat rise, a fire in a basement can quickly cause exits and exit discharges located on the street floor to be unusable.

26-3.2 Protection from Hazards.

26-3.2.1 Any area used for general storage, boiler or furnace rooms, fuel storage, janitor closets, maintenance shops including woodworking and painting areas, and kitchens shall be separated from other parts of the building by construction having a fire resistance rating of not less than 1 hour, and all openings shall be protected with self-closing fire doors.

Exception: Areas protected by an automatic extinguishing system.

26-3.2.2 High hazard content areas, as defined in Section 4-2, shall be protected by both fire-rated construction and automatic extinguishing equipment.

Paragraphs 26-3.2.1 and 26-3.2.2 follow the general pattern (but not the specific requirements) of Section 6-4 which calls for either separation of the hazardous area by construction from the remainder of the occupancy, or minimization of the hazard by the installation of an automatic extinguishing system in the hazardous area.

26-3.3 Interior Finish.

26-3.3.1 Interior finish on walls and ceilings of exits and of enclosed corridors furnishing access thereto or ways of travel therefrom shall be Class A or Class B in accordance with Section 6-5.

26-3.3.2 In office areas, Class A, Class B, or Class C interior finish shall be provided in accordance with Section 6-5.

26-3.3.3 Interior Floor Finish.   No requirements.

26-3.4 Alarm and Communication Systems.   A manual fire alarm system shall be provided in accordance with Section 7-6 in any business occupancy where:

(a) The building is two or more stories in height above the level of exit discharge, or

(b) The occupancy is subject to 100 or more occupants above or below the level of exit discharge, or

(c) The occupancy is subject to 1,000 or more total occupants.

Exception No. 1:   In buildings protected throughout by an approved automatic fire detection and alarm initiation system in accordance with Section 7-6.

Exception No. 2:   In buildings protected throughout by an approved automatic sprinkler system in accordance with Section 7-7, which provides alarm initiation in accordance with Section 7-6.

If *any* of the three conditions in 26-3.4 exist, a manual alarm system is required for the building. Note that there is no difference between the three basic conditions of 26-2.9.1 and 26-3.4.

The reasoning behind Exception Nos. 1 and 2 is that manual alarm systems are required under the fundamental requirements of the *Life Safety Code* (see Section 2-7) if a building has a size and arrangement which would allow a fire to develop without the occupants being aware of the event. In such a case, a manual fire alarm system is used to warn the occupants. However, Exception Nos. 1 and 2 recognize that both automatic sprinkler systems and automatic fire detection systems sounding an alarm preclude the possibility of a fire taking place without the occupants being warned in time to evacuate the building safely. In addition, the extinguishing action of the automatic sprinkler system will in most cases control or hold down the size of the fire, reducing the threat posed to the occupants of the building. For these reasons, the requirement for manual fire alarm pull stations was removed.

26-3.5 Extinguishment Systems.   (*See Section 26-4.*)

26-3.6 Corridors.

26-3.6.1   Where access to exits is limited to corridors, such corridors shall be separated from use areas by partitions having a fire resistance rating of at least 1 hour.

Exception No. 1:   Where exits are available from an open floor area, corridors need not be separated.

Exception No. 2:   Corridors need not be separated within a space occupied by a single tenant.

Exception No. 3:   Corridors need not be separated within buildings protected throughout by an approved automatic sprinkler system.

The requirement in 26-3.6.1 is quite straightforward.

Exception No. 1 provides for the now popular "office landscape" or "open office" arrangements. If there is direct access to exits from the open area, it is not necessary to require separated corridors. This recognizes that a fire in an open space is more rapidly observed and reacted to than a fire in an enclosed room or office.

Exception No. 2 recognizes that in areas occupied by a single tenant there is a high level of familiarization with the space and that the partitioned offices or spaces are frequently monitored. It is the intent of "occupied by a single tenant" that simultaneous hours of operation exist so that a fire would not occur in a closed area and expose an occupied area.

Exception No. 3 recognizes the value of automatic sprinklers as a life safety feature.

26-3.6.2   Doors and frames, each with a minimum 20-minute fire protection rating, equipped with a positive latch and closing device, shall be used to protect openings in 1-hour partitions separating the corridor from use areas.

Note that 26-3.6.2 does require closing devices and positive latching devices on the doors but does not require all hardware on the door to be rated. It does require a 20-minute rating for the door frame and for the door itself.

This set of requirements should not be confused with those of a "fire door" which would require rated hardware for every door component (such as the latch, the keeper, the hinges, and the closer). The committee responsible for business occupancies felt that a rated door and frame would be sufficient for these purposes, and that is the limit and extent of the requirements of 26-3.6.2.

26-3.6.3 Glass vision panels within 1-hour fire-rated partitions, or doors therein, shall be limited to fixed wired glass in approved steel frames and shall be 1,296 sq in. (.84 sq m) or less in size per panel.

Note that there is no upper limit on the number of glass vision panels that may be installed in a corridor, only a limit of 1,296 sq in. (.84 sq m) on the area of each individual panel.

SECTION 26-4   SPECIAL PROVISIONS

26-4.1 Windowless or Underground Buildings.   (*See Section 30-7.*)

26-4.2 High-Rise Buildings.

In the design of high-rise buildings, special consideration should be given to a system for life safety which includes the following elements: movement of occupants to safety; control of fire and smoke; psychological features; communications; elevators (see 7-3.1); emergency planning; and overall system reliability.

The problems which high-rise buildings pose for life safety, fire fighting, and fire protection in general are covered in *High-Rise Building Fires and Fire Safety,*[3] *Fighting High-Rise Building Fires — Tactics and Logistics,*[4] and *Fires in High-Rise Buildings.*[5] All three publications contain extensive bibliographies on the subject.

26-4.2.1   All business occupancy buildings over 75 ft (22.86 m) in height shall be protected throughout by an approved automatic sprinkler system, fully electrically supervised and designed in accordance with *Standard for the Installation of Sprinkler Systems,* NFPA 13, or shall be designed with a system that will provide equivalent life safety as permitted by the provisions of Section 1-5. Building height shall be measured from the lowest level of fire department access to the floor of the highest occupiable story.

The requirement for the installation of automatic sprinkler protection in high-rise buildings [those over 75 ft (22.86 m) in height] recognizes the life safety problems encountered in this class of buildings. The committee on mercantile and business occupancies chose not to write a detailed set of requirements for safely arranging a high-rise business occupancy. Instead, the committee specified automatic sprinkler protection as the single most important element of a design that ensures a high level of life safety from fire. The committee also wished to allow the authority having jurisdiction to allow an equivalent life safety system. This is spelled out in the reference to Section 1-5.

26-4.2.2 In addition to the above requirements, all buildings regardless of height shall comply with all other applicable provisions of this chapter.

Paragraph 26-4.2.2 emphasizes that the provision for the installation of automatic sprinkler protection does not preclude the need for meeting the other requirements in the *Code* unless specific exceptions are granted to the *Code*'s text for the presence of automatic sprinklers.

26-4.3 Atriums.

26-4.3.1 Atriums are permitted provided they comply with Section 6-2 and 26-4.3.2 through 26-4.3.6.

26-4.3.2 The occupancy within the atrium meets the specifications for classification as low hazard contents. (*See 4-2.2.2.*)

Note that this is more restrictive than 6-2.2.3.1, Exception No. 2(c).

26-4.3.3 The automatic sprinkler system required by 6-2.2.3.1 Exception No. 2(e) shall be electrically supervised.

26-4.3.4 The atrium is provided with an automatic ventilation system operated by all of the following:

(a) Approved smoke detectors located at the top of the space and adjacent to each return air intake from the atrium, and

(b) The required automatic fire extinguishing system, and

(c) Manual controls which are readily accessible to the fire department.

The intent of 26-4.3.4 is to require a smoke control system as noted in Exception No. 2(f) to 6-2.2.3.1, and to modify the provisions of Exception No. 2(g) to not require the manual alarm to activate the smoke control system. Note that 26-4.3.5 does not require manual pull stations.

The reason for not permitting the manual alarm to activate the system is the possibility of persons pulling a manual alarm on other than the fire floor, thus possibly causing the smoke control system to improperly function.

26-4.3.5 Fire Alarm System. A fire alarm system shall be provided for the building in accordance with Section 7-6.

(a) The initiation of the fire alarm shall be by the activation of any smoke detectors or the automatic sprinkler system.

(b) Manual pull stations are not required.

26-4.3.6 All electrical equipment essential for smoke control or automatic extinguishing equipment for buildings more than six stories or 75 ft (22.86 m) in height containing an atrium shall be provided with an emergency source of power in accordance with *National Electrical Code*, NFPA 70, Section 700-12(b), or equivalent.

Section 700-12(b) of NFPA 70, *National Electrical Code*,[6] requires a generator set.

SECTION 26-5   BUILDING SERVICES

26-5.1   Utilities shall comply with the provisions of Section 7-1.

26-5.2   Heating, ventilating and air conditioning equipment shall comply with the provisions of Section 7-2.

26-5.3   Elevators, dumbwaiters and vertical conveyors shall comply with the provisions of Section 7-4.

Referral to Section 7-4 and its referenced document, ANSI A17.1,[7] will provide design criteria and specifications for the proper arrangement of an elevator control system, which will allow both automatic recall during a fire and fire department use exclusive of the normal automatic control mode of the elevator system.

26-5.4   Rubbish chutes, incinerators and laundry chutes shall comply with the provisions of Section 7-5.

REFERENCE CITED BY CODE

(These publications comprise a part of the requirements to the extent called for by the Code.)

NFPA 13, *Standard for the Installation of Sprinkler Systems*, NFPA, Boston, 1980.
NFPA 70, *National Electrical Code*, NFPA, Boston, 1981.

REFERENCES CITED IN COMMENTARY

[1]NFPA 13, *Standard for the Installation of Sprinkler Systems*, NFPA, Boston, 1980.
[2]NFPA 220, *Standard Types of Building Construction*, NFPA, Boston, 1979.
[3]*High-Rise Building Fires and Fire Safety*, NFPA SPP-18, NFPA, Boston, 1973.
[4]Robert F. Mendes, *Fighting High-Rise Building Fires — Tactics and Logistics*, NFPA FSP-44, NFPA, Boston, 1975.
[5]*Fires in High-Rise Buildings*, NFPA SPP-25, NFPA, Boston, 1974.
[6]NFPA 70, *National Electrical Code*, NFPA, Boston, 1981.
[7]ANSI A17.1-1978, *Safety Code for Elevators, Dumbwaiters, Escalators, and Moving Walks; and Supplement*: ANSI A17.1a-1979, American Society of Mechanical Engineers, 345 East 47th Street, New York, NY 10017.

27

EXISTING BUSINESS OCCUPANCIES

(See also Chapter 31.)

Business occupancies are those used for the transaction of business, for the keeping of accounts and records, and similar purposes. Minor office occupancies incidental to operations in another occupancy are considered as part of the predominating occupancy and are subject to the provisions of this *Code* as they apply to the predominating occupancy. The commentary for 27-1.4 in this chapter discusses classification of business occupancies in more detail.

SECTION 27-1   GENERAL REQUIREMENTS

27-1.1 Application.

27-1.1.1   Existing business occupancies shall comply with the provisions of this chapter. (*See Chapter 31 for operating features.*)

See Section 1-4 for application provisions. The comments on existing mercantile occupancies in 25-1.1 also apply to business occupancies.

27-1.1.2   This chapter establishes life safety requirements for existing buildings. Specific requirements for high-rise buildings [buildings over 75 ft (22.86 m) in height] are contained in paragraphs pertaining thereto.

New buildings are discussed in Chapter 26.

27-1.1.3 Modernization or Renovation.   No construction in either modernization or renovation projects shall diminish the fire safety features of the building below the level of new construction as described elsewhere in this *Code*. Alterations or installations of new building services equipment shall be accomplished as nearly as possible in conformance with the requirements for new construction. (*See Section 1-5 for equivalency concepts.*)

27-1.1.4   Additions to existing buildings shall conform to the requirements for new constructon. Existing portions of the structure need not be modified, provided that the new construction has not deminished the fire safety features of the facility.

689

27-1.2 Mixed Occupancies.

27-1.2.1 Combined Business and Mercantile Occupancy.

27-1.2.1.1 In any building occupied for both business and mercantile purposes, the entire building shall have exits in accordance with 1-4.5.

Exception: If mercantile occupancy sections are effectively segregated from business sections, exit facilities may be treated separately.

The exception to 27-1.2.1.1 is for emphasis only. A review of 1-4.5 shows that only if two different occupancies are "so intermingled that separate safeguards are impracticable," is it necessary for special consideration to be taken beyond the requirements of Chapter 27. Those considerations involve two steps:
1. The exit capacity of each room and section and of the entire building must be determined by careful calculations of the maximum occupant load applicable based on whether a room or section is used primarily for mercantile or business purposes.
2. The *Code*'s requirements for construction, protection, and related safeguards must meet those requirements imposed for the more hazardous occupancy. Or, to phrase it differently, the more stringent requirements for construction, protection, and for safeguards (extinguishing systems, emergency lighting, etc.) must apply *to the entire facility.*

Note that the exception to 27-1.2.1.1 *applies only to the means of egress* and permits designs based on a clearly defined separation of the mercantile portion from the business portion of a mixed occupancy. No. 2 above would still apply to the entire building.

27-1.3 Special Definitions.   None.

27-1.4 Classification of Occupancy.

27-1.4.1   Business occupancies shall include all buildings and structures or parts thereof with occupancy described in 4-1.8.

In reviewing the *Code*'s definition (see 4-1.8) of what constitutes a business occupancy, note that the definition *does not include* types of stores which, though a "business," are covered under the provisions of Chapter 25; e.g., supermarkets, department stores, and other occupancies which display and sell merchandise to large numbers of people. Doctors' offices, and treatment and diagnostic facilities not meeting the definition of a health care occupancy are included in business occupancies. (See Chapter 13.) Also not included are the public assembly portions of city halls, town halls, and courthouses which are covered under Chapter 9.

The following constitute business occupancies and are covered by the provisions of Chapter 27:
1. Those occupancies used for the transaction of business (other than those classified as mercantile occupancies).
2. Occupancies used for the keeping of accounts and records and for similar purposes.

Included in (1) and (2) are: doctors' offices, dentists' offices, general offices, and outpatient clinics, as well as city halls, town halls, and courthouses, all of which have areas for keeping books, records, and transacting public business. Other occupancies included under the definition of business occupancies are service facilities usual to office buildings such as newsstands, lunch counters (serving fewer than 50 people), barber shops, and beauty parlors.

Also, by reference from Chapter 11, college classroom buildings are considered office buildings.

27-1.5 Classification of Hazard of Contents.

27-1.5.1 The contents of business occupancies shall be classified as ordinary hazard in accordance with Section 4-2.

It should be pointed out that the classification of hazard of contents under the definitions in Section 4-2 of the *Life Safety Code* has no bearing or relationship to the hazard classification in NFPA 13, *Standard for the Installation of Sprinkler Systems*.[1]

27-1.5.2 For purposes of the design of an automatic sprinkler system, a business occupancy shall be classified as "light hazard occupancy," as identified by *Standard for the Installation of Sprinkler Systems*, NFPA 13.

Paragraph 27-1.5.2 was placed in the *Code* to show that contents classed as ordinary under the *Code* for life safety purposes are not classified as ordinary under NFPA 13, *Standard for the Installation of Sprinkler Systems*.[1] As indicated in 27-1.5.2, for purposes of sprinkler design, the anticipated fuel load of business occupancies in Chapter 13 is classed as "light hazard."

27-1.6 Minimum Construction Requirements. No requirements.

The provisions of a local building code may apply.

27-1.7 Occupant Load.

27-1.7.1 For purposes of determining required exits, the occupant load of business buildings or parts of buildings used for business purposes shall be no less than one person per 100 sq ft (9.29 sq m) of gross floor area.

27-1.7.2 In the case of a mezzanine or balcony open to the floor below or other unprotected vertical openings between floors as permitted by 27-3.1, the occupant load of the mezzanine or other subsidiary floor level shall be added to that of the street floor for the purpose of determining required exits. However, in no case shall the total number of exit units be less than would be required if all vertical openings were enclosed.

Since the number of people expected to occupy certain types of office buildings can be determined with a great degree of accuracy, e.g., through a company's detailed arrangement of its office space, it may prove beneficial to compare such a figure with one calculated on the basis of one person per 100 sq ft (9.29 sq m) of gross floor area (see 27-1.7.1). In concentrated office occupancies (particularly those used for government operations), the actual number of people found in a space may exceed the figure calculated by gross area. As emphasized in Section 5-3, when this is the case, the exit capacity must be designed on the basis of the actual occupant load. Note that the converse is not true; namely, if the actual occupant load is less than the gross area calculation, the *Code* still requires that the gross area calculation be used to determine the required exit capacity.

The requirements of 27-1.7.2 are identical to those of 25-1.7.2 for mercantile occupancies. The examples in Figures 25-2 and 25-3 of how to determine the exit capacity for the street floor of a mercantile occupancy apply equally well to a business occupancy. Note that 27-2.3.3 is consonant with 25-2.3.2; in both mercantile and business occupancies, the street floor needs to provide 1½ units of exit width for every 2 units required for stairways discharging through the street floor.

SECTION 27-2   MEANS OF EGRESS REQUIREMENTS

27-2.1 General.

27-2.1.1 All means of egress shall be in accordance with Chapter 5 and this chapter. However, only types of exits specified in 27-2.2 may be used as required exit facilities in any business occupancy with access thereto and ways of travel therefrom in accordance with Chapter 5.

27-2.1.2 If, owing to differences in grade, any street floor exits are at points above or below the street or ground level, such exits shall comply with the provisions for exits from upper floors or floors below the street floor.

Figure 25-4 illustrates a case where two street floors of a mercantile occupancy are at ground level at one side of a building, but either above or below ground level at the other side. Many business occupancies have a similar configuration. The two "street" floors must have their exits arranged to allow horizontal travel to the exterior on one end of the floor and vertical travel (either up or down to ground level) at the other end of the floor. This means that the exit capacity to the exterior must be able to accommodate, in the case of Floor 1, people from the higher floors who may need to travel down to and through the exits to the exterior on Floor 1. The reverse holds true for Floor 2, which must size its exterior exit capacity to accommodate occupants who may travel up from Floor 1 as well as occupants who may have to travel down to, and through, the exterior exits on Floor 2. Paragraphs 5-3.1.4, 27-1.7.2, and 27-2.3.3 demonstrate how to add exit capacity based on expected occupant use from floors above the street floor. (This method is equally valid for adding exit capacity based on expected occupant use from floors below the street floor.) Figure 25-5 provides an example of how to calculate exit capacity for a street floor, such as Floor 2 in Figure 25-4.

27-2.1.3 Where a stairway, escalator, outside stair, or ramp serves two or more upper floors, the same stairway or other exit required to serve any one upper floor may also serve other upper floors.

Exception: No inside open stairway, escalator, or ramp may serve as a required egress facility from more than one floor.

Under 27-2.1.3, if the second and third floor of a business occupancy were each required to have three stairways, the second floor could use the stairways serving the third floor so that the total number of stairways required would be three, not six.

Note that the exception prohibits the use of *open* stairways, escalators, or ramps as an egress facility for more than one floor.

27-2.1.4 Where two or more floors below the street floor are occupied for business use, the same stairways, escalators or ramps may serve each.

Exception: No inside open stairway, escalators or ramp may serve as a required egress facility from more than one floor level.

The explanation to 27-2.1.3 also applies to 27-2.1.4. The only difference is that these floors are *below* the street floor. In both 27-2.1.3 and 27-2.1.4, it is important to remember to base the width of the stair, escalator, or ramp on the floor with the largest occupant load. In this way it can be expected that a stair or other component of a means of egress will accommodate the population of *any* floor it serves. Again, note the prohibition in 27-2.1.4 against open stairs, escalators, or ramps serving more than one floor.

27-2.1.5 Floor levels below the street floor used only for storage, heating, and other service equipment, and not subject to business occupancy, shall have exits in accordance with Chapter 29.

A significant reduction in the number and size of exits is allowed for floors used for the purposes specified in 27-2.1.5, since the expected population of such floors will be well below that of the typical business floor.

27-2.2 Types of Exits.

27-2.2.1 Exits shall be restricted to the following permissible types:

  (a) *Doors (see 5-2.1).*
  (b) *Interior stairs, Class A or B (see 5-2.2).*
  (c) *Smokeproof towers (see 5-2.3).*
  (d) *Outside stairs (see 5-2.5).*
  (e) *Horizontal exits (see 5-2.4).*
  (f) *Ramps (see 5-2.6).*
  (g) *Exit passageways (see 5-2.7).*
  (h) *Escalators (see 5-2.8).*
  (i) *Revolving doors (see 5-2.1).*
  (j) *Fire escape stairs (see 5-2.9).*

Note that 5-2.9.1.1.1 permits *existing* buildings to continue to use fire escape stairs for no more than 50 percent of their required exit capacity.

27-2.2.2 An existing interior stair or outside stair not complying with 5-2.2 or 5-2.5 may be continued in use subject to the approval of the authority having jurisdiction.

The authority must determine if equivalent life safety is being provided.

27-2.2.3 Slide escapes, elevators or other types of exit facility not specified in 27-2.2.1 shall not be used to provide required exits from any business occupancy.

27-2.3 Capacity of Means of Egress.

27-2.3.1 The minimum width of any corridor or passageway shall be 44 in. (111.76 cm) in the clear.

27-2.3.2 The capacity of a unit of exit width shall be as follows:

(a) Doors, including those leading outside the building at the ground level, or three risers above or below the ground level — one unit for 100 persons.

(b) Class A or Class B stairs, outside stairs or smokeproof towers — one unit for 60 persons.

(c) Ramps: Class A — one unit for 100 persons; Class B — one unit for 60 persons.

(d) Escalators — one unit for 60 persons.

(e) Horizontal exits — one unit for 100 persons, but no more than 50 percent of the required exit capacity.

> For an escalator to count as a means of egress and be assigned a capacity of 1 unit of exit width for 60 people, it is required that the escalator be enclosed in the same manner as an interior exit stair. (See 5-2.8 and Section 6-2.) Note that escalators protected in accordance with the sprinkler-vent method, the spray nozzle method, the rolling shutter method, or the partial enclosure method do not constitute an acceptable exit and cannot be used in calculating the required exit capacity.

27-2.3.3 Any street floor exit, arranged as required by 27-2.4 and 27-2.6, shall be sufficient to provide the following numbers of units of exit width:

(a) One unit for each 100 persons capacity of the street floor, plus

(b) One and one-half units for each two units of stairway, ramp or escalator from upper floors discharging through the street floor, plus

(c) One and one-half units for each two units of stairway, ramp or escalator from floor levels below the street floor.

> Refer to 27-1.7.2 and 27-2.1.2 when considering the requirements of 27-2.3.3. The committee, in 27-2.3.3, was attempting to provide the exit discharge for the street floor of a business occupancy with sufficient capacity to handle the people who, in exiting the building during an emergency, must travel up from the basement or down from the upper floors, and mix with the occupants who are already on the first, or street, floor.
>
> Since people move more quickly in the horizontal than in the vertical direction (by a factor of 4 to 3, i.e., 60 people a minute through a horizontal exit as opposed to 45 a minute down stairs — see commentary for 5-3.3), it is permissible to provide *less* door width than stair width. Thus, the *Code* requires doors of 1½ exit units for every 2 units of exit width provided by stairs, ramps, or escalators which discharge into the street floor. (Note that 2 to 1½ = 4 to 3.) Figure 25-5 provides an example of how to calculate the required exit capacity for the street floor.
>
> An alternative method is to total the units of exit width for any stairs, ramps, or escalators (where the escalators conform to the requirements of 5-2.2) which discharge through the street floor. Multiply the total by ¾ and add the results to the units of exit width (at 100 people per unit) required to handle the population of the street floor. This total will provide a door capacity for the street floor which meets the requirements of 27-2.3.3.

27-2.4 Number of Exits. Not less than two exits shall be accessible from every part of every floor, including floor levels below the street floor occupied for business purposes or uses incidental thereto.

> **Paragraph 27-2.4 would require the 19 units calculated in Figure 25-5 to be divided into at least two groupings of 9½ units located at opposite or remote points on the street floor. Similarly, the required stair capacity from the upper and lower floors must be separated into at least two groupings remote from each other.**

Exception No. 1:   For a room or area with a total occupant load of less than 100 persons (or less than 50 if a place of assembly — see Chapter 9), having direct exit to the street or to an open area outside the building at the ground level, with a total travel distance from any point of not over 100 ft (30.48 m), a single exit may be permitted. Such travel shall be on the same floor level or, if the traversing of stairs is required, such stairs shall not be more than 15 ft (457.2 cm) in height, and they shall be provided with complete enclosures to separate them from any other part of the building, with no door openings therein.

> **Figures 27-1 and 27-2 illustrate two cases where a single exit is allowed from a room or area in a business occupancy (see Exception No. 1 to 27-2.4). In the first case, the travel distance from the area is on the same floor level as the exit. In the second, stairs must be traversed.**
> **The criteria for allowing the single exit are:**
>   1. **Occupant load less than 100 (less than 50 if a place of assembly),**
>   2. **Direct exit to a street or to an open exterior area at ground level,**
>   3. **Total travel distance no more than 100 ft (30.48 m) from anywhere in the room to the exterior,**
>   4. **Any stairs no more than 15 ft (457.2 cm) in height, and**
>   5. **Any stairs completely enclosed with no door openings between the stair enclosure and the rest of the building.**
> **If *any* of Conditions 1 to 5 are not met, two exits are required from the room or space in question.**

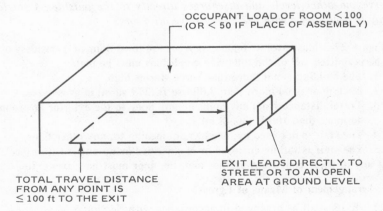

OCCUPANT LOAD OF ROOM < 100
(OR < 50 IF PLACE OF ASSEMBLY)

EXIT LEADS DIRECTLY TO STREET OR TO AN OPEN AREA AT GROUND LEVEL

TOTAL TRAVEL DISTANCE FROM ANY POINT IS ≤ 100 ft TO THE EXIT

Figure 27-1. Single Exit from an Area or Room in a Business Occupancy. Travel from area to exit is horizontal.

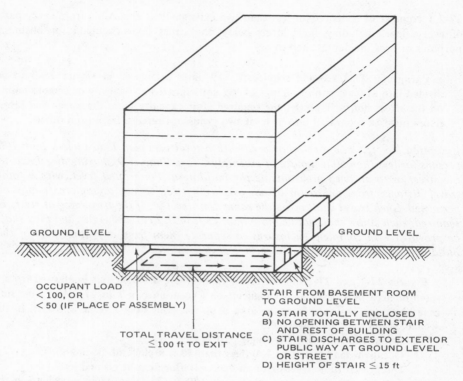

GROUND LEVEL   GROUND LEVEL

OCCUPANT LOAD
< 100, OR
< 50 (IF PLACE OF ASSEMBLY)

STAIR FROM BASEMENT ROOM
TO GROUND LEVEL
A) STAIR TOTALLY ENCLOSED
B) NO OPENING BETWEEN STAIR
   AND REST OF BUILDING
C) STAIR DISCHARGES TO EXTERIOR
   PUBLIC WAY AT GROUND LEVEL
   OR STREET
D) HEIGHT OF STAIR ≤ 15 ft

TOTAL TRAVEL DISTANCE
≤ 100 ft TO EXIT

Figure 27-2. Single Exit from an Area or Room in a Business Occupancy Where Stairs Must Be Traversed.

Exception No. 2: Any business occupancy not over three stories and not exceeding 3,000 sq ft (279 sq m) gross floor area per floor may be permitted with a single separate exit to each floor if the total travel distance to the outside of the building does not exceed 100 ft (30.48 m) and if such exit is enclosed in accordance with 5-1.3 and serves no other levels and discharges directly to the outside. A single outside stairway in accordance with 5-2.5 may serve all floors.

Figure 27-3 illustrates a single exit from the third floor of a business occupancy. To be permitted, *all* of the following conditions must be met:
1. The building is not more than three stories high,
2. Each floor is no more than 3,000 sq ft (279 sq m) in gross area,
3. Travel distance from any point on any floor to the exterior at ground level is no more than 100 ft (30.48 m),
4. The stair is not used by, nor has an opening to, any other floor,
5. The stair is totally enclosed or is classified as an outside stair (see 5-2.5).

If any of these conditions are not met, the floor must have two exits.

27-2.5 Arrangement of Means of Egress.

27-2.5.1 Exits shall be arranged in accordance with Section 5-5.

Required exits must be suitably located to allow access without passage through areas which might be locked.

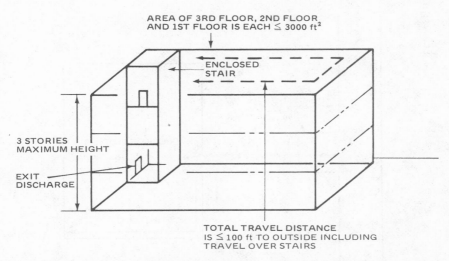

AREA OF 3RD FLOOR, 2ND FLOOR
AND 1ST FLOOR IS EACH ≤ 3000 ft²

ENCLOSED
STAIR

3 STORIES
MAXIMUM HEIGHT

EXIT
DISCHARGE

TOTAL TRAVEL DISTANCE
IS ≤ 100 ft TO OUTSIDE INCLUDING
TRAVEL OVER STAIRS

Figure 27-3. Single Exit from Third Floor of a Business Occupancy. Stair is totally enclosed, has opening only at third floor, and discharges directly to street with no communication at second and first floors. A similar arrangement could be provided for the second floor of the same building.

27-2.5.2   No dead-end corridor shall exceed 50 ft (15.24 m).

Exception: A common path may be permitted for the first 50 ft (15.24 m) from any point.

The exception to 27-2.5.2 allows room to be located along the ends of corridors so that travel to an exit is possible in only one direction for the first 50 ft (15.24 m) from the doorway of a room. After the 50-ft (15.24-m) point the corridor, or exit access, must provide at least two paths to two separate exits. This assumes that, in accordance with 5-6.4, each room will not be occupied by more than six people and that the distance between any point in a room and the door to the corridor does not exceed 50 ft (15.24 m). Common paths of travel are illustrated in Figures 27-4A and 27-4B.

27-2.6 Measurement of Travel Distance to Exits.   Travel distance to exits, measured in accordance with 5-6, shall be no more than 200 ft (60.96 m).

Exception: An increase in the above travel distance to 300 ft (91.44 m) shall be permitted in a building protected throughout by an approved automatic sprinkler system in accordance with Section 7-7.

Paragraph 5-6.4 allows travel distance to an exit to be measured from the corridor door of a room occupied by not more than six people if the distance between the door to the corridor and the most remote point in the room is not more than 50 ft (15.24 m). This allowance leads to possible cumulative travel distances of up to 250 ft (76.20 m) [350 ft (106.68 m) in a building completely protected by an automatic sprinkler system].

A review of 5-6.2 will show that the travel distance requirements apply to only the first (or nearest) exit from a point in a building. For example, the 200-ft (60.96-m)

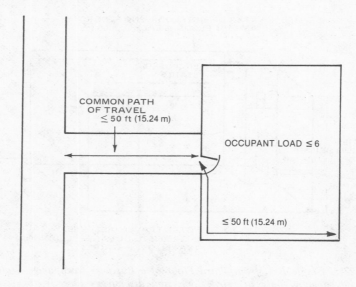

Figure 27-4A. Allowed Common Path of Travel in a Business Occupancy. Measure from room door to point where corridor provides access to two separate exits. The travel distance from any point in the room to the corridor door must not exceed 50 ft (15.24 m) and the occupant load must be six or fewer.

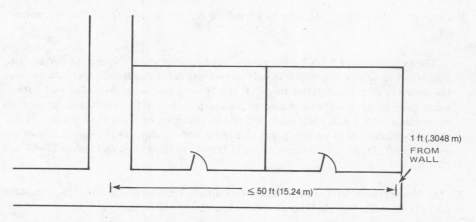

Figure 27-4B. Allowed Dead End in a Business Occupancy. Measure from a point 1 ft (30.48 cm) in from end of corridor to point where access to two separate and remote exits is provided. Measurement is made in the same fashion as travel distance (see 5-6.2).

travel distance limit means that at least one exit must be within 200 ft (60.96 m) of a point in the building, not that all exits must be within 200 ft (60.96 m) of that point in the building.

27-2.7 Discharge from Exits.

27-2.7.1   At least half of the required number of units of exit width from upper floors, exclusive of horizontal exits, shall lead directly to the street or through a yard, court, or passageway with protected openings and separated from all parts of the interior of the building.

Paragraph 27-2.7.1 requires that at least 50 percent of the exits from the upper floors of a business occupancy discharge directly to the exterior. If such an exit does not discharge directly to a "public way," 27-2.7.1 requires an exit passageway. For the remaining exits (of which there can be a maximum of 50 percent) which do not discharge directly to the exterior or through an enclosed passageway, see 27-2.7.2.

27-2.7.2 A maximum of 50 percent of the exits may discharge through areas on the level of discharge provided:

(a) Such exits discharge to a free and unobstructed way to the exterior of the building, which way is readily visible and identifiable from the point of discharge from the exit.

(b) The floor into which the exit discharges is protected throughout by an approved automatic sprinkler system and any other area with access to the level of discharge is provided with automatic sprinkler protection or separated from it in accordance with the requirements for the enclosure of exits (*see 5-1.3*).

(c) The entire area on the floor of discharge is separated from areas below by an assembly(ies) having a minimum of 2-hour fire resistance rating.

It is important to note that *all three* of the conditions in 27-2.7.2 must be met for any exit (of which there may be a maximum of 50 percent of the total required for the upper floors of the building) to discharge through a street floor *in less than a protected enclosed passageway*. These conditions are:
1. Free unobstructed passage through the floor of discharge from the base of the stair, ramp, or other allowed type of exit,
2. Automatic sprinkler protection for the floor of discharge and all spaces with direct access to the floor of discharge, or separation of the exit by means of an exit passageway, and
3. Separation of lower floors (basements) from the floor of discharge by 2-hour fire-resistant construction (see NFPA 220, *Standard Types of Building Construction*).[2]

27-2.8 Illumination of Means of Egress. Exit illumination shall be provided in accordance with Section 5-8. For the purposes of this requirement, exit access shall include only designated aisles, corridors, and passageways leading to an exit.

27-2.9 Emergency Lighting.

27-2.9.1 Emergency lighting in accordance with Section 5-9 shall be required in any business occupancy building where:

(a) The building is two or more stories in height above the level of exit discharge, or

(b) The occupancy is subject to 100 or more occupants above or below the level of exit discharge, or

(c) The occupancy is subject to 1,000 or more total occupants.

For the purpose of this requirement, exit access shall include only designated aisles, corridors, and passageways leading to an exit.

If any of the three conditions of 27-2.9.1 are met, emergency lighting as specified in Section 5-9 is required for the building. Note that in item (a), the provision states that the building have two floors *above* the level of exit discharge or a minimum of three floors.

27-2.9.2   Emergency lighting in accordance with Section 5-9 shall be provided for all windowless or underground structures meeting the definition of 30-1.3.

27-2.10 Marking of Means of Egress.   Signs designating exits and ways of travel thereto shall be provided in accordance with Section 5-10.

27-2.11 Special Features.

27-2.11.1   Locks in accordance with the Exception stated in 5-2.1.2.1.1 shall be permitted only on principal entrance/exit doors.

The term principal entrance/exit doors is intended to imply doors which the authority having jurisdiction can be reasonably assured will be unlocked in order for the facility to do business.

27-2.11.2   Special locking arrangements in accordance with 5-2.1.2.1.5 are permitted.

This paragraph permits the time delay lock.

27-2.11.3   Where horizontal or vertical security grills or doors are used as a part of the required means of egress from a tenant space, such grills or doors shall be used in accordance with the provisions of 5-2.1.1.4.1.

27-2.11.4   Spiral stairs in accordance with 5-2.2.1.6 are permitted.

Note that spiral stairs can only serve an occupant load of five or fewer.

27-2.11.5   Winders in stairs in accordance with 5-2.2.2.4 are permitted.

SECTION 27-3   PROTECTION

27-3.1 Protection of Vertical Openings.

27-3.1.1   Every stairway, elevator shaft, escalator opening, and other vertical opening shall be enclosed or protected in accordance with Section 6-2.

Exception No. 1: Unprotected vertical openings connecting not more than three floors used for business occupancy only may be permitted in accordance with the conditions of Section 6-2.2.3.1 Exception No. 1.

Note that one of the requirements of 6-2.2.3.1, Exception No. 1 is that occupancies with ordinary hazard contents must be protected throughout by

automatic sprinklers. Per 26-1.5, business occupancies are considered ordinary hazard.

See 27-4.3 for atrium provisions.

Exception No. 2: In buildings protected throughout by an approved automatic sprinkler system in accordance with Section 7-7, vertical openings may be unprotected if no unprotected vertical opening serves as any part of any required exit facility and all required exits consist of smokeproof towers in accordance with 5-2.3, outside stairs in accordance with 5-2.5, or horizontal exits in accordance with 5-2.4.

In Exception No. 2 to 27-3.1.1, not only must the building be protected with complete automatic sprinkler protection, but *all* building exits must consist of either smokeproof towers, outside stairs, horizontal exits, or a door directly to the outside at ground level. Otherwise, the unprotected vertical openings must be suitably enclosed.

Exception No. 3: A vertical opening enclosure will not be required for a vertical opening where:

(a) The vertical opening connects only two adjacent floors, neither of which is a basement, and

(b) The vertical opening is not a required means of egress, and

(c) The vertical opening is not connected with corridors or other stairways, and

(d) The building is protected throughout by an approved automatic sprinkler system, or the connected floors are protected throughout by an approved automatic smoke detection system installed in accordance with Section 7-6.

Exception No. 3 to 27-3.1.1 allows the two-level office or reference library in an office building. Item A restricts the use to only two levels. Item B requires that the stairs not be part of the means of egress; therefore, the space would have to have access to exits on both levels. Item C requires that the areas connected by the opening be separated from corridors and other stairways. Item D requires either total building sprinkler protection or total smoke detection on the levels connected.

27-3.1.2 Floors below the street floor used for storage or other than business occupancy shall have no unprotected openings to business occupancy floors.

Enforcing 27-3.1.2 prevents the possibility that a fire in a hazardous area with a high fuel load, e.g., areas used for shops, repairs, storage of maintenance supplies, files, or records, might directly expose the floor of exit discharge through an unprotected vertical opening. Studies have shown that there is a higher rate of fire incidence in basements than in other areas of business occupancies. Because smoke and heat rise, a fire in a basement can quickly cause exits and exit discharges located on the street floor to be unusable.

27-3.2 Protection from Hazards.

27-3.2.1 Any area used for general storage, boiler or furnace rooms, fuel storage, janitor closets, maintenance shops including woodworking and painting areas, and kitchens shall be separated from other parts of the building by construction having a fire resistance rating of not less than 1 hour, and all openings shall be protected with self-closing fire doors.

Exception: Areas protected by an automatic extinguishing system.

27-3.2.2 High hazard content areas, as defined in Section 4-2, shall be protected by both fire-rated construction and automatic extinguishing equipment.

> **Paragraphs 27-3.2.1 and 27-3.2.2 follow the general pattern (but not the specific requirements) of Section 6-4 which calls for either separation of the hazardous area by construction from the remainder of the occupancy, or minimization of the hazard by the installation of an automatic extinguishing system in the hazardous area.**

27-3.3 Interior Finish.

27-3.3.1 Interior finish on walls and ceilings of exits and of enclosed corridors furnishing access thereto or ways of travel therefrom shall be Class A or Class B in accordance with Section 6-5.

27-3.3.2 In office areas, Class A, Class B, or Class C interior finish shall be provided in accordance with Section 6-5.

27-3.3.3 Interior Floor Finish.   No requirements.

27-3.4 Alarm and Communication Systems.   A manual fire alarm system shall be provided in accordance with Section 7-6 in any business occupancy where:

(a) The building is two or more stories in height above the level of exit discharge, or

(b) The occupancy is subject to 100 or more occupants above or below the level of exit discharge, or

(c) The occupancy is subject to 1,000 or more total occupants.

Exception No. 1:   In buildings protected throughout by an approved automatic sprinkler system in accordance with both Sections 7-6 and 7-7.

Exception No. 2:   In buildings protected throughout by an approved automatic fire detection system in accordance with Section 7-6.

> **If *any* of the three conditions in 27-3.4 exist, a manual alarm system is required for the building. Note that there is no difference between the three basic conditions of 27-2.9.1 and 27-3.4.**
>
> **The reasoning behind Exception Nos. 1 and 2 is that manual alarm systems are required under the fundamental requirements of the *Life Safety Code* (see Section 2-7) if a building has a size and arrangement which would allow a fire to develop without the occupants being aware of the event. In such a case, a manual fire alarm system is used to warn the occupants. However, Exception Nos. 1 and 2 recognize that both automatic sprinkler systems and automatic fire detection systems sounding an alarm preclude the possibility of a fire taking place without the occupants being warned in time to evacuate the building safely. In addition, the extinguishing action of the automatic sprinkler system will in most cases control or hold down the size of the fire, reducing the threat posed to the occupants of the building. For these reasons, the requirement for manual fire alarm pull stations was removed.**

27-3.5 Extinguishment Systems.   (*See Section 27-4.*)

SECTION 27-4   SPECIAL PROVISIONS

27-4.1 Windowless or Underground Buildings. *(See Section 30-7.)*

27-4.2 High-Rise Buildings.

In the design of high-rise buildings, special consideration should be given to a system for life safety which includes the following elements: movement of occupants to safety; control of fire and smoke; psychological features; communications; elevators (see 7-3.1); emergency planning; and overall system reliability.

The problems which high-rise buildings pose for life safety, fire fighting, and fire protection in general are covered in *High-Rise Building Fires and Fire Safety,*[3] *Fighting High-Rise Building Fires — Tactics and Logistics,*[4] and *Fires in High-Rise Buildings.*[5] All three publications contain extensive bibliographies on the subject.

27-4.2.1 All business occupancy buildings over 75 ft (22.86 m) in height shall be protected throughout by an approved automatic sprinkler system, fully electrically supervised and designed in accordance with *Standard for the Installation of Sprinkler Systems,* NFPA 13; or shall be designed with a system that will provide equivalent life safety as permitted by the provisions of Section 1-5. Building height shall be measured from the lowest level of fire department access to the floor of the highest occupiable story.

The requirement for the installation of automatic sprinkler protection in high-rise buildings [those over 75 ft (22.86 m) in height] recognizes the life safety problems encountered in this class of buildings. The committee on mercantile and business occupancies chose not to write a detailed set of requirements for safely arranging a high-rise business occupancy. Instead, the committee specified automatic sprinkler protection as the single most important element of a design that ensures a high level of life safety from fire. The committee also wished to allow the authority having jurisdiction to allow an equivalent life safety system. This is spelled out in the reference to Section 1-5.

27-4.2.2 In addition to the above requirements, all buildings regardless of height shall comply with all other applicable provisions of this chapter.

Paragraph 27-4.2.2 emphasizes that the provision for the installation of automatic sprinkler protection does not preclude the need for meeting the other requirements in the *Code* unless specific exceptions are granted to the *Code*'s text for the presence of automatic sprinklers.

27-4.3 Atriums.

27-4.3.1 Atriums are permitted provided they comply with Section 6-2 and 27-4.3.2 through 27-4.3.3.

27-4.3.2 The occupancy within the atrium meets the specifications for classification as low hazard contents. *(See 4-2.2.2.)*

Note that this is more restrictive than 6-2.2.3.1, Exception No. 2(c).

27-4.3.3   The automatic sprinkler system required by 6-2.2.3.1 Exception No. 2(e) shall be electrically supervised.

27-4.3.4   The atrium is provided with an automatic ventilation system operated by all of the following:

(a) Approved smoke detectors located at the top of the space and adjacent to each return air intake from the atrium, and

(b) The required automatic fire extinguishing system, and

(c) Manual controls which are readily accessible to the fire department.

The intent of 27-4.3.4 is to require a smoke control system as noted in Exception No. 2(f) to 6-2.2.3.1, and to modify the provisions of Exception No. 2(g) to not require the manual alarm to activate the smoke control system. Note that 27-4.3.5 does not require manual pull stations.

The reason for not permitting the manual alarm to activate the system is the possibility of persons pulling a manual alarm on other than the fire floor, thus possibly causing the smoke control system to improperly function.

27-4.3.5 Fire Alarm System.   A fire alarm system shall be provided for the building in accordance with Section 7-6.

(a) The initiation of the fire alarm shall be by the activation of any smoke detectors or the automatic sprinkler system.

(b) Manual pull stations are not required.

27-4.3.6   All electrical equipment essential for smoke control or automatic extinguishing equipment for buildings more than six stories or 75 ft (22.86 m) in height containing an atrium shall be provided with an emergency source of power in accordance with *National Electrical Code*, NFPA 70, Section 700-12(b), or equivalent.

Section 700-12(b) of NFPA 70, *National Electrical Code,*[6] requires a generator set.

SECTION 27-5   BUILDING SERVICES

27-5.1   **Utilities** shall comply with the provisions of Section 7-1.

27-5.2   **Heating, ventilating, and air conditioning equipment** shall comply with the provisions of Section 7-2.

27-5.3   **Elevators, dumbwaiters and vertical conveyors** shall comply with the provisions of Section 7-4.

Referral to Section 7-4 and its referenced document, ANSI A17.1,[7] will provide design criteria and specifications for the proper arrangement of an elevator control system, which will allow both automatic recall during a fire and fire department use exclusive of the normal automatic control mode of the elevator system.

27-5.4   **Rubbish chutes, incinerators and laundry chutes** shall comply with the provisions of Section 7-5.

REFERENCES CITED BY *CODE*

(These publications comprise a part of the requirements to the extent called for by the Code.)

NFPA 13, *Standard for the Installation of Sprinkler Systems*, NFPA, Boston, 1980.

NFPA 70, *National Electrical Code*, NFPA, Boston, 1981.

REFERENCES CITED IN COMMENTARY

[1]NFPA 13, *Standard for the Installation of Sprinkler Systems*, NFPA, Boston, 1980.

[2]NFPA 220, *Standard Types of Building Construction*, NFPA, Boston, 1979.

[3]*High-Rise Building Fires and Fire Safety*, NFPA SPP-18, NFPA, Boston, 1973.

[4]Robert F. Mendes, *Fighting High-Rise Building Fires — Tactics and Logistics*, NFPA FSP-44, NFPA, Boston, 1975.

[5]*Fires in High-Rise Buildings*, NFPA SPP-25, NFPA, Boston, 1974.

[6]NFPA 70, *National Electrical Code*, NFPA, Boston, 1981.

[7]ANSI A17.1-1978, *Safety Code for Elevators, Dumbwaiters, Escalators, and Moving Walks and Supplements*: ANSI A17.1a-1979; American Society of Mechanical Engineers, 345 East 47th Street, New York, NY 10017.

28

INDUSTRIAL
OCCUPANCIES

(See also Chapter 31.)

Industrial occupancies is a broad classification. The types of activities included in this classification are indicated by the following examples of some industrial occupancies:

Factories of all kinds	Creameries
Laboratories	Gas plants
Dry-cleaning plants	Refineries
Power plants	Sawmills
Pumping stations	Smokehouses
Laundries	

SECTION 28-1   GENERAL REQUIREMENTS

28-1.1 Application.   The requirements of this chapter apply to both new and existing Industrial Occupancies. Industrial occupancies include factories making products of all kinds and properties used for operations such as processing, assembling, mixing, packaging, finishing or decorating, repairing and similar operations.

Unlike the previous occupancy chapters, industrial occupancies cover both new and existing occupancies in one chapter.

The potential for loss of life from fire in an industrial occupancy is directly related to the hazard of the industrial operation or process. Records show that the majority of industrial fires that result in multiple deaths are the result of (1) flash fires in highly combustible material or (2) explosions involving combustible dusts, flammable liquids, or gases.

Although industrial fire losses constitute a high percentage of the annual fire loss in property, such fires have not, as a general rule, resulted in extensive loss of life. A number of operating features common to industrial occupancies have contributed to this favorable experience. Continued emphasis on proper exit design and maintenance, and day-to-day attention to industrial safety and training programs can help to continue this trend.

707

One of the major elements to consider in the design of an industrial building's life safety system is the widespread utilization of automatic sprinkler protection. Originally developed for industrial property protection, the automatic sprinkler has also been largely responsible for an excellent life safety record in industrial occupancies. This record has been recognized by fire protection engineers and other authorities, as evidenced by the recent widespread use of automatic sprinkler systems for life safety protection in buildings with significant hazards to life. Automatic sprinkler protection in industrial occupancies has been a principal factor in ensuring life safety through the control of "fire spread." Limiting the size of a fire by the operation of sprinklers provides sufficient time for the safe evacuation of people exposed to a fire. The contribution of the automatic sprinkler to life safety can only be fully appreciated when one recognizes the wide range of fire risks related to the variety of processes used in an industrial plant.

Employees and other occupants of industrial buildings are generally ambulatory and fully capable of a quick response to fires, and are also able to exit rapidly once properly alerted. To capitalize on this employee capability, many industrial plants include life safety measures in their emergency preplanning. A well-thought-out plan provides a valuable tool for helping to prevent loss of life. Provisions which should be included in the emergency preplan include measures for alerting employees, identification and posting of exit access routes, establishing group assembly areas for evacuees outside the building, plus procedures for determining if all employees have safely exited. Responsibilities are usually established in the preplan to ensure that necessary tasks to facilitate safe exiting of the building are accomplished. The preplan should be routinely evaluated by simulated fire exercises and fire drills. Only through such drills can weaknesses in the preplan be recognized and the plan modified.

Although life safety experience in industry has been relatively good, a major problem may be emerging in the trend toward constructing large industrial plants housing hazardous operations. The introduction of new materials, such as extensive quantities of plastics, has increased the need for additional measures to help ensure the life safety of employees from fire. Compared with industrial buildings of the early twentieth century, the modern industrial complex has placed a larger number of employees in a more complex and increasingly hazardous environment. This trend has increased the need for industrial management to concentrate on life safety principles not only during design but also during day-to-day plant operations.

Most industrial firms include in the employee training program an orientation in the use of first aid fire fighting equipment such as in-plant standpipes, hose, and fire extinguishers. Industrial training of this type, where fully utilized, has resulted in a major reduction in property loss and loss of life. Although first aid fire fighting measures are primarily a property protection measure, there is also a significant life safety benefit. In any situation where the spread of a fire is checked through effective employee action, employee life safety is also provided. If fire spread is restricted to the incipient stages, there is no significant threat to life safety.

28-1.2 Mixed Occupancies.   In any building occupied for both industrial and other purposes, exits shall comply with 1-4.5.

28-1.3 Special Definitions.   None.

28-1.4 Classification of Occupancy.   (*See 4-1.9, and for open industrial structures, see Chapter 30.*)

28-1.4.1 General Industrial Occupancy. Ordinary and low hazard manufacturing operations, conducted in buildings of conventional design suitable for various types of manufacture. Included are multistory buildings where floors are rented to different tenants or buildings suitable for such occupancy and, therefore, subject to possible use for types of manufacturing with a high density of employee population.

The method for determining the degree of hazard to life safety of an industrial occupancy is at best a result of personal judgment and not an exact science. The authority having jurisdiction must use judgment based on past personal experience, a review of the reference materials, and full discussion with third parties to evaluate the life safety measures in an industrial occupancy. The *Code* establishes broad categories of occupancy classification so that the relative risks to life safety of various types of buildings can be assessed.

One mistake common to occupancy hazard classification in industrial buildings is the use of risk categories for automatic sprinklers from NFPA 13, *Standard for the Installation of Sprinkler Systems*,[1] in determining the hazard to life safety. While the guidelines in NFPA 13[1] may not differ greatly when considering high hazard occupancies, the remaining NFPA 13[1] categories are usually not suitable for the general industrial occupancy classification of the *Code*. This is particularly true when considering low hazard occupancies, which are classified differently by the sprinkler standard and by the *Code*. The difference is that a life safety classification is concerned with the overall hazard to occupants in the manufacturing building while the NFPA 13[1] classification system is concerned with sprinkler system design.

To examine the conflicts between life safety occupancy classification and other fire codes, consider a metalworking plant with a flammable solvent in a dip-tank coating operation. The normally low hazard classification of the metalworking plant, from a life safety standpoint, should not be changed to high hazard solely because of a dip-tank coater located in the plant. Adequate means of safe egress away from the coater is needed to ensure the safety of the occupants, but additional exits and a reduction in travel distance to an exit, as specified for a high hazard occupancy, are not required. However, should the coater be the principal piece of equipment in a separately enclosed area, then that area should be considered as a high hazard occupancy.

When determining the life safety hazard classification for an industrial occupancy, the authority having jurisdiction should carefully analyze the nature of an industrial operation to ensure a correct interpretation of the hazard to occupants. A number of resources are available as aids in correctly determining the degree of risk to life safety. One useful aid, which should not be overlooked, is the expertise of the industrial plant operator. The operator has available a wealth of hazard information. However, the information may be treated as confidential material so that competitors will not learn the details of a process. An enforcing authority should work to build the trust of the operator by the careful handling of such material. It is vital that process data be kept confidential since once an enforcing authority is known to be a source of data on industrial secrets, further cooperation will be difficult to obtain.

Another resource is the engineering department of the insurance company responsible for a plant's insurance coverage. Also, discussions with officials in jurisdictions with similar plants and a review of NFPA literature will lead to further information on the process and its associated hazards.

To assist in determining the risk to the life safety of an industrial occupancy, a number of factors should be considered.

Determine if the manufacturing process includes the handling of flammable, reactive, or explosive materials in a quantity that could expose most of the occupants to an initial fire or explosion. If so, the occupancy is a strong candidate for a high hazard classification.

Determine if the manufacturing process requires many people, or if it is basically a large collection of machines or equipment occasionally attended by operators. In some instances the operators will even be clustered in one location, such as a control room. If a building is predominantly occupied by machinery or equipment and has a minimum of employees, the building can be classified as a special purpose industrial occupancy (see 28-1.4.2).

If an industrial building is used mostly for storage of materials (such as preparatory stock for assembly or finished goods), then the occupancy meets the requirements for a storage area (see Chapter 29).

Occupancy classification is dependent on the burning characteristics of the materials in a building, not on the quantity of combustibles. For example, there would be no reason to change the life safety classification of a building to high hazard simply because a manufacturing process included extensive quantities of ordinary combustible materials distributed in such a manner that the process would be considered a "high combustible loading."

The classification of an industrial occupancy for life safety purposes does not depend on the type of structure housing the process. The basic purpose of the hazard classification in Chapter 4 is to evaluate the risk of contents. The classification is determined by an evaluation of the contents for rate of fire spread, development of toxic fumes, and other factors of a fire's development which control the time available to safely evacuate the occupants. Once employees are evacuated to a safe location, the extent of fire spread in the structure becomes a problem of property protection. As long as life safety measures are met, the fact that a building can be heavily damaged by fire is beyond the scope of this *Code*.

28-1.4.2 Special Purpose Industrial Occupancy.
Includes ordinary and low hazard manufacturing operations in buildings designed for and suitable only for particular types of operations, characterized by a relatively low density of employee population, with much of the area occupied by machinery or equipment.

A special purpose industrial occupancy can be difficult to determine. For example, a structure is often erected to protect a large machine or equipment from weather. Once constructed, authorities may impose exit requirements applicable to a general industrial occupancy, even though there is to be only a handful of personnel in the building. Steel mills, paper plants, telephone switch buildings, and other operations with large machines are examples of the type of industrial occupancy requiring massive structures for process control and weather protection. Often, these structures represent minimum hazards to life safety and may be classed as a special purpose industrial occupancy. In many of the more modern operations, all process control is conducted from a control room by remote control which further reduces the number of occupants likely to be exposed to a fire.

On the other hand, the special purpose industrial occupancy classification cannot be applied to a building simply to reduce exit requirements. Economic considerations, or staffing limitations resulting in a smaller than normal number of occupants, cannot be used as justification to reduce life safety features; the full exits should be maintained. Closing of aisles, exit doors, stairways, and other components of the means of egress cannot be justified by the temporary classification of a building as a special purpose industrial occupancy.

28-1.4.3 High Hazard Industrial Occupancy. Includes those buildings having high hazard materials, processes or contents. Incidental high hazard operations in low or ordinary occupancies and provided in accordance with Section 4-2 and 28-3.2 shall not be the basis for overall occupancy classification.

The high hazard occupancy classification includes occupancies where gasoline and other flammable liquids are handled, used, or are stored under conditions which might result in the release of flammable vapors; where explosive dusts from grain, wood flour, plastic, aluminum, magnesium, or other dust-generating materials may be produced; where hazardous chemicals or explosives are manufactured, stored, or handled; where cotton or other combustible fibers are processed or handled under conditions which might produce combustible flyings; and other situations of similar hazard.

A high hazard occupancy classification is limited to those industrial buildings housing extremely hazardous operations. Incidental use of restricted quantities of flammable liquids in a building does not constitute a high hazard occupancy, although some extra life safety precautions may be required during the limited period of use. Refer to Chapter 5 of NFPA 30, *Flammable and Combustible Liquids Code*,[2] for guidance. Storage of flammable liquids, such as paint, in sealed containers would not require a high hazard occupancy classification unless the operation included mixing or blending operations involving the opening of containers. Mixing and blending of flammable liquids could be conducted in a separate room with a fire barrier between the storage and mixing areas. In such an operation, the mixing and blending room would be a high hazard occupancy while the adjacent, fire-separated storage area would be considered a general purpose industrial occupancy, or possibly a storage area subject to the requirements of Chapter 29.

Combustible dusts released from an industrial or manufacturing process constitute a significant life safety problem and require a high hazard classification. Major loss of life has occurred in industrial occupancies releasing extensive quantities of combustible dusts. Every opportunity should be given for the quick escape of employees working in operations releasing combustible dust to prevent injury or loss of life should a dust explosion occur. In high hazard occupancies with an explosion potential, provisions of 28-3.2 require special consideration of techniques for explosion suppression or venting to ensure the life safety of a building's occupants. Full utilization of fire protection engineering techniques should be employed in such occupancies to minimize the potential risk to life safety.

The most obvious industrial occupancy requiring classification as a high hazard occupancy is one associated with the production of explosives or highly reactive chemicals. In some especially hazardous operations extra exits will be necessary to ensure rapid occupant egress to prevent loss of life should an explosion or fire occur. Where installation of the preventive or protective measures specified in 28-3.2 is not possible, due to the nature of the industrial operation, consideration should be given to operating procedures which restrict access to a limited number of people during the hazardous portion of the operation. The procedure would limit life safety exposure to those trained personnel fully aware of the extent of the hazard.

Procedures should also include a record of the personnel who have signed in or out to ensure prompt determination of the number of personnel exposed to a hazardous operation and thus the number who may require rescue.

28-1.5   Classification of hazard of contents shall be as defined in Section 4-2.

28-1.6 Minimum Construction Standards.   No occupancy requirement.

28-1.7 Occupant Load.   The occupant load of industrial occupancies for determination of exits shall be one person per 100 sq ft (9.29 sq m) of gross floor area.

Exception: In special purpose industrial occupancy, the occupant load shall be the maximum number of persons to occupy the area under any probable conditions.

The occupant load of an industrial building is based on an average of 100 sq ft (9.29 sq m) of gross floor area per occupant. Many industrial users of the *Code* confuse this concept with the actual number of employees. The usual complaint is that the number of potential employees determined for exit purposes by the 100-sq ft (9.29-sq m) criterion far exceeds the anticipated or actual number of employees. Many industrial managers argue that using the larger number as a basis for exit design requires more exits, wider doors, and more passageways than are needed for exit purposes, all at a penalty to productive work space and resulting in increasing costs.

The concept of determining occupant load actually is not related to the number of anticipated or actual employees, but is a means of calculating the minimum exit requirements based on the needs of an average industrial occupancy. While actual conditions may vary in a specific location, the amount of exit width determined by the occupant load calculation will normally provide the necessary, adequate, and required exits for a typical industrial building with little or no penalty to the building's occupant.

In most cases the requirements for maximum travel distance to exits (see 28-2.6), rather than the occupant load, are the deciding factor in determining the number of exits needed. Exits provided to satisfy travel distance requirements should be sufficient to provide exit capacity for all occupants, except when a building is arranged in an unusual manner or in the case of a general manufacturing occupancy with a high occupant load.

SECTION 28-2   MEANS OF EGRESS REQUIREMENTS

28-2.1 General.

28-2.1.1   Each required means of egress shall be in accordance with the applicable portions of Chapter 5.

28-2.1.2   Any floor below the street floor used only for storage, heating, and other service equipment, and not subject to industrial occupancy, shall have exits in accordance with Chapter 29.

The intent of 28-2.1.2 is to minimize the number of exits required from locations which contain a minimum number of occupants and are below the street floor. Since utility and storage areas are usually located in basement areas, it was determined that special mention should be made of these locations so that enforcement of other sections in the *Code* would not impose exit provisions too strict and also unnecessary for these minimum use areas. Utility areas, such as boiler rooms, storage areas, and shops, contain a minimum number of employees. Occupants are fully aware of the layout of the room or area, and the nature of the occupancy presents a minimum risk to life safety.

28-2.2 Types of Exits.   Exits shall be restricted to the following permissible types:

Doors (*see 5-2.1*).

Smokeproof towers (*see 5-2.3*).

Interior stairs (*see 5-2.2*). In existing buildings Class A or B.

Outside stairs (*see 5-2.5*).

Horizontal exits (*see 5-2.4*).

Ramps (*see 5-2.6*).

Exit passageways (*see 5-2.7*).

Escalators (*see 5-2.8*).

Exception No. 1:   Any existing stairway or fire escape not complying with 5-2.2 and 5-2.5 may be continued in use, subject to the approval of the authority having jurisdiction.

The authority should be confident that an equivalent level of life safety has been achieved.

Exception No. 2:   Approved slide escapes may be used as required exits for both new and existing high hazard industrial occupancies. Slide escapes shall be counted as exits only when regularly used in drills or for normal exit so that occupants are, through practice, familiar with their use.

The intent of Exception No. 2 to 28-2.2 is to allow the use of slide escapes, which are a common means of egress from areas housing explosives or other highly hazardous materials in chemical industry buildings. The exception allows consideration of slide escapes as the required exit from high hazard occupancies and modifies the limitations in Chapter 5; in 5-2.11.2 only 25 percent of the required exits may be provided by slide escapes. In many high hazard industrial occupancies, slide escapes are the only practical means of ensuring safe egress prior to an explosion or flash fire. To restrict the use of slide escapes to only 25 percent of the required exits would create an unsafe condition and possibly result in injury or loss of life.

28-2.3 Capacity of Means of Egress.

28-2.3.1   The capacity of a unit of exit width shall be as follows:

(a) Doors including those leading outside the building at the ground level or three risers above or below the ground level — one unit for 100 persons.

(b) Class A or Class B stairs, outside stairs or smokeproof towers — one unit for 60 persons.

(c) Ramps: Class A — one unit for 100 persons; Class B — one unit for 60 persons.

(d) Escalators — one unit for 60 persons.

(e) Horizontal exits — one unit for 100 persons but no more than 50 percent of the required exit capacity.

Exception: In special purpose industrial occupancies, means of egress shall be provided at least for the persons actually employed; spaces not subject to human occupancy because of the presence of machinery or equipment may be excluded from consideration.

The exception to 28-2.3.1 places practical limits on the number of required exits and on the arrangement of the means of egress in a special purpose industrial occupancy. There is no life safety purpose served by providing exits from the center of a large machine or equipment installation where there are no occupants under normal operating conditions. A number of industries provide weather shelter for large processes and equipment. Typical examples include steel rolling mills, paper extruders, and metalworking machines, all of which occupy a majority of the floor space in the sheltered building. In many of the more sophisticated operations, full process control is conducted from a remotely located control room. Personnel are normally in the building only for maintenance and adjustment purposes, and then only on a limited basis. To provide exits from such special purpose industrial occupancies would serve no useful purpose and would impose a severe economic penalty in the name of safety.

The large areas normally enclosed by special purpose structures would require an excessive number of units of exit width if the occupant load were calculated on the basis of 100 sq ft (9.29 sq m) per person. If provisions for travel distance and the capacity of the means of egress in a special purpose industrial occupancy were based on the requirements specified for general industrial occupancies, the result would be extensive egress facilities for nonexistent occupants. Such arrangements might actually result in exits being required from the interior of machinery and equipment, an idea incompatible with the equipment's design. In many cases the exits would be from locations which even under normal operating conditions would be considered dangerous for humans. Poorly conceived exit facilities serve no life safety purpose and detract from an otherwise well-designed exit system.

28-2.3.2   Required means of egress for multistoried buildings may serve floors other than the level where required. For multistory buildings, means of egress shall be designed in accordance with the provisions of 5-3.1.4 and 5-3.1.5.

Exception: No inside open stairway, escalator, or ramp may serve as a required egress facility from more than one floor level.

Under 28-2.3.2, if the second and third floor of a building were each required to have three stairways, the second floor could use the stairways serving the third floor so that the total number of stairways required would be three, not six.

28-2.4 Number of Exits.

28-2.4.1   No less than two exits shall be provided for every story or section, including stories below the floor of exit discharge used for general industrial purposes or for uses incidental thereto.

Exception: For rooms or areas with a total capacity of less than 25 persons having a direct exit to the street or to an open area outside the building at ground level, with a total travel distance from any point of not over 50 ft (15.24 m), a single exit may be permitted. Such travel shall be on the same floor level or, if the traversing of stairs is required, there shall be a vertical travel of no more than 15 ft (457.2 cm) and such stairs shall be provided with complete enclosures to separate them from any other part of the building, with no door openings therein. This exception shall not apply to high hazard industrial occupancies.

The intent of the exception to 28-2.4.1 is to allow the construction of small meeting or conference facilities in an industrial occupancy. It is common practice to provide small areas for shift safety meetings, production scheduling, coffee breaks, etc. Occupants are normally limited in number and are quite familiar with the industrial occupancy's layout and construction. The appropriate occupant load factor [for example 100 sq ft (9.29 sq m) per person] is used to determine if the space will have a capacity of less than 25 people. Since the number of occupants is limited to 25, these areas represent a minimum risk to life safety, as contrasted with a place of assembly where larger groups of people are anticipated.

28-2.4.2 There shall be at least two separate means of egress from every high hazard area regardless of size.

The provisions of 28-2.4.2 are vital to life safety in high hazard occupancies. The requirement for two means of egress for all high hazard occupancies recognizes that there is always the possibility that a fire or explosion can occur which could block or destroy one of the two exits. Two separate and equal means of egress from high hazard areas provide a necessary redundancy to ensure the evacuation of occupants under fire or explosion condition and to minimize the potential for injury or loss of life. It is not the intent of this paragraph to require two means of egress from very small high hazard areas, such as a paint spray room, if the single path of travel is not through or towards the hazardous operation.

28-2.5 Arrangement of Means of Egress.

28-2.5.1 Measurement of Width of Means of Egress. The minimum width of any corridor or passageway serving as a required exit, exit access, or exit discharge shall be 44 in. (111.76 cm) in the clear.

It is not the intent of 28-2.5.1 to limit the width of a corridor or passageway to 44 in. (111.76 cm). Where there are more than 2 units of exit width served by a corridor, a greater corridor width is required. The width of a corridor must be at least as wide as the exit to which it leads.

28-2.5.2 Where two or more exits are required, they shall be so arranged as to be reached by different paths of travel in different directions.

Exception: A common path of travel may be permitted for the first 50 ft (15.24 m) from any point.

The requirements of 28-2.5.2 must be considered by designers, inspectors, and authorities having jurisdiction, particularly where sections of a building are occupied by more than a single tenant. Obviously, uncontrolled access between areas of different ownership is not desirable from a tenant's point of view. However, security provisions between separate facilities must never be allowed to restrict the use of a required means of egress. Where multiple tenants occupy the same building and use common exit facilities, careful consideration is required to ensure continued use of the means of egress over the life of a building. Often a tenant will close off an exit corridor with a door subject to locking and treat the corridor on that side of the door as part of the manufacturing space. If such a practice eliminates another tenant's access to an exit, alternate exits will have to be provided.

28-2.5.3   No dead end may be more than 50 ft (15.24 m) deep.

See discussion of dead ends and common paths of travel in Chapter 5.

28-2.6 Measurement of Travel Distance to Exits.

28-2.6.1   Travel to exits shall not exceed 100 ft (30.48 m) from any point to reach the nearest exit.

Exception No. 1:   In a building protected throughout by an approved automatic sprinkler system in accordance with Section 7-7, travel distance may be increased to 150 ft (45.72 m).

Exception No. 2:   As permitted by 28-2.6.2.

Exception No. 3:   Travel distance to exits in high hazard industrial occupancies shall not exceed 75 ft (22.86 m).

28-2.6.2   In a building used for low or ordinary hazard, general industrial occupancies or special industrial occupancy requiring undivided floor areas necessitating travel distances exceeding 150 ft (45.72 m), distance to exits shall be satisfied by providing stairs leading to exit tunnels, overhead passageways or through horizontal exits through firewalls, arranged in accordance with Chapter 5. Where such arrangements are not practicable, the authority having jurisdiction may, by special ruling, permit travel distances up to 400 ft (121.92 m) to the nearest exit. Distances shall be based on meeting the following additional provisions in full:

   (a) Shall limit application to one-story buildings only.

   (b) Shall limit interior finish to Class A or B (*see Section 6-5*).

   (c) Shall provide emergency lighting (*see Section 5-9 and 28-2.9*).

   (d) Shall provide automatic sprinkler or other automatic fire extinguishing systems in accordance with Section 7-7. The extinguishing system shall be supervised.

   (e) Shall provide smoke and heat venting by engineered means or by building configuration to ensure that employees shall not be overtaken by spread of fire or smoke within 6 ft (182.88 cm) of floor level before they have time to reach exits. Smoke and heating venting shall be in accordance with *Guide for Smoke and Heat Venting*, NFPA 204.

The provisions of 28-2.6.2 are meant to provide a flexibility for determining layout of exits in an industrial building with a large floor area housing low or ordinary hazards. The provisions apply to both general and special purpose industrial occupancies.

The construction of tunnels and elevated means of egress from the center of an industrial building with an extensive floor area is rarely attempted. Only a handful of buildings have ever been provided with such an exit facility, and most were World War II airframe manufacturing buildings of massive size. In most industrial buildings it is not practicable or economical to construct exit tunnels or overhead passageways. These special types of means of egress are not easily changed if modifications are necessary to adjust to changes in an industrial plant's layout. Additionally, the construction costs for tunnels and elevated passageways are high due to the special design features required to make them safe, including fireproofed supports for the elevated passageways and waterproofing and other features necessary to maintain the integrity of the underground tunnels. Another negative factor in constructing such facilities is the confining nature of a tunnel or elevated passage, which will tend to divert employees away from such means of egress.

The use of horizontal exits through firewalls is common in many industrial occupancies. Full consideration of the provisions in Chapter 5 is required to ensure the safe use of these types of exits. A common discrepancy is the failure to provide the proper type of door in a fire wall. The sliding and roll-up types of fire doors cannot be considered as acceptable elements of a means of egress. Since a horizontal exit may be used from both sides of a fire wall, careful consideration of the direction of door swing is required so that the doors can be used from both sides of the fire wall. In many instances, two doors swinging in opposite directions will be required so that the exit may be used as a means of egress from both sides of the fire wall. (See 5-2.4.2.3.)

A common example of travel distance to an exit in a general purpose industrial occupancy, classified as a low or ordinary hazard, is 400 ft (121.92 m) under the provisions of items (a) through (e) of 28-2.6.2.

Item (a) limits the provisions to one-story buildings to utilize horizontal movement of the occupants through the means of egress. Any stairs or other impediments to the rapid movement of people would result in slower evacuation times from the building and increase the possibility of exposure to smoke or fire.

The intent of limiting the interior finish to Class A or B materials [item (b)] is to minimize the chance of a fire spreading through the structure beyond the area of origin and cutting off the means of egress before employee evacuation.

Item (c) requires emergency lighting to ensure full illumination of the means of egress during the time of occupant exit from the building. With this illumination occupants will be able to see, even in the event of a power failure.

Installation of a complete automatic extinguishing system as required by item (d) is intended to ensure control and extinguishment of incipient fires, thus minimizing the exposure of the occupants to a fire. It is not the intent of this paragraph to require automatic sprinkler protection since a number of equally effective extinguishing agents and systems may be utilized for specific fire hazards. What is important in this provision is the necessity for automatic initiation of the fire control and extinguishing system to minimize the extent of the occupants' exposure to fire. The installed system is required to be fully supervised to ensure that it will operate when a fire occurs. Adequate procedures must be provided by the building's owner or tenant to ensure the prompt correction of any impairments to the extinguishing systems. In some facilities, the degree of fire risk during the impairment period may require limitations on hazardous operations and the number of occupants so that the level of life safety will be equivalent to that provided when the extinguishing system is operational.

To satisfy the intent of item (e), a great deal of judgment must be exercised in the design of systems for smoke and heat venting. The provisions in the *Code* to utilize the requirements of NFPA 204, *Guide for Smoke and Heat Venting*,[3] should be, in most instances, sufficient. The limitation on the accumulation of smoke is a key factor in the design of the smoke removal system. The average evacuation speed of a person walking is normally considered to be 250 ft (76.20 m) per minute or a little over 4 ft (122 m) per second. When applied to the 400-ft (121.92-m) travel distance allowed by the *Code*, the maximum time to reach an exit should not exceed 2 minutes. It is an extremely rare situation where the smoke which could accumulate in an industrial building will be so extensive that it fills the structure and descends to less than 6 ft (182.88 cm) above the floor level in 2 minutes. With the added benefit of a properly designed system for smoke and heat venting, there will be little chance of blocking the means of egress with smoke.

28-2.7 Discharge from Exits.   A maximum of 50 percent of the exits may discharge through areas on the level of discharge arranged in accordance with 5-7.2.

The purpose of 28-2.7, along with 5-7.2, is to control the arrangement of exits from upper stories which discharge to the outside through a lower floor level. The basis for this exception to the general rule on complete enclosure of exits up to their point of discharge to the outside of the building is that with the safeguards specified in 5-7.2 (especially automatic sprinkler protection for the level of discharge), reasonable safety is maintained. In evaluating the arrangement of exits, a stairway is not considered to discharge through the level of discharge if it leads to the outside through a fire-resistive enclosure separating it from the level of discharge, even though there are doors between the stairway landing and the level of discharge.

Discharge from exits will not require any special arrangement when all exits go directly to the outside from a one-story building. (Paragraph 28-2.7 should not be used to require the installation of automatic sprinklers in single-story buildings.)

28-2.8 Illumination of Means of Egress.

28-2.8.1   Illumination of means of egress shall be provided in accordance with Section 5-8. For purposes of this requirement, exit access shall include only designated aisles, corridors, and passageways leading to an exit.

Exception: Means of egress illumination may be eliminated in structures occupied only in daylight hours with skylights or windows arranged to provide, during these hours, the required level of illumination on all portions of the means of egress.

Paragraph 28-2.8.1 is not meant to require the installation of extensive and unneeded illumination systems in industrial structures. Illumination is required for the exit access, which is limited to designated aisles, corridors, and passageways leading to an exit. There is no requirement to provide illumination throughout the entire building, which in many industrial occupancies would involve lighting an extensive floor area. The purpose of the lighting system is to ensure that people be able to see the means of egress and not to illuminate the operation of production facilities.

The *Code* also does not require illumination of the means of egress if the building is occupied only during the daylight hours, except under the provision of 28-2.6.2(c). To meet the requirements of the exception to 28-2.8.1, the building, including stairways, must have sufficient windows and skylights to ensure natural illumination. The authority having jurisdiction should make certain that the building is not occupied during the night.

28-2.9 Emergency Lighting.

28-2.9.1 All industrial occupancies shall have emergency lighting in accordance with Section 5-9. For purposes of this requirement, exit access shall include only designated aisles, corridors, and passageways.

Exception No. 1: Special purpose industrial occupancies do not require emergency lighting when routine human habitation is not the case.

Exception No. 2: Emergency lighting may be eliminated in structures occupied only in daylight hours with skylights or windows arranged to provide, during those hours, the required level of illumination on all portions of the means of egress.

Exceptions to the requirement for emergency lighting are included in the *Code* for the same reasons that permit not illuminating the means of egress (see 28-2.8.1). An additional exception has been made for special purpose industrial occupancies which do not have routine human habitation, since there is no need to install an extensive and costly lighting system where there are no occupants. See also the commentary on 28-2.6.2(c).

28-2.10 Marking of Means of Egress.

28-2.10.1 Signs designating exits or ways of travel thereto shall be provided in accordance with Section 5-10.

28-2.11 Special Features.

28-2.11.1 Special locking arrangements in accordance with 5-2.1.2.1.5 are permitted on exterior doors.

This permits the time delay lock.

28-2.11.2 Spiral stairs in accordance with 5-2.2.1.6 are permitted.

Note that spiral stairs can only serve an occupant load of five or fewer.

28-2.11.3 In existing buildings winders in accordance with 5-2.2.2.4 are permitted.

SECTION 28-3 PROTECTION

28-3.1 Protection of Vertical Openings.

28-3.1.1 Every stairway, elevator shaft, escalator opening, and other vertical opening shall be enclosed or protected in accordance with Chapter 5 and Section 6-2.

Exception No. 1: In existing buildings with low or ordinary hazard contents and protected throughout by an approved automatic sprinkler system in accordance with Sections 7-6 and 7-7, vertical openings may be unprotected providing the vertical opening does not serve as a required exit. All required exits under such conditions shall consist of smokeproof towers in accordance with 5-2.3, outside stairs in accordance with 5-2.5, or horizontal exits in accordance with 5-2.4.

Exception No. 1 to 28-3.1.1 recognizes that an existing industrial occupancy may contain unprotected vertical openings and still provide a reasonable level of life safety

if the building contains only low or ordinary hazards and is protected by a complete automatic sprinkler system. Smokeproof towers and outside stairways (the only types of vertical exits allowed by this exception) must be fully enclosed or protected against vertical fire spread and meet the requirements of Chapter 5. The unenclosed vertical openings must not be used in any way as a means of egress, although they can remain as convenience stairways for normal operations.

While the major reason for allowing this provision is economic, due to the high cost of enclosing all vertical openings in existing buildings, there is actually little effect on the life safety of occupants where the building houses low or ordinary hazards. There will be some problems, however, in fire control since unprotected vertical openings can contribute to fire spread in buildings and result in extensive property damage. This is the reason for the requirement for a complete automatic sprinkler system.

Exception No. 2: In special purpose and high hazard occupancies where unprotected vertical openings are in new or existing buildings and necessary to manufacturing operations, they may be permitted beyond the specified limits, provided every floor level has direct access to one or more enclosed stairways or other exits protected against obstruction by any fire or smoke in the open areas connected by the unprotected vertical openings.

Exception No. 2 to 28-3.1.1 strictly limits the use of unprotected vertical openings in high hazard and special purpose industrial occupancies. Direct access to one or more enclosed stairways or to other exits is required from any areas connected by unprotected vertical openings. This provision recognizes that many high hazard and special purpose industrial occupancies require openings between floor levels to accommodate piping, conveyors, and other devices and equipment essential to the orderly operation of the business. In most of these situations full enclosure is not practical or feasible. In high hazard occupancies, the provision of two means of egress will, in most situations, be sufficient to comply with this exception. In special purpose occupancies, additional exits or other special arrangements will normally be required to comply with the provision that stairways and exits be protected against obstruction from fire and smoke in the open areas connected by the unprotected vertical openings.

28-3.2 Protection from Hazards.   Every high hazard industrial occupancy, operation, or process shall have automatic extinguishing systems or such other protection as may be appropriate to the particular hazard, such as explosion venting or suppression, for any area subject to an explosion hazard, designed to minimize danger to occupants in case of fire or other emergency before they have time to utilize exits to escape.

The intent of 28-3.2 is to provide for the life safety of the occupants of industrial buildings through control of the explosion risk associated with highly hazardous operations. The alternatives in the paragraph are not meant to be inclusive, and a proper fire protection engineering solution might not incorporate the listed provisions. The *Code* is intended to allow for engineering judgment in a wide range of potential high hazard occupancies, some where protection may be limited. The intent of the paragraph is also broad in application since in many high hazard occupancies, an explosion may be immediately preceded by a fire or other emergency such as an overheated reactor vessel, an exothermic reaction, and increased pressure. Since such conditions may be initiators of an explosion, depending on the process and arrangement of the equipment, immediate egress from the facility may be necessary. If fire or other emergencies are likely to proceed rapidly to an explosion, adequate precautions will be necessary for life safety. Emergency lighting should be considered where operations require lighting to perform orderly manual emergency operation or shutdown, maintain critical services, or provide safe start-up after a power failure.

In many modern facilities, provisions may already be included for process control and property protection which will prove adequate for the life safety of a building's occupants, and any additional measures will not increase to any appreciable degree the life safety of operators.

Section 15, Chapter 7, of the *Fire Protection Handbook*[4] discusses the basic principles of explosion prevention, venting, and suppression. The section also contains an extensive bibliography on the subject. Recommendations for the design and utilization of vents to limit pressures developed by explosions are contained in NFPA 68, *Guide for Explosion Venting*.[5] Standards for explosion prevention systems are found in NFPA 69, *Standard on Explosion Prevention Systems*.[6]

28-3.3 Interior Finish.

28-3.3.1   Interior finish on walls and ceilings shall be Class A, B or C in accordance with Section 6-5, in operating areas, and shall be as permitted by Chapter 5 in exits.

28-3.3.2 Interior Floor Finish.   No occupancy requirements.

28-3.4 Fire Alarm System.

28-3.4.1   Industrial occupancies shall be provided with a manual or automatic fire alarm system in accordance with Section 7-6. The alarm system shall sound an audible alarm in a continuously manned location for purposes of initiating emergency action.

Exception: If the total capacity of the building is under 100 persons and less than 25 persons are employed above or below the level of exit discharge.

28-3.4.2   In all high hazard industrial occupancies, the fire alarm system shall automatically initiate an evacuation alarm signal. The alarm shall also sound at a continuously manned location.

Paragraph 28-3.4 contains two separate and distinct provisions for audible alarms from fire alarm systems. In low and ordinary hazard occupancies, the system is not required to activate an evacuation alarm but is required to sound an alarm in a continuously manned location to initiate emergency action. The intent of this provision is to allow an interface between the alarm system and the plant's emergency organization. The alarm system may be controlled from a central security console or a similar location. The key factor is that the point where the alarm sounds must be a continuously manned location. This requirement need not be interpreted as requiring installation of supervisory service, such as to a central station, but the location must be fully manned during all periods when the building is occupied. In high hazard occupancies, the alarm must be arranged to sound an evacuation alarm since the safety of the occupants of these areas requires immediate notification of a fire.

REFERENCES CITED BY *CODE*

(This publication comprises a part of the requirement to the extent called for by the Code.*)*

NFPA 204, *Guide for Smoke and Heat Venting*, NFPA, Boston, 1968.

REFERENCES CITED IN COMMENTARY

[1]NFPA 13, *Standard for the Installation of Sprinkler Systems*, NFPA, Boston, 1980.
[2]NFPA 30, *Flammable and Combustible Liquids Code*, NFPA, Boston, 1981
[3]NFPA 204, *Guide for Smoke and Heat Venting*, NFPA, Boston, 1968.
[4]*Fire Protection Handbook*, 14th ed., NFPA, Boston, 1976, pp. 15-44 to 15-55.
[5]NFPA 68, *Guide for Explosion Venting*, NFPA, Boston, 1978.
[6]NFPA 69, *Standard on Explosion Prevention Systems*, NFPA, Boston, 1978.

29

STORAGE
OCCUPANCIES

(See also Chapter 31.)

Storage occupancies include all buildings or structures utilized primarily for the storage or sheltering of goods, merchandise, products, vehicles, or animals. Included in this occupancy group are:

Warehouses | Parking garages
Cold storage | Hangars
Freight terminals | Grain elevators
Truck and marine terminals | Barns
Bulk oil storage | Stables

Minor storage incidental to another occupancy is treated as part of the other occupancy.

SECTION 29-1   GENERAL REQUIREMENTS

29-1.1 Application.   The requirements of this chapter apply to both new and existing storage occupancies. Storage occupancies include all buildings or structures used primarily for the storage or sheltering of goods, merchandise, products, vehicles or animals.

Note that this chapter applies to both new and existing facilities.

29-1.2 Mixed Occupancies.   *(See 1-4.5 and 29-1.4.)*

29-1.3 Special Definitions.   None.

29-1.4 Classification of Occupancy.   Storage occupancies shall include all occupancies defined in 4-1.10. Incidental storage in another occupancy shall not be the basis for overall occupancy classification.

Exception: Storage occupancies or areas of storage occupancies which are used for the purpose of packaging, labeling, sorting, special handling or other operations requiring an occupant load greater than that normally contemplated for storage shall be classified as industrial occupancies (see Chapter 28).

Life safety provisions for storage locations are not extensive since the number of occupants is generally low and many of those in such a structure are present for only a short duration. Further, occupants of storage occupancies do not normally remain in one location; instead, their assignments have them moving about and performing activities of a temporary nature.

Fire records indicate a minimum of life safety problems in storage occupancies. A study by the NFPA Fire Records Department found that during a four-year period, 123 deaths occurred in storage occupancies, which was 1.4 percent of the total number of fatalities from fires recorded during the same period. The number is not totally conclusive since the data did not distinguish between those deaths due to fire-associated injuries and those due to lack of proper exit facilities.

Due to the special characteristics of storage occupancies, a number of provisions have been included in the *Code* to modify, as required, provisions normally applicable to occupancies with larger populations.

The purpose of the exception to 29-1.3 is to provide suitable exit facilities for storage occupancies or portions of storage occupancies with a population greater than normally expected in a storage building. It is sometimes common practice to place large numbers of people in a storage building to conduct an industrial type of operation, such as labeling, sorting, or packaging; this will require extra exit facilities in accordance with the provisions in Chapter 28.

29-1.5 Classification of Hazard of Contents.   Contents of storage occupancies shall be classified as high hazard, ordinary hazard, or low hazard in accordance with Section 4-2, depending upon the character of the materials stored, their packaging, and other factors.

In the past few years, a great deal of fire protection literature has concentrated on the risk associated with rack storage facilities. Although NFPA 231C, *Standard for Rack Storage of Materials*,[1] was developed because of the increased awareness of the fire potential inherent in rack storage methods, there is no basis for comparison between the hazard categories in NFPA 231C[1] and those of the *Life Safety Code*. NFPA 231C[1] hazard categories are established for the design of automatic sprinkler systems. For determining hazards to life safety, all commodity classifications in NFPA 231C[1] can be considered as low or ordinary hazards. Particular attention should be paid to the scope (Paragraph 1-1) of NFPA 231C[1] which excludes commodities that could be classified as highly hazardous materials.

There is a great temptation to use the potential for rapid fire growth inherent in high-piled or racked storage as justification for establishing strict life safety provisions. However, the typical arrangement of buildings with this type of storage is adequate to allow safe and rapid egress at the first notification or discovery of fire. Should a building not be protected by automatic sprinklers, then the *Life Safety Code* contains adequate provisions (such as those for travel distance to an exit) to ensure the survival of the occupants.

29-1.6 Minimum Construction Standards.   No occupancy requirements.

29-1.7 Occupant Load.   No requirements.

SECTION 29-2   MEANS OF EGRESS REQUIREMENTS

29-2.1 General.   Every required means of egress shall be in accordance with the applicable portions of Chapter 5.

29-2.2 Types of Exits.   Exits shall be restricted to the following permissible types:

Doors (*see 5-2.1*).
Smokeproof towers (*see 5-2.3*).
Interior stairs (*see 5-2.2*). In existing buildings Class A or B.
Outside stairs (*see 5-2.5*).
Horizontal exits (*see 5-2.4*).
Ramps (*see 5-2.6*).
Exit passageways (*see 5-2.7*).
Fire escape stairs (*see 5-2.9*).
Ladders (*see 5-2.10*).
Slide escapes (*see 5-2.11*).

Exception: Any existing stairway or fire escape not complying with 5-2.2 and 5-2.5 may be continued in use, subject to the approval of the authority having jurisdiction.

29-2.3 Capacity of Means of Egress.   The capacity of a means of egress shall be in accordance with Chapter 5.

29-2.4 Number of Exits.

29-2.4.1   Every building or structure used for storage and every section thereof considered separately shall have at least two separate means of egress, as remote from each other as practicable.

Exception: One means of egress may be provided from rooms or enclosures within storage buildings, structures or sections of a storage building not exceeding 10,000 sq ft (929 sq m) and not occupied normally by more than ten persons, and not containing high hazard material. Travel distance in that means of egress in an unsprinklered building shall not exceed 50 ft (15.24 m) and 100 ft (30.48 m) in a building protected throughout by an approved automatic sprinkler system.

The intent of 29-2.4.1 is to require at least two means of egress from every storage building or structure. The exits should be located as remote from each other as possible, preferably in opposite walls of a building or in diagonally opposite corners. The exception recognizes the existence of bonded storage of goods under different ownership in the same building. The separate enclosures used in public warehouses are examples of such an arrangement. Occupancy is infrequent in the separate enclosures and, due to the limitation of size, there is no need for more than one exit. Should the enclosure contain high hazards or house an industrial type of operation, then two means of egress would be required. (See 29-2.5.2 and 29-2.6.1.)

29-2.4.2   Locked exit doors are permissible when arranged in accordance with 5-2.1.2.

29-2.5 Arrangement of Means of Egress.

29-2.5.1 Measurement of Width of Means of Egress. The minimum width of any corridor or passageway serving as a required exit or means of travel to or from a required exit shall be 44 in. (111.76 cm) in the clear.

29-2.5.2 Travel from all locations in a storage occupancy of high hazard contents shall be via at least two separate routes to exits remote from each other.

> Paragraph 29-2.5 does not include limitations on exit arrangement normally found in other chapters of the *Code*, such as those on length of dead ends. The reason such measures have been omitted is that the minimal population of storage buildings does not require the more explicit provisions specified for occupancies with large numbers of people.

29-2.6 Measurement of Travel Distance to Exits.

29-2.6.1 Travel to exits shall not exceed 200 ft (60.96 m) from any point to reach the nearest exit.

Exception No. 1: In a building protected throughout by an approved automatic sprinkler system in accordance with Section 7-7, travel distance may be increased to 400 ft (121.92 m).

Exception No. 2: There shall be no limitations on travel to exits for low hazard storage occupancy.

Exception No. 3: Every area used for the storage of high hazard commodities shall have an exit within 75 ft (22.86 m) of any point in the area where persons may be present. Travel distance shall be measured in accordance with 5-6.2.

Exception No. 4: In areas used for the storage of high hazard commodities and protected throughout by an approved automatic sprinkler system in accordance with Section 7-7, distances to an exit shall be within 100 ft (30.48 m) of any point in the area where persons may be present.

> Paragraph 29-2.6.1 and its exceptions establish the limitations on travel distance for storage occupancies. Note that the provisions make a direct relationship between the hazard of contents and the life safety requirements for a building. Thus, in low hazard storage occupancies, there is no limitation on travel distance. As the hazard of contents increases, travel limitations are required. Storage buildings housing ordinary hazards and lacking protection are limited to 200 ft (60.96 m) of travel distance to an exit. A distance of 400 ft (121.92 m) is permissible if complete automatic sprinkler protection is provided. In high hazard storage occupancies, travel distance is restricted to a maximum of 75 ft (22.86 m) if unsprinklered and 100 ft (30.48 m) if the building is equipped with a complete automatic sprinkler system.
>
> The elimination of travel distance restrictions for low hazard storage occupancies is realistic since the small fire risk represented by such materials, coupled with the low occupant population, provides a minimal risk to life safety. Imposing restrictive provisions would not be consistent with good fire protection and reasonable life safety requirements since the possibility of fire is very low and little difficulty is expected for occupants exiting the building.

29-2.7 Discharge from Exits. A maximum of 50 percent of the exits may discharge through areas on the level of discharge arranged in accordance with 5-7.2.

29-2.8 Illumination of Means of Egress.

29-2.8.1 Illumination of means of egress shall be provided in accordance with Section 5-8. For purposes of this requirement, exit access shall include only designated aisles, corridors, and passageways leading to an exit.

Exception: In structures occupied only in daylight hours with windows arranged to provide, during daylight hours, the required level of illumination of all portions of the means of egress may be eliminated by special permission of the authority having jurisdiction.

The provisions of 29-2.8.1 are not intended to require the installation of extensive and unneeded exit illumination systems in storage occupancies. Illumination *is* required for the exit and for the exit access, which is limited to designated aisles, corridors, and passageways leading to an exit. Limiting the extent of the lighting system to a building's egress areas eliminates the necessity of placing specialized lighting systems throughout storage areas, a practice which would be extremely costly with little or no return in life safety.

The exception allows a waiver of the requirement for installing illumination systems if a building, including stairways, is sufficiently lighted during periods of occupancy by means of natural lighting. The term "windows," as used in the text of the exception, should not be interpreted literally. The term is meant to include skylights, open wall sections, and similar means of providing illumination by natural sources. Provisions are based on the fact that there is no need for a lighting system if the building is unoccupied during nondaylight hours.

29-2.9 Emergency Lighting.

29-2.9.1 All storage occupancies shall have emergency lighting in accordance with Section 5-9.

Exception No. 1: Storage occupancies do not require emergency lighting when not normally occupied.

Exception No. 2: In structures occupied only in daylight hours with skylights or windows arranged to provide, during these hours, the required level of illumination on all portions of the means of egress, emergency lighting may be eliminated.

Exceptions to the requirement for the installation of emergency lighting are included for the reasons stated in 29-2.8.1. Exception No. 1 allows circuit arrangements which disconnect power from emergency lighting systems when the building is unoccupied. In many warehouses, power is turned off during periods when occupants are not in the building. The power disconnect serves fire prevention, energy conservation, and security purposes.

29-2.10 Marking of Means of Egress. Signs designating exits or ways of travel thereto shall be provided in accordance with Section 5-10.

29-2.11 Special Features.

29-2.11.1 Special locking arrangements in accordance with 5-2.1.2.1.5 are permitted on exterior doors.

This permits the time delay lock.

29-2.11.2   Spiral stairs in accordance with 5-2.2.1.6 are permitted.

Note that spiral stairs can only serve an occupant load of five or fewer.

29-2.11.3   In existing buildings winders in accordance with 5-2.2.2.4 are permitted.

SECTION 29-3   PROTECTION

29-3.1 Protection of Vertical Openings.

29-3.1.1   Every stairway, elevator shaft, escalator opening, manlift opening and other vertical opening shall be enclosed or protected in accordance with Section 6-2.

Exception: In existing buildings with low and ordinary hazard contents and protected throughout by an approved automatic sprinkler system in accordance with Sections 7-6 and 7-7, vertical openings may be unprotected when they do not serve as required exits. All required exits under such conditions shall consist of smokeproof towers in accordance with 5-2.3, outside stairs in accordance with 5-2.5, or horizontal exits in accordance with 5-2.4.

29-3.2 Protection from Hazards.   No occupancy requirements.

29-3.3 Interior Finish.

29-3.3.1   Interior finish on walls and ceilings shall be Class A, B, or C, in accordance with Section 6-5.

29-3.3.2 Interior Floor Finish.   No occupancy requirements.

29-3.4 Fire Alarm Systems.   Occupancies with ordinary or high hazard contents exceeding an aggregate floor area of 100,000 sq ft (9,290 sq m) in unsprinklered buildings shall be provided with a manual or automatic fire alarm system in accordance with Section 7-6. The alarm system shall sound an audible alarm in a continuously manned location for purposes of initiating emergency action.

Paragraph 29-3.4 requires the installation of a fire alarm system in unsprinklered occupancies with an aggregate floor area of over 100,000 sq ft (9,290 sq m). Visibility is limited in buildings with large floor areas, and personnel working in the storage areas could be unaware of a fire for a long period of time. As the fire spreads, which is a good possibility in an unprotected storage building, means of exit access could be blocked. The alarm system will provide a means of alerting all occupants to the fire and allow for timely exit. The alarm is required to sound in a continuously manned location as a precaution in case it is necessary to alert additional fire fighting personnel or initiate search and rescue procedures. The *Code* does not specify an alarm system as a property protection requirement, although the probability of property loss is reduced in any occupancy when an alarm system is installed. In buildings provided with an automatic sprinkler system, it is anticipated that an alarm will sound in a continuously manned location upon operation of the system.

SECTION 29-4   SPECIAL PROVISIONS
(RESERVED)

SECTION 29-5   BUILDING SERVICES
(RESERVED)

SECTION 29-6   SPECIAL PROVISIONS FOR GARAGES

29-6.1 General Requirements.

29-6.1.1 The following provisions apply to parking garages of closed or open type, above or below ground, but not to mechanical or exclusively attendant parking facilities, which are not occupied by customers and thus require a minimum of exits.

The intent of the special provisions for garages is to provide adequate life safety for the customers of parking facilities who will probably not be familiar with the garage or its arrangement. Where only attendants enter the parking area, the *Code*'s intent is to provide exits in accordance with the previous sections of Chapter 29. In such instances, the provisions for ordinary hazard occupancies apply.

For further information on garages, including a definition of "open garage," see NFPA 88A, *Standard for Parking Structures.*[2] The basic criterion for classifying a garage as "open" is that not less than 25 percent of the total wall area must be open to the atmosphere at each level, utilizing at least two sides of the structure.

29-6.1.2   In areas where repair operations are conducted, the exits shall comply with Chapter 28, Industrial Occupancies.

29-6.1.3   Where both parking and repair operations are conducted in the same building, the entire building shall comply with Chapter 28.

Exception: If the parking and repair sections are separated by 1-hour fire-rated construction, the parking and repair sections may be treated separately.

The exception to 29-6.1.3 allows a building to house parking and repair operations if they are separated by fire-resistive construction. The repair operation would be governed by the provisions of Chapter 28 and the parking facilities by Chapter 29. Guidelines on the rating of construction assemblies can be found in NFPA 220, *Standard Types of Building Construction.*[3] Special requirements for repair garages can be found in NFPA 88B, *Standard for Repair Garages.*[4]

29-6.2 Means of Egress Requirements.

29-6.2.1 General.   Means of egress shall be in accordance with Section 29-2.

29-6.2.2 Types of Exits.   Exits shall be restricted to the following permissible types:

Doors, in accordance with 5-2.1.

Interior stairs, in accordance with 5-2.2.

Smokeproof towers, in accordance with 5-2.3.

Outside stairs, in accordance with 5-2.5.

Horizontal exits, in accordance with 5-2.4.

Exception No. 1:   In a ramp-type open garage with open ramps not subject to closure, the ramp may serve in lieu of the second exit from floors above the level of exit discharge, providing the ramp discharges directly outside of the street level.

Exception No. 2:   For garages extending only one floor level below the level of exit discharge a ramp leading directly to the outside may serve in lieu of the second exit, provided no door or shutter is installed therein.

Exception No. 3:   An opening for the passage of automobiles may serve as an exit from a street floor, provided no door or shutter is installed therein.

The exceptions to 29-6.2.2 allow the designer to take advantage of the garage ramps as part of the means of egress. Properly arranged ramps can facilitate safe egress to an extent well in excess of what is required for the number of occupants.

Exception No. 1 allows consideration of ramps as an alternate secondary means of egress from floors above the street level when arranged so that discharge to the street level is clear and unobstructed. Ramps from floors above the street level are required to be open and not subject to closure by walls or some other means for confining smoke and heat in the ramp structure. Under Exception No. 1, it is only possible to use a ramp as part of the exit design if a parking garage is an open-type structure. Ramps in closed garages cannot be considered as part of the exit system, and normal means of egress (listed in 29-6.2.2) should be installed.

Exception No. 2 allows a ramp to be used as an alternate secondary means of egress in a closed or open garage which extends not more than one floor level below the level of exit discharge. The ramp must not have a door or a shutter and must lead directly outside.

29-6.2.3 Capacity of Means of Egress.

29-6.2.4 Number of Exits.   Every floor of every garage shall have access to at least two separate exits.

29-6.2.5 Arrangement of Means of Egress.

29-6.2.5.1   Exits shall be so arranged that from any point in the garage the paths of travel to the two exits will be in different directions.

Exception: A common path of travel may be permitted for the first 50 ft (15.24 m) from any point.

29-6.2.5.2   If any gasoline pumps are located within any closed parking garage, exits shall be arranged and located to meet the following:

(a) Travel away from the gasoline pump in any direction will lead to an exit, with no dead end in which occupants might be trapped by fire or explosion at any gasoline pump.

(b) Such exit shall lead to the outside of the building on the same level, or stairs; no upward travel shall be permitted unless direct outside exits are available from that floor.

(c) Any story below that story at which gasoline is being dispensed shall have exits direct to outside via outside stairs or doors at ground level.

Paragraph 29-6.2.5.2 specifies the special conditions necessary to protect the occupants of closed parking garages from fires which may occur from gasoline-dispensing operations located in the building. Item (c) requires that direct access to the outside be provided from floors below a story on which gasoline is dispensed. This eliminates the possibility of gasoline vapors, which are heavier than air, accumulating in enclosed portions of a means of egress, such as inside exit stairways.

The hazards associated with dispensing gasoline inside buildings are avoided with outdoor dispensing, as in ordinary gasoline filling stations.

29-6.2.6 Measurement of Travel Distance to Exit. Exits in garages shall be so arranged that no point in the area will be more than 150 ft (45.72 m) (measured in accordance with 5-6.2) from the nearest exit other than a ramp on the same floor level.

Exception No. 1: Travel distance may be increased to 200 ft (60.96 m) for open floors of unsprinklered, open garages and 300 ft (91.44 m) in open garages protected throughout by an approved automatic sprinkler system.

Exception No. 2: Travel distance may be increased to 200 ft (60.96 m) for enclosed parking garages protected throughout by an approved automatic sprinkler system in accordance with Section 7-7.

29-6.2.7 Discharge from Exits.   No special occupancy provisions.

29-6.2.8 Illumination of Means of Egress.   Every public space, hall, stair enclosure, and other means of egress shall have illumination in accordance with 29-2.8.

29-6.2.9 Emergency Lighting.   Every public space, hall, stair enclosure, and other means of egress shall have emergency lighting in accordance with 29-2.9.

29-6.2.10 Exit Marking.   Signs in accordance with 5-2.10 shall be provided for all required exits and exit access.

SECTION 29-7   SPECIAL PROVISIONS FOR AIRCRAFT HANGARS

29-7.1   Exits from aircraft storage or servicing areas shall be provided at intervals of not more than 150 ft (45.72 m) on all exterior walls. There shall be a minimum of two exits serving each aircraft storage or servicing area. Horizontal exits through interior fire walls shall be provided at intervals of not more than 100 ft (30.48 m) along the wall.

Exception: Dwarf or "smash" doors in doors accommodating aircraft may be used to comply with these requirements.

Paragraph 29-7.1 provides two alternate methods of providing exit from aircraft hangars. Where exit is possible through the outside wall, a spacing of 150 ft (45.72 m) is adequate between exit doors. In larger hangars, the servicing bay may be provided with offices and shops along one or more sides, with the wall construction having a fire-resistant rating. In cases where the wall has a fire-resistant rating, exit spacing of up to 100 ft (30.48 m) is specified. Should the wall not be rated, then access to the outside is required. Large hangar doors cannot be left open in poor weather to ensure a means of egress, so it is common procedure to provide small personnel access doors in the larger aircraft hangar door. The small door can be considered a normal means of egress from an aircraft hangar. If possible, the door should swing in the direction of egress; however, this may not be possible due to the design of the aircraft door. For further information on aircraft hangars, see NFPA 409, *Standard on Aircraft Hangars.*[5]

29-7.2 Exits from mezzanine floors in aircraft storage or servicing areas shall be so arranged that the maximum travel to reach the nearest exit from any point on the mezzanine shall not exceed 75 ft (22.86 m). Such exits shall lead directly to a properly enclosed stairwell discharging directly to the exterior, to a suitable cutoff area, or to outside stairs.

29-7.3 Signs. Exit signs shall be provided over doors and exitways in accordance with Section 5-10.

SECTION 29-8 SPECIAL PROVISIONS FOR GRAIN OR OTHER BULK STORAGE ELEVATORS

29-8.1 There shall be at least two means of egress from all working levels of the head house. One of these means of egress shall be a stair to the level of exit discharge which is enclosed by a dust resistant 1-hour rated enclosure in accordance with 5-1.3. The second means of egress may be either:

(a) An exterior stair or basket ladder-type fire escape accessible from all working levels of the head house which provides a passage to ground level, or

(b) An exterior stair or basket ladder-type fire escape accessible from all working levels of the head house which provides access to the top of adjoining structures which provide a continuous path to the means of egress described in 29-8.2.

Exception: Stair enclosures in existing structures may have non-fire-rated dust resistant enclosures.

It is not the intent of 29-8.1 to require a fully dusttight shaft since the door will allow passage of some limited amounts of dust during the normal course of day-to-day operations. The shaft should, however, be separated from the operating areas by fire-resistant construction and be as free of dust as possible.

29-8.2 There shall be an exterior stair or basket ladder-type fire escape which provides passage to ground level at the top of the end of the adjoining structures such as silos, conveyors, galleries, gantries, etc.

29-8.3 Underground spaces shall have at least two means of egress, one of which may be a means of escape. The means of escape shall be arranged to eliminate dead ends.

Section 29-8 provides three basic requirements:
1. Two means of egress from all working levels of the head house.
2. A means of egress at the end of all galleries, etc., thereby eliminating dead ends.
3. Means of escape provided to eliminate dead ends in underground areas.

Paragraph 29-8.1 requires that one means of egress from the head house shall be an enclosed stair. The alternate means of egress can be either an outside stair or basket ladder-type fire escape connecting all working levels and going either to the ground or to the top of an adjoining structure which complies with 29-8.2.

The principal hazard of elevator storage structures which handle combustible materials is a dust explosion. A dust explosion can be violent enough to damage or destroy the primary means of egress required in 29-8.1.

For further information on preventing fire and dust explosions in grain elevators and bulk grain handling facilities, see NFPA 61B, *Standard for the Prevention of Fires and Explosions in Grain Elevators and Facilities Handling Bulk Raw Agricultural Commodities.*[6]

REFERENCES CITED IN COMMENTARY

[1]NFPA 231C, *Standard for Rack Storage of Materials*, NFPA, Boston, 1980.

[2]NFPA 88A, *Standard for Parking Structures*, NFPA, Boston, 1979.

[3]NFPA 220, *Standard Types of Building Construction*, NFPA, Boston, 1979.

[4]NFPA 88B, *Standard for Repair Garages*, NFPA, Boston, 1979.

[5]NFPA 409, *Standard on Aircraft Hangars*, NFPA, Boston, 1979.

[6]NFPA 61B, *Standard for the Prevention of Fires and Explosions in Grain Elevators and Facilities Handling Bulk Raw Agricultural Commodities*, NFPA, Boston, 1980.

30

OCCUPANCIES IN UNUSUAL STRUCTURES

(See also Chapter 31.)

Occupancies in unusual structures include any building or structure which cannot be properly classified in any of the other occupancy groups, either by reason of some function not encompassed or some unusual combination of functions necessary to the purpose of the building or structure. Such miscellaneous buildings and structures must conform to the fundamental principles stated in Chapter 2 as well as the provisions of this chapter.

SECTION 30-1   GENERAL REQUIREMENTS

30-1.1 Application.   The requirements of this chapter apply to both new and existing occupancies in unusual structures. Unusual structures are those buildings or structures occupied for purposes not regulated by Chapters 8 through 29.

Occupancies in unusual structures present a special challenge to life safety. Many of the structures covered by the provisions of Chapter 30 are also governed by provisions in other chapters of the *Code*. As a basic requirement, the provisions for specific occupancies in Chapters 8 through 29 take precedence over the provisions in Chapter 30. However, all occupancies in windowless and underground buildings must comply with the additional provisions of 30-7.1 for complete automatic sprinkler protection, emergency lighting, and smoke venting.

Although the *Code* is essentially complete, providing adequate means of egress from many unusual structures will require unique solutions. Obviously, engineered solutions in many instances will exceed the minimum provisions in Chapter 30. Still, the uniqueness of a structure should not become an excuse for excessive or unneeded requirements. The *Code*'s user is cautioned to exercise judgment when determining the exit requirements for unusual structures not included in the scope of Chapter 30.

30-1.2 Mixed Occupancies.   *(See 1-4.5.)*

30-1.3 Special Definitions.

30-1.3.1 Tower. Independent structure or portion of a building occupied for observation, signaling or similar limited use and not open to general use.

30-1.3.2 Vehicles and Vessels. Any house trailer, railroad car, street car or bus, ship, barge or vessel or similar conveyance no longer mobile and permanently fixed to a foundation or mooring.

30-1.3.3 Underground Structure. A structure in which there is no direct access to outdoors or to another fire area other than by upward travel.

30-1.3.4 Windowless Structure. A building lacking any means for direct access to the outside or outside openings for light or ventilation through windows.

30-1.3.5 Water Surrounded Structure. A structure fully surrounded by water.

30-1.3.6 Open Structures. Operations and equipment conducted in open air and not enclosed within buildings, such as found in oil refining and chemical processing plants. Roofs or canopies providing shelter without enclosing walls may be provided and shall not be considered an enclosure.

Section 30-1.3 defines the unusual structures considered in Chapter 30. If an occupancy in one of these structures is regulated by Chapters 8 through 29, then the provisions of the appropriate chapter apply. One frequently confused arrangement is a place of public assembly, such as a restaurant or sightseeing lookout point on a tower structure. A number of towers have been constructed for promotional purposes in cities and amusement centers, many reaching heights of 500 ft (152.40 m). Despite such unusual arrangements, the placement of a public place of assembly on a tower requires consideration of the provisions in Chapters 8 and 9 in addition to the requirements of Chapter 30. However, towers serving special purposes, such as fire observation, radio or TV transmission, or some other similar purpose, need only meet the requirements of Chapter 30.

30-1.4 Classification of Occupancy. Occupancies in unusual structures, but meeting purposes regulated by Chapters 8 through 29, shall meet requirements of those chapters.

30-1.5 Classification of hazard of contents shall be as defined in Section 4-2.

30-1.6 Minimum Construction Standard. No special occupancy provisions.

30-1.7 Occupant Load. The occupant load of unusual structures shall be as determined by the maximum actual design occupant load.

Exception: Any unusual structure or part of an unusual structure utilized for an occupancy regulated by Chapters 8 through 29, in which case the requirements of the appropriate chapter shall apply.

SECTION 30-2   MEANS OF EGRESS REQUIREMENTS

30-2.1 General. Each required means of egress shall be in accordance with the applicable portions of Chapter 5.

30-2.2 Types of Exits. Exits shall be restricted to the following permissible types:

Doors (see 5-2.1).

Smokeproof towers (see 5-2.3).

Interior stairs (see 5-2.2). In existing structures, Class A or B.

Outside stairs (see 5-2.5).

Horizontal exits (see 5-2.4).

Ramps (see 5-2.6).

Exit passageways (see 5-2.7).

Escalators (see 5-2.8).

Exception No. 1:   Any existing stairway not complying with 5-2.2 and 5-2.5 may be continued in use, subject to the authority having jursidiction.

Exception No. 2:   Towers, such as a forest fire observation or railroad signal tower designed for occupancy by not more than three persons employed therein may be served by ladder instead of stairs.

Exception No. 3:   Open structures.

30-2.3 Capacity of Means of Egress.

30-2.3.1 The width and capacity of a means of egress shall be in accordance with Chapter 5.

Exception No. 1:   The means of egress for towers shall be provided for the persons actually employed. Where towers utilize ladders in accordance with 30-2.2, Exception No. 2, the ladders shall comply with ANSI A14.3, Safety Code for Fixed Ladders.

Exception No. 2:   Open structures.

Exception No. 3:   Structures fully surrounded by water and arranged in accordance with U.S. Coast Guard regulations.

Exception No. 4:   Spaces not subject to human occupancy because of machinery or equipment may be excluded from consideration.

Exception No. 2 to 30-2.3.1 recognizes the multiple means of egress possible from open-air structures, such as those found in petrochemical and process industries. An open-air structure actually is an access platform to the equipment which it surrounds or supports. Normal occupancy is very limited and occasional in nature. If a fire should block one means of egress, a number of alternate means of egress still remain accessible. In addition to the fixed means of egress, rescue is possible from any portion of the structure by the emergency procedures of fire fighting personnel. Potential exposure of portions of the structure not involved in a fire is minimal since in open-air platforms flames, heat, and smoke are safely dispersed directly to the atmosphere and not into the uninvolved portions of the structure.

Exception No. 3 to 30-2.3.1 recognizes the regulations of the U. S. Coast Guard which specify the means of egress from water-surrounded structures. Special requirements for egress from structures surrounded by water are necessary due to poor weather, tidal variations, and other risks to life safety imposed by sea conditions.

30-2.3.2 Required means of egress for multistoried unusual structures may serve other floors than the level where required. However, an interior egress facility shall serve only one floor for purposes of designing means of egress.

Exception No. 1: No inside open stairway, escalator or ramp may serve as a required egress facility from more than one floor level.

Exception No. 2: Open structures.

30-2.4 Number of Exits. No less than two exits shall be provided for every story or section, including stories below the floor of exit discharge.

Exception No. 1: Piers used exclusively to moor cargo vessels and to store materials where provided with proper exit facilities from structures thereon to the pier and a single means of access to the mainland as appropriate with the pier's arrangement.

Exception No. 2: Any building or tower surrounded by water, such as a light house, off shore oil platform or vessel mooring point when designed and arranged in accordance with U.S. Coast Guard regulations.

Exception No. 3: The grade level of open air structures which by their very nature contain an infinite number of exits.

Exception No. 4: Towers may be provided with single exits if the following conditions are met:

(a) The tower is subject to less than twenty-five persons on any one floor level.

(b) The tower is not used for living or sleeping purposes and is subject to occupancy by only able-bodied persons.

(c) The tower is of Type I, II or IV construction.

(d) The tower interior finish is Class A or B.

(e) The tower has no combustible materials in, under, or in the immediate vicinity, except necessary furniture.

(f) There are no high hazard occupancies in the tower or immediate vicinity.

Exception No. 5: Open structures.

The intent of Exception No. 1 to 30-2.4 is to recognize the open nature of a pier and equate a pier to a public way for purposes of exit arrangement. Note that the exception applies mainly to cargo and storage piers which are occupied by a limited number of people, most of whom are accustomed to a pier's arrangement. Under these conditions the risk to life safety of the pier is considered to be minimal, and one exit is acceptable.

Exception No. 4 to 30-2.4 restricts the provisions for a single means of egress from a tower. Calculation of the number of people [fewer than 25, see item (a) of this exception] should be based on the actual number expected to occupy the facility. This method of determination is valid since the facility is not subject to the provisions for calculating occupant load specified in Chapters 8 through 29. Limitations on the combustibility and interior finish of the structure are established so that the potential exposure of the occupants of the tower to fire is minimal. Types I, II, and IV construction [see item (c)] are defined in NFPA 220, *Standard Types of Building Construction.*[1]

One of the difficult aspects of the requirements is determination of the exposure of the tower to combustible materials under or in the immediate vicinity of the structure. Judgment should be used by the authority having jurisdiction and other users of the *Code* to ensure that arbitrary limitations are not established which restrict the use of the tower too severely. As an example, a forest fire tower is usually placed in a clearing in a large forest. The proximity of trees to the tower could be interpreted as being combustible materials in the "immediate" vicinity of the tower. Reasonable clearances [such as a clear space of 50 ft (15.24 m) to 100 ft (30.48 m) between the tower and forest] could be considered adequate separation for the life safety of the tower's occupants. Similar judgment will be needed when evaluating the clearance between high hazard occupancies and towers.

30-2.5 Arrangement of Means of Egress.

30-2.5.1 Measurement of Width of Means of Egress. The minimum width of any corridor or passageway serving as a required exit, or means of travel to or from a required exit, shall be 44 in. (111.76 cm) in the clear.

Exception: Where ladders are permitted by 30-2.2.

30-2.5.2 Where two or more exits are required, they shall be arranged so as to be reached by different paths of travel in different directions.

Exception: A common path of travel may be permitted for the first 50 ft (15.24 m) from any point.

30-2.5.3 No dead end may be more than 50 ft (15.24 m) deep.

30-2.5.4 Piers.

30-2.5.4.1 Piers not meeting requirements of 30-2.4, Exception No. 1, and occupied for other than cargo handling and storage shall have exits arranged in accordance with Chapters 8 through 29. In addition, one of the following measures shall be provided on piers extending over 150 ft (45.72 m) from shore to minimize the possibility that fire under or on the pier may block escape of occupants to shore.

30-2.5.4.2 The pier shall be arranged to provide two separate ways of travel to shore as by two well-separated walkways or independent structures.

30-2.5.4.3 The pier deck shall be open and fire resistive on noncombustible supports.

30-2.5.4.4 The pier shall be open and unobstructed and is 50 ft (15.24 m) or less in width if less than 500 ft (152.4 m) long, or its width is not less than ten percent of its length if over 500 ft (152.4 m) long.

30-2.5.4.5 The pier deck shall be provided with automatic sprinkler protection for combustible substructure and all superstructures, if any.

The provisions of 30-2.5.4.1 through 30-2.5.4.5 apply to all pier structures except those structures controlled by Exception No. 1 of 30-2.4. Note that the provisions are in addition to those contained in Chapters 8 through 29, for those piers exceeding 150 ft (45.72 m) in length from shore. For further information on constructing and protecting piers and wharves, see NFPA 87, *Standard for the Construction and Protection of Piers and Wharves*.[2]

30-2.6 Measurement of Travel Distance to Exits.   Travel to exits, when not regulated by Chapters 8 through 29, shall not exceed 100 ft (30.48 m).

Exception No. 1: In a building or structure protected throughout by an approved automatic sprinkler system in accordance with Section 7-7, travel distance may be increased to 150 ft (45.72 m).

Exception No. 2: Where ladders are permitted in 30-2.2, Exception No. 2.

Exception No. 3: Structures surrounded by water with exits arranged in accordance with U.S. Coast Guard regulations.

Exception No. 4: Open structures.

30-2.7 Discharge from Exits.   A maximum of fifty percent of the exits may discharge through areas on the level of discharge arranged in accordance with 5-7.2.

Exception: Towers or other structures provided with one exit, as permitted by 30-2.4 and arranged in accordance with 30-2.5, may have 100 percent of the exit discharge through areas on the level of discharge.

30-2.8 Illumination of Means of Egress.   Illumination of means of egress shall be provided in accordance with Section 5-8.

Exception No. 1: Open structures.

Exception No. 2: Towers with ladders for exits as permitted by 30-2.2, Exception No. 2.

Exception No. 3: Structures surrounded by water with exits arranged in accordance with U.S. Coast Guard regulations.

30-2.9 Emergency Lighting.   Emergency lighting shall be provided in accordance with Section 5-9.

Exception No. 1: Open structures.

Exception No. 2: Towers with ladders for exits as permitted by 30-2.2, Exception No. 2.

Exception No. 3: Structures surrounded by water with exits arranged in accordance with U.S. Coast Guard regulations.

Exception No. 4: Locations not routinely inhabited by humans.

Exception No. 5: Structures occupied only in daylight hours with windows arranged to provide, during daylight hours, the required level of illumination on all portions of the means of egress, upon special approval of the authority having jurisdiction.

30-2.10 Marking of Means of Egress.   Signs designating exits or ways of travel thereto shall be provided in àccordance with Section 5-10.

Exception No. 1: Towers with ladders for exits as permitted by 30-2.2.

Exception No. 2: Open structures.

Exception No. 3: Structures surrounded by water with exits arranged in accordance with U.S. Coast Guard regulations.

Exception No. 4: Locations where routine human habitation is not provided.

30-2.11 Special Features.

30-2.11.1   Spiral stairs in accordance with 5-2.2.1.6 are permitted.

30-2.11.2   In existing buildings winders in accordance with 5-2.2.2.4 are permitted.

SECTION 30-3   PROTECTION

30-3.1 Protection of Vertical Openings.   Every stairway, elevator shaft, escalator opening, and other vertical opening shall be enclosed or protected in accordance with Chapter 5 and Section 6-2.

Exception No. 1: In towers where there is no occupancy below the top floor level, stairs may be open with no enclosure required or fire escape stairs may be used when the structure is entirely open.

Exception No. 2:   Towers with ladders for exits as permitted by 30-2.2, Exception No. 2.

Exception No. 3:   Open structures.

Exception No. 4:   Structures surrounded by water with exits arranged in accordance with U.S. Coast Guard regulations.

30-3.2 Protection from Hazards. Every unusual structure shall have automatic, manual or such other protection as may be appropriate to the particular hazard designed to minimize danger to occupants in case of fire or other emergency before they have time to utilize exits to escape.

Exception: Unusual structures, such as open structures, with only occasional occupancy.

The provisions of Section 30-3 require careful analysis by the *Code*'s user to ensure that fire protection required for life safety is provided. The key element of the requirement is that the protection be adequate to safeguard occupants during the time required to reach exits. Fire protection systems which may be needed for property protection or to control fire losses in a process or occupancy will, in many cases, be excessive for life safety of occupants, and are beyond the scope of this *Code*.

30-3.3 Interior Finish.

30-3.3.1 Interior finish on walls and ceilings shall be Class A, B or C, in accordance with Section 6-5, and as required in Chapter 5 for exits.

30-3.3.2 Interior Floor Finish. No special occupancy requirements.

30-3.4 Fire Alarm System. A manual or automatic fire alarm system shall be provided in accordance with Section 7-6. The alarm system shall sound an audible alarm in a continuously manned location for purposes of initiating emergency action.

Exception No. 1:   Towers with ladders for exits as permitted by 30-2.2, Exception No. 2.

Exception No. 2:   Open structures.

Exception No. 3:   Structures surrounded by water with exits arranged in accordance with U.S. Coast Guard regulations.

SECTION 30-4   SPECIAL PROVISIONS

(RESERVED)

SECTION 30-5   BUILDING SERVICES

(RESERVED)

SECTION 30-6   SPECIAL PROVISIONS FOR VEHICLES
AND VESSELS

30-6.1   Any vehicle which is subject to human occupancy and is prevented from being mobile shall comply with the appropriate requirements of this *Code* which are appropriate to buildings of similar occupancy.

30-6.2   Any ship, barge or other vessel, permanently moored or aground and occupied for purposes other than navigation, shall be subject to the requirements of this *Code* applicable to buildings of similar occupancy.

Standards for exits and other requirements for fire safety in mobile homes will be found in NFPA 501A, *Standard for the Installation of Mobile Homes Including Mobile Home Park Requirements*,[3] and in the federal mobile home construction and safety standards.

SECTION 30-7   SPECIAL PROVISIONS FOR UNDERGROUND
STRUCTURES AND WINDOWLESS BUILDINGS

30-7.1 General.

30-7.1.1   Windowless or underground areas occupied by 100 or more persons shall be protected throughout by an approved automatic sprinkler system in accordance with Section 7-7.

30-7.1.2   Windowless or underground buildings, structures and areas shall be provided with emergency lighting in accordance with Section 5-9.

30-7.2 Underground Structures.

30-7.2.1   Where required, exits from underground structures involving upward travel, such as ascending stairs or ramps, shall be cut off from main floor areas per Section 5-1 and shall be provided with outside smoke venting facilities or other means to prevent the exits from becoming charged with smoke from any fire in the area served by the exits.

Exception: As modified by Chapters 8 through 29.

30-7.2.2   Underground buildings, structures, and areas having combustible contents, interior finish or construction shall have automatic smoke venting facilities in accordance with Chapter 7 in addition to automatic sprinkler protection.

The provisions contained in 30-7.1.1 through 30-7.2.2 for control of life safety deficiencies in windowless or underground buildings are minimal and are considered to be in addition to those contained in Chapters 8 through 29. It is not the intent of these sections to provide a means of reducing the life safety provisions contained in other chapters of the *Code*. If a building in consideration is windowless or underground and, due to its occupancy classification, subject to stricter requirements than those contained in Chapter 31, then the strictest provisions of the *Code* should be followed.

Windowless and underground structures pose special risks to life safety since the buildings cannot be easily vented of products of combustion. In an area from which there is no direct access to the outside and no windows to permit outside fire department rescue operations and ventilation, any fire or smoke may tend to produce panic. Therefore, additional corrective measures such as complete automatic sprinkler protection and automatic smoke venting systems must be provided where necessary to ensure an adequate level of life safety.

It must be noted that a windowless area is defined as an area lacking *any* means for *direct* access to the outside either by windows or other openings.

"Fire Hazards of Windowless Buildings"[4] discusses the life safety problems encountered in underground buildings; "Underground Buildings"[5] contains a detailed review of the fire experience in windowless structures.

REFERENCES CITED BY CODE

(This publication comprises a part of the requirements to the extent called for by the Code.)

ANSI A14.3 — 1974, *Safety Code for Fixed Ladders*, American National Standards Institute, 1430 Broadway, New York, NY 10018.

REFERENCES CITED IN COMMENTARY

[1]NFPA 220, *Standard Types of Building Construction*, NFPA, Boston, 1979.

[2]NFPA 87, *Standard for the Construction and Protection of Piers and Wharves*, NFPA, Boston, 1980.

[3]NFPA 501A, *Standard for the Installation of Mobile Homes Including Mobile Home Park Requirements*, NFPA, Boston, 1977. Also see the federal Mobile Home Construction and Safety Standards (Code of Federal Regulations, Title 24, Part 280).

[4]E. E. Juillerat, "Fire Hazards of Windowless Buildings," *NFPA Quarterly*, Vol. 58, No. 1, July 1964, pp. 22-30.

[5]Horatio Bond, "Underground Buildings," *Fire Journal*, Vol. 59, No. 4, July 1965, pp. 52-55.

31

applies to all occupancies

OPERATING FEATURES

Chapter 31 serves a unique purpose in the *Life Safety Code.* It specifies activities to complement the structural features mandated by the *Code* to ensure a minimum acceptable level of life safety. Usually codes and standards restrict themselves to proper building arrangements with no emphasis or advice on such subjects as maintenance, inspections, drills, or the contents (furniture or furnishings) of a structure.

These items are germane to the scope and content of the *Life Safety Code* because, as stated in Section 2-1, "...the design of exits and other safeguards shall be such that reliance for safety to life in case of fire or other emergency will not depend solely on any single safeguard; additional safeguards shall be provided for life safety in case any single safeguard is ineffective due to some human or mechanical failure."

Prevention of "human or mechanical failure" puts the *Code* into the areas of care, operation, maintenance, and inspection of equipment. Further, since life safety depends upon proper human actions at the time of an emergency, drills and checklists of what is to be done at the time of the event become critical. Because the protection safeguards built into a building may be defeated by the introduction of hazardous material, it is necessary to address the aspects of a building's contents which have a bearing on life safety (such as their arrangement, flammability, or toxicity under combustion).

In Chapter 31, these factors are covered in general for all occupancies, and are then reinforced for each specific occupancy. Section 31-1 applies to all occupancies; Sections 31-2 through 31-8 cover each individual occupancy. Since some of the factors are critical for only certain specific occupancies, e.g., stage scenery applies only to occupancies that have stages, they are not emphasized.

Finally, Chapter 31 focuses on the things that people (occupants, owners, tenants, and maintenance personnel) can do to assist the *Code* in achieving life safety. This allows for involvement of people in providing for their own safety and security. If properly addressed in the public sector, the enthusiasm generated could conceivably ensure total, or near total, compliance with all *Code* requirements.

SECTION 31-1   GENERAL REQUIREMENTS

(See also Sections 31-2 through 31-8 for special occupancy requirements.)

31-1.1 Construction, Repair, Improvement Operations.

31-1.1.1 Adequate escape facilities shall be maintained at all times in buildings under construction for the use of construction workers. Escape facilities shall consist of doors, walkways, stairs, ramps, fire escapes, ladders or other approved means or devices arranged in accordance with the general principles of the *Code* insofar as they can reasonably be applied to buildings under construction. See also *Standard on Building Construction and Demolition Operations*, NFPA 241.

31-1.1.2   Flammable or explosive substances or equipment for repairs or alterations may be introduced in a building of normally low or ordinary hazard classification while the building is occupied, only if the condition of use and safeguards provided are such as not to create any additional danger or handicap to egress beyond the normally permissible conditions in the building.

31-1.2 Means of Egress Reliability.

31-1.2.1   Every required exit, exit access or exit discharge shall be continuously maintained free of all obstructions or impediments to full instant use in the case of fire or other emergency.

> Paragraph 31-1.2.1 does not specify who will be responsible for keeping exits free and clear. The person responsible for each facility, whether manager, owner, or operator, must ensure that required exit components are maintained in usable condition. The authority having jurisdiction has the responsibility to ensure that this is being accomplished.

31-1.2.2 Furnishings and Decorations in Means of Egress.

31-1.2.2.1   No furnishings, decorations, or other objects shall be so placed as to obstruct exits, access thereto, egress therefrom, or visibility thereof.

31-1.2.2.2   Hangings or draperies shall not be placed over exit doors or otherwise located as to conceal or obscure any exit. Mirrors shall not be placed on exit doors. Mirrors shall not be placed in or adjacent to any exit in such a manner as to confuse the direction of exit.

> Paragraphs 31-1.2.2.1 and 31-1.2.2.2 provide guidance for the interior decoration and maintenance of such places as restaurants and theaters where excessive decoration, needed to establish a "style" or "theme," often totally obscures, and in some cases obstructs, exits. Here the authority having jurisdiction must take care to ensure that normal access to a free and unobstructed exit is not lost in the pursuit of authenticity of period or style.

31-1.2.2.3   There shall be no obstruction by railings, barriers, or gates that divide the open space into sections appurtenant to individual rooms, apartments, or other uses. Where the authority having jurisdiction finds the required path of travel to be obstructed by furniture or other movable objects, he may require that they be fastened out of the way or he may require that railings or other permanent barriers be installed to protect the path of travel against encroachment.

> Paragraph 31-1.2.2.3 relates primarily to the arrangement of furniture (and to railings, gates, or barriers) found in lobbies, foyers, waiting spaces, or staging areas of businesses, hospitals, health care clinics, hotels, and apartments. Because these large spaces are often subdivided by furniture (chairs, tables, and plants) or by

railings and gates, assurance must be given that the furnishings will not block the access to exits. This paragraph suggests fastening the objects out of the way or placing railings around them to ensure that they will be held in a fixed location and cannot be easily moved or rearranged, possibly blocking access to an exit.

31-1.3 Equipment Maintenance and Testing.

31-1.3.1 Every required automatic sprinkler system, fire detection and alarm system, exit lighting, fire door, and other item of equipment required by this *Code* shall be continuously in proper operating condition.

31-1.3.2 Any equipment requiring test or periodic operation to assure its maintenance shall be tested or operated as specified elsewhere in this *Code* or as directed by the authority having jurisdiction.

31-1.3.3 Systems shall be under the supervision of a responsible person who shall cause proper tests to be made at specified intervals and have general charge of all alterations and additions.

31-1.3.4 Systems shall be tested at intervals recommended by the appropriate standards listed in the references at the end of this chapter.

The standards referred to in 31-1.3.4 appear in the "References Cited by *Code*" section at the end of this chapter.

31-1.3.5 Automatic Sprinkler Systems.
All automatic sprinkler systems required by this *Code* shall be continuously maintained in reliable operating condition at all times, and such periodic inspections and tests shall be made as are necessary to assure proper maintenance.

NFPA 13A, *Recommended Practice for the Care and Maintenance of Sprinkler Systems,*[1] gives detailed information on the care and maintenance of sprinkler systems.

31-1.3.6 Alarm and Fire Detection Systems.
Fire alarm signaling equipment shall be restored to service as promptly as possible after each test or alarm and shall be kept in normal condition for operation. Equipment requiring rewinding or replenishing shall be rewound or replenished as promptly as possible after each test or alarm.

Paragraphs 31-1.3.1 through 31-1.3.6 emphasize that any system or mechanical device installed to ensure life safety must be maintained. Maintenance should be performed according to a set schedule established either by code (this *Code* or other referenced codes) or by the authority having jurisdiction. If this maintenance is not performed, failure of these systems is a possibility. Thus, lack of maintenance is comparable to providing a non-*Code*-complying facility, particularly if the unmaintained system was required by the *Code* or installed to provide an equivalency to the *Code*'s requirements.

31-1.4 Furnishings, Decorations, and Treated Finishes. *(See also 31-1.2.2.)*

31-1.4.1 Draperies, curtains, and other similar furnishings and decorations shall be flame resistant where required by the applicable provisions of this chapter. These materials required herein to be tested in accordance with *Standard Method of Fire Tests for Flame Resistant Textiles and Films*, NFPA 701, shall comply with both the small- and large-scale tests.

Although NFPA 701, *Standard Methods of Fire Tests for Flame-Retardant Textiles and Films*,[2] does an adequate job of measuring the level of hazard presented by draperies and the outermost upholstered surface of a piece of furniture, it does not address the hazard of the underlayment or the cushioning material. NFPA 701[2] does not predict how these objects will perform in a fire because the interface of the outer layer of material combined with a variety of underlayments or cushions will produce a variety of different hazard levels, some insignificant, but some severe. There is no standard available at the national level that truly assesses the hazard level of a complete piece of furniture, nor is there a recommended test procedure for determining a realistic assessment.

31-1.4.2   Furnishings or decorations of an explosive or highly flammable character shall not be used.

Christmas trees not treated effectively with flame retardants, ordinary crepe paper decorations, and pyroxylin plastic decorations may be classed as highly flammable. The *Code* relies on the authority having jurisdiction to exercise judgment in enforcing 31-1.4.2.

31-1.4.3   Other furnishings, such as furniture and bedding, do not require additional flammability regulations under this *Code*.

Resistance of mattresses to small ignition sources such as cigarettes is regulated by federal law. Studies regarding their resistance to large ignition sources such as waste basket fires are presently being conducted by the National Bureau of Standards. Many furniture manufacturers are voluntarily complying with small ignition resistance requirements for chairs, sofas, and similar furnishings. Test methods for these are still being studied.

31-1.4.4   Fire retardant paints or solutions shall be renewed at such intervals as necessary to maintain the necessary flame retardant properties.

See NFPA 703, *Standard for Fire-Retardant Impregnated Wood and Fire-Retardant Coatings for Building Materials*.[3]

31-1.5 Fire Exit Drills.

Paragraphs 31-1.5.1 through 31-1.5.6 serve as a primer on how to conduct a fire exit drill. Sections 31-2 through 31-8 provide specific details that apply or relate a drill directly to the characteristics of the occupancy in question.

The term "fire exit drill" is used to avoid confusion between drills held for the purpose of rapidly evacuating buildings and drills of the fire fighting practice which, from a technical viewpoint, are correctly designated as "fire drills," although this second term is, by common usage, applied to egress drills in schools.

The purpose of fire exit drills is to ensure the efficient and safe use of the available exit facilities. Proper drills ensure orderly exit under control and help prevent panic.

Order, control, and familiarity with exits are the primary purposes of the drill. Speed in emptying buildings, while desirable, is not in itself an object, and should be made secondary to the maintenance of proper order and discipline.

The usefulness of a fire exit drill and the extent to which it can be carried depend upon the character of the occupancy. The drill is most effective where the occupants of the building are under discipline and subject to habitual control. For example, schools offer possibilities of more highly developed and valuable fire exit drills than other types of occupancies.

In buildings where the occupant load is of a changing character and under no program of discipline (for example, in hotels or in department stores), no regularly organized fire exit drill, such as that which may be conducted in schools, is possible. In such cases the fire exit drills must be limited to the regular employees who, however, can be thoroughly schooled in the proper procedure and can be trained to direct other occupants of the building in case of fire. In occupancies such as hospitals, regular employees can be rehearsed in the proper procedure in case of fire; such training is always advisable in all occupancies whether or not regular fire exit drills can be held.

If a fire exit drill is considered merely as a routine exercise from which some persons may be excused, there is a grave danger that in an actual fire the drill will fail in its intended purpose.

31-1.5.1   Fire exit drills conforming to the provisions of this chapter of the *Code* shall be regularly conducted in occupancies where specified by the provisions of this chapter, or by appropriate action of the authority having jurisdiction. Drills shall be designed in cooperation with the local authorities.

31-1.5.2   Fire exit drills, where required by the authority having jurisdiction, shall be held with sufficient frequency to familiarize all occupants with the drill procedure and to have the conduct of the drill a matter of established routine.

31-1.5.3   Responsibility for the planning and conduct of drills shall be assigned only to competent persons qualified to exercise leadership.

31-1.5.4   In the conduct of drills emphasis shall be placed upon orderly evacuation under proper discipline rather than upon speed.

31-1.5.5   Drills shall include suitable procedures to make sure that all persons in the building, or all persons subject to the drill, actually participate.

31-1.5.6   Drills shall be held at unexpected times and under varying conditions to simulate the unusual conditions obtaining in case of fire.

Fire is always unexpected. If the drill is always conducted in the same way at the same time, it loses much of its value, and when in an actual fire it is not possible to follow the usual routine of the fire exit drill to which occupants have become accustomed, confusion and panic may ensue. Drills should be carefully planned to simulate actual fire conditions. Not only should they be held at varying times, but they should use different means of exit. Assume, for example, that some given stairway is unavailable due to fire or smoke, and that all the occupants must be led out by some other route. Fire exit drills should be designed to familiarize the occupants with all available means of exits, particularly emergency exits that are not habitually used during the normal occupancy of the building.

SECTION 31-2 PLACES OF ASSEMBLY

31-2.1 Drills. The employees or attendants of places of public assembly shall be schooled and drilled in the duties they are to perform in case of fire, panic, or other emergency in order to be of greatest service in effecting orderly exit of assemblages.

Attention is directed to the importance of having an adequate number of competent attendants at all times when the place of public assembly is occupied.

31-2.2 Open Flame Devices. No open flame lighting devices shall be used in any place of assembly.

Exception No. 1: Where necessary for ceremonial or religious purposes, the authority having jurisdiction may permit open flame lighting under such restrictions as are necessry to avoid danger of ignition of combustible materials or injury to occupants.

Exception No. 2: Open flame devices may be used on stages where a necessary part of theatrical performances, provided adequate precautions satisfactory to the authority having jurisdiction are taken to prevent ignition of any combustible materials.

Exception No. 3: Gas lights may be permitted provided adequate precautions, satisfactory to the authority having jurisdiction, are taken to prevent ignition of any combustible materials.

Exception No. 4: As permitted in 31-2.3.

Securely supported altar candles in churches, well-separated from any combustible material, may be permitted by 31-2.2. On the other hand, lighted candles carried by children wearing cotton robes present a hazard too great to be permitted even for the most worthy cause. There are many other situations of intermediate hazard where the authority having jurisdiction will have to exercise judgment.

31-2.3 Special Food Service Devices. Portable cooking equipment, not flue-connected, shall be permitted only as follows:

(a) Equipment fueled by small heat sources which can be readily extinguished by water, such as candles or alcohol-burning equipment (including "solid alcohol"), may be used provided adequate precautions satisfactory to the authority having jurisdiction are taken to prevent ignition of any combustible materials.

(b) Candles may be used on tables used for food service if securely supported on substantial noncombustible bases, so located as to avoid danger of ignition of combustible materials, and only if approved by the authority having jurisdiction. Candle flames shall be protected.

(c) "Flaming Sword" or other equipment involving open flames and flamed dishes such as cherries jubilee, crepes suzette, etc., may be permitted provided necessary precautions are taken, and subject to the approval of the authority having jurisdiction.

The list of tragic fires in places of assembly where the cause was a "friendly" fire (alcohol or sterno fires in restaurants, flames used for dramatic effects in theaters,

etc.) is well-documented. Paragraph 31-2.3 and its exceptions provide a fundamental exercise in fire prevention, whereby the use of these open flame devices is tightly controlled. The first step in fire prevention, which 31-2.2 and 31-2.3 try to achieve, is prevention of ignition. This section has been interpreted to allow decorative candles under the same conditions as candles used for food warming.

31-2.4 Smoking.

31-2.4.1 Smoking in places of assembly shall be regulated by the authority having jurisdiction.

31-2.4.2 In rooms or areas where smoking is prohibited, plainly visible "NO SMOKING" signs shall be posted.

31-2.4.3 No person shall smoke in prohibited areas which are so posted.

Exception: The authority having jurisdiction may permit smoking on a stage only when it is a necessary and rehearsed part of a performance and only by a regular performing member of the cast.

31-2.4.4 Where smoking is permitted, suitable ash trays or receptacles shall be provided in convenient locations.

31-2.5 Decorations and Stage Scenery.

31-2.5.1 Combustible materials shall be treated with an effective flame retardant material. Stage settings made of combustible materials shall likewise be treated with flame retardant materials. Flame retardant treatments shall be as specified in 31-1.4.

31-2.5.2 Only noncombustible materials, limited-combustible materials, or fire retardant pressure treated wood may be used for stage scenery or props, on the audience side of the proscenium arch.

31-2.5.3 The authority having jurisdiction shall impose controls on the amount and arrangement of combustible contents (including decorations) in places of assembly to provide an adequate level of safety to life from fire.

The scenery found stored in the fly sections of a stage, plus that used in a stage production, represent a sizable (and usually highly combustible) fuel load. Classic theater fires (for example, the Iroquois Theater, Chicago, 1903) involved the ignition of the scenery on stage and subsequent exposure to the audience by this sizable amount of burning fuel. Chapters 8 and 9 provide for a curtain of noncombustible material to drop, thus separating the fuel from the audience, and for the installation of extinguishing systems (both automatic and manual) on or around the stage. In 31-2.5.1 through 31-2.5.3, the *Code* controls the hazard of fuel stored or placed outside the proscenium arch and attempts to limit the flammability of all the scenery, thus minimizing the level of exposure (hazard) to the audience.

31-2.6 Seating.

31-2.6.1 Seats in places of assembly accommodating more than 200 persons shall be securely fastened to the floor except when fastened together in groups of not less than three nor more than seven and as permitted by 31-2.6.2. All seats in balconies and galleries shall be securely fastened to the floor, except in churches.

31-2.6.2   Seats not secured to the floor may be permitted in restaurants, night clubs, and other occupancies where the fastening of seats to the floor may be impracticable, provided that in the area used for seating (excluding dance floor, stage, etc.), there shall be not more than one seat for each 15 sq ft (1.39 sq m) of net floor area and adequate aisles to reach exits shall be maintained at all times.

Exception: Seating diagrams shall be submitted for approval of the authority having jurisdiction to allow increase in occupant load per 8-1.7.2 and 9-1.7.2.

The function of 31-2.6.1 and 31-2.6.2 is to prevent the movement of seats so that aisles, rows, and access to the exits do not become blocked in a place of assembly during the jostling that occurs when people flee from a fire.

31-2.6.3   Every room constituting a place of assembly and not having fixed seats shall have the occupant load of the room posted in a conspicuous place, near the main exit from the room. Approved signs shall be maintained in a legible manner by the owner or his authorized agent. Signs shall be durable and shall indicate the number of occupants permitted for each room use.

31-2.7 Projection Room.   Unless the projection room is constructed in accordance with the applicable standard listed in Appendix B, there shall be posted on the outside of each projection room door, and within the projection room proper, a conspicuous sign with 1-in. (2.54-cm) block letters stating: "Safety Film Only Permitted in This Room".

The standard referenced in 31-2.7 is NFPA 40, *Standard for the Storage and Handling of Cellulose Nitrate Motion Picture Film.*[4]

SECTION 31-3   EDUCATIONAL OCCUPANCIES

Firesafety, including an approved fire evacuation plan, should be included in the curriculum of all educational occupancies. This part of the curriculum should be approved by the authority having jurisdiction.

The requirements of Section 31-3 are of necessity general in scope, since they must apply to all types of schools, such as truant schools; schools for the mentally retarded; schools for the blind, deaf, and dumb; and public schools. It is fully recognized that no one code can meet all the conditions of the various buildings involved, and it will be necessary for some school authorities to issue supplements to these requirements; however, all supplements should be consistent with these requirements.

31-3.1 Drills.

31-3.1.1   Fire exit drills shall be conducted regularly in accordance with the applicable provisions of the following paragraphs.

Drills for educational occupancies, particularly at the grade school level, are essential to ensure an orderly response during a fire. Unfortunately, the predictability of such drills often leads to their becoming self-defeating. When an alarm bell sounds and a fire department monitor is seen in a corridor, some teachers ignore the bell,

assuming that it is a false alarm. Or, if the bell sounds and a fire department monitor is not seen, teachers opt for a "we all go or we all stay" posture which is decided upon in the hallway while the bell continues to ring and while the students stay in class. Thus, when a bell sounds, primary emphasis should be placed on evacuation, regardless of who is or is not present in the hallways, or whether or not fire equipment is parked in front of the school. Essentially, the fire department and the school should vary the timing and arrangement of the drills, but not vary the required response, which is orderly evacuation.

31-3.1.2 There shall be at least eight fire exit drills a year in schools through grade 12. In climates where the weather is severe during the winter months, weekly drills should be held at the beginning of the school term to complete the required number of drills before cold weather so as not to endanger the health of the pupils.

"Practice drills" may be held during inclement weather. Such drills would be held at the regular dismissal time, when the pupils are properly clothed, by using the exit drill alarm signal. With such drills, there would be no necessity of a return signal.

31-3.1.3 Drills shall be executed at different hours of the day or evening; during the changing of classes; when the school is at assembly; during the recess or gymnastic periods; etc., so as to avoid distinction between drills and actual fires. If a drill is called when pupils are going up and down the stairways, as during the time classes are changing, the pupils shall be instructed to form in file and immediately proceed to the nearest available exit in an orderly manner.

Cards of instruction should be conspicuously posted describing the procedure of the drills.

31-3.1.4 Every fire exit drill shall be an exercise in school management for principal and teachers, with the chief purpose of every drill complete control of the class so that the teacher will form its ranks quickly and silently, may halt it, turn it, or direct it as desired. Great stress shall be laid upon the execution of each drill in a brisk, quiet and orderly manner. Running shall be prohibited. In case there are pupils incapable of holding their places in a line moving at a reasonable speed, provisions shall be made to have them taken care of by the more sturdy pupils, moving independently of the regular line of march.

If, for any reason, a line becomes blocked, some of the pupils should be countermarched to another exit in order to prevent panic arising from inactivity.

31-3.1.5 Monitors shall be appointed from the more mature pupils to assist in the proper execution of all drills. They shall be instructed to hold open doors in the line of march or to close doors where necessary to prevent spread of fire or smoke, per 5-2.1.2.3. There shall be at least two substitutes for each appointment so as to provide for proper performance in case of absence of the regular monitors. The searching of toilet or other rooms shall be the duty of the teachers or other members of the staff. If the teachers are to do the searching, it should be done after they have joined their classes to the preceeding lines.

31-3.1.6   As all drills simulate an actual fire condition, pupils shall not be allowed to obtain clothing after the alarm is sounded, even when in home rooms, on account of the confusion which would result in forming the lines and the danger of tripping over dragging apparel.

31-3.1.7   Each class or group shall proceed to a predetermined point outside the building and remain there while a check is made to see that all are accounted for, leaving only when a recall signal is given to return to the building, or when dismissed. Such points shall be sufficiently far away from the building and from each other as to avoid danger from any fire in the building, interference with fire department operations, or confusion between different classes or groups.

31-3.1.8   Where necessary for drill lines to cross roadways, signs reading "STOP! SCHOOL FIRE DRILL", or equivalent, shall be carried by monitors to the traffic intersecting points in order to stop traffic during the period of the drill.

Wherever possible, drill lines should not cross a street or highway, especially where the traffic is heavy. It is recommended that where drill lines must cross roadways, a police officer, school janitor, or a teacher acting as a traffic officer be on duty to control traffic during drills.

31-3.1.9   Fire exit drills in schools shall not include any fire extinguishing operations.

Instructors and employees should be trained in the function and use of fire extinguishing equipment to meet an emergency; however, their primary responsibility is to lead the students to safety.

31-3.2 Signals.

31-3.2.1   All fire exit drill alarms shall be sounded on the fire alarm system and not on the signal system used to dismiss classes.

31-3.2.2   Whenever any of the school authorities determine that an actual fire exists, they shall immediately call the local fire department using the public fire alarm system or such other facilities as are available.

31-3.2.3   In order that pupils will not be returned to a building which is burning, the recall signal shall be one that is separate and distinct from, and cannot be mistaken for, any other signals. Such signals may be given by distinctive colored flags or banners. If the recall signal is electrical, the push buttons or other controls shall be kept under lock, the key for which shall be in the possession of the principal or some other designated person in order to prevent a recall at a time when there is a fire. Regardless of the method of recall, the means of giving the signal shall be kept under a lock.

31-3.3 Inspection.

31-3.3.1   It shall be the duty of principals and teachers to inspect all exit facilities daily in order to make sure that all stairways, doors, and other exits are in proper condition.

Particular attention should be given to keeping all doors unlocked and to having doors closed which serve to protect the safety of paths of egress (such as doors on stairway enclosures). Under no conditions should doors be blocked open. Outside

stairs and fire escape stairs should be kept free from all obstructions and clear of snow and ice, allowing no accumulation of snow or ice or materials of any kind outside exit doors which might prevent the opening of the door or interfere with rapid escape from the building.

Any condition likely to interfere with safe exit should be immediately corrected if possible, or reported at once to the appropriate authorities.

31-3.3.2 Open-plan buildings require extra surveillance to ensure that exit paths are maintained clear of obstruction and are obvious.

31-3.4 Day-Care Centers.

31-3.4.1 Fire prevention inspections shall be conducted monthly by a trained senior member of the staff. A copy of the latest inspection form shall be posted in a conspicuous place in the day-care facility.

Paragraph 31-3.4.1 does not intend to eliminate inspections by the personnel of fire prevention bureaus where they exist, but to supplement such inspections. Where no fire department inspections are made or where they are made infrequently, monthly inspections must be made by a senior member of the staff who has been trained to make such inspections by the authority having jurisdiction.

31-3.4.2 An approved fire evacuation plan shall be executed not less than once per month.

Fire safety, including an approved fire evacuation plan, should be included in the curriculum of all day-care centers, group day-care homes, and family day-care homes. This part of the curriculum should be approved by the authority having jurisdiction.

31-3.4.3 Furnishings and decorations in day-care centers shall be in accordance with the provisions of 31-1.4.

31-3.4.4 Flammable and combustible liquids shall be stored in areas accessible only to designated individuals and as recommended in the appropriate standard listed in the references at the end of this chapter.

To ensure that only designated individuals have access to flammable or combustible liquids, such materials should be kept in locked areas.

NFPA 30, *Flammable and Combustible Liquids Code*,[5] is the "appropriate standard" referred to in 31-3.4.4.

31-3.4.5 Wastebaskets and other waste containers shall be made of noncombustible materials.

31-3.4.6 Child-prepared artwork and teaching materials may be attached directly to the walls and shall not exceed 20 percent of the wall area.

It is necessary not only to limit the quantity of child-prepared materials, but also to avoid locating these materials near the exit access doors in a room. Where possible, such materials should be fastened to the wall at the top and bottom of displays.

31-3.5 Group Day-Care Homes.   At least one operable flashlight shall be provided for each staff member in a location accessible to the staff for use in the event of a power failure.

31-3.6 Family Day-Care Homes.   At least one operable flashlight shall be provided in a location accessible to the staff for use in the event of a power failure.

SECTION 31-4   HEALTH CARE OCCUPANCIES

31-4.1 Attendants, Evacuation Plan, Fire Exit Drills.

31-4.1.1   The administration of every hospital, nursing home and residential-custodial care facility shall have in effect and available to all supervisory personnel written copies of a plan for the protection of all persons in the event of fire and for their evacuation to areas of refuge and from the building when necessary. All employees shall be periodically instructed and kept informed respecting their duties under the plan. A copy of the plan shall be readily available at all times in the telephone operator's position or at the security center.

The provisions of 31-4.1.3 to 31-4.2.6 inclusive shall apply.

Health care occupants have, in large part, varied degrees of physical disability; their removal to the outside, or even disturbance by moving, is inexpedient or impractical in many cases, except as a last resort. Similarly, recognizing that there may be an operating necessity for the restraint of the mentally ill occupant (often by use of barred windows and locked doors), exit drills are usually extremely disturbing, detrimental, and frequently impracticable.

In most cases, fire and exit drills as ordinarily practiced in other occupancies cannot be conducted in health care occupancies. Fundamentally, superior construction, early discovery and extinguishment of incipient fires, and prompt notification must be relied upon to reduce to a minimum the occasion for evacuation of buildings of this class.

31-4.1.2   Every bed intended for use by health care occupants shall be easily movable under conditions of evacuation and shall be equipped with the type and size casters to allow easy mobility, especially over elements of the structure such as expansion plates and elevator thresholds. The authority having jurisdiction may make exceptions in the equipping of beds intended for use in areas limited to patients such as convalescent, self-care, or mental health patients.

Although the function of 31-4.1.2 is to provide for the horizontal movement of patients in their beds, normal hospital practice is to move patients through the hospital in narrow carts or wheelchairs. Thus, hospitals have little or no practice in moving patients in the larger beds. In addition, the furniture (chairs, nightstand, food tray/table) in a room must be moved out of the way to allow a bed to be turned and moved out. This requires extra time that is usually unavailable to the staff at the time of a fire. Emphasis should be placed on moving patients who are in the "room of fire origin" and others who are directly exposed to the fire, and on maintaining in their rooms the patients who are not immediately threatened during the fire.

31-4.1.3 Fire exit drills in health care occupancies shall include the transmission of a fire alarm signal and simulation of emergency fire conditions except that the movement of infirm or bed-ridden patients to safe areas or to the exterior of the building is not required. Drills shall be conducted quarterly on each shift to familiarize facility personnel (nurses, interns, maintenance engineers, and administrative staff) with signals and emergency action required under varied conditions. At least twelve drills shall be held every year. When drills are conducted between 9:00 p.m. (2100 hours) and 6:00 a.m. (0600 hours) a coded announcement may be used instead of audible alarms.

Many hospitals conduct fire exit drills without disturbing patients by planning the choice of location of the simulated emergency and by closing doors to patients' rooms or wards in the vicinity, prior to the initiation of the drill. The purpose of a fire exit drill is to test the efficiency, knowledge, and response of institutional personnel, not to disturb or excite patients.

Convalescent patients should be removed from involved zones lest their curiosity or anxiety cause them injury or hamper fire brigade activity. All sections should be ensured of a necessary complement of doctors, nurses, attendants, and other employees in reserve, ready to assist in the transfer of bed patients to less exposed areas or sections.

31-4.2 Procedure in Case of Fire.

31-4.2.1 Upon discovery of fire, personnel shall immediately take the following action:

(a) If any person is involved in the fire, the discoverer shall go to the aid of that person, calling aloud an established code phrase. The use of a code provides for both the immediate aid of any endangered person and the transmission of an alarm. Any person in the area, upon hearing the code called aloud, shall transmit the interior alarm using the nearest manual alarm station.

(b) If a person is not involved in the fire, the discoverer shall transmit the interior alarm using the nearest manual alarm station.

(c) Personnel, upon hearing the alarm signal, shall immediately execute their duties as outlined in the facility firesafety plan.

31-4.2.2 The telephone operator shall determine the location of the fire as indicated by the audible signal. In a building equipped with an uncoded alarm system, a person on the floor of fire origin shall be responsible for the prompt notification of the fire location to the facility telephone operator.

31-4.2.3 If the telephone operator receives a telephone alarm reporting a fire from a floor, the operator shall regard that alarm in the same fashion as an alarm over the fire alarm system. The operator shall immediately notify the fire department and alert all facility personnel of the place of fire and its origin.

31-4.2.4 If the interior alarm system is out of order, any person discovering a fire shall immediately notify the telephone operator by telephone. The operator shall then transmit this to the fire service and alert the building.

31-4.2.5 A written facility firesafety plan shall provide for:

(a) Use of alarms

(b) Transmission of alarm to fire department

(c) Response to alarms

(d) Isolation of fire

(e) Evacuation of area

(f) Preparing building for evacuation

(g) Fire extinguishment.

31-4.2.6 All facility personnel shall be instructed in the use of, and response to, fire alarms; and, in addition, they should be instructed in the use of the code phrase to ensure transmission of an alarm under the following conditions:

(a) When the discoverer of a fire must immediately go to the aid of an endangered person.

(b) During a malfunction of the interior alarm system.

Personnel hearing the code announced shall first transmit the interior alarm using the nearest manual alarm station and shall then immediately execute their duties as outlined in the firesafety plan.

In addition to the requirements of 31-4.2, evacuation plans should stress closing doors of as many patient rooms as possible in order to shut out smoke spreading from a fire and, if possible, to confine the fire in a room. This single event of the staff's manually closing the doors completes the *Code*-mandated level of safety found in Chapters 12 and 13. In studies of fires in health care institutions in which the staff closed doors, the fire spread was readily confined and the life loss was either nil or small.

In many recent serious loss-of-life fires in health care facilities, staff either did not close doors or else reopened them. The fire spread was sizable, and the life loss was high. Enough emphasis cannot be given to training staff on sounding an alarm (first!), rescuing patients (as needed), and closing all doors. The last item has the most significant effect on the spread of a fire.

31-4.3 Maintenance of Exits.   Daily inspection and proper maintenance shall be provided to ensure the dependability of the method of evacuation selected. Facilities which find it necessary to lock exits shall at all times maintain an adequate staff qualified to release and conduct occupants from the immediate danger area to a place of safety in case of fire or other emergency.

31-4.4 Smoking.   Smoking regulations shall be adopted and shall include the following minimal provisions:

(a) Smoking shall be prohibited in any room, ward, or compartment where flammable liquids, combustible gases, or oxygen are used or stored and in any other hazardous location. Such areas shall be posted with "NO SMOKING" signs.

(b) Smoking by patients classified as not responsible shall be prohibited.

Exception: When the patient is under direct supervision.

(c) Ashtrays of noncombustible material and safe design shall be provided in all areas where smoking is permitted.

(d) Metal containers with self-closing cover devices into which ash trays may be emptied shall be readily available to all areas where smoking is permitted.

Smoking in bed or discarding smoking materials into ordinary waste containers not designed for receiving them lead the list of causes of fires in health care occupancies. The requirements of 31-4.4 must be adhered to in order to minimize the chance of ignition.

The most rigid discipline with regard to prohibition of smoking may not be nearly as effective in reducing incipient fires from surreptitious smoking as the open recognition of smoking and the providing of suitable facilities for smoking. Proper education and training of the staff and attendants in the ordinary fire hazards and their abatement are unquestionably essential. The problem is a broad one, variable with different types of arrangements of buildings, and the effectiveness of rules of procedure, necessarily flexible, depends in large part upon the management.

31-4.5 Draperies. Window draperies, curtains for decorative and acoustical purposes and cubical curtains shall be noncombustible or rendered and maintained flame resistant as per *Standard Method of Fire Tests for Flame Resistant Textiles and Films*, NFPA 701.

31-4.6 Furnishings and Decorations.

31-4.6.1 Furnishings and decorations in health care occupancies shall be in accordance with the provisions of 31-1.4.

Furniture, including mattresses, are recognized as providing combustibles for the support of fire. As such, appropriate measures should be taken to protect the facility and occupants from immediate danger. Also see commentary following 31-1.4.3.

31-4.6.2 Combustible decorations are prohibited in any health care occupancy unless flame retardant.

To meet the requirements of 31-4.6.2, decorations should pass both the large- and small-scale tests of NFPA 701, *Standard Methods of Fire Tests for Flame-Resistant Textiles and Films.*[2]

31-4.6.3 Wastebaskets and other waste containers shall be of noncombustible or other approved materials.

The purpose of 31-4.6.3 is to try to contain any fire that may start in a waste container. A combustible container or container that collapses during fire exposure will help spread the fire. If the trash container is adjacent to a bed, there is a high probability that the bed linens will ignite regardless of whether or not the container is approved. This fire spread scenerio is very common in health care facilities.

SECTION 31-5   DETENTION AND CORRECTIONAL OCCUPANCIES

31-5.1 Attendants, Evacuation Plan, Fire Exit Drills.

31-5.1.1 Detection and correctional facilities, or those portions of facilities having such occupancy, must be provided with 24-hour staffing on any floor level having residency and located within 100 ft (30.48 m) of the accessway to any housing area. Under Use Conditions III, IV and V, as defined in 14-1.4, audio monitoring shall be provided for every sleeping space.

Use Conditions III, IV, and V rely on staff action to protect residents; therefore, the staff needs to be aware of conditions immediately, as residents may discover a fire before automatic detection devices react.

31-5.1.2 The administration of every detention or correctional facility shall have in effect and provided to all supervisory personnel written copies of a plan for the protection of all persons in the event of fire and for their evacuation to areas of refuge and from the building when necessary. All employees shall be periodically instructed and kept informed respecting their duties under the plan.

A properly planned and well-tested plan is of great importance, especially in a detention and correctional occupancy where residents depend heavily on staff performance in order to survive a fire.

31-5.2 Books, clothing and other combustible personal property allowed in sleeping rooms shall be stored in closable metal lockers or fire resistant container.

31-5.3 The amount of heat producing appliances (such as toasters, hot plates, etc.) and the overall use of electrical power within a sleeping room shall be controlled by facility administration.

31-5.4 Furnishings and Decorations.

31-5.4.1 Furnishings and decorations in detention and correctional occupancies shall be in accordance with the provisions of 31-1.4.

31-5.4.2 Combustible decorations are prohibited in any detention or correctional occupancy unless flame retardant.

Decorations meeting the requirements of this paragraph should pass both the large- and small-scale tests of NFPA 701, *Standard Methods of Fire Tests for Flame-Resistant Textiles and Films.*[2]

31-5.4.3 Wastebaskets and other waste containers shall be of noncombustible or other approved materials.

31-5.4.4 Furnishings, such as mattress and upholstered or cushioned furniture, shall not be of a highly flammable character.

Use of foam plastic mattresses and pads must be carefully reviewed.

31-5.4.5 Draperies. Window draperies, curtains for decorative or acoustical purposes and privacy curtains shall be noncombustible or rendered and maintained flame resistant as per *Standard Method of Fire Tests for Flame Resistant Textiles and Films*, NFPA 701.

31-5.5 All keys necessary for unlocking doors installed in means of egress shall be individually identified by both touch and sight.

Loss of keys, broken keys, wrong keys, etc., have played a major role in several multiple-death detention and correctional occupancy fires.

SECTION 31-6 RESIDENTIAL OCCUPANCIES

31-6.1 Hotel Emergency Organization.

31-6.1.1 All employees of hotels shall be instructed and drilled in the duties they are to perform in the event of fire, panic, or other emergency.

The exact nature of the emergency organization specified in 31-6.1 must of necessity be governed by such factors as the number of available employees, the structural conditions, the degree of compliance with this *Code*, and other elements pertinent to the individual situation. To be efficient, any such organization must depend upon:
1. A definite working plan,
2. Competent leadership,
3. Rigid discipline,
4. Maintenance of necessary apparatus, and
5. A schedule of sufficient training under discipline with such apparatus.

It is advisable to secure the cooperation of local fire department officials in developing and training employees.

31-6.1.2 Drills of the emergency organization shall be held at monthly intervals, covering such points as the operation and maintenance of the available first aid fire appliances, the testing of guest alerting devices, and a study of instructions for emergency duties.

In order to train employees in logical procedure, it is recommended that emergencies be assumed to have arisen at various locations in the occupancy.

31-6.2 Emergency Duties.

31-6.2.1 Upon discovery of fire, some or all of these duties will become immediately imperative, the number and sequence depending upon the exact situation encountered

Alarms
Notify office.
Notify public fire department.
Notify private fire brigade.
Guests
Warn guests or others who are or may become endangered.
Assist occupants to safety, with special attention to aged, infirm, or otherwise incapacitated persons.
Search rooms to be sure all occupants have escaped.
Man all elevators (including those of automatic type) with competent operators.
Extinguishment
Extinguish or control the fire, using available first aid equipment.
Send messenger to meet public fire department upon arrival in order to direct latter to exact location of fire. (The public fire department is in full command upon arrival.)

Special Equipment

Fire Pumps — stand by for instant operation.

Ventilating Equipment — in case of dense smoke, stand by, operate under proper instructions to clear area affected.

Refrigerating Equipment — if machines are definitely endangered, shut them down and blow refrigerant to sewer or atmosphere to prevent explosion.

Generators and Motors — protect against water damage with tarpaulins — shut down motors not needed — keep generators operating to furnish lights, elevator power, etc.

Boilers — if necessary to abandon boiler room, extinguish or dump fire and lower steam pressure by blowing to sewer or atmosphere to prevent possible explosion.

31-6.3 Dormitories.

31-6.3.1 Drills.   Fire exit drills shall be regularly conducted in accordance with 31-1.5.

SECTION 31-7   MERCANTILE OCCUPANCIES

31-7.1 Drills.   In every Class A store, employees shall be regularly trained in fire exit drill procedures, in general conformance with 31-1.5.

SECTION 31-8   BUSINESS OCCUPANCIES

31-8.1 Drills.   In any building subject to occupancy by more than 500 persons or more than 100 above or below the street level, employees and supervisory personnel shall be instructed in fire exit drill procedures in accordance with 31-1.5 and shall hold practice drills periodically where practicable.

REFERENCES CITED BY *CODE*

(These publications comprise a part of the requirements to the extent called for by the Code.)

NFPA 10, *Standard for Portable Fire Extinguishers*, NFPA, Boston, 1978.

NFPA 11, *Standard on Foam Extinguishing Systems*, NFPA, Boston, 1978.

NFPA 11A, *Standard for High Expansion Foam Systems (Expansion Ratios from 100:1 to 1000:1)*, Boston, 1976.

NFPA 12, *Standard on Carbon Dioxide Extinguishing Systems*, NFPA, Boston, 1980.

NFPA 12A, *Standard on Halon 1301 Fire Extinguishing Systems*, NFPA, Boston, 1980.

NFPA 12B, *Standard on Halon 1211 Fire Extinguishing Systems*, NFPA, Boston, 1980.

NFPA 13, *Standard for the Installation of Sprinkler Systems*, NFPA, Boston, 1980.

NFPA 14, *Standard for the Installation of Standpipe and Hose Systems*, NFPA, Boston, 1980.

NFPA 15, *Standard for Water Spray Fixed Systems for Fire Protection*, NFPA, Boston, 1979.

NFPA 16, *Standard for the Installation of Foam-Water Sprinkler Systems and Foam-Water Spray Systems*, NFPA, Boston, 1980.

NFPA 17, *Standard for Dry Chemical Extinguishing Systems*, NFPA, Boston, 1980.

NFPA 20, *Standard for the Installation of Centrifugal Fire Pumps*, NFPA, Boston, 1980.

NFPA 70, *National Electrical Code*, NFPA, Boston, 1981.

NFPA 71, *Standard for the Installation, Maintenance and Use of Central Station Signaling Systems*, NFPA, Boston, 1977.

NFPA 72A, *Standard for the Installation, Maintenance and Use of Local Protective Signaling Systems*, NFPA, Boston, 1979.

NFPA 72B, *Standard for the Installation, Maintenance and Use of Auxiliary Protective Signaling Systems*, NFPA, Boston, 1979.

NFPA 72C, *Standard for the Installation, Maintenance and Use of Remote Station Protective Signaling Systems*, NFPA, Boston, 1975.

NFPA 72D, *Standard for the Installation, Maintenance and Use of Proprietary Protective Signaling Systems*, NFPA, Boston, 1979.

NFPA 72E, *Standard on Automatic Fire Detectors*, NFPA, Boston, 1978.

NFPA 74, *Standard for the Installation, Maintenance and Use of Household Fire Warning Equipment*, NFPA, Boston, 1980.

NFPA 241, *Standard for Safeguarding Building Construction and Demolition Operations*, NFPA, Boston, 1980.

NFPA 701, *Standard Methods of Fire Tests for Flame-Resistant Textiles and Films*, NFPA, Boston, 1977.

REFERENCES CITED IN COMMENTARY

[1]NFPA 13A, *Recommended Practice for the Care and Maintenance of Sprinkler Systems*, NFPA, Boston, 1978.

[2]NFPA 701, *Standard Methods of Fire Tests for Flame-Resistant Textiles and Films*, NFPA, Boston, 1977.

[3]NFPA 703, *Standard for Fire-Retardant Impregnated Wood and Fire-Resistant Coatings for Building Materials*, NFPA, Boston, 1979.

[4]NFPA 40, *Standard for the Storage and Handling of Cellulose Nitrate Motion Picture Film*, NFPA, Boston, 1974.

[5]NFPA 30, *Flammable and Combustible Liquids Code*, NFPA, Boston, 1981.

APPENDIX A

The material contained in Appendix A of the 1981 *Life Safety Code* is for the most part included in the commentary within this *Handbook*, and therefore Appendix A is not repeated here.

APPENDIX B

The referenced publications listed in Appendix B of the 1981 edition of the *Life Safety Code* are for the most part listed at the end of the respective chapters in this *Handbook*. Therefore, Appendix B is not repeated here.

It is important to note, however, that the Committee recognizes that it is sometimes not practical to continually upgrade existing buildings or installations to comply with all the requirements of the referenced publications. Existing buildings or installations which do not comply with the provisions of the referenced publications may be continued in service, subject to approval by the authority having jurisidiction and provided that the lack of conformity with those standards does not present a serious hazard to the occupants.

APPENDIX C

Fire Safety Evaluation System for
Health Care Occupancies

Appendix C of the 1981 *Life Safety Code* contains the Fire Safety Evaluation System for Health Care Facilities, otherwise known as FSES. This system provides a methodology to assist in developing equivalencies for health care facilities (hospitals and nursing homes only in this case) in order to comply with the *Life Safety Code*. This system was developed by the National Bureau of Standards of the U.S. Department of Commerce in cooperation with the U.S. Department of Health and Human Services (formerly Health, Education and Welfare) for the 1973 edition of the *Code*. That system has been modified for inclusion with the 1981 edition. It should be noted that previous editions of the Fire Safety Evaluation System which were based on the 1973 and modified for the 1967 editions of the *Code* should not be used to determine equivalent compliance with the 1981 edition.

Section 1-5, Equivalency Concepts, of the *Code* specifically allows "the use of systems, methods or devices of equivalent or superior quality, strength, fire resistance, effectiveness, durability and safety to those prescribed by this *Code*..." This is the basis for Appendix C. It should be noted that the *Code* requires the approval of the authority having jurisdiction to use equivalent protection. In other words, it is up to the authority having jurisdiction to determine whether the equivalency is actually obtained. The Subcommittee on Health Care Occupancies and the Committee on Safety to Life were quite specific with regard to this subject and any equivalent protection developed under the use of Appendix C is subject to approval by the authority having jurisdiction. Since this system is a numeric one there is always the possibility of juggling and using numbers such that, numerically, equivalency is shown to exist when, in fact, an unsafe condition is being permitted to exist and equivalency is not obtained. In such cases, the authority having jurisdiction retains the right to not allow the "equivalent" system.

Appendix C is a tool to use with the *Code* and is not a replacement for the requirements contained within the *Code*. A thorough understanding of the *Code* is still necessary in order to work with the FSES methodology. For example, in order to check off that a smoke partition serves the zone in row 9 of Table C-4, the user must have a thorough understanding of the *Code* requirements for a smoke partition.

Before attempting to fill in the worksheet the user must read and study the instructions contained in Appendix C. These instructions are self-explanatory and, in combination with the commentary contained within the *Code*, should allow the user to prepare the material without much difficulty. At the time of the printing of this *Handbook* there were several different organizations offering or preparing to offer seminars on the subject of this evaluation system. These would be most helpful and, in some cases, necessary to apply the system properly.

This appendix describes a system for determining the relative level of safety for new or existing health care facilities as compared to explicit conformance with the applicable requirements of Chapters 1 through 31. This system considers mixes and arrangements of safeguards most of which are described in detail in Chapters 1 through 31.

Contents

Procedure for Determining Equivalency.

1. Using the "Fire/Smoke Zone Evaluation Work Sheet for Health Care Facilities" (dated 1/81, 1981 *Life Safety Code*), evaluate every fire zone.* Use the manual portion of this appendix as a guide.

2. Using the "Facility Fire Safety Requirements Work Sheet," determine any nonconformance with the requirements listed on the work sheet.

3. Equivalency is achieved if the fire/smoke zone evaluations show equivalency or better in each and every fire zone and the requirements on the facility requirements work sheet are met.

This appendix is provided to assist in completion of the Fire/Smoke Zone Evaluation Work Sheet for Health Care Facilities. The step by step instructions for the mechanics of completing the work sheet are included in the work sheet itself. They are not repeated in this appendix. This appendix provides expanded discussion and definition of the various items in the work sheet to assist the user when questions of definitions or interpretation arise. The manual is organized to progressively follow the format of the work sheet.

---

*A fire/smoke zone is a space separated from all other space by floors, horizontal exits, or smoke barriers. Where a floor is not subdivided by horizontal exits or smoke barriers the entire floor is a single zone. The entire facility shall be divided into zones. There shall be no areas that are not in a zone.

NOTE: The paragraph references within this manual are to this edition of the *Life Safety Code*.

Fire/Smoke Zone.   A fire/smoke zone (zone) is a space which is separated from all other spaces by floors, horizontal exits, or smoke barriers. Where a floor is not subdivided by horizontal exits or smoke barriers the entire floor is the zone.

NOTE: Patient sleeping rooms or suites exceeding 1,000 sq ft (92.9 sq m) of floor area should be evaluated as follows:

(a) If the room or suite has a single exit access door, it should be evaluated as a single dead-end zone.

(b) If the room has two or more exit access doors, it should be evaluated as either a room in a zone or as a separate zone, whichever gives the better (higher) rating.

Selection of Zones to Be Evaluated.   For a complete evaluation, every zone in the health care facility should be evaluated individually. From a practical standpoint most health care facilities have repetitive arrangements so that a complete picture can be developed by evaluating typical zones until all combinations are evaluated. The zones selected should include:

(a) Each type of patient zone having a different type of mobility, density, or attendant ratio as classified in Table 1 of the work sheet.

(b) Each zone that represents a significantly different type of construction, finish or protection system.

(c) Zones containing special medical treatment or support activities (operating suites, intensive care units, laboratories).

(d) Zones not involving housing, treatment, or customary access for patients as follows:

1. Any zone, whether used for patient egress or not, may be evaluated on the same basis as a patient use zone. In such case the value of factor F in Table 2 shall be assigned the value of factor L (Fire Zone Location) from Table 1. In such cases, Item 10, Emergency Movement Routes shall be graded "Deficient Capacity" if the exit capacity is less than that prescribed for the actual occupancy of the space as "< two routes" if less than 75 percent of the prescribed exit capacity is present.

2. If the zone is separated from all patient use zones by 2-hour fire-resistive construction (including any members that bear the load of a patient zone and with Class B fire doors on any communicating openings), it may be excluded from evaluation. In such case, that space shall conform with the portion of the *Life Safety Code* appropriate to its use. In addition, appropriate charges under Item 8, Hazardous Areas, in Table 4 shall be charged against other zones in the facility.

Maintenance.   Any protection system, requirements, or arrangement which is not maintained in a dependable operating condition or is used in such a manner that the intended fire safety function or hazard constraint is impaired should be considered as defective and receive no credit in the evaluation.

Occupancy Risk (*General Discussion*).   In establishing a system for evaluating occupancy risk, it is recognized that:

(1) There is a basic level of risk inherent in every health care facility;

(2) The fuel characteristics of furniture, equipment, and supplies vary with time; and

(3) The arrangement of these items within the space available also may vary with time.

Consequently, these three factors are not included as parameters in a safety equivalency measurement. To account for these factors, the occupancy risk base line is set at the inherent risk level with the presumption that the furniture, equipment, and supplies will be the most combustible and adversly located (from a fire safety standpoint) of those normally found in health care facilities.

1. *Patient Mobility*.

The single most important factor controlling risk in a health care facility is the degree to which patients must be assisted in taking actions necessary for their safety. The level of capability in health care facilities will vary from patients who, if informed or directed, will be able to take positive self-protecting actions to those patients who have no ability to move or even to take the simplest actions to safeguard themselves. In some cases, patients may be directly connected to a fixed life support system and so intimately dependent upon it that regardless of their physical condition or the availability of assistance they cannot be moved without jeopardy of death or serious harm. In the measurement of occupancy risk factors, the least mobile category of patient expected in the zone determines the risk factor for that zone. The rationale for this approach is that if a zone accepts any patient with a reduced mobility status it may at any time increase the number of those patients. The impact of this approach will be that most health care facilities will be rated in the "not mobile" risk category.

Mobility Status. Patient mobility status is based on the capability of each patient to take actions necessary to protect himself. The four classes are defined as follows:

(a) *Mobile.* Capable of readily rising from bed and taking self-protecting actions at approximately the same rate as a healthy adult. In order to be classified as mobile the patient must not require assistance in getting out of bed and must be able to open a closed or locked door. Mobile persons when sleeping shall be considered as mobile if they are not restrained or in any other way reduced in response capabilities so that the type of arousal mechanism that would normally awaken an adult would not be affected.

(b) *Limited Mobility.* Those patients who have all of the capabilities of a mobile person except that their rate of travel will be significantly less.

(c) *Not Mobile.* Incapable of removing themselves from danger exclusively by their own efforts. Examples would include persons who are totally bedridden, who require assistance to get out of bed or to move, or who are restrained, locked in their rooms, or otherwise prevented from taking complete emergency self protection evacuation actions without assistance. Mobility status should be based on the minimum level of mobility in an average 24-hour period.

(d) *Not Moveable.* Not capable of being moved from the room in which they are housed through the course of a fire. Examples would include patients attached to life support systems or involved in medical or surgical procedures that prohibit their immediate relocation without extreme danger of death or serious harm.

2. *Patient Density*.

The occupancy risk evaluation for occupancy density (number of patients within the zone) measures both the inherent increase in the maximum fire death potential that occurs as the number of patients in a zone increases, and the problems involved by a limited staff in handling larger numbers of patients during an emergency.

Patient Factor. The density of patients is the number of patients that could potentially be housed in the zone. The patient count should be based on the number of assignable beds in the zone on the assumption that they may all be occupied at the time of the fire emergency.

3. *Zone Location.*

This risk factor relates to fire department accessibility to a fire. The rating system recognizes the inherent advantages for the first floor zone. It also recognizes the problems of evacuation from higher floors and the virtual impossibility of using external fire fighting efforts above the sixth floor in any building.

Floor Factor. The measured zone's location shall be considered to be on floor one if the floor has direct access to the exterior at or within less than one-half floor height above or below grade. If a building is on a sloping grade, each floor that has such exterior access shall be considered as a first floor situation for measurement of fire zones on those floors. The measured zone shall be considered on the second to third floor range, and the fourth to sixth floor range, based on the height of the zone above the nearest grade floor. The zone shall be considered to be above the sixth floor if it is more than six floors above the nearest grade floor. The risk factor value for zones in basements is the same as for zones at or above the seventh floor. The problems involved in emergency internal access, fire fighting and rescue, and the inability to make external attack in basements is approximately equivalent to that in upper stories of buildings.

4. *Ratio of Patients to Attendants.*

This risk factor recognizes the importance of patient safety of a staff immediately available to respond in an emergency. The emergency actions that may be undertaken by the staff include detection, alarm, fire extinguishment, confinement of the fire, establishing barriers between the patients and the fire (closing patient room doors), rescue, emergency medical aid, and other related functions. A few of these functions, such as detection and alarming, may not be critically related to the ratio of nursing staff to patients while those related to rescue and the closing of patient room doors have a strong relationship to the staffing ratio. The staff ratio considered is based on the minimum staffing level immediately available (normally night hours).

Patient-Attendant Factor. The ratio of patients to attendants is based on those patients in the fire/smoke zone and the immediately available attendant staff. In calculating the ratio, it shall be based on the minimum staffing level (usually occurring in the night shift). Where nursing stations or other positions of attendants are located at the junction of two or more zones and the location of the station is such that each of the zones has immediate access and view of the nursing station, then the total staffing assigned to the nursing station can be credited to each of the zones. An exception is where staff members are bound by duty assignments (cardiac care units, infant nurseries, operating suites, etc.) that prevent them from responding to other than their assigned zone.

The evaluation system assesses a charge of 4.0 to this risk factor in any case where there are periods when there are no attendants immediately available to a zone that houses patients.

5. *Patient Average Age.*

This risk factor recognizes the increased susceptibility of the elderly and of infants up to one year of age to physical harm by smoke particles, gaseous combustion products and heated air. This rating assigns a larger risk factor to zones occupied by a population whose average age is above 65 or below one year. Basically, imposition of this charge demands additional safety protection in nursing homes for the aged and nurseries.

Age Factor.   The mode value is used to arrive at the age factor for the patients in the zone. The calculation should be based on the past record of occupants assigned to the zone. Patients under one year old are classified at the same risk level as those over 65. This is in recognition of the fire susceptibility of infants.

Safety Parameters (*General Discussion*).   The safety parameters are a measure of those building factors that bear upon or contribute to the safety of those persons (patients, staff, visitors, others) who may be in the particular zone at the time of a fire.

Each of the safety parameters was analyzed. Where the current *Code* requirements recognize several different approaches to the parameter, the most important alternatives were listed. In addition, conditions likely to be encountered in situations failing to meet the explicit *Code* requirements and conditions exceeding those required by the *Code* but available for increased protection were also listed.

1. *Construction.*

Construction types are classified in accordance with the definitions of *Standard Types of Building Construction*, NFPA 220. Major revisions have been made in the titles and definitions in *Standard Types of Building Construction*, NFPA 220, as compared to prior editions of that standard.

NOTE: Prior editions of NFPA 220 include requirements for "interior partitions enclosing stairs or other openings through floors." The current edition deletes this requirement. This change is fully accounted for in this system through Safety Parameter Item 7, Vertical Openings.

Where the facility includes additions or connected structures of different construction, the rating and classification of the structure shall be based on (a) separate buildings if a 2-hour or greater fire-resistive separation exists between the portions of the building, (b) separate buildings if the additions and connected structure conform to the provisions of applicable sections of Chapter 12 or 13, whether or not separation is provided, and (c) the lower safety parameter point score involved if such a separation does not exist.

The floor level used to determine the parameter value is the floor of the fire zone being evaluated. The "floor of zone" is the story height above the floor of primary level of exit discharge as defined by 12-1.6.1 and 13-1.6.1.

When the zone is on a floor below the floor of lowest discharge, the construction value shall be based on the distance of that floor from the closest level of discharge, i.e., one floor below discharge = "Second"; two floors below discharge = "Third"; three or more floors below discharge = "Fourth and above."

2. *Interior Finish (Corridor and Exit).*

The classification of flame spread for corridor and exits is in accordance with the categories specified in 6-5.1. The flame spread classification shall be based on the most combustible surface after deleting trim. No allowance is made in the safety parameter values for Class D or E interior finishes. It is not anticipated that such material will be used in health care facilities. In the rare case such high flame spread interior finish material is involved, an individual appraisal outside the capability of this evaluation system will be required.

3. *Interior Finish (Rooms).*

The same classification of interior finish applies to rooms as applies to corridors and exits. The specific definitions are given in 6-5.1. The flame spread classification shall be based on the most combustible surface after deleting trim. No consideration is included in the safety parameter values for Class D or E interior finishes. It is not anticipated that such material will be used in health care facilities. In the rare case such high flame spread interior finish material is involved, an individual appraisal outside of the capability of this evaluation system will be required.

4. *Corridor Partitions/Walls.*

For the purpose of this evaluation, the fire-resistive partitions considered are as defined in 12-3.6 for new buildings and 13-3.6 for existing buildings. All elements of the partition, except the door (considered as a separate element in this evaluation), must be included in the determination of its time-rated fire resistance classification, according to *Standard Methods of Fire Tests of Building Construction and Materials*, NFPA 251. An exception to the general rule of evaluating doors separate from walls occurs when one or more rooms has no door (*see Safety Parameter Item 5*). In this instance it is considered that the worth of the fire resistance capabilities of the corridor partition wall is so reduced that the wall should be graded as having no fire resistance. The mechanism for doing this is incorporated into the Fire Safety Evaluation Work Sheet.

Walls shall be considered as incomplete if they have unprotected openings (louvers, gaps, transfer grills) between the floor and the ceiling, or have ordinary glass lights.[1] If openings exist above the ceiling level (or even if the partitions stop at the ceiling level), the walls shall be considered as complete if the ceiling within the fire/smoke zone is of monolithic construction designed to resist the passage of smoke and there is a smoke tight joint between the top of the partition and the bottom of the ceiling. The fire resistance rating in this parameter shall be based on the lowest fire resistance level involved in the corridor partition or the monolithic ceiling. In such cases, the ceiling and the corridor walls jointly perform the fire and smoke barrier functions normally expected of a corridor wall which extends from the floor slab to the underside of the floor or roof slabs above.

Walls shall be considered to have less than a one-third hour fire resistance rating if they are not equivalent to ½-in. (1.27-cm) gypsum wall board on both sides of studs (even if they extend at least from floor to ceiling) or if they are not continous above the ceiling to the underside of the floor or roof (or floor or roof assembly) above, through any concealed space such as above a suspended ceiling and through interstitial stucture and mechanical spaces. Partitions shall also be rated as less than one-third hour if they are not incomplete but other defects are involved, or if the criteria in 12-3.6 and 13-3.6 are not met.

Fire-resistive partitions shall be considered as between one-third and 1 hour if they meet all the criteria for continuity of construction and the criteria of 12-3.6 and 13-3.6 and have a fire resistance of between 20 minutes and 1 hour.

5. *Doors to Corridor.*

The classification of doors to the corridor shall be based on the minimum quality of any door in the zone, and the classification shall be determined in accordance with

---

[1]Ordinary glass lights shall not be considered as making a partition incomplete in locations where both sides of the glass light are fully protected by automatic sprinker systems.

Standard Methods of Fire Tests of Door Assemblies, NFPA 252. Doors for protection of hazardous areas and stairwells are not included in this evaluation. They are covered separately in Safety Parameter Items 7 and 8.

(a) *No Door.* A room shall be considered as not having a door if there is no door in the opening or if there is some other mechanism which prevents closing of the door or otherwise leaves a significant opening between the patient room and the corridor. Doors with louvers or ordinary glass lights[2] shall be classified as "no door." Doors which have been blocked open by door stops, chocks, tie backs or other devices which require manual unlatching or releasing action to close the door shall be classified as "no door." Also, doors that are not provided with a latch suitable for keeping the door tightly closed shall be classified as "no door."

(b) *Door Less than Twenty Minutes of Fire Resistance.* Doors which are not deficient as described in A, but which do not meet the requirements for C below, will be classified as less than 20 minutes of fire resistance.

(c) *Door Twenty Minutes or More Fire Resistance.* Doors shall be considered as having 20 minutes or greater fire resistance if they are of 1¾-in. (4.45-cm) thick solid core wood construction or any other arrangement of equal or greater stability and fire integrity. The thermal insulation capability of the door is not considered. Hollow or sheet steel doors therefore meet the 20-minute requirement.

(d) *Twenty Minutes or More Fire Resistance and Automatic Closing.* Automatic closing devices shall be considered present if the door has an arrangement which holds them open in a manner such that they will be released by a smoke detector operated device (e.g., magnetic or pneumatic hold open device) prior to the passage of significant smoke from a room of fire origin into the corridor or from the corridor into a room not involved in the fire. Smoke detectors for operation of such doors may be integral with the door closers, mounted at each opening, or operated from systems meeting the requirements for 2 or more point credit under Safety Parameter Item 12, Smoke Detection and Alarm. The requirement for 20 minutes of fire resistance is the same as in C above.

Self-Closing Patient Room Doors. Traditional self-closing doors on individual patient rooms shall be evaluated in the following manner:

(1) If it can be established that the doors are constantly kept in the normally closed position except when persons are actually passing through the openings, the self-closing device shall be considered as equal to an automatic closing device and credited accordingly.

(2) If the self-closing doors are blocked open they shall be classified as "no door" and a charge of (−10) invoked.

6. *Zone Dimensions.*

Zone length is the greatest straight line dimension of the fire/smoke zone. (*See 12-3.7.1 or 13-3.7.1.*)

The length of a corridor "dead end" shall be measured from the point at which a person egressing from the dead end would have an option of egressing in two separate directions.

In assessing the values for this parameter, a single value will be chosen based on the

---

[2]Ordinary glass lights shall not be considered as making a partition incomplete in locations where both sides of the glass light are fully protected by automatic sprinkler systems.

poorest safety level in the zone. For example, if one or more dead ends in excess of 50 ft (15.24 m) exists, the charge for dead ends (−4) shall be applied regardless of the actual corridor lengths.

Since dead-end corridors and single emergency movement routes (covered in Item 10, Emergency Movement Routes) will each confine the occupants of a fire zone to a single means of egress, the charges for these two items are not cumulative. As indicated by the footnote on the safety parameter values page in the Fire Safety Evaluation Work Sheet, the charge for dead-end corridors is to be a value of 0 instead of either (−2), (−4) or (−6) in the special case where a charge of (−8) is assessed under Item 10 for single emergency movement routes.

7. *Vertical Openings.*

These values apply to vertical openings and penetrations including exit stairways, ramps and other vertical exits of the type recognized by the *Life Safety Code*, pipe shafts, ventilation shafts, duct penetrations, and laundry and incinerator chutes. Enclosures shall be of construction having fire resistance not less than that prescribed for vertical openings (*see Safety Parameter Item 7*). In addition, they shall be equipped with fire doors or acceptable protection of openings into the shafts, all designed and installed so as to provide a complete barrier to the vertical spread of fire or smoke. A vertical opening or penetration shall be considered open if it is: (a) unenclosed; (b) is enclosed but does not have doors; (c) is enclosed but has openings other than doorways; and (d) is enclosed with cloth, paper or similar materials without any sustained flame-stopping capabilities.

Where vertical openings are located outside the fire/smoke zone and the separation between the zone and the vertical opening is of 1-hour or greater fire resistance and is of higher fire resistance than the protection of the vertical opening itself (for example: an open shaft separated from the zone by a 2-hour fire-resistive partition with Class B self-closing fire doors), the rating of this factor for the zone being measured shall be based on the higher of the two fire resistant categories. In the above example, a safety parameter value of 3 would be given for the 2-hour fire resistance. When this occurs, however, the space with the vertical opening cannot be considered as an exit route or refuge area for that zone when considering Safety Parameter Item 10, Emergency Movement Routes.

A vertical opening shall be considered as open for greater than three floors if there is unprotected penetration of four or more floors on the same shaft without an intervening slab or other cutoff. (*See also same area as an unprotected penetration covered in the discussion of Item 13, Automatic Sprinklers.*) If a shaft is enclosed at all floors but one and this results in an unprotected opening between that shaft, and one and only one fire/smoke zone, the parameter value assigned for that shaft opening in that fire/smoke zone shall be zero.

8. *Hazardous Areas.*

Hazardous area protection is determined in accordance with Section 6-4 of the *Life Safety Code*. In assessing the charge for hazardous areas only, one charge shall be made. It shall be the most severe charge corresponding to the deficiencies present. A double deficiency can exist only where the hazard is severe and the space is not sprinkler protected. Double protection consists of both a fire-resistive enclosure and automatic sprinkler protection of the hazardous area. If both of these are lacking in a severe hazardous location, the double deficiency charge shall be made. If double deficiencies exist both in the zone and outside the zone, the higher charge (−11) for the condition inside the zone shall be made. The charges are not cumulative, regardless of how many hazardous areas are present.

Where the hazard is not severe, the maximum deficiency that can occur is a single deficiency which may be countered by either a fire-resistive enclosure or automatic extinguishing equipment.

A single deficiency situation will also be considered to exist when a severe hazard is either protected by automatic extinguishing systems or by fire-resistive enclosure, but not by both.

The term "adjacent zone" as used in the evaluation form means any zone, either on the same floor or on the floor immediately below, that physically abuts the zone being evaluated and is not separated by 2-hour fire-resistive rated construction.

The term "outside zone" as used in the evaluation form means any place within the building other than the fire/smoke zone being measured.

9. *Smoke Control.*

Smoke Control.   The smoke control definitions are as follows:

(a) *No Control.*   There are no smoke barriers (or horizontal exits) on the floor and there is no mechanical smoke control system.

(b) *Smoke Partition.*   A smoke partition consists of a partition extending across the entire width of the zone equipped with doors that are either self-closing or are closed upon detection by smoke detectors located at the door arches or other release mechanism as described in 5-2.1.2.3. To be credited as a smoke partition an existing partition must also conform with the requirements of 13-3.7.2 through 13-3.7.7 of the *Life Safety Code*. New smoke partitions in either new or existing buildings must meet the more stringent requirements of 12-3.7.2 through 12-3.7.8 of the *Life Safety Code*. A horizontal exit will act as a smoke partition and is credited as both a smoke partition (Item 9) and an emergency movement route (Item 10).

(c) *Mechanically Assisted Systems — by Zone.*   Mechanically assisted smoke control on a zone basis must include a smoke partition, as in B above, supported by a mechanism of automatic controlled fans, smoke vent shafts, or a combination thereof to provide a pressure differential that will assist in confining the smoke to the zone of origin. The fans involved may be special smoke control fans or special adjustment of the normal building air movement fans.

10. *Emergency Movement Routes.*

A movement route is any means of egress meeting the requirements for such means in 5-2.2 through 5-2.7 of Chapter 5 of the *Life Safety Code*. Horizontal exits shall also meet the requirements stated below. Doors exiting directly to the exterior shall also constitute a movement route from the room containing such a door.

(a) < *Two Routes.*   The emergency movement means from a zone is classified as less than two routes if there are not two or more movement routes serving it. Movement routes may be outside the physical limits of the zone.

(b) *Multiple Routes.*   The emergency movement route is multiple if the zone occupants have the choice of two or more distinctly separated movement routes from the zone.

(c) *Deficient.*

NOTE: The charges for deficient emergency movement routes are in addition to any values assessed in Safety Parameter Item 7, Vertical Openings.

An emergency movement route is deficient if it is of a type described by 12-2.2 or 13-2.2 but (1) the door to a patient room or passage through a smoke barrier is less than 34 in. (86.36 cm) [44 in. (111.76 cm) in new buildings] in clear width or if the corridor in the zone between patient rooms and smoke barriers and exits is less than 48 in. (121.92 cm) [8 ft (243.84 cm) in new buildings] in clear width. These figures are based on the minimum width for a wheelchair to egress a room and the minimum width for the passage of a wheelchair in one direction and an ambulatory person in the opposite direction. Exit routes shall also be considered deficient if any of the dimensional details are less than that required by the *Life Safety Code* for the egress route involved. However, any route where the doors from rooms or through partitions or walls are less than 32 in. (81.28 cm) in the clear, where the corridor(s) involved are less than 34 in. (86.36 cm) wide or where stair access is less than 28 in. (71.12 cm) in the clear shall not be credited as an egress route. Exit routes shall also be considered deficient in capacity if they are not provided with emergency lighting in accordance with 12-2.8.1 or 13-2.8.1, or if beds for health care use are not easily moveable as defined by 31-4.1.2 or (2) the route does not otherwise conform to the requirements of 5-2.2 through 5-2.9 but the routes have been or are acceptable to the authority having jurisdiction.

(d) *Horizontal Exit.*   The presence of a single horizontal exit from the zone being evaluated shall be considered to meet this requirement provided the space on the opposite side of the horizontal exit is capable of handling all of the patients from affected zones. To be credited as a horizontal exit, the existing arrangement must also conform with the requirements of 13-2.2.5 of the *Life Safety Code.* New horizontal exits in new or existing buildings must meet the more stringent requirements of 12-2.2.5 of the *Life Safety Code.*

(e) *Direct Exits.*   To be credited with direct exits, each patient use space (except bath rooms, restrooms, and corridors) in the zone shall have a door operable by the room occupant(s) that opens directly to the exterior at grade or onto an exterior balcony with direct access to an exterior exit or a smoke proof tower. To be credited, the direct exit must be ramped or otherwise without steps or changes in elevation that would prevent or obstruct the movement of wheelchairs or wheel-littered patients through the direct exits to a place of safety and refuge.

11. *Manual Fire Alarm.*

The manual alarm systems for new construction shall be in accordance with the requirements of 12-3.4.2 and 12-3.4.5 through 12-3.4.8. Existing construction shall be in accordance with 13-3.4.2 through 13-3.4.5. Connection to the Fire Department shall be considered as being met if the fire alarm system is connected directly to the Fire Department, through an approved central station, or through other means acceptable to the authority having jurisdiction.

12. *Smoke Detection and Alarm.*

A detection system as used here is one based on use of smoke detectors. No recognition is given for thermal detectors. The detection system categories are as follows:

(a) *None.*   There are no smoke detectors in the zone or, if present do not meet any of the following categories.

(b) *Corridor Only.*   Smoke detectors located in the corridor shall be considered as meeting the requirement if the detectors are within 15 ft (457.2 cm) of each end of the corridor and not more than 30 ft (914.4 cm) apart throughout the corridor. All such detectors shall be electrically interconnected with the fire alarm system. If the facility does not have a fire alarm system, no credit shall be given to the detectors unless they include an alarming system that meets the requirements for alarming that would be involved with a manual fire alarm system. This includes audible alarm devices throughout the building.

(c) *Rooms Only.* Smoke detectors shall be considered as meeting this requirement when there is at least one smoke detector in each room occupied or used by patients. In rooms having a dimension in excess of 30 ft (914.4 cm), additional detectors shall be provided so that detector spacing does not exceed approximately 30 ft (914.4 cm). Detectors are not required in restrooms or closets. Detectors intended for operation of door closing mechanisms that are located on the patient's side of the door or in the door opening are considered as meeting this requirement for rooms of 500 sq ft (46.45 sq m) or less.

(d) *Corridor and Habitable Spaces.* Detection systems installed throughout the corridors of the zone involved and in the habitable spaces (patient rooms, nurses stations, and other areas basically used for human occupancy) shall be considered as meeting the requirements for a corridor and habitable spaces detection system. Closets, toilet rooms, and other auxiliary spaces as well as ceiling voids, interstitials and other building space not used by humans as a normal part of their regular occupancy are not required to have detectors.

(e) *Total Spaces.* Total space provision of detectors includes detector coverage of all spaces except noncombustible building voids which contain no combustible materials. The total space credit is to be given if the zone measured meets this criteria, regardless of the presence or lack of detectors in other portions of the building.

13. *Automatic Sprinklers.*

In evaluating sprinkler protection within the zone, the protection or lack of protection of hazardous areas is considered separately and covered under Safety Parameter Item 8. For all other areas in the zone, sprinklers shall be graded on the following basis:

(a) *None.* No charge is applied if there are no sprinklers or if sprinklers, though present, are not sufficient to qualify for one of the other categories listed herein.

(b) *Corridor and Habitable Space[3].* This credit is based on standard sprinkler spacings in the areas covered and is conditional on the classification of construction type as covered in Safety Parameter Item 1, Construction, as follows:

(1) Item 1, Construction, is based on a "protected" or "fire-resistive" type of construction.[4] This credit is based on a system that effectively provides coverage for all corridor and habitable space in the zone, plus the establishment of water distribution patterns or other protection in a manner to prevent advance of fire from non-sprinklered spaces into the sprinklered spaces. In buildings of protected or fire-resistive construction, the credit is to be applied to any zone where the above conditions are met whether or not areas outside the zone are similarly protected.

---

[3]Habitable space includes patient rooms, nurses stations, and other areas basically used for human occupancy. Habitable space does not include closets, bath rooms, toilets, elevators, and similar spaces.

[4]"Protected" or "fire-resistive" types of construction include Types I; II (222) or (111); III (211); and V (111). "Unprotected" types of construction include Types II (000); III (000); and V (000).

(2) Item 1, Construction, is based on an "unprotected" type of construction.[4] In any unprotected type of construction the credit for corridor and habitable space protection is to be given only if, in addition to the conditions described in (1) above, sprinkler protection is also provided in all spaces in the building (including attic or loft spaces) with construction elements that are not sheathed enclosed, or otherwise protected with fire resisting materials such as gypsum board, plaster, or masonry block.

(c) *Total Space.* Total space automatic sprinkler protection is to be credited only if the entire structure is protected by automatic sprinklers in accordance with Section 7-7 of the *Life Safety Code.*

Wherever sprinkler protection is involved in an area having an unprotected vertical opening, the sprinkler protection around that vertical opening must conform with one of the following methods outlined either in Chapter 6 of the *Life Safety Code* or in *Standard for the Installation of Sprinkler Systems,* NFPA 13. This protection is required to allow the credit for sprinkler protection but shall in no way reduce any charge under Safety Parameter Item 7 resulting from an unprotected vertical opening.

In Table 5 of the Fire Safety Evaluation Form (Individual Safety Evaluations), the value for sprinkler protection credited to the people movement safety (S_3) category is divided by 2. This produces a safety value only one-half the value credited in other categories.

Each sprinkler system shall be provided with supervision. Each sprinkler system shall be electrically interconnected with the fire alarm system and the main sprinkler control valve shall be electrically supervised so that at least a local alarm shall sound in a constantly attended location when the valve is closed.

FIRE/SMOKE ZONE* EVALUATION WORK SHEET
FOR HEALTH CARE FACILITIES
(1981 *Life Safety Code*)

FACILITY_____ BUILDING_____

ZONE(S) EVALUATED_____

EVALUATOR_____ DATE_____

Complete this work sheet for each zone. Where conditions are the same in several zones, one work sheet can be used for those zones.

Step 1: Determine Occupancy Risk Parameter Factors — Use Table C-1.
  A. For each Risk Parameter in Table C-1, select and circle the appropriate risk factor value. Choose only one for each of the five Risk Parameters.

*FIRE/SMOKE ZONE is a space separated from all other spaces by floors, horizontal exits, or smoke barriers.

TABLE C-1.	OCCUPANCY RISK PARAMETER FACTORS				

RISK PARAMETERS	RISK FACTOR VALUES				
1. PATIENT MOBILITY (M)	MOBILITY STATUS	MOBILE	LIMITED MOBILITY	NOT MOBILE	NOT MOVABLE
	RISK FACTOR	1.0	1.6	3.2	4.5
2. PATIENT DENSITY (D)	PATIENT	1-5	6-10	11-30	>30
	RISK FACTOR	1.0	1.2	1.5	2.0
3. ZONE LOCATION (L)	FLOOR	1ST	2ND OR 3RD	4TH TO 6TH	7TH AND ABOVE	BASE-MENTS
	RISK FACTOR	1.1	1.2	1.4	1.6	1.6
4. RATIO OF PATIENTS TO ATTENDANTS (T)	PATIENTS ATTENDANT	$\frac{1-2}{1}$	$\frac{3-5}{1}$	$\frac{6-10}{1}$	$\frac{>10}{1}$	ONE OR† MORE NONE
	RISK FACTOR	1.0	1.1	1.2	1.5	4.0
5. PATIENT AVERAGE AGE (A)	AGE	UNDER 65 YEARS AND OVER 1 YEAR		65 YEARS & OVER 1 YEAR & YOUNGER	
	RISK FACTOR	1.0		1.2	

†RISK FACTOR OF 4.0 IS CHARGED TO ANY ZONE THAT HOUSES PATIENTS WITHOUT ANY STAFF IN IMMEDIATE ATTENDANCE

(Dated 1/81, 1981 *Life Safety Code*)

Step 2: Compute Occupancy Risk Factor (F) — Use Table C-2.
  A. Transfer the circled risk factor values from Table C-1 to the corresponding blocks in Table C-2.
  B. Compute F by multiplying the risk factor values as indicated in Table C-2.

TABLE C-2.	OCCUPANCY RISK FACTOR CALCULATION

OCCUPANCY RISK   M [ ] X D [ ] X L [ ] X T [ ] X A [ ] = F [ ]

Step 3: Compute Adjusted Building Status (R) — Use Table C-3A or C-3B.
  A. If building is classified as "New" use Table C-3A. If building is classified as "Existing" use Table C-3B.
  B. Transfer the value of F from Table C-2 to Table C-3A or Table C-3B as appropriate. Calculate R.
  C. Transfer R to the block labeled R in Table C-7.

TABLE C-3A. (NEW BUILDINGS)	TABLE C-3B. (EXISTING BUILDINGS)
F R 1.0 X [ ] = [ ]	F R 0.6 X [ ] = [ ]

(Dated 1/81, 1981 *Life Safety Code*)

Step 4: Determine Safety Parameter Values — Use Table C-4.
  A. Select and circle the safety value for each safety parameter in Table C-4 that best describes the conditions in the zone. Choose only one value for each of the 13 parameters. If two or more appear to apply, choose the one with the lowest point value.

TABLE C-4.		SAFETY PARAMETERS VALUES					
PARAMETERS		PARAMETERS VALUES					
1. CONSTRUCTION		COMBUSTIBLE TYPE III, IV AND V				NON-COMBUSTIBLE TYPE I AND II	
FLOOR OF ZONE	000 (U)	111	200 (U)	211 + 2HH	000 (U)	111	222, 332, 443
FIRST	-2	0	-2	0	0	2	2
SECOND	-7	-2	-4	-2	-2	2	4
THIRD	-9	-7	-9	-7	-7	2	4
4TH & ABOVE	-13	-7	-13	-7	-9	-7	4
2. INTERIOR FINISH (Corr. & Exit)	CLASS C	CLASS B		CLASS A			
	-5	0		3			
3. INTERIOR FINISH (Rooms)	CLASS C	CLASS B		CLASS A			
	-3	1		3			
4. CORRIDOR PARTITIONS/WALLS	NONE OR INCOMPLETE	<1/3 HR.		≥1/3 <1.0 HR.	≥1.0 HR.		
	-10 (0)*	0		1 (0)*	2 (0)*		
5. DOORS TO CORRIDOR	NO DOOR	<20 MIN. FR		≥20 MIN. FR	≥20 MIN. FR & AUTO CLOS.		
	-10	0		1 (0)†	2 (0)†		
6. ZONE DIMENSIONS	DEAD END			NO DEAD ENDS >30' & ZONE LENGTH IS:			
	>100'	50'-100'	30'-50'	>150'	100'-150'		<100'
	-6 (0)**	-4 (0)**	-2 (0)**	-2	0		1
7. VERTICAL OPENINGS	OPEN 4 OR MORE FLOORS	OPEN 2 OR 3 FLOORS		ENCLOSED WITH INDICATED FIRE RESIST.			
				<1 HR.	≥1 HR. <2 HR.		>2 HR.
	-14	-10		0	2 (0)††		3 (0)††
8. HAZARDOUS AREAS	DOUBLE DEFICIENCY		SINGLE DEFICIENCY		NO DEFICIENCIES		
	IN ZONE	OUTSIDE ZONE	IN ZONE	IN ADJACENT ZONE			
	-11	-5	-6	-2	0		
9. SMOKE CONTROL	NO CONTROL	SMOKE PARTITION SERVES ZONE		MECH. ASSISTED SYSTEMS BY ZONE			
	-5 (0)***	0		3			
10. EMERGENCY MOVEMENT ROUTES	<2 ROUTES	MULTIPLE ROUTES					
		DEFICIENT	W/O HORIZONTAL EXIT(S)	HORIZONTAL EXIT(S)	DIRECT EXIT(S)		
	-8	-2	0	3	5		
11. MANUAL FIRE ALARM	NO MANUAL FIRE ALARM		MANUAL FIRE ALARM				
			W/O F.D. CONN.	W/F.D. CONN.			
	-4		1	2			
12. SMOKE DETECTION & ALARM	NONE	CORRIDOR ONLY	ROOMS ONLY	CORRIDOR & HABIT. SPACE	TOTAL SPACE IN ZONE		
	0	2	3	4	5		
13. AUTOMATIC SPRINKLERS	NONE	CORRIDOR & HABIT. SPACE	ENTIRE BUILDING				
	0	8	10				

NOTE: *Use (0) when item 5 is -10.   †Use (0) when item 4 is -10.
    **Use (0) when item 10 is -8.   ††Use (0) when item 1 is based on first floor zone or on an unprotected type
    ***Use (0) on floor with less than 31 patients (existing buildings only).   of construction (columns marked "U").
                                †††Use (0) when item is based on an unprotected type of construction (columns
                                marked "U").

(Dated 1/81, 1981 *Life Safety Code*)   Conversion: ft × .3048 = m.

Step 5: Compute Individual Safety Evaluations — Use Table C-5.

   A. Transfer each of the 13 circled safety parameter values from Table C-4 to every unshaded block in the line with the corresponding safety parameter in Table C-5. For Safety Parameter Item 13 (Sprinklers) the value entered in the (People Movement Safety) is recorded in Table C-5 as one-half the corresponding value circled in Table C-4.

   B. Add the four columns, keeping in mind that any negative numbers deduct.

   C. Transfer the resulting total values for S_1, S_2, S_3, S_G to the blocks labeled S_1, S_2, S_3, S_G in Table C-7.

TABLE C-5.	INDIVIDUAL SAFETY EVALUATIONS			
SAFETY PARAMETERS	CONTAINMENT SAFETY (S_1)	EXTINGUISHMENT SAFETY (S_2)	PEOPLE MOVEMENT SAFETY (S_3)	GENERAL SAFETY (S_G)
1. CONSTRUCTION			▨	
2. INTERIOR FINISH (Corr. & Exit)		▨		
3. INTERIOR FINISH (Rooms)		▨	▨	
4. CORRIDOR PARTITIONS/WALLS		▨	▨	
5. DOORS TO CORRIDOR		▨	▨	
6. ZONE DIMENSIONS	▨			
7. VERTICAL OPENINGS		▨		
8. HAZARDOUS AREAS			▨	
9. SMOKE CONTROL	▨	▨		
10. EMERGENCY MOVEMENT ROUTES	▨	▨		
11. MANUAL FIRE ALARM	▨		▨	
12. SMOKE DETECTION & ALARM	▨			
13. AUTOMATIC SPRINKLERS			÷ 2 =	
TOTAL VALUE	$S_1 =$	$S_2 =$	$S_3 =$	$S_G =$

(Dated 1/81, 1981 *Life Safety Code*)

Step 6: Determine Mandatory Safety Requirement Values — Use Table C-6.
  A. Using the classification of the building (i.e., New or Existing) and the floor where the zone is located, circle the appropriate value in each of the three columns in Table C-6.
  B. Transfer the three circled values from Table C-6 to the blocks marked S_a, S_b, and S_c in Table C-7.

TABLE C-6.	MANDATORY SAFETY REQUIREMENTS					
	CONTAINMENT S_a		EXTINGUISHMENT S_b		PEOPLE MOVEMENT S_c	
ZONE LOCATION	New	Exist.	New	Exist.	New	Exist.
FIRST FLOOR	9	5	6 (4)*	4	6 (4)*	1
ABOVE OR BELOW FIRST FLOOR	14	9	8 (6)*	6	9 (7)*	3

*Use value in parentheses ( ) for hospitals.

(Dated 1/81, 1981 *Life Safety Code*)

Step 7: Evaluation Fire Safety Equivalency — Use Table C-7.
  A. Perform the indicated subtractions in Table C-7. Enter the differences in the appropriate answer blocks.
  B. For each row check "Yes" if the value in the answer block is zero or greater. Check "No" if the value in the answer block is a negative number.

TABLE C-7.	ZONE SAFETY EQUIVALENCY EVALUATION				YES	NO
CONTAINMENT SAFETY (S_1)	less	MANDATORY CONTAINMENT (S_a)	≥ 0	S_1 □ − S_a □ = C □		
EXTINGUISHMENT SAFETY (S_2)	less	MANDATORY EXTINGUISHMENT (S_b)	≥ 0	S_2 □ − S_b □ = E □		
PEOPLE MOVEMENT SAFETY (S_3)	less	MANDATORY PEOPLE MOVEMENT (S_c)	≥ 0	S_3 □ − S_c □ = P □		
GENERAL SAFETY (S_G)	less	OCCUPANCY RISK (R)	≥ 0	S_G □ − R □ = G □		

(Dated 1/81, 1981 *Life Safety Code*)

```
┌─────────────────────────────────────────────────────────────────────────────────┐
│                              CONCLUSIONS:                                         │
├─────────────────────────────────────────────────────────────────────────────────┤
│                                                                                   │
│  1. ☐  All of the checks in Table 7 are in the "Yes" column. The level of fire    │
│         safety is at least equivalent to that prescribed by the Life Safety       │
│         Code®. *                                                                  │
│                                                                                   │
│  2. ☐  One or more of the checks in Table 7 are in the "No" column. The level of  │
│         fire safety is not shown by this system to be equivalent to that          │
│         prescribed by the Life Safety Code. *                                     │
│                                                                                   │
│  *The equivalency covered by this worksheet includes the majority of              │
│  considerations covered by the Life Safety Code. There are a few considerations   │
│  that are not evaluated by this method. These must be separately consid-          │
│  ered. These additional considerations are covered in the "Facility Fire Safety   │
│  Requirements Worksheet." One copy of this separate worksheet is to be            │
│  completed for each facility.                                                     │
└─────────────────────────────────────────────────────────────────────────────────┘
```

TABLE C-8.
FACILITY FIRE SAFETY REQUIREMENTS WORKSHEET

COMPLETE ONE COPY OF THIS WORKSHEET FOR EACH FACILITY
FOR EACH CONSIDERATION SELECT AND MARK THE APPROPRIATE COLUMN

		MET	NOT MET	NOT APP.
A.	Building utilities conform to the requirements of Section 7-1.			▓
B.	In new facilities only, life support systems, alarms, emergency communication systems and illumination of generator set locations are powered as prescribed by 12-5.1.2 and 12-5.1.3.			
C.	Heating and air conditioning systems conform with the air conditioning, heating, and ventilating systems requirements within Section 7-2.			▓
D.	Fuel burning space heaters and portable electrical space heaters are not used.			
E.	There are no flue fed incinerators.			
F.	An evacuation plan is provided and fire drills conducted in accordance with Subsections 31-1.5, 31-4.1, and 31-4.2.			▓
G.	Smoking regulations have been adopted and implemented in accordance with Subsection 31-4.4.			▓
H.	Combustible draperies, furnishings and decorations are prohibited in accordance with Subsections 31-4.5 and 31-4.6.			
I.	Fire extinguishers are provided in accordance with the requirements of 12-3.5.5 and 13-3.5.5.			▓
J.	Exit signs are provided in accordance with the requirements of 12-2.10.1 and 13-2.10.1.			
K.	In new facilities without mechanically assisted smoke control systems, each patient room has an openable outside window or door as described by 12-3.8.1.			

(Dated 1/81, 1981 *Life Safety Code*)

This system has been prepared by the Fire Safety Engineering Division, Center for Fire Research, NBS, as part of the HEW/NBS Life Safety project.

CROSS REFERENCE TO 1973 AND 1976 EDITION

1973	1976	1981	1973	1976	1981
	Chapter 1			**Chapter 2**	
1-1111	1-1.1	1-1.1	2-1111	2-1	2-1
1-2111	1-2.1	1-2.1	2-1112	2-2	2-2
1-2111	1-2.2	1-2.2	2-1113	2-3	2-3
	1-3	1-3	2-1114	2-4	2-4
1-3111	1-3.1	1-3.1	2-1115	2-5	2-5
1-3111	1-3.2	1-3.2	2-1116	2-6	2-6
1-3111	1-3.3	1-3.3	2-1117	2-7	2-7
1-3111	1-3.4	1-3.4	2-1118	2-8	2-8
1-3116	1-3.5	A-1-3.1	2-1119	2-9	2-9
1-3114	1-3.6	1-3.5	2-1120	2-10	2-10
1-3118	1-3.7	1-5.1			
1-3113	1-3.8	1-3.6		**Chapter 3**	
		1-3.7		3-1	3-1
1-3115	1-3.9	1-3.7		3-1.1	3-1.1
	1-4	1-4		3-1.2	3-1.2
	1-4.1			3-1.3	3-1.3
1-4111	1-4.1.1	1-4.1		3-2	3-2
	1-4.1.2				
1-3117	1-4.1.3	1-4.2		**Chapter 4**	
1-5111	1-4.1.4	1-4.3		4-1	4-1
	1-4.1.5	1-4.5	4-111	4-1.1	4-1.1
	1-4.1.5.1	1-4.5	4-112	4-1.2	4-1.2
	1-4.1.5.2	1-4.5	4-113	4-1.3	4-1.3
	1-4.1.5.3	1-4.5	4-114	4-1.4	4-1.4
	1-4.2	1-5	4-114	4-1.5	4-1.5
	1-4.2.1	1-5.1	4-115	4-1.6	4-1.6
1-4113	1-4.2.2	1-5.2	4-116	4-1.7	4-1.7
1-3112	1-4.3	1-4.6	4-117	4-1.8	4-1.8
1-6111	1-4.4	1-5.2	4-118	4-1.9	4-1.9
	1-5	1-6	4-119	4-1.10	4-1.10
1-4113			4-120	4-1.11	4-1.11
1-4112	1-5.1	1-6.1	4-121	4-1.12	4-1.12
		1-6.2		4-2	4-2
	1-5.2	1-6.3		4-2.1	4-2.1
1-5111	1-5.3	1-6.4	4-2111	4-2.1.1	4-2.1.1
	1-5.4	1-6.3	4-2112	4-2.1.2	4-2.1.2

1973	1976	1981
4-2113	4-2.1.3	4-2.1.3
	4-2.2	4-2.2
4-2121	4-2.2.1	4-2.2.1
4-2122	4-2.2.2	4-2.2.2
4-2123	4-2.2.3	4-2.2.3
4-2124	4-2.2.4	4-2.2.4

Chapter 5

1973	1976	1981
	5-1	5-1
	5-1.1	5-1.1
5-1111	5-1.1.1	5-1.1.1
5-1112	5-1.1.2	5-1.1.2
5-1113	5-1.1.3	5-1.1.3
	5-1.2	5-1.2
5-1121	5-1.2.1	5-1.2.1
5-1121	5-1.2.2	5-1.2.2
5-1121	5-1.2.3	5-1.2.3
5-1121	5-1.2.4	5-1.2.4
5-5111	5-1.2.5	5-1.2.5
	5-1.3	5-1.3
5-1141	5-1.3.1	5-1.3.1
5-1251	5-1.3.2	5-1.3.2
5-1142	5-1.3.3	5-1.3.3
5-1231	5-1.4	5-1.4
5-1241	5-1.5	5-1.5
	5-1.6	5-1.6
5-1261	5-1.6.1	5-1.6.1
5-1263	5-1.6.2	5-1.6.2
	5-2	5-2
	5-2.1	5-2.1
	5-2.1.1	5-2.1.1
	5-2.1.1.1	5-2.1.1.1
5-21111	5-2.1.1.1.1	5-2.1.1.1.1
5-2112	5-2.1.1.1.2	5-2.1.1.12
	5-2.1.1.2	5-2.1.1.2
5-2141	5-2.1.1.2.1	5-2.1.1.2.1
5-2142	5-2.1.1.2.2	5-2.1.1.2.2
5-1206	5-2.1.1.3	5-2.1.1.3
5-2151	5-2.1.1.3.1	5-2.1.1.3.1
5-2152	5-2.1.1.3.2	5-2.1.1.3.2
5-2153	5-2.1.1.3.3	5-2.1.1.3.3
	5-2.1.1.4	5-2.1.1.4
5-2121	5-2.1.1.4	5-2.1.1.4
5-2122	5-2.1.1.4.2	5-2.1.1.4.1

1973	1976	1981
		5-2.1.1.4.2
	5-2.1.1.4.3	5-2.1.1.4.2
5-2123		
5-1202	5-2.1.1.4.4	5-2.1.1.4.1
5-2124	5-2.1.1.4.5	5-2.1.1.4.3
5-2191	5-2.1.1.4.6	5-2.1.4.4
	5-2.1.2	5-2.1.2
	5-2.1.2.1	5-2.1.2.1
5-2131	5-2.1.2.1.1	5-2.1.2.1.1
5-2132	5-2.1.2.1.2	5-2.1.2.1.2
5-2171	5-1.1.2.1.3	5-2.1.2.1.4
	5-2.1.2.2	5-2.1.2.2
5-2161	5-2.1.2.2.1	5-2.1.2.2.1
		5-2.1.2.2.2
5-2162	5-2.1.2.2.2	5-2.1.2.2.2
5-2163	5-2.1.2.2.3	5-2.1.2.2.3
	5-2.1.2.2.4	5-2.1.2.2.4
5-2134		
5-2133	5-2.1.2.3	5-2.1.2.3
	5-1.2.3	5-2.1.3
	5-2.1.3.1	5-2.1.3.1
5-2181	5-2.1.3.1.1	5-2.1.3.1.1
5-2182	5-2.1.3.1.2	5-2.1.3.1.2
	5-2.1.3.2	5-2.1.3.2
5-2201	5-2.1.3.2.1	5-2.1.3.2.1
5-2202	5-2.1.3.2.2	5-2.1.3.2.2
5-2203	5-2.1.3.2.3	5-2.1.3.2.3
5-2204	5-2.1.3.2.4	5-2.1.3.2.4
	5-2.1.3.3	5-2.1.3.3
5-2211	5-2.1.3.3.1	5-2.1.3.3.1
5-2211	5-2.1.3.3.2	5-2.1.3.3.2
5-2212	5-2.1.3.3.3	5-2.1.3.3.3
5-2213	5-2.1.3.3.4	5-2.1.3.3.4
5-2214	5-2.1.3.3.5	5-2.1.3.3.5
5-2221	5-2.1.3.4	5-2.1.3.4
	5-2.2	5-2.2
	5-2.2.1	5-2.2.1
5-3111	5-2.2.1.1	5-2.2.1.1
5-3121	5-2.2.1.2	5-2.2.1.2
5-3141	5-2.2.1.3	5-2.2.1.3
5-3181	5-2.2.1.4	5-2.2.1.4
	5-2.2.2	5-2.2.2
5-3151	5-2.2.2.1	5-2.2.2.1
5-3156	5-2.2.2.2	5-2.2.2.2
5-3152	5-2.2.2.3	5-2.2.2.3

1973	1976	1981	1973	1976	1981
5-3157	5-2.2.2.4	5-2.2.2.4	5-5135	5-2.4.3.5	5-2.4.3.5
5-3158	5-2.2.2.5	5-2.2.2.5	5-5136	5-2.4.3.6	5-2.4.3.6
5-3155	5-2.2.2.6	5-2.2.2.6	5-5137	5-2.4.3.7	5-2.4.3.7
5-3131	5-2.2.2.7		5-5138	5-2.4.3.8	5-2.4.3.8
5-3132	5-2.2.2.8	5-2.2.2.7		5-2.5	5-2.5
	5-2.2.2.9	5-2.2.2.8		5-2.5.1	5-2.5.1
5-3153	5-2.2.2.10	5-2.2.2.9	5-4111	5-2.5.1.1	5-2.5.1.1
5-3154	5-2.2.2.11		5-4113	5-2.5.1.2	5-2.5.1.2
	5-2.2.2.12	5-2.2.2.11		5-2.5.1.3	5-2.5.1.3
	5-2.2.3	5-2.2.3	5-4121	5-2.5.1.3.1	5-2.5.1.3.1
5-3161	5-2.2.3.1	5-2.2.3.1	5-4122	5-2.5.1.3.2	5-2.5.1.3.2
5-3162	5-2.2.3.2	5-2.2.3.2	5-4112	5-2.5.1.3.3	5-2.5.1.3.3
5-3163	5-2.2.3.3	5-2.2.3.3	5-4123	5-2.5.1.3.4	5-1.6.3
5-3164	5-2.2.3.4	5-2.2.3.4	5-4123	5-2.5.2	5-2.5.2
5-3165	5-2.2.3.5	5-2.2.3.5		5-2.5.3	5-2.5.3
	5-2.3	5-2.3	5-4131	5-2.5.3.1	
5-3171	5-2.3.1	5-2.3.1	5-4132	5-2.5.3.2	5-2.5.3.1
5-3172	5-2.3.2	5-2.3.2	5-4133	5-2.5.3.3	5-2.5.3.2
5-3173	5-2.3.3	5-2.3.3	5-4134	5-2.5.3.4	5-2.5.3.3
5-3174	5-2.3.4	5-2.3.4	5-4135	5-2.5.3.5	5-2.5.3.4
5-3175	5-2.3.5	5-2.3.5	5-4136	5-2.5.3.6	5-2.5.3.5
5-3176	5-2.3.6	5-2.3.6		5-2.6	5-2.6
5-3177	5-2.3.7	5-2.3.7		5-2.6.1	5-2.6.1
5-3178	5-2.3.8	5-2.3.8	5-6111	5-2.6.1.1	5-2.6.1.1
	5-2.4	5-2.4	5-6121	5-2.6.1.2	5-2.6.1.2
	5-2.4.1	5-2.4.1		5-2.6.1.3	5-2.6.1.3
5-5112	5-2.4.1.1	5-2.4.1.1	5-6131	5-2.6.1.3.1	5-2.6.1.3.1
	5-2.4.1.2	5-2.4.1.2	5-6132	5-2.6.1.3.2	5-2.6.1.3.2
5-5122	5-2.4.1.2.1	5-2.4.1.2.1	5-6133	5-2.6.1.3.3	5-2.6.1.3.3
5-5121				5-2.6.1.4	5-2.6.1.4
	5-2.4.1.2.2	5-2.4.1.2.2	5-6141	5-2.6.1.4.1	5-2.6.1.4.1
5-5123	5-2.4.1.2.3	5-2.4.1.2.3	5-6142	5-2.6.1.4.2	5-2.6.1.4.2
5-5124	5-2.4.1.2.4	5-2.4.1.2.4	5-6143	5-2.6.1.4.3	5-2.6.1.4.3
	5-2.4.2	5-2.4.2	5-6144	5-2.6.1.4.4	5-2.6.1.4.4
5-5151	5-2.4.2.1	5-2.4.2.1	5-6145	5-2.6.1.4.5	5-2.6.1.4.5
5-5152				5-2.6.2	5-2.6.2
5-5141			5-6211	5-2.6.2.1	5-2.6.2.1
5-5142	5-2.4.2.2	5-2.4.2.2		5-2.6.2.2	5-2.6.2.2
5-5143	5-2.4.2.3	5-2.4.3.3	5-6221	5-2.6.2.2.1	5-2.6.2.2.1
5-5144	5-2.4.2.4	5-2.4.2.4	5-6222	5-2.6.2.2.2	5-2.6.2.2.2
	5-2.4.3	5-2.4.3	5-6212	5-2.6.2.2.3	5-2.6.2.2.3
5-5131	5-2.4.3.1	5-2.4.3.1	5-6223	5-2.6.2.2.4	5-1.6.3
5-5132	5-2.4.3.2	5-2.4.3.2	5-6223	5-2.6.2.2.5	5-2.6.2.2.4
5-5133	5-2.4.3.3	5-2.4.3.3		5-2.6.2.3	5-2.6.2.3
5-5134	5-2.4.3.4	5-2.4.3.4	5-6231	5-2.6.2.3.1	5-2.6.2.3.1

1973	1976	1981	1973	1976	1981
5-6232	5-2.6.2.3.2	5-2.6.2.3.2	5-9224	5-2.10.2.4	5-2.10.2.4
5-6233	5-2.6.2.3.3	5-2.6.2.3.3		5-2.10.3	5-2.10.3
	5-2.7	5-2.7	5-9231	5-2.10.3.1	5-2.10.3.1
5-7111	5-2.7.1	5-2.7.1	5-9232	5-2.10.3.2	5-2.10.3.2
5-7122	5-2.7.2	5-2.7.2	5-9233	5-2.10.3.3	5-2.10.3.3
5-7121			5-9234	5-2.10.3.4	5-2.10.3.4
5-7131	5-2.7.3	5-2.7.3		5-2.1.1	5-2.1.1
5-7141	5-2.7.4	5-2.7.4		5-2.11.1	5-2.11.1
	5-2.8	5-2.8		5-2.11.1.1	5-2.11.1.1
	5-2.8.1	5-2.8.1	5-9321	5-2.11.1.2	5-2.11.1.2
5-8111	5-2.8.1.1	5-2.8.1.1	5-9314	5-2.11.1.3	5-2.11.1.3
	5-2.8.1.2	5-2.8.1.2		5-2.11.2	5-2.11.2
	5-2.8.2	5-2.8.2	5-9312	5-2.11.2.1	5-2.11.2.1
5-8121	5-2.8.2.1	5-2.8.2.1	5-9313	5-2.11.2.2	5-2.11.2.2
5-8122	5-2.8.2.2	5-2.8.2.2		5-3	5-3
5-8123	5-2.8.2.3	5-2.8.2.3		5-3.1	5-3.1
5-8124	5-2.8.2.4	5-2.8.2.4	5-1161	5-3.1.1	5-3.1.1
5-8125	5-2.8.2.5	5-2.8.2.5	5-1161	5-3.1.2	5-3.1.2
5-8126	5-2.8.2.6	5-2.8.2.6	5-1162	5-3.1.3	5-3.1.4
5-8127	5-2.8.2.7	5-2.8.2.7	5-1162	5-3.1.4	5-3.1.5
	5-2.8.3	5-2.8.3		5-3.2	5-3.2
5-8131	5-2.8.3.1	5-2.8.3.1	5-1152	5-3.2.1	5-3.2.1
5-8132	5-2.8.3.2	5-2.8.3.2	5-1153	5-3.2.2	5-3.2.2
5-8133	5-2.8.3.3	5-2.8.3.3	5-9155	5-2.9.3.5	5-2.9.3.5
	5-2.9	5-2.9	5-9131	5-2.9.4	5-2.9.4
	5-2.9.1	5-2.9.1		5-2.9.5	5-2.9.5
	5-2.9.1.1	5-2.9.1.1	5-9171	5-2.9.5.1	5-2.9.5.1
5-9111	5-2.9.1.1.1	5-2.9.1.1.1	5-9172	5-2.9.5.2	5-2.9.5.2
5-9111	5-2.9.1.1.2	5-2.9.1.1.2	5-9173	5-2.9.5.3	5-2.9.5.3
5-9111	5-2.9.1.1.3	5-2.9.1.1.3		5-2.9.6	5-2.9.6
5-9112	5-2.9.1.2	5-2.9.1.2	5-9161	5-2.9.6.1	5-2.9.6.1
5-9121	5-2.9.1.3	5-2.9.1.3	5-9162	5-2.9.6.2	5-2.9.6.2
	5-2.9.2	5-2.9.2	5-9163	5-2.9.6.2	5-2.9.6.3
5-9141	5-2.9.2.1	5-2.9.2.1	5-9164	5-2.9.6.4	5-2.9.6.4
5-9143	5-2.9.2.2	5-2.9.2.2	5-9165	5-2.9.6.5	5-2.9.6.5
5-9142			5-9166	5-2.9.6.6	5-2.9.6.6
	5-2.9.3	5-2.9.3		5-2.9.7	5-2.9.7
5-9151	5-2.9.3.1	5-2.9.3.1	5-9181	5-2.9.7.1	5-2.9.7.1
5-9152	5-2.9.3.2	5-2.9.3.2	5-9182	5-2.9.7.2	5-2.9.7.2
5-9153	5-2.9.3.3	5-2.9.3.3	5-9183	5-2.9.7.3	5-2.9.7.3
5-9154	5-2.9.3.4	5-2.9.3.4	5-9184	5-2.9.7.4	5-2.9.7.4
	5-2.10.2	5-2.10.2	5-9185	5-2.9.7.5	5-2.9.7.5
5-9221	5-2.10.2.1	5-2.10.2.1	5-9186	5-2.9.7.6	5-2.9.7.6
5-9222	5-2.10.2.2	5-2.10.2.2	5-9187	5-2.9.7.7	5-2.9.7.7
5-9223	5-2.10.2.3	5-2.10.2.3	5-9188	5-2.9.7.8	5-2.9.7.8

1973	1976	1981	1973	1976	1981
5-9189	5-2.9.7.9	5-2.9.7.9	5-10113	5-8.1.3	5-8.1.3
	5-2.10	5-2.10	5-10114	5-8.1.4	5-8.1.4
5-9211	5-2.10.1	5-2.10.1	5-10115	5-8.1.5	5-8.1.5
5-1151	5-3.3	5-3.3		5-8.2	5-8.2
	5-3.4	5-3.4	5-10121	5-8.2.1	5-8.2.1
	5-3.4.1	5-3.4.1	5-10122	5-8.2.2	5-8.2.2
	5-3.4.2	5-3.4.2	5-10123	5-8.2.3	5-8.2.3
	5-4	5-4	5-10124	5-8.2.4	
	5-4.1	5-4.1		5-9	5-9
5-1201	5-4.1.1	5-4.1.1		5-9.1	5-9.1
	5-4.1.2	5-4.1.2	5-10213	5-9.1.1	5-9.1.1
	5-5	5-5	5-10211		
	5-5.1	5-5.1	5-10211	5-9.1.2	5-9.1.2
	5-5.1.1	5-5.1.1		5-9.2	5-9.2
5-1171	5-5.1.2	5-5.1.2	5-10212	5-9.2.1	5-9.2.1
5-1181	5-5.1.3	5-5.1.3	5-10214	5-9.2.2	5-9.2.2
	5-5.2	5-5.2	5-10215	5-9.2.3	5-9.2.3
5-1203	5-5.2.1	5-5.2.1	5-10216	5-9.2.4	5-9.2.4
5-1204	5-5.2.2	5-5.2.2	5-11	5-10	5-10
5-1205	5-5.3	5-5.1.4	5-1111	5-10.1	5-10.1
	5-5.4	5-5.3	5-11111	5-10.1.1	5-10.1.1
5-1211	5-5.4.1	5-5.3.1	5-11111	5-10.1.2	5-10.1.2
5-1214	5-5.4.2	5-5.3.2	5-11115	5-10.1.3	5-10.1.3
5-1214	5-5.4.3	5-5.3.3	5-11113		
5-1215	5-5.4.4	5-5.3.4	5-11131	5-10.2	5-10.2
	5-5.4.5	5-5.3.5	5-11121	5-10.3	5-10.3
5-1212	5-5.4.6	5-5.3.6			5-10.3.1
5-1213	5-5.4.7	5-5.3.7			5-10.3.2
5-1216	5-5.4.8	5-5.3.8			5-10.3.3
	5-6	5-6			5-10.3.4
5-1181	5-6.1	5-6.1			5-10.3.5
5-1191	5-6.2	5-6.2			5-10.3.6
5-1192	5-6.3	5-6.3	5-11122	A-5-10.3	
5-1192	5-6.4	5-6.4		5-10.4	5-10.4
5-1193	5-6.5	5-6.5		5-10.4.1	5-10.4.1
5-1194	5-6.6	5-6.6	5-11114	5-10.4.1.1	5-10.4.1.1
	5-7	5-7		5-10.4.1.2	5-10.4.1.2
5-1221	5-7.1	5-7.1		5-10.4.2	5-10.4.2
5-1222	5-7.2	5-7.2	5-11112	5-10.4.2.1	5-10.4.2.1
5-1223	5-7.3	5-7.3		5-10.4.2.2	5-10.4.2.2
5-1224	5-7.4	5-7.4	4-213	5-11	5-11
5-1225	5-7.5	5-7.5	4-2131	5-11.1	5-11.1
	5-8	5-8	4-2132	5-11.2	5-11.2
5-10111	5-8.1.1	5-8.1.1		5-11.3	5-11.3
5-10112	5-8.1.2	5-8.1.2		5-11.4	5-11.4

1973	1976	1981	1973	1976	1981
			6-1312	6-1.3.2	6-2.3.2
		Chapter 6		6-2	6-5
	6-1	6-2.2		6-2.1	6-5.1
		6-2.3	6-2111	6-2.1.1	6-5.1.1
	6-1.1		6-2112	6-2.1.2	6-5.1.2
6-1111	6-1.1.1	6-2.2.3.1		6-2.1.3	6-5.1.3
6-1112	6-1.1.2	6-2.2.3.1	6-2113	6-2.1.4	6-5.1.4
6-1113	6-1.1.3	6-2.2.3.1	6-2114	6-2.1.5	6-5.1.5
6-1114	6-1.1.4	6-2.2.9	6-2115	6-2.1.6	6-5.1.6
	6-1.2	6-2.2.3	6-2116	6-2.1.7	6-5.1.7
6-1211	6-1.2.1	6-2.2.3.3	6-2117	6-2.1.8	6-5.1.8
6-1212	6-1.2.1.1	6-2.2.3.4		6-2.2	6-5.3
	6-1.2.2	A-6-2.2.3.4	6-2121	6-2.2.1	6-5.3.1
6-1221	6-1.2.2.1	A-6-2.2.3.4	6-2122	6-2.2.2	6-5.3.2
6-1222	6-1.2.2.2	A-6-2.2.3.4	6-2131	6-2.3	6-5.4.1
6-1223	6-1.2.2.3	A-6-2.2.3.4	6-2141	6-2.4	6-5.5
6-1224	6-1.2.2.4	A-6-2.2.3.4	6-2151	6-2.5	6-5.6.1
6-1225	6-1.2.2.5	A-6-2.2.3.4	6-3	6-3	7-6
6-1226	6-1.2.2.6	A-6-2.2.3.4	6-3111	6-3.1	7-6.1.1
6-1227	6-1.2.2.7	A-6-2.2.3.4	6-312	6-3.2	7-6.2
6-1228	6-1.2.2.8	A-6-2.2.3.4	6-3121	6-3.2.1	7-6.2.1
6-1229	6-1.2.2.9	A-6-2.2.3.4	6-313	6-3.3	
	6-1.2.3	A-6-2.2.3.4	6-3131	6-3.3.1	
6-1231	6-1.2.3.1	A-6-2.2.3.4	6-3132	6-3.3.2	
6-1232	6-1.2.3.2	A-6-2.2.3.4	6-3133	6-3.3.3	
6-1233	6-1.2.3.3	A-6-2.2.3.4	6-314	6-3.4	7-6.3.3
6-1234	6-1.2.3.4	A-6-2.2.3.4	6-3141	6-3.4.1	7-6.3.3.3
6-1235	6-1.2.3.5	A-6-2.2.3.4	6-3142	6-3.4.2	7-6.3.3.4
6-1236	6-1.2.3.6	A-6-2.2.3.4	6-3143	6-3.4.3	7-6.3.3.6
6-1237	6-1.2.3.7	A-6-2.2.3.4	6-3144	6-3.4.4	7-6.3.3.1
6-1238	6-1.2.3.8	A-6-2.2.3.4	6-3145	6-3.4.5	7-6.3.3.2
6-1239	6-1.2.3.9	A-6-2.2.3.4	6-32	6-3.5	
	6-1.2.4	A-6-2.2.3.4	6-3211	6-3.5.1	7-6.1.3
6-1241	6-1.2.4.1	A-6-2.2.3.4	6-3212	6-3.5.2	7-6.1.2
6-1242	6-1.2.4.2	A-6.2.2.3.4	6-3213	6-3.5.3	7-6.1.2
6-1243	6-1.2.4.3	A-6-2.2.3.4	6-3214	6-3.5.4	7-6.1.2
6-1244	6-1.2.4.4	A-6-2.2.3.4	6-3215	6-3.5.5	7-6.3.2
6-1245	6-1.2.4.5	A-6-2.2.3.4	6-3216	6-3.5.6	7-6.4.1
6-1246	6-1.2.4.6	A-6-2.2.3.4			7-6.4.2
6-1247	6-1.2.4.7	A-6-2.2.3.4			7-6.4.3
	6-1.2.5	A-6-2.2.3.4		6-3.6	7-6.2
6-1251	6-1.2.5.1	A-6-2.2.3.4	6-3311	6-3.6.1	7-6.2.2
6-1252	6-1.2.5.2	A-6-2.2.3.4	6-3312	6-3.6.2	7-6.2.3
	6-1.3	6-2.3			7-6.2.5
6-1311	6-1.3.1	6-2.3.1	6-3313	6-3.6.3	7-6.2.4

1973	1976	1981	1973	1976	1981
			6-5113	6-5.2	6-4.2
6-3314	6-3.6.4		6-5116	6-5.3	6-4.3
6-3315	6-3.6.5	6-6.2.5		6-6	6-2
6-3316	6-3.6.6	7-6.1.2		6-6.1	6-2.1
6-34	6-3.7	7-6.2	6-6	6-6.2	6-3
6-3411	6-3.7.1	7-6.2.1	6-611	6-6.2.1	6-3.2
6-3412	6-3.7.2	7-6.1.3	6-6131		
6-3413	6-3.7.3	7-6.1.2	6-6132		
6-3414	6-3.7.4	7-6.1.2	6-6134		
6-35	6-3.8	7-6.2	6-6135	6-6.2.2	6-3.3
6-3511	6-3.8.1	7-6.2.1	6-6133	6-6.2.3	6-3.4
6-3512	6-3.8.2	7-6.1.3		6-6.2.4	6-3.5
6-3513	6-3.8.3	7-6.1.2		6-6.2.5	6-3.6
6-3514	6-3.8.4	7-6.1.2		6-6.3	
6-36	6-3.9	7-6.1		6-6.3.1	6-2.2.4
6-3611	6-3.9.1	7-6.2.6		6-6.3.2	6-2.2.1.1
6-3612	6-3.9.2	7-6.2.1	6-711	6-6.3.3	6-2.2.6
6-3613	6-3.9.3	7-6.1.3		6-6.3.4	6-2.2.7
6-3614	6-3.9.4	7-6.1.2		6-6.3.5	6-2.2.8
6-3615	6-3.9.5	7-6.2.1		6-6.4	
6-37	6-3.10			6-6.4.1	6-3.2 Exception
6-3711	6-3.10.1			6-6.4.2	6-2.2.10
6-3712	6-3.10.2			6-6.4.3	6-2.2.10
6-3713	6-3.10.3				6-3.2
6-3714	6-3.10.4			6-6.4.4	6-2.2.10
6-3175	6-3.10.5			6-6.4.5	6-2.2.2
6-38	6-3.11	7-6.3.3			6-3.2
6-3811	6-3.11.1	7-6.3.4.1			
6-3812	6-3.11.2	A-7-6.3.4.1(c)			
6-4	6-4	7-7			
6-41	6-4.1	7-7.1		**Chapter 7**	
6-4111	6-4.1.1	7-7.1.1			
6-4112	6-4.1.2	7-7.1.2		7-1	7-1
6-4113	6-4.1.3	7-7.1.3		7-1.1	7-1.1
6-4132	6-4.2	7-7.2		7-1.2	7-1.2
6-4132	6-4.2.1	7-7.2.1		7-2	7-2
6-4132	6-4.2.2	7-7.2.2	7-1111	7-2.1	7-2.1
6-4132	6-4.2.3	7-7.2.3		7-2.2	7-2.2
6-4211	6-4.3	7-7.3		7-2.3	7-2.3
6-43	6.4.4	7-7.4		7-3	7-4
6-4311	6-4.4.1	7-7.4.1		7-3.1	7-4.1
6-4312	6-4.4.2	7-7.4.2		7-3.2	7-4.2
6-5	6-5	6-4		7-3.3	7-4.3
6-5115	6-5.1	6-4.1		7-4	7-5
6-5112			7-1141		
6-5111			7-1131	7-4.1	7-5.1

1973	1976	1981
7-1132	7-4.2	7-5.2
	7-4.3	7-5.3

Chapter 8

1973	1976	1981
	8-1	8-1
		9-1
	8-1.1	8-1.1
		9-1.1
	8-1.1.1	8-1.1
		9-1.1
	8-1.1.2	8-1.2
		9-1.2
8-1121	8-1.1.2.1	8-1.2.1
		9-1.2.1
	8-1.1.2.2	8-1.2.2
		9-1.2.2
8-1411	8-1.1.2.3	8-1.2.3
		9-1.2.3
8-1412	8-1.1.2.4	8-1.2.4
		9-1.2.4
8-1511		
8-1131	8-1.2	8-1.3
		9-1.3
	8-1.3	8-1.4
		9-1.4
8-1132	8-1.3.1	8-1.4.1
		9-1.4.1
	8-1.4	8-1.5
		9-1.5
	8-1.5	8-1.7
		9-1.7
8-5111		
8-1133		
8-1134	8-1.5.1	8-1.7.1
		9-1.7.1
8-1135	8-1.5.2	8-1.7.2
		9-1.7.2
8-1311	8-1.5.3	8-1.7.3
		9-1.7.3
8-5121		
8-1111	8-1.6	
	8-2	8-2
		9-2
	8-2.1	8-2.1

1973	1976	1981
		9-2.1
	8-2.2	8-2.2
		9-2.2.2
8-1251	8-2.2.1	8-2.2.1
		9-2.2.1
8-1252	8-2.2.2	8-2.2.2
		9-2.2.2
	8-2.3	8-2.3
		9-2.3
8-1211	8-2.3.1	8-2.3.1
		9-2.3.1
8-1231	8-2.3.2	8-2.3.2
		9-2.3.2
8-1232	8-2.3.3	8-2.3.3
		9-2.3.3
	8-2.4	8-2.3.4
		9-2.4
8-1221	8-2.4.1	8-2.4.1
		9-2.4.1
8-1222	8-2.4.2	8-2.4.2
		9-2.4.2
8-1223	8-2.4.3	8-2.4.3
		9-2.4.3
	8-2.5	8-2.5
		9-2.5
	8-2.5.1	8-2.5.1
		9-2.5.1
8-1271	8-2.5.2	8-2.5.3
		9-2.5.3
8-1272	8-2.5.3	8-2.5.4
		9-2.5.4
8-1241	8-2.6	8-2.6
		9-2.6
	8-2.7	8-2.7
		9-2.7
8-1112	8-2.7.1	8-2.7.1
		9-2.7.1
8-1113	8-2.7.2	8-2.7.2
		9-2.7.2
	8-2.8	8-2.1.1
		9-2.1.1
8-1261	8-2.8.1	8-2.11.1
		9-2.11.1
8-1273	8-2.8.2	8-2.11.2
		9-2.11.2

1973	1976	1981	1973	1976	1981
	8-2.9	8-2.8	8-1519	8-3.5.1.7	8-3.2.1.6
		9-2.8			9-3.2.1.6
	8-2.9.1	8-2.8.1		8-3.5.2	8-3.2.2
		9-2.8.1			9-3.2.2
8-1282	8-2.9.2	8-2.8.2	8-1611	8-3.5.2.1	8-3.2.2.1
		9-2.8.2			9-3.2.2.1
8-1281	8-2.10	8-2.9		8-3.5.2.2	8-3.2.2.2
		9-2.9			9-3.2.2.2
	8-2.1.1	8-2.10	8-6111	8-3.5.2.2.1	8-3.2.2.2.1
		9-2.10			9-3.2.2.2.1
	8-3	8-3	8-6112	8-3.5.2.2.2	8-3.2.2.2.2
		9-3			9-3.2.2.2.2
8-1711	8-3.1	8-3.1	8-6113	8-3.5.2.2.3	8-3.2.2.2.3
		9-3.1			9-3.2.2.2.3
	8-3.2	8-3.3	8-6114	8-3.5.2.2.4	8-3.2.2.2.4
		9-3.3			9-3.2.2.2.4
8-5131			8-6115	8-3.5.2.2.5	8-3.2.2.2.5
8-1721	8-3.2.1	8-3.3.1			9-3.2.2.2.5
		9-3.3.1	8-6116	8-3.5.2.2.6	8-3.2.2.2.6
8-1722	8-3.2.2	8-3.3.2			9-3.2.2.2.6
		9-3.3.2		8-3.5.3	8-3.2.3
8-1723	8-3.2.3	8-3.3.3			9-3.2.3
		9-3.3.3	8-1731	8-3.5.3.1	8-3.2.3.1
8-1724	8-3.2.4	8-3.3.4			9-3.2.3.1
		9-3.3.4	8-1731	8-3.5.3.2	8-3.2.3.2
	8-3.3	8-3.4			9-3.2.3.2
		9-3.4		8-3.5.3.3	8-3.2.3.3
	8-3.4	8-3.5			9-3.2.3.3
		9-3.5		8-3.5.4	8-3.2.4
	8-3.5	8-3.2			9-3.2.4
		9-3.2		8-3.5.4.1	8-3.2.4.1
	8-3.5.1	8-3.2.1			9-3.2.4.1
		9-3.2.1	8-1832	8-3.5.4.2	8-3.2.4.2
8-1512	8-3.5.11	8-3.2.1.1			9-3.2.4.2
		9-3.2.1.1		8-3.6	
8-1513	8-3.5.1.2	8-3.2.1.2		8-3.7	
		9-3.2.1.2		8-4	8-5
8-1515					9-5
8-1514	8-3.5.1.3	8-3.2.1.3		8-4.1	8-5.1
		9-3.2.1.3			9-5.1
8-1516	8-3.5.1.4		8-1821	8-4.2	8-5.2
8-1517	8-3.5.1.5	8-3.2.1.4			9-5.2
		9-3.2.1.4	8-1811	8-4.3	8-5.3
8-1518	8-3.5.1.6	8-3.2.1.5			9-5.3
		9-3.2.1.5		8-5	8-4

1973	1976	1981	1973	1976	1981
		9-4	9-2112		
8-3111	8-5.1	8-4.1	9-2113		
		9-4.1	9-2114		
	8-5.2	8-4.2	9-2115		
		9-4.2	9-2116		
8-2111			9-2117	9-1.2	10-1.3
8-2112	8-5.2.1	8-4.2.1			11-1.3
		9-4.2.1		9-1.3	10-1.4
	8-5.3	8-4.3			11-1.4
		9.4.3	9-1111	9-1.3.1	10-1.4.1
8-4111	8-5.3.1	8-4.3.1			11-1.4.1
		9-4.3.1	9-1112	9-1.3.2	10-1.4.2
8-4112	8-5.3.2	8-4.3.2			11-1.4.2
		9-4.3.2	9-1113	9-1.3.3	10-1.4.3
8-4113	8-5.3.3				11-1.4.3
8-4113	8-5.3.4	8-4.3.3	9-1114	9-1.3.4	10-1.4.4
		9-4.3.3			11-1.4.4
				9-1.4	10-1.5

Chapter 9

1973	1976	1981	1973	1976	1981
				9-1.5	10-1.7
	9-1	10-1			11-1.7
		11-1	9-1121	9-1.5.1	10-1.7.1
	9-1.1	10-1.1			11-1.7.1
		11-1.1	9-1122	9-1.5.2	10-1.7.2
9-6111					11-1.7.2
9-6121	9-1.1.1	10-1.1.1	9-1123	9-1.5.3	10-1.7.3
		11-1.1.1			11-1.7.3
9-3111	9-1.1.2	10-1.1.2	9-1124	9-1.5.4	10-1.7.4
		11-1.1.3			11-1.7.4
	9-1.1.3	10-1.1.3		9-2	10-2
		11-1.1.4			11-2
	9-1.1.4	10-1.2		9-2.1	10-2.1
		11-1.2			11-2.1
	9-1.1.4.1	10-1.2.1	9-1251	9-2.1.1	10-2.1
		11-1.2.1			11-2.1
9-5111	9-1.1.4.2	10-1.2.2		9-2.1.2	
		11-1.2.2	9-6131	9-2.1.2.1	
9-5121	9-1.1.4.3	10-1.2.3	9-6132	9-2.1.2.2	
		11-1.2.3		9-2.2	10-2.2
	9-1.1.4.4	10-1.2.4			11-2.2
		11-1.2.4		9-2.3	10-2.3
9-5131	9-1.1.4.4.1	10-1.2.4.1			11-2.3
		11-1.2.4.1	9-1221	9-2.3.1	10-2.3.1
9-5132	9-1.1.4.4.2				11-2.3.1
9-2111			9-1222	9-2.3.2	10-2.3.2

1973	1976	1981	1973	1976	1981
		11-2.3.2			11-2.10
	9-2.3.3	10-2.5.3	9-1511	9-2.1.2	10-2.11.5
		11-2.5.3			11-2.11.5
9-1252	9-2.3.3.1	10-2.5.3.1		9-3	10-3
		11-2.5.3.1			11-3
9-1254	9-2.3.3.2	10-2.5.3.2		9-3.1	10-3.1
		11-2.5.3.2			11-3.1
9-1253	9-2.3.3.3	10-2.5.3.3	9-1611	9-3.1.1	10-3.1.1
		11-2.5.3.3			11-3.1.1
	9-2.4	10-2.4	9-1612	9-3.1.2	10-3.1.2
		11-2.4			11-3.1.2
	9-2.4.1	10-2.4.1	9-6141		
		11-2.4.1	9-1631	9-3.2	10-3.3
9-1231	9-2.4.2	10-2.4.2			10-3.3.1
		11-2.4.2			11-3.3
	9-2.5	10-2.5			11-3.3.1
		11-2.5		9-3.3	10-3.4
	9-2.5.1	10-2.5.4			11-3.4
		11-2.5.4	9-1641	9-3.3.1	10-3.4.1
9-1261	9-2.5.1.1	10-2.5.4.1			11-3.4.1
		11-2.5.4.1	9-1642	9-3.3.2	10-3.4.2
9-1262	9-2.5.1.2	10-2.5.4.2			11-3.4.2
		11-2.5.4.2	9-6151	9-3.3.3	11-3.4.3
9-1271	9-2.5.2	10-2.5.1	9-1651	9-3.4	10-3.5
		11-2.5.1			11-3.5
9-1272	9-2.5.3	10-2.5.2		9-3.5	10-3.2
		11-2.5.2			11-3.2
9-1241	9-2.6	10-2.6	9-1661	9-3.5.1	10-3.2.1(a)
		11-2.6			11-3.2.1(a)
	9-2.7	10-2.7		9-3.5.2	10-3.2.3
		11-2.7			11-3.2.3
	9-2.8	10-2.11		9-3.6	
		11-2.11		9-3.6.1	10-3.6
9-1311	9-2.8.1	10-2.11.1			11-3.6
		11-2.11.1	9-1621	9-3.6.1.1	10-3.6.1
9-1321	9-2.8.2	10-2.11.2			11-3.6.1
		11-2.11.2	9-1622	9-3.6.1.2	10-3.7.1
9-1331	9-2.8.3	10-2.11.3			11-3.7.1
		11-2.11.3		9-3.7	
9-1411	9-2.9	10-2.8		9-4	10-5
		11-2.8			11-5
9-1411	9-2.10	10-2.9	9-1731	9-4.1	10-5.1
		11-2.9			11-5.1
9-1413			9-1721	9-4.2	10-5.2
9-1412	9-2.11	10-2.10			11-5.2

1973	1976	1981	1973	1976	1981
9-1711					11-6.3.2
9-1712	9-4.3	10-5.3	9-2123	9-5.2.3.4.1	10-6.3.2.1
		11-5.3			11-6.3.2.1
	9-5	10-4	9-2124	9-5.2.3.4.2	10-6.3.2.2
		11-4			11-6.3.2.2
9-4111	9-5.1	10-4.1		9-5.2.3.5	10-6.3.8
		11-4.1			11-6.3.8
	9-5.2	10-4.2	9-2131	9-5.2.3.5.1	10-6.3.8.1
		11-4.2			11-6.3.8.1
	9-5.2.1		9-2132	9-5.2.3.5.2	10-6.3.8.2
9-2121	9-5.2.1.1	10-4.2			11-6.3.8.2
		11-4.2		9-5.3	10-7
	9-5.2.2	10-6.2			11-7
		11-6.2		9-5.3.1	10-7.1
	9-5.2.2.1	10-6.2.1			11-7.1
		11-6.2.1		9-5.3.1.1	
9-2141	9-5.2.2.1.1	10-6.2.1.1	9-7111	9-5.3.1.1.1	10-7.1.1.2
		11-6.2.1.1			11-7.1.1.2
9-2142	9-5.2.2.1.2	10-6.2.1.2	9-7113	9-5.3.1.1.2	10-7.1.1.3
		10-6.2.1.3			11-7.1.1.3
		11-6.2.1.2	9-7114	9-5.3.1.1.3	10-7.1.1.4
		11-6.2.1.3			11-7.1.1.4
9-2171	9-5.2.2.1.3	10-6.2.1.4	9-7115	9-5.3.1.1.4	10-7.1.1.5
		11-6.2.1.4			11-7.1.1.5
9-2172	9-5.2.2.1.4	10-6.2.1.5	9-7321		
		11-6.2.1.5	9-7322		
9-2151	9-5.2.2.2	10-6.2.2	9-7116		
		11-6.2.2	9-7323	9-5.3.1.1.5	10-7.1.2
	9-5.2.3	11-6.3			11-7.1.2
		11-6.3		9-5.3.1.1.6	10-7.1.6.2
	9-5.2.3.1	10-6.3.1			11-7.1.6.2
		11-6.3.1		9-5.3.1.2	10-7.1.3
	9-5.2.3.1.1	10-6.3.1.1			11-7.1.3
		11-6.3.1.1	9-7112	9-5.3.1.3	10-7.1.4
9-2122	9-5.2.3.1.2	10-6.3.1.2			11-7.1.4
		11-6.3.1.2		9-5.3.1.4	10-7.1.5
9-2161	9-5.2.3.2	10-6.3.3			11-7.1.5
		11-6.3.3	9-7121	9-5.3.1.5	10-7.1.7
	9-5.2.3.3	10-6.3.5			11-7.1.7
		11-6.3.5		9-5.3.2	10-7.2
9-2181	9-5.2.3.3.1	10-6.3.5.1			11-7.2
		11-6.3.5.1		9-5.3.2.1	10-7.2.1
9-2182	9-5.2.3.3.2	10-6.3.5.2			11-7.2.1
		11-6.3.5.2		9-5.3.2.2	10-7.2.2
	9-5.2.3.4	10-6.3.2			11-7.2.2

1973	1976	1981	1973	1976	1981
9-7242			9-7351	9-5.3.3.2.1	10-7.3.3.1
9-7241	9-5.3.2.2.1	10-7.2.2.1			11-7.3.3.1
		11-7.2.2.1	9-7352	9-5.3.3.2.2	10-7.3.3.2
9-7251	9-5.3.2.2.2	10-7.2.2.2			11-7.3.3.2
		11-7.2.2.2	9-7353	9-5.3.3.2.3	10-7.3.3.3
	9-5.3.2.3	10-7.2.3			11-7.3.3.3
		11-7.2.3		9-5.3.3.3	10-7.3.4
	9-5.3.2.4	10-7.2.4			11-7.3.4
		11-7.2.4	9-7362	9-5.3.3.3.1	10-7.3.4.1
9-7211	9-5.3.2.4.1	10-7.2.4.1			11-7.3.4.1
		11-7.2.4.1	9-7361	9-5.3.3.3.2	10-7.3.4.2
9-7212	9-5.3.2.4.2	10-7.2.4.2			11-7.3.4.2
		11-7.2.4.2		9-5.3.3.4	10-7.3.5
	9-5.3.2.5	10-7.2.5			11-7.3.5
		11-7.2.5	9-7364	9-5.3.3.4.1	10-7.3.5.1
	9-5.3.2.6	10-7.2.6			11-7.3.5.1
		11-7.2.6	9-7364	9-5.3.3.4.2	10-7.3.5.2
	9-5.3.2.6.1	10-7.2.6.1			11-7.3.5.2
		11-7.2.6.1	9-7371	9-5.3.3.5	10-7.3.2
9-7221	9-5.3.2.6.2	10-7.2.6.2			11-7.3.2
		11-7.2.6.2		9-5.3.3.6	10-7.1.6
9-7221	9-5.3.2.6.3	10-7.2.6.3			11-7.1.6
		11-7.2.6.3	9-7331	9-5.3.3.6.1	10-7.1.6.1
	9-5.3.2.7	10-7.2.7			11-7.1.6.1
		11-7.2.7	9-7311		
	9-5.3.2.8	10-7.2.11	9-7312	9-5.3.3.6.2	10-7.3.7
		11-7.2.11			11-7.3.7
9-7231	9-5.3.2.8.1	10-7.2.11.1		9-5.3.4	10-7.5
		11-7.2.11.1			11-7.5
9-7232	9-5.3.2.8.2	10-7.2.11.2		9-5.3.4.1	10-7.5.1
		11-7.2.11.2			11-7.5.1
9-7233	9-5.3.2.8.3	10-7.2.11.3	9-7421	9-5.3.4.1.1	10-7.5.1.1
		11-7.2.11.3			11-7.5.1.1
	9-5.3.2.9	10-7.2.8	9-7422	9-5.3.4.1.2	10-7.5.1.2
		11-7.2.8			11-7.5.1,2
9-7261	9-5.3.2.10	10-7.2.9		9-5.3.4.1.3	10-7.5.1.3
		11-7.2.9			11-7.5.1.3
	9-5.3.2.11	10-7.2.10	9-7411	9-5.3.4.2	10-7.5.2
		11-7.2.10			11-7.5.2
	9-5.3.3	10-7.3		9-5.4	10-8
		11-7.3			11-8
9-7341	9-5.3.3.1	10-7.3.1		9-5.4.1	10-8.1
		11-7.3.1			11-8.1
	9-5.3.3.2	10-7.3.3		9.5.4.1.1	10-8.1.1
		11-7.3.3			11-8.1.1

1973	1976	1981	1973	1976	1981
9-8111	9-5.4.1.1.1	10-8.1.1.1			11-8.2.11.2
		11-8.1.1.1		9-5.4.2.9	10-8.2.8
9-8113	9-5.4.1.1.2	10-8.1.1.2			11-8.2.8
		11-8.1.1.2		9-5.4.3	10-8.3
9-8114	9-5.4.1.1.3	10-8.1.1.3			11-8.3
		11-8.1.1.3	9-8331	9-5.4.3.1	10-8.3.1
9-8311					11-8.3.1
9-8312				9-5.4.3.2	10-8.3.3
9-8115	9-5.4.1.1.4	10-8.1.2			11-8.3.3
		11-8.1.2	9-8341	9-5.4.3.2.1	10-8.3.3.2
	9-5.4.1.2	10-8.1.3			11-8.3.3.2
		11-8.1.3	9-8342	9-5.4.3.2.2	10-8.3.3.1
9-8112	9-5.4.1.3	10-8.1.4			11-8.3.3.1
		11-8.1.4	9-8351	9-5.4.3.3	10-8.3.4
	9-5.4.1.4	10-8.1.5			11-8.3.4
		11-8.1.5	9-8361	9-5.4.3.4	10-8.3.5
	9-5.4.1.5	10-8.1.7			11-8.3.5
		11-8.1.7	9-8321	9-5.4.3.5	10-8.1.6
	9-5.4.2	10-8.2			11-8.1.6
		11-8.2		9-5.4.4	10-8.5
	9-5.4.2.1	10-8.2.1			11-8.5
		11-8.2.1		9-5.4.4.1	10-8.5.1
	9-5.4.2.2	10-8.2.2			11-8.5.1
		11-8.2.2	9-8421	9-5.4.4.1.1	10-8.5.1.1
	9-5.4.2.3	10-8.2.3			11-8.5.1.1
		11-8.2.3	9-8422	9-5.4.4.1.2	10-8.5.1.2
	9-5.4.2.4	10-8.2.4			11-8.5.1.2
		11-8.2.4	9-8423	9-5.4.4.1.3	10-8.5.1.3
9-8211	9-5.4.2.4.1	10-8.2.4.1			11-8.5.1.3
		11-8.2.4.1		9-5.4.4.2	10-8.5.2
9-8212	9-5.4.2.4.2	10-8.2.4.2			11-8.5.2
		11-8.2.4.2	9-8411	9-5.4.4.2.1	10-8.5.2.1
9-8213	9-5.4.2.4.3	10-8.2.4.3			11-8.5.2.1
		11-8.2.4.3	9-8412	9-5.4.4.2.2	10-8.5.2.2
	9-5.4.2.5	10-8.2.5			11-8.5.2.2
		11-8.2.5		9-5.5	10-9
	9-5.4.2.6	10-8.2.6			11-9
		11-8.2.6		9-5.5.1	10-9.1
	9-5.4.2.7	10-8.2.7			11-9.1
		11-8.2.7		9-5.5.1.1	10-9.1.1
	9-5.4.2.8	10-8.2.11			11-9.1.1
		11-8.2.11	9-9111	9-5.5.1.1.1	10-9.1.1.1
9-8221	9-5.4.2.8.1	10-8.2.11.1			11-9.1.1.1
		11-8.2.11.1	9-9113	9-5.5.1.1.2	10-9.1.1.2
9-8222	9-5.4.2.8.2	10-8.2.11.2			11-9.1.1.2

1973	1976	1981	1973	1976	1981
9-9114	9-5.5.1.1.3	10-9.1.1.3			11-9.2.10
		11-9.1.1.3		9-5.5.3	10-9.3
9-9115	9-5.5.1.1.4	10-9.1.2			11-9.3
		11-9.1.2		9-5.5.3.1	10-9.3.1
	9-5.5.1.2	10-9.1.3			11-9.3.1
		11-9.1.3		9-5.5.3.2	10-9.3.3
9-9112	9-5.5.1.3	10-9.1.4			11-9.3.3
		11-9.1.4	9-9321	9-5.5.3.2.1	10-9.3.3.2
	9-5.5.1.4	10-9.1.5			11-9.3.3.2
		11-9.1.5	9-9322	9-5.5.3.2.2	10-9.3.3.1
	9-5.5.1.5	10-9.1.7			11-9.3.3.1
		11-9.1.7	9-9331	9-5.5.3.3	10-9.3.4
	9-5.5.2	10-9.2			11-9.3.4
		11-9.2	9-9341	9-5.5.3.4	10-9.3.5
	9-5.5.2.1	10-9.2.1			11-9.3.5
		11-9.2.1	9-9311	9-5.5.3.5	10-9.1.6
	9-5.5.2.2	10-9.2.2			11-9.1.6
		11-9.2.2		9-5.5.4	10-9.5
	9-5.5.2.3	10-9.2.3			11-9.5
		11-9.2.3		9-5.5.4.1	10-9.5.1
	9-5.5.2.4	10-9.2.4			11-9.5.1
		11-9.2.4	9-9421	9-5.5.4.1.1	10-9.5.1.1
9-9211	9-5.5.2.4.1	10-9.2.4.1			11-9.5.1.1
		11-9.2.4.1	9-9422	9-5.5.4.1.2	10-9.5.1.2
9-9212	9-5.5.2.4.2	10-9.2.4.2			11-9.5.1.2
		11-9.2.4.2	9-9423	9-5.5.4.1.3	10-9.5.1.3
9-9231	9-5.5.2.4.3	10-9.2.4.3			11-9.5.1.3
		11-9.2.4.3		9-5.5.4.2	10-9.5.2
	9-5.5.2.5	10-9.2.5			11-9.5.2
		11-9.2.5	9-9411	9-5.5.4.2.1	10-9.5.2.1
	9-5.5.2.6	10-9.2.6			11-9.5.2.1
		11-9.2.6	9-9412	9-5.5.4.2.2	10-9.5.2.2
	9-5.5.2.7	10-9.2.7			11-9.5.2.2
		11-9.2.7			
	9-5.5.2.8	10-9.2.11		**Chapter 10**	
		11-9.2.11			
9-9221	9-5.5.2.8.1	10-9.2.11.1		10-1	12-1
		11-9.2.11.1		10-1.1	12-1.1
9-9222	95.5.2.8.2	10-9.2.11.2		10-1.1.1	12-1.1.1
		11-9.2.11.2	10-0001	10-1.1.1.1	12-1.1.1.3
9-9223	9-5.5.2.8.3	10-9.2.11.3		10-1.1.1.2	
		11-9.2.11.3	10-0001	10-1.1.1.3	12-1.1.1.4
	9-5.5.2.9	10-9.2.8	10-0001	10-1.1.1.4	12-1.1.1.6
		10-9.2.10	10-0002	10-1.1.1.5	12-1.1.1.10
		11-9.2.8	10-0004	10-1.1.1.6	12-1.1.1.7

1973	1976	1981	1973	1976	1981
10-0004	10-1.1.1.7	10-1.1.1.8	10-1211	10-2.2.2.3	12-2.2.3
10-0004	10-1.1.1.8		10-1211	10-2.2.2.4	12-2.2.4
10-0003	10-1.1.2	12-1.1.3	10-1261		
	10-1.1.3	12-1.1.4	10-1211	10-2.2.2.5	12-2.2.5
10-2132			10-1271		
10-1121	10-1.1.3.1	12-1.1.4.1	10-1211	10-2.2.2.6	12-2.2.6
10-1121	10-1.1.3.2	12-1.1.4.2	10-1211	10-2.2.2.7	12-2.2.7
10-1121	10-1.1.3.3	12-1.1.4.3	10-1213	10-2.2.2.8	
10-1121	10-1.1.3.4		10-1214	10-2.2.2.9	
10-2131				10-2.2.2.10	
10-1122	10-1.1.4	12-1.1.4.4		10-2.2.3	12-2.3
10-2133	10-1.1.5	12-1.1.4.5	10-1221	10-2.2.3.1	12-2.3.1
10-1123	10-1.1.6	12-1.1.4.6	10-1221	10-2.2.3.2	12-2.3.2
10-3121				10-2.2.4	12-2.4
10-0005	10-1.2	12-1.3	10-1212	10-2.2.4.1	12-2.4.1
	10-1.3	12-1.4		10-2.2.4.2	12-2.4.2
10-0001	10-1.3.1		10-1212	10-2.2.4.3	12-2.4.2
	10-1.3.2	12-1.2		10-2.2.5	12-2.5
10-2142			10-1233	10-2.2.5.1	12-2.5.1
10-1132	10-1.3.2.1	12-1.2.1	10-1234	10-2.2.5.2	12-2.5.2
	10-1.3.2.2	12-1.2.2	10-1234	10-2.2.5.3	12-2.5.3
10-2141			10-1235	10-2.2.5.4	12-2.5.5
10-1131	10-1.3.2.3	12-1.2.3	10-1237	10-2.2.5.5	12-2.5.6
10-1131	10-1.3.2.4	12-1.2.4		10-2.2.5.6	12-2.5.7
10-2143			10-1236	10-2.2.5.7	12-2.5.8
10-1133	10-1.3.2.5	12-1.2.5		10-2.2.6	12-2.6
10-1131	10-1.3.2.6	12-1.2.6		10-2.2.6.1	12-2.6.1
10-1131	10-1.3.2.7	12-1.2.7	10-1232	10-2.2.6.2	12-2.6.2
10-3133	10-1.4	12-1.5		10-2.2.7	12-2.7
10-2144				10-2.2.7.1	12-2.7.1
10-1134	10-1.5	12-1.7	10-1241	10-2.2.8	12-2.11
	10-2.1	12-1	10-1242	10-2.2.8.1	12-2.11.1
	10-2.1.1	12-1.1.1	10-1242	10-2.2.8.2	12-2.11.2
10-1111	10-2.1.1.1	12-1.1.1.1	10-1243	10-2.2.8.3	12-2.11.5
	10-2.1.1.2	12-1.1.1.2	10-1244	10-2.2.8.4	12-2.11.6
	10-2.1.2	12-1.3		10-2.2.9	12-2.8
	10-2.1.3	12-1.4		10-2.2.9.1	12-2.8.1
	10-2.1.4	12-1.5		10-2.2.9.2	12-2.8.2
	10-2.1.5	12-1.7		10-2.2.10	12-2.9
	10-2.2	12-2	10-1282		
10-2231			10-1281	10-2.2.10.1	12-2.9.1
10-1231	10-2.2.1	12-2.1	10-1281	10-2.2.10.2	12-2.9.2
10-1211	10-2.2.2	12-2.2		10-2.2.11	12-2.10
10-1211	10-2.2.2.1	12-2.2.1	10-1283	10-2.2.11.1	12-2.10.1
10-1211	10-2.2.2.2	12-2.2.2		10-2.2.11.2	12-2.10.2

1973	1976	1981	1973	1976	1981
	10-2.3	12-3		10-2.3.6.6.9	12-3.7.9
	10-2.3.1	12-3.1		10-2.3.6.7	12-3.6
10-1341			10-1331	10-2.3.6.7.1	12-3.6.1
10-1251	10-2.3.1.1	12-3.1.1	10-1331	10-2.3.6.7.2	12-3.6.2
10-1341			10-1331	10-2.3.6.7.3	12-3.6.3
10-1245	10-2.3.1.2	12-3.1.2	10-1331	10-2.3.6.7.4	12-3.6.4
	10-2.3.2	12-3.3	10-1342	10-2.3.6.7.5	12-1.6.7
10-1351	10-2.3.2.1	12-3.3.1		10-2.3.7	12-3.8
10-1352	10-2.3.2.2	12-3.3.2	10-1325	10-2.3.7.1	12-3.8.1
	10-2.3.2.3			10-2.4	12-5
	10-2.3.3	12-3.4		10-2.4.1	12-5.1
10-1363	10-2.3.3.1	12-3.4.1			12-5.1.2
10-1361	10-2.3.3.2	12-3.4.2		10-2.4.2	12-5.2
	10-2.3.3.3	12-3.4.3	10-1411	10-2.4.2.1	12-5.2.1
10-1361	10-2.3.3.4	12-3.4.4	10-1412	10-2.4.2.2	12-5.2.2
10-1361	10-2.3.3.5	12-3.4.5	10-1413	10-2.4.2.3	
10-1362	10-2.3.3.6	12-3.4.6		10-2.4.3	12-5.3
	10-2.3.3.7	12-3.4.7		10-2.4.4	12-5.4.1
	10-2.3.3.8	12-3.4.8	10-1414	10-2.4.4.1	12-5.4.2
	10-2.3.4	12-3.5	10-1414	10-2.4.4.2	12-5.4.3
10-1364	10-2.3.4.1	12-3.5.1	10-1414	10-2.4.4.3	12-5.4.4
10-1366	10-2.3.4.2	12-3.5.2		10-2.5	12-4
10-1366	10-2.3.4.3	12-3.5.3	10-1511	10-2.5.1	12-4.1
10-1368				10-3	Chapter 13
10-1367	10-2.3.4.4	12-3.5.4		10-3.1	13-1
10-1369	10-2.3.4.5	12-3.5.5		10-3.1.1	13-1.1.1
	10-2.3.5	12-3.2	10-3162		
10-1371	10-2.3.5.1	12-3.2.1	10-3161	10-3.1.1.1	13-1.1.1.1
10-1372	10-2.3.5.2	12-3.2.2	10-2111	10-3.1.1.2	13-1.1
	10-2.3.5.3	12-3.2.3			13-1.1.1.2
	10-2.3.6	12-1.6		10-3.1.1.3	13-1.1.5
10-1321	10-2.3.6.1	12-1.6.1	10-2121	10-3.1.1.3.1	13-1.1.5.1
10-1321	10-2.3.6.2	12-1.6.2	10-2122	10-3.1.1.3.2	13-1.1.5.2
10-1322	10-2.3.6.3	12-1.6.3	10-2123	10-3.1.1.3.3	13-1.1.5.3
10-1323	10-2.3.6.4	12-1.6.4		10-3.1.2	13-1.3
10-1324	10-2.3.6.5	12-1.6.5		10-3.1.3	13-1.4
	10-2.3.6.6	12-3.7		10-3.1.4	13-1.5
10-1311	10-2.3.6.6.1	12-3.7.1		10-3.1.5	13-1.7
10-1312	10-2.3.6.6.2	12-3.7.2		10-3.2	13-2
10-1313	10-2.3.6.6.3	12-3.7.3		10-3.2.1	13-2.1
10-1314	10-2.3.6.6.4	12-3.7.4	10-2211	10-3.2.2	13-2.2
10-1315	10-2.3.6.6.5	12-3.7.5	10-2211	10-3.2.2.1	13-2.2.1
10-1316	10-2.3.6.6.6	12-3.7.6	10-2251		
10-1317	10-2.3.6.6.7	12-3.7.7	10-2211	10-3.2.2.2	13-2.2.2
10-1318	10-2.3.6.6.8	12-3.7.8	10-2211	10-3.2.2.3	13-2.2.3

1973	1976	1981	1973	1976	1981
10-2211	10-3.2.2.4	13-2.2.4		10-3.3.3	13-3.4
10-2261	10-3.2.2.5	13-2.2.5		10-3.3.3.1	13-3.4.1
10-2252			10-2351	10-3.3.3.2	13-3.4.2
10-2211	10-3.2.2.6	13-2.2.6		10-3.3.3.3	13-3.4.3
10-2211	10-3.2.2.7	13-2.2.7		10-3.3.3.4	13-3.4.4
10-2213	10-3.2.2.8		10-2351	10-3.3.3.5	13-3.4.5
10-2214	10-3.2.2.9			10-3.3.3.6	13-3.4.7
	10-3.2.2.10			10-3.3.4	13-3.5
	10-3.2.3	13-2.3	10-2352	10-3.3.4.1	13-3.5.1
10-2221	10-3.2.3.1	13-2.3.1	10-2353	10-3.3.4.2	13-3.5.2
10-2221	10-3.2.3.2	13-2.3.2	10-2353	10-3.3.4.3	13-3.5.3
	10-3.2.4	13-2.4	10-2354	10-3.3.4.4	13-3.5.4
10-2212	10-3.2.4.1	13-2.4.1	10-2354	10-3.3.4.5	13-3.5.5
10-2212	10-3.2.4.2	13-2.4.2		10-3.3.5	13-3.2
	10-3.2.5	13-2.5	10-2361	10-3.3.5.1	13-3.2.1
10-2233	10-3.2.5.1	13-2.5.1	10-2362	10-3.3.5.2	13-3.2.2
10-2234	10-3.2.5.2	13-2.5.2		10-3.3.5.3	13-3.2.3
10-2235	10-3.2.5.3	13-2.5.3		10-3.3.6	13-1.6
10-2236	10-3.2.5.4	13-2.5.5	10-2321	10-3.3.6.1	13-1.6.1
10-2236	10-3.2.5.5	13-2.5.5	10-2322	10-3.3.6.2	13-1.6.2
		exception	10-2323	10-3.3.6.3	13-1.6.3
	10-3.2.6	13-2.6	10-2324	10-3.3.6.4	13-1.6.4
10-2232	10-3.2.6.1	13-2.6.1	10-2325	10-3.3.6.5	13-1.6.5
10-2232	10-3.2.6.2	13-2.6.2		10-3.3.6.6	13-3.7
	10-3.2.7	13-2.7	10-2311	10-3.3.6.6.1	13-3.7.1
	10-3.2.7.1	13-2.7.1	10-2313	10-3.3.6.6.2	13-3.7.2
10-2241	10-3.2.8	13-2.11	10-2312	10-3.3.6.6.3	13-3.7.3
10-2242	10-3.2.8.1	13-2.11.1	10-2314	10-3.3.6.6.4	13-3.7.4
10-2242	10-3.2.8.2	13-2.11.2	10-2315	10-3.3.6.6.5	13-3.7.5
10-2243	10-3.2.8.3	13-2.11.3	10-2316	10-3.3.6.6.6	13-3.7.6
10-2244	10-3.2.8.4	13-2.11.4		10-3.3.6.6.7	13-3.7.7
10-2245	10-3.2.8.5	13-2.11.5		10-3.3.6.7	13-3.6
	10-3.2.9	13-2.8	10-2327	10-3.3.6.7.1	13-3.6.1
	10-3.2.9.1	13-2.8.1	10-2329	10-3.3.6.7.2	13-3.6.2
	10-3.2.10	13-2.9		10-3.3.6.7.3	13-3.6.3
10-2271	10-3.2.10.1	13-2.9.1	10-2328	10-3.3.6.7.4	13-3.6.4
	10-3.2.11	13-2.10	10-2333	10-3.3.6.7.5	13-1.6.7
10-2272	10-3.2.11.1	13-2.10.1		10-3.3.7	13-3.8
	10-3.3	13-3	10-2326	10-3.3.7.1	13-3.8.1
	10-3.3.1	13-3.1		10-3.4	13-5
10-2331				10-3.4.1	13-5.1
10-2332	10-3.3.1.1	13-3.1.1		10-3.4.2	13-5.2
	10-3.3.1.2	13-3.1.2	10-2411	10-3.4.2.1	13-5.2.1
10-2341	10-3.3.2	13-3.3	10-2412	10-3.4.2.2	13-5.2.2
		13-3.3.1	10-2413	10-3.4.2.3	

1973	1976	1981	1973	1976	1981
	10-3.4.3	13-5.3			19-1.4
	10-3.4.4	13-5.4			20-1.4
10-2334	10-3.4.4.1	13-5.4.1			22-1.4
10-2414	10-3.4.4.2	13-5.4.2	11-0001	11-1.3.1	16-1.4.1
10-2414	10-3.4.4.3	13-5.4.3			17-1.4.1
10-2414	10-3.4.4.4	13-5.4.4			18-1.4.1
	10-3.5	13-4			19-1.4.1
10-2511	10-3.5.1	13-4.1			20-1.4.1
	10-4	All Section 10-			22-1.4.1
		4—Chapters 14		11-1.3.2	16-1.2.1
		& 15			17-1.2.1
					18-1.2.1
					19-1.2.1
	Chapter 11				20-1.2.1
					22-1.2.1
	11	Chapters 16-22		11-1.4	16-1.5
	11-1	16-1			17-1.5
		17-1			18-1.5
		18-1			19-1.5
		19-1			20-1.5
		20-1			22-1.5
		22-1		11-1.4.1	16-1.5.1
	11-1.1	16-1.1			17-1.5.1
		17-1.1			18-1.5.1
		18-1.1			19-1.5.1
		19-1.1			20-1.5.1
		20-1.1			22-1.5.1
		22-1.1			
	11-1.1.1		11-111	11-1.5	16-1.7
	11-1.1.2				17-1.7
	11-1.1.3				18-1.7
	11-1.2	16-1.3			19-1.7
		17-1.3			20-1.7
		18-1.3			22-1.7
		19-1.3	11-1111	11-1.5.1	16-1.7.1
		20-1.3			17-1.7.1
		22-1.3			18-1.7.1
	11-1.2.1	16-1.3.1			19-1.7.1
		17-1.3.1		11-1.6	
		18-1.3.1	11-1121	11-1.6.1	
		19-1.3.1	11-113	11-1.7	
		20-1.3.1	11-1131	11-1.7.1	16-2.11.1
		22-1.3.1			17-2.11.1
	11-1.3	16-1.4			18-2.11.1
		17-1.4			19-2.11.1
		18-1.4			20-2.3

1973	1976	1981
		22-2.6
11-2	11-2	Chapters
		16 & 17
11-211	11-2.1	16-1
		17-1
11-2111	11-2.1.1	
11-212	11-2.1.2	
11-2121	11-2.1.2.1	16-1.2.3
		17-1.2.3
11-22	11-2.2	16-2
		17-2
11-221	11-2.2.1	
11-2221	11-2.2.1.1	16-2.4.2
		17-2.4.2
11-2212	11-2.2.1.2	16-2.1.1
		17-2.1.1
11-2213	11-2.2.1.3	16-2.1.2
		17-2.1.2
11-2214	11-2.2.1.4	16-2.1.3
		17-2.1.3
	11-2.2.2	16-2.2
		17-2.2
11-2221	11-2.2.2.1	16-2.2.1
		17-2.2.1
11-2222	11-2.2.2.2	17-2.2.2
	11-2.2.3	16-2.3
		17-2.3
11-2231	11-2.2.3.1	16-2.3.2
		17-2.3.2
11-2232	11-2.2.3.2	16-2.3.3
		17-2.3.3
11-2233	11-2.2.3.3	16-2.3.4
		17-2.3.4
	11-2.2.4	16-2.4
		17-2.4
11-2241	11-2.2.4.1	16-2.4.1
		17-2.4.2
	11-2.2.5	16-2.5
		17-2.5
11-2261	11-2.2.5.1	16-2.5.1
		17-2.5.1
11-2262	11-2.2.5.2	16-2.5.2
		17-2.5.2
	11-2.2.6	16-2.6
		17-2.6

1973	1976	1981
11-2251	11-2.2.6.1	16-2.6.1
		17-2.6.1
	11-2.2.6.2	16-2.6.2
		17-2.6.2
	11-2.2.7	16-2.7
		17-2.7
11-2271	11-2.2.7.1	16-2.7.1
		17-2.7.1
11-2272	11-2.2.7.2	16-2.7.2
		17-2.7.2
	11-2.2.8	
11-2263	11-2.2.8.1	16-3.6.3
		17-3.6.3
	11-2.2.9	16-2.8
		17-2.8
11-2281	11-2.2.9.1	16-2.8.1
		17-2.8.1
	11-2.2.10	16-2.9
		17-2.9
11-2281	11-2.2.10.1	16-2.9.1
		17-2.9.1
	11-2.2.11	16-2.10
		17-2.10
11-2282	11-2.2.11.1	16-2.10.1
		17-2.10.1
	11-2.3	16-3
		17-3
	11-2.3.1	16-3.1
		17-3.1
11-2311	11-2.3.1.1	16-3.1.1
		17-3.1.1
11-2312	11-2.3.1.2	16-3.1.2
		17-3.1.2
11-2313	11-2.3.1.3	16-3.1.3
		17-3.1.3
	11-2.3.2	16-3.3
		17-3.3
11-2331	11-2.3.2.1	16-3.3.1
		17-3.3.1
	11-2.3.3	16-3.4
		17-3.4
11-2341	11-2.3.3.1	16-3.4.1
		17-3.4.1
11-2342	11-2.3.3.2	16-3.4.2
		17-3.4.2

1973	1976	1981
	11-2.3.3.3	16-3.4.3
11-2343	11-2.3.3.4	16-3.4.4
		17-3.4.3
11-2344	11-2.3.3.5	16-3.4,4
		17-3.4.4
	11-2.3.4	16-3.5
		17-3.5
	11-2.3.4.1	16-3.5.1
		17-3.5.1
	11-2.3.4.2	16-3.5.2
		17-3.5.2
	11-2.3.5	16-3.2
		17-3.2
11-2351	11-2.3.5.1	16-3.2.1
		17-3.2.1
11-3341		
11-2352	11-2.3.5.2	16-3.2.2
		17-3.2.2
	11-2.3.6	16-3.6
		17-3.6
11-2321	11-2.3.6.1	16-3.6.1
11-2322	11-2.3.6.2	16-3.6.2
		17-3.6.4
11-2323	11-2.3.6.3	16-3.6.4
		17-3.6.4
	11-2.3.7	16-3.8
		17-3.8
	11-2.3.7.1	16-3.8.1
		17-3.8.1
11-4412		
11-2412	11-2.3.7.2	16-3.6.5
		17-3.6.5
	11-2.4	16-5
		17-5
	11-2.4.1	16-5.1
		17-5.1
	11-2.4.1.1	16-5.1
		17-5.1
	11-2.4.2	16-5.2
		17-5.2
11-2411	11-2.4.2.1	16-5.2
		17-5.2
	11-2.4.3	16-5.3
		17-5.3
	11-2.4.3.1	16-5.3

1973	1976	1981
		17-5.3
11-3	11-3	Chapters 18 & 19
11-31	11-3.1	18-1
		19-1
11-3111	11-3.1.1	18-1.1.2
		19-1.1.2
	11-3.1.2	
11-3112	11-3.1.3	18-1.1.4
		19-1.1.4
	11-3.2	18-2
		19-2
11-3212	11-3.2.1	18-2.1
		19-2.1
11-3221		
11-3211	11-3.2.1.1	
	11-3.2.2	18-2.2
		19-2.2
	11-3.2.2.1	18-2.2.1
		19-2.2.1
	11-3.2.3	18-2.3
		19-2.3
	11-3.2.3.1	18-2.3.1
		18-2.3.2
		18-2.3.3
		18-2.3.4
		19-2.3.1
		19-2.3.2
		19-2.3.3
		19-2.3.4
	11-3.2.4	18-2.4
		19-2.4
11-3231	11-3.2.4.1	18-2.4.1
		19-2.4.1
	11-3.2.5	
	11-3.2.5.1	18-2.11.1
		19-2.11.1
	11-3.2.5.2	18-2.6.1
		19-2.6.1
11-3233		
11-3232	11-3.2.6	18-2.6
		19-2.6
	11-3.2.6.1	18-2.6.2
		19-2.6.2
	11-3.2.6.2	18-2.6.3

1973	1976	1981	1973	1976	1981
		19-2.6.3			19-3.5
	11-3.2.7	18-2.7		11-3.3.4.1	
		19-2.7		11-3.3.4.2	18-3.5.5
11-3241	11-3.2.7.1	18-2.7.1			19-3.5.6
		18-2.7.2		11-3.3.4.3	
		19-2.7.1		11-3.3.5	18-3.2
		19-2.7.2			19-3.2
	11-3.2.8	18-3.6	11-3342	11-3.3.5.1	18-3.2.1
		19-3.6			18-3.2.2
11-3234	11-3.2.8.1	18-3.6.2			19-3.2.1
		19-3.6.2		11-3.3.6	18-3.7
	11-3.2.8.2	18-3.6.3			19-3.7
		19-3.6.3		11-3.3.6.1	18-3.7.1
	11-3.2.9	18-2.8			19-3.7.1
		19-2.8		11-3.3.7	18-3.7.3
11-3251	11-3.2.9.1	18-2.8.1			19-3.7.2
		19-2.8.1		11-3.3.7.1	18-3.7.3
	11-3.2.10	18-2.9			19-3.7.2
		19-2.9		11-3.3.7.2	18-3.8.1
11-3251	11-3.2.10.1	18-2.9.1			19-3.8.1
		19-2.9.1		11-3.4	18-5
	11-3.2.11	18-2.10			19-5
		19-2.10		11-3.4.1	18-5.1
11-3252	11-3.2.11.1	18-2.10.1			19-5.1
		19-2.10.1		11-3.4.1.1	18-5.1
	11-3.3	18-3			19-5.1
		19-3		11-3.4.2	18-5.2
	11-3.3.1	18-3.1			19-5.2
		19-3.1	11-3411	11-3.4.2.1	18-5.2
11-3311	11-3.3.1.1	18-3.1			19-5.2
		19-3.1		11-3.4.3	18-5.3
	11-3.3.2	18-3.3			19-5.3
		19-3.3		11-3.4.3.1	18-5.3.1
11-3321	11-3.3.2.1	18-3.3.1			19-5.3
		19-3.3.1		11-3.4.4	18-5.4
	11-3.3.3	18-3.4			19-5.4
		19-3.4		11-3.4.4.1	18-5.4
	11-3.3.3.1	18-3.4.1.1			19-5.4
		19-3.4.1.1		11-3.5	Chapters
11-3331	11-3.3.3.2	18-3.4.2.1			18 & 19
		19-3.4.2.1		11-3.5.1	18-1.1.2
	11-3.3.3.3	18-3.4.2.3			19-1.1.2
		19-3.4.2.3		11-3.5.2	18-2
	11-3.3.3.4				19-2
	11-3.3.4	18-3.5		11-3.5.2.1	18-2.1

1973	1976	1981	1973	1976	1981
		19-2.1			19-3.4
	11-3.5.2.2	18-2.2		11-3.5.3.3.1	18-3.4.3
		19-2.2			19-3.4.3
	11-3.5.2.3	18-2.3		11-3.5.3.4	18-3.5
		19-2.3			19-3.5
	11-3.5.2.4	18-2.4		11-3.5.3.5	18-3.2
		19-2.4			19-3.2
	11-3.5.2.5			11-3.5.3.5.1	18-3.2.1
	11-3.5.2.5.1				19-3.2.1
	11-3.5.2.5.2	18-2.6.1		11-3.5.3.6	18-3.7
		19-2.6.1			19-3.7
	11-3.5.2.6	18-2.6		11-3.5.3.6.1	18-3.7.1
		19-2.6			19-3.7.1
	11-3.5.2.6.1	18-2.6.2		11-3.5.3.7	18-3.7.3
		19-2.6.2			19-3.7.2
	11-3.5.2.6.2	18-2.6.3		11-3.5.3.7.1	18-3.7.3(a)
		19-2.6.3			19-3.7.2(a)
	11-3.5.2.7	18-2.7		11-3.5.3.7.2	18-3.8.1
		19-2.7			19-3.8.1
	11-3.5.2.8	18-3.6.2		11-3.5.3.7.3	18-2.1.1.2
		18-3.6.3			19-2.1.1.2
		19-3.6.2		11-3.5.4	18-5
		19-3.6.3			19-5
	11-3.5.2.9	18-2.8		11-3.5.4.1	18-5.1
		19-2.8			19-5.1
	11-3.5.2.10	18-2.9		11-3.5.4.2	18-5.2
		19-2.9			19-5.2
	11-3.5.2.11	18-2.10		11-3.5.4.3	18-5.3
		19-2.10			18-5.3.1
	11-3.5.3	18-3			19-5.3
		19-3		11-3.5.4.4	18-5.4
	11-3.5.3.1				19-5.4
	11-3.5.3.1.1	18-3.1.1(a)		11-3.6	Chapters
		19-3.1.1(a)			18 & 19
	11-3.5.3.1.2	18-3.7.2(a)		11-3.6.1	18-1.1.2
		19-3.7.2(a)			19-1.1.2
	11-3.5.3.1.3	18-3.6.1(a)		11-3.6.2	18-2
		19-3.6.1(a)			19-2
	11-3.5.3.2	18-3.3		11-3.6.2.2	18-2.2
		19-3.3			18-2.2.1
	11-3.5.3.2.1	18-3.3.1(a)			19-2.2
		19-3.3.1(a)			19-2.2.1
	11-3.5.3.2.3	18-3.3.1(a)		11-3.6.2.3	18-2.3
		19-3.3.1(a)			19-2.3
	11-3.5.3.3	18-3.4		11-3.6.2.4	18-2.4

1973	1976	1981	1973	1976	1981
		18-2.4.1			19-3.1.1
		19-2.4			19-3.1.2
		19-2.4.1			19-3.1.3
	11-3.6.2.5			11-3.6.3.1.1	18-3.1.1
	11-3.6.2.5.1	18-2.11.1			19-3.1.1
		19-2.11.1		11-3.6.3.1.2	18-3.7.2
	11-3.6.2.5.2	18-2.6.1(b)			19-3.7.1
		19-2.6.1(b)		11-3.6.3.1.3	18-3.6.1
	11-3.6.2.6	18-2.6			19-3.6.1
		19-2.6		11-3.6.3.2	18-3.3
	11-3.6.2.6.1	18-2.6.2			19-3.3
		19-2.6.2		11-3.6.3.2.1	18-3.3.1(a)
	11-3.6.2.6.2	18-2.6.3(b)			19-3.3.1(a)
		19-2.6.3(b)		11-3.6.3.2.2	18-3.3.1(a)
	11-3.6.2.7	18-2.7			19-3.3.1(a)
		18-2.7.1		11-3.6.3.2.3	18-3.3.1(a)
		18-2.7.2			19-3.3.1(a)
		19-2.7		11-3.6.3.3	18-3.4
		19-2.7.1			18-3.4.1.1
		19-2.7.2			18-3.4.2.1
	11-3.6.2.8	18-3.6			18-3.4.2.3
		18-3.6.2			19-3,4
		18-3.6.3			19-3.4.1.1
		19-3.6			19-3.4.2.1
		19-3.6.2			19-3.4.2.3
		19-3.6.3		11-3.6.3.3.1	18-3.4.5
	11-3.6.2.9	18-2.8			19-3.4.6
		18-2.8.1		11-3.6.3.4	18-3.5
		19-2.8			18-3.5.5
		19-2.8.1			19-3.5
	11-3.6.2.10	18-2.9			19-3.5.6
		18-2.9.1		11-3.6.3.5	18-3.2
		19-2.9			19-3.2
		19-2.9.1		11-3.6.3.5.1	18-3.2.1
	11-3.6.2.11	18-2.10			19-3.2.1
		18-2.10.1		11-3.6.3.6	18-3.7
		19-2.10			19-3.7
		19-2.10.1		11-3.6.3.6.1	18-3.7.1
	11-3.6.3	18-3			19-3.7.1
		19-3		11-3.6.3.7	18-3.7.3
	11-3.6.3.1	18-3.1			19-3.7.2
		18-3.1.1		11-3.6.3.7.1	18-3.7.3(b)
		18-3.1.2			19-3.7.2(b)
		18-3.1.3		11-3.6.3.7.2	18-3.8.1
		19-3.1			19-3.8.1

1973	1976	1981	1973	1976	1981
	11-3.6.3.7.3	18-2.11.2			19-2.7
		19-2.11.2			19-2.7.1
	11-3.6.4	18-5			19-2.7.2
		19-5		11-3.7.2.8	18-3.6
	11-3.6.4.1	18-5.1			18-3.6.2
		19-5.1			18-3.6.3
	11-3.6.4.2	18-5.2			19-3.6
		19-5.2			19-3.6.2
	11-3.6.4.3	18-5.3			19-3.6.3
		18-5.3.1		11-3.7.2.9	18-2.8
		19-5.3			19-2.8
	11-3.6.4.4	18-5.4		11-3.7.2.10	18-2.9
		19-5.4			19-2.9
	11-3.7	Chapters		11-3.7.2.11	18-2.10
		18 & 19			19-2.10
	11-3.7.1	18-1.1.2		11-3.7.3	18-3
		19-1.1.2			19-3
	11-3.7.2	18-2		11-3.7.3.1	18-3.1
		19-2			18-3.1.1
	11-3.7.2.1	18-2.1			18-3.1.2
		19-2.1			18-3.1.3
	11-3.7.2.2	18-2.2			19-3.1
		18-2.2.1			19-3.1.1
		19-2.2			19-3.1.2
		19-2.2.1			19-3.1.3
	11-3.7.2.3	18-2.3		11-3.7.3.1.1	18-3.1.1(a)
		19-2.3			19-3.1.1
	11-3.7.2.4	18-2.4		11-3.7.3.1.2	18-3.7.2(a)
		18-2.4.1			19-3.7.1(a)
		19-2.4		11-3.7.3.1.3	18-3.6.1(b)
		19-2.4.1			19-3.6.1(b)
	11-3.7.2.5			11-3.7.3.2	18-3.3
	11-3.7.2.5.1	18-2.11.1			19-3.3
		19-2.11.1		11-3.7.3.2.1	18-3.3.1(a)
	11-3.7.2.5.2	18-2.6.1(a)			19-3.3.1(a)
		19-2.6.1(a)		11-3.7.3.2.2	18-3.3.1(a)
	11-3.7.2.6	18-2.6			19-3.3.1(a)
		19-2.6		11-3.7.3.2.3	18-3.3.1(a)
	11-3.7.2.6.1	18-2.6.2			19-3.3.1(a)
		19-2.6.2		11-3.7.3.3	18-3.4
	11-3.7.2.6.2	18-2.6.3(b)			19-3.4
		19-2.6.3(b)		11-3.7.3.3.1	18-3.4.3
	11-3.7.2.7	18-2.7		11-3.7.3.3.2	18-3.4.6
		18-2.7.1			19-3.4.5
		18-2.7.2		11-3.7.3.4	18-3.5

1973	1976	1981	1973	1976	1981
		18-3.5.5			19-2.2.1
		19-3.5		11-3.8.2.3	18-2.3
		19-3.5.5			19-2.3
	11-3.7.3.4.1	18-3.5.1		11-3.8.2.4	18-2.4
		19-3.5.1			19-2.4
	11-3.7.3.4.2	18-3.5.2		11-3.8.2.5	
		19-3.5.2		11-3.8.2.5.1	18-2.11.1
	11-3.7.3.4.3	18-3.5.3			19-2.11.1
		19-3.5.3		11-3.8.2.5.2	18-2.6.1(b)
	11-3.7.3.5	18-3.2			19-2.6.1(b)
		19-3.2		11-3.8.2.6	18-2.6
	11-3.7.3.5.1	18-3.2.1			19-2.6
		19-3.2.1		11-3.8.2.6.1	18-2.6.2
	11-3.7.3.6	18-3.7			19-2.6.2
		19-3.7		11-3.8.2.6.2	18-2.6.3(b)
	11-3.7.3.6.1	18-3.7.1(c)			19-2.6.3(b)
		19-3.7.1		11-3.8.2.7	18-2.7
	11-3.7.3.7	18-3.7.3			19-2.7
		19-3.7.2		11-3.8.2.8	18-3.6
	11-3.7.3.7.1	18-3.7.3(b)			18-3.6.2
		19-3.7.2(b)			18-3.6.3
	11-3.7.3.7.2	18-2.11.1			19-3.6
		19-2.11.2			19-3.6.2
	11-3.7.4	18-5			19-3.6.3
		19-5		11-3.8.2.9	18-2.8
	11-3.7.4.1	18-5.1			19-2.8
		19-5.1		11-3.8.2.10	18-2.9
	11-3.7.4.2	18-5.2			19-2.9
		19-5.2		11-3.8.2.11	18-2.10
	11-3.7.4.3	18-5.3			19-2.10
		18-5.3.1		11-3.8.3	18-3
		19-5.3			19-3
	11-3.7.4.4	18-5.4		11-3.8.3.1	18-3.1
		19-5.4			19-3.1
	11-3.8	Chapters 18 & 19		11-3.8.3.1.1	18-3.1.1(b)
					19-3.1.1
	11-3.8.1	18-1.1.2		11-3.8.3.1.2	18-3.6.1(c)
		19-1.1.2			19-3.6.1(c)
	11-3.8.2	18-2		11-3.8.3.2	18-3.3
		19-2			18-3.3.1
	11-3.8.2.1	18-2.1			19-3.3
		19-2.1			19-3.3.1
	11-3.8.2.2	18-2.2		11-3.8.3.2.1	18-3.3.1(b)
		18-2.2.1			19-3.3.1(b)
		19-2.2		11-3.8.3.2.2	18-3.3.1(b)

1973	1976	1981	1973	1976	1981
		19-3.3.1(b)	11-4242	11-4.2	16-6.2
	11-3.8.3.2.3	18-3.3.1(b)			17-6.2
		19-3.3.1(b)		11-4.2.1	16-6.2.1
	11-3.8.3.3	18-3.4			17-6.2.1
		19-3.4	11-4211	11-4.2.1.1	16-6.2.1.1
	11-3.8.3.3.1	18-3.4.7			17-6.2.1.1
		19-3.4.6		11-4.2.2	16-6.2.2
	11-3.8.3.4	18-3.5			17-6.2.2
		18-3.5.5	11-4231	11-4.2.2.1	16-6.2.2.1
		19-3.5			17-6.2.2.1
		19-3.5.6	11-4212	11-4.2.3	16-6.2.3
	11-3.8.3.4.1	18-3.5.4			17-6.2.3
		19-3.5.5	11-4221	11-4.2.3.1	16-6.2.3.1
	11-3.8.3.5	18-3.2			17-6.2.3.1
		18-3.2.1		11-4.3	16-6.3
		19-3.2			17-6.3
		19-3.2.1		11-4.3.1	16-6.3.1
	11-3.8.3.5.1	18-3.2.2			17-6.3.1
		19-3.2.1(b)	11-4311	11-4.3.1.1	16-6.3.1.1
	11-3.8.3.6				17-6.3.1.1
	11-3.8.3.6.1			11-4.3.3	16-6.3.2
	11-3.8.3.7				17-6.3.2
	11-3.8.3.7.1		11-4331	11-4.3.3.1	16-6.3.2.1
	11-3.8.4	18-5			17-6.3.2.1
		19-5		11-4.4	16-6.5
	11-3.8.4.1	18-5.1			17-6.5
		19-5.1		11-4.4.1	16-6.5.1
	11-3.8.4.2	18-5.2			17-6.5.1
		19-5.2		11-4.4.1.1	16-6.5.1.1
	11-3.8.4.3	18-5.3			17-6.5.1.1
		18-5.3.1		11-4.4.2	16-6.5.2
		19-5.3			17-6.5.2
	11-3.8.4.4	18-5.4	11-4411	11-4.4.2.1	16-6.5.2.1
		19-5.4			17-6.5.2.1
	11-4	16-6		11-5	Chapter 20
		17-6		11-5.1	20-1
	11-4.1		11-5111	11-5.1.1	20-1.1.2
	11-4.1.1		11-5112	11-5.1.2	20-1.1.4
	11-4.1.2			11-5.2	20-2
	11-4.1.2.1	16-6.1.1		11-5.2.1	20-2.1
		17-6.1.1	11-5211	11-5.2.1.1	20-2.1.1
11-4321				11-5.2.2	20-2.2
11-4112			11-5212	11-5.2.2.1	20-2.2.1
11-4111			11-5213	11-5.2.2.2	
11-4241				11-5.3	20-3

1973	1976	1981
	11-5.3.1	20-3.1
11-5311	11-5.3.1.1	20-3.1.1
	11-5.3.2	20-3.2
	11-5.3.2.1	20-3.2.1
	11-5.4	20-5
	11-6	Chapter 22
	11-6.1	22-1
11-6111	11-6.1.1	22-1.1.2
	11-6.2	22-2
	11-6.2.1	22-2.1
11-6211	11-6.2.1.1	22-2.1.1
	11-6.2.2	22-2.2
11-6212	11-6.2.2.1	22-2.2.1
	11-6.2.3	22-2.3
11-6213	11-6.2.3.1	22-2.3.1
	11-6.2.4	22-2.4
11-6221	11-6.2.4.1	22-2.4.1
11-6222	11-6.2.4.2	22-2.4.2
11-6223	11-6.2.4.3	22-2.4.3
	11-6.2.4.4	22-2.4.4
	11-6.2.5	22-2.5
11-6231	11-6.2.5.1	22-2.5.1
	11-6.3	22-3
	11-6.3.1	22-3.1
11-6311	11-6.3.1.1	22-3.1.1
	11-6.3.2	22-3.2
	11-6.3.2.1	22-3.2.1
	11-6.4	22-5
	11-6.4.1	22-5.1
11-6411	11-6.4..1.1	22-5.1.1

Chapter 12

1973	1976	1981
	12-1	24-1
		25-1
	12-1.1	24-1.1.1
		25-1.1.1
	12-1.2	24-1.4
		25-1.4
12-111	12-1.2.1	24-1.4.1
		25-1.4.1
	12-1.2.2	24-1.4.2
		25-1.4.2
12-1121	12-1.2.2.1	24-1.4.2.1
		25-1.4.2.1

1973	1976	1981
12-1122	12-1.2.2.2	24-1.4.2.2
		25-1.4.2.2
12-1123	12-1.2.2.3	24-1.4.2.3
		25-1.4.2.3
12-1124	12-1.2.2.4	24-1.4.2.4
		25-1.4.2.4
	12-1.2.3	24-1.2
		25-1.2
	12-1.2.3.1	24-1.2.1
		25-1.2.1
12-531	12-1.2.3.1.1	24-1.2.1.1
		25-1.2.1.1
12-532	12-1.2.3.1.2	24-1.2.1.2
		25-1.2.1.2
12-1211	12-1.3	24-1.5
		25-1.5
	12-1.4	24-1.7
		25-1.7
12-1311	12-1.4.1	24-1.7.1
		25-1.7.1
12-1312	12-1.4.2	24-1.7.2
		25-1.7.2
	12-2	24-2
		25-2
	12-2.1	24-2.1
		25-2.1
12-2111	12-2.1.1	24-2.1.1
		25-2.1.1
12-2112	12-2.1.2	24-2.1.2
		25-2.1.2
12-2113	12-2.1.3	24-2.1.3
		25-2.1.3
12-2114	12-2.1.4	24-2.1.4
		25-2.1.4
	12-2.1.5	24-2.1.5
		25-2.1.5
	12-2.2	24-2.2
		25-2.2
12-2211	12-2.2.1	24-2.2.1
		25-2.2.1
12-2212	12-2.2.2	25-2.2.2
	12-2.3	24-2.3
		25-2.3
12-2311	12-2.3.1	24-2.3.1
		25-2.3.1

1973	1976	1981	1973	1976	1981
12-2312	12-2.3.2	24-2.3.2	12-3113	12-3.1	24-3.1
		25-2.3.2			25-3.1
	12-2.4	24-2.4	12-321		
		25-2.4	12-322		
12-2411	12-2.4.1	24-2.4.1	12-323		
		25-2.4.1	12-324	12-3.2	24-3.3
12-2412	12-2.4.2	24-2.4.2			25-3.3
		25-2.4.2	12-331	12-3.3	24-3.4
	12-2.5	24-2.5			25-3.4
		25-2.5	12-341	12-3.4	24-3.5
12-2511	12-2.5.1	24-2.5.1			25-3.5
		25-2.5.1		12-3.5	24-3.2
12-2512	12-2.5.2	24-2.5.3			25-3.2
		25-2.5.3	12-351	12-3.5.1	24-3.2.1
12-2513	12-2.5.3	24-2.5.4			25-3.2.1
		25-2.5.4	12-352	12-3.5.2	24-3.2.2
12-2514	12-2.5.4	24-2.5.5			25-3.2.2
		25-2.5.5		12-3.6	24-1.6
12-2515	12-2.5.5	24-2.5.6			25-1.6
		25-2.5.6		12-3.7	
12-2516	12-2.5.6	24-2.5.7		12-4	24-5
		25-2.5.7			25-5
12-2611	12-2.6	24-2.6		12-4.1	24-5.1
		25-2.6			25-5.1
12-2711	12-2.7	24-2.7	12-41	12-4.2	24-5.2
		25-2.7			25-5.2
	12-2.8	24-2.11		12-4.3	24-5.3
		25-2.11			25-5.3
12-2811	12-2.8.1	24-2.11.1	12-42	12-4.3.1	24-5.3
		25-2.11.1			25-5.3
12-2812	12-2.8.2	24-2.11.2	12-42	12-4.3.2	24-5.3
		25-2.11.3			25-5.3
12-2813	12-2.8.3	24-2.11.3		12-4.4	24-5.4
		25-2.11.4			25-5.4
12-291	12-2.9	24-2.8		12-5	24-4
		25-2.8			25-4
12-292	12-2.10	24-2.9		12-5.1	24-4.1
		25-2.9			25-4.1
	12-2.11	24-2.10		12.5.2	
		25-2.10	12-511	12-5.2.1	24-2.5.7
	12-3	24-3			25-2.5.7
		25-3	12-512	12-5.2.2	24-2.5.8
12-3111					25-2.5.8
12-3114				12-5.3	24-4.2
12-3112					25-4.2

1973	1976	1981
12-521	12-5.3.1	24-4.2.1
		25-4.2.1
12-522	12-5.3.2	24-4.2.2
		25-4.2.2
	12-5.4	24-4.3
		25-4.3
12-541	12-5.4.1	24-1.3(d)
		25-1.3(d)
12-542	12-5.4.2	24-4.3.1
		25-4.3.1
	12-5.4.3	24-4.3.2
		25-4.3.2
12-5431	12-5.4.3.1	24-4.3.2.1
		25-4.3.2.1
12-5432	12-5.4.3.2	24-4.3.2.2
		25-4.3.2.2
12-5433	12-5.4.3.3	24-4.3.2.4
		25-4.3.2.4
12-5434	12-5.4.3.4	

Chapter 13

1973	1976	1981
	13-1	26-1
		27-1
	13-1.1	26-1.1.2
		27-1.1.2
	13-1.2	26-1.4
		27-1.4
13-1111	13-1.2.1	26-1.4.1
		27-1.4.1
	13-1.2.2	26-1.2
		27-1.2
	13-1.2.2.1	26-1.2.1
		27-1.2.1
13-51	13-1.2.2.1.1	26-1.2.1.1
		27-1.2.1.1
	13-1.3	26-1.5
		27-1.5
13-1211	13-1.3.1	26-1.5.1
		27-1.5.1
13-1212	13-1.3.2	26-1.5.2
		27-1.5.2
	13-1.4	26-1.7
		27-1.7
13-1311	13-1.4.1	26-1.7.1

1973	1976	1981
		27-1.7.1
13-1312	13-1.4.2	26-1.7.2
		27-1.7.2
	13-2	26-2
		27-2
	13-2.1	26-2.1
		27-2.1
13-2111	13-2.1.1	26-2.1.1
		27-2.1.1
13-2112	13-2.1.2	26-2.1.2
		27-2.1.2
13-2113	12-2.1.3	26-2.1.3
		27-2.1.3
13-2114	13-2.1.4	26-2.1.4
		27-2.1.4
13-2115	13-2.1.5	26-2.1.5
		27-2.1.5
	13-2.2	26-2.2
		27-2.2
13-2211	13-2.2.1	26-2.2.1
		27-2.2.1
13-2212	13-2.2.2	27-2.2.2
13-2213	13-2.2.3	26-2.2.2
		27-2.2.3
	13-2.3	26-2.3
		27-2.3
13-2311	13-2.3.1	26-2.3.1
		27-2.3.1
13-2312	13-2.3.2	26-2.3.2
		27-2.3.2
13-2313	13-2.3.3	26-2.3.3
		27-2.3.3
13-2411	13-2.4	26-2.4
		27-2.4
	13-2.5	26-2.5
		27-2.5
13-2511	13-2.5.1	26-2.5.1
		27-2.5.1
	13-2.5.2	26-3.6.1
	13-2.5.2.1	26-3.6.2
	13-2.5.2.2	26-3.6.3
13-2611	13-2.6	26-2.6
		27-2.6
	13-2.7	26-2.7
		27-2.7

1973	1976	1981	1973	1976	1981
13-2711	13-2.7.1	26-2.7.1			27-5.3
		27-2.7.1	13-42	13-4.2.1	26-5.3
13-2712	13-2.7.2	26-2.7.2			27-5.3
		27-2.7.2	13-42	13-4.2.2	26-5.3
13-2811	13-2.8	26-2.8			27-5.3
		27-2.8		13-4.3	26-5.4
	13-2.9	26-2.9			27-5.4
		27-2.9		13-5	26-4
13-2812	13-2.9.1	26-2.9.1			27-4
		27-2.9.1		13-5.1	26-4.1
	13-2.9.2	26-2.9.2			27-4.1
		27-2.9.2		13-5.2	26-4.2
13-2813	13-2.10	26-2.10			27-4.2
		27-2.10		13-5.2.1	26-4.2.1
	13-3	26-3			27-4.2.1
		27-3		13-5.2.2	26-4.2.2
	13-3.1	26-3.1			27-4.2.2
		27-3.1			
13-3111	13-3.1.1	26-3.1.1		**Chapter 14**	
		27-3.1.1			
13-3112	13-3.1.2	26-3.1.2		14-1	28-1
		27-3.1.2	14-1111	14-1.1	28-1.1
	13-3.2	26-3.3		14-1.2	28-1.3
		27-3.3		14-1.3	28-1.4
13-3211	13-3.2.1	26-3.3.1	14-1111	14-1.3.1	28-1.4.1
		27-3.3.1	14-1111	14-1.3.2	28-1.4.2
13-3212	13-3.2.2	26-3.3.2	14-1111	14-1.3.3	28-1.4.3
		27-3.3.2		14-1.3.4	28-1.2
13-3311	13-3.3	26-3.4		14-1.4	28-1.5
		27-3.4	14-1121	14-1.5	28-1.7
	13-3.4	26-3.5		14-2	28-2
		27-3.5		14-2.1	28-2.1
	13-3.5	26-3.2	14-2111	14-2.1.1	28-2.1.1
		27-3.2	14-2115	14-2.1.2	28-2.1.2
13-3411	13-3.5.1	26-3.2.1	14-2121		
		27-3.2.1	14-2122		
13-3412	13-3.5.2	26-3.2.2	14-4211		
		27-3.2.2	14-2113	14-2.2	28-2.2
	13-4	26-5		14-2.3	28-2.3
		27-5	14-3211		
13-41	13-4.1	26-5.1	14-2141	14-2.3.1	28-2.3.1
		26-5.2	14-2114		
		27-5.1	14-2112	14-2.3.2	28-2.3.2
		27-5.2	14-4221	14-2.4	28-2.4
	13-4.2	26-5.3	14-2163		

1973	1976	1981	1973	1976	1981
14-2151	14-2.4.1	28-2.4.1	14-1221	15-2.6.1	29-2.6.1
	14-2.4.2	28-2.4.2		15-2.7	29-2.7
	14-2.5	28-2.5		15-2.8	29-2.8
14-2131	14-2.5.1	28-2.5.1		15-2.8.1	29-2.8.1
	14-2.5.2	28-2.5.2		15-2.9	29-2.9
14-4231	14-2.6	28-2.6		15-2.9.1	29-2.9.1
14-2161	14-2.6.1	28-2.6.1		15-2.10	29-2.10
14-2162	14-2.6.2	28-2.6.2		15-3	29-3
14-2171	14-2.7	28-2.7		15-3.1	29-3.1
	14-2.8	28-2.8		15-3.1.1	29-3.1.1
14-2182	14-2.8.1	28-2.8.1		15-3.2	29-3.3
	14-2.9	28-2.9			29-3.3.1
	14-2.9.1	28-2.9.1		15-3.3	29-3.4
	14-2.10	28-2.10		15-4	29-4
14-2181	14-2.10.1	28-2.10.1		15-4.1	29-6
	14-3	28-3		15-4.1.1	29-6.1
14-4311	14-3.1	28-3.1	15-2111	15-4.1.1.1	29-6.1.1
14-3311			15-2111	15-4.1.1.2	29-6.1.2
14-2211	14-3.1.1	28-3.1.1	15-2112	15-4.1.1.3	29-6.1.3
14-2221	14-3.2	28-3.3		15-4.1.2	29-6.2
		28-3.3.1		15-4.1.2.1	29-6.2.1
	14-3.3	28-3.4	15-2211	15-4.1.2.2	29-6.2.2
14-2183	14-3.3.1	28-3.4.1	15-2211	15-4.1.2.3	29-6.2.4
	14-3.3.2	28-3.4.2		15-4.1.2.4	29-6.2.5
14-4321	14-3.4	28-3.2	15-2312	15-4.1.2.4.1	29-6.2.5.1
			15-2313	15-4.1.2.4.2	29-6.2.5.2
	Chapter 15		15-2311	15-4.1.2.5	29-6.2.6
				15-4.1.2.6	29-6.2.7
⋅	15-1	29-1	15-2411	15-4.1.2.7	29-6.2.8
	15-1.1	29-1.1	15-2411	15-4.1.2.8	29-6.2.9
	15-1.2	29-1.3	15-2511	15-4.1.2.9	29-6.2.10
15-1111	15-1.3	29-1.4		15-4.2	29-7
15-1121	15-1.4	29-1.5	15-3111	15-4.2.1	29-7.1
	15-1.5	29-1.7	15-3112	15-4.2.2	29-7.2
	15-2	29-2	15-3121	15-4.2.3	29-7.3
	15-2.1	29-2.1		15-4.3	29-8
	15-2.2	29-2.2	15-4111	15-4.3.1	29-8.1
	15-2.3	29-2.3	15-4112	15-4.3.2	
	15-2.4	29-2.4	15-4113	15-4.3.3	29-8.1(a)
15-1212			15-4114	15-4.3.4	29-8.1(b)
15-1211	15-2.4.1	29-2.4.1			
	15-2.4.2	29-2.4.2		**Chapter 16**	
	15-2.5	29-2.5			
	15-2.5.1	29-2.5.1		16-1	30-1
	15-2.5.2	29-2.5.2	16-0001	16-1.1	30-1.1
	15-2.6	29-2.6		16-1.2	30-1.3

1973	1976	1981
	16-1.2.1	30-1.3.1
	16-1.2.2	30-1.3.2
	16-1.2.3	30-1.3.3
16-1111	16-1.2.4	30-1.3.4
	16-1.2.5	30-1.3.5
	16-1.2.6	30-1.3.6
	16-1.3	30-1.4
	16-1.4	30-1.5
	16-1.5	30-1.7
16-1113		
16-1112		
16-2113	16-2	30-2
	16-2.1	30-2.1
16-1114	16-2.2	30-2.2
	16-2.3	30-2.3
	16-2.3.1	30-2.3.1
	16-2.3.2	30-2.3.2
	16-2.4	30-2.4
	16-2.5	30-2.5
	16-2.5.1	30-2.5.1
	16-2.5.2	30-2.5.2
16-2112		
16-2111	16-2.5.3	30-2.5.4
		30-2.5.4.1
16-2112	16-2.5.3.1	30-2.5.4.2
16-2112	16-2.5.3.2	30-2.5.4.3
16-2112	16-2.5.3.3	30-2.5.4.4
16-2112	16-2.5.3.4	30-2.5.4.5
	16-2.6	30-2.6
	16-2.7	30-2.7
	16-2.8	30-2.8
	16-2.9	30-2.9
	16-2.10	30-2.10
	16-3	30-3
	16-3.1	30-3.1
	16-3.2	30-3.3
		30-3.3.1
	16-3.3	30-3.4
	16-3.4	30-3.2
	16-4	30-4
	16-4.1	30-6
16-3111	16-4.1.1	30-6.1
16-3112	16-4.1.2	30-6.2
	16-4.2	30-7
16-4112		

1973	1976	1981
16-4111	16-4.2.1	30-7.1
	16-4.2.1.1	30-7.1.1
16-4113	16-4.2.1.2	30-7.1.2
	16-4.2.2	30-7.2
16-4211	16-4.2.2.1	30-7.2.1
	16-4.2.2.2	30-7.2.2
16-4311	16-4.2.3	

Chapter 17

1973	1976	1981
	17-1	31-1
	17-1.1	31-1.1
	17-1.1.1.1	31-1.1.1
	17-1.1.2	31-1.1.2
	17-1.2	31-1.3
	17-1.2.1	31-1.2
	17-1.2.1.1	31-1.2.1
	17-1.2.1.2	31-1.2.2
17-1211	17-1.2.1.2.1	31-1.2.2.1
17-1611	17-1.2.1.2.2	31-1.2.2.2
	17-1.2.1.2.3	31-1.2.2.3
	17-1.2.2	31-1.3
	17-1.2.2.1	31-1.3.1
	17-1.2.2.2	31-1.3.2
17-1411	17-1.2.2.3	31-1.3.3
17-1412	17-1.2.2.4	31-1.3.4
17-1311	17-1.2.2.5	31-1.3.5
17-1413	17-1.2.2.6	31-1.3.6
	17-1.3	31-1.4
17-1212	17-1.3.1	31-1.4.1
17-1213	17-1.3.2	31-1.4.2
17-1511	17-1.3.3	31-1.4.4
	17-1.4	31-1.5
17-1111	17-1.4.1	31-1.5.1
17-1112	17-1.4.2	31-1.5.2
17-1114	17-1.4.3	31-1.5.3
17-1115	17-1.4.4	31-1.5.4
17-1116	17-1.4.5	31-1.5.5
17-1113	17-1.4.6	31-1.5.6
	17-2	31-2
17-2111	17-2.1	31-2.1
17-2121	17-2.2	31-2.2
17-2131	17-2.3	31-2.3
	17-2.4	31-2.4
17-2141	17-2.4.1	31-2.4.1

1973	1976	1981	1973	1976	1981
17-2142	17-2.4.2	31-2.4.2			31-5
17-2143	17-2.4.3	31-2.4.3		17-4.1	31-4.1
17-2144	17-2.4.4	31-2.4.4'			31-5.1
	17-2.5	31-2.5	17-4111	17-4.1.1	31-4.1.1
17-2151	17-2.5.1	31-2.5.1			31-5.1.2
17-2152	17-2.5.2	31-2.5.2	17-4112	17-4.1.2	31-4.1.2
17-2153	17-2.5.3	31-2.5.3	17-4113	17-4.1.3	31-4.1.3
	17-2.6	31-2.6		17-4.2	31-4.2
17-2161	17-2.6.1	31-2.6.1	17-4121	17-4.2.1	31-4.2.1
17-2161	17-2.6.2	31-2.6.2	17-4122	17-4.2.2	31-4.2.2
	17-2.6.3	31-2.6.3	17-4123	17-4.2.3	31-4.2.3
	17-2.7	31-2.7	17-4124	17-4.2.4	31-4.2.4
	17-3	31-3	17-4125	17-4.2.5	31-4.2.5
	17-3.1	31-3.1	17-4126	17-4.2.6	31-4.2.6
17-3111	17-3.1.1	31-3.1.1	17-4131	17-4.3	31-4.3
17-3112	17-3.1.2	31-3.1.2	17-4141	17-4.4	31-4.4
17-3113	17-3.1.3	31-3.1.3	17-4152		
17-3114	17-3.1.4	31-3.1.4	17-4151	17-4.5	31-4.5
17-3115	17-3.1.5	31-3.1.5			31-5.4.5
17-3116	17-3.1.6	31-3.1.6		17-4.6	31-4.6
17-3117	17-3.1.7	31-3.1.7			31-5.4
17-1118	17-3.1.8	31-3.1.8	17-4161	17-4.6.1	31-4.6.1
	17-3.1.9	31-3.1.9			31-5.4.1
	17-3.2	31-3.2	17-4162	17-4.6.2	31-4.6.2
17-3121	17-3.2.1	31-3.2.1			31-5.4.2
17-3122	17-3.2.2	31-3.2.2		17-4.6.3	31-4.6.3
17-3123	17-3.2.3	31-3.2.3			31-5.4.3
	17-3.3	31-3.3		17-5	31-6
17-3131	17-3.3.	31-3.3.1		17-5.1	31-6.1
17-3132	17-3.3.2	31-3.3.2	17-5111	17-5.1.1	31-6.1.1
	17-3.4	31-3.4	17-5112	17-5.1.2	31-6.1.2
17-3141	17-3.4.1	31-3.4.1		17-5.2	31-6.2
17-3142	17-3.4.2	31-3.4.2	17-5121	17-5.2.1	31-6.2.1
17-3143	17-3.4.3	31-3.4.3		17-5.3	31-6.3
17-3144	17-3.4.4	31-3.4.4	17-5211	17-5.3.1	31-6.3.1
17-3145	17-3.4.5	31-3.4.5		17-6	31-7
17-3146	17-3.4.6	31-3.4.6	17-6111	17-6.1	31-7.1
17-3151	17-3.5	31-3.5		17-7	31-8
17-3161	17-3.6	31-3.6	17-7111		
	17-4	31-4	17-8111	17-7.1	31-8.1

INDEX

— A —

Addition
defined 3–2
Air conditioning
as building service equipment 7–2
in ambulatory health care
facilities 12–6.5.2.1, 13–6.5.2.1
in apartment buildings 18–5.2, 19–5.2
in assembly occupancies 8–5.2, 9–5.2
in business occupancies 26–5.2, 27–5.2
in child day care centers 10–7.5.2, 11–7.5.2
in detention and correctional
occupancies 14–5.2.1, 15–5.2.1
in dormitories 16–6.5.2, 17–6.5.2
in educational occupancies . 10–5.2, 11–5.2
in health care occupancies . 12–5.2, 13–5.2
in hotels 16–5.2, 17–5.2
in mercantile occupancies . . 24–5.2, 25–5.2
Aisles
for assembly occupancies . 8–2.5.4, 9–2.5.4
Alarm devices
for doors 5–2.1.2.1
Alarm initiation
of protective signaling
systems 7–6.2
Alarm systems
in ambulatory health care
facilities 12–6.3.4, 13–6.3.4
in apartment buildings 18–3.4, 19–3.4
in assembly occupancies 8–3.4, 9–3.4
in business occupancies 26–3.4, 27–3.4
in child day care centers 10–7.3.4, 11–7.3.4
in detention and correctional
occupancies 14–3.4, 15–3.4
in dormitories 16–6.3.2, 17–6.3.2
in educational occupancies . 10–3.4, 11–3.4
in health care occupancies . 12–3.4, 13–3.4
in hotels 16–3.4, 17–3.4
in lodging or rooming houses 20–3.1
in mercantile occupancies . . 24–3.4, 25–3.4
maintenance of 31–1.3.6
requirements for 7–6
Alterations
building 1–4.3
Ambulatory health care facilities
air conditioning in . 12–6.5.2.1, 13–6.5.2.1
alarm systems in 12–6.3.4, 13–6.3.4
arrangement of means of
egress in 12–6.2.5, 13–6.2.5
capacity of means of
egress in 12–6.2.3, 13–6.2.3
classification of

occupancy 12–6.1.4, 13–6.1.4
communication
systems in 12–6.3.4, 13–6.3.4
corridors in 12–6.3.6, 13–6.3.6
detection systems in . . . 12–6.3.4, 13–6.3.4
discharge from exits in . 12–6.2.7, 13–6.2.7
elevators in 12–6.5.3, 13–6.5.3
emergency lighting in . . 12–6.2.9, 13–6.2.9
extinguishing requirements
for 12–6.3.5, 13–6.3.5
general requirements for . . . 12–6.1, 13–6.1
heating in 12–6.5.2.1, 13–6.5.2.1
illumination of means of
egress in 12–6.2.8, 13–6.2.8
incinerators in 12–6.5.4, 13–6.5.4
interior finish in 12–6.3.3, 13–6.3.3
laundry chutes in 12–6.5.4, 13–6.5.4
locks in 12–6.2.11.1, 13–6.2.11.1
marking of means of
egress in 12–6.2.10, 13–6.2.10
means of egress
requirements for 12–6.2, 13–6.2
measurement of travel
distance to exits in 12–6.2.6, 13–6.2.6
minimum construction
requirements 12–6.1.6, 13–6.1.6
modification of retroactive
provisions for 13–6.1.1.3
number of exits in . . 12–6.2.4, 13–6.2.4
occupant load in 12–6.1.7, 13–6.1.7
protection of 12–6.3, 13–6.3
protection from hazards
in 12–6.3.2, 13–6.3.2
protection of vertical
openings in 12–6.3.1, 13–6.3.1
rubbish chutes in 12–6.5.4, 13–6.5.4
subdivision of building
space in 12–6.3.7, 13–6.3.7
types of exits in 12–6.2.2, 13–6.2.2
utilities in 12–6.5.1, 13–6.5.1
ventilating in 12–6.5.2.1, 13–6.5.2.1
Apartment buildings
air conditioning for 18–5.2, 19–5.2
alarm systems in 18–3.4, 19–3.4
building compartmentation
requirements for 18–3.7, 19–3.7
building services for 18–5, 19–5
capacity of means of egress
for 18–2.3, 19–2.3
communication systems in . 18–3.4, 19–3.4
detection systems in 18–3.4, 19–3.4
discharge from exits in 18–2.7, 19–2.7
distance from apartment

Chapters 1-7 and 31 reference general requirements. Chapters 8, 10, 12 14, 16, 18, 24 and 26 reference requirements for new occupancies. Chapters 9, 11, 13, 15, 17, 19, 25 and 27 reference requirements for existing occupancies. Chapters 20, 22, 29 and 30 reference requirements for both new and existing occupancies.

Chapters 1-7 and 31 reference general requirements. Chapters 8, 10, 12 14, 16, 18, 24 and 26 reference
requirements for new occupancies. Chapters 9, 11, 13, 15, 17, 19, 25 and 27 reference requirements for existing
occupancies. Chapters 20, 22, 29 and 30 reference requirements for both new and existing occupancies.

— C —

Chapters 1–7 and 31 reference general requirements. Chapters 8, 10, 12 14, 16, 18, 24 and 26 reference requirements for new occupancies. Chapters 9, 11, 13, 15, 17, 19, 25 and 27 reference requirements for existing occupancies. Chapters 20, 22, 29 and 30 reference requirements for both new and existing occupancies.

— F —

— G —

— H —

Chapters 1–7 and 31 reference general requirements. Chapters 8, 10, 12 14, 16, 18, 24 and 26 reference requirements for new occupancies. Chapters 9, 11, 13, 15, 17, 19, 25 and 27 reference requirements for existing occupancies. Chapters 20, 22, 29 and 30 reference requirements for both new and existing occupancies.

— I –

1–7 and 31 reference general requirements. Chapters 8, 10, 12 14, 16, 18, 24 and ence
nts for new occupancies. Chapters 9, 11, 13, 15, 17, 19, 25 and 27 reference requiremeting
ies. Chapters 20, 22, 29 and 30 reference requirements for both new and existing occupa

— L —

— M —

— I —

Chapters 1-7 and 31 reference general requirements. Chapters 8, 10, 12 14, 16, 18, 24 and 26 reference requirements for new occupancies. Chapters 9, 11, 13, 15, 17, 19, 25 and 27 reference requirements for existing occupancies. Chapters 20, 22, 29 and 30 reference requirements for both new and existing occupancies.

Chapters 1–7 and 31 reference general requirements. Chapters 8, 10, 12 14, 16, 18, 24 and 26 reference
requirements for new occupancies. Chapters 9, 11, 13, 15, 17, 19, 25 and 27 reference requirements for existing
occupancies. Chapters 20, 22, 29 and 30 reference requirements for both new and existing occupancies.

— P —

— S —

Chapters 1-7 and 31 reference general requirements. Chapters 8, 10, 12 14, 16, 18, 24 and 26 reference requirements for new occupancies. Chapters 9, 11, 13, 15, 17, 19, 25 and 27 reference requirements for existing occupancies. Chapters 20, 22, 29 and 30 reference requirements for both new and existing occupancies.